THE Great Movie Stars

2 The International Years

The Stars of The International Years . . .

The stories of other stars, who made their names before the beginning of World War II, are contained in the companion to this volume, THE GREAT MOVIE STARS – THE GOLDEN YEARS

Anouk Aimée
June Allyson
Dana Andrews
Julie Andrews
Pier Angeli
Eve Arden
Alan Arkin
Arletty
Richard Attenborough
Lauren Bacall
Anne Bancroft
Brigitte Bardot
Alan Bates
Anne Baxter
Warren Beatty
Barbara Bel Geddes
Jean-Paul Belmondo
William Bendix
Claire Bloom
Ann Blyth
Dirk Bogarde
Shirley Booth
Ernest Borgnine
Marlon Brando
Charles Bronson
Mel Brooks
Yul Brynner
Ellen Burstyn
Richard Burton
James Caan
Michael Caine
Leslie Caron
Jack Carson
Jeff Chandler
Cyd Charisse
Julie Christie
Montgomery Clift
James Coburn
Sean Connery
Joseph Cotten
Jeanne Crain
Broderick Crawford
Tony Curtis
Zbigniew Cybulski
Linda Darnell
Danielle Darrieux
Doris Day
James Dean
Sandra Dee
Alain Delon
Catherine Deneuve
Diana Dors
Kirk Douglas
Paul Douglas
Faye Dunaway
Clint Eastwood
Edith Evans
Mia Farrow
Fernandel
José Ferrer
Edwige Feuillère
Peter Finch
Albert Finney
Louise Fletcher
Jane Fonda
Glenn Ford
Jean Gabin
Ava Gardner
Betty Garrett
Vittorio Gassmann
Mitzi Gaynor
Ben Gazzara
Elliott Gould
Gloria Grahame
Farley Granger
Stewart Granger
Kathryn Grayson
Sydney Greenstreet
Joan Greenwood
Alec Guinness
Gene Hackman
Julie Harris
Richard Harris
Kathleen Harrison
Rex Harrison
Laurence Harvey
Susan Hayward
Audrey Hepburn
Charlton Heston
William Holden
Judy Holliday
Celeste Holm
Trevor Howard
Rock Hudson
Tab Hunter
Glenda Jackson
Glynis Johns
Celia Johnson
Van Johnson
Jennifer Jones
Louis Jouvet
Danny Kaye
Howard Keel
Gene Kelly
Grace Kelly
Kay Kendall
Deborah Kerr
Burt Lancaster
Angela Lansbury
Mario Lanza
Jack Lemmon
Jerry Lewis
Gina Lollobrigida
Sophia Loren
Peter Lorre
Shirley MacLaine
Gordon MacRae
Anna Magnani
Jayne Mansfield
Jean Marais
Dean Martin
Lee Marvin
Giulietta Masina
Marcello Mastroianni
Walter Matthau
Victor Mature
Dorothy McGuire
Steve McQueen
Melina Mercouri
Toshiro Mifune
Ann Miller
Hayley Mills
John Mills
Robert Mitchum
Marilyn Monroe
Yves Montand
Agnes Moorehead
Kenneth More
Jeanne Moreau
Michèle Morgan
Robert Morley
Patricia Neal
Paul Newman
David Niven
Kim Novak
Maureen O'Hara
Ryan O'Neal
Tatum O'Neal
Peter O'Toole
Geraldine Page
Gregory Peck
Anthony Perkins
Gérard Philipe
Sidney Poitier
Jane Powell
Elvis Presley
Robert Preston
Vincent Price
Anthony Quinn
Raimu
Robert Redford
Lynn Redgrave
Vanessa Redgrave
Oliver Reed
Lee Remick
Debbie Reynolds
Thelma Ritter
Jason Robards
Cliff Robertson
Gail Russell
Jane Russell
Margaret Rutherford
Robert Ryan
Eva Marie Saint
Maximilian Schell
Romy Schneider
Paul Scofield
Geroge C. Scott
Jean Seberg
George Segal
Peter Sellers
Omar Sharif
Simone Signoret
Alastair Sim
Jean Simmons
Frank Sinatra
Rod Steiger
Barbra Streisand
Elizabeth Taylor
Rod Taylor
Terry Thomas
Gene Tierney
Richard Todd
Jean-Louis Trintignant
Liv Ullmann
Peter Ustinov
Alida Valli
Raf Vallone
Vera-Ellen
Monica Vitti
Robert Walker
Clifton Webb
Raquel Welch
Tuesday Weld
Richard Widmark
Cornel Wilde
Esther Williams
Shelley Winters
Natalie Wood
Joanne Woodward
Jane Wyman
Susannah York

THE Great Movie Stars

2 The International Years

DAVID SHIPMAN

Little, Brown and Company
BOSTON NEW YORK TORONTO LONDON

Volume 2 Little, Brown edition

First US edition 1995

ISBN 0 316 78488 5
10 9 8 7 6 5 4 3 2 1

Printed in Great Britain

Acknowledgements

The illustrations have been supplied by several individuals, and with the magnanimous co-operation of many film companies and distributors: Frances Clarke, The Cinema Bookshop, Bob Fournier, John Kobal, Tracey Lee, André Vannier, the author and the British Film Institute; A.I.P., Anglo-Amalgamated, Avco-Embassy, British Lion, C.I.C., Cinema Center, Cinerama Releasing (U.K.) Ltd., Columbia-E.M.I.-Warner, Columbia Pictures, Connoisseur Films, Curzon Film Distributors, Ealing Studios, E.M.I.-Films, Film Polski, Films André Paulvé, Fox-Rank Distributors, Luxosfilm, M.G.M., National General, Paramount, the Rank Organisation, Screen Gems, Titanus, Toho, 20th Century-Fox, United Artists, Universal, Unifrance, Waloria Films, Walt Disney, Warner Bros. and Woodfall.

Introduction

The coming of Sound to the motion-picture medium killed it as a means of almost effortless international communication. Hitherto, it had been a simple matter to slip in titles in the appropriate language. Once it became clear that audiences wanted Talkies, Talkies and nothing but Talkies, there was – because of the primitive dubbing techniques – nothing for it but to abandon the foreign markets. The American industry – by far the most powerful – for a while made simultaneous foreign-language versions of some of their films. This was not an expensive practice (obviously, the same sets were used) but it was a time-consuming one – and certainly the financial returns did not justify it, especially when (because of the Depression), some countries raised tariffs on foreign goods. In time, most countries accepted dubbing, and the smaller countries – where the cost of dubbing was not justified by the takings – accepted the use of sub-titles.

The only country to go in for dual-language versions in a big way was Germany. The German companies made films in German, English and French. The English versions were abandoned because they could not compete in Britain or the US with American movies; but until the war the Germans made simultaneous French versions of their important films. Similarly there were occasional co-productions between Italy and France, with each version filmed separately.

The rift between the European and American industries was almost complete. The US continued to dominate world markets; but European films were not expected or welcomed in the US. For one thing they were mainly bad (Hollywood had poached from Germany, for instance, almost every film-maker of note); at first they talked far too much; and many of them featured new players unknown to American audiences. The common language between Britain and the US did not help much, because British films were slow and invariably of inferior quality – for which, ironically, Hollywood was partly to blame: the quota system inaugurated by the British government meant that British cinemas needed a supply of cheap pictures and the Hollywood companies were glad to cash in by producing them in Britain – not only for the money, but to protect their product in that country. The producers concerned were not necessarily traditional Hollywood people sent to Britain, but sometimes entrepreneurs who could not get a foothold in Hollywood. Since its inception the film industry had been, and still is, marked by the sharks and charlatans attracted to it; but they almost buried the British film industry in the 30s. A few people, notably Michael Balcon and Alexander Korda, kept it alive.

In France, the situation was worse, for it attracted people not capable of getting a foothold in Britain, let alone Hollywood. Some of these people were refugees from Hitler; others were men who had departed their own minor industries in Eastern Europe. That the French cinema survived is due to a few men whose creative genius could not be denied – artists who made films for France and for the world. The first of these, chronologically, is René Clair, with his early Talkie comedies; then, more marginally, Marcel Pagnol. Later, four French films, still memorable, came to mean something abroad and above all others opened the market for French films, at least in New York and London. These were *La Kermesse Héroïque*, made by Jacques Feyder, a Belgian-born director who had worked in Hollywood; *Mayerling*, directed by a Russian, Anatole Litvak, who went to Hollywood; *Un Carnet de Bal*, directed by Julien Duvivier; and *La Grande Illusion*, directed by Jean Renoir. Flushed with success, and with due regard to the language-barrier, the French industry by 1939 confidently expected to gain a fair share of the world market (it would never be great: in 1938 France produced 120 films to Hollywood's 550 – at an average cost of $75,000, compared with Hollywood's $1,500,000).

There was little competition from the other European industries, most of which aped the American product with indifferent results. Russia was occupied with propaganda. So, by and large, was the German industry. The Third Reich maintained cinemas and distribution facilities in New York and London, but the films were recognized for what they were and not welcomed. The Italian industry was equally under the dominance of the government – but its films were mainly escapist and not of a quality to compete with the limited market for foreign films in London or New York.

After the war, Hollywood was as strong as ever. In Britain, the war brought some sort of national pride to the fore and the quality of movies improved; after the war, Olivier's *Henry V* brought tremendous prestige and opened up all markets for Britain's 'quality' product. Its entertainment films still could not compete with Hollywood's in the US, but in Europe they were pushing American films off the screen. By 1951 at least, there were so many British films on American television that British players became known and sometimes popular in the US (at that time the only American films on home television were curiosities like *The Eagle* with Valentino or old B series like the Charlie Chans. It was not till 1956 that the Hollywood studios began selling their old films to TV *en masse*).

Germany's industry was annihilated by defeat and by the Allies' determination to see that it never again amounted to much – and even when the Allies relinquished control of it, it did not recover. From that day to the 60s, German films were mainly for home consumption – *gemütlich* musicals and comedies, sleazy thrillers.

The French industry had the advantage of its pre-war reputation: the intelligentsia awaited its resuscitation with impatience. French films were more mature than Hollywood's – they provided sustenance: fortunately, although Duvivier and Carné did very little that was memorable after 1946, some other directors came up: René Clément, Jacques Becker, Max Ophüls, Claude Autant-Lara (the first new French film shown in New York after the war was Becker's *Goupi Mains Rouges* – the first Italian feature was *Open City*). This period of French films, roughly between 1937 and 1952, seems to evoke more nostalgia among film buffs than any other except Hollywood in the 30s. Columbia was the first major company to distribute a foreign film in the US – *Fanfan-la-Tulipe* in 1951. But the immediate postwar scene was dominated by Italy and especially by the films of Roberto Rossellini and Vittorio de Sica. They offered a new realism – called at the time 'neo-realism'.

It would be the last time there would be any sort of 'national' movement. The breakthroughs in the 50s would be made by individual directors: Akira Kurosawa, who was Japanese; Luis Buñuel, a Spaniard who had not made a major film for almost two decades; Ingmar Bergman, from Sweden; Satyajit Ray, from West Bengal, etc., etc. The way foreign films infiltrated the American and British markets is told to some extent in this book, under the guise of the leading players, but it should be borne in mind that the stars were merely pawns. The ground was broken by directors whose work the critics told the public they ought to see; the second factor was that European films were in general much more free and frank about sex – and the attempt to censor or ban these was, commercially, a more powerful impetus to the cause of foreign-language films than any other.

And thus Hollywood was beset. It was beset from within, in the first place, by rigid rules, by more old hacks than seemed humanly possible and by ideas which had not changed since 1930. It was beset from without by television, by critics who lambasted it almost every time a new film appeared from abroad and by the freer approach to sex – and it was not only where sex was concerned that the imported film was superior. Hollywood seemed to have lost the vivacity and vitality of the 30s and the war years, so that one often had the feeling (especially with the films of 20th Century-Fox) that American films consisted mainly of people standing about in rooms talking. Audiences dwindled, costs rose astronomically: the picturegoer who went indiscriminately to his local movie-house found it more convenient and comfortable to be indiscriminate before his television screen. The average-budget, average film no longer turned a profit automatically. In 1951 Hollywood produced over 400 movies; in 1959 it made only 177. The big American companies began to invest in films in Britain, France and Italy – anywhere where there might be good pickings for American distribution – and the results were sometimes so good in the local market that they took to backing films without much world-potential. As costs in Hollywood rose, more and more films were made in Europe and elsewhere: also, audiences would no longer tolerate model sets or back-projections. The old Hollywood fell apart; stars and directors and writers left the fold; a series of financial crises culminated in a general débâcle in 1969/71, when every one of the famous old, Hollywood studios lost money and new patterns began to emerge. With the ending of censorship, pornography began to flourish – in the end, in the US, hard-core pornography. Cinema which had once relied for their attractions on unwanted films – those the major circuits rejected – found it more profitable to go over to sex. The major studios noted the returns; bare buttocks abounded and, as a sort of bonus, blood-letting became common. Whenever a 'family' movie flopped, the industry thought it proved that it was blood and/or breasts and buttocks the public wanted: but the truth is probably that the industry was still dominated by the same old hacks. And, sadly, too many directors, talented and not, became self-indulgent when no longer reined in by the moguls of the past. Critics, by and large, did not help: divining, rightly, that there were many current movies which did not interest the public, the same few fashionable films got chewed over *ad nauseam* – and many of these proved to be very small beer when you got to them. Their commercial success, however, proved that the cinema public was still there – and will be there as long as there is a good chance it will not be bored.

The star system was pronounced dead by almost everyone, but when this book was first published everyone was talking about Liza Minnelli in *Cabaret* and she made the covers of 'Time' and 'Newsweek' simultaneously. Contrast the unfortunate Julie Ege, a Scandinavian starlet. The 'Sunday Times' reported in February 1971 that in less than two years 1,657 column inches had been devoted to her, of which only 31 inches consisted of 'critical appraisal of her film roles'. The movie world may have endured a series of convulsions which now and then seemed fatal: but some things do not change.

This book is a sequel to THE GREAT MOVIE STARS: THE GOLDEN YEARS. The project was originally envisaged as covering about 100 stars but when we (my editor and I) tried to reach a conclusion about which 100, we never managed to make a list of less than 150. These were 150 people we liked. Beyond this, there were scores of others claiming our attention – Oscar-winners, box-office favourites, famous stars of the Silent era whose names have lingered on. Thus the project grew until it was quite clear that one book would not be enough, or, rather, that a book with all our 400 names would hardly be an economic proposition. With some reluctance we decided that if the material had to be divided, World War II was as good a time as any: there were stars before the war and stars afterwards, but it seemed to us that *films* after the war were different. Also it had become accepted that the 30s in Hollywood was the cinema's golden decade, and the stars of that era and of the Silent period would sit very comfortably together. As I said in my introduction to that book, there has to be some overlapping, and there are probably a dozen people in both volumes whom some moviegoers would expect to see in the other book.

There was never any question that foreign performers would be more at ease in this second volume, which covers the period in which Hollywood's domination of the world's film markets began to ebb away or was eroded by local film industries. What we have tried to do is include all those performers whose names would be known in most households in the US and Britain. This has led to some odd anomalies: apart from British and American names, there are several from France and Italy, but only one from Germany. There are none from Spain. After long consideration, we decided that, with the exception of Liv Ullmann, Ingmar Bergman's marvellous stock-company did not come within our definition; but we were able to include one name from Japan and one from Poland. A name or two from Russia was suggested, but too few of their films have been seen in the West for a fair assessment.

In Volume One we applied the word 'great' rather more rigidly than we are doing here. I wrote then: 'The choice has been guided by the box-office figures, by popularity polls and the reputation that remains.' That meant that I was bound to include artists like Abbott and Costello, while leaving out an artist of charm and ability like Nancy Carroll. In that book, it must be said, there were more outstanding names clamouring to be included than there is in the present circumstances. With many less 'great' names to deal with, we have been able to include many others whose careers seem either interesting, or who were representative of the times or particularly famous without being much liked. And as to the two or three reviewers who questioned the selection in Volume One, might I hopefully silence them this time by suggesting that if they think I prefer Jayne Mansfield to Annie Girardot or Janet Leigh they must be out of their minds. Hopefully, too, this book will be regarded in a measure as a panoramic history of world cinema in the postwar years – at least of those industries which were tied to the star system.

As to the individual entries, we have followed the same pattern as Volume One; each feature is listed in chronological order, except where otherwise stated (it was particularly difficult to do this in the case of those French stars whose work was affected by the disruption of war). The dates used are of the first known preview or public showing, with all ensuing titles belonging to the same year – until the next date. It should again be remembered that by the time the film is shown the star might have done other work either on the stage or TV; and that, if you are sometimes trying to tie in the dates with box-office results, a December release will produce results the following year, as the film pays off. Once again, I have not tried to be exhaustive on the matter of stage work or television; films made for television seem to be regarded by both the industry and the public as different kettles of fish from films made for cinemas, but I have tried to include all of those in syndication, including mini-series – but in the case of the latter, however, pressure of space does not permit me to differentiate between those shown over two nights or many more. Other television work detailed is that which I think will most readily strike a chord: it is easier to imagine Miss X in an old-hat but well-known Broadway play than in an imaginative but forgotten play written specially for television.

A more contentious point is the matter of titles. All film titles are given as in their country of origin. For aesthetic reasons I have forborne to list the English and American titles given to many foreign features – we must each have our own favourites of movies mistitled in the hope of drawing in extra patrons. Most of these offences are committed in the name of sex (*Hungry for Love*, *Love is My Profession*) but others are simply mistakes, however well-meaning: *Children of the Gods* is not quite the same thing as *Les Enfants du Paradis*. Also, to be blunt, I have tried to make the text as economical as possible. Is it worth explaining that *Les Quatre Vérités* became *Three Kinds of Love* because an episode was omitted? Continental films often are retitled differently in Britain and the US, and what to make of *Los Olvidados* (admittedly not in this book), known variously as *Pity For Them*, *The Lost Ones* and *The Young and the Damned*? – but finally best known by its original title. Some continental features revert to their original-language titles on reissue and some get a new title when shown on television. Anyone with an elementary knowledge of French, German or Italian – and a dictionary – should have no difficulty; just occasionally, for reference, I have used the English-language title if the picture is thus better-known (this is true of some films shown in the 30s and 40s, e.g. *Four Steps in the Clouds*).

In the case of the Polish, Scandinavian and Japanese films – because these are relatively unknown languages in the US and Britain – I have seen fit to provide either the title by which it is known in the West or a literal translation. Otherwise, the title of 'international' productions is often a difficult matter – and it is difficult to be consistent. Once again, for reasons of economy, I have taken the shortest way out. It is just not possible to put all the titles when a film is a Franco-German-Spanish-Italian co-production and I have settled for either the country or the language in which it was filmed. In the case of American or British performers in European films, it is not quite so simple. If, say, the film is an American film made in Italy I have given it the American title; if it is an Italian film made in English in Italy I have given it both the Italian and English-language title; if it is an Italian film made in Italy I have given it the Italian title only – unless it is clear that the American star concerned acted his part in English (as opposed to merely dubbing it later). The point is not how much is acted in which language – the sets of most of these pictures are like Towers of Babel – but status: I hope I have made it clear of the importance or otherwise of these co-productions. 'Otherwise' is probably the operative word: Robert Ryan appears in *Uno Minuto per Pregare Uno Secondo per Morir*, which is the Italian title of a Spanish-Italian Western; as there are other English-speaking actors in it, it is probable that most of it was filmed in English. But to baldly call it *A Minute to Pray A Second to Die* only tells part of the story – in any case, in Britain it was called *Dead or Alive*. As very few people ever heard of it by any of these titles, it seemed best to simply give it its one (Italian) title. A list of the major British and American title-changes appears at the back of the book, plus the more generally known English-language titles of European films.

★ ★ ★ ★ ★

My grateful thanks are due to reviewers and others I have quoted, and to the following, all of whom read at least some of the manuscript: Felix Brenner, Mary Davies, Christopher Davis, David Holland, Ann Wilson and Michael Stapleton. My special thanks to André Vannier, who put his vast knowledge of the French cinema at my disposal, despite his confessed preference for American films. Also, my thanks for help and suggestions to Frances Clarke of Unitalia, to Linda Davis, Julian Fox, David Meeker, Peter Seward and his colleagues in the Information section of the British Film Institute, Brian Wood, and Fred Zentner, to Film Polski and Unijapan.

Anouk Aimée

From time to time Anouk Aimée has been on the verge of great success in American or British films. She has been flirted with more than most of her compatriots, but she has never responded with much enthusiasm: 'I was never an actress with a flame,' she said once. She admits to having lost all interest in her career when her daughter was born in 1951 and probably would not have persevered at all had her romantic life gone smoothly (she was married four times). She might have disappeared from public view years ago had not producers and directors sought her out: for, even when she is not trying, she has something of the same magical femininity as Ingrid Bergman.

Her lack of concern might be due to the fact that success came by chance and easily. She was born Françoise Sorya in Paris in 1932, studied dancing at the Marseilles Opéra and drama under René Simon in Paris. Both her parents were actors. She was with her mother one day in the Rue du Colisée when they were greeted by director Henri Calef, seeking a girl to play a servant in a Viviane Romance vehicle, *La Maison Sous la Mer* (47), a love-and-jealousy melodrama. In the part she showed a timid but definite presence, a pretty, willowy girl with large limpid eyes. She took her professional name from this character and her next director, Marcel Carné, added the 'Aimée' (later dropped for a while). The Carné film, *La Fleur de l'Age*, with Arletty, was never completed, but its writer, Jacques Prévert, was so struck with Aimée that he wrote a film for her, *Les Amants de Vérone* (49), about the stand-in of a film Juliet tragically in love with a studio carpenter (Serge Reggiani). This brought her to the notice of Rank, seeking a French girl to partner Trevor Howard in a romantic thriller, *The Golden Salamander*. Her name was lopped back to 'Anouk' and as this was the time of snoek there were some journalistic jokes – but not in the film reviews, which gave her a warm welcome. She was reportedly under contract to Rank for three years and to Herbert Wilcox, but a Rank film with Michael Redgrave, *Dangerous Meeting*, was cancelled and the Wilcox film, *Into the Blue*, was made with Odile Versois.

She married (for the first time), and did not film again till *Noche de Tormenta* (51), in Spain, as a Spanish gangster's moll. Then Alexandre Astruc selected her for his short (¾ hour), elegant, neo-Gothic *Le Rideau Cramoisi* (52) and British producer Raymond Stross remembered her when Simone Simon wisely turned down *The Man Who Watched the Trains Go By* with Claude Rains – she had two brief scenes as a rebuffed seductress. In 1953 she did a play in Paris, Julien Green's 'Sud', and then there was silence till another call from Britain, *Contraband Spain* (55), a wretched thriller with Richard Greene. She was stilted as a cabaret girl. A TV film she did with Douglas Fairbanks Jr, *Forever My Heart*, played a few cinemas and around the same time she returned temporarily to French films, in Astruc's arty policier, *Les Mauvaises Rencontres*, with Jean-Claude Pascal, as a provincial girl caught up in high society Paris. It was a critical success after a fashion, but not one with the public. The next offers were from Germany: *Ich Suche Dich*, directed by and starring O.W. Fischer, as a French doctor; *Nina* (56), in the title-role, with Karlheinz Böhm; and *Stresemann*, with Wolfgang Preiss. While making the last she sustained a serious car accident.

Her hold on stardom, always precarious, had gone and in Duvivier's *Pot-Bouille* (57) she had only a brief role and no billing. Gérard Philipe was the star, however, and he wanted her for *Montparnasse 19*, to play the wealthy girl seduced by him, as Modigliani, away from her parents. She was lovely in an unfilmstarlike way, but hardly incisive, and she was wan indeed – in a thin role – in Decoin's *Tous Peuvent Me Tuer* (58), the fiancée of one of a gang of crooks, André Versini. But directors continued to see in her a quality of tenderness that was virtually erotic and Georges Franju used this well in *La Tête Contre les Murs*, as the girl who loves and protects Jean-Pierre Mocky, consigned by his father to a mental home. She went from that to what was only a bit part in Litvak's made-

Anouk Aimée and Trevor Howard in The Golden Salamander *(50). She had made a couple of French movies, but this was reckoned to be her big chance – and it was widely believed she would be one of the big British stars of the 50s.*

in-Europe *The Journey* (59), but Mocky, now turned director, cast her as one of the several women (others: Dany Robin, Belinda Lee) involved with Jacques Charrier in *Les Dragueurs*. She was sympathetically cast as a girl with a club-foot, but she played the part in a conventional manner. Offscreen she was seen much with Maurice Ronet and several co-starring ventures were announced – but none came to fruition.

Instead, she went to Italy to make *La Dolce Vita* (60), playing a loose lady for Fellini. She adored working with him; he taught her, she said, to enjoy film-making for the first time. The film was further important to her in that it was both her first to enjoy a worldwide success and she was easily the most fetching of the generally lustreless females in it. She had at last begun to flower; her screen presence, always elusive, now suggested that 'enigma' which has been the desired accompaniment of screen beauty since Garbo. Philippe de Broca (his second film) cast her as a mysterious woman in *Le Farceur*, the glamorous wife of a tycoon and idolized by Jean-Pierre Cassell – who unexpectedly wins her, whereupon she becomes merely bored and spoilt. Another young director, Jacques Demy (his first feature), had come up with a subject which he hoped would exploit her special qualities, *Lola* (61). It was first and foremost a study of Proustian time slips and changing relationships, but Aimée was the catalyst, a dance-hall girl who was, as it turned out, one of those women who are all things to all men. Or something like that. Dilys Powell called hers an 'exquisite performance, a breathless, electric, vulnerable, supremely sensuous being'. There was no longer any question that Aimée was one of the screen's leading enchantresses, but the film did not get its deserved public success in France or elsewhere.

Instead, Mlle Aimée spent the decade in semi-eclipse – emerging, very definitely, with her entrancing performance in Jacques Demy's Lola *(61).*

This was doubly a pity because Aimée now was offered parts in lots of films, all of them vastly inferior: Lattuada's *L'Imprevisto*, as the wife of professor/kidnapper Thomas Milian, with Raymond Pellegrin as the baby's father; *Quai Notre-Dame*, as a chic boutique-owner on whom a young junk-dealer gets a crush – referred to as 'elle' on the cast-list and the film's sole star; *Il Giudizio Universale*, one of the several stars in De Sica's first major mistake (unaccountably one of his own favourite films); *Sodoma e Gomorra/Sodom and Gomorrah* (62), as the lesbian queen – virtually the film's sole contact with the delights promised by its title; *Les Grands Chemins*, as a mysterious widow involved with Robert Hossein, directed by Christian Marquand from a novel by Jean Giono set near Grenoble – but publicized as France's first 'Western'; and Fellini's *Otto e Mezzo* (63), a small role as Mastroianni's rather dry wife.

She remained in Italy for the next few years: *Il Terrorista*, a wartime Resistance story set in Venice, with Gian Maria Volonte; *Il Successo*, as the wife of Vittorio Gassmann in this comedy; *Liola* (64), as Pierre Brasseur's supposedly barren wife, in this study of Sicilian mores based on Pirandello and directed by Blassetti, with Ugo Tognazzi; *Le Voci Bianche*, a period farce about the castrati; *La Fuga* (65), as an interior decorator locked in lesbian love with Giovanna Ralli; and *La Stagione del Nostro Amore* (66), in all the flashbacks when ageing journalist Enrico Maria Salerno reflected on his past love(s). That film failed to get accepted for the Cannes festival that year. Another film – at the festival – made Aimée a world name.

This was Claude Lelouch's first feature, *Un Homme et Une Femme*, which was hardly more complicated than its title – a love story of a widow and a widower (Jean-Louis Trintignant). Some of it was – or seemed – improvised; all of it was smothered in high-class gubbins, a hit theme tune, elegant colour photography. Because it did resemble (and was imitated by) TV commercials and because it was overpraised (an Oscar for best foreign film) a reaction later set in, but in the meantime it had a gigantically successful career worldwide. The backlash did not affect Aimée, whom Hollywood had now begun to pursue with ruthlessness. Hollywood waited while she fulfilled contracts in Italy – *Lo Scandalo* with Philippe Leroy and *Il Morbidonne* with Paolo Ferrari – and announced several projects, of which the most consistently mentioned was *The Bliss of Mrs Blossom*, eventually done by Shirley MacLaine. None of the others worked out either and in the meantime *Un Soir Un . . . Train* (68) appeared from Belgium, a fuzzy philosophical drama in which she had brief footage opposite Yves Montand – in her usual role as the sad-eyed loving mistress.

Also at this time when she was in peak demand Aimée was involved with *Justine* (69), whose filming was a protracted affair. First, earlier that year, appeared *Model Shop*, in which she was Lola again under Demy's direction, in Los Angeles now and less interesting if more enigmatic; and *The Appointment* – which was with Omar Sharif in Rome, under Sidney Lumet's direction, and equally disappointing. The studio's accountants were no happier (Aimée's fee was $150,000) though in fact MGM, who made it, did not bother to release it in most countries. *Justine* was simply unlucky: it had been planned 10 years earlier with Elizabeth Taylor and there were script as well as casting difficulties. Lawrence Durrell, who wrote the original novel(s), 'The Alexandria Quartet', thought Aimée would be 'perfect . . . under the surface sweetness and haunting beauty [she] has an inner structure of tensile steel; one feels that she could switch from angel to demon at any point.' This Aimée apparently did, not only on the set. There were stories of temperament and rumours that she preferred to be on Albert Finney's yacht. The film in any case was stopped under Joseph Strick's direction and restarted under George Cukor; and Cukor managed to make a vigorous picture, utilizing to the full both Durrell's expatriate characters and the (Oriental) settings. But the film, much underrated, had no success and lost a mint for 20th. For that company Aimée was also signed to do a film of Simone de Beauvoir's 'The Mandarins', but she begged off because she was too tired. 'Variety' commented that Mr Finney was probably the real reason; they were married in 1970 and divorced in 1978. She returned to France to make *Si C'Etait à Refaire* (76) for Claude Lelouch and on the set met Elie Chouraqui, with whom she was living when he directed her in *Mon Premier Amour* (78), a drama about a son and a mother, the latter with only a short time to live. In Italy for Marco Bellocchio, at much below his best, she did *Salto nel Vuoto* (80) with Michel Piccoli, the two of them trying to bring life to the roles of a judge and his somewhat batty sister who discovers sex in middle age. She was Best Actress at the Cannes Festival for that.

Anouk Aimée and Michael York in Justine *(69), both ideally cast: he as a young British diplomat, and she as the mysterious wife of a somewhat shady entrepreneur (John Vernon).*

After *Une Page d'Amour*, from Zola for TV, she returned to the peninsula for Bertolucci's *La Tragedia di un Uomo Ridicolo* (81). The film was ridiculous, too. And a flop. She and Ugo Tognazzi played parents whose son is kidnapped by terrorists. She was the ex-mistress of a Jewish film-maker (Francis Huster) in *Qu'est-ce qui Fait Courir David?* (82) and was reunited with Piccoli for *Le Général de l'Armée Morte* (83), which also starred Marcello Mastroianni, and Lelouch's *Viva la Vie* (84). The two of them were also in Skolimowski's inept autobiographical piece, *Success is the Best Revenge*, she trying to help a Polish film director (Michael York) present his homeland's problems to the British. It was a small role, with co-star billing. She continued to be selective and throughout this period films were announced for her that were made with lesser actresses or with names less potent in the international market. She retrieved an old role in *Un Homme et une Femme: Vingt Ans Déjà* (86), with Trintignant, in which Lelouch showed little of his customary vulgarity, much of his cinema mastery and some tricks old and new – and, not least, a joke or so at the expense of the original. It was a movie deserving the cheers it received at festival screenings, but poor reviews in both France and the US effectively killed its commercial career. Aimée's only subsequent credit has been *Arrivederci e Grazie* (88) with Tognazzi.

JUNE ALLYSON

In her heyday June Allyson seemed just about the nicest thing on two legs. More than any other big star since the advent of Talkies, she was the campus sweetheart – pretty, unassuming, uncomplicated, with a delicious husky voice and a twinkling smile. Men dreamt of that smile. Today, the memory of it makes strong men cringe: the niceness of June Allyson has gone out of fashion. Watching an Allyson movie on TV is like drowning in sugar. She has no successors: the girls since then are the heiresses of Monroe and Clara Bow rather than of Allyson and Mary Pickford. They are no longer virginal; and would rather be seen dead than baking an apple-pie.

This is the sort of thing Van Johnson remembered when shipwrecked in the Pacific – apple trees and June Allyson. The film was High Barbaree *(47).*

She was born in the Bronx in 1917 (some sources say 1923). In her teens she became a dancer and began getting the breaks when she was around 20: she had a part in *Swing for Sale* (37), a Vitaphone short, which led to other two-reelers. She appeared in a Broadway revue, 'Sing Out the News', and had featured roles in several other shows, including 'Panama Hattie' (40), where she also understudied Betty Hutton. She went on for Hutton one night, which led to a star part in 'Best Foot Forward' (41) with Rosemary Lane and Nancy Walker. MGM saw her, liked her, and signed her as their answer to Hutton; and they gave her a Hutton-style song in the Garland-Rooney *Girl Crazy* (43), listed in the cast as 'Speciality'. Shown first, however, was the film of *Best Foot Forward* (41), an equally inauspicious start, though she got to sing a couple of songs and the Hutton impersonation was dropped. Later, she seldom sang on the screen, but MGM for years used her as a threat whenever Garland became difficult. She stayed in musicals for a while, however: *Thousands Cheer*, *Meet the People* (44), in a strictly minor role supporting Virginia O'Brien in a song, and *Two Girls and a Sailor*, teamed in the title-roles with Gloria de Haven and Van Johnson. She and Johnson became America's favourite sweethearts – though MGM ignored pleas to reunite them until 1947.

In the interim she progressed through a series of innocuous pictures: *Music for Millions* – it was José Iturbi's; *Her Highness and the Bellboy* (45) and *The Sailor Takes a Wife*, two comedies with Robert Walker; and two musicals, *Two Sisters from Boston* (46) with Kathryn Grayson and *Till the Clouds Roll By*, guesting in a couple of numbers. An excursion into drama, *The Secret Heart* – she was Claudette Colbert's neurotic daughter trying to pinch Mommy's beau Walter Pidgeon – proved that her talents did not lie in that direction. In 1946 the Harvard Lampoon named her the year's worst actress, along with Joan Crawford and Alexis Smith – Van Johnson was named sole worst actor. The long-awaited film with Johnson was *High Barbaree* (47), a sticky portrait of small-town life as recalled by a sailor to his buddy shipwrecked in the Pacific. *Good News*, however, was just that – a bright collegiate musical with a flock of 20s tunes. She and Johnson did a comedy, *The Bride Goes Wild* (48), and she rounded out the year as Constance in *The Three Musketeers*, opposite Gene Kelly, and memorably rendering 'Thou Swell' in *Words and Music*.

MGM's remake of *Little Women* (49) almost duplicated the box-office success of the 1933 Cukor-Hepburn version, but critics were unanimous in finding Allyson's Jo inferior to Hepburn's. She was as high-spirited and ingratiating as ever – but Hepburn had not tried to be ingratiating (later, when Allyson did four remakes in a row, they confirmed the impression that one of the things which separated Allyson from the stars of the 30s was that the earlier ladies did not care about being lovable). After Jo, she found her niche – as James Stewart's eager, loyal, loving wife in *The Stratton Story*, a sentimental baseball drama which became her favourite film – though she had only been in it because husband Dick Powell urged it on her. She and Powell had been married not long after they had appeared together in *Meet the People*, not greatly to the pleasure of the studio, who did not care to have a bright new star wed to a fading one from a former generation; and when MGM was finally talked into co-starring them in *The Reformer and the Redhead* (50) and *Right Cross*, the films were thrown away on double-bills (which was probably the best place for them anyway).

She was in two more programmers, *Too Young to Kiss* (51), posing as an infant prodigy to ensnare Johnson, and *The Girl in White* (52), as a lady doctor. She was a nurse in *Battle Circus* (53), opposite Humphrey Bogart, a teaming which reputedly amused him greatly (she replaced Shelley Winters, who was pregnant). Things were not going well. A last film with Johnson, *Remains To Be Seen*, a dim comedy-thriller, played B dates; then she was one of the stars asked to take a salary cut. She refused and said she would retire when her contract was up shortly. Meanwhile, Universal borrowed her for *The Glenn Miller Story* (54), again opposite James Stewart, again in sequences of cloying, even tearful, domesticity. Back at MGM she completed her contract in Robert Wise's excellent drama set in an *Executive Suite*, one of several names in the cast. At 20th she was again one of many stars and again involved with big business, in *A Woman's World*, probably her best performance, gauche and anxious to please the boss of husband Cornel Wilde. Her performance as Mrs Glenn Miller had pushed her at last into the front rank of stars; the film was one of the year's top grossers and she won both the 'Photoplay' and 'Woman's Home Companion' awards as 1954's favourite actress (US). The following year she made a fleeting appearance – at 9th – in the box-office top 10 list.

Still freelancing, she was the patient and understanding wife of Stewart again and Alan Ladd in, respectively, *Strategic Air Command* (55) and *The McConnell Story*. She was José Ferrer's wife in *The Shrike*, a nagging wife who almost destroys her husband. Ferrer had insisted on her for the part and some interest was engendered by this flagrant casting against type; but she reaped only limited kudos and the film itself was a flop.

MGM were now offering $150,000 per film – more than she had got from them in a year when under contract. She elected to do *The Opposite Sex* (56), which was *The Women* remade – badly – as a musical; and she got the songs and dances, thus wasting Ann Miller and Dolores Gray, who did not. It was clearly a mistake to take on Norma Shearer's old role, but Allyson then compounded it by taking on parts once played perfectly by Claudette Colbert, Irene Dunne and Carole Lombard respectively: *You Can't Run Away From It*, a musical version of *It Happened One Night* directed by her husband; *Interlude* (57) with Rossano Brazzi, which was *When Tomorrow Comes* relocated in and around Munich; and *My Man Godfrey*. All three films found critics hostile and audiences indifferent. The last two were part of a new multiple deal with Universal, but after a silly sudser with Jeff Chandler, *A Stranger in My Arms* (59), there were not any more.

Allyson had her own TV series in 1960 and has guested on other shows since, looking plump but as cheerful as ever. She was widowed in 1963 and remarried: it lasted two years, but the couple were remarried in 1966. She had done nightclub work and in 1968 appeared in a play in Chicago with her son, Dick Powell Jr. The following year it was announced that she would make two Spanish Westerns, but instead she took over from Julie Harris in Broadway's long-running 'Forty Carats' (70). In 1972 she appeared in the touring version of 'No No Nanette' and in 1974 she toured with Powell Jr in 'My Daughter, Your Son'. On screen she has been seen in *See the Man Run* (71), a TV thriller starring Robert Culp, as Eddie Albert's wife; *Three on a Date* (72) for TV, as a quiz-show winner in Hawaii; *They Only Kill Their Masters* at MGM and starring James Garner, as a lesbian murderess; *Letters From Three Lovers* (73), sharing her episode with Barry Sullivan and Robert Sterling, for TV; *Curse of the Black Widow* (77) and *Vegas* (78), both tele-movies; the Canadian *Blackout* (78) with Jim Mitchum; and *The Kid With the Broken Halo* (82), a TV fantasy.

Domestic June Allyson: as Mrs Glenn Miller in The Glenn Miller Story *(54), with James Stewart.*

DANA ANDREWS

In *Crash Dive* Dana Andrews was Tyrone Power's submarine commander, playing, said the 'New York Times', 'with commendable second lead charm'. The chief requirement of second leads was that they did not swamp the star and Andrew's experiences *not* overpowering Mr Power and others may well have conditioned his subsequent star career. he served his purpose; he never got in anybody's way and his sober-citizen appearance made its own mild contribution to the texture of the films in which he appeared. He projected a certain authority, grave-faced and grave-voiced, a certain masculine concern and an air of restrained heroism – all qualities used well in his two best films, *The Ox-Bow Incident* and *A Walk in the Sun.* He is so good in both (in each, curiously, as a doomed leader) that one must assume he only reacted with enthusiasm to the tougher assignments. Most of his parts were routine, and maybe it is a pity – you cannot be sure: there is a case to be made that no one who started as a second lead ever amounted to much *as a star.* What one recalls best about Andrews is a wry chuckle. It is hardly a very individual characteristic.

He was born in Collins, Mississippi, in 1909; at Sam Houston College he wanted to be an actor and after a spell as an accountant with Gulf Oil he hitchhiked to Los Angeles to try to get a job in show business. He spent several years working in a gas station in an LA suburb, but studied with the Pasadena Playhouse: finally, he made his pro début in a small part in 'Cymbeline' in 1935. His parts got bigger, until one night he was spotted by a Goldwyn agent and given a studio test which resulted in a contract starting at $150 a week. In nine months he had only a few lines in *The Westerner* (40), but was considered promising enough for Goldwyn to sell half his contract to 20th. He worked for both studios over the next 11 years.

20th put him into two Bs and loaned him out for a third: *Lucky Cisco Kid*, one of the series starring Cesar Romero, as a sergeant of the US Cavalry; *Sailor's Lady*, a comedy about a baby stowaway; and *Kit Carson*, as a captain in the Cavalry. Jon Hall starred in both the latter: Andrews was second lead. He was the juvenile in *Tobacco Road* (41), John Ford's dull film version of a long-running play about life in a hillbilly community, adapted in turn from a salacious bestseller by Erskine Caldwell; and was in another A picture, *Belle Starr* (who was Gene Tierney), when Henry Fonda refused to do it – the leads were shuffled and he supported Randolph Scott. He put on a city suit on screen for the first time in *Ball of Fire*, in a small role as Barbara Stanwyck's gangster boyfriend, but was back in the backwoods in Jean Renoir's *Swamp Water* (42), one of the least successful of the Master's Hollywood films and one of his least typical.

He starred in a B, *Berlin Correspondent*, uncharacteristically moustached in the title-role, with Virginia Gilmore, and then did his stint with Power in *Crash Dive* (43). The next gave him his best chance so far, William A. Wellman's tense tale of an attempted lynching, *The Ox-Bow Incident.* Bosley Crowther in the 'New York Times' spoke of 'a heart-wringing performance by Dana Andrews as the stunned and helpless leader of the doomed trio'. There were rave notices in general and 20th, who had disliked it, began belatedly to 'push' it (Darryl F. Zanuck later claimed it was one of the films he was most proud of). Henry Fonda was the star and now that he followed Power to the wars there were greater chances for those handsome hunks who were medically unfit. Andrews reached stardom in three war films: Goldwyn's *The North Star*, as a Russian student; Lewis Milestone's *The Purple Heart* (44), much criticized for its brutality; and *A Wing and a Prayer.* Still in uniform, he was the romantic lead in Danny Kaye's *Up in Arms.* He did not give off a very romantic aura and yet was now cast in films which might appeal more to the women in the audience: *Laura*, as a detective fascinated by Gene Tierney; *State Fair* (45), as a journalist wooing Jeanne Crane; and *Fallen Angel*, as a layabout marrying Alice Faye for her money.

The next was another of which 20th were distinctly unproud, *A Walk in the Sun*, from Harry Joe Brown's slight tale of one platoon during the invasion of Italy. It failed to get raves in the US or do good business and 20th sold it off to a very minor British distributor, who showed it eventually in 1951 – to reviews which saluted it unequivocally as the best war film since *All Quiet on the Western Front*, made by the same director 20 years before: twin peaks in Lewis Milestone's uneven career.

After a Western at Universal with Susan Hayward, *Canyon Passage* (46), Andrews was in a contemporary subject of which everyone was very proud and which was a huge commercial success – Goldwyn's production of Wyler's *The Best Years of Our Lives.* He was the flyer who returns from the war to realize that his wife is a tramp (Virginia Mayo in her

Henry Fonda and Dana Andrews as two men unhappily caught up in a lynching: Wellman's The Ox-Bow Incident *(43). 'It stands in my memory very firm, respectable and sympathetic' wrote James Agee later.*

one good screen portrayal). Under Wyler he was good: as he was under Kazan, as the prosecuting DA in *Boomerang* (47), then much praised for its semi-documentary approach to a factual trial (today it seems demi-semi at best). As it turned out, it was almost his last decent film.

He was a blind pianist loved by Merle Oberon in *Night Song* and a married man loved by Joan Crawford in *Daisy Kenyon*. He was a Russian again, a cipher clerk, in Wellman's factual spy story, *The Iron Curtain* (48), notable only for its use of the newly coined phrase as its title and for being the first postwar anti-Red film. 20th finally decided that audiences would accept him as a romantic hero: *Deep Waters* with Jean Peters, as a fisherman; Milestone's *No Minor Vices*, losing wife Lilli Palmer to Louis Jourdan; and *Britannia Mews* (49), romancing Maureen O'Hara in two different roles and dubbed in one of them (an impoverished artist) by an English actor. 20th made the last in Britain and in that country Andrews's next was withdrawn quickly after protests about its bias: *Sword in the Desert*, Ben Hecht's interpretation of the Palestine troubles. No one, except some critics and perhaps J.D. Salinger, objected much to a Goldwyn romance with Susan Hayward, *My Foolish Heart* – it was a padded adaptation of Salinger's 'Uncle Wiggley in Connecticut'. And indifference was the order towards this batch: *Where the Sidewalk Ends* (50), a sludgy melodrama – 'Street Scene' during the credits – with Gene Tierney, as a brutal cop who kills a suspect while beating him up; *Edge of Doom*, one of Goldwyn's biggest flops, as a priest who redeems Farley Granger; and *Sealed Cargo* (51), a World War II drama, as a New England fishing skipper. *The Frogman*, with Richard Widmark, was his last for 20th and *I Want You* his last for Goldwyn, a horrendously sentimental recruiting poster (for the Korean War) which its producer considered as 'relevant' as *The Best Years of Our Lives*. According to 'Picturegoer' in 1952 Andrews paid Goldwyn $100,000 to get out of his contract. His earnings had been reported as about $200,000 a year.

More people went to My Foolish Heart *(49) than it deserved – mainly because of its very popular theme-song (it was not until fairly recently that producers finally realised what a significant effect this could have on a film's receipts). The stars were Susan Hayward and Dana Andrews.*

In the next two years he made only one film, *Assignment Paris* (52), a poor spy thriller, made in Paris, as a reporter; and toured the New England straw-hat circuit in 'The Glass Menagerie', as Tom. Freelancing was less easy than supposed: most studios had their pre-war stalwarts still under contract (Power, Gable, etc.) but the big talk anyway was the new breed of forceful independents like Kirk Douglas and Burt Lancaster. In parenthesis, it might be noted that no ex-20th contractee had it easy as a freelance. Andrews did get to be the Other Man, the plantation manager, in *Elephant Walk* (54) with Elizabeth Taylor at Paramount; then did some dreary actioners: the British *Duel in the Jungle* with Jeanne Crain; *Three Hours To Kill*, a Western with Donna Reed; *Smoke Signal* (55) at Universal – because Charlton Heston was too expensive; *Strange Lady in Town*, another Western, straight-faced despite Greer Garson's shenanigans; and *Comanche* (56), as an Indian scout. He was city-suited again, for Fritz Lang, in the last (and least) of Lang's Hollywood thrillers, *While the City Sleeps* and *Beyond a Reasonable Doubt*, as a TV commentator and a writer respectively. In *Spring Reunion* (57) he romanced Betty Hutton.

In Britain he did a well-thought-of but little-seen horror film, Jacques Tourneur's *Night of the Demon* (57), with the faded Peggy Cummins; and then co-starred, in the US, with two other fading veterans – Linda Darnell in *Zero Hour*, an unambitious cliff-hanger about a plane-full of food-poisoning, based on a Canadian TV play by Arthur Hailey; and Jane Powell in a feeble version of Melville's 'Typee', *Enchanted Island* (58). Earlier in 1958 he was in another Tourneur-directed piece, *The Fearmakers* (the title referred to opinion-pollsters), as a confused war veteran. Maybe that induced him to try Broadway, taking over from Henry Fonda in 'Two for the See-Saw', and TV, 'The Right-hand Man'.

He returned to films in *The Crowded Sky* (60), a slightly changed remake of *The High and the Mighty*, and was absent again till another programmer, *Madison Avenue* (62), once again with Jeanne Crain. On the stage he was one of 'The Captains and the Kings' and then, after another break, in a slew of (mainly undistinguished) films: *A Crack in the*

World (65), a sci-fier, as a mad scientist; John Sturges's *The Satan Bug*, as a general, with Anne Francis; *In Harm's Way*, a supporting role in this big-budgeter, as an admiral; *Brainstorm* with Anne Francis again, as a sadist/masochist tycoon who drives his wife's lover to madness and gets murdered by him; *Town Tamer*, an A.C. Lyles Western; and *The Loved One*, a bit as a (licentious) general. He was a colonel in *The Battle of the Bulge*, made in Europe, and he stayed in Europe for an Italian film with Pier Angeli, *Berlino Appuntamento per le Spie/Spy in Your Eye*. In the US he had the title-role in one of the last Lyles Westerns, *Johnny Reno* (66), and was in one of the movies made by MGM mainly for ABC TV, a film known (if at all) as both *Hot Rods to Hell* and *52 Miles to Terror* (67). In Europe: *Super Colpa da Sette Miliardi*; a British low-budgeter, *The Frozen Dead* – the title referred to 12 Nazi officers in an English mansion and Andrews was a mad German scientist; an Italian-Spanish thriller, *Il Cobra*, with Anita Ekberg, helping to smash a narcotics gang; and *Il Diamante Che Nessuno Voleva Rubare* (68) in a cameo part.

In 1967 he toured the US hinterland in 'The Odd Couple'; then was promoted, in screen terms, to Brigadier-General in *The Devil's Brigade*, starring William Holden. In 1969 he began a daytime sudser on NBC TV, 'Bright Promise', and he was later in a movie for that medium, *The Failing of Raymond* (71). In 1972 he talked frankly about his bouts with alcoholism and made a film in Britain, *Innocent Bystanders*, as the head of the American Secret Service. He was the cause of all the trouble in *Airport 1975* (74), an ailing pilot; and after supporting roles in two tele-movies, *A Shadow on the Streets* (75) and *The First 36 Hours of Dr Durant* was guest-starred in an exploitation Western, *Take a Hard Ride*. Then: *The Last Tycoon* (76), as the harassed but calm film director; the television remake of *The Last Hurrah* (77); *Good Guys Wear Black* (78), as a 'Government Man'; *Born Again* as a board chairman, supporting Dean Jones, the Nixon aide who found God; and *Ike* (79), a mini-series, as General Marshall. He was widowed in 1935; he has been married since 1939 to ex-actress Mary Todd.

Julie Andrews

Julie Andrews was once the subject of a panegyric in 'Time Magazine': 'She's everybody's tomboy tennis partner and their daughter, their sister, their mum. . . . She is Christmas carols in the snow, a companion by the fire, a laughing clown at charades, a girl to read poetry to on a cold winter's night.' Yeah. Still, more hard-boiled critics were united as to no star since Shirley MacLaine 10 years before. In New York: 'the most enchanting and compleat performer to come to the screen in years' (Judith Crist). In London: 'If this is the Girl Next Door, I'm moving. Next door' (John Coleman). In Hollywood: 'This lady is not just a great star, she is a whole whirling constellation. . . . She is very likely going to be the object of the most intense and sustained love affairs between moviegoers and a star in the history of motion pictures' (James Powers in the 'Hollywood Reporter'). The intensity of the affair was clear to all when three Andrews pictures became the biggest money-makers yet for their respective studios: *Mary Poppins* for Disney, *The Sound of Music* for 20th (at one point it overtook *Gone With the Wind* as the highest-grossing film of all time) and *Thoroughly Modern Millie* for Universal. But it was brief: neither of the next two, to put it mildly, got their costs back.

When she came along there was only a handful of female stars with any appeal at all; most of the others were the same tired hopefuls, manufactured if not by the studios, by their own PR firms. With Julie, the genuine thing was back and everyone knew it. She embodied some of the best qualities of the great stars of the 30s: on the surface the same common sense, underneath hints of other things – the gaiety of Irene Dunne, the independence of Hepburn, the irreverence of Carole Lombard, the vulnerability of Margaret Sullavan. And what they had and what she has is style: discipline. She knows instinctively what to do, what she can do (unlike, say, Barbra Streisand). She is what she seems to be.

She had learnt the old way – probably the last great star to be trained 'on the halls', perhaps the reason for her consummate professionalism. She had been waiting in the wings almost since she was born (1935 in Walton-on-Thames, Surrey). It was a showbiz family: mother and (subsequently) stepfather were a music-hall act. He had the child taught singing – a freak four-octave voice – and she appeared sometimes in their act. She made her London bow in a revue, 'Starlight Roof' (47), singing the Polonaise from 'Mignon'. She played principal girl in panto – and was the London Palladium's Cinderella (53) when she was selected for the New York production of Sandy Wilson's mock-20s musical 'The Boy Friend' (54). She scored a bigger success than any British musical star since Gertrude Lawrence and was engaged for 'My Fair Lady' (after Mary Martin had turned it down because she did not care for the score). She

In 1965 a helicopter high in the Austrian Alps swooped down to find a pretty girl singing about the hills being alive with the sound of music: and thus began one of the most popular films ever made. It had so much drama and sentiment that the funny moments were easily forgotten – but they were mainly due, anyway, to the skill of Julie Andrews.

did three years as Eliza, including one in London, and there were TV shows: 'High Tor' (56) with Bing Crosby, Rodgers and Hammerstein's 'Cinderella' (57) and a BBC series (59). Then the creators of 'Lady', Lerner and Loewe, wrote 'Camelot' (60) for her; during its run she learnt that the film Eliza would be Audrey Hepburn (at a million dollars instead of the $75,000 for which her agents would have traded her).

But Disney liked her and cast her (at a fee of $125,000) as the flying governess in his version of P.L. Travers's *Mary Poppins* (64). Word went round that he had something special and two other studios made firm deals on the strength of some rushes. When the film was shown – an overlong one-joke fantasy – it was a smash and she won a popular Best Actress Oscar. During 1965 she seemed to be collecting one award or another every week. MGM's *The Americanization of Emily* gave her a good role as a nice English girl who jumps into bed with GI James Garner; then came *The Sound of Music* (65).

This had been a particularly maudlin Broadway musical, based on fact, with Mary Martin; in an effort to make a less sentimental film 20th had offered it first to Billy Wilder and then to William Wyler; Robert Wise eventually took it and did a magnificent job. Four factors made it the most popular film, apparently, yet made: (1) Andrews, (2) the Rodgers and Hammerstein score, (3) the Austrian locations and (4) a Cinderella story, grafting nuns, kids and Nazis on to a youth-middle-age romance (*cf* Daphne du Maurier's 'Rebecca'). And the greatest of these was the star: 'But it is Julie Andrews of the soaring voice and thrice-scrubbed innocence who makes me, even in guarded moments, catch

Andrews's comic skill was again apparent in Thoroughly Modern Millie *(67), alongside Beatrice Lillie, left, and Mary Tyler Moore. If you're wondering about the cloche hat – it was set in the 20s.*

my breath' (Kenneth Tynan). At the end of 1965, she was reckoned the fourth biggest draw in the US; in 1966 and 1967, top and in 1968, third. In Britain an 'Evening Standard' poll found her overwhelmingly the most popular star in 1967 and 1968.

She got $700,000 for *Hawaii* (66), an epic wrought expensively from James A. Michener's novel (Fred Zinnemann had laboured on it for some years). As directed by George Roy Hill, it was a fairly intelligent and absorbing account of the effect of civilization on Hawaii and Andrews was affecting as the pastor's long-suffering wife. At $750,000 plus a percentage she did Hitchcock's *Torn Curtain* – but he later declared she was miscast. Co-star Paul Newman called her 'the last of the really great dames'. Both films were among the year's top grossers. She was abetted by two great female drolls in *Thoroughly Modern Millie* (67), Beatrice Lillie and Carol Channing, but this loud imitation of 'The Boy Friend' wasted all of them. In 1967 Andrews won a Golden Globe as the world's most popular star.

In 1968 came *Star!*, a much-vaunted life of Gertrude Lawrence, and well received in Britain: Clive Hirschhorn in the 'Sunday Express' said that the star's 'presence on this occasion is breathtaking'. The film itself had a witless screenplay and was unmistakably old-fashioned: a wounded and astonished 20th discovered that the public were not coming in the expected numbers. Market research proved that Andrews's popularity was unimpaired, but her fans did not want to see her as Gertrude Lawrence. The film was withdrawn, re-edited and reissued as *Those Were the Happy Times*, but it did no better.

Andrews's fee had been $220,000, in a deal made before *The Sound of Music*, but 'Variety' thought it would be $1 million for MGM's *Say It With Music*; that was cancelled in 1969 after several years' preparation at an

Since Gertrude Lawrence was one of the legendary stage stars, Julie Andrews was a sound choice to play her on the screen, even if her own magic isn't quite the same. Star! *(68) was a treat whenever she was singing – or doing some excerpts from Noël Coward plays: the dialogue in between was not too hot, however.*

estimated cost of $3 million. Then under another change of management at MGM a substitute project, *She Loves Me*, was cancelled. *Star!* was not the only recent musical to fail and industryites were watching the fate of *Darling Lili* (70), a dangerously expensive one at Paramount, with Andrews as a World War I spy. Blake Edwards directed (and during its making became her second husband; the first was designer Tony Walton); there were cheers for her but none for this dinosaur of a film. Said 'Time Magazine' (Stefan Kanfer): 'A major talent is still settling for that vanilla species, the common, overproduced, underinspired feature (Cinema vulgaris).'

When the film failed at the box-office, she did her own TV series, which 'Variety' rightly predicted was too good for the medium; but in which she herself was always superb, extending her versatility in all directions – as if aware that she was the only star around fit to be ranked with the great ones of the past. The contract for this Anglo-American series stipulated two films and one was made, directed by her husband, *The Tamarind Seed* (74), an enjoyable Cold War thriller set mainly in Barbados – but perhaps a mite old-fashioned in the then cinema market. In 1976 she scored a personal triumph at the London Palladium and in Las Vegas and other arenas; and she seemed leery of films: though one could hardly blame her for turning down roles such as Tatum O'Neal's mother in *Six Weeks*, which was never made, and in *International Velvet*, which was. Minor talents were in movies a-plenty: she was never more needed. She finally returned in *10* (79): her co-star should have been George Segal, who reneged at the last minute – which is a pity (or in today's terms, a tragedy) since he is one of the few players able to match her comedy technique. Among replacements, one might have wished for Burt Reynolds, who might also have matched her irreverence towards her image: instead, they got Dudley Moore, who must surely have been the last resort. Ideal teaming found her with Walter Matthau in the new version of *Little Miss Marker* (80), her first film in 10 years not directed by her husband. The teaming could have worked better – the classy lady and the slob – but she had little to do.

The commercial success of *10* made Edwards a 'hot' director again and he found backing for an old script, *S.O.B.* (81), a semi-autobiographical comedy about a film-maker who makes one of the greatest movie duds of all time. In this version its star – Andrews – has to bare her boobs to make a musical number more commercial, and swear offscreen. For this unrewarding chore Edwards did present Julie with a huge role in a real musical, *Victor/Victoria* (82), as a down-and-out singer persuaded by Robert Preston (they had an engaging song-and-dance at one point) to earn a living as a drag artist – and thus perplex James Garner when he falls in love with 'him'. Despite generally favourable notices, the film's box-office performance was not greatly above average. Edwards claimed $180 million from MGM/UA for not exploiting this and the last two Pink Panthers properly, and the company retaliated by demanding $340 million from him for, inter alia, 'extravagance'. As his wife's role in *10* was subordinate to the now-forgotten Bo Derek, so it was to a succession of starlets in *The Man Who Loved Women* (83), but as Burt Reynolds's psychiatrist she was still the best thing in the film. As much may be said of *'That's Life'* (86), another autobiographical piece, filmed at the Edwards mansion with Jack Lemmon as a surrogate Edwards, undergoing a midlife crisis. It may not take a miracle to play yourself so beautifully, but the effect was something like that. She replaced the fortunate Faye Dunaway in Cannon's *Duet for One*, as a concert violinist who develops multiple sclerosis. Andrei Konchalovsky directed the appalling script, which reduced her and the entire cast (rumour had it that Edwards tried to buy up copies of the film to prevent it being seen). The two films, however, brought her Golden Globe nominations, one for comedy and one for drama, to emphasize that one of the greatest of all stars has spent most of her career being either misused or undercast. She returned to the screen playing the villainess in *Annie 2* (89).

Said Andrews a few years ago: 'What I suppose I'd like to be, one day, is someone who is fascinating. You know – a person you want to look at or see no matter what they're doing. I think what I'm trying to say is that I'd like to be an original, to be myself and not a pale copy of anyone else. You know, the really marvellous actors and actresses we admire have qualities that can't be pinned down. I suppose I'd like to be that type of performer if I were to leave a mark.'

PIER ANGELI

When Pier Angeli made her first American film there was a flurry of excitement. Paul Holt's comment was entirely typical: 'Pier Angeli, sloe-eyed, solemn and boyish, is the best discovery the screen has made since Garbo was a girl.' Throughout the reviews for this film, *Teresa*, there is a consistent reference to Garbo. They were not a bit alike: Angeli was an 18-year-old Italian and like the young Garbo only in that she was European, gentle and unglamorous. In the film she played a GI bride confronting life in a New York tenement – 'with exceptional charm and feeling' (Gavin Lambert in 'Sight and Sound'). From there, it seemed, there was nowhere to go but down.

She was born in Cagliari, Sardinia, in 1932, the daughter of a construction engineer and a mother who was an enthusiastic amateur actress. In 1935 they moved to Rome where the girl later studied art. She was seen at the home of a friend by director Leonide Moguy, who chose her to play with Vittorio de Sica and Gabrielle Dorziat in *Domani è Troppo Tardi* (49). The title referred to sexual enlightenment and was basically a tale of chattering teenagers, one of whom (Angeli) is destroyed when she is wrongly suspected of having had carnal knowledge of a young man. Still under her own name (Anna Maria Pierangeli – it was MGM who shortened it) she appeared in Moguy's similar *Domani è un Altro Giorno* (51), three stories of suicide – she was in the last of them.

It was Stewart Stern, who co-authored *Teresa* with Alfred Hayes, who 'discovered' her for MGM; while in Italy looking for a girl to play the title-role, she was recommended on the strength of her first film by the head of a Rome acting school. MGM signed her and when the reviews were out it looked as though they had never done a wiser thing. Under Fred Zinnemann's direction she was eloquent without being histrionic, using only slight movements of hands and eyes to express bewilderment and confusion at her new circumstances. In *The Light Touch* she brought something magical to the old story about a cad – con-man Stewart Granger – reforming for the love of an innocent young girl; but she was a little less effective as a German B-girl in *The Devil Makes Three* (52), opposite Gene Kelly. MGM announced a *Romeo and Juliet* to co-star Marlon Brando, but while they hesitated a British-Italian one was made. Also, MGM had discovered another continental charmer, Leslie Caron, possibly more appealing. Certainly the next three did nothing to further her career and the first two had production difficulties. *The Story of Three Loves* (53) – the 'Equilibrium' episode, was begun with Ricardo Montalban, who was replaced by Kirk Douglas when the film was rescheduled after Angeli broke her wrist doing one of the trapeze sequences. She only did *Sombrero* because Ava Gardner refused to play the heroine of this lurid drama, along with such Mexican villagers as Montalban, Cyd Charisse, Nina Foch and Rick Jason. *The Flame and the Flesh* (54) was another clinker, only more so, and Angeli had another nebulous role, losing her man to Lana Turner.

Pier Angeli in her second American film, The Light Touch *(51), playing an art student who unwittingly helps crooked art dealer Stewart Granger.*

Studio and star were both discouraged, but she was nevertheless surprised when they agreed to let her go to France to make *Mam'zelle Nitouche* with Fernandel, a version of the old operette with him as the convent organist and she as one of its inmates. It did not reach the US or Britain for some years. She was loaned out again, to Warners, for *The Silver Chalice*, symbolizing 'Christian Conscience' said the MFB but representing only 'empty naiveté'. At MGM she began *Green Mansions*, but it was abandoned (and later made with Audrey Hepburn). For Paramount she should have had the ingénue role in *The Rose Tattoo* but motherhood intervened and it went to her sister, Marissa Pavan. (Pavan had accompanied her and their mother to Hollywood and had made her début in *What Price Glory?* in 1952. Her talent was stronger than her sister's and until she married Jean-Pierre Aumont and retired it looked as though she might have had an important career.) Angeli was loaned to Columbia for a silly British melodrama, *Port Afrique* (56), with Phil Carey and Dennis Price, and seemed ill-at-ease as a Spanish café singer. Returning somewhat to the territory of *Teresa* she showed a return to her old form in *Somebody Up There Likes Me*, as Paul Newman's long-suffering Italian wife. But she was insipid in *The Vintage* (57) – with Mel Ferrer and John Kerr as fellow Italians – another of the melodramas with which MGM almost bankrupted itself during this period. There was mutual dissatisfaction between star and studio, and she finished her contract lamely in *Merry Andrew* (58), somewhat cute as Danny Kaye's leading lady.

Her marriage (1954–58) to singer Vic Damone had been instigated by her mother in response to her passion for James Dean, which apparently did not die with his death; when she broke with Damone there were headlined court battles over the custody of the child. After playing St Bernadette for the Desilu Playhouse (TV) she returned to Europe and began a brief career in Britain, first in a tiresome melodrama, *S.O.S. Pacific* (59), as an air hostess. The 'all-star' cast included Eddie Constantine, John Gregson and Richard Attenborough, and Attenborough cast her in his *The Angry Silence* (60), playing – very well – his Italian wife. Her travels then led her back to Italy where she was reunited with Stewart Granger for the English-language *Sodoma e Gomorra/Sodom and Gomorrah* (62): he played Lot and she got turned into a pillar of salt. Before it was released she appeared with two other erstwhile names: with Edmund Purdom in a convict-ship melodrama, *L'Ammutinamento* (61), and with Aldo Ray in a pirate tale, *I Moschettieri del Mare*. In 1952 she married bandleader Armando Trovajoli, but this was equally unsuccessful. The sons of both marriages were taken from her and European fan magazines occasionally noted further upsets in her *vie sentimentale*.

She reverted to her original name, Anna Maria Pierangeli, and this now hard-faced girl hardly looked like MGM's white hope: as a Eurasian in *Banco à Bangkok pour OSS 177* (64), one of a French series, this time starring Kerwin Matthews. *M.M.M. 83 – Missione Morte Molo 83* (65) with Gerard Blain was a very minor effort despite being a Spanish-French-Italian co-production. She had a brief role in *The Battle of the Bulge*, her only major film of the decade, but after *Per Mille Dollari al Giorno* (66) she snared two one-time Hollywood names as leading men – Dana Andrews in *Berlino Appuntamento per le Spie/Spy in Your Eye* and *Rey de Africa/One Step to Hell* (67) with Ty Hardin, George Sanders and Rossano Brazzi. She was a saloon girl who got tortured to death. She made an Israeli film, in English, *Every Bastard a King* (68), a story of the Six Days' War and, said 'Variety', 'decisively un-acts her un-role'. Then: *Rose Rosse per il Führer* based on a story by Dumas starring Jaques Perrin (68); *La Scelta* (69); *La Vera Storia di Frank Mannata* co-starring Jeffrey Hunter; *Nelle Pieghe della Carne* (70) with Eleonora Rossi Drago; and *Icaro* which seems to have been abandoned. In *Addio Alexandra* she was often naked: this sexploiter is adequately described by its English title, *Love Me Love My Wife*.

She died of an overdose of barbiturates, in 1971, not long after writing, 'I'm so afraid to get old – for me, being 40 is the beginning of old age . . . Love is now behind me, love died in a Porsche.' She was in Hollywood, making a come-back in a minor film, *Octamon* (72). It was reckoned to be suicide; she never adjusted to Hollywood in the first place or to stardom, and could not later adjust to the decline in her fortunes. Leonide Moguy blamed himself for her death simply because, he said, he had discovered her.

She was the most unspoilt and natural female to appear in movies since the advent of Ingrid Bergman ten years earlier. But the years were not kind: in Sodom and Gomorah *(62).*

Eve Arden

One of the reasons that the movies of today are not as much fun as those made in the first two decades of Talkies is because they jettisoned their great army of supporting players. At one time when people reminisced about movies, they were more likely to be talking about Eve Arden than Doris Day or Jane Wyman, whose friends she played on some funny occasions. Her first appearance always caused an appreciative buzz and her slightest glance was treasured more than all the star's vapourings. She could do a lot with a glance, suggesting surprise, disapproval and distaste all at the same time. And she could make almost any line funny, though her forte was the sort of lines that went with the look – elegant bitchery or advice she knows the heroine is too stupid to accept. Her standards were high: she might on the side do a bit of gold-digging and man-hunting, but always with a sensible air of tart resignation. 'I'm getting awfully tired of men talking to me man-to-man,' she says in *Mildred Pierce*, a film that contains perhaps her most famous line – commenting on Joan Crawford's awful daughter – 'Alligators have the right idea, they eat their young.' As a guide for the spectator, she was more eloquent than all the choruses in Euripides. Her whole act is skilled and lovely and justly famous.

She was born in Mill Valley, California, in 1912. On leaving school she joined a stock company in San Francisco and got nowhere fast. Under her own name of Eunice Quedens she had bit parts in *Song of Love* (29) and *Dancing Lady* (33), but as Eve Arden in 1933 she appeared successfully in a revue at the Pasadena Playhouse, 'Lo and Behold', which led to a Broadway chance the following year in the first posthumous 'Ziegfeld Follies'. She was also in the 1936 edition, which again starred Fanny Brice. Her work attracted the attention of Hollywood and she headed the supporting cast of *Oh Doctor!* (37) at Universal, a small-town comedy starring Edward Everett Horton. She did not set the place on fire, but worked steadily at most major

Gossip-time in a theatrical boarding-house. Talking to Eve Arden, in the chair, are Katharine Hepburn and Ginger Rogers: Stage Door *(37).*

studios over the next few years: *Stage Door*, wise-cracking as the wisest of the stage aspirants; *Coconut Grove* (38), supporting Fred MacMurray and Harriet Hilliard; *Having Wonderful Time*, with Ginger Rogers, husband-hunting at a holiday camp; *Letter of Introduction*, with Edgar Bergen and Adolphe Menjou; and *Women in the Wind* (39), as one of Kay Francis's fellow flyers.

She had established herself to the extent that she startled filmgoers when she appeared in a serious role (and it was to be almost the only time on film): *Big Town Czar*, a gangster story with Barton MacLane in the title-role. She was top-featured as the florist's assistant Who Knew Him When. *The Forgotten Woman* was, cruelly enough, Sigrid Gurie – sent to gaol: Arden was her best friend. In *Eternally Yours* she solaced David Niven when he left Loretta Young. She was treacherous in *At the Circus*, as the bare-back rider who walks on the ceiling and persuades Groucho Marx to accompany her. On Broadway she was in 'Very Warm for May' and, starring with a particular glitter, 'Two for the Show' (40), a revue with Keenan Wynn. She did not care for Hollywood, she said, because the star got everything and the comedians 'what's left'. She did not aspire to stardom herself and when later she was nominated for an Oscar (for *Mildred Pierce*) commented, 'That'll spoil everything.'

Still, she was back on the Coast for *A Child is Born* (40), a remake of *Life Begins* starring Geraldine Fitzgerald: *Slightly Honorable*, ending up a corpse, a whacky murder mystery with Pat O'Brien; *Comrade X*, as Clark Gable's hard-boiled journalist colleague; and *No No Nanette*, where her acidulous asides (she was a gold-digger) were a relief from the winsomeness of Anna Neagle. Warners took a chance and starred her in *She Couldn't Say No* (41), a farce with Roger Pryor, but it was a poor thing even for a B. She made 10 other films that year: *That Uncertain Feeling*, as a secretary; *Ziegfeld Girl*, wise-cracking this time as the wisest of the showgirls; *She Knew All the Answers* as Joan Bennett's room-mate; *San Antonio Rose*, a Universal B musical; *Manpower*, with Dietrich, as a dance hostess; *Whistling in the Dark*, an enjoyable comedy-thriller starring Red Skelton; *The Last of the Duanes*, the fourth screen version of this Western, with George Montgomery; *Sing For Your Supper*, a B with Jinx Falkenburg; *Obliging Young Lady*, a farce with Ruth Warrick and Edmond O'Brien; and, last but not least, *Bedtime Story* – a poor film, but she was superb in it, as the temperamental actress 'used' by Fredric March when he is having wife-trouble.

She returned to Broadway to appear with Danny Kaye in 'Let's Face It', which became her second film on returning to Hollywood. The first was *Hit Parade of 1943* (43), in which she was responsible for the quips between the acts. The film of *Let's Face It* starred Bob Hope, a comedy about an army barracks and some neglected wives, of whom she was the most vocal: 'Twenty thousand lonely men' she reflected, 'yum-yum'. It might fairly be said that she stole both the next two from their respectively pleasant casts: *Cover Girl* (44), as the assistant of fashion editor Otto Kruger, commenting succinctly on Rita Hayworth's progress; and *The Doughgirls* at Warners, as a rifle-toting Russian guerrilla leader with a penchant for double-features. Warners had always liked Arden and signed her to a non-exclusive featured contract, though first she wasted her time in three second-string musicals: at Republic, *Earl Carroll Vanities* (45), supporting Dennis O'Keefe and Constance Moore, and *Pan-Americana*, supporting Philip Terry and Audrey Long (with Robert Benchley they were touring journalists); and at Universal, *Patrick the Great*, supporting Peggy Ryan and Donald O'Connor.

The writers at Warners knew how to write dialogue for Eve Arden, even at their most what-the-hell (well, so was she most of the time); there was a tradition at the studio and in the 30s they had been writing similar quips for Ruth Donnelly and Aline MacMahon – though Arden was superficially different from both, with her chic career-women clothes and preposterous headpieces. The Warner stock company had completely changed, but was still strong. Arden settled in, with *Mildred Pierce*, as Joan Crawford's knowing friend, and *My Reputation* (46), as one of Barbara Stanwyck's neighbours. At Goldwyn she supported Danny Kaye in *The Kid from Brooklyn* and, back at Warners, in *Night and Day*, played a French chanteuse. She was virtually the only bright spot in *Song of Scheherazade* (47), as a campy Spanish madam, the mother of Yvonne de Carlo – with Jean-Pierre Aumont as Rimsky-Korsakov; and in *The Arnelo Affair*, a mediocre melodrama with John Hodiak and George Murphy. She had an unsympathetic part, as Ann Sheridan's bitchy sister-in-law, in *The Unfaithful* and then probably her best part to date in *The Voice of the Turtle*, catty this time, as the busy-body actress friend. The response was so favourable that in her two 1949 Warner films she had as much footage as the stars, though first she gamely trotted through *One Touch of Venus* (48), with Ava Gardner, and *Whiplash*, a prize-fighting melodrama with the Warner stock company, Zachary Scott, Dane Clark and Alexis Smith.

The 1949 films were *The Lady Takes a Sailor*, as Jane Wyman's best pal, and *My Dream is Yours* with Doris Day, as Jack Carson's eyes-wide-open but long-suffering fiancée. In *Paid in Full* (50) she was relief again, intervening in a plot about two sisters in love with Robert Cummings, the bad one (Diana Lynn) he marries and the good one (Lizabeth Scott) who willingly dies giving birth to his child. *Curtain Call at Cactus Creek* was a programmer which found her trouping with Donald O'Connor and Vincent Price, and *Tea for Two* was a sort of remake of *No No Nanette*, with Doris Day, with Arden less involved in the plot now than commenting on the action. She returned to the stage, 'Over Twenty-One' in stock, and then starred in *Three Husbands* with Emlyn Williams, which was an attempt to reverse the situation of Mankiewicz's *A Letter to Three Wives* and about one-hundredth less successful. Then she supported Joan Crawford again, in *Goodbye My Fancy* (51), her last film under her contract.

Miss Arden is clearly looking for something to gossip about: in The Voice of the Turtle *(47), with Eleanor Parker and Ronald Reagan.*

She starred again, with a host of others but with Paul Douglas in particular, in *We're Not Married* (52); and in *The Lady Wants Mink* (53), but both scripts were weak and in the latter she had not much to do as a rapacious neighbour of Ruth Hussey and Dennis O'Keefe. Motherhood occupied her increasingly, two children by the first marriage (1939–47) and two by the second (1951); also in 1953 she went into TV with a version of the radio series she had done since 1948, 'Our Miss Brooks' – a schoolteacher. The Hollywood front offices more or less refused to employ film talent that had gone into TV, but in 1956 Warners made a film called *Our Miss Brooks*. It was the first time Arden had carried a film since her Bs in 1941 and she gave, said the 'MFB', 'an exaggerated but

S.Z. Sakall; Patrice Wymore, Doris Day, Eve Arden and Bill Goodwin in Tea for Two *(50), which used some of the songs of 'No No Nanette' – and some of its plot.*

determined performance, receiving little help from the supporting players or the script'. It is in the nature of such artists that they cannot carry a whole film, but even Garbo could not have overcome this script. Arden proceeded to wow 'em on stage however, acknowledged as one of the best Auntie Mames (58). She returned to films, *Anatomy of Murder* (59) – again relief – as James Stewart's secretary; and she had a big part and a serious role in *The Dark at the Top of the Stairs* (60), as Dorothy McGuire's bossy and talkative sister.

She toured in 'Goodbye Charlie' (60), 'Plain and Fancy' (65), 'Butterflies Are Free' (70) and other plays, and did another TV series, 'Mothers-in-Law', with Kaye Ballard. Her one film in a decade was *Sergeant Deadhead* (65), starring Frankie Avalon; as a WAF officer she had little to do, but as ever (in this case, more than ever) one was grateful to have her there. There were a number of movies for TV: *In Name Only* (69), which reprised the idea of *We're Not Married*; *A Very Missing Person* (72), in the role of Miss Withers, the spinster detective played by Edna May Oliver in the 30s; and *All My Darling Daughters*, with Robert Young. Other films gaining from her participation include the Disney Studio's *The Strongest Man in the World* (75), third-billed as the head of a cornflake company, and certainly *Grease* (78), guest-starred as the school principal. In a tele-movie, *A Guide for the Married Woman,* she was an employment officer. In 1980 she did 'Little Me' in St Louis with Donald O'Connor and played a Hollywood gossip columnist in a TV mini-series, *The Dream Merchants*. *Under the Rainbow* (81) and *Grease 2* (82) were not among her happier credits, though the former gave her a large role as a German duchess staying at the same hotel as the Munchkins (making *The Wizard of Oz*). Around this time she also played the Queen of Hearts in a Broadway 'Alice in Wonderland', based on the old Paramount film; not a success (again) in this incarnation, it nevertheless made it to video – and surrounded Arden with some other considerable talents, e.g. Maureen Stapleton, Kaye Ballard. *Pandemonium*, made in 1981 as *Thursday the 12th*, was released in 1987 on video. Ballard and O'Connor are among the other guest stars in this horror spoof.

Alan Arkin

Alan Arkin had a varied career in show business, a Jack of all trades, before coming to films. With one film he proved himself a master.

He was born in 1934 in Brooklyn of Russian-German-Jewish parents and wanted to act from childhood, but 'I guess they didn't need a 12-year-old character star'. His goal was always the cinema – he was a compulsive moviegoer (favourite actors – Tracy, Laughton, Walter Huston, the young Brando, Jouvet, Raimu, Gabin and Michel Simon). He studied acting while at college in California (where the family were living) and at Bennington College in Vermont, but he dropped out to join a folk-trio, 'The Tarriers'. After a tour of Europe he quit (though he still collects royalties from songs he wrote for them). In 1958 he was in stock in the Adirondacks; in 1959 in an off-Broadway production, 'Eloise'. The same year he had some short stories published. He joined an improvisation theatre group in St Louis, from where he went to Chicago and joined the Second City company. After the New York stand with that company, he had Broadway successes in 'Enter Laughing' (63), as a terrified and talentless drama student, and 'Luv' (64), directed by Mike Nichols, who called him 'the best actor in America'.

During this time he made his film début in two shorts based on his Second City sketches, *That's Me* and *The Last Mohican* (in 1970 he made another 'personal' short, *People Soup*). His feature-film début was outstanding and brought an Oscar nomination, as the timorous but resourceful Russian lieutenant in *The Russians are Coming, The Russians are Coming* (66), directed by Norman Jewison and written by William Rose, an elaborate and hysterical comedy (the faults were inherent in the matter – a Russian submarine aground off the coast of Maine). Despite cool reviews, it did great business; and anyone who missed it was quite likely individually to 'discover' Arkin in the unpublicized parts he did after-

The Russians are Coming, the Russians are Coming (66) *was not a comedy to cherish – with the distinct exception of Alan Arkin's performance as a harassed Russian seaman.*

The novels of Carson McCullers have, on the whole, been well treated by movies. The least good is perhaps The Heart is a Lonely Hunter *(68), although it contained excellent performances by Sandra Locke and Alan Arkin.*

wards: *Sept Fois Femme/Woman Times Seven* (67), with Shirley MacLaine, as a meek French workman bent on suicide – the best episode in that film; *Wait Until Dark*, in three disguises as the terrifying villain out to kill Audrey Hepburn; and *Inspector Clouseau* (68), taking over Peter Sellers's old part as the Gallic gumshoe and not profiting much thereby. Then he played the deaf-mute in a generally prosaic version of Carson McCullers's *The Heart is a Lonely Hunter*, filmed at last after years of trying to wrench a screenplay from it. The 'New York Daily News' called Arkin's performance 'a masterpiece' and John Coleman in the 'New Statesman', after referring to him as 'that superlatively generous actor', said 'a great performance, proceeding from a central stillness and control that commands the attention'. It won the New York critics' Best Actor award; but at the Oscar ceremony the statuette went to Cliff Robertson.

There were more raves for him in *Popi* (69): Wanda Hale in the 'New York Daily News' said she wanted to 'go up to the screen, to hug him and say "You're wonderful"' and 'Time Magazine' said, 'as a comedian, he clambers over the film to reach the front rank of American performers'. He played a poverty-pinched Puerto Rican widower in New York who thinks up a scheme to get his kids brought up in luxury: an odd film, part harsh, part sentimental, part critical and always likeable. It was critically underrated and a disappointment to United Artists – in Britain some critics did not bother to go, as though that is the way to treat one of the world's best actors. Nor did many go to *Catch-22* (70), despite its being directed by Mike Nichols from Joseph Heller's bestselling novel: and a good one, albeit a bit sententious, cleverly rendering that intractable anti-military masterpiece. Arkin played the self-seeking survivor, Yossarian, with his usual understated attention to detail. Said 'Time Magazine': 'Arkin's complex, triumphant performance is due in part to good genes – he looks more like Yossarian than he does like Arkin. In part it is due to a virtuoso player entering his richest period.'

The virtuoso player rested on his laurels and took to directing 'Little Malcolm' off-Broadway and *Little Murders* (71), with Elliott Gould; in the latter he did a cameo as a paranoid detective – but too late in the film to save this hopelessly heavy attempt at satire. There was a less deserved failure when he played *The Last of the Red Hot Lovers* (72), one of the few Neil Simon pieces to flop on the screen; between the two, for Paramount, he made *Deadhead Miles*, which had a few scattered showings 10 years later; Arkin played a truck-driver. At a loss, he tried two more commercial-seeming chores: *Freebie and the Bean* (74), sharing the title-roles with James Caan, the two of them comic Frisco cops; and *Rafferty and the Gold Dust Twins* (75), as Rafferty, a driving instructor picked up at gunpoint by two female vagrants. He

Alan Arkin in Fire Sale *(77), a comedy about a department store, and his second unsuccessful stab at direction.*

was top-billed in both and both were, again, failures: so he accepted strong supporting roles in *Hearts of the West*, as an old-time Hollywood director – of Jeff Bridges; and *The Seven-Per-Cent Solution* (76), as Sigmund Freud – trying to cure Sherlock Holmes (Nicol Williamson). The reception of both did nothing to revive Arkin's standing, though his participation brightened both films: the first brought him a Best Supporting award from the New York critics – and the second sorely needed brightening.

Directing again, he did a crazy comedy about a department store, also playing the leading role, the owner's son: but *Fire Sale* (77), like *Little Murders*, only proved that he should stick to acting. And since, through all these reverses, he remained one of the few American screen actors whose talent was really rewarding, it was good to have him in a superior TV movie, *The Defection of Simas Kurdika*, based on the true story of a Lithuanian seaman who had jumped ship hoping for asylum in the US, and in the leading role in *The Magician of Lublin* (79), an Israeli version – in English, made in Germany – of the novel by Isaac Bashevis Singer. Before it was completed he had begun *The In-Laws*, co-starring effectively with Peter Falk and sharing the title-roles. They were often said to be reteaming, but did not for some years – which is a pity, since Arkin picked so badly for some years that he lost whatever box-office standing he had had.

These are the films concerned; *Simon* (80), written and directed by Marshall Brickman (former collaborator of Woody Allen), as a professor brainwashed into believing he is an extra-terrestrial; *Improper Channels* (81), made in Canada, as an architect – a put upon little man, separated from his wife and suspected of child abuse after his cute little daughter has been hospitalized; and *Chu Chu and the Philly Flash*, as a bum, involved with Carol Burnett and some government documents. One of the writers of the second of these was Arkin's son Adam, who played a role in the third picture – and *that* was written by Barbara Dana, who is the second Mrs Alan Arkin. Dad guested when Adam starred in a silly horror spoof directed by Larry Cohen, *Full Moon High*. In 1982 he appeared in 'Le Malade Imaginaire' in Washington, then took off for Australis to star in *The Return of Captain Invincible* (83), as a comic-book hero, now a drunk in Sydney, who is restored to his former glory – and New York – to amusingly right some wrongs. After *A Matter of Principle*, for pay-cable, he was in Montreal playing a small-time gangster, father to James Woods in *Joshua Then and Now* (85), based on an autobiographical novel by Mordecai Richler. Arkin's performance brought him a Best Supporting Actor award from the Canadian Academy. But few people liked either of the next two: *Bad Medicine*, in which he was the disciplinarian head of a banana republic medical school attended by Steve Guttenberg (because no one at home would take him); and *Big Trouble*, a reteaming with Peter Falk, directed by Falk's friend John Cassavetes. The co-producers had their names taken off the credits after some test screenings.

His subsequent credits have been in TV (though he was at one point announced for a British picture, *Beyond Therapy*): *A Deadly Business*, a movie for CBS; *Escape from Sobibor* (87), as the leader of those escaping from a Jewish concentration camp – and his most distinguished movie in years; and 'Harry', starring in this ABC sitcom as the wheeler-dealer head of purchasing for a hospital. *Necessary Parties* (88) – one of PBS's 'Wonderworks' – was a family affair, with Arkin and his wife Barbara Dana playing divorcing parents; she co-scripted from her own book, and their sons Adam and Anthony were also in it. Then Arkin was in *Coup de Ville* (89).

ARLETTY

There is, she herself thinks, only one other screen role comparable and that is the one played by Dietrich in *The Blue Angel*. This role, Arletty's role, is not one she sought. It was written for her: Garance in *Les Enfants du Paradis*, first discovered modelling a side-show Beauty with a hand-mirror in a revolving barrel, and subsequently sought, desired and loved by four very different men – Lacenaire (Marcel Herrand), blackmailer, receiver, pickpocket, sexually ambiguous; Frédérick-Lemaître (Pierre Brasseur), master actor, charlatan, egoist, who sleeps with her but regards her more as a *copine*; Baptiste (Jean-Louis Barrault), the whey-faced, timid mime of the Funambules, who loves her to the exclusion of wife and work; and Métray (Louis Salou), the aristocrat who keeps her but cannot get an admission of love. The part, like that in *The Blue Angel*, requires no ordinary actress; in Arletty-Garance the screen found one of its few goddesses, as mysterious as Garbo. Arletty discounts the analogy: 'Dans notre métier, qu'on ne me parle pas de mystère, je n'admire pas ça du tout, c'est la bêtise, tout ça. . . . Garbo? Oui, c'est Metro-Goldwyn-Mayer qui a trouvé ça. . . .' But when you come to analyse it, you do not get much beyond physical description – the deep-black eyes, slightly hooded, the alabaster skin and the jet-black hair drawn straight back; the voice, thin and grating, with its accent *du faubourg*, raucous in laughter; the gentle movement, like a flower. Her gaze is half-mocking (of course), knowledgeable, never ardent, never desperate. She knows too much.

She was born Léonie Bathiat in Courbevoie (Seine) in 1898, the daughter of a miner. When he was killed (accidentally) in 1916 she quit studying shorthand/typing and went to work in a munitions factory, living with her mother in extreme poverty till she met a foreigner who promised to keep her. Before the war was over she was working as a mannequin – for Poiret – and posing for painters – Matisse, among others. By chance she met Paul Guillaume the art-dealer, who thought she should be on the stage and introduced her to Armand Berthez, manager of the Capucines. Berthez changed her name to 'Arlette' and then they changed the final 'e' to 'y' to make it sound more English. She was to make the new name famous in the series of caustic revues written by Rip at the Capucines. After seeing one of them, 'Si Que Je Serais Roi' (22), Colette said: 'Cette Lavallière un peu gouape fait de nous ce qu'elle veut. Rein de plus dangereux que ce regard chaviré et sa grâce à peine dessaoulée.' Arletty had already appeared in 'L'École des Cocottes' (20), in a small role, a comedy about the training of a courtesan, and during the next decade she occasionally left the Capucines to play in comedies and operettes: 'Mon Gosse de Père' (25), 'Knock-Out' (27) and 'Yes' (28).

She made her film début in *Un Chien qui Rapporte* (31), directed by Jean Choux, a vaudeville piece about a dog, in the leading role. It was not at all a success, so she decided to do what she had done on the stage – to start at the bottom and work her way up. The films were pretty low, too, a series of very stagey comedies: *Mais n' te Promène donc pas Toute Nue*, a version of Feydeau directed by Léo Joannon; *Enlevez-moi* (32) starring Roger Tréville, another doggie piece; two more Feydeaus, *Un Fil à la Patte* with Robert Burnier and *Feue la Mère de Madame* with René Lefèvre. In Germany she made *La Belle Aventure* with Käthe von Nagy, who also starred in the simultaneous German version; then made *Une Idée Folle* (33), directed by Max de Vaucorbeil, with Lucien Baroux; and *Un Soir de Réveillon*, directed by Karel Anton, with Henry Garat. Her parts were so small that if you blinked you might have missed her, but playwright Yves Mirande, with whom she had worked on the stage, gave her a good part in his *Je te Confie ma Femme*, a comedy about a wife loaned to her lover by her husband: she was a tart employed to impersonate the wife when hubby returns. (During most of her career she played tarts – but then, it often seemed, so did most French actresses.)

On the stage she played Sacha Guitry's wife in 'O Mon Bel Inconnu', with Jacqueline Delubac, who became Mme Guitry. Guitry was very fond of Arletty (once, in the 40s, between marriages, he proposed to her) and later she would appear in his films. At this time she was in *Le Voyage de Monsieur Perrichon* (34), a version of Labiche's classic comedy with Alerme as Perrichon. In Berlin she did the French version of *Walzerkrieg*, called *La Guerre des Valses* (35) starring Fernand Gravey and Madeleine Ozeray; but she was unhappy under director Ludwig Berger (who later made *Trois Valses* with Yvonne Printemps). Jacques Feyder engaged her for *Pension Mimosas*, set on the Côte d'Azur, a pleasant fable about a gambler saved from himself by godmother Françoise Rosay (Feyder's wife); Arletty played a lady parachutist called Parasol. She was less felicitously involved in *La Fille de Madame Angot* starring André Baugé, from the operette set during the Directoire; *L'École des Cocottes* with Raimu; Raymond Bernard's *Amants et Voleurs* with Michel Simon, Florelle and Pierre Blanchar; and *Le Vertige* with Henri Rollan, probably the least known of France's character actors.

La Garçonne (36), again with Rollan, was adapted from a novel which had scandalized the country, about a woman (Marie Bell) who wanted to live like a man – and had sexual troubles on the side: it was a mild thing, but was banned outright in Britain. Arletty played one of Bell's friends. She was now playing second leads, the Other Woman or the heroine's friend: *Un Mari Rêvé* with Pierre Brasseur; Marc Allégret's *Aventure à Paris* with Jules Berry and Lucien Baroux. She did a bit part in Guitry's *Faisons un Rêve*, to please him, and took a small part in *Messieurs les Ronds-de-Cuir*, starring Simon, a turn-of-the-century stage farce about bureaucracy. She had continued to work in revue despite offers from Jouvet, Dullin, among others; 1936, however, saw her in what she considered her real début in legit, 'L'École des Veuves' at the ABC, a sketch that Cocteau had written for her. Later that year she, Michel Simon and Victor Boucher were the stars of 'Fric-Frac', an astonishing play to have been written by the director of the Comédie-Française (Édouard Bourdet), a study of the *gens du milieu* written mostly in their argot.

Guitry asked her to do a small role – the Queen of Ethiopia, in blackface – in his celebration of the English coronation, *Les Perles de la Couronne* (37), a series of sketches involving François Ier (Guitry), Henry VIII (Lyn Harding), Bonaparte (Jean-Louis Barrault) and other royals. She was very amusing; and she also livened up *Aloha le Chant des Îles*, as the film star wife of an explorer (Jean Murat) who falls for a British aristocrat (Danièle Parola). She and Michel Simon were friends of Barrault and Jeanne Aubert in *Mirages*, a romance with a music-hall setting; and she was a maid and Guitry a valet, the title-role, in *Désiré*, a theatrical comedy about servant and mistress. On the stage she was in 'Cavalier Seul' and then in Maurice Cloche's charming version of Daudet's *Le Petit Chose* (38), considered to be the best romantic film yet made in France,

Jean Gabin and Arletty in Le Jour se Lève *(39), one of the great, haunting French movies of the immediate pre-war period.*

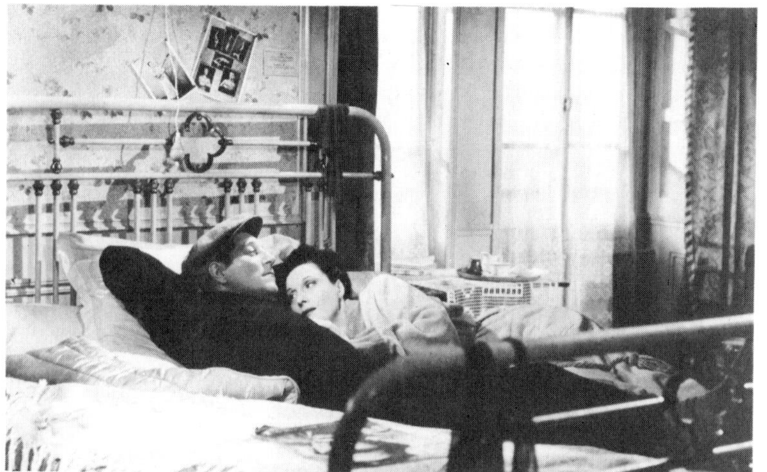

as a Second Empire courtesan loved by Robert Lynen, in the title-role. *La Chaleur du Sein* was yet another filmed play – by Jean Boyer of a comedy by André Birabeau – with Arletty as one of three step-mothers tending a would-be suicide while father (Michel Simon) is away.

She had met Marcel Carné when he was Feyder's assistant and for some time he had been looking for the right role for her: in *Hôtel du Nord* he found it, written by Henri Jeanson and Jean Aurenche, a study of some derelicts in a shabby Paris hotel, including Annabella and Jean-Pierre Aumont. Arletty was a whore living with Jouvet, full of fun and spirit but aware of her status, longing for something better, not quite resigned – a *poule* written with more depth than her previous ones, and played that way. Carné gave her a similar part, written this time by Jacques Prévert, in *Le Jour se Lève* (39), sad and sensual, old and girl-like, instantly attracted to both a kind stranger (Jean Gabin) and her 'protector' Jules Berry.

A film was made (by Claude Autant-Lara, though credited to Maurice Lehmann) of *Fric-Frac*, so Arletty remained On the Game, with Fernandel replacing Boucher as her pimp. Simon had his stage role; and he was in *Circonstances Atténuantes*, as a judge forced by a breakdown to stay in a hotel full of crooks – one of whom was Arletty, as a whore called Marie-qu'a-d'ca. The film was made in only two weeks and was another big success for both of them. She was now (at last) a movie star of the front rank and was signed for what was to be (like others before it) the first French film in Technicolor, *Madame Sans-Gêne*; but the war aborted this, as well as Carné's *École Communale*, for which she was also scheduled. Because of the war, too, *Tempête sur Paris* (40) was released as *Tempête*, a screenplay by André Cayatte based loosely on Balzac, in which she was an agent-provocateur/singer, accoutred like Dietrich in feathers and garters. Von Stroheim was in the film, but most of her scenes were with Dalio.

For propaganda reasons she and Simon toured – Brussels, Geneva – in 'Fric-Frac'; and when the Germans occupied Paris she did not work. She claimed to be lazy and uninterested in working unless the script was good (her poor films, she said, were made when she needed money). But Roger Richebé claimed her for *Madame Sans-Gêne* (41), not now in colour, from Sardou's play about the washerwoman who becomes the mistress of Napoleon (Albert Dieudonné, who had played that part in Abel Gance's Silent *Napoléon*). Wrote Cocteau of her performance: 'S'il fallait incarner les mystères de Paris à tous les étages, depuis les grandes dames de Balzac jusqu'aux larves d'Eugène Sue, s'il fallait essayer de rendre visibles à un étranger les contrastes, les détresses, le luxe, la misère, la malice et le crime de notre ville, je désignerais Mlle Arletty.' Mirande then engaged her again for *La Femme que J'ai le Plus Aimée* (42), a sketch-film where she and Noël-Noël had the best sequence. Then there were two filmed plays, *Boléro* with André Luguet and *L'Amant de Bornéo* with Jean Tissier.

Carné and Prévert collaborated again on *Les Visiteurs du Soir*, with Arletty and Alain Cuny in the title-roles, sent by the Devil (Jules Berry) to disturb the lives of some medieval people. Considered a masterpiece at the time, it has dated, curiously, more grievously than the Carné-Prévert contemporary subjects and is most notable for the work of Berry and of Arletty, enslaver of men mortal and immortal. After returning to the stage, in 'Voulez-Vous Jouer avec Môa?' (43), she began work on *Les Enfants du Paradis* (45), Carné-Prévert again, a long film made with difficulty during the last days of the German occupation. It ran an unprecedented nine months in Paris and was worldwide the most successful French film up to that time, to the French cinema what *Gone With the Wind* is to the American, the apotheosis of romantic film-making. (There are other similarities: both were very long, both recreated a vanished epoch – in this case the boulevards of the time of Louis-Philippe – and both centred on a woman to whom all men paid court.) Critically, it was the more highly regarded and, now that the style of both films is extinct, it is, because of the maturity of its dialogue, the more persuasive.

Arletty in the role for which most people remember her: as the courtesan Garance in Marcel Carné's Les Enfants du Paradis *(45). With her is Jean-Louis Barrault.*

According to journalist Sam White, Arletty was an exception among French actresses in not having a wealthy 'protector', but during the war years she fell deeply in love with a German officer. In 1944 she heard that the tribunal in Algiers had condemned her to death. After the Liberation she was arrested for collaboration and spent two months in gaol, followed by more than a year under surveillance. It was announced that she would return to films in *Contre-Enquête*, but the part went to Jany Holt; then she began *La Fleur de l'Age* for Carné and Prévert, with Paul Meurisse and Serge Reggiani – but that was abandoned after two months due to poor weather and the money running out (by the time they could start again, the many child actors had grown too much). The following year, 1948, she started *Madame et ses Cowboys* or *Buffalo Bill et la Bergère*, but that also was unfinished – for reasons she would not discuss. She finally returned in a thriller that was more puzzling than intended, *Portrait d'un Assassin* (49), as Pierre Brasseur's wife in a cast also including Erich von Stroheim, Dalio, Jules Berry and Maria Montez. Around the same time she scored a big success as Blanche in 'Un Tramway Nommé Désir' adapted by Cocteau. In 1950 she appeared in a revue at the Empire and in 1952 was in Marcel Archard's 'Les Compagnons de la Marjolaine', with Melina Mercouri.

Few of her subsequent films left France: *L'Amour Madame* (52), as herself ('dynamic and appealing in a roisterous take-off' – 'Variety') in a sleeping-car with François Périer; *Gibier de Potence*, a psychological drama with Georges Marchal; *Le Père de Mademoiselle* (53), a comedy where she – as an actress – changed places with her secretary to fool the girl's father; and *Le Grand Jeu* (54) with Gina Lollobrigida, in Françoise Rosay's old part (she did not believe in remakes and did it because she needed money). Carné directed *L'Air de Paris* – she was Gabin's wife – but the air was hardly fresh and it was not shown abroad. *Huis-Clos* (55) was – Jacqueline Audrey's film version of Sartre's theory that hell is other people. Arletty was Inez the lesbian, scathing and taunting, and horribly fascinating. There was *Mon Curé chez les Pauvres* (56), an outdated tale with Yves Deniaud, and *Vacances Explosives* (57) with Andrex. Then *Le Passager Clandestin* (58), a small part, again as a whore – in a brothel with Martine Carol: a weird Franco-Australian co-production from a story by Simenon, filmed in the South Seas (she did it for the trip) and with Roger Livesey, Reggiani and Karkheinz Böhm also in the cast.

On stage she starred in another play by Tennessee Williams, 'La Descente d'Orphée', but in films she was now a supporting actress: *Et ta Sœur?*, a comedy with Pierre Fresnay; *Maxime*, as a retired courtesan, with Michèle Morgan and Charles Boyer; *Drôle de Dimanche* with Danielle Darrieux; *La Gamberge* (61), a comedy with Jean-Pierre Cassel, as his mother; and *Les Petits Matins*, the adventures of a girl hitchhiker (Agathe Aems), who met not only Arletty, but a host of names from past movies – Noël-Noël, Brasseur, Gravey, Daniel Gélin, Jean-Claude Brialy, Gilbert Bécaud, Francis Blanche, Lino Ventura and Pierre Mondy. After playing a princess in *La Loi des Hommes* (62), a detective story in which Micheline Presle was a reporter, she was one of the many names in *The Longest Day*.

She had become almost blind (due to an accident with eye-drops). Nevertheless, she worked on stage in 'L'Étouffe-Chrétien' (61) and 'L'Otage' (62); and accepted parts in films that required little movement (her parts she learnt by tape-recorder): *Tempo di Roma* (63) with Charles Aznavour and *Le Voyage à Biarritz* with Fernandel, as a bourgeois couple who were definitely not older versions of the parts they had played in *Fric-Frac*. But a part for her in *Du Mouron pour les Petits Oiseaux* was taken on by Suzy Declair.

Apart from revivals of her best films (38–45) she has been lost to British and American audiences. She had had offers from abroad and might have had an international career had she been willing to leave Paris: 'Sans Paris, je suis très malheureuse. Etre loin de Paris, pour moi c'est l'exil.' Oriana Fallaci, who interviewed hr in 1963, found her blind and 'also the loneliest woman I have ever met'. She wrote too: 'cynical, atheist, brave Arletty'. Some French artists had expressed concern about her condition, and Jean-Claude Brialy wanted her for his second film as a director, *Les Volets Fermés* (72), as a madam, but Marie Bell played the role when it was found impossible to use her.

A studio portrait of Arletty taken in the early 60s, not long before her sad blindness caused her to retire.

Richard Attenborough

Richard Attenborough's survival in the perilous world of the British cinema has been an admirable achievement. He has done it, too, on a modest talent – no glamorous film star he, no rugged good looks, no aura, no dash; just a conscientious lightweight actor, best in character-roles and in them best in the coward parts in which he was once type-cast. He has simply battled on, head unbowed after some of the most bloody films ever made.

He was born in Cambridge in 1923 and educated in Leicester, where his father was head of the University College. He won a scholarship to RADA and while there was so striking that he was taken on by Al Parker, at that time perhaps the biggest agent in London. He made his first professional appearance at the Intimate, Palmers Green, in 'Ah Wilderness!' (41) and was auditioned by Noël Coward for a good cameo role in *In Which We Serve* (42) and got it – the stoker who loses his nerve under fire (in films, he was almost always below decks). He had another small part in *Schweik's New Adventures* (43), and a rather bigger one in *The Hundred Pound Window* (44), a slight wartime drama with David Farrer and Anne Crawford. On the stage he had his first taste of success playing Leo in 'The Little Foxes' (42), but really made his name as Pinkie in an adaptation of Graham Greene's 'Brighton Rock' (43). The run over, he joined the RAF, whose Film Unit put him into a propaganda training film, *Journey Together* (45), directed by John Boulting. The war over, the Boultings signed Attenborough to a personal contract.

He was loaned out for small roles in *A Matter of Life and Death* (46) and *School for Secrets*; and for his first star roles – in *The Man Within* (47), as another blubbery coward, with Michael Redgrave, and *Dancing with Crime*, a programmer about black marketeers, with Sheila Sim (his wife; they married in 1944; she retired in the early 50s). The Boultings then filmed *Brighton Rock* and Attenborough repeated as the vicious young

Richard Attenborough as Pinkie, the memorable teenage thug of Graham Green's 'Brighton Rock'. The film was made in 1947.

gang-leader – ultimately cowardly: 'a performance of scarifying nervous tension' (Dilys Powell). He was a crook again in *London Belongs to Me* (48), a studio-bound version of Norman Collins's Priestleyesque bestseller. For the Boultings he was a schoolboy – sent from a grammar to a public school as an experiment, *The Guinea Pig* (49), supposedly based on a topical problem (it was adapted from a West End play). It must be the most specious of all Attenborough's films, but could be challenged by the next two: *The Lost People*, about displaced persons, and *Boys in Brown* (50), about Borstal boys. A mite more encouraging would be *Morning Departure*, an up-periscope down-periscope drama with John Mills and one of the year's biggest hits in Britain.

Attenborough's impact on the British public up to this point might best be described as nil. It was hardly a surprise when he took a supporting role, as the chum of romantic lead Herbert Lom in *Hell is Sold Out* (51), with Mai Zetterling, an inept comedy. He guested in *The Magic Box*. With slightly more effect he had returned to the stage, in 'The Way Back' (49) and a long-running comedy, 'To Dorothy a Son' (50). He played an ordinary seaman in *The Gift Horse* (52), with Trevor Howard, and then had the lead in a hopeless minor comedy, *Father's Doing Fine*, with such starlets of the time as Virginia McKenna and Mary Germaine. He did two plays in a row, the second of which was Agatha Christie's 'The Mousetrap', starting on its inexplicable long career. He stayed with it two years, during which time he did one film, *The Eight o'Clock Walk* (54), as a taxi-driver on trial for murder. He was a nasty, cocky little smuggler in *The Ship That Died of Shame* (55).

But now, in the middle of the decade, Attenborough's career took impetus. The Boultings put him into *Private's Progress* (56), one of Britain's better attempts at service comedy. Ian Carmichael was the nervous recruit and Attenborough, supporting, an old lag. This was the best indication yet that his forte might be character acting; moreover, it was the first really successful film he had been in since his first, and the first film since then to have any wide distribution overseas. He was in a second successful service comedy, *The Baby and the Battleship*, with John Mills, and then in another comedy with Carmichael, *Brothers in Law* (57), as a know-it-all young lawyer. The Boultings again produced and directed, the second of their 'satirical' looks at British institutions. Attenborough did his last stage work to date – 'Double Image' in 1956, 'The Rape of the Belt' in 1957 – and began to accept the many offers he was now getting: *The Scamp*, a minor melodrama, as a schoolteacher who adopts the title-character, Colin Petersen; and *Dunkirk* (58), another war film with John Mills, one of the fruits of the brief and unhappy liaison between Ealing and MGM. Attenborough was not in uniform this time, but a garage-man who answered the country's call with his own small boat.

He was much more interested in *The Man Upstairs*, where he was trapped in a situation very much like that of Gabin in *Le Jour se Lève*; a modest film, modestly liked – and no one went to see it. But it strengthened his desire to produce his own pictures – to avoid, perhaps, pictures like this batch: *Sea of Sand*, a war film whose cast included Dermot Walsh as 'guest star'; *Danger Within* (59), a POW drama, promoted to (army) captain; *I'm All Right Jack*, the Boultings' look at the trade unions, as a shady businessman; *Jet Storm*, a cliché-ridden drama about a bomb on board, with Attenborough the possessor of the bomb, frightening Stanley Baker, Diane Cilento, Mai Zettling and others; and *S.O.S. Pacific*, another idiot melodrama, as the vicious blackmailing villain.

He moved into production with Bryan Forbes, scriptwriter and actor, when British Lion agreed to back *The Angry Silence* (60), a story of a man (Attenborough) ostracized after a factory strike. It reflected the new honesty and awareness just introduced into British films by *Room at the Top* and *Look Back in Anger*, but the critics found it difficult to be more than lukewarm. Despite its box-office failure, it did Attenborough's reputation a power of good. He and Forbes were able to form their own company, Beaver, for whom Forbes made *Whistle Down the Wind* and *The L-Shaped Room*; meanwhile, Forbes wrote, and they both appeared in, *The League of Gentlemen*, along with Jack Hawkins, Nigel Patrick and others – all shady ex-officers planning a robbery. Attenborough did a guest appearance in *Only Two Can Play* (61), very funny as a smoothie literary gent, and had a similarly brief role in the overheated *All Night Long* (62), as a dilettante jazz patron. He was type-cast again in *The Dock Brief*, as a seedy little murderer, and was back in uniform, as the Group Captain, in *The Great Escape* (63), his first American assignment, with Steve McQueen.

With Forbes again, and for Beaver, he did *Séance on a Wet Afternoon* (64), as a weak little husband involved by his wife (Kim Stanley) in a child kidnapping; she played a medium, and medium might also describe the film (and low its box-office performance). He was weak again as a vain little art-dealer in *The Third Street*, a rotten thriller starring Stephen Boyd and Jack Hawkins; but transformed himself into a martinet sergeant-major in *Guns at Batasi*. For this and for *Séance* the BFA voted him Best British Actor: the sort of conscious, conscientious character acting which has *au fond* no character in it. Hollywood, however, offered him good character parts – and second-billed in both instances to the star: *The Flight of the Phoenix* (65), as James Stewart's nerve-shattered navigator; and *The Sand Pebbles* (66), as Steve McQueen's best buddy. He did a successful cameo – and sang one song – as a showman in *Doctor Doolittle* (67), but back home was involved in two of the year's flop comedies, *The Bliss of Mrs Blossom* (68), as Shirley MacLaine's bra-manufacturing husband, and *Only When I Larf*, as a master-crook with a penchant for impersonation.

The latter was written and co-produced by Len Deighton, who became the producer of Attenborough's first project as a director, *Oh What a Lovely War!* (69) – only in the event he had his name removed from the credits. Attenborough had long spoken of retreating behind the camera and had angled for some years to get backing for a film on Gandhi; in the end he was offered this screen adaptation of Joan Littlewood's 'revue' – a moving indictment of World War I told in terms of a pierrot show. From a risky commercial venture it became a success – due in part to the illustrious names he had persuaded to appear in it – which might suggest a future at least as a diplomat, if not as a director, for the film was in truth a chocolate-box travesty of the original, as unmoving as that had been moving. In the US the press did not agree with (the majority of) their British colleagues and the film quietly disappeared.

He returned to acting: *David Copperfield* (70), as Laurence Olivier's cringing, fawning assistant; *The Magic Christian*, guesting, as an Oxford coach; *The Last Grenade*, an adventure tale with Alex Cord, as British commander in Hong Kong; *A Severed Head* (71), with

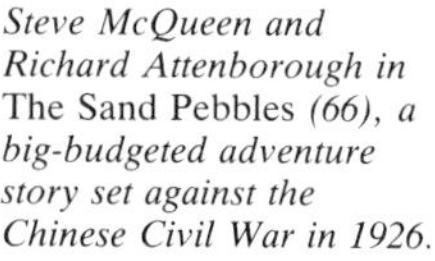

Steve McQueen and Richard Attenborough in The Sand Pebbles *(66), a big-budgeted adventure story set against the Chinese Civil War in 1926.*

Lee Remick, as a smoothie psychiatrist; and *Loot*, again with Remick, as a comic police inspector, in that good film version of Joe Orton's play. Unlike a disastrous earlier effort to film Orton (*Entertaining Mr Sloane*), this cast and crew had the style for the thing – with the exception of Attenborough, too self-consciously 'funny'. His calculation, his willingness to please, always get between him and the character; he tried too hard. He should not have tried at all with *10 Rillington Place*, a totally unnecessary resurrection of John Christie, mass-murderer of the early 50s – for one thing, because he had played these squalid killers too often before and for another, because the film was hysterical. After that, he returned to direction; *Young Winston* (72), which failed.

So it was back to acting – in supporting roles in four of the year's worst films: *Ten Little Indians* (75), a re-hash of Agatha Christie which was hardly seen; *Brannigan*, as a Scotland Yard chief helping John Wayne in London; Otto Preminger's *Rosebud*, as an English fanatic wanting to destroy Israel and Peter O'Toole; and *Conduct Unbecoming*, as the real villain of the piece in this stagey tale of army life. However, all four seemed masterpieces beside *A Bridge Too Far* (77), which he directed for Joe Levine, an all-star account of the Battle of Arnhem which managed to beat *Oh What a Lovely War!* in the manner of pretension and the matter of boring its audience. He redeemed himself partly by participating in *Shatranj Ke Khilari*/*The Chess Players*, the first film made in Hindi (and English) by the great Bengali director, Satjayit Ray: but his performance as a Victorian officer was banal. Seemingly unperturbed by the reception of his last film for him, Levine engaged him to direct *Magic* (78), which received even worse notices than that. Returning solely to performing, he was in *The Human Factor* (79), Otto Preminger's version of Graham Greene's novel. He has since directed *Gandhi* (82), which won several Oscars, including Best Picture and Best Director, *A Chorus Line* (85) and *Cry Freedom!* (87), perhaps the best – certainly the most honorable – film with which he has been associated.

Lauren Bacall

'Slinky! Sultry! Sensational!' was how Lauren Bacall came to the screen, along with press releases as to how her husky voice had been developed by making her shout across a canyon for six months. But she was not a joke at all. James Agee described her: '[she] has cinema personality to burn, and she burns both ends against an unusually little middle. Her personality is compounded partly of percolated Davis, Garbo, West, Dietrich, Harlow and Glenda Farrell, but more than enough of it is completely new to the screen. She has a javelinlike vitality, a born dancer's eloquence in movement, a fierce female shrewdness and a special sweet-sourness. With these faculties, plus a stone-crushing self-confidence and a trombone voice, she manages to get across the toughest girl a piously regenerate Hollywood has dreamed of in a long while. . . . She does a wickedly good job of sizing up male prospects in a low bar, growls a *louche* song more suggestively than anyone in cinema has dared since Mae West.'

She was born (Betty Pepske – she hates the name Hollywood gave her) in New York City in 1924 and was brought up by a divorced mother, who had her study dancing and acting and enrolled her at the AADA – which she quit after one term. She was an usherette briefly, then got a couple of minor stage jobs and – she was strikingly handsome – several modelling assignments. One 'Harper's Bazaar' cover was seen by Howard Hawks, who tested her and signed her to a seven-year contract, 32 weeks a year. (Columbia asked her to be the 'Harper's Bazaar' girl in *Cover Girl*, but she knew his was likely to provide a better future.) He showed the test to Warners – who promptly bought half her contract – and trained her for a year. While coaching her, Hawks began to see her potential more clearly, and when he and Warners cast her opposite Humphrey Bogart in *To Have and Have Not* (44) he moulded her into a younger, a female Bogart – though he let her often make her own decisions. She was even more cynical than Bogie and more coolly independent: to his second kiss she responds 'It's even better when you help.' The sexual antagonism between them worked sufficiently to carry this mangled version of Hemingway to success; and they married the following year. Warners were so pleased with her that they bought the other half of her contract from Hawks and raised her weekly pay from $550 to $1,000, the start of a new seven-year contract, to go to $1,250 in the second year and thence to $1,500 with $500 weekly annual increases to a ceiling of $3,500. She was to be paid 52 weeks a year instead of the usual 42, but they believed she was a strong actress who should not be overexposed; the sales force was calling for a reteaming with Bogart and indeed one was in the can, but release was delayed till after the next one, since it was more topical and Jack Warner thought her better in it.

Confidential Agent (45) was in fact set in pre-war Britain, with Bacall as a local girl who

Bogart and Bacall in The Big Sleep *(46). She finds the door locked but he assures her it was not intentional. 'Try it some time' she offers. 'Bogart and Bacall will be all washed up if they make any more like this one' said one showman ('What The Picture Did For Me') to the 'Motion Picture Herald' in 1947.*

aids Spanish Republican Charles Boyer. The 'New York Times' thought her performance 'close to becoming an unmitigated bore. . . . Miss Bacall starts out brusque and surly, obtuse and emotionally cold – and she ends up that way, with nary a flicker of responsiveness or "give" in between.' It is curious that Warners should have preferred that to Hawks's *The Big Sleep* (46), the one with Bogart; the magic between them worked again, he as a private eye and she as a wealthy, insolent divorcée. She did two more with him, *Dark Passage* (47) and *Key Largo* (48), but these were roles which any competent actress might have played. She was a strongly individual heroine, but clearly less effective than before. Meanwhile, Hollywood had proliferated with imitators, from the variable Lizabeth Scott downwards. Encouraged by Bogart – who wanted her to be as independent of Warners as he now was – she quarrelled frequently with the studio over roles; but not, alas, over those in *Young Man with a Horn* (50) and *Bright Leaf*, both old favourites. In the former, she was the wealthy socialite who seduces Kirk Douglas from his music and Doris Day; in the second, the madam who comforts Gary Cooper on excursions from wife Patricia Neal. The sixth suspension in six years was over the co-starring role with Errol Flynn in *Rocky Mountain* (Patrice Wymore – his wife – played it); then she bought herself out of her contract, just a few months before Warners dropped many players in a panic at the threat from TV.

She signed a long-term contract with 20th, but made only two films for them over a two-year period; after a long absence, *How To Marry a Millionaire* (53), as a gold-digger, and *A Woman's World* (54), as the bored wife of executive Fred MacMurray. Not surprisingly, she proved to be a stylish light comedienne, incisive and elegant, a shrewd woman-about-town who knows the answers before the questions are asked. In the former she stole scenes from Marilyn Monroe and Betty Grable; in the latter there was little competition from June Allyson or Arlene Dahl. Changing mood again, she embarked on a quiet romance with Richard Widmark in *The*

Three memorable Hollywood ladies modelling in a sequence from How To Marry a Millionaire *(53): Marilyn Monroe had top-billing and the best role; Betty Grable was second-billed and had the biggest role; but it was, of the three of them, only Lauren Bacall who had the style for this sort of comedy.*

Cobweb (55) at MGM, the only good 'serious' film she made – but not a success. It would be more difficult to divine her motives in taking on conventional parts in either *Blood Alley*, a mediocre John Wayne vehicle, or *Written on the Wind* (56), a lurid melodrama with Rock Hudson, especially as the Wayne film was a silly anti-Red drama, and Bogart and Bacall were considered to be on Hollywood's Left. Still, Wayne admired her and made one of his rare comments on a co-star: 'One of the smartest of all Hollywood's tempting women. Betty never flaunts her loveliness, nor her intellect. A man in her presence is conscious only of her charm.'

When Grace Kelly departed for Monaco, MGM substituted Bacall in *Designing Woman* (57), a comedy about spouses with different interests, with Gregory Peck – an actor whom Bogart particularly despised. Bogart died while she was completing it and working to forget (she had been, by all accounts, a particularly devoted wife) might explain her acceptance of *The Gift of Love* (58) at 20th, with Robert Stack. That one was a two-time loser, having failed 10 years earlier as *Sentimental Journey* with Maureen O'Hara. She went to Britain to play another action-tale heroine in *North West Frontier* (59), with Kenneth More, and then had a Broadway success in 'Goodbye Charlie'. In 1961 she married Jason Robards Jr (they were divorced in 1969). Films were not too kind: the unsuccessful *Shock Treatment* (64), as a mixed-up psychiatrist; *Sex and the Single Girl* (65), as Henry Fonda's quarrelsome wife; and *Harper* (66), with Paul Newman, as the enigmatic wealthy woman. That film had some in-jokes – Newman was a Bogart-like private-eye – but Bacall's striking apparition was warmly welcomed for its own sake. Despite the infrequency of her appearances she had, like all strong players, kept her hold.

There was another stage role and in 'Cactus Flower' (67) for a couple of years she was, literally, the toast of Broadway; and she was again when she did the musical version of *All About Eve* called 'Applause!' (70). She said at this time: 'Bogie always told me not to relive the past. . . . Sometimes I've thought that if the public didn't stop taking these trips down Memory Lane about me, I was going to lose my mind. . . . Being a widow isn't exactly a profession. I've had thirteen years of bad luck, and I mean desperately bad luck. But now I feel the cycle of life is changing. This musical is like a second chance, as if my life is beginning again.' She played it in London two years later, and filmed it there for American TV; and in England she was one of the several stars suspected of *Murder on the Orient Express* (74). Opposite John Wayne in *The Shootist* (76) she was his landlady, their friendship ripening as the film progressed. A TV movie, *Perfect Gentlemen* (78), co-starred her with Sandy Dennis; and a memoir, 'By Myself', found its way to the bestseller lists and redirected Hollywood attention to her: *Health* (80), as an 80-year-old food expert, with Carol Burnett and James Garner; and *The Fan* (81), as a Broadway star menaced by a psychotic admirer. Bacall's own particular glitter could not hide the fact that the piece was unworthy of her. She would like to work more, she has said, but she turns down much: 'I've been sent an average of two or three plays a year lately – one worse than the other. They're awful. It's all well and good to do things for money if occasionally you have to, but not a film that's going to come back to haunt you. And certainly not a play that you have to do eight times a week. I couldn't bear it.'

She returned to Broadway in 1981 in 'Woman of the Year', a musical based on the Tracy-Hepburn film, for a long run – and a Tony Award. In 1985 she played 'Sweet Bird of Youth' in London, subsequently taking it to Australia and the West Coast. It was not, frankly, one of her finest moments, for she totally lacked the vulnerability essential to the role. Films then again beckoned: an Agatha Christie thriller, *Appointment with Death* (87), directed by Michael Winner; *Mr North* (88), directed by Danny Huston after his father John died, as a boarding-house keeper; *The Tree of Hands* (89) in Britain, from a novel by Ruth Rendell; and *The Actor*, made in France, with Anthony Quinn.

ANNE BANCROFT

Hollywood, in the fallow 60s, was suddenly blessed with a group of talented ladies in their middle years, actresses who literally bridged the gap between the new ingénues and the older stars like Davis and Hepburn. Most of them had made their reputations in the theatre and were just as experienced in TV – Geraldine Page, Julie Harris, Kim Stanley (though the last has made only a few films because she dislikes the medium). But not all: Anne Bancroft, like Patricia Neal, was a Hollywood failure who went away and returned a star.

Born in the Bronx in 1931 of Italian parentage, she wanted to act professionally after the lead in a high school play and studied at the AADA. One of the teachers there arranged a TV audition and she made her pro debut, on TV, in an adaptation of Turgenev's 'Torrents of Spring'. She made a small impact in TV under the name of Anne Marno, particularly in 'The Goldbergs'. A 20th scout saw her; she was tested and signed to a contract. 20th tried her out as Richard Widmark's girlfriend, a cabaret singer, in *Don't Bother to Knock* (52). She appeared only at the beginning and end (the rest was Marilyn Monroe) but created a sympathetic impression – though girls who could play slightly tarnished singers were 10 a penny in Hollywood at the time. She had a bit – the false heroine – in a Cornel Wilde action picture, *Treasure of the Golden Condor* (53), and then a good part in *Tonight We Sing*, which purported to celebrate the achievements of impresario Sol Hurok (David Wayne) – as his wife. Despite guest appearances (Toumanova as Pavlova, Pinza as Chaliapin) it did nothing for the cause of Serious Music on the Screen and Bancroft's own cause was not furthered by it nor by another of specialized interest, *The Kid from Left Field* with Dan Dailey. There was a part in *Demetrius and the Gladiators* (54), the horrendous sequel to *The Robe*, and then another lead, as a trapeze artist, in *Gorilla at Large*, a penny-pinching thriller in 3-D (it came at the end of the craze and was mostly shown flat). She played a young Civil War widow in *The Raid* opposite Van Heflin, but when her next option came up, 20th did not renew it.

Most of these movies, and the batch that followed, went unnoticed by major critics, but the specialized and trade press gave Bancroft reviews that varied between the warm and the respectable. She was 'excellent' said the 'MFB', as a Mexican in *A Life in the Balance* (55), which 20th asked her back to make; and she did not have difficulty getting work as a freelance. In *New York Confidential* she was Broderick Crawford's daughter and, said the ads, 'the teen-age problem all rolled into one'; in *The Naked Street* she was the sister on whom Anthony Quinn is fixated (in the way that screen gangsters have); in *The Last Frontier* the Colonel's lady and then widow, marrying Sgt Victor Mature at the end; and in *Nightfall* (56) a model who takes up with fugitive Aldo Ray. Then she was revealed as a murderess (again) in a good B with Lex Barker, *The Girl in Black Stockings*. Still, no matter how much she showed her versatility, or how often those notices spoke of her as 'spirited' and 'intelligent', she was considered only programmer material: *Walk the Proud Land*, with Audie Murphy, as an Apache squaw, and *The Restless Breed*, with Scott Brady, as a half-breed stray. She gave up: 'I'm going back to New York, where an over-sized bosom [this was the time of Jayne Mansfield] doesn't take priority over reading your lines.'

In fact, she went East expressly to try for one of the parts in William Gibson's two-character play, 'Two For the See-Saw' (58): once they had auditioned her, Gibson and director Arthur Penn were as sure as she was that she was the perfect choice to play the kookie Jewish girl Gittel (co-star Henry Fonda had wanted a name). The critics and public concurred. Gibson and Penn then cast her as Annie Sullivan, Helen Keller's teacher, in 'The Miracle Worker' (59) and she won a second Tony Best Actress award; when they negotiated the film rights they insisted on her, Penn directing. As a film, *The Miracle Worker* (62) was not entirely satisfactory, but was often extraordinarily moving, and the battles between the child Keller (Patty Duke) and the part-blind, stubborn, Irish teacher were astonishing stuff. Both actresses won Oscars and Bancroft's Best Actress award was a popular

There have been few movies with a theme as vital as that of The Miracle Worker *(62): the recovery of a human being from a state of savagery. Anne Bancroft was memorable as the teacher of the child concerned, Helen Keller.*

one. Not that Hollywood atoned: after 'Mother Courage' in New York, her next film was British, *The Pumpkin Eater* (64), Jack Clayton's version of the Penelope Mortimer novel, playing marvellously a somewhat neurotic baby-producing London housewife. She was Best Actress at Cannes and the British Film Academy voted her a second Best Foreign Actress award.

In Hollywood, she was another unhappy wife, saved from suicide long-distance by Good Samaritan psychologist Sidney Poitier, in *The Slender Thread* (65). It was too slight, artificial, but she was impeccable, as she was again as the cocky realistic doctor (replacing Patricia Neal), one of the *Seven Women* (66) holed up in a Chinese mission during the Civil War. Because John Ford directed, some excused it as cod. Stinking fish, anyway, what with Bancroft sacrificing herself at the end to save the others, sipping poison after submitting to the drunken lust of warlord Mike Mazurki.

The original choice for Mrs Robinson in *The Graduate* (67) was Jeanne Moreau, but director Mike Nichols felt that that would give it too much the old 'Old Europe *v.* Young America' slant; Bancroft was an obvious choice to play the older woman who seduces Dustin Hoffman and then bitches him when she discovers he is in love with her daughter. The only scenes which had any charm or humour were those involving her, but this extended anecdote became a huge success, third among the all-time box-office champs (approx. $40 million at the end of 1968), till overtaken by the even more meretricious *Love Story*. Its success had no visible effect on Bancroft's film career. She was soon on Broadway in 'A Cry of Players' and then inactive for a while. She returned to the screen (unwillingly – she turned down the part several times) as the mother of *Young Winston* (72).

After playing Jack Lemmon's wife in *The Prisoner of Second Avenue* (74), the two of them facing grim New York with gritted teeth and one-liners, she made two films as bad as those of her contract days: *The Hindenburg* (75), involved with George C. Scott in a disaster film too many; and *Lipstick* (76), guest-featured as a lawyer involved with a raped Margaux Hemingway, an actress whose chief claim to attention is an ancestor. Bancroft must have felt more at home in Zeffirelli's TV *Gesu di Nazaret/Jesus of Nazareth* – at least, her Mary Magdalene was one of its outstanding performances. And presumably she enjoyed doing her guest cameo in *Silent Movie* since its star/writer/director was her husband, Mel Brooks (they married in 1964; earlier, 1953–57, she had been married to a real estate man). On Broadway, she thickened herself up to play the Israeli prime minister, 'Golda', and around the same time she thinned herself down to play a Margot Fonteyn-like ballerina in *The Turning Point* (77), a much-admired performance – as was that of Shirley MacLaine, playing an old buddy.

Anne Bancroft in a rare happy moment from The Pumpkin Eater *(64).*

After a run of buddy-buddy pictures Hollywood returned to the women in The Turning Point *(77), giving big roles to Shirley MacLaine and Anne Bancroft. They played buddies, and the film had some fair things to say about the world of ballet.*

She wrote and directed *Fatso* (80), a starring vehicle for Dom DeLuise, and supported him 'unusually shrill' ('Variety') as his sister. It was not a success, but many liked *The Elephant Man*, also produced by Brooks's own company. John Hurt played the title-role, a Victorian 'freak'/curiosity, and Bancroft was the actress Dame Madge Kendal who (in this version) was so kind to him. She was then scheduled to play Joan Crawford in *Mommie Dearest*, but she asked for a script rewrite: the second version, she thought, was even worse than the first. Instead, she went to Broadway to do 'Duet for One', a quick failure despite her participation and that of Max Von Sydow (who would play the same role in the film version, with Julie Andrews). She died and did little more than that in a TV mini-series, *Marco Polo* (82), after which she appeared opposite her husband in the remake, produced by him, of *To Be or Not To Be* (83). They did not eliminate memories of Benny and Lombard, but in her case the comparison was not fatal. Lumet's *Garbo Talks* (84) was another failure, perhaps because the idea was too slim and not developed – about a dying New York woman whose son (Ron Silver) wants to bring Garbo to meet her. *Agnes of God* (85) was no more substantial, though ye gods it thought it was, as Mother Superior Bancroft and shrink Jane Fonda pondered the whys and wherefores of one of the nuns being pregnant. There was more fine acting in *'night Mother* (86), in which Sissy Spacek was her daughter, and again in *84 Charing Cross Road* (87), in which she was an American corresponding with a London bookseller (Anthony Hopkins). Although successful as novel and play (in London but not New York) it was an unlikely subject for a movie – and it did not work on the screen. At the same time it was more worth while than most of the films produced by Brooksfilm. She had splashy but smallish roles in *Torch Song Trilogy* (88), as the Jewish mother of transvestite star Harvey Feinstein, and *Bert Rigby You're a Fool* (89), as a Hollywood producer's vapid wife attracted to star Robert Lindsay.

Brigitte Bardot

People have heard of Brigitte Bardot who have never heard of any other French star, and people have seen Brigitte Bardot movies who have never seen any other French movie. When she rose to world prominence in 1956 she was the first non-Hollywood star ever to make it – and no one was surprised that she was French, because the French are always so sexy or sex-obsessed or whatever. The French themselves were not, originally, especially turned on by Bardot, but they were flattered to have a world star who belonged solely to the native film industry; the bourgeois did not like her and even fans failed to see her as a national treasure like the Louvre. She was not very good at acting – but then, for most of the time she was about to make love or had just finished making it.

She pouted, she smiled (marvellously), she sprawled on a bed with bits of her strategically covered by a sheet, she wiggled her bottom as she walked across the room clad only in a towel. She was amorously inclined towards any male in the film who fancied her. Like Clara Bow, men are to her a constant source of delight, but unlike Miss Bow the consequences are to be seen (or, at least, the immediately before- and after-). In *En Cas de Malheur* she blatantly sets out to seduce Jean Gabin by raising her skirt to display her stocking-tops (they used the scene in the adverts): she was playful, guiltless. The film contrasted her with Gabin's wife (Edwige Feuillère), bourgeoise, middle-aged, discreet – and hypocritical. Bardot was the child of the gutter, *gamine* – and honest in her sexual relations.

She was miraculously exploited – she was not so much discovered as invented – but what made her legendary (Bardolatry) was her life-style, wholly in keeping with her screen image: much-publicized love affairs, a wilful, fickle temperament, skimpy dresses and a penchant for Saint-Tropez which in the 50s became for a while the glamour-capital of the world. Saint-Tropez was a fishing village on the Côte d'Azur which became famous at the same time – when they were both featured in *Et Dieu Créa la Femme*: it became a haven of smart restaurants, smoky night-*boîtes* (literally *boîtes*) and boutiques. She had a house there and was much pictured enjoying every aspect of the town's new existence. Not only France but the Western world became chock-a-block with imitation Bardots. Few stars so well symbolized their era. In 1960 Simone de Beauvoir wrote a treatise, 'Brigitte Bardot and the Lolita Syndrome', claiming as much for her. Writers are prone to see movie stars as representative of their time, whereas most of them are merely reflective; the few really great stars forced fashion on us and nothing Bardot did on screen identified her as a great star. But her identity as the female exponent of the new permissiveness is entirely sure.

She was born in Paris in 1934 into a wealthy middle-class family (father was an industrialist). She studied at a ballet school, where she was approached by a visiting photographer to do some modelling. By 1949 she was a popular model and in 1950 director Marc Allégret noticed her on the cover of 'Elle'. She reminded him of the young Simone Simon, whom he had discovered, and he charged his assistant, Roger Vadim, to contact her for a film called *Les Lauriers Sont Coupés.* In the event he did not use her but Vadim was much taken with her: she was sent to study acting under René Simon and in 1952 she and Vadim married. She was put on the stage in a revival of 'L'Invitation au Château'. Allégret recommended her to Jean Boyer for *Le Trou Normand* (52), which starred Bourvil as a stupid student hoping to inherit an inn; she made her film début therein, as a pretentious teenager. She starred in a B, *Nanina la Fille sans Voiles*, as an innkeeper's daughter involved with smugglers, and then had a bit in *Les Dents Longues*, starring and partly directed by Daniel Gélin. She had a huge close-up as a courtesan who attracts the attention of Louis XV (Jean Marais) in *Si Versailles m'était Conté* (53), and similarly insubstantial parts in the US-French *Act of Love* (54) with Kirk Douglas, *Le Portrait de Son Père* starring Jean Richard as a peasant in Paris, the Italian *Tradita* and *Le Fils de Caroline Chérie* with Jean-Claude Pascal. She was more in evidence as the maid of *Helen of Troy* (55) – the Trojan War in comic strip, with Rosanna Podesta (Helen) and Jacques Sernas (Paris). Warners, who presented it, were sufficiently impressed to offer a seven-year contract, which was refused. She was very much in evidence with Isabelle Pia as the *Futures Vedettes*: they were music students both having affairs with opera-singer Jean Marais.

Britain called, in the shape of the Rank Organization, looking for a piece of sexy manbait (replacing Kay Kendall) to tempt Dirk Bogarde, the *Doctor at Sea*; after which she had an ingénue role supporting Michèle Morgan in *Les Grandes Manœuvres.* It was her last supporting part: next she was the focal point of a gloomy triangle drama, attracted to the *garagiste* over the road, *La Lumière d'en Face* (56), while husband Raymond Pellegrin goes bonkers. Although this was much revived later (the adverts conveniently pictured a lamp-post) she was not good: she did little but pout and change her clothes. Still, it was her first dramatic role; and it also provided her with another mentor, for Christine Gouze-Renal, who worked on the production side, was to help guide her career for years.

When the film was premièred in Paris Bardot was still virtually unknown; by the end of the year a succession of hits had pushed her to the forefront of French stars and she had toppled Martine Carol as the national sex-symbol: *Cette Sacrée Gamine*, a comedy, as the precocious and scatterbrained daughter of a Pigalle nightclub owner; the Italian *Mi Figlio Nerone*, a comedy with Alberto Sordi as Nero, as Poppea; and *En Effeuillant la Marguerite*, directed by Allégret and written by him and Vadim, a witless rigmarole about a girl who writes a bestseller and runs away to Paris where she gets involved with, among other things, a striptease context – it became *Mam'selle Striptease* in Britain, *Please Mr Balzac* in the US. There was a weak comedy about the fashion world, *La Mariée est Trop Belle*, with Micheline Presle and Louis Jourdan, about which 'Variety's' Paris correspondent (Gene Moskowitz) wrote: 'Perhaps for lack of anybody else, Brigitte Bardot seems to be the No 1 star here these days. . . . Possessed of a pouting pigeon personality, she does not seem up to dishing out either the beauteous firebrands or the wavering virgins. She appears to have been pushed too fast for her real thespic talents.'

An astute producer, Raoul J. Levy, saw a couple of these films and offered Vadim a chance of directing Bardot, in a story to be written by himself and Vadim. The result was *Et Dieu Créa la Femme*, a hot-blooded melodrama about an over-sexed girl-wife running the gamut in Saint-Tropez. The style was lush and lyrical, and yet to some extent the film was realistic – a combination of opposites which, plus the eroticism, got this poor little piece much attention. Further, there were censorship troubles and the press was encouraged to believe that the love scenes with Jean-

Before she became a star Brigitte Bardot crossed the Channel to play in one of Britain's immensely popular 'Doctor' series – Doctor at Sea *(55). The doctor was Dirk Bogarde.*

Louis Trintignant were the real thing. Bardot and Vadim were divorced the following year, though their names were to remain linked in the same way as those of Dietrich and von Sternberg. Certainly he *made* Bardot and he was to continue to exploit, less successfully, screen eroticism almost up to the present.

When the film opened in New York in 1957, 'Time Magazine' observed that Bardot was now worth about 30 million francs – or more than $70,000 – per film. The film was to take more than $4 million in the US and was to be one of the first foreign language films ever to be generally released in Britain. Hollywood inevitably wanted Bardot and other reports in 1957 speak of offers of $25,000 – though it was believed that her asking price for a Hollywood film was $150,000. Levy made a deal with Columbia for three films (in French) with Bardot, which would reputedly pay her $225,000. Beyond that, to what extent Levy negotiated is not known, but she was undoubtedly commercial in the US: her films were achieving a penetration afforded no previous foreign star and in 1958 she was seventh at the US box-office. Meanwhile, she was making *Une Parisienne* (57), with Charles Boyer and Henri Vidal. She undressed a lot, but otherwise this was a depressed soufflé about a diplomat's wife who flirts with a foreign prince. More murky drama followed and indeed she was killed off at the end of *Les Bijoutiers du Clair de Lune* (58), directed by Vadim and produced by Levy for Columbia. The budget was big enough to allow an 'international name', Stephen Boyd (not that it helped). She did *En Cas de Malheur*, directed by Autant-Lara, her best film even if, artistically, the experienced Gabin and Feuillère wiped the floor with her. She was up against no such competition in the next – her co-star was Antonio Vilar – but the film again was dreadful: *La Femme et le Pantin* (59), Duvivier's remake of *The Devil is a Woman.*

It was customary in Bardot's films to find someone of an older generation shocked by her attitude towards morality. In Les Bijoutiers du Clair de Lune *(58) it was Alida Valli as her aunt – though they quarrelled over the same man (Stephen Boyd).*

Plans were finally announced for her first big English-speaking film, a musical with Frank Sinatra and directed by Vadim, *Paris by Night.* It did not happen: it was reported that Sinatra considered she had been overexposed on US screens. Instead, Columbia announced a British war picture to co-star David Niven. This was eventually made without Niven, in France, and was now about a girl parachuted into France to help the Resistance, *Babette s'en va-t-en Guerre.* The co-star was Jacques Charrier, who married Bardot; they had a son but the marriage did not last, partly because Charrier did his *service militaire* shortly afterwards and as Bardot's spouse found life difficult. Then she did a mild comedy, *Voulez-Vous Danser avec Moi?* with Henri Vidal. Wrote Dwight Macdonald: 'The toucan has its bill and Bardot has her hair. Unhappily she has nothing else, dramatically speaking. Unlike her American opposite number, Miss Monroe, she has no lightness, no verve, no womanly softness, no change of pace, nothing but the petulant defiance of a depraved child.'

Early in 1960 de Beauvoir's book was published and in September – on her 26th birthday – Bardot tried to commit suicide. Filming was held up on *La Vérité* (60), with Sammy Frey (who was involved in a street scuffle with Charrier). The film was directed by Clouzot and was said to reveal Bardot as a great actress. It did not; but it was a good court-room drama, if less popular outside France (where it was the year's top money-maker) than was hoped. It was the last of Levy's deals with Columbia and as Bardot's appeal in both the US and Britain had considerably lessened there were no longer automatic bids for her films. In any case, *La Bride sur le Cou* (61) was another parochial comedy (part-directed by Vadim, who took over when Bardot sacked the original director). The episodic *Les Amours Célèbres* boasted some big names – but Bardot's section with Alain Delon, 'Agnès Bernauer', as medieval lovers, found them at their most inept. French audiences laughed, American audiences did not go and the British were not given the chance.

Her next picture was announced as a remake of *Private Lives* with MGM backing. By a series of reversals, what MGM got in the end, *Vie Privée* (62), bore no relation to Coward's play. Louis Malle directed, Marcello Mastroianni co-starred and it was frankly biographical, with Bardot trying to cope with stardom. 'Cinema '61' called it 'une minutieuse radiographie du mythe Brigitte Bardot', but it turned out to be the same old Bardot vehicle. Outside France it was written off. Vadim directed *Le Repos du Guerrier*, a gaudy version of a bestseller, Christiane de Rochefort's, with Robert Hossein. This was considered to be Bardot's farewell film – there had been many rumours of retirement – but Joe Levine talked her and Jean-Luc Godard into a collaboration based on a novel by Moravia, *Le Mépris/Il Disprezzo* (63), for which her stipend was said to be $500,000. Godard was given a free hand but there were disputes about the version to be shown outside France and this again, when later shown, turned out to be a commercial disaster. In France, Bardot was overtaken by Sophia Loren as the country's most popular star (Claudia Cardinale was third, followed by Jeanne Moreau and Michèle Morgan). She turned again to a purely 'fun' picture, *Une Ravissante Idiote* (64), with Anthony Perkins, but few got any fun watching it (they had tried to shoot locations in London but were so mobbed they gave up).

In 1964 Canada's 'Weekend Magazine' thought that her films had drawn $50 million into France. At last she made an American movie: she appeared briefly, as herself, in *Dear Brigitte*, a James Stewart comedy (his son writes Bardot a fan letter). The next garnered much publicity. She was to co-star with Jeanne Moreau, considered France's best actress and an exponent of more mature and passionate sex: *Viva Maria!* (65), Louis Malle's comedy about two soubrettes caught up in a Mexican revolution. As expected, Bardot was no match for Moreau's magnetism, but time had not dimmed her charm. In France the film was a wow, but was considered to have failed elsewhere; in fact, it did not do badly for such a confused, overlong event. There had never been any doubt that it had been intended for

Brigitte Bardot and Jeanne Moreau in Viva Maria! *(65). With the possible exception of Olivier and Marilyn Monroe, this teaming created more publicity than for any other movie within recent memory.*

the international market and Bardot now did an Anglo-French movie, playing a model who meets Laurent Terzieff in London, Serge Bourguignon's *A Coeur Joie/Two Weeks in September* (67) – which was about as long as it played in Britain and the US. No more successful was the three-part *Histoires Extraordinaires* (68), which teamed her again with Delon, under Malle's direction, in 'William Wilson', from a story by Poe.

She made her full-scale English début as a French countess in a British 'Western', filmed in Spain, *Shalako*, with Sean Connery, unconvincingly brave in the face of danger. The casting looked more like opportunism than anything else – but it did not lead anywhere. At least, 'Ciné-Revue' commented that from the 250 million old francs she was paid for that she went down to a reputed 80 million only for *Les Femmes* (69), a mild comedy with Maurice Ronet (*cf* Louis de Funes 350 million, Delon 250 million, Belmondo 150 million, Michèle Mercier 120 million). Better was Michel Deville's *L'Ours et la Poupée* (70), which, aided by Jean-Pierre Cassel, attempted to change her image to comedienne and provided her first hit in France since *Viva Maria!* Then: *Les Novices*, a tasteless comedy where she and Annie Girardot were whores impersonating nuns; *Boulevard du Rhum* (71), as a Silent movie star with Lino Ventura as a gangster; and *Les Pétroleuses* with Claudia Cardinale, a sort of re-vamp of *Viva Maria!* (which in itself was a re-vamp of Preston Sturges's *The Beautiful Blonde From Bashful Bend*).

Bardot has appeared on TV in her own spectaculars. In 1966 she married a wealthy German, Gunther Sachs, but interviews with her early on suggested that it would not last. It didn't. Her last two films were failures: *Don Juan 1973 ou Si Don Juan Etait une Femme* (73), directed by Vadim, and *L'Histoire Très Bonne et Très Joyeuse de Colinot Trousse-Chemise*, a historical romp. Her salary made her the 15th highest-paid among French players, but she announced her retirement, and has reiterated that she does not want to act again; she turned down *The Fan Club*, which was not made, and *Someone is Killing the Grand Chefs of Europe*, in which Jacqueline Bisset replaced her. She still makes headlines supporting good causes.

Alan Bates

Others may well have had the publicity and the tele-interviews, but during his first decade in films Alan Bates steadily advanced until he was perhaps the key British actor of his generation. He is one of the successful few who has eschewed the limelight, perhaps because his work is All or perhaps because he is uncertain of the image he wants to convey. He is neither the actual toothpaste-ad film star of yore nor one of the rollicking ravers with their (over-publicized) working-class origins. He is simply a fine, inevitably classless, actor; when he started he was rather like an office or factory chum, but after moving through a period of Housman-like heroes he enters middle-age with a wide range.

He was born in Allestree, Derbyshire, in 1934 and was grammar-school educated. He wanted to act while still at school and after national service (with the RAF) studied at RADA. He made his professional début with the Midland Theatre Co. in Coventry, in 'You and Your Wife' (55), and joined London's Royal Court Co. as it was about to enjoy its first flush of success; after playing in Angus Wilson's 'The Mulberry Tree', he played Cliff in 'Look Back in Anger' – a part he also played in New York (and in Moscow). He was in the British première of 'Long Day's Journey Into Night' (58), as Edmund, and the first production of Harold Pinter's 'The Caretaker' (60). Meanwhile, the Royal Court team of Tony Richardson and John Osborne were filming Osborne's *The Entertainer* (60) and they cast Bates as the pacifist son, the one Laurence Olivier uses as a 'feed'. Then he gave a sturdy performance in *Whistle Down the Wind* (61) in what was a sticky part – a crook on the run whom Hayley Mills believes to be Christ. But as a film player he first became well known as the boy in *A Kind of Loving* (62), a young draughtsman who somehow gets hitched to the girl (June Ritchie) he has got pregnant, and thereby to her horrible suburban mum (Thora Hird) as well. Said 'Playboy': 'Alan Bates turns in an eminently winning performance as the loser. Not as feisty as Albert Finney nor as hammy as Laurence Harvey, Bates gives a touch of pavement poetry to the Lancashire lad whose rough edges are ground down by propriety and poverty so that he can be slipped into his slot in the scheme of things.' John Schlesinger directed (his first feature), from Stan Barstow's novel and, coming towards the end of a run of similar films, its virtues were overlooked till it took the top award at the Berlin festival. It was just that bit more honest and better observed than its predecessors; and became big box-office.

The Caretaker (63) did not, even by the minority standards expected of it: the play had done well, but the few people who saw the movie must have decided it was a put-upon – and a verbose one at that – for it soon disappeared from view. After that, Bates decided to do a 'commercial' picture with a name director – Carol Reed's *The Running Man*, as an insurance agent in pursuit of Laurence Harvey and Lee Remick. Then there was a black comedy written by Frederic Raphael about a climber who wanted *Nothing But the Best* (64): it was a bit too agreeable but otherwise winning and he was well partnered by Millicent Martin as a deb. He was the young Englishman impressed by *Zorba the Greek* Anthony Quinn – Prince Hal to his Falstaff, after which he returned to the theatre: 'Poor Richard' in New York and 'The Four Seasons' in London. He was the amoral lover of both *Georgy Girl* (65) Lynn Redgrave and her room-mate (Charlotte Rampling), from which he went to France for one of the less successful frolics of Philippe de Broca, *Le Roi de Cœur* (66), in the title-role as a man who finds more sanity within a lunatic asylum than without.

The next two impressively indicated his maturing talent: *Far From the Madding Crowd* (67), doing forcefully under Schlesinger's direction that old standby, the dog-like, patient and faithful lover – Julie Christie's; and *The Fixer* (68), John Frankenheimer's version of Bernard Malamud's novel, which brought him rave reviews and an Oscar nomination – as a victim of Russian anti-Semitic tyranny. He returned to the stage, playing Richard III and Master Ford in Stratford, Ontario, and much later, Hamlet in Nottingham and London. In films he was D.H. Lawrence under his alias of Birkin in *Women in Love* (70), with its unjustly famous male nude wrestling sequence. He was Vershinin in the National Theatre's filmed theatre, *Three Sisters*, at Laurence Olivier's request, deputizing for Robert Stephens when he fell ill. Then he was Julie Christie's farmer-lover in *The Go-Between* (71) and this second excursion into rural England for them was a critical and box-office success. It was, however, much inferior to their earlier trip, a vulgarization by Pinter (script) and Joseph Losey (director) of L.P. Hartley's delicate novel about a child (Dominic Guard) who acts as postman between the daughter of the big house and a tenant farmer. Bates's own performance was as uncertain as his Norfolk accent.

Things were redeemed by *A Day in the Death of Joe Egg* (72), with Janet Suzman, the two of them as a couple with a spastic daughter: as directed with sensitivity by Peter

Far From the Madding Crowd (67) *was the first of Thomas Hardy's novels to be filmed since the Silent days. Producers were afraid of Hardy, and the reception accorded this – excellent – film did not prove them wrong. Julie Christie was Bathsheba and Alan Bates the faithful Gabriel Oak.*

As a play, A Day in the Death of Joe Egg (72) *was a success in London, New York and elsewhere, but the subject-matter – the stress caused to a marriage by a spastic child – was uncongenial to cinema audiences, despite fine work by Alan Bates and Janet Suzman.*

Medak, Peter Nichols's superb play lost nothing in coming to the screen – but the subject-matter was too downbeat for both the company handling it and audiences. *The Impossible Object* (73) was hardly seen at all: made in English by Frankenheimer in France, it was not liked enough to make its début in the markets for which it was intended. *Butley* (74) and *In Celebration* (75) were versions of plays he had done on the stage, hardly altered, and meant for limited screenings: which was just as well. *Royal Flash* was George MacDonald Fraser's cod Victorian hero, as played by Malcolm McDowell, and Bates was an unscrupulous Hungarian adventurer. In London he starred in 'Otherwise Engaged' and in New York he played Jill Clayburgh's sympathetic artist lover in *An Unmarried Woman* (78), for which he is 'perhaps best known to American audiences' – said 'Newsweek', previewing the BBC's seven-part 'The Mayor of Casterbridge', in which Bates showed new form in the title-role.

If he was not fully employed in the British cinema, that was because the industry was in a bad way – a situation unlikely to be rectified by films like *The Shout*, an artsy-crafty effort in which he shouted and went berserk. For sanity, Bates returned to the US to make his second film there, *The Rose* (79), playing Bette Midler's manager, a deceptively nice man, since he is in reality another of the monsters feeding off her. As Diaghilev, he managed *Nijinsky* (80), while discreetly (oh ever so!) lusting after him. Herbert Ross directed this first-realized of the many, many film projects on this celebrated couple announced over the years. It was critically underrated, but it could still have been better done. After the televised *Very Like a Whale*, with a John Osborne script, he played another autocratic monster, based on the novelist Ford Madox Ford, in the Merchant-Ivory *Quartet* (81), from Jean Rhys's autobiographical novel of expatriate British society in the Paris of the 20s. *The Return of the Soldier* (82) was a second inadequate rendering of another semi-classic novel, in this case by Rebecca West: in it, Bates returns from the War (World War I) to find himself preferring Glenda Jackson to wife Julie Christie. Imagine! He played James Mason's old role in the remake of *The Wicked Lady* (83), meant to be a rollicking commercial production – though it probably took less at the box-office than Bates's last two movies, aimed at the art-houses. The experience kept him away from cinemas for four years.

In 1982 he had played Olivier's son in an acclaimed tele-film, *A Voyage Round My Father.* He continued to appear on the stage, most notably as a homosexual spy in 'A Patriot for Me' (83) in Chichester and London, in 'The Dance of Death', Shaffer's 'Yonadab' at the National and 'Melon'. Television work included: *An Englishman Abroad* (83), written by Alan Bennett and directed by John Schlesinger for the BBC, as the spy Philby (a role meant for Bates in at least two cinema films which never materialized); *Separate Tables* opposite Julie Christie and playing Eric Portman's old role(s) with aplomb; and *Pack of Lies* (87) for CBS in the US, as the police inspector in this transfer of a successful West End play about a suburban family discovering that their neighbours are Soviet spies. Bates returned to cinemas with a dire performance as Julie Andrews's husband in *Duet for One* (86), followed by *A Prayer for the Dying* (87), third-billed after Mickey Rourke and Bob Hoskins, as an English mobster who employs an IRA man for a hit killing. He had another gay role in *We Think the World of You* (88), based on J.R. Ackerly's autobiographical account of a man who becomes attached to a dog after his lover has been sent to prison; and he had third billing in a French movie, *Force Majeure* (89), as a lawyer trying to persuade two youngsters, Patrick Bruel and François Cluzet, to return to Asia to help a friend condemned to death for drug trafficking. In 1989 he played Benedick opposite Felicity Kendall's Beatrice in the West End. He married in 1970.

ANNE BAXTER

In her best-remembered role Anne Baxter was matched against Bette Davis, playing an actress who hoped to supplant her and did. The film was named for her and not Davis: *All About Eve*. It was an entirely competent performance – guile hidden by sweetness, and baleful in a mild way. But it was not entirely believable: even if Davis had not been at her best you could not imagine Baxter supplanting her. She was just not individual or forceful enough. Baxter was no slouch as an actress and her (Best Supporting) Oscar was well deserved: it is just that on most outings she has been middle-of-the-road. What one thinks of first is a shy smile – a lesser gift for actresses.

She was born in Michigan City, Indiana, in 1923, the daughter and granddaughter of architects (her mother's father was Frank Lloyd Wright). The family moved to Bronxville, New York, and she was put to study at the Theodora Irvine School. At age 11 she landed a leading role in 'Seen but not Heard'; then came Broadway assignments in 'There's Always a Breeze' and 'Madame Capet' (38) with Eva le Galliene; she also acted in stock. Hollywood showed interest and Selznick tested her twice – once for *Rebecca*, but he considered her too young. 20th did sign her and she made her screen début on loan to MGM in *Twenty Mule Team* (40), starring Wallace Beery, as 'an attractive little desert-flower' ('New York Times'). She was the timid, gentle heroine of *The Great Profile* who was John Barrymore and *Charley's Aunt* (41) ditto Jack Benny, but was replaced as the barefoot girl by Linda Darnell in *Chad Hanna* when Zanuck did not think she could manage the change to someone more determined: but that was a role she did play in Renoir's *Swamp Water*, in which she was harassed as well. Orson Welles at RKO borrowed her to play the girl courted by Tim Holt, one of *The Magnificent Ambersons* (42). She worked conscientiously and gradually achieved star-status: in *The Pied Piper*, from Nevil Shute's novel about Nazi refugees, as a French girl with Monty Woolley; *Crash Dive* (43), opposite Tyrone Power; and both on loan (and both with Erich von Stroheim), *Five Graves to Cairo*, as a French serving-maid, and *The North Star*, as a Russian peasant.

Three Home Front movies refined her image – the girl the Boys Remembered when They Went Off to Fight: *The Sullivans* (44), *The Eve of St Mark*, from Maxwell Anderson's play, and *Sunday Dinner for a Soldier*. The last in particular was admired – for its quiet charm – but it seems too cute today. The soldier concerned was John Hodiak, to whom Baxter was married in 1946. She was the disrupting *Guest in the House* at UA, the first of her smiling schemer roles, and the ingénue of *A Royal Scandal* (45) starring Tallulah Bankhead. *Smoky* (46) was a horse. After another loan-out – for *Angel on my Shoulder* with Paul Muni – she was the unfortunate Sophie (taking to drugs and drink) in *The Razor's Edge*, a touching performance which brought her her Oscar. Alice Faye, Judy Garland and Betty Grable had turned down the role and Baxter had asked to test for it after hearing that it was to go to a freelance player, Bonita Granville. She was loaned to Paramount for *Blaze of Noon* (47), playing William Holden's loyal wife, and to MGM for *Homecoming* (48), losing Clark Gable to Lana Turner.

20th were not yet certain of Baxter's appeal. Of her next four films, three had been abandoned by other actresses: *The Walls of Jericho*, as a lawyer, with Cornel Wilde, had been turned down by Gene Tierney; *The Luck of the Irish* was a whimsy with Tyrone Power; a Western, *Yellow Sky*, had been planned for Paulette Goddard; and *You're My Everything* (49) had been planned for the pregnant Jeanne Crain. The last was a musical about Hollywood in the 30s with Baxter as a Clara Bow-type star: she showed little aptitude for the medium but was nevertheless put into another musical, with Dan Dailey, *A Ticket to Tomahawk* (50), set out West.

Then came *All About Eve* and 20th finally and jubilantly decided to build Baxter – but she became pregnant and lost *People Will Talk* to Jeanne Crain. Both *David and Bathsheba* and *White Witch Doctor* were

Sunday Dinner for a Soldier *(44) was an anecdote about a poor Florida family who invite a soldier, John Hodiak, to lunch. Inevitably the daughter, Anne Baxter, falls in love with him.*

Gay Merrill, Anne Baxter and Bette Davis in All About Eve *(50): the airport scene where Eve (Miss Baxter) first proves how useful she can be. Her rise has begun.*

announced for her soon but the studio decided that Susan Hayward was a bigger draw. The opportunities Baxter did get allowed her little chance to shine: *Follow the Sun* (51), as Glenn Ford's faithful wife; *The Outcasts of Poker Flats* with Dale Robertson, from Bret Harte's story; *My Wife's Best Friend* with Macdonald Carey, more sophisticated than usual in a dim comedy; and *O. Henry's Full House*, in a sensitive performance as the dying girl in 'The Last Leaf' episode.

As her marriage broke up (they were divorced in 1953; Hodiak died of a heart attack two years later) a new Baxter emerged – with martini-coloured hair and a penchant for cigars (it was admitted later, for publicity purposes). Said John Gold in the 'Evening News': 'In Hollywood Miss Baxter is known for three things – driving ambition, unlimited energy and a completely honest if occasionally withering tongue.' She had gone blonde, it was said, in order to get the lead in *Gentlemen Prefer Blondes* – but that went to Marilyn Monroe, as did *Niagara*, once announced for Baxter. Instead, 20th loaned her to Warners for Hitchcock's *I Confess* (53), though he had not wanted her – he had brought Anita Bjork over from Sweden for the part but WB sent her home and imposed Baxter on him. Still, Baxter was good in the part. She asked 20th for and got release from her contract (when asked to test for *How to Marry a Millionaire*) and stayed at Warners for Fritz Lang's poor *The Blue Gardenia*, as an amnesiac murder suspect, with Richard Conte. Her freelance fee was reported to be $75,000.

In Europe she made a mistake – *Carnival Story* (54) with Steve Cochran, a rehash of Dupont's *Variété* (a concurrent German version was made with Eva Bartok). In Paris she was *Bedevilled* (55) for MGM at $60,000, with Steve Forrest; then back in Hollywood she had only *One Desire* with Rock Hudson – to move from the other side of the tracks into high society. This was at Universal and also there she was in what is probably the poorest of the several versions of *The Spoilers*. Said the 'MFB': 'Coy, arch and overdressed, her performance verges on caricature.'

She was not accustomed to bad notices, but both she and *The Come-On* (56) reaped a harvest (and the film was banned in Britain). In it she was glamorous again, as an ambitious con-woman. The film was produced by Russell Birdwell, her publicist (he was also Jane Russell's; and it was he who had 'invented' Baxter the vamp) and one-time fiancé. That out of the way, her career took a faint upward curve when she went to Paramount to obey *The Ten Commandments*; and there, with Charlton Heston, she was one of the *Three Violent People*, a hooker who becomes a loving wife. In Britain she was a South African heiress in *Chase a Crooked Shadow* (57) with Richard Todd. She enjoyed filming in Britain and returned to do a West End play,

Anne Baxter and Tom Tryon in Three Violent People *(56): he played her brother-in-law and was somewhat more sympathetic than a gloomy Charlton Heston as the spouse. (Tryon retired from acting and became a best-selling novelist.)*

'The Joshua Tree' (58), but it did not run. An appearance in New York, in Carson McCullers's 'The Square Root of Wonderful', was no more successful. After an absence she, along with Angela Lansbury, was game as a jolly tart in *Summer of the Seventeenth Doll* (59), but as the film stripped the original character of its sluttishness she became merely enigmatic. It was made in Australia and while there she met and in 1960 married a rancher – about which she wrote a book, 'Intermission'.

She honoured two commitments – *Cimarron* (60), as an Oklahoman bar-girl, and *A Walk on the Wild Side* (61), as an Italian bar-girl – and then went into semi-retirement. She left it for the British *Mix Me a Person* (63), a thriller in which she was a psychiatrist – having twice already turned down the film as unlikely to appeal to American audiences (or, indeed, any). She was divorced in 1968, by which time she had tentatively returned to films: a guest spot as a movie star in Jerry Lewis's *The Family Jewels* (65), and a supporting role among several names in a B, *The Busy Body* (67), producer William Castle's second attempt to make a film star out of comic Sid Caesar. After a indifferent Spanish Western, *Las Siete Magnificas*, she began to appear frequently on television: *Stranger on the Run*, opposite Henry Fonda; *Companions in Nightmare* (68) with Gig Young; *Marcus Welby MD* (69) with Robert Young; *The Challengers* (70), guest-starring along with Richard Conte and Farley Granger; and *Ritual of Evil* with Louis Jourdan. She returned to films proper to play a madam in *Fools' Parade*, which starred James Stewart, but was back on the small screen in *If Tomorrow Comes* (71) and *The Catcher* (72). *The Late Liz* found her as a movie star who gives up booze for religion, but like *Lapin 360*, another independent production, bookings were few. She and John Forsythe were the parents of *Lisa Bright and Dark* (73), a tele-movie about a teenager (Kay Lenz) with mental problems, and she played a movie star again, on Broadway, in the musical based on *All About Eve*, 'Applause!', taking over from Lauren Bacall. Kirk Douglas and Christopher Plummer battled it out in a mini-series, *The Moneychangers* (76), while she looked on, and she played the lead in 'The Little Foxes' in Palm Beach; then she replaced Lana Turner as the mother of tennis player *Little Mo* (78), with Glynis O'Connor in the title-role of this tele-movie. Another followed: *Nero Wolfe* (79), and she was the tycoon employing him, Thayer David.

The Merchant-Ivory *Jane Austen in Manhattan* (80) must rank as one of her least distinguished efforts, though her stylish presence – attempting to stage an Austen play (!) – contrasted with the muddle around her. She appeared in a mini-series version of *East of Eden* (81) starring Timothy Bottoms and played Gertrude in 'Hamlet' (82) at Stratford, Connecticut. *Blake: a Marriage of Heaven and Hell*, a docudrama with George Rose, was televised a few months later. She went to London to play Irene Adler in a Sherlock Holmes (Peter Cushing) pastiche, *The Masks of Death* (84), and then replaced a sick Bette Davis in a TV series, *Hotel.* She died of a heart attack in 1985.

WARREN BEATTY

Warren Beatty came to films on a wave of publicity as high as it was wide. These were murky waters, colouring him 'the new Brando' or 'the new James Dean'. The tide retreated, leaving him high and dry and friendless on the shore. For a while,

He was born in 1937 in Richmond, Virginia, the brother of Shirley MacLaine. At school his prowess as a footballer suggested he would make a career at that, but he wanted to act. He studied for a year at Northwestern University, where he did college plays; then he studied with Stella Adler, doing manual work to support himself. He began to get parts in radio and TV, and was in stock in a New Jersey 'Compulsion' when William Inge and Joshua Logan spotted him. Logan asked him to test for *Parrish* but when he could not get Vivien Leigh and Clark Gable for the leads he left the project and Beatty was passed over for Troy Donahue. On the strength of his test MGM signed him for one movie, but that was abandoned; Inge thereupon cast him in his 'A Loss of Roses' (59) on Broadway.

His film début followed, in the Inge-written Kazan-directed *Splendor in the Grass* (60), with Natalie Wood, a silly picture about teenage lovers torn apart by parental disapproval (it was set in the 20s). He was sullen, little more. His price was an astonishing fee for a newcomer – $200,000. Inge helped him get the part of Vivien Leigh's Italian gigolo in Tennessee Williams's *The Roman Spring of Mrs Stone* (61) – a portrayal considerably inferior to that of George Hamilton in a similar part in the concurrent *The Light in the Piazza*. After that he was unlucky. *All Fall Down* (62) was from a good novel (James Leo Herlihy's, screenplayed by Inge) and was well made (by John Frankenheimer), but it came much too late in the Unhappy American Family cycle. He did not – he said later – like his own performance as the centrepiece. Bosley Crowther said he played it as a cretin, 'surly, sloppy, slow-witted, given to scratching himself . . . being rude beyond reason'. He should have done *Youngblood Hawk* for Warners, but demanded so many changes that Warners replaced him with James Franciscus. Other projects did not work out and his next two movies were even less popular than the first three: Robert Rossen's study of life in a mental institution, *Lilith* (64), with Jean Seberg, over which Beatty and Rossen disagreed throughout production; and Arthur Penn's *Mickey One* (65), a study of a night-club entertainer. In an attempt to retrieve his career, Beatty made (in Britain) a couple of commercial pieces: *Promise Her Anything* (66) ('but don't take her to this' ran Judith Crist's review), with Leslie Caron, as a Greenwich Village porno movie-maker; and *Kaleidoscope*, with Susannah York, as a master gambler/crook. Neither did much either, but amid the shenanigans could be discerned Beatty's amiable, lazy, boyish charm.

Then came *Bonnie and Clyde* (67). The script, based on fact and concerning a couple of hoodlums in the late Depression era, had

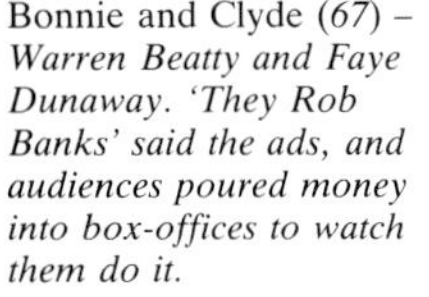

Bonnie and Clyde (67) – *Warren Beatty and Faye Dunaway. 'They Rob Banks' said the ads, and audiences poured money into box-offices to watch them do it.*

been hanging around for some time (at one time Jean-Luc Godard was offered it). Beatty took it up, to produce and star, and assigned Arthur Penn to direct. (Penn later paid tribute to Beatty's work as producer.) Dismissed in the US (apart from some strictures on excessive violence) it was recognized as a masterpiece in Britain: '1967 is the year of *Bonnie and Clyde*', declared the 'Queen Magazine', righter than it knew. American critics reassessed it and after initially poor business it went on to gross over $19 million over the next year. The title became a byword – appropriately, for this was a watershed among American films. Beatty's performance as Clyde Barrow (Faye Dunaway was Bonnie), insolent and uncertain like a small boy, brought him world fame and a personal fortune of $6 million ('Variety' estimate).

Now he was greatly in demand again. He turned down *Bob & Carol & Ted & Alice*, *Butch Cassidy and the Sundance Kid* and *Getting Straight*, and was able to command $750,000 when he next ventured to film, taking over the part Sinatra had abandoned in George Steven's *The Only Game in Town* (69), opposite Elizabeth Taylor. It failed and a similar fate seemed in store for *McCabe and Mrs Miller* (71), though directed by Robert Altman (then still riding high from his *M-A-S-H* success). But this tale of life in a primitive Western town was saved by some critics. As usual alternating between good films and bad, he went on to do *$* (72), which deserved no better title, one of a slew of current movies about bank-heists. During this period he turned down roles in *The Godfather*, *The Sting*, *The Great Gatsby*, *Last Tango in Paris* and *The Way We Were*; the one that he chose to do was both better and less successful than any of them, *The Parallax View* (74), a sharp account of political assassination and rare among contemporary thrillers in a) having a hero – Beatty – who is neither thug, thief, whacko or embezzler and b) a well-developed plot.

Beatty's biggest success to date was *Shampoo* (75), which he also produced, playing a randy coiffeur in this foul-tongued but not disagreeable attack on Californian mores. Partnered by Jack Nicholson, *The Fortune* proved neither of them box-office if the formula was not right: making a shiftless *ménage à trois* with the marvellous Stockard Channing, the two men were thrown time after time into Laurel & Hardy situations, but the director (Mike Nichols) had not understood the vulgarity of the L & H connection. The conjunction of these two films indicated to Beatty only to star in films he himself produced: and *Heaven Can Wait* (78) was also co-written and co-directed by him, in collaboration with Elaine May and Buck Henry respectively: but good intentions could not make more than a mild diversion from this remake of *Here Comes Mr Jordan*, its undead hero now a football player. Its public acceptance (there were not many light-hearted films around that year) meant a hat-trick for Beatty the producer; a flock of Oscar nominations but only one non-major award seemed fair comment on a film which will not be around as long as the original (or Lubitsch's film with the same title). Anyway, Beatty was encouraged to attempt a project that had long daunted Hollywood, *Reds* (81), the story of the American communist John Read and his relationship with Louise Bryant – played by Diane Keaton (the latest in an over-publicized series of romances). A long, riveting film, positively approving of Reed and Bryant, if eventually a little ambiguous when it could have been straightforward, it returned $21 million of its $35 million cost in the domestic market. It is unequivocably one of Hollywood's best serious films in its poorest period,

McCabe and Mrs Miller *(71) – Warren Beatty and Julie Christie. Beatty was still up to no good – a possible gunfighter, an inveterate gambler, and owner of the town's first bordello. Miss Christie ran it for him – and they ended up no happier than Bonnie and Clyde.*

bringing Beatty an Oscar for Best Direction.

Projects considered and rejected over the next few years included some new adventures for Dick Tracy and *The Slugger's Wife* by Neil Simon. Anything would have been better than *Ishtar* (87), in which he and Dustin Hoffman took on the mantle of Hope and Crosby – dismally, at salaries of $5½ million each. Director Elaine May's quest for perfection was one reason the budget escalated from $27½ million to $40 million, little of which was recovered from any market, domestic or otherwise. Undoubtedly the three principals were justified in suing Columbia for $2 million each for unpaid salaries, but they also asked for another $5 million each in damages because the film was not properly exploited: odd, that, since its failure was famous enough for it to become a joke for comedians. In 1989 Beatty at last began *Dick Tracy*.

Barbara Bel Geddes

One of the things wrong with *Vertigo* was that it was difficult to believe that any normal man could prefer Kim Novak to Barbara Bel Geddes; but then, Hollywood has preferred any number of cute blondes to actresses like her (say, Margaret Sullavan, Betty Field, Dorothy McGuire). She in turn has shown no great love for the place, picking her rare films with some discrimination, a warm actress whose teddy-bear-like beauty somewhat disguises a strong acting intelligence.

She was born in New York City in 1922, the daughter of designer Norman Bel Geddes. Being around show people from childhood it was perhaps natural that she wanted to act; and while still at school she did a walk-on in 'The School for Scandal' at the Clinton Playhouse, Connecticut. The following year she made her Broadway début in 'Out of the Frying Pan' (42), after which she toured army installations for the USO in 'Junior Miss'. She was tested for a lead in *Guest in the House* without success. She worked again in stock and in some Broadway flops, and finally hit it big in the successful 'Deep Are the Roots'. When the run finished she went to Hollywood to star in Anatole Litvak's remake of his own *Mayerling*, but the film was never made. Litvak put her instead into *The Long Night* (47) with Henry Fonda, also a remake of a French movie (*Le Jour se Lève*), as the understanding girl. RKO produced and signed her to a contract which specifically included the lead in *I Remember Mama* (48) – the 13-year-old Katrin. Mama was Irene Dunne.

Critics lauded Bel Geddes as a sensitive actress and a spectacular career seemed assured. But she was not perhaps the type of actress to appeal to Howard Hughes, who had taken over RKO: after playing a rancher's daughter in *Blood on the Moon*, with Robert Mitchum, she left the studio. One flop left her vulnerable: *Caught* (49), haplessly married to neurotic millionaire Robert Ryan. She went to 20th for two good pictures, *Panic in the Streets* (50), as Richard Widmark's wife, and Henry Hathaway's *Fourteen Hours* (51), as the girlfriend of Richard Basehart up there on that ledge. Already she had signed to return to Broadway: 'Burning Bright' (50) and 'The Moon is Blue' (51). There followed, among others: 'The Living Room' (54), 'Cat on a Hot Tin Roof' (55) and 'The Sleeping Prince' (56). She was a big Broadway attraction and Hollywood made occasional overtures. At one time she was reported as signed for *The Man with the Golden Arm*, but she did not return till *Vertigo* (58): Hitchcock as director was the lure, but it was only a featured role. She then played Danny Kaye's wife in *The Five Pennies* (59) and was back on Broadway in 'Silent Night Holy Night'.

Her next two films were mistakes: *Jovanke e le Altre/Five Branded Women* (60), an international effort directed by Martin Ritt with Silvana Mangano and Jeanne Moreau, among others, a drama set in the aftermath of World War II; and *By Love Possessed* (61), a mediocre version of James Gould Cozzens's novel, in a supporting part as the estranged wife of Efrem Zimbalist Jr. Then, 'Mary Mary' (61) provided her with her biggest stage triumph. She was also on television, but had become as fussy about Broadway plays as

Richard Widmark and Barbara Bel Geddes in Panic in the Streets *(50), one of the rare films made by this actress.*

about film scripts. She lived in semi-retirement with second husband Windsor Lewis, stage director and writer (at one time they lived in Ireland). She was wooed back to films for *Summertree* (71), as the bewildered mother of draft-dodging Michael Douglas, and then did *The Todd Killings*, as the murderer's mother. In 1973 she was on Broadway in 'Finishing Touches'; in 1974 her husband died. For TV she did a mother-role in 'Our Town' (77) and then the matriarch in 'Dallas', which began in 1979 and is still running. Bel Geddes's Miss Ellie made her very famous. When she left due to ill-health she was replaced by Donna Reed, who filed suit – despite a huge pay-off – when Bel Geddes indicated her willingness to return. There really was only one Miss Ellie.

JEAN-PAUL BELMONDO

'New blood, new looks, new vitality, new *fluidum*, new eroticism, new normality for that malady-ridden strain of today's neurotic actors' – Marlene Dietrich's 'ABC', under B for Belmondo.

Jean-Paul Belmondo was born in Neuilly-sur-Seine, Paris, in 1933, the son of a sculptor. As a boy his main achievements were in sport. He knew he wanted to act and was sent to study under Raymond Giraud, whence he went to the Conservatoire. He first made news when he failed to carry off first prize (which would have guaranteed a contract with the Comédie-Française): his fellow students booed the winner and the Paris papers carried a picture of Belmondo being chaired in triumph by them. This auspicious beginning resulted in some provincial tours with friends (including Annie Girardot and Guy Bedos), playing sometimes to a handful of people in run-down village halls. He returned to Paris and as the result of one small role was signed to star in 'Oscar' (58): both he and the play got good notices.

He was already appearing in films. His first role, in a scene with Jean-Pierre Cassel, was cut from *A Pied à Cheval et en Voiture*, which starred Noël-Noël. He appeared briefly in *Sois Belle et Tais-toi* (57), with Mylène Demongeot and Henri Vidal, then was tested by Marcel Carné for one of the leads in his old-hat look at modern youth, *Les Tricheurs* (58) – but he gave the part to Jacques Charrier and made Belmondo merely one of the gang. Belmondo was engaged by Jean-Luc Godard for a short, *Charlotte et son Jules* (his voice was dubbed), and given a small role in *Drôle de Dimanche* with Bourvil. He did star in *Les Copains du Dimanche*, which was never shown (he has described it as an agreeable location-made piece and thinks it might later have had a modest success on the strength of his name). There was a role in *Ein Engel auf Erden/Mademoiselle Ange* (59), as Henri Vidal's mechanic; then a very good one in Claude Chabrol's *A Double Tour* – which he asked for after bumping into Jean-Claude Brialy who had just turned it down on doctor's orders. He disliked the part (he does not like playing umsympathetic characters) and feels he was not good in it. Certainly he was not restrained – but neither was the film, an incredible thriller. By this time 'Oscar' had made him known and he was offered two star parts in films which opened in Paris the same week (before *A Double Tour*).

Director Claude Sautet had cast him in *Classe Tous Risques* only after a battle with the producers, who had wanted Dario Moreno for the part – a last loyal supporter of ageing gangster Lino Ventura. The friendship between these two crooks appealed to Belmondo, who found it pure, like the heroes in Westerns, and *implied* (unlike Jules and Jim, who were forever talking about theirs). This 'amitié virile de deux hommes' was a theme he was to return to time and again (*not* a theme many of his contemporaries were capable of handling). He admired the film enormously: 'le meilleur film policier français,' he said 10 years later, and he overestimates but a little. At the time it was overlooked in the rush to praise *A Bout de Souffle* – a film in which he had little confidence.

Nor had the producer, Georges de Beauregard, whose name hitherto had been associ-

Jean-Paul Belmondo as the young hoodlum around whom Jean-luc Godard constructed A Bout de Souffle *(59) – or* Breathless, *as it was called in the US. It was the film which made them both famous, and as with Byron, it happened overnight. The girl is Jean Seberg, whose career was also boosted by the film.*

ated with some not too successful 'commercial' films. But the success of Chabrol's films and Truffaut's *Les 400 Coups* had opened the floodgates for the *nouvelle vague*: he gave the go-ahead provided that Chabrol supervise and Truffaut provide the script. In effect, Chabrol considered Godard entirely capable and the script was a five-line résumé. The film, made in chronological sequence, was mainly an improvisation between Godard, Belmondo and Jean Seberg – the story of a petty hood and an American girl. They strove for spontaneity, for flippancy, for the attitudes people have in life – and in so doing both provided the 60s with its archetypal hero and extended the vocabulary of the cinema (no one, once involved with it, doubted that it would revolutionize the cinema – even if, outside France, it took time: without it, *M-A-S-H*, 10 years later, would not have been possible). The analysts went to work. 'L'Express' thought Belmondo represented all the anguish of a Youth so uncertain that its only refuge is murder and crime. Belmondisme was described thus: 'Un petit peu voyou, un petit peu anarchiste, mauvais garçon mais cœur sensible.' This author wrote (in 1963): 'If Belmondo's contribution was little more than allowing his personality to be exploited, it wouldn't be the first film in history to commend itself for such a reason. . . . I don't, myself, care much for cult figures, but there is no doubt that Michel (Belmondo) did respond to the restlessness of the atom-age. While Belmondo, himself, is presumably incapable of Michel's anarchy or his capacity for destruction, Godard found some inner conviction, perhaps some sort of reasoning in a mad world, to suggest that he could do such things. If some of Michel's other qualities look like a bit of Godard, a bit of Belmondo, a bit of luck – his carelessness, opportunism, romanticism, his *je m'en fichisme*, it is not by chance that his hero is Humphrey Bogart, who also represented a maverick in a dangerously conformist world. Belmondo might be dangerous and impulsive, but he always trusts his intuition and fists to the words of others. The audience trusts him, he is always one step ahead – and when he isn't, he dies.'

He had already done *Les Distractions* (60), as a reporter who hides a friend (Claude Brasseur), shares his girl with him and commits suicide when forced to betray him: a feeble effort as directed by one Jacques Dupont, his first film. (In his book – '30 Ans et 25 Films' – Belmondo implies that his incompetence was due to his extreme right-wing views.) He was then offered films with Bardot (*La Vérité*) and Jeanne Moreau; while deciding, he went to Italy for *Lettere di una Novizia*, playing an impoverished aristocrat wooing the daughter while carrying on with the mother (all told in flashback after the girl has shot him and entered a convent).

He wanted to act with Moreau, so signed for *Moderato Cantabile*, though in fact he liked neither Marguerite Duras's original

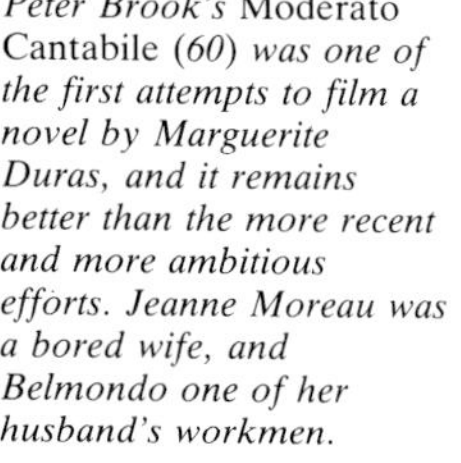

Peter Brook's Moderato Cantabile *(60) was one of the first attempts to film a novel by Marguerite Duras, and it remains better than the more recent and more ambitious efforts. Jeanne Moreau was a bored wife, and Belmondo one of her husband's workmen.*

novel nor, later, the finished film. As the workman who befriends the lonely Moreau his dog-like understanding was touching, the characterization the antithesis of his film persona to date. Then he played comedy for the first time on screen, as the lover coming between Dany Robin and Paul Meurisse in the 'Adultery' sketch of *La Française et l'Amour*, an otherwise soggy entertainment. Then he played two Italian country boys: bookish, bespectacled and gently adoring Sophia Loren in *La Ciociara* (61) and lazy, loutish and ineloquently devoted to prostitute Claudia Cardinale in *La Viaccia*, Mauro Bolognini's dazzling evocation of 19th-century Florence. Godard reclaimed him for *Une Femme est une Femme*, one of those films that was primarily a love-song to his then wife, Anna Karina: a thin idea (she wanted a baby, husband Brialy did not) which left much time for her cavorting, plus a look-in by Belmondo as the friend who realizes he might bed her after all. He was lusting again in one sketch of *Les Amours Célèbres*, in moustache and full-bottom wig, after one of Louis XIV's mistresses – an anecdote that proved he could play theatrical comedy with cinematic reticence.

He then made a wise move: he accepted the title-role in *Léon Morin Prêtre*. He liked the part if not the film; his participation enabled Jean-Pierre Melville to get backing (his last two films had failed); and he was superb as the priest, beautifully matched by Emmanuèle Riva as a one-time communist and lesbian drawn to the Church by what might be his sympathy but is more likely his sex-appeal. Melville said later that he was the most accomplished actor of his generation – that he could play any given scene in 20 different ways and all of them would be right. When 'Ciné-Revue' announced its poll of readers' favourite stars he led the field by miles (followed by Anthony Perkins, Charlton Heston, Alain Delon and Jean-Claude Brialy). Abroad, commentators were wondering about Hollywood offers. Henry Fonda called him one of the three best actors in the world and Jean Gabin said he was the only one who could take *his* place. Truffaut went further; after saying 'Pour moi, cela ne fait aucun doute, Jean-Paul Belmondo est le meilleur acteur actuel, le meilleur et le plus complet', he added that he could take on – without effort or fear of comparisons – not only the old roles of Gabin, Fernandel and Gérard Philipe, but those of Jules Berry, Michel Simon and Pierre Brasseur.

Only Belmondo's name brought any kudos to *Un Nommé la Rocca* (62), directed by Jacques Becker's son Jean, which reprised the themes of gangsterism and friendship (for Pierre Vaneck); but Philippe de Broca's sprightly *Cartouche* was a great hit, a Robin-Hood-type tale which did slip Philipe's mantle on his shoulders (at least, the Philipe of *Fan-fan-la-Tulipe*), though the 'New York Times' found him, rather, 'a latter-day Harold Lloyd'. The next was also a hit – *vieille vague* and therefore underestimated – *Un Singe en Hiver* with Gabin, from Antoine Blondin's novel about a young alcoholic whose friendship with an ex-drunk (Gabin) is a danger to the older man. Their scenes together were models of underplayed virtuosity, notably their parting. The sympathy between them was manifested by Gabin's professed admiration of Belmondo and the latter's pride in this; but it began to look as though the remarks were ill-judged – for in the films that followed, Belmondo played Belmondo as ruthlessly as Gabin had for years been playing Gabin. Not that audiences minded.

An old story: the country boy enslaved by a heartless whore. But it all seemed new enough as acted by Belmondo and Claudia Cardinale in La Viaccia *(61), set in a rainy Florence some many years ago.*

In 1961, 1962 and 1963 he was voted France's best actor by a consortium of the readers of 'Cinémonde', 'Figaro' and 'Le Film français'. He should have made *Fahrenheit 451*, but while Truffaut sought backing he did a couple for Melville: *Le Doulos* (63), with trilby, trench-coat and revolver again, and with Serge Reggiani; and *L'Ainé des Ferchaux*, from a novel by Simenon, set in the US, with Charles Vanel. In both, friendship was the motif. He remarked at this time that he had chosen a diversity of roles to escape from the *A Bout de Souffle* image – but he was in a rut. He was merely lumpish in Castellani's solemn *Mare Matto*, with Gina Lollobrigida – though he was very funny in *Dragées au Poivre* as a moronic legionnaire trying to date call-girl Simone Signoret, a good episode in an otherwise disastrous sketch-pic. He did a gay comedy with Moreau, *Peau de Banane*, but it had too much violence and too little wit to recall the Loy-Powell movies it was emulating; because of the stars it was a big success in France. But he was marvellous in *L'Homme de Rio* (64) – if not 'le nouveau Gabin' or 'le Brando français', at least the heir of Fairbanks Sr. '1,001 Exploits Belmondoesques!' said the ads as the public lined up (it was his biggest commercial hit). The critics were no less happy with this super-Tintin, a parody of all the chase films that ever were. It was also funny, beautiful (Rio and Brasilia in colour) and a triumph for de Broca, who directed.

Abroad it was Belmondo's most popular film since *A Bout de Souffle*, but these were hardly exportable: *100,000 Dollars au Soleil*, a fatigued actioner; *Echappement Libre*, a crooks-and-cons thriller with Jean Seberg; and *La Chasse à l'Homme*, in a guest cameo. *Weekend à Zuydcoote* (65) was based on a novel by Robert Merle about some events leading up to Dunkirk: a minor but valid statement on war, handsomely photographed by Henri Decae. In France, a huge success: in Britain and the US, dubbed and cut, nothing. *Par un Beau Matin d'Été*, another confused melodrama: nothing either, except in France on the strength of his name. He continued to head the popularity polls and great things were expected of a follow-up to *L'Homme de Rio* called *Les Tribulations d'un Chinois en Chine* with Ursula Andress, based on Jules Verne – but de Broca had not brought it off a second time.

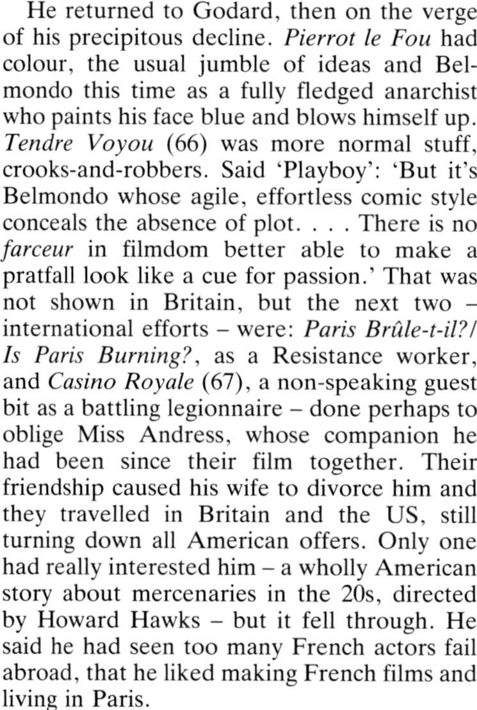

He returned to Godard, then on the verge of his precipitous decline. *Pierrot le Fou* had colour, the usual jumble of ideas and Belmondo this time as a fully fledged anarchist who paints his face blue and blows himself up. *Tendre Voyou* (66) was more normal stuff, crooks-and-robbers. Said 'Playboy': 'But it's Belmondo whose agile, effortless comic style conceals the absence of plot. . . . There is no *farceur* in filmdom better able to make a pratfall look like a cue for passion.' That was not shown in Britain, but the next two – international efforts – were: *Paris Brûle-t-il?/Is Paris Burning?*, as a Resistance worker, and *Casino Royale* (67), a non-speaking guest bit as a battling legionnaire – done perhaps to oblige Miss Andress, whose companion he had been since their film together. Their friendship caused his wife to divorce him and they travelled in Britain and the US, still turning down all American offers. Only one had really interested him – a wholly American story about mercenaries in the 20s, directed by Howard Hawks – but it fell through. He said he had seen too many French actors fail abroad, that he liked making French films and living in Paris.

At the same time he curtailed his activity; he had taken as much work as he could fit in because he did not think it would last. His best film in a long while was Louis Malle's elegant turn-of-the-century thriller, *Le Voleur*, though it was *déjà* more *vu* than any good film in an age, with that peculiarly romantic French criminal milieu where the whores are all healthy and pretty and friendly and the crooks loyal, steadfast and daring. Belmondo, more restrained than for some while, was that outsider – drifter/dreamer – that had been Gabin, Gérard Philipe and was now Lino Ventura, Jean-Louis Trintignant or indeed himself. He was again a crook in *Ho!* (68), a good gangster novel by José Giovanni directed by Robert Enrico: but it went wrong in filming and Belmondo felt let down by it. *Le Cerveau/The Brain* (69) was a heist story, with David Niven. Belmondo did not like his part – it required not an iota of his ability – but thought the film might be fun to make. He did not think he would become involved in a similar project, even though the film was a giant hit – in France. For love he appeared in a semi-documentary, *Dieu a Choisi Paris*, and then at last made a film with Truffaut, *La Sirène de Mississippi*, co-starring Catherine Deneuve, a mystery story set in La Réunion. The next was set in the US, Claude Lelouch's *Un Homme qui me Plait*, with Annie Girardot, the story of two expatriates who have an affair while and because far from home.

Belmondo in Le Voleur *(67), a study of a compulsive house-breaker. Louis Malle's direction gave style to some familiar themes.*

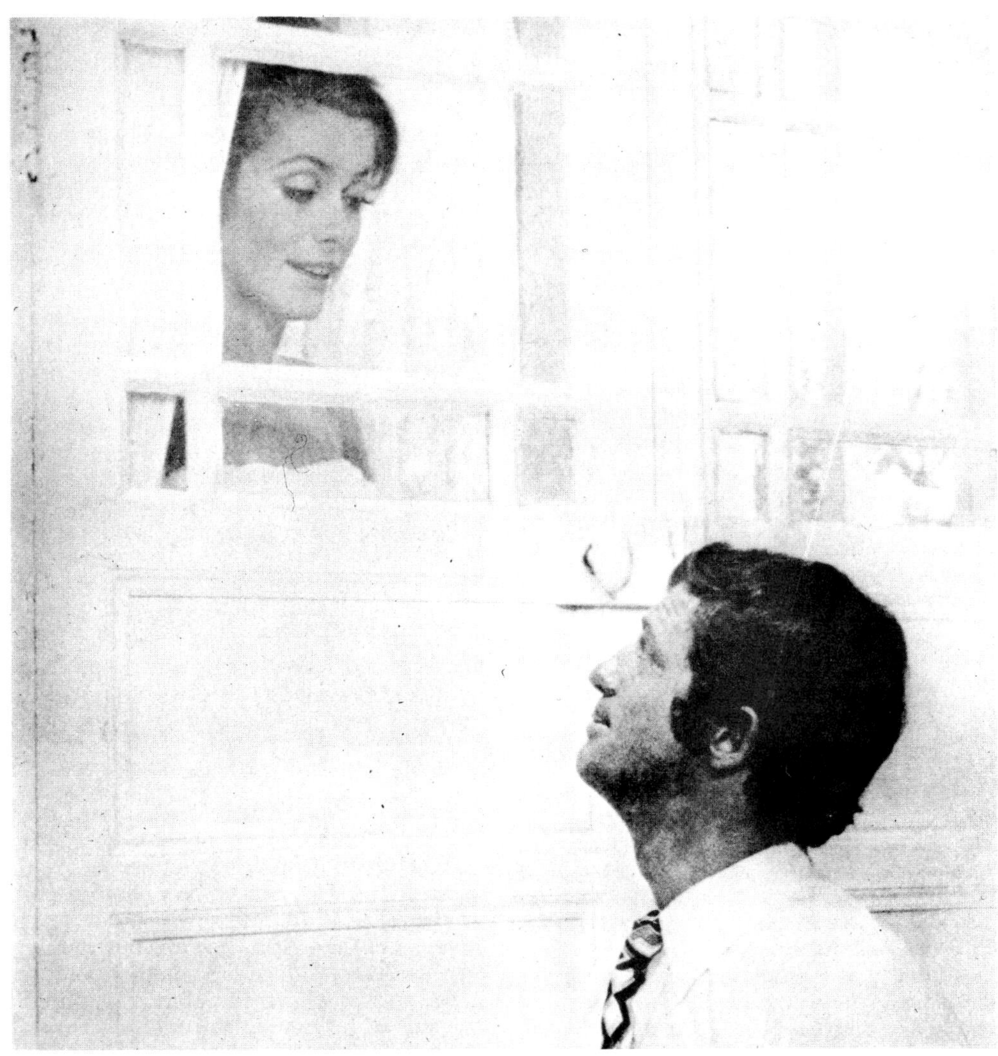

Catherine Deneuve and Belmondo in La Sirène de Mississippi *(69), a thriller directed by Truffaut. He has ordered a bride by mail, and she turns up: the mystery deepens from there.*

Borsalino (70) was an ersatz gangster piece, set in Marseilles, with a cliché a minute. Producer/co-star Delon plastered Paris with posters and was rather surprised when Belmondo took out an injunction, claiming that his contract was violated if Delon as producer had his name twice in the same size letters. Perhaps it mattered, but if the posters were Delon's the reviews were all Belmondo's. *Les Mariés de l'An Deux* (71) was another tongue-in-cheek swashbuckler, with Marlène Jobert, and *Le Casse*, yet another heist film, with Omar Sharif and Dyan Cannon, set in Greece. And yet another huge success. He had a second American leading lady, Mia Farrow, in one of Chabrol's clumsier comedies about murder, *Docteur Popaul* (72), in which he played the title-role. *La Scoumone* was virtually a remake of *Un Nommé la Rocca*, set back to the days of *Borsalino*: and Labro's *L'Héritier* (73) was equally Belmondo-formula stuff, with our hero as a sexual athlete chased by crooks from jet-liners to penthouse to fast sports cars. In de Broca's *Le Magnifique* he doubled as a shabby, meek writer and his dare-devil hero, but it did not match their best earlier films together.

Belmondo served as executive producer on most of these films and in that capacity he got Alain Resnais's backing for his *Stavisky* (74), playing the title-role, the Russian-born financial swindler of the 30s: and once more working with a good director, he again found the French public indifferent. These films with Malle, Chabrol, Godard, Truffaut, etc., found none of these directors at their best, but since they provided him with only poor to fair box-office he can hardly be blamed for increasingly eschewing prestige productions. In the US and Britain he became a lost cause: his big popular films arrived dubbed and without his voice Belmondo is lost – it is an undistinguished voice (unlike, say, Gabin's or Boyer's), but when it goes so do his skill and presence. Had it not been dubbed, there should have been a warm welcome for Verneuil's *Peur sur la Ville* (75), if only for its stunning chase sequence over the roofs near the Opéra: as it is, it failed to repeat its huge success in France. It was, not incidentally, the first time he had played a *flic*. And he continued to turn down English-language films, including *The French Connection II* and *March or Die*.

In 1973 'France-Soir' reported his salary as the highest in French films, at the equivalent of $600,000 per film (*cf* Delon and de Funes, $500,000; Montand $260,000 or a deferment; Girardot and Deneuve, $250,000; Gabin, Signoret and Trintignant $160,000); and he would certainly have at least equalled that working with his most trusted directors: *L'Incorrigible* for de Broca, *L'Alpaquer* (76) for Labro and *Le Corps de Mon Ennemi* for Verneuil. Indeed, he probably took more since he also decreased his activity to one film a year – which only increased his popularity, as witness the queues for *L'Animal* (77), with Raquel Welch, in which he did another double-role, as a stunt-man and an effeminate movie star. *Flic ou Voyou* (79) broke all box-office records and after a slight hiatus with *Le Guignolo/I Piccioni di Piazza San Marco* (80) – though it did well – so did these: *Le Professionel* (81), *L'As des As* (82) and *Le Marginal* (83). Cinemas were closing, but since French box-office statistics are based on attendances rather than receipts Belmondo's achievement is remarkably impressive. He refused to sell his films to television, but the last seven were released to video in 1981.

Not that everyone was pleased. When Demy's *La Chambre en Ville* flopped, Belmondo, who was not in it, was blamed; the critics took an ad citing *L'As des As* as a film made by publicity. The ploy rebounded, not only because it was now customary for the public to flock to Belmondo's films, but because he took an ad in both 'Figaro' and 'Le Monde' which stated, inter alia, that he had not blamed James Bond when *Stavisky* flopped. The film concerned showed Belmondo's care in giving variety to his vehicles: he played a man helping a Jewish family escape the Nazis. In *Les Morfalous* (84) he was a French legionnaire in Tunis in 1943, trying to get some gold bullion from a deserted bank. As a change of pace he did a comedy, *Joyeuses Paques*, based on a popular play by Jean Poiret, in which he was a middle-aged man whose difficulties mount when he tries to pass off his mistress as his long-lost daughter. Business was only fair and did not improve for *Hold Up* (85), although it was his best film for years, a French-Canadian production in which he masterminded a heist. *Le Solitaire* (87) was a comparative failure, though he remained on top form as a lone wolf cop in pursuit of the man who had killed one of his colleagues. Unperturbed by his falling status, Belmondo announced a heavy future schedule (which included a remake of *Le Bossu*). But for the moment the theatre occupied him: he revived Sartre's version of Dumas's 'Kean' and triumphed. The limited season was extended several times and to judge by the reception the tour that followed could have lasted for years. He cut it short to commit the role to video and to return to films, in Lelouch's *L'Itinéraire d'un Enfant Gâté* (88), playing a wanderer who befriends the child of the title – a performance which won him the French equivalent of the Best Actor Oscar.

The last Belmondo film to be seen in Britain and the US is *Peur dans la Ville*. Belmondo's 'commercial' films are preferable to most of the French films which are imported. But thank your lucky stars that *La Chambre en Ville* was not among them.

WILLIAM BENDIX

William Bendix was Neanderthal man reincarnated in Brooklyn, with a lantern-jaw, a Durante-like nose and eyes ablaze with wonder that life could be so different from what was learnt on the stoop. But not fazed: Brooklyn kids are never fazed, not as long as there is a crack to be made, half-rueful, half-cynical. Similar actors enlivened movies as cab-drivers, thugs, mugs, barmen and salesmen, but Bendix was somehow more disarming than such contemporaries as Allan Jenkins and Frank Jenks. Two other players climbed to stardom in ox-like roles, Jack Carson and Broderick Crawford, but Bendix was more likeable – he certainly had a much more subtle gift for comedy. In *Wake Island* he makes a withering retort as the island is blown up: 'Whad'you care? It ain't your island, is it?' Not many actors could have made that line funny. There was no particular finesse in his occasional forays into villainy, where his main asset was a tendency to act like a gorilla – though, still, not badly. He was one of the great natural actors.

He acted first at the age of five, in a Silent short made at the Vitagraph studio in Brooklyn, not far from where he was born (in 1906). His first job was as batboy with the New York Giants and he played minor league baseball. He worked as a singing waiter and did other such jobs on the fringe of show business, but when he married (in 1928) he became the manager of a grocery store. When the business failed he returned to show business, mainly in cabaret. He joined the New Jersey Federal Project, where he got a number of small roles and attracted the attention of the Theater Guild, who engaged him to play Policeman Krupp in 'The Time of Your Life' (39). He was in it for two years, and then signed a contract with Hal Roach at $300 a week plus 50 per cent of everything that Roach earned in excess of $600, if he loaned him out. But if Roach saw Bendix primarily as a comic, Hollywood saw him as an actor: instead of becoming Roach's top banana he was much in demand at other studios. Roach was mainly inactive anyway and Bendix made only one film for him at this time, *Brooklyn Orchid* (42), a B, released a couple of weeks after his first film, *Woman of the Year*, where he was one of Spencer Tracy's buddies.

Paramount put him into a couple: *Wake Island*, a sober account of that unhappy event in the Pacific campaign, as a tough marine, with Brian Donlevy; and *The Glass Key*, superb as an over-willing hired thug ('You mean, I don't get to smack baby?'). Paramount signed him to a non-exclusive contract and for the rest of the 40s he also worked regularly at 20th, UA and Universal. In *Who Done It?* he was a dimwit cop unable to cope with Abbott and Costello; in *Star Spangled Rhythm* a dumb husband in the Bob Hope sketch; and in *The Crystal Ball* (43) Ray Milland's tough valet. He starred in a B for Roach, *Taxi Mister?*, as the guy asking the question, and then supported Alan Ladd, as his sidekick, in *China*. Paramount were so convinced of Bendix's ability that they made him a Hungarian Resistance leader in *Hostages*, with Luise Rainer. *Guadalcanal Diary* was his first for 20th and as adapted from the book by Richard Tregaskis one of the best war films made during the hostilities; the cross-section was bound to include a Bendix, with wise-cracks full of Brooklyn pride (as well as 'human' Irish padre Preston Foster and Mexican Anthony Quinn to represent the ethnic groups – there were no Negroes to be seen).

He was outstandingly good in Hitchcock's *Lifeboat* (44), as the seaman who has to have his leg amputated therein, and in the title-role of the film version of Eugene O'Neill's *The Hairy Ape* – it was his biggest part yet, as the stoker who falls for hooker Susan Hayward, and it brought him his best reviews. Said the 'New York Times': 'His work rarely falls short of excellent and at times touches several degrees higher.' As a definite change, he – and Dennis O'Keefe – spent most of *Abroad with Two Yanks* in drag in order, so it went, to pursue Helen Walker: an amusing piece of flapdoodle. He was back on home ground, nearly, in *Greenwich Village*, a Carmen Miranda musical, and then did a guest stint as a gang boss in *It's In the Bag* (45). He was *Don Juan Quilligan*, a barge-carrier with a mother complex and two wives – one in Brooklyn and the other in Buffalo: a comedy-thriller that did not quite come off. After which, he returned to supporting roles: in *A Bell For Adano*, as the cynical sergeant; *Sentimental Journey* (46), as the chumpish family friend, the only believable character in the film; *The Blue Dahlia*, as Alan Ladd's sidekick again, trigger-tempered and slug-happy; and *The Dark Corner*, as 'White Suit', a singularly vicious hired killer.

William Bendix and Joan Blondell in Don Juan Quilligan *(45).*

He did not relinquish star-billing, but he seldom again was in any but subsidiary roles, as in *Two Years Before the Mast*, as one of the maltreated crew, and *White Tie and Tails*, as a tough guy tangling with Ella Raines and her butler Dan Duryea (essaying a comedy role in Universal's bid to make him, Duryea, into a star instead of just a prize baddie). He was Deanna Durbin's self-appointed guardian in *I'll Be Yours* (47), and then one of William Holden's buddies in *Blaze of Noon* and one of Ladd's again in *Calcutta*; the police lieutenant who unravels *The Web*, with Edmond O'Brien; a guest in *Variety Girl*; a New York cop plagued by Bob Hope in *Where There's Life*; and the barman (not his stage role) in *The Times of Your Life* (48). After an indifferent crime melodrama with George Raft, *Race Street*, as a detective, he was twice top-starred again – though neither film was

William Bendix was usually an amiable, simple soul in movies, but on occasion he was a very good heavy – as here, in The Dark Corner *(46). It was a relief to find Mark Stevens getting the better of him.*

any great shakes. In *The Babe Ruth Story* he was unable, intentionally or not, to suggest that the great baseball player had any intelligence, before the film degenerated into tear-jerking; and *The Life of Riley* (49) was merely a modest version of a radio show he had done since 1944 – a suburban husband and father beset by family. Rosemary de Camp was Riley's wife and remained so in the subsequent TV series, when Jackie Gleason played Riley; Bendix took over his old part in 1953, with Marjorie Reynolds as his wife, and played it on TV for another eight seasons.

Streets of Laredo was his first Western and he was one of Holden's gang of outlaws; then was a good foil to Crosby in *A Connecticut Yankee at the Court of King Arthur*, as Sir Sagramore. He hindered insurance agent Dennis O'Keefe in *Cover-Up*; competed with Robert Mitchum to get Patric Knowles and the swag in *The Big Steal* – one of his best villains; and was a tough reform-school sergeant in *Johnny Holiday*, a sentimental *Boy's Town* tale. He was top-billed in that and in a B, *Kill the Umpire* (50), as an obstreperous fan who becomes an umpire, with Una Merkel as his wife. At RKO he was a gang boss who framed Victor Mature for a killing he had done, in *Gambling House*, and while there Howard Hughes signed him to a contract – seven years, two films a year, plus the right to do TV (a remarkable concession at that time). He went back to Paramount to play a non-com in *Submarine Command* (51) and a sympathetic cop in *Detective Story* – but once he began to do TV the other studios were no longer interested. Hughes used him in just four films before he folded RKO, starting with *Macao* (52), as a shady merchant who turns out to be a US undercover man. He was Groucho Marx's buddy in *A Girl in Every Port*, and an admirable foil to that Marxist gob; but was only too much at sea as an evil crony of *Blackbeard the Pirate*, who was Robert Newton at his most hammy. He had a brief role in *Dangerous Mission* (54), as a Glacier National Park guardsman.

Busy in TV, he made only three films over the next four years: *Crashout* (56), an independent venture, as a ruthless convict escaping with Arthur Kennedy; *Battle Stations* with John Lund, as a tough bosun; and *The Deep Six* (58), alongside Alan Ladd for the last time, a tasteless drama wherein Ladd conquers his Quaker training in order to return home a hero. Bendix made a deal to make three pictures in Britain and they were all poor – but two of them gave him parts way off his usual beat: and the first, if it put back stripes on his arm, well, it was the British army and he was barking at pop idol Anthony Newley, *Idle on Parade* (59). In Robert Siodmak's drear *The Rough and the Smooth* he was the love-sick voyeuristic elderly boss of Nadja Tiller, a nympho married to Tony Britton. And in *Johnny Nobody* (61) he was an alcoholic writer of bestsellers murdered by religious fanatic Aldo Ray, in Ireland. Meanwhile, back in the US, he had starred in a short-lived TV series, 'Overland Trail', and he took over from Jackie Gleason in Broadway's 'Take Me Along'. Then he put on his sergeant's jacket again for a German film about the Berlin airlift, *Toller Hecht auf Krummer Tour* (62), starring Christine Kauffman.

There was a cameo part, a barman, in *Boys' Night Out* (63) and then he was a staff sergeant in *The Young and the Brave* with Rory Calhoun, a low-budget (Korean) war drama, produced by A.C. Lyles for MGM. There was another small role in a film with Kirk Douglas, *For Love or Money*, and A.C. Lyles gave him supporting parts in two of his low-budget Westerns, *Law of the Lawless* (64), as a sheriff, and *Young Fury* (65), as a blacksmith. Before it was shown he had died (in 1964) of pneumonia. Not long before, he had toured in 'Never Too Late' and had sued CBS TV for cancelling a series planned for him and Martha Raye. CBS claimed his health was not up to it and the matter was settled out of court.

Claire Bloom

For someone whose career began with such lustre, Claire Bloom has had a difficult path. Overlauded at first as the most winsome thing on four wheels, it later seemed that she was merely the leading representative of a rather ghastly sect, the English Rose. It is a species whose individuals (the word is used loosely) seldom endure. But this one was hardy; she really was talented; when they let her break from type she was liable to give a superb performance. She may continue to surprise.

She was born in London in 1931 and studied for the stage at the Guildhall School of Music and Drama and at the Central School; she made her début with the Oxford rep in 'It Depends What You Mean' (46) and her London bow six months later walking-on in 'The White Devil'. She came to the attention of the Rank Organization – this was their Charm School era – and was signed for five years starting at £25 a week. She was obviously different from the other starlets, so instead of having her advertise soap or hair-brushes they actually put her in a film: *The Blind Goddess* (48), a small role as the fiancée of advocate hero Michael Denison. Her verdict: 'I was terrible', but she did get favourable mentions. At all events, she asked Rank to release her and they complied. At Stratford-upon-Avon she played Ophelia (to Scofield's Hamlet) and Perdita; in London she was the ingénue in Christopher Fry's 'The Lady's Not For Burning' (49), with Richard Burton. She starred in Fry's adaptation of an Anouilh play, 'Ring Round the Moon' (50), and was seen in it by dramatist Arthur Laurents, who recommended her to Charlie Chaplin, then looking for a new heroine. She flew to Hollywood to test and Chaplin signed her.

Few of Chaplin's leading ladies had independent careers, but Bloom could be more hopeful because of the tremendous publicity at this time and because for *Limelight* (52) she got glowing notices, playing the ballerina the old clown adores. Also at the time the film came out she was a highly acclaimed Juliet at the Old Vic (her success saved the company from bankruptcy). Offers poured in, but she did not want to play another dewy heroine, so chose a comedy, *Innocents in Paris* (53): it was British, and episodic, and seemed a good indication that she wanted to wreck her own career. Carol Reed came to her rescue by offering her the lead opposite James Mason in *The Man Between*. She did another Old Vic season, with Burton, playing Helena in 'All's Well', Viola, Ophelia and Miranda. She has described this as a 'difficult period' and says she turned down parts wholesale. She allowed herself to be wooed, however, by two monarchs, Olivier as *Richard III* (55) and Burton as *Alexander the Great* (56); after which, she said, there were no offers at all.

She returned to the stage – Juliet again and Cordelia; on TV in the US she did 'Cyrano de Bergerac' with José Ferrer, and 'Caesar and Cleopatra' with Cedric Hardwicke and Farley

Laurence Olivier's first Lady Anne was Joyce Redman, a lovely actress still too little known despite a distinguished career, when he first played Richard III for the Old Vic; Vivien Leigh was his second, when he took on the role again in the late 40s. Claire Bloom was the only choice when he put the role on the screen in 1955.

Granger. She returned to Hollywood for *The Brothers Karamazov* (58), with Yul Brynner, playing the wealthy heiress Katya, and *The Buccaneer*, also with Brynner, as the spitfire heroine who is won by him in the end. There have been better spitfire heroines. Back in London she agreed to star with Vivien Leigh in 'Duel of Angels' but declined at first to appear in the film of *Look Back in Anger* (59) with Burton; the part offered was not, as she had supposed, the submissive wife, but the smarty actress who supplants her. Bloom was certain she could not do this, but was eventually talked into it – and was fine. Thereafter she was less timid in selecting parts, but the parts offered over the next decade were not greatly numerous. In 1959 she played in a Broadway adaptation of 'Rashomon' with Rod Steiger, whom she married.

She played a ballerina again, in a German film with Curt Jurgens, *Schnachnovelle* (60), based on a Stefan Zweig story. In 1961 she appeared in London in Sartre's 'Altona' and went back to Hollywood to play the wife of Grimm Laurence Harvey in *The Wonderful World of the Brothers Grimm* (62). Her career seemed to take an upsurge: *The Chapman Report* (63), a febrile performance as a pathetic nympho, and *The Haunting*, as good if not better, as a *chic* lesbian mocking Julie Harris. Richard Johnson was also in it and Bloom was married to him in *80,000 Suspects*, a platitudinous study of how a smallpox scare can cure a marriage, among other things.

None of these films was successful, so Bloom's good work in the best of them (*The Chapman Report*, *The Haunting*) went for little. She accepted two offers from Italy, both from director Elio Petri: *Il Maestro di Vigevano* (64), from a bestseller, as the ambitious money-mad wife of professor Alberto Sordi, and *Alta Inedeltà*, in the episode with Charles Aznavour, 'Peccato nel Pomeriggio' (which had the same idea as Harold Pinter's play 'The Lover'). Back in the US she was in another box-office clinker – though it was no fault of hers or co-star Paul Newman: *The Outrage*, which was *Rashomon* again, transferred to a Western setting and directed by Martin Ritt, who cast her in *The Spy Who Came in From the Cold* (65), opposite Burton again, as the communist librarian who loves him. In London she appeared in 'Ivanov'.

After another long absence from the screen she played musical chairs with a couple of actresses who had been later Rank starlets and were not, in those days, likely ever to be in the same league: she had signed for *Shalako* but ceded to Honor Blackman when Anne Heywood left *Charly* (68) at the last moment after script differences – a good chance for Bloom as the therapist who falls for Cliff Robertson. By this time her husband, Steiger, had reached the top of the Hollywood heap and it was probably he who insisted on her as his leading lady in the sci-fi *The Illustrated Man* (69) and in *Three Into Two Won't Go*. It was uxoriousness to no point: neither film was up to much and during the second, a study of a decaying marriage, their own marriage was

The Chapman Report *(63) had previously been a best-seller about some women who answer a sex-questionnaire. Here are the actresses who played four of them on the screen: Claire Bloom, Glynis Johns, Jane Fonda and Shelley Winters.*

breaking up, which may account, sadly, for her superb work in it. Before it was shown she married Hillard Elkins, Broadway and movie entrepreneur.

Her next film made her a sleek monster again, a kinky Oxford don, but the part was a joke: the film, *A Severed Head* (71) was not. As a change she played a loving wife in *Red Sky at Morning*; and in New York alternated two Ibsen women, Norah in 'A Doll's House' and Hedda Gabler. It was generally agreed she was great as Norah, so-so as Hedda. And then on Broadway she played Mary Stuart in 'Vivat! Vivat Regina!' (72). She put her Norah on screen, in a competent film version of *A Doll's House* (73), which beat the Jane Fonda version into cinemas; and there was premièred a film she had made in Israel with Topol and Melvyn Douglas, *The Going Up of David Lev*. A play with Anthony Quinn, 'The Red Devil Battery Sign' by Tennessee Williams, folded without reaching New York and a similar fate met her marriage to Elkins. In London in 1974 she failed to erase memories of Vivien Leigh in 'A Streetcar Named Desire', but as the first wife of the Hemingway hero in *Islands in the Stream* (77) her 'few moments on screen are terrific' – said 'Variety'. Turning to TV, she was the second Mrs Wilson in a mini-series, *Backstairs at the White House* (79), and the first wife of Henry VIII in the BBC's attempt to put on record all the plays of the Bard; for the BBC she was one of several names entrapped in a literally hysterical version of the Oresteia. Staying with the classics, sort of, she played Hera to the Zeus of Olivier in *Clash of the Titans* (81).

In 1981 she was in 'The Cherry Orchard' at Chichester; the following year she published an autobiography and had a notable success in Granada TV's *Brideshead Revisited*. Also for TV she was the boarding-house manageress in *Separate Tables* (83), starring Julie Christie and *The Ghost Writer* (84), based on a novel by Philip Roth, whose life she shares. Her only cinema movie in a while was *Déjà* (85), a one-week flop directed by a former assistant of Nicholas Roeg, Anthony Reynolds, in his master's style. The stars were Jaclyn Smith and Nigel Terry, a young couple who become obsessed with a dead ballerina; Bloom played that lady's possessive mother, ultimately discovered to be the source of the movie's horrors. You could hardly blame her for returning to TV: the mini-series, *Ellis Island*; the Priestley play, *Time and the Conways*, for the BBC; a tele-movie for NBC, *Florence Nightingale*, as her mother (Jaclyn Smith had the title-role); *Promises to Keep* with Robert Mitchum; *Shadowlands*, an award-winning drama for the BBC, as an American divorcee falling in love with confirmed bachelor and writer C.S. Lewis (Joss Ackland); *Liberty* (86), which celebrated the centenary of the statue of same, as the wife of its sculptor, Frank Langella; *Anastasia: the Mystery of Anna* (86), in the role played by Helen Hayes in the movie; *Consenting Adults* (87), a British mini-series with Daniel Massey as her husband, a victim of AIDS; *Queenie*, an American mini-series based on a fictionalized life of Merle Oberon, as her mother; and yet another such, *Hold the Dream*, in support of Deborah Kerr and Jenny Seagrove. Movies reclaimed her with *Sammy and Rosie Get Laid*, when Shashi Kapoor revisited her after years away, the two of them representing an older generation of Anglo-Indian relationships than Sammy or Rosie. Then, for TV: *Beryl Markham, A Shadow in the Sun* (88), the tale of a once-famous aviatrix (Stephanie Powers), as an aristocratic Brit in Kenya; and *The Lady and the Highwayman* (89), some lush Barbara Cartland nonsense, with Oliver Reed. She would be better employed in Woody Allen's next film, untitled as yet.

Ann Blyth

Ann Blyth was one of the ugly ducklings of show business. As a teenage star she was one of the least attractive of that unprepossessing species; then she suddenly emerged as one of the screen's better soubrettes, shed of the affectation that had marked her earlier work and now very pretty. Then, just as she looked like taking her place among the top stars, she disappeared.

She was born in Mount Kisco, New York, in 1928 and was a child prodigy: she made her professional début at five, singing and reciting on the air, and was soon an established radio actress. She studied at the Children's Professional School and later with the San Carlos Opera Company. She made her Broadway bow in 'Watch on the Rhine' (41) as Babette and toured with that play. While in Los Angeles she was offered a test by Universal and they signed her to a contract. She quickly became the girl whom Donald O'Connor dotes upon in *Chip Off the Old Block* (44) and *The Merry Monahans*, two of Universal's cheapie imitations of the successful Garland-Rooney musicals. Indeed, the title of the next, *Babes on Swing Street*, was reminiscent of them, though O'Connor was not around that time. Blyth was no Garland, nor was she the second Deanna Durbin for whom Universal were now seeking desperately, as that lady grew up. So Blyth went into another Grade B musical with O'Connor (and Susannah Foster and Maria Montez and others of the stock company), *Bowery to Broadway*, the *n*th film that year with the Good Old Tunes.

So far, so bad; but Warners borrowed her to play Joan Crawford's vicious daughter in *Mildred Pierce* (45) and for the first time on screen she impressed. Unfortunately, she then broke her back tobogganing – it was thought at one point she might be an invalid for life. When she recovered, she was cast in more stern stuff: *Swell Guy* (47), with Sonny Tufts as the ex-war hero who turns out to be anything but; *Brute Force*, a prison melodrama with Burt Lancaster; and *Killer McCoy* at MGM opposite Mickey Rooney himself. She had grown up; but as the minx who breaks up Charles Boyer's home and becomes his second wife she was clearly out of her depth – *A Woman's Vengeance.* Nor was she any more convincing a villainness in *Another Part of the Forest* (48), a sequel (earlier in time) to *The Little Foxes* – impossible to imagine this spoiled kitten growing into the panther-like Bette Davis. She sported a tail to vamp William Powell in *Mr Peabody and the Mermaid* (around the same time as Glynis Johns in an even wetter British picture, *Miranda*) and then played a Zane Grey heroine in the Utah-locationed *Red Canyon* (49), with Howard Duff. She was a teenager with a crush on movie star Robert Montgomery in *Once More My Darling.*

Bing Crosby's contract allowed him to choose his leading ladies and he chose Blyth for *Top o' the Morning* – but it was one of his worst films. She was with Robert Cummings in *Free For All*: 'Miss Blyth looks startled and wide-eyed which she mistakenly thinks is the only way to play comedy' – Steven H. Scheuer. Her career looked up somewhat, temporarily, when Goldwyn borrowed her for a knee-deep sudser, *Our Very Own* (50), playing the adopted daughter of Jane Wyatt and discovering her real mother lives on the other side of the tracks – Ann Dvorak. 'See It With Someone You Love Very Much,' said the ads, advice countermanded by the critics. Farley Granger was her sweetheart and for a second film running she had a leading man of more or less the same age: Mark Stevens in *Katie Did It* (51), a small-town comedy.

What saved her was *The Great Caruso* with Mario Lanza. Presumably the part of Mrs C. was not acceptable to any of their own stars, so MGM borrowed Blyth – who was delighted. They experimented with her make-up, they let her sing, they revealed her as charming and attractive; and as an actress, she was not at all bad in a poor part. Back at Universal she was a condemned murderess holed-up in a convent in the wretched *Thunder on the Hill*, with Claudette Colbert, and a Levantine princess wooed by crusader David Farrar in *The Golden Horde*: but *Caruso* had made her a fairly hot property. Meanwhile 20th was having trouble with British actress Constance Smith, signed on a new long-term contract; she had replaced Maureen O'Hara on *The Thirteenth Letter*, but was now to be replaced by Blyth, whom 20th were only too pleased to get: *I'll Never Forget You*, opposite Tyrone Power. Universal caught on and gave her to the equally important Gregory Peck for *The World in His Arms* (52) – not, as in the posters, as the World, but a Russian countess. She worked out her contract in a folksy comedy with Edmund Gwenn, *Sally and Saint*

Ann Blyth and Farley Granger in Our Very Own *(50), one of Sam Goldwyn's occasional sagas of American family life – in this case, one of the soppier ones.*

Ann Blyth and Fernando Lamas in the 1954 version of Rose Marie. *Some of the film, refreshingly, looked like this; at other times, the wide screen only emphasized the painted back-drops.*

Anne, and was then rushed into *One Minute to Zero* when Claudette Colbert caught pneumonia. It was a war film with Robert Mitchum and she was a nurse.

MGM had been waiting patiently and now signed her. They planned to star her mainly in musicals, but first put her opposite Robert Taylor in an adventure opus, *All the Brothers Were Valiant* (53). She did sing in *Rose Marie* (54) with Howard Keel, and her performance and voice were among the good things in a generally poor remake – and she was certainly the nicest thing about *The Student Prince*, the tavern wench listening to Mario Lanza's voice as it emerged from Edmund Purdom. MGM put these young lovers again (Purdom without the Voice) in *The King's Thief* (55). She was top-billed. Then she was the ingénue in *Kismet*, again with Keel, the film which virtually killed off the MGM musical. After a year's absence MGM gave her an innocuous part in *Slander* (56) opposite Van Johnson and, along with most of their stars, let her go.

She did not mind. She had married a doctor in 1953 and had embarked on a family. Still, there were offers, one from Paramount to play with her old co-star, Donald O'Connor, in *The Buster Keaton Story* (57). The other was from Warners to play another of the unfortunates of showbiz, the title-role in *The Helen Morgan Story*; announced for many actresses, and for which 32 of them tested. Of them all, Blyth had to be the most unsuitable. Even so, aided by the voice of Gogi Grant (though her own singing voice was nearer to Morgan's: Judy Garland had originally been scheduled for the role and Jack Warner wanted a Garland-like voice) she might have pulled it off – but the script insisted on every cliché in the book (showbiz alcoholic); further, Morgan was too well remembered and revered for Blyth to get anything but dreadful notices. She retired, but does make occasional guest appearances on TV and in summer stock. For instance, in Milwaukee between 1966 and 1978 she appeared in 'Showboat', 'The Sound of Music', 'South Pacific' and 'Bitter Sweet'. In 1985 she did some nostalgia concerts.

Dirk Bogarde

Dirk Bogarde began as a particularly uninteresting *jeune premier* and for a while looked like having a career playing spivs; but he surfaced as a romantic hero with a huge female following, one of the top box-office stars in Britain. He refused to go to Hollywood and even when he did start appearing in American-backed films, few of them were good. He surmounted 20 years of mainly poor films, not one of which was not the better for the care and integrity of his performance. Most of the time the only aura he gave off was an anxiousness to please, but his reputation was rising all the time because he was always so reliable; his range was restricted but he moved within it with more subtlety and sensitivity than actors more showily equipped. When finally he gave a great performance, in *Death in Venice*, there was much satisfaction among those who had watched him grow.

He was born in Hampstead in 1920, the son of a Dutchman who was art correspondent for 'The Times'. He began a career as scenic designer and commercial artist but wanted to act and was given the chance at a small suburban theatre, the Q, as the juvenile in 'When We Are Married' (39). Some small parts followed, including a spell in rep and extra-work on *Come on George* (40), but nothing important till after his war service, when he was at another small theatre, in 'Power Without Glory' (46) with Kenneth More; the play transferred to the West End and was televised. In films he had one line in *Dancing with Crime* (47). He was also one of the leads in a TV 'Rope'. His notices in the play with More brought him a long-term Rank contract and the small part of a priest in an adaptation of George Moore's *Esther Waters* (48), starring Kathleen Ryan and Stewart Granger; but when Granger decided not to do it the lead was given to Bogarde in desperation. He followed it with 'The Alien Corn' episode in a collection of Somerset Maugham stories, *Quartet*, the one about the would-be pianist – which survives only on the strength of Françoise Rosay's participation; with *Once a Jolly Swagman*, a back-streets story of speedway tracks; *Dear Mr Prohack* (49), a mild comedy from a play by Arnold Bennett; and *Boys in Brown*, as a reform-school inmate. He was a cheap little crook in *The Blue Lamp* (50), a schmaltzy tribute to the boys on the beat which was the most successful British film of that year. Its director, Basil Dearden, was the first, he has said, to give him any guidance. He was still appearing in the theatre, notably in Anouilh's 'Point of Departure' ('Eurydice'), but after a revival of Coward's 'The Vortex' in 1952 he has only done two plays. Ugo Betti's 'Summertime' (55) in London, and Anouilh's 'Jezebel' (58) in Oxford.

He was Jean Simmons's romantic interest in *So Long at the Fair* and one of several that Jean Kent had as *The Woman in Question*, Anthony Asquith's study of a murder victim as seen by her friends. Neither did much for him and still less was done by *Blackmailed* (51), a hapless little thriller. His film career really began to move with *Hunted* (52), an intelligent thriller about an escaped convict saddled with a small boy (Jon Whiteley). It opened in London the week George VI died, which did not help it, but the trade and press noted how good Bogarde was ('The discipline involved in playing with and to a child seems to have found new reserves of strength in Dirk Bogarde's acting,' wrote C.A. Lejeune) – which was fortuitous, because the next one was *Penny Princess* starring Yolande Donlan (an American who had done 'Born Yesterday' in the West End, but who did not make it in films). Bogarde later described his attempted comedy performance as 'terrible'.

There was a crisis, as usual, in the British film industry and Rank dropped several artists. Bogarde was offered a cut in salary instead and reckoned he was only kept because he was scheduled for *The Gentle Gunman*, a melodrama about IRA activities during the war years. Like all British male stars of the 50s, he could not escape being in uniform and it was a wing commander's in *Appointment in London* (53), a better than average war drama. He was hunted again, a wrongly convicted murderer, in *Desperate Moment* and in uniform again, a lieutenant's, in Lewis Milestone's disappointing war story, made in Rhodes, *They Who Dare* (54).

Four more Bogarde pictures were released that year, none of much interest, but *Doctor in the House* turned out to be a blazing popular hit. Adapted from a laboured comic novel by Richard Gordon about a group of medical students, it had a certain zest; but the others in the series that followed had little to offer. They were all highly popular and this

Pursued by the police: Dirk Bogarde in The Blue Lamp *(50), a tribute to the London bobby that was – alas – nearer in style to* Rebecca of Sunnybrook Farm *than* The French Connection.

first emanation as Dr Simon Sparrow made Bogarde a box-office star. No one, however, bothered much with *The Sleeping Tiger*, a ludicrous drama about psychiatry, made by the exiled Joseph Losey under a pseudonym, or *For Better For Worse*, a comedy about young marrieds. He was a flight-sergeant in *The Sea Shall Not Have Them*.

Simba (55) was a surprisingly good film about the Mau Mau troubles – 'surprisingly', because Rank pictures, never very good, had become amorphous as well. If any of them had any merit, the secret was well kept. Like *Doctor at Sea*. Bogarde was the only Rank star to have script approval, but as he said later, there were few good scripts to approve. He went out on loan for *Cast a Dark Shadow*, a theatrical melodrama with Margaret Lockwood, returned for the title-role in *The Spanish Gardener* (56), from a novel by A.J. Cronin, and *Ill Met by Moonlight* (57), yet more war, from a book by Patrick Leigh-Fermor – played by Bogarde in the film. Some of these movies were popular. Like *Doctor at Large*. In 1955 and again in 1957 he was Britain's top box-office star. 'Picturegoer' readers voted him the year's best actor for *Campbell's Kingdom*, presumably because in that he only had six months to live.

Plaguing Rank for better vehicles, he was offered a remake of *A Tale of Two Cities* (58), capably remade, but hardly shown outside Britain. He played Sidney Carton with a dignity that did not go much beyond a melancholy expression and one raised eyebrow. *The Wind Cannot Read* was a love-story (RAF officer and Oriental maiden) from a facile bestseller. Then: *Lawrence of Arabia*, directed by Anthony Asquith, written by Terence Rattigan, budgeted at £1½ million. Three days before it was due to begin it was cancelled. More than ever Bogarde wanted to leave Rank, but because he had had time off for stage work they had a hold on him for some years more. However, he started to break hesitantly into the international market. He had had American offers ever since *Hunted* (*The Egyptian* and *Gigi*, among others – he observed once that each time he refused *The Egyptian* the money went up) and now MGM backed Asquith's version of Shaw's *The Doctor's Dilemma*, in the hope, it was said, that the British public would think it was another *Doctor* film. Leslie Caron co-starred. Bogarde hit Louis off to a T, spineless, charming and ruthless, but the piece itself was slow. Asquith also directed, also for MGM, *Libel* (59), a hoary old court-roomer with Olivia de Havilland and Bogarde in a double role.

The ads for *Song Without End* (60) read, curiously, 'the story of Liszt's life with Dirk Bogarde', but in fact he played Liszt, in Hollywood, under George Cukor's direction (the film was credited to Charles Vidor, who died during shooting). Cukor 'really did teach me everything,' said Bogarde later, but little of Cukor's elegance was on the film and it was a flop (thus confirming Columbia's doubts, having planned the subject 16 years earlier, after the success of their film on Chopin; concurrent with the failure of Liszt to lure was a flop about Wagner, *Magic Fire*). Back in Britain, for Rank, Bogarde was a Mexican bandit with an unspoken crush on John Mills in *The Singer Not the Song*. Wrote Peter John Dyer: 'A Dirk Bogarde picture is rarely a guarantee of a work of art, yet it has come to promise, certainly of late, a film of definite morbid interest. . . . It is a strangely compelling film. This is mainly due to the presence of Bogarde himself, intelligent, quietly sardonic, his restraint (apart from an over-indulged left eyebrow) verging on the hieratic, his hints of inner *angoisse* . . . boyishly appealing yet at the same time oddly reminiscent of Joan Fontaine in *Ivy*, his wardrobe (60 per cent black leather) a fetishist's dream, his aptness for a part requiring Marlon Brando approximately nil.' In Italy he made *La Sposa Bella/The Angel Wore Red* with Ava Gardner and this time Dyer wrote: 'The abounding impression of gloomy incompetence is reinforced by the deep involvement of Nunnally Johnson, who wrote and directed it.' He was a Spanish priest who loves a whore in the Civil War.

Bogarde was probably the first major screen actor to accept the part of a homosexual (overt, this time) in the first ever film to deal mainly with that problem, *Victim* (61).

Dirk Bogarde being dragged out of the closet in Victim *(61), after telling his wife (Sylvia Sims) that he is being blackmailed by a rentboy. An eternal bachelor, Bogarde was then writing articles in the magazines claiming that he was probably going to marry Capucine.*

He was a nice young lawyer ('Roger, you really do *care* for people, don't you') having to confess to his wife a strange infidelity ('I wanted him, I tell you, I wanted him') and he tackled the subject rather in the way he had confronted recalcitrant patients and enemy squadrons. The film itself was styled as a thriller and was glib even on that level, but it had a *succès d'estime* and was popular. Looking for similarly gutsy material, Bogarde took options on Osborne's 'Epitaph for George Dillon' and John Harris's 'Covenant With Death' but could get neither financed; so he donned uniform again, even if in *HMS Defiant* (62) it was 18th-century naval (another subtle study in nastiness) and in *The Password Is Courage* that of a POW. *The Mind Benders* (63) was an insubstantial film about brain-washing and *I Could Go On Singing* an emotional vehicle for Judy Garland. Bogarde's selfless performance as her boorish ex-husband brought him his best notices to date.

He had said on many occasions that he would never do another *Doctor* film and the last one had had Michael Craig in the lead, *Doctor in Love*. He had done a guest shot as Simon Sparrow in *We Joined the Navy* in 1962, for laughs, but he capitulated now and made *Doctor in Distress*. He did it, he said, to stay 'in' with the box-office, but it also looked as though he was rushing from film to film because he felt his luck was waning. There were precedents: very few British screen actors had made the transition from leading man to mature star actor with any success. 'The trouble is' he said, 'I've never yet managed to be brilliant in a brilliant film. I've done some good work in bad films, and been awful in some good films, but the two excellences have hardly ever come together.' His wish was granted by *The Servant*, a Losey-directed, Pinter-scripted enigma of a reversing master-valet relationship. Bogarde's wily, slimy Cockney servant was a beautiful job and brought him the BFA award as the year's Best Actor.

For the box-office he did an inept thriller for Rank, *Hot Enough for June* (64), and then another for Losey, *King and Country*, a World War I drama on the lines of *Paths of Glory* but more explicit and infinitely less effective. It cost only £80,000 and five years later had not made back its cost. There was another Rank thriller, *The High Bright Sun* (65), and then *Darling*, where his performance as Julie Christie's most stable lover brought him a second BFA award. This and *The Servant* opened up new audiences for Bogarde, and he and Losey tried for a hat-

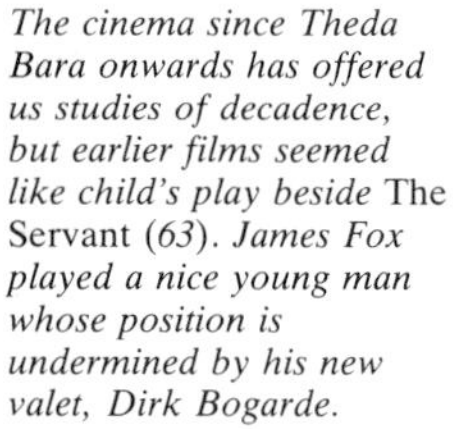

The cinema since Theda Bara onwards has offered us studies of decadence, but earlier films seemed like child's play beside The Servant *(63). James Fox played a nice young man whose position is undermined by his new valet, Dirk Bogarde.*

trick, but *Modesty Blaise*, based deliberately on a comic strip, turned out to be camp nonsense, though Bogarde was fine as a very effete villain. Pinter scripted *Accident* (66), and Losey again directed, but this time they were even more overwhelmed by Enigma. Bogarde was an Oxford don.

He was an opportunist father returning to his orphaned kids in Jack Clayton's *Our Mother's House* and an Oxford professor, involved with computers, in *Sebastian* (68), a modish thriller. He was acting now with a modulated subtlety, foreshadowing his work in *Death in Venice*: in *Oh What a Lovely War!*, as a blasé aristocrat; in *The Fixer*, as a fashionable but idealistic lawyer; and in *Justine*, as the unhappy, incestuous diplomat Pursewarden. Like all good actors, he was part of the fabric, each of these parts unimaginable with any other actor – which is true also of the next one, although he was miscast, as a strong, ambitious executive married into a family based on the Krupps: *The Damned/La Caduta degli Dei*. Visconti presumably meant this as an allegory, the study of one (important) family during the rise to power of the Nazis, but it emerged as a grandiloquent catalogue of most of the perversions known to man. Warners had backed it during production when money ran out – and were not to regret it. They backed Visconti again in his film of Thomas Mann's *Death in Venice* (71), as good as the other film was bad, with Bogarde (at a fee of $100,000) as the dying composer (based on Mahler – in the book he was a writer) obsessed by a youth staying at the same hotel on the Lido: a superb study, hardly dialogued, of a sick, haunted man.

Between the two films Bogarde moved to Italy and then to France to live. He said that he was getting no offers from British producers except for the sort of 'rubbish' he had done in the past: but if his two big Hollywood films (*The Fixer* and *Justine*) had been disappointing, the two with Visconti made him an actor the world respected. He played a Kim Philby-like agent in the French-German-Italian *Le Serpent/The Serpent* (73), with Yul Brynner, and Bonnie Prince Charlie in *Upon This Rock*, a study of the Vatican made some years earlier and premièred on US TV around this time. In the absurdly overblown *Il Portiere di Notte/The Night Porter* (74) he had the title-role, an ex-SS officer who staged orgies reminiscent of those days, and in the weakly scripted *Permission to Kill* (75) he was once again a British agent. *Providence* (77) was made in English by Alain Resnais, almost the only person on the unit who took the thing seriously: 'There is a sort of Harold Pinter ambiguity and menace plus the ranting of John Osborne' said 'Variety', but it won golden opinions and awards, predictably, in France – which brought a belated booking in London (earlier, distributors had turned it down). If you missed these films – and there were good reasons why you should – you would have found Bogarde changed, doing his libellous portrait of Lt-Gen. Browning in Richard Attenborough's disastrous *A Bridge Too Far*: from being an actor of subtlety, he had become as mannered and as overemphatic as Ralph Richardson – and clearly as much to be avoided. Since German whizzkid Rainer Werner Fassbinder directed *Despair* (78) there was no problem: in this adaptation from Nabokov Bogarde was, in the words of 'Time Magazine', 'a middle-aged Berlin chocolate

Dirk Bogarde as the camera starts to turn on Death in Venice *(71), Visconti's version of the Thomas Mann novella. Bogarde's performance confirmed his standing as one of the half-dozen best actors in films.*

manufacturer who, seeking escape from sexual problems and his failing business, retreats into a world of schizophrenic fantasy'.

For CBS TV he played Roald Dahl in *The Patricia Neal Story* (82) opposite Glenda Jackson. The two stars were to have been reunited for a film based on Arnold Bennett's 'Buried Alive', on salaries of £40,000 each, but illness intervened. Director Mike Hodges, without mentioning this figure, later said the film was cancelled because they were asking too much money. Bogarde was earning splendid royalties from a novel and a series of self-serving autobiographies. He was wont to tell interviewers that he now regarded himself primarily as a writer – but also that he had been a star for 40 years and was not prepared to take supporting roles. When he did return to acting it was in a prestigious tele-film, *May We Borrow Your Husband?* (86), based on a Graham Greene tale of a writer observing a homosexual couple woo away a newly married man. Bogarde also wrote it, quite faithfully, except that the role of the writer had grown till on screen it became a very festival of Bogarde; and it showed an unpleasant contempt for gay men. For the BBC he co-starred with Lee Remick – they would have been a box-office team 20 years earlier – in *The Vision* (87), the tale of an over-the-hill media man manipulated and destroyed by the head of a new TV channel aiming to sell American-style revision. The role was played by Lee Remick and Eileen Atkins was Bogarde's wife: confronted with two superior talents, he did an awful lot of acting, but was more restrained than other recent occasions. He claimed in an interview that there were other offers, but he had no intention of trading years of stardom 'to go under the title'.

Shirley Booth

Back in 1951 reviewing 'A Tree Grows in Brooklyn', the 'New York Post' observed that Shirley Booth was 'one of the wonders of the American stage; a superb actress, a magnificent comedienne and an all-round performer of seemingly endless variety'. Had she wanted to be, she might have been one of the wonders of the American screen.

She was born in New York City in 1907 and made her first professional stage appearance at Hartford, Connecticut, in 'The Cat and the Canary' (23). Two years later she made her New York bow, in 'Hell's Bells' (Humphrey Bogart also had a small part). She acted regularly in New York and in stock, but without notable success until she played Mabel in 'Three Men on a Horse' in 1935. She starred in 'Too Many Heroes' (37) and supported Katharine Hepburn in 'The Philadelphia Story' (39), in the role Ruth Hussey played in the movie. She also became nationally famous by virtue of being Miss Duffy in 'Duffy's Tavern', a radio show compèred by her husband, Ed Gardner (1929–41; she married again in 1943 and was widowed in 1951). On Broadway she played Ruth in 'My Sister Eileen' (40), which ran two years; and had another long run in 'Tomorrow the World' (43). In 1945 she played Louhedda Hopsons in 'Hollywood Pinafore'; was in 'Land's End', 'The Men We Marry' and 'Goodbye My Fancy' (48). She was normally cast as a sardonic career girl, but in 1950 she played Lola in 'Come Back Little Sheba', William Inge's study of a rather unusual suburban marriage – he is an ex-alcoholic, she is blowsy, shabby, careless and good-natured. It eclipsed her previous personal successes and brought her just about every Broadway award. The following year she was in the musical version of 'A Tree Grows in Brooklyn' and when that came off she went into Arthur Laurents's 'The Time of the Cuckoo', the romance of a spinster school-marm in Venice.

Meanwhile, Hall Wallis had decided to film *Come Back Little Sheba* (52) and, although the official line later was that only she could play the part, it had earlier been reported that Bette Davis had declined it. Wallis signed her on a four-film deal. Of her playing of Lola, Richard Winnington wrote: 'Miss Booth is a magnificent actress of patently wide range, who accomplishes the miracle of making Lola at once repulsive and beneath her load of pain, longing and stupidity, oddly beautiful.' She took the New York Critics' award and the Best Actress Oscar.

She played herself in *Main Street to Broadway* (53), an odd little film about the theatre which was hardly seen outside the US. On Broadway she did another musical, 'By the Beautiful Sea', and Wallis found another film for her, *About Mrs Leslie* (54) with Robert Ryan, a wistful tale about an illicit romance kept alive over the years via one annual shared holiday. There was a taste of soap opera about it, but she was again splendid, making it work. It failed at the box-office and Wallis dropped plans to film 'The Time of the Cuckoo' (when it was finally clear that she would not do it, Katharine Hepburn accepted it). In 1955 she was in William Marchant's play 'The Desk Set' and toured in it, at one point interrupting the tour to give a few tips to Hepburn, who was (again) to do the film version.

She was in Hollywood again some months later for two films for Wallis: *Hot Spell* (58),

Shirley Booth and Burt Lancaster in Come Back Little Sheba *(52). The film itself is a patchy version of William Inge's play, but it preserves for posterity Miss Booth's beautiful performance.*

a family drama with gleanings from a hundred other such, and – on loan to Paramount – *The Matchmaker*, from the Thornton Wilder comedy that was to become 'Hello Dolly'. Both were a bit bleak and Booth had to dig into her capacious bag of tricks ro make her character work. There were other virtues (Shirley MacLaine was in both) but neither clicked. Also, the Paramount distributing arm did not know what to do with two films starring a dumpy, middle-aged lady. She has not filmed since and Robert Ryan later told 'Films in Review' that she was 'uncomfortable working in movies. She is a very timid woman and walked part of the way to work before someone told her she could park her car on the Paramount lot. In fact, *I* told her.' Among the films she turned down are *A Pocketful of Miracles* and *Airport*.

In 1961 she was approached to star in a TV series based on 'Hazel', the 'Saturday Evening Post' comic-strip maid. Despite the advice of friends she agreed to do it; it ran for years and brought her a couple of Emmy awards. Among other TV appearances was 'The Glass Menagerie' (67), as the mother, but she has made only one tele-movie, *The Smugglers* (68), as a tourist caught up with same in Europe (the first and only telecast was not seen complete, for it was interrupted to show preparations for the first landing on the Moon). And among later stage appearances: 'Juno and the Paycock' (59), as Juno; 'A Loss of Roses'; a revival of 'The Desk Set' (69), an unsuccessful 'Hay Fever' in New York and a revival of 'Harvey' (71) with Gig Young.

Ernest Borgnine

Ernest Borgnine won an Oscar with his first leading role, in *Marty*, playing an ugly, past-30 butcher who courts and wins a faded schoolteacher (Betsy Blair), resigned to life on the shelf. He woos her thus: 'Dogs like us. . . . We're not such dogs as we think we are,' and the line might have recurred to him at the Oscar ceremony, for he is one of the least likely leading actors on record. Before the Oscar, he was mainly a slob-like heavy in Westerns, with a ferocious growl of a frown – even the teeth were chilling. He was not, physically, one of nature's successes, being round and having a face which has been likened to both a pug's and a toad's. Thus of course he got *Marty*, but it was not for looks (i.e. the lack of them) that he won an Oscar; this was a warm, confident portrait of a nice man. In all his sympathetic parts he projects a concern for humanity and, without ever falling into the Zorba-traps, a huge expansiveness.

He was born in Hamden, Connecticut, in 1917 and acted in school – but became a truck-driver. He joined the navy and finished the war as a CPO gunner's mate; he applied under the GI Bill of Rights for a grant to study acting and was enrolled at the Randall School of Dramatic Art in Hartford, Connecticut. He was several years with the Barter Theater in Virginia; then there were several TV plays in New York. He tried Hollywood and got a leading role in a cheap Columbia B, *China Corsair* (51), starring Jon Hall as a pirate. He stayed at that studio for a couple of films: *The*

Whistle at Eaton Falls, a study of labour-management relations in a New England town produced in familiar style, with Lloyd Bridges; and *The Mob* starring Broderick Crawford.

He went to Broadway to appear in 'Mrs McThing' (52) starring Helen Hayes. Columbia called him back for *From Here to Eternity* (53), to play the loud-mouthed and sweaty Sergeant Fatso who beats Frank Sinatra to death in the stockade. It was not a big part but was showy enough to ensure regular work: *The Stranger Wore a Gun*, a Randolph Scott Western, as a member of George Macready's gang, along with Lee Marvin; *Johnny Guitar* (54), as one of Scott Brady's gang; *Demetrius and the Gladiators*; *The Bounty Hunter*, another Scott Western, as a bank robber; *Vera Cruz*, as a particularly vicious adventurer; and *Bad Day at Black Rock*, again in a dirty double-act with Marvin. Both were so strikingly sinister, and one-armed Spencer Tracy's triumph over them was so welcome that both were established. He was a bank robber in *Run for Cover* (55) and Marvin was thus employed in *Violent Saturday* but this time they were not buddies – indeed, Borgnine was a respectable Quaker. He was the heavy in *The Last Command*, a silly Alamo epic directed by Frank Lloyd (his last picture), with Sterling Hayden as Jim Bowie, and Tony Curtis's trainer in *The Square Jungle*. His salary was $750 a week.

By this time he was famous. Indeed, *Marty* was released around the same time as *Run for Cover*, but despite its having taken the Grand Prix at Cannes it took some time to have any effect on Borgnine's career. It had been a naturalistic TV play by Paddy Chayevsky and legend has it that Hecht-Hill-Lancaster only took it on because they thought its eventual flop could be set off against taxes. Delbert Mann directed and the film swept into the convention-bound movie world of that time like a new broom. Public response was enthusiastic and as well as the Best Actor Oscar

Ernest Borgnine and Lee Marvin making trouble for Spencer Tracy in Bad Day at Black Rock *(54). They were not then stars, and had been noticed in some good supporting roles: but as a duo they were so deadly that both careers received a boost. The man on the left is John Ericson.*

Betsy Blair and Ernest Borgnine in Marty *(55). It came as a surprise to find a Hollywood picture built around two plain, ordinary people falling in love – and that in itself drew attention to it. Beyond that, it was as honest as it aspired to be.*

Borgnine won the New York Critics' award; and both he and Betsy Blair won the BFA awards for Best Foreign players. To get the part he had signed a five-year contract with H-H-L and his fee for it was $5,000, plus 21 per cent of the net for five years.

Jubal (56) reflected his new status, second-billed after Glenn Ford and in a sympathetic part, as a rancher Othello spurred on to jealousy by Rod Steiger. Then he was reunited with Chayevsky and Mann for the film version of another TV drama, *The Catered Affair*, with Bette Davis as his wife: shenanigans surrounding a Bronx-Irish wedding and a mite less likeable than *Marty*. At 20th he played songwriter Lew Brown (of de Sylva, Henderson and Brown) in an agreeable musical, *The Best Things in Life Are Free*; at which point he sued H-H-L for $142,500 damages and breach of contract, claiming also that they were getting $75,000 from 20th for his services and paying him only $17,500. He refused to report to them for *The Sweet Smell of Success* (the matter was settled out of court) and returned to 20th for *Three Brave Men* (57), as a civilian employee in the US Navy Dept accused of being a security risk. Then he was villainous again as a chieftain – who gets thrown to the wolves – in *The Vikings* (58). He supported Alan Ladd in *The Badlanders*, as an ex-convict settler, one of his best performances. The cast also included Mexican actress Katy Jurado, who became his second wife, 1959–64. (Other marriages: 1949–58; 1964–Ethel Merman; 1965–72.)

After another supporting stint, in *Torpedo Run* with Glenn Ford, he went to do a film in Australia for H-H-L, *Summer of the Seventeenth Doll* (59), about two cane-cutters on vacation (John Mills was the other). Then he starred in three low-budgeters: *The Rabbit Trap*, another quiet 'social realist' drama that originated on TV; *Man on a String* (60), based on a true story – Boris Morros's life as a double agent, given documentary treatment by Louis de Rochement, but unconvincingly played throughout and a flop at the box-office; and *Pay or Die* as a detective – another factual tale, based on Mafia activities in New York in the early years of the century. From these he moved to the ripe absurdities of *Go Naked in the World* (61), as Anthony Franciosa's millionaire father, driving call-girl Gina Lollobrigida to suicide.

This film may well have driven him to Italy: *Il Re di Poggio Reale* (62) with Lino Ventura; De Sica's *Il Giudizio Universale*, about the end of the world in Naples; in English, *Barabba/Barabbas*, starring Anthony Quinn, and down to ninth on the cast-list; and *I Briganti Italiani*, as a bandit chief, with Katy Jurado, Micheline Presle and Vittorio Gassmann. He turned to TV and had a successful series called 'McHale's Navy'; and that spawned a couple of films, only the first of which starred him: *McHale's Navy* (64). Then, all as a supporting actor: *The Flight of the Phoenix* (65), as an oil-driller crazed by the crash of the aircraft; *The Oscar* (66), as a crooked private eye; *The Dirty Dozen* (67), as the general who sends them on their mission, with Marvin; *Chuka*, as a tough sergeant in this medium Rod Taylor adventure; *Ice Station Zebra*, as a supposed Russian defector but in fact a spy; *The Legend of Lylah Clare*, as a film executive; and *The Split* (69), with Julie Harris. There were two Westerns, *A Bullet for Sandoval* and the absurd Spanish-Italian *Quei Disperati che Puzzano di Sudore e di Morte/Los Desesperados*.

Borgnine was one actor not affected by the crisis in the industry at the turn of the decade: *The Wild Bunch*, as a member of William Holden's gang; *The Adventurers* (70), as a millionaire; *Suppose They Gave a War and Nobody Came*, with Tony Curtis; two pilots for Western tele-series which did not materialize, *Sam Hill, Who Killed the Mysterious Mr Foster?* (71), in the title-role, and *The Trackers*, partnered with Sammy Davis Jr; *Willard*, as a nasty boss who is attacked by rats trained by employee Bruce Davison – one of the biggest financial successes he had been in; *Bunny O'Hara*, robbing banks with Bette Davis; *Rain for a Dusty Summer*, a US-Spanish production directed by Arthur Lubin; *Hannie Caulder*, with Raquel Welch; *Pelle Dura/Tough Guy* (72), an Italian prison drama made in the US, with Robert Blake; and *The Poseidon Adventure*, playing a belligerent cop in this highly successful shipwreck thriller. Around this time his fifth marriage began.

He made: *The Neptune Factor, An Undersea Odyssey* (73), in Canada, as an aquanaut; *Emperor of the North Pole*, a vicious Depression-era drama, as a brutal train-guard terrorizing hobo and co-star Lee Marvin; *Twice in a Lifetime* (74), another busted pilot, as an old salt; *Law and Disorder*, co-starring with Carroll O'Connor, the two of them as auxiliary cops in this duff attempt to satirize the problem of urban violence; *A Sunday in the Country* (75), in Canada again, with Michael Sarrazin, as a bloody avenger; and *The Devil's Rain*, as the leader of a Satanist cult. In that he had top billing, but he moved well down the cast-list – for the first time in years – in *Hustle*, as a police chief. Early in 1975 he sued producer Adrian Gaye for $6 million punitive damages plus $250,000 for lost salary: the film not made was *Ronnie and Leo*, with Michael York, which should have started in Canada the previous summer. *Future Cop* (76), for TV, found him as a streetwise cop whose new partner is an alien and *Shoot*, with Cliff Robertson, back in Canada as a fascist; in Italy he was a client of a bordello, in *Natale in Casa d'Appuntamento*. He was a sympathetic centurion in the TV *Jesus of Nazareth/Gesu di Nazaret* (77) and he starred, as a kindly millionaire, in a tele-movie, *Fire!*, which was shown in cinemas abroad. In *The Prince and the Pauper/Crossed Swords* he was the ruffian father of the pauper; and then the trainer of *The Greatest*, Muhammed Ali; he had the title-role in another tele-movie, *The Ghost of Flight 401* (78). Paramount had liked the idea of *Future Cop* so much that it had become a TV series; it did not run, but the studio put him back into uniform yet again for a sequel, *The Cops and Robin*, also for television. Borgnine continued to have leading roles, in: *Convoy*, as a corrupt sheriff; *The Double McGuffin* (79); *Ravagers*, as a benevolent dictator discovered by Richard Harris in this looney sci-fi thriller; *All Quiet on the Western Front*, a TV mini-series wrought from Remarque's novel; Disney's *The Black Hole*, as a journalist – one of the crew – who is sucked into it; and *When Time Ran Out . . .* (80), as a New York cop on the trail of Red Buttons.

He played a Miami police sergeant in *Poliziotto Superpiu/Superfuzz*, opposite Terence Hill – the Bud Spencer role, since this popular Italian team seldom appear separately. The next three are best forgotten: *High Risk* (81), one of several names in small roles, as a gun dealer; John Carpenter's cautionary tale of future horrors, *Escape from New York*, as a mad cabbie; and *Deadly Blessing*, as the fanatical leader of a religious sect. In 1981 he was in a solo-play, 'An Offer You Can't Refuse', which played Buffalo and other towns, but did not make it to New York. After a well-deserved rest, he was in two tele-movies, *Blood Feud* (83), as J. Edgar Hoover, and *Carpool*; *Young Warriors* was a sequel to the equally dire *Malibu High* and he was a police officer in this exploitation piece. Yet again on TV, he was teaching gladiators to do their thing in a mini-series, *The Last Days of Pompeii* (84), and he was a Senator in a Disney jape, *Love Leads the Way. The Dirty Dozen, the Next Mission* (85) was a reunion in reduced circumstances (i.e. for TV) with his old partner-in-crime, Lee Marvin, and *Alice in Wonderland* (also for TV) was a semi-all-star (Donald O'Connor, Carol Channing, Eydie Gorme, Beau and Lloyd Bridges, Red Buttons, Imogene Coca, Karl Malden, Anthony Newley, Roddy McDowall, etc.) version of that story: he played a lion. The next two took a while to get to the world's attention, which they occupied minimally: *Caccia all'Uomo/The Manhunt* (86), as a nasty ranger, co-starring with John Ethan Wayne in this Italian-funded Arizona-filmed tale which went direct to video; and *Codename Wild Geese*, as a drug enforcement official, supporting Lewis Collins, Lee Van Cleef and Klaus Kinski in this German/Italian-funded Philippines-filmed adventure. *Jungle Raiders* has been advertised in the trade press but not seen. Borgnine turned up in a TV series, 'Airwolf', and was then in Italy playing Billy Bones in a sci-fi mini-series based on Robert Louis Stevenson, *L'Isola del Tesoro* (87), starring Anthony Quinn. Though no one much noticed it, he continued to work: *The Dirty Dozen, the Fatal Mission* (88), for TV; *The Opponent*, as a boxing promoter; *Spike of Bensonhurst*, as a mobster; and *Skeleton Coast*, looking for his son in Angola. All decent work, undoubtedly, but during these last years, there are some other titles which do not seem to have surfaced: *Qualcuno Paghera*, *Any Man's Death*, *Turnaround*, *Moving Target* and *Laser Mission*.

Marlon Brando

Probably no actor ever enjoyed such acclaim as Marlon Brando. There have been dissenters – Cary Grant was a very vocal one in the early days – but since he first appeared in Hollywood he overshadowed all discussions on screen-acting. In terms of stardom, he was unique – both a 'great' actor and a hunk of sex-appeal. His ability has been considered alongside Olivier's, his picture pasted up beside that of Rock Hudson. His name eventually lost its lustre as he failed to live up to his early achievements; but since they were so remarkable the rest of his career was bound to be something of an anticlimax.

He was born in Omaha, Nebraska, in 1924 and was sent to a military academy, from which he was expelled. He tried digging ditches – till his father offered to finance whatever education he fancied. He chose the theatre (his mother ran a local drama group) and went to New York where he studied with Stella Adler, a follower of Stanislavsky's principles, and with the Actors' Studio (whose most famous pupil he continues to be). He made his New York début in a play for children, 'Bobino' (43), and had small parts in stock on Long Island. His Broadway début was in John Van Druten's 'I Remember Mama' (44) and he had his first success two years later in 'Truckline Café', for which the critics voted him Broadway's Most Promising Actor. Also in 1946, he played Marchbanks to Katherine Cornell's Candida and toured briefly in 'The Eagle Has Two Heads' with Tallulah Bankhead; in 1947 came Tennessee Williams's 'A Streetcar Named Desire', as Stanley Kowalski, the mumbling, inarticulate brute who sees through, taunts and finally rapes his ladylike, nymphomaniac sister-in-law. His performance in what was withal a fine play made him the rage of Broadway.

In keeping with the contradictions, both professional and personal, which would pursue him through the years, he announced that he was not interested in Hollywood while at the same time secretly seeking a film role. It was said that every studio made overtures whereas in fact his crass behaviour both on and off stage had made Hollywood wary. It was the independent Stanley Kramer who finally approached him – with $50,000 and a sympathetic study of paraplegic war victims, *The Men* (50), directed by Fred Zinnemann. 'The film', said Richard Winnington, 'depends a good deal, of course, on Marlon Brando, whose combination of style, depth and range comes like a blood transfusion into cinema acting.' Great reviews for Brando and good ones for the film did not save it at the box-office; nor did publicity about the new 'anti-star'. He was rude to influential columnists; appeared at functions – if he came at all – in jeans and a T-shirt; and made no bones about despising Hollywood and its inhabitants. He was dismissed as an exhibitionist and only tolerated because it was clear he would be a top-ranking star.

Elia Kazan, who had directed it on stage, was called upon to direct the movie of *A Streetcar Named Desire* (51) and Brando repeated his stage performance, at a fee of $75,000. Kim Hunter and Karl Malden also came from the Broadway production, Vivien

Marlon Brando as Kowalski in A Streetcar Named Desire *(51), directed by Elia Kazan. Kazan said twenty years later: 'He's full of deep hostilities, longings, feelings of distrust, but his outer front is gentle and nice. . . . [He is] the only genius I've ever met in the field of acting.'*

Leigh from the London one. C.A. Lejeune wrote that Brando 'exacts the same sort of pity as Caliban, [in] one of the strongest and most selfless performances I remember seeing in a cinema'. The film was a box-office smash and the New York film critics voted it the year's Best Film (but their Best Actor award went to Arthur Kennedy for *Lights Out* and the Oscar to Humphrey Bogart for *The African Queen* – though Leigh, Hunter and Malden all won Oscars). Brando years later considered it his most satisfactory film.

The critics reached for superlatives again when – for $100,000 – he did a second film for Kazan, *Viva Zapata!* (52), written by John Steinbeck. Brando was the Mexican peasant/revolutionary leader, though some observers found the performance a variation on his Kowalski. Winnington said this: 'Arguments as to whether Brando can act in the theatrical sense or not are irrelevant, Brando conveys power, which, in the cinema, can transcend acting. . . .'

Wilfully, he turned his back on Hollywood to make a film in France, *Le Rouge et le Noir*, but walked out a few days before it was due to start because, it was said, he could not get on with director Claude Autant-Lara. Producer Paul Graetz sued for $150,000 (presumably the return of salary) and later made the film with Gérard Philipe. Again attracted to a classic, Brando agreed to play Mark Antony in the MGM-Mankiewicz *Julius Caesar* (53), with James Mason and John Gielgud. So many commentators scoffed that producer John Houseman defended his choice – 'he is one of the very great actors of our time' – and Gielgud went on record as being an admirer. In the event, he did slur the verse occasionally but was impressive and at ease (to appreciate his range, the 'Observer' pointed out, one would have to imagine Gielgud in *Streetcar*).

He returned to slob-like parts, but the variations he brought to two different roles were astounding. Kramer's *The Wild One* (54) was a study of two motor-cycle gangs that terrorize a small town (it was banned in Britain for 12 years) and Brando was the leader of one of them. In Kazan's *On the Waterfront* he was an ex-pug/longshoreman who fights The System. He won the New York critics' Best Actor award and the Best Actor Oscar; in Britain he won the BFA Best Foreign Actor award – for the third consecutive year – and the 'Picturegoer' Gold Medal. The film itself won the Academy's Best Picture Oscar and was a huge popular success. Brando was the hottest property in films (and he stopped talking of leaving Hollywood and began dressing more conventionally).

Up to this time, as Kramer later remarked, he had done everything right, 'his instincts were faultless'. Now, under the terms of an arrangement with 20th (said to be two films a year), he agreed to do a historical subject called *The Egyptian*; but – presumably after reading the script – he changed his mind. 20th replaced him with Edmund Purdom and slapped a $2 million lawsuit on him. The matter was resolved when he agreed to do *Desirée* instead, from another bestseller. It was marginally the better of the two films – because he was in it – and much publicity accrued because he played Napoleon, though, in the event, with diminished power and finesse. He expressed a wish to appear in a projected French version of 'Lady Chatterley's Lover' but even with a huge salary cut the budget could not accommodate him.

Instead, he was in two films of Broadway hits: Goldwyn's *Guys and Dolls* (55), kinging it as a singing gambler gone on Salvation Army lass Jean Simmons; and *The Teahouse of the August Moon* (56), as a fly Japanese interpreter. Then there were two films from bestsellers: *Sayonara* (57), as an air force officer in love with a Japanese actress (at a salary of $300,000 plus a percentage); and *The Young Lions* (58), as a blond, idealistic Nazi officer. These were all popular, and in 1955 and 1958 Brando was voted among the top 10 box-office stars. His admirers were sustained by his versatility in what were considered overly commercial vehicles and looked for a return to the sort of films in which he had made his name.

But the next three were financial disasters. The first to be shown was *The Fugitive Kind* (60), Sidney Lumet's screen version of William's 'Orpheus Descending' (the part, as in most of Williams's plays, had been originally written for Brando). Brando was a wanderer come to roost in Anna Magnani's store and, like the film, was good; but there were wild stories of friction between him and Magnani; and then the film failed at the box-office. Then there was Brando's first independent production. For years there had been rumours of plans and when one finally jelled Hollywood gasped at the terms – Paramount would finance completely but take only 27 per cent of the gross for distributing. Brando would get 100 per cent of all receipts after the cost had been recouped. He signed Stanley Kubrick to direct but took over the reins when they had differences. Sam Peckinpah also worked on the film for a while. He said later: 'Very strange man, Marlon. Always doing a number about his screen image, about how audiences would not accept him as a thief, how audiences would only accept him as a fallen sinner – someone they could love.' The film was *One-Eyed Jacks* (61), a Western. Brando described it as a frontal attack on the clichés of the genre, which it was not quite; but his performance was, even if for the first time he seemed to be reprising bits of earlier performances – his cowboy was cunning, vain, sentimental, vicious, masochistic and rather stupid. The film was praised and did well, but even had it done spectacularly it would hardly have got back its huge cost.

But what went on behind the scenes pales into insignificance beside the (re)making of *Mutiny on the Bounty* (62): Carol Reed was replaced by Lewis Milestone and among several published accounts both co-stars, Trevor Howard and Richard Harris, spoke of difficulties. Brando had artistic control and spent weeks brooding on the script. Much talent – including the likes of Billy Wilder – was brought in to satisfy the star's requirements and it was reported that 12 varying endings were shot. Such gossip was grist to the mill of those who prophesied that it would not come up to the first version. Certainly you might long for Clark Gable after a couple of reels of Brando's prissy, dandified, very English Fletcher Christian, but at least he was again trying to prove his versatility. The film grossed a healthy $9 million, but this was no solace to an MGM that had sunk a record $19 million into it – including Brando's $1¼ million (the deal had included a percentage). There was a strong move to kick him out of Hollywood.

He survived and for a while there was no more talk of tantrums. Old rumours that he was only in the business for the dough were confirmed by him – but he added that his attitude had changed somewhat. Either way, his work continued to be interesting: as the slick, moustached US ambassador in *The Ugly American* (63); as a con-man in the slapstick *Bedtime Story* (64); as a spy in a good melodrama, *Morituri* (65); as a harassed, beset and beaten-up sheriff in a small Southern town in *The Chase* (66); as a Mexican peasant in a Western, *The Appaloosa*; and as a diplomat in Chaplin's (supposedly) sophisticated comedy, *A Countess from Hong Kong* (67). However, most of this batch lost a packet, due probably to poor reviews. Press reaction to Brando remained standard, compounded one part of carping, one part of honest bewilderment that things were not better and one part the raves as ever. The only time there was unanimity was over the Chaplin film.

It was not only Brando's acting that was under scrutiny, but his personality and career. Right from the start he had been an easy target: some attacked him because his screen character was anti-Establishment, others chided him for deserting the purple of Broadway for Hollywood gold. There was disagreement among his colleagues as to the extent he was 'difficult' or merely meticulous. Some directors he treated with contempt, while fellow-actors were disconcerted by the habit he had developed of reading his dialogue from cue-cards.

Opinion remained divided over *Reflections in a Golden Eye*, directed by John Huston from Carson McCullers's novel. In the US the film did badly with critics and public but in Britain it was much admired – and Brando amazed some, as the priggish Southern army officer who unwillingly acknowledges his homosexuality. It was a portrait so precise and full of nuances – great care had gone into its structure. Like Olivier, Brando is a great observer and like him he takes great risks, physically and temperamentally: he pushes each performance as far as it will go.

It is possible that his career would have been less patchy had he *not* had a free choice of material. Actors are not necessarily the best judge of scripts and Brando was, apparently, the guiding-force behind *Candy* (68), which his friend Christian Marquand wanted to direct. Taken from a piece of spoof

Later, Brando seldom acted under directors of the calibre of Kazan, so that very often his performance was the most interesting feature of the films he made: here he is as Fletcher Christian in the 1962 version of Mutiny on the Bounty.

1

2

5

6

3

4

7

8

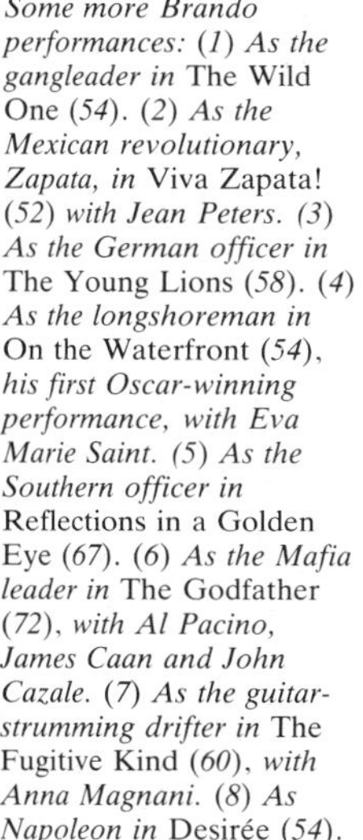

Some more Brando performances: (1) As the gangleader in The Wild One *(54). (2) As the Mexican revolutionary, Zapata, in* Viva Zapata! *(52) with Jean Peters. (3) As the German officer in* The Young Lions *(58). (4) As the longshoreman in* On the Waterfront *(54), his first Oscar-winning performance, with Eva Marie Saint. (5) As the Southern officer in* Reflections in a Golden Eye *(67). (6) As the Mafia leader in* The Godfather *(72), with Al Pacino, James Caan and John Cazale. (7) As the guitar-strumming drifter in* The Fugitive Kind *(60), with Anna Magnani. (8) As Napoleon in* Desirée *(54).*

pornography, this cosmopolitan, multi-star effort brought discredit to all connected with it: the unreadable became the unwatchable. Brando had 20 minutes as an Indian guru. Somewhat better was a French-locationed thriller, *The Night of the Following Day* (69), which, after poor notices, played the lower half of double-bills. The critic of 'Time Magazine' was one of the few who did not accuse Brando of self-parody: 'Once again, in a film good enough to match his talents, he demonstrates conclusively . . . that his powers remain undiminished by intervening years of sloppiness and self-indulgence.'

When Kazan told Warners that he wanted Brando for the lead in *The Arrangement* they told him to run some of his recent films, to prove that he was paunchy and only 'going through the motions'. Kazan believed that he could get a good performance out of Brando, but in the event Brando relinquished the role, due, he said, to the assassination of Martin Luther King: but as the columnist Sheilah Graham sagely observed, if he failed with Kazan 'there would be nothing left'. He is a leading spokesman on Civil Rights and he said at the time that he only wished to make films with a strong social message. Because he had also said that he considered acting a neurotic, unimportant job, his future became uncertain. Further, around that time 'Variety' listed him, because of his string of flops, as a decided box-office risk – though it added that he would probably ride through better than the others on the list because of his reputation as *the* American actor.

The 'Sunday Telegraph' summed it up when it described him as 'the great, baffling mystery of the American cinema' and quoted Rod Steiger: 'Marlon was in a unique position. He could have done anything, *anything*, however difficult or uncommercial, on the screen and taken the critics, the industry, the fans with him. But he didn't choose to. I don't know why.' And James Mason said in conversation that George C. Scott was the No 1 actor in the US 'now that Brando has presumably conceded and retired. Brando has made such a balls-up of his career.'

That career revived after a spell, if only gingerly, perhaps because of alimony problems. Although he has always believed his private life to be sacred, his first marriage, to Anna Kashfi (1957–59) broke up with bitter recriminations and the custody battles for their son Christian were equally well-publicized. Less, accordingly, is known of his apparently legal liaisons Movita (1960–61) and with Tarita, whom he met while making *Mutiny on the Bounty* and the mother of two of his children. Books about him by Kashfi and his friend Carlo Fiore indicate an uncertain emotional life and in 1976 he told a French journalist that he had had 'like everyone' homosexual experiences. He returned to films with Pontecorvo's interesting but unsatisfactory *Queimada/Burn* (70), as an English milord involved in a South American revolution (and there were again reports of dissension on the set); and the British *The Night Comers* (71), a concocted sequel to Henry James's 'The Turn of the Screw', in which his foul-mouthed, scruffy and sloppy groom is a violation of all we know of men in service at the turn of the century. The director was the unesteemed Michael Winner and it is significant that Brando had spoken of his refusal to work again with Kazan and Mankiewicz, in the first case because of Kazan's stand during the McCarthy era and in the second because Mankiewicz refused quite to agree that there was only one romantic lead in *Guys and Dolls* (as Mankiewicz said, he did not feel inclined to tell Sinatra how to sing). At this time Huston offered him *Fat City*, another of his best late films, but he heard no more from Brando after giving him the script.

It was Francis Coppola who brought him back to the Hollywood mainstream, after testing him privately and over Paramount's objections: his enormously successful film of a meretricious bestseller about the Mafia, *The Godfather* (72). Brando played the title-role, that of a Mafia chieftain – much older than himself: and it was generally agreed that this marked the renaissance of a great actor. Paramount emphasized that he was 'co-operation itself' but were mute on the question of salary: Brando himself – when questioned on what had attracted him to the part – said it was $250,000 plus a percentage, but 'Variety' reported it as being a percentage only. That journal reported his next salary as being $250,000 plus a percentage, for a European film reluctantly backed by United Artists: *Ultimo Tango a Parigi/Last Tango in Paris*, about an American widower who screws a young Frenchwoman (Maria Schneider) – and the coarseness of expression is appropriate to a film which was all coarseness and nothing else. Although the director called Brando 'an angel of a man but a monster as an actor' Brando co-operated with him to the extent that his contribution would appear to be autobiographical, perhaps a public penance for being a world-famous movie star. The furore it caused brought a certain cachet and he continued to be talked about when he refused his Best Actor Oscar for *The Godfather*, sending to the ceremony instead a small-part actress who pretended to be a Red Indian woman, there to plead the cause of her people.

If his work in *Last Tango* was self-indulgent, that in *The Missouri Breaks* (76) seemed designed to give offence to the audiences and critics who had admired him; playing an admittedly eccentric lawman, he indulged in all his worst tricks. As Kazan said, he must despise his profession to have given that performance. His co-star, Jack Nicholson, had earlier said 'He's still the one to beat'; and he had a walk-over victory. Brando received $1 million for five weeks' work and Nicholson $1¼ for 10, with Brando getting 10 per cent of the gross receipts after $10 million and Nicholson the same percentage after $12½ million. In fact its domestic gross reached only $7 million.

As if to prove his assertion that he worked only for money, Brando abdicated artistically by doing *Superman* (78), playing father to that comic-strip hero (Christopher Reeves) – at a salary reliably reported to be $3.7 million; since his role was small, this was, as publicized, 'the highest salary ever paid a performer' – a fact which, to judge from his performance, had thoroughly bemused him. To the backward, his participation meant Class; it certainly helped this entertaining film to be taken seriously – and it was also a commercial success. His salary for Coppola's troubled, long-in-filming and dangerously expensive *Apocalypse Now* (79) was $2 million; and Coppola was grateful to him since other names had turned him down. Whether he was as grateful in view of Brando's weird performance is another secret – the obese, bald jungle commander Kurtz in this Vietnamized version of Conrad's 'The Heart of Darkness'. Before it was shown, Brando lost some weight and regained some prestige by playing American Nazi Nelson Rockwell in the second session of TV's 'Roots'. Around this time it was reported that his terms for a movie with Barbra Streisand were $3 million plus 25 per cent of receipts.

It was not made. Brando did get $1 million for just three sequences in *The Formula* (80), with co-starring billing and the role of the villain, the boss of an energy conglomerate. Its writer, Steve Shagan, observed of Brando and co-star George C. Scott: 'I sensed a loss of purpose, a sense of betrayal, a feeling that they don't want to work any more, a sense that they have come to think of acting as playing with choo-choo trains.' The film failed at the box-office and in 1982 'Variety' reported that Brando's recent record meant that he was 'dead' in Hollywood. He was nevertheless offered (and refused) $5 million for three weeks' work in Michael Cimino's *The Sicilian*, based on the book by Puzo. Paramount wanted him for *The Presidio*, for the role played by Sean Connery, and he did eventually return to the screen in a tale of apartheid, *A Dry White Season* (89), but yet again in a cameo role, as a lawyer. Elliott Kastner, producer of some of Brando's lesser films, found backing for a script Brando had written, *Jericho*, in which he would play a CIA man in Mexico; Brando had discussed the project for years with an old friend and sometime film-maker, Donald Cammell, who was to direct, but he changed his mind on the eve of filming and the picture was cancelled. Said Cammell, 'He's so ambitious and idealistic. But being an idealist and a perfectionist can become very destruction . . . a crazy self-defeating limitation.'

Charles Bronson

Charles Bronson is a surprising star; he was a bit player and character actor of no distinction for years – till elevation finally came. As he puts it himself: 'I guess I look like a rock quarry that someone has dynamited. A dozen years or so ago mine was the kind of face nobody wanted to see in the movies. At least, not the good guy's face. But times have changed. I seem to have the right face at the right time.'

He was born Charles Buchinski (which name he kept, sometimes with a final y, for his first four years in films) in Ehrenfeld, Pennsylvania, in 1921, the ninth of 15 children born to Lithuanian immigrant parents. At 16 he followed his family into the mines and did not envisage any other life for himself till he went into the army; determined not to return to the pits he took advantage of the GI Bill of Rights to study art in Philadelphia, which led to scene-painting and then acting. He had small roles in neighbourhood companies – and did odd jobs – for three years, till 1949, when he enrolled as a student at the Pasadena Playhouse in California, where he played the lead in a 'balcony' production of 'The Last Mile'. One of his instructors was up for a role in *You're in the Navy Now* (51) and he recommended Buchinski for a role as a brawling Polish sailor – and Buchinski was cast after an interview with the director, Henry Hathaway. On the set he met an agent, who got him a number of small roles: *The People Against O'Hara*, sharing one scene with Spencer Tracy; *The Mob*, as a longshoreman; *Red Skies of Montana* (52), as a firefighter; *My Six Convicts*, as another convict; and *The Marrying Kind*, unbilled. The director of the latter, George Cukor, gave him an important supporting role, as a pugilist, in *Pat and Mike* and Hathaway sent for him to do a bit in *Diplomatic Courier*. After *Bloodhounds of Broadway* he changed his agent and made the

As Charles Buchinski, Charles Bronson was on the periphery of movies for a long time. The others in this scene from Pat and Mike *(52) are Spencer Tracy and Katharine Hepburn, of course, and on the far right, George Mathews.*

first of many TV appearances; his new agent got him a job as Vincent Price's gruesome assistant in *House of Wax* (53), though not with the billing as it appears in the current TV print. Andre de Toth directed and after playing one of Aldo Ray's buddies in *Miss Sadie Thompson*, de Toth cast him as a convict in *Crime Wave* (54), upped to sixth billing in this B starring Gene Nelson. He had equally good roles in: *Tennessee Champ*, as the boxer Keenan Wynn thinks he has killed; *Riding Shotgun*, a Randolph Scott Western, as a bungling bad guy; and, as a result of a TV drama with Robert Aldrich directing, in Aldrich's *Apache*. He changed his name to Bronson for another Western, *Drum Beat*, playing the leader of a gang of renegade Indians, and then Aldrich made him one of Burt Lancaster's gang in *Vera Cruz*.

On TV he began to do the same sort of 'heavy' roles – convicts, fighters – and he was a gun-toting con in *Big House USA* (55), starring Broderick Crawford, and a sergeant in *Target Zero*, a Korean war tale with Richard Conte. He was 'outstanding' – said the 'Hollywood Reporter' – as Glenn Ford's pal in *Jubal* (56), but did not film again till he played a 'good' Indian in *Run of the Arrow* (57). He was refusing roles he did not like and he changed his agent, which led to the leading role in two Bs at 20th, *Gang War* (58), as a high school teacher who becomes involved in same, and *Showdown on Boot Hill*. He played the title-role in AIP's bigger-budgeted *Machine Gun Kelly* and had the lead in another B, *When Hell Broke Loose*, as a gambling soldier. He headed a TV series, 'Man With a Camera', and returned to films as a sergeant in *Never So Few* (59), directed by John Sturges, who cast him as one of *The Magnificent Seven* (60) – the paternal one – and it was in this spectacular hit that the large cinema public first became aware of him. Between the two films he had changed agents again, to Hollywood's biggest, MCA, and they got him a fee of $50,000.

According to one biographer (Steven Whitney), Bronson had set his sights on becoming a major star. The only other 'ugly' supporting actor to make it to the top, Jack Palance, had not found public favour for long; but on the other hand, the public was no longer responding to the very handsome stars being foisted on them – so that regardless of their talent, later Universal acquisitions found the going tough. Both Ernest Borgnine and Broderick Crawford had become stars via a lucky role and an Oscar apiece, but both had stayed in leading roles. And TV had made stars of a number of faces very much unlike Ronald Colman's – Lee Marvin, Richard Boone, Jack Webb, Ward Bond. It is not coincidental that Bronson had worked with most of these people and indeed Marvin had started off in a small role, like himself, in *You're in the Navy Now*. Bronson, however, chose the wrong films at this point: *Master of the World* (61), as the hero who outwits Vincent Price; *A Thunder of Drums*, a cavalry Western that starred Boone, as a trooper; *X–15* (62), a sci-fier, as a test pilot; and *Kid Galahad*, with Elvis Presley, as a prize-fighter. Directed again by Sturges, he was in another hugely successful film, *The Great Escape* (63), where he was excellent as the Polish tunneller who goes to pieces at the end. Also in the film was David McCallum, whose wife, Jill Ireland, became the second Mrs Bronson. He played occasional leads in two TV series, 'Empire' (63) and 'Jamie McPheeters' (63–64), in both sharing or alternating with other actors. At his usual fee of $50,000 he had lead featured roles in a number of duff ventures: *Four for Texas*, as a gang boss outwitted by Frank Sinatra and Dean Martin; *The Sandpiper* (65); *Battle of the Bulge*, made on location in Spain, as a battle-hard Polish officer – and another of Bronson's outstanding performances; and *This Property Is Condemned* (66), as the middle-aged man married by Natalie Wood out of pique.

He returned to Europe for another war film, directed by Aldrich, *The Dirty Dozen* (67), with Lee Marvin, and since it was a success of the order of *The Magnificent Seven* and *The Great Escape*, stardom was at last within Bronson's grasp; but he chose two films which failed, the French-Italian-Mexican *La Bataille de San Sebastian/Guns for San Sebastian*, as a Mexican Indian, and Paramount's made-in-Spain *Villa Rides!* (68), as a sadistic Mexican. The star of the first was Anthony Quinn and Bronson supported Yul Brynner and Robert Mitchum in the second: soon, and unexpectedly, the middle-aged Bronson would be a bigger star than any of them – and it would happen in Europe. He had turned down an approach by Sergio Leone to do the spaghetti Western which was subsequently offered to Clint Eastwood and which made him a star; Leone approached Bronson later twice to appear with Eastwood, but on the first occasion he chose to do *The Sandpiper* and on the second he was committed to *The Dirty Dozen*. But since Eastwood had become a star in Europe (which had revitalized Quinn's career, among others) Bronson listened to overtures from Serge Silberman, visiting him in Spain, to partner Alain Delon in *Adieu L'Ami*: he would get equal billing with Delon and twice his usual fee, i.e. $100,000. Delon and he played parachutist-adventurers, to popular approval in France, but it was not seen in the US. When it was finished, Bronson was able at last to film for Leone, in *C'era una Volta il West/Once Upon a Time in the West* (69), as a good guy – a laconic avenger – to Henry Fonda's bad guy; and then he returned to Silberman for one of the later, lesser films of René Clément, *Passager de la Pluie/Rider on the Rain*. It was, in fact, a dreadful film: Bronson, as some sort of enigmatic American (detective? undercover agent?) mooned around with rape victim and murderess Marlène Jobert, both of them – despite acting in English – badly dubbed. His wrinkled *désinvolture* apparently moved huge European audiences to ecstasy – to the extent that he regarded this as his 'breakthrough' film, but on its few US and British bookings audiences recognized bloody awful movie-making and two anodyne personalities in the leads. As a change of pace he played a novelist, in Britain, in *Twinky* – a soft-porn writer who has an affair with a teenager (Susan George): and as directed by Richard Donner the film was as bad as it sounds. And equally poor was the Anglo-American *You Can't Win 'em All* (70), in which he and Tony Curtis were soldiers of fortune in 1922 Turkey: like all this batch, it had few bookings Stateside. But these were successful in Europe: *Città Violenta/Cité de la Violence/The Family*, set in New Orleans, about a hit man who falls for the same fatal lady (Ireland, in her first film opposite her husband) as his boss (Telly Savalas); *De la Part des Copains/L'Uomo dalle Due Ombre/Cold Sweat*, set on the Côte d'Azur, about an ex-con and his wife (Liv Ullmann) sought out by an old enemy (James Mason); *Quelqu'un Derrière la Porte/Someone Behind the Door* (71), set in England, about a murderer tricked up to the nines by a psychiatrist (Anthony Perkins); and *Soleil Rouge/Red Sun*, set in Arizona, about an outlaw, a samurai (Toshiro Mifune), a gambler (Delon) and some Comanches. During these last four movies Bronson's salary went up to $500,000, and in 1972 he trailed Delon and Belmondo in the 'Ciné-Revue' poll of favourite actors in France.

His return to the US was engineered by Michael Winner, an opportunist producer-director if ever, who persuaded United Artists to back Bronson in a Western, *Chato's Land* (72) filmed in Spain – for cheapness – and co-starring Jack Palance; and Winner followed it with a Mafia (Mafia dramas were very big at that point), *The Mechanic*, filmed in Italy and Hollywood, with Jan-Michael Vincent. Despite UA's handling, neither was of a quality to establish Bronson in the US, but the Foreign Press Association at this time decreed that Bronson – with Sean Connery – was the world's most popular actor and since this meant a Golden Globe awarded in Hollywood, the American industry could no longer shrug off Bronson. First he did two more films in Europe, both for producer De Laurentiis, *Cosa Nostra/The Valachi Papers*, as Mafia leader Joe Valachi, ageing from young man to old in the course of the film; and *Valdez il Mezzosangue/The Valdez Horses* (73), directed by Sturges, in the title-role. The first of these was directed by Terence Young, with Winner Bronson's most consistent director at this time: but it did not matter, since now that he was a star he was no longer required to act. He did not need to, since these were star vehicles needing only a presence: a rather dour, rootless loner who was only ruthless when roused. Stardom had been achieved with the aid of a PR man, engaged around the time of the Leone film, with specific instructions to make Bronson a star in the US: Bronson is quite frank about this in interviews, but of course stardom of this kind can only be achieved if the public approved.

For American distributors voted Bronson the eighth biggest draw at the box-office in 1973, despite the fact that his only other film that year met with mediocre audience response: *The Stone Killer*, a De Laurentiis-Winner effort in which he was a detective. And Bronson remained in the top 10 list for the next three years, without being in any very popular films: they were made to a formula at a time when the public had clearly tired of formula films – even if that formula included violence, supposedly a crowd-pleaser. The publicity on *Mr Majestyk* (74) was that he had entered the million dollar salary bracket, but according to Whitney the sum paid was $602,500. The story concerned a poor melon-farmer fighting the syndicates; Winner's *Death Wish* concerned a New York businessman who takes revenge into his own hands – and it was Bronson's most successful film in the US since becoming a star. There was a much more muted welcome for the next pair: *Breakout* (75), with Bronson as a helicopter pilot helping a prisoner down Mexico way; and Walter Hill's effective *Hard Times* (75) also titled *The Streetfighter*, as a streetfighter at the time of the Depression. *Breakheart Pass* (76) and *From Noon Till Three* were both Westerns, the first a screen original by novelist Alistair MacLean and the latter supposedly funny; and *Raid on Entebbe*, an all-star TV movie in which Bronson played General Dan Shomron. Before that, he did a private-eye thriller, *St Ives*, directed by J. Lee Thompson, who also made *The White Buffalo* (77), both so bad that neither reached Britain – and indeed the latter was one of the year's biggest flops. Bronson's wife was his co-star in most of these films, but with a popular player – Lee Remick – and a good director for once, Don Siegel, a Cold War thriller, *Telefon*, failed to take off. Neither did *Love and Bullets* (79), for Lew Grade. He was to have played in *Firepower*, but refused the role when the producer, Grade, would not give the lead to Ireland – though Bronson himself denied this as the reason he did not do the film.

In 1979 he gave an interview to 'Photoplay', speaking of his recent flops and his loss of popularity; he was not pleased about either. If his face was no longer 'right' for the American screen, he retained some standing

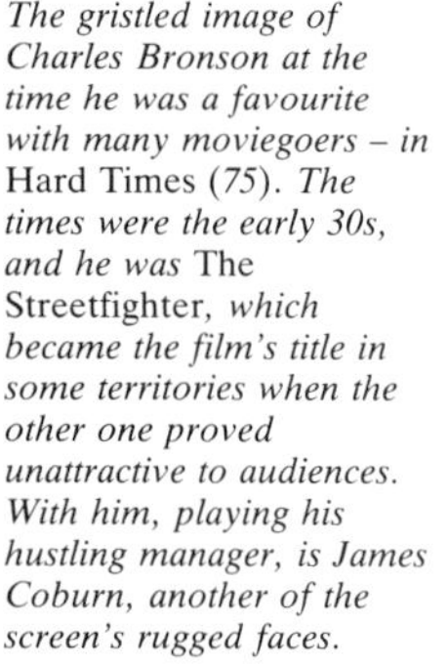

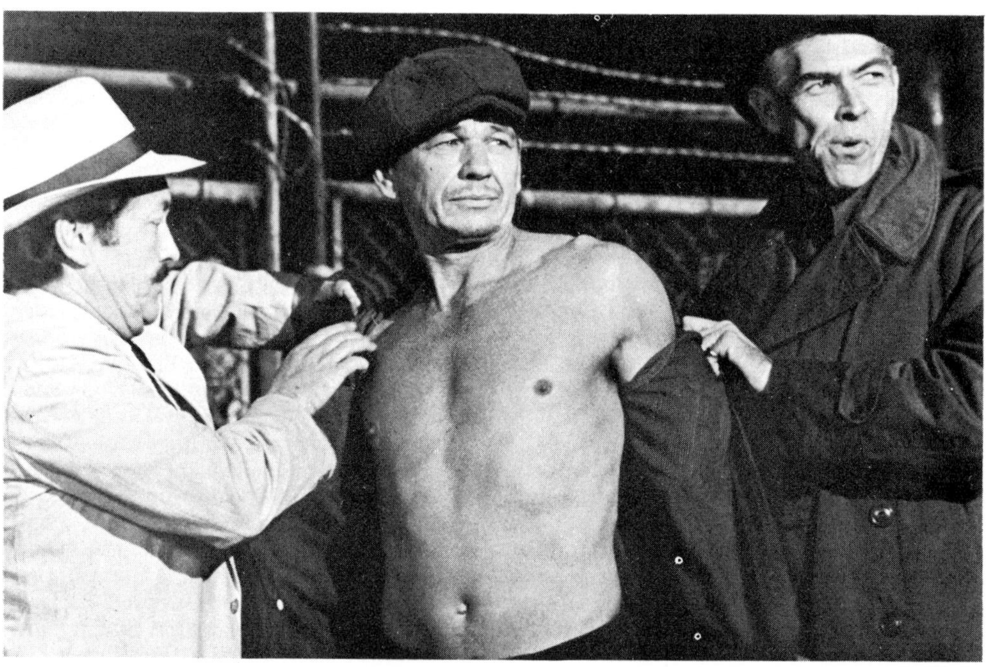

The gristled image of Charles Bronson at the time he was a favourite with many moviegoers – in Hard Times *(75). The times were the early 30s, and he was* The Streetfighter, *which became the film's title in some territories when the other one proved unattractive to audiences. With him, playing his hustling manager, is James Coburn, another of the screen's rugged faces.*

in Europe. His popularity within the industry had never been legendary; he is widely regarded as unapproachable except by his family – and Eddie Constantine, among others, has spoken of 'misanthropy'. After an independent effort, *Cabo Blanco* (80) with Dominique Sanda, which failed everywhere, he played a border patrolman in *Borderline*, the last of his four-picture $6 million contract with Grade, whose company went into bankruptcy. He moved to another downmarket set-up, Golden Harvest, for *Death Hunt* (81), as a settler pursued across the Arctic by mountie Lee Marvin, and then to yet another, Cannon, for Winner's *Death Wish 2* (82). Said the normally generous critic of the 'Miami Herald': 'Impossible to imagine worse performances than those of Charles Bronson and Jill Ireland, or worse direction.' He remained with Cannon for *Ten to Midnight* (83), playing a cop who takes the law into his own hands when a psychopathic killer strikes, and he went to Grade's successor at ITC for *The Evil That Men Do* (84), as a hit man amidst the usual vigilante violence, set this time in Central America. J. Lee Thompson directed both. Winner was back for *Death Wish 3* (85), after which was a much-needed change of pace: *Act of Vengeance*, based on fact, about Jack Yablouski, who ran for the presidency of the miners' union in order to expose corruption at the top. It was made for cable, for HBO. Said 'Variety', paraphrasing the company's publicity: 'Last year HBO did *Draw* with Kirk Douglas as star. But no one was knocking down doors to get Douglas as a theatrical film star. . . . But Bronson is hot!' You could have fooled me, as the man said. *Murphy's Law* (86) – the star as a veteran LA cop framed for the murder of his ex-wife – came and went speedily, but Cannon signed Bronson to an exclusive pact for six years, beginning with *The President's Assassin* (87). It was hard not to feel that Cannon, Bronson and Winner were natural bedmates, but Bronson announced that he wanted Thompson to direct *Death Wish 4* – just what the world needs – because Winner had allowed too much violence into Part 3. After that came *Messenger of Death* (88), as a detective, and *Kinjite* (89), both to go, like most of this batch, quickly to video.

Mel Brooks

'To be the funniest has always been my aim' said Mel Brooks to 'Newsweek' in 1975, or so Kenneth Tynan wrote in his 'New Yorker' profile of Brooks in 1978, which manages much information about 'top-grossing comedies' with admiration on the part of the writer. For instance, Tynan tells us that a 'Playboy' interview 'deserves a place in any anthology of modern American humour. The Master is back on his home ground. Brooks is showing off his own invention – the interview as comic art – and doing so with a virtuosity that makes one wonder how any other form could ever put his talents to better use.' Of the Master's films, Tynan is more guarded: 'in order to enjoy *The Producers*, you have to cultivate a taste for grotesque and deliberate overstatement.' In other words, you have to be a sucker for the 'anything-goes' school of comedy, a genre that started with desperate TV writers. Brooks had been one of the writers on a well-thought-of series, 'Your Show of Shows', and he tried for a similar creative atmosphere when he made his 'breakthrough comedy', as he called it, *Blazing Saddles*: '. . . it carried the audience into territory that film comedy had never entered before – kinds of satire, kinds of special vulgarity.' The vulgarity was as much in evidence as the satire was missing: film comedy had not entered this territory because paddling around in such murky waters had previously been denied to it. In the Old West it was probably common to kick your opponent in the balls, which happens a lot in *Blazing Saddles*, along with a lot of other 'humour' which would not seem funny in the dying embers of a rowdy stag-night. Tynan says that Brooks's humour is mainly vocal, and quotes chunks of it: case unproven.

Brooks was born Melvin Kaminsky in Brooklyn in 1926, of immigrant parents and 'Russian-Ukranian-Jewish intellectual heritage'; but poor. He changed his name when he went from high school to the borscht-belt circuit in 1942, as drummer and occasional comic. There he met Sid Caesar, who much later – after army service – asked him to write for him; except for one season, he was one of Caesar's writers from 1950 to 1959. Carl Reiner was one of his fellow-writers and one of their improvised routines, about The Two-Thousand-Year-Old Man, was set down and recorded by them, to considerable success. A year later, in 1961, Jerry Lewis hired Brooks to work on *Ladies' Man*, but kept in little of his material; in 1962 he wrote the book of a flop Broadway musical, 'All American', and he was divorced. In 1964 he married Anne Bancroft, whose fame considerably outweighed his, but that year he won an Oscar for a short cartoon which he had conceived with Ernest Pintoff, 'The Critic'; the following year with Buck Henry he wrote a TV sitcom about a hopeless private eye, 'Get Smart'. He wrote a play, which became a screenplay: Joseph E. Levine backed it and allowed

Brooks to direct: *The Producers* (68), a lethally funny idea about an accountant (Gene Wilder) who persuades an unprincipled impresario (Zero Mostel) to put on a flop show for tax purposes. With reason, the screenplay brought Brooks an Oscar, but his stately direction and the heavy mugging by the principals kept the customers away: but the sequenes of the flop show – 'Springtime for Hitler' – guaranteed a cult following.

The Producers' producer, Sidney Glazier, set up *The Twelve Chairs* (71), which was filmed in Yugoslavia since the original novel by the Petrovs had been set in Russia: the 1945 version with Fred Allen, *It's in the Bag*, was updated and set in New York – and it was a damnsight funnier than this version. True, Brooks appeared to be making a Statement and true he again had an unlikeable lead, Ron Moody, and an inadequate one, Frank Langella; the film was stolen by Dom DeLuise as Moody's priestly rival in the matter of pursuing the jewels hidden in one of the chairs, and Brooks himself was funny in a cameo as a servile and drunken caretaker. His all-round fee for the film was $50,000, possibly more than the film took at the box-office, but it was reissued and got some foreign showings after Brooks had his first big success. This was not *She Stoops To Conquer*, with Albert Finney as Tony Lumpkin, since Finney changed his mind, but a script by Andrew Bergman which Warners invited him to rewrite. With several other writers this became *Blazing Saddles* (74), with Wilder as an over-the-hill gunfighter (a role intended for Dan Dailey); Brooks directed and played the way-out self-aggrandizing Governor. He was one of the pluses, as were Madeline Kahn as a Dietrich-like chantoosie and Harvey Korman as a conniving speculator. Korman had done funnier movie spoofs on TV in 'The Carol Burnett Show' and this movie lacked the real bad taste stuff which might have been explored at this particular time; but at this particular time the movie public was starved of comedy and it patronized – hugely – this ragbag.

It doesn't look funny to me either: Mel Brooks and companion in a sequence from the highly successful comedy, Blazing Saddles *(74). It did not appear in the finished film, which might have been even more successful if they had cut some of the rest of it.*

It came out while Columbia was dickering over the budget of *Young Frankenstein*, which consequently went to 20th, for whom it became a huge earner, though it was no funnier on horror movies than its predecessor had been on Westerns (as Jason Robards put it, 'I thought we did better jokes in high school'). Wilder and Marty Feldman were in it, and they went away and did their own movie spoofs, respectively *The Adventures of Sherlock Holmes' Smarter Brother* and *The Last Remake of Beau Geste*, proving in the process that movie-spoofing was not their bag. There is a tendency in this school of film-maker to claim prejudice and/or misunderstanding on the part of critics who thumbs-down their work: since critics like to laugh as much as the public, and have frequently been kind to the second-rate in the field of comedy, this view is untenable – and in these two cases critics and public concurred, almost to a man. Thus, Brooks has been luckier: *Silent Movie* (76) was warmly welcomed. True, it had a roster of popular guest stars, but Brooks did prove that he had learnt, from his days as a movie buff, the sort of construction which made the great Silent comedies work. As Mel Funn in this film he made one – an alcoholic ex-director thus saving the studio from being taken over by a conglomerate. Seemingly unable to get away from movies about movies, he spoofed Hitchcock in *High Anxiety* (78) and the Hitchcock connection enabled it to do better than his disciples' connections to Sherlock Holmes and Beau Geste. Still, after a poor press (even 'Photoplay' referred to it as 'a clinker' while it was still going the rounds), it was touch and go, not restoring Brooks to box-office eminence as predicted by him in the 'New Yorker' profile: in 1976 he was fifth and in 1977 he was seventh. He was one of the guest stars in *The Muppet Movie* (79).

Then 20th Century-Fox put up the $10 million budget of *History of the World Part I* (81) and Brooksfilm the completion guarantee); Brooks took only a nominal fee as producer/director/writer in exchange for the

Let us ask not why so many Hollywood movies have portrayed film directors as drunks, but at least Silent Movie (76) *was a comic variation. The director with the shaking hand is Mel Brooks, and helping to sober him up are Dom DeLuise, Bernadette Peters and Marty Feldman.*

foreign rights. Columbia handled in most territories and Brooks went to tub-thump. Consequently the film did better overseas than at home – but that would not have been difficult. It was time perhaps for a change of pace and *To Be or Not to Be* (83) was a relatively straight comedy, co-starring his wife. It was not much appreciated, but then Brooks could not have expected it to be: why remake one of the funniest, most enduring comedies in the history of the cinema? There was a well-earned silence, till Brooks returned, via MGM, with the sort of 'zany' comedy for which he was once famous, *Spaceballs* (87). Good grosses the first weekend: after that the notices had effect.

Yul Brynner

Yul Brynner shaved his head to play the King in 'The King and I' on Broadway and he kept it shaved for the film version. Once or twice, shortly afterwards, he sported hair, but he stayed bald for the rest of his career.

There are several versions of his early life, none of which he would confirm or deny: 'Just call me a nice, clean-cut Mongolian boy' was his response. Let's say: he was born in 1915 on the island of Sakhalin off the coast of Siberia. His birth was recorded at Vladivostock. He was brought up in Paris and either studied at the Sorbonne or started work at 13, singing for sous with a guitar; or both. At some time he worked as a trapeze artist. In 1934 he was with the Pitoeff company, unpaid, doing odd jobs and apparently earning his living as a life-guard on the Côte d'Azur during the summer months. In 1941 he arrived in the US and at first did one-night stands with his guitar; he then joined Michael Chekov's company in Connecticut, with whom he made his US début, as Fabian in 'Twelfth Night' (41), learned phonetically. He sometimes drove the bus for the company, till it disbanded; then he got a job with the USO War Information Dept as a radio commentator. Also in 1943 he married Virginia Gilmore, a second-string leading lady at 20th, then almost at the end of her film career. In 1944 he was in a pre-Broadway try-out, 'The House in Paris', and in 1945 in a Broadway success, 'Lute Song' with Mary Martin; in 1947 he was in London in a flop gypsy musical, 'Dark Eyes'.

He had worked a little with CBS TV in its pioneer days and in 1949 he returned there, acting and directing, during which time he got a film chance in a B made by Eagle-Lion in New York, *The Port of New York* (49), as a particularly nasty villain, a drug-smuggler, whose come-uppance from Scott Brady was greeted by cheers. He was, however, happily settled directing in TV when Mary Martin recommended him for the role of the King of Siam opposite Gertrude Lawrence in 'The King and I' (51). He got raves and went on to win almost every award open to a Broadway actor; he would have preferred to have remained a TV director, but the acclaim was too great. In 1952 Paramount signed him to a seven-year contract, one film a year, and they 'bought' him from the run of 'The King and I' for 12 weeks to make either *A New Kind of Love* for Billy Wilder or a South Seas story, but neither was made, though Brynner collected $75,000 for the commitment. When, in 1953, De Mille and Paramount announced that he would play the Pharaoh in *The Ten Commandments* no reference was made to that contract (De Mille chose Brynner on the strength of his Siamese King). The film took so long to make, and Brynner was committed to tours of 'King', that it was not till 1956 that the film public saw him – in 20th's film version of *The King and I*, opposite Deborah Kerr. He was still superb: disarmingly stubborn and autocratic, playing with some subtlety and much magnetism. He won a Best Actor Oscar and the film was enormously popular, certainly the best of the gargantuan versions of Broadway musicals that Hollywood made in the 50s. Released soon afterwards, *The Ten Commandments* was equally popular, though the press thought it as crass as most of De Mille's work.

20th cast him opposite Ingrid Bergman in *Anastasia*, as the severe Russian general who claimed to have discovered that unfortunate lady. It was also a big one and producers were falling over themselves to cast the no-haired actor: he was Dmitri in Richard Brooks's valiant shot at *The Brothers Karamazov* (58) and then *The Buccaneer*, in wig and moustache, an old De Mille remake by Anthony Quinn (replacing Brynner himself as director when he decided not to try to act and direct at the same time). In 1957 and 1958 he just scraped into the top 10 lists. It was announced that he had a $25 million deal with UA for 11 films, some of which he would direct, but nothing seemed to come of this.

He was a Russian officer in *The Journey* (59), which blatantly used the tragic Hungarian Revolution of 1956 for an exceptionally banal romance (the original script had been set in China); and, again hirsute, was Joanne

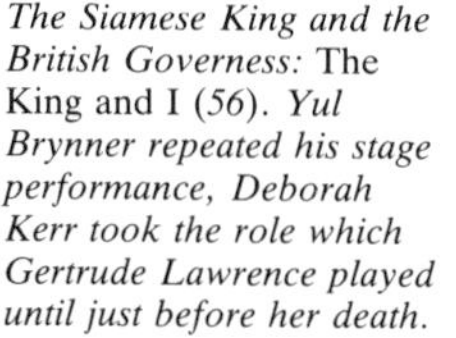

The Siamese King and the British Governess: The King and I (*56*). *Yul Brynner repeated his stage performance, Deborah Kerr took the role which Gertrude Lawrence played until just before her death.*

Woodward's stern guardian in *The Sound and the Fury*, an adaptation of Faulkner which came out more like a Deep South *Seventh Veil*. He was as commanding as ever, but these had only candlepower at the box-office. It was decided the public would not accept him with hair, but he had hair when rushed into *Solomon and Sheba* to replace the deceased Tyrone Power, at a reputed fee of $1 million; marginally less tedious than the previous occasion on which he had played a biblical monarch, it burned almost as brightly at the box-office. As a favour to his friend Jean Cocteau, Brynner did a guest bit in *Le Testament d'Orphée*. He was then in a couple that failed to ignite – director Stanley Donen has taken full responsibility, and why not as he saw the rushes, revealing, presumably, a comedy touch as light as a stone-crusher? – as a temperamental conductor in *Once More With Feeling* (60), with Kay Kendall, and as a gangster in *Surprise Package*, with Mitzi Gaynor.

He was much more happily cast as the black-garbed leader of *The Magnificent Seven*, John Sturges's excellent Western based on Kurosawa's even better *Seven Samurai*. It was his last big success. In 1968 'Variety' was to list him, because he was still highly paid, as a liability to producers, but most of the films were a liability to him – though whether his participation improved them is a moot point: as a Middle East revolutionary in *Escape From Zahrain* (62) 'Variety' said he 'plays with a characteristic stoicism of emotional expression'. It changed its mind, though, when it inspected his performance as the Cossack leader in *Taras Bulba*: 'He's allowed plenty of space in which to chew the scenery and there's precious little of it in which he doesn't leave teethmarks.' The 'MFB' observed that he could 'chalk up yet another part that calls for a well-shaven head'. The others: *Kings of the Sun* (63), as a Mayan chieftain, with George Chakiris; *Flight From Ashiya* (64), as a Japanese parachute expert; *Invitation to a Gunfighter*, as a hired gunman and all in black again; *Morituri* (65) with Marlon Brando, as the humane German captain; *The Poppy is Also a Flower* (66), a warning against narcotics made by the UN for TV but shown in cinemas, in a cameo (one of many stars) as a police chief; and *Cast a Giant Shadow*, another cameo, as a Jewish Resistance leader.

He was the only one of the original seven to return, still black-garbed, in *Return of the Seven*, his most popular film around this time. He had moved to Switzerland with his second wife (1960) and accepted three offers for British films (indeed, he did not film in the US again till 1972; and became a Swiss citizen): *The Double Man* (67), an inexplicably poor thriller directed by Franklin Schaffner; *Triple Cross* with Christopher Plummer, as a monocled Nazi; and *The Long Duel* with Trevor Howard, as an Indian rebel leader, one of the periodic, vain attempts by Rank to make a blockbuster for the world market. In Spain he played Pancho Villa in *Villa Rides!* (68) with Robert Mitchum; in Britain he did a poor thriller that played B dates, *The File of the Golden Goose* (69). He got good notices again for his forceful performance as the top baddie agin Katharine Hepburn in *The Madwoman of Chaillot*, around which time he was filming a cameo in the hardly shown *The Picasso Summer*. In Yugoslavia he was a demolitions expert in *Bitka na Neretvi/The Battle of Neretva*; then, unbilled, he sang 'Mad About the Boy' in *The Magic Christian* (70), in drag, to Roman Polanski.

After that, the next logical step was towards spaghetti Westerns: *Sai Che ti Dico tu Sei un Gran Figlio di . . ./Indio Black* (71), dressed from head-to-toe in guess-what again, getting $250,000 up front in this 100 per cent Italian-financed film plus 15 per cent of the net after twice the negative cost had been recouped. Then: *Romance of a Horse Thief*, made by Abraham Polansky in Yugoslavia, with Eli Wallach, a return to 'class' films, but it flopped badly; *Adios Sabata*, in a part played originally by Lee Van Cleef – this was a sequel (both Italian); *Catlow* in Spain; and *The Light at the Edge of the World*, in Spain with Kirk Douglas. He returned to the US to make a thriller about the New York police, *Fuzz* (72), written by Evan Hunter, with Raquel Welch. In 1972 he played the Siamese King again in a TV series based on 'Anna and the King of Siam', with Samantha Eggar.

The Magnificent Seven *(60). The cast was not magnificent, but it was certainly pretty good: Steve McQueen, James Coburn, Horst Buchholtz, Yul Brynner, Brad Dexter, Robert Vaughan and Charles Bronson. Although McQueen had above-the-title billing, the only real name at that time was Brynner. Only Dexter did not make it.*

He married for the third time in 1971. After playing a Russian defector in *Le Serpent/The Serpent* (73), Brynner made his first Hollywood movie in a while, playing a mechanical monster in a science fiction job, *Westworld*; and *The Ultimate Warrior* (75) was not dissimilar, with Brynner as a sort of superman defying the future. *Con la Rabbia Agli Occhi/ Shadow of a Thriller* was a gangster story and after touring in a play called 'The Odyssey', he returned to Italy for *Gli Indesiderabili* (76). In 1977 he was in a very successful New York revival of 'The King and I', which he took to London in 1979. After a two-year run, he toured for another two, returning to New York in the show in 1985, where he was breaking house records till his sudden death a few months later.

ELLEN BURSTYN

Ellen Burstyn is probably a terrific actress: she has won a ton of awards; we loved her in *Alice Doesn't Live Here Anymore*, as the young widow who wants a life of her own instead of living only through her men. Her Alice was the most ordinary of women and if you start to call her plucky or humorous, you are still not near. We had not seen this sort of pluck on the screen, born of despair; nor this sort of humour, moving from gentle sarcasm to self-mockery to play-acting. It was a big chance and she grabbed it, contributing as much to the end result as any actress since Garbo. But whereas you could not forget Garbo in anything, or Ingrid Bergman, or Margaret Sullavan, it is difficult indeed to recall Burstyn in any of her other film appearances.

More than Alice's, it was a long and winding road. She was born in Detroit in 1932, as Edna Rae Gillooly, of Irish parents who divorced when she was six; in her teens she was married to a man described as both a poet and an automobile salesman; she also studied dancing and was part of an acrobatic troupe. In Detroit and then in Texas she modelled; she danced in Montreal; in New York she modelled for paperbacks and became a Gleason Girl on 'The Jackie Gleason Show' on TV. That was in 1954. In 1957 she auditioned for the lead opposite Sam Levene in 'Fair Game' and won the role over such established names as Mona Freeman and Terry Moore; but she found it was not much fun being in a Broadway show without experience and began to study under Stella Adler. She married the play's director, Paul Roberts, did TV in Los Angeles and then returned to study with the Actors Studio. There were two film offers: *For Those Who Think Young* (64), a teenage frolic with James Darren and Pamela Tiffin, as a disapproving sociology professor; and *Goodbye Charlie*, supporting Debbie Reynolds. She did not enjoy either of them and found herself able to work more creatively in a TV soap opera, 'The Doctors'. Till this time she had acted as Ellen McRae; for the next role she took the name of her third husband, actor Neil Burstyn: they were in Rome when Joseph Strick invited her to Paris for his film of Henry Miller's autobiographical *Tropic of Cancer* (69): Rip Torn was Miller, she was his wife and the film was a series of flat, pointless adventures. Paul Mazursky saw it and asked her to play the wife of a movie writer, Donald Sutherland, in *Alex in Wonderland* (70), a self-indulgent and mainly pretentious homage to jokes and movies old and new. There was more obeisance to the cinema's past in Peter Bogdanovich's overrated *The Last Picture Show* (71), but at least the Texas tanktown folks under examination were beautifully acted: as Cybill Shepherd's sluttish mother Burstyn was chosen Best Supporting Actress by the New York critics. An old friend, Bob Rafelson, had considered her for *Five Easy Pieces*, but had decided that the role needed a younger actress – Karen Black; but he did put Burstyn into his rich, ambiguous *The King of Marvin Gardens* (72), as one of the women involved with Jack Nicholson and Bruce Dern, 'a champagne-bubbly, fading beauty, whose effervescence has gone flat' (Burstyn). Then, William Friedkin wanted her for his show-off version of a meretricious occult thriller, *The Exorcist* (73), as the actress mother of the young victim, Linda Blair; after which Mazursky used her again, as Art Carney's daughter in *Harry and Tonto* (74), an odyssey of an old man and his cat, sometimes bright, sometimes folksy, which brought Carney a Best Actor Oscar. A TV movie, *Thursday's Game*, found her wife to Gene Wilder, whose fellow poker-player was Bob Newhart.

That year the Academy awarded Burstyn the Best Actress Oscar for *Alice Doesn't Live Here Anymore*. Despite the popularity of both *The Last Picture Show* and *The Exorcist*, it could not be said that she had succeeded in imposing herself on the public, but for both she had been nominated for a Best Supporting Oscar – which was why Warners let her persuade them into laying out a $2.1 million budget for *Alice*. Robert Getchell's script had originally been a TV Movie of the Week project for David Susskind (who, according to Burstyn, loathed the film, despite a producer credit and a share of the profits), but she got hold of it and was determined to do it for cinemas: it took her two years. She took the

Ellen Burstyn in her Oscar-winning role in Alice Doesn't Live Here *(75).*

script to Francis Ford Coppola, who suggested as director another Corman alumnus, Martin Scorsese, who made of it one of the few ingratiating movies of the time – though in essence it was like many movie tales of people drifting through an America of one part kindness, one part heartbreak and one part hopelessness; it was also, if you like, the best film statement on Women's Lib. For Burstyn her Oscar was part of a double triumph: for her role in a two-character Broadway play, 'Same Time Next Year', she won a Tony award, the first actress to score thus since Audrey Hepburn in 1954 (not, of course, that the two awards in one season is more than a coincidence).

But times had changed in the meantime. After the New York run there was no long-term Hollywood contract awaiting: though it was Burstyn's intention to 'avoid doing the things that would make me well known' she could surely have chosen better than Alain Resnais's *Providence* (77), which threatened to render her unknown. Joanne Woodward had sensibly turned down the role; and Burstyn, groping around the idiocies of set and script, seemed – like most of the cast (Elaine Stritch was the exception) – an amateur at first rehearsal. She hardly chose better with one of Jules Dassin's updatings of Greek tragedy, *A Dream of Passion* (78), as a modern Medea visited in prison by Melina Mercouri. Help was needed and it was at hand – with the film of *Same Time Next Year*, repeating her role of the woman restricted to one annual reunion with her lover (Alan Alda). Ageing over the years, both players were good – as they had to be, given the improbable situations of this Broadway schlock. *Resurrection* (80), a drama about faith-healing with Sam Shepard, proved that Burstyn's box-office appeal was severely limited and she was pleased to get a plum role in a tele-movie, *The People vs. Jean Harris* (81), an account of the schoolteacher who murdered her lover, the author of the 'Scarsdale Diet' book. It was transmitted only five weeks after the trial, perhaps the reason for Burstyn's monotonous performance, but she was not any better as a Canadian pioneer woman in *Silence of the North*, made a couple of years earlier and now going direct to cable. A Broadway role in '84 Charing Cross Road' (82) did not detain her long, nor was much notice taken of *The Ambassador* (84) despite the presence of Robert Mitchum and Rock Hudson: she was the former's wife, having an affair with an Arab (Fabio Testi). Gene Hackman was unfaithful to her (with Ann-Margret) in *Twice in a Lifetime* (85), her last film for cinemas for a while. But she had been busy: *Act of Vengeance*, opposite Charles Bronson, for HBO; *Into Thin Air*, a tele-movie in which she is a mother whose son disappears; 'The Ellen Burstyn Show' (86), which did not run; *Something in Common*, as a woman whose son falls in love with Tuesday Weld; and *Pack of Lies* (87) with Alan Bates, in the role played in London by Judi Dench and in New York by Rosemary Harris. Returning to movies, she had top-billing, but only a supporting role, as the heroine's mother in *Hanna's War* (88).

Richard Burton

'Make up your mind,' Laurence Olivier is supposed to have said to Richard Burton, '. . . a household word or a great actor.' Burton's offscreen adventures plus a reputation as an embryo 'great actor' contributed to a position unjustified by any of his screen work. BC ('Before *Cleopatra*' – one of his jokes), he gave monotonous performances in a series of mainly terrible films; afterwards, in many better films, he was often only marginally better. His stock-in-trade was to gaze mournfully just to right or left of the camera and let his great actor's voice bark at some hapless fellow player.

It was a great voice. John Coleman wrote in the 'Weekend Telegraph': 'From the outset, his major capital has lain in that huge, instrumental voice, capable of thrilling switches from whisper to roar, with every syllable an honest transaction between you and him.' Burton did have other useful attributes. He always looked interesting – as a young man idealistic and soulful, later dissipated and soulful. He had arrogance and authority. On the stage, in his late twenties and early thirties he tackled some of the great classical roles and emerged with credit (he once complained to a reporter that he was always described as a promising actor rather than a great one – but an examination of the reviews of his Stratford and Old Vic seasons produces no other conclusion).

He was born in 1925 in Pontrhydfen, South Wales, the son of a miner and the twelfth of 13 children. He was raised by a sister and while at Port Talbot Secondary School came under the influence of a teacher who saw great possibilities for a theatrical or scholastic future. When he was 16 he answered an advert for a Welsh boy that Emlyn Williams had put in a local paper; as a consequence he played with him in London in 'The Druid's Rest' for a run before going up to Oxford (on a scholarship). There he made such a mark in an OUDS 'Measure for Measure' that the London theatrical firm H.M. Tennent offered him a contract, and it was with Tennents that he began to work after national service with the RAF, 1944–47. Success came quickly. In 1949 he had a featured role in 'The Lady's Not For Burning' with John Gielgud – they took it to New York in 1950. But he was established by the Stratford season of 1951, where he was a memorable Prince Hal. Meanwhile, he had brought a needed masculine grace to some weak little films, of which the first was easily the best, *The Last Days of Dolwyn* (49), written and directed by Emlyn Williams, with Edith Evans. Korda produced and unsuccessfully tried to get Burton to sign a long-term contract. He had small parts in *Now Barabbas Was a Robber . . .* as a prisoner with a homosexual bent; *Waterfront* (50) as Robert Newton's prospective son-in-law; *The Woman With No Name* (51) as a Norwegian pilot who is killed just after marrying Phyllis Calvert; and – a bigger part in a B film – *Green Grow the Rushes* as a village smuggler.

Korda had never given up hope of getting Burton to sign with him and renewed his efforts after the acclaim which greeted his 1951 Stratford work. On Broadway Burton did 'Legend of Lovers'. In May 1952 he signed a five-year contract with Korda, starting at £100 a week. Around the same time Daphne du Maurier was selling her new novel to 20th and she recommended Burton for the male lead; so 20th negotiated with Korda to borrow him for that film and two others, at $50,000 per film. Olivia de Havilland was the star of this pseudo-Gothic romance, *My Cousin Rachel* (52), and reports went that she did not get on with Burton. But the critics loved him – Jympson Harman in the 'Evening News': 'I would say he is the most exciting thing in movies since the advent of Gregory Peck eight years ago.' He also impressed American televiewers in 'Anna Christie' with June Havoc, and a jubilant 20th hastened Burton into two more films (the second of which had been destined for Peck or Tyrone Power) and negotiated with Korda to buy the rest of Burton's contract. He turned down their offer of one film a year for 10 years at $100,000 each but did sign for seven years on those terms.

Meanwhile, *The Desert Rats* (53), a war picture, had not been warmly received; and Peter Myers wrote in 'Picturegoer' of Burton's performance: 'If you met this officer off the screen you would at once take him for a leading man, with a commission kindly granted for ENSA purposes, fresh from the

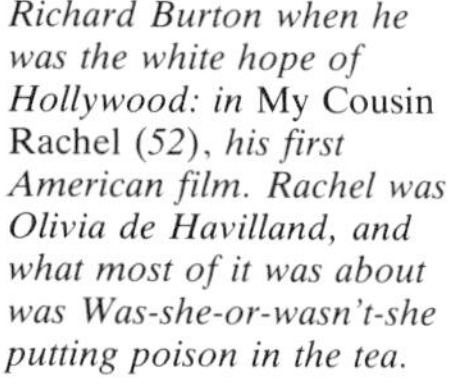

Richard Burton when he was the white hope of Hollywood: in My Cousin Rachel *(52), his first American film. Rachel was Olivia de Havilland, and what most of it was about was Was-she-or-wasn't-she putting poison in the tea.*

best agents and the best towns.' In *The Robe*, a dreadful Roman religioso that was the first CinemaScope film and a giant grosser, Burton was merely wooden. The filming prevented him accepting MGM's offer of Mark Antony in *Julius Caesar*, but he returned to Britain then to do Shakespeare in an Old Vic season, playing, among other parts, Hamlet, Coriolanus and the Bastard in 'King John'.

A second Hollywood sojourn was even less interesting than the first. He played Edwin Booth in a simplistic biopic of that actor, *Prince of Players* (55), which became known as the first flop in CinemaScope. Said 'Time Magazine': 'Actor Burton shows a pretty talent though not exactly for Shakespeare. In almost every scene, this one-time junior colleague of Laurence Olivier (*sic*) . . . does more a parody of his senior than an imitation of life.' (The film had been intended originally for Olivier or Brando.) *The Rains of Raunchipur* was a tedious remake of *The Rains Came* with Burton in blackface in Tyrone Power's old part of the Indian prince. *Alexander the Great* (56) was at least an intelligent attempt, by Robert Rossen at UA, to tell it like it was and Burton was regally graceful in the under-written title-role; but only some critics liked it, the public shunned it – and today it is as dull as the rest of Burton's early films. Back at the Old Vic Burton was again in blackface, as Othello, alternating that part and Iago with John Neville. Neville won on points but the gambit – plus a rousing Henry V – salvaged Burton's reputation after the Hollywood débâcle.

At least on paper *Sea Wife* (57) looked okay: from a bestseller about a shipwrecked couple (she turns out to be a nun – Joan Collins), directed by Roberto Rossellini. But Rossellini left after a few days. The film sank without trace and 20th and Burton called it quits. *Amère Victoire/Bitter Victory* also flopped, a French war film made in English by Nicholas Ray. Negotiations to play Warwick in *Saint Joan* broke down: John Gielgud played it. Burton went to Broadway to appear in 'Time Remembered' with Helen Hayes and was a success; on TV he played Heathcliff to Yvonne Furneaux's Cathy; but was considered washed-up in Hollywood. However, he had offers to appear in *The Miracle* and *Solomon and Sheba*, which he turned down for a British movie, *Look Back in Anger* (58). The success of this on the stage had brought industry interest, but author John Osborne and director Tony Richardson rejected all offers in order to retain autonomy over the film version; it was Burton's encouragement which enabled them to get it off the ground. They repaid the debt by giving him by far his best film to date – and he was quite perfect as that prototypical but accurate 50s figure, Jimmy Porter. Unlike the play, the film was too soon for its audiences and did only so-so business. Warners had had a small hand in the financing and that company was appalled when they learnt that producer Milton Sperling had signed Burton for two films – and the box-office results proved them right: *The Bramble Bush* (60), as a New England doctor, and *Ice Palace*, as an Alaskan adventurer. Both were from bestsellers.

His career was rescued when he was offered the role of King Arthur in a Broadway musical, 'Camelot' (61), which he did quite beautifully; but he became tired of it and jumped at the chance of being bought out to play Mark Antony in *Cleopatra* (63). This had begun abortively in England with Stephen Boyd as Antony and Peter Finch as Caesar; but when it was restarted in Rome after Elizabeth Taylor's illness Rex Harrison was engaged as Caesar. Boyd's inexperience beside Harrison was thought to jeopardize the film, so 20th doubtfully settled on the more capable Burton. It turned out that the actor they had once written off was to provide – unwillingly – more publicity for this film than any before or since. He and Taylor fell in love, watched or at least spied upon by what seemed to be the world's entire press corps. Filming was prolonged for other reasons as well and finally cost more, at $35 million, than any other film before or since. Predictably, it turned out to be a giant bore (whatever had gone on offscreen was not reflected by this dreary Antony and Cleopatra) and only slipped into the black, years later, via a TV sale. Burton in the meantime had done a cameo in *The Longest Day* (62), but there were now indications that neither he nor Taylor would get further film offers: there were accusations that their behaviour – both moral and financial – had alienated the public as much as the industry, but it became clear that this was not so. After a hiatus, offers began to pour in.

The first was from Anatole de Grunwald, who had been connected with Burton's first film, and Burton demanded, hopefully, $500,000 (twice his basic *Cleopatra* salary). He got it, but despite it was in jaded form as Taylor's tycoon husband in *The V.I.P.'s*; it was an all-star film and a box-office hit. But what re-established him was the title-role in *Becket* (64) with Peter O'Toole, a facile reconstruction (after a play by Anouilh) of the events which led up to the martyrdom of Henry II's archbishop; and he had another big one with *The Night of the Iguana*, as Tennessee Williams's unfrocked priest. He made both parts variations on his role in *The V.I.P.'s* but in *Iguana* it worked surprisingly well – indeed a superb performance, cleverly

The Night of the Iguana *(64) was the usual woozy Tennessee Williams blend of melodrama, eroticism, morality and sentiment – and, as usual, it worked more than tolerably, due in no small part to fine performances by Ava Gardner and Richard Burton.*

balancing the pathos and comedy. He and Taylor, their divorces through, got married, and played lovers in *The Sandpiper* (65). He was yet again a priest, if a rather unorthodox one, and she was a beatnik. Awful notices had no visible effect on the box-office, where the figures justified the huge salary that Burton now demanded.

He did 'Hamlet' on Broadway (assisted by his wife's nightly appearances in the audience) and a film of the stage performance was shown briefly in the US (September 1964) and even more briefly in London in 1972. The next two were good. *The Spy Who Came in From the Cold* was not only the most realistic but by far the best of the 60s espionage-fad films. From a superior bestseller by John Le Carré, Martin Ritt drew a spine-chilling film and from Burton drew his best qualities of misanthropy, determination and sardonic humour. For the second year running Burton came in at tenth on the box-office lists and he was to stay in the list for two more years. He and his wife had a big hit in *Who's Afraid of Virginia Woolf?* (66), finely directed by Mike Nichols from Edward Albee's play about a warring campus couple.

The Spy Who Came in From the Cold *(65) stood out head-and-shoulders above the other spy films of the 60s. Richard Burton was the sadly used British agent, Leamas; and Claire Bloom played the girl who loved him.*

They were similarly cast in Zeffirelli's rumbustious version of *The Taming of the Shrew* but this time to only moderately favourable reviews; then, still on a culture kick, he co-directed and played the lead in a film version of an OUDS production which he had just done for philanthropic reasons – Marlowe's *Doctor Faustus* (67). Both film and performance were panned and it did badly even by the modest standards expected of it. A sadly mediocre version of Graham Greene's *The Comedians* did appropriate business; and a fifth consecutive venture with Taylor, *Boom!* (68) – directed by Joseph Losey from a play by Tennessee Williams – was described by 'Variety' as one of the biggest money-losers of all time. The public were perhaps surfeited with the Burtons: each day the papers carried stories of their antics – of rows in public, of purchases of a yacht, an aeroplane, of jewellery and paintings and furs. Their press agent must have been pleased – but few people were surprised when they appeared near the top of the 'Time Magazine' 1970 list of famous bores. And they guested too often on TV: when David Frost interviewed them the 'Daily Mail' referred to them and him as 'This grotesque trio'.

There was a disastrous 10-minute appearance as a Welsh pop poet in *Candy*; then Burton recovered his box-office somewhat with *Where Eagles Dare* (69), though his performance did little to lift a conventional war thriller. As for *Staircase*, where he and Rex Harrison were an ageing queer ménage, there were dreadful reviews: 'Newsweek' accused the film of 'opportunism' and described its two actors as 'plainly and simply bad'. He began *Laughter in the Dark* under Tony Richardson's direction, but left after two weeks' work, with allegations of lateness and not knowing his lines (Nicol Williamson played it). However, Hal Wallis, who had produced *Becket*, wanted Burton to play Henry VIII – but Paramount chief Charles Bluhdorn had declared that Burton would never work at the studio again. (Burton had agreed to do a voice-over for a modest sum, but changed his mind at the last minute,

unless Bluhdorn bought Taylor 'a pair of diamond-and-emerald ear-rings she's taken a fancy to'). So Wallis moved from Paramount (after 30 years) to Universal. The film was *Anne of the Thousand Days*, historical fustian of undreamt depths – but quite successful. However, said Penelope Mortimer in the 'Observer': 'Richard Burton plays Henry like a man who has promised to buy another diamond before Easter, using himself like an acting machine that will, if flogged, produce another million dollars.' Burton got a million, plus a percentage, and a sixth Oscar nomination. He appeared on TV with his wife as a consequence: the Burtons 'came to town, quite candidly, for him to win an Oscar' ('Variety').

However, he then began to work for small fees and/or large percentages – *Raid on Rommel* (71), a programmer directed by Henry Hathaway, and, in Britain, *Villain*. On the former indeed, Robert Stack had already been paid $175,000 when Burton said he would do it for less. Both films flopped in the US and they occasioned some vicious attacks on Burton, notably in the 'New York Times' and in 'Time Magazine'. The latter wrote: 'Burton's voice remains one of the most distinctive and controlled in the world. But he is no longer in charge of his face. The little piggy eyes glisten and swivel in a seamed and immobile background. Dissipation, alas, now seems less a simulacrum than a portrait.' This review was regarded with alarm by the film industry, which saw it as marking a new low in its relations with critics, but it was the sort of review which Burton's sort of fame was liable to incite. In Britain, *Villain* was attacked mainly for its violence, but Burton's performance as a queer thug was not much liked; still, it did well enough there for him to be voted the No 1 star at the box-office. As if in the hope that one success might restore his rating in the US, he shortened the odds by working non-stop; *Under Milk Wood*, as the narrator in this version of Dylan Thomas's radio play, with his wife; and *Hammersmith Is Out*, also with his wife, and directed by Peter Ustinov, who later said that since he had twice worked with the Burtons he felt that 'having both of them in a film, regarded as a rare "coup" by financiers, in fact lacked mystery.' In Yugoslavia, Burton played Marshal Tito in an epic, *Sujetska*, which does not seem to have been seen outside that country except for a few showings at the New York Cultural Center in 1976. Nor was there a much warmer welcome for the French-Italian-British *The Assassination of Trotsky*, in which he was Trotsky, or the French-Italian-German *Barbe-Bleue/Bluebeard* (73), made in Hungary, in the title-role – 'more monotonic than manic' (Clyde Jeavons in the 'MFB') as the Austrian aristocrat with a penchant for marrying and murdering.

There were two Italian pictures: *Rappresaglia/Massacre in Rome*, as a German colonel quarrelling over hostages with priest Marcello Mastroianni, and *Il Viaggio/The Trip* (74), romancing with Sophia Loren; the latter was seen briefly in London, the other seems never to have left Italy. On TV (in Britain and the US) he played Winston Churchill in a dramatized biography and appeared with Miss Loren in a new version of *Brief Encounter*, widely viewed as a ludicrous undertaking. *The Klansman*, a Southern drama with Lee Marvin, got some of the worse notices of the decade – and so did Burton's own performance as an embittered aristocrat; just after it came out Burton began *The Jackpot*, under the same director, Terence Young, but money ran out and it was abandoned when Paramount dropped its option. In 1975 Burton remarried Taylor, in Botswana, after a brief divorce: but the remarriage was also brief. It had failed the first time, it was reported, because of his drinking; it was at this time that he told an interviewer (David Lewin in 'Ciné-Revue') that he drank because he had once been a homosexual; in 1976 he was reputed to have bought up all copies of *Hammersmith Is Out*. Since his career needed a shot in the arm, more than somewhat, he returned, as before, to the theatre – taking over the leading role in 'Equus' on condition, said 'Variety', that he played the same role in the movie version. His reception and box-office reawakened Hollywood interest and he was cast as a Jesuit priest in *The Exorcist II The Heretic* (77), sequel to an earlier, highly popular film. This one flopped miserably, due to the different approach by the new director, John Boorman: but since, in the words of 'Newsweek', Burton's performance was 'a dispiriting spectacle' he clearly did not help. He was excessively dull in Sidney Lumet's film of *Equus*, but managed to get Oscar-nominated: and again anyone following that business knew how desperately he wanted to win.

He spoke of playing Lear on Broadway, but instead moved into those action pictures which are the refuge of fading stars: *The Medusa Touch* (78) and *The Wild Geese*, both in Britain. The first one, a thriller, was summed up by Barry Took in 'Punch': 'You remember what Lew Grade did to television – well, he's doing it to films now'; unlike it, the second, a patronizing and irresponsible romp about mercenaries in Africa, did find a certain audience. The remainder of Burton's film career was a prolonged fiasco. *Breakthrough* (79) was a sequel to *Cross of Iron*, with Burton replacing James Coburn as Sergeant Steiner; the original had not been too successful except in Germany – hence this one was German-financed – but those responsible found no distributors interested in Britain or Germany (despite the presence of Robert Mitchum and Rod Steiger). *Tristan and Iseult*, made in Ireland, has never to date surfaced, while the Canadian *Circle of Two* (80), directed by Jules Dassin, had the briefest of careers; Burton was an ageing artist fascinated by nymphette Tatum O'Neil. The British *Absolution* (81) was no luckier, but in this case it had been sitting on a shelf for almost three years. It was a horror film, with Burton in a role turned down by Michael Caine, a teacher-priest at a Catholic school. By this time he had returned to 'Camelot', but ill-health forced him from the tour (he was replaced by Richard Harris). He guested on TV's 'The Fall Guy' (83), starring Lee Majors, and was reunited with Taylor on Broadway for 'Private Lives', which reaped them both some of the worst notices in theatrical history. With his daughter Kate in the title-role, he was the White Knight in a tele-movie, *Alice in Wonderland*, and then he was a tired and expressionless *Wagner*, a slow plod through the facts delivered in a sock-it-to-'em style. Made in a five-hour cinema version and seven for TV, its backers had difficulty in getting bookings for either, despite the presence of distinguished names among Burton's back-up.

His drinking by now had affected his life as much as his work and he was advised by doctors that he must give up: but it was hardly a revitalized Burton who played the interrogator in the new version of George Orwell's *1984* (84). John Hurt was equally monotonous and lugubrious as the protagonist, so it was hardly surprising that it had difficulty finding a distributor in the US – where, when it did arrive, the critics quickly put paid to any chance of success. Burton was one of many names, playing a senator, in a mini-series, *Ellis Island* (85), a role he completed two weeks before his death, of a cerebral haemorrhage, in August of that year. He had married his fourth wife, a journalist, only a year earlier. His will stated that anyone who contested it was automatically disqualified.

James Caan

James Caan is undoubtedly a star, but whether he is a superstar is another matter. You may dislike the word 'superstar', but its use became necessary when the word 'star' became devalued; the connotation has particular relevance to Caan, since he has so often been claimed either as our 'newest superstar' or our 'next big superstar'. He is, said 'Time Magazine' in 1975, 'one of the five top box-office draws in the country' – a contention not borne out by any of the exhibitors' polls which officially designate these things; and in fact he has not, in 20 years of stardom, made the Golden 10. The simple reason would seem to be that he has lacked that one right, special vehicle which makes all the difference. He has a large, screen-filling personality of exceptional amiability; he is capable of versatility, at ease both as man of thought and of action. He was not very good when he started, but after a number of mediocre films he was in *The Rain People*, giving the sort of performance that other actors get Oscars for.

He was born in Sunnyside in suburban New York in 1940, the son of a meat wholesaler; his schooldays consisted of much sport and scrapping, and include one explusion; at vacation time he was a lifeguard on Rockaway Beach. During his university days he decided that he wanted to act and was accepted by Sanford Meisner at the Neighborhood Playhouse, from which he went into an off-Broadway play called 'I Roam'. There was a leading Broadway role in 'Mandingo' (61), but he left after four performances after differences with the star, Franchot Tone. He began to do TV and achieved a formidable list of credits; and he turned down a seven-year contract offered by Universal. His first film work, however, was not much: an unbilled bit in *Irma La Douce* (63), as a sailor waiting to go into Irma's hotel. He married (it lasted four years); and achieved his screen break as one of the thugs terrorizing the *Lady in a Cage* (64) – it was actually an elevator and she was Olivia de Havilland. He supported Tom Tryon and Harve Presnell, *The Glory Guys* (65), playing a cavalryman hiding his fear under a veneer of banter; and then Howard Hawks gave him the star role in his mediocre study of the life and loves of racing drivers, *Red Line 7000*. Hawks did much better by him with *El Dorado* (67), supporting old hands Wayne and Mitchum; he was the young greenhorn learning the ropes from them – if deadly with a knife, useless with a gun. It was he and Simone Signoret who played those horrific *Games* at Universal, he as the tacky, mysterious husband of a frightened Katharine Ross. In Robert Altman's *Countdown* (68) he was an astronaut; in *Journey To Shiloh* the leader of a gang of young Texans who want to join the Confederates; and in the British *Submarine X-1* (69) a submarine commander. *The Rain People* was, according to the credits, 'A Film by Francis Ford Coppola' and it was also pretty good – about a mixed-up New

York housewife (Shirley Knight (Hopkins)) who goes on the lam and gets to meet a number of oddities, including a cop and a high school drop-out reduced to sweeping leaves after a football injury. As the cop, Robert Duvall was superb; but as the dummy it was Caan who held the film together. Warners, in the midst of a power struggle, did not bother to sell it, but it perhaps had little box-office potential; when it eventually premièred in London in 1978 it went unnoticed – though it had in the interim been on British TV. *Man Without Mercy*, co-starring Sammy Davis Jr, was not theatrically released – and does not even appear to have reached TV; and Caan was again unlucky with *Rabbit, Run* (70), based on John Updike's bestselling novel about a former athlete who finds that marriage – to Melodie Johnson – is not quite so easily played. The director, Jack Smight, wanted his name removed from the credits and the film was a disaster with critics and public.

Caan several times turned down *Brian's Song*, because he did not want to return to TV; but he did it to splendid personal notices and it enjoys a reputation as one of the best-ever tele-movies. Based on fact, it tells of a football player (Caan) with the Chicago Bears, of his fatal illness and of his friendship with a black team-mate (Billy Dee Williams). *T.R. Baskin* (71) was Candice Bergen, the director was Herbert Ross and its subject was loneliness in a wintry city – Chicago; Caan had good billing but only a supporting role as the guy who gives T.R.'s address to a pal, Peter Boyle. The good popular film Caan needed was Coppola's *The Godfather* (72), playing one of that gentleman's sons – the extrovert, boisterous one, contrasting neatly with Al Pacino as his more dour brother. Caan-fever started – of sorts, anyway – but he lumbered himself with *Slither* (73), one of the seemingly endless stream of 'road' movies concerning ex-cons or drop-outs. Howard Zieff directed stylishly and Caan was relaxed as the car-thief who gets involved with kookie Sally Kellerman; but you could have put in a reel from any of the other road movies and not noticed the difference. *Cinderella Liberty* seemed more promising, the story of a gentle (moustached) gob who marries a prostitute (Marcia Mason), but with the exception of the central performances the ingredients did not quite jell. And the same might be said of *Freebie and the Bean* (74), in which he and Alan Arkin were cops: Caan called it '*The Odd Couple* in a squad car'. There were too many cop movies around that year.

In *The Gambler*, he was a compulsive one, during working hours a university teacher; director Karel Reisz took to the New York scene with old-fashioned skill (and the film to see on the subject was Altman's *California Split*, around at the time). 'Newsweek's' review encapsulates the vices and virtues: 'The movie nearly succeeds through the sheer kinetic energy of James Caan, whose virtuoso performance establishes him as one of the most dynamic actors in films today. . . . It is Caan's instinct and intelligence as the symbolically named Freed that overcomes the script's pretentiousness and comes close to capturing Dostoevsky's vision of existential man striving to become free. . . .' After existential man, Billy Rose, to the Fanny Brice of Barbra Streisand in *Funny Lady* (75) – though, Jewishness excepted, two men had less in common (Rose, for instance, was short and dark). Caan observed that several of his songs and dances had been cut: 'I'm not saying it was Barbra's fault, but some people felt that since it was her film, no one else should stand out.' And after Billy Rose, *Rollerball* player – a game of violence in a future society in which violence is banned: the film was Norman Jewison's grandiose attempt at significance, disliked at the time by those who saw it – for whom it has soured even more in the memory. Publicity brought in some viewers: but the next two brought few pennies to the box-office – *The Killer Elite*, Sam Peckinpah's jokey, opportunist mixture of Kung Fu and CIA thrillerdom; and *Harry and Walter Go to New York* (76), more jokiness, turn-of-the-century kind, with Elliott Gould. The failure of both films made Caan less of a hot property and his only two films in a while were *Silent Movie*, in a guest role, and *A Bridge Too Far* (77), one of many names in small roles, that of an American sergeant. In the old West, in English opposite Geneviève Bujold, he did *Un Autre Homme, une Autre Chance*, Lelouch's virtual reworking of *Un Homme et une Femme* – which, retitled *Another Man, Another Woman*, was another failure.

Nevertheless it was reported that Coppola would not meet his terms for *Apocalypse Now* – and that was perhaps just as well for Caan, though in view of his track record it is a pity he turned down *One Flew Over the Cuckoo's Nest*, *Superman* and *Kramer vs. Kramer*. He was billed over Jane Fonda in *Comes a Horseman* (78), playing a World War II veteran helping her, a lone cattlewoman, fight big bad Jason Robards. It did nothing to revive the Western, alas, nor Caan's standing at the box-office. Perhaps he was the first victim of the new era, when stars were dispensable: for he was as likeable as ever in *Chapter Two* (79), again playing a real-life character whose looks were infinitely more comely – Neil Simon, for this was his hardly

Jane Fonda and James Caan in Comes a Horseman *(78): they were business partners in a Montana cattle ranch, and United Artists' original caption speaks of them finding romance in this scene. Clearly there has been a change from the way stars used to find romance in movies.*

disguised account of his courtship and (second) marriage to Marsha Mason, here playing herself. Also based on fact was *Hide in Plain Sight* (80) with Caan as a Buffalo factory worker tackling the big guys – in this case the authorities who have spirited away his kids, together with his ex-wife and her new man, given immunity for squealing on the Mafia. It was also very well done – by Caan, who directed. Michael Mann over-directed *Thief* (81) – called *Violent Streets* overseas – and tried to make jewel thief Caan into a super-hero, the sort to floor audiences and win Academy Awards, but the film lost on both counts. Caan returned to work with Lelouch – for no salary but a cut of the American takings. He also played two roles, an American bandleader of the 30s and 40s, moustached, and his gay son, bespectacled – the latter a sympathetic and unflamboyant job. Almost everyone in *Les Uns et les Autres* had dual roles, for it was a vast extravaganza encompassing several nations and characters, all of them reunited at the end for a celebration of Ravel's 'Bolero' under the Eiffel Tower. As absurd as it was awful, you could not look away because it kept on going in even more outlandish directions. Lelouch's faith in the project (he mortgaged himself to the hilt, to the equivalent of £5 million) was justified by its success at home and in Canada; but as *Bolero* it did poorly in the US and no better when retitled *Within Memory*. It was not released in Britain, and after flopping at home *Kiss Me Goodbye* (82) went direct to video in that country. It was not Caan's fault, for he was on top form as a dead Broadway whizzkid who pops up again to bother wife Sally Field and her second husband, Jeff Bridges, whom he considers a wimp: three bright stars landed with only feeble material in the second half.

He was off the screen for several years – though before pulling out of *The Holcroft Covenant* (Michael Caine replaced him) his fee was said to be \$1½ million. He had a cocaine problem and checked into the Cedars-Sinai Chemical Dependency Center: 'I wasn't in the gutter or anything.' He observed that he turned down so much at this time that the offers stopped coming; he also became the manager of a prize-fighter. There were eventual financial problems and he took only a quarter of his former fee when offered *Gardens of Stone* (87) – by its director, Francis Coppola, over the objections of Tri-Star, who produced it. Caan and James Earl Jones played Vietnam veterans assigned to Arlington National Cemetery. In *Alien Nation* (88) he is a hard-bitten alcoholic detective and his partner is Mandy Patinkin – in fact an android in this recycling of the idea behind *Future Cop*. Caan was then scheduled for *Dad* (89) with Jack Lemmon, but was replaced by Ted Danson.

MICHAEL CAINE

Michael Caine is one of several bright, pugnacious, unactorish British actors who rose to fame in the 60s. None of them is exactly overendowed with star quality but, unless that returns as a prerequisite, they should remain all right. Caine is perhaps the most individual. His initial success was probably due to the fact that there was never a screen hero before like him. The Elephant and Castle vowels were refreshing after years of Eton-bred heroes. His heroic qualities were part real, part assumed: basically unassuming, he had learnt the hard way that if you wanted to survive you had to be a bit arrogant, boast a bit. He was recognizably the fellow who served you on the barrow, or stood next to you downing a pint, friendly, glib and myopic (the first hero since Harold Lloyd to wear glasses).

He was born in South London in 1933 and started acting as an amateur in his teens. He liked it so much that he gave up a steady job to work with a minor rep – Horsham – for 50 bob a week. After three and a half years there, he began to get small parts in TV (about 125 over a seven-year period) and worked also with Joan Littlewood's Theatre Workshop and with Sam Wanamaker's company in Liverpool. In films he got an unbilled bit as a national serviceman in *A Hill in Korea* (56), a war film with Harry Andrews and the Bakers, George and Stanley. Reputedly he was in over 30 films uncredited before being discovered. In the following – traceable – list he was unbilled except where noted: *How To Murder a Rich Uncle* (57), billed 10th; *The Key*, with one line; *The Two-Headed Spy*, starring Jack Hawkins; *Blind Spot* (58), a B; *Foxhill in Cairo* (60), an espionage tale, 16th on the cast-list; *The Bulldog Breed*, starring Norman Wisdom; *The Day the Earth Caught Fire* (61), a minor sci-fier; and *Solo for Sparrow* (62), one of a B series based on Edgar Wallace stories. In 1959 he understudied Peter O'Toole in 'The Long and the Short and the Tall'. In 1963 he appeared in a West End play, 'Next Time I'll Sing to You'.

Stanley Baker saw that play and asked Caine to test for the role of a Cockney soldier in *Zuzu* (63). James Booth got the part, but Cy Endfield, Baker's partner, thought Caine would be fine as the very aristocratic young officer; and the notices singled him out for praise. Embassy, who produced, announced that they had signed him for five years (but he did not film for them). Meanwhile, he went straight from locations in South Africa to Denmark, where the BBC were filming a 'Hamlet' for TV; he played Horatio to Christopher Plummer's prince. Plummer, as it happened, was the actor finally set for the film of Len Deighton's popular thriller *The Ipcress File* (65) – when he plumped for *The Sound of Music* instead. Caine was offered it and it was much touted at the time because its secret agent hero – called Harry Palmer in the film – was as different from 007 James Bond as chalk from cheese. Again, his notices were fine and, coupled with the film's box-office success, made him the most discussed new star of the year. And that solved a problem for Lewis Gilbert, who could not get a star for the film of Bill Naughton's play *Alfie* (66). It had been turned down by, among others, Anthony Newley, James Booth, Terence Stamp and Laurence Harvey – the part of a Cockney tearaway who loves 'em and leaves 'em till retribution sets in and he has to settle for no birds and lots of loneliness. Clad winningly in 1966 modishness it was old hat except for an abortion sequence and a mammoth tastelessness (characterized by its smirking exploitation of what it purported to condemn). However, in Britain it trailed *Thunderball* as the year's biggest money-maker and was one of the most successful British pictures ever to play the US – thanks, one trusts, to Caine's likeable personality.

The producer of *The Ipcress File*, Harry Saltzman, had put Caine under an exclusive seven-year contract, guaranteeing him a minimum of £50,000 per year; but he generously broke it when he realized how much Caine could earn. Caine, incidentally, refused a percentage on *Alfie*, which would probably have brought him in £3 million; his salary was £75,000. The following year he signed a non-exclusive pact with 20th, but nothing much came of it.

He was much in demand: *The Wrong Box*, as the young hero in this swinging Victorian comedy, out of RLS by Bryan Forbes; *Gambit*, as a con-man in this comedy-thriller with Shirley MacLaine; *Funeral in Berlin* (67), again as Harry Palmer; and Otto Preminger's *Hurry Sundown*, with Jane Fonda, as a wicked Southern landowner – the accent was convincing but nothing else was. The third

Harry Palmer, *Billion Dollar Brain*, proved the law of diminishing returns – but then, it was even less good than the second one (Ken Russell directed); indeed, damaged by poor reviews, none of these films did outstanding business. Still, Caine, was voted into Britain's top 10 in 1966, stayed there in 1967. The failure of his next three pictures ensured his omission the following year: *Sept Fois Femme/ Woman Times Seven* (68), where his silent sequence shadowing Shirley MacLaine was one of the few good episodes; *Deadfall*, a thriller botched by writer-director Bryan Forbes, as a jewel-thief; and *Play Dirty*, a war film, directed initially by René Clément but taken over by André de Toth. 'Variety' observed that Caine 'seems lately to have lost much of the spark which launched his career so promisingly. Could be it's a case of over-exposure. Or maybe he's simply underplaying too much.'

About the same time he was telling 'Film and Filming': 'Whilst the star system lasts, I shall do everything in my power to be a star, at the highest price that I can screw out of anybody, and then, when it collapses (if indeed it does), it may only collapse for me.' His fee at the time was reported at £250,000 per film. This he presumably got for *The Magus*, miscast in a travesty of John Fowles's novel, with Anthony Quinn. It is doubtful whether the film took as much. More successful was *The Italian Job* (69), a crook comedy where he (as a ludicrously incompetent crook) and Noël Coward came second to a series of car chases. 'Time Magazine' observed that Caine played 'with his bag of stock accessories: Cockney locutions, drooping eyelids and acute satyriasis'. These were somewhat less in evidence in *The Battle of Britain*, as a squadron leader, and also in *Too Late the Hero* (70), playing the cynical Cockney there is in every platoon. Then he did a story of the Thirty Years War, *The Last Valley* (71), with Omar Sharif, as the leader of a band of marauding mercenaries. Caine's fee was $750,000, because Sharif had suggested to him that first billing should go to the highest paid; and Caine asked for that on learning that Sharif was getting $600,000. The film itself lost over $7 million. There was more modern crime at hand in *Get Carter*, a thriller of gratuitous violence and some box-office appeal. Then for US TV, but for cinemas in Britain, he did *Kidnapped* (72) – but it turned out to be so good, due in part to his fine swashbuckling performance, that it was shown first in the US in cinemas. In *Zee and Company* he was the husband of Elizabeth Taylor, having an affair with Susannah York.

He played a *Pulp* writer in another thriller for the *Get Carter* team and held his own in the two-character *Sleuth* against Laurence Olivier: the latter did not quite repeat the London-Broadway success of Anthony Shaffer's original play, since the material looked thinner than ever on the screen, despite elegant direction by Joseph L. Mankiewicz. Caine's fee was $250,000 plus a percentage; but the profits were meagre. He continued to be directed by American directors – but not in Hollywood: Don Siegel made *The Black Windmill* (74) in Britain, a thriller about an undercover agent (Caine) whose child is kidnapped; Robert Parrish made *The Marseille Contract* in France, a thriller about

Michael Caine as detective Harry Palmer in Funeral in Berlin *(67). 'And the way Palmer lives, the funeral may be his,' said the original caption to this picture. Below, in one of the few movies where he has left off his specs,* Play Dirty *(68): he played the dilettante commander of a unit of ex-criminals.*

drug-smuggling and a professional killer (Caine); Ralph Nelson made *The Wilby Conspiracy* (75) in Kenya, a thriller about apartheid with Sidney Poitier as a revolutionary and Caine as his reluctant aide; and Joseph Losey made *The Romantic Englishwoman* in Britain and Germany, with Caine and screen-wife Glenda Jackson buried beneath the ambiguities. Liked even less than this batch was *Peeper*, a 40s private-eye thriller with Natalie Wood; that was filmed in Hollywood but earlier, with delayed release. Caine, needing a good film, got it when John Huston partnered him with Sean Connery to play Kipling's soldier-adventurers in *The Man Who Would Be King*, but 'Variety' thought his contribution single-handedly almost sank the film: he had been 'strong', cocky and cockney before, but this time he was dull in all three qualities. His wife Shakira (they married in 1973) had a role, though she is not a professional actress; Caine and Connery were both paid £250,000 plus a percentage, for which they later sued. That was filmed in Morocco; Cain went to the US to do *Harry and Walter Go to New York* (76), playing a master safecracker aped by James Caan and Elliott Gould. Since the film did not work, it did not help Caine's career, and the same is true of the next batch: *The Eagle Has Landed*, as a German officer sent to kidnap Winston Churchill; *A Bridge Too Far* (77), still fighting old battles, in charge of the tanks; and a comedy-thriller (it was neither) about con-men, *Silver Bears*. As for *The Swarm* (78), a Hollywood disaster movie, it quickly established a reputation as the worst film ever made – or so a number of commentators claimed, having to eat their words when *Ashanti* (79) turned up, a so-called adventure drama in which Caine's native wife is abducted by Arab slave-traders. In view of both, it is a shame that *Philby*, in which he should have played the title-role, did not get made; but he was again gainfully employed, in the US, in Neil Simon's *California Suite*, as the homosexual husband of Maggie Smith – who paid warm tribute to Caine in accepting her Oscar. Remaining in the US, he was in another terrible disaster film, *Beyond the Poseidon Adventure*, beating vile Telly Savalas to the salvage. The next two were horrors – and no better, despite directors who were or would be capable of distinguished work: Oliver Stone's *The Hand* (80), which belonged to Caine, and it became homicidal after he lost it in an accident; and Michael Ritchie's *The Island*, which is where Caine and young son turn up after being captured in the Bermuda Triangle by primitive pirates. Caine's fee was $650,000. It was he who was *Dressed to Kill* (after Sean Connery turned it down) as a psychiatrist who donned frocks to go out slashing: which is giving quite a lot away, but who cares with films of this quality? He had a cheerful film for a change with John Huston's *Victory* (81), by which the director tried to revitalize the POW movie – and by and large did so; Caine showed humour and authority above the norm as a British soccer international who heads the team playing the Germans in Paris.

Then it was back to killing and homosexuality again in Lumet's *Deathtrap* (82) – or, come to that, *Sleuth*-like games as taken from Ira Levin's play about a playwright bent on stealing a play by a student (Christopher Reeve). He was the (bearded) professor *Educating Rita* (83) – and she a simple-minded hairdresser, Julie Walters, opting for the Open University. She had played the role on the stage and because director Lewis Gilbert insisted on using her, every US major turned the film down. Rank put some money in, its first investment in years, and certainly did not regret it. Gilbert had given Rank some successes a quarter-century earlier and the piece seemed to belong to that era, superficial and manipulative. It is amazing that it was liked more than *The Honorary Consul*, an honourable transcription of Graham Greene's novel about political and religious loyalties in Argentina. Caine, though he had the title-role, was basically supporting Richard Gere; but like Trevor Howard before him (in *The Heart of the Matter*) he gave a powerful performance as a basically decent man in a world which no longer wanted him. There were three clear failures: *Blame it on Rio* (84), a tame remake of *Un Moment d'Egarement*, as the philanderer, with Joseph Bologna in the Lanoux role; *The Jigsaw Man*, a British thriller, as a Philby-type spy, co-starring Olivier and directed by Terence Young, which ran out of money while filming and which, when eventually completed, went direct to video in its country of origin; and *Water* (85), an under-written, overacted comedy in the Ealing vein, with Caine as the governor of a British Caribbean island. The only person who may have enjoyed the experience was Valerie Perrine, because Caine was 'the nicest human being' she had ever worked with. When James Caan left the cast of Frankenheimer's *The Holcroft Covenant*, he took over, to play a New York architect who returns to Germany to search for the money stashed away by his Nazi father.

About this time he sued two European companies for replacing him with Sean Connery in *The Name of the Rose*, when it was revealed that his fee should have been $1,500,000 plus 10 per cent of the gross above break-even point. The suit was dismissed and had he done it he might have missed *Hannah and her Sisters* (86), which brought him a Best Supporting Oscar, playing Hannah's second husband – the first was Woody Allen, who wrote and directed – now intent on seducing one of said sisters. Caine also came in for kudos for what amounted to a guest role, as a British gang boss in *Mona Lisa*, starring Bob Hoskins, but he gave his most inventive performance for years in Alan Alda's underrated and aptly named *Sweet Liberty*, playing a terribly nice major movie star who rather bores his colleagues because his games and affairs are chiefly done to live up to his legend.

No other actor of his stature was in employment so constantly, 'the hardest working man in show business' as 'Variety' said, but the next few credits added little to his lustre: *Half Moon Street* (87), from Paul Theroux's novel, as an aristocratic client of callgirl Sigourney Weaver; yet two more tales of the British security services *The Fourth Protocol* and *The Whistleblower*; and *Jaws, the Revenge*, which brought that series to an ignominious end, as love interest for Lorraine Gray. He observed that the fee paid him for this had enabled him to do the more worthwhile but less well-paid movie which preceded it. He played a mystery writer in a romantic comedy with Sally Field, *Surrender*, and few did: which may be why another, *Switching Channels*, went to Burt Reynolds and not him, as first announced. *Without a Clue* (88) was an unfunny send-up of the Sherlock Holmes industry, with Ben Kingsley as Watson hiring Caine, an unemployed actor, to play you-know-who. Said Vincent Canby in the 'New York Times': 'The actor goes through the film as if held hostage by a terrorist talent agent. He does the slapstick business and says the terrible lines with a minimum of conviction and no sense of fun. He is both gloomy and patronising.' It was clearly a move-up to do a mini-series (his first TV work for over 20 years), *Jack the Ripper*, and to take on David Niven's old role in a remake of *Bedtime Story, Dirty Rotten Scoundrels*, teamed with Steve Martin.

'Our Love is Here to Stay': Gene Kelly and Leslie Caron in An American in Paris *(51). No one was deceived into thinking this was really the bank of the Seine, and it is one of the most memorable of all studio settings.*

Leslie Caron

'Made her first appearance as an actress in Paris, 1955,' says 'Who's Who in the Theatre' of ex-dancer Leslie Caron, grandly overlooking half a dozen film appearances. She possibly approved: once Hollywood gave her the chance to leave ballet, she wanted to be an actress at all costs. She derided the sort of films MGM put her in, though she later changed her mind and decided that her best films were indeed those which the public liked best – *An American in Paris* and *Lili.* Certainly she was at her best in them. Later appearances suggest that behind the remnants of the once-famed *gamine* charm there is steely calculation, but a good actress she certainly is.

She was born in Paris (Boulogne-Billancourt) in 1931 and convent-educated. From the age of 10 she studied ballet, later doing two years with the Conservatoire National de Danse. From 1947 to 1951 she was with the Ballets des Champs-Elysées and it was there that Gene Kelly saw her, in a leading role in 'La Rencontre', when looking for a soubrette for *An American in Paris* (51). She spoke English (her mother was American); at his request MGM tested her and signed her; and in the film she was a success, not only because of her dancing. Half the world was entranced by this *jolie laide*, with her butch haircut and buck teeth (later fixed; after a spell as a beatnik, reacting against Hollywood, she became offscreen *soignée* in the best French way). MGM tried her as a straight actress in a period mystery with Barbara Stanwyck, *The Man With the Cloak*, as a French orphan in New York; and then in *Glory Alley* (52), a mild prize-fighting yarn set in New Orleans, with Ralph Meeker – she had some stunningly sexy dances. She had the middle episode of *The Story of Three Loves* (53), a whimsical tale about a boy who dreams he is grown up and in love with his strict governess – Caron in the title-role, 'Mademoiselle'. Two other European beauties, Moira Shearer and Pier Angeli, were the centrepieces of the other two stories. Angeli had been originally announced for *Lili*, a fey commercial piece about an orphan loved by a puppeteer (Mel Ferrer), but it was Caron who played it; she was delightful in it and its success made her one of the studio's brightest stars. She superseded Angeli as MGM's leading continental heroine.

A follow-up was attempted, again directed by Charles Walters, *The Glass Slipper* (55), a more or less straight version of 'Cinderella'. Again there was a dull leading man (Michael Wilding as the Prince) and the whole thing was not noticeably less leaden – but this time neither public nor critics liked it. Over at 20th, they had jettisoned one of their own hopes, Mitzi Gaynor, to get Caron to play the orphan in *Daddy Long Legs* opposite Fred Astaire. Astaire wrote in his memoirs: 'Leslie Caron is a fine artist, conscientious, apt, serious. She hesitates to attempt anything either in dance or acting unless she is absolutely sure of herself. Leslie will hold up production for many minutes (or hours) on some occasions, until she feels complete control of what she's about to do. I consider that a most commendable trait.' Obviously it paid off: 'Variety' thought her 'beguiling all the way. This Gallic import is a pixie charmer who gives the film much of its warmth and delightful merriment.'

She returned to Paris to appear in a play by Jean Renoir, 'Orvet'; flew back to Hollywood for *Gaby* (56), which was less a *Lili* than a repaint job on *Waterloo Bridge*, with John Kerr: a bad idea in its own right and rendered ludicrous by attempts to bring it up to date. In London she played 'Gigi', adapted from Colette's novel, and married the play's director Peter Hall. (Earlier, 1951–54, she had been married to meat-heir George Hormel.) To MGM's annoyance she refused to leave the play to co-star with Gene Kelly in *Les Girls*; her contract had some years to run but she said she did not care if she never went back. She returned when MGM decided to film *Gigi* (58) – Audrey Hepburn had done it in New York, but Caron was under contract, and cheaper. Still, no expense was spared – Lerner and Loewe music, Cecil Beaton costumes, Minnelli directing: the film was popular (except in France) and won a Best Picture Oscar. She was again enchanting as an orphan – in *fin-de-siècle* Paris, wooed away from her training as a courtesan by dashing Louis Jourdan – but, like the film, there was a hint of mechanism. It was, said Caron later, the greatest mistake of her career – because she was type-cast.

In London she was due to star with Jourdan in a film for Rank, *Anna*, but it was cancelled ostensibly because she was pregnant (Rank cancelled a batch of films that year). Eventually for MGM-British she played Mrs Dubedat opposite Dirk Bogarde in *The Doctor's Dilemma* (59), her first good non-musical film. In the States she did a couple of clinkers, *The Man Who Understood Women*, with Henry Fonda at 20th, and *The Subterraneans* (60), based on a novel by Jack Kerouac. That concluded her Metro contract, not to her displeasure. To celebrate, she did a guest role in the French movie that marked Abel Gance's return to filming, *Austerlitz*, as a Napoleonic mistress, and then a play in London, Giraudoux's 'Ondine' (for the Royal Shakespeare Company, now directed by her husband).

She returned to Hollywood for a part that Audrey Hepburn had turned down, *Fanny* (61). It was an odd fish: a Broadway musical filmed without the songs, in turn adapted from three Marcel Pagnol films of the early 30s (Caron in the Orane Demazis role, Horst Buchholz in Pierre Fresnay's). Critics loathed it, but it did quite well. Her appearance in a thriller with David Niven, *Guns of Darkness* (62), went unnoticed, as did the René Clair sequence of *Les Quatre Vérités*, 'Les Deux Pigeons' with Charles Aznavour. She

Hollywood was ever addicted to whimsy, without much response from the public. One exception was Lili *(53), with Leslie Caron as a waif who is loved by a puppeteer. Against the studio's wishes she insisted on looking as plain and drab as possible, thus adding an edge and draining out some of the treacle.*

returned to the limelight in *The L-Shaped Room* (63), a modish reprise of that old Shaftesbury Avenue staple, the boarding-house drama. Her performance as the lonely pregnant girl in a bedsitter was affecting and brought her a second BFA award as the year's Best Actress (the other was for *Lili*).

Hollywood reclaimed her for three comedies: *Father Goose* (64), as a starchy schoolteacher melted by Cary Grant; *A Very Special Favor* (65), as a prissy psychoanalyst melted by Rock Hudson; and *Promise Her Anything* (66), as a French Greenwich Village widow melted by Warren Beatty – with whom her name was at that time linked by columnists (she persuaded him to buy *Bonnie and Clyde* as a starring vehicle for the two of them; she and Hall were divorced in 1966). The critics decided she could not play comedy, but her dramatic bit in what was then the biggest-budgeted ($6½ million) French film yet made, *Paris Brûle-t-il?/Is Paris Burning?*, was one of its few bright spots. In Italy she did *Il Padre di Famiglia* (67), Nanni Loy's clever comedy with Nino Manfredi and Ugo Tognazzi, but that was hardly shown abroad. In 1968 she went to Canada to make *The Beginners*, but walked out before filming commenced and was replaced by Jacqueline Bisset. She married producer Michael S. Laughlin, who produced her two next films: *Chandler* (71), a private-eye thriller with Warren Oates; and *Madron* (72), a Western made in Israel with Richard Boone, whom she found a difficult colleague. In 1974 she was one of many star names in a very long TV movie about a libel case, *QB VII*, and her marriage ended; in France she began a movie with Albert Finney for Jacques Rivette which was abandoned after a few days' shooting, but 'I discovered that I really liked being in Paris and that I acted better in France'. She also said that since there were few roles in Hollywood for American actresses of her age there were clearly less for any French one.

Her new career in Europe has not been dazzling: Eduardo de Gregario's enigma-happy *Sérail* (76), as the rather butch housekeeper running the mansion where lodges English writer Corin Redgrave; Truffaut's emaciated *L'Homme qui Aimait Les Femmes* (77), as a woman once loved by the man, Charles Denner; and the revolting *Valentino*, which sank Rudolf Nureyev's chances of a screen career. 'Leslie Caron goes in for Fellini-like grotesqueness in her limning of Alla Nazimova' said 'Variety': but since the director was Ken Russell it probably was not her fault. She returned to Hollywood for *Goldengirl* (79), a vapid tale of a girl training to be an Olympic gold medallist, in a cameo as a doctor. She played the mother of an aspiring star in *Tous Vedettes* (80), a French attempt at a musical and even worse than usual. After touring Australia in a Feydeau farce with Louis Jourdan, '13, rue de l'Amour', she made two films for Krzysztof Zanussi, *Kontrakt/The Contract* (80) in Poland, which centred on a wedding, as the groom's aunt by marriage, a foreigner speaking no Polish and an ageing ballerina, a role requiring self-parody, and *Die Unerreichbare* (82) in West Germany for television (but filmed in English), as an ex-movie star, now a recluse, who is visited by a strange young man who stays on and on. The first was dense, rich; the second was not. In 1983 she toured Britain in a revival of Anouilh's 'The Rehearsal' and the following year she committed herself to a six-month US tour of 'On Your Toes', but it was cancelled after three weeks due to illness; around the same time she appeared in an American mini-series, *Master of the Game*, which starred Ian Charleson. She was Robert Powell's mother in another Zanussi film made in English in Germany, *Imperativ* (84), and Michel Piccoli's wife in a Swiss movie, *La Diagonale du Fou* (85), which as *Dangerous Moves* won a Best Foreign Movie Oscar, doubtless for trying to say something about the Cold War in a chess metaphor. There was another American tour in 1985, in 'One for the Tango', and *Courage Mountain* (87) with Charlie Sheen, of which nothing seems to be known, except that it is available on video. In *Il Treno di Lenin* (88), for TV, she played the wife of Lenin (Ben Kingsley); and then she was in a Western filmed in Argentina, *Guerriers et Captives* (89) with Dominique Sanda.

Jack Carson

Jack Carson was a leading exponent of the dumb-ox school of comedy. He was hail-fellow-well-met, always around, dull and steady. It is what you might call inverse comedy. He thought himself a decent sort of guy, go-ahead, amiable, bright; but nobody else did. He frequently winced with pain when others failed to understand how good and well-meaning he was. Everything he thought he was, he was not. Everything he thought they were, he was, 'Wise guy' and 'smart aleck' were terms he used in derision – but that was the way others thought of him. He was well cast as a travelling salesman or a cop on the beat. In some of the jobs he assumed, either bigotry or stupidity – or both – was some sort of prerogative. It may not be coincidental that both he and William Bendix became stars after the outbreak of war, when many spectators had become familiar with the non-com mentality. Because of his ineffable conceit he was a plausible heel. He was a fairly nice guy in *Mildred Pierce* but he had a line which explains why he was never nicer: 'I'm a nice guy up to a certain point but don't get me sore.' It was this menace, this lack of innocence, which prevented him from reaching the top flight of stardom.

He was born in Carman, Manitoba, in 1910 and was educated in Milwaukee, at military school in Delafield, Wisconsin, and at Carleton College in Northfield, Minnesota. At 19 he went into vaudeville and for a while was MC in vaude in the Middle West; he worked as a salesman and railway construction worker, and later established himself as an all-round actor in radio and on the stage. He began in films with an unbilled bit in *You Only Live Once* (37). RKO offered him a featured-player contract and gave him small parts mainly in Bs: *Too Many Wives* with Anne Shirley; *The Toast of New York* starring Frances Farmer; *It Could Happen To You* with Andrea Leeds; and *Reported Missing* at Universal with William Gargan. Three good parts in big pictures helped: *Stage Door*, as a blind date; *Music for Madame*, with Joan Fontaine, as an assistant director of the Hollywood Bowl; and notably, *Stand-In* for Wanger, as a hard-boiled press agent. He was also in: *High Flyers* – Wheeler and Woolsey; *Crashing Hollywood* (38) with Lee Tracy; *She's Got Everything* with Ann Sothern; *Quick Money* with Fred Stone; *Everybody's Doing It* with Sally Eilers; *Night Spot* with Allan Lane; *Go Chase Yourself* with Joe Penner; *Law of the Underworld* with Chester Morris; *The Saint in New York*, with Louis Hayward in the title-role, as one of the baddies; *Vivacious Lady* with Ginger Rogers, as a waiter captain; *This Marriage Business* with Victor Moore and a girl who foolishly took the name Vicki Lester; and *Maid's Night Out* with Joan Fontaine. Then he stepped into the niche he was to occupy over the next few years – hero's friend or heroine's ex: *Having Wonderful Time*, as a noisy holiday-maker, Ginger Rogers's old flame, and *Carefree*, as a pal of Fred Astaire's. RKO were not about to give him anything more important to do: after another smallish part in *Mr Doodle Kicks Off*, a campus comedy with Joe Penner, he had only a few minutes' exposure in *Holiday*, as a roustabout. He and RKO called it quits.

He freelanced: *The Kid From Texas* (39) with Dennis O'Keefe; *Mr Smith Goes to Washington*, as a breezy newshound; *The Escape*; *Legion of Lost Flyers*; *Destry Rides Again*, as a saloon blowhard; *The Honeymoon's Over* with Stuart Erwin; *I Take This Woman* (40) with Spencer Tracy; *Shooting High*, a silly programmer with Gene Autry and Jane Withers; *Young As You Feel*; *Enemy Agent* with Richard Cromwell; *Parole Fixer* with William Henry; *Typhoon*, again as a tavern trouble-maker; a remake of *Alias the Deacon* with Bob Burns; *The Girl in 313* with Florence Rice and Kent Taylor; *Queen of the Mob*, an FBI story with Blanche Yurka; *Lucky Partners*, third-billed and his best role yet, as Ginger Rogers's fiancé; *Sandy Gets Her Man* with Baby Sandy and Stuart Erwin; and *Love Thy Neighbour* with Jack Benny, as a cop. Most of these parts were small – indeed, some were minute; but RKO offered him a good role, fourth-billed, in *Mr and Mrs Smith* (41), as Robert Montgomery's friend. Then Warners gave him an excellent role in *The Strawberry Blonde*, as the heavy – the friend who pinches Rita Hayworth from James Cagney. At MGM he was the man Myrna Loy dallies with when she leaves William Powell, in *Love Crazy*.

Until the Cagney picture, Warners was the only studio in which Carson had not worked; it was now the studio which offered a long-term contract, with top-featured roles. As in: *The Bride Came COD*, as Bette Davis's stuffy fiancé; *Navy Blues* with Ann Sheridan, as a gob; *Blues in the Night*, memorable mainly for its title-song – the melodramatic adventures of a jazz quintet, with Carson appropriately cast as the hornblower; *The Male Animal* (42), as the superannuated football star, on the verge of turning to blubber; and *Larceny Inc*, as a travelling salesman who makes off with Jane Wyman. Warners, with singular lack of imagination, saw Carson and Wyman as a team; and they also began to see Carson and Dennis Morgan as a team, no doubt influenced by the success of Bob Hope and Bing Crosby at Paramount. However, they were rivals in the first they did together, *Wings for the Eagle*, with Carson married to Sheridan and Morgan after her. In *The Hard Way* they were a team of itinerant hoofers who elope with sisters Ida Lupino and Joan Leslie. Carson was Errol Flynn's buddy in *Gentleman Jim*; did a vaudeville act with Alan Hale in *Thank Your Lucky Stars* (43); and was teamed again with Wyman, second leads, in *Princess O'Rourke*.

He was billed over the title in *Shine On Harvest Moon* (44), with Sheridan and Morgan, teamed with the latter in a vaudeville act. And he was sole star-billed in *Make Your Own Bed*, a spy spoof, as a muddle-headed detective, with Jane Wyman below the title. The ads proclaimed 'He's Our No 1 Comedy Star' – but it was hardly a No 1 comedy. He played Wyman's husband in *The Doughgirls*, but only had a small role in *Arsenic and Old Lace* (it was made a couple of years earlier) as the friendly but dumb corner cop. He and Wyman sang a duet in *Hollywood Canteen*,

Arsenic and Old Lace (44) was directed by Frank Capra, a funny version of the Broadway hit about two lovable poisoners. Josephine Hull played one of the sweet old ladies, seen here with John Alexander, as the brother who thought he was Teddy Roosevelt. Jack Carson and Edward McNamara played the friendly local cops.

then he co-starred with Rosalind Russell in *Roughly Speaking* (45), as one of her husbands, a fast-talking salesman. He supported Joan Crawford in *Mildred Pierce*, as an old admirer, rejected but still hopeful (can you imagine?), raising his eyebrow and getting her restaurants in the end. He became a stock figure in that Warner Bros repertory group, soon to be depleted: *One More Tomorrow* (46), with Sheridan, Morgan and Wyman, as an ex-pug turned Brooklyn butcher; *Two Guys from Milwaukee*, a comedy with Morgan and Janis Paige, as a cab-driver; *The Time the Place and the Girl*, a musical with Morgan and Paige, as a night-club owner; *Love and Learn* (47), a comedy with Paige, as a songwriter; *April Showers* (48), a musical, with Ann Sothern, about a vaudeville act whose male member takes to drink; *Two Guys From Texas* with Morgan – they were actually from New York and *in* Texas, as a vaudeville team; and *Romance on the High Seas*, a musical with Doris Day and Paige.

Real stardom eluded him. He was always second banana, as in *John Loves Mary* (49), as the guy for whom Ronald Reagan is transporting an English bride. He was the huckster trying to get Doris Day on to radio in *My Dream Is Yours* and he was with her again in *It's a Great Feeling*, a Hollywood story where he and Morgan co-starred as themselves – Carson being amiably depicted as bullying, vain and obtuse. He then did a straight role, as Gary Cooper's loyal friend in *Bright Leaf* (50). That completed his contract and Warners did not renew it.

He freelanced again and got three good roles in three not very good films: *The Good Humor Man*, in the title-role, a slapstick comedy about an ice-cream salesman, with Lola Albright, whom he married a couple of years later, his third wife; *Mr Universe* (51), a satire on the wrestling game, as a hard-case manager; and *The Groom Wore Spurs*, as a fake cowboy, opposite Ginger Rogers as an

This was Doris Day's first movie and she got Jack Carson as her leading man. It was called Romance on the High Seas *(48) –* It's Magic *in Britain – and here they are arriving in Rio.*

attorney. In 1951 he topped the bill at the London Palladium and some months later opened in a flop Broadway revival of the Gershwins' 'Of Thee I Sing'. He returned to films as Esther Williams's manager in *Dangerous When Wet* (53). Paramount then brought him in as part of their $250,000 rescue-operation on *Red Garters* (54). The first sign of trouble was when Pat Crowley replaced Anna Maria Alberghetti; then George Marshall replaced Mitchell Leisen as director, at which time the footage with Don Taylor was scrapped and he was replaced by Carson. It was hardly worth it; it flopped at the box-office and as entertainment it suffered from stylized stage sets and galumphing cuteness. And Carson lacked charm and believability as the town boss loved hopelessly by saloon singer Rosemary Clooney.

He lacked charm but was certainly believable in *A Star Is Born*, possibly the best work of his career, as the press agent loaded with false bonhomie – as good as Lionel Stander had been in the original version. He engaged the attention of Judy Holliday when her marriage to Jack Lemmon went *Phffft!*, but few of his subsequent films were of much consequence: *Ain't Misbehavin'* (55), with Piper Laurie and Rory Calhoun, as a PR director; *The Bottom of the Bottle* (56) with Van Johnson; *The Magnificent Roughnecks*, partnered with Mickey Rooney in a hoary drama about oil-men; *The Tattered Dress* (57) as a scheming sheriff, with Jeff Chandler; and *The Tarnished Angels*, as Rock Hudson's mechanic, Jiggs. He left Hollywood to tour in tent shows and returned to a good part, as Gooper, the hero's aggressively virile brother, in *Cat on a Hot Tin Roof* (58). In *Rally Round The Flag Boys* he was the cocky space-station commander, who gets accidentally sent up in a rocket, providing that film with a 'hilarious' climax, and in *The Bramble Bush* (60) an ambitious lawyer. He was a ruthless political bossman in *King of the Roaring Twenties* (61), a biopic of Arnold Rothstein, with David Janssen in the title-role. His last film was Disney's *Sammy the Way Out Seal* (62).

Carson was married four times in all. During the latter years he often worked in TV. He collapsed while rehearsing for a stock production of 'Critics' Choice' in 1962 and died the following year, of cancer.

Jeff Chandler

Jeff Chandler looked as though he had been dreamed up by one of those artists who specialize in male physique studies or, a little further up the artistic scale, he might have been plucked bodily from some modern mural on a biblical subject. For that he had the requisite Jewishness (of which he was very proud) – and he was not quite real. Above all, he was impossibly handsome. He would never have been lost in a crowd, with that big, square, sculpted 20th-century face and his prematurely grey wavy hair. If the movies had not found him the advertising agencies would have done – whenever you saw a still of him you looked at his wrist-watch or his pipe before realizing that he was not promoting something. In the coloured stills and on posters his studio showed his hair as blue, heightening the unreality. His real name was Ira Grossel; his film-name was exactly right.

He was born in Brooklyn in 1918. His father was connected with the restaurant business and got him a job as a restaurant cashier; he stuck this for some years, but sought an out via art or acting. He studied art and then got a scholarship to the Feagin School of Dramatic Art in New York. He got a few small roles in stock and started his own company with a friend – studio publicity later insisted that this was on the verge of being hugely successful when disbanded because of the war. On leave in Hollywood, Mervyn LeRoy promised him a role in his eventual film of *The Robe*; Hunt Stromberg promised to test him – but was in an accident. He spent four years in the army, ending up as a first lieutenant, and on being demobbed went to Los Angeles, where he married (1946; divorced 1959 but the marriage seems to have been brief). He was a while getting resettled in his old profession, but finally got bit parts in *Johnny O'Clock* (47) at Columbia and then, some months later, in a couple at 20th, *The Invisible Wall* and *Roses are Red*. He worked in radio ('Mr Dana', 'Michael Shayne Detective') waiting for another film break – but his part in *Mr Belvedere Goes to College* (49) was not much bigger (he was a cop) than his earlier film parts. It was while playing Eve Arden's boyfriend in 'Our Miss Brooks' that he was brought to the attention of Universal, looking for someone to play the rebel Israeli leader in *Sword in the Desert*; after a day's work he was signed to a seven-year exclusive contract.

They put him in a programmer with Gale Storm and Dennis O'Keefe about unwanted babies, *Abandoned* (rechristened *Abandoned Woman* when the title proved only too apt), as a DA. Then 20th, who had failed to notice him when he had worked there earlier, borrowed him to play the Red Indian leader, Cochise, in a James Stewart Western, *Broken Arrow* (50), which was enormously popular (a year after release 'Picturegoer' readers voted it their favourite film after *Gone With the Wind*, *The Best Years of Our Lives*, *Hamlet*

Jeff Chandler, whose looks were so charismatic that his acting ability was seldom ever questioned.

and *The Way to the Stars*). It made Chandler a star and 20th kept him on for *Two Flags West*, competing with fellow cavalrymen Joseph Cotten, Cornel Wilde and Dale Robertson for immobility of expression. At Universal he was a gangster *Deported* to the land of his fathers (Italy), with Marta Toren; then 20th claimed him again, to play another native son, in *Bird of Paradise* (51) with Debra Paget – an odd choice for a remake and, as it turned out, an unpopular one.

The films with which Universal lumbered him somewhat dimmed the impression he had made as Cochise: *Smuggler's Island*, dirty work in the China Seas; a remake, *Iron Man*, as a punch-drunk prize-fighter, played earlier by Lew Ayres; *Flame of Araby* with Maureen O'Hara, a Western with turbans and yashmaks; *The Battle of Apache Pass* (52), as Cochise again, with John Lund; *Red Ball Express*, as the officer in charge of supplies for Patton's tanks; *Yankee Buccaneer*, in the title-role; and *Because of You*, as the husband who loves, leaves and finally returns to Loretta Young. In return for his stoicism Universal tore up his old contract and offered new terms, four years to go with a guarantee of one film a year. There was no improvement in the films, however: *The Great Sioux Uprising* (53), as an ex-Yankee officer opposed to it; *East of Sumatra*, as an engineer involved there with Marilyn Maxwell; *War Arrow*, again in the US Cavalry; *Taza Son of Cochise* (54), in – briefly – as Rock Hudson's pa; *Yankee Pasha*, as a fur-trapper, ideally teamed with Rhonda Fleming; and *Sign of the Pagan*, as a Roman centurion, with Jack Palance as Attila the Hun. That one had a bigger budget as it was supposed to launch Ludmilla Tcherina into big-time stardom.

Indeed, Chandler now moved into Universal's (slightly) more ambitious products, like *Foxfire* (55), as an ambitious working-class boy married to Social Register wife Jane Russell, and *Female on the Beach*, as an ambitious beach-boy married to Joan Crawford and maybe wanting to murder her. Then he was in the *n*th remake of *The Spoilers*, with Rory Calhoun and Anne Baxter. He was not only fighting on the screen but with the studio. He was not a docile star. Of all Universal's stock company only he, Hudson and Tony Curtis really became big stars (around this time he also had some hit records and sang in a nightclub act). Like Curtis he was ambitious: he had refused films (*Five Bridges to Cross*, *Lady Godiva* – though these were no worse than most he did do) and had a number of suspensions. The studio gave way and let him do a comedy, *Toy Tiger* (56), a remake of *Mad About Music*, in the Herbert Marshall role of the 'adopted' father: Tim Hovey was Deanna Durbin and Laraine Day his mother. Hastily Universal put him back into action stuff: *Away All Boats*, a war movie, and *Pillars of the Sky*, where he was a cavalryman again and an Indian scout to boot.

His contract was up and he moved over to UA to produce himself in a Western, *Drango* (57) – and he also directed it for a couple of

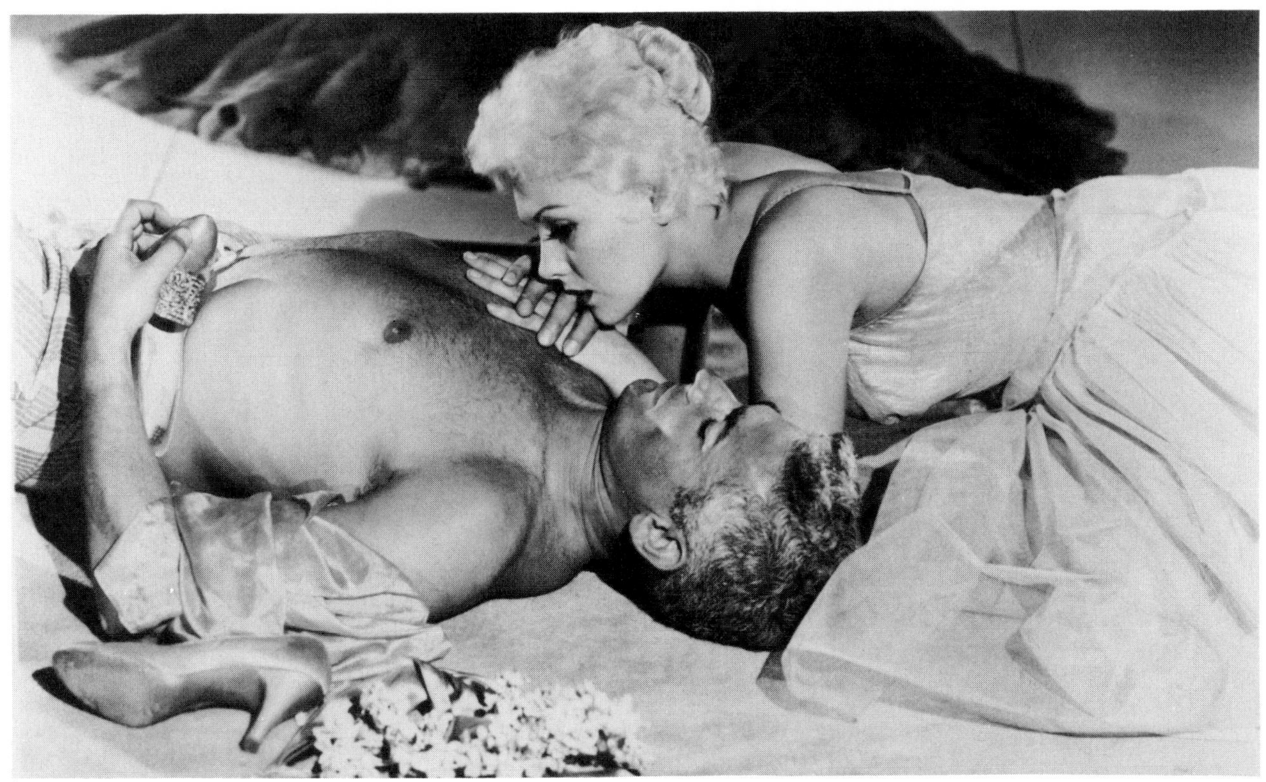

Jeanne Eagles (57) *purported to be a biography of that actress of the 20s who killed her career and then herself via liberal dosages of booze and pills. As interpreted by Kim Novak and Jeff Chandler, the film was resolutely unpainful. And quite pretty.*

weeks. It did not reveal any desire to get away from the standardized films he had been making (he played an ex-Union officer taming a Southern town), so it was no surprise that he signed again with Universal, two films a year for three years. Now he could do outside films and, after playing a criminal lawyer framed by Jack Carson in *The Tattered Dress*, he went to Columbia for *Jeanne Eagels*, to play a Yiddish showman. After that, his box-office, never sensational, began to dip slowly: *Man in the Shadow* (58) with Orson Welles and produced by Albert Zugsmith, as a sheriff in a corrupt small town; *The Lady Takes a Flyer*, a so-called 'romantic' comedy with Lana Turner; *Raw Wind in Eden* with Esther Williams, as a man of mystery; and *Stranger in my Arms* (59), falling for the widow (June Allyson) of his army buddy. Still, Chandler was proving that to survive bad material in Hollywood is easier with looks than with talent.

This lot, if possible, were worse: Robert Aldrich's *Ten Seconds to Hell* with Jack Palance and Martine Carol, a co-production between Britain's Hammer and the American 7-Arts; *Thunder in the Sun* with Susan Hayward; *The Jayhawkers*, a Western; and *The Plunderers* (60), produced by his own company, a dreadful film about a one-armed Civil War veteran coping with the 19th-century equivalent of juvenile delinquents. In *Return to Peyton Place* (61), he was the publisher who published 'Peyton Place'. He was about to start *Operation Petticoat* when he was taken ill (Cary Grant took the part) and he died in 1961 of blood-poisoning contracted in hospital after spinal surgery. His last film was shown later, but extracted no posthumous tributes because, like most of his films (at least, those for Universal), it was not shown to the press: *Merrill's Marauders*, a Burmese war tale directed by Samuel Fuller. Also, in 1962 there turned up in a few cinemas an independent production he had made in Britain in 1960, *A Story of David*, more like a Sunday-school lecture than a film. Chandler was nevertheless surprisingly good, as if this was the one part he had done that he cared about.

Cyd Charisse

If you were in an air-force cinema, *circa* 1952, you will never forget the sound which greeted the appearance of Cyd Charisse halfway through the climatic ballet in *Singin' in the Rain*. The audience to a man greeted this sinuous leggy beauty with a loud and prolonged 'Ooooaah!'. As she slithered round an understandably bewildered Gene Kelly, there was uproar in the cinema. Cyd Charisse did not do more than dance in *Singin' in the Rain* and people remember her in it. You cannot remember her acting, which at best could be described as 'friendly'. Dancing, she is unforgettable.

She was born – Tula Ellice Finklea – in Amarillo, Texas, in 1921, and began ballet lessons when she was eight. Four years later she left Texas to learn advanced dancing in Hollywood under Nico Charisse. He introduced her to Colonel de Basil who signed her – she was 14 – for his Ballet Russe. With it she toured in the US and in Europe; Charisse later joined the company and she married him in France in the autumn of 1939. They returned to Los Angeles where Mr Charisse reopened his school. There was a baby in 1942, but Mrs Charisse was restless and was glad to get engaged – as Lily Norwood – to dance in *Mission to Moscow* (43), as Ulanova, and *Something to Sing About.* When she went to MGM to test, she came out with a contract and a new name. Metro were looking for a 'classical' dancer for *Ziegfeld Follies* (46) and she could certainly dance (she had a few steps with Fred Astaire) and had looks. She then put in a pleasing appearance – she had a dozen or so lines and a song or so (dubbed) – with Judy Garland as one of *The Harvey Girls.* She could at least speak, and became the wan grown-up heroine – another minor role – in a Margaret O'Brien vehicle, *Three Wise Fools.* She danced in *Till the Clouds Roll By* – with Gower Champion. Dancing and acting, she supported Esther Williams in *Fiesta* (47), as a señorita, Margaret O'Brien in *The Unfinished Dance* and Williams again in *On an Island With You.* She danced in *Words and Music* (48). She supported Kathryn Grayson in *The Kissing Bandit*, with Ricardo Montalban as her romantic vis-à-vis, and got her first star-billing in a neat murder mystery with Richard Basehart and Audrey Totter, *Tension* (49). She had a brief straight role in *East Side West Side* as one of James Mason's girlfriends. She was pregnant (she had married Tony Martin in 1948) and was off the screen for over a year. MGM had nothing for her, so loaned her and Montalban to Universal for *Mark of the Renegade* (51), where he was a gay caballero and she a señorita. She was a half-breed Indian girl opposite Stewart Granger in *The Wind North* (52), after which came the sensational dance in *Singin' in the Rain* and a reunion with Montalban in the tacky circumstances of *Sombrero* (53).

Fans, if not critics, were imploring MGM to give her better roles and MGM had the good idea of putting her opposite Fred Astaire, in *The Band Wagon.* She had to wear flat shoes but who cared? – certainly not Astaire, who called her 'beautiful dynamite' and added, 'That Cyd! When you've danced with her you stay danced with.' Plotwise, she had little to do except indicate a classical dancer who thought herself slumming in musical comedy (at first). The film itself was a last peak among the great MGM musicals and Charisse starred in most of the others that finished off

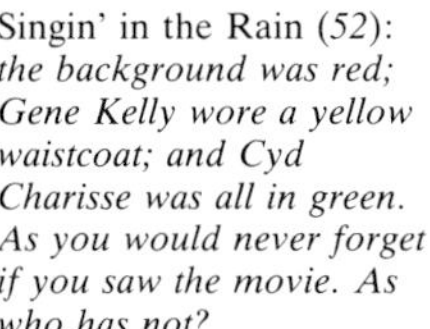

Singin' in the Rain (*52*): *the background was red; Gene Kelly wore a yellow waistcoat; and Cyd Charisse was all in green. As you would never forget if you saw the movie. As who has not?*

the range: *Brigadoon* (54), opposite Kelly, as a Scots lassie; *Deep in My Heart*, guesting in a ballet based on 'One Alone'; *It's Always Fair Weather* (55) again with Kelly; *Meet Me in Las Vegas* (56) opposite Dan Dailey, a film described by the 'MFB' as 'a musical of stupefying banality' – though she danced a sizzling 'Frankie and Johnny'; and *Invitation to the Dance* (57), Gene Kelly's ballet film. Then there was *Silk Stockings* opposite Astaire, based on a Broadway musical that Cole Porter had based on *Ninotchka*: Charisse as Garbo just was not funny.

Curiously, she was one of the last great contract-players left at Metro. She was loaned to Universal to team with Rock Hudson in a drama about sailing-ships, *Twilight for the Gods* (58), improbable as a fugitive from the fleshpots of Hawaii. Her last for MGM was *Party Girl*, a gangster movie with Robert Taylor, and with screen musicals few and far between she worked in films only intermittently afterwards. There were two offers from Europe. *Five Golden Hours/Cinque Ore in Contati* (60) was an unfunny *comédie noire* – she was a husband-killer – with George Sanders and Ernie Kovacs. *Un Deux Trois Quatre/Black Tights* was a collection of Roland Petit ballets transferred to film, more successful than Gene Kelly's ballet film, but colder; two starred Petit's wife Zizi Jeanmaire, one featured Moira Shearer and Charisse was in 'Deuil en 24 Heures', at her most elegant as a merry widow. In Italy, she did another for MGM, *Two Weeks in Another Town* (62), as the nympho ex-wife of Kirk Douglas, and *Assassino Made in Italy* (63) – also known as *Il Segreto del Vestito Rosso* – with Hugh O'Brien, which never reached the US. There was a Matt Helm picture with Dean Martin, *The Silencers* (66), in which she danced a bit. Then a British thriller with fellow American Gene Barry, *Maroc 7* (67), where her appearances as a famous fashion editor brightened an otherwise drab effort. She was one of the old star-names in *Won Ton Ton, the Dog That Saved Hollywood* (76); she did a nightclub act with her husband and when they took it to London she was offered a guest role, as an important citizen, one of the *Warlords of Atlantis* (78). In 1986 she returned to London to do some rather stately dances in a revival of 'Charlie Girl'.

Julie Christie

Julie Christie's entrance in *Billy Liar* is one of the most beguiling things in 60s cinema: a long fugue in which she wanders gaily through the streets of a Northern town, swinging a large handbag. The sequence owes something to the *nouvelle vague* and as that was a liberating movement, so is she a liberating spirit. She is Billy's escape route. He can pour out his troubles to her. She is the girl who has been around, who takes off when she feels like it and returns just as simply to the nest. She throws the film off balance, she adds a touch of stardust, but she is so strong and bewitching that it does not matter. She has a quality of love. She looks at George C. Scott in the same way in *Petulia*, she is warm and protective, she is sunny and desirable. Momentarily, there is a pinched, hurt look in her eyes, then she smiles that marvellous smile again. It was said, when she appeared, that she represented the new young girl of the 60s. Maybe; but none of the subsequent imitations came anywhere near her.

Billy Liar was not quite her first movie. She was born in Assam, India, where her father had a tea-plantation, in 1941. She was sent back to Britain to school and at 16 decided that she wanted to study art in Paris. After a while she changed her mind, returned to London and enrolled at the Central School of Music and Drama. She made her professional bow with the Frinton-on-Sea rep and stayed there three years, 1957–60. Her break came with a big part in a TV serial, 'A for Andromeda', around which time she had small roles in a couple of film comedies, *Crooks Anonymous* (62) and *The Fast Lady* (it was a car). Apart from the fact that comic Stanley Baxter was in both there was nothing at all remarkable about either, including her performances. But director John Schlesinger saw her and decided she was just the girl for *Billy Liar* (63), with Tom Courtenay.

The notices were ecstatic and occasioned much publicity. She was already contracted for a small role in *Young Cassidy* (65), as a whore (in the only sequences John Ford directed before becoming ill). And she went back to rep, in Birmingham, to try to learn her craft. Meanwhile, Schlesinger, with writer Frederic Raphael, was fashioning a film for her, *Darling*, a very moral and contemporary tale of a young model who did not know what she wanted, apart from a good time. They had difficulty raising the backing (they could have got it for Shirley MacLaine), but its eventual financiers were well paid when it became a worldwide success. It was nominated for several Oscars and Christie won the Best Actress award; the film itself was the New York critics' Best and she their Best Actress. In Britain she was the BFA's Best Actress. But Stanley Kauffman was cautious in the 'New Republic': 'She has an expressive, unusual face and an attractive voice, but she is not yet a controlled or subtle actress. Her

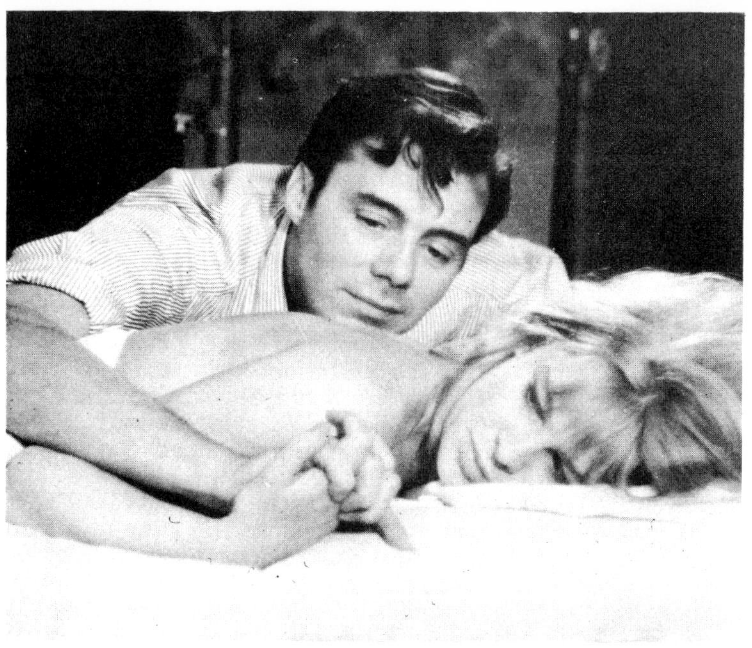

Above, Dirk Bogarde and Miss Christie in Darling *(65): she offered him sex and companionship but not, as it turned out, very much else. Below, Christie in* Petulia *(68).*

chief effects come from her vivid personality in this tailor-made part.' *Darling* in itself would have been enough – but an Oscar was too much: there was a crescendo of publicity which in the end began to turn sour. She gave ammunition to the mockers by turning in three indifferent performances, in David Lean's gigantesque *Doctor Zhivago*, as Lara, and in a dual role in Truffaut's *Fahrenheit 451* (66), opposite Oskar Werner. Truffaut had wanted to film Ray Bradbury's science-fiction story for years and finally set it up in Britain with Universal's backing – ironically, in Christie's case, for that company had refused to pay her £50,000 fee when Charlton Heston had wanted her for *The War Lord*, just before her Oscar. Now they paid her far more, but it

was probably unjustified, for Truffaut misfired somewhere and the film was not widely shown.

Schlesinger sent for her again when he finally found backing for *Far From the Madding Crowd* (67), an adaptation of Thomas Hardy's novel about a Victorian female farmer and the three men who loved her. It was an old-fashioned subject, said the critics, complaining that it was slow and she was too modern. It was not and she was not: they were gentle pleasures among the year's blood and violence. The reviews killed it in the US, but in Britain it picked up and survived to strong business. Reviewers also mauled *Petulia* (68), directed by Richard Lester for a British company in San Francisco, the tale of a British girl who wants to have an adulterous affair, preferably with George C. Scott. It was not as profound as it hoped about the various malaises of modern society, but it was by far the best of several films on that theme, with a performance by Christie of an indolent sadness. With much less *éclat* than was customary, she made *In Search of Gregory* (69), an English-Italian melodrama *à la* Antonioni, directed by Peter Wood. It was shown, briefly, with even less *éclat.*

After three failures there were perhaps less offers; but she returned in two prestige films. Joseph Losey chose her to play the young milady in love with farmer Alan Bates in his version of L.P. Hartley's novel *The Go-Between* (71). MGM, who had the US rights, disliked it so much they they sold it to Columbia, but after a Grand Prix at Cannes it went on to worldwide success. The other picture was *McCabe and Mrs Miller*, in which she played a warm-hearted madam in the old West, opposite Warren Beatty. She had been living with Beatty for some years and it was he who brought her into the film – to some of the best notices either of them had ever got. 'And Julie shows that she's a funny, plucky character actress as well as the owner of an extraordinarily photogenic face' ('Playboy'). The director, Robert Altman, said: 'Julie doesn't like being a movie star. All she wants is to act. If she had her way, she'd like a nice role to play in a film that doesn't require a lot of recognition' – quoted by the 'News of the World' in the course of an article to prove that till this day Beatty carries a torch for her.

Truth to tell, her subsequent career is notable only for the two films she made with him. She was in a singularly unsinister wintry Venice with Donald Sutherland in the aptly-named *Don't Look Now* (73) – though you were certainly supposed to notice the flashy tricks of the director, Nicolas Roeg (and they were marginally more interesting than the enigma-laden plot). In *Shampoo* (75) she was in California with Beatty, as one of the women in his life; and she was in *Nashville* for Altman, very briefly as herself. There was talk of her being in *L'Innocente* for Visconti, in a film for Chabrol and in an Italian film on Rosa Luxemburg; in Hollywood she was sexually assaulted by a machine in *The Demon Seed* (77) – which, quite predictably, the public did not want to see. The public did want to see Beatty's *Heaven Can Wait* (78) and Christie's frank performance as his romantic interest was virtually the film's sole merit. She was to have been in *Agatha*, but was taken ill; and *Sophie et le Capitan* was abandoned after two weeks' shooting. This story of a man who turns into a transvestite because of his wife's liberalism would not be, said 'Variety', 'a viable vehicle worth finishing'. And she did not think *American Gigolo* viable, since she turned down the lead.

As finished, it was surely preferable to *Memoirs of a Survivor* (81), a poorly realized version of Doris Lessing's novel about a drab woman carrying on after nuclear devastation. She was the English wife of Jacques Perrin in *Les Quarantièmes Rugissants* (82), based on the story of Donald Crowhurst, who cheated his way to become the winner of the 'Sunday Times' round-the-world race and then disappeared from his craft. The film's cost was 'astronomical' for a French project (the equivalent of over $4 million), but the film to date has not been seen publicly in Anglo-Saxon countries. Christie chose to play Alan Bates's cold, prissy wife in *The Return of the Soldier* (82), losing him to Glenda Jackson, after which she had her best movie in a good while, *Heat and Dust* (83), visiting India in the modern section of the story. Although the last was a success, all of these were away from the mainstream of industry production. *Gold* was a BFI production with a large budget (for the BFI) – £100,000. It had been made two years earlier and finally managed some showings at the BFI's own NFT, with a late and hopeful title change to *The Gold Diggers*. It was a feminist tract made entirely by women: indeed, it was all tract and no plot, with Christie's star image utilized when the black heroine carries her off from a ballroom to explain women to her. Around the same time she turned down *Under Fire* (Joanna Cassidy played the role). 'Yes' she said firmly, 'that was a mistake.'

She was stunning in her two roles in a *Separate Tables* for TV, showing a range only hinted at in some of her film; Schlesinger directed and Bates was her co-star. She played Richard Gere's ex-wife, an investigative reporter in *Power* (86), partly because she and director Sidney Lumet wanted to work together: but she said of the result 'I don't think it quite zings off': neither did the critics, but it is a considerable entertainment and she is excellent in it. After that, the bags were packed for Argentina, to play a British governess, *Miss Mary*, to a wealthy family: but as directed by Maria-Luisa Bemberg the tale lacked both cohesion and conviction. Still on the move, she was in three further productions, all of which surfaced a while later: the French-Tunisian *La Mémoire Tatouée* (88), forming an estranged couple with Ben Gazzara, to be called *Silent Memory* in the US, where it went direct to video, 'acquired from MGM'; a German mini-series, *Sins of the Fathers*, as Burt Lancaster's daughter-in-law, blackmailed by her lover into letting him control her shares in the family business; and an Australian one, *Dadah is Death*, based on fact, as an Australian woman trying to save her son, a drug-smuggler, from the mandatory death penalty in Malaysia. These are honourable credits, witness to her political involvement, but we are far from the days when she was the darling of the film industry: but her personality and performing were as refreshing as they ever were.

Montgomery Clift

Montgomery Clift died at the age of 45, the recipient of as much publicity and praise as most actors get in a full lifetime. He attracted attention partly because he was a fine actor, partly because he was very handsome and partly because he refused to conform. He appears to have been unconcerned about making any sort of effect – to that extent he and Brando were the only 50s originals, the forerunners of today's actors. He did not choose to work unless he felt like it, he did not choose to be tied by long-term contracts, he did not go to premières, did not indulge in fake romances, did not marry. For flouting these and other Hollywood rules he defended himself: 'I am neither a young rebel nor an old rebel, nor a tired rebel but quite simply an actor who tries to do his job with the maximum of conviction and sincerity.' Where it mattered, there was respect. Spencer Tracy once said: 'He makes most of today's young players look like bums.' Yet there remains an aura of failure – his early promise did not move on to achievement and it is very clear that somewhere along the way things went very wrong.

He was born in Omaha, Nebraska, in 1920. When he was 14 his parents, through friends, got him a job in summer stock in Stockbridge, Massachusetts, in 'Fly Away Home' which starred Thomas Mitchell. It transferred to Broadway for a seven months' run – and till he went into movies Clift was seldom away from the New York boards. His second show was Cole Porter's 'Jubilee' (35), as Prince Peter, and he went on to do 'Yr Obedient Husband' (38), 'Eye on the Sparrow', 'Life With Father' – from which he was quickly fired – and two long runs, 'There Shall Be No Night' (40), with the Lunts, and 'The Skin of Our Teeth' (42). A big success in Lillian Hellman's 'The Searching Wind' brought Hollywood offers, but he turned them down to do 'The Foxhole in the Parlor' and then Tennessee Williams's 'You Touched Me'.

He finally accepted an offer from Howard Hawks to play John Wayne's protégé in *Red River* (48), an introverted cowboy – and an unconvincing one. The film was so long in production, however, that cinemagoers had had their first glimpse of Clift earlier that year, in *The Search*, Fred Zinnemann's careful study of displaced children. Clift was a GI and his performance, said C.A. Lejeune, 'can hardly be faulted. Never for a moment does he allow sentiment to blur the outlines of a character that is tough as well as tender; a kind man with enough dispassion to be a natural-born teacher. The relationship between the man and the boy is beautifully done altogether, and one of the most delicate achievements of a moving film.'

This sort of praise made him the hottest young property in films and Paramount offered a very open contract for three pictures (of which he only made two). In Wyler's *The Heiress* (49) he was the archetypal Henry James fortune-hunter, with the requisite charm and weakness – if little sense of the style. At the very last minute he turned down *Sunset Boulevard*, only to do an infinitely less distinguished film, *The Big Lift* (50) at 20th, about the then current Berlin airlift. Again he was a GI. He returned to Paramount for the second film version of Dreiser's 'An American Tragedy', rechristened *A Place in the Sun* (51) and directed by George Stevens. Chaplin described it as the best movie ever to come out of Hollywood, but after generally great reviews the carpers moved in (there is still no unanimity as to how good it is). Clift's own press was excellent: 'But it is Montgomery Clift's performance to which the film owes the greatest debt: his playing of George as a weak, rather blunt, quietly charming drifter, if it pleads too much sympathy for Dreiser's novel, seems to be precisely what was required of him by the script' (Karel Reisz in 'Sight and Sound').

Montgomery Clift and Wendell Corey in The Search *(48), a film about GIs working on the problem of 'lost' children in the aftermath of war.*

Hitchcock's *I Confess* (53) ended an unexpected two-year absence. Its initial premise – that a priest (Clift) is bound by his vows not to reveal a murderer who has confessed to him – was not sustained on a suspenseful level and the film was not very popular. Zinnemann insisted on Clift to play the victimized GI hero of *From Here to Eternity* against Columbia's opposition (they wanted Aldo Ray). The book had been a bestseller, the film was the New York critics' Best Picture and the Academy's Best Picture (eight Oscars in all): it was a giant box-office film, Clift's biggest success, and gained him his third (and last) Oscar nomination. His career then took a step backward.

Stazione Termini/Indiscretion of an American Wife (54) had been written by Zavattini and had at one time been earmarked by Claude Autant-Lara for Ingrid Bergman and Gérard Philipe (who actually began work on it). Later Brando planned to do it in English and it was finally bought by Selznick for his long-projected liaison with Vittorio De Sica; he cast his wife, Jennifer Jones, and Clift – and all concerned emerged with reputations diminished (for all that, its treatment of love, via a protracted farewell at Rome's main station, was considerably more mature than in most English-speaking films of that time). Clift's offers, however, did not diminish: over the next few years, he turned down, among others, *On the Waterfront*, *East of Eden*, *Not As a Stranger* and *Moby Dick* (as Ishmael). He went to New York instead to play Konstantin in 'The Seagull' (54) for £100 a week – and that impressed Hollywood, because at that time his fee was $160,000 per film.

He returned in MGM's *Rainbow County*

(57), a period piece with Elizabeth Taylor, playing – in mannered fashion – a man seeking his destiny. Despite off-putting reviews, the film did great business. The offscreen events were more dramatic: on location there were two occasions when he was found wandering at night in the nude – as well as an overdose of sleeping-pills. His drinking was said to be caused by guilt over his homosexuality. More seriously, perhaps, there was an automobile accident which scarred his face and made it difficult for him to move his face muscles. Nevertheless, he gave a sensitive performance, again as a GI, in *The Young Lions* (58), a goodish war film with Marlon Brando. Edward Dmytryk, who directed both films, said that after the accident Clift was 'impossible', so drunk that he could not work in the afternoons. He added, 'He was an exceptionally bright man who liked to pretend he wasn't, unlike Marlon Brando who likes to pretend he's bright, whereas in fact he isn't very'. The next one did not make it. *Lonelyhearts* (59) was an emasculated version of Nathaniel West's novel, with Clift suggesting less a journalist with a Christian conscience than one after too many sleepless nights. He was, however, of benefit to *Suddenly Last Summer*, as Elizabeth Taylor's understanding doctor, and was as quiet and as forceful as ever in Kazan's *Wild River* (60), as a TVA official 'working on' obstinate widow Jo Van Fleet. All the same, there were times when he seemed to be carrying naturalism too far – though Huston controlled him in *The Misfits* (61), playing Clark Gable's nut-headed and lonely buddy. (On the set he remained difficult – perhaps only Katharine Hepburn's intervention saved him from being sacked from *Suddenly Last Summer*.)

Stanley Kramer offered him a key cameo (one of the witnesses) in *Judgment at Nuremberg* – two days' work. His agent demanded his usual huge fee, so Clift did the part (movingly) for nothing and sent his agent an empty paper-bag containing, he said, his commission. Either this one, or a new agent, got him only two more offers. Huston cast him as Freud in his worthy attempt at a screen study of that gentleman, *Freud* (62) – hastily rechristened *Freud the Secret Passion* by a frightened Universal, not without reason: poor reviews killed whatever box-office potential it had (today, it is a film very much admired). Also, it had been costly: there were delays when Clift was operated on for the removal of cataracts in both eyes (it was rumoured that he was going blind). But that was not all: he sued Universal for the balance of his $200,000 fee and they counter-sued for nearly $700,000, alleging excessive drinking. The matter was settled out of court.

Clift had a less essential problem in Stazione Termini *(54) – in the person of Jennifer Jones as a married woman who could not bear to be parted from him. Hence its American title,* Indiscretion of an American Wife *(54).*

Montgomery Clift in John Huston's Freud *(62), an ambitious and worthy screen biography, though curiously reminiscent of Warners' biographical series made more than two decades earlier – even if Huston had worked as a writer on a couple of them.*

Almost certainly an offer from Raoul Levy was the first major one he had had in some years: a Franco-German spy film, with some American backing, *L'Espion/The Defector* (66). After that, at Elizabeth Taylor's insistence, he was cast in *Reflections of a Golden Eye*, but died (1966) of a heart attack before it started. *The Defector* was finally shown in a few spots in 1968, a good counter-espionage tale spoilt by the direction and much hacking in the cutting-room. Clift's initial entrance, the taut, unsmiling loner, is moving, but not as sad as his subsequent performance – mechanical, somnambulant, with no hint of his former charm and ability.

JAMES COBURN

Duffy was a particularly tiresome film about two English boys who plan to rob their millionaire father of his fortune. It was all cross and double-cross, set in one of the new Mediterranean fun-spots, Tangier, with every modish device available to its creators – pop-art, pop-music, pop-art photography, Susannah York and a new superstar, James Coburn. Coburn played a con-man who helps the boys, a carefree grinning, stubbornly heterosexual, lone Belmondoesque American; and the film, because it had no higher inspiration, kept him as firmly at the centre as anything that Theda Bara ever made. He was decidedly not tiresome.

He was born in Laurel, Nebraska, in 1928, of Swedish-Irish-Scottish parentage; when his father's business collapsed because of the Depression they moved to Los Angeles. After military service as a radio operator, he studied at the Los Angeles City College, where he became interested in acting. He moved on to the Motion Picture Dept of the University of Southern California; and the La Jolla Playhouse gave him a part in 'Billy Budd'. In New York he studied under Stella Adler, but there was a long period before he got any work – and then it was in a TV commercial. Later he appeared in shows like 'Studio One' and 'General Electric Theater'. In 1958 he married Beverly Kelly and headed back to the Coast. He began to get small parts in pictures, beginning with three Westerns: *Ride Lonesome* (59), with Randolph Scott, as an outlaw; *Face of a Fugitive*, with Fred MacMurray; and *The Magnificent Seven* (60). His performance as the laconic, bandy-legged knife-man in the last really set him up.

Paramount took both him and Steve McQueen from that film and put them into *Hell is for Heroes* (62), Coburn as the bespectacled member of the platoon; and United Artists cast them both in *The Great Escape* (63), Coburn still in a subsidiary role, but mightily effective as a nonchalant Australian – and his geniality compensated for his poor attempt at an Aussie accent. Coincidentally, he was as enjoyable as McQueen in his attitude towards their Nazi captors and would later, like him and Lee Marvin, be at his best as a restless opponent of conformist society (but unlike them: the strength of this new breed was in their rangy individuality).

A TV film, *The Murder Men* (made in 1962), was shown in European cinemas around this time; Mark Richman and Dorothy Dandridge co-starred and Coburn was a particularly leering villain. He stayed that way as one of the three particularly convincing toughs in *Charade* – the others were George Kennedy and Walter Matthau. He was upped to third-billing in *The Man from Galveston* (64), as a hapless deputy marshal in this courtroom Western starring Jeffrey Hunter (also made originally for TV, as a pilot for 'Temple Huston'). He continued in supporting parts: *The Americanization of Emily*, as James Garner's girl-mad buddy; and *Major Dundee* (65), bearded, as a one-armed scout. He finally got a big role, second-billed, as Anthony Quinn's amiable pirate-mate in *A High Wind in Jamaica*; then he did a cameo as an awkward Customs officer in *The Loved One*.

20th then starred him, and paid him $75,000, for *Our Man Flint* (66), one of the numerous James Bond spoofs – and a damp squib, lit only by his presence; but it brought them in. He starred in *What Did you Do in the War Daddy?*, an inept piece of hanky-panky written by William Peter Blatty and directed by Blake Edwards; and *Dead Heat on a Merry-go-round*, a 'perfect crime' story that depended less on machinations than on this personality. Neither was successful, but a second Flint film, *In Like Flint* (67), was extremely popular. Coburn was not interested in continuing the series – he neither liked the films nor found the part interesting. Instead, he produced himself in *Waterhole No 3*, as a jolly rapist-cardsharp-gunman, and in *The President's Analyst*, in the title-role, beset by foreign agents. While making the latter, he told an interviewer that he was getting $450,000 per film. Unfortunately, it was the only one of his starring films to get good notices and even then many critics found it unsatisfactory. It was clear that the public liked Coburn, but it was still waiting to see him in a really good film. It did not, therefore, go to either *Duffy* (68) or *Hard Contract* (69), a somewhat similar yarn, where he was a hired killer, or to *Blood Kin* opposite Lynn Redgrave. He told 'Variety' in 1970: 'I was living it up on big salaries for a long time but about a year ago activity slowed and nothing came along for six months.'

The film crisis could not affect him for long. He went to Europe to make a Western for Sergio Leone, with Rod Steiger, *Giù la Testa/ Duck You Sucker/A Fistful of Dynamite* (72); then appeared in the carefully budgeted *The Honkers* and *The Carey Treatment*, directed by Blake Edwards again. 'Variety' said that it was 'written, directed, timed, paced and cast like a feature for TV' – perhaps the most biting judgment ever offered on any movie. *Una Ragione per Vivere e una per Morire/A Reason to Live A Reason to Die* was an Italian venture which never got very far. And he was hardly luckier with *The Last of Sheila* (73), getting murdered while dressed up as Raquel Welch; or *Pat Garrett and Billy the Kid*, the film that was supposed to restore the reputation of director Sam Peckinpah, as Garrett; or *Harry in Your Pocket*, as Harry, a pickpocket; or a British thriller, *The Internecine Project* (74), as a former Harvard professor and multinational tycoon. It is doubtful whether many but its makers heard of the latter – or *Bite the Bullet* (75), a Richard Brooks Western that was warmly received by some sections of the press. He and Gene Hackman made a fine team; and his partnership with Charles Bronson was equally happy in *Hard Times*, playing a small-time hustler and fight promoter. Up to no good again, he was a smuggler in *Sky Riders* (76), a mishmash of Greek locations and hang-gliding, and he was the half-breed villain of *The Last Hard Men*, with Charlton Heston. Like the Brooks film, it proved that Westerns were out of fashion; and *Midway* did the same for war films: Coburn was one of several names, in one scene, as a captain. He appeared as himself to link *White Rock* (77), 'the official film of the 1976 Winter Olympic Games': and was a German sergeant in *Cross of Iron*. He was a Dashiell Hammett private eye in *The Dain Curse* (78), a long thriller for TV; was in France for *Crimes Obscurs en Extrème-Occident*; and was in *Firepower* (79) with Sophia Loren, a thriller so desperate that once or twice he turned up as his own twin-brother. He also made a guest appearance in *The Muppet Movie*.

He managed *Goldengirl* Susan Anton, an Olympic hopeful, and fell in love with her; he matched Omar Sharif grin for grin, both of them pool hustlers, in *The Baltimore Bullet* (80); and he was *Mr Patman*, an Irish orderly in a psychiatric ward. Kate Nelligan co-starred in the last of these, John Guillerman directed (in Canada) and as it went nowhere was said at one point to be re-edited: whereupon nothing more was heard of it. Coburn had his best chance in a while opposite Shirley MacLaine in *Loving Couples*, both of them doctors in an 'open' marriage. As in the past with inferior material their insouciance tended to be irritating. He was one of three guest stars in cameo roles in a daft action-adventure starring James Brolin, *High Risk* (81), as a drug dealer. Jacqueline Susann's *Valley of the Dolls*, a tele-movie in two parts, was marginally superior to its earlier cinema manifestation. *Looker* found him as a conglomerate chief acquiring ever more power by using computer graphics of famous people whom he then murdered; Albert Finney investigated, in Los Angeles. The film was no more successful than any of the others, so he returned to television to play a lawyer in a starry mini-series, *Malibu* (83). He guested in *Digital Dreams*, an autobiographical fantasy by Bill Wyman of the Rolling Stones; Coburn was a sort-of father figure. He returned to Westerns (actually, in Alberta) for HBO, opposite Kirk Douglas, old sparring partners naturally: *Draw!* (84). Still in Canada he had his son

James Coburn in expansive mood as an Irish explosives expert in Sergio Leone's tale of the Mexican revolution, known variously as Giù la Testa, Duck You Sucker *and* A Fistful of Dynamite (72).

kidnapped by Richard Harris in *Martin's Day* (85). And he practised law again in *Sins of the Father* and *Death of a Soldier* (86). The first was a tele-movie in which he has an affair with his ex-partner's daughter. The second, filmed in Australia, concerned an incident in 1942 when a GI (Reb Brown) murdered three women in Melbourne. Coburn's role made him the investigating cop and then the defence counsel, the voice of liberalism throughout – and always, with ease and confidence, holding this slackly imagined film together. He was a Gringo hobo in *Tag till Himmel/El Tren al Cielo* (88), a co-production between Sweden and Ecuador; and there have been ads in the trade press for *Walking After Midnight*, unseen as yet, in which he is billed after Martin Sheen, Willie Nelson and Rae Dawn Chong.

Sean Connery

The success of the James Bond novels and movies was one of the key events in the communications media in the 60s. Everyone, everywhere, it seemed, was reading them or seeing them. Inevitably, the actor playing Bond became a big star. The lucky man was Sean Connery, hitherto an undistinguished actor mainly in second features. He was born in Edinburgh in 1930; became a milk-roundsman on leaving school at 15 and then joined the navy. Later he was a swimmingpool life-guard, a bricklayer, an undertaker's assistant and a plasterer. In his spare time he went in for body-building and that led to a chance in 'South Pacific' (51) in London – as one of the chorus of sailors – and also to modelling swimming-trunks. After 18 months in 'South Pacific' he went into rep and later began getting small parts in movies: *No Road Back* (57), a B starring Skip Homeier and Patricia Dainton; *Hell Drivers*, a Rank actioner about truck drivers; *Time Lock* with Robert Beatty; and *Action of the Tiger* with Van Johnson. But he got big roles on TV: 'Anna Christie' opposite Diane Cilento (who became his first wife); and, when the BBC could not get Jack Palance, the lead in 'Requiem for a Heavyweight', a remarkable performance, predicting a great future. He played Vronsky to Claire Bloom's TV Anna Karenina.

In 1957, around the time of his success in 'Requiem . . .', 20th signed him to a long-term contract; they considered him for the role that Curt Jurgens eventually played in *The Inn of the Sixth Happiness* and loaned him out to play Lana Turner's lover in the British film she made, *Another Time Another Place* (58). He was loaned out again for the lead in a minor Disney frolic, *Darby O'Gill and the Little People* (59), and a supporting role in *Tarzan's Greatest Adventure* starring Gordon Scott. He turned down a role in *El Cid* to do Pirandello's 'Naked' at Oxford with Cilento; played an Irish crook in *The Frightened City* (61), a protection-racket thriller starring Herbert Lom; and (agreeably) a comedy cook in a filler army farce, *On the Fiddle*. 20th used him finally as a private in *The Longest Day* (62), though whether he was still under contract is a bit muddy: 'Picturegoer' in 1959 had speculated whether they would drop him; Connery himself has said he broke his contract because they would not use him.

Several well-known actors (Trevor Howard, Richard Burton, James Mason, Peter Finch) were mentioned for the role of Bond, Ian Fleming's ultra-virile, ultra-smart (What sort of man reads 'Playboy'?) secret service agent (007). Harry Saltzman and Albert Broccoli were producing *Dr No* (63) for United Artists – and by the look of the finished film Connery was chosen out of budgetary considerations (he got $15,000). It was badly made into the bargain and Connery, a solid clod-hopping lump, was grossly miscast. Both British and American critics gave it its due and business in both countries initially was only medium. Then it began to snowball: it wound up as the fifth biggest hit in Britain that year (it eventually made a packet in the US, reissued later). A second – and better – Bond film proved it was no fluke and *From Russia With Love* (64) racked up huge grosses worldwide. Connery was now enormously in demand – but neither of the two films he did out of his Bond suit was

Sean Connery in his pre-Bond days – as an airman in On the Fiddle *(61), called in the US* Operation Snafu. *In any case, its sole claim to fame is his presence in the cast.*

successful: *Woman of Straw*, inveigling Gina Lollobrigida to help him murder Uncle Ralph Richardson; and Hitchcock's *Marnie*, besotted with Hitchcock's discovery Tippi Hedren: it was not top-flight Hitchcock, but when they kissed it was light years away from Cary Grant and Grace Kelly. His fee was $200,000 plus a 5 per cent percentage; without a percentage his fee at that time was $400,000.

With *Goldfinger*, the third Bond film, critics and sociologists were falling over themselves to analyse the appeal. By this time the original novels were going over the million mark in paperback. Fleming himself said of Connery, 'He is the character as I envisaged him', and Bond was completely identified with Connery. The suave Bond of the books had disappeared: Connery was Bond and Fleming's well-constructed and sometimes witty books became roaring, gimmicky cinema thrillers, an artful blend of 'Boy's Own' and 'Playboy'. *Goldfinger* had been expensive to make and looked it, and it did finally take over $20 million in the US market. *Thunderball* (65) cost more and took more – $27 million: then one of the 10 all-time box-office champs.

It was not to be expected that *The Hill* (65) – made between the two to get away from the Bond image – would do great business, a study of brutality in a Middle East army detention centre, directed by Sidney Lumet. It enjoyed fine reviews and Connery's ox-like rebel – harking back to his 'Requiem . . .' role – proved that in the right part he could be a formidable actor. He was not, however, up to the role of the poet-rebel in the Hollywood *A Fine Madness* (66), but he indicated that he was more engaging than the dour Bond allowed. Neither did significant business, though in 1965 he was considered the top star draw in both Britain and the US (he had entered the British list in 1963 and had been first already in 1964; in 1965 he shot from nowhere to head the US list; in 1966 remained the top male in both countries). *You Only Live Twice* (67) did less well than the previous two Bonds (at the end of 1968, $18 million) and Connery dipped in the US list to seventh – but remained top in Britain.

Increasingly, the Bond suit had fitted him better – during which time he increasingly wanted out. He was fed up with the double identification, especially as regards Bond's potent sex image. The producers wanted him to stay on and there were frequent reports of his contract being negotiated and his salary upped ('Variety' in 1969 said his fee per film had been $1 million in recent years, plus a small participation). As reported, the affair became squalid, with Connery making accusations of greed and the producers claiming they did not want him anyway. Meanwhile, he was determined to change the image: he left off his toupee and grew a full moustache for *Shalako* (69), with Brigitte Bardot, advertised as 'A devastatingly different kind of Western' (the difference was, it was British and made in Spain). He followed with *The Molly Maguires* (70), as their leader, a group of striking miners in Pennsylvania during the last century, with Richard Harris. It was a nebulous picture, but his screen presence had become positively strong and sure. 'Time Magazine' thought it proved he was 'one of the screen's most underrated stars, an actor of tightly controlled power and technical accomplishment'. It was not a success. Meanwhile, the new Bond, an Australian ex-model called George Lazenby, had been difficult on the set of *On Her Majesty's Secret Service* and uninteresting on screen: long before the film made its comparatively poor ($8 million, US) showing, the producers announced that it was his first and last Bond. Connery was engaged on the Russian-Italian *The Red Tent* (71), with Peter Finch, and then a successful thriller for Lumet, *The Anderson Tapes.* That film brought him back to the US box-office list – at ninth (1971).

Neither had been shown when he agreed to do another Bond, on his own terms – possibly the best granted a player since the days of Mary Pickford: $1,200,000 (mostly to go to Scottish charities), plus two films of Connery's own choosing. *Diamonds are Forever* was the first Bond made in Hollywood. It broke records worldwide and restored Connery to his former position. One of the films he chose to do was *The Offence* (72), based on a play

Connery as James Bond. It would be wrong to say that he is the only conceivable actor in the role, or even that he is the definitive Bond. So let us settle for saying that he did not seem too well cast in the first of the series but by this time, Diamonds are Forever *(71), he had made the role his own.*

by John Hopkins, directed by Lumet, in which he played a policeman of dubious ethics. He was a man of the future – 2293 AD – in *Zardoz* (74), written, produced and directed by John Boorman, and had better luck with *Murder on the Orient Express*, best of all the strong all-star suspects – an Indian Army colonel with a Scottish accent. They each were paid $100,000, except the Poirot, Albert Finney, and Connery, who were also on a percentage. He was the head of Norwegian National Security in a poorly received British thriller, *Ransom* (75), and was an Arab warlord and Indian Army soldier-of-fortune respectively in *The Wind and the Lion* and *The Man Who Would be King*. Both were old-fashioned adventure stories set at the turn of the century in North Africa, and the costs and risks were such that MGM and Columbia shared them on the first and Allied Artists and Columbia on the latter. Both were reasonably successful; but Connery and co-star Michael Caine sued for their percentage on the latter. They had received $250,000 salary and were due to receive 5 per cent of the gross receipts over $5 million and 7½ per cent thereafter.

Neither, however, kept Connery's position at the box-office; nor could the help of Audrey Hepburn in a foolish, foul-mouthed and brutal revamping of an old legend, *Robin and Marion* (76), in which they were ageing Hoods. Richard Lester directed. He played a Saudi-Arabian diplomat for Allied Artists in *The Next Man*, which was so badly received on its New York première that it has hardly surfaced since; but his professionalism was a solace amidst the wastes of *A Bridge Too Far* (77), once again as a Scottish officer. Bearded, he masterminded *The First Great Train Robbery* (78) in Victorian London with Donald Sutherland; and then he was up to his neck in New York mud, literally, in a disaster tale, *Meteor* (79); indeed the film was a disaster at the box-office. Then he was off to *Cuba* for a reunion with Lester, but the result did little better. It was a fascinating, if flawed, account of (chiefly) expatriate reactions to the Castro coup. Connery, as a well-meaning British mercenary, was not at his best, but his sequence in *Time Bandits* (81) towered above the others in what was a generally messy enterprise; he was Agamemnon, befriending the boy hero as he journeyed through space and time. Made in Britain by some of the Monty Python team, it failed – despite the 'name' cast – to find an American distributor till the last minute, accordingly opening just after *Outland*, which was made before it. This sci-fi reworking was Connery's best chance in years. He knew it, turning in an outstanding job of a man slow to action but dangerous when roused. Though capably directed by Peter Hyams, it emphasized that Connery had built his career without benefit of many major film-makers. He jumped at the chance of working with Fred Zinnemann on *Five Days One Summer*, but it was one of this director's lesser films, though Connery was relaxed as a Glaswegian shipowner on vacation in Switzerland with his 'wife'. He told an interviewer that he did not entirely care for the character, but 'You have to be indifferent to the reaction of the audience. Some actors will send out little signals indicating "I am not really like this". I cannot bear that ploy.' He had a more deserved failure with *Wrong is Right* (82), though in fine form himself as a reporter up to his neck in mayhem in North Africa. The culprit was writer-director Richard Brooks, trying to stuff in too many political allusions. A quick title-change to *The Man With the Deadly Lens* proved no better.

The question for years was whether Connery would play Bond again. He did at this point, remaking *Thunderball* as *Never Say Never Again* (83) – the title suggested by his (second) wife, since he had sworn that he would not. He was one of the guiding forces behind the production, along with Kevin McClory, who had planned the story with Fleming as a script before it became a novel. When the rights reverted, and despite suits on both sides, McClory approached Connery and Warners assigned a huge budget, $34 million. It took $2 million less than that in the US market, as opposed to a budget of $30 million and a take of $34 million for the rival Bond, *Octopussy*. Connery's successor, Roger Moore, had never enjoyed critical favour and

Sean Connery in The First Great Train Robbery *(78). Connery escaping more and more from James Bond, gets better than ever.*

looked more insipid than ever now that Connery was back: but *Octopussy* was the better of the two. The following year Connery sued Broccoli and MGM/UA for $225 million for profits due (including the merchandizing of the character) on all the Bonds he did from *From Russia With Love* onwards, according to the 5 per cent allotted to him in his contract of the time. His suit also alleged 'fraud, deceit, conspiracy, breach of contract and inflicting emotional distress'.

Never Say Never Again proved that Connery as Bond was infinitely more saleable than Connery the serious actor, even if there were now few better ones working in films. He may have decided to choose more carefully, for he did guest spots with special billing in two action adventures, *Sword of the Valiant* (84) and *Highlander* (86). He was paid $1 million for six days' work on the first of these, playing a feisty Green Knight to the dull Gawain of Miles O'Keeffe. The director, Stephen Weeks, had made a movie on this subject in 1972 which was never released. There was general agreement that cinemagoers would have been no worse off if this had met the same fate. *Highlander* was little more liked, an eclectic mixture of swashbuckler, science fiction and New York-is-hell, with Connery once again crossing the centuries to help its young hero, Christopher Lambert. He took over a role unwillingly vacated by Michael Caine in a West German-Italian-French co-production, *Der Name der Rose* – or in its English version, *The Name of the Rose.* Umberto Eco's novel, a story of murder and detection in an Italian Benedictine monastery in the 14th century, had been an international bestseller. The European returns echoed this success, but lethal reviews greeted the film in Britain and the US – which was a pity, since Connery's monk Sherlock was an impressive job. So was his Irish Chicago cop, one of *The Untouchables* (87), Eliot Ness's band which brought down Al Capone. Like Robert DeNiro, Connery was in support of Kevin Costner, with special billing, but his authority was essential to the quality of the film – and, many would say, to its considerable success; his Best Supporting Actor at the Oscar ceremony was clearly a popular win. While the film was still riding high, he played a high-ranking US army officer in *The Presidio* (88) with top-billing, but the role was subsidiary to that of Mark Harmon, who was a cop courting his daughter and investigating a break-in. Then he was Harrison Ford's father in *Indiana Jones and the Last Crusade* (89). He was again directed by Sidney Lumet in *Family Business*, where he had the unlikely part of Dustin Hoffman's father. Films he did not make during this period include: *Tai-Pan*, *High Spirits*, in the Peter O'Toole role; *The Adventures of Baron Munchausen*; and *Rosencrantz and Guildenstern Are Dead.* He indeed worked on these last two, but left the one because of the delays and the other because of a throat ailment, to be replaced respectively by Robin Williams and Richard Dreyfuss.

Joseph Cotten

Considering that he was once a drama critic, Joseph Cotten should have tried harder. He started impressively, on stage and on screen with Orson Welles, and developed into a strong romantic star. But he rose or sank with his material. He could be genuinely light-hearted, marching to the sound of a very debonair drummer; at other times he simply trudged forward, never varying his step. He once expressed his philosophy: 'Movies and the theatre aren't life. They're only part of it. We make a living out of acting and pray we don't get associated with too much junk.' Very little of what he made after 1950 was not junk. His disdain was apparent. Earlier he lent distinction to some of Hollywood's most popular films. Withal, he was always handsome, with his tooled-leather face (and voice) a dead ringer for the illustrated heroes of women's magazines.

He was born in 1905 in Petersburg, Virginia, studied for the stage at the Hickman School of Expression in Washington, DC, and, between whiles, was a professional footballer and a paint-salesman. For a time he sold space for the 'Miami Herald' and did occasional drama criticism for it; at the same time he did his first acting, for a little theatre in Miami. In 1930 he was engaged by David Belasco as ASM and understudy for his last two productions, 'Dancing Partner' and 'Tonight or Never'. He had a small role in 'Absent Father' (32); other plays in New York included 'Jezebel' (33), 'Accent on Youth' (35) and 'The Postman Always Rings Twice' (36). He joined Orson Welles's Mercury Theater Co. in 1937 and stayed with it two years, when he was offered the lead opposite Katharine Hepburn in 'The Philadelphia Story'. Strictly speaking, he made his film début at this time, in a mock French farce, *Too Much Johnson* (38), in the title-role: it was made by Welles to go with a stage production. It was Welles who brought him to Hollywood, to play his friend and right-hand man in *Citizen Kane* (41). Alexander Korda engaged him to play one of the men in the life of *Lydia* (Merle Oberon); then he returned to Welles for the leading roles in *The Magnificent Ambersons*

Citizen Kane (*41*): *Joseph Cotten, Orson Welles and Everett Sloane. This is the moment when Kane realizes that the rival 'Chronicle' has a greater circulation, and proceeds to poach their writers.*

(42), as the patient admirer of Isabel (Dolores Costello), and *Journey into Fear*, as an engineer unwittingly involved in some nefarious plots in the Middle East.

In 1942 David O. Selznick signed him to a seven-year contract and his first loan-out kept him at altitude: Hitchcock's *Shadow of a Doubt* (43), which the director – and others – think his best film. Cotten was nice, suave Uncle Charlie – Teresa Wright's – with a neat line in bumping off wealthy widows. He looked young enough to play the lead opposite the 20-year younger Deanna Durbin in *Hers To Hold*, one of the better patriotic romances; he then did another conventional chore in *Gaslight* (44) with Ingrid Bergman, as a Scotland Yard man. The first film he did for Selznick was *Since You Went Away*, as an old family friend still hoping to make it with Claudette Colbert, and easily the film's most likeable performance. Also for Selznick he did *I'll Be Seeing You*, as a shell-shocked soldier rehabilitated by Ginger Rogers, a parolee from the clink. Then Selznick loaned him and Jennifer Jones out for *Love Letters* (45), in which he was the soldier who had written them for her (conveniently) dead husband., He was also mad about Jones in *Duel in the Sun* (46). He deserted her temporarily for Loretta Young, *The Farmer's Daughter* (47), as her senator-employer, and was back being obsessed again in *Portrait of Jennie* (48), as a penniless artist who paints her – a performance which was prized at Venice.

Selznick sent him to Europe for a co-production with Korda, *The Third Man* (49), with Alida Valli, as the puzzled thriller-writer looking for old pal Welles. He was fine, but was dour in another British picture, Hitchcock's *Under Capricorn*, as an ex-convict who has run off with Ingrid Bergman and made it big in Australia. If that was unworthy of the creative talents involved, even more so was King Vidor's *Beyond the Forest*, with Bette Davis, as her doctor husband. After that he was a crook in *Walk Softly Stranger* (50), a thriller with Valli; a Confederate colonel in

Two Flags West; and an unhappily married executive in love with Joan Fontaine in the lush *September Affair*.

It was his last good film for some time. Now free of the Selznick link, the offers were much less good; and though he looked little different from when he started, he was old – 45 – by movie standards. He moved immediately into programmers: *Half Angel* (51), as a lawyer loathed by Loretta Young during the day but loved by her at night; *Peking Express*, as a doctor in this routine reworking of the old Shanghai rolling-stock with Corinne Calvet inept as Dietrich; *The Man With A Cloak*, in the title-role (Edgar Allan Poe), with Barbara Stanwyck; *Untamed Frontier* (52), as a cattle baron, with Shelley Winters; and Andrew Stone's *The Steel Trap* with Teresa Wright, a taut melodrama with one of his best performances, as a bank executive who steals from the vault and then has second thoughts. *Niagara* (53) found him fallen hopelessly in love with Marilyn Monroe ('I guess it was the way she slopped the beer on the tables') and in *A Blueprint for Murder* he was accusing Jean Peters of murdering his brother. After such experiences, he returned to Broadway for 'Sabrina Fair'.

On TV he appeared in 'State of the Union' with Margaret Sullavan and 'Broadway' with Piper Laurie. He returned to films in a cheap US-German comedy, *Special Delivery/Von Himmel Gefallen* (55), made in both languages. He was a US diplomat and his leading lady was Eva Bartok. The next leading lady was Rhonda Fleming (a far cry from his co-stars of the 40s!) in *The Killer Is Loose* (56), in which he was a detective, a performance

Hitchcock's Shadow of a Doubt *(43), and it is Patricia Collinge – in a lovely performance – looking admiringly at her brother Charlie, played by Joseph Cotten. If he looks far less happy it is because he knows (as we do) that he is wanted for murder.*

Joseph Cotten in Carol Reed's film of a Graham Greene story, The Third Man *(49), pausing in his quest in Vienna for his pal Harry Lime. Mr Lime's theme, played on a zither, was ubiquitous and inescapable for anyone with a radio in the Autumn of that year.*

described as 'listless' by 'Variety'. He had a drink problem in *The Bottom of the Bottle*, which, after the cracks of American critics, became *Beyond the River* for Britain – where most critics overlooked it. A similar fate everywhere overtook *The Halliday Brand* (57), again as a proud prairie boss, and *From The Earth to the Moon* (58), an earthbound version of Jules Verne, with George Sanders. Between the two he did a guest cameo in Welles's *Touch of Evil* and then he returned to Broadway, in 'Once More With Feeling'.

In 1960 his wife (since 1931) died and he married Patricia Medina, who had been married to Richard Greene. He accepted a supporting role in *The Angel Wore Red/La Sposa Bella* (60) with Ava Gardner, as a hard-bitten one-eyed war correspondent, and another in *The Last Sunset* (61) with Kirk Douglas, as an alcoholic. He worked on the stage, 1962-64, returned to films in *Hush Hush Sweet Charlotte* (65) with Bette Davis, as a scheming doctor. He stepped up his activity: *The Great Sioux Massacre*, top-billed again, as a drunken army major; *The Oscar* (66), as the studio head; *The Money-Trap* with Glenn Ford, as a society doctor involved in a drugs racket; and *Brighty of the Grand Canyon*. In Italy he made Two Westerns, *Gli Uomini dal Passo Pesanti/The Tramplers*, starring Gordon Scott, and *I Crudeli/The Hellbenders* (67). He remained in Europe: the US-German *Jack of Diamonds*, with George Hamilton in the title-role and Cotten as the Ace, 'the greatest jewel-thief of his time'; and *Some May Live*, a British B with Martha Hyer, as an intelligence officer in Saigon. And he then did a British film in the US *Petulia* (68), a riveting performance as Richard Chamberlain's neurotic father.

He made his TV drama début in *Split Second to an Epitaph*, which featured Raymond Burr as Ironside, and returned to Europe for another Western, *Comanche Blanco/White Comanche* in Spain. In Japan he played an American scientist in *Ido Zero Daisakusen/Latitude Zero* (69), an underwater sci-fier, made in English; he returned to Hollywood for *The Grasshopper*, starring Jacqueline Bisset. *The Lonely Profession* was a superior tele-movie with an all-star cast, headed by Harry Guardino as a private eye. Cotten was one of the few 'names' in 20th's huge panorama of the Pearl Harbor event, *Tora Tora Tora* (70), as Secretary of War Stimson, a film that hoped to duplicate the success of *The Longest Day*, but did not. In *Cutter's Way*, a tele-movie Western, he was an army officer.

In January the following year you could not escape from him on television: *Assault on the Wayne* (71), as an admiral; and *Do You Take This Stranger?* and *City Beneath the Sea*, in both playing a doctor. He was a surgeon in *The Abominable Dr Phibes*, who was Vincent Price, and then Frankenstein in *La Figlia di Frankenstein/Lady Frankenstein*; he moved up-market for *Lo Scopone Scientifico/The Scientific Cardplayer* (72) – at least, Bette Davis was also in it and he was an old admirer who played cards with her. *Gli Orrori del Castello di Norimberga/Baron Blood* does not seem to have left Italy; and *Doomsday Voyage* should never have been made – the sort of inept little thriller which simply disappears in today's market. He replaced Ray Milland as Olivia de Havilland's lawyer in a tele-movie, *The Screaming Woman*, and was promoted to judge in another, *The Devil's Daughter* (73).

Cotten's late fortunes improved with *Soylent Green*, supporting Charlton Heston, as a millionaire; and with *A Delicate Balance*, supporting Katharine Hepburn – though the film itself had restricted showings. He was a doctor again, one of a distinguished cast, in a tele-movie, *The Lindbergh Kidnapping Case* (76); returned to Italy for *Un Sussurro nel Buio/A Whisper in the Dark*; was Secretary of State in an American thriller filmed in Munich, *Twilight's Last Gleaming* (77), and was one of the passengers who left *Airport 77*, meeting up with old flame Olivia de Havilland. Television reclaimed him for a mini-series, *Aspen*, and *Return to Fantasy Island* (78). In France with several other names – Bruno Cremer, Donald Pleasance, Dennis Hopper, Michel Bouquet – he did *L'Ordre et la Sécurité du Monde* (78), whose director was quoted by 'Metro' as saying that he could not act but was what the role required; and he was in the Iran-backed *Caravans*, as the American ambassador, after which he was in Italy for *Concorde Affaire 79* (79) with James Franciscus, as the head of the airline. He was General Marshall in a BBC tele-film, *Churchill and the Generals*, in a distinguished cast: one may wonder at the BBC spending licence money on such lifeless hagiography.

Guyana (80), alternatively subtitled *Cult of the Damned* and *Crime of the Century*, was one of two concurrent films about the religious leader, Jim Jones, who willed almost a thousand of his followers to commit suicide in the jungle. Stuart Whitman played the lead, inferior to Powers Boothe in the better rendering, made for TV. It is typical of Cotten's career at the time that he got into the wrong one. He supported Mike Connors, new boss of *Casino*, a tele-movie taking off from the old 'Mr Lucky' series, and Tish Van deVere, the frightened lady of *The Hearse*; then he had the further misfortune of making it to *Heaven's Gate* – or rather *not*, since he did his three-minute stint in the prologue, speechifying as 'The Reverend Doctor' in Oxford's Sheldonian, passing itself off as Harvard. *The Survivor* (82) was directed by David Hemmings in Australia and co-starred Robert Powell and Jenny Agutter; Cotton played a priest. *Screamers* had originally started out as an Italian film made in 1978, *The Fish People*, with Cotten as the professor who invented them, and had gone through many title changes before Roger Corman bought it, adding a prologue and the new title; Richard Johnson was the mad island owner not at all unlike Dr Moreau. Another uncertain Cotten credit is *Delusion*, starring Patricia Pearsy and David Hayward, picked up for US distribution in 1980 and last heard of as *The House Where Death Lives*, set to open in 1984. He was scheduled to support Charles Bronson in *My President's Wife*, but ill-health intervened. In 1987 he published an autobiography, 'Vanity Will Get You Somewhere'.

Jeanne Crain

Youth played a considerable part in Jeanne Crain's success. She came to the screen before she was 20 and was fresh, enthusiastic and pretty, with a direct approach to her lines. She developed into a capable actress, but as she grew older was hardly distinguishable from a hundred others.

She was born in Barstow, California, in 1925 and was still a schoolgirl when Orson Welles saw her in the RKO restaurant and tested her for *The Magnificent Ambersons* (for the part Anne Baxter played). Fired now with a desire to act, she began entering beauty contests – and won several, which led to modelling jobs. Her beauty brought her to the attention of 20th – though reputedly when a talent scout spotted her in an audience – and they signed her for their school of starlets. Her only work in over a year was posing in a bathing-costume in *The Gang's All Here* (43); then one day Darryl F. Zanuck spotted her on the lot and had her tested for *Home in Indiana* (44), a folksy tale about horses, a boy (Lon McCallister) and two girls – the other one was another débutante, June Haver. She was the gentle heroine, Crain the hoydenish one. She starred in a B, *In the Meantime Darling*, as the wife of soldier Frank Latimore; and was a soldier's wife again – Barry Nelson's – in *Winged Victory*, George Cukor's film version of Moss Hart's patriotic stage success (all the men in the cast were billed with their army rank – viz. Pvt Lon McCallister, Sgt Edmond O'Brien).

State Fair (45) made her a star, in Janet

Much ado about Blue Boy, who – as it happened – was a prize pig. His owner, Charles Winninger, is seen here with his proud family – Fay Bainter as his wife, Dick Haymes and Jeanne Crain as his children. The movie was the 1945 version of State Fair.

Gaynor's old role in this musical remake; Luanne Hogan dubbed her songs and Dana Andrews romanced her. The Rodgers and Hammerstein tunes were good and the film was a huge success. Today it is 40s kitsch, with a self-conscious air of niceness that affects even Fay Bainter and Charles Winninger as the parents. And Crain, sugary and breathless in dirndl skirts and bouffant sleeves, is as hard to take as contemporaries like June Allyson. (One who found her captivating then was businessman Paul Brinkman: they were married in 1945 and have seven children.) She was the equally winsome heroine of *Leave Her to Heaven*, as opposed to Gene Tierney, who was the lady left; and of *Centennial Summer* (46), which became a musical (with Jerome Kern songs) at the last moment, after the success of *State Fair*. Her leading man in both was Cornel Wilde, but she was now big enough to be billed alone above the title – as *Margie*, a high-school girl with a crush on the French master (Glenn Langan) and a tendency to lose her bloomers. Her tendency to saccharine was cleverly used and the film, with its 20s songs and accurate evocation of that period, was a big success for her and for the studio.

20th kept her in that period for *You Were Meant For Me* (48), but they knew it was weaker and filmed it in monochrome: the story of a small-town girl and the roving bandleader (Dan Dailey) she marries. She had further marital problems in *Apartment For Peggy*, a sentimental comedy with William Holden, and the three-part *A Letter to Three Wives* with Jeffrey Lynn, directed by Joseph L. Mankiewicz. Of the three wives, she was of course the silly loving ninny. Matrimonially speaking, things were not entirely smooth when she played Lady Windermere in *The Fan* (49), a botched version of Oscar Wilde that got few bookings. Then, rather unexpectedly, she made a good film, playing *Pinky*, Ethel Water's granddaughter. Elia Kazan, the director, later observed that 'it stirred up all kinds of hell, but it was a phony picture. If I made it now, I'd never try to make the Fox back lot look like the South, or use Jeanne Crain, the blandest person I ever worked with, as a black girl trying to pass herself off as white.' Mankiewicz successfully fought Zanuck's proposal to cast her in *All About Eve*, as Eve, and he later said that she was always cooperative, but of all the people he had met in show business she seemed to have the least business there. For *Pinky* Crain got an Oscar nomination – but 20th did not let it turn their collective head; they cast her as a gushing teenager in *Cheaper by the Dozen* (50), daughter of Myrna Loy and Clifton Webb. She guested, as herself, in *I'll Get By*.

She was back at college for *Take Care of My Little Girl* (51), a peep at sororities, and, though married to Cary Grant in Mankiewicz's *People Will Talk*, was still a (medical) student. She was the model in *The Model and the Marriage Broker*, a good comedy directed by George Cukor, and one of the *Belles on Their Toes* (52) – a sequel to *Cheaper by the Dozen*, but was furious because Zanuck made her do it instead of loaning her to appear opposite Laurence Olivier in *Carrie*. In *O. Henry's Full House* she and Farley Granger were the sad young married couple, in 'The Gift of the Magi' sequence. The next three were strictly from the studio's oddbox; *City of Bad Men* (53) – Carson City – with Dale Robertson; *Dangerous Crossing*, a thriller with Michael Rennie; and *Vicki* with Jean Peters, a remake of *I Wake Up Screaming*. With that, she asked for release from her contract and got it.

There was a British offer, *Duel in the Jungle* (54): Dana Andrews also crossed the Atlantic for it, but perhaps no one but its sponsors appreciated their effort. Then she signed a five-year contract with Universal, to begin with the role of a tough dance-hall hostess in *One Desire* – but the part, more sensibly, later went to Anne Baxter. She was certainly miscast as a bold cattlewoman in *Man Without a Star* (55), with Kirk Douglas, and hardly more at ease in *Gentlemen Marry Brunettes* at UA with Jane Russell. Both ladies showed their legs, but Crain was no substitute for Russell's earlier partner, Marilyn Monroe. A second musical also owed something to an earlier one: *The Second Greatest Sex*, a flattering but inferior copy of MGM's *Seven Brides for Seven Brothers* – based this time on 'Lysistrata' and enlivened by the participation of Bert Lahr. She was Glenn Ford's wife in *The Fastest Gun Alive* (56) at MGM and Jeff Chandler's in *The Tattered Dress* (57), her last for Universal. She was a society beauty in *The Joker is Wild* with Frank Sinatra, her last 'class' film.

After three years' absence she played a ranch-owner in *Guns of the Timberland* (60), opposite Alan Ladd, and then took the European trail: *Nefertite Regina del Nilo* (61), corn in Egypt, as its queen, with Edmund Purdom; the French-Italian-Yugoslav *Col Ferro e col Fuoco*, as a royal ward in Old Poland, with John Drew Barrymore; and *Ponzio Pilato*, as Pilate's wife, with Jean Marais. In none of them did she seem very likely. Back in the US she rushed into *Twenty Plus Two*, a cheapie drama with David Janssen, and *Madison Avenue* (62). Over the next few years she worked from time to time in TV and made a couple of pilots which did not become series (she was turned down for one because she did not look sufficiently matronly). In the late 50s she had begun to do some summer stock, notably in 'Claudia' and 'The Philadelphia Story'. Her last screen appearance for some time was in *Hot Rods to Hell* (67), once again with Dana Andrews; she kept her hand in in a horror film, *The Night God Screamed* (71) and she was one of the first-class passengers *Skyjacked* (72) in Charlton Heston's plane.

Broderick Crawford

Broderick Crawford, like Ernest Borgnine, won an Oscar with his first really important lead role. Within a year or so he was back in supporting parts, not perhaps very much missed. He was a good actor, if a shade strident and monotonous. His characterization of the junk-merchant in *Born Yesterday* is a bit too good. The sympathy is all Judy Holliday's, but his Harry Brock, bawling, ignorant ('Ya know the trouble with you, Harry? – you're just not couth'), abrasive, is all too unlikeable; it needed the touch of humour that Paul Douglas brought to it on stage. (Crawford had turned down the play as it happened: and got the film when Douglas turned it down – in one of the early scripts the part had been reduced.) Before and after this and the Oscar-winning film – *All the King's Men* – Crawford specialized in heavies, mainly gang-leaders of the underworld or out on the prairie. His bulky presence could on occasion suggest a bull-like danger. Few of the parts gave him much to do except rant: one recalls a more genial presence in some of his earlier films.

He was born in Philadelphia in 1911, the son of Helen Broderick, who became a popular supporting player in the 30s. He started his career very young, as a radio actor, and then went to London to appear at the Adelphi in 'She Loves Me Not' (32). In London he met the Lunts, who offered him a role in 'Point Valaine' (35) in New York; and he was in 'Punches and Judy' when Goldwyn saw him and offered a contract. He was cast in *Woman Chases Man* (37), one of the leads, as one of the jobless young along with Miriam Hopkins and Ella Logan; and then loaned to WB to play one of the crew of *Submarine D-I*, along with George Brent and Pat O'Brien. Then he was at Columbia with Jimmy Durante in *Start Cheering* (38), a comedy about a Hollywood star (Charles Starrett) who goes to college. He played a student, Biff, ninth on the cast-list – hardly a progression; so he was delighted by the offer of a Broadway play, an adaptation of Steinbeck's 'Of Mice and Men'. As the moronic, pitiable Lennie, he scored a big success and returned to Hollywood confident of better roles. He did not get them – and the part of Lennie in the film version went to Lon Chaney Jr.

For a while he was at Paramount: *Sudden Money* (39), a B; *Ambush*, starring Gladys Swarthout in a straight role, as a bankrobber; *Undercover Doctor* with Lloyd Nolan, as a gunman; *Beau Geste*, as the American legionnaire; and *Island of Lost Men*, one of several kept prisoner in the jungle lair of J. Carroll Naish. He returned to Goldwyn for *The Real Glory*, as an orchid-fancying junior officer, and then comforted Loretta Young on the rebound from David Niven in *Eternally Yours*. He was lawyer Pat O'Brien's partner in *Slightly Honorable* (40) – and a surprise killer, by implication because of World War I ('For three years I killed guys I didn't have anything against'). Then he signed a long-term contract with Universal: *I Can't Give You Anything But Love Baby*; *When the Daltons Rode*, as one of them along with Brian Donlevy, defying Randolph Scott; *Seven Sinners*, as Marlene Dietrich's self-appointed and rather vicious bodyguard; *Trail of the Vigilantes*, as Franchot Tone's sidekick; *Texas Rangers Ride Again* at Paramount, starring John Howard; and *The Black Cat* (41), a B mystery with Basil Rathbone and Bela Lugosi, as comedy relief. He starred in a B with Binnie Barnes, *Tight Shoes*, moustached as a shady operator in this Damon Runyon comedy. Said the 'New York Times': 'Broderick Crawford plays the pedal-ponderous mugg with a charming lack of lucidity.'

Then he returned to prop up some more actioners: *Badlands of Dakota*, with Richard Dix as Wild Bill Hickok and Robert Stack and Crawford as the Holliday brothers; *South of Tahiti* with Maria Montez, brawling with fellow pearl-diver Andy Devine; and *North to the Klondike* (42), starring. He was loaned to Warners to play Edward G. Robinson's simple-minded accomplice in *Larceny Inc*; then had another good role in *Butch Minds the Baby*, another Runyon story, as Butch, co-starring. There were three more roles before he left for war service: *Broadway* with George Raft, as a killer; *Men of Texas*, with Stack; and *Sin Town*, opposite Constance Bennett as a team of con-artists putting to rights a Western town.

He spent three years in the USAAF and returned to Universal to complete his contract: *The Runaround* (46), a B comedy, vying with fellow detective Rod Cameron in pursuit of heiress Ella Raines; *Black Angel*, a murder mystery with Dan Duryea, as a police lieutenant; and *Slave Girl* (47), an Oriental skit with Yvonne de Carlo, as George Brent's bodyguard. He freelanced: *The Flame*, a pallid melodrama with Vera Hruba Ralston; *The Time of Your Life* (48), supporting James Cagney, as the reflective cop; *Sealed Verdict* with Ray Milland, again as a cop, military kind; *Bad Men of Tombstone*, a low-budget Western with Barry Fitzgerald; and *A Kiss in the Dark* (49), supporting Jane Wyman, as a loud-voiced quarrelsome neighbour. For a change he was sympathetic in *Night unto Night*, as a kindly artist, a bluff and blunt friend to heroine Viveca Lindfors – whose first film this was under her Warner contract and in fact made in 1947; two years' delay did not improve it, a sluggish, talky psychological drama, also starring Ronald Reagan. Crawford was his usual screen self again in *Anna Lucasta*, as Paulette Goddard's thuggish, greedy brother-in-law.

Meanwhile, Robert Rossen was preparing to film *All the King's Men*, Robert Penn Warren's novel based on the life of Southern demagogue Huey Long, here called Willie Stark. Columbia boss Harry Cohn wanted Spencer Tracy, but Rossen stuck out for Crawford because he thought he had more brute force and a less sympathetic film persona. Stark had to be loathsome, a tinpot politician who used and abused democracy for his own aggrandizement. Crawford bullied his way through the part, his only virtue a slight oleaginous charm; and won a Best Actor Oscar and the New York critics' award. The film won the Best Picture Oscar.

Columbia had placed him under contract and now found themselves in a dilemma: what to do with an important, respected star, but one of limited appeal. He was not beefcake material or likely to be convincing as a romantic lead. So he was put into a couple of actioners: *Cargo To Capetown* (50), battling the elements alongside John Ireland, and

Walter Burke, Broderick Crawford and Ralph Dumke in All the King's Men *(49), Robert Rossen's study of graft and corruption at State Governor level. Much praised in the US, it opened in Britain to damp notices, most of which accused it of over-simplification.*

Convicted with Glenn Ford, as an incorruptible DA. Then came *Born Yesterday*, followed by *The Mob* (51), an exposé of gangland methods, as an undercover man. In *Scandal Sheet* (52) he was an erring editor; in *Lone Star* with Clark Gable, a politically ambitious tycoon (MGM borrowed him for that, in exchange for Gene Kelly, whom Columbia then thought they wanted for *Pal Joey*). At Warners he took over Edward G. Robinson's old role in the musical remake of *A Slight Case of Murder* called *Stop You're Killing Me*, but the performance, like the film, was charmless and heavy-handed. Columbia then put him into two Westerns which quickly sank, *The Last of the Comanches*, a Cavalry-*v*-Indians with Barbara Hale, and *The Last Posse* (53), as a drunken sheriff, with John Derek – who was also failing to make any dent at the box-office.

Crawford quarrelled with Columbia and was off the screen till *Night People* (54) at 20th, as an American businessman whose son is kidnapped in Berlin – and he played in overemphatic style. Back at Columbia – his last film for them – he was driven to murder by the fickleness of wife Gloria Grahame: *Human Desire* (a remake of *La Bête Humaine*, in the part taken originally by Fernand Ledoux). In *Down Three Dark Streets* he was an FBI agent; in *New York Confidential* (55) a top mobster, with Richard Conte as his chief henchman; and in *Big House USA* a brutal homicidal convict. He returned to top-budget material as one of several names in *Not As a Stranger*, 'absurdly miscast as a tough-sentimental Jewish pathologist' ('MFB'). However, he was at his best – though poorly dubbed into Italian – as the most experienced and jaded of the swindlers in Fellini's enjoyable and least pretentious film, *Il Bidone*, along with Richard Basehart (then resident in Italy). Unlike some others, his Italian trip was not due to a career lull; and back in Hollywood he was featured in *The Fastest Gun Alive* (56), as a belligerent bandit, and *Between Heaven and Hell*, with Robert Wagner, as a fanatical and probably queer army commander. Besides which, he now embarked on a TV series, 'Highway Patrol', as a cop, and that would keep him busy over the next four years. During this time he made only one film, *The Decks Ran Red* (58), as a mutinous deckhand, more than a thorn in the flesh of captain James Mason.

He went to Europe for a TV series which failed to materialize; in Italy played a vile scar-faced king in *La Vendetta di Ercole/Goliath and the Dragon* (60), directed by Vittorio Cottafavi and starring Mark Forest (even dubbed, badly, it did not seem to be about either Hercules or Goliath). He then did *Nasilje na Trgu/Square of Violence* (61), a Yugoslav-American resistance drama, as a super-patriot, with Valentina Cortese and Bibi Andersson; and returned to Hollywood for *Convicts Four* (62), in a cameo as an obstinate 'treat-'em-rough' warden. He was in *The Castilian* (63), an American film made in Spain, a poor man's *El Cid* with Cesar Romero, as the King of Navarre. In the US he was featured in *A House Is Not a Home* (64), with Shelley Winters, and *Up from the Beach* (65), as an MP major. Back in Spain he played the heavy in *Kid Rodelo*, one of actor Richard Carlson's occasional directing jobs, and an amateurish one at that; Carlson also appeared in it, with Don Murray and Janet Leigh. Crawford played a Cornish squire in *The Vulture*, a pitiful attempt at a horror film made by a British-US-Canadian consortium, then went to Hollywood for *The Oscar* (66). There were two more low-budget Westerns – *El Tejano/The Texican*, made in Spain with Audie Murphy, and *Red Tomahawk* – and a Spanish-Italian Western, *Per Un Dollaro di Gloria* (67) with Elisa Montes. *Smashing the Crime Syndicate* (68), with Scott Brady, was retitled *Hell's Bloody Devils* – but few heard of it under either title. Then he did *Wie Kommt ein so Reizendes Mädchen zu diesem Gewerbe?/How Did a Nice Girl Like You Get into This Business?* (70); a tele-movie about nuclear war starring Darren McGavin, *The Challenge*; a drab American independent production, *Ransom Money* (71); and a TV movie with Lloyd Bridges, *The Tattered Web*. He was at his best in *Embassy* (72), with Richard Roundtree, as a wise-cracking security chief, and around this time he was in a TV movie. *The Adventures of Nick Carter*. In 1970 he was in a brief TV series, 'The Interns'.

With Ray Milland he was in Victorian London in *Terror in the Wax Museum* (73), as the American showman who wanted to buy it; and the following year he was in fact in London to play the coach in 'That Championship Season', but it failed to duplicate its Broadway success. A TV film, *The Phantom of Hollywood* (74), found him on the MGM lot, and he was on the Paramount lot as a Special Effects Man in *Won Ton Ton, the Dog That Saved Hollywood* (76). *Look What's Happened to Rosemary's Baby* and *Mayday at 40,000 Feet!* were both tele-movies in which Crawford and Ray Milland were veterans supporting much brighter talents. He and George Kennedy starred in *Ningen No Shómei/Proof of a Man* (77), a Japanese film – the first to be made in the US; and he played Hoover in *The Private Files of J. Edgar Hoover*, one of a number of names in a film described by 'Variety' – only part truthfully – as 'cheap, lurid, sensational'. That was followed by George Roy Hill's *A Little Romance* (79), playing himself in weary fashion, made in Paris with Laurence Olivier; and a feeble British farce filmed in the US, *There Goes the Bride* (80), in a guest appearance as a gas station attendant. He supported Matt Dillon in *Liar's Moon* (81) and was killed off before the credits of *Den Tüchtigen Gehort die Welt/The Uppercrust* (82), a US co-production made in Vienna with Nigel Davenport. Crawford suffered a series of strokes at the end of 1984 and died penniless in 1986. He was married three times, 1940–55, 1962–67 and 1973.

Tony Curtis

Among the least likely candidates for a prolonged screen career was the young Tony Curtis. As he flowered into a strictly PR-made star he was the pretty boy *par excellence*, the head of the gang – what you might call the Hollywood delinquent syndrome. The rest of the gang fell by the wayside, just as Curtis was finding within himself some talent. He emerged, curiously, as less pushy than the other actors of his generation. On most outings he simply tried very hard and, when he had a good script, succeeded, a mite less amiable and somewhat more chirpy than his avowed idol, Cary Grant: 'I would be happy if I could equal his career and his lasting power' he has said. In that respect, he did very well for a while.

He was born in New York City in 1925, the son of a Hungarian immigrant – and was indeed a juvenile delinquent, or so studio publicity used to emphasize. He served in the navy, straight from school, during the war, and on demobilization set about fulfilling his acting ambitions. He studied at a drama school for a year and toured the borscht circuit, then got the lead in a Greenwich Village revival of 'Golden Boy' when an agent saw him and recommended him to Universal. A seven-year contract was arranged, starting at $100 a week and rising to $1,500 at the end of that period. Universal were the last of the studios training young talent in a thorough manner (in the 60s they, and 20th, revived the idea – briefly) and Curtis (ex-Bernie Schwartz) joined the stable of young hopefuls. He underwent training in voice, dramatics, gymnastics, horsemanship, etc., but it was a long time before anything he learnt showed up on the screen. He made his début, unbilled, dancing with Yvonne de Carlo in *Criss Cross* (48) and had bits in some programmers: *City Across the River* (49), *The Lady Gambles*, *Johnny Stool-Pigeon*, as a mute killer, *Francis*, a film about a talking mule, starring Donald O'Connor, *Sierra* (50) and *I Was a Shoplifter*. He was 15th on the cast-list (still as Anthony Curtis) of *Winchester 73* but rose to fifth for *Kansas Raiders*; all the same, he was still better known than that film's nominal star, Brian Donlevy – at least to teenagers.

Universal at that time were assiduous in publicizing their youngsters and fan-magazine editors liked Curtis because their readers could identify with him: he was the slick, greasy-haired yob who stood around outside

What a little Hollywood grooming can do: on the left Anthony Curtis in 1948, in one of the first stills Universal issued of him, and Tony Curtis just three years later. Actually, it looks like a lot of Hollywood grooming. . .

poolrooms or chatted up the girls at the Saturday night hop. His haircut was famous and the studio announced they were getting 10,000 letters weekly asking for his lopped-off locks. There was a contest called 'Win Tony Curtis for a week' with, as consolation prize, 'Talk to a movie star' – 245 girls reputedly talked to him by phone within the space of one hour. Clearly, he was ready to star: *The Prince Who Was a Thief* (51), a swashbuckler based on a Theodore Dreiser story, with Piper Laurie, who could be said to be his female counterpart (years later, in *The Hustler*, she proved she had much more talent than Universal ever let her show). The film found the market it was aimed at, but the fact that it was the only film that Curtis made that year, despite the demand, suggests that he was still undergoing extensive training.

He returned to the screen in *Flesh and Fury* (52) as a deaf-and-dumb boxer who simultaneously wins the championship and is cured. He was itching to do comedy: in *No Room for the Groom* he was a groom with mother-in-law trouble. Laurie was the bride and they were teamed again in another cheap escapist piece, *Son of Ali Baba*. His agent was negotiating for a revised contract – reckoning him worth $50,000 a film: a view strengthened when Paramount wanted to borrow him to play *Houdini* (53), a biopic of the famous magician, with Janet Leigh (his wife; also borrowed - from MGM). The budget was somewhat bigger than Universal allotted to Curtis films and he was doubtless depressed to return to *The All American*, a football story with Mamie van Doren, and *Forbidden*, set in Macao, as a hood. Still, his reviews were poor, like the 'MFB''s on the later film, describing his performance as 'very inept'. He continued to churn out formula pictures of no interest whatsoever: *Beachhead* (54), a World War II story; *Johnny Dark* – motor-racing; and *The Black Shield of Falworth* with Janet Leigh, as a medieval English knight.

Universal unashamedly pinched from other studios' successes and *So This is Paris* was patterned after *On the Town* – but further than Paris is from New York (not that it looked remotely like Paris). There was some verve in the direction, though, and Curtis was spirited as one of the sailors, if not much in the dancing department. Then: *Six Bridges to Cross* (53), about the Brinks robbery; *The Purple Mask*, set in Paris under Napoleon; and *The Square Jungle* – boxing. An offer from Burt Lancaster and UA brought him his first important film – and a fee of $150,000: *Trapeze* (56). It was also his first big box-office picture and it brought a new seven-year contract offer from Universal. 'Picturegoer' a year later reckoned his salary at $25,000 a week: given a 30-week year, this would make $750,000, which seems about right at this point for a top Hollywood star. In any case, his salary would have taken the biggest slice from the budgets of these programmers: *The Rawhide Years*, where he was falsely accused of murder; *Mister Corey* (57), as a small-time opportunist; and *The Midnight Story*, as an ex-cop. Whatever the terms of the contract, he had to fight, reputedly, for his next loan-out.

Lancaster had liked him in *Trapeze* and wanted him for *The Sweet Smell of Success*, to play his chief hanger-on, a fawning, opportunistic creep. It was a characterization of some skill and netted Curtis his first good notices; more than that, it established him as an actor of ability and seriousness. Still on loan, he was an Anglo-Saxon princeling in *The Vikings* (58), with a terrific climactic duel with Kirk Douglas; in a war film with Frank Sinatra, *Kings Go Forth*; and handcuffed to Sidney Poitier – they were both convicts, *The Defiant Ones*. The last was again a big plus and when he returned to Universal for a Blake Edwards film with his wife, *The Perfect Furlough*, it was now conceded that he could play comedy. Certainly he was finding the right style. In *Some Like It Hot* (59) his drag act was more or less a match for Jack Lemmon's and he was amusing in a long sequence when he put on pants and tried to seduce Marilyn Monroe by pretending to be impotent. He dared – and brought off – a parody of Cary Grant – and he and Grant were co-starred in the next one, again a big money-maker, *Operation Petticoat*. (After that, unfortunately, there were intimations of Grant in almost every performance he gave.)

After a guest spot in *Pepe* (60), he made *Who Was That Lady?* with Dean Martin and Janet Leigh; *The Rat Race* with Debbie Reynolds; and *Spartacus*, andother big one and *most* unlikely as a Roman. *The Great Impostor* (61) was based on the career of Ferdinand Waldo Demara, who masqueraded in a variety of disguises and literally triumphed or escaped in all of them – a good subject which degenerated into another star vehicle. Much better was another factual story, *The Outsider*, about the Indian Ira Hayes who left his reservation and became a hero at Iwo Jima, but who could not cope with fame or the paleface world – and Curtis was very fine in it. The film was a failure, even in a butchered version which finished with the unveiling of the Iwo Jima memorial instead of the scenes of joblessness and alcoholism. Who could blame Curtis if he retreated into sentimental comedy, *Forty Pounds of Trouble* (62), and mindless adventure, *Taras Bulba*, with Yul Brynner? In 1961 he should have

Tony Curtis and Jack Lemmon in a publicity shot for Some Like It Hot *(59). There is no scene like this in the film, for, as the whole world knows, they spent all but a few moments in frocks and bangles – to escape some gangsters.*

been in *Lady L* at MGM with Gina Lollobrigida but it was abandoned (at a great loss, including his $300,000 fee) when he walked out. His agreement gave him script approval and the final revised script had considerably minimized his role.

Between two guest appearances, *The List of Adrian Messenger* (63) and *Paris When It Sizzles* (64), he was in a comedy with Gregory Peck, *Captain Newman MD* (63) – and very winning as a fly wheeler-dealer. He had continued to work spasmodically for Universal but there was a break after *Wild and Wonderful* (64), another comedy, with wife No 2, German actress Christine Kauffman. It was reported that he would not work there again. He concentrated on comedy: *Goodbye Charlie* with Debbie Reynolds; *Sex and the Single Girl* with Natalie Wood; the big-budgeted *The Great Race* (65), unsuccessfully reunited with Jack Lemmon; *Boeing-Boeing* with Jerry Lewis, as a philandering airline pilot; and *Not With my Wife You Don't* (66), with Virna Lisi. He made a guest appearance in *Chamber of Horrors*, shown in cinemas but originally a TV pilot.

He went to Britain for a comedy that had title trouble during its making – and after flopping in the US as *Arrivederci Baby* it turned up in its country of origin as *Drop*

Dead Darling. Indeed, all of Curtis's recent comedies had dropped dead at the box-office and *Don't Make Waves* (67) with Claudia Cardinale did not make it either. In 1968 Curtis was listed by 'Variety' as one of the high-priced talents who might not be worth the money; and the Italian *La Cintura di Castità* (68) with Monica Vitti did not help – at least, not in Britain, where it was translated literally as *The Chastity Belt*, nor in the US, where it became *On My Way to the Crusades I Met a Girl Who . . .* (radio and TV stations refused to advertise it under its original title). It was no secret in Hollywood that Curtis was in considerable career trouble and according to 'The Studio' by John Gregory Dunne he went to great trouble to get the part of *The Boston Strangler*, based on some nefarious doings in that city some years earlier – and was excellent in the title-role. Another international comedy also flopped out: *Quei Temerari Sulle Loro Pazze Scatenate Scalcinate Carriole/Monte Carlo or Bust* (69), an attempt by Ken Annakin to cash in on the success of his *Those Magnificent Men in Their Flying Machines*. (In the US it was called *Those Daring Young Men in Their Jaunty Jalopies*.) Both in the next two had, from the point of view of audiences, unfortunate titles: *Suppose They Gave a War and Nobody Came* (70) and *You Can't Win 'Em All* With Charles Bronson, filmed in Yugoslavia. 'Variety' said the latter had 'forced gags with Curtis pouring on the Cary Grant imitation'. Before the accounts were in on both of them Curtis had signed for a TV series with Roger Moore, 'The Persuaders', which failed.

In 1973 he toured in a play, 'Turtlenecks', which failed to reach New York, and he had a good TV film, *The Third Girl on the Left*; in June he announced that he had quit movies, but in March 1975 he was suing independent producer Max J. Rosenburg for $75,000 – for failure to pay, or start a projected *Man in the Iron Mask*. He also thereabouts played the title-role in *Lepke* (75) for Israeli director Menahem Golan, but there were few takers for this biopic of the American Jewish gangster of the 20s, nor many for another Dumas, *The Count of Monte Cristo* (76), made in Britain: Richard Chamberlain had the title-role and Curtis was the arch-villain, Mondego. Prior to its appearance he had been on US TV in *The Big Rip-Off* and in the rotating Sunday Mystery Movie as 'McCoy'. He was one of the many stars sunk in a big movie, *The Last Tycoon*, playing a 30s film star and anomalously wearing the skin-tight pants he had worn in most of his roles. He published a novel, 'Kid Cody and Julie Sparrow', and starred in the French-Italian-Austrian-West German *Casanova and Company* (77), as Casanova: it was rushed to the screens before the Fellini film on the same subject, but the public wisely decided it wanted little to do with either. Curtis's next three ventures were equally exploitive: he was a con-man in the Canadian *The Manitou* (78), which offered an Exorcist-type tale of the supernatural; he was a guest in *Sextette*, which offered a very aged Mae West as a sexy bride; and he was a trainer in *Bad News Bears Go to Japan*, second sequel to a comedy about a kids' baseball team. Unlike the earlier two films, this one failed to find a public. Curtis was singularly unlucky in the films he did over the decade; but the cinema had changed. The public did not want middle-aged or over-age stars, and Curtis was simply not a good enough actor to compete when there was a large role for a 'character'-player. He must have wondered why a contemporary like Burt Lancaster had slightly better luck during this time; but he could console himself with TV, as in a series, 'Vegas', in a tele-movie about Hollywood, *The Users*, or in more Canadian films, *It Rained All Night the Day I Left* (79) and *Title Shot*, about Mafia involvement in boxing, as a ring owner.

He was back in Hollywood, but below the title, to play a mobster in *Little Miss Marker* (80), which starred Julie Andrews and Walter Matthau, and about this time he played the role Matthau would take in the movie version of Neil Simon's 'You Ought to Be in Pictures', but according to 'Variety' he 'was replaced' before it reached Broadway. He appeared in the French-Canadian-Israeli *Deux Affreux sur le Sable* with Lou Gossett and Sally Kellerman, but it did not cross other frontiers; and he was a movie producer in the next two – an unconvincing David O. Selznick in an inept telefilm, *Moviola: The Scarlett O' Hara War*, and in *The Mirror Crack'd*, married to Kim Novak. That returned him to star-billing in a major movie, but his fellow-players were also passé names supporting Angela Lansbury. He also starred in a tele-movie, *The Million Dollar Face* (81), a busted pilot, as the head of a cosmetics firm, but supported in two more: *Inmates: a Love Story* (82) starring Kate Jackson and Perry King, as a small-time hood, and *Portrait of a Showgirl*, one of a series of 'Portraits', starring Lesley Ann Warren and Rita Moreno, the three of them employed in Las Vegas. He was Iago in an updated *Othello*, made in Spain and starring Max H. Boulois, who also wrote and directed; he was a mastermind doctor in *Brainwaves* (83), directed by Ulli Lommel and starring Keir Dullea. He was lured to Britain for a couple, *Where Is Parsifal?* (84), top-billed as an impoverished inventor who hopes to retrieve his fortunes with a sky-writing machine, and *Insignificance* (85), as a Senator, supposedly Joseph McCarthy, talking endlessly with someone like Marilyn Monroe, another like Einstein and another like Joe diMaggio. This quartet sank without trace and swiftly; the last made a little noise before disappearing, due to the (inexplicable) cult for its director, 'Nic' Roeg. It was sad to see Curtis move from dumb downmarket movies to a dumb 'art' movie. It was true that his personal notices were usually dreadful, which could not have helped; interviewers and co-workers spoke of his 'courtesy' – but he did not have that, Sheilah Graham remarked, when he was one of the biggest stars in Hollywood. He guested in a tele-movie, *The Half-Nelson*, and had two further failures, *The Last of Philip Banter* (86), aka *Banter*, and *Balboa*. But do not blame him: he was only in the supporting cast. He was also up for a CBS series, 'Spies', but the role went to George Hamilton. *Mafia Princess* and *Midnight*, from this period, have yet to be seen.

Welcome to Germany/Der Passagier (88) was said by its German and Swiss producers to be his 'come-back' vehicle; he played an émigré European director who returns to Germany to make a World War II story. And he remained in the movies in *Lobster Man From Mars* (89), playing a mogul who is trying to make a flop for tax purposes: his fee was $50,000 – for one and a half days' work.

Zbigniew Cybulski

In general the cinema of the Soviet bloc has not greatly relied on the star system. In films from behind the Iron Curtain there has been a face from time to time, behind the proletarian murk, which suggested the glamour of a Gable – a personality one would like to experience again. But the only undisputed star to cross the barrier was a young Polish actor called Zbigniew Cybulski, who stunned audiences and critics in the third, if not the first, of his films to be shown this side of the Curtain.

Zbigniew Cybulski (far right) in Ashes and Diamonds, *directed by Andrzej Wajda in 1958 – and still the most successful Polish film shown in the West. Like most of Wajda's films, one could spot derivations from other directors, fake symbolism and crass effects: all done with crushing confidence and a variety of ideas going off in all directions. And as usual, the effect was dazzling. With Cybulski (right) is Ewa Krzyzanowska, who offered him, in the film, some moments of relaxation and perhaps undying love.*

He was born in 1927, the son of a minor civil servant, and educated secretly during the Nazi occupation, being trained in commerce and journalism. He did not, however, care for journalism and left to study at the Cracow Theatre School. In 1953 he began acting in provincial rep and in 1954 with a colleague, Bogumul Kobiela, founded the student theatre, Bim Bom, in Cracow. Its aims were avant-garde and its eventual fame considerable. Cybulski was commissioned to produce and act in Warsaw; and he began to get small parts in films. *Pokolenie/A Generation* (54) was the first of Andrzej Wajda's trilogy on the Polish Resistance: Cybulski had a brief role as a Resistance fighter and was not noticed by Western critics. Nor did the West see the next four: *Trzy Starty/Three Starts* (55), in the episode on cycling; *Tajemnica Dzikiego Szybu/The Secret of the Old Mine* (56), in a supporting part; *Koniec Nocy/The End of the Night* (57), in the lead; and *Wraki/Wrecks*.

Osmy Dzien Tygodnia/Der Achte Wochentag (58) was a Polish-West German production directed by Alexander Ford and written by Marek Hlasko, about the love between a shy student (Cybulski) and a self-willed girl (Sonia Ziemann); there was a scene where she gets drunk and seduced just as he finds an apartment for them and this, together with its relentless portrait of Poland as grim and sleazy, caused it to be completely suppressed in that country. It was seen in Germany, and at the Cannes festival, but not otherwise widely in the West.

The second of Wajda's trilogy was *Kanal*, which took place almost wholly in the sewers of Warsaw. Cybulski was not in it, but he had the lead in part three, *Popiól y Diament/Ashes and Diamonds*, a work of considerably more weight than the other two: Poland during the first uneasy day of peace, with several factions struggling for the vacant leadership, including Cybuylski as a disillusioned Resistance worker, uncertain – in the continuing nightmare of the quasi-peace – whether to go on killing or let a casual promise of love provide a better future. It is a world of seedy hotel bedrooms, bars, empty streets, where impulse and mad jokes hide the despair and anxiety. Cybulski brilliantly realized the complexity of the character, this 'Hamlet in windcheater and dark glasses' (David Robinson) – dressed deliberately to recall not 1945 but the Hollywood 'rebels' of the 50s (Brando, etc.).

In Poland the film was one of the most successful ever made there. In the West, after it was shown at the Venice festival in 1959, Cybulski became a name – indeed a draw – on the art-house circuit; about half the other films he made were exploited on his name. There were difficulties, however, beyond the quality of the films: he was not always in the star part and he was not always good. As he grew older he was increasingly undisciplined and only strong direction could keep him in check. He was in the third and last episode of *Krzyz Waleczhych/The Cross of Valour* – 'The Widow' – as a foot-loose philandering veterinary surgeon; and he had only a small role in Jerzy Kawalerowicz's *Pociag/Night Train* (59), a fascinating piece about a woman (Lucyna Winnicka) sharing a sleeping-berth with a stranger (male). Cybulski appeared from time to time as her ex-lover. Around this time he returned to the stage, in two plays directed by Wajda, 'A Hatful of Rain' in Gdansk and 'Two for the See-Saw' in Warsaw.

He wrote the scenario of *Do Widzenia do Jutra/See You Tomorrow* (60) and played the lead, the director of a little theatre in Gdansk, clearly modelled on the Bim Bom. Like *Ashes and Diamonds*, the film was permeated with the feeling of youth, elegiac and afraid: a couple destined to be separated by the exigencies of a world divided into East and West (the girl was an envoy's daughter). And *Niewinni Czarodzieje/Innocent Sorcerers*, directed by Wajda, also had the authentic tang – bored, uncertain young people, getting high on jazz records and vodka. Tadeusz Lomnicki played the lead; Cybulski – and Roman Polanski – were two of his friends, with Cybulski displaying the high comic skill which Polish film-makers were to utilize so seldom. He wore as ever his dark glasses – and if this was an affectation he was also short-sighted. Otherwise, he made only a guest appearance in *Rozstanie/Partings* (61).

To what extent there were offers from the West was not disclosed, but he elected to do three French movies. The first was another guest appearance in *Le Thé à la Menthe* (62); the second was in fact a multilingual production, *L'Amour à Vingt Ans*, with episodes set in Paris, Rome, Munich, Tokyo and Warsaw. The French (Truffaut) and Polish (Wajda) sketches were fine, the others dreadful (perhaps the reason it was not shown in Britain). Cybulski was a lovable bear of a man, a minor bureaucrat adopted – because of an act of bravery at the zoo – by wealthy Barbara Lass (in real life at that time married to Polanski). He was a war hero and her young friends are at first fascinated; then they mock him as the wine flows. The maturity of this piece was rendered in inverse proportion by Jacques Baratier's *La Poupée*, a trite fantasy purporting to be about a Latin American revolution. The leading role was taken by a female impersonator and Cybulski, in a double role (revolutionary and a corrupt general), was shamelessly wasted.

After *Spoznieni Przechodnie/Those Who Are Late* he made two of his best films. Wojciech Has's *Jak Być Kochana/How To Be Loved* (63) was a wartime recollection by an actress (Barbara Kraftowna) of the egocentric actor (Cybulski) she had sheltered throughout the war. His 'act of heroism' had been to insult a collaborator, but in the years of boredom his deeds burgeoned, till, free at last, he drifted boasting from bar to bar. *Ich Dzien Powszedni/Their Everyday Life* also examined a claustrophobic relationship. He had a supporting role in *Milczenie/Silence*, a village drama about a boy whose blindness is thought to be heavenly justice because he persecuted the priest; and then made three which were not exported to the West: *Zbrodniarz i Panna/The Criminal and the Girl*, *Rozwodów nie Bedzie/No More Divorces* (64), an episoder, and *Giuseppe w Warszawie/An Italian in Warsaw*, a comedy.

In Sweden he played a foreigner working in a travel agency in *Att Älska/To Love*, a drawn-out anecdote directed by Jörn Donner and co-starring his wife, Harriet Andersson, about a couple living together. In Poland again he did an ambitious picture directed by Has, *Rekoopis Znaleziony w Saragossie/ The Saragossa Manuscript*, based on an 18th-century classic novel by Jan Potocki, the exotic adventures of a Walloon captain in Spain. Cybulski, without his dark glasses, was merely bemused in that part. He made: *Pingwin/Penguin* (65), a tale of student lovers, in a supporting part as an older rival; *Salto/*

Salto, as a moody intruder in a small town, causing its inhabitants to examine their illusions; *Sam Pośród Miasta/Alone in the City;* and *Jutro Meksyk/Mexico . . . Soon* (66), as an Olympics swimming trainer coaching one particular girl. He was invariably at his best playing a complicated man and the one in *Szyfry/The Enigma* was quite weird, a mystic young man unable – because of the war – to face reality (he was, in fact, the son of the focal character, a man returning to Poland for the first time since the war). There was another comedy, *Cala Naprzód/Full Steam Ahead*, in a supporting role; and *Jowita* (67), adapted from a Polish bestseller,'Disneyland', supporting Barbara Lass, in this romance set against a sporting background.

He was becoming fat, he was drinking more than heavily and spending all night, and every night, if not drinking and talking, in womanizing (although he was married). He was in a way the 60s Polish equivalent of the fading matinée idol played by John Barrymore in *Dinner at Eight*. His friends watched his disintegration helplessly and were, it was said, hardly surprised when he was killed in an accident at the beginning of 1967 – he died late at night trying to board the Wroclaw–Warsaw express. He left unfinished *Morderca Zostawia Ślad/The Murderer Leaves a Clue* (photography had been completed but there was the dubbing to be done), in which he played a businessman, with moustache, spectacles, homburg and rolled umbrella: a different Cybulski from the one who had once become overnight the idol of the young. A national hero had departed; Dilys Powell spoke for foreign cinemagoers: '. . . the disappearance of a personality both appealing and powerful leaves one with a feeling of bereavement'. There was an epilogue when Wajda made *Wszystko Na Sprzedaz/ Everything For Sale* (68), which was inspired by his death.

LINDA DARNELL

Acting ability was never a prerequisite for Hollywood stardom, but in the 40s when the studios scratched around for new stars it was just about the least-looked-for commodity. Linda Darnell had other attributes: a sultry, dark-eyed beauty and a sort of gleaming sincerity which had nothing to do with any dictionary definition of that quality. In the same way, she was seductive – in the way that Hollywood had falsified sex by the time she arrived there. She could be fiery, in a hoity-toity way that had nothing to do with real temper. As Tyrone Power's beloved in *The Mark of Zorro* schoolboys adored her, but it is difficulty to imagine grown men finding her flesh and blood. She could act a bit, but it is significant that her career hardly survived the coincidental ending of her long-term contract and the decade – and a pity: by the time she was capable of playing interesting characters she was no longer being offered them. She was born in 1923 in Dallas, Texas, to a mother with abnormal – even by the standards of show-business mothers – ambitions for her children. This one was considered the most likely and was taught dancing; she was also put to modelling and into amateur dramatics. Encouraged by the interest of a visting 20th talent scout, they entrained for Hollywood where the 16-year-old Linda entered the RKO 'Gateway to Hollywood' competition – but the aforementioned talent scout found them there and got Darnell signed by 20th. She got a lead immediately, in *Hotel for Women* (39), as an innocent whose virtue is threatened by some wealthy older men. Zanuck was so pleased with her that – at great expense – he yanked her out of *Drums Along the Mohawk*, where she had a small role, and into the title-role of *Day-Time Wife* and Tyrone Power's arms (jettisoning on the way Nancy Kelly, who was signally failing as star material). Thus she was hardly appropriately cast as a Hollywood hopeful in *Star Dust* (40).

Back she went to Power for *Brigham Young Frontiersman* and *The Mark of Zorro;* she was Henry Fonda's (first) wife in *Chad Hanna;* then Power's childhood sweetheart and long-suffering wife in *Blood and Sand* (41). After *Rise and Shine* – loosely based on Thurber's 'My Life and Hard Times' – with Jack Oakie and George Murphy, she was consigned to Bs: *The Loves of Edgar Allan Poe* (42) and *City Without Men* (43). In the latter, a prison drama, she became a nun at the end, from which it was only a step up to play the vision of the Virgin in *The Song of Bernadette*. She was unbilled but publicity ensured that the public knew it was her and naturally her stock rose – within the studio also, especially with her marriage to cameraman Peverell Marley, for that removed mother's powerful influence. A loan-out also proved beneficial, René Clair's *It Happened Tomorrow* (44), with Dick Powell.

Her parts improved again, as in the concurrent *Buffalo Bill*, as a doomed Indian maid. For a while she seldom finished a film alive, as in *Summer Storm*, where her beauty proved fatal to George Sanders and then herself; Edward Everett Horton in a serious role was the third side of the triangle and the Chekhovian mood (an adaptation of 'The Shooting Party') was surpisingly well caught. There was a respite while she decorated a Benny Good-

Linda Darnell started her career playing pretty little ingénues, but later became type-cast as a Bad Lot. She practised her wiles on Laird Cregar in Hangover Square *(45), and quite appropriately was murdered by him. The same fate awaited the same wiles in* Fallen Angel, *later that year, when it was Dana Andrews who was suspected of murder.*

man vehicle, *Sweet and Low Down*, and then she got it again – from Laird Cregar – in *Hangover Square* (45), and deservedly! Cregar might have been psychopathic, but she was a mighty convincing slut (neither the first nor last actress more at ease as a whore than as a dewy-eyed heroine). She was a stage star, one of the two loves of *The Great John L.* (Sullivan, the boxer, played by Greg McClure) at UA, dying conveniently so that he could return to first love Barbara Britton; and again a tramp in *Fallen Angel* – it was Dana Andrews this time who did her in. She made the fade-out of *Centennial Summer* (46), as Jeanne Crain's flighty sister, but was burned at the stake in *Anna and the King of Siam* and shot in Ford's *My Darling Clementine* – in which she was conspicuously modern.

She was originally passed over for *Forever Amber* (47), an expensive version of a wartime bestseller. Details of Amber's amours at the court of Charles II had given the book a notorious reputation and the search for Amber was manna to the 20th publicity dept. Vivien Leigh and Margaret Lockwood, among others, turned it down and 20th, in their bid to get a British actress, signed Peggy Cummins, who had been doing prissy junior missy parts on the West End stage. Predictably, she proved to be unsuitable, but was not replaced till filming was under way and a million dollars had been expended. Of the available contract stars Darnell was the most obvious replacement (Preminger had wanted Lana Turner, but Zanuck could see no reason why he should do MGM such a favour) – but she did nothing for the film, nor it for her. Preminger's direction was turgid even for him,

but the film had a certain box-office – and absolutely no critical – success.

However, her status was enhanced and after *The Walls of Jericho* (48), as Kirk Douglas's vicious conniving wife, she actually made a couple of good films: Preston Sturges's *Unfaithfully Yours* as Rex Harrison's wife, and Mankiewicz's *A Letter to Three Wives*, in its best episode, as Paul Douglas's gold-digging wife. That one, said Richard Winnington, 'shows Linda Darnell to be an actress when encouraged'. She was not encouraged – or so it seemed– with *Slattery's Hurricane* (49), but did nicely as an opera star vamping Paul Douglas in *Everybody Does it*.

She was also good in *No Way Out* (50) with Richard Widmark, as a tramp – the sort of good performance a second-rate actress can give, but will spoil by overemphasis because she is hoping for an Oscar. She played conventional parts in a conventional way: *Two Flags West*, a Western; *The Thirteenth Letter* (51), top-billed, though in a small part, with Michael Rennie; and *The Guy Who Came Back*, a programmer with Douglas and Joan Bennett. After that, 20th did not renew her contract.

Like other falling stars at that time she found a haven at Universal – if briefly: *The Lady Pays Off* with Stephen McNally, a comedy about a schoolteacher (Darnell) in Las Vegas. She was marooned on the British *Saturday Island* (52) with one-armed Donald Gray and young marine Tab Hunter, and their rivalry for her had audiences rolling about in the aisles. For what audiences there were, the next one, *Night Without Sleep*, was inaptly named, a psychological thriller at 20th with Gary Merrill. *Blackbeard the Pirate* was Robert Newton and Darnell returned to her early job as helpless heroine. Her marriage ended in divorce in 1952 and she remarried twice subsequently (1954-55 and 1957-63).

When Susan Hayward did not like the costumes she got a good part in a good thriller at RKO, *Second Chance* (53), filmed in 3-D, and RKO liked her enough to ask her back for *This Is My Love* (54), a trite soap opera where she showed marked ability in one spectacular emotional outburst. A couple of Italian ventures paid poor results: *Donne Proibite* (55) did not reach the US or Britain till years later (ineptly dubbed and rechristened *Angels of Darkness*) and *Gli Ultimi Cinque Minuti* seems never to have been exported. The former was a drama about whores (what else?) with Anthony Quinn, the latter a version of a popular Italian stage comedy with Vittorio De Sica and Rossano Brazzi. She replaced Anne Baxter in a Republic Western, *Dakota Incident* (56), with Dale Robertson and John Lund, and tried Broadway – 'Harbor Lights'. It was not a success, but she liked the stage and turned down a part in *Drango* to tour in 'Tea and Sympathy'. That she was getting stout was clear from *Zero Hour!* (57), a low-budget drama with former co-star Dana Andrews. Hers was a nothing part that she did rather well. However, she retired on remarriage and did not return till they were divorced – TV guest stints, a nightclub act, some stage work. In 1965 she received an offer from A.C. Lyles, who at that time packaged B Westerns with as many old-timers as his minute budget would allow. This one, *Black Spurs*, came out after her death. She was killed when her cigarette (apparently) set fire to the friends' living-room where she was sleeping. It was disclosed that she had been plagued for some time by weight problems and alcoholism.

Danielle Darrieux

As a young girl, petulant, fragile, a coquettish creature in a cotton dress, meltingly romantic but always somewhat caustic; as a woman, with diamonds at her throat and a mink not far away, elegant, poised, always beautiful, always very knowing, never taken in. It was an unpleasant surprise to young men when they first went to France that all Frenchwomen were not like Danielle Darrieux. For 40 years she represented to many the ideal Frenchwoman. Beyond the *chic*, there was a gaiety. She was the best *femme du monde*, less etheral than Michèle Morgan, less primeval than Jeanne Moreau. She looked at men quizzically and sceptically and her voice rose a tone or two: no actress – not even Myrna Loy – was as adept at light sarcasm.

She was born in Bordeaux in 1917, the daughter of an army doctor who died when she was seven. The family had lived in Paris from the time Danielle was two; at 14 she was studying the cello at the Conservatoire when her mother saw a newspaper advertisement asking young girls to audition for *Le Bal* (32), with André Lefaur, the French version of a German film directed by Wilhelm Thiele, based on a novel by Irene Nemirowsky. Dolly Haas had played the part in the original, that of an adolescent who, instead of delivering her parents' ball invitations, deposits them down a drain. Darrieux was a plain little girl at that point, but she got the part; producer Marcel Vandal signed her to a five-year contract. She had supporting roles in the films that followed: *Coquecigrolle* (32), a period piece starring Max Dearly; *Panurge* with Gérard Sandoz; *Le Coffret de Laque* with René Alexandre; and *Château de Rêves* (33) with Jaque Catelain. *Mauvaise Graine* (34) was directed by Alexander Esway and Billy Wilder, from a story by Wilder, about a gang of boys who steal cars: Darrieux was the sister of one of them, the decoy, and it was made entirely on location to save money.

She went to Prague to make *Volga en Flammes*, about revolution in Russia, with Albert Préjean. After a chance meeting back in Paris Préjean recommended her for his leading lady in Robert Siodmak's *La Crise est Finie*, a jubilant musical detailing the adventures of a troupe of strolling players in Paris. It was a great success and he asked for her again, to play the title-role in *Quelle Drôle de*

Gosse – a title which described her on-screen and off. Préjean found her 'a child of the devil: intolerable' – but 'adorable'. She later said it took her four years to realize what it was like to be an actress. Meanwhile, she and Préjean were engaged briefly in 1935 and made a whole series of films: *Dédé*, another musical; *L'Or dans la Rue* (35), a comedy directed by Curtis Bernhardt; and *Le Contrôleur des Wagons-Lits*. In *J'aime Toutes les Femmes* she played opposite Polish tenor Jan Kiepura in the role played in the concurrent German version, *Ich Liebe alle Frauen*, by his wife, Martha Eggert. She did her first really dramatic role, in *Le Domino Vert*, with Maurice Escande, and then the pleasant *Mademoiselle Mozart*, in the title-role, the bankrupt owner of a music-store wooed by a wealthy boy (Pierre Mingand) she does not want. *Mon Coeur t'Appelle* (36) was another Kiepura vehicle, called in its German version *Mein Herz Ruft nach Dir*.

It was *Mayerling* which first brought her to world attention, playing the tragic Marie Vetsera to Charles Boyer's Prince Rudolph: Anatole Litvak's densely romantic tale of what led to the dual suicide in the hunting-lodge. It was Boyer who insisted on her (producers said she could only play comedy) and as a result the world was at her feet. In the 'New York Times' Frank S. Nugent described her as 'unbelievably lovely' and he later referred to 'one of the hauntingly charming performances of the year'. The New York critics voted the film the year's Best Foreign movie; it was the most successful foreign Talkie shown in that city; and it played the Paramount circuit (dubbed into English). Meanwhile, she played in another of the industry's biggest pictures, *Tarass Boulba*, based on Gogol's novel about the classic Cossack victory over the Poles, with Harry Baur in the title-role and Jean-Pierre Aumont as his son. It flopped at the box-office. She did a gay comedy with Henry Garat, *Un Mauvais Garçon*, based on a play by Louis Verneuil, and then another spectacle, *Port-Arthur*, made in Prague and set in 1905, a routine spy story in which she was a Japanese bride involved with Russian officer Anton Walbrook. At the end of the year, she was voted the second most popular star in France, after Gaby Morlay, and before Annabella, Shirley Temple and Garbo.

She signed an exclusive contract with Grégor Rabinovitsch of Ciné-Alliance, but after the US success of *Mayerling*, Hollywood wooed her; in January 1937 she signed a nine-year contract with Universal, with options, at $4,000 a week. She was at that time making her stage début, in a play by Henri Decoin, whom she had married in 1935, 'Jeux Dangereux'. She did it in both Paris and Brussels, and then appeared in the scandalous *Club de Femmes* (37), written by Jacques Deval, with Betty Stockfield and Josette Day. She played a girl who smuggles her fiancé into her hostel room and later has a baby by him (in the US, a subtitle made him her husband). Also somewhat shocking was *Mademoiselle ma Mère* in the part that Gaby Morlay had played on stage (another adaptation from Verneuil), that of a spoilt brat who marries an old man to spite her father and then falls in love with his son (Pierre Brasseur). Said 'Le Figaro': 'Danielle Darrieux joint le talent à la grâce, la jeunesse à l'élégance. Elle est une de nos vedettes la plus accomplies.' In Hollywood, Universal waited impatiently, but her contract

A Habsberg tragedy as interpreted by the movies: Charles Boyer as the Crown Prince Rudolf and Danielle Darrieux as Marie Vetsera, in Mayerling *(36).*

permitted her seven months a year in France and she dallied to do *Abus de Confiance*, specially written for her by Pierre Wolff, a comedy about an orphan who lies her way into a benefactor's home in order to continue her law studies. At the end of the year she was voted France's favourite female star, over Annabella, Garbo, Miss Temple and Edwige Feuillère.

She was not the only French star to go to Hollywood at this time. Annabella went and so, less successfully, did Mireille Balin, Tino Rossi, Georges Rigaud and Jacqueline Laurent. But she was certainly the most illustrious of those who went then. Under its top producer, Joe Pasternak, Universal fashioned for her *The Rage of Paris* (38), the story of a penniless French girl stranded in New York and searching for a rich husband, aided and subsidized by a head waiter and an ex-chorine. After announcing Melvyn Douglas, Franchot Tone and then Joel McCrea as her co-star, Douglas Fairbanks Jr co-starred and the ads challenged: 'Fifty Million Frenchmen Can't Be Wrong!' It was a fine film and her notices were good; but before it was shown she had shaken the Hollywood dust from her feet and was back in Paris. Universal offered her $300,000 to stay, but she claimed that she had signed contracts for her next two French films. The first was *Katia*, made in Hungary, a reasonably successful return to the mood and romance of *Mayerling*: her tragic partner this time was John Loder, as Tsar Alexander II, and she was the countess who loved him till his assassination. Maurice Tourneur directed. Her husband directed *Retour à l'Aube*, from a Vicki Baum novel, about the wife of a Hungarian station-master who has 24 hours of adventure on a shopping expedition to Budapest.

She had preferred that to *French Can-Can* and the company which had announced that film sued her. Simultaneously, RKO sued her, in Paris, for breach of contract. Finally, in July 1939, Universal lost patience and sued. At first it refused to believe that she did not want to return, but since October they had been waiting for her to arrive to start *Rio*. They claimed that their contract gave them exclusive right to her services, but Darrieux and Decoin countered that there was a clause to the effect that it did not become exclusive till the matter of her earlier contract with Ciné-Alliance was settled. Litigation dragged on, while Ciné-Alliance produced her next vehicle, a remoulding by Decoin of an Italian comedy made a few months earlier (Mario Camerini's *Batticuore*, with John Lodge and Assia Norris): a delightful comedy about a girl in a school of pickpockets, *Battement de Coeur* (40). Claude Dauphin was the nice young millionaire who made her heart beat faster. Before it was made, Rabinovitsch announced that the following Darrieux film would be made in French and English, but the war put paid to that – as well as the differences with Universal.

The Germans occupied Paris, and Decoin and Darrieux made their next film for them – for their company, Continentale – the first film to be made under the Occupation: *Premier Rendezvous* (41), about an orphan who runs away to join her pen-pal but finds him middle-aged (Fernand Ledoux) but with an attractive young nephew (Louis Jourdan). All the Decoin-Darrieux comedies were fresh and confident – this particular one was sentimental, a species at which the French were not very good. It was also permeated with sadness, for it was known that after this the team would split. Leo Joannon directed *Caprices* (42), with François Périer, Paul Meurisse – and Albert Préjean, who thought the magic of the old partnership no longer worked. It was a comedy *à l'Américaine* and it did not work either. André Cayatte made his début as a director on *La Fausse Maîtresse*, a modernization of Balzac in which the star, to her credit, seemed lost. It was made by Continentale and so bad that she decided not to film till the war was over. She and Decoin were divorced and in 1942 she married playboy and diplomat Porfirio Rubirosa.

She returned to show business in 1945 in 'Tristan et Iseult' with Alain Cuny, which played 50 performances despite vociferously vocal audiences objecting to Lucien Favre's treatment of the legend. In films her place remained unusurped. Michèle Morgan returned from Hollywood, Arletty and Viviane Romance were there from the pre-war years, but of the new ingénues (Madeleine Sologne, Giselle Pascal, Odette Joyeux) only Micheline Presle had imposed herself. The public welcomed her back in *Adieu Chérie* (45), with Louis Salou, exactly the sort of light entertainment sought by the liberated French, but the next two flopped: Marcel L'Herbier's *Au Petit Bonheur* (46), with Périer and André Luguet, as a jealous wife, a stagy version of a successful stage comedy; and *Bethsabée* (47), a pretentious drama with Georges Marchal, as an adventuress on a Foreign Legion outpost. On the stage she had a big success in 'L'Amour Vient en Jouant', with Pierre Louis, who was briefly her fiancé. In 1948 she and Rubirosa were divorced and she married her present husband, a non-professional. On screen she looked ravishing in Christian Bérard's costumes as the Spanish queen in *Ruy Blas* (48), with Jean Marais, and she was enchanting in Madeleine Renaud's old part in a new version of Marcel Achard's

Danielle Darrieux as a Parisian cocotte in Occupe-toi d'Amélie *(49) – advice, that is, given by a foolish young officer to his best friend, Jean Desailly, who decides that they should go through a mock wedding for his own selfish ends. This being based on a farce by Feydeau, the complications do not end there; they were handled in glittering, imaginative style by the director, Claude Autant-Lara.*

fantasy, *Jean de la Lune* (49), with Périer and Dauphin. On-stage she did Anouilh's 'Leocadia' and her screen career revived with an unexpected role, in *Occupe-toi d'Amélie*, Autant-Laura's cunning version of a Feydeau farce – frankly theatrical, taken at breakneck speed, with Darrieux perfect as the doll-like Amélie.

She enhanced her reputation by her witty playing of The Married Women in Max Ophüls's version of Arthur Schnitzler's 'Reigen', *La Ronde* (50), sharing her scenes with Daniel Gélin (student) and Fernand Gravey (husband); then she left to make *Romanzo d'Amore* in Italy, playing Princess Louise of Saxony whose affair with composer Toselli (Rossano Brazzi) once scandalized all Europe. MGM – her old producer, Pasternak – beckoned for a musical, *Rich Young and Pretty* (51), in the part of Jane Powell's mother (Hollywood did not let its own 34-year-old stars play mother roles). She walked off with it, deliciously warbling a couple of songs as well as a duet with Fernando Lamas. In France, there was a play called 'Evangéline' and then Carlo Rim's excellent period piece, *La Maison Bonnadieu*, as Bernard Blier's flighty wife. Then she did her first screen prostitute – one of the *pensionnaires* of the Maison Tellier in the middle episode of Ophüls's three-part *Le Plaisir*, based on stories by de Maupassant: beautifully done, a small part, partnered by Jean Gabin as her 'admirer'. After 20 years' stardom apiece this was their first teaming; they made up for lost time by co-starring in *La Vérité sur Bébé Donge* (52), directed by Decoin from a novel by Simenon, a harsh and fascinating study of an unhappy marriage. In Hollywood she was the double-crossing countess in *Five Fingers*, opposite James Mason, and in France one of the *Adorables Créatures* in the life of Daniel Gélin (others: Renée Faure, Martine Carol, the present and future wives of the director Christian-Jaque). Then she did Autant-Lara's interesting *Le Bon Dieu sans Confession* (53), with Henri Vilbert in the title-role – a series of flashbacks, with Darrieux as the mistress of the deceased.

There were and are times when she rarely seems to bother, especially in drama, but Ophüls knew how to use her in her passive

Danielle Darrieux as Madame De . . . *(53), who starts off a sad sequence of events when she pawns her ear-rings. Her husband retrieves them, gives them to his mistress, who sells them; they are bought by an Italian diplomat who will present them to Madame De . . .*

mood. She acknowledged once that she did her best work for him; she liked working with him and admitted that he made her work harder. She was probably never more of an enchantress than in his lovingly made *Madame De ...*, taken from an ironic/ sentimental *conte* by Louise de Vilmorin, about a lady of fashion, her husband (Boyer), her lover (Vittorio De Sica) and a pair of pawned diamond ear-rings. With that she probably reached the highest point of her postwar prestige outside France. The next two were not exported: *Châteaux en Espagne* (54), with Maurice Ronet, as a French secretary involved with a bullfighter; and *Escalier de Service*, an all-star comedy centred upon Etchika Choureau as a maid. Autant-Lara used her again in *Le Rouge et le Noir* with Gérard Philipe, playing Mme de Renal – her favourite role – with a serenity and some slight ardour. Then she did another for her ex-husband, *Bonnes à Tuer* (55), an engaging thriller, as the intended victim of philanderer Michel Auclair (Corinne Calvet was another). She put in a brief fictional appearance in Sacha Guitry's *Napoléon* and then was wasted as Richard Burton's mother in *Alexander the Great*. Decoin directed her in *L'Affaire des Poisons* (originally to have been made by Autant-Lara with Michèle Morgan and Madeleine Robinson), an account of the scandal which rocked the Court of Louis XIV and indeed the nation; she played Mme de Montespan and Viviane Romance was the chief of the accused. Marc Allégret directed *L'Amant de Lady Chatterley* (56), a shabby version of a certain English novel, with Leo Genn as Sir Clifford and Erno Crisa as the famous game-keeper. She was Agnès Sorel in *Si Paris Nous Était Conté*, another of those panoramic slices of Guitry history so popular in France; and then in *Typhon sur Nagasaki*, the first French-Japanese co-production, as the former mistress of Jean Marais, trying to woo him back from Nippon customs and a girl. It was considerably more rewarding than any Hollywood excursion into the Orient.

Le Salaire du Péché was a tense thriller with Jean-Claude Pascal and Jeanne Moreau, and *Pot-Bouille* (57) was a comedy based on Zola, with Darrieux as the widowed employer of Gérard Philipe. There followed a run of competent entertainments: *Le Septième Ciel*, a comedy with Noël-Noël; *Le Désordre et la Nuit* (58), with Gabin, in what was basically a supporting role; *La Vie à Deux*, an episode in this all-star movie, with Robert Lamoureux; *Drôle de Dimanche* with Bourvil; and *Marie-Octobre* (59), directed by Duvivier, a wan thriller about a reunion of ex-Resistance workers – Blier, Serge Reggiani, Lino Ventura, Paul Guers, Paul Meurisse, etc. She was the widow who knew which one had betrayed her husband and the film was a big success. After playing a middle-aged woman looking after blind Jean-Claude Brialy in *Les Yeux de l'Amour* she did another thriller as ingenious – and as dull: *Meurtre en 45 Tours* (60), from a Boileau and Narcejac novel about a husband who sends his recorded voice from the grave. She co-starred with Mel Ferrer in *L'Homme à Femmes* and guested in another frivolous look at history, *Vive Henri IV, Vive L'Amour* (61) – and if you blinked, you missed her. There was an offer from Britain, *The Greengage Summer*, as Kenneth More's bad-tempered and possibly lesbian mistress. She gave the part what it deserved.

Les Lions sont Lâchés was basically the same formula as *Adorables Créatures* (and a dozen other French movies) with Brialy this time as the young man set loose among several female stars. They included Michèle Morgan, whose popularity remained extraordinary. That is one reason why there were so many roles for middle-aged actresses; Darrieux, Feuillère, Signoret, Presle all remained popular and cynical producers knew that what one turned down another would take. In *Les Bras de la Nuit* (62) Darrieux murdered her husband and had detective Roger Hanin fall in love with her; after which she, Morgan, Feuillère and Annie Girardot had an episode each of *Le Crime ne Paie pas*, of which Darrieux's – with Richard Todd – was the worst: quite an achievement. Nor was she better served by *Le Diable et les Dix Commandements*, briefly in a sketch as Alain Delon's Maman; nor by Chabrol's *Landru* (63), where she and Morgan were two of that gentleman's victims. If there were better parts for ladies *d'un certain âge*, they were not to be found in *Méfiez-vous Mesdames* with Paul Meurisse, where she played an ageing swindler; the all-star *Pourquoi Paris?*; or *Du Grabuge chez les Veuves* (64), a *comédie noire* with Dany Carrel, as a fading beauty trying to hang on to her gigolo. All the same she was good in the last and she was at the same time delighting Paris in 'La Robe Mauve de Valentine', a boulevard comedy with aspirations (by Françoise Sagan). She began to branch out as a singer, both on record and in concert.

There was another ordinary film, *Patate*, with Marais and Pierre Dux, but then came Jean Cayrol's interesting *Le Coup de Grâce* (65), about a collaborator (Michel Piccoli) returning to the town where he betrayed his colleagues to the Germans; Darrieux was his wife. *L'Or du Duc*, with Pierre Brasseur, was indifferent stuff, but then there was the good *Le Dimanche de la Vie*, sympathetically directed by Jean Herman from a novel by Raymond Queneau – a study of a *quartier* of Paris on the verge of World War II, with Françoise Arnoul and Darrieux as her older sister. Some years earlier she had turned down the role of the mother in Demy's successful *Les Parapluies de Cherbourg*; when Demy came to do the follow-up, *Les Demoiselles de Rochefort* (67), she agreed to play the mother (of the Dorléac sisters): it was a smaller role and, ironically, the film flopped. Her luck was out also with *L'Homme à la Buick* (68), co-starring at last with another hero of longevity, Fernandel; but it was in (sort-of) with *24 Heures de la Vie d'une Femme*. Zweig's story had been filmed many times before, but never so ravishingly – in colour, in the Italian lakes; it was about the love affair between an ageing beauty and a young man, but the director, Dominique Delouche, seemed only interested in the young man and Darrieux reacted accordingly. Equally uninterestedly, she played a lesbian madame in *Les Oiseux Vont Mourir au Pérou*, with Jean Seberg. *La Maison de Campagne* (69) was a farce about a couple who want a country cottage – a contrasting couple, he (Jean Richard) down-to-earth, she a bourgeois snob.

In 1970 she replaced Katharine Hepburn on Broadway in 'Coco' but despite excellent personal notices the show did not run. The following year she appeared in a musical adaptation of Henry James, 'Ambassador', with Howard Keel, in London: a show quite unworthy of either of them. In Paris she appeared on the stage in 'Folie Douce' (72) and her subsequent film appearances were not memorable: *No Encontre Rosas para mi Madre* (73), in Spain; *La Divine* (75), a dim tale about a star, directed by Delouche; and *L'Année Sainte* (76), in a smallish role as an old flame of Jean Gabin. In 1978 she was in a Feydeau double-bill, 'On Purge Bébé' and 'Mais ne te Promène Donc pas Toute Nue', and in a TV series, 'Miss'. She had another subsidiary role in *Le Cavaleur* (79), Philippe de Broca's sequel to his *Le Farceur*, but with Jean Rochefort in the Jean-Pierre Cassel role because Cassel was not suitable. After returning to the stage in a revival of 'La Bonne Soupe' (80), she starred in *En Haut des Marches* (82), in a role written for her by producer Paul Vecchiali whose favourite actress she is: a woman in Toulon in 1963 who wants vengeance for her husband, killed in 1945 for supposed Pétainist sympathies. Then Demy called for her again to play a mother in another film entirely sung, but *Une Chambre en Ville* was meant to be the reverse of his earlier pretty musicals – very dark, with Darrieux as a petty, frustrated woman whose lodger (Richard Berry) has an affair with her daughter (Dominique Sanda). The result was even

Danielle Darrieux in the late '60s.

worse – incredibly – than *Les Demoiselles de Rochefort*. She looked glamorous as the courtesan in 'Gigi' (85), Colette's translation of Anita Loos's play based on her novel, and then anything but in *Le Lieu de la Crime* (86) as Catherine Deneuve's mother (again). It was not a question of looking frumpish, but of having decided that this countrywoman would just be absolutely ordinary. It was odd to think that this old lady could be seen in her old movies as a girl – perhaps the only star to rival Lillian Gish in that respect. She received excellent notices for her playing an alcoholic amateur detective in *Corps et Bien*, an otherwise humourless exercise in style based on 'Deadlier Than the Male'. There was another play, 'Adorable Julia', the ever-ready role for ageing actresses (based on Maugham's 'Theatre'), and a TV series about lawyers with Georges Wilson, 'Bonjour Maître'. *Le Font dans les Nuages* (88) was a tele-movie with Annie Girardot; it was followed by Claude Sautet's *Quelques Jours Avec Moi*, in which Darrieux was the mother of supermarket heir Daniel Auteuil; and *Bille en Tête* (89), with Kristin Scott-Thomas.

Doris Day

Warner Bros were singularly unlucky with their star-making in the 40s and this was nowhere more apparent than in their musicals: they seemed either to rely on – the always reliable – Janis Paige or to borrow June Haver from 20th. Doris Day was probably their happiest accident. They had one of their routine musicals on the stocks and had negotiated to borrow Betty Hutton, who became pregnant. Day was at that time a fairly successful band-singer and her agent took her to Warners for a test, conducted by Michael Curtiz who was due to direct the Hutton musical. She cried throughout, but at Curtiz's urging she got the part at an unenthusiastic $500 a week. He signed her to a personal contract and when later WB bought up his company, she was its major asset. Her agent knew she had something: 'People could identify themselves with Alice (Faye), and they can with Doris. Because any girl in the world could be Doris Day, and she could be any girl.'

She was born Doris Kappelhoff in Cincinnati in 1924. She had hoped to be a dancer but in her teens was involved in an automobile accident which kept her in hospital for over a year; she began singing on local radio stations, graduated to vocalist with Bob Crosby's band and then with Les Brown – with whom she had a hit record, 'Sentimental Journey'; in the late 40s she sang with Frank Sinatra on the radio-networked 'Saturday Night Hit Parade'. Artie Shaw thought she had film potential and recommended her to RKO but they were not interested.

The film she tested for was *Romance on the High Seas* (48), a farce with Jack Carson and Janis Paige. It owed its (mild) success to Day's hit recording of one of its songs, 'It's Magic', and to nice notices from the press. The London 'Sunday Express' described her as a blend of Hutton, Judy Garland and Dolores Gray, which was not accurate but made people sit up. She was peppy, gay and sincere; and she loathed the Hutton hair and bounce they made her have. Warners rushed her into *My Dream is Yours* (49), a *Star is Born*-type musical, set in the radio studios, with Lee Bowman as an alcoholic singer; and *It's a Great Feeling*, in which she played the same part but was trying to crash Hollywood instead of radio. Little was required of her except to be sunny and sing (away from the stuidos at this time she also had a series of hit records) but she had a chance at straight acting in *Young Man With a Horn* (50), as a band-singer who befriends Kirk Douglas. *Tea for Two* was an enjoyable rehash of 'No No Nanette' with Gordon MacRae and they were teamed again in the James Cagney musical, *The West Point Story*. She did not sing at all in *Storm Warning*, where she was Ginger Rogers's sister and got bumped off by the Ku Klux Klan.

Warners had planned to borrow June Haver for *Lullaby of Broadway* (51), but Day was clearly a bigger star – and was becoming the biggest one of the lot. At the end of the year she would be trailing Betty Grable as the most popular female star in the US and in 1952 the box-office lists would reveal her as the biggest female attraction (and she began to make the popularity polls in Britain). She was helped possibly by Marty Melcher who was her agent and became her third husband around this time – and who was to guide her career until his death in 1968. Certainly he saw to it that her salary had reached $2,500 a week in 1952. The films that helped her to the top were nothing special, including this *Lullaby of Broadway*, where she innocently believed that has-been mother Gladys George was still a famous singer. *On Moonlight Bay* was based on Booth Tarkington's 'Penrod' stories (Billy Gray was Penrod) and it managed, in the words of Richard Winnington, 'to last for 95 minutes with one song, no plot, an air of faint family charm and Doris Day as an exponent of teenage love'.

Of *Starlift*, where Day was much in evidence as herself, Winnington wrote: 'Several gallant stars are seen distributing a portion of their glamour to the boys on the way to and back from the Korean front – while being paid to act in the film which you pay to see. As in *Hollywood Canteen* the stars (and Warner Bros) glow with emotion at their own generosity while the boys and their officers swoon with gratitude. "Operation Nausea".' The level hardly rose with two tearful biopics: *I'll See You in My Dreams* (52), cliché-packed but likeable, about songwriter Gus Kahn (Danny Thomas), and *The Winning Team*, about baseball star Grover Cleveland Alexander (Ronald Reagan). *April in Paris* had Ray Bolger, a tastaeless plot about a couple who think they are married and are not, and every possible joke about Gay Paree. *By the Light of the Silvery Moon* (53) was a sequel to *On Moonlight Bay*, again with Gordon MacRae.

Today on TV these films inevitably look even worse than they did then; and Day's fluffy, eager-to-please, ingenuous charm is not always easier to take than they are. Ironically, the one film where she was good, and which was fairly good itself, was not a hit in the US when it came out: *Calamity Jane* with Howard Keel. It was indeed a pseudo-'Annie Get Your Gun' but in Britain the critics liked it and it was one of the year's top box-office films (a hit song, 'Secret Love', helped). Paul Dehn wrote that its success was due to Day 'who, emerging in a stinging temper from the honeycomb of sickly sweet pictures that have recently been her lot, gives the performance of her life as a wild Western shrew magnificently worth the taming. . . . She takes the script between her perfect teeth and makes off at a graceful gallop for the foothills of real stardom. By the end, she is within hailing distance of Ginger Rogers and Judy Garland.'

Warners signed her to a lucrative new contract and put her into *Lucky Me* (54), a 'putting-on-a-show' musical with Phil Silvers

Gordon MacRae and Doris Day were co-starred in a series of unpretentious musicals in the early 50s. This is a better moment from the least of them, Starlift *(51), all about a crowd of Warner Bros stars going to entertain the troops in Korea.*

Doris Day's perky charms and real abilities as a singer-actress were often wasted in adolescent romances or tear-jerking biopics. Allowed to let go in Calamity Jame *(53) she proved her ability. She, of course, was Calam, feudin' and lovin' Howard Keel as Wild Bill Hickock.*

and Robert Cummings. 'Lucky you!' lied the advertisements, adding 'it's Doris Day in the first CinemaScope musical' (in fact, it was only shot in that process at the last minute and looked like it). Slightly better was *Young at Heart* with Frank Sinatra, a musical remake of *Four Daughters*. WB announced another remake, *The Jazz Singer*, with Danny Thomas, but Day balked. To her reported fury the part went to another blonde singing star, Peggy Lee, who went on to get an Oscar nomination for *Pete Kelly's Blues* but did not make it in films – though she proved to be a more durable star on disc than Day. Also in 1952 WB had under contract another fine record star, Jo Stafford, but never used her. Melcher negotiated to free Day from the contract and it was finally dissolved with four years to go.

MGM signed her for one film at $150,000 plus 10 per cent of the gross after costs had been recouped; *Love Me or Leave Me* (55). It had once been planned for Ava Gardner, so it was not surprising when MGM advertised it as the 'Dawn of a new Day!' – she was painted up as a torch-singer getting heart-burn over being married to big-time hoodlum James Cagney (a not entirely accurate biography of 20s vocalist Ruth Etting). It was a big success and MGM signed her for five films for a total of $900,000 – to be spread over 10 years if necessary. However, she went to Paramount for Hitchcock's remake of his own *The Man Who Knew Too Much* (56), as James Stewart's worried wife – a state she reprised in *Julie*, where she discovered that second husband Louis Jourdan had murdered her first and had like plans for her. She returned to musicals and Warners – for $250,000 – for *The Pajama Game* (57), a lively version of the Broadway hit with the same cast except for her role (Janis Paige, ironically, had done it on stage). Then she jumped to comedies: *Teacher's Pet* (58), a clash between old-hand reporter Clark Gable and a young teacher of journalism; *The Tunnel of Love* – a long dark slog and a mile from Peter de Vries's novel, with Richard Widmark; and *It Happened to Jane* (59) with Jack Lemmon, a Capraesque comedy which was perhaps the best she made.

But it was not by any means a hit. *Pillow Talk*, which she did at Universal with Rock Hudson, was: a candy-coated concoction about an interior decorator chased by the wolf who shares her party line. At MGM there was another comedy, *Please Don't Eat the Daisies* (60), which, predictably, concocted a plot about a dramatist (David Niven) and his wife from Jean Kerr's bestselling and light-hearted essays; and at Universal a frightened-wife thriller, *Midnight Lace*. Day stayed at Universal to make another comedy with Hudson, *Lover Come Back* (62). She was now in the midst of a series of comedies which were to make box-office history – her profit participation is reckoned to have brought her $1 million per film, for the early ones, at least. There was a big one with Cary Grant, *That Touch of Mink*. But at that point she decided she wanted to sing again and MGM dusted off *Billy Rose's Jumbo*, which they had had on the shelf for years – it turned out to be the one sour note in this box-office melody, despite sterling work by her, Jimmy Durante and Martha Raye (male lead Stephen Boyd was no help). As a result Day lost both *The Sound of Music* and *The Unsinkable Molly Brown*. (MGM had bought the latter for her.)

In the latter part of the 50s, Doris Day demonstrated both versatility and talent: then she got mired down again, in a series of successful but rather tired comedies. This is the first of the series, Pillow Talk *(59), with Rock Hudson.*

The comedies were virtually indistinguishable, and even though made at three different studios – Universal, 20th and MGM – seemed to have the same expensive cars and furnishings. Wit was purely secondary. They were vaguely salacious and completely vacuous. Publicists hopefully talked of Carole Lombard, Myrna Loy or Irene Dunne, but critics did not. Day could certainly play comedy, but the situations made her crisp style seem positively arch. She – and more particularly her apparent regard for her virginity – became a butt for comics, a cruel fate for the cheery heroine of her best old musicals. Not that the public cared; after some years' absence she had returned to the top 10 draws in 1959 and stayed through to 1966. She was top on four of these occasions, a remarkable achievement, and one which might entitle her to be considered the most successful of the stars who came up after the war. Norman Jewison, who directed *The Thrill of It All* (63), with James Garner, said: 'Some critics branded her as a kind of artificial girl-next-door, but I found Doris an extremely exciting actress to work with. For instance, she's marvellous at improvisation.'

Day and Garner were also teamed in *Move Over Darling*, which had originally done service as *My Favorite Wife*, and had been started under a different title by Marilyn Monroe before her death. Day reteamed with

Doris Day about the time she quit movies for television.

Hudson for *Send Me No Flowers* (64) and then with Rod Taylor for a couple, *Do Not Disturb* (65) and *The Glass-Bottom Boat* (66); but the series was grinding to a box-office halt. *Caprice* (67), with Richard Harris, did not help, and *The Ballad of Josie* (68), a comedy Western, bypassed the press and went straight out on double bills. 'Time Magazine''s review of *Where Were You When the Lights Went Out?* contained a phrase which surprised no one: 'Doris Day's fans, if there are any left . . .' However, this one, based on the New York power failure of 1967, did stop the rot and the next one was not a disaster, *With Six You Get Eggroll* (69), with Brian Keith and the same premise as Lucille Ball's concurrent *Yours Mine and Ours*.

Melcher produced it and died after completion. Miss Day's first shock was to find that he had committed her to a TV series, 'The Doris Day Show', with a concept she loathed. It was so successful that she did it for five years, until she told CBS that she was leaving in 1974. She later said that she was glad to be working, since there were a number of other shocks – including the fact she was virtually penniless; as she says in her bestselling autobiography (75), she learnt what the rest of Hollywood had known for years – that Melcher had been ripping her off during all the years he had managed her, even taking $50,000 for himself whenever he arranged a deal. She quotes Les Brown: 'Melcher was an awful man, pushy, grating on the nerves, crass, money-hungry. He lived off Patty Andrews; then, when Doris came along and looked like a better ticket, he glommed onto her.' Fortunately, she had redress and she sued Jerome Rosenthal, who had been attorney for herself and Melcher: and in 1974 the courts awarded her over $22 million damages against Rosenthal and others. Her memoir discloses that her relationship with Melcher was 'without physical love', and bears witness to his mishandling of her career except for his own financial gain; it regained for her America's respect, lost when he had forced her into films she had not wanted to do (one he turned down was *The Graduate* – the Anne Bancroft role). She remarried briefly in 1976 and devoted herself to animal causes. She said that she had not retired, but was in no hurry to return to work – which would seem to be in a 1989 tele-movie, *Running Mates*.

James Dean

There is not much to be said about James Dean beyond the fact that, like Queen Anne, he is dead. He was a shuffling, mumbling actor and because of that was branded Brando's successor – but in his three films he displayed little of the power and less of the versatility that had distinguished Brando's first three film ventures. He was very intense, but always in full command of his limited range. He had something of the innocence and defencelessness of a puppy, but despite this was a kicker – a somewhat inarticulate one, admittedly – against the pricks of parental and other authority. It is not perhaps surprising that with his sudden death a cult arose – the Cult of Youth in full cry. This has tended to obscure his genuine promise. Had he lived, he might have been (unlike Queen Anne) good at his job.

He was born in Fairmount, Indiana, in 1931. His mother died when he was nine and he was brought up by an aunt. While at high school he won the Indiana State Dramatic Contest doing a monologue. He went on to UCLA and while there joined a drama group run by actor James Whitmore – and got bit parts in three movies, *Fixed Bayonets* (51), *Sailor Beware* and *Has Anybody Seen My Gal?* (52). Whitmore encouraged him to study for the Actors' Studio, but in New York Dean could only get work as an extra on TV, just another bisexual adventurer. He signed on as a sailor on Lemuel Ayer's sloop and Ayers put him on Broadway in 'See the Jaguar', which

James Dean and Raymond Massey in East of Eden *(55), one of several father-son confrontations in Kazan's film. Kazan didn't like Dean, but he commented later: 'There was a value in Dean's face. His face is so desolate and lonely and strange.'*

led to TV parts and the role of the blackmailing Arab lover in the play made from Gide's 'The Immoralist'. Elia Kazan saw him and signed him at $18,000, for the role of Cal in *East of Eden* (55), which might have been the Original Mixed-up Kid – a boy suffering the pangs of despis'd love (parents, brother). It was overdirected by Kazan from part of a novel by Steinbeck. Hedda Hopper sat through it 'spellbound. I couldn't remember ever having seen a young man with such power, so many facets of expression, so much sheer invention as this actor'. 'Picturegoer' readers voted him their Best Actor award.

Nicholas Ray's *Rebel Without a Cause* had the same theme, but transferred to modern California. A whole generation, reputedly, found it mirrored their conflicts (it was not a patch on *The Young Stranger*, shown around the same time). William Whitebait found Dean's performance 'wholly his own, more electric to my mind than any of Marlon Brando's'. There had been friction between Ray and Dean, between the studio and Dean, and there would be between him and his next director, George Stevens. (His biographer and room-mate for five years, William Bast, admits that Dean was difficult and uncooperative.) Steven's *Giant* (56) was a saga of three generations of Texans, from a novel by Edna Ferber. Dean had to age from youthful cowhand to menacing old oil tycoon, and he did it with some resource. The day after his own part was completed, in September 1955, he ran into another car in his brand-new Porsche and was killed instantly. *East of Eden* had just begun to go the rounds (all three films did good business, especially *Giant*).

He had been due to start rehearsals two days later for 'The Corn is Green' on TV; and was scheduled for *Somebody Up There Likes Me* (at a fee of $100,000) and *The Sea Wall*. Warners, who had made his three films and had him under a six-year contract, were inundated with mail – letters of mourning, requests for souvenirs (a year after his death they were still receiving 5,000-6,000 a week). There had been nothing like it since the death of Valentino. Hundreds of James Dean Appreciation Societies sprang up and to appease them Warners put together a compilation documentary, *The James Dean Story* (57); and they netted considerable amounts from reissues of the three films over the next 10 years.

His following has not decreased with the

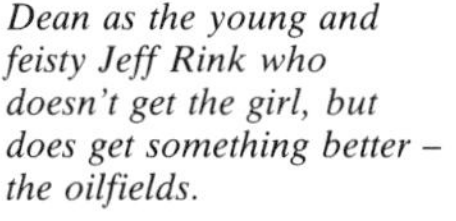

Dean as the young and feisty Jeff Rink who doesn't get the girl, but does get something better – the oilfields.

James Dean in classic Rebel Without a Cause *pose.*

years. Unlike, say, Valentino, who soon seemed horribly old-fashioned, Dean appeals to each new generation, despite revelations about his life in the many, many books about him. As 'Modern Screen' once put it: 'There were reports of a wild lifestyle including visits to S&M clubs, constant use of marijuana and bizarre sexual liaisons. His rude behaviour was well known and it was obvious to many an observer he was on his way downhill.' Kazan recalled: 'What I disliked was the Dean legend. He was the glorification of hatred and sickness. When he got success he was victimized by it. He was a hero to the people who saw him only as a little waif, when actually he was a pudding of hatred.'

Sandra Dee

In the 30s the teenage element in films was more or less restricted to the likes of Deanna Durbin and Mickey Rooney in agreeable family comedies. After World War II the teenage delinquent – though by no means a new discovery (what else was Rooney in *Boy's Town*?) – took on supremacy, from Ann Blyth's nastiness in *Mildred Pierce* to the young thugs of *The Blackboard Jungle*. But Youth, increasingly important in the eyes of the studio accountants, yearned to see itself portrayed more sympathetically. The teenage film became common fare in the later 50s, a wide spectrum that went from drag-car gangs via surf-parties to the 1920ish *Tammy*. As most of them were low-budget, it was hardly to be expected that their players had staying power. But one teenage star, Sandra Dee, was astonishingly successful.

She was born Alexandra Zuck in Bayonne, New Jersey, in 1942. A successful Conover model at the age of 12, she was subsequently one of the country's top models and cover girls. Her agency got her into TV and TV commercials. Meanwhile, in Hollywood, Universal producer Ross Hunter balked at paying Warners $200,000 to borrow Natalie Wood for the remake of *Imitation of Life*: he resolved to find his own teenager and pay her infinitely less. He discovered Sandra Dee on a New York sidewalk. Universal did not like her, so Ross put her under personal contract at $300 a week. However, officially: 'A producer at Universal was attracted by some photographs of the young girl, as he was searching for just such a girl to star in a new film.'

Hunter managed to persuade MGM to borrow her for the role of the youngest sister in *Until They Sail* (57): she turned out to be pert, pretty and indistinguishable from a million other girls. All the same, MGM kept her for *The Relulctant Débutante* (58), in the title-role, an American-educated girl being launched into London society. She was partnered by John Saxon, also from Universal, and they were both inadequate. At some point Hunter managed to sell her contract to the company which liked them together and put them into a teenage soap opera with Teresa Wright as her mother: *The Restless Years* – which became *The Wonderful Years* in Britain, for unfathomable reasons. Helmut Kautner directed it and he also made *A Stranger in My Arms* (59), where Dee supported June Allyson. She finally made the film she had been signed for, *Imitation of Life*, as Lana Turner's neglected daughter, and it was a big success. She left behind her cute and cuddly personality to play a hellcat in *The Wild and the Innocent*, an Audie Murphy Western, but had it back with a vengeance as Columbia's *Gidget*, the teenage film to end all teenage films. Only it did not: it was so successful that Columbia planned a sequel, *Gidget Goes Hawaiian* – but Universal refused to loan her as they wanted her for their Tammy, a role vacated by Debbie Reynolds. Meanwhile, she was loaned to Warners to co-star with Troy Donahue in *A Summer Place*; she was Lana Turner's step-daughter in *Portrait in Black* (60) and Juliet, the American ambassador's daughter in *Romanoff and Juliet* (61).

In 1960 she married singer Bobby Darin (it ended in divorce in 1967) and was voted one of the top 10 money-makers – as she was again the following year, due to *Tammy Tell Me True* (61) and *Come September*, though in the latter she and Darin were second leads (it starred Rock Hudson and Gina Lollobrigida). Thousands of girls saw her as their ideal representative and Dee's agent jubilantly negotiated a new seven-year deal with Universal. They put her into another innocuous comedy with Darin, *If a Man Answers* (62), notable only for the presence of Micheline Presle as her mother, and then into *Tammy and the Doctor* (63) with Peter Fonda as the doctor. 20th borrowed her to play James Stewart's daughter in *Take Her She's Mine* and then she did a literal remake of *It Started With Eve* called *I'd Rather Be Rich* (64), with Andy Williams and Robert Goulet. She was supposed to do a serious film for Hunter, *The Twelfth of Never*, but instead did another comedy with her husband, *That Funny Feeling* (65), a title which did not exactly tie in with what was happening on screen. Further, it did even less business than the last three Dee films and, after a supporting role in *A Man Could Get Killed* (66), a thriller with Melina Mercouri, she and Universal parted company. She said she would seek 'more challenging roles' as a freelance.

After an interval, she did one of these more challenging roles, in MGM's *Doctor You've Got To Be Kidding* (67), a comedy interchangeable with those she had been doing. Ross Hunter asked her back to play Rosalind Russell's chummy granddaughter in *Rosie!* (68); then after a TV movie, *The Man Hunter* (69), she was in an unimportant – but good – AIP picture, *The Dunwich Horror* (70) with Dean Stockwell. Then she did one in Italy, *Ad Est di Marsa Matruh* (71), and she was in a TV movie, *Daughters of Joshua McCabe* (72). In 1976 she toured in 'Sabrina Fair.' There was another tele-movie, *Fantasy Island* (77), as a guest there of Ricardo Montalban, and she was later in an episode of 'Police Woman' (79). In 1982 she was reported to be in Utah making an independent film, *Skipper*, but it seems never to have been shown.

Sandra Dee in one of the sophomoric romances she made during her brief career in films: A Summer Place *(59), with Troy Donahue (another forgotten name).*

ALAIN DELON

'I am not a star. I am an actor. I have been fighting for ten years to make people forget that I am just a pretty boy with a beautiful face. It's a hard fight but I will win it. I want the public to realize that above all I am an actor, a very professional one who loves every minute of being in front of the camera, but who becomes very miserable the instant the director shouts "Cut!" ': Alain Delon, quoted in 'Films and Filming'.

Delon was born in Sceaux, a suburb of Paris, in 1935. His parents were divorced when he was four and he was farmed out to foster-parents. When they died, his parents shared him, but the arrangement proved unsatisfactory and he was sent away to school. He was expelled from several and once tried to run away; in the end he worked in his stepfather's delicatessen. At 17 he joined the marines and served in Indo-China as a parachutist. On demobilization he frequented, he said, 'les gangsters' of Marseilles. He went to Paris, where he was introduced to Jean-Claude Brialy and Brialy, than a budding actor, invited Delon to accompany him to the Cannes Film Festival of 1957. At Cannes he made friends and was reputedly offered a screen test which carried with it a seven-year contract with David O. Selznick; he was also offered a small role in an Edwige Feuillère vehicle, *Quand la Femme s'en Mêle* (58), and he accepted the latter. This brought a role in *Sois Belle et Tais-toi* starring Henri Vidal and Mylène Demongeot, followed by the lead opposite Romy Schneider in a period romance, *Christine* (59). Michel Boisrond chose him for two mediocre comedies, *Faibles Femmes*, top-billed with Pascale Petit, as a philanderer whom the women of the title want to murder, and *Le Chemin des Ecoliers* with Françoise Arnoul.

His luck held: René Clément chose him for one of the leads in a clever thriller adapted from a novel by Patricia Highsmith, *Plein Soleil* (60) – and it was considerably successful. Neither he nor Maurice Ronet were convincing as Americans, but he was okay as the impostor/murderer. After Clément, Visconti: *Rocco e i Suoi Fratelli*, as Rocco, one of a Sicilian family in Milan, the one who becomes a boxer – a monumental piece of miscasting in a melodrama with delusions of grandeur, and an old-fashioned one despite a graphic rape scene and a homosexual seduction. Said the 'MFB': 'Alain Delon's interpretation is totally unconvincing – a dreamy-eyed mediator, a puppy-fat masochist, all silent-suffering, guilt complexes and Ganymedean charm.' Visconti's patronage included a production of Ford's ' 'Tis Pity She's a Whore' in Paris for which he also did the décor and costumes. Opposite Delon was Romy Schneider, with whom his name was linked romantically: neither of them was ready for the stage. Nor was he any better as an Italian again in Clément's *Che Gioia Vivere* (61), a comedy set in the early days of Fascism: he was glum, straining hard to be an Italian rip. And his sequence with Brigitte Bardot in *Les Amours Célèbres* was inept every whichway.

Still, the big directors kept coming after him: now, Antonioni with *L'Eclisse* (62), a barren account of a bored couple in Rome (she was Monica Vitti). And Then Duvivier (if no longer very big) in his sketch film *Le Diable et les Dix Commandements*, with Danielle Darrieux in 'L'Inceste'. This run of mainly prestige films had ensured him fame and a certain popularity: he consolidated both with *Mélodie en Sous-Sol* (63), a big-budgeted gangster film with Jean Gabin. Delon bought the distribution rights in a couple of foreign territories – which, especially after some personal appearances to drum up business, gave him a taste for producing. Meanwhile, he had started *L'Echiquier de Dieu* for Raoul Levy, playing Marco Polo, but it was abandoned (Horst Buchholz later took on the part). And he worked for Visconti again, on *Il Gattopardo/The Leopard*, as the *jeune premier*, partnered by equally anodyne Claudia Cardinale. Said Dwight Macdonald: 'Alain Delon creates the same vacuum he did in *Purple Noon* [*Plein Soleil*] and *The Eclipse*'. After a new version of Dumas with Virna Lisi, *La Tulipe Noire* (64) swashbuckling in a double role, he returned to Clément for *Les Félins/Joy House/The Love Cage* as the intruder who inveigles himself into the affections of Jane Fonda. Then he became a producer, with *L'Insoumis*, directed by Alain Cavalier from a screenplay by himself and Jean Cau: he played an ex-legionnaire mixed up with the OAS, a young man gradually dying of a bullet wound. Legal difficulties caused the withdrawal of the film after a brief run and a revised version did badly, which was a pity, for this was his first good performance.

Meanwhile, his sights were beyond being a mere *French* film star. Neither *Il Gattopardo* nor *Les Félins*, in their English versions, had achieved the hoped-for success. He was offered the part of a gigolo who courts Shirley MacLaine in *The Yellow Rolls-Royce* (65) and then a couple of films in Hollywood. To his credit, he managed to get much publicity mileage from this and confidently predicted a big American future. He observed that he was equipped for an international career, while Jean-Paul Belmondo was not. He made *Once a Thief/Les Tueurs de San Francisco*, a Franco-US melodrama with Ann-Margret; *The Lost Command* (66) with Anthony Quinn, as an idealistic soldier sickened by war; *Paris Brûle-t-il?/Is Paris Burning?*, in France, directed by Clément; and *Texas Across the River*, a Western with Dean Martin.

Suddenly he was back in France: Robert Enrico's *Les Aventuriers* (67), a restating of that favourite French theme, masculine friendship, with Lino Ventura; and Jean-Pierre Melville's *Le Samourai*, as a ruthless killer in an ambitious gangster film whose cast included his wife, Nathalie. Also at this time he did a play in Paris, 'Les Yeux Crevés'. Then, still keeping up a terrific pace: Duvivier's last film, *Diaboliquement Vôtre* (68), a thriller in which Delon was an amnesiac; Louis Malle's episode 'William Wilson' in *Histoires Extraordinaires; La Motocylette/Girl on a Motorcycle*, a Franco-British co-production which had Marianne Faithfull, a one-time pop-star, in the title-role, Delon as a schoolteacher, poetic photography and infinite pretension; and *Adieu l'Ami*, a film about the friendship between two ex-legionnaires – the other was Charles Bronson.

In 1969, in the words of 'Photoplay', 'Alain and Nathalie were central figures in a scandal that threatened to expose some of the best-known figures in French show business and politics. His bodyguard was found dead from a bullet-wound and left on a rubbish-dump. Fantastic stores of drugs, murders and orgies floated around the French capital. . . . Gradually the furore died down . . . ' Delon, however, was cleared of all suspicion. At first the scandal threatened to destroy him, but he turned it to his own account, with that sharp intelligence which had distinguished his career and his public image. He had already made it clear that he felt most at home in the thrillers and gangster films he was now making and he emerged in interviews not only as a 'tough' actor, but a tough cookie in real life. On British TV he admitted that he had been homosexual, but his succeeding remarks suggested that this was one facet of a bizarre existence.

There was no harm done, either, when he was very publicly reunited with his ex-fiancée, Schneider, for *La Piscine* (69), a *dolce-vita* crime tale in which he again murdered Maurice Ronet. And the four films that followed were all gangster stories: *Jeff*, which he produced himself; *Le Clan des Siciliens*, again with Jean Gabin; and *Borsalino* (70), again producing, with Belmondo. Said 'Time Magazine': 'Delon moves through the picture like a still-warm stiff *en route* to a comfortable slab in the morgue, but Belmondo, mugging furiously and retaining just the right air of detachment, compensates by providing enough energy for this and at least three other movies.' The fourth was *Le Cercle Rouge*, with Yves Montand, directed by Melville, who observed, 'of course, he [Delon] is the cleverest actor in France today'.

These last three films were wild successes in France, and were expected to do as well abroad. They did not; but Delon still yearned for Hollywood success, saying that he was too young before. In 1970 he said, 'Now I'll be ready to go in two years, and I know what I'm going to do.' His ambition would not be helped by 'Variety''s comment on *Madly* (71), a feeble *ménage-à-trois* comedy: 'Delon lacks the timing and charm for this sort of role and clouds it by his more complex intimations of underlying violence.' The film flopped – but not quite as badly as *Doucement les Basses*, a comedy about a priest and his ex-wife (played by ex-wife Nathalie Delon). It was quite apparent that the French public would only go to see this former pretty boy as a *dur*. He returned to action in *Soleil Rouge/Red Sun*, a French 'Western' directed by Terence Young,

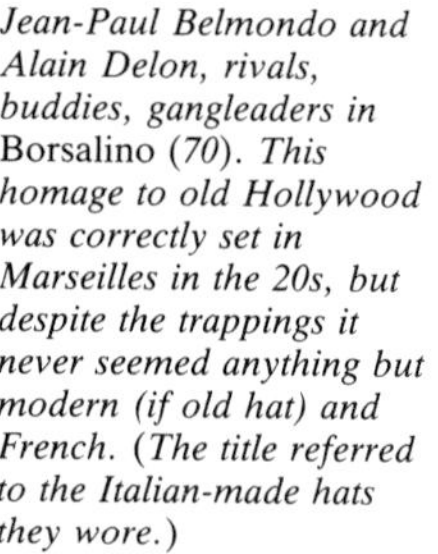

Jean-Paul Belmondo and Alain Delon, rivals, buddies, gangleaders in Borsalino *(70). This homage to old Hollywood was correctly set in Marseilles in the 20s, but despite the trappings it never seemed anything but modern (if old hat) and French. (The title referred to the Italian-made hats they wore.)*

as the villain, with Toshiro Mifune, and was suitably tough in *La Veuve Couderc*, opposite Simone Signoret (with whom, during shooting, he did not get on), playing a farmer who protects him from the police. He was against the law in *The Assassination of Trotsky* (72), as the murderer, with Richard Burton, but on the right side of it for once as *Un Flic*, a commissioner of police; Melville directed and Catherine Deneuve co-starred. In *La Prima Notte di Quiete*, in Italy, he was a professor involved in an adulterous affair; and in *Traitement de Choc* (73) a small town doctor who gives Annie Girardot rejuvenation treatment. The latter was directed by Alain Jessua, but it was such a falling-off from his earlier films that one could not too much regret the British release title, *Doctor in the Nude*. Delon was a hit man in a duff spy thriller, *Scorpio*, with Burt Lancaster; and as it was his last English language film for several years it was clear that Hollywood success was as far off as ever.

However, he remained a potent box-office name in his own and other countries: *Les Granges Brûlées*, once again on a farm with Signoret; the Franco-Italian *Tony Arzenta è Big Guns/Les Grands Fusils*, with Richard Conte, as a former hit man at bloody war with his Mafia bosses; *Deux Hommes dans la Ville*, reunited with Gabin; *Les Seins de Glace* (74), a complicated thriller, as a TV writer who meets a girl (Mireille Darc: his offscreen companion) who is the dead image of his own heroine; and *La Race des Seigneurs*, as a politician who sacrifices ambition for love. *Borsalino et Cie* was a sequel and since Belmondo was not in it (he had been killed off in the earlier one) it did not find its way to Britain or the US; but in France it was Delon at this time who headed the list of most popular actors, with Belmondo just behind. *Zorro* (75) was one of the swashbuckler remakes that have punctuated Delon's career; *Flic Story* and *Le Gitan* were two more of his run-of-the-mill thrillers: he was a detective in the former and in the latter of gypsy with a grudge against life. He had the title-role in *Mr Klein* (76), a case of confused identity between a Paris art dealer and a Jew the Nazis want to deport: in France this chic enigma had won a César for the year's best film, but in Britain and the US it was quicky recognized as the same lousy movie Losey had been making for years. Really, it was better to stick to straightforward thrillers, like *Comme un Boomerang*, playing a respectable man whose past is revealed when his son is found to be crooked, or *Le Gang* (77) – though 'Variety' was distinctly unappreciative of the latter: 'Delon plays a sort of neurotic chieftain with nervous giggles, watered-down menace and a curly fright-wig. There is no depth to hs characterisation.' At the end of the year he was the favourite actor in the 'Ciné-Revue' poll, but the other films were nothing much: Jessua's *Armaguedon*, as a nerve specialist curing Jean Yanne; *L'Homme Pressé* and *Mort d'un Pourri*. Activity slowed down to *Attention les Enfants Regardent* (78), as a crook threatened by TV-orientated kids, and *Opium*, but Hollywood unexpectedly called for Delon to play a pilot in *Airport 790 Concorde* (79): since the series was clapped out anyway, and since the co-star was the equally cardboard Sylva Kristel, it looked as though all Universal hoped for was some quick returns in Europe.

He had a change of pace with *Le Toubib*, a wartime romance between a surgeon and a nurse, but returned to thrillers with *Trois Hommes à Abattre* (80) and *Pour la Peau d'un Flic* (81), both based on books by Jean-Patrick Manchette; in the first he was a professional gambler sought by killers and in the second, which he directed and co-wrote, an ex-cop who becomes a private eye. Not long before it was premièred there was released a Russian film made a year earlier, *Teheran '43* (81), in which he was a French police inspector investigating a plot to kill the Allied leaders. *Le Choc* (83) found him as a hit man hiding out on Catherine Deneuve's turkey farm, after which he was *Le Battant* (83). Said 'Variety' this time: 'His new film proudly bears his name as producer, director, co-screenwriter and, of course, star, leaving no doubt about who's to blame for the numbing mediocrity of this thriller without thrills, drama or anything else usually associated with good commercial entertainment. Delon continues to be faithful to the image he thinks the public wants to see. But to judge from early box office returns, the public may be tired of his refrigerated magnetism and scrappy suspense vehicles.' He was reduced to third-billing, after Jeremy Irons and Ornella Muti, in Schlöndorff's *Un Amour de Swann* (84), but it was the most prestigious production with which he had been associated since his work with Visconti; and his performance as the painted homosexual Baron Charlus was expected to establish him as a character actor. He did win a César for *Notre Histoire*, co-producing with co-star Nathalie Baye, the story of a marriage directed by Bertrand Blier. It was not, however, a success, but *Parole de Flic* (85) was – though not of the measure being enjoyed by his erstwhile rival Belmondo. *Farewell Waltz*, to co-star Philippe Noiret, Isabelle Huppert and Burt Lancaster, based on a Milan Kundera novel, was cancelled weeks before shooting when its prospective director, Marc Grunebaum, died – thus making 'Variety''s comment on *Le*

Passage (86) even more poignant: 'Film's only mystery surrounds Delon's reason for choosing to produce and star in such cinematic infantilism. The star's confused quest for renewal is one of the saddest sights on the domestic scene.'

So the star decided to lie low for a while, eventually returning in *Ne Reveillez pas un Flic qui Dort* (88), but it was sleepy time at the box-office as well. He did four 90-minute films for TV, under the generic title of 'Cinéma', and was then said to be planning a film with Jean-Luc Godard.

Catherine Deneuve

These arises, from time to time, a player born under a lucky star. The best directors want them; if they are European Hollywood beckons; reams are written about them and they get on all the best magazine covers. All these things happened to Catherine Deneuve, easily the most successful French film actress of her generation. Why her? Why not Juliette Mayniel, Marie Dubois, Marie Laforêt, Bernadette Laffont, Mireille Darc, Françoise Brion, Sophie Daumier, Catherine Spaak? Why not Annie Girardot or Emmanuèle Riva, both incomparably better actresses? Then, why *not* her? She is beautiful. 'Time Magazine' once spoke of her 'exquisite face and presence – eerily evocative of a warmer Grace Kelly', but that misses the point (Kelly's *manner* was cool, nothing else). Deneuve's heart temperature can be little warmer than a piece of Arctic ice. She is the screen's ice maiden. (Manny Farber called her Catherine Deadnerve.) She has been cleverly used by a couple of directors who needed her reserve and suggestion of melancholy – surface qualities for characters with fires down below. The finished effect (in *Repulsion* and *Belle de Jour*) was interesting, but there was no indication that as an actress she understood what she was doing.

Her sister, Françoise Dorléac, was more readily accessible – even prettier, vivacious, wont to charm where Catherine mooned. They came from a theatrical family: father (Maurice) Dorléac worked as an actor dubbing foreign films into French. Françoise, the elder sister (Catherine was born in 1943, in Paris), was successful in films first, though Catherine (then a brunette) had small parts while still at school, in *Les Collégiens* (56) and *Les Petits Chats* (60). She believes her career really began with *Les Portes Claquent*, when called upon to play her sister's sister, a chore she undertook again in Michel Deville's *Ce Soir ou Jamais*, an agreeable light comedy with Marina Vlady and Claude Rich. There were more small parts in *L'Homme à Femmes* with Danielle Darrieux and *Les Parisiennes* (62), a sketch-film made by Marc Allégret, with pop star Johnny Halliday.

Around this time Deneuve met Roger Vadim, mentor (and ex-husband) of Brigitte Bardot, and would-be mentor (and husband) of a girl called Annette Stroyberg. He became the mentor of Deneuve and would-be husband (she had his baby in 1963 but refused to marry him). Vadim, nothing if not an opportunist, was continuing his career as a purveyor of fashionable film eroticism and he made (a blonde) Deneuve the centrepiece of two such subjects. He directed her in *Le Vice et la Vertu* (63), de Sade brought up to date, with Robert Hossein and Annie Girardot as Nazis and Deneuve as the victimized – almost masochist – Justine, a part for which she was insufficiently experienced. *Et Satan Conduit le Bal . . .* was produced by Vadim and directed by a protégé, a singularly pointless addition to those current exposés of life among the *fils à papa* and their equally spoilt girls. (Françoise Brion stole the film.) The reviews, and the Vadim-oriented publicity, merely left Deneuve standing pathetically on the fringe of the film business; and she was not helped by Pierre Kast's *Vacances Portugaises*, with Bernhard Wicki, about some *chic* couples on holiday.

However, another encounter saved her – with Jacques Demy, who made her the star of *Les Parapluies de Cherbourg* (64), opposite Nino Castelnuovo, a story of lovers who part, marry each on his side and meet again too late. The difference here was the non-cloying charm, the delicacy of the emotion and the fact that it was all sung – to lilting melodies by Michel Legrand. The film-going world was enchanted and Deneuve herself found that Demy had given her the confidence she had hitherto lacked. Chabrol directed her in his sequences of *Les Plus Belles Escroqueries du Monde* – a minuscule joke (and her part was no bigger), 'L' Homme qui Vendit la Tour Eiffel' with Jean-Pierre Cassel and Francis Blanche. There were two diffuse comedies: Molinaro's *La Chasse à l'Homme* with her sister, Claude Rich, Belmondo, etc.; and de Broca's *Un Monsieur de Compagnie*, with Cassel as almost-a-gigolo, a very variable piece. She was a very pallid heroine. In Italy she made *La Constanza della Ragione* with Sammy Frey.

Her next director further increased her confidence, Roman Polanski, who cast her as a sexually inhibited Belgian girl – living in London – who takes first to self-induced loneliness and then, crazily, to murder: *Repulsion* (65), a grand guignol masterpiece, with

something repulsive for everyone. She was frighteningly believable, though she had not so much to act as merely to *appear*. It was the sort of role that kills careers, but she was already contracted for Marcel Camus's *Le Chant du Monde*, with Hardy Kruger, an old-fashioned tale – by Jean Giono – of vendetta in the Midi. She had signed also for Jean-Paul Rappeneau's diverting *La Vie de Château* (66), some misadventures during the Occupation as a bored wife who discovers that her stolid husband is a hero (Philippe Noiret, in one of his best performances).

In Austria she appeared with Gert Fröbe in an episode of a ponderous sex comedy, *Liebeskarusell* (not shown in France); and then was a deaf-mute in the pretentious *Les Créatures*, with Michel Piccoli, for Agnès Varda (Demy's wife). It was not a success. Nor, after the initial good will, was Demy's *Les Demoiselles de Rochefort* (67), a miscalculated follow-up to *Les Parapluies de Cherbourg*. Difficult to say what went wrong – the earlier film was just as studied – but one had only crumbs of comfort, like the dances and duets of Deneuve and Dorléac. It was the last time they would play sisters: some months later Françoise was killed in a car accident near Nice airport (a cruel blow to Deneuve; after an early rivalry they had become very close). In 1968 her three-year marriage to English photographer David Bailey broke up: they were, apparently, separated too often.

She herself was on the verge of her biggest success. When Joseph Kessel sold the rights of his novel *Belle de Jour* he insisted on her for the lead. Luis Buñuel was engaged to direct and the film became his biggest commercial success in over 35 years of film-making – due partly to good reviews (but he usually got those) and partly due to the public taste for films about prostitution. But whereas such films hitherto barely bothered with the mechanics of the trade and always had the poor whore faithful (in spirit) to her true love, this one had some graphic black-comic scenes and actually depicted Deneuve enjoying herself. She played, in fact, a bourgeois wife on

High on the list of films which worked against all odds is Les Parapluies de Cherbourg *(64) – because, for one thing, every word was sung. Nino Castelnuovo and Catherine Deneuve were the couple who swear eternal love but do not keep their pledge.*

Catherine Deneuve in Benjamin, ou les Mémoires d'un Puceau *(68), a jeu d'esprit with echoes of Fragonard. With her in this picture are Pierre Clementi and Michèle Morgan (who played her aunt).*

the game as a way of whiling away her afternoons. Buñuel did not direct Deneuve in the established sense, but again her behaviour was exactly right.

Her role in Deville's *Benjamin, ou les Mémoires d'un Puceau* (68) was on the surface a turnabout – an innocent, like the hero (Pierre Clémenti), in this 18th-century world of libertines; but she callously robs him of his virginity so that hers shall not go to the rake she really craves, Michel Piccoli. It was her best performance to date, in a film that was a giant hit in France, a mild one in the US and, killed by the press, a flop in Britain. *Manon 70*, a new version – by Jean Aurel – of one of the cinema's perennials, was a flop in France and disappeared. She then took a giant step into big-budget international filming, playing Danielle Darrieux's old part in Terence Young's remake of *Mayerling*, with Omar Sharif. She did not care for the finished result – nor did many other people (and Sharif did not care for her; he observed sourly that she believed herself 'la Greta Garbo des temps modernes'). She was much more at home in a typical Françoise Sagan piece, *La Chamade*, as a kept woman (Piccoli's) attracted to a younger man – till laziness and selfishness send her back to Square One. Her vague, dreamy, simple personality made her ideal for the part.

But she was not good as the siren luring Jack Lemmon from his wife in *The April Fools* (69); when critics spoke of her 'coldness' it was not in any admiring sense. But Truffaut knew what he wanted from her in *La Sirène de Mississippi*, with Belmondo. And so did Buñuel, who chose her for *Tristana* (70), a girl seduced by her guardian, leaving him for a younger lover (Franco Nero), but returning – as an invalid – to destroy him. It was also, along the way, a compendium of Buñuelisms and a haunting picture of Toledo in 1929. Buñuel called her the 'Anglo-Saxon' – but Anglo-Saxon actresses were by now more sexy. She had developed a quality of mystery, but Demy hardly needed that in his version of a Perrault fairy-tale, *Peau d'Âne*, in which she played both mother and daughter. It was not one of the cinema's most successful fantasies and her name did not help it to success in the international market – which it needed to get its money back. No more successful was *Ça N'arrive qu'aux Autres/It Only Happens to Others* (71), an autobiographical piece written and directed by Nadine Marquand Trintignant, about the death of a child and its effect on the parents. Neither Deneuve nor Marcello Mastroianni were able to command the needed audience sympathy. They were seen together offscreen; and together went into a curious desert island tale directed by Marco Ferreri, *Lisa* (72), for which she eschewed Chabrol's *La Décade Prodigieuse*, once announced for her. After *Un Flic*, with Alain Delon, she did two more with Mastroianni, *L'Evènement le Plus Important Depuis que l'Homme a Marché sur la Lune* (73) and *Touchez Pas à la Femme Blanche* (74), but neither was the sort of comedy to which her style was remotely suited. Nor were they, despite their ambitions, cinema events of any importance; and the same is true of *La Femme aux Bottes Rouges*, in which Juan Buñuel tried to make of her the sort of perverse sex-lady she had been for his father.

The following year Deneuve was busy: *Zig Zig* (75); Bolognini's excellent *Fatti di Gente Perbene*, with Giancarlo Giannini and Fernando Rey, all of them involved in scandal and socialism in Turin at the end of the last century; *L'Agression*, having an affair with brother-in-law Jean-Louis Trintignant; and *Le Sauvage*, on a desert island with Yves Montand – a crazy comedy that was liked in France, but which bewildered on its few export dates. Exported herself, for *Hustle*, Deneuve was a high-class call-girl in San Francisco, but it was difficult to see why Burt Reynolds was so hung up on her. In *Si c'était à Refaire* (76) her co-star was Anouk Aimée, both of them as ex-convicts up to their ears in trouble, *amour* and banality: Claude Lelouch directed – in his usual manner, unable despite odd felicities to disguise the weirdness of his material. She was Vittorio Gassmann's young wife in *Anima Persa* (77), directed by Dino Risi – and it was due to him, thought 'Variety', that her work 'rises above her usual standard'. Few critics were even as kind as that for Deneuve's second return to English-language movies, *March or Die*, in which she was the pride of the Foreign Legion. *Coup de Foudre* co-starred Philippe Noiret and was directed by Robert Enrico; it was also one of the most expensive films ever made in France – or, rather, unmade, since the money ran out and it was abandoned. *Ecoute Voir . . .Mon Lapin* (78) was described thus by 'Variety': 'The winsome idea here is to have the alabaster, inexpressive French star Catherine Deneuve play a distaff private eye in the mold of Sam Spade.' However, she was in a big success, *L'Argent des Autres*, if in a 'guest' role, as the wife of Trintignant: outstanding in the cast – as usual – was Claude Brasseur (son of Pierre), who took co-starring status with Deneuve in *Ils Sont Grands ces Petits* (79), a psychological drama. She and Jacques Dutronc were bankrobber lovers in Lelouch's Franco-Canadian *A Nous Deux*, which may have suggested the title for the next, *Courage, Fuyons*, except that the plot concerned a mild but married man (Jean Rochefort) who falls in love with a nightclub singer. Show business was also the subject of Truffaut's desperately thin *Le Dernier Métro* (80), in which she ran her (Jewish) husband's theatrical troupe in wartime Paris, for which she was accorded a Best Actress César. In *Je Vous Aime* (81) with Trintignant, she was a sexually ambitious businesswoman; in *Le Choix des Armes* she was Yves Montand's wife, killed off before the end. She shared a banal romance in Biarritz with Patrick Dewaere in André Techiné's *Hotel des Ameriques* and shacked up with Alain Delon for *Le Choc* (82). Her best film in a while was de Broca's *L'Africain* (83), in which she meets up with ex-spouse Philippe Noiret in Africa, where he has become a shopkeeper; and her worst was Tony Scott's *The Hunger*, a a bisexual vampire in league with David Bowie. After a reunion with Trintignant for a comedy, *Le Bon Plaisir* (84), he as the President of the Republic, she as the mother of his son, she guest-starred in Alain Corneau's ambitious *Fort Saganne*, cause of dalliance for Gérard Depardieu as he moves from peasant youth to heroism in the Sahara. In *Paroles et Musiques* she starred again with one of the younger actors, when she embarked on a new life with pop singer Christophe Lambert.

Moving into middle age, she continued to deliver her trade-marked glamour – in Monicelli's *Speriamo che sia Femmina* (86): it was easier to believe that she was a movie/TV star than it was that Liv Ullman was an Italian countess, or that the two of them were sisters. It was not very good, but it was better than Techiné's *Le Lieu du Crime*, a traditional (or, if you prefer, corny) tale of a café-owner (her) who takes one look at a homicidal teenage punk and falls madly in love with him. It was not a success. *Agent Trouble* 987) was her, a bespectacled, brunette museum worker solving the mystery of her nephew's disappearance. Then she was a radio psychiatrist receiving threatening calls in *Fréquence Meurtre* (88), directed by the veteran screenwriter Elisabeth Rappeneau, after which she was due to co-star with Gérard Depardieu in *Drole d'un Endroit pour un Rencontre* (89).

Diana Dors

Diana Dors was living demonstration that the British cannot make sex queens. In her heyday, sex on the British screen was mostly a matter of plastic macs and low necklines; but as real eroticism has little to do with either tarts or the amount of flesh exposed it can be said with certainty that she did not have much. She herself agreed; but she listened sufficiently to her advisers to let the 'blonde bombshell' tag get in the way of a real ability as a character actress. When she was young, she was very funny: she did a neat parody of the man-mad teenager, the nubile cousin who ogles the best man at the wedding breakfast, the office junior ready for a bit of slap-and-tickle behind the filing cupboard. She was the best thing about most of her early films.

She was born in Swindon, Wiltshire, in 1931 (real name: Diana Fluck). She studied at RADA, was seen in a play there and given spot in the film version of a West End thriller, *The Shop at Sly Corner* (46), starring Oscar Homolka. Her agent got her a similar cameo in *Dancing with Crime* (47) and she was in Rank's *Holiday Camp*, ready for anything in trousers. Rank's production head, Sydney Box, was impressed and signed her for the lead in *Streets Paved with Water*. The film was not made, but she emerged with a 10-year Rank contract, starting at £10 a week and rising to a maximum of £200. There was a succession of small parts: *Good Time Girl* (48), as one of Jean Kent's cronies; *The Calendar*, from an old Edgar Wallace play, as a maid; *My Sister and I*, a pale theatrical romance, as a flighty young actress; *Oliver Twist*, in very briefly as a scullery maid; and a B, *Penny and the Pownall Case*, her first big role. She was delicious as the sexy cousin in *Here Come the Huggets* and *Vote for Huggett* (49), and, briefly, as a secretary in *It's Not Cricket*, a corny comedy starring the urbane

Diana Dors, temporary typist, sets her sights on Basil Radford in a British comedy of 1949, It's Not Cricket. *Radford's co-star was Naunton Wayne, as happened frequently since their teaming in* The Lady Vanishes.

team of Basil Radford and Naunton Wayne. In *A Boy, A Girl and A Bike* she joined a cycling club for the boys rather than for the bikes. She then starred in a film claimed to be (as so many since) Britain's first Western: *Diamond City*, set in South Africa, as a saloon-girl battling with pure Honor Blackman for digger David Farrar. She had not the age or weight for the part and was better cast as one of the *Dance Hall* (50) girls. The truth was that though the Rank Organization knew how to put Dors through its Charm School paces they had no idea how to handle such an individual talent. She did a play, 'Man of the World', in a (vain) attempt to enhance her burgeoning reputation and in September 1950 had her option dropped.

She was in uniform for a feeble film version of a long-running farce about an RAF billet, *Worm's Eye View* (51), and then returned to Rank to play a professional beauty-contest winner in *Lady Godiva Rides Again*. According to the press she spent months contemplating a seven-year Hollywood contract – before declining in favour of Exclusive, a minor British company who made shoddy thrillers utilizing their country-house studio, often with passé Hollywood names, such as George Brent and Marguerite Chapman, who were in *The Last Page* (52). In that, Dors was a blackmailer. For another small firm, Adelphi, she was in *My Wife's Lodger*, an inept farce co-starring Dominic Roche, playing a character called Willie Higginbotton. Also that year she was in two West End flops, 'Rendezvous' and 'Remains To Be Seen'. She turned to the music hall and in 1953 sang sexy songs in Glasgow, Blackpool and other places. Her film career continued downbeat: *The Great Game* (53), an idiotic football film; *Is Your Honeymoon Really Necessary?*, another poor version of a West End long-runner; and, playing a man-hungry corporal, *It's a Grand Life*, the last film of Frank Randle, a Lancashire comedian whose films were not projectionable below The Wash. She was 'guest star' in *The Saint's Return*, with Louis Hayward reprising a role he had last done in 1938.

It is always darkest before the dawn. She got a part in an A picture, co-starring with Glynis Johns, *The Weak and the Wicked* (54), as a girl who takes the rap for her bloke. This vapid prison flick was directed by J. Lee Thompson, who gave her a guest role in *As Long As They're Happy* starring Jack Buchanan. It could not be said – then or later – that she was worth an ounce of beans at the box-office, but she had an uncanny knack of making headlines, sometimes with rather mild scandals, or, as in 1954, when questions were asked in Parliament about her expenses. The publicity line on her was that she was Britain's Marilyn Monroe and although she rebutted this she got a lot of mileage out of it. Her hair had been platinum blonde for a couple of years now and her pin-up poses were poor revamps of Monroe's: vamping poor Jack Buchanan, she copied Marilyn's most famous gestures. She was certainly one of the most famous women in Britain and it was not surprising that Rank offered a new contract, reputedly worth £100,000. She turned it down, and could afford to, as the prestigious Carol Reed had just chosen her to star in *A Kid for Two Farthings* (55), with Celia Johnson. 'No more Bs for me,' she said (unwisely). Rank, however, used her in a couple of namby-pamby comedies, *Value for Money*, as a bouncy showgirl after John Gregson's money, and *An Alligator Named Daisy*, as a film star involved with a man (Donald Sinden) saddled with the title-character. Lee Thompson directed the latter, and he and Dors were reunited for *Yield to the Night* (56), supposedly a plea for the abolition of capital punishment but no less specious than their last prison film. Much publicity accrued from the deglamorization of Dors, but the performance was effective only in parts.

Hollywood and she now felt ready for each

Diana Dors at the time she was making a bid to be both a serious actress and Britain's answer to Marilyn Monroe. With her is Glynis Johns in The Weak and Wicked *(54), a title which does suggest its subject, life in a women's prison.*

other and she signed a long-term deal with RKO. The result was two colossal flops: *I Married a Woman* (57), starring TV comic George Gobel but enlivened by bits from Jessie Royce Landis and Nita Talbot; and *The Unholy Wife*, about a B-girl who plots to murder her husband (Rod Steiger) after falling in love with Tom Tryon. In Hollywood she was no less adept at getting publicity (there was a swimming-pool episode – did she fall or was she pushed?) but American columnists were bewildered by the tag of the British Marilyn: this cheery but synthetic blonde had nothing in common with the spiritual Monroe. RKO folded, but it is doubtful whether she could have overcome the starting handicaps. She later (December 1958) sued RKO for $1,275,000, charging that she had 'become an object of disgrace, ill-will and ridicule' fomented by the company because they did not want to honour the contract (she settled out of court in 1960 for $200,000). Meanwhile, she returned to her native land to make an American-backed film, *The Long Haul*, as a blonde menace and home-wrecker (Victor Mature's). In Italy she was *La Ragazza del Palio* (58), a Texan gas-station girl courted by impoverished prince Vittorio Gassmann who thinks she is an heiress (she gets her revenge during the Siena palio). In Britain again she did a couple of programmers, *Tread Softly Stranger*, a triangle crime tangle with George Baker and Terence Morgan, and *Passport to Shame* (59), a prostitute film made with dedicated simple-mindedness. Though top-billed, her part in the latter was small: it was mainly a vehicle for Eddie Constantine (the producers were trying to cash in on his French popularity) plus Odile Versois, with Herbert Lom and Brenda de Banzie as white-slavers.

Her next assignment was hardly more distinguished: *Scent of Mystery* (60), a thriller produced by Mike Todd Jr, with assorted smells under the seats let off at appropriate intervals. After flopping in some countries it was shown in Britain six years later without smells. Those years did not see an amelioration of Dors's screen hopes, despite another trip to Hollywood to appear, again in uniform (as a sergeant), in Danny Kaye's *On the Double* (61). Also in the US she did *King of the Roaring Twenties*, as a moll; in Spain, *Encontra a Mallorca* with Alfredo Kraus, apparently not exported. There were character roles in a couple of programmers, *Mrs Gibbon's Boys* (62), starring Kathleen Harrison, and *West Eleven* (63), with Harrison and Alfred Lynch, as an ageing doxy. But Dors looked her old 'glamorous' self, playing herself, in Robert Dhéry's *Allez France* (64), a comedy about French football supporters in London, which was a success in France only. Buxom now, she played a Billingsgate fisherwoman in a flop comedy starring a score of British comedians in cameo parts, *The Sandwich Man* (66).

Stage work continued, mostly in Northern working-men's clubs. The film roles offered were small, usually as an ageing woman of the underworld: *Berserk* (67), with Joan Crawford, where she was sawn in half by her conjurer husband; *Danger Route*, a massively absurd spy thriller starring Richard Johnson, as a housekeeper; *Hammerhead* (68), starring Vince Edwards, as a resort operator; *Baby Love* (69), a silly sex film, seen briefly in the prologue as Baby Love's mother; *There's a Girl in my Soup*, as a janitor's wife; and Jerzy Skolimowski's Anglo-German *Deep End* (70), as a fat blonde who wants to rape the hero. In 1970 a stage part, in 'Three Months Gone', brought her excellent notices and seemed to presage a new career; but a TV series, 'Queenie's Castle', negated the good that that had done. Now frankly stout – but still posing for pin-ups – she played a madame, in a role much cut, in *Hannie Caulder* (71) with Raquel Welch, and was in Jacques Demy's virtually unseen *The Pied Piper* (72), as the burgomaster's wife. In Sweden she decorated yet another bordello in the American-backed *The Groove Room*. She played a madame – throughout the film in a wheelchair. As *What the Swedish Butler Saw* it turned up in Britain in 1980. She then made *Nothing but the Night*, with those two stand-bys of cut-rate horror films, Peter Cushing and Christopher Lee; and *The Amazing Mr Blunden*, plotting in Dickensian fashion against its child heroes.

Below, Miss Dors in Baby Love (69).

She was killed Othello-style by her actor-husband (Jack Hawkins) in *Theatre of Blood* (73); and she tempted Harry H. Corbett in the second of two poor films from an excellent TV series, *Steptoe and Son Ride Again*. She was again one of several names in two more horror films, From *Beyond the Grave* (74), as a murder victim, and *Craze*, starring Jack Palance. She appeared from time to time on TV, buxom and gruesome in slit skirts and lots of cleavage, and as far as cinemagoers were concerned was forgotten except by the most arduous seekers out of British rubbish: *Bedtime with Rosie* (75), as the heroine's Aunt Annie; *Three For All; The Amorous Milkman*, as an amorous client; *Keep It Up Downstairs* (76), as an American ex-actress trying to marry her daughter to the scion of a stately home; *Adventures of a Taxi Driver*, as the hero's nagging mother; and, in the same series, *Adventures of a Private Eye* (77). With the exception of *Three For All*, a pop comedy, these were soft-core sex comedies – to which her name was presumably an asset.

She married three times and various articles ('Out of Dors', 'Swinging Dors') filled in the details behind the headlines. In 1970 husband No 3 was sent to gaol after an affray outside a pub. He, Alan Lake, started later to make films, and she supported him in *Confessions from the David Galaxy Affair* (79). The title was later changed to *Star Sex* but bookings were still meagre. Since she was RKO's last contract player it seemed appropriate that she was offered a (supporting) role in the company's first film for 25 years, *Dick Turpin*, but it was never released. There followed a long battle with cancer, which she lost in 1984, only a few weeks after completing *Steaming* (85). She was the cheerful, realistic manageress of a ladies' Turkish Bath, a role within her range: but looking better than for years, exquisitely made up and speaking 'nicely', she gave a stilted performance. Obituarists noted her fame and the paucity of good films. It is a pity she turned down *Saturday Night and Sunday Morning*.

Kirk Douglas

There are people who cannot tell margarine from butter, and there are people who cannot tell Kirk Douglas from Burt Lancaster. It is odd, because they are not really very much alike. Maybe it is because they have co-starred together on several occasions or because they both represent more than any other the postwar male movie star: powerful and inflexible, producers and executives who appear in films – rather than actors. Sheilah Graham paired them in one of her books, in a chapter headed 'The Terrible-Tempered Twins'. John Frankenheimer directed them both in *Seven Days in May*; 'Kirk Douglas was very jealous of Lancaster; he felt he was playing a secondary role to Lancaster, which indeed he was. . . . He wanted to be Burt Lancaster. He's wanted to be Burt Lancaster all his life.' Douglas later commented on the partnership: 'I've finally got away from Burt Lancaster. My luck has changed for the better. I've got nice-looking girls in my films now.'

Douglas's remark gives ample indication of

why 'Photoplay' once called him 'The most hated man in Hollywood'. Miss Graham describes him offscreen as 'boastful, egotistical, resentful of criticism – if anyone dare give it'. She adds that he 'has rarely been successful on the screen as a nice guy'. Maybe it is the Russian strain in him, but he is unapproachable, even formidable. His personality has no elasticity. He is at his best as a driving egotist, propelled on some inner motor. One critic wrote (reviewing *There Was a Crooked Man*): 'Douglas is maybe the least relaxed of enduring screen stars. He's *on* all the time; he holds your attention without really interesting you. But he's a commanding presence, and Mankiewicz uses him for that cocky magnetism.' When he started he enjoyed a measure of critical success, but he has never been considered by exhibitors, when they vote on these things, as one of the most popular stars. Lancaster has been more popular, as well as more versatile. Well, they both have teeth and dimples; they both arrived around the same time, and it looks as though their fortunes dimmed together: 'Both Douglas and Lancaster, it is said in Hollywood these days, are unbankable for any picture budgeted at more than $2,000,000' said 'Playboy' in 1971.

Douglas was born Issur Danielovitch Demsky in Amsterdam, New York, in 1916, and was educated at St Lawrence University where, between wrestling bouts (he was intercollegiate champion), he began to take an interest in dramatics. Like a John Garfield character, he was variously a professional wrestler, an usher, a parking-lot attendant and a bell-hop, all to pay his way through the AADA. He also jerked soda, nights, at Schrafft's. Studies completed, he got a Broadway role as a singing messenger-boy in 'Spring Again', which starred Sir C. Aubrey Smith, followed by stage-manager and understudy with Katharine Cornell's 'The Three Sisters' (42). After war service with the navy he did some radio soap operas and was the juvenile lead (taking over from Richard Widmark) opposite Joan Caulfield in 'Kiss and Tell'. He was in a stage version of Dorothy Baker's 'Trio', and then in 'The Wind is Ninety': on Lauren Bacall's recommendation Hal Wallis went to see him and he signed him starting at $500 a week.

Wallis gave him a showy part as Barbara Stanwyck's alcoholic husband in *The Strange Love of Martha Ivers* (46) and he was impressive. Then he loaned him to RKO for a couple: *Mourning Become Electra* (47), as Peter Niles, the lover of Lavinia (Rosalind Russell); and *Out of the Past* starring Robert Mitchum, as a big-time hoodlum. Wallis had him support Burt Lancaster, as his nightclub owner pal, in *I Walk Alone*, and with that the association with Wallis came to an end. Douglas went over to 20th to play a newspaper proprietor in *The Walls of Jericho* (48) and then got hs first real star part in a programmer opposite Laraine Day, *My Dear Secretary*. At 20th he was Ann Sothern's husband in *A Letter to Three Wives*; then Stanley Kramer engaged him for the modestly budgeted *Champion* (49), in the title-role, a ruthless, unscrupulous pug. Mark Robson directed and the film was a big, big hit. Douglas became *the* big new star of 1949-50. Everyone was after him. 20th, who had not taken up their option for a second film after *A Letter to Three Wives* (at less than $50,000), now offered $200,000 for a projected film about Rommel.

Warners won; they signed Douglas for seven years, with the right to do one outside film a year. For them he was the *Young Man With a Horn* (50), a title that pleased Miss Graham ('It should be cinch, he never stops blowing it'). It was in fact a fictionalized account of trumpeter Bix Beiderbecke, with Doris Day, and he was another go-getter till drink ruined him. He was the Gentleman Caller in *The Glass Menagerie* and his conscious charm gave a new dimension to that role. He admitted later that he had only signed the contract for these two roles and to get out of it he did for no salary a Western, *Along the Great Divide* (51), with Virginia Mayo. At Paramount he did *The Big Carnival*, based on the Floyd Collins case of the 20s, when a miner was trapped for days: Douglas was the cynical reporter who uses the disaster

Kirk Douglas in Wilder's The Big Carnival (*51*), *originally released as* Ace in the Hole. *The title change offered no improvement at the box-office – an attack on yellow journalism considered too acrid, too vicious and more than somewhat harrowing.*

Kirk Douglas and Lana Turner in a Hollywood roman-à-clef, The Bad and the Beautiful *(52), in which she played a movie star based partly on herself and partly on Diana Barrymore. His role was an amalgam of Selznick, Thalberg and Val Lewton plus all the unpleasant characteristics of the Broadway producer Jed Harris. The result was so loathsome that Clark Gable had turned it down; he of course would have given it far more charm than Douglas. It would also have been a much better film than most he made about this time.*

for his own ends and Billy Wilder made good use of his drive and intensity. Still at Paramount he was an ambitious detective in Wyler's film of Sidney Kingsley's play *Detective Story*, a performance which won for him the 'Picturegoer' Gold Medal. He returned to Warners for *The Big Trees* (52), an actioner, and for Howard Hawks he did another, *The Big Sky*, based on A.B. Guthrie Jr's bestseller. Neither of them was big at the box-office; he turned down *Stalag 17*, which won William Holden an Oscar.

At MGM for Vincente Minnelli he was one of *The Bad and the Beautiful*, a movie producer (pronounced 'heel'), 'presented one-dimensionally and with all the aggressiveness at the command of Kirk Douglas' (Richard Winnington). Also at that studio he was a trapeze artist in the Pier Angeli episode of *The Story of Three Loves* (53). For Kramer he was a Jewish refugee, the title-role of *The Juggler*: 'Kirk Douglas plays yet again the neurotic fugitive from justice and, as usual, gives the part a certain unexpected depth' (Karel Reisz in the 'MFB'). The film was made partially in Israel and Douglas stayed out of the US for a further period to qualify for tax exemption. Still planning to produce, he had a hand in the production of the two films he made in Europe: *Act of Love*, a GI love story, heavily directed by Anatole Litvak from a delicate novel by Alfred Hayes; and the Italian *Ulisse/Ulysses* (54), or What's a nice Jewish boy doing in a place like this? – cardboard Homer and a flop outside Italy. In 1954 he married his second wife, his – French – press agent at the time. In 1955 back in the US, he founded his own production company, Bryna.

For Disney, and a fee of $175,000, he did *20,000 Leagues Under the Sea*, a version of Jules Verne that was his first unqualified success since *Champion*. At Universal on a participation basis he did a Western for King Vidor, *Man Without a Star* (55); at 20th he was one of the *The Racers*, with Bella Darvi;

then came the first for Bryna, *The Indian Fighter*. It was not a success. When Minnelli came to make *Lust for Life* (56), he found Douglas 'the only possible choice' to play Van Gogh, because of his physical appearance, 'and then for his great violence . . . because Van Gogh, like Douglas, was very fierce in his loves and hates: a wonderful performance'. The New York critics agreed – at least, they designated him the year's Best Actor. To some, his accent jarred and he had not, said Catherine de la Roche, 'quite the right style', but, she went on, 'his tremendous temperament, combined here with a gravity not evident in his other roles, enabled him to create a portrait which has authority, truth and moments of genuine tragedy. . . .' The film was MGM's 'quality' movie of the year and great care had been taken with the sets and locations – but for all its sympathy the creators' creed was so alien from Van Gogh's that the final result was negative. The public stayed away. Douglas was compensated by the highly successful *Gunfight at the OK Corral* (57), a reunion with Lancaster for Wallis, as Doc Hollliday to Lancaster's Wyatt Earp. Between these two, *Top Secret Affair* with Susan Hayward was not very top and fairly secret.

Stanley Kubrick then approached him to do *Paths of Glory* – at a fee of $350,000, more than one-third of the budget. This was an adaptation of Humphrey Cobb's novel about the French army mutiny in World War I. The book had been a success in the 30s though pacifism was then unpopular; 20 years later Kubrick found no studio would touch it till Douglas agreed to star, as the army lawyer whose idealism is is incomprehensible to his fellow officers (Adolphe Menjou and George Macready, among others). Reaction to the film was lukewarm from those critics who had just been raving about *The Bridge on the River*

Paths of Glory *(57) was a grim, grainy picture about what happened when a French regiment refused to leave the safety of the trenches to take an almost impregnable ant-hill. Kirk Douglas was their commander and defence counsel at the subsequent court martial; George Macready a fanatical senior officer. Kubrick directed; and the film was banned in France for almost twenty years.*

Kwai, but it became recognized as the best war film since *All Quiet* in 1931; to some it remains a strong contender for the best movie ever to come out of Hollywood.

Douglas's own company also produced *The Vikings* (58), in which he had an eye torn out and was the most villainous amongst them. Richard Fleischer directed vigorously and achieved a sort of cross between Homer, the Brothers Grimm and Li'l Abner. It was a big hit and so was a Wallis Western, *Last Train to Gun Hill* (59), with Anthony Quinn. For Lancaster's company he co-starred with him in *The Devil's Disciple*, as Dick Dudgeon, made in Britain. Then he produced *Spartacus* (60) and Kubrick came in to direct it – returning a favour – after Douglas had a falling out with Anthony Mann. As Howard Fast's slave-hero he himself for some reason seemed monumentally uninterested in the goings on, but the film was regarded as one of the better Roman film epics and eventually proved lucrative. Curiously, he worked much more conscientiously – and was in the end likeable – in *Strangers When We Meet* with Kim Novak, a love story after (a long way after) the *Brief Encounter* idea. *The Last Sunset* (61) was virtually the last film in which Bryna was a major production partner; Robert Aldrich directed this Western and later described Douglas's behaviour as 'impossible' – in contrast to co-star Rock Hudson, with whom he found it a pleasure to work.

Town Without Pity/Stadt ohne Mitleid was medium stuff – what happened when a German girl is raped by four GIs; Douglas was the defence attorney. He was a modern cowboy in *Lonely Are the Brave* (62), a much-liked picture which did not do well. These were not liked – and they did not do well either: Minnelli's *Two Weeks in Another Town*, from an Irwin Shaw novel, as a has-been movie director making a come-back; *The Hook* (63), a Korean war drama, as a sergeant; *The List of Adrian Messenger*, a thriller made by John Huston, with Douglas as the only one of the five advertised guest stars to have a considerable part; and *For Love or Money* with Mitzi Gaynor, a misguided excursion into comedy. In 1963 he appeared briefly on Broadway in 'One Flew over the Cuckoo's Nest'; and he failed to interest anyone in filming it. He eventually passed the rights in Ken Kesey's novel to his son Michael, whose film version (with Jack Nicholson) netted Poppa Kirk a percentage of the profits. The next batch all had military settings: Frankenheimer's *Seven Days in May* (64) with Lancaster, as a scheming air force colonel; *In Harm's Way* with John Wayne, as an embittered naval commander (at a fee of $400,000); *The Heroes of Telemark* (65), as a Norwegian patriot in this Resistance drama; *Cast a Giant Shadow* (66), as Colonel Mickey Marcus in this fictionalized biopic of one of the founders of the state of Israel – and a horrendous flop, despite the participation of names like Wayne and Frank Sinatra; and *Paris Brûle-t-il?/Is Paris Burning?*, in a guest shot as General Patton.

The dismal box-office level continued through a couple of Westerns, *The Way West* (67) with Mitchum and Widmark, and *The War Wagon* with John Wayne; through a thriller that sank without trace, *A Lovely Way to Die* (68), and a drama about the Mafia, *The Brotherhood* (69). When it was suggested to Elia Kazan that Douglas take on Marlon Brando's abandoned role in *The Arrangement* he was, he said, appalled – but he liked working with Douglas and liked his performance. The film was not successful and even less so was the Western that Mankiewicz directed, *There Was a Crooked Man* (70), with Henry Fonda. After that it was a question of taking what parts were offered: in a good Western, *A Gunfight* (71), an independent venture totally financed by the Jicarilla, an Apache Indian tribe of New Mexico; a cosmopolitan venture made in Spain, *La Luz del Fin del Mundo/The Light at the Edge of the World*, with Yul Brynner, from a Jules Verne story; and a British thriller, *Catch Me a Spy*. In Germany he did a dual-nationality thriller, *Un Uomo da Rispettare/A Man to Respect* (72), and in Yugoslavia he directed a co-production between his own company and an Italian one, *Scalawag* (73), also acting in this badly received pirate yarn. An Italian-German heist movie, filmed in English with Florinda Bolkan as *The Master Touch*, did no better. He was a singing 'Dr Jekyll and Mr Hyde' for NBC TV; and that medium had the US première of a British drama originally meant for cinemas, *Cat and Mouse* (74), retitled *Mousey*, in which he was cast against type – as a meek teacher driven to murder his wife. He produced, directed and acted in *Posse* (75); and for the first time for years – apart from TV – was seen by a vast public in *Once Is Not Enough*, a junk movie from Jacqueline Susann's junk novel. As a movie producer he was one of several talents wasted and as much could be said for his participation in the TV *Victory at Entebbe* (76), as the father of one of the hostages. The British-Italian *Holocaust 2000* (77) was a quick flop in the US as *The Chosen*, but around the same time there was a warmer welcome for *The Fury* (78), directed by Brian de Palma. There was a TV mini-series *The Moneychangers*, after Arthur Hailey, and a comic Western, *The Villain* (79), vainly retitled *Cactus Jack* in some overseas territories. He was on equally (over) familiar territory in a British sci-fier, *Saturn 3* (80), and *The Final Countdown*, which started similarly but then via a time warp managed to return to 1941 just before Pearl Harbor. It was the last cinema production to date of Bryna, but he did invest – and guest-starred – in *Home Movies*, a semi-amateur effort made by Brian DePalma and his students. Douglas played an egotistic director. In 1981 he played an ageing Tom Sawyer in 'The Boys in Autumn' with Lancaster, in San Francisco, and walked out of *First Blood* after 'creative differences', presumably with the star, Sylvester Stallone. *The Man From Snowy River* (82) was an Australian film about a boy proving his manhood out in the Outback with horses; Jack Thompson had the title-role and Douglas played – not well – subsidiary roles as two old ranchers revealed to be brothers, 'a dual star turn as unnecessary as it is incongruous', according to the Australian critic David Stratton. HBO invested in return for US première rights on Cable, which presumably accounts for the Douglas participation, but in foreign cinemas generally its success was the reverse of the huge one it enjoyed on its home ground.

Remembrance of Love, made for TV on locations in Israel, made him a survivor of the Warsaw Ghetto reunited with the girl he loved there, after which he was another of the ageing stars propping up a TV name in his movie début – in this case John Schneider, *Eddie Macon's Run* (83). Douglas was the vindictive cop doing the pursuing. HBO was also behind *Draw!* (84), a Western with James Coburn, and also for the home screen Douglas was *Amos*, an old baseball coach confined to a mental home. His son Peter produced it, not dampening several similarities to *One Flew Over the Cuckoo's Nest*. Then someone at Disney thought it might be good box-office to reunite him with Douglas, *Tough Guys* (86) both, capitalizing on their years. It was not a good idea. Nor was he right for the Korda role in a mini-series built around Merle Oberon, *Queenie* (87) – not that it mattered, though it was uninteresting type-casting. A TV remake of *Inherit the Wind* (88) was a much better idea: Douglas had Fredric March's old role and Jason Robards was his opponent in court.

Paul Douglas

Paul Douglas was a burly, big-mugged actor whose appearances in most films somewhat improved them. He was one of those actors who did not fit easily into any category. He was not a supporting actor because he always had star-billing, yet he was not exactly what is called a leading man; and he was not a character actor because he invariably played himself – a gruff, gravel-voiced, middle-aged man. If he was not exactly box-office attraction, audiences liked his way with a line and his genial personality.

He was born in 1905, the son of a Philadelphia physician. At West Philadelphia High School he was active in both dramatics and athletics; he went to Yale, but left to play professional football with the Fighting Yellow Jackets. Later he became a radio sports commentator, which led to straightforward announcing, and that led in turn to stints as straight-man to Jack Benny and Burns and Allen. Garson Kanin had once seen him hit one of his wives in public and could not get it out of his head that he wanted him to play the loud-mouthed scrap tycoon in his play 'Born Yesterday'; he persuaded him to turn actor and Douglas scored a personal success and met Jan Sterling, Judy Holliday's understudy (in 1950 she became his fifth wife – and later, widow. Wife No. 4 was Virginia Field).

During the play's run he turned down several film offers, but eventually accepted a part in *A Letter to Three Wives* (48), with Linda Darnell, and a short-term contract with 20th. When the film opened his notices were so gratifyingly good that he was upped to star-billing in *It Happens Every Spring* (49) – baseball does, and he was a star-catcher – with Ray Milland. And the next one was a star vehicle, *Everybody Does It*, a remake of *Wife Husband and Friend*, in Warner Baxter's old part as the executive who turns out to have a better singing voice than his socialite wife (Celeste Holm), who has aspirations in that

Celeste Holm and Paul Douglas reunited at the end of Everybody Does It *(49), a marital comedy based on the neat idea that she wanted to sing Grand Opera and could not – and he did not but could.*

direction. He did *The Big Lift* (50), as a German-hating sergeant, with Montgomery Clift, and then did another remake, *Love That Brute*, which had been *Tall Dark and Handsome* in its previous incarnation – Douglas had a good, typical part, as a tough Runyonesque gang-leader with a Runyonesque heart of gold. Jean Peters was the girl. He turned down *Father of the Bride* and moved to the right side of the law for a couple of films: Kazan's exciting *Panic in the Streets*, as a detective trying to track down a killer with bubonic plague in New Orleans; and *Fourteen Hours* (51), as a traffic cop trying to persuade Richard Basehart to come down off that ledge. The latter was a critical but not a popular success. *The Guy Who Came Back* was neither, a weepie for man-sized Kleenex, about a former football player trying to make it back to the big time.

His contract was up and MGM wanted him for a couple of films which two of their big names could not, or would not, do – Clark Gable and Spencer Tracy respectively: *Angels in the Outfield*, a title (alas!) to be taken literally, with Douglas as the Muggsy McGraw-type manager of the Pittsburgh Pirates; and *When In Rome* (52), more religion, with Douglas as a con-man posing as a priest but reforming at the behest of real priest Van Johnson. Likely, it wasn't: one of Douglas's great virtues as an actor was his Bogart-like impatience of bull – and Hollywood bull, you felt, more than that. However, he was gently tolerant of three tiresome screen wives: restless Barbara Stanwyck in *Clash by Night*; Zsa Zsa Gabor, just plain tiresome, in *We're Not Married*; and wacky Rosalind Russell in *Never Wave at a WAC*. And he put up with Ginger Rogers's whims in *Forever Female* (53).

He was one of several tycoons in *Executive Suite* (54); and played a similar part in very different circumstances – Scotland, as a blustering American outwitted by the locals – Ealing's *The Maggie*. It was one of his most ingratiating performances. He was Stewart Granger's business partner in *Green Fire*, after which he returned to Britain for a much less profitable excursion, *Joe Macbeth* (55), a gangster melodrama based on guess-what, with Ruth Roman as Lady M. He was a promoter in *The Leather Saint* (56), a nondescript boxing yarn with John Derek; and a tycoon again in *The Solid Gold Cadillac*, his best part for years and playing beautifully with his old partner Judy Holliday. Another trip to Britain yielded a sluggish science-fiction piece, *The Gamma People*. Then MGM wanted hm once more for a part meant originally for another actor (in this case, James Cagney) – a Runyonesque club-owner/gang-leader in *This Could Be the Night* (57), an agreeable comedy with Jean Simmons.

He was Bob Hope's sidekick in *Beau James*, a wily politician; then a drunken professor trooping with some strolling players in the Italian *Fortunella* (58), a Felliniesque tale with Giulietta Masina in the title-role, a junk-merchant who falls for Douglas. Hollywood offers may not have been numerous, for he planned an independent production to be directed by himself; instead he was Debbie Reynolds's father in *The Mating Game* (59). He died, not long afterwards, of a heart attack as he was about to begin *The Apartment* (in the role Fred MacMurray played): a loss to the upper echelons of film comedy.

Faye Dunaway

Faye Dunaway's screen career started about the time there began the decline of interest in female stars in films. It would be churlish to suggest that she was a contributory factor, but it must be said that she did nothing to stop the rot. Handed some good roles in a number of very popular pictures - *Bonnie and Clyde*, *The Thomas Crown Affair*, *Chinatown*, *The Towering Inferno* – she succeeded in imposing herself on neither the industry nor the public. She conveys a steely sensuality, but she does not have, in a word, warmth. She finally hit her stride, and won an Oscar, playing an ambitious career woman in *Network* and if you can shift your mind about you can see in the character the sorts of roles once played by Bette Davis, Barbara Stanwyck, Rosalind Russell and Katharine Hepburn. Ah!

She was born in Tallahassee, Florida, in 1941, the daughter of an army officer; her parents divorced when she was 13, leaving her, in her own words, 'a lonely, frightened child.' She studied Theatre Arts at the University of Boston, auditioned for the Lincoln Center Repertory Company and was taken on by Robert Whitehead and Elia Kazan. The latter directed her in 'After the Fall'; and she had her first big success in 'Hogan's Goat' (which she later did for TV). Otto Preminger signed her to play the role of a Mississippi dirt farmer in *Hurry Sundown* (67), with an option on six more films; but she found him a difficult taskmaster and after litigation later when she refused (wisely) to do *Skidoo* she bought herself out of her contract. Launched in a large role in a major film, she starred in *The Happening*, as one of the beach bums who kidnap Anthony Quinn: which made two flops in a row. But in the role refused by any number of actresses, gangster Bonnie Parker opposite Warren Beatty in *Bonnie and Clyde*

(68), she had the world at her feet – a position it did not keep after *The Extraordinary Seaman* (69) with David Niven, in which she was a gun-toting garage owner. She was an insurance investigator in *The Thomas Crown Affair*, a role conceived after the Grace Kelly character in *Rear Window*: but playing footsy with Steve McQueen, Dunaway was merely high-fashion – a quality essential to her role as a dying woman in *Amanti/A Place for Lovers*, in love with Marcello Mastroianni. Their offscreen romance was 'hotter . . . than anything visible on screen' said 'Playboy', before turning its attention to the next: 'Faye was no less long-suffering, and possibly even more dreary, as a party to *The Arrangement*, the pretentiously boring adaptation that Elia Kazan made of his own novel.'

The career momentum had been lost. Her salary had gone to $200,000 for *Thomas Crown* from the $25,000 she had received for being Bonnie. That second success brought her asking price of $400,000, but it was to drop again. After guesting as a whore Out West in *Little Big Man* (70), she played a one-time fashion model in *Puzzle of a Downfall Child* (71), directed – and it looked like it – by a one-time fashion photographer, Jerry Schatzberg, to whom she was engaged at the time. It was reputedly the first of a four-picture deal with Warner Bros., but the others were not made; indeed, Dunaway was reduced to the rubbishy *La Maison Sous les Arbres/The Deadly Trap*, directed by the once excellent René Clément: she and Frank Langella were an American couple living in France suddenly deep in skulduggery – she with more troubles than poor Bella in 'Gaslight', but at least with a shrink to help her. She was another whore Out West, Katie Elder to Stacy Keach's Doc Holliday – another film to waste the talent of that actor. In life she was helped by appearing in Harold Pinter's 'Old Times': 'trying to find a philosophy', as the London 'Evening Standard' put it. 'Pinter taught me there are no answers, no labels, just an investigation.' On TV, she played Mrs Simpson to the Edward VIII of Richard Chamberlain in 'The Woman I Love', and in Los Angeles she played Blanche du Bois. She had the misfortune to be in one of Stanley Kramer's late flops, *Oklahoma Crude* (73), as a fanatical oil woman, and to be lost in the jolly junketings of Richard Lester's *The Three Musketeers*, as Milady. So much material was shot on that film that it was released with a subtitle, *The Queen's Diamonds*, and the rest turned up as *The Four Musketeers: The Revenge of Milady* (74). She married – rock-star Peter Wolf – and was reduced to auditioning, for *The Great Gatsby*: she did not get the role, but was taken on for a second role originally intended for Ali McGraw by her then-husband, Robert Evans. The film was *Chinatown* and she was the mystery woman who draws private eye Jack Nicholson into deeper waters: it was her best work since *Bonnie and Clyde*, but the director, Roman Polanski, called her 'a gigantic pain in the arse', adding that he had 'never known an actress take her work so seriously – she's a maniac'. However, there was not much to act in *The Towering Inferno*, which had McQueen, Paul Newman and a blazing skyscraper to make it one of the year's most popular films. *Three Days of the Condor* (75) had Robert Redford and she was the lonely, mixed-up girl forced to shelter him.

Then came *Network* (76), where the calmness of her thrusting TV backroom-person was a relief from the rest of it; and, in Britain, *Voyage of the Damned*, billed over all the other star names, monocled and booted, as the wife of Oskar Werner. She was bland as Aimee Semple McPherson in *The Disappearance of Aimee*, for TV. The Best Actress Oscar for *Network* at least did something for her salary: she had received $100,000 for that film and was reported six months later as asking $500,000. That she did not film was due to turning down offers, including *Fun With Dick and Jane* and *Julia*, both of which were made with Jane Fonda. She made a thriller, *The Eyes of Laura Mars* (78), and before it came out 'Variety' reported that if successful

Faye Dunaway as a professional photographer in a murder mystery, The Eyes of Laura Mars *(78): the combination of actress and subject encouraged its makers to go all out for chic – at the expense of entertainment. It was reported that the paperback rip-off was more profitable than the film.*

her salary would go to $1 million per film.

'With her bulging, teary eyes and fluttery voice, this actress is a one-woman band of neurotic gestures', said Frank Rich in 'Time Magazine'. 'It is a tiresome performance that will be particularly grating on anyone who has seen the mannerisms previously in *Chinatown* and *Network*. Dunaway does, however, have the only credible line in the movie. It occurs midway through her love scene, when she announced, "I'm completely out of control".' Something was not right, since this much-touted star had a very uninteresting role – the mother – in *The Champ* (79), for Franco Zeffirelli, with whom relations during filming were reported as 'strained'. Nor was she better served by *The First Deadly Sin* (80), which required her to be comatose for most of its length, as Frank Sinatra's fatally ill wife. Accordingly she seized her chance with two biographies, *Evita Peron* (81), for TV, and *Mommie Dearest*. 'Variety' liked her work in neither. It spoke of her 'cold, humorless (though technically accomplished) performance' in the first and 'high camp Faye Dunaway playing [female impersonator] Charles Pierce playing Joan Crawford' in the second. Both pieces were mediocre and to make matters worse relations were not good backstage: when Robert Mitchum walked off the Peron movie he echoed Polanski's opinion, adding, 'When I got here I walked in thinking I was a star and then I found out I was supposed to do everything the way she says. . . .'

She had a Broadway flop with 'The Curse of an Aching Heart' and should have been in Laurence Olivier's television *King Lear*, as Regan, but was replaced by Diana Rigg when she was offered a movie: Michael Winner's execrable remake of *The Wicked Lady* (83), which provided her with another deserved flop. Staying with Cannon she did an Agatha Christie mystery (only it was not), *Ordeal by Innocence* (84) with a singularly unnattractive cast (Donald Sutherland, Christopher Plummer, Sarah Miles). Though made in Britain it was not released there. Still on that side of the Atlantic she replaced Dolly Parton (who at the last minute changed her mind) as the villainess in the cynically motivated *Supergirl*. After two mini-series, *Christopher Columbus* and *Ellis Island*, she remained on the small screen with *Thirteen for Dinner* (85), another Christie tale, as a movie star and her imitator, and *Beverly Hills Madam* (86), in the title-role. There was a play in Hampstead, 'Circe and Bravo', only done because a West End transfer was guaranteed; she wanted the movie rights, but the author, Donald Freed, said he hoped for someone with more box-office appeal. Jane Fonda perhaps. 'Ouch' said 'The Times', reporting this. Dunaway's notices ranged from the ecstatic to the unimpressed. She supported Richard Chamberlain, an unlikely *Casanova* (87), for TV, and returned to Cannon opposite fellow *Barfly* Mickey Rourke. The company had bought *Duet for One* at her insistence but after two consecutive failures had preferred Julie Andrews. The attraction this time may have been that she took no salary, since she was 'desperate' to get back into films. Around this time she was divorced from her second husband, British photographer Terry O'Neill.

She played the wife of Daniel J. Travanti in the supposedly frightening *Midnight Crossing*, which went direct to video, and was a mother who embarks on an affair while staying in a sanatorium with her son, in *The Burning Secret* (88): the man was Klaus-Maria Brandauer, who in life threatened to withdraw 'if she continues to act in this fashion . . . '. Notwithstanding colleagues' opinions, there were many offers: *La Partitia/The Match* (89) in Italy, with Matthew Modine and Jennifer Beals; *Wait Until Spring Bandini*, with Joe Mantegna; and *The Handmaid's Tale*, scripted by Harold Pinter from Margaret Atwood's novel, with Robert Duvall.

Clint Eastwood

No one was more surprised than those Italian film executives when their cheap spear-and-sandal epics made inroads into the world markets, in a way undreamed of in the heyday of De Sica and Castellani. When the fad faded, Italian producers seized on that particularly indigenous American product, the Western, to prolong the profits. Soon they were turning them out at the same rate. Someone tagged them 'spaghetti Westerns'. Like the muscle-man movies most of them had an American 'name' in the lead – and indeed many of them Anglicized the complete credits in order to disguise the origins (unsuccessfully). When Italy was raked and found wanting as a substitute for Texas or New Mexico, the crews shifted to Spain and so, near Almeria, on a day in 1964, shooting commenced on *Per un Pugno di Dollari*. The total budget was $200,000 and the leading man, a TV star called Clint Eastwood, was being paid $15,000 of it. This was not the first of the spaghetti Westerns, but it was by far the most successful – indeed, its success accelerated the species. There were two sequels, with Eastwood, who then returned to the States as one of the top box-office stars in the world.

His earlier brushes with Hollywood were

not rewarding. He was born in San Francisco in 1933, the son of an itinerant accountant, and educated at Oakland Technical High School. He worked as a lifeguard and for a while as a lumberjack in Oregon, and then joined the army, where he became an athletics coach and taught swimming. After the army he entered Los Angeles City College (where he met his wife Maggie) and worked as a delivery man. He delivered trucks to Universal and an army buddy there got him a test: Universal offered the standard option, starting at $75 a week. They dropped him 18 months later, during which period he appeared – according to their later bulletins – in 14 pictures. However, his only *credits* for this period were: *Revenge of the Creature* (55), *Francis in the Navy*, *Lady Godiva*, *Tarantula* and *Never Say Goodbye* (56). He went over to RKO for two small parts: in *The First Travelling Saleslady* and *Escapade in Japan* (57). Then he got a good role in *Ambush at Cimarron Pass* at 20th – second lead to Scott Brady in what he called 'the lousiest Western ever made'. He was also in a small part in *Lafayette Escadrille* at Warners. Between whiles he tried New York, getting an occasional bit part on TV while eking out a living as a labourer. On a chance visit to CBS TV he was picked out by a director casting a new 30-minute Western series, 'Rawhide', and signed for the lead. CBS dithered, finally put it out in 1959 and it ran for eight years. Presumably between seasons Eastwood was up for grabs, but normally he did not work – till, between the sixth and seventh season, his agent came up with an offer from Italy. The producers did not like his somnambulant manner – the Italian cast were in contrast very active – but director Sergio Leone knew what Eastwood was aiming at. He came on strong as the traditional primitive cowboy, a bounty-hunter, silent, violent, The Man With No Name, in poncho and sombrero, with a short black cheroot clenched between his teeth. The film, *Per un Pugno di Dollari* (64, dubbed, *A Fistful of Dollars*), was distinguished only by Leone's visual gift and his taste for violence, but there must have been something charismatic about the combination of these and Eastwood. After a slow start the film took Italy by storm and then the rest of Europe. Britain and the US had to wait because the plot was based on *Yojimbo* and the Japanese company brought a lawsuit (settled out of court).

Eastwood returned to Spain (these were Spanish-Italian-West German productions) for *Per Qualche Dollari in Più* (65; dubbed, *For a Few Dollars More*), at $50,000 plus a percentage, plus Lee Van Cleef, another American semi-name destined to find fame in

Clint Eastwood as The Man With No Name in the first of Sergio Leone's famous Spaghetti Western trilogy A Fistful of Dollars *(64).*

such films. When Eastwood returned to Europe for the next one his salary would be $250,000 plus a percentage. First he did a sketch-film, *Le Streghe* (67), about witches – the De Sica episode, as Silvana Mangano's husband; then *Il Buono, il Brutto, il Cattivo* (dubbed, *The Good, the Bad and the Ugly*), again directed by Leone, again with Van Cleef – plus Eli Wallach. And again to big grosses. By this time he had accepted a Hollywood offer, at $400,000 plus 25 per cent of the net: *Hang 'Em High*, a Western every bit as brutal as the Italian ones. As this played off, the three Italian Westerns arrived and the four films did so well in the Anglo-American market that Eastwood turned up at fifth in the 1968 US box-office list and seventh on the British list.

He did a programmer for Universal, *Coogan's Bluff* (68), called a New York Western, about a sheriff hunting his quarry in Manhattan; as directed by Don Siegel it was punchy and exciting, and Eastwood for the first time established his screen personality – the laconic, deadpan Westerner who is just too smart to let the townsfolk take him for a ride. It was a wholly engaging character, with something of the purity of the great Western heroes. He agreed later that part of his appeal was in his self-sufficiency: 'A superhuman character who has all the answers, is doubly cool, exists on his own without society or the help of society's police forces.' He did a World War II adventure story, *Where Eagles Dare*, helping a sagging Richard Burton at the box-office, and then a musical, *Paint Your Wagon* (69), where his taciturn determination contrasted effectively with the ebullience of Lee Marvin. He was No 5 at the box-office that year and No 2 in 1970. He returned to the Western, one directed by Siegel with Shirley MacLaine, *Two Mules for Sister Sara* (70), playing what he called 'the ironic cowboy, selfish, but with a tinge of compassion'. Then Brian G. Hutton, who had directed his previous war film, guided him through another, jollier, one *Kelly's Heroes*, in which he led a looting expedition behind enemy lines. Telly Savalas, playing the sergeant in this goof-up gang, was not the first person to compare Eastwood to Gary Cooper: 'Cooper was perhaps more a man of instinct than Clint, but they both project one thing beautifully: pure Americanism.'

The two actors are not much alike – but one has to look backwards to find anyone comparable. For one thing, he is the only contemporary star whom it is difficult to imagine in the midst of agents and advisers, wheeling and dealing. Probably he does, but he seems to belong rather to the movies' age of innocence. He is an anomaly. He has his own production company, but is known to have turned down several $1 million offers to make the films he wants to make: *The Beguiled* (71), directed by Siegel, the adventures of a badly wounded Union soldier towards the end of the Civil War – a horror story rather than a Western; and *Play Misty for Me*, an okay thriller directed by himself about a disc-jockey pursued by an amorous fan (Jessica Walter). When Frank Sinatra sprained a wrist he replaced him in what would have been Sinatra's last film, *Dirty Harry*, and when Siegel was ill, directed some of it. He played the title-role, a tough Frisco cop using the same methods as his opponents. In 1971 he had again been second at the box-office and as *Dirty Harry* played off in 1972 that made him Numero Uno that year: the industry at last regarded him as more than a passing phenomenon. John Sturges directed *Joe Kidd* (72) and he himself directed – no less well – *High Plains Drifter* (73): both concerned the stranger who rides in to help the villagers and except in quality are virtually interchangeable. Some cinemagoers began to find the laconic gunfighter and the violence increasingly monotonous.

Eastwood directed, but did not appear in, *Breezy*, a romance with William Holden; and appeared in a sequel to *Dirty Harry*, called *Magnum Force*, which was liked much less by the press but was equally popular. In 1973 he was again the box-office Champ and in subsequent years never far down the list. He attempted to change the formula with *Thunderbolt and Lightfoot* (74), a caper tale with Jeff Bridges, and *The Eiger Sanction* (75), a mountain drama; he directed the latter and

Clint Eastwood in Dirty Harry *(72), a title which referred to the most ruthless cop in San Francisco. It was good to meet him again in the four sequels (so far), but in truth only the first two came within distance of being as exciting and accomplished as the first.*

also directed *The Outlaw Josey Wales* (76) after parting company with the original director. Like *The Enforcer*, the third and least of Dirty Harry's adventures, this was formula stuff and it is a pity that he turned down *The Towering Inferno* and, later, *Apocalypse Now*; there seemed no very good reason to go to see *The Gauntlet* (77), another cops-and-violence tale – especially as the reviews were not too hot. He said that he had no desire to branch out, though TV interviews suggested that he had a lot more to offer – could he play comedy as well as Cooper did? *Every Which Way But Loose* (78) was touted as a different Eastwood film; he played a hard-drinking truck-driver in a series of comic adventures with a pet orangutan, but, said 'Variety', disliking it, 'For Eastwood fans, the essential elements are there. Lots of people get beat up. Eastwood walks tall and looks nasty, lots of cars are smashed.' Some reviewers noticed the resemblance to some of the films of Burt Reynolds – with whom, earlier that year, Eastwood had shared a 'Time Magazine' cover; but that journal, in the person of Frank Rich, found it 'almost impossible to sit through'. For the second film running, the female lead was Sondra Locke, reputed to be the cause of the Eastwoods' separation. For years, he had filmed only at Warners, swearing that he would not return to Paramount after his experiences on *Paint Your Wagon*: but *Escape From Alcatraz* (79) was made there.

He was *Bronco Billy* (80), which he also directed, a knife-thrower who takes into his act a runaway heiress (Locke); with more care, it might have become one of the classic mismatings of screwball comedy, but it lacked even the joy of the Reynolds-Field relationship of *Smokey and the Bandit*. It did not do very well, but why anyone went to *Any Which Way You Can* is a puzzle: but in fact that took $39 million domestic, only $9 million less than its rather less horrible predecessor. Eastwood directed the next three, explaining that his decision about directing himself depended on liking the story, seeing it clearly or not wanting 'to have to work with another guy and explain it to him'. In *Firefox* (82) he was an embittered war veteran required to pose as a businessman in the USSR in order to spirit out the ultimate weapon; in *Honkytonk Man* he had leukaemia but was hoping to get to Grand Ole Opry before being called upstairs (accompanying him was his son, Kyle, playing his nephew); and *Sudden Impact* (83) as Dirty Harry. Cynics suggested that he returned to the role because of falling box-office – *Honkytonk Man* did particularly badly – and it has to be said that *Tightrope* (84) smacked of desperation. The fourth Dirty

Clint Eastwood's movies are an annual treat – and sometimes more – for his fans, and sometimes more than just them. This one is Every Which Way But Loose *(78).*

Harry had gratuitous violence to spare and then some; so did this, plus a fetid plot about a New Orleans cop identifying with hs prey, a sadistic whore-killer. *City Heat* was the long-delayed teaming with Reynolds and they were paid $5 million and $4 million respectively for a take of $21 million – which was $4 million less than it cost. Audiences fell away quickly when word-of-mouth indicated that this tale of Kansas City Depression gangsters – our heroes were on the other side of the law – had nothing new to offer. It had always been obvious that Eastwood tried to be faithful to his image while wanting, if only by small degrees, not to repeat himself: but it was certainly time to return to the Western, though now a genre long out of favour. *Pale Rider* (85), which he also directed, suggested a study of *Shane* and, more hopefully (and surprisingly), the surviving oeuvre of W.S. Hart. The result was tonic, if studied, and though some sceptics placed the Eastwood icon alongside Redford, he was to most audiences a reassuring figure – and along with Eddie Murphy, perhaps the only genuine box-office draw of this time. Certainly there was a warm welcome for a gung-ho marine movie, *Heartbreak Ridge* (86), with Eastwood directing and playing a Vietnam veteran sergeant training recruits to invade Grenada (ostensibly to rescue American citizens). His fee was said to be $6 million.

He was elected mayor of Carmel, the town

in which he lives, and was off the screen for a while. He returned with the fifth and least impressive of the Dirty Harries, *The Dead Pool* (88), and received excellent notices for a biography of Charlie Parker which he produced and directed, *Bird*. He then went into *The Pink Cadillac* (89) and is interestingly cast as a director based on John Huston in *Black Hunter White Heart*.

EDITH EVANS

Long regarded as one of the most distinguished figures of the British theatre, Edith Evans was 60 before she made her first starring film. She and her contemporary, Sybil Thorndike, had for years been considered the leading British actresses. Dame Sybil had starred in some Silent pictures and early Talkies (*Dawn, To What Red Hell?, Hindle Wakes*) and during the 40s and 50s was a major supporting actress (*Major Barbara, Nicholas Nickleby, The Prince and the Showgirl*). Dame Edith, whose theatrical career began in 1914, except for two early tries, did not enter films till 1948.

She was born in London in 1888 and on leaving school was apprenticed to a milliner. She studied acting at night school and was playing Beatrice in 'Much Ado About Nothing' at Streatham Town Hall when William Poel, the Elizabethan theatre specialist, saw her. He persuaded her to play Cressida with a professional company and after that she was unwilling to return to making hats. She began to play supporting parts in the West End – mostly character roles which led to two roles supporting the movies' first star, Florence Turner, in two of her British productions, *A Welsh Singer* (15) and *East Is East* (16), as her aunt. In 1918 she was invited by Ellen Terry to join her in a tour of music halls in scenes from 'The Merchant of Venice' and 'The Merry Wives of Windsor'. She established herself in the early 20s, notably as the Serpent and the She-Ancient in the original production of 'Back to Methuselah' and as Millamant in 'The Way of the World'. In 1925 she joined the Old Vic Company for the first time and played, among other parts, Cleopatra, Portia, Katherine in 'The Taming of the Shrew', Mrs Page, Beatrice and Rosalind. She made her New York bow in 1931 as Florence Nightingale in 'The Lady With a Lamp'.

As actresses age, their mannerisms increase and their range narrows. Edith Evans was an outstanding exception. Here is her celebrated Lady Bracknell in the film version of The Importance of Being Earnest *(52), with Joan Greenwood as Gwendoline and Michael Denison as Algernon.*

Other highlights of her career: Orinthia in 'The Apple Cart' (a part she created); Irela in 'Evensong' (London and New York); Gwenny in 'The Late Christopher Bean'; the Nurse in 'Romeo and Juliet', on several occasions, including one in New York; Agatha in 'The Old Ladies'; Arkadina in 'The Seagull'; an Old Vic season in 1936 and 'Old Acquaintance' in 1940. During the war she entertained the troops and appeared notably in revivals of 'Heartbreak House', as Hesione, and 'The Importance of Being Earnest', as Lady Bracknell, stunningly self-righteous and self-confident. In 1945 she played Mrs Malaprop (and was created a Dame) and the following year was Cleopatra again. With the Old Vic in 1948-49 she played Lady Wishfort in 'The Way of the World' and Ranevska in 'The Cherry Orchard'; she was 'Daphne Laureola' in London and New York, 1949-50; played in 'Waters of the Moon', 'The Dark is Light Enough' and 'The Chalk Garden'; and was with the Royal Shakespeare Company in 1959 – the Countess in 'All's Well . . .' and Volumnia in 'Coriolanus'.

She succumbed to the cinema when the producers of *The Queen of Spades* (48) promised her, if not a good film, a quality one. It was both. Thorold Dickinson directed from the Pushkin novella about a gambler (Anton Walbrook) who prises from an old lady her winning secret. Evans wore a rubber mask to age her and it did somewhat hamper her acting. A few months later she gave a beautiful performance as a Welsh peasant woman in Emlyn Williams's *The Last Days of Dolwyn* (49). She was the obvious choice for Lady Bracknell in Anthony Asquith's film of *The Importance of Being Earnest* (52), though the performance was too theatrical in a film already theatrical enough. There was but small hint of greasepaint in her work in *Look Back in Anger* (58), as Jimmy Porter's elderly friend, Ma Tanner, a Cockney char she otherwise delineated without patronage or a single false note. Some idea of her range was indicated by her playing of the bigoted but understanding Mother Superior in *The Nun's Story* (59), conceived entirely in terms of cinema and one of the outstanding performances in the medium (incredibly, not nominated for a Best Supporting Oscar). The more familiar Edith Evans, invincibly patrician, was on display in *Tom Jones* (63) – for which she was nominated – and *The Chalk Garden* (64). The latter had as a play contained one of her notable parts; in the diminished circumstances of the film she salvaged what she could.

She acted Judith Bliss in Noël Coward's 'Hay Fever' with the National Theatre and made her last major West End appearance in 'The Chinese Prime Minister'. In films, she played Lady Gregory in *Young Cassidy* (65) with Rod Taylor, a version of the early life of Sean O'Casey; and a lonely old working-class woman living in poverty in *The Whisperers* (66). This was a downbeat subject and, despite plot contrivances, the best film made by writer-director Bryan Forbes. 'But,' said 'Time Magazine', 'Dame Edith, 79, gives a superb performance that soars above the script. Hobbling on thick ankles that can no longer bear their burden, querulously demanding a new pair of shoes. . . . She has created new proof that for great actresses there is still no age limit.' The film was indeed a triumph for her and brought a bevy of awards, including the New York critics' Best Actress (the Oscar went to her friend Katharine Hepburn). But it was not popular. In the wake of it, she went to Hollywood to play a daffy old lady in a Dick Van Dyke comedy, *Fitzwilly* (67), and then did another poor comedy, *Prudence and the Pill* (68), as Deborah Kerr's mother. She was one of the old girls clucking round Katharine Hepburn in *The Madwoman of Chaillot* (69) and then an old lady beset by crooks in *Crooks and Coronets*, a belated American attempt to resurrect Ealing comedy, with Telly Savalas and Warren Oates.

Then, Charles Dickens: Betsy Trotwood in *David Copperfield* (70), a part she had longed to play, but the film was dire; and The Ghost of Christmas Past in *Scrooge* – to hear her announce herself, 'I am the Ghost . . .', in those inimitable tones, gave one a *frisson* of misplaced pleasure. In 1971 she appeared in 'Dear Antoine' at the Chichester Festival, but on medical advice relinquished the part after a few days. Unable to act on the stage again – except to read poems – she did a number of small roles in films, almost all of them unworthy of her: *Upon This Rock* (73), as Queen Christina in this semi-documentary for TV; *A Doll's House* – the Claire Bloom version, as the old nurse; and *Craze* (74), being murdered by Jack Palance. It was sad to see her propped up in *The Slipper and the Rose* (76), presumably being used for her name value, as the Prince's grandmother; her last appearance was as the dying abbess in *Nasty Habits*, with Glenda Jackson. She herself died before it was seen. A one-time companion, Jean Batters, published a perceptive account of her life with Evans, which made clear that she had subordinated everything in life to her ambition – including, perhaps, the brief marriage which left her a widow.

In stark contrast to Lady Bracknell, here is the lonely old woman she played in The Whisperers *(66), a performance which contained not a hint, not a whisper, of Lady Bracknell or the other aristocratic ladies she often played.*

Mia Farrow

Mia Farrow is the daughter of Hollywood parents. Father was writer-director John Farrow, whose work ranged from the accomplished (*The Big Clock*) to the banal (*John Paul Jones*).He was a drinker in the Hollywood tradition. Mother is Maureen O'Sullivan, dimity MGM star of the 30s (Kitty in Garbo's *Anna Karenina*, Weissmuller's Jane and assorted B pictures). Mia was born in Hollywood in 1945, the third of seven children. Following father's filmic chores, she had a peripatetic existence, but was brought up mostly in Britain, well away from the public glare. She decided she wanted to be an actress and managed to get some TV roles as well as a part in an off-Broadway production of 'The Importance of Being Earnest'. Around the same time 20th were having trouble with a British movie, *Guns of Batasi* (64): it was alleged that Peter Sellers withdrew his wife, Britt Ekland, from the role of the ingénue (20th sued and the Sellers counter-sued). Farrow was taken on to play it and as a result 20th offered the part of Alison in their continuing 'Peyton Place' on TV. She did it for two years and it made her mildly famous; what made her very famous was that Frank Sinatra courted her and made her his third wife in 1966. Much (too much) was written about the marriage and its break-up (1968), but it seems partly to have been due to her insistence on pursuing her career. During the marriage she made one picture, *A Dandy in Aspic* (68), partnered by Laurence Harvey. He, she and it got terrible notices; she seems to have quit a small part in *The Detective*, with her husband, on grounds of discretion.

The rather fey quality of Mia Farrow's screen personality has limited her appeal, though in recent years Woody Allen has managed to show other facets of the lady. Among the best of her earlier performances is the one in Altman's A Wedding *(78), as the bride. Howard Duff plays the doctor examining her.*

A better film awaited her: *Rosemary's Baby*, Roman Polanski's devilishly good adaptation of Ira Levin's story of witchcraft and diabolism in Manhattan. Frail and fawn-like, Farrow may not so much have been performing as permitting herself to be manipulated; whatever, audiences were caught up in her dilemma as with the best Hitchcock heroines and the film was a gigantic, deserved success. *Secret Ceremony* (69) confirmed that she could act – a startling study of a fey young thing who attaches herself to a has-been whore (Elizabeth Taylor); Joseph Losey directed and the film was liked by neither press nor public. (Co-star Robert Mitchum convinced her that Henry Hathaway was a hard taskmaster, so she turned down *True Grit*.) Nor was *John and Mary*, a not-delicate-enough tale of a couple of New Yorkers (he was Dustin Hoffman) who pick each other up for the weekend; and Farrow's hesitant swinger soon became cloying. In 1970 she gave birth to twins via André Previn – jazz musician, film composer, symphony conductor – and when his divorce came through they were married. In London together they did 'Joan of Arc at the Stake' and in Britain she made a minor horror film, *Blind Terror* (71; US title *See No Evil*), about a blind girl terrorized by the man who has slain her family. In a tele-movie, *Goodbye, Raggedy Ann*, she was a neurotic Hollywood starlet. For Hal Wallis in London she played a part once announced for Julie Andrews, Elizabeth Taylor and several others: *Follow Me* (72), with Michael Jayston and Topol. In France she made a picture with Belmondo, *Docteur Popaul*, after which she made her English stage début, in Manchester, in 'Mary Rose'.

She was one of the several aspirants to the role of Daisy in *The Great Gatsby* (74) and was paid $100,000 – as against Robert Redford's $250,000 and Bruce Dern's $75,000. She said afterwards that she was more interested in motherhood than filming and indeed the film, overblown and over-publicized, did nothing for her reputation (or anyone else's). The following year she was in 'The Marrying of Ann Leyte' for the RSC and she was off the screen till the British-Canadian *Full Circle* (77), presumably her only film offer – otherwise why would she want to play yet another fey waif up to her ears in horror? It was reported that her marriage was in not-too-good state and she embarked on a number of films: *Avalanche* (78), as Rock Hudson's ex-wife; Altman's *A Wedding; Death on the Nile*, as a neurotic trouble-maker; and the remake of *Hurricane* (79) – shown about the time of the divorce. She played the Dorothy Lamour role, now white, so that the match more fashionably was one of miscegenation. On Broadway she and Anthony Perkins made an ideal (for some) team in 'Romantic Comedy'.

In 1981 she was announced for an Australian film, but instead Woody Allen chose her to be one of those playing *A Midsummer Night's Comedy* (81). They fell in love and she has been his muse ever since – apart from an appearance in an unseen animated feature made in 1982, *Sarah*. The Allen films: *Zelig*

(83), as that gentleman's shrink; *The Purple Rose of Cairo* (85), as an unhappily married waitress whose dreams materialize at the local cinema during the Depression; *Broadway Danny Rose* (84), showing unexpected range as a Bronx-voiced moll with Mafia connections – 'a revelation' as Janet Maslin said in the 'New York Times'; *Hannah and her Sisters* (86), as Hannah, the nice normal one, an actress making a come-back, married to Michael Caine and with her mother playing her mother; *Radio Days* (87), as a one-time floozy, now a gossip columnist; and *September*, as a lady in mid-life crisis. There was trouble on that one: Elaine Stritch replaced Maureen O'Sullivan as Farrow's mother and Sam Waterston's role had at one time been played by Sam Shepard and then Christopher Walken. On top of all that, the box-office was not good. For Allen, Farrow was not *Another Woman* (88), Gena Rowlands was; though she looked in as a pregnant woman talking to a shrink; but she was his Gentile girlfriend in his episode of the three *New York Stories* (89). She also had a few lines as the mother of *Supergirl* (84).

FERNANDEL

The films of Fernandel were for 40 years the targets of critics. 'L'Écran Français' once observed that each time a journalist questioned him on the mediocrity of his films, he vainly reassured them: 'Oh, mais maintenant je vais être très difficile sur le choix des scénarios.' When, in the early 50s, he did escape from run-of-the-mill Fernandel fare, he made a considerable name for himself in the US and Britain. Few comics can breach national boundaries: every country has its comedies for home consumption. France has quite a few. Fernandel's own long and enormous popularity was somewhat eaten into in the late 50s by Bourvil, who was succeeded in turn by Louis de Funès.

De Funès was funny as a featured player, but as a star actor had no success with either critics or public outside France. Too few of Bourvil's films were seen – and then mainly those in which he had a straight part. His comedies were old-fashioned, but in his quiet loon-faced way he was an agreeable actor. Fernandel was also no mean actor, though the fact was obscured as he mugged his way from one forgettable farce to the next. One French critic in 1947 reckoned that of the 70 odd films he had made till then only six were any good. It was said with regret. Throughout this phenomenal career (in French films, only Gabin's can compare in longevity) he was never confined to the scrap heap often reserved for popular favourites – though no French critic would go as far as 'Life Magazine', which once used his face to epitomize France.

Undoubtedly, he was an actor with whom audiences identified, a plain man, reminiscent of Disney's Horace Horsecollar. His face, literally, was his fortune. It was a generous face, though at times it seemed capable of only two expressions – wide-eyed surprise and smug satisfaction (accompanied by a breathless voice, interminably wheedling). But there must have been something more to have carried it through more than 150 films.

He was born Fernand Contandin in 1903, the son of a man who entertained part-time at various music halls in the neighbourhood. As a boy Fernandel also entertained in the evenings and carried off prizes at amateur concerts. When he left school he worked as a junior commissionaire in the bank where his brother was employed; and then joined the wholesale grocery firm that his father set up when he left the army. After a spell as a docker he became a bank-teller, while continuing as an amateur singer. In 1992 he turned professional, appeared on vaudeville bills and toured in an operette called ' Le Cavalier Lafleur'. In 1925 he married the sister of an ex-bank colleague. His *tour-de-chant* was successful in the Midi and he was engaged to appear at the Bobino in Paris: success was immediate and he was engaged to star in a revue at the Concert Mayol, 'Vive le Nu' (30). As a result he was offered a small part in *Le Blanc et le Noir* (30), as a virgin messenger boy who helpfully offers to deflower Raimu's wife. He was thus launched into a series of (mainly) farces – including several shorts – where husbands were compromised, wives were found in unlikely beds and lovers in cupboards: *La Meilleure Bobonne; J'ai Quelque Chose à Vous Dire; Attaque Nocturne; Paris-Béguin* (31); *Vive la Classe; Coeur de Lilas* starring Gabin; *La Fine Combine; Pas un Mot à ma Femme; Bric-à-Brac et Cie*; and *La Veine d'Anatole*. Among these was Renoir's first Talkie, *On Purge Bébé*, with Michel Simon, adapted from Feydeau, filmed in four days and a considerable box-office success. Some of the others were directed by Maurice Cammage, who was to direct about 50 per cent of his films over the next decade.

Bernard Deschamps was convinced that Fernandel was the only actor to play the virtuous Isidore in his adaptation of de Maupassant, *Le Rosier de Madame Husson* (32), opposite Françoise Rosay. It was a serious role that scared Fernandel but he did it with pathos and dignity – that of a grocer's imbecile son who is elected to receive Mme

Husson's cheque for virtue (there being no suitable maidens that year), then rushes off to lose it – his virtue that is. Basically a study in small-town hypocrisy, it was also funny; there were rave notices, queues at the box-office and Fernandel became a national favourite. It was one of the first and one of the few French Talkies to be shown in New York and London at this time. After another farce, *Pas de Femmes*, Fernandel was invited to Berlin by UFA to support Firmin Gémier in *L'Homme sans Nom*, a desperate tale about an amnesiac (Werner Krauss played Gémier's role in the German version). He returned to France to play with Raimu again and Gabin in *Les Gaîtés de l'Escadron*, a successful army comedy. He was the eternal grumbler who, wrote Maurice Bourdet in 'Vu', 'n'est pas de deuxième classe, mais, tout de bon, hors classe. Plus qu'une réussite passagère. . . .'Apart from two-reelers, he made two more films that year. He had a small role, as a baker's boy, in *La Porteuse de Pain*, a hoary old stage melodrama modernized, about a wrongly convicted girl (Germaine Dermoz) who escapes to find the real killer; and a big one, as a shady lawyer, in *Le Jugement de Minuit*, an adaptation of an Edgar Wallace story.

After a stint in his home town in a revue, he got his first star-billing (name alone above the title): *Le Coq du Régiment* (33). That was followed by two more miliary tales, *Lidoire* and *L'Ordonnance*. The latter was adapted from a de Maupassant story – life in a garrison town – and gave Fernandel the chance to play a stupid brute, having a kitchen flirtation with Paulette Dubost. He returned to the Bobino and co-starred with Mistinguett at the Folies-Bergère; then did a succession of comedies: *D'Amour et d'Eau Fraiche* (34), as the chauffeur of Renée Saint-Cyr; *La Garnison Amoureuse* with Colette Darfeuil; the hugely successful *Adémai Aviateur*, in which he and Noël-Noël were novice airmen in a plane neither could fly – one of a series starring Noël-Noël as Adémai; *Une Nuit de Folie* with Dolly Davis; *Le Chéri de sa Concierge* with Alice Tissot; and another – but unsuccessful – version of Feydeau, *L'Hôtel du Libre-Échange*.

Angèle was written and directed by Marcel Pagnol from a novel by Jean Giono, the story of a village girl (Orane Demazis) seduced and betrayed, rescued from harlotry by family retainer Fernandel and imprisoned by a vengeful father till a Good Man (Jean Servais) comes along to forgive her. Due to its scandalous nature, the complete version was not shown in Paris till three years later; almost 60 years later, it still works – due to the Provençal locations and the performances of Demazis and Fernandel, he touching as the baboon-jawed handyman, called 'imbécile' by most of the cast. He returned to comedy, playing a matelot in *Les Bleus de la Marine*, written by his brother-in-law (the ex-bank clerk; he also wrote much of his music-hall material). Then: *Le Train de 8 h. 47* (33), after Courteline, with Bach as his comrade-in-arms, the two of them stuck in Bar-le-Duc; *Le Cavalier Lafleur*, which he had done on stage – now in the leading role; *Ferdinand le Noceur*, with Paulette Dubost as his bride; *Jim la Houlette* with Marguerite Moreno; and *Les Gaîtés de la Finance* (36), with Raymond Cordy.

In 1935 he had reappeared in vaudeville, at the ABC, and in the winter of that year had a big success, in Marseilles and in Paris in 'Ignace', an operette written by his brother-in-law; in accustomed French tradition it had a military setting and he was a conscript batman shaking up the dust in his colonel's mansion. He remained in uniform for *Un de la Légion*, which combined the farce of 'Ignace' with the pathos of *Angèle*, about an unwilling legionnaire who comes to like the life. Christian-Jaque directed Fernandel for the first time – on location in Morocco. The producers (and the public) liked the film so well that they were reunited for three successive films: the sentimental *Josette* – played by Fernandel's own daughter, Josette; *François Ier*, a historical burlesque – he dreams himself back in time – which was quite funny; and *Les Dégourdis de l'Onzième*, another 'casernes en folie' effort (set in 1906) which proved, quite conclusively, that the public was sick of the genre. *François Ier* was not shown in New York till 1947, the first film of Fernandel's, save the Pagnols, to reach there in more than a decade – not to the approval of the 'New York Times', who said that he 'hams, mugs

Angèle *(34) was a typical Marcel Pagnol melodrama about a nice girl seduced and abandoned. The film was made memorable by the sunny Provençal locations and most of the acting, and contained a notable portrait of a simpleton, touchingly played by Fernandel.*

and chews the scenery in a fashion which is disastrously unfunny'. (However, a few weeks later in that same paper a different critic, reviewing *Fric-Frac*, referred to 'the rich and robust comic talents of that horse-faced actor. . . .')

Meanwhile, there was a mild welcome for *Les Rois du Sport* (37), a weak joke about two waiters who become boxers; Raimu co-starred and, though he was billed over Fernandel, the latter was better paid – indeed, he was now the highest-paid actor in France. They were both in *Carnet de Bal*, but Fernandel's episode was one of the weakest – as the hairdresser who has become the happy father of several kids. He needed a good film – so did the screen version of *Ignace*, which was successful; but whatever it was like then, it is now totally unfunny and rather like a cheap imitation of a British imitation of a Hollywood musical of the period. His 'serious' reputation was retrieved by *Regain*, which Pagnol directed from a Giono original. He played – beautifully – a knife-grinder who loses his mistress (Demazis) to his best friend. The 'New York Times' called it 'an enduring work of art' and the critics in that city voted it the Best Foreign Film of the year; it was banned in Britain till 1956 (probably because it implied that the girl had been forced into a gang-bang). Fernandel played on the stage in an operette constructed from 'Le Rosier de Madame Husson' and had a second good film, *Hercule*, with Gaby Morlay, a fable especially written by Carlo Rim – about a naive fisherman who inherits a Paris newspaper and, taking over as editor, turns the tables on the mockers. Said Alexandre Arnoux in 'Les Nouvelles Littéraires': 'Acteur grossier et fin en même temps, Fernandel domine toujours son public; il possède sa manière du génie et se tire des pas les plus difficiles sans trébucher, si bien qu'on ne s'avis pas toujours de son adresse infaillible. Ici, il avait un rôle en or, et plus nuancé que ceux qu'il joue d'ordinaire. Il y fait merveille.'

As far as the public was concerned, he dominated the French film scene. In 1936, he had been third at the box-office, trailing Charles Boyer and Pierre-Richard Wilm; in 1937 he was first with over 11,000 points (Gabin, who was second, got 4,000). His position was so strong that he did not need to work with the charlatans and passing foreigners who dominated the French film industry and permanently threatened to ruin it (they certainly bankrupted not themselves but various companies they formed). He worked again with Pagnol, directing a story he had written for him: *Le Schpountz* (38), about a yokel who fancies himself a tragedian and is taken to Paris as a joke by a film company – there he stars in a film parody which is a riot with the public; but his heart is broken. The real film public were not so taken by this corny but enjoyable film and he went back to farces: *Barnabe*, a case of mistaken identity (they think he's a count); *Tricoche et Cacolet*, from an old comedy about two private sleuths – Duvallès was the other and Elvire Popesco was also in it; *Ernest le Rebelle*, directed by Christian-Jaque, about a French jazz musician

Fernandel was the eternal optimist – at least in the films he made for Pagnol. This one is Regain *(37), and he plays an itinerant knife-grinder cheerfully surviving the blows of fate.*

Fric-Frac (39) was an amusing and very popular slice of low-life, recounting the adventures of a respectable jeweller's assistant, Fernandel, after he has fallen for a tough lady of the milieu, Arletty.

Fernandel still smiling for Pagnol: La Fille du Puisatier *(40).*

involved in a Latin-American revolt; and *Raphael le Tatoué*, about a night-watchman who deserts his post and invents a twin brother when he is seen by his boss. During the making of this, he recalled later, the producers told him he was finished.

Still, there was work to be had and typical stories like *Les Cinq Sous de Lavarède*, in which he was a blowhard who will inherit a fortune if he can go round the world on five sous. (It had been made only three years earlier with Albert Préjean; this version was not shown till the German occupation, when the authorities hacked chunks out of it; so when finally shown complete in 1951 it was advertised as the unexpurgated version.) There followed *Berlingot et Cie* (not shown till 1940), with Suzy Prim; *Fric-Frac* (39), in the role played on the stage by Victor Boucher; and *L'Héritier des Mondésir* (40), made in Berlin for UFA just before the outbreak of war, with Fernandel in a quadruple role, as the old baron and as his bastard, the village postman who inherits – and in a dream, their ancestors. When hostilities commenced he abandoned the film he was making for Pagnol and joined the army – but that turned out to be a brief interlude. He returned to finish the film, *La Fille du Puisatier*, where he and Raimu were marvellous *copains*. Then he was again a valet, mistaken for his master and in love with a maid mistaken for her mistress: *Monsieur Hector*.

In Marseilles he appeared in an operette, 'Hughes', and in Vichy France made a series of poor films: *L'Acrobate*, as a maître d'hôtel who fakes amnesia to get even with his mistress; *La Nuit Merveilleuse* with Madeleine Robinson; the aptly named *Les Petits Riens* (41), in a sketch as an undertaker, with Suzy Prim; and *Le Club des Soupirants*. He directed *Simplet* (42), made by the German-backed Continentale, only too happy to try new directors. Carlo Rim wrote it: Fernandel was the village mascot expelled when he gets above himself and sheltered in a rival village, where he watches catastrophes rain on his native heath. *La Bonne Étoile* (43) was a sentimental tale about a Provençal fisherman who loses his girl to a wealthy playboy. Then: *Une Vie de Chien*, in which he dragged-up in order to marry the woman he loves (!); *Ne le Criez pas sur les Toits*, in search of a secret formula; *La Cavalcade des Heures*, in one sketch, singing for his supper; *Adrien*, which he also directed, as a cashier who invents motorized roller-skates; and *Un Chapeau de Paille d'Italie* (44), a remake of René Clair's famous Silent comedy. By this time he had returned to Paris, on the principle that there were now as many Germans in Marseilles as in Paris. He returned to vaudeville in 1944 and 1945; and quietly returned to filming.

Le Mystère Saint-Val (45) was an old-dark-house mystery. Among the critics who put it down was 'L'Écran Français': 'Fernandel, qui est souvent drôle au milieu de situations absurdes, n'est pas cette fois dans ses bons jours; il vit sur son vieux stock d'expressions, sur ses tics comiques dont l'efficacité s'émousse un peu plus chaque jour.' Pagnol wrote *Naïs*, from Zola's 'Naïs Micoulin', and managed to include all his clichés (unmarried mother, etc.). Fernandel was a pathetic hunch-backed farmhand desperately adoring the flighty Naïs (Jacqueline Bouvier/Pagnol – she soon married the director): roaring melodrama, only just two-dimensional. He was again with Raimu in an unsuccessful fantasy, *Les Gueux au Paradis* (46), and then in another flop, Marc Allégret's *Pétrus*, from a play by Marcel Achard that Louis Jouvet had done. He played a photographer and it was mainly notable for the return of Simone Simon after her sojourn in Hollywood. After a short, *Escale au Soleil*, he appeared in 'Le Chasseur d'Images', an operette. There was *L'Aventure de Cabassou* (47), produced by Pagnol's brother, René, in Marseilles, a film about a cuckold and a ghost. Said 'L'Écran Français': 'Et il fait ce qu'il peut, le malheureux, tellement qu'au milieu de cet océan de platitude et de vulgarité, il arrive même à être drôle l'espace de dix secondes au moins.'

But *Coeur de Coq* must be his, or anybody's, worst film, a musical about an amorous typographer wth a heart transplant which makes him crow each morning. *Emile l'Africain* (48) was more suitable, with Fernandel as a film-studio worker who gets the chance to pass himself off as a great explorer. He was already involved with this when Pagnol wanted him for the lead in one of the first French colour films, *La Belle Meunière* (the part went to Tino Rossi). Another project which did not come to fruition was a modern *Candide*, directed by René Clément (conceived when Marcel Carné's version with Gérard Philipe fell through). And it was reported that David O. Selznick had asked him to play a part in *Portrait of Jenny* in New York. Instead, he did *Si Ça Peut Vous Faire Plaisir*, a study of Marseilles life, as a barker who helped a friend in marital difficulties. He did go to New York, and to Canada, with his music-hall act (48) and appeared there on TV.

But, in general, his reputation overseas depended on the Pagnol films. Then *L'Armoire Volante* (49) was successful abroad, a black comedy about a very proper bureaucrat hunting for a cupboard containing his aunt's corpse. He played it entirely straight and without a smile – to confound those critics, he said, who claimed his talent lay in his gums. The level was maintained with the Italian *Botta e Risposta*, in which Suzy Delair hunted for a dress through the music halls of Rome, encountering among the unclad girls pious pilgrim Fernandel; and *On Demande un Assassin*, a farce where he loaned his apartment for assignations. Then *L'Heroïque Monsieur Boniface*, as a *petit employé* involved in a police raid; the poor *Casimir* (50), as a vacuum-cleaner salesman; *Tu m'as Sauvé la Vie*, a farce written and directed by, and co-starring, Sacha Guitry, that they had done in Paris the pevious year. They even used the stage settings, which caused the public to cold-shoulder it: Fernandel, however, was at his best as a *clochard* adopted as heir by a baron – to the distress of his family. There was another filmed play, *Topaze*, a remake of Jouvet's famous vehicle, directed now by its author, Pagnol.

Fernandel had been considered a funny man for so long that his appearance in *Meurtres* (51) surprised his admirers. He was a farmer driven to the mercy killing of his wife, but what started as high drama finished, not disagreeably, as low comedy. He was much praised, though 'Variety' thought he had 'a tendency to declaim his histrionic scenes'. *Uniformes et Grandes Manoeuvres* was a return to an old formula and so was *Boniface Somnambule*, but there he was at his very best as a store detective. And he was superb, if eventually a trifle wearing, in Autant-Lara's grisly black comedy, *L'Auberge Rouge*, as an itinerant monk to whom innkeeper Françoise Rosay confesses her habit of murdering her guests. *La Table aux Crevés* (52) might be considered his first wholly serious film, an adaptation of a novel by Marcel Aymé about a feud in a village of the Midi, centred on a man (Fernandel) suspected of murdering his wife. Henri Verneuil directed, the first of several with Fernandel. His stock rose and was not seriously hurt by another shot at direction, *Adhémar ou le Jouet de la Fatalité*, wiith Jacqueline Pagnol, from a play by Guitry.

International fame came in a big way with Julien Duvivier's *Le Petit Monde de Don Camillo*, adapted from Giovanni Guareschi's

Fernandel's biggest successes outside France were the Don Camillo films, where he played a kindly, if idiosyncratic, village priest – seen here talking to his sworn enemy, the Communist mayor, in Le Petit Monde de Don Camillo *(52).*

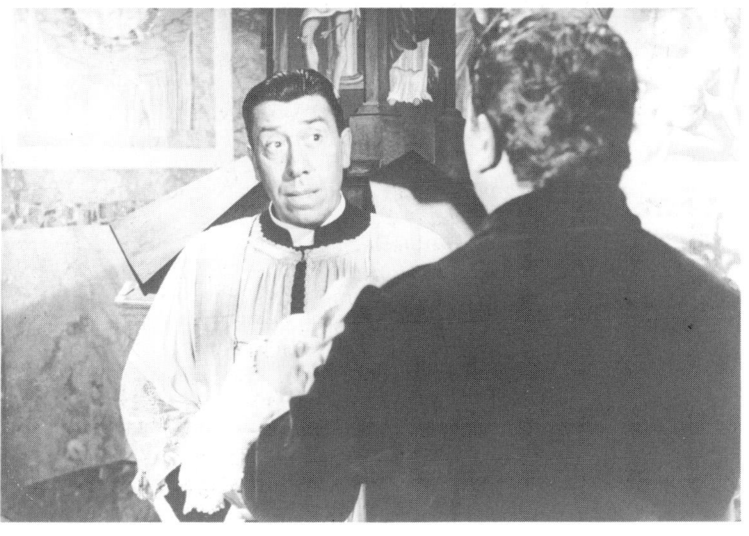

fables about the rivalry of two lovable bigots, the Communist mayor (Gino Cervi) and the village curé (Fernandel) – irascibly turning to God for inspiration in direct confrontation. These serio-comic adventures were a big success overseas (somewhat to Fernandel's consternation, as he had preferred a salary to a percentage; Duvivier had a percentage and became quite rich). At least temporarily this success assured an export market for each film Fernandel made. In France, the next was his biggest postwar success apart from the Don Camillo films – though it was a feeble-minded thing, *Coiffeur pour Dames*, a farce about a sheep-shearer who makes it big on the Champs-Elysées, adapted from a play and originally filmed in 1932 with Fernand Gravey. *Le Fruit Défendu* was serious – based on a Simenon story about a country doctor infatuated with Françoise Arnoul. Verneuil directed, as he did *Le Boulanger de Valorgue*, a more typical vehicle about a baker who defends the honour of his son by denying bread to the villagers. Then another Guareschi book was adapted, *Le Retour de Don Camillo* (53), which had almost as much success as the original. Duvivier directed, but the several inferior sequels were done by other hands (and mainly made in Italy).

After taking Raimu's old part in the remake of *Mam'zelle Nitouche* with Pier Angeli (his producers could now – just about – afford international names) he did three for Verneuil; the poor *Carnaval*, written by Pagnol, with Jacqueline Pagnol, a comedy about cuckoldry; *L'Ennemi Public No 1* (54) – a New York salesman mistaken for a gangster, with Zsa Zsa Gabor; and *Le Mouton à Cinq Pattes*, playing father and quintuplets, a black comedy whose possibilities went mainly undeveloped. The latter was a success abroad; not so *Ali-Baba et les 40 Voleurs*, partly written by Zavattini and directed by Jacques Becker – then at the height of his prestige. Great things were expected of this fantasy – filmed on location in North Africa – but director and star did not get on, a fact apparent in the finished film. Then: *Le Printemps, l'Automne et l'Amour* (55), a romance which partnered him wtih the young Nicole Berger; *Don Camillo e l'Onorevole Peppone; Le Couturier de ces Dames* (56), as a philanderer uneasily married to Suzy Delair; and *Don Juan*, a comic swashbuckler directed by John Berry from Hollywood, as Sganarelle, with Erno Crisa in the title-role.

Mike Todd badly wanted him to play the valet in *Around the World in 80 Days*, but Fernandel insisted that his English was not up to it and did a cameo part instead. The Mexican Cantinflas played the part; but Fernandel promised Todd that he would learn English for his projected *Don Quixote*. (Todd was killed and the film was not made.) Then: *L'Homme à l'Imperméable* (57) a tired gangster piece directed by Duvivier; *Sous le Ciel de Provence*, pretending to marry a girl (Giulia Rubini) who is pregnant – a remake by Mario Soldati of the Italian *Four Steps in the Clouds; Sénéchal le Magnifique*, with Nadia Gray, as a small-time actor getting to the top by his own devious means; and *Honoré de Marseille*.

For some time it had become practice in certain journals to invoke the name of Fernandel to castigate British and American comics; and it was assumed that in the unlikely event of his going to Hollywood he would knock them all silly. Several comedians said they would like to partner him and it was Bob Hope who nabbed him: *Paris Holiday*. Fernandel was not enthusiastic, but agreed to do it provided he got top-billing in France. Alec Guinness wisely turned down the chance to make it a trio, so Hope and Fernandel were a couple of globe-trotting rival actors, the former wise-cracking and the latter (in the role of Fernydel) mostly miming. He was mildly effective in what was, anyway, a weakly scripted film. At all events, producers concurred that he was at his best in native products and his international reputation began to tail away – helped on its way, no doubt, by a run of poor films: a comedy, *Le Chômeur de Clochemerle* (58), in the title-role, the only unemployed man in the village; *La Loi est la Loi*, as a French customs officer involved in a racket with Italian smuggler Toto (an actor who in Italy had a position akin to his own in France); *La Vie à Deux*, in that film's weakest episode, a joke about a cuckold; *Les Vignes du Seigneur* (59), with some drunk scnes; *Le Grand Chef*, with Cervi, echoes of their Don Camillo battles as two kidnappers lumbered with a frightful child – an O. Henry story, filmed before with Fred Allen and Oscar Levant; and *Le Confidant de ces Dames* with Sylva Koscina, as a vet who becomes a famous ladies' doctor. Much better was *La Vache et le Prisonnier* (60), the adventures of an escape from a German prison camp trying to reach Paris – and one of the most successful of all his films.

Jean Giono wrote and directed *Crésus*, a rambling tale about a shepherd who finds some stolen money and generously gives it away. It reinforced the impression that Fernandel had abandoned his old ebullient style for a quieter approach, so that the eloquence of his expressions was more effective than ever. His popularity remained extraordinary, but the acclaim that might have been generously offered was denied him because he still made too many films – and too many bad ones. Too many of them echoed films he had made years before: *Le Caid*, a thriller, as a professor mistaken for a sinister gangster: *Cocagne* (61), with Dora Doll; *Dynamite Jack*, in a dual role, as a nervous French visitor to the Far West and as a hired killer; *Don Camillo Monseigneur*; and *L'Assassin est dans l'Annuaire* (62), a who-dunnit with Edith Scob. He went to Italy to appear in De Sica's dreadful, all-star *Il Giudizio Universale* and, with Cervi again, *Avanti la Musica*, set in that country just before the Americans landed and notable – to its star at any rate – for the screen début of his son, Franck Fernandel. He was promoted from Don Camillo to God in Duvivier's episodic *Le Diable et les Dix Commandements* – but turned out to be mental, something unsurprising in a film whose general tone was relentlessly facetious. *Le Voyage à Biarritz* was a bourgeois comedy with Arletty, somewhat more enjoyable than *Le Bon Roi Dagobert* (63), a historical romp with Cervi, in the title-role. The next was his biggest success in years, *La Cuisine au Beurre* – it teamed him with Bourvil, who in the plot had married his wife (Claire Maurier) during his 10-year absence. After that: *Relaxe-toi Chérie* (64) with Sandra Milo; *Blague dans le Coin* with Perrette Pradier; and *L'Age Ingrat* (65), the first film of Gafer, a production company he had formed with Jean Gabin. They played parents trying to marry off their offspring, one of whom was Franck Fernandel. There was another in the series, *Il Compagno Don Camillo/Don Camillo à Moscou*.

Virtually none of these was exported; one that slipped through was *La Bourse et la Vie*, written and directed by Jean-Pierre Mocky, and infinitely worse than any of them – a tedious, childish 'chase' comedy involving a cache of money and three accountants – Jean Poiret, Fernandel and Heinz Rühmann (a middle-aged man who was a big star in his native Germany – and on this showing, inexplicably). Fernandel had fattened, had mellowed and was less agile. He made only one picture the following year, *Le Voyage du Père* (66) and was then inactive due to ill-health. He returned in an indifffferent comedy, *L'Homme à la Buick* (68), and also made his way back to the theatre, in 'Freddy le Clown'. There were high hopes for *Heureux qui comme Ulysse* (70) because it was directed by Henri Colpi; but it was disappointing, a slight comedy about a labourer's love for his horse. Then he began another Camillo, *Don Camillo Peppone e i Giovanni d'Oggi*; it was held up for months because he was ill and was still unfinished when he died of cancer in 1971 (it was finally made with Gastone Moschin in his part). Every so often a new comic is said to be taking his place in the affections of the public. It is unlikely to happen.

José Ferrer

In the theatre, José Ferrer has been producer, director, writer, actor: Jack of all trades and master of most of them. In films he has won an Oscar, but films are not really his medium. Here is an obviously versatile and highly intelligent actor, but not versatile or intelligent enough to prevent monotony creeping in; if you are a 'strong' actor, you need to coast sometimes, you must not be always 'on'. Ferrer's own idols were Walter Huston and Louis Jouvet, but if he learned from them, it does not show in films – he forces too much, seldom relaxes. And they both had something he lacks and it is something that makes the vital difference between good acting and great acting – a sense of humanity, i.e. a sense of humour, a sense of pity. 'Picturegoer' once called him ' a morbidly precise actor'.

He was born in 1912 in Santurce, Puerto Rico, and was educated in New York and later at Princeton, where he did amateur dramatics; he soon abandoned his intended profession – architecture – to make his stage début on a showboat on Long Island; in 1935 he joined Joshua Logan's straw-hat group in Suffern, NY, and later that year had one line in a Broadway play,'A Slight Case of Murder', as a cop. After that he was seldom out of work and his parts got bigger all the time: among others, 'Brother Rat' (36), 'Missouri Legend' (38) and 'Key Largo' (39). His first major role was the lead in 'Charley's Aunt' (40), which made him a name; in 1943 he demonstrated his ability first by taking over from Danny Kaye in 'Let's Face It' and then by playing Iago to Paul Robeson's Othello. Billy Wilder saw him and tried to persuade Paramount to cast him in *The Lost Weekend* – but Paramount insisted that that subject needed an attractive 'name'-star. Ferrer toured as Iago and later as Richard III and Cyrano de Bergerac; he did 'Design for Living' in stock and several notable revivals at the City Center – 'Volpone', 'The Alchemist', 'Angel Street' and 'The Long Voyage Home'. Not long afterwards he made his movie début, as the Dauphin to Ingrid Bergman's *Joan of Arc* (48). After another play, 'The Silver Whistle', he went to Hollywood for three films, starting with *Whirlpool* (49), as a hypnotist who employs murder to get what he wants, including Gene Tierney. He did a bit part, unbilled, just for fun, in *The Secret Fury* (50) and was then a South American dictator in *Crisis*, a thriller with Cary Grant. The third

José Ferrer in the Hollywood version of Edmond Rostand's famous play, Cyrano de Bergerac *(50), the tragicomedy of a soldier of fortune whose nose prevented him from wooing the lady he loved – except on another's behalf.*

picture was *Cyrano de Bergerac.* After his early tour he had played the part in New York (46) and on TV (49); (he did it again on TV in 1955, with Claire Bloom): Stanley Kramer was among those impressed and he dreamed of filming it. Earlier projects (Olivier, Laughton) had come to naught and the version for which Kramer got backing had to be made cheaply – and it looked like it; but it was redeemed by Ferrer's bravura interpretation, or at least it was to the Hollywood Academicians, who voted him a Best Actor Oscar.

Among the resulting Hollywood offers was one to play Androcles in the film of Shaw's play, but he was appearing in a revival of 'Twentieth Century' with Gloria Swanson and her contract stipulated that she appear only with him. Then he directed three plays, the first of which he also presented and in the third of which he starred: 'Stalag 17', 'The Fourposter' and 'The Shrike'. He returned to Hollywood finally for *Anything Can Happen* (52), a folksy comedy about a Georgian immigrant, with Kim Hunter. The 'MFB' referred to Ferrer's 'over-calculated, chilly playing'; the film was not a success. The next one was: *Moulin Rouge*, John Huston's elaborate reconstruction of the Paris of Toulouse-Lautrec – notably played by Ferrer on his knees (his legs strapped up to enable him to play this dwarf). He also at full height played his own father. Because of the décor and a notable can-can sequence, the film was much praised, but to some it was monotony in Montmartre, what with Zsa Zsa Gabor as Jane Avril. . . .

Ferrer was now a Hollywood star. He played the Rev. Davidson to Rita Hayworth's *Miss Sadie Thompson* (53) and then, after reviving most of his famous roles in a season at the City Center, devoted himself to films: *The Caine Mutiny* (54), as the defending officer, a performance described by Lindsay Anderson in the 'MFB' as 'self-satisfied and shallow'; *Deep in My Heart*, much too heavy as Sigmund Romberg in this biopic, among a host of guest stars, which included his then wife, Rosemary Clooney (earlier he had been married to Uta Hagen, 1938-48, and Phyllis Hill, 1948-53); and *The Strike* (55), wedded to a monstrous June Allyson. He also directed that one, and in Britain he directed and starred in a war film, *Cockleshell Heroes* (56), at a fee of £50,000 for the double assignment. The producer, Irving Allen, told Thomas Wiseman: 'When Ferrer finished the film we found that he had made it a *tour de force* for Joe Ferrer. But he seems to have forgotten about the rest of the cast. . . . I've been doing close-ups of Trevor Howard that Joe forgot to do.'

He certainly hogged the camera as a reporter in *The Great Man*, which he co-wrote as well as directed, a *Kane*-like examination of a TV star/heel that was all talk and poor talk. Despite a few critical mitts, it flopped and so did *I Accuse!* (58), in which he directed himself as Dreyfus, as written up by Gore Vidal. A comedy in which he appeared, and directed, *The High Cost of Loving* with Gena Rowlands, was also a flop. For the next few years he was occupied mainly with directing, though he did co-author a Broadway musical, 'Oh Captain!' (58) from *The Captain's Paradise*; toured in a flop play about Edwin Booth; and at one point in Santa Fe sang the title-role in 'Gianni Schicchi'. He directed a couple of films without success, *Return to Peyton Place* and *State Fair*, but returned to film-acting with an effective minor role, that of the Turkish bey in *Lawrence of Arabia* (62). He stayed with the betel-juice in *Nine Hours to Rama* (63), as the inspector out to trap Gandhi's assassin (Horst Buchholz), and then crossed the Channel. In Germany he did a thriller, *Verspätung in Marienborn*, and in France a comic swashbuckler, *Cyrano contre d'Artagnan* (64), with Jean-Pierre Cassel sharing the title. In New York he did a musical with a Noël Coward score, 'The Girl Who Came to Supper' (née 'The Sleeping Prince'), but it did not run. He was a hammy Herod in *The Greatest Story Ever Told* (65) and hardly better as the incipient Nazi in *Ship of Fools*. That year also he played Coppelius in the ballet 'Coppelia' and, in stock, the several different roles in 'Little Me'.

He had his first leading role in 10 years in an American film, as a hard-drinking ham actor in *Enter Laughing* (67), directed by Carl Reiner, from Joseph Stein's play based on Reiner's novel. It was not a success, nor was a French-Italian-Spanish *Cervantes* – played by Buchholz, with Ferrer again as a Turkish bey. In 1967 he was the 'Man of La Mancha' in New York and on tour. When he was in London in 1968 to direct 'You Know I Can't Hear You When the Water's Running' he cheerfully told reporters: 'Hollywood doesn't want me.' Consequently, he worked in TV: *The Aquarians* (70), which starred Ricardo Montalban; *Banyon* (71) and *The Cable Car Murders*, both pilots for detective series with, respectively, Robert Forster (which took) and Robert Hooks (which did not); *The Marcus-Nelson Murders* (73), a three-hour movie which was not exactly a pilot, but it did mark Telly Savalas's first appearance as Kojak. Ferrer played Cyrano again in a musical which failed to reach Broadway and then accepted a Spanish-Italian co-production made in the Dominican Republic, *El Clan de los Immorales/Order to Kill*, as an American inspector bumped off by Helmut Berger. After a tele-movie, *The Missing Are Deadly* (75) he was in South Africa as an Italian priest in *e'Lollipop*, a tear-jerker about black and white kids which became *Forever Young Forever Free* in the US – if briefly; and in Columbia he and Allen Garfield were two of the adults encountered by a small boy called *Paco*. He was one of several doctors in a pilot which went nowhere and remained in TV with *The Art of Crime*. Movies showed an interest again and he was one of several names in both *The Big Bus* (76) and *Voyage of the Damned*, in the former as its chief saboteur, trapped in an iron-lung, and in the latter as the corrupt head of Cuban immigration.

After *The Sentinel* (77), a horror film in which he was seen as a robed figure, he returned to TV for a mini-series, *The Rhinemann Exchange*, and *Exo-Man*, which starred David Ackroyd. But yet again there was a flurry of films for the big screen: *Who Has Seen the Wind*?, in Canada, as the town drunk; *The Private Files of J. Edgar Hoover* (78), as one of Hoover's aides; *Dracula's Dog*, as an expert on vampire lore; *The Swarm*, as the director of a nuclear plant; and *Fedora*, as a once-famous beauty surgeon. In 1978 he produced and starred in an off-Broadway flop, 'White Pelicans': as the chief investor he lost over $40,000. *The Fifth Musketeer* (79) – he was Athos – did not help him recoup, as it had been made in Austria some time earlier.

Understandably, he seemed to work without stopping: *Natural Enemies*, which starred Hal Holbrook; *The French Atlantic Affair*, a mini-series, as a French president; *The Murder That Wouldn't Die*, a busted pilot; *Gideon's Trumpet*, as Henry Fonda's lawyer; *The Dream Merchants*, a mini-series, as a movie producer; and *Pleasure Palace*, which was run by Omar Sharif. Except for the first, all these were for TV; this same year for the big screen he was a gangland boss in both *Brawl*, whch starred the Hong Kong star Jackie Chan, and *The Big*. He supported Faye Dunaway in *Evita Peron* (81), Richard Thomas in *Berlin Tunnel 21* and Anthony Hopkins in a Biblical, *Peter and Paul*, all for TV, and in that medium should have been Sadat in *Golda* (two weeks' work for $40,000); but after Sadat's assassination he was so afraid of being killed himself he relinquished the role. He had his best film in a very long while with *A Midsummer Night's Sex Comedy* (82), as the all-knowing professor who falls for Julie Hagerty, and he kept his spirits up, presumably, by doing 'The Dresser' in Miami, as well as the gambling boss who employs Robert Mitchum in *The Shoe Makes It Murder*, for TV.

And They're Off, co-starring Tab Hunter, seems never to have been shown, while it was touch and go for *Blood Tide*, filmed in Greece and described by its writer-producer Nico Mastorakis as an 'underwater horror film' – made in 1980, there was litigation both before and after its American première in October 1982. Ferrer's co-stars were James Earl Jones and Lila Kedrova. *Blood Feud* (83) was a very different matter, a superior mini-series about the Teamsters Union boss, Jimmy Hoffa (Robert Blake); but *The Being* was another misbegotten horror movie, having been made three years earlier as *Easter Sunday*. Ferrer was mayor of an Idaho town whose inhabitants include Martin Landau, Dorothy Malone and, newly spawned, the creature of the title. In *This Girl for Hire*, a tele-movie, the girl concerned, a detective, had to discover who had murdered him, playing an unpleasant thriller writer. After being a quisling in the Brooks *To Be or Not To Be* he was involved with several historical characters for TV: *Christopher Columbus* (84), *George Washington*, both mini-series, and *Samson and Delilah*, as a high priest. He was the Guatemala-based sadistic torturer whom Charles Bronson is hired to kill in *The Evil That Men Do* and then he hired himself back to TV to be *Seduced* (85). Two films made at this time seem never to have been released, *The Violins Came With the Americans* and *Romance Language*, but he had another respectable credit with a mini-series, *Blood and Orchids* (86), as a high-powered lawyer whose wife, Sean Young, has an affair with the star, Kris Kristofferson. Then his gory past returned to haunt him: *Bloody Birthday* had been filmed six years earlier, as *Creeps*. . . . His next credit would seem to be *Young Harry Houdini* (87) and then he was announced for the Franco-Spanish *Rosa*. He did appear in *Strange Interlude* (88) as Glenda Jackson's father, for TV, and took over for Douglas Fairbanks Jr when he left the cast of *Old Explorers* (89).

Edwige Feuillère

'La Dame aux Camélias' is hardly a play that appeals today. It is best seen as transformed by Garbo and the camera (*Camille*) or by Maria Callas and the music of Verdi ('La Traviata'). The third great Marguerite Gautier of our time is an actress who played the old drama quite straight, a French actress who is a pupil of a pupil of Sarah Bernhardt: Edwige Feuillère. There is a mortal glow about Feuillère's Marguerite: the haughty elegance of her humour, the panache of her movements – even the gentle half-turn to hide the tubercular cough. She is incandescent; and there is not the slightest gesture or intonation which has not been carefully calculated and wrought. In plays somewhat poorer (even) than 'La Dame aux Camélias' her technique is revealed as about as interesting as Mother Hubbard's cupboard; there is surface polish, there is glitter and not much else (like many of the big-name American stage actresses: for some reason British actresses, the best of them, are seldom superficial).

Feuillère's screen work has suffered less from glibness. She started out as a vamp and soon developed a comic style which suited the heartless creatures she played. Later she played the *femme du monde*, coquettish and desirable, disillusioned and falsely gay. Her plots made of her a French Garbo. In Ophüls's heavily romantic *Sans Lendemain* she was an impoverished striptease dancer who pretends to be a lady of means to win back a lover; and when he goes away with their son she commits suicide rather than continue the deception. She was *La Duchesse de Langeais*, Balzac's tragic heroine, who discovered too late that she really loved the man she had vengefully forced to love her. Garbo, who was to have remade that (directed by Ophüls), is reputed to have hesitated because she thought Feuillère 'incomparable'; but Feuillère, at that time at her peak, had Garboesque qualities. This was no attempt at imitations; she simply was, by nature and inclination, a similar personality – with the same melancholy, the same brief grasping of happiness, the same indolence; with mystery, beauty and grace.

She was born in Vesoul, in Haute-Saône, in 1907, the only child of an Italian architect (her real name is Vivette Cunatti) and his Alsace-born wife, and was brought up mainly in Dijon. She studied drama there at the Conservatoire and at the age of 20 enrolled at the Paris Conservatoire. In her spare time she studied also under René Simon and began getting minute parts on the professional stage; under the name Cora Lynn she appeared as one of the harem in an operette (music by Honegger), 'Les Aventures du Roi Pausole' (30), and in a small part – with a nude scene – in a short, *La Fine Combine* (31) starring Fernandel. She married a fellow pupil, Pierre Feuillère, and took her present name (the marriage lasted two years; she never remarried; he committed suicide in 1940). She won a first prize at the Conservatoire and was engaged by the Comédie-Française, who started her off with a small role in 'Le Sicilien'; her first good role came some months later, Suzanne in 'Le Mariage de Figaro'. Two years later, in 1933, she resigned, fed up with mainly minor roles. There were other offers and she was moving ahead in films. (Not long after she had signed with the Maison de Molière, Paramount had offered a Hollywood contract which she had had to refuse.)

She had appeared in *Le Cordon Bleu* starring Pierre Bertin, made at Joinville, which specialized in *théâtre en conserve* – of which this was a prime example; followed by *Le Beau Rôle* (32), with Dranem; *Monsieur Albert*, vamping Noël-Noël; *La Perle* with Robert Arnoux; *Une Petite Femme dans le Train* with Henry Garat; and *Maquillage*, again with Arnoux. She had her first sympathetic moments on screen as Louis Jouvet's mistress in *Topaze* (33) and then was the favourite of the king in the film of *Les Aventures du Roi Pausole*; André Berley was the king (played in the German version by Emil Jannings). Then: *Matricule 33*, more glamorous than ever, with André Luguet; *Toi que J'adore* (34), a comedy with Jean Murat; and *Ces Messieurs de la Santé*, which starred Raimu. She recalls with awe his temper, but says that he was always 'adorable' towards her. She did her first leading stage role away from the Comédie, in Louis Verneuil's 'Mon Crime', and then went to Berlin to make a French film for UFA, *Barcarolle*, set in Venice, with Pierre-Richard Wilm, who was to partner her often in the future. She was, as usual, a vamp, the object of a wager between the two protagonists. She played the wife of Pontius Pilate (Jean Gabin) in Duvivier's *Golgotha* (35); dyed her hair blonde for *Le Miroir aux Alouettes* with Pierre Brasseur; and co-starred with Wilm in a love story, *Stradivarius*, again made by UFA, at the same time as a German version. She was also on the stage that year, in 'La Prisonnière' and 'La Dame de Solitude'.

Abel Gance chose her to be his *Lucrèce Borgia*, which had a bath-tub scene. Her breasts were clearly visible – at that time a spectacle daring enough to ensure a degree of fame. Not that – even for a glimpse of the lady in the buff – the film was very popular; and it was a cheap thing, a schoolboy fantasy of the Borgias, whitewashing them. She made *La Route Heureuse* (36), with Claude Dauphin, and its Italian version, *Amore*, with Gino Cervi. She was with Jouvet again in Siodmak's *Mister Flow*, from a story by Jeanson, as a gay lady tossed between him and Fernand Gravey. It could not be said that she was widely popular, but producers were now announcing Feuillère's vehicles – like Marc Allégret's *La Dame de Malacca* (37), made in French and German, a Maugham-type tale about a poor Irish beauty forced by her weak civil servant husband (Jean Debucourt) to divorce and marry the Hindu prince (Wilm) whom up till then she has treated with haughty disdain. Somewhat more restrained was *Marthe Richard*, as a World War I spy (it was based on fact), with Erich von Stroheim; but what to make of *Feu!*, where she was, in the words of Robert Kemp, 'une aventurière de grande classe' – a gun-runner in Tangier who confesses to her lover (Victor Francen) and is drowned when he sinks one of her boats? It was a remake of a Silent and seemed like it every step of the way.

At least *J'étais une Aventurière* (38) was light-hearted about it all: she was a con-woman and jewel-thief, with Raymond Rouleau, Jean Tissier and Jean Murat as her partners. Ciné-Alliance, who produced, announced that they had her under exclusive contract and plans were made to have her play Charlotte Corday, Elizabeth of Austria and La Tosca. Instead she was *L'Emigrante* (40), owner of a *louche* bar in Antwerp who flees from her lover to South America. *Sans Lendemain*, with Georges Rigaud, stands out from her films of this period like a peak; and another film with Ophüls must have raised her spirits – though filmed quickly in the shadow of war, with funds running low, and in fact premièred the day the Germans invaded Belgium and Luxembourg. She liked working

Edwige Feuillère as a sad lady reunited with a former lover: Sans Lendemain *(40), directed by Max Ophüls, with Georges Rigaud, the Argentine-born French actor.*

with Ophüls and has recalled the warmth and teamwork which she says no longer exists. The film was *De Mayerling à Sarajevo*, inspired perhaps by the abdication of Edward VIII but impregnated with the sense of a world dying – a study of the morganatic marriage of Crown Prince Ferdinand (John Lodge). Both stars were eclipsed by Gabrielle Dorziat and the film, if not too convincing, has a certain charm.

In the autumn of 1940 she played for the first time in Paris 'La Dame aux Camélias' (she had done it in Brussels in 1937, along with 'La Parisienne') with Wilm as Armand. From thence she was generally regarded as the leading French actress of her generation. After the trifling *Mam'zelle Bonaparte* (42), in which she was Cora Pearl, she received some sort of consecration with *La Duchesse de Langeais*, with dialogue by Giraudoux and with Wilm as the scorned lover. If she was perfect, the film was much less so and is pedestrian today.

Because of her the next one was a success: *L'Honorable Catherine* (43), a farce about an intriguer who falls for one of her victims (Raymond Rouleau). Foreigners found it tiresome; The 'New York Times' noted that Feuillère 'proceeds to grimace and shout from one cliché to the next'. She was more sedate as *Lucrèce*, a love-jaded actress who unwillingly falls for a student who has boasted of loving her (Jean Mercanton, who died of polio a year later). On the stage she appeared in Giraudoux's 'Sodome et Gomorrhe', then stayed away from both mediums for almost two years. She returned in Delannoy's *La Part de l'Ombre* (45), as gloomy a piece as it sounds, with Jean-Louis Barrault as a self-destructive musician and Feuillère as the woman who saves him on three occasions, in 1920, 1928 and 1936. There followed *Tant que Je Vivrai* (46), as an adventuress briefly loved by tubercular Jacques Berthier and *Il Suffit d'une Fois*, with Fernand Gravey, as a sculptress in this comedy directed by a woman, Andrée Feix.

Outside France, she was known less via her films than reports of her stage performances. One of the films which changed that situation

Filmed Dostoevsky: Edwige Feuillère as Nastasia and Gérard Philipe as Prince Myshkin in Georges Lampin's version of L'Idiot, *(46).*

was *L'Idiot*, with Gérard Philipe. Said 'Time & Tide': 'As for Mme Feuillère, her Nastasia, black-haired and flashing-eyed, tempestuous, tender and tormented, is of a calibre we seldom see on the screen. But then Mme Feuillère is evidently the actress of the greatest feminine charm, grace and artistry to be seen on the screen today.' C.A. Lejeune: 'This magnificent actress . . . this imperial creature, who is not afraid to act as if acting were the privilege of princes, plays what is known as a "fallen woman" and makes her so bright and shining that she brings a radiance even to the sullen world from which she fell.'

On the stage she was playing the queen in 'L'Aigle à Deux Têtes', specially written for her by Jean Cocteau. This was some tosh about a Ruritanian monarch who falls for a mysterious young peasant (Jean Marais) sent to assassinate her. Done with seeming conviction, its deep-seated romanticism appealed greatly to postwar audiences. In London the play was equally successful with Eileen Herlie (it was a star-vehicle *par excellence*) and Korda planned a film of it; but Cocteau made the film himself (48), with Feuillère and Marais, and it was taken quite seriously in some quarters. Feuillère's triumph caused her to be much debated abroad. In 1948 she played Ysé in Claudel's 'Partage de Midi' for the first time and when she played it in London (in French) in 1951 some critics thought they had seen the light beyond. Meanwhile, she was solicited for a British film, *Woman Hater* (49), playing a Hollywood star opposite Stewart Granger. The ads carefully explained how to enunciate her name but the film – though she enjoyed making it – was an endurance test for audiences. Hollywood was not deterred; for the second time in her career there were overtures from that direction, but she refused for 'des raisons sentimentales'.

She made the dark but not disagreeable *Julie de Carneilhan*, from a minor novel by Colette, enslaving Pierre Brasseur and audiences: this was Feuillère again as the Eternal Woman. And it was Brasseur who was trapped with her in a portmanteau film, *Souvenirs Perdus* (50): old lovers meeting again, spending the night and parting. *Olivia* was adapted from the novel by 'Olivia' and directed by another female director, Jacqueline Audrey: memoirs of Belle Epoque schooldays and the beautiful, kind, lesbian headmistress (Feuillère). The film was considered a plea for sanity on such matters: it was delicately done. She was an ageing beauty running a bar and trying to keep her lover (Franck Villard) in *Le Cap de L'Espérance* (51) and then one of Daniel Gélin's *Adorables Créatures* (53). After that she set about debauching the young again, only it was a boy this time, in *Le Blé en Herbe*, another Colette story, stagily directed by Autant-Lara: an evocation of lazy childhood summers, with Feuillère as every precocious boy's ideal Older Woman. On the stage she starred in Giraudoux's 'Pour Lucrèce', and in London in 1955 she played Marguerite Gautier. She did a farce, *Les Fruits de l'Eté* (55), which started off with a teenage orgy, continued with mother trying to seduce her estranged husband for the sake of family honour and finished with both mother and daughter pushing prams. Somewhat more palatable was an elongated rejig of *J'étais une Aventurière* called *Le Septième Commandement* (56), Balmain-clad in this thriller which piled ingenuity on ingenuity to no worthwhile purpose.

Filmed Cocteau: Jean Marais as Stanislas and Edwige Feuillère as the Queen, in Cocteau's filming of his play L'Aigle à Deux Têtes (*48*).

A young man's initiation into the ways of sex by an older woman has been the subject of countless novels, but it is a theme rarely touched upon by film-makers. It was, however, tenderly handled in 1953, in Le Blé en Herbe, *by Edwige Feuillère and Pierre-Michel Beck.*

Neither film affected her reputation in Britain, where in 1957 she did a season of plays (in French) including 'La Parisienne' and 'Phèdre'. She made another indifferent film, Yves Allégret's *série noire, Quand la Femme s'en Mêle* (58), as a classy gun-moll, and appeared in a stage version of the novel 'Lucy Crown'. She was Gabin's wife in *En Cas de Malheur* (59), but the film parts available for ladies of her age went mainly to Mlles Morgan and Darrieux. On the stage with her own company she revived past successes as well as appearing in 'Constance' (60), a version of Maugham's 'The Constant Wife'. Other stage appearances in the 60s include 'Eve et Line' by Pirandello, 'Le Placard' ('Oh Dad Poor Dad Mother's Hung you in the Closet', etc.) and 'La Folle de Chaillot'. There were two appearances, of little moment, in films both adapted from comic strips – *Les Amours Célèbres* (61), as an ageing actress, and *Le Crime ne Paie pas* (62), as an ageing Venetian countess losing her lover. She took a supporting role – that of an aunt – and was very funny in a black comedy written by Roman Polanski, *Aimez-vous les Femmes?* (64); and played a silly woman, very *seizième,* in *La Bonne Occase* (65), the adventures of a second-hand motor-car. In Italy she did another trifle, written and directed by actor Vittorio Caprioli, *Scusi Facciamo L'Amore* (68), as one of the victims of Pierre Clémenti, a well-born Neapolitan who tries to seduce himself into the aristocracy and makes it, finally, with a man. For reasons best known to herself she elected to do one of a series of secret agent films, *Tous les Coups sont Bons pour OSS 117* (69), starring Lux Merenda, but this was compensated for by *Clair de Terre* (70), where she shared the *générique* with Annie Girardot and Micheline Presle, in a good role as a teacher who guides a young expatriate Tunisian on his return home.

She made her television début in 'L'Échange' (69); and was on the stage in 'Les Bonshommes' (70) and the French version of 'Sweet Bird of Youth' (71). Her only film in several years was *La Chair d'Orchidée* (75), a sequel to 'No Orchids for Miss Blandish', as Charlotte Rampling's villainous aunt.

In 1977 she had a long run in 'Le Bateau pour Liparia', which she also did on TV. In 1980 she and Marais appeared in a translation of 'Dear Liar'. *Le Chef de Famille* (81) was a tele-movie with Fanny Ardant and Francis Huster. Since then she has appeared in 'L'Amour an Eté' (82), a revival of Anouilh's 'Léocadia' (84) and, again with Marais, in a translation of 'On Golden Pond' (86). And also in 'Cinéma' (88), a television series with Alain Delon.

PETER FINCH

Peter Finch said once: 'I've been lucky. My agent might have hoped that I'd be a bigger name – as they call it – in America, but I'm very happy. I like what I do and I choose what I do. . . .' He did not always choose what he did, and he did not always choose wisely. He was marked for the heights of stardom when he made his first film in Britain, but for a while the real peaks eluded him – too many bad films and that kiss of death, a long-term Rank contract. In the right material he always looked good – he had a good actor's voice and stance, a touch of arrogance, a touch of humour, some warmth, leading man's looks and the same sort of gritty dependability that characterized the male stars of Hollywood's golden age.

He was born in London in 1916, the son of an Australian physicist. His parents were divorced when he was two and he was brought up in France and then Madras, India, by a grandmother; he moved on to Australia – Sydney – where he had relatives, and worked at many jobs, including waiter, journalist and jackaroo. He had acted at school, but turned professional because of economic need during the Depression when, after auditioning, he was taken on as stooge by a small-time comedian. From vaudeville he went into legit and toured NSW and Queensland in 'While Parents Sleep' (35); and he began getting small parts in the – poor – Australian films of the period, *Dad and Dave Come to Town* (36) and *Red Sky at Morning*. His first important film part was as the delinquent son of Cecil Kellaway in *Mr Chedworth Steps Out* (38), a naive domestic drama. Later he had good parts in *The Power and the Glory* (42), *A Son is Born* (46) and *Rats of Tobruk*, a war film that was considered to be the best Australian movie up to that time.

By this time he had become probably the best-known radio actor in the country and had formed his own theatre company, the Mercury (named after Orson Welles's group), which played the classics, mainly in factories – because no one else would house them; all the same, it was sufficiently famous for Laurence Olivier to visit when touring Australia with the Old Vic in 1947. Finch asked him about the possibilities of a career in Britain and Olivier said that if he went he would try to help him. He did not know till much later that Finch had started an affair with his wife, Vivien Leigh, which would last intermittently for the next 10 years. Meanwhile, Ealing had made a very successful film in Australia, *The Overlanders*, directed by Harry Watt, and Watt cast Finch in a good part, heavily bearded, in a sort of follow-up, *Eureka Stockade* (48). In London Finch looked for work, till Watt persuaded Ealing to cast him in the role of a homicidal maniac in an episode of *Train of Events* (49) and he impressed at least C.A. Lejeune, who commented that he was 'likely to become a cult'. During its making Olivier contacted him and cast him as a romantic young man with a crush on Edith Evans in 'Daphne Laureola'. During its run he got two small but good film roles: an Australian soldier in sick-bay in *The Wooden Horse* (50) and a Polish officer in *The Miniver Story*. He was the evil Sheriff of Nottingham in Disney's *The Story of Robin Hood* (51), but was continuing in star roles under Olivier's management: the title-role in 'Captain Carvallo' and Iago to Orson Welles's Othello. In 1952 he was briefly at the Old Vic, in 'An Italian Straw Hat' and as Mercutio.

Thereafter for some years films claimed him: *The Story of Gilbert and Sullivan* (53), as their impresario, D'Oyly Carte; and *The Heart of the Matter*, as the understanding cleric. His first film lead was at the suggestion of Vivien Leigh, then scheduled to appear in *Elephant Walk* (54), a silly Maugham-like drama about a plantation overlord (Finch) whose wife (not Leigh but Elizabeth Taylor) tires of him and has an affair with his foreman (Dana Andrews). Hollywood neither retained him nor asked him back (the film flopped) and instead of returning to Britain a star he played support to Alec Guinness in *Father Brown*, as the foppish villain Flambeau. He had the lead in a B, *Make Me an Offer* (55), an inept little drama about the antique trade, and then was a villainous French count in one of Errol Flynn's sad British swashbucklers, *The Dark Avenger*. He said later: 'I was very depressed . . . because I realized after a week's shooting that I was in a very crumby picture . . . Often people said to me "You're an intelligent guy – however did you get mixed up in that thing?" They forget that actors have to eat.' Worse, according to 'Picturegoer', he was embroiled in it when Olivier offered him the role of Buckingham in *Richard III* and he had to turn it down.

However, Rank starred him in several of their more important films of the time: *Passage Home*, as a martinet sea captain coping with storms and Diane Cilento; *Josephine and Men*, for the Boultings, a comedy with Glynis Johns; and *Simon and Laura*, another comedy, with Kay Kendall, where his playing was very heavy. He was an Australian in a competent version of Nevil Shute's novel *A Town Like Alice* (56), which was extremely popular and which won for him and co-star Virginia McKenna BFA Best Acting awards. *The Battle of the River Plate* was more British war stuff and, though poor, again popular; but Finch was 'vacuous' (Stanley Kauffman) as the bearded German commander. Two Australian subjects somewhat dissipated the popularity he had gained with *A Town Like Alice*: *The Shiralee* (57), as a swagman ('lively, uninhibited playing' – the 'MFB'); and *Robbery Under Arms*, as a notorious outlaw, in this crass version of Rolf Boldrewood's classic novel. Finch turned down both *Dangerous Exile* and *Floods of Fear* but accepted one even worse, *Windom's Way* (58), playing a doctor in the Far East fighting Commie infiltration, an adaptation of a cheap American novel disdained by Hollywood. The inevitably poor box-office was not bettered by *Operation Amsterdam* (59), a daft tale about diamond-smuggling with Eva Bartok, and Rank dropped Finch from their big-budgeted *Ferry to Hong Kong* and replaced him with Curt Jurgens. (It was one of their periodic attempts to storm world markets, but it flopped.)

Peter Finch and Audrey Hepburn, doctor and nurse, in The Nun's Story (59).

In London, however, he had begun to restore his crumbling reputation, in 'Two for the See-Saw' with Gerry Judd; and it was retrieved internationally when Fred Zinnemann chose him to support Audrey Hepburn in *The Nun's Story* – a strong and attractive performance as the agnostic Congo doctor. After a stint in Scotland playing Alan Breck in Disney's *Kidnapped* (60), with James MacArthur, he directed a short called *The Day* and played poor Oscar in one of the two concurrent films about that writer's love life, *The Trials of Oscar Wilde*, fattened and padded and acting most movingly. It had been felt that an obviously heterosexual actor would create more sympathy and Finch did, to the extent of winning a second BFA award. The film itself, though restricted by both budget and censor, was a modified triumph, but for several reasons bookings were limited. Warners had liked Finch's work in *The Nun's Story* and had been waiting to get him back; but *The Sins of Rachel Cade* (61) was a poor rehash of the Congo scenes of that film, with Finch as the Belgian commissioner and Angie Dickinson as a military nurse. It set both careers back years, but Finch was luckier than she, for he won a third BFA award for *No Love for Johnnie*, though the film itself was dim – the old story about a ruthless climber with the 'novel' twist that he was a Labour MP. It was his last film for Rank.

There were two more unfortunate Hollywood-backed ventures: *I Thank a Fool* (62), as a lawyer secretly in love with his wife's nurse, Susan Hayward, and *In the Cool of the Day* (63), as a publisher illicitly in love with Jane Fonda. On stage he played Trigorin in 'The Seagull' with Vanessa Redgrave and on film concurrently he was a worldly writer loved by a waif (Rita Tushingham), in Desmond Davis's *Girl With Green Eyes* (64), some attractive variations on that old theme. He had a guest spot in *First Men in the Moon* (a day's work, because the actor engaged did not turn up and he happened to be on the neighbouring set) and was then in another good film of that year, *The Pumpkin Eater*, as Anne Bancroft's husband – and another writer. If Finch seldom in these parts suggested any literary aura, he looked the sort of author publishers like to have on the back of their jackets, the ideal man of women's magazines; he projected authority easily, so to add to his various doctors and administrators he played a kibbutz leader in *Judith* (65) with Sophia Loren, and a British army officer in Aldrich's *The Flight of the Phoenix* (66) with James Stewart. Neither film did much for him and even less was done by Jules Dassin's flop, *10.30 p.m. Summer*, playing Melina Mercouri's puzzled husband, as who wouldn't be?

He did wonders with a stodgy part, that of the squire in *Far From the Madding Crowd* (67), aided by director John Schlesinger, and then returned to Hollywood to play a corny movie director in Aldrich's *The Legend of Lylah Clare* (68) with Kim Novak, not released in Britain. Much of the next two years was taken up with *The Red Tent* (71), an Italo-Russian colossus, filmed in English, in which he played the unfortunate Arctic explorer, General Nobile. Ian Bannen was originally cast as the homosexual Jewish doctor in Schlesinger's highly successful *Sunday Bloody Sunday* and Finch took it on at short notice – getting his best reviews to date and another BFA Best Actor award – a sensitive performance, not unlike the one he had given in *Girl with Green Eyes*, coping with a younger lover. He then played a seedy man disintegrating in *Something to Hide* (72) and a tycoon in *England Made Me* with Michael York, a version of an early novel by Graham Greene. His performance in the Schlesinger film reawakened the interest of Hollywood and he returned there to play Ronald Colman's old part in the musical remake of *Lost Horizon* (73), which quite deservedly reaped the worst notices of the decade. And two slated historicals made three consecutive flops: *A Bequest to the Nation*, from a play by Terence Rattigan, as Nelson to Glenda Jackson's Emma; and *The Abdication* (74), as the glamorous cardinal who interrogates and befriends the Queen Christina of Liv Ullmann. He turned down the male lead in what turned out to be another flop musical, *A Little Night Music*, and played a TV pundit in *Network* (76). His last role was that of the Israeli prime minister in an all-star TV film, *Raid on Entebbe* – for he dropped dead of a heart attack early in 1977. He had been nominated for a Best Actor Oscar for *Network*, and won it: the first player to be awarded a posthumous Academy Award – which was accepted by his second, Jamaican, wife on his behalf.

Peter Finch in The Red Tent *(71). '. . . every contour and crevice of that familiar face reflecting the awareness of a tragic destiny' – Julian Fox in 'Films & Filming'.*

ALBERT FINNEY

Albert Finney projects virility, a North of England bluntness and a certain considered *joie de vivre*: his later film roles have not suggested a greater range than he displayed in his first major movie, *Saturday Night and Sunday Morning*. 'With his jutting fighter's chin, drinker's jowl and watchful, moody eye,' said Peter John Dyer in 'Sight and Sound', he exactly fitted the part: 'with the tension and over-exuberance of inexperience, he somehow magnifies it into a figure brimming over with vitality, one who earns more and womanizes more than his mates, who prides himself on having everyone "summed up" and who frequently lies the same way he gambles, to put snap judgements to the test.' It remains the definitive portrait on film of a British working-class hero (at least, one would have to think hard to find a better one).

He was born in Salford, Lancashire, the son of a bookmaker, in 1936. He did a considerable amount of acting at grammar school and was encouraged by his headmaster to try for a scholarship at RADA. After RADA he went to Birmingham rep, where he made his début as Decius Brutus in 'Julius Caesar' (56); he remained there two years, playing, among other roles, Henry V and Macbeth. Charles Laughton saw him as Macbeth and invited him to join his London production of 'The Party'. He followed Laughton to Stratford-upon-Avon, where he played Lysander, Edgar and Cassio. He made a considerable

Albert Finney as a factory worker in Saturday Night and Sunday Morning *(60)*.

impression when he went on for Olivier in 'Coriolanus' and Tony Richardson chose him to play Olivier's son in the brief prologue to *The Entertainer* (60). Richardson produced *Saturday Night and Sunday Morning*, directed by Karel Reisz from a novel by Alan Sillitoe, a study of a young factory worker and his two women. The press quickly labelled it a real milestone among British films and an equally enthusiastic public, pleased at the unaccustomed accuracy, turned it into one of the biggest hits of the year.

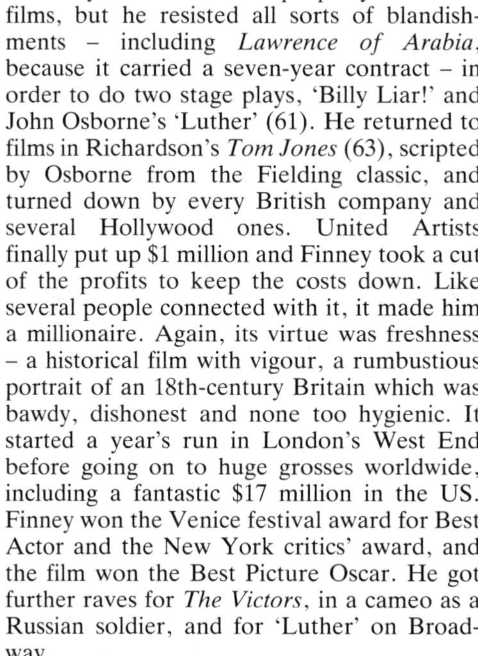

Finney was the hottest property in British films, but he resisted all sorts of blandishments – including *Lawrence of Arabia*, because it carried a seven-year contract – in order to do two stage plays, 'Billy Liar!' and John Osborne's 'Luther' (61). He returned to films in Richardson's *Tom Jones* (63), scripted by Osborne from the Fielding classic, and turned down by every British company and several Hollywood ones. United Artists finally put up $1 million and Finney took a cut of the profits to keep the costs down. Like several people connected with it, it made him a millionaire. Again, its virtue was freshness – a historical film with vigour, a rumbustious portrait of an 18th-century Britain which was bawdy, dishonest and none too hygienic. It started a year's run in London's West End before going on to huge grosses worldwide, including a fantastic $17 million in the US. Finney won the Venice festival award for Best Actor and the New York critics' award, and the film won the Best Picture Oscar. He got further raves for *The Victors*, in a cameo as a Russian soldier, and for 'Luther' on Broadway.

He joined up with Reisz to produce a remake of Emlyn Williams's *Night Must Fall* (64), with the idea, presumably, of making an old-fashioned horror film which would be convincing in the light of present psychological knowledge. Finney's performance as the psychopathic killer was sinister and forceful, but the film was generally regarded as a failure. With his *Tom Jones* profits he took off on a world trip, telling reporters that he was bored with acting and did not know what to do next. In the event, he went to Britain's National Theatre for two seasons (1965–66) and confirmed his position as one of the finest young actors of his generation. He did make one film, Stanley Donen's *Two for the Road* (67) with Audrey Hepburn, because, he said, he wanted to make a film like that and it was the best example he was offered. He was short on the charm the piece called for, but the film was liked and did well.

For his own company, Memorial, he directed as well as starred in *Charlie Bubbles* which, after a brief US showing, became a *cause célèbre* when it failed to get either a West End showing or a circuit booking. When it finally opened in London it was much praised, but turned out to be an unexceptional series of anecdotes about a wealthy and world-weary writer (Finney) which stopped when an already feeble script could think of nowhere to go. Finney's own performance was strong and his direction sufficiently accomplished. He then elected to appear in a reputedly odd trifle, *The Picasso Summer*, scripted by Ray Bradbury, directed by Serge Bourguignon – twice: it was almost entirely refilmed and was never shown in cinemas.

Albert Finney as an eighteenth-century aristocrat bastard in Tom Jones *(63), with Susannah York.*

Finally it was sold direct to television. He said he did it because he hoped to meet Picasso. Over the next few years he occupied himself with his production company and for them did 'A Day in the Death of Joe Egg' (70) in New York. He married Anouk Aimée (his first wife was actress Jane Wenham, divorced 1961). Then, when Rex Harrison and then Richard Harris could not play *Scrooge* (70), he jumped at the chance, looking too well fed but otherwise competent in a film that often looked right but seldom sounded it (the songs were dire). More impressively, he played a Liverpool bingo-caller with a hang-up on Bogart in *Gumshoe* (71), a good mystery whose *raison d'être* seemed to be its frequent references to pop culture of the 40s and 50s. In 1972 he returned to the Royal Court, in 'Alpha Beta' with Rachel Roberts, and they filmed it – in 10 days: a prolonged marital quarrel which had a few US cinema bookings in 1973 and a sole British showing, on TV, two years later. He had the leading role, Hercule Poirot, investigating the *Murder on the Orient Express* (74), a disappointingly heavy performance – and over made-up – which did not help to make this verbose thriller any more entertaining. Two years later he was reported as signing a four-picture deal with Memorial, but nothing emerged. He did do a 'guest' supporting role in *The Duellists* (77), a British film with Keith Carradine and Harvey Keitel in the title-roles. During this time he was busy at the National, playing some of the titanic roles – Tamburlaine, Hamlet, Macbeth – to medium response. He was a good Lopahin (78), but as a Shakespearian actor he had little beyond stage presence: he had neither the temperament nor an ability to seem at home with the verse.

You would be forgiven if you had not heard of the Finney films which were released in 1981. He was a safe-cracker in a tired British heist movie, *Loophole*, which went direct to Cable in the US; a busted New York detective in *Wolfen*, hopefully described by its director, Michael Wadleigh, as 'the first thinking man's horror film'; and an LA plastic surgeon in a thriller, *Looker*. 1982 was more promising, but Alan Parker's *Shoot the Moon* was practically sabotaged by Finney himself, in a truck-heavy performance as a Marin County-based man of letters who ups and leaves his wife (Diane Keaton). It could be argued that his contribution to *Annie* was sour, when what was needed – for the role of 'Daddy' Warbucks – was a gruff but genial type like Guy Kibbee. John Huston directed this version of a mediocre Broadway musical based on a cartoon strip, 'Little Orphan Annie'; it cost over $37 million (which was not evident on screen, even given a record sum for the rights) but managed to appeal to the 'family' market to the extent of $51 million domestic – infinitely less than Columbia had expected. Finney's next outing was something else again – doing salvage work this time, as a 'great' actor leading a tatty touring company (the

Albert Finney questioning the suspects of the Murder on the Orient Express *(74), from left to right, Jean-Pierre Cassel, Anthony Perkins, Vanessa Redgrave, Sean Connery, Ingrid Bergman, George Coutouris, Rachel Roberts, Wendy Hiller, Dennis Quilley, Michael York, Jacqueline Bisset, Lauren Bacall and Martin Balsam. This still is typical of the film, so you can probably tell that it was not much fun.*

role was based on Donald Wolfit); helping him on this version of a feeble play were director Peter Yates and Tom Courtenay in the title-role, *The Dresser* (83). Finney himself had the title-role in a tele-movie, *Pope John Paul II* (84), then went to the extreme as the drunken ex-consul in a small Mexican town *Under the Volcano*. Huston directed Finney to a powerful and subtle performance of a role which, in the original novel, allows little scope for either quality. He returned to the stage, to the Old Vic, to 'Sergeant Musgrave's Dance', which he had done there 20 years earlier, and on TV in Britain did *The Biko Trial.*

Alan J. Pakula invited him to Hollywood for *Orphans* (87), based on a play he had earlier done in the West End: so he repeated his performance as a Chicago gangster who starts game-playing with two lonely, misfit brothers (Matthew Modine, Kevin Anderson). These were three splendid performances in a hypnotic entertainment, but despite good notices very few came: a $15 million investment was almost entirely lost, which did little for Finney's standing in the industry. He eventually worked with another whose talents were no longer greatly in demand, writer-director Bryan Forbes, whose *The Endless Game* (89) mini-series was backed by Italian television. Then Finney was to repeat his Daddy Warbucks in *Annie 2*.

Louise Fletcher

There were for a while so few good roles for women in films that the selectors of Oscar nominees had a job to come up with five names. When Louise Fletcher was nominated for *One Flew Over the Cuckoo's Nest*, the previous year's winner, Ellen Burstyn, appeared on TV to ask the members of the Academy not to vote in this category – since in fact, she said, the five nominees had all played supporting roles. In the case of Miss Fletcher, this may, strictly speaking, be true: but her superb portrayal of Nurse Ratched seemed to dominate the film. It was a notably well acted movie: but Fletcher's performance, had it been on stage, was one that you would want to tell your grandchildren about.

She was born in Birmingham, Alabama, in 1936, of deaf-mute parents – her father was an Episcopalian missionary to the deaf. In 1957 she graduated from the University of Southern California and got a job in summer stock, as Helen in 'Tiger at the Gates' (Robert Redford was also in the cast). With friends, she set out for Los Angeles and worked as a doctor's receptionist; she studied acting with Jeff Corey (Jack Nicholson was also in the class) and found some TV assignments – in 'Wagon Train', 'Lawman' and 'The Untouchables', among others. In 1962 she married a TV producer, Jerry Bick, and since there was no great demand for her services as an actress she retired to raise a family; and during this time lived for six years in London. When Bick turned to films, he gave her a small role in *Thieves Like Us* (74), which Robert Altman directed: she was the woman in the motel who turns the lovers (Keith Carradine, Shelley Duvall) over to the police. The editor of that film, Lou Lombardo, directed *Russian Roulette* (75) and Bick produced it: she had another small role. Determined to take up her career again, she says no agent would handle her: she had always been too tall – 5ft 10 in – and now she was too old. Altman fashioned a role for her in *Nashville*, after watching her with her parents, but he eventually gave it to Lily Tomlin.

Among the players who turned down the role of the nurse in *One Flew Over the Cuckoo's Nest* are Anne Bancroft, Geraldine Page, Angela Lansbury, Colleen Dewhurst and Miss Burstyn – any of whom, you would have thought, would have jumped at working with director Milos Forman. He called Fletcher after viewing *Thieves Like Us*, looking at another actress for another role; but co-star Nicholson also said that it was he who recommended Fletcher for the role of Ratched, a woman whose life has stood still for 20 years, a woman without imagination or feeling – which is where the cruelty of her lies. It is a haunting performance.

It was also a very popular Oscar. With success, her marriage took a tumble and her

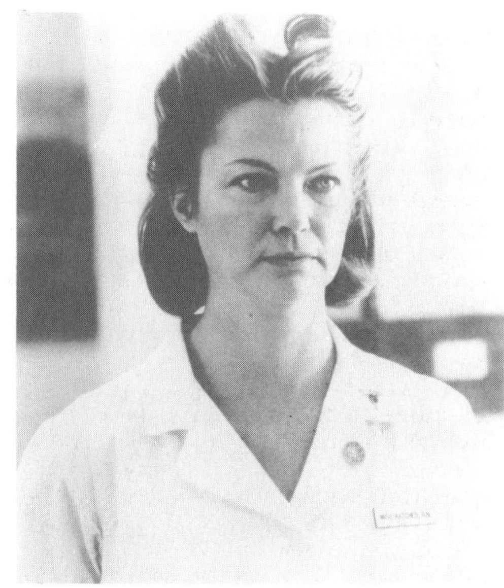

When Louise Fletcher, Jack Nicholson and One Flew Over the Cuckoo's Nest *(75) all won Oscars, it was quickly pointed out that the three top awards had not all gone to the same film since* It Happened One Night: *two very different films for different times, but the unexpected public affection for both may tell us something.*

career did no better with *The Exorcist II The Heretic* (77), a role – as a psychiatrist – she took because she wanted to work with Richard Burton. In Neil Simon's cod Bogart thriller, *The Cheap Detective* (78), she had to model herself on the heroine of *Casablanca,* which was not easy for her – nor would it be for any of today's actresses. A TV movie, *Thou Shalt Not Commit Adultery*, found her doing just that, with the consent of her husband, a paraplegic. She was an old mistress of Alan Arkin in a West German-Israeli co-production, *The Magician of Lublin* (79), which proved conclusively that the stories of Isaac Bashevis Singer are not movie material – not, anyway, as directed by Menahem Golan. *The Lady in Red* was Dillinger's mistress and Fletcher was the Madam who shopped him; the *Natural Enemies* were she and spouse Hal Holbrook, who suddenly one morning felt a desire to murder her and the kids. They were, said 'Variety' of this Canadian movie, 'perfect casting for the roles of Mr and Mrs John Q. Dullsville'. She was *Mama Dracula* (80) in this English-language French-Belgian comedy and then a wealthy Dutch farm-owner in a wartime drama with Rod Steiger, *The Lucky Star*, made in Canada. Also with an identity crisis was *Dead Kids* (81), an Anzac co-production about a series of murders set in a small town in the Mid-West – where, if it was seen at all, it would have been under its new title, *Strange Behavior*. Michael Laughlin directed. *Talk to Me* (82) was financed by the Hollins Communications Research Institute, which had found a cure for stuttering; Fletcher was the mother of Austin Pendelton, a chronic stutterer. Again under Laughlin's direction she was in the Mid-West, for *Strange Invaders* (83), a spoof of 50s sci-fi movies: this time the producers were Canadian.

The next three were more promising, but did not do well – nor did they do anything to prevent this actress from settling into supporting roles: *Brainstorm*, a sci-fier in which she and top-billed Christopher Walken were research scientists; *Firestarter* (84), in which she and farmer husband Art Carney shelter the little girl who gives the film its title – and another daft concept from horror merchant Stephen King; and *Invaders from Mars* (86), more of same in this feeble remake, as the science teacher who gets eaten by the monsters. She supported Vanessa Redgrave in the tele-movie, *Second Serve*, and then did two more which did nothing to recall the world's attention to her – *The Boy Who Could Fly*, as a psychiatrist, and *Nobody's Fool*, as Rosanna Arquette's mother. *Flowers in the Attic* (87) was not up to much, but she was top-billed – and in terrific form, as the grandmother of four children kept hidden while their widowed mother tries to get her father to love her! She had a similar role, that of a matriarch, in *Two Moon Junction* (88), a silly tale of sexual obsession in an unconvincing Alabama.

JANE FONDA

Jane is Henry's daughter, so it was perhaps natural that she became an actress. Recent decades have seen a reversal of the old show-business maxim that the talents of the offspring are in inverse proportion to those of the parents – but it was not natural that she should be so good. So very, very good.

She was born in 1937 in New York, of Fonda's marriage to Frances Brokaw, and raised unlike other kids. When her father left the Coast to appear on Broadway in 'Mister Roberts' she went with him and was raised by her grandmother in Connecticut. She was educated at Vassar and acted there; with her father she did 'The Country Girl' (55) in his home town of Omaha and a year later was in 'The Male Animal' in Connecticut. She did not think she was very good and went to Paris to study painting. Then she took up the piano in New York. But when staying with her father in Hollywood she met Lee Strasberg, who encouraged her to study at his (The) Actors' Studio. She did some modelling on the side. Her father's friend, Joshua Logan, screen-tested her and cast her in *Tall Story* (60), as Tony Perkins's cheer-leading college bride. Having a famous name did not hurt

Jane Fonda and her father, Henry Fonda, off-set, in 1968. He was to say later, after her Oscar: 'She isn't good, she is sensational . . . the best actress of her generation.'

her, but in this instance it did not help much either. She appeared in a couple of Broadway plays, neither of them successful, 'There was a Little Girl' and 'The Fun Couple': the latter provided the occasion for a good hour-long documentary about her, *Jane* (62).

She returned to Hollywood for a couple of contrasting parts: *A Walk on the Wild Side,* with Laurence Harvey, as a hooker not long on the game; and *The Chapman Report*, as a female frigidaire. Said Stanley Kauffman in the 'New Republic': 'I have now seen Miss Fonda in three films. In all of them she gives performances that are not only fundamentally different from one another but are conceived without acting cliché and executed with skill. Through them can be heard, figuratively, the hum of magnetism without which acting intelligence and technique are admirable but uncompelling.' No one else took much notice of her till her sprightly playing of a brand-new bride (Jim Hutton's) undergoing a *Period of Adjustment*, from Tennessee Williams's only comedy (and a minor one). Logan had put her under personal contract before *Tall Story*, starting at $250 a week plus expenses. Andreas Voutsinas, her lover and business manager, thought that Logan exploited her and she paid Logan $250,000 to get out of the contract – the sum, in fact, paid by MGM for the Williams film. Any good that that may have done was undone by some tosh where she and Peter Finch where adulterous lovers, *In the Cool of the Day* (63). That year the 'Harvard Lampoon' voted her 'the year's worst actress'. She appeared on Broadway in a revival of 'Strange Interlude' with Geraldine Page, Ben Gazzara and Pat Hingle; then did a filmed play, *Sunday in New York* (64), as a virtuous – but curious – country mouse at odds with wolf Rod Taylor.

There were quibbles about whether Barbarella *(68) fully utilized Jane Fonda's acting ability; but as she appeared semi-nude most of the time who was worrying?*

She crossed the Atlantic to make, in French and English, René Clément's *Les Félins/Joy House/The Love Cage*, a neat thriller where she was super and sexy as a housebound girl who lets in Alain Delon. She stayed in France to take on Danielle Darrieux's old role of the philandering wife in Roger Vadim's *La Ronde*, a sorry effort, especially when considered beside the earlier Max Ophüls version. She married Vadim (1965) and became, in Sheilah Graham's words, 'The American girl gone to sex'. Meanwhile, in the States, she had fun – as did audiences – as a gun-totin' schoolmarm, *Cat Ballou* (65), with Lee Marvin. Somewhat more severe was *The Chase* (66), as a rich girl in love with Robert Redford. Vadim directed *La Curée*, a trashy effort about a girl who plays kinky games with her same-age stepson (Peter McEnery). Said 'Time Magazine' (later): 'Such Vadim-witted flicks were 25 per cent titillation, 75 per cent marzipan; but because they were 100 per cent Jane, they were worthwhile.'

In the US she did not enhance her reputation with either *Any Wednesday*, another filmed play – as Jason Robards's once-a-week mistress – or *Hurry Sundown* (67), as Michael Caine's wife. Yet another filmed play, however, Neil Simon's *Barefoot in the Park* – proved a glorious exception for Fonda-lovers. It was funny, and she and Robert Redford as newly-weds played with a style and charm not seen snce the days of Powell/Loy and Hepburn/Tracy. It broke box-office records, but turned out to be a flash-in-the-pan. The next one to come along was Vadim's *Barbarella* (68), based on a sci-fi comic strip, and hardly more noteworthy; but David Robinson ('Financial Times'), noting that her 'immense gift for comedy has incomprehensibly been neglected', thought her 'an ideal comic strip heroine with an affectation of naivety . . . constantly startled by the accidents of fate which rob her indifferently of her clothing and her honour.' Vadim also directed *Histoires Extraordinaires* – the episode 'Metzengerstein' with Peter Fonda, her brother; it turned up in New York late in 1969 (but was hardly seen in Britain), by which time she and Vadim had separated.

She turned down many offers, including *Bonnie and Clyde* and *Rosemary's Baby*, and made headlines mainly for her work on behalf of underprivileged Indians. Later she campaigned tirelessly against the war in Vietnam. She cared little, she said, whether she alienated either cinemagoers or the industry; as it happened, she gave a couple of performances which both cinemagoers and the industry could do with more of. The first (at a fee of $400,000 plus a percentage) was in *They Shoot Horses Don't They?* (69), a grim allegory of the Depression, as a hard-bitten marathon dancer – a performance which brought her the New York critics' Best Actress award. The second was in a New York thriller, *Klute* (71), with Donald Sutherland. He was a detective, Klute, and she a call-girl, Bree; and the film itself was the cinema's old standby – a fallen woman and a pure hero with a climactic will-he-won't-he-save-her-from-the-villain last reel. 'Variety' said that up to now there had been momentary magnetism, but now 'there is something coming off the screen'; 'Time Magazine' called it 'her best performance to date, she is profoundly and perfectly Bree . . . it is a rare performance'. She won a second New York critics' award and the Best Actress Oscar.

She returned to France to make *Tout Va Bien* (72) for Jean-Luc Godard and with co-star Yves Montand took only a token salary, since they wanted to help Godard; they were also due to get 23 per cent of the gross, but by this time there were very few filmgoers in the world likely to pay to see a Godard film. For the record, she was an American journalist and Montand a film-maker who became involved with strikers. With Sutherland, she toured army bases with a revue and they filmed it, *F.T.A.* or *Free the Army*; and with him she did a daft film about drop-outs, *Steelyard Blues* (73), playing a fizzy-haired whore. She spoke out against Nixon and because of her political views considered herself 'grey-listed' by the industry; but another reason may have been the publicity given to the making of *A Doll's House*. 'I hated every bloody minute of it' said the director, Joseph Losey, of the filming in Norway; most of the trouble sprang from Fonda's insistence, in the words of 'Time Magazine', on improving Ibsen. To little avail: for few saw it. Preceded to Britain by a version with Claire Bloom, it was damply received and when no US distributor would take it, it was sold direct to TV. She married Tom Hayden, alumnus of the Chicago Seven, and she campaigned for him in his unsuccessful bid for the Senate; together they made a documentary, *Introduction to the Enemy* (75). It was possible that the only film offer at this time was *The Blue Bird* (76), a Russian-American co-production filmed in Leningrad, and conceivably better not to have been accepted: filming was apparently nightmarish and when the result opened at Radio City it was killed stone-dead by the notices.

Jane Fonda as the tough hooker in Klute *(71), which brought her the first of her two Best Actress Oscars.*

However, Fonda's career was about to revive miraculously – and it is tempting to view that as not coincidental with the fall of Nixon. The revival started with *Fun With Dick and Jane* (77), a comedy about improvident but enterprising young-marrieds with George Segal; and it reached a peak with *Julia*, directed by Fred Zinnemann from part of Lillian Hellman's 'Pentimento'. Vanessa Redgrave had the title-role and Fonda was the young Hellman, in a tingling and touching performance which reminded everyone that she was one of the best actresses in Hollywood. The film was also big box-office and it was reported that Fonda's fee had risen to $750,000; but Fonda-watchers could take note from interviews how soundly she reconciled fame and big money with being a political activist. She turned down the title role in *An Unmarried Woman* as she found the film 'not relevant' – and one might wish for her the decision of Gian Maria Volonte in Italy, who has said that he will not make films unless they have some political content. In his case, that has resulted in some films at least interesting and Fonda's careful choice of subject has resulted in a group of films both more worthwhile and more entertaining than any in the first phase of her career. In *Coming Home* (78) she was an army wife (Bruce Dern's), who falls for a wounded Vietnam veteran (Jon Voight); she had a hand in the production and the Best Actress Oscar she won for it made her specially happy, for she considered it the most important film she had made. For our part, we might note it the first Oscar awarded for a role requiring an on-screen orgasm: since few commented on this it is a definite advance in the cause of sensible sexuality on screen. In *Comes a Horseman*, with James Caan, she was a fierce lady of the plains; in Neil Simon's *California Suite* a New York divorcée at odds with her now-Californian ex-husband (Alan Alda) – a less happy outing into the works of this writer than the last time; and an investigative TV reporter in *The China Syndrome* (79), with Jack Lemmon and Michael Douglas, and co-produced with the latter's company. Fonda's aim to make 'responsible films . . . movies that explore choices that people make' was once again justified – coincidentally, when shortly after its opening there was grave danger at a Pennsylvania nuclear-energy factory, but also commercially. She herself was 'downright terrific' said David Ansen in 'Newsweek'. 'There's a new simplicity in her acting that impresses all the more because it isn't calculated to impress. It's a pleasure to watch a superb actress continually refining her art'.

She was a reporter again in *The Electric Horseman*, exploiting over-the-hill cowboy Robert Redford: but like Jean Arthur with Gary Cooper she had doubts about this, and they are soon sharing the same sleeping-bag. She, Lily Tomlin and Dolly Parton worked from *Nine to Five* (80), so exasperated by MCP boss Dabney Coleman that they kidnap him; she worked *on* it for $2 million plus a percentage – which must have been considerable, since the public flocked, apparently not caring that it was so keen to make a joke at any price that it threw away chances wholesale. *On Golden Pond* (81) was even more popular – ironically, since it would not have been given a theatrical release with the interest of HBO, or so one of its executives claimed. Old age had never been box-office and though well expressed by Katharine Hepburn and Henry Fonda it had nothing interesting to say on the subject. Jane had been looking for a vehicle for herself and her father (who had not long to live) for many years. Her own role was small; Coleman played her live-in lover. More irony here – since *Rollover* was (by far) Jane's best picture of this batch and it died at the box-office.

Jack Lemmon and Jane Fonda acting marvellously in The China Syndrome *(79), towards the shattering climax when an explosion at a nuclear power plant becomes a possibility. Michael Douglas was the third star, and, with Miss Fonda, the producer: since this was the best American film in years, they have every reason to be proud of it.*

Maybe spectators were deterred by the intrigues of high finance, in which banker Kris Kristofferson and ex-movie star Fonda were involved; they missed an expert thriller directed by Alan Pakula, who had made both *Klute* and *Comes a Horseman*. It seemed to prove that audiences had not gone to *On Golden Pond* for her and she stayed away from the studios – while not incidentally making herself very rich with her series of 'Work-Out' books and video-cassettes. They also brought her renewed popularity – so she may have felt that *The Dollmaker* (84) was only suitable for the small screen: after all, how many people are interested in the lives of the deprived in Detroit in World War II? Fonda played an indomitable Kentucky wife and mother seeing it through and, though it had more fire and guts than most tele-movies, you yourself might not have felt deprived if you dropped off. And you missed little if you missed *Agnes of God* (85) – only some bravura encounters between psychiatrist Fonda and Mother Superior Anne Bancroft, debating why a nun has had a baby. Several reviewers commented that America's most famous health fanatic was playing a chain-smoker.

She played an ex-movie star again in Lumet's *The Morning After* (86), but not like the one in *Rollover*: this one was a drunk and had not really made it in the first place ('They were grooming me to be the new Vera Miles' – 'The new who?' – 'Exactly. They were grooming me to replace someone the audience didn't even know was missing.'): the man asking the question was Jeff Bridges and the film was an efficient murder mystery. She was off the screen for a while and her marriage broke up. She returned in *Old Gringo* (89) with Gregory Peck and *Union Street* opposite Robert DeNiro.

Glenn Ford

Glenn Ford was not the most stimulating or individual of players, nor – despite a brief showing among the top 10 money-making stars – does he seem to have had either a clique or a mass following. He was instead a good – if not the best – example of that second-string group, the dependable and efficient actor. It was always a pleasure to renew acquaintance with him, especially in comedy, where his relaxed and impish performances as a bumbling ordinary guy have been much underrated. In drama he remained the Little Man, often victimized and battling grimly against the forces of fate. Everyone likes him – except perhaps his directors. Frank Capra's memoirs are eloquent on Ford and David Swift, working with him on *Love is a Ball*, found that he approached 'his craft like a twelve-year-old temperamental child. Were he mine I would have spanked him physically' (quoted by Paul Mayersberg in 'Hollywood the Haunted House').

Ford was born in 1916 in Quebec, Canada, where his father was a railway executive. He was taken to Santa Monica, California, at the age of seven and later worked as a stable-boy for Will Rogers. This may well have imbued him with acting aspirations for though on leaving high school he did several jobs – salesman, bus-driver, telephone repair man, etc. – he continued to plan an acting career. He was working in a paint-shop when he got a chance to play the very minor role of the grocer's boy in 'The Children's Hour' with the Santa Monica Players. Not long afterwards he was engaged for a Paramount short, *Night in Manhattan* (37). He went to New York and appeared in 'Soliloquy' (38), 'Broom For the Bride' and 'Golden Boy'. 20th tested him but were unimpressed. He returned to the Coast to play in Elmer Rice's 'Judgment Day', which resulted in a Columbia contract; at the same time 20th had rerun the test that they had made and they signed him for a sentimental B directed by Ricardo Cortez, *Heaven With a Barbed Wire Fence* (40), in which he and Jean Rogers were impoverished sweethearts.

Columbia put him in a slew of Bs: *My Son is Guilty*, starring Bruce Cabot; *Convicted Women* and its companion piece, *Men Without Souls* – a prison drama, both with Rochelle Hudson; *Babies for Sale*; and *Blondie Plays Cupid*, one of the series based on the comic strip. He had a good part in *The Lady in Question* and, as Brian Aherne's son, got to kiss Rita Hayworth; but stardom came on loan-out to UA, *So End Our Night* (41) as Margaret Sullavan's companion, the Jewish couple befriended by anti-Nazi Fredric March. The films Columbia assigned him to were mainly programme-fillers: *Texas*, as William Holden's rival for Claire Trevor; *Go West Young Lady* as a young sheriff, with Penny ('Blondie') Singleton; *The Adventures of Martin Eden* (42) with Trevor, Jack London's tale much softened in this version; *Flight Lieutenant*, a conventional service drama with Pat O'Brien and Evelyn Keyes; and *The Desperadoes* (43) with Randolph Scott, Keyes and Trevor. He was a cocky young bo'sun pitted against Edward G. Robinson in *Destroyer*, after which he joined the navy in earnest.

When he returned, Columbia, grateful to a veteran, decided to showcase him for the first time in a top-budget production, *Gilda* (46),

as an adventurer opposite their cherished Rita Hayworth. And he got some more publicity mileage when Bette Davis chose him to co-star with her in *A Stolen Life* at Warners. Columbia loaned him on condition he signed a new seven-year pact with them, but they clearly did not know what to do with him: after *Gallant Journey*, one of William A. Wellman's aviation dramas, they kept him idle for a year. He returned in a sentimental comedy with Evelyn Keyes, *The Mating of Millie* (48).

Hayworth's sagging career needed a boost and as she and Ford had been a wow in *Gilda* they were reunited – in *The Loves of Carmen*. He was Don José (no one could accuse Columbia of obvious casting). After that lush pasture, back to barren ground: *The Return of October*, a horse story with Terry Moore; *The Man From Colorado* with Holden, as a sadistic Federal judge whose psychological problems he indicated by a 'frozen expressionless mask' ('New York Times'); *The Undercover Man* (49), with Nina Foch; *Lust for Gold* with Ida Lupino; and *Mr Soft Touch* with Keyes. Like his Columbia classmate, Holden, Ford's career – after a decade at that studio – was to get an impetus from films at other studios. But not quite yet: *The Doctor and the Girl* at MGM, with Janet Leigh, was medium stuff and there were not enough thrills in *The White Tower* (50), a Technicolored mountaineering drama at RKO. Columbia *Convicted* him though innocent (a remake of *The Criminal Code*): then Paramount made of him and Rhonda Fleming *The Redhead and the Cowboy* – or 'The Deadhead and the Cowboy' as one wag called it. *The Flying Missile* was a World War II story.

William Holden and Glenn Ford when they were just two junior leading men at Columbia. This was a publicity still issued to celebrate a 1941 Western called Texas.

There were two Bette Davises in love with ferryman Glenn Ford in A Stolen Life *(46) – and it was the bad one who married him. However, in the end . . .*

Ford was rising to the top of the heap and his very niceness – by turns brash and diffident – fitted him well to play contemporary heroes. 20th wanted him to play golfer Ben Hogan in their biopic, *Follow the Sun* (51), announced as the first of a five-year contract. At 20th he did *The Secret of Convict Lake*, another factual story reduced to fakery; again wrongly convicted, with Gene Tierney as the wife of his betrayer and reluctantly in love with him. Neither film was successful and no more was heard of the 20th contract. He went off to Europe to make a French film, made in English with mainly US players, *The Green Glove* (52), a melodrama set on the Côte d'Azur; the result did not accelerate the demand for 'international' films.

Meanwhile, his commitment to Columbia had been adjusted at the time he had signed with 20th to one film a year for the next four years. He and Hayworth were reunited for an *Affair in Trinidad*, a title that promised far more than was delivered. Ford was as discontented as audiences; he had not got the contracted equal billing with Hayworth. The matter was resolved by cutting his Columbia commitment to two. He did a couple of programmers for MGM: *Young Man With Ideas*, as an ambitious but bumbling lawyer, and *Time Bomb* (53), an efficient thriller made on location in the English Midlands. As *The Man From the Alamo* he fought against the Mexicans; in *Plunder of the Sun* he journeyed among them, looking for buried treasure. Warners paid him $125,000 for that.

Back at Columbia he made what is almost certainly his best film, Fritz Lang's masterly *The Big Heat*, fine as an ex-cop out to find who killed his wife and bust a crime-ring – with the aid of moll Gloria Grahame. It was not at the time a smash and had only a coterie following. Still, Columbia let Lang follow it up with *Human Desire* (54), a remake of *La Bête Humaine*, with Ford in the Gabin part, dangerously attracted to trollop Grahame. It was by no means as good as *The Big Heat*. Between the two Ford had an *Appointment in Honduras* (53) with Ann Sheridan; and then was *The Americano* (55) in Brazil, another illustration of his tendency to retreat South of the Border (perhaps because *Gilda* had been set in South America). This was not a happy occasion – an independent production which stalled when the money ran out. RKO took it over, replaced leading lady Ursula Theiss by Sarita Montiel and filed suit against Ford for damages because he was unable to finish it. He did, though working concurrently on *The Violent Men*, a Western with Barbara Stanwyck.

A couple of films at MGM shifted his career into top gear. *The Blackboard Jungle* was adapted from a bestseller by Evan Hunter about a teacher threatened by the delinquents in his class. The film's success was due mainly to a song in it, 'Rock Around the Clock' (which inaugurated the Rock 'n Roll era in films), but for the first time Ford's name began to carry weight at the box-office. *Interrupted Melody* did not achieve the same success, but it proved that Ford was at home in lavish MGM drama – in this case the sad story of opera singer Marjorie Lawrence (Eleanor Parker). MGM offered a long-term contract and he thus became the last major star to be tied to one studio (with the exceptions of Jerry Lewis at Paramount and Rock Hudson and Tony Curtis at Universal, all of whom had been nurtured by those studios). He also became the last of the big MGM male stars – though he was allowed to do outside films (all of which, for five years, he did at his old alma mater, Columbia). MGM put him in two more contemporary dramas in the manner of *Blackboard Jungle*: *Trial* and *Ransom!* (56). There were two Westerns, *Jubal* and *The Fastest Gun Alive*, and then *The Teahouse of the August Moon*, based on an artful Broadway hit about the tribulations of the US army while grappling with the (peacetime) Japanese, who included Marlon Brando. The film made the top 10 that year and was partly responsible for Ford

The Teahouse of the August Moon (56), *with Marlon Brando as the local – Japanese – interpreter and master-of-all-tricks, and Glenn Ford as the American captain in charge of rehabilitation. Relations on the set were not cordial, since both actors suspected that the other had the most important and most sympathetic role.*

jumping up to fifth among star moneymakers. Its success led to a series of service comedies in which Ford played a blend of Mister Roberts and Santa Claus – tolerant of his superiors, kind to the enlisted men and the natives: a real democratic guy (in one of them he blackmails Keenan Wynn with a tape-recording in order to get $1,000 to rebuild the native school).

He turned villain for a good Western, *3.10 to Yuma* (57), as a killer dedicated to getting Van Heflin, and then did *Don't Go Near the Water*, notable mainly for Wynn's journalist and Fred Clark's bumbling, officious CO. Both were popular, but Ford himself did not make the box-office listings. Paradoxically, he did in 1958 – at No 1 – though none of the films that year was very popular: two attempts at comedy Westerns, *Cowboy* with Jack Lemmon and *The Sheepman* with Shirley MacLaine; *Imitation General*, a comedy; and *Torpedo Run*, which was more serious. Then he shared a couple of comedies with Debbie Reynolds, MGM's last female star: *It Started With a Kiss* (59), again in uniform, as an air force sergeant; and *The Gazebo*. At the end of 1959 he was fifth among the top 10.

The box-office descent began with a disastrous remake of *Cimarron* (60), heavy, long-winded and lifeless. Ford could do nothing with either his character or leading lady Maria Schell. *Cry For Happy* (61) did not do much to retrieve the situation, a poor thing about the US navy and some geishas, with Donald O'Connor. *A Pocketful of Miracles*, at UA with Bette Davis, was another remake, by Frank Capra of his own *Lady for a Day*; Ford was fine as a Runyonesque gang-leader, neatly abetted by girlfriend Hope Lange (his companion in real life and, according to Capra, in this film only because Ford insisted; Ford's marriage to Eleanor Powell, 1943–59 had ended in divorce, in 1965 he married Kathy Hayes). His fee was $350,000 plus a hefty percentage. Another remake emerged after rumours of troubles, Vincente Minnelli's *The Four Horsemen of the Apocalypse* (62), to be greeted by even worse reviews than was *Cimarron*. The leading lady, Ingred Thulin, had to be dubbed (there is a case to be made for all recent continental ladies – even as talented as this one – being the kiss of death on Hollywood films).

There was an agreeable *Experiment in Terror*, with Lee Remick; then a couple of comedies, *Love Is a Ball* (63) with Hope Lange and *The Courtship of Eddie's Father* with Shirley Jones. None of them undid the damage done by *Cimarron* and *The Four Horseman*. . . . The next one played B dates, known alternatively as *Advance to the Rear* (64) and *A Company of Cowards?* At 20th, there was an actioner, *Fate Is the Hunter*, the last of Ford's films to play the A slot on double bills. The rest were lucky to get B dates, even if most of them were top-budget productions: *Dear Heart*, a romantic tale with Geraldine Page; *The Rounders* (65) with Henry Fonda; *The Money Trap* (66), a reunion with Hayworth that no one heeded; *Paris Brûle-t-il?/Is Paris Burning?*, a guest appearance as General Omar Bradley; and *El Mal/ The Rage* made in Mexico.

Ford did three Westerns in a row: *A Time for Killing* (67), begun by Roger Corman and completed by Phil Karson; *The Last Challenge* with Angie Dickinson; and *Day of The Evil Gun* (68). The first and third of these titles were made by MGM for ACT TV – i.e. they were expected to have only a brief career in cinemas, in B slots, before going to TV.

It was not surprising that Ford was placed on 'Variety's' list of overpriced stars published in 1968 and he probably got much less than his normal fee for two more Westerns, *Heaven With a Gun* (69) and Disney's *Smith*. It was almost as if Ford was dogged by fate, for *Smith* was one of the few Disney films to fail. It *is* almost inexplicable, for Ford's work had not deteriorated in quality and he remained a more attractive talent than others of his generation still operating. Perhaps the trouble was that the films he had been making were just the sort of fare being shown nightly on TV, just as there were so many nice-guy actors like him on TV. . . . On TV he did *The Brotherhood of the Bell* (70), as a distinguished economist, and the following year he began a successful TV series, 'Cade's County'.

His film career never really got going again. In *Santee* (73) he was a bounty hunter softened by a child, but the film was not widely shown. Instead, his agent was able to keep him in leading roles on television: *Jarrett*, in the name part, as an arts investigator; *The Disappearance of Flight 412* (74), as the flight commander; *The Greatest Gift*, as a dedicated priest in the 40s, with Julie Harris as his wife; and *Punch and Jody*, as a circus grifter, with his own new wife – Cynthia Hayward – among the cast. The last-named was a pilot for a series which no one picked up; instead, in 1975 the one with Harris became a short-lived series, 'The Family Holvak', with the action moved back to the Depression. Then he was one of several names playing high-ranking officers in two pieces set during World War II, *Midway* (76) and *Once an Eagle*, a mini-series in which he was starred with four youngsters while the other veteran names were guest-starred; after that one he finally accepted one of the many offers from Europe: *Goodbye e Amen* (77), based on a thriller by Francis Clifford, with Tony Musante.

For television, he accompanied Cliff Young on *The 3,000 Mile Chase* and starred in three important mini-series: *Evening in Byzantium* (79), Louis l'Amour's *'The Sacketts'* and *Beggarman Thief*. The second of these was a Western top-lining Tom Selleck and Sam Elliott; the other two were unrelated other than being both based on novels by Irwin Shaw, but both plots sent Ford to the Cannes Film Festival. Ford turned character actor with a vengeance for a superior tele-film with Miss Harris again as his wife, *The Gift*, playing sailor Gary Frank's hard-drinking, peg-legged Brooklyn Irish father. His popularity had gone and there were few subsequent offers. He played a detective in an Italian horror movie set in Atlanta, *Il Visitore* (80) and the American president in a Japanese disaster tale, *Virus* – in fact of largish budget with locations all over the world, but the presence of Ford, George Kennedy and Robert Vaughan brought it few bookings anywhere. There was a job in Canada, as psychiatrist to student Melissa Sue Anderson, who would seem to be systematically murdering her classmates: *Happy Birthday to Me* (81). *Day of the Assassins*, made the previous year in Mexico City with Chuck Connors and Richard Roundtree, would seem never to have been shown.

JEAN GABIN

Few screen images have been so completely and consistently realized as that of the pre-war Gabin. Written mainly by Jacques Prévert, Henri Jeanson or Charles Spaak, directed often by Renoir, Duvivier and Marcel Carné, he has sometimes been seen to be an allegorical statement of the Third Republic. He was beautifully summed up by Penelope Houston in 1951: 'The Gabin hero is perhaps the the archetype of the 30s. He is anti-romantic (yet so defiantly so as to suggest a romantic atmosphere of his own); anti-heroic, a victim-hero. His enemy is not an individual who can be fought, but the remote, inhuman and unshifting form of society itself. [He] is cut off by his own actions; he tries to escape (into his happier past or, more positively, by actual flight), he is pulled back and punished, and he accepts his punishment with fatalistic expectancy. His ambitions have been abandoned before the picture even opens, and his only aim, as we see it, is to survive somehow, through human contacts, against the impersonal forces. Yet it is these contacts, arising more from pity than from love . . . that eventually trap and destroy him.'

Physically, Gabin was hardly more expressive than in his later career. He looked hunted but never furtive, neither resigned nor apprehensive. He rarely if ever smiled. He was stoic and world-weary, a man whom life had used, leftist but neither agitator nor underdog. When not in uniform and *képi* – he was often an army deserter – his clothes were nondescript, with a nod towards the criminal classes: trench-coat and cap or trilby, pulled down over the eyes; Italian striped suit and a black shirt with a white silk tie.

The war killed the character – just as it almost killed Gabin's career – though some essentials lived on. Before the war, when Hollywood remade Gabin's *Pépé le Moko* the central character became a somewhat *déclassé* romantic (though partly because Charles Boyer's personality was too strong to even suggest Gabin); but the Humphrey Bogart character in *Casablanca*, though American-born, was clearly inspired by Gabin. Gabin himself was to move over to the Establishment, though in all his enormously successful later career there were glimmerings of the old doom-haunted fugitive.

He was born in the La Villette *quartier* of Paris in 1904, the seventh son of a couple who entertained in cabarets and music halls. Gabin (born Jean-Alexis Moncorgé) was brought up partly by relatives in the country, until after World War I when he was apprenticed to a construction company in La Chapelle, in the north of Paris. After two more jobs he decided to follow his parents' profession and he eked out a living over the next few years. Shortly after his 18 months' *service militaire* he was taken on for some Rip revues, followed by two operettes, 'La Dame en Décolleté' and 'Trois Jeunes Filles Nues' (26), after which he joined a troupe that toured South America. It was on his return he took the name Gabin (his father's stage-name). He got a small part at the Moulin Rouge and was seen socially with Mistinguett – though in 1928 he married his mistress of four years, Gaby Basset. Work now began to come to him; he was appearing not only in music halls but in plays like 'Arsène Lupin Banquier' (which starred his father) and 'Flossie'. A German film company offered him a contract to make French versions of German Talkies but he turned it down because he considered that he now had a 'standing' in Paris; he accepted, however, an offer from Pathé-Natan to make films – most of which turned out to be the French versions of co-productions with Germany.

His first picture, *Chacun sa Chance* (30), was the French version of *Kopfüsser ins Glück*, with Gaby Basset as a dancer being wooed by boulevardier Gabin. There followed: *Mephisto* (31), a thriller with France Dhélia, directed by the actor Henri Debain;

Paris-Béguin, directed by Augusto Genina, a drama of life backstage, with Jane Marnac as a music-hall star and Gabin (second-billed) and Fernandel as gangsters; *Gloria*, made in Germany with Brigitte Helm, with Gabin as a pilot who pursued her across the Atlantic; *Tout ça ne vaut pas l'Amour*, directed by Jacques Tourneur, with Josseline Gaël; and *Coeur de Lilas* (32), directed by Anatole Litvak, with Frehel, the great music-hall singer, and the beautiful Marcelle Romée (who committed suicide as soon as the film was over). This was an atmospheric picture of the *quartier* around the Porte des Lilas, with Gabin as a petty crook; and here, with bored expression and dangling Gauloise, was the beginning of the Gabin image. He was equally *louche*, singing in waterfront cafés, in *La Belle Marinière*, from a play by Marcel Achard, with Madeleine Renaud, but was an upright recruit to the cavalry, supporting Raimu, in *Les Gaités de l'Escadron*.

He made: *La Foule Hurle* (33) with Hélène Perdrière, which included some footage from James Cagney's auto-racing thriller of the previous year, *The Crowd Roars*; *L'Etoile de Valencia*, as a Spanish police chief fighting the white-slave traffic, with Simone Simon and Brigitte Helm; and *Adieu les Beaux Jours* again with Helm, in the parts played in the remake, *Desire*, by Gary Cooper and Marlene Dietrich. *Le Tunnel* was also remade by a British company: this was a Franco-German production, directed by Curtis Bernhardt, about the building of a tunnel under the Atlantic. Pabst directed *De Haut en Bas*, another look at Paris low-life, with Michel Simon and Janine Crispin; and *Au Bout du Monde* saw Gabin similarly placed – but with ideas above his station in the person of Kate de Nagy. He played a sailor in *Zouzou* (34), primarily a vehicle for Josephine Baker, a crude backstage story which was vaguely autobiographical, directed by Marc Allégret; and then had his first big success in *Maria Chapdelaine*, a tragic romance between a girl (Renaud) and a happy-go-lucky fur-trapper on the run from the police. The film quite preserved the spirit of Louis Hémon's novel, but there were two more significant factors: it was directed by Julien Duvivier (it won the Grand Prix du Cinéma that year) and Gabin died during the action. Duvivier was so struck with Gabin's potentialities that he looked for another subject for him, while the Gabin death scene was to become obligatory in his pre-war movies. Rumour had it that this was written into his contracts.

Passage Interdit (35) was written apparently by Jacques Prévert but is now completely forgotten. So – and it is just as well – is *Variétés*, a French remake of the German Silent classic, with Gabin, Annabella and Fernand Gravey as the tragic triangle. It was, however, a huge success at the time. Duvivier directed *Golgotha*, notable for the presence of Harry Baur as Herod and Gabin's highly uncomfortable Pontius Pilate (Robert Le Vigan was Christ). Duvivier and writer Charles Spaak then came up with *La Bandéra* (36), which shook together vigorously all the Foreign Legion clichés and propelled Gabin forward as a great romantic hero. He was a suspected murderer hiding out in the Legion (the Spanish, not the French as in Pierre MacOrlan's original novel) who dies a hero's death. Annabella was the native girl he loved. The 'MFB' thought its chief virtues the 'atmosphere' and Gabin's 'powerful performance'. It was a great success and so was *La Belle Équipe* (36), another collaboration between Duvivier and Spaak, a bitter variation on the money-doesn't-bring happiness theme. The *équipe* were five layabouts who win a lottery and start a restaurant, till almost sundered by the arrival of Viviane Romance, as the sexy wife of Charles Vanel. Alternative endings were shot: in one Gabin kills Vanel and is arrested, in the other both men turn their backs, emotionally, on Romance. Both were consistent with the Gabin creed, as now formulated.

The rules were rejected, however, in *Les Bas-Fonds*, the first of the four films he made for Jean Renoir: he was the pickpocket who flirts with Suzy Prim but goes off with waiflike Junie Astor. *Pépé le Moko* (37) was scripted by Jeanson, directed by Duvivier and had Gabin as a master-crook who falls for society girl Mireille Balin: when he leaves his kingdom – the Algiers casbah – to follow her to France he is gunned down. The film was another hit, and more than anything hitherto established Gabin's name in foreign markets (though it disappeared for a while when Hollywood remade it as *Algiers* with Charles Boyer). The next one ran an unprecedented six months in New York, whose critics voted it the Best Foreign Film of the year: *La Grande Illusion*, Renoir's deeply felt study of interned officers during World War I, with Erich von Stroheim as the German commandant, and Pierre Fresnay and Gabin as contrasting officers – Fresnay refined and aristocratic, Gabin rugged and bourgeois. In France, it was the year's most successful film.

And Gabin was now the biggest box-office actor. With the degree of autonomy allowed him he chose Raymond Rouleau to direct *Le Messager*, with Gaby Morlay repeating her stage role (it was a play by Henri Bernstein) as the wife seduced by the messenger (Jean-Pierre Aumont) of absent husband Gabin. It was nowhere as strong as the six which

Jean Gabin as he was when world cinemagoers began to realise that France had a romantic leading man as effective as any then starring in films: in the title-role of Pépé le Moko *(37), a fugitive from justice hiding out in the casbah and falling fatally in love with a socialite (Mireille Balin) who went slumming there.*

surrounded it. To Gabin must go much of the credit for these: he was known to put subject-matter over money and he turned down several Hollywood offers (one film he wanted to do, *Casque d'Or*, did not get made till 14 years later, with Serge Reggiani). The least of the following films was perhaps Grémillon's *Gueule d'Amour*, written by Spaak – filmed in Berlin but set mainly in the Midi – about a spahi who falls hopelessly for the 'cold' Mireille Balin who laters marries his best friend. (Balin, in life, was Gabin's offscreen companion – and later a tragic figure: she became a drug addict and died not long after effecting a cure.) Marcel Carné and Jacques Prévert then made the first of their – considerable – additions to the Gabin legend: *Quai des Brumes* (38), again adapted from a novel by MacOrlan, with the action transferred from 1914 Paris to present-day Le Havre – fog-bound, menacing. Gabin was a pessimistic deserter waiting to ship out illegally, till he finds happiness with the mysterious Michèle Morgan, met by chance in a café; he murders her 'guardian' Michel Simon and is killed in turn by Simon's aide, Pierre Brasseur. The film was, after Disney's *Snow White*, France's most popular film that year. Renoir's *La Bête Humaine* was also an updating – of Zola – with Simone Simon as the tramp who inveigles engine-driver Gabin into murdering her husband and in turn cuckolds him with another man: a film of trains and seedy stations, with an unforgettable ending – the speeding express after Gabin has jumped from the cabin.

Morgan and Gabin were seen together socially and together made the minor *Le Récif de Corail* (39), in which he was again a fugitive. The Carné and Prévert cast him in *Le Jour se Lève*, as a factory hand who kills, in justified anger, the evil Jules Berry; through one night he is holed up in a hotel room while the police await with guns. The film was pessimistic, even defeatist, and its allegorical relevance was not lost on contemporary audiences – it was banned by Daladier and then by the Germans, but via a copy which reached North Africa was seen in Allied countries in 1943. It disappeared again when Hollywood (i.e. the French producer brothers Hakim) bought the remake rights and in its absence acquired a reputation which proved to be unjustified when it reappeared in the late 50s. Like all the pre-war Gabin films – except the Renoirs – it had dated in every way; but its pervading romanticism was almost intoxicating. As 1939 ended, Gabin was again the most popular male draw in France. There was one more to come, Grémillon's *Remorques*, a triangle story (Renaud as his wife, Morgan as his mistress) set against a background of the sea. Filmed under difficulties (it was started before the war, then abandoned for some months while Gabin was mobilized), it was finally finished and premièred late in 1941; but what emerged was still a notable addition to the Gabin legend.

Meanwhile, in 1940, Gabin had reached the US via Lisbon and in Hollywood signed a contract with 20th, who looked high and low for a suitable vehicle. The one they came up with, *Moontide* (42) with Ida Lupino, set among the California docks, pleased neither his fans (despite a plethora of close-ups) nor the 20th accountants. He moved over to Universal where Duvivier was to direct *The Impostor*, playing an escaped murderer who dies heroically while fighting with the Free French. Then: RKO signed Renoir to direct him and Luise Rainer in *The Temptress*. At the last minute Gabin insisted that Marlene Dietrich be his co-star. The head of RKO paid their salaries, cancelled the film and swore that Gabin would never work in Hollywood again. Without waiting for the (unenthusiastic) reviews of *The Informer*, Gabin sailed to North Africa to join his compatriots. He had found himself dull in English and so had the Americans; and his conscience would not permit him to sit out the rest of the war in California. He was decorated (Croix de Guerre, etc.) and was one of the forces who marched through Paris at the Liberation in 1944.

His projected come-back film was calculated to stand the French film industry on its ears: *Les Portes de la Nuit*, directed by Carné, written by Prévert and co-starring no less than Dietrich, still his current offscreen companion and a national heroine due to her ceaseless singing to the troops – plus Serge Reggiani, Pierre Brasseur, Carette, etc. There were delays when finance was not forthcoming (Korda partially backed it) and then Gabin complained that the script was too intellectual; Dietrich walked out because her part was too small. There were further delays while he complained about his new co-star. During all this time he was on full pay while everyone else was at 50 per cent. In the end he was sacked and able to do a second film planned with Dietrich, a property he owned – and in which he had failed to interest Carné and Prévert. *Les Portes de la Nuit* was made with Yves Montand and was a failure; so was *Martin Roumagnac* (46), some variations on old themes (Dietrich was the mistress of Marcel Herrand but was in love with Gabin, who kills her when he discovers she is unfaithful; then letting himself be killed by her new admirer, Daniel Gélin). It was a foredoomed failure: the public had followed the quarrels over the Carné project with bated breath and had cast Gabin as the villain; his career dived into such opprobrium that it took him years to climb back. The next flopped, *Miroir* (47), a flat piece with Gisèle Préville in which he was a self-made man – made by crime, to be unmasked by his own confederates.

In 1949 he returned to the stage, unsuccessfully, in 'La Soif' by Henry Bernstein, and remarried (his second wife had divorced him during the war) – in the 50s he became a father thrice-over. His only good film offer was from Italy – *Le Mura di Malapaga/Au delà des Grilles* (49), directed by René Clément and written by Cesare Zavattini with more than a backward glance at *Quai des Brumes*. He was a murderer who jumps ship in Genoa to visit a dentist and falls for the waitress (Isa Miranda) who knows he cannot pay for his meal; they love desperately as the police move in. The film was well received (it won the Best Foreign Film Oscar in 1951) but did not do well in French cinemas. Gabin and Carné were encouraged to rejoin forces and again great things were expected of them: *La Marie du Port* was based on a Simenon story, about a middle-aged man who falls for his mistress's young sister (Nicole Courcel). The result has nothing in common with their earlier triumphs.

Clearly Gabin, more image-conscious than most actors, was searching for a new one and Zavattini provided another idea: *E più Facile che un Camello* (50), directed by Luigi Zampa, a fantasy about an industrialist sent back to earth for 12 hours to find salvation. He did a mediocre version of a boulevard comedy, *Victor* (51), as the scapegoat of two rapacious friends. In *La Nuit est mon Royaume* he was once more the SNCF driver, this time adjusting to blindness: not one of his better performances but prized at Venice that year. He was a lecherous farmer in the Maison Tellier sequence of *Le Plaisir* – a small role – with Danielle Darrieux; and he was the unfaithful husband poisoned by her in *La Vérité sur Bébé Donge* (52). *La Minute de Vérité* was another study of marriage, but it was the wife (Michèle Morgan) who was unhappy this time – with Daniel Gélin as the lover in the French version and Walter Chiari in the Italian (for some reason the version shown in Britain was the Chiari one dubbed into French). *La Fille Dangereuse/Bufere* (53) was also a co-production, a crude sex drama about a famous surgeon who goes to the dogs after breaking up a trapeze act (Serge Reggiani, Silvana Pampanini). Shades of Emil Jannings. *La Vierge du Rhin* was a revenge melodrama and he was again the older man; the title referred neither to Andrée Clément, Nadia Gray nor to Elina Labourdette, but to a barge; and the film was only notable because it was directed by Gilles Grangier, to become one of Gabin's favourite directors.

Leur Dernière Nuit might be considered the

Le Plaisir *(51) was Max Ophüls's re-telling of three stories by Guy de Maupassant. The best one was 'La Maison de Madame Tellier', the story of a day's outing by Madame and her young ladies. Madame (Madeleine Renaud) can be seen in the front row, and Ginette Leclerc in the second – as well as Danielle Darrieux, here being accosted by Jean Gabin.*

watershed of his career, with elements of the old (young) Gabin and of the (old) Gabin of the 50s and 60s, the bourgeois Gabin, the paterfamilias, the family favourite. He was a conscientious librarian by day, a wanted gangster by night; betrayed by one of his henchmen he spends a last night with Madeleine Robinson and is gunned down before her eyes as he is escaping across the border. He is care-worn but resigned, inflexibly aware of his failings, magisterial and tough. He was a gangster again in *Touchez pas au Grisbi* (54), a superior underworld story built round a big heist, directed by Jacques Becker. He was not friendless now, but loyal to his friends and fascinating to women, though his old passion for both had gone. The film was a hit everywhere and re-established him as the leading French actor. At Venice this and *L'Air de Paris* resulted in a second Best Actor award. The latter was a boxing yarn – he was a manager attempting a come-back – indifferently directed by Carné. Then he did: *Napoléon* (55) as a dying soldier, one of the 50 names in the cast; Renoir's *French Can-Can*, a celebration of that dance, as the proprietor of the cabaret where it was invented; *Razzia sur la Chnouff* with Lino Ventura and Magali Noël, as a narcotics investigator working within the gang, Paris-sin-city propaganda; *Le Port du Désir*, as an ageing diver – it was Andrée Debar who was desired; and *Chiens Perdus sans Collier*, as a judge in this well-received but elementary study of juvenile delinquents. He was a truck-driver in the next two: *Des Gens sans Importance* (56), falling for the hotel maid on his overnight stop, and *Gas-Oil*, foiling a gang of hijackers. The former was directed by Henri Verneuil, also to become a Gabin regular; the latter directed by Grangier and written by Michael Audiard, who was to script most of Gabin's later films.

Duvivier directed *Voici le Temps des Assassins*, another Jannings-type melodrama about an elderly restaurateur in the thrall of a promiscuous girl (Danièle Delorme) and nagged by both her and her mother. Much better was Autant-Lara's *La Traversée de Paris*, an engaging study of occupied Paris, in which Gabin was a wealthy painter in uneasy liaison with a proletarian black-marketeer (Bourvil). After the Grangier-Audiard *Le Sang à la Tête*, based on Simenon, he was in an ambitious modernization of Dostoevsky, *Crime et Châtiment*, directed by Georges Lampin and scripted by Charles Spaak, as the inspector, with Marina Vlady as the whore and Robert Hossein as Raskolnikov. There followed: *Le Rouge est Mis* (57), as a gang-leader who sacrifices himself for a child, with Lino Ventura; *Les Misérables*, adapted by Audiard, directed (badly) by Jean-Paul Le Chanois, as Valjean with Bernard Blier as Javert; *Le Cas du Docteur Laurent* (58), a well-made drama about a Paris doctor trying to convince some Alpine villagers of the benefits of natural childbirth; *Le Désordre et la Nuit*, as a vice detective in love with dope addict Nadja Tiller, with Danielle Darrieux; and Delannoy's *Maigret Tend un Piège*, fine as Simenon's detective in one of the best screen versions of that author's work. Said the 'MFB': 'Gabin's Maigret, heavy with the years and the stress of his profession, is one of his finest recent achievements.'

After a co-starring stint with Brigitte Bardot, *En Cas de Malheur* (another Jannings situation), he did two pictures which only served to increase his popularity: *Les Grandes Familles*, by Audiard based on Maurice Druon's Prix Goncourt novel, directed by Denys de la Patellière (the third of Gabin's late, favourite directors), about a *Kane*-like millionaire and his possessive love for his son (Jean Desailly), with Pierre Brasseur and Bernard Blier; and *Archimède le Clochard* (59), directed by Grangier from an idea by Gabin – about a lovable old hobo – and nicely enjoyable. But while he increased his hold on family audiences he was rejected by buffs, in France at least. 'Cahiers du Cinéma' and other journals tended, not entirely without reason, to belittle or overlook the Gabin vehicles and his reputation tumbled (unlike that of Spencer Tracy – considered by the French his American counterpart – whose prestige never diminished).

There was another good Simenon, again directed by Delannoy, *Maigret et l'Affaire Saint-Fiacre*, and a slight comedy, *Rue des Prairies*, about a widower trying to bring up his children. *Le Baron de l'Ecluse* (60) was a three-star comedy, however, a bright piece (again after Simenon) about a monocled nobleman living on his wits, with Micheline Presle. And there was more comedy – plus a bit of pathos – in *Les Vieux de la Vieille*, about three scrappy old man (Noël-Noël, Pierre Fresnay, Gabin) who manage – in the end – not to go into an institution. Verneuil's *Le Président* (61) was an interesting view of life at Cabinet level, with Gabin as a Clemenceau-like ex-president and Blier as his rival. In *La Cave se Rebiffe* he was a crook brought out of retirement who double-crosses his double-crossing associates – Blier, Frank Villard and Antoine Balpetré (a strong cast also included Françoise Rosay, Martine Carol and Ginette Leclerc). Then he was an old ex-drunk in Verneuil's *Un Singe en Hiver* (62) with Belmondo, who said that Gabin 'quoi qu'en dise la jeune critique, a toujours représenté pour moi, l'acteur de cinéma accompli. Celui à qui l'on n'en remontre plus. Celui qui sait tout et qui accepte toujours d'apprendre. . . . Bref, celui qui a une gueule irremplaçable: notre Bogart, notre Laughton, notre Edward G. Robinson. . . .' But whatever Belmondo said, Gabin would not take direction. Like Raimu, he was not interested in working with directors stronger than himself. Consequently, few of his pictures of the 60s reached the US or Britain. They were solid, old-fashioned entertainments, but the limited market abroad could not absorb them as well as the younger, more vital movies being made in France.

His salary for them, in 1962, was 100 million francs a film. However, after *Le Gentleman d'Epsom* (he was a con-man) he was in a worldwide success, Verneuil's *Mélodie en Sous-sol* (63), a gangster piece co-starring Alain Delon. It was followed by: *Maigret voit Rouge; Monsieur* (64), a comedy about a gentleman's gentleman (actually a banker) who straightens out the family problems; *L'Age Ingrat* (65) with Fernandel (they co-produced it); and *Le Tonnerre de Dieu*, about a childless couple (Lilli Palmer was the wife) who adopt a prostitute (Michèle Mercier). He played a retired vet, anarchistic and mostly soused, and there must have been something about this corny melodrama to make it his biggest hit of three decades (but only in France). He had little to do as an ageing smuggler in *Du Rififi à Paname* (66), one of the endless follow-ups to the original *Rififi*, with George Raft in support; and he went listlessly through his chores in *Le Jardinier d'Argenteuil*, again as a recluse forced back into action. But, said 'Variety', 'Gabin stands around looking old and is not even given a chance to do his stock anger scene.' There was another gangster piece, *Le Soleil des Voyous* (67), with Robert Stack, and then *Le Pacha*, with Dany Carrel, as a police commissioner, his least successful film in some time. *Le Tatoué* (68) made up for it, a comedy about a count with a Modigliani and the crafty art-dealer (Louis de Funès) who is after it.

He had finally cut his activity to one movie a year: *Sous le Signe du Taureau* (69), as a missile-manufacturer at odds with the money-men, with Suzanne Flon; Verneuil's *Le Clan des Siciliens*, a very successful Mafia story with Delon; and *La Horse* (70), another crime story. No matter: Gabin retained his huge following. In 1970 for the third year running he was the most popular male star in France, according to L'Institut Français D'Opinion Publique, with 35 per cent of the votes (Belmondo was second, with 17 per cent; Fernandel third at 15 per cent; Bourvil fourth with 12 per cent; Alain Delon fifth with 11 per cent; and Jean Marais and Louis de Funès tied sixth with 6 per cent). However, *Le Drapeau Noir Flotte sur la Marmite* (71), a comedy about an old sea-dog, was only mildly popular; after a domestic drama with Simone Signoret, *Le Chat*, he played yet another police commissioner, in *Le Tueur* (72). Since again patrons were not forthcoming, he made a film less tried and true than his usual run: *L'Affaire Dominici* (73), based on that incident in 1952 when a peasant family was

Except for a brief period Gabin enjoyed a long popularity in France and so, like most stars, he only played variations of himself. It was not till past middle age that he attempted character acting, as here, in L'Affaire Dominici *(73), when he played the patriarch of a peasant family which had murdered some British tourists.*

accused of murdering three English tourists; he played the patriarch. He also said it would be his last film, but was tempted to do another with Delon, *Deux Hommes dans la Ville* (one was a social worker and the other a delinquent), and then one – and who can blame him? – with Sophia Loren, *Verdict* (74), as the President of the Court in which her son is being tried. Nor could he resist a tailor-made role in *L'Année Sainte* (76), as a master-criminal who knows it all and then some, wearily foiling some clumsy young hijackers whose lack of professionalism he despises. He did indeed seem weary; and he died later that year.

It was a career spanning 35 years, but almost certainly he will be remembered best looming out of the Carné mists. . . .

Ava Gardner

Ava Gardner has seldom been accused of acting. She is of what might be termed the genus Venus, stars who are so beautiful that they need not bother to act. It is enough if they just stand around being desirable. In films, unsurprisingly, it is a common or garden species, notably proliferating in the 40s with Rhonda Fleming, Adele Jergens, Arlene Dahl and other half-forgotten names. Gardner is a hardy survivor. The public made her a star, she was a star, and she is a star. 'Whatever it is, whether you're born with it, or catch it from a public drinking cup, she's got it and the people with the money in their hands put her there,' said Edmond O'Brien in *The Barefoot Contessa*. When she was a starlet just out of the mould, she was sexy and attractive, like the others; but not long after there began to appear that quality which in cinema terms is more important than ability – the 'it' that O'Brien spoke of, consciously or subconsciously paraphrasing Elinor Glyn, the magic something that makes Gardner so much more exciting to watch than the other vacuous beauties. It is sensuality, perhaps: watch her light a cigarette – not actress ever smoked as erotically. Perhaps she always belonged to the nether side of men's desires – smoking, booze, late nights, strange ladies in faraway places; never quite a lady but never cheap; warm and sympathetic but not immediately attainable. Whatever, as she aged she had/has the fascination of the courtesan, the older woman, the woman who has lived. Ravaged, but still beautiful.

She was born on a tenant-farm in Grabtown, Smithfield, North Carolina, in 1922. When she was two her father was deprived of his holding, so the Depression was particu-

larly tough; he died when she was 14. At 17 she went to New York to visit her sister, who had married a professional photographer, Larry Tarr; he took hundreds of pictures of her, some of which were seen by an employee of MGM in New York. He arranged a screen test and she was signed to a seven-year contract starting at $50 a week. The studio detected no star potential, but at this time all the studios had lots of extra pretty girls under contract – useful for pin-up pictures, for being decorative at studio functions, for entertaining visiting celebrities. Or for walking on in films when required: after a year she was given an unbilled bit in *We Were Dancing* (42). As that was being premièred she made the public prints for the first time, as the new wife of Mickey Rooney. During the 18 months of their marriage Rooney tried to promote her, but she continued to get only bits, most of them unbilled: *Joe Smith American, This Time for Keeps, Kid Glove Killer, Sunday Punch, Calling Dr Gillespie, Reunion (in France), Pilot No 5* (43), *Du Barry Was a Lady, Hitler's Madman* as a Czech patriot, *Ghosts on the Loose* at Monogram, *Young Ideas, Lost Angel* as a hat-check girl and *Swing Fever*. She eventually got yanked right up the cast-list to fifth: *Three Men in White* (44), as a suffering but brave lady who visits Dr Gillespie. There followed three more duallers: *Maisie Goes to Reno*, as a fellow divorcée; *Blonde Fever*, briefly attracting Philip Dorn; and *She Went to the Races* (45), involved with nice professor Edmund Gwenn in a gambling scheme.

In 1945 she married Artie Shaw, but the marriage did not last long; at the same time her career took an upward turn when United Artists borrowed her for an action melodrama with George Raft, *Whistle Stop* (46): it was she who got off there, swathed in mink, his ex-girlfriend. The reaction was strong enough for Universal to borrow her to play the vamp who double-crosses Burt Lancaster in *The Killers*. They plugged her as the new sex sensation, but MGM was not having any of that (after all, Garland, Garson, Margaret O'Brien and June Allyson were the big ones there), so she was Gable's ex-flame in *The Hucksters* (47), a small part, and losing him for good and all to the respectable Deborah Kerr. Not that she was unrespectable – just not the vamp Universal liked. That studio, sensing MGM's disinterest, borrowed her for two more films: *Singapore*, filmed on the back-lot, as an amnesiac who marries again when hubby Fred MacMurray is away; and *One Touch of Venus* (48), as a statue of that goddess who comes to life in a department store and falls for Robert Walker. Based on a Broadway hit, it was too whimsical for wide acceptance – and in any case, who in 1948 wanted to see a black and white musical?

Its failure caused Universal to lose interest, but MGM had at last started to pay attention, due to the requests for publicity stills, etc. Already Gardner's name was a byword for Hollywood glamour and the fact that she was being extensively trained by dramatic teachers (later screen absences would be because she turned down so many films). Critics remained unimpressed, through: *The Bribe* (49), as the honky-tonk singer wife of John Hodiak, falling for Robert Taylor; *The Great Sinner*, as the mysterious Russian countess who lures Gregory Peck to the gambling tables; and *East Side West Side*, seducing James Mason from Barbara Stanwyck. She tempted Mason again in *Pandora and the Flying Dutchman* (51), finally loving him enough to rid him of the 800-year curse. In the film Nigel Patrick and Mario Cabre also loved her and she was driftless, an American playgirl in Europe (Tossa del Mar); presumably writer-director Albert Lewin based part of the character on her (or she based part of her later life on it) – at any rate, she had never been so ravishingly photographed (in colour for the first time, by Jack Cardiff) so that the film was at least in one way an anatomy of Gardner. And she did wonders with a song, 'How Am I to Know?' But she was no Garbo, nor even a Shearer; she read her lines well but without much feeling. She was not a vital screen presence, but she was already charismatic. The film, overlong and ambitious, had no wide appeal.

MGM had loaned her out for it in return for United States rights. Still not knowing what to do with her, they loaned her to RKO for *My Forbidden Past*, to play a vengeful Southern belle jilted by impecunious doctor Robert Mitchum. Then they had a very bright idea:

Nothing can prevent Ava Gardner from looking like one of the world's most exciting women – not even the standard Hollywood glamour props used in the picture on the left to publicize The Killers (*46*).

Ava Gardner as Julie and Kathryn Grayson as Magnolia in MGM's sumptuous version of Show Boat (*51*). *Julie has just sung 'Can't Help Lovin' Dat Man' and they break into a little dance as they contemplate the nature of love.*

the half-caste, unhappy Julie in *Show Boat*, originated on stage by Helen Morgan. Lena Horne was once cast, but Metro had not the guts and it went to Judy Garland and, when she fell ill, to Gardner. MGM dubbed both her songs – though let her voice go out on the soundtrack album, and on the 78 rpm single, which was hugely successful. The dubbing disillusioned her, she said later, because this was one film where she really *tried*. Certainly it marked a turning-point in her relationship with the critics – thereafter she could do little wrong. All the same MGM wasted her in a couple of Westerns: *Lone Star* (52), with Clark Gable, and *Ride Vacquero* (53), as Howard Keel's wife and falling for his brother, Robert Taylor. Between the two she went to 20th for *The Snows of Kilimanjaro* (52) and gave an excellent account of a Hemingway woman.

MGM teamed her again with Gable, sparring with him in the remake of *Red Dust* called *Mogambo* (53), in Jean Harlow's old role – a wise-cracking hard-bitten showgirl, taking what chance had to offer. It may be the only film to reflect her offscreen personality – she's 'a bright, witty and intelligent person,' says David Hanna, who wrote a book about her. The film brought her her only Oscar nomination, but there would only have been a wooden spoon award for her Guinevere in *Knights of the Round Table*, particularly poor

It is a principle of movies like Mogambo *(53) that girls like Ava Gardner can turn up in the African bush without anyone wondering why.*

At her best, with Gregory Peck in The Snows of Kilimanjaro *(52).*

after she had taken the veil. Her popularity was at its peak. She never made the 'Motion Picture Herald' list, but was No 3 in the 'Box Office Magazine''s 1953 poll, behind Gary Cooper and Bing Crosby, ahead of Susan Hayward, Marilyn Monroe, John Wayne, Jane Wyman, Esther Williams, June Allyson and Montgomery Clift. In private, her stormy marriage to Frank Sinatra (1951–57) was over.

The Barefoot Contessa (54) was about a Spanish gypsy dancer discovered by a film director (Humphrey Bogart) and turned into a Hollywood legend. Partly because Joseph L. Mankiewicz wrote and directed, most Hollywood actresses wanted to do it; but he stuck out for Gardner, and met MGM's stiff terms (due, it was said, to Mankiewicz once having quarrelled with studio chief Nicholas Schenck): $200,000 plus 10 per cent of the gross after the first million. She herself got $60,000 (Bogart got $100,000) but was philosophical: 'That's Metro, they'll louse you up every time.' Of the role: 'Hell, Joe, I'm not an actress, but I think I understand this girl. She's a lot like me.' Said 'Variety' of her work: 'Miss Gardner is ideal in her spot, looking every inch the femme magnetism around which the action revolves. She's a beautifully dimensioned knock-out. . . .' More succinctly, the ads proclaimed her 'The World's Most Beautiful Animal' and, as photographed again by Cardiff, it seemed so; but the film meandered endlessly and was not a big hit.

Her feuding with MGM now intensified, mainly over terms; she was suspended for several months and the matter was finally resolved by a new contract and a film she wanted to do, *Bhowani Junction* (56) with Stewart Granger, George Cukor's superb version of John Masters's novel about the partition of India. She loved working with Cukor and was good as, again, a half-caste. The film over, she moved to Madrid, from whence came rumours of retirement and several reports of romances; the press pursued her relentlessly and fans became familiar with most of the facts about her expatriate life. It was considerably more colourful than her films: *The Little Hut* (57), a flop comedy with Granger. 'I hated it, that's all. Every minute of it. It was a lousy story . . . but what could I do? If I took another suspension they would keep me at Metro the rest of my life.' At 20th, another Hemingway part, Lady Brett, in *The Sun Also Rises*; and her salary was rising too, from $240,000 to $350,000 for *La Maja Desnuda/The Naked Maja* (59), though she only got $90,000 of it, on loan to Titanus of Italy, with MGM distributing as her last commitment to them. She was the Duchess of Alba, Anthony Franciosa was Goya and the film was awful. She got $400,000 for her brief footage in *On the Beach* with Gregory Peck, but much coverage when she arrived in Australia and said: 'I'm here to make a film about the end of the world and this sure is the place for it.' Her salary went down to $300,000 for another incompetent Italian venture, *La Bella Sposa/The Angel Wore Red* (60), written and directed by Nunnally Johnson for MGM, as a whore in love with a priest (Dirk Bogarde).

Again she was a Russian countess, in *55 Days at Peking* (63), with Charlton Heston, produced in Madrid by Samuel Bronston, one of the spectacular flops which put him out of business. She had a key role – but a small one – in *Seven Days in May* (64) with Burt Lancaster, but made a come-back in glory with *The Night of the Iguana*, as the earthy and sexually ambitious hotel-owner, adding much to one of the best of the films made from Tennessee Williams material. John Huston directed and she trusted him enough to do *The Bible* (66) for him, mildly touching in the insignificant part of Sarah. She told Rex Reed after the première: 'What did I ever do worth talking about? Every time I tried to act they stepped on me. That's why it's such a goddam shame. I've been a movie star for 25 years and I've got nothing, nothing to show for it. . . . But I never brought anything to this business and I have no respect for acting. Maybe if I had learned something it would be different. But I never did anything to be proud of. Out of all those movies, what can I claim to have done?' Reed suggested two titles. 'Hell, baby, after 25 years in this business, if all you've got to show for it is *Mogambo* and *The Hucksters* you might as well give up.'

She did not; presumably for money she played the Empress Elizabeth in *Mayerling* (68) and most critics kindly commented that she was miscast. She then did a British picture directed by former child star Roddy McDowall, *Tam Lin*, as a wealthy woman using all means including witchcraft to hang on to her looks and loves. It had a few bookings in the US in 1971 before disappearing; it resurfaced – very briefly – in its country of origin in 1977, as *The Devil's Widow*. Meanwhile, she had returned to Hollywood briefly for a few days' work and $50,000 – to play Lillie Langtry in *The Life and Times of Judge Roy Bean* (72), with Paul Newman. In the US again she was one of the people affected by the *Earthquake* (74); in Vienna she decorated *Permission to Kill* (75), with Dirk Bogarde. None of these experiences could be described as fortunate, but worse was to come: the US-Russo *The Blue Bird* (76), appropriately as Luxury, and a bright spot in this banal entertainment – directed by Cukor, but no one could have done much with this abysmal conception; *The Cassandra Crossing* (77), as one of the passengers – a wealthy one, with gigolo – along with Sophia Loren and Burt Lancaster; and *The Sentinel*, as an estate agent in this 'grubby, grotesque excursion into religioso psychodrama' ('Variety'). After a break she joined Henry Fonda in Canada for *City on Fire* (79), to play a drink-happy TV personality. Also in Canada she was Van Johnson's wife in *The Kidnapping of the President* (80) – and Hal Holbrook was the President. In Britain – where she has lived for the past 20 years – she played a much-married American admirer of D.H. Lawrence (Ian McKellan) in *Priest of Love* (81), an insensitive and vulgar interpretation of that writer's life. Probably she never went to see any of these. Had she done so she might have felt doubly aggrieved – for seldom did any of them show the great beauty she retained – in middle age – in life. Whether *Regina* (82) did better in that respect is a question the Italians could answer, for it has not been exported; her co-star was Anthony Quinn. There were two TV mini-series, a laughable Biblical, *A.D.* (85), and a new version of *The Long Hot Summer*, in Angela Lansbury's old role. As Jason Robards's mistress she was, said 'Variety', 'a constant delight and a reminder that a top-class actress is not being used as much as she should be'. Also for TV she was the Grande Dame of Omar Sharif's *Harem* (86) and guest star in *Maggie*, a one-hour pilot for Stephanie Powers.

'We're going on the town' they sang at the top of the Empire State Building: Jules Munshin, Ann Miller, Frank Sinatra, Betty Garrett and Gene Kelly in On the Town *(49).*

Betty Garrett

In the old days – especially in the 40s, when the screen seemed overcrowded with wishy-washy females – there was always a chance that the heroine's best friend would be one of those whacky dames with a neat line in deflating wisecracks. There is a long and honourable line of them, from Glenda Farrell through Eve Arden to Nita Talbot. One particularly remembers Betty Garrett, who brightened a couple of Esther Williams vehicles. She was one of the few who made it to stardom – just.

She was born in St Joseph, Missouri, in 1919. A varied education finally brought her, via a scholarship, to the Neighbourhood Playhouse in New York and she made her first professional appearance at the Mercury, New York, in 'Danton's Death' (38). She appeared at the World's Fair and sang in nightclubs until her big break, in a revue, 'Let Freedom Sing' (42). At the end of the Broadway run she was engaged for 'Something for the Boys' with Ethel Merman, whom she also understudied. Her starring role in 'Call Me Mister' (46) brought her a Donaldson award and an MGM contract. Her husband, Larry Parks (they had married in 1944), was a Columbia featured player who had achieved stardom in *The Jolson Story* (46).

She made her début in *The Big City* (48), where her agreeable combination of vivacity and astringency was a welcome relief in that Margaret O'Brien schmaltz – just as her poise and sense of fun alleviated some of the more maudlin bits of *Words and Music*. She was then the second female in the two Williams films, *Take Me Out to the Ball Game* (49), as Frank Sinatra's clinging vine, and *Neptune's Daughter,* as Red Skelton's (they had a fine duet, 'Baby It's Cold Outside'). She was not a star yet, but her reception indicated that she soon would be. Critics thought her notably good in *On the Town* (49); as the man-hungry cab-driver – again after Sinatra; she brought new qualities of warmth and self-mockery to this sort of part.

At this upbeat moment she and MGM came to the parting of the ways – and what happened must be among the saddest of all Hollywood stories. Her agent had asked release from her contract when Judy Garland left *Annie Get Your Gun*, the plum role in a musical in many a moon: she was approached, but her agent's demands were so extreme that the studio did not even bother to negotiate. Her version is that she had completed three years of a seven-year contract, and MGM wanted to start her again for seven years, at less money. It would have been a small price to pay for Annie – and the stardom that thereafter eluded her. Husband Parks was riding high as a result of the second Jolson film and they planned to make independent films of their own choosing. The titles were announced – then Garrett became pregnant. MGM offered him a role in *Love Is Better Than Ever* and Columbia lined up parts to keep him busy to the end of his contract, by which time he was *persona non grata* in Hollywood. (In March 1951 he had admitted before the Un-American Activities Committee that he had been a Communist Party member, 1941–45. John Wayne, no less, said he should be forgiven – for which Louella Parsons castigated him: Wayne apologized.) Work in films became difficult to get. The Parks had already toured Britain and played the Palladium (50); in 1952 they toured the US in 'The Anonymous Lover'.

Garrett did not get a film offer until Judy Holliday had to have foot surgery and thus missed out on *My Sister Eileen* (55), a musical remake of an old Rosalind Russell comedy. (The property had just been done on Broadway as 'Wonderful Town', but Columbia, who owned the film rights, preferred to commission a new score than buy the one that Leonard Bernstein had composed.) The film was sprightly and fun, and Garrett, in a star part at last, was marvellous as the elder of two sisters trying to make out in New York. Columbia promptly signed her to a contract – one film a year; but she told reporters when she and her husband toured Britain again that she would not do a film that separated them. In fact, she made only one more film, a B with her husband, *The Shadow on the Wall* (57), playing a young mother held captive by delinquents.

She has appeared occasionally on TV and on the stage – notably in a reading of 'Spoon River Anthology' and in a tour of 'Plaza Suite' (71) with Parks. He had been little more in demand, but had a successful business in Los Angeles (he had invested in real estate) till he died in 1975. Interviewed a few years ago, Garrett said that she remained optimistic about working again in Hollywood. In 1975 she had a supporting role in TV's 'All in the Family'. Later she was in 'Laverne and Shirley' for a while. She left the acting school she runs in Hollywood to tour in 'Betty Garrett and Other Songs' (80) and again to star on Broadway in 'The Supporting Cast' (81), when 'Variety' described her as 'superb'.

Vittorio Gassmann

The official publicity line on Vittorio Gassmann is that he is the Laurence Olivier or Louis Jouvet of Italy – a great stage actor who makes movies for divertissement and/or money. The critic Silvio d'Amico once wrote that he was the finest actor of the contemporary Italian theatre. In films he has been intermittently impressive, but has been so rigidly type-cast that one can make no ready assessment. During his first few years in films, he was an athletic, lithe hero. There was something bombastic and egocentric about him and it was not surprising when he became typed as a heel. Later, by accident, he turned to comedy and it is as a comedian that he achieved a vast popularity in Italy.

He was born in Genoa in 1922, to a mother of Florentine origin and an Austrian father. His father died when he was young, but the family was comfortably off; in school his interest vacillated between journalism and law, and at 17 he represented Italy in its national basketball team. His mother, without much reference to him, entered him in the Accademia Nazionale di Arte Dramatica, where he met Nora Ricci, the daughter of the actor Renzo Ricci; they were married in 1944. The previous year he had made his stage début in Milan with the Alda Borelli company, in 'La Nemica'. He made his Rome début in 'L'Albergo dei Poveri', with the Merlini-Gialente company, and later returned to Milan, where he and his wife joined the Laura Adani company, which specialized in comedy. He achieved fame in 'Tre Rosso, Dispari', one of the company's biggest successes. By the time he went into films he had appeared in over 40 plays.

His first film was *Preludio d'Amore* (46), directed by Giovanni Paolucci, a melodrama about two sailors, the good one (Gassmann) and the bad (Massimo Girotti) and two girls, Marina Berti and Maria Michi, who had been unfaithful during the war. It was not very good. However, it was better than the film of Fogazzaro's novel *Daniele Cortis* where, with blond hair and false beard, he loved from childhood his cousin Sarah Churchill – a love which involved them in many a misfortune and a tragic end. And he was not at all good in it. The film took an unbelievable seven months to make and he had to cancel a contract with the Teatro Quirino company. Undeterred, he went into Mario Camerini's version of a Pushkin story, *La Figlia del Capitano* (47), with Amadeo Nazzari as the usurper who became Tsar Peter III. Gassmann took on the role of the villain, which appealed to him; a little later, he published a piece on the villain in art. He was in a poverty-stricken version of Carlo Collodi's classic, *Le Avventure di Pinocchio,* and then played *L'Ebreo Errante*, directed by Alessandrini, as our old friend the Wandering Jew, brought up to date and set mainly in a concentration camp. Valentina Cortese was in it and it completely failed to arouse pity or sympathy. He joined Eva Maltagliati's company and began to play the classics. His films were not classic: *Il Cavaliere Misterioso* (48), directed by Riccardo Freda, as Casanova; and *Riso Amaro*, Giuseppe de Santis's murky study of lust amidst the rice-fields, with Silvana Mangano. That one, however, was shown abroad – and was condemned by the Legion of Decency, which made Mangano, if not Gassmann, somewhat famous (he played her lover). Mangano starred in *Il Lupo delle Sila* (49) and he agreed to do a brief role in the prologue – as a man who prefers to die rather than compromise the woman he loves.

On the stage his work was distinguished: in Visconti's production of 'Tobacco Road' and in 'Peer Gynt' in 1950; and in 1952 he would play Hamlet for the first time. His films were uninteresting, with the possible exception of *Una Voce nel Tuo Cuore*, as a war correspondent trying to get his girlfriend into opera

In Riso Amaro (*48*) – Bitter Rice – *Vittorio Gassmann was bothered by Silvana Mangano, but then, she was enough to handle.*

(Gigli and Gino Bechi were in it). The others: *Ho Sognato il Paradiso; Lo Sparviero del Nilo*; *I Fuorilegge* (50); *Il Leone di Amalfi*; *Ka Corona Nera*; and *Il Tradimento* (51), in which he and Amadeo Nazzari were double-crossing crooks. He was the villain in *Anna*, with Mangano, which was a considerable success abroad, and then – after *Il Sogno di Zorro* (52) – a wily, cowardly opportunist in *La Tratta delle Bianche*, a silly white-slave drama with Silvana Pampanini, a sequel to a movie successful abroad as *Behind Closed Doors*.

Outside Italy, his name was known – if at all – for his work on the stage. When producer Sam Zimbalist went to Rome to make *Quo Vadis?* he found Gassmann so famous and respected that he cabled his boss at MGM, Doré Schary. Schary cautiously said that if Gassmann ever went to the US he would have him tested. His trip to the States was precipitated by a meeting in Rome with Shelley Winters; according to publicity she later sent him a cable saying she was lonely and as a result they were married (in 1952; his first marriage had lasted a year). In the US he duly tested for MGM, who signed him for seven years (with permission to spend six months every year in Italy). They loaned him to Columbia to play a Hungarian immigrant in *The Glass Wall* (53), with Gloria Grahame; then he was a Mexican in *Sombrero*, with Yvonne de Carlo; then a tough, savage creature in *Cry of the Hunted*, with Barry Sullivan. Whatever the intention, the three of them played B dates. Hardly more prominent was *Rhapsody* (54), with Elizabeth Taylor, in which he played a neurotic violinist. He was announced for the role which Robert Taylor played in *Valley of the Kings*, but instead was home touring as Amleto, with Anna Maria Ferrero as his Ophelia; gossip said it was on account of her that he and Winters were divorced. Articles on Gassmann dwelt on his conceit and vanity and temperament, as if these were qualities unexpected in actors. MGM were certainly no happier with him offscreen than on, and were happy to loan him to Paramount for their made-in-Italy *Mambo*, playing a black marketeer. Winters was in it and Michael Rennie, as a haemophiliac Italian count, and Mangano; it was patterned after *Riso Amaro* and *Anna*, but, as usual when Hollywood meddles with a European formula, the result was neither art nor box-office.

MGM loaned him to play Lollobrigida's Russian princely lover in *La Donna più Bella del Mondo* (55), which had (vain) aspirations in the international market. After that, the association with MGM quietly came to an end. Gassmann played Anatole in *War and Peace* (56) and then starred in another picture with ideas above its station (it was directed by

Vincent Sherman), *Difendo il Mio Amore*, with Martine Carol and Gabriele Ferzetti – he was a muck-raking reporter out to expose their unhappy marriage. His films hit a new low with *Giovanni dalle Bande Nere* (57), but on the stage he had retrieved his reputation. He played in 'Edipe Re' (Oedipus), 'I Persiani', in his own translation of 'Tieste', and in Sartre's version of an old play by Dumas – 'Kean' – a story of the 19th-century English tragedian; he played Otello, Ornifle and Oreste. He started his own company, the Teatro Popolare Italiano. With renewed confidence he attacked the film of *Kean Genio o Sregolatezza* (Genius or Scoundrel, as it was subtitled). He directed (with Francesco Rosi) but the film was no more than respectfully received, and it does not appear to have played in the US or Britain. At another cinematic low ebb, he romanced Diana Dors in *La Ragazza del Palio* (58).

Then Mario Monicelli offered him a full-blooded comedy role in *I Soliti Ignoti*, as a stuttering, cunning ex-boxer involved with some other incompetent crooks (including Renato Salvatori and Marcello Mastroianni) in a grandiose robbery masterminded by a wily old lag (Toto). His excellence was accepted along with the excellence of the film – the first Italian comedy to be successful outside Italy within memory. He was also seen abroad in a couple of misguided epics: *La Tempesta/The Tempest*, the de Laurentiis remake – directed by Lattuada – of the same Pushkin story that Gassmann had made 10 years earlier, though now in a much smaller role; and *The Miracle* (59), as the gypsy Carroll Baker would have married if he had not got murdered. Monicelli directed *La Grande Guerra*, but offered only a superficial view of it (World War I), with Gassmann and Alberto Sordi as two awkward and unwilling recruits – too much a mixture of Martin & Lewis and Flagg & Quirt to have any vitality. Monicelli did not direct the sequel to his big success, *Audace Colpo dei Soliti Ignoti*, which did not do well. Nor did *La Cambiale* (60). But Gassmann did have a hit with *Il Mattatore*, based on a TV series he had done, a picaresque story of a con-man, from his start in a tatty vaudeville to grand larceny. Dino Risi directed; and, when he film was shown in New York a while later, 'Variety' said: 'It's now obvious that Gassmann's talents were never fully utilized by his former Hollywood employers. He's a gifted comic actor, buoyant and light of touch.' At the same time (1963), Gassmann observed: 'I've made fifty-five (*sic*) movies. I'd say forty of them were dreadful and the four I made in Hollywood were probably the most dreadful of all.' (He added that life in Hollywood was 'so artificial and spiritually dry'.)

He was now – for the first time – becoming a popular favourite in Italy. Audiences liked him in comedy, so he stayed in comedy: *Fantasmi a Roma* (61), as Marcello Mastroianni's forger-painter friend, and *Crimen*, a *comédie noire* set in Monte Carlo, with Sordi, Mangano and Nino Manfredi. The latter was produced by Laurentiis, who signed him to an exclusive contract. It began disastrously when he participated in De Sica's *Il Giudizio Universale* (62); and if *Barabba/Barabbas* was poor, he was good in it, in the best role, as a determined Christian who gets chained to Anthony Quinn. He was comic again in *I Briganti Italiani*, with Ernest Borgnine, as a cowardly corporal who redeems himself. Then he had the chance of working with Roberto Rossellini, whose reputation was then having a renaissance: *Anima Nera*, from a play by Giuseppi Patroni-Griffi, about a marriage in peril when the husband receives a legacy from a homosexual friend. Gassmann achieved the equivocal nature of the husband, but it was poor material, not improved by Rossellini (the renaissance was temporary). Dino Risi

Il Sorpasso (62) *was a free-wheeling comedy about a man, Vittorio Gassmann, who has failed at everything he has tried, but who still views life with gusto. For instance, he likes hitch-hikers – Jean-Louis Trintignant (left) and a hobo.*

directed *Il Sorpasso*, a tale about a meek student (Jean-Louis Trintignant) who is taken in hand for a weekend by an egotistical braggart (Gassmann) – the title referred to his insistence on overtaking the car in front, a clue to his character. The film attempted to suggest a man with a hollow and unhappy heart, but was superficial; it was, however, a great success in Europe and confirmed Gassmann's popularity in this sort of part.

He played a defending lawyer in *La Smania Andosso*, a serio-comic tale about two Sicilians (Gérard Blain and Nino Castelnuovo) who have compromised Annette Stroyberg; and was a miserly suitor for the hand of Nadja Tiller in 'L'Avaro', an episode of *L'Amore Difficile* (63). He and Ugo Tognazzi were involved in *La Marcia su Roma*, a good ironic comedy based on that historical event. Meanwhile, producer Mario Cecchi Gori was preparing a sequel to *Il Sorpasso*, again for his Fairfilm Company, released by Titanus: *Il Successo*. Gassmann was a likeable scoundrel bound for the top, Trintignant was his bemused friend. Again it was a great success. Fairfilm hurried Gassmann into *I Mostri*, co-starred with Tognazzi, where in 20 vignettes, partnered and single, they portrayed various Italian eccentrics. Tognazzi's engaging charm was lost and Gassmann's histrionics were strained; but it was a third success for Fairfilm. To all intents and purposes Gassmann's career since has been tied to that company. Their films together were so successful that he had little time for the theatre or indeed anything else. He was one of the country's popular favourites – along with Tognazzi, Alberto Sordi and, to a lesser extent, Nino Manfredi. The films were resolutely second-rate and mainly unexportable – except to the South American market. Cecchi Gori was enabled, by their success, to employ international names and from that point on they were *filmed* in English (and dubbed for Italy). It made no difference: foreign interest was still slight.

But Italians flocked to see: *Parliamo di Donne* (64), a series of sketches with Gassmann partnering various female players; *Frenesia d'Estate*, directed by Mario Zampi, with Gassmann as an army officer and Michèle Mercier, subbing in a drag show, trying to convince him she is a woman; *Il Gaucho*, directed by Risi, a co-production with Argentina, with Gassmann as the bluffing head of a delegation of Italians at a film festival in Buenos Aires; *Una Vergine per il Principe* (65), a facetious treatment of that incident when one of the Gonzaga heirs was subjected to a Papal examination of his virility; *La Congiuntara*, produced by Cecchi Gori but not for Fairfilm, with Joan Collins, about an indolent Roman nobleman engaged in smuggling; *La Guerre Secrète*, a sketch-film about spies with Henry Fonda, etc., in the Italian sequence; and *Slalom*, about a battle between international counterfeiters – but still a one-man show. The derivative nature of these films was taken one stage further with *L'Armata Brancaleone* (66): Monicelli, who directed, borrowed from his own *I Soliti Ignoti* as well as from every historical spoof and swashbuckler he could think of. Gassmann and sidekick Gian Maria Volonte were feudal soldiers of fortune. It was the official Italian entry at Cannes and such a success that a follow-up was hastily ordered: *Il Diavolo Innamorato/The Devil in Love*, filmed in English with Mickey Rooney, about an emissary from hell in Renaissance Italy.

He seemed to work non-stop: *I Piacevoli Notti* (67), three stories by the 16th-century writer Gianfranco Straparola, with Lollobrigida in a different episode; *Il Profeta*, with Ann-Margret; *Sept Fois Femme*, chatting trouserless (no reason given) to Shirley MacLaine; *Lo Scatenato/Catch as Catch Can*, with Martha Hyer, as a male model disliked by animals; *Il Tigre/The Tiger and the Pussycat*, as an industrialist on an extramarital fling with Ann-Margret; *Questi Fantasmi*, for Ponti, with Sophia Loren (a flop for both of them); and *La Pecora Nera* (68), as twins who change places – one a civil servant and the other a cheap con-man. He did not get artistic satisfaction from this stuff and embarked on a very personal effort with two old freinds, Adolfo Celi and Luciano Lucignani: *L'Alibi*. They wrote and directed and played in the three episodes, about three old friends facing up to crises in their middle-aged lives (Vides produced). Gassmann played an actor much like himself, but, for all their integrity, it did not come off. Gassmann returned to Fairfilm for two comedies: *Dove Vai Tutta Nuda?* (69), in a featured role as the boss of Thomas Milian, who discovers he has married the nude girl beside him the night before when drunk; and *L'Arcangelo*, as a lawyer who has never won a single case, getting caught up in the machinations of Pamela Tiffin and Irina Demick. Another wheezy old plot got a working-over in *Una su Tredici* – the one about the legatee whose fortune is in one of the 13 chairs he has already sold. He was an American-Italian barber looking for the chair in Britain, among such British types as Orson Welles, Sharon Tate and Vittorio De Sica. Then: *La Contestazione Generale*, directed by Luigi Zampa; *Il Divorzio* (70), with Anna Moffo and Anita Ekberg; *Scipione detto anche l'Africano*; *Brancaleone alle Crociate* (71); *I Fakiri*, co-starring Tognazzi and Manfredi; and *In Nome del Popolo Italiano* (72), again with Tognazzi

Vittorio Gassmann's acting continues to astonish Italian audiences, and it is a shame that we get to see so few of his films. We did see Profumo di Donne *(74), in which he was a blind retired military man; Agostina Belli is the much younger woman trying to persuade him that she loves him.*

and with Risi at the helm. He returned to directing; *Senza Famiglia Nullatenenti Cercano Affetto*, in which he also appeared, as an ebullient circus magician who befriends Paolo Villaggio. *L'Audienza* concerned a young man who hoped to see the Pope; Gassmann was a well-born priest, Tognazzi a police inspector and Claudia Cardinale a prostitute.

After playing Scarpia to Monica Vitti's *La Tosca* (73) he was Othello in the deep South, hiding from a lynch-mob with a priest: *Che C'entriamo Noi con la Rivoluzione?* He was a one-armed, blind ex-cavalry captain in Risi's *Profumo di Donne* (74), accompanied on a journey South by an inexperienced batman, who inevitably learns much of life. Gassmann's masterly, sympathetic impression of this rather unpleasant man brought him a Best Actor award at the Cannes festival, clinching the film's success in Europe; one would have understood better its damp reception in Britain and the US had the critics not welcomed films yet more contrived and superficial – and less entertaining. The US certainly welcomed Ettore Scola's lightly charming *C'Eravamo Tanti Amati* (75), a study of several friendships over the years, including lawyer Gassmann's with Nino Manfredi; and it is a shame that few foreign audiences have had a chance to see *A Mezzanotte Va la Ronda del Piacere*, in which Gassmann's bourgeois marriage to Cardinale is compared, outside the courtroom, to the humble one between Vitti and Giancarlo Giannini. Risi's *I Telefoni Bianchi* (76) concerned an ambitious starlet in the 30s with Gassmann as an alcoholic 'great' star she encounters; it was much liked in France, where it was thought that the public success of the last Risi-Gassmann collaboration had caused resentment among Italian critics and hence undervaluation. *Signore e Signori Buonanotte* was yet another sketch-pic, with Gassmann as both a CIA man and an inspector; and *Come una Rosa al Naso* was yet another of his films founded on an amusing precept – that a Sicilian crime boss should hide out in Britain, uneasily pretending to be a phlegmatic Londoner: but despite its being a co-production with that country, as *Pure as a Lily* it has not been theatrically shown there.

Il Deserto dei Tartari was also a co-production, with France, Germany and Iran (where the locations were done); and with 10 stars – four French (Jacques Perrin, Trintignant, Philippe Noiret, Laurent Terzieff), two Italian (Gassmann, Giuliano Gemma), two Spanish (Fernando Rey, Francisco Rabal), one German (Helmut Griem) and one Swedish (Max von Sydow) – and one of them might have been British, if Olivier had accepted the Gassmann role of the weak commandant. Olivier was right: despite assorted neuroses, this study of an imperial army outpost never amounts to much. To be preferred was Risi's spine-chilling Venetian tale, *Anima Persa* (77), as the mysterious uncle, but not a sequel with Tognazzi, *I Nuovi Mostri* (78). This time they were joined by Alberto Sordi, and rechristened *Viva Italia!* it had a certain success in the States.

But it was *Profumo di Donne* which had awakened international interest in Gassmann and he was announced for *The Silver Bears* – in the role which Louis Jourdan eventually played. His first American film in two decades was Robert Altman's *The Wedding*, in which he was the groom's father; and for the same director he was among the barbarities of *Quintet* (79), with Paul Newman. With Noiret he did *Due Pezzi di Pane* and they were musicians loved equally by the same woman. After that, he returned to Risi for *Caro Papa*, a generation gap story, in the title-role; followed by *Armonia*, also directing, and a reunion with Tognazzi, *La Terrazza* (80), playing a Communist deputy. He had a dual role as the villains (they were, in fact, clones) of a secret service spoof, *The Nude Bomb*, one of his worst Hollywood outings; the star was Don Adams, one-time star of a dated TV series, 'Get Smart', and this was – incredibly – a long-while-after sequel, which is why it is aka *The Return of Maxwell Smart*. After Monicelli's *Camera d'Albergo* (81) and Tonino Cervi's *Il Turno*, from a story by Pirandello, Hollywood asked him to sneer again, at Burt Reynolds this time, in *Sharkey's Machine*: the role required him to be both political manipulator and white slaver. He was a shady casino boss in Mazursky's *Tempest* (82), supporting John Cassavetes, and a drunken, impoverished prince who passes off a carpenter's son (Enrico Montesano, who starred) as his own, in *Il Conte Tacchia*. He moved to a château in the Ardennes for Resnais's puzzling *La Vie est un Roman* (83), playing an architect, and although André Delvaux's *Benvenuta* was chiefly Belgian, Gassmann was a Neapolitan lawyer domiciled in Milan – and in love with Fanny Ardant. He directed and starred in *Di Padre in Figlio* (83) and in 1984 toured the US in a one-man-show, 'Via Vittorio'. There was a guest role in Zanuzzi's *Paradigme* (85), as the wealthy man who befriends a medical student till the boy meets a suicidal Marie-Christine Barrault. *I Soliti Ignoti . . . Vent' Anni Doppo* (86) was not a good idea and Gassmann returned to the stage, in Milan, in Pasolini's 'Affabulazione'. Scola's *La Famiglia* (87) traced the history of one Roman over the past 80 years and Gassmann's performance in that role (he also played his own grandfather) brought him a Donatello for Best Actor. After that marathon, he had only a cameo in Monicelli's *I Picari*, as an impoverished baron who befriends Giancarlo Giannini in this revamping of the Don Quixote stories – a role meant for Gassmann when the film was planned some years earlier.

Nora Ricci died in 1975: since Italy did not recognize divorce, she remained his legal wife despite Miss Winters and other alleged relationships, including Annette Stroyberg and Juliette Mayniel, the latter the mother of his son; in 1970 he underwent a civil ceremony with Diletta D'Andrea.

Mitzi Gaynor

Mitzi Gaynor flashed but briefly on cinema screens, a happy, chirpy girl seemingly hurt once musicals stopped being staple product at each studio. She was born in Chicago in 1931, of Austro-Hungarian ancestry. Her father was a musical director and her mother a dancer; she was taught dancing as a child. She also acquired proficiency in imitating Carmen Miranda and during the war toured army camps (with a troupe) doing just that. In her teens she was taken on as a dancer by the Los Angeles Light Opera Co., to appear in musicals like 'Roberta' and 'Naughty Marietta'. She was starred in a rivival of 'The Great Waltz' – and was seen by a 20th scout.

She made her début as a showgirl in *My Blue Heaven* (50) and stole the notices from the star, Betty Grable. While deciding what to do with her they put her into Jeanne Crain's college film, *Take Care of My Little Girl* (51), and then into a musical, *Down Among the Sheltering Palms*, which pinched at least its setting from 'South Pacific'. Gaynor was just one of a generally young cast – Jane Greer, William Lundigan, Gloria de Haven – and 20th decided to withhold it till after she had achieved stardom; in fact it was a lousy film and was not released till 1953 – by which time she had made her bid for stardom and made it three times over. 20th were delighted with her – the more so as Grable's box-office light was flickering dangerously; they put her in the appropriately titled *Golden Girl*, playing Lotte Crabtree, a vaudeville artist who toured the Old West. It was a slight musical, co-starring Dale Robertson, and brought her nice notices but no stampedes to the box-office. She was simply one of the names in *We're Not Married* (52), (not) married to Eddie Bracken, and then had two more star vehicles: *Bloodhounds of Broadway* with Scott Brady, from a Damon Runyon story about a country girl who becomes a star; and a biopic of one-time Broadway star Eva Tanguay, *The 'I Don't Care' Girl* (53), with David Wayne. The trouble was, the public did not either; it was by now heartily sick of the clichés of showbiz biographies, of which there had been a plethora, and Gaynor's co-stars were not strong enough to help her at the box-office. 20th's own indecision resulted in their releasing the last two pictures in reverse order of their making. When the *Sheltering Palms* film also failed, they paused.

After months of inactivity, Gaynor's new (first and only) husband, Jack Bean, got her into an independent production distributed by 20th, *Three Young Texans* (54), with Jeffrey Hunter and Keefe Brasselle, which played B dates. Still nothing happened. Rodgers and Hammerstein wanted her for the ingénue in a revival of 'Annie Get Your Gun' and then the role of Ado Annie in *Oklahoma!*; but 20th refused to loan her. Then, during the production of *There's No Business Like Show Business* (she was billed last of the six stars), they announced that they were dropping her. However, they liked what she was doing and her part was built up: she got excellent notices. Her dancing was more lithe, more skilled than ever and she flashed her long sexy legs, but she had lost a little of the effervescent individuality with which she had started.

At Paramount, for a fee of $100,000, she was an efficient partner for Bing Crosby in *Anything Goes* (56), but indequate as Barbara Stanwyck's replacement in a musical remake of *The Lady Eve* called *The Birds and the Bees* (but not as much as was George Gobel in the Henry Fonda part). 20th had wanted her back for *The Best Things in Life Are Free*; but she did not go, and the part went to Sheree North. Gaynor consolidated her new position in *The Joker Is Wild* (57), opposite Frank Sinatra, and *Les Girls*, opposite Gene Kelly, playing show-girls in both. Then she got the plum screen musical role of the decade: Nellie Forbush in *South Pacific* (58). Broadway's Mary Martin was turned down and so, among others, was Elizabeth Taylor, who auditioned; Judy Garland and Doris Day were other names mentioned. So Gaynor played the part – nicely, a performance which brought to mind Bing Crosby's ad-lib in *High Society*:

In 1989 Mitzi Gaynor was touring in 'Anything Goes', proving herself a box-office attraction almost thirty years after her film career came to an end. She is best remembered, if not too kindly, for South Pacific, *and you may sometimes catch her earlier pictures, when she was the white hope of the 20th Century-Fox musical: this one is* The 'I Don't Care' Girl *(53).*

'Game girl. Got up and finished fourth.' Leading man Rossano Brazzi, however, did not begin to measure up to the part and the film was long and south-soporific, punched in by Joshua Logan's vulgar fist. What with the score and the locations and Todd AO it did great business; but – perhaps because of the bad reviews – it virtually spelled 'finis' to the Hollywood career of both stars.

Next, Gaynor played with David Niven in *Happy Anniversary* (59); then with Yul Brynner in *Surprise Package* (60); then in a third comedy, with Kirk Douglas, *For Love or Money* (63). It was not her fault, but no fires were lit at the box-office. She has worked since in clubs, on TV and in tent shows, and always gets stunning notices. In 1972 she was reported as returning to films in *Hollywood! Hollywood!*, a musical about the 30s with Carol Burnett. The film was never made.

Ben Gazzara

Ben Gazzara is probably best known for his work in two television series – 'Arrest and Trial' and 'Run for Your Life' – which is ironic, because he does TV only for the money. He cares enough about films (or did) that in 1956 he turned down one of the leads in King Vidor's *War and Peace* because he did not want to be merely part of a spectacle. He was then one of the cinema's most promising new stars – and to date that promise has been largely unfulfilled. He is a sympathetic actor – but at that time he gave one of the great definitive performances of evil.

He was born in New York City in 1930 to Sicilian immigrant parents and became determined to be an actor after seeing Laurette Taylor in 'The Glass Menagerie'. After an abortive start studying engineering he got a scholarship to study under Erwin Piscator and then moved on to the Actors' Studio, where a group of students improvised a play from Calder Willingham's novel about life in a Southern military academy, 'End As a Man' (53). This finally reached Broadway in somewhat altered form with Gazzara still in the lead; it made him a star and he went on to play the leads in 'Cat on a Hot Tin Roof' and 'A Hatful of Rain'. Sam Spiegel bought the rights to 'End As a Man' and it emerged on screen as *The Strange One* (57), brilliantly recreating the heated, perverted atmosphere of that military school – especially in Gazzara's portrait of Jocko de Paris, an upper-class Iago, a quiet, mocking sadist who gets his kicks from seeing other people squirm. 'Time Magazine' observed that he was 'the most huggable heavy' since Bogart (huggable for boa constrictors, possibly). Seen today the film has an edge unlike any other; at the time, not surprisingly, it did not have a mass appeal.

Ben Gazzara in The Strange One (57), *the film of Calder Willingham's 'End As a Man'. He played a character called Jocko de Paris, a name suggesting a fetishism not at odds with the spirit of the film.*

He had a similar part in *Anatomy of a Murder* (59), as the army lieutenant on trial for killing a man who had tried to rape his wife (Lee Remick); the two of them suggested the doubtful nastiness of this tacky couple, giving the film the only interest it had. Then he went to the land of his forebears to make a comedy with Anna Magnani, *Risati di Gioia* (61), which surfaced briefly in the US as *The Passionate Thief* and not at all in Britain. This was a career setback, not offset by a couple of Hollywood ventures: *The Young Doctors*, a soap opera clash between him and old doctor Fredric March; and *Reprieve* (62) – or *Convicts Four* as it was later retitled – a dull biography of John Resko, a lifer (for murder), later rehabilitated. In Italy he made *La Città Prigioniera/The Captive City/Conquered City*, a war movie, with David Niven. After that, there was nothing for it but to turn back to the theatre and television. A return to films was flunked by the quality of the film concerned, a version of John O'Hara's novel *A Rage to Live* (66), as the poor unfortunate who breaks up the marriage of nympho Suzanne Pleshette.

He spent the next few years in TV and returned to filming quietly with a role in *The Bridge at Remagen* (69), with George Segal. He did a minute guest appearance in *If It's Tuesday It Must be Belgium* with John Cassavetes, who directed and co-starred with him in *Husbands* (70), the important picture Gazzara had been looking for since his first one. It did not do much for him, for he was announced for an Italian film called *Diary of a Police Commissioner*, at a salary of $60,000 plus 50 per cent of the US takings – but at the last minute changed his mind and Martin Balsam played it. Instead, he was in a slew of movies for television: *When Michael Calls* (72), a thriller; *Fireball Forward*, as a major general with the help of some footage from *Patton* (both were produced by Frank McCarthy); *The Family Rico*, a remake of *The Brothers Rico*, based on a novel by Simenon, as a Mafia man whose brother (Sal Mineo) has chickened out of a hit killing; and *Pursuit*, directed by Michael Crichton from his own novel, as a government agent desperate to outwit a terrorist. Gazzara did make an Italian film, *Afyon Oppio* (73), and then did an equally undistinguished tele-movie, *Maneater* with Sheree North, as one of two couples in danger from an escaped tiger. Looking, perhaps, for a popular film, he played a rescue expert in *The Neptune Factor An Undersea Odyssey*, but this was one of the disaster films the public did not want to see. He was the American writer sued for libel in the British courts by Polish doctor Anthony Hopkins in Leon Uris's semi-autobiographical *QB VII* (74), made as a six-hour (two-part) TV movie; he owned part of it and said he hoped that it could be cut down to make a cinema feature. He also hoped to direct himself in *Funzy and the Holy Name Society*; but that plan came to naught. So he was *Capone* (75), for producer Roger Corman, still trying and failing to make good exploitation movies out of old gangsters. Cassavetes was in it and he gave Gazzara another good role in *The Killing of a Chinese Bookie* (76), as an LA strip-show operator involved with the Mob: but, like all Cassavetes's films, it was long on earnestness and short on narrative drive. See-sawing still, Gazzara was in another exploitation film, *High Velocity*, filmed in Manila, as a Vietnam hero involved in the shady business of a banana republic; in *Voyage of the Damned*, as the American head of the Jewish agency in Europe; and then in Cassavetes's *Opening Night* (77), as a stage director – directing Gena Rowlands (Mrs Cassavetes). In *The Death of Richie*, for TV, he was the father of a drug-addicted teenager. After a mini-series, *The Trial of Lee Harvey Oswald*, he returned to the Far East – to Singapore – for *Saint Jack* (79), directed by Peter Bogdanovich, who needed a success after a run of flops. Commercially, it did fairly, but it was a tonic for admirers of both gentlemen: as an all-embracing no-holds-barred expatriate pimp, Gazzara took his best chance in 20 years, proving how often he has been wasted; from which it was a retrogressive step to *Sidney Sheldon's Bloodline*, which boasted a third-rate director working on a bestseller by a fourth-rate novelist. True, Audrey Hepburn was in it, but Gazzara's American executive had little to do but look suspicious.

He continued to keep excellent company: with Olivier (as General MacArthur) in *Oh Inchon* (81) and, as a detective trailing Miss Hepburn, in Bogdanovitch's *They All Laughed*; but both were regrettable credits. Matters hardly improved with Marco Ferreri's *Storie di Ordinaria Follia/Tales of Ordinary Madness*, made in English in New York – on a wasteland, in fact; it was based on stories by the underground writer Charles Bukowski and Gazzara played a self-destructive poet involved with several women. He was an incorruptible cop, one of the few, apparently, in New York's Finest, in a tele-movie, *A Question of Honor* (82) – and this was a huge step up, if not as good as some of the reviews suggested. A trip to Italy brought the fair *La Ragazza di Trieste* (83), playing an American strip cartoonist obsessed with a neurotic Ornella Muti, and two potboilers, *La Donna delle Meraviglie* (84) and *Uno Scandolo Perbene* (85), which were followed by the better *Figlio mio Infinimente Caro. . .*, in which he took to drugs in order to cure his drug addict son. He had more paternal troubles in a superior tele-film, *An Early Frost*, because his son (Aidan Quinn) is a gay man with AIDS. And the troubles were marital in the inferior remake of *A Letter to Three Wives*, in the Paul Douglas role. He had the title part in *Il Camorrista* (86), which was about the rise to power of a Mafia boss (him); and also in Europe he was in the French-Spanish *Fatale*, the Swiss-French *Quicker Than the Eye* and the Italian *Don Bosco*, as a priest. None of these appears to have been shown, a fate which almost befell *La Mémoire Tatouée*, also made at this time, with Julie Christie.

Police Story: The Freeway Killings (87) was a three-hour tele-movie and *Road House* (89) has Patrick Swayze and Gazzara as a brutal patriarch.

He has been married three times, the first two times to actresses Louise Erickson and Janice Rule (1961–79). He is now married to Elke Krivat.

Elliott Gould

For Elliott Gould, in 1970, the time had come. Audiences immediately recognized him as the sort of man they knew, had met at parties but had not yet encountered in Hollywood movies. In *Bob & Carol & Ted & Alice* he was a corporation lawyer in a three-piece suit – but that suit was all he had in common with movie executives of the past (it was not a surprise to find him in later films with a hippie haircut and a generally unkempt appearance). He had the authority and confidence of the old-time star, but most importantly he had the hang-ups of his generation – in this film, several neuroses about adultery, group sex and kindred matters. He had large startled eyes and a drooping jaw, but he was funny, with a probing self-deprecatory wit. He was not pretty; he was real, kinetic and shaggy. With women, he came on rather like a bear. Audiences, said 'Time Magazine', see in Gould 'all their tensions, frustrations and insecurities personified and turned into nervous comedy that both tickles and stings with the shock of recognition'. It seemed that every newspaper in the world examined him in such terms: he became the representative of his generation as Brando had been of his, etc. A likeable talent was being analysed to death; it might have proved fatal had not a run of flops reduced him to mere leading man status.

He was born in 1938 in Brooklyn, of Jewish parents – the first major actor since Al Jolson to use the Jewish ethos in his work and publicity (but in a much more sympathetic way than those boring New York Jewish heroes of those innumerable Jewish novels). His mother enrolled him in a school for child actors when he was 8½ and he grew up doing things on amateur TV shows, at neighbourhood concerts, etc. As a teenager, he got experience in the borscht belt and played one of the leads in a show at Woodstock, 'Some Little Honor'. He made his Broadway début in the chorus of a flop called 'Rumple' and was in the chorus of 'Irma la Douce', which resulted in an audition for understudy in 'I Can Get it for You Wholesale' (62). What he got was the lead, as well as one of the featured performers, Barbra Streisand. In London he played in 'On the Town' and then toured the US in 'The Fantasticks' with Liza Minnelli. He was in two Broadway failures, 'Drat the Cat' and Jules Feiffer's comedy 'Little Murders'; and in a film failure, *Quick, Let's Get Married*, as a deaf-mute: the stars were Ginger Rogers and Ray Milland – names which helped it to a few bookings years later. He toured in 'Luv' with Shelley Winters and was seen in it by someone who recommended him for *The Night They Raided Minsky's* (69), an affectionate look back at the old stripper-house, flawed by a weak plot and pallid leads – Jason Robards, Britt Ekland, Norman Wisdom. In that company, Gould's cameo as the fast-talking, indolent lessee of the theatre stood out; he got good notices, some consolation for being generally known around show business as Mr Barbra Streisand. They split up around this time.

Unexpectedly, his fame was about to overtake hers. There was another play in New York which clunked out, 'A Way of Life', and then he auditioned for the role in *Bob & Carol & Ted & Alice*, an unpalatable and ultimately sententious comedy about wife-swapping. The subject-matter made it a giant hit – plus the performances of Gould and Dyan Cannon, by far the nicer of the two couples. They managed to get away with scenes like the he-wants-it-she-doesn't bit and both were Oscar-nominated. He at once went into *M-A-S-H* (70), an irreverent battle-front farce which 20th backed in a forgetful moment; they thought it might just get back its costs, but it soared to $22 million: Gould and Donald Sutherland were medics interested less in surgery than in wine, women and song, and in bucking all military authority. As directed by Robert Altman, it was the most invigorating US film in years, despite the gouts of blood (which led some into believing it an anti-war film).

As a cinema property, Gould was at white heat. He did an over-extended campus comedy with good movements, *Getting Straight*, as a bolshie teaching assistant, and Judith Crist thought we all might be 'shilled into it, courtesy of the irresistible Mr Gould'. However, not many people went to the critically panned *Move*, despite the presence of the delectable Paula Prentiss as his wife; he was a fantasy-ridden, rebellious writer of dirty books. Little better liked was *I Love My Wife. . .* , a tale so similar – and coming along so precipitously after – that within a while you had forgotten which film was which. Both films failed miserably, victims of the star's over-exposure. He was still voted into the

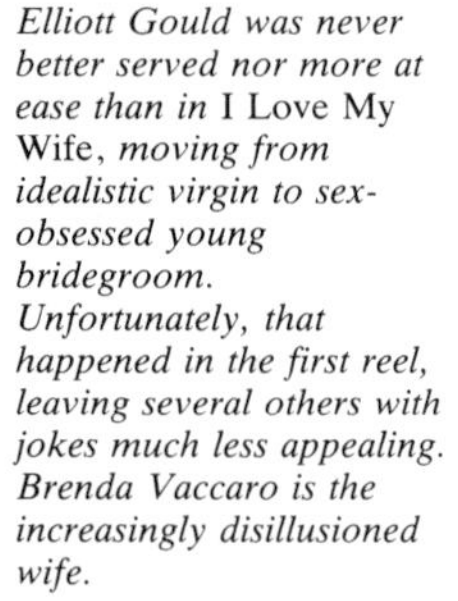

Elliott Gould was never better served nor more at ease than in I Love My Wife, *moving from idealistic virgin to sex-obsessed young bridegroom. Unfortunately, that happened in the first reel, leaving several others with jokes much less appealing. Brenda Vaccaro is the increasingly disillusioned wife.*

box-office 10 in 1970, at fifth. Gould had formed his own company with Jack Brodsky and endless projects were announced. The first to arrive, *Little Murders* (71), with Alan Arkin, cast Gould again as the urban prisoner and was greeted with icy good will. A similar welcome awaited *The Touch/Beröringen*, made in two versions, Swedish and English, by Ingmar Bergman. Every critic pays lip-service to Bergman's greatness but few of them like him; and when there is a question of Homer nodding, he is done in. It happened in this case and Gould – who had got publicity out of being the first American star to be directed by Bergman (in his first English-speaking film) – in the end reaped little benefit. But he was good – if outclassed by the Swedes – as a rootless Jewish archaeologist involved in an impossible affair with Bibi Andersson, wife of Max von Sydow.

Before this was shown, he had begun and abandoned *A Glimpse of Tiger*. It folded after a week's location in New York, after reported differences between Gould and co-star Kim Darby, director Anthony Harvey and his partner Brodsky (the partnership was dissolved). 'Playboy' later spoke of 'Elliott's oafish behaviour . . . the rigours of a too strenuous programme' and added, 'There were rumours of a drug problem.' After a year, in which he was said to be recuperating, he played Marlowe in Robert Altman's not-disagreeable mangling of Raymond Chandler, *The Long Goodbye* (73). This Marlowe was a shuffling near-hippie, but his affection for the deprived as against the rich lot he was investigating was neatly arranged. Still fighting crime, he and Robert Blake were cynical LA vice cops in *Busting* (74); and still partnered, he and Sutherland were spies in *Wet Stuff* – an appropriate title, but since it never looked like doing much at the box-office its title was changed pre-première to *S-P-I-E-S*. But no one was fooled into thinking it was another *M-A-S-H*. There was a more felicitous partnership, with George Segal, in Altman's fine, funky *California Split*, both of them as compulsive gamblers.

With the possible exception of the two Altmans, Gould had not been in a box-office film in years . . . and things got worse. He was an FBI man in *Who?* for director Jack Gold in Britain, but to date it has not been publicly shown (it was trade-screened at the end of 1978); and around the same time 'Variety' carried an ad for *The Hero*, where he is second-billed to Fred Williamson, but if it was ever made it has also stayed under drapes. In *Whiffs* (75) he was an impotent and rebellious outsider-soldier who takes to robbing banks – a film hopefully retitled *C-A-S-H* for overseas audiences; and in *I Will I Will For Now* (76) he was the opposite of impotent and thus having marital trouble with Diane Keaton. Brut produced both these flops; and hence cancelled Gould's plan to direct and star in *A New Life*. Indeed, Hollywood had lost interest and after a guest appearance as himself in Altman's *Nashville* he went to Britain to play – ineffectively – an ebullient, cigar-smoking American officer in *A Bridge Too Far* (77). *Capricorn One* (78), a sci-fier, was made in the US, but with money from Britain; and it was followed by two in former dominions of that country, *The Silent Partner*, a thriller set in Canada in which he was a bank-teller (at a fee of $325,000), and *Matilda*, an Australian whimsy in which he promoted a boxing kangaroo. Hollywood seemed uninterested – though Gould had turned down *King Kong* since its makers could not decide which of the two leading roles they wanted him for – but apparently the British did not find him anachronistic in their seemingly endless stream of movies about World War II. These two were particularly unnecessary: *Escape to Athena* (79), in which Gould was a USO entertainer interned on a Greek island under commandant Roger Moore until rescued by partisan Telly Savalas; and *The Lady Vanishes*, romping and rowing with Cybil Shepherd through most of Europe in August 1939. It may also be said that Gould was the last person one expected to see in one

There was absolutely no need for a new version of The Lady Vanishes *(78), and it was entirely typical of the Rank Organisation that the leads should now go to two American players, Cybill Shepherd and Elliott Gould, though it must be said that they coped very nicely with them.*

of Michael Redgrave's old roles – now transformed into a 'Life Magazine' photographer. Around the same time he was one of the cameo performers in *The Muppet Movie*.

The Disney Organization, astute in its use of neglected talent – Gould was no longer box-office – engaged him to play a pilot who comes down in the Pacific with animals, children and Geneviève Bujold: *The Last Flight of Noah's Ark*. However, *Dirty Tricks* (80) and *Falling in Love Again* were most unspectacular credits. The first was a Canadian chase 'comedy' in which he was a Harvard professor; the second title referred to him and Susannah York – ineffectively, as produced, written and directed by Steven Paul (just out of his teens), who also played a supporting role. *The Devil and Max Devlin* (81) were Bill Cosby and him, being sent back to earth to corrupt three innocents – the revamping of an ancient piece of whimsy which did not revive Gould's career or that of the Disney studio, at a low ebb at this stage. They did not use him again. In 1983 he went to New York to appear in 'The Guys in the Trunk', but left and was replaced by the actor who had played the role in the off-off-Broadway production (this one lasted only one night). He had his best role in a while as the Jewish boy who shocks his family by wanting to marry a schiksa (Margaux Hemingway) in *Over the Brooklyn Bridge* (84), but it was not exactly a crowd-pleaser; however, it is hard to imagine *anyone* being pleased by *The Naked Face*, unless it be director Bryan Forbes, who also scripted from a novel by Sidney Sheldon, about two cops (Gould, Rod Steiger) trying to nail a psychiatrist (Roger Moore). In the Austrian-West German *Strawanzer* Gould (who was dubbed) was an architect who leaves his family to go on almighty drunks. He guested in *The Muppets Take Manhattan* and had his own TV series, 'E/R' (85), which did not run. In that medium he did an excellent film, *Vanishing Act* (86), playing a slow-witted police lieutenant, but he was dropped from the cast of another TV series, 'Together We Stand'. In an independent production, *Inside Out*, he was a New York agoraphobic recluse, but there followed an upper-case credit, *Conspiracy: the Trial of the Chicago Seven* (87) for HBO. Shelved definitely, it seems, is *The Myth* with Peter Cook, which Gould also co-scripted.

He went to Italy to do *I Miei Quarant' Anni/The Story of a Woman*, based on the explicit memoirs of Marina Ripa di Meara, who was played by Carol Ault; he had a cameo as one of her lovers, what else? After another cameo performance in *The Telephone* (88), starring Whoopi Goldberg, he was the ex-jock father of Shelley Duvall (also the executive producer) in *Frog* for PBS; and he had only a tacked-on role in *Der Joker*, in Germany, which starred Michael York and which was renamed *Lethal Obsession* when it went direct to video in the US. A career now in low gear was not helped by a low-budget thriller, *Dangerous Love*, playing a detective: his 'presence adds a touch of class to the project' said 'Variety', 'but he ultimately seems lost and a bit sad in a role that is so far below the level achieved in his heyday.'

Gloria Grahame

The screen floozie – as opposed to the moll – did not really arrive till the *films noirs* of the 40s. Till then – in American films at least – the ladies of easy virtue came in a few stereotypes, none of which was ever seen near a bed. There was the whore-heroine, a victim of circumstance, waif-like, to all intents and purposes true to her true love; there was her first cousin, the courtesan, another lady seldom seen to be sullied; there was the tart with the heart of gold, whose role was merely functional – to advance the plot; and there was the gangster's moll and kept woman, dressed in silks and satins, sassy and slapped-around. They were biffed but never kissed and – like the tarts-with-the-hearts-of – often got theirs in reel 10 as a result of turning-coat and helping the hero. Once out of the cloud-cuckoo-land of the 30s, more realism was brought to bear on the screen's tarnished ladies; they were still cheap and kind-hearted but also sexy and sometimes libidinous. They were seen reclining on beds – at least, on the coverlets – not (yet) on the sheets.

The best of the 40s floozies was Gloria Grahame. She was so good that she eased herself out of supporting roles into star parts – though not many of much variation. She was usually cast as your friendly neighbourhood nympho. She was both tough and vulnerable, a combination not rare but here at its most winning.

She was born in Pasadena, California, in 1925, daughter of an industrial designer and a British-born actress (Jean Grahame). An agent saw her in a school play and got her a job – under her real name, Gloria Hallward – understudying Miriam Hopkins in 'The Skin of Our Teeth' on Broadway (43). She then got a small part in 'A Highland Fling', where Louis B. Mayer saw her and signed her to an MGM contract. She was photographed in bathing costumes, but in two years got only two parts, a good one as a vamp in a triangle story, *Blonde Fever* (44), and a minute one in *Without Love* (45). Her agent got her taken on also at Paramount and RKO but nothing happened till an MGM casting director recommended her to Capra for his film at RKO, *It's a Wonderful Life* (46), as a platinum blonde wanting a loan in order to make a new start in New York (in his vision of the future James Stewart sees her being bundled into a police-wagon). MGM gave her bigger parts: *It Happened in Brooklyn* (47), as a nurse; *Crossfire* at RKO, attracting favourable attention as a sympathetic bar-room singer; *Song of the Thin Man*, vamping William Powell; and *Merton of the Movies*, as the temperamental movie star who uses Red Skelton and almost woos him from extra Virginia O'Brien.

She left MGM and did not film in 1948, being busy getting divorced from actor Stanley Clements (married 1945) and marrying director Nicholas Ray. Ray directed the next film she was in, *A Woman's Secret* (49), with Melvyn Douglas; and she returned to RKO to play the lead in a low-budget Western, *Roughshod*, as a saloon-girl herded by Robert Sterling over the passes. She and Ray moved over to Columbia for *In a Lonely Place* (50), where she played opposite Bogart, as the girl in the next-door bungalow who befriends him when he is suspected of murder. She was as cynical as he was and they made a mighty successful team. At that point she took a long sabbatical and in 1952 was divorced from Ray. She signed a contract with Paramount and was one of several stars in De Mille's *The Greatest Show on Earth* (52), as the elephant girl. However, she shook herself free of it and freelanced, in supporting roles: *Macao*, with Jane Russell, in a small role as the villain's girl; *Sudden Fear*, as the pouting, sulky moll for whose sake Jack Palance wants to murder Joan Crawford; and Minnelli's *The Bad and the Beautiful*. In the last she had a good part, as an irritating Southern belle bored with screenwriter husband Dick Powell and amusing herself with big star Gilbert Roland. It brought her a Best Supporting Oscar.

The Oscar brought her starring parts again: in *The Glass Wall* (53), as the New York girl who loves Vittorio Gassmann; and in *Man on a Tightrope*, as Fredric March's unfaithful wife – filming took so long that she lost *East of Sumatra* to Marilyn Maxwell. Then in Fritz Lang's *The Big Heat* she was the moll who befriends Glenn Ford and for her pains has hot coffee thrown in her face by Lee Marvin. Real stardom eluded her. Said 'Picturegoer': 'If she were more synthetic, producers might not be so wary of her particular kind of explosive sex-appeal. But she's very real, too real perhaps.' But she and her agent alone knew why she did *Prisoners of the Casbah*, a Sam Katzman Arabian Night with Turhan Bey and Cesar Romero, as a pouting princess. She rejoined Lang and Ford for *Human Desire*, as Broderick Crawford's playgirl wife inveigling Ford into murder (a part intended for Barbara Stanwyck, then Rita Hayworth and offered to Olivia de Havilland, who said she would do it if her leading man was Brando, Mitchum, Montgomery Clift, Kirk Douglas or Burt Lancaster). It was she who ended up dead, as she did as a saloon-singer in *The Naked Alibi* (54), a mediocre melodrama with Sterling Hayden.

She went to Britain to make *The Good Die Young* (55), playing the film-extra wife of GI John Ireland; and then returned to Minnelli for *The Cobweb*: 'It's simply not as good a script as the other film I did with him . . . I had Richard Widmark and Charles Boyer as co-stars. One as my husband, one as my lover. As it happens Widmark hated me and Boyer was a drunk. It was a disaster.' After playing an amorous widow in *Not As a Stranger*, she had another unpleasant experience, on *Oklahoma!* – she did not want to do it, since she could not sing a note (she recorded them one at a time) and had thought Celeste Holm

Gloria Grahame in the process of winning an Oscar – in The Bad and the Beautiful *(52), with Dick Powell. He was a Pulitzer-prize-winning author who gets the Hollywood call, and she was his Southern belle of a wife who lets the whole business get way, way over her head.*

'great' on Broadway: still, she got $100,000 for being Ado Annie, the girl who cain't say no, and gave a performance of impish charm. She had a conventional leading role, war-film type, in *The Man Who Never Was* (56), and got poor notices for her part. She refused to meet the press, etc., and 'Picturegoer' quoted 20th as being 'embarrassed and disgusted' by her attitude. She decided to leave films and went to live in Paris; she was off the screen 18 months till a shoddy B for Kirk Douglas's company, *Ride Out for Revenge* (57) as a man-crazy tramp opposite Rory Calhoun. She had a small part as a sluttish neighbour in *Odds Against Tomorrow* (59) and then worked mainly in TV. She was divorced from Cy Howard (1954–59), then a radio and TV writer, and in 1961 married assistant director Tony Ray; they had three children and she stayed at home to bring them up.

She returned to films in a minute role in a good low-budget Western, *Ride Beyond Vengeance* (65), with Chuck Connors and Michael Rennie; and a few years later began working again with a will – but still in small parts: *Blood and Lace* (71); *Escape* and *Black Noon*, an occult Western, both for television; *The Todd Killings*; *Chandler* (72), a private eye thriller with Warren Oates; and *The Loners*, as the heroine's widowed mother in this kids-against-society tale. There was another tele-film, *The Girl on the Late, Late Show* (74), playing a one-time movie star who has vanished; she was surrounded, when she reappeared, by some other veterans – Don Murray, Van Johnson, Yvonne de Carlo, Cameron Mitchell, Walter Pidgeon and Ralph Meeker. She then journeyed to Spain for *Tarot*, supporting Fernando Rey as a blind millionaire hung up on 'sexy' Sue Lyon; she did have star roles in two American Bs, made on Z budgets, *Mama's Dirty Girls* (75), as Mama, and *Mansion of the Doomed* (76), also titled *Eyes*. There were two mini-series, *Rich Man Poor Man* and *Seventh Avenue*, but she was well down the cast-list in the second. In an attempt to regain stardom she turned up in London with mother in 1978, to do two plays in the suburbs, 'Rain' and 'A Tribute to Lily Lamont', the latter about an ageing Hollywood star and her fan-club. She spoke to reporters about playing Shakespeare – perhaps Juliet – but instead did a movie, *Head Over Heels* (79), not helping the romance between John Heard and May Beth Hurt because as his mother she is forever threatening suicide. She did do 'Private Lives' (80), in Geneva, NY, after which there were some more brief appearances as a mother – Mary Steenbergen's – in *Melvin and Howard*. She was wasted in her last film, *The Nesting* (81), a horror tale in which she was a Madam and a phantom. She died in 1981, but could be seen a year later in a piece made in 1979 but shelved till it went direct to cable, *A Nightingale Sang in Berkeley Square*. It was one of her better late outings, as Richard Jordan's brash mother.

Farley Granger

Farley Granger was once under contract to Sam Goldwyn, who thought he would become the biggest star in movies. It did not happen. He was a nice-looking kid with a neat line in both underprivileged heroes and wealthy weaklings. Another Clark Gable he was not.

He was born in San José, California, in 1925 and straight out of school was recommended to Goldwyn for a small role in *The North Star* (43). He followed with a big part in *The Purple Heart* (4), third-billed, and then joined the army. For a while after his release he pounded in vain on studio doors, till at RKO Nicholas Ray cast him in *They Live By Night* (48), a low-budget drama about a sad little *ménage* – Cathy O'Donnell, plain, harassed, as the girl, Granger, embittered, semi-criminal, as the breadwinner. Howard Hughes as head of the studio held it up for a year, but rumours of quality leaked out (and were confirmed by critics). By the time it was shown Granger was making a picture for Hitchcock and had been signed by an impressed Goldwyn to a five-year contract. The Hitchcock movie was *Rope*, about two rich homosexual undergraduates who play at murder; John Dall was the other one and Granger the one who cracks when professor James Stewart suspects the truth. Granger's first for Goldwyn was *Enchantment* which interwove his own romantic complication (Evelyn Keyes) with flashbacks of granddad David Niven's (Teresa Wright).

His big launching was to be *Roseanna McCoy* (49), a story of the famous feud between two hillbilly families, with Joan Evans, another Goldwyn discovery, in the title-part. But it flopped. He was loaned to MGM for *Side Street*, a neighbour to *They Live By Night*, with O'Donnell, as newlyweds terrorized by gangsters. While he was gone, Goldwyn prepared two more pictures destined to launch Granger and Miss Evans as the screen lovers of the 50s: *Our Very Own* (50), a soap opera which also involved Ann Blyth, and *Edge of Doom*, in which he murdered a priest. Both failed conspicuously and a fourth co-starring film, *All for Love*, was cancelled. Evans quietly disappeared from the Goldwyn contract list. Goldwyn was no happier with Granger, who refused to be loaned out for a new version of *Lorna Doone*. Goldwyn suspended him; but while the unfortunate Richard Greene was landed in this dreadful *Lorna*, Granger was being sought by Hitchcock for *Strangers on a Train* (51), as the socialite tennis-champ embroiled by Robert Walker in his lethal plottings. It was a competent performance, though Hitchcock said later that the situations might have been more effective with a 'stronger' actor. He was loaned out again for *Behave Yourself*, a comedy with Shelley Winters, reputedly his offscreen interest; and back in the Goldwyn fold was wanted in *I Want You*, with Dana Andrews.

That he had not 'made it' was clear from the next two: *O. Henry's Full House* (52), as Jeanne Crain's selfish sensitive husband in the episode 'The Gift of the Magi'; and *Hans Christian Andersen*, starring Danny Kaye, as the juvenile lead. It was his last for Goldwyn. At MGM he was the wealthy orphan loved by Leslie Caron in the episode 'Mademoiselle' of *The Story of Three Loves* (53) and a playboy in a B musical with Jane Powell, *Small Town Girl*. His contribution to all these – admittedly poor – pictures was little more than an anguished expression. Goldwyn then let him go to Italy for a film, at a fee of $85,000, on the curious condition that he had the *right* to re-sign him to a new long-term contract when the present one expired in 1955. The film was Visconti's *Senso* (54), as the worthless Austrian soldier who betrays Alida Valli, and by far his best screen work. It took a long time to make; when it was completed Granger bought a house in Rome, but in 1955 did a Broadway play, 'The Carefree Tree'. In Hollywood, he was a weak young punk 'befriended' by underworld boss Anthony Quinn in *The Naked Street* (55), a Crime Does Not Pay-type tale; and then Harry Thaw in *The Girl in the Red Velvet Swing*, the rich roué who had shot his wife's lover (50 years earlier) in a Manhattan nightclub. This was a pedestrian reconstruction of the case, not helped by a less than glittering cast (Ray Milland, Joan Collins).

Strangers on a Train (*51*), *literally: Farley Granger as the tennis champion approached by a fellow-traveller who does not so much want to chat as to suggest they 'swop' murders. He is appalled, if not yet in this still, but the trouble is that Walker has a screw or two loose.*

Over the next 10 years Granger worked on the stage, mainly in stock. He reappeared in films without fuss in an A.C. Lyles B – the last that producer made for Paramount – *Rogue's Gallery* (67), with Dennis Morgan, and Roger Smith as a private eye. Granger had a small role as the henchman of evil *boîte*-owner Edgar Bergen. It was shown in a couple of cinemas and then put up for sale to TV. An independent venture, *Maharlika* (68), also seems to have had only a few bookings. He appeared in the memorably bad TV 'Laura', with Lee Radziwill and George Sanders, then went to Italy where he made several potboilers: *Shadows* (69); *Violence* (70), with Susan Strasberg, directed by Damiano Damiani; *La Tela del Ragno*, with Edwige Fenech; *The Challengers,* in the US with Anne Baxter for TV; *Qual Cosa Striscia nel Buio*; *Lo Chiamavano Trinità* (71); *Il Posso dell' Assassino*, with Rosalba Neri; *La Rossa dalla Pelle che Scotta* (72); and *Replica di un Delitto*. The *Trinità* film was one of a hugely successful Western series. In 1972, in Sicily, Granger made *Rivelazione di un Maniaco Sessuale al Capo della Squadro Mobile*, with Sylva Koscina. He supported Shirley Jones, glammed-up to meet the requirements of producer Ross Hunter (in his first film for TV), in *The Lives of Jenny Dolan*; Jenny was a reporter caught up in political assassinations. He was due to support Richard Burton in *Bluebeard*, but this co-production required

Farley Granger was a good actor too-soon type-cast as romantic but unreliable young lovers: here he is as the Austrian officer who will desert the Italian countess, Alida Valli, who has betrayed her country for him. The film is Senso *(54), directed by Luchino Visconti, who had wanted Brando for the role, till persuaded by his producers that Granger would be a bigger attraction.*

an Italian actor to qualify as a part-Italian film.

In the US there were more supporting roles on television, in *Seventh Avenue* (77) and *Black Beauty* (78), both mini-series. In another attempt to revitalize his career he returned to the stage: off-Broadway in 'A Month in the Country' (79) and in stock in Boucicault's 'The Streets of New York' (80). Film offers continued to be negligible: *The Prowler* (81), a horror movie; *Deathmask* (84), trying to discover who killed his daughter; and *The Imagemaker* (86), a political thriller, as an ambassador. During this period he appeared off-Broadway in a revival of 'Outward Bound' and with former co-star Joan Collins stepped out in 'Night of a Hundred Stars' at Radio City Music Hall: these were her pre-'Dynasty' days and they probably received less applause than any of those appearing. Also, *Very Close Quarters*, a sex-comedy set in Moscow with Miss Winters, went direct to video (86, filmed in 85).

STEWART GRANGER

When Stewart Granger was the hottest male property around the British studios he was seldom taken seriously. He was just too good-looking, involved in too many junky films and – by his own admission – too arrogant. His relationship with the press was poor, so he was irritatingly labelled 'glamour boy'. The name hardly stuck, but he never managed to get away from the dimpled teeth-flashing he-man roles he started with and only in glimpses has he been able to suggest that there is something more in him.

He was born in London in 1913 and was educated at Epsom College and then at the Webber-Douglas School of Dramatic Art. He started out under his own name, James Stewart, but changed it when another James Stewart appeared in the West. Meanwhile, he had carried a spear at the Old Vic and worked as a film extra (*A Southern Maid* in 1933, *Giver Her a Ring* in 1934). He was Ben Lyon's stand-in on *I Spy* (33). He began to get leading roles in rep at Hull and Birmingham, and played at the Malvern Festival; he was in London in 1937, in a small part in 'Autumn' starring Flora Robson, and again in 1938, in 'Serena Blandish' starring Vivien Leigh. He got a good film chance when 20th cast him as the romantic lead in their British remake of and old George M. Cohan vehicle, *So This Is London* (39), starring the West End farceurs Alfred Drayton and Robertson Hare. When the war started he was touring with the Old Vic in 'Saint Joan', as Dunois, and after a small part in *Convoy* (40) he joined the Black Watch Regiment. Invalided out two years later, he got a small part in *Secret Mission* (42) starring James Mason; and a better one in *Thursday's Child* (43), written and directed by Rodney Ackland, with Wilfred Lawson, a suburban drama which had a certain *succès d'estime* after being disdained by distributors.

James Mason was originally set to play the romantic young hero of *The Man in Grey*, but, when he moved up to play the villain, Granger was taken on (he was in 'Rebecca' at the time) – for £1,000 for 12 weeks' work. The success of the film swept the two of them, plus co-stars Margaret Lockwood and Phyllis Calvert, to top stardom in Britain. Granger played a factory owner who when visiting his fiancée falls in love with her nurse (Rosamund John) in *The Lamp Still Burns* and then with his *Man in Grey* co-stars became the cornerstone of Gainsborough Pictures (soon to be part of the Rank Organization). For Gainsborough he did some highly popular romances: *Fanny By Gaslight* (44), who was Calvert, with Granger again the nice hero and Mason the baddie; a mawkish *Love Story* with Margaret Lockwood; and *Madonna of the Seven Moons*, a film dear to the hearts of connoisseurs of camp, as an Italian gypsy in love with a schizophrenic Calvert. *Waterloo Road* (45) was an improvement, but it did not help his image, playing a foppish wide-boy who dallies with John Mills's wife while he is away at the front.

Mason had been sought for the role of Apollodorus in *Caesar and Cleopatra*, but did not want to do it – so Granger played it; in return Mason played a role that Granger should have done (in *The Wicked Lady*), when the latter went off on an ENSA tour with Deborah Kerr, playing 'Gaslight'. Later, Granger took over Mason's role in *The Magic*

Phyllis Calvert and Stewart Granger in Madonna of the Seven Moons *(44), one of the Gainsborough romances which made him a top star.*

Bow (46) when Mason realized this Paganini biopic had been reduced to just another Gainsborough romance – certainly no more adult than Granger's other, earlier, film that year, the slow-moving *Caravan*, some malarkey set in Spain where he was torn between high-born Anne Crawford and gypsy Jean kent. Critical scorn had absolutely no effect on the box-office: austerity Britain queued to see this stuff and Granger was well to the fore in all the box-office lists, though always trailing Mason, as in the Granada poll of 1946, second – but only 8 per cent of the votes compared to Mason's 27 per cent.

The next three were not made by Gainsborough, but by other Rank units – and if they had more class, they were even duller: *Captain Boycott* (47), as a rebel farmer on the captain's Irish estate; *Blanche Fury* (48), as a bastard scion scheming, killing and loving Valerie Hobson to get back the ancestral home; and *Saraband for Dead Lovers*, as a soldier of fortune, with Joan Greenwood. Rank's big stars were in fact tired of these flummeries; like Margaret Lockwood, Granger wanted to try comedy, so he became the *Woman Hater* who succumbed in the end to the wiles of Edwige Feuillère. 'That got spat at,' he commented later. A second attempt was a minute improvement, *Adam and Evelyne* (49), a *Daddy Long Legs*-type tale with Jean Simmons as the ward. He and Simmons appeared in a flop revival of Tolstoy's 'The Power of Darkness' and a year later she became his second wife (the first was actress Elspeth March).

Stewart Granger not long after he had become one of MGM's leading stars.

By that time they were settled in Hollywood. There had been much speculation as to what would happen when his Rank contract expired: Korda offered the perennial project, *The King's General*, already turned down by Mason, but MGM wanted him for one film: the salary was a drop – only $25,000 – but it would help to pay for his losses on the Tolstoy venture. The film was the very popular remake of *King Solomon's Mines* (50), with Deborah Kerr and a British director, Compton Bennett, who found Granger 'very diffi-

Ever since Trader Horn *MGM had had dreams of another successful jungle movie. Finally in 1950 they re-made* King Solomon's Mines: *Stewart Granger was Allan Quartermain; Deborah Kerr a widow in search of her husband. Richard Carlson was her brother, along for the thrills.*

cult' to work with. Nevertheless, a jubilant Metro signed him to a seven-year contract reputedly worth $1½ million and announced a hoard of films for him, developed to exploit his gift for playing gallant but ruthless adventurers. According to his own account he was blackmailed into it: Metro had an option on a second movie and threatened either to put him into a small role or charge him with the expense incurred during filming (during the negotiations he lost *An Outcast of the Islands* when that was postponed). However, the next one was a flop: *Soldiers Three* (51), Kipling's boys, with David Niven and Robert Newton (an old MGM property, once scheduled for Gable, Tracy and Beery). And the one after that just broke even: *The Light Touch*, a comedy about art forgers, with Pier Angeli. MGM hurried him back into actioners: *The Wild North* (52), as a French-Canadian fur-trapper suspected of murder, and *Scaramouche*, a new version of the Rafael Sabatini novel that bore little resemblance to the original. As that immortal jester Granger did some spectacular duelling, but did not find the right note of parody. Said 'Variety': 'Granger is handsome enough, but never seems quite able to keep from letting his smirk show through. . . . ' Another remarke, *The Prisoner of Zenda*, with Deborah Kerr and Mason (now in a supporting role), found Granger again swashbuckling vigorously, but it proved that he was no Ronald Colman.

In more ways than one. There were persistent reports in the British press that Granger was not MGM's most docile star, like this in the 'Daily Mirror' in 1952: 'his manner is making him a most unpopular Englishman in Hollywood'. His films did not get better either – and indeed there was a distinct falling off in the next two, where he played the beloveds of a couple of princesses: *Salome* (53), Rita Hayworth, at Columbia, and *Young Bess*, Jean Simmons, at MGM, as Seymour (while making the former he was offered the role Burt Lancaster eventually played in *From Here to Eternity*). He partnered Robert Taylor in another remake, *All the Brothers Were Valiant*, a whaling drama, and then essayed a part once played by John Barrymore, *Beau Brummell* (54), but the film itself was awful. Hardly better was *Green Fire*, an adventure tale with Grace Kelly, but *Moonfleet* (55) was fine, certainly the best film that Granger was ever in. A British smuggling yarn from a boy's classic novel, it was acted with gusto by a good cast and directed by Fritz Lang with a nice emphasis on Strawberry Hill Gothic. MGM disliked it so much that it played the lower half of double bills, but when it finally arrived in France the press voted it the Best Foreign Film of the year.

Granger and Simmons returned to Britain to do an Edwardian thriller, *Footsteps in the Fog*, and then he was in another good one, *Bhowani Junction* (56) with Ava Gardner, as one of the last of the Raj colonels. Then, as all action heroes must, he finally went West, partnering Robert Taylor for *The Last Hunt*. His contract finished with a couple that did not do well, *The Little Hut* (57), a so-called comedy with Ava Gardner, and *Gun Glory*, a Western with Rhonda Fleming. It was announced that Granger would not re-sign because he wanted more money; and he decamped to England to make an indifferent murder mystery with Donna Reed, *The Whole Truth* (58). There he told the 'Sunday Express': 'Acting now bores the hell out of me. I know I haven't a nutshell of talent compared to my wife Jean Simmons.' In 1960, divorced and with his career on the slide, he rationalized to the same newspaper: 'I accepted all sorts of rubbish to pay the bills so that Jean could sit it out and wait for better parts.' The films he presumably meant: the British *Harry Black* (58), jungly larks that added *and the Tiger* for American marquees; *North to Alaska* (60), as one of John Wayne's sidekicks; and *The Secret Partner*, a British thriller that played as a B. Reputedly he turned down Messala in *Ben Hur*.

There was, however, a biblical spectacle on his horizon, *Sodoma e Gomorrah/Sodom and Gomorrah* (62), as Lot, filmed in English by a Franco-Italian company. Granger continued to work on the Continent, presumably in the language of the producing company – for when they turned up in Britain or the US (if at all) they were invariably dubbed. Released before *Sodom* was *Lo Spadaccino di Siena/Le Mercenaire*, which drew a half-admiring comment from the 'MFB': 'Stewart Granger may not be everyone's second-best Fairbanks, but he gives edge to the odd witty line, and shows that he at least realizes what the director could have done if he had had a sense of style.' Also in Italy he did a Foreign Legion story, *Marcia o Crepa*. After two years' absence from the cameras he faced them again for a couple in Yugoslavia: AIP's *The Secret Invasion* (64), as a British major persuading five criminals to venture behind the lines to rescue a general; and the British-Yugoslav *The Crooked Road* (65), as a Balkan dictator, with Robert Ryan.

He was to remain in Yugoslavia for three German-Yugoslav-Italian Westerns, part of a series revolving round Apache chief Winnetou (Pierre Brice) and all taken from (German) novels by Karl May; the earlier ones had employed Lex Barker and Guy Madison and had been so successful on the Continent that the producers could afford to pay Granger's fee. He played Old Surehand in *Unter Geiern*, in *Old Surehand – I Teil* and in *Der Ölprinz* (the latter made in Italy). Also that year he made a German-Italian thriller, *Das Geheimnis der drei Dschunken/A009 Missione Hong Kong*, with Rosanna Schiaffino, and then some Austrian-Italian thrillers; *Das Geheimnis der Gelben Mönche* (66) with Curt Jurgens; *Gern Hab Ich die Frauen Gekillt/Spie Contro Il Mondo*, a three-episode film with Lex Barker and Pierre Brice; *Requiem per un Agente Segreto*, with Peter Van Eyk; and *Wie Tötet Man Eine Dame/Tiro a Segno per Uccidere* (67), as a secret agent involved with an heiress. He returned to Britain for a couple of modest-budgeters, *The Trygon Factor*, as a Scotland Yard man, and *The Last Safari*, again as an intrepid hunter but dismally directed by Henry Hathaway. In that one Granger was billed after someone called Kas Garas. The following year he told the 'Daily Express' again: 'I've never done a film I'm proud of.' In 1969 he was trying to murder his wife in a TV movie, *Any Second Now*. His third marriage (1964–68), to a Belgian girl, broke up, but his career was revitalized by an American TV series in 1970, 'The Men From Shiloh'. There was also a TV movie, *The Hound of the Baskervilles* (72). In 1975 he was reported making a Western in the Canary Islands, *The Long Hard Ride*, with Jim Brown and Lee Van Cleef but nothing seems to have come of this; cinemagoers saw him again when he left his real estate interests in Spain and Arizona to play the man who recruits the mercenaries in *The Wild Geese* (78).

He said in an interview that he had decided to quit at the time of *Any Second Now*, because it was so bad. In view of his subsequent credits it is a pity he did not: *The Royal Romance of Charles and Diana* (82), one of two rival tele-movies on that matter – neither shown in Britain – as Prince Philip; a mini-series, *Crossings* (86), described by 'Variety' as 'bilge', playing Cheryl Ladd's interfering uncle; *Rage to Kill* (87), which starred Maude Adams, as a sort of Nazi-type; and *A Hazard of Hearts* for television, a romantic double threat from Lew Grade/Barbara Cartland.

He is scheduled to make his Broadway début at the Brooks Atkinson Theater in November 1989, where he will join Rex Harrison and Glynis Johns in a revival of Somerset Maugham's 'The Circle'.

Kathryn Grayson

When MGM lost Deanna Durbin to Universal, urgent instructions went out to the studio's talent scouts to find another girl soprano (every studio wanted a Durbin and Universal itself signed two more both as insurance and to prevent other studios getting them, Gloria Jean and Susanna Foster; but no one wanted one as much as Louis B. Mayer). The result was Kathryn Grayson, born in 1923 in Winston-Salem, North Carolina, and then still in high school. The official publicity line was that she used to wander on to the deserted stage of the St Louis Opera House and sing, and was one day heard by the star of the company who coached her and introduced her to an MGM executive. At all events, MGM was in such a hurry that she was signed without a test; but though her youth was an asset she was kept under wraps for two years being trained. In the end, she was launched tentatively – like other MGM hopefuls – as one of Mickey Rooney's girlfriends (actually in the title-role) in *Andy Hardy's Private Secretary* (41). (Rooney says in his autobiography that he wanted to date her in real life, but she had a friend among the top executives.) The company continued to doubt her appeal and put her into supporting parts: *The Vanishing Virginian* starring Frank Morgan and *Rio Rita* (42) with Abbott and Costello, an updating of the old musical with fifth columnists instead of bandits.

Finally, *Seven Sweethearts* was fashioned to do for her what *Three Smart Girls* had done for Durbin, but this family musical – directed by Frank Borzage – was overly cute for public taste; so it was not till *Thousands Cheer* (43) that audiences were much aware of Grayson. She was with Gene Kelly in the story which framed the turns by the studio's big stars. MGM liked the teaming with Kelly, but not too much, presumably, because it was two years before *Anchors Aweigh* (45) was released. She guested in both *Ziegfeld Follies* (46) and *Till the Clouds Roll By*, in the latter in the 'Show Boat' sequence with Tony Martin, in between which she co-starred with June Allyson as *Two Sisters From Boston* – working in a Bowery saloon. Jimmy Durante was their boss and he was also a solid prop in *It Happened in Brooklyn* (47). Frank Sinatra was in that, and he and Grayson were teamed, even less felicitiously, in *The Kissing Bandit* (48), one of MGM's all-time flops.

Many of Grayson's films had a rough passage at the box-office and because MGM used her only about once a year it must be concluded that she never achieved any marked degree of popularity. Both *That Midnight Kiss* (49) and *The Toast of New Orleans* (50) did poorly – till co-star Mario Lanza became popular and they were reissued on the strength of his appeal. A comedy with Van Johnson, *Grounds for Marriage*, quickly disappeared from view.

Her chance was to come, however, as the

In the great age of MGM musicals Kathryn Grayson was an asset, for she was pretty, she could sing a sweet soprano, and she could play both demure maidens and sophisticated ladies: but unlike her rivals at the same studio, Jane Powell and Ann Blyth, she seemed unable to lose that hint of archness which marred her work. That their films are still shown is comment enough on the fact that their film careers finished as that great age declined.

MGM musical was to turn towards the operette; and of all the stars under contract she was the most suitable to play the winsome soprano heroine of *Show Boat* (51) – or at least the studio thought so, despite her failure with the songs some years previously. Said 'Time Magazine': 'Actress Grayson is less than entrancing as the belle of the Cotton Blossom.' Howard Keel co-starred and they were teamed again in another lush piece, *Lovely to Look At* (52). Grayson, however, was complaining about the material she was offered and stated that she wanted to leave Metro (her salary at this time was $4,000 a week). She was loaned to WB for a couple of films, *The Desert Song* (53) with Gordon MacRae and *So This is Love*, as Grace Moore in this biopic. The 'MFB' found her acting 'coy and mannered', which was true, alas, throughout her career, though she was somewhat better, cast against type, as the tantrum-prone actress in *Kiss Me Kate*, again with Keel. In fact, MGM were so pleased with her that they announced her for musical versions of *Trilby* and *Camille*, and for *Brigadoon*; but *Kate* was the last film under her contract and she did not film for that studio again.

Or hardly anybody. Paramount engaged her to co-star in *The Vagabond King* (56) with Oreste (Kirkop), a singer whom they were launching with a great show of publicity: 'Remember the name – you'll never forget the voice.' Both film and Oreste disappeared with record speed, which neither Grayson nor Paramount found very encouraging. She went into semi-retirement, emerging from time to time for tent musicals, summer stock, TV, nightclubs – and opera ('La Traviata' – Phoenix, Arizona, in 1960). Rumours of a film come-back were confirmed in 1977 when she was reported making *How I Lay Me Down to Sleep*: but she did not.

Her first husband was actor John Shelton (1940–46) and the second Johnny Johnston, the singer (1947–51).

Sydney Greenstreet

In all movie-lore, there are probably few lines as well recalled (if not always accurately) as those spoken by Sydney Greenstreet to Bogart in *The Maltese Falcon*: following his jovial laugh – more like a farmyard grunt – 'By gad, sir, you're a one, you're an amazing character' and his deceptively good-humoured, 'I'm a man who likes to talk to a man who likes to talk.' Greenstreet is one of the great classic villains and was so recognized in his lifetime: an urbane fat man, a favourite client of the *maître d'* in all the best restaurants in this world and the underworld. The devil alone knew what sinister schemes were being plotted within those mounds of flesh or how quickly the bon viveur's smile could fade when frustrated.

Like many of the best character actors, he came to films after a lifetime in the theatre. He was born in Sandwich, Kent, in 1879, the son of a leather-merchant. He began his career as a tea-planter in Ceylon, but abandoned that after two years when there was a slump in the market. In Britain, he did a number of jobs, including managing a brewery. But he wanted to act and studied under Ben Greet; he made his début as the murderer in 'Sherlock Holmes' in Ramsgate in 1902. He went to the US with Greet in 1904 and remained there for the rest of his life, except for visits. With Greet, he was a notable Sir Toby Belch. He made his Broadway début in 'Everyman' (04), then toured Canada and parts of Europe. In 1908 he toured with Julia Marlowe in 'The Goddess of Reason'. Among his other appearances: 'Lady Windermere's Fan' (13), 'The Merry Wives of Windsor' (16), with Beerbohm Tree; 'The Rainbow Girl' (18, in which year he married); 'The Student Prince' (25); 'Much Ado About Nothing', as Dogberry, on tour; on tour, 1928–29, with Mrs Fiske; 'R.U.R.' (30); 'Lysistrata', with Miriam Hopkins; 'The Admirable Crichton', with Walter Huston; and 'Roberta' (33). Then he joined the Lunts in 'Idiot's Delight' and remained with them at the Theater Guild till he entered films. He went with them to London in 1938, in 'Amphitryon 38', and was with them in Los Angeles on tour in 'There Shall Be No Night' when John Huston saw him and asked him to play Mr Guttman in *The Maltese Falcon* (41), the ruthless cosmopolitan who would do almost anything to get hold of that valuable reliquary, and a possibly homosexual one (there is something over-familiar in the way he squeezes Bogart's arm on first meeting).

He was well received and Warners signed him to a long-term contract. They wasted him in *They Died With Their Boots On*, as General Winfield Scott, but allowed him another full-scale portrait of villainy, again Bogart's enemy, in *Across the Pacific* (42), a pro-Japanese fellow traveller (it was set before the war). Said the 'New York Times' 'Mr Greenwood is entirely an enigma – malefic yet dignified, urbane and full of enviable refinement, yet hard and unpredictable underneath.' He had a brief role in another Bogart vehicle, *Casablanca*, as a rival saloon-keeper

Greenstreet and Ingrid Bergman in Casablanca *(42).*

with illegal connections. Also in that, as in *The Maltese Falcon*, was Peter Lorre and Warners featured them again in *Background to Danger* (43), Lorre as a Russian agent, Greenstreet as an agent provocateur working for the Nazis (in Turkey). After that, it was often a question of Wherever Sydney Goes, Mr Lorre is bound to follow. They were both in *Passage to Marseilles* (44), again with Bogart, with Greenstreet as a pro-Vichy French colonial governor. He played the Ultimate Examiner in *Between Two Worlds* and was then matched against Lorre in the good film version of Eric Ambler's clever thriller *The Mask of Dimitrios* – Greenstreet was the villain, cropping up inopportunely and importunate in the most unlikely places. They were the *Conspirators*, plotting along with Dutch guerrilla Paul Henreid in Lisbon; and they appeared, as themselves, in *Hollywood Canteen*.

Greenstreet longed to play comedy and was pleased when he was loaned, along with Ida Lupino, to play in *Pillow to Post* (45), where he was a colonel staying for health reasons in a tourist camp. But it was not very good. He was a psychiatrist, the suspicious friend of murderer Bogart in *Conflict* and was Barbara Stanwyck's editor-boss in *Christmas in Connecticut*. Then: *Three Strangers* (46), as an embezzler, locked in unholy alliance with Lorre and Geraldine Fitzgerald; the unforgettable *Devotion*, made a couple of years earlier, as Thackeray; *The Verdict*, with Lorre, as an Edwardian Scotland Yard inspector, predictably working in swirling fog; *That Way With Women* (47), another dim comedy, a remake of *The Millionaire*, in George Arliss's old part, but with the emphasis shifted to the top-billed Dane Clark; and *The Hucksters*, at MGM with Clark Gable, as a testy, vicious-tempered, soap tycoon. He was loaned out again to play another magnate, losing his young wife, Lucille Bremmer, to *Ruthless* (48) Zachary Scott; and was then one of the great villains of literature, Count Fosco, in Warners' Hollywoody, eccentric – but still enjoyable – version of *The Woman in White*. On loan, he was a detective in *The Velvet Touch*; and then a death's-head politician, the lethal power behind-the-scenes of a Southern town, *Flamingo Road* (49).

After playing himself in *It's a Great Feeling* he was loaned again to Metro for *Malaya*, playing the Dutchman, a saloon-keeper with wide-ranging connections. It completed his contract. In 1952 he announced his retirement, but indicated that he might be willing to carry on if he was offered a good comedy role. He died two years later, in 1954.

Joan Greenwood

Think of Kristin Scott Thomas in the disastrous film of Evelyn Waugh's *A Handful of Dust*: she is supposed to be a covetous, scheming, selfish bitch, a silly little ninny and absolutely adorable all at the same time. Joan Greenwood could have played her effortlessly and indeed did have a similar role in *Kind Hearts and Coronets*. The British cinema has nurtured so few talents of her order that she was hugely missed during the latter part of her career. 'That formidable enchantress,' Frank Marcus once called her. She was not, of course, of the stuff of which British female stars were made: she had sex appeal, style and a striking individuality. She had a husky voice that liked to pounce on certain vowels, speaking her lines, as Karel Reisz said once, 'as if she dimly suspected some hidden menace in them which she can't quite identify' – 'Variety' once described it as 'one of the wonders of the modern world'. She was of diminutive stature and moved like a cat – to watch her sit down is like watching a cat settle itself, as she wittily poses hands, feet, knees and elbows. Obviously, she was mannered, but her range was by no means narrow. With all the fastidiousness, the strange enquiring stare, the voice and the exquisite postures, this was an actress who played many parts, all of them beautifully.

She was born in Chelsea in 1921 and studied at RADA. She made her stage début in 'Le Malade Imaginaire' at the Apollo in 1938 and continued in the West End, in among other plays, 'Peter Pan' (as Wendy) and 'The Women'. Her first three films were undistinguished: *John Smith Wakes Up* (40), wartime propaganda directed by Jiri Weiss, the refugee Czech director; *My Wife's Family* (41), a version of the old farce; and *He Found a Star*. In all of them she played a child. In Leslie Howard's *The Gentle Sex* (42) she was old enough to be in the ATS (a very small part), but she was back in a gym-slip for *They Knew Mr Knight* (44), a family drama. She continued to work in the theatre, including a season at Worthing rep and a spell with Donald Wolfit's company; in 1945, at Oxford, she played Lady Teazle, Cleopatra and Norah in 'A Doll's House'.

British National gave her her first star role in pictures. This was a minor company with ideas above its station; its films were mainly panned, but *Latin Quarter* (46) was quite cordially received, an 'atmospheric' melodrama set in a phoney Paris. Derrick de Marney was a sculptor and Greenwood his mysterious model. Sydney Box liked her and cast her as *A Girl in a Million*, a not disagreeable comedy about a mute girl in a household of bachelors (the joke was that when she was cured she could not stop talking).

Box then took over production at the Rank studios and Greenwood signed a Rank contract. Her first film for them was an extremely feeble smuggling story, *The Man Within*, with Michael Redgrave. *The October Man* (47) was much better, an Eric Ambler story about an amnesiac (John Mills). Greenwood was the girl who helps him, from which it was a plummet to *The White Unicorn*, where she was poor and Margaret Lockwood was rich

Joan Greenwood – an MGM portrait taken in 1955.

but they still had the same problems underneath. Ealing, which frequently used the best of the Rank star stable (and the choice was not wide), then came to her rescue – though the part had been intended for Mai Zetterling till she became pregnant. Perhaps for that reason Greenwood did not seem at ease, but it was a stolid affair, *Saraband for Dead Lovers* (48), with spectacle smothering the love story of George I's consort and Koenigsmark (Stewart Granger). She was perfectly cast as Lady Caroline Lamb in *The Bad Lord Byron* (49) – Dennis Price – but the film itself defied belief – and received some of the worst notices of any film ever made.

Ealing, however, then put her into two of three comedies which revolutionized British film humour: *Whisky Galore*, as a Scots lassie; and *Kind Hearts and Coronets*, as the wife of one of the Alec Guinnesses, a *fin-de-siècle* comedy of manners that provided her with the perfect setting. *Flesh and Blood* (50) was another period piece and she was wilful and seductive – but it was infinitely less rewarding. She returned to Ealing for another fine comedy with Guinness, *The Man in the White Suit* (51), as the admiring and eccentric heroine. *Young Wives' Tale* was much more modest stuff, but gave her one of her best film parts, that of a dizzy young wife (she had done it on the stage). Then she took it into her head to go off to France to play a luscious lady burglar in *La Passe Muraille/Mr Peek-a-Boo* (52), filmed in French and English, with Bourvil – but it was not up to the standard to get the British bookings its promoters hoped for. There was another good part – Gwendolen in *The Importance of Being Earnest* – and she was good in this curate's egg of a film. Her reading of '. . . I asked for bread and butter and you have given me cake', climaxing the one delightful sequence (Dorothy Tutin was Cecily), rendered this the definitive Gwendolen.

She was similarly fortunate with *Knave of Hearts/Monsieur Ripois* (54), singularly touching as the suburban girl seduced and then abandoned by Gérard Philipe, from which she returned to the aristocracy for

Gérard Philipe and Joan Greenwood in Knave of Hearts/Monsieur Ripois *(54) ; and Miss Greenwood with Stewart Granger in* Moonfleet *(55). Both were among the rarer movie-going pleasures of the time – and both were poorly received by the press.*

Ealing's *Father Brown* with Guinness. It was a smallish part and so was her mocking villainess in *Moonfleet* (55) with Stewart Granger; when John Houseman was asked why he had brought her all the way to Hollywood for that, he said he had wanted the role played with style. MGM threw the film away and equally cold-shouldered was *Stage Struck* (57) with Henry Fonda, in which she was very funny as a Broadway actress *à la* Tallulah. Americans also saw her on TV with Maurice Evans in 'Man and Superman' (56) and on Broadway in 'The Confidential Clerk' (54). British stage appearances during the decade included 'Bell, Book and Candle' (55), taking over from Lilli Palmer; and Nigel Dennis's 'Cards of Identity' and 'Lysistrata' (57), both at the Royal Court. She also appeared in 'A Doll's House' (54) in Helsinki and Copenhagen. In 1960 she was an adorable *femme fatale* in 'The Grass is Greener' and four years later was a surprisingly convincing Hedda in the best interpretation of that play that London has seen.

In 1959 she married André Morell, an agreeable supporting actor, and she later became a mother. She had never been a career actress, but with marriage – as with many other good actresses – she seemed no longer to care about status and appeared frequently on TV and in stock productions in the provinces. London stage apperances included revivals of 'Fallen Angels' (67) and 'The Chalk Garden' (71). In films, she was in a Charles Schneer version of Jules Verne, *The Mysterious Island* (62), deliciously incongruous as a lady companion; *The Amorous Prawn*, a dizzy milady once more in an inept farce; *Tom Jones* (63), as one of Albert Finney's willing conquests; and Disney's *The Moonspinners* (64), as Hayley Mills's aunt. After another gap she appeared in a flop film version of a flop West End play, *Girl/Boy* (71) though getting, with Michael Horden, the only kind words going in the press notices. For the next few years she appeared mostly on TV, returning to films to be wasted in *The Hound of the Baskervilles* (78) and *The Uncanny*. *The Water Babies* (79) was a Polish-British semi-animated version of Charles Kingsley's classic tale which got few bookings; it might have been better had it had more of James Mason, and of Greenwood and David Tomlinson as the eccentric aristocratic couple who befriend the orphan hero. *The Flame is Love* was an American tele-movie based on a novel by Barbara Cartland. Greenwood's last stage appearance, opposite Ralph Richardson, was a failure – 'The Understanding' (82). TV apperances included a BBC soap opera, 'Triangle', and an American mini-series, *Ellis Island* (84). She died in 1987 of a heart attack. Her son said she had her favourite roles and films but regarded her greatest achievement as becoming a popular and much loved star. Shown posthumously were two three-hour movies of *Little Dorrit* (87), which had started filming two years earlier: she played Mrs Clannam.

Alec Guinness

Apart from Olivier, none of the serious, highly regarded top-drawer British actors has had such a successful career in films as Alec Guinness. He has been in many very popular films, most of them enhanced by his performance. His versatility has been a byword over the past 30 years and perhaps it is the diffidence in his character which has prevented him from being a really magical actor.

He was born in 1914 in Marylebone, London. On leaving school he became a copywriter, but gave it up to study at Fay Compton's acting school; he made his first London appearance walking-on in 'Libel' (34) and later that year had a small part in 'Queer Cargo'. In 1935 John Gielgud took him into his company on the basis of a letter of introduction and it was Gielgud, he has said, who first gave him confidence. His training was impeccable; when he was not with Gielgud's company, he was probably at the Old Vic and it was there, 1938–39, that he began to play leading roles, including a full-length modern-dress Hamlet. He married around the same time. In 1939 in an off-West End hall he played Herbert Pocket in his own adaptation of 'Great Expectations'. He joined the navy in 1941, but was released to appear in New York in 'Flare Path': during its brief run 20th offered a screen test in Hollywood but he felt obliged to refuse.

His first postwar appearance was at the Lyric, Hammersmith, as Mitya in 'The Brothers Karamazov' (46); he rejoined the Vic and played, among other parts, the Fool to Olivier's Lear, the Dauphin in 'Saint Joan', Richard II and 'The Government Inspector'. Meanwhile, David Lean was filming *Great Expectations* (46) and remembered the Guinness Pocket; repeating, he got good notices and certainly was not hurt by opinions like Richard Winnington's, who called it 'probably the best British film yet made'. When Lean was preparing to film another novel of Dickens, *Oliver Twist* (48), Guinness begged for the role of Fagin. Lean considered him too light, but Guinness insisted on testing. He proved a loathsome villain – superbly made-up, but good in his own right. In Britain the film was a success in every way, but in the US it ran into conflict with Jewish societies – so fine notices did nothing to help it.

He signed to make one film a year for Rank. His feat in playing nine different characters in *Kind Hearts and Coronets* (49) made him nationally famous – considered more remarkable then than it seems on reviewing. They were all killed off by Dennis Price in order to succeed to the family seat, a comedy of murders both stylish and funny. It was Guinness's first film for Ealing Studios, with whom his name – particularly in the US – was to become synonymous. Ealing comedy was insular, demotic and surprising: the British comic tradition examined afresh as outrageous concepts were carried logically through – by the same old types but newly observed. Most of them were genuinely witty, even if they enshrine what later became cliché. He remained at Ealing to play a meek gardening correspondent involved with some Welsh rugger fans in *A Run for Your Money* and then appeared in some J.B. Priestley sentiment about a man with a few months to live, *Last Holiday* (50), looking more or less like his offscreen self. That was liked better in the US than in Britain, but *The Mudlark* was a disaster there, an American-backed film with Irene Dunne as Queen Victoria. Guinness's Disraeli won him a 'Picturegoer' Gold Medal. He returned to Ealing for two of their best and most popular comedies: *The Lavender Hill Mob* (51), as a myopic, lisping bank clerk who turns to organizing large-scale crime; and *The Man in the White Suit* with Joan Greenwood, as a boffin who invents a cloth that won't wear out. These really began the worldwide admiration and the period when he could do little wrong either commercially or artistically. In 1951 he was Britain's favourite British star, and fifth of all box-office stars – after Bob Hope, James Stewart, John Wayne and Abbott and Costello.

Alec Guinness as bigamist and celibate: top, with Celia Johnson, one of his two wives in The Captain's Paradise *(53) ; and in the title-role of* Father Brown *(54), battling wits with mastercrook Peter Finch.*

Unlikely bank-robbers: Alec Guinness and Stanley Holloway, heads of The Lavender Hill Mob *(51). The comedies which Guinness made for Ealing depended a great deal on the unlikely.*

He was Arnold Bennett's *The Card* (52), very happily, but looked ill at ease in a tedious war picture he did as a change of pace, *The Malta Story* (53). *The Captain's Paradise* was, despite a virtually witless script, the first of his films to be widely distributed in the US – mainly because Yvonne de Carlo was one of his wives (Celia Johnson was the one in the other port). *Father Brown* (54), G.K. Chesterton's impish clerical detective (impish at least in this interpretation), provided another civilized entertainment, but, still at Ealing, their *To Paris With Love* was a real ham-fisted job. *The Prisoner* (55), with Jack Hawkins, was a stark if banal drama based on the imprisonment of Cardinal Mindzenty which he had recently done on the stage. Other theatre work of this period: 'The Cocktail Party' (50), in Edinburgh and New York; 'Hamlet' (51), 'Richard III' (53) at Stratford, Ontario; and Feydeau's 'Hotel Paradiso' (56).

After that he devoted himself to films for four years. He was knighted in 1959.

The Ladykillers proved that there was still life in the old Ealing. With a clever script by William Rose, Guinness as a crook made up as something out of Charles Addams, plus a fine cast, it was and is a perfect *comédie noire* – about an inept, ill-assorted gang of burglars. He should then have done a film of *Arms and the Man*, but it fell through, just at the moment he was offered the part of a European princeling opposite Grace Kelly in MGM's *The Swan* (56), made in Hollywood. There was another Ealing comedy, *Barnacle Bill* (57), his only flop with that company; then, after Noël Coward turned the role down, David Lean engaged him to play the colonel in *The Bridge on the River Kwai*, based on Pierre Boulle's novel about the building of the Burma railway. The role was virtually unplayable, that of a commander who stands up to the Japs and wins the loyalty of his men – but he won a Best Actor Oscar and the New York critics' award. The film, indeed, was hugely popular with a press and public anxious to believe that war and service life were just like that.

He was in one of the last films Ealing made, *The Scapegoat* (59), co-producing and playing a dual role, a weak mystery by Daphne du Maurier further diluted in this version. His relationship with Ealing concluded on a 'disappointing' note: 'I would have been willing to launch out into much harder and sharper things than they were willing to do.' Thus, he wrote the screenplay of Joyce Cary's novel *The Horse's Mouth* and played the lead: another attempt to stretch his talents, but its lovable rogue-hero-painter was not funny enough – by design – for audiences convinced that Guinness as an eccentric had to be funny; his performance did, however, win a prize at Venice. *Our Man in Havana* (60) was another version of a good book, Graham Greene's, but Carol Reed lacked the former mastery he had had of Greeneland; and Guinness's 'little man' impersonation had by now been overexposed. But his next performance was beyond his accepted range and possibly his most brilliant and moving characterization: the vain, blustering, dense, red-headed martinet CO of *Tunes of Glory*, from James Kennaway's Walpole-ish novel of rivalry in the Mess. John Mills was conventional as his opponent.

He returned to the stage in Rattigan's 'Ross', a chronicle of T.E. Lawrence, but left the cast to play a Jap in Hollywood, to Rosalind Russell's Jewish matron, in *A Majority of One* (61). It was damned by the press and thus marks a turning-point in his career, for hitherto he had been treated with infinite respect. Also, most of his subsequent film roles were in supporting parts and he was not, in general, considered an extraordinary supporting actor. Nor did he hold his old position in the theatre; in New York he had a success playing 'Dylan' (64) Thomas, but in London his Von Berg in Arthur Miller's 'Incident at Vichy' (66) was damply received. He appeared in drag in the modishly enigmatic 'Wise Child' (67), conceivably one of the worst plays in which any major actor ever appeared – and this just after being trounced for his Macbeth. He had repeatedly said that he would not appear on the stage again, so one must assume these plays were done for want of better screen offers.

Many of the films he now selected to do were unfortunate. He gave a good performance as a weak-willed but kindly captain savaged by the evil Dirk Bogarde in *H.M.S.*

Some more portraits in the Guinness gallery: right, as the colonel in The Bridge on the River Kwai *(57); below, as the commanding officer in* Tunes of Glory *(60), with Alec McCowen, Alan Cuthbertson and John Mills; and far right, in* Star Wars *(77).*

Defiant (62) and was superb as the wily Feisal in *Lawrence of Arabia*; but he was ineffectual as another ruler, Marcus Aurelius in *The Fall of the Roman Empire* (63) – a mighty title for a minuscule epic. He played a German nutcase in *Situation Hopeless But Not Serious*, a version of Robert Shaw's 'The Hiding Place', which was hardly shown anywhere; and he was poor in a small role, as a commissar, in Lean's *Doctor Zhivago* (65). He made a film of *Hotel Paradiso* (66) under the direction of Peter Glenville, who directed it on stage, but it got dreadful reviews in the US and does not appear to have had more than a couple of – belated – showings in Britain. *The Quiller Memorandum* was just another spy film; and *The Comedians* (67) made another such out of Greene's novel – Greene did the screenplay himself, but Glenville again directed. On the stage Guinness appeared in a revival of 'The Cocktail Party' and did not film again till *Cromwell* (70) as the King, looking right but letting a Scots accent come and go; and *Scrooge*, as Marley's Ghost. An on-set sprain kept him inactive for more than a year, when he accepted a role declined by Laurence Olivier, the Pope in *Brother Sun and Sister Moon* (72), Zeffirelli's personal account of Saint Francis of Assisi. Filming over, Guinness played a blind man in John Mortimer's 'A Voyage Round My Father'. Other stage work included two plays by Alan Bennett, 'Habeas Corpus' in 1973 and 'The Old Country' in 1977. He played Hitler in *Hitler: The Last Ten Days* (73), but before it opened expressed 'disappointment. I thought at the time it was my best work.' Few saw it; and though many went to *Murder by Death* (76) it was also dreadful – Neil Simon's idea of spoofing old detective stories. It was filmed in Hollywood, with several names, and Guinness was a blind butler – but without an iota of the wit he had brought to his grotesque in *The Lady Killers*.

He has been the only major British actor to turn down cameo roles (in *The Greatest Story Ever Told, The Battle of Britain*, etc.) because he disapproves of star-spotting; and he is the only major British actor to become a dollar millionaire – by virtue of his participation in *Star Wars* (77). He had turned down the role of the warrior knight/sage and George Lucas, producer and director, offered him a minute percentage – 2½ per cent – in gratitude for his eventual acceptance: but the film's gross was so huge that that percentage made Guinness wealthy. In terms of success, everything about the film – at the time the biggest money-maker in cinema's history – is exceptional, all the more so since it must be one of the most mindless of all science-fiction tales. In 1980 he was honoured with a special Oscar.

On reason for rejecting *Star Wars* was that he was killed halfway through, but now gratitude found him reprising the role, if only of brief footage, in the sequel, *The Empire Strikes Back* (80) – able to do so, of course, because the action pre-dated it. He played an old sea-dog in *Raise the Titanic*, the culmination of all Lew Grade's dreams of becoming a movie mogul, i.e. it was even worse than the awful films he had produced till then and lost even more money, driving him out of the business. Guinness's scenes, dotted throughout the film, relieved the monotony – and it was good to see him in a leading role again, as the grandfather in *Little Lord Fauntleroy*, an American tele-movie which was shown in some foreign cinemas. But he returned to a cameo role in *Lovesick* (83), as a Sigmund Freud materializing to advise the horrendously unfunny Dudley Moore in perhaps Guinness's poorest film. *The Return of the Jedi* was a further sequel to *Star Wars* – and a third gigantic hit. If these ventures were hardly worthy of this actor, he had meanwhile had a huge success playing John Le Carré's spy in *Tinker, Tailor, Soldier, Spy* in 1979 and *Smiley's People* in 1982, both BBC mini-series. In 1985 he published his autobiography, 'Blessings in Disguise', in which he forestalled the universally bad notices (the book was written before the film came out) for his performance in *A Passage to India* (84): 'the fact that my bizarre Hindu song and dance were cut. . . left me presenting Professor Godber as a comic-cuts character without the necessary oriental mystery.' He mentioned that it was his sixth film with David Lean, that they had got along 'swimmingly' on three but not on the others. He played the title-role in a British tele-movie, *Monsignor Quixote* (85), Graham Greene's unenchanting reworking of Zorba the Greek meets Don Camillo. The very long, two-part *Little Dorrit* (87) must have been a more satisfying credit, for he played alongside one of his own favourite actors, Cyril Cusack, and his performance as William Dorrit was regarded as his best film work in many years. He was personally good in *A Handful of Dust* (88), but came in too late to save it. He played the part of the eccentric jungle-dwelling Mr Todd who makes the unfortunate Tony Last (James Wilby) read Dickens out loud for the rest of his days. Waugh's bitter novel was interpreted rather badly in the film, offering only drippy nostalgia rather than anger and wit. Later in the year Guinness returned to the stage in 'A Walk in the Woods', a US-Soviet duologue with Edward Herrmann.

Gene Hackman

'Dependable' was a good word to use about Gene Hackman as a supporting actor (and John Simon did, about his performance in *Downhill Racer*). And then, by virtue of a role turned down by at least seven other actors and its accompanying Oscar, he became a star. His acting, if anything, became more finely honed – but stardom brought its problems. As Bart Mills wrote in London in the 'Guardian', 'It's not easy being a star who knows he has no right to be a star. Gene Hackman never got near the honey pot till he was past 40. He has about as much sex appeal as your balding brother-in-law. He dreams fondly of retiring. He's aware that somebody, somewhere made a big mistake.' The mistakes, as it happened, were all his.

He was born in Danville, Illinois, in 1930 and ran away from home at 16 to join the Marines, to which he returned later for the Korean War. He studied journalism at the University of Illinois and went into TV as technician and administrator; but decided to study acting – at a drama school in Pasadena, with Dustin Hoffman also in the cast. It took time to get a Broadway role; he made his name off-Broadway in Irwin Shaw's 'Children at their Games', which won him the Clarence Derwent award for a supporting actor. He progressed, via 'Barefoot in the Park', to a lead role in 'Any Wednesday' in 1964. Meanwhile, he had married, in 1956, Fay Maltese and had made his first film, *Mad Dog Call* (61), in a small role as a cop in a dud B picture.

Broadway leads, however, led to a goodish supporting role in *Lilith* (64), which starred Warren Beatty; and he was also seen to advantage in *Hawaii* (66), as the doctor-priest who becomes a successful priest in those islands. At Warner Bros. he was in *A Covenant with Death* and they kept him on to play a sergeant in a flop World War II tale, *First to Fight* (67). Hoffman got him the role of Mr Robinson in *The Graduate*, but he was sacked during rehearsals. Then Beatty chose him to play his brother in *Bonnie and Clyde*: an Oscar nomination and that film's success brought him to the forefront of supporting actors – but he certainly was not helped by *Banning*, a story of golf-pros with Robert Wagner. *Shadow on the Land* (68) was made for TV; and there were two films starring Jim Brown, *The Split*, in which Hackman was a crooked detective, and *Riot* (69), upped to second billing as the convict who started it. He shared billing with Robert Redford on *Downhill Racer*, as the team's coach, and with Burt Lancaster on *The Gypsy Moths*, as the old hand sky-diver. Obviously very active, he was an astronaut in *Marooned*, which starred Gregory Peck.

He received another Supporting Oscar nomination for *I Never Sang for My Father* (70), but it was in fact the leading role (and a difficult one which he played superbly) – that of a middle-aged man worrying about his father's becoming a widower and dying. That was not a subject the public found attractive and Gilbert Cates's film was not seen as widely as it should have been. *Doctors' Wives* (71) was one of Hackman's films that he has never seen – in common with most of the world; he was a doctor who forgives wife Rachel Roberts after she has confessed to a lesbian affair. He was a Texas cattle baron in *The Hunting Party*, with Oliver Reed, filmed in Spain. And he won his Best Actor Oscar for playing Popeye Doyle, a weary, dogged and sadistic detective, in *The French Connection*; the film itself, which in the old days would have been a good B-picture thriller, walked off with Best Picture Oscar. Since it took a while for it to build into a success, Hackman had done before the Oscar both *Cisco Pike* (72), as another corrupt cop, out to get rock star Kris Kristofferson; and *Prime Cut*, in which Lee Marvin was out to nail him – as a gangland boss who grounds his opponents into sausages. These are two more of his films he has not seen.

After the Oscar, he elected to do a popular 'family' film, *The Poseidon Adventure*, as the Reverend who leads the passengers to safety: the success of that brought him in at No 3 at the box-office that year. Unfortunately, the exhibitors were wrong: the public did not go to *Scarecrow* (73), with Al Pacino, and described by Hackman as 'a combination of *Of Mice and Men* and *Midnight Cowboy*'; nor, despite admiring notices, to Coppola's essentially phoney *The Conversation* (74); nor to *Zandy's Bride*. In the Coppola film Hackman was head of a bugging operation; in the other he was Zandy and Liv Ullmann was his immigrant bride. He did a guest stint in *Young Frankenstein* and was a private eye in Arthur Penn's part-brilliant *Night Moves* (75), made a year earlier but held up since Warners were 'uncertain' about it. In the event the public did not care for it, or for *Bite the Bullet*, in which Hackman was a compassionate cowboy; but they liked *The French Connection II* well enough for him to come in at No 10 that year at the box-office. Again the exhibitors were wrong: *Lucky Lady* laid a gigantic egg at the box-office. When at the last minute George Segal ankled the role, Hackman's agent managed to get him an astronomical $1,250,000 – as against Burt Reynolds's $500,000 and Liza Minnelli's $350,000.

The following year Hackman's salary was reported at $700,000 – which is presumably what he got for his role as an escaping convict in *The Domino Principle* (77), another flop (it was hardly seen overseas). However, when Coppola was badly needing names to help him get going with *Apocalypse Now*, Hackman's demanding price was $2 million – according to Joe Levine, who was happy to pay Hackman

The Conversation *(74) was an unsatisfactory film about bugging devices, but Gene Hackman was superb as the lonely man who ran the operation.*

whatever he was demanding for his cameo as a Polish officer in *A Bridge Too Far*. It was a British company prepared to pay out for *March or Die*, in which Hackman was a Foreign Legion major; and the money-happy Salkinds paid him $2 million for another British film, *Superman* (78), in which he was that gentleman's eccentric opponent. The Foreign Legion film was another commercial failure. It is not surprising that there were virtually no reports of Hollywood offers and late in 1978 Hackman was reported as saying that he wanted to go back to work. In retrospect it is a shame about that Oscar, and about Hackman's expressed wish to play romantic roles: we lost an excellent character actor, but did not gain a star.

After *Superman II* (80) he embarked upon what he regarded as his 'last chance', *All Night Long* (81), playing the night manager of a supermarket who puts his marriage into jeopardy by embarking on an affair with Barbra Streisand. It did not play long in cinemas. Unbilled and well down the cast-list he had two scenes as a New York newspaper editor in Beatty's *Reds*, but 'Warren always calls me up for these things because I owe him'. Top-billed, he had a splendid role in *Eureka* (83), as a Canadian gold prospector who becomes very rich in the Caribbean and ends up very dead in Florida – or so did Sir Harry Oates, on whose unsolved murder in 1943 the script was based: but alas, the obfuscation of this one was not helped by the direction. Said the producer, Jeremy Thomas, 'It's the negative Midas touch. How can anyone deny that there is an audience for a Nik Roeg film starring Hackman, Rutger Hauer and Teresa Russell', trying to explain why bookings were few (a fate met by most of Roeg's films). UA, who produced, refused to release it in the US, but its Classics division got it some dates two years later. If Hackman looked washed up, he played a role others would not touch in *Under Fire* – the veteran 'Time Magazine' war correspondent who loses the girl (Joanna Cassidy) to a colleague (Nick Nolte) and who is killed off well before the end. But it was an exceptional film, as directed by Roger Spottiswoode, and did much to revive Hackman's career.

He was in an action film, *Uncommon Valor*, as an army veteran leading others to look for his son in the POW camps of Laos, and then in an old-fashioned weepie, *Misunderstood* (84), as a diplomat (the film was made in Tunisia, in 1982) too preoccupied with work and the death of his wife to notice that his son (Henry Thomas) needs him. The source was Florence Montgomery's 'classic' novel, last filmed in Italy in 1967 with Anthony Quayle, when the setting was Florence. Bookings were again limited; and when every distributor turned down Bud Yorkin's *Twice in a Lifetime* (85) he sold it individually after fine notices and business. But British critics were unimpressed – significantly, for author Colin Welland had taken an old British TV play and reset it among Seattle steelworkers. Hackman played a middle-aged man leaving his wife (Ellen Burstyn) for a younger woman (Ann-Margret). In Arthur Penn's thriller *Target* he was combing Europe for his kidnapped wife, helped by his grown-up son (Matt Dillon). Both *Power* (86) and *Hoosiers* were underrated: Lumet directed the first, in which Hackman was former mentor to media figure Richard Gere, while in the second he was a bellicose basketball coach. After *Superman IV: The Quest for Peace* (87) – he missed out on Number Three – he played Charles Laughton's old role in the remake of *The Big Clock*, now titled *No Way Out*, and like his predecessor relishing his villainy as he tries to pin a murder he has committed on to one of his Pentagon employees.

It is not quite clear why Gene Hackman was such a poor villain in Superman *(78), or why the scenes involving him were so drear: much of it was, however, enchanting, putting it light-years ahead of the* Star Wars *illustrated on page 231.*

He was now working harder, even, than Michael Caine and in general in much better films: *Split Decisions* (88), as the oldest of three generations of Irish working-class prizefighters; *Full Moon in Blue Water*, as a saloon owner who cannot reconcile himself to the death of his wife; *BAT-21* with Danny Glover, as an intelligence man stuck in the Malaysian jungle; *Another Woman*, as a figure in Gena Rowlands's past; and *Mississippi Burning*, in which he and Willem Dafoe are FBI men investigating down there in the 50s. To come are: *I Banchieri di Dio/Bankers of God* with Gian Maria Volonte as Calvi and Cardinal Marcinkus; and *The Von Metz Incident*.

Julie Harris

Probably the only people who have not minded the infrequency of Julie Harris's film appearances are New York theatregoers. In that city, one is likely to find her on the boards gratifyingly often. She is not perhaps a great actress, but she is perhaps a witch, a skinny Lorelei calling to the smitten with a giggle and a coo like a love-sick dove. She casts a spell in films as well, but her parts have been uneven.

She was born in Grosse Pointe, a suburb of Detroit, in 1925 and began acting at high school. She acted at summer camp and studied for the stage in Steamboat Springs, Colorado, in New York and at the Yale Drama School; she eventually got a small part in 'It's a Gift' (45), which did not run. She was taken on by the visiting Old Vic Co. to walk-on and got small parts in 'Alice in Wonderland', as the White Rabbit, and Michael Redgrave's 'Macbeth' (48), among other plays. She studied at the Actors' Studio and did a play with them which ran a week, 'Sundown Point'; but Harold Clurman saw it and many moons later offered her the role of Frankie in 'The Member of the Wedding' (50), an adaptation of Carson McCullers's novel about a fey, lonely pre-adolescent girl, her young friend John Henry (Brandon de Wilde) and the Negro mammy (Ethel Waters). It ran for over a year. She was the toast of Broadway again with her next play, 'I Am a Camera' (51), John Van Druten's version of two of Christopher Isherwood's Berlin stories. After the run, she toured with it.

When Stanley Kramer came to film *The Member of the Wedding* (53), he engaged the stage cast and Fred Zinnermann to direct; given the material, none of them could have done better, but it was too slight and pixilated a piece to be of wide appeal. Dilys Powell saluted Harris's 'superb performance' and added that her 'extraordinary understanding of the restlessness, the uncertainty and the violence of closing childhood' made you forget that she was too old for the part. Harris returned to Broadway as Anouilh's Colombe and filmed again in *East of Eden* (55), as James Dean's buddy – their scenes together were played with an intimacy that was quite new to films. She was Joan of Arc in another Anouilh, 'The Lark', and then went to Britain to play Sally Bowles again in the film of *I Am a Camera* (56), a show-off performance entirely too good for the leading man (the greatest disparity of talents since Garbo and Taylor in *Camille*) and the shabby job made of the material. 'She is extravagantly mannered, never achieves an appropriate accent, and is cast in a milieu quite alien to the real Sally; but with her plain, cunning yet open

The Member of the Wedding *(53) was originally a novel and then a play. Re-creating their memorable stage performances were Brandon de Wilde, Julie Harris as the 12-year-old Frankie who dreamed about her sister's wedding, and Ethel Waters.*

Julie Harris in the poor film version of I Am a Camera *(56) – she was the only reason for seeing the film, but a good enough one.*

face and her responsive alertness, she is . . . the schoolgirl shocker with grubby hands and green fingernails, the would-be whore who is always a bit surprised when it happens' (David Robinson). The film, because it featured this happy half-whore and an abortion, was denied a Production Code seal in the US, which limited its commercial chances.

On Broadway, she did 'The Country Wife' (58) and 'The Warm Peninsula' (59). At Stratford, Ontario, she played Blanche in 'King John' and Juliet (60); on Broadway she had a qualified success in 'Little Moon of Alban' (which she had done earlier on TV with George Peppard and Christopher Plummer) and a big one in 'A Shot in the Dark' (61). Her only movies during this period were resolutely mediocre: *The Truth About Women* (58), a 'comedy' with Laurence Harvey; and *Sally's Irish Rogue*, made in Ireland, as a poacher's daughter and surrounded by the Abbey Players. She tried again some years later: *Requiem for a Heavy-weight* (62), a delicate performance as the employment counsellor trying to help Anthony Quinn; and *The Haunting* (63), a mannered one as the victim of that manifestation – but, as directed by Robert Wise, the best ghost film in many a year.

In New York she played June Havoc in 'Marathon '33' and Ophelia; did a light comedy, 'Ready When You Are C.B.' and a musical, 'Skyscraper', a version of Elmer Rice's 'Dream Girl'. In films, she played supporting roles in *Harper* (66), with Paul Newman, and *You're a Big Boy Now* (67), in both as a neurotic spinster. She was married, but still neurotic, in *Reflections in a Golden Eye*, a strong and sensitive performance in another version of a novel by McCullers. Surprisingly, she turned up as the brains behind a gang of crooks (which included Jim Brown) in a dualler, *The Split* (68). On Broadway she won another clutch of Broadway awards for her performance in a smash comedy, 'Forty Carats'. *The House on Greenapple Road* (69) was made for cinemas, but went straight to TV. *The People Next Door* (70) had been originally a TV play, but it was a flop in cinemas, a drama about the generation gap, with Eli Wallach; director David Greene thought it so distorted after he had left it that he asked for his name to be removed. *How Awful About Allan*, for TV, was little better, a thriller in which she protected her blind neurotic brother, Anthony Perkins. Other times she was seen on TV included: 'The Good Fairy' (56), 'The Lark', 'Johnny Belinda.' 'Ethan Frome', 'A Doll's House', 'The Power and the Glory', 'Victoria Regina' and 'Pygmalion'. She returned to Broadway in 'And Miss Reardon Drinks a Little' (71) and was there again in 'The Last of Mrs Lincoln', 'In Praise of Love' and in a one-woman play about Emily Dickinson, 'The Belle of Amherst', which in 1977 brought about her fourth Tony Award and her London début. She continued to make the occasional film: *Home for the Holidays* (72) for TV, married to Walter Brennan, who is convinced that because she is much younger she is trying to murder him; *The Greatest Gift* (74) also for TV, with Glenn Ford; *The Hiding Place* (75), filmed in the Netherlands by Billy Graham's evangelical organization, as a courageous Christian woman who was sent to a concentration camp for helping the Jews (Miss Harris is herself Jewish); and *The Belljar* (79), Larry Peerce's wretched kitsch version of Sylvia Plath's harsh autobiographical novel. Harris played the mother, fighting a losing game against the Esther of Marilyn Hassett. In a mini-series, *Backstairs at the White House*, Harris was Mrs Taft, around which time she was involved in a rare (for her) Broadway disaster, 'Break a Leg', which closed after one performance.

The Gift was a tele-movie with Glenn Ford; and 'Under the Ilex', produced in St Louis in 1983, a play about Lytton Strachey (Leonard Frey) and Carrington. Staying literary, Harris was the sole player in *Brontë* (83), directed by Delbert Mann in Eire. A spell in 'Knott's Landings' from 1986 onwards was more mundane, but she left there for a return to the big screen in *Gorillas in the Mist* (88), but in a small role as an Africa-domiciled American woman who is a friend of Signourney Weaver. She toured in 'Driving Miss Daisy' and appeared in two tele-movies: *Too Good to Be True*, a remake of *Leave Her to Heaven*, in a supporting role; and *The Christmas Wife* opposite Jason Robards.

She was married, 1946–54, and remarried in 1954.

Richard Harris

The career of Richard Harris has been milestoned by a series of noisy headlines – nightclub squabbles, on-set brawls with actors he does not like. It would be tempting to assume that he takes seriously his usual on-screen role of rebel. Oddly, the industry has tolerated his peccadilloes without being compensated with either great reviews or a stampede to the box-office. That Harris was larger-than-life, a 'character', was evident, but it was not so immediately obvious on film. In a way, he crept up on us in stealth, like the great stars of the 30s, getting better and better, more authoritative, more interesting, more varied.

He was born in Limerick, Eire, in 1933, was educated at a Jesuit college and studied for the stage – RADA turned him down – at the London Academy of Music and Dramatic Art. He got his first chance immediately after leaving, in Joan Littlewood's production of 'The Quare Fellow' (56). He worked mainly with Littlewood's company over the next few years and established himself as a name in the West End production of 'The Ginger Man' in 1959. Meanwhile, he played a young Irish lover in a comedy with Kathleen Harrison, *Alive and Kicking* (58). Associated British, who produced, were so impressed that they signed him to a seven-year contract. (A year later he was reported as trying to get out of it; he made only one other film for them.) He got another part which required an Irish accent, in *Shake Hands With the Devil* (59), but it was small; then had a good part as the villain in *The Wreck of the Mary Deare*, as that ship's first mate, smiling sarcastically at Gary Cooper and Charlton Heston and, later, trying to harpoon them. He seized his chance and was uncommonly effective. Then he was a member of the IRA, Robert Mitchum's harum-scarum chum in *A Terrible Beauty* (60).

Associated British gave him second-billing, under Laurence Harvey, in *The Long and the Short and the Tall* (61), their poor version of Willis Hall's good play about some soldiers stranded in the jungle; he did a stereotype as the bullying corporal. He was somewhat more effectual in *The Guns of Navarone*, at which point MGM assigned him to play the leading mutineer, after Marlon Brando, in *Mutiny on the Bounty* (62). He did not get on with Brando *at all*, he told reporters, but in view of the quality of his performance, he would have done better to have kept quiet. He was certainly fine in *This Sporting Life* (63) – a strong performance, if not a very interesting

Richard Harris on a Northern rugger pitch; and getting married in Camelot. Left, in This Sporting Life *(63) ; and below, with Vanessa Redgrave in* Camelot *(67).*

one, as a North Country rebel, a rugger player. The film itself was a misanthropic and derivative attempt at a Great Tragic Love Story, with a heroine (Rachel Roberts) just as egotistical and humourless as the hero. Lindsay Anderson directed and the film was violently overpraised by British critics – and suffered accordingly at the box-office. It brought Harris an acting award at Cannes and to the attention of Antonioni, who cast him as Monica Vitti's long-suffering lover in *Il Deserto Rosso* (64). He loathed making it and, with some minor shots still to be done, refused to complete it; but his performance, though dubbed (by an Italian), adds much to the final effect of this hugely personal study of inertia within marriage. However, he did not dislike Italy and returned at once to do one of the episodes – 'Gli Amanti Celebri' – in *I Tre Volti* (65), the unsuccessful attempt to make a film star out of ex-Empress Soraya (he played her lover). The film does not seem to have reached beyond the frontier, despite other high-voltage talent (Antonioni directed the first episode; the third co-starred Alberto Sordi).

He went to Hollywood to co-star with Charlton Heston in *Major Dundee*, as his implacable foe, mean-eyed and tight-lipped – but was altogether too 'small' for the part. He was a Norwegian resistance leader in *The Heroes of Telemark*, co-starring with Kirk Douglas (with whom, reputedly, he got on as badly as with Brando and Heston). He then got involved in a couple of epics: *La Bibbia/The Bible . . . In the Beginning* (66), as Cain, a performance described by the 'MFB' as 'epileptic'; and *Hawaii*, as Julie Andrew's true light-of-love – a boorish performance and only lively beside that of Max von Sydow as her husband. Nor was he much at ease opposite Doris Day in a comedy, *Caprice* (67), which he considers the low point of his career. He auditioned for *Camelot* because, he said, he desperately wanted to play Arthur – and in the unhappy overblown circumstances was admirable. Indeed, the only time that dramatic musical worked as drama was in his performance, in his nobility, his idealism and his love for Guinevere (Vanessa Redgrave). More of it and the film might have done better at the box-office.

In 1968 he walked out of *Play Dirty* a few days before shooting and was replaced by Nigel Davenport. He also changed his mind about *Flap*, for which his salary was announced as $325,000 against 20 per cent of the gross. Anthony Quinn played the part. Nor did he do *Scrooge*, for which he was announced. He did do *The Molly Maguires* (69), with Sean Connery, a strong, sympathetic performance as the Pinkerton detective who infiltrates that band of rebels. Then he was *Cromwell* (70) for Ken Hughes, allowing

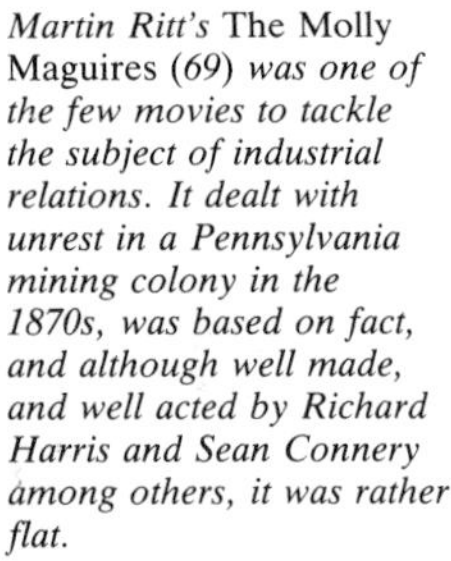

Martin Ritt's The Molly Maguires *(69) was one of the few movies to tackle the subject of industrial relations. It dealt with unrest in a Pennsylvania mining colony in the 1870s, was based on fact, and although well made, and well acted by Richard Harris and Sean Connery among others, it was rather flat.*

Hughes to realize a pet project. It was a dull child's guide to the Great Rebellion and not even – which might have justified it – historically accurate. Nothing in Harris's performance suggested he was the sort of man interested in democracy, or indeed anything. His Cromwell was at one extreme snarling cur and at the other hangdog in the soulful manner of Richard Burton; and there was nothing in between. Somewhat more usefully he played an English milord initiated as a member of the Sioux in *A Man Called Horse*, a pretentious Western.

He had announced some ambitious projects, including a *Hamlet* with Faye Dunaway and an *Antigone*. He produced and starred in *Bloomfield* (71), made on location in Israel, playing an ageing footballer. After a few days' shooting he took over from the Israeli director and he made of the material an inferior *Sporting Life*; when the film was booed at the Berlin Film Festival, he booed back. Then he starred in *A Man in the Wilderness*, once more a lone man against adversity, this time Nature's. On television he appeared to good effect as the hunch-backed artist in 'The Snow Goose', from Paul Gallico's bestseller, and then embarked on a concert tour, singing.

He was married (1957–69) to the Hon. Elizabeth Rees-Williams, who later married Rex Harrison. His second wife was Ann Turkel, who appeared in several of his films.

In 1972 he began *Riata* in Spain under the direction of Samuel Fuller from his own story, but it was abandoned after five weeks' shooting; Warner Bros. looked at the footage and sent in another director to complete it. It emerged as *The Deadly Trackers* (73) and sank. Harris was a widower bent on revenge. He was a bespectacled trouble-shooter in John Frankenheimer's daft film about the mobs, *99 and 44/100% Dead* (74), and the head of a bomb disposal unit on shipboad in *Juggernaut*. In *Echoes of Summer* (76) he was a writer – and the film's producer: but like all this batch it found little public or press favour. As King Richard he died early in *Robin and Marion*, leaving the rest of it to Sean Connery and getting special billing. *The Return of a Man Called Horse* was not one the public wanted; and Harris was probably glad to get the role of the doctor-'hero' vacated by Peter O'Toole in *The Cassandra Crossing* (77), ex-husband to Sophia Loren. He missed Bergman's *The Serpent's Egg* due to a virus and was further unlucky with two films virtually laughed off the screens of Britain, the part-cartoon *Gulliver's Travels* and *Golden Rendezvous*, which caused a mild controversy when it became known that money had not been forthcoming for a scene to make the plot intelligible (it was then filmed, but with little discernible improvement). In that year's round-up of films, John Coleman in the 'New Statesman' decided that he 'saw far too much of a fellow by the name of Richard Harris . . . His three expressions hardly changed.'

He was one of the mercenaries in *The Wild Geese* (78), after which he did *The Last Word* (79) with Karen Black, *Ravagers* with his wife and *A Game for Vultures*. While filming the latter in South Africa, the producer of *Golden Rendezvous* sued for 1.4 million rand (approx. $1½ million), the sum lost on production, he claimed, due to the actor's 'drinking habits'; he also sought to prevent him leaving the country. Harris counter-sued for a sum mentioned as $28 million, claiming, among other things, that he had been so cooperative that he had been asked to take over direction; and he was supported in his petition by the man who had directed. He sued, he said, because he wanted to protect his new salary of $1 million plus 10 per cent of the gross – this due, he said, to the success of *The Wild Geese* in he US. Interestingly enough, the producer of *Golden Rendezvous* did not file his claim till he had repeatedly failed to sell it in the US to either a distributor of a TV company. In fact, *The Wild Geese* bombed in the US, continuing a run of cinematic bad luck. There were to have been three films in Canada, but the third (*The Burning Bush*, with Christopher Plummer and David Warner) was shelved and then cancelled. The others should have been as lucky: *Your Ticket is No Longer Valid*, based on a Romain Gary novel, with Jeanne Moreau, Christopher Plummer and Harris as an impotent, impoverished tycoon, and *Highpoint* (80), which was anything but, with him as an out-of-work accountant mixed up with the CIA. That was re-edited at a cost of $2 million in 1982 and eventually reviewed by the trade press in 1984. Harris was at last in a film people heard about, *Tarzan the Ape Man* (81), even if they did not actually go to see it; he was Bo Derek's intrepid explorer father, a role played in wildly over the top manner. *Triumphs of a Man Called Horse*, another mis-titling, was a sequel to an earlier film; it was filmed in 1982 and eventually premièred on HBO in 1984. *Martin's Day* (85) was another Canadian venture, co-starring James Coburn.

In 1981, as his marriage was ending, he was invited to take over from the ailing Richard Burton in 'Camelot' and he has been playing Arthur intermittently ever since – on two American tours, in 1981 and 1985, in London for a year in 1982, for video (who on earth would want it?) and for the bus-and-truck company, also directing it, in 1987. He owns the property outright and it has made him a millionaire several times over. It was a pity therefore that he went to Scranton, New Jersey, for a gimmicky mishmash of 'Julius Caesar', with a cast of over 100 but only one other professional actor. Then he played Mr Peachum in the new version of *The Beggar's Opera* (89). He said during this period, 'I consider a great half of my career a total failure. I went after the wrong things – got caught in the 60s. I picked pictures that were way below my talent, just to have fun.'

KATHLEEN HARRISON

In a long career, Kathleen Harrison was rigidly type-cast, kept firmly below stairs. On the few occasions she was not a maid or the daily she was a nosy neighbour or a Cockney mum – clearly the British character actress *par excellence*. She has been loyal, cheeky, vague ('I dunno, dear' is one of her stock remarks) and chin-up cheerful – 'common' to use a word she (the screen Harrison) uses about others but never dreamt applied to herself. There have been other actresses of this vernacular – Thora Hird, Dandy Nichols and the more eccentric and divinely funny Irene Handl – but Harrison is the only one who achieved real film stardom. In her own modest way she was as accomplished a screen artist as any.

She was born in Blackburn in 1898, but soon moved with her mother to London, where she was educated at Clapham High School; afterwards she went to RADA. She married before making any stage appearance and went to live in Argentina and in Madeira; back in Britain, she returned to RADA and got a job at the Pier Theatre, Eastbourne, as Mrs Judd in 'The Constant Flirt' (26). She made her first London appearance the following year in 'The Cage' and soon established a small reputation as an interpreter of Cockney maids. In her first film, however, she was a native of her own native county, Lancashire: *Hobson's Choice* (31), the second film version of Harold Brighouse's play. She worked consistently in both films and theatre thereafter. The films: *Happy Ever After* (32) with Lilian Harvey, as a maid; *Aren't We All?*, a version of Frederick Lonsdale's play, starring Gertrude Lawrence; *The Man from Toronto* (33), a good role as Jessie Matthews's maid; *The Ghoul* with Boris Karloff, probably her biggest role before stardom, as Dorothy Hyson's maid, caught along with the others in the 'haunted' house; *The Great Defender* (34), directed by Thomas Bentley; *Line Engaged* (35), as the maid (she had played it on stage); and *Broken Blossoms*, the (dreadful) remake with Dolly Haas and Emlyn Williams. Williams offered her the role of the housekeeper in his play 'Night Must Fall', her best role to date. She continued playing her chars and maids in films: *The Tenth Man* (36), as the servant-girl, a version of Somerset Maugham's play directed by Brian Desmond Hurst; *Everybody Dance* with Cicely Courtneidge; *Aren't Men Beasts* (37), a version of a stage farce, with most of the same farceurs (Robertson Hare, etc.); and *Wanted* starring Zazu Pitts.

When MGM came to film *Night Must Fall* they engaged her to repeat her stage role; and she had another good role in *Bank Holiday* (38), as a Cockney mum by the sea. Her success in both movies – and on the stage in Williams's 'The Corn is Green' – led to a flurry of film parts: *Jane Steps Out*, with Judy Kelly; *Almost a Gentleman*, starring comic Billy Bennett; a B, *Lovers Knot*; *Convict 99*, a brief role as Will Hay's sister; *I Got a Horse*; *Home from Home* (39), as Sandy Powell's nagging wife; *The Outsider* with George Sanders, in a minute role; *A Girl Must Live* with Margaret Lockwood, as a Cockney drudge; *Discoveries*, which was built round a BBC radio show; *I Killed the Count*, again in a part she had done on stage; *They Came By Night* (40), written by Launder and Gilliatt, with Will Fyffe; *The Flying Squad*; the third film version of *Tilly of Bloomsbury*, as Tilly's mother; *The Girl in the News* with Margaret Lockwood; *The Ghost Train* (41) with Arthur Askey, a very funny version of the old farce, as a prissy frightened spinster; *Major Barbara*, in a one-line part; *Kipps*, unbilled, as a customer in the shop where Kipps works; *Once a Crook* with Gordon Harker; and *I Thank You*, which was another vehicle for Arthur Askey.

Noël Coward cast her as the wife of Bernard Miles in *In Which We Serve* (42) and she was again an NCO's wife, but with a different service, in Terence Rattigan's 'Flare Path'. After two more films – *Much Too Shy*, opposite George Formby, and *Dear Octopus* (43) – she toured the Middle East for ENSA in 'Flare Path', plus 'Blithe Spirit' and 'Night Must Fall' (with a company which included Emlyn Williams). She was back in films in *It Happened One Sunday* (44), a minor romance with Barbara White and Robert Beatty, and *Meet Sexton Blake* (45), with David Farrar. The small parts continued: *Caesar and Cleopatra*, unbilled: *Wanted for Murder* (46), with Eric Portman, as a maid; *I See a Dark Stranger*, as a waitress; *The Shop at Sly Corner*, a version of a stage thriller with Oscar Homolka; and *Temptation Harbour* (47), a version of Simenon with Robert Newton and Simone Simon, as a neighbour.

At that point Rank decided to make a

Grand Hotel/Bank Holiday kind of film based on a postwar innovation, the *Holiday Camp*. Among the motley crew there for love and melodrama was a Cockney family, the Huggetts, played by Harrison and Jack Warner. The film was a huge success and so was the Harrison-Warner team. There was a genuine demand for a sequel. Meanwhile, Harrison did her last three small parts: *Oliver Twist* (48), in a very brief role, as Mrs Sowerby; *Bond Street*, a portmanteau film, in an episode about a lady (Adrienne Allen) and her dressmaker; and *The Winslow Boy*, as the excitable maid. That was another part she had done on stage and there could be no other casting – a jewel of a performance. At last Rank obliged with the three Huggett films: *Here Come the Huggetts, Vote for Huggett* (49) and *The Huggetts Abroad,* all directed again by Ken Annakin. The offspring now were Petula Clark, Susan Shaw, Jimmy Hanley and Jane Hylton. Unfortunately, the third went into production before the critics had got at the first – in fact, they were no more atrocious than *Holiday Camp*, but that had been fun in the way its title indicated. With a red face, Rank stopped the series; it found a home on BBC radio.

Harrison was now a star; she would henceforth be billed mainly above the title, though her task was to find good playable parts within her limitations. She could no longer play maids and chars, so she would have to rely on her box-office draw to get good character parts – especially as she was a very shy and retiring woman. In the few interviews she gave, she made it quite clear that she could not, after 20 years in the business, think of herself as a star. She had two scenes in a (men's) prison picture, *Now Barabbas Was a Robber* (49), and had a good part in *Landfall*, as Patricia Plunkett's mother – a dreadful film from a Nevil Shute novel with Michael Denison. And she was the only good thing in the dire *Golden Arrow*, as an ardent film fan (it was made in 1949, not released till 1953). Then: *Double Confession* (50) with Peter Lorre; *Trio*, three Somerset Maugham stories, in 'The Verger', as his, James Hayter's, wife; *Waterfront*, a Liverpool story, again as the heroine's mother, married to Robert Newton; *The Magic Box* (51), as one of a family group; *Scrooge* with Alastair Sim; and *The Happy Family* (52), a weak comedy with Stanley Holloway about a family dispossessed because of the Festival of Britain (Sydney Box's return to independent production after leaving Rank).

James Hayter played Mr Pickwick, in a flawed production with most of Britain's eccentric players (Hermione Gingold, Hermione Baddeley, Joyce Grenfell, Nigel Patrick, etc.): *The Pickwick Papers*. Said Richard Winnington: 'In actual truth there is only one player in the entire film who carries the flavour of Dickens and is able to equate the human and grotesque – Kathleen Harrison as that symbol of coy spinsterhood, Miss Wardle.' She was even more desperately needed in the mainly awful films she made after that: *Turn the Key Softly* (53), what happens when women leave prison, with Yvonne Mitchell; *Lilacs in the Spring* (54), as a barmaid and Anna Neagle's dresser; *The Dog and the Diamonds*, as the owner of a pet-shop, a film made for the Children's Film Foundation and not shown except at children's matinées; *Where There's a Will* (55), a Grade Z comedy; and *Cast a Dark Shadow*, again as the housekeeper. On the stage she had co-starred with Edith Evans and Sybil Thorndike in 'Waters of the Moon' (51) and in 1954 she had

Before achieving stardom Kathleen Harrison invariably portrayed domestics, and she was invariably sent for if the role was large, as gratifyingly in The Winslow Boy *(48) with Sir Cedric Hardwicke. She had played the role on stage, and indeed Terence Rattigan had written it with her in mind.*

After years of minor roles – many of them uncredited, and usually as a maid – Kathleen Harrison became a star playing a working-class mum in Holiday Camp. *This is a scene from one of the follow-ups:* Here Come the Huggetts *(48), with Petula Clark playing her daughter.*

a big West End success in 'All for Mary', as an enthusiastic and officious nurse mothering two grown men. She repeated in the film version (55). She appeared in Noël Coward's 'Nude With Violin', in a part written specially for her, but her films around this time were not good. Indeed, *The Big Money* was so bad that it was reportedly scrapped – but it turned up two years later, re-edited, with the producer's name removed (Joseph Janni); she played Ian Carmichael's mother. The others: *It's a Wonderful World*, a musical starring Ted Heath and his Band, as a housekeeper; and *Home and Away*, with Jack Warner, another clinker from the same bunker as *Where There's a Will*. She was a Cockney married to a Marseilles docker in *Seven Thunders* (57), a Rank melodrama with the doubtful benefit of Stephen Boyd and Tony Wright in the leads, and the mother of a deprived child in *A Cry from the Streets* (58), with the even more doubtful Max Bygraves. Then she had another star role, with Sybil Thorndike and Estelle Winwood, as three old ladies very much *Alive and Kicking*.

In 1960 she took over the Peggy Mount character of the bossy mother in 'Watch It Sailor' – but did not play it in the film version. In 1962 she was one of the distinguished company Laurence Olivier invited to open the first Chichester Festival; in 1965 she was in a revival of 'Thark', among other plays. During the decade she made very few films and all of them were bad: *On the Fiddle* (61), married – again – to Stanley Holloway; *Mrs Gibbons's Boys* (62), starring, as a widow with three loutish sons; *The Fast Lady*, as a housekeeper; *West II* (63), as the mother of the drifting hero, Alfred Lynch; and *Lock Up Your Daughters* (69), as a *nouveau-riche* milady. In the meantime she had a hugely popular TV series 'Mrs Thursday'. In 1972 she said 'I'm sad and depressed. I'm fit and I want to work but there doesn't seem to be anything for me. It's not as though I'm asking for star parts. I'm a character actress and always have been.' She had one last role, as an elderly lady bystander in a Disney chase comedy, *The Omega Connection* (79), a tele-film starring Jeffrey Byron and Larry Cedar, upright Americans set down among the Limeys, and unaccountably shown in cinemas in Britain retitled *The London Connection*.

Rex Harrison

In an interview once, Rex Harrison referred to Alan Jay Lerner, the writer of 'My Fair Lady': 'I owe that man such a great deal.' Few actors are so in debt: 'My Fair Lady' came to him when he was past middle age and transformed him from leading man to superstar. He had ever been a formidable light comedian, but a fairish run of poor films had kept this Rolls-Royce of actors going in only a low gear. He is a player of strong personal style, presumably achieved by much work but looking deceptively easy: the aristocratic, elegant Englishman, with ingratiating hints of well-being and devilry. He can play with real bite. Noël Coward's famous crack is not quite fair: 'If, next to me, you were not the finest light-comedy actor in the world, you'd be good for only one thing; selling cars in Great Portland Street.' It suggests that behind Harrison's smooth surface bravado, there is not very much – which is intriguingly possible; but it also suggests his superb self-confidence and it was that, deepened into arrogance, which made him such a marvellous Higgins. To the extent that 'My Fair Lady' put him right in the forefront of actors, with roles to match, we all owe Alan Jay Lerner a great deal.

Harrison was born in Huyton, Lancashire, in 1908 and educated at Liverpool College for a while. When he left, at 16, instead of joining the steel firm where his father worked, he got a job with Liverpool rep and had a variety of small parts, starting with a one-acter, '30 Minutes in a Street'. In 1927, after three years, he left and toured with various companies, till he got a part in London, at the Everyman, in 'Getting George Married' (30). He landed small parts in *The Great Game* (30) and *The School for Scandal*, and later in three quota quickies, *Get Your Man* (34), *Leave It to Blanche* and *All at Sea* (35), a comedy with Googie Withers. His parts on the stage grew, through 'No Way Back', Anthony in 'Anthony and Anna', 'Man of Yesterday' – his first real success, 'Sweet Aloes' (36) in New York and 'Heroes Don't Care'. Around the time that he began the long run of 'French Without Tears', in the leading role, Korda offered him a £2,500-a-year contract.

He started with Korda in *Men Are Not Gods* (37), starring Miriam Hopkins, in a featured role as a breezy journalist; and starred in *Storm in a Teacup*, opposite Vivien Leigh, as a journalist again – and breezy. He was an odd-looking man at this time, wiry, thin-faced, with rather bulbous eyes: he did not look like a romantic leading man and it was not till he filled out physically that he began to be popular with audiences. Korda made him the poor doctor who waits for heiress Merle Oberon while she dallies with high life, in *Over the Moon* – which was not released till Korda's creditors put it on the market, to minimal interest, in 1940. He was then loaned out for a quartet: *School for Husbands* (38), a bedroom farce co-starring the lovely Diana Churchill; *St Martin's Lane*, again as Vivien Leigh's boyfriend; *The Citadel*, in a featured role as an unconscientious society doctor; and *The Silent Battle*, with Valerie Hobson, as a mystery man on the Simplon-Orient express. There was a West End hit, Coward's 'Design for Living', and two more contemporary adventure tales, *Ten Days in Paris* and Carol Reed's *Night Train to Munich* (40), in which he was a government agent 'guarding' refugee Margaret Lockwood. In that he impersonated a seaside song-plugger and a Nazi officer, risking his neck with great aplomb. Unusually for a British film, it broke records in New York (20th, however, had produced it, as part of their British programme). It also interested Hollywood in him.

But the war was on; after playing 'Dolly' in Gabriel Pascal's version of Shaw's *Major Barbara* (41), he joined the RAF. He was released to fall in love with Anna Neagle in *I Live in Grosvenor Square* (45). Then he did the two films which not only prevented him from making *Piccadilly Incident* with her, but which established him as the best British light comedian of his generation: *Blithe Spirit*, a literal version of the Coward play, with Constance Cummings, Margaret Rutherford and, above all, Kay Hammond in her stage role of that obstreperous ghost, Elvira; and *The Rake's Progress*, a serious and hackneyed story of a cad who dies a hero's death. C.A. Lejeune wrote: 'His sense of timing is so delicate, and his sense of showmanship so disciplined, that he can make the flattest line seem knowing, and give an illusion of soundness and depth to a part that is hollow as a rotten apple.'

Of the Hollywood offers, the most attractive was from 20th – seven years at $4,500 a week, with the choice of working in Britain. It further stipulated that his first US film would be *Anna and the King of Sian* (46), opposite Irene Dunne. He had another success as the imperious king; and another as the spectral sea-captain in *The Ghost and Mrs Muir* (47) with Gene Tierney. But the next three were not good: *The Foxes of Harrow*, as a foxy Irish adventurer in a dull spectacle about the very old very Deep South – no cliché left unturned – from a novel by Frank Yerby; Mankiewicz's filmed-in-Britain remake of Galsworthy's *Escape* (48) as an escaped convict; and Preston Sturges's unfunny *Unfaithfully Yours*, as a monstrously egotistical orchestral conductor. 20th were increasingly unhappy with the grosses and he loathed Hollywood and the constraint of being under contract; the career of his (second) wife, Lilli Palmer, was not flourishing there, either; and he was unwittingly involved in a scandal (when Carole Landis committed suicide; he had dined with her alone a few hours previously). The contract was dissolved by mutual agreement.

He went to Broadway and played Henry VIII in 'Anne of a Thousand Days' – for almost as long as that; had another success there, with his wife, in 'Bell, Book and Candle' (50), and one in London in T.S. Eliot's 'The Cocktail Party'. In Britain he produced a thriller which he later described, accurately, as 'a dreadful film', *The Long Dark Hall*, playing a man unjustly condemned to death, with his wife. In 1952 he was on Broadway again, in 'Venus Observed'; then he and Palmer were offered a Hollywood movie, *The Fourposter* (52). It had been a drear two-character play chronicling a marriage and neither they, nor director Irving Reis, did anything to improve the material. Cheap as it was, it lost a packet. They played themselves in a sequence of *Main Street to Broadway* (53) and appeared on Broadway in 'The Love of Four Colonels'; then he returned to Hollywood to play Saladin – the only

Rex Harrison and Margaret Lockwood in Night Train to Munich *(40).*

Rex Harrison's Henry Higgins – see next page – made him one of the most eminent exponents of Shavian wit. In his late 70s he was playing Captain Shotover in 'Heartbreak House', but here early in his film career he is in Major Barbara *(41) with Wendy Hiller.*

consolation in a flop epic, *King Richard and the Crusaders* (54).

Korda had been trying to lure him back to Britain: abortive plans had included new versions of *The Scarlet Pimpernel* and *The Admirable Crichton*. When he and Palmer were in London doing 'Bell, Book and Candle' Korda signed him for *The Constant Husband* (55), an inconsequential comedy about an amnesia victim and his wives, Margaret Leighton and Kay Kendall. As an experiment, and at a huge fee, it was premièred in the US on TV, but 'Variety' thought this particular film would do the cause of British films in the US more harm than good. In 1957 he and Palmer divorced and he married Kendall.

He was not the first choice for Higgins (several more eminent British actors were approached) in the musical version of 'Pygmalion', 'My Fair Lady' (56), but, as it turned out, he was the right one. The show itself was at that time the greatest financial – and perhaps critical – success of the century, in no small way due to Harrison. He played the part for two years in New York and for one in London. He might have returned to the screen in the film of *Bell, Book and Candle* but repeatedly refused it after Kim Novak was cast. Thus it was MGM who cashed in on the now great fame of Harrison, when they starred him and Kendall in *The Reluctant Débutante* (58), from a popular British matinée play. Universal then cast him as the meanie-husband of Doris Day in a second-hand thriller, *Midnight Lace* (60), but he kept his end up in a couple of superior plays, Anouilh's 'The Fighting Cock' in New York and Chekhov's 'Platonov' in London (the cast of which included Rachel Roberts, who became his fourth wife). Then he surprised everyone by doing a minor comedy in Spain with Rita Hayworth, *The Happy Thieves* (62) – not that everyone, by any means, went to see it.

On the strength of Mankiewicz as director-writer, he was next involved in the *Cleopatra* (63) débâcle, described by him as a 'bizarre' experience; but Caesar gave him more satisfaction than any other role during his career and he was the only one of the principals to emerge with any credit. When Warners came to film *My Fair Lady* (64) he was not, again, the first choice. Among others, Cary Grant was approached, but he told Warners: 'Not only will I not play Higgins, but if you don't put Rex Harrison in it I won't go and see it.' Warners gave in and Harrison's celluloid Higgins won him a Best Actor Oscar, a BFA award and the New York critics' award. The

Rex Harrison's famous performance as Professor Higgins was repeated in the film version, with Audrey Hepburn as his new Eliza: My Fair Lady (*64*).

film trailed *Cleopatra* and the *Mutiny on the Bounty* remake as the most expensive film yet made, but within three years it had taken $30 million domestic, one of the all-time top 10 box-office champions. He did an episode film, *The Yellow Rolls Royce* (65), and then another epic, *The Agony and the Ecstasy*, for 20th, a sprightly Pope Julius to Charlton Heston's Michelangelo. Carol Reed directed; the critics found it reverent but dull and it was not popular. Nor was *The Honey Pot* (67), Mankiewicz's updated and over-verbose version of 'Volpone', though he was good as the wily fox. Nor was Harrison luckier with *Dr Doolittle*, a musical version of Hugh Lofting's children's classic that also, somehow, wound up among the 10 most expensive movies ever made. Great drum-banging by 20th proved ineffective in the face of reviews which praised him but otherwise niggled (derivative music, etc.) and it lost a fortune.

In his 1969 account of 20th ('The Studio') John Gregory Dunne says that Harrison was considered 'difficult'; relations between star and studio must have cooled further as two more 20th movies bit the dust. So far Harrison's reputation had remained unscathed; but he was not successful in a dual role in *A Flea in Her Ear* (68), as stuffy lawyer and drunken janitor. Directed by Jacques Charon, translated by John Mortimer, this Feydeau farce had been a hit at Britain's National Theatre; but 20th, still employing Charon and Mortimer, jettisoned the very qualities (pace, timing, élan) which had made it a success. And Harrison's own notices were bad for *Staircase* (69), the first real character performance of his career, as an ageing gay married to Richard Burton. He had liked the play, but thought the film ruined by over-emphasis: 'We had a great time making it but I don't think anyone had a great time watching it.' He was paid $1 million to do it and said later that he wished he had given $1 million not to do it. He should then have made *Scrooge*; but doctors ordered him to rest. During his absence from the screen he planned some independent productions in which he would not appear; and married (after a divorce from Miss Roberts) the ex-wife of Richard Harris, who left him shortly afterwards and wrote a nasty book on the experience of being married to both of them.

In 1973 Harrison played 'Don Quixote' in a co-production between the BBC and Universal; and since he is reported to have refused supporting billing his films were limited – *The Prince and the Pauper/Crossed Swords* (77), as the Duke of Norfolk, and *The Fifth Musketeer* (79), as Colbert. Both were made in Vienna and the latter took a couple of years to surface. Meanwhile, Harrison did a cameo role in *Ashanti*, oddly cast as a representative of an anti-slave society; and he was in an even stranger 'international' venture, *Shalimar*, an Indian-British effort with Swiss backing. He was a retired jewel thief in this piece, made three years earlier. *Seven Graves to Rogan* fared no better: filmed in 1978 it was released on video in Britain in 1982 and retitled *A Time to Die* for US release the following year. He played a German politician. Stage performances during these years included Pirandello's Enrico IV in New York (73), M. Perrichon at Chichester (76), and 'The Kingfisher' on Broadway with Claudette Colbert. During the run of the latter he married for the sixth time and it was announced (following Yul Brynner as the Siamese King) that he would play Higgins again – on tour, in New York and in London, on a 22-month contract which brought him in $2 million. A tele-movie, co-starring Wendy Hiller, was made of *The Kingfisher* (82), but Miss Colbert bore him no grudge for they were reunited – after he had played Shotover in 'Heartbreak House' (83) in London and New York – for a revival of 'Aren't We All?' (84), which they subsequently took to New York, Australia, etc.

The success of Mary Poppins *and* The Sound of Music *suggested to Hollywood a huge market for 'family' musicals – and Harrison was engaged to appear in* Doctor Doolittle *(67), right, which promptly proved that there was not. At least, not for this particular musical.*

During this period he made a tele-film, *Anastasia: the Mystery of Anna* (86) and returned to the West End as Lord Loam in 'The Admirable Crichton' (88). He is scheduled to appear at The Brooks Atkinson Theater in November 1989, where he will join Stewart Granger and Glynis Johns in a revival of Somerset Maugham's 'The Circle'.

LAURENCE HARVEY

Laurence Harvey's career should be an inspiration to all budding actors: he demonstrated conclusively that it is possible to succeed without managing to evoke the least audience interest or sympathy – and to go on succeeding despite unanimous critical antipathy and overwhelming public apathy. His 20-year career of mainly unprofitable films is a curiosity of film history.

According to studio hand-outs, he was born in 1928 in Yonishkis, Lithuania, but raised in South Africa from the age of six. He served with the South African army in Egypt and Italy during the war (regardless of his youth, apparently) and appeared in an army show, 'The Bandoliers', and then on the stage in Johannesburg. He turned up in Britain, studied three months at RADA and worked for a while at the Manchester Library Theatre; he was also a male prostitute. Then, as 'Picturegoer' put it later, 'Forcefulness and ability to back up his own self-selling resulted in a role in a second-feature film', *House of Darkness* (48). Associated British produced and offered a two-year contract: *Man on the Run*, fourth-billed, as a detective; *The Dancing Years*, in a minute role; *Man From Yesterday* (49); and *Cairo Road*, a leading role in this film starring Eric Portman, an offscreen companion. He had the lead in a B made by Butcher's, *The Slender Thread*, with Kathleen Byron, was in a small role in *Landfall* and was bottom of the cast-list of 20th's British-made biggie, *The Black Rose* (50). Things were not going well: the following year he was in a disastrous West End revival of 'Hassan' and again he only had one film part, in a Butcher's B, *There Is Another Sun* (51), as Maxwell Reed's staunch buddy. Also in the cast was Hermione Baddeley, offscreen a great chum.

Then things picked up. Associated British gave him a part in *A Killer Walks* (52) and Ealing gave him a break as a juvenile delinquent in *I Believe in You*, with Joan Collins. Romulus took him on to play a con, the boyfriend of one of the *Women of Twilight*, a horrendously shoddy melodrama based on a West End play. That was Harvey's break. The film went unnoted, but one of the brother-founders of Romulus, James Woolf, believed in Harvey and was prepared to promote him. He was given the part of an amorous waiter in an equally ghastly comedy, *Innocents in Paris* (53), and despite reviews like Penelope Houston's, which referred to his 'inadequacy', was sent to Hollywood to test for a role in MGM's *Knights of the Round Table*. He got it and top supporting roles in three other important films. Meanwhile, he had done a season with the Memorial Theatre at Stratford (52) – to generally poor notices. His response was to give interviews patiently explaining that the critics were wrong and pointing out that he was a great actor. The game went on for years, till Fleet Street finally grew tired of it. Despite the complete failure of his Shakespeare performances Renato Castellani chose him to play Romeo in his British-Italian, Rank-financed *Romeo and Juliet* (54). He was paid $20,000 for it. Castellani was accustomed to getting good performances in his films from amateurs and opposite Harvey he cast Susan Shentall, who had never acted before – casting 'too rash, too sudden, too unadvis'd'. But Harvey's performance, said the 'MFB', 'fails more profoundly . . . it stands out as incongruous' – being virtually without expression.

To do that one Harvey had cancelled those Hollywood films, but there was another offer from that direction: Warners wanted him for *King Richard and the Crusaders*, a version of Sir Walter Scott's 'The Talisman', as the hero ('Fight, fight, fight! That's all you think of, Dick Plantagenet' quoth Virginia Mayo). According to 'Picture Show', he returned with a contract to make one film a year for Warners, but none was ever made: he reputedly turned down the role of Paris in their *Helen of Troy* in order to return to Stratford (1954, including another Romeo), but it is more likely that WB were frightened off after examining the receipts for *Richard*. Romulus, however, were loyal. They had made enough money from two John Huston films to employ some semi-big Hollywood names in *The Good Die Young* (55) and they added Harvey, who in the film married wealthy Margaret Leighton in order to pay his gambling debts. He married her in real life too. Then they brought over Julie Harris to play in *I Am a Camera* and cast Harvey opposite as Herr Issyvoo – 'a flat and insensitive performance' said David Robinson.

He was loaned out to play the sun-blinded soldier in *Storm Over the Nile* (56), with Anthony Steel, a movie whose main virtue was the footage inserted from the earlier version, *The Four Feathers*. Another popular old novel, *Three Men in a Boat* (57), co-starred a popular TV comedian, Jimmy Edwards, and that showed up on statistics as one of the most popular British films of the year; but *After the Ball* disappeared after one week's première run and was never heard of again (till a TV showing). It was a life of Marie Lloyd – gallantly played by Pat Kirkwood, with Harvey as one of the men in her life. Then, *The Truth About Women* (58), which elicited this comment from the 'MFB': 'Apart from Laurence Harvey's heavy and charmless Humphrey, the performances are good.' Nor did *The Silent Enemy*, an underwater drama, do much to brighten the evenings that year. But Romulus had bought the rights to John Braine's bestselling novel about a North Country opportunist, *Room at the Top*, and they got a goodish director for it (Jack Clayton), plus an outstanding co-star (Simone Signoret). Harvey's impassive and unfeeling young climber was the best thing he had done; the film was a big hit and revived Hollywood's interest in him. After a commitment to play in *Expresso Bongo* (59) – the part of the pushy pop-promoter which Paul Scofield had done on the stage – he went.

For John Wayne, he played an effete Englishman in *The Alamo* (60) and signed multi-picture deals with both Hal Wallis and MGM. At Metro he played opposite Elizabeth Taylor in the huge-grossing *Butterfield 8*; then returned to Britain to play the smart-aleck soldier in the disappointing film version of *The Long and the Short and the Tall* (61). There were two more Hollywood flops: *Two Loves*, with Shirley MacLaine and *Summer and Smoke*, with Geraldine Page. American critics were echoing the British: 'Laurence Harvey, who once found room at the top, continues his descent to the bottom; as John, he adds another still life to his growing gallery' ('Playboy'). Of *A Walk on the Wild Side* (62), Bosley Crowther observed that 'Harvey is barely one-dimensional'; co-star Jane Fonda said, 'Acting with Harvey is like acting by yourself – only worse.'

Such comments were reflected at the box-office. *The Wonderful World of the Brothers Grimm* hoped to emulate the success of *Hans Christian Andersen*, made 10 years earlier; it was one of two Cinerama features launched simultaneously on the market, the first 'fictions' in that huge-screen process. The other (*How the West Was Won*) took $23 million; this one limped to a poor $6.1 million. Wallis's *A Girl Named Tamiko* (63) – Harvey as a Eurasian, with France Nuyen – never looked like making it; and 'Variety' reported that *The Manchurian Candidate* did disappointing business despite Frank Sinatra and rave reviews. Harvey's role required him to act like a zombie and several critics cited it as his first convincing performance. More disasters followed, beginning with *The Running Man*, with Lee Remick, who said, 'The tales I can tell of working with him are too horrendous to repeat.' Then, *The Ceremony*, a pretentious plea against capital punishment, produced and directed by himself, with Sarah Miles ('He's a rude man – a horrible man'), and *Of Human Bondage* (64), with Kim Novak. He played in that, said 'Variety', 'in such a stiff, martyred manner as to forfeit any sympathy or liking in the audience'. Then *The Outrage*, with Paul Newman, most of whose length he spent bound and gagged.

Laurence Harvey in his best-known role, in Room at the Top *(58). The film was mainly notable for the performance of Simone Signoret as the mistress he threw over for a wealthy wife.*

At that point he had, reported 'Variety', two more films to make for Wallis and one for MGM. Instead, Britain reclaimed him and he played Arthur in the Drury Lane 'Camelot'. He was a playboy in *Darling* (65), with Julie Christie, directed by John Schlesinger – and it was mainly on account of his 'name' that Schlesinger got financial backing. It was a huge success, but his role was small; there was a moderate welcome for *Life at the Top*, a sequel to his earlier success, this time with Jean Simmons. Little was heard of a spy spoof, *The Spy With the Cold Nose* (66), or of a more serious venture in the same genre, *A Dandy in Aspic* (67), which he finished directing when Anthony Mann died and where he acted 'on a monotonous note of expressionless gloom' (Tom Milne). Then there cropped up (for two weeks) an oddity made two years earlier, *The Winter's Tale* (68), a record of a stage production he had done. The reviewers were mystified because – as the 'MFB' put it – 'the performances are not of a standard that would seem likely to commend them to posterity.'

He hit the European trail and made *Rebus* in Italy with Ann-Margret, playing an alcoholic croupier on the verge of suicide; then did a big German-Romanian historical co-production, *Kampf um Rom* (69), shown in two parts; in Italy he produced and acted in *L'Assoluto Naturale/He and She*, with Sylva Koscina. The last ran two weeks at a minute London cinema; the others do not seem to have reached Britain or the US. In 1969 he played in 'Arms and the Man' at Chichester. He put in a guest appearance in *The Magic Christian* (70), doing a striptease while reciting 'To be or not to be', and had a five-minute role in Paul Newman's *W.U.S.A.* (71), as a shyster priest. He was billed below the title. After doing 'Child's Play' in London he did an Israeli-French-German production, *Habricha El Hashemesh/Escape to the Sun* (73), as a KGB man trying to prevent Soviet Jews from escaping. 'Nothing can bring alive Laurence Harvey's wooden performance,' said 'Variety' and it was almost his last bad notice. At Elizabeth Taylor's request he supported her in *Night Watch*, a resistible blending of talents. He directed and starred in *Welcome to Arrow Beach* (74), a ponderous horror film; but before it was shown he died of cancer, in October 1973. There also might crop up one day a movie he made for Orson Welles in Yugoslavia, with Jeanne Moreau.

He had been divorced from Miss Leighton in 1961; for most of the subsequent decade he was the constant companion – and briefly (1968–72) the husband – of Joan Cohn, widow of Harry Cohn.

Susan Hayward

It is easier for a man. For women to have a long career in films requires superhuman energy, guts and determination. The longest surviving ladies usually betray in their performances something of their offscreen battles: impossible not to believe that Joan Crawford had not browbeaten producers the same way she harried her leading men. Susan Hayward was a small-scale Crawford. The final effect is less of domination than of pugnacity. Ability is not lacking, though it did not have the individuality of Bette Davis at her peak. Like Crawford, and to a lesser degree Barbara Stanwyck, Hayward was an entirely predictable actress. It was the aggressive, meaty roles of these actresses that she tried to inherit and in the 50s she had the field to herself. She was lucky: fans with a *faiblesse* for the grand manner liked her, but if she is at her best in *I'll Cry Tomorrow* (she won an acting award at Cannes for it) she still is not good. Whenever she is on screen with Jo Van Fleet – playing her screen mother – you do not notice her; she is colourless in a plastic part, wrapped in cellophane; whereas Van Fleet, if not exactly flesh and blood, at least does her job in an interesting way (for instance, no reference is made to their being Jewish, but Van Fleet's intonation and mannerisms suggest it). Later in the film, Hayward has to portray an alcoholic – admittedly without help from either script or direction – and she just cannot supply what they lack. Davis, Stanwyck and even Crawford were given equally difficult tasks – their villainesses – but they could always suggest some motivation for their actions.

She was born (Edythe Marriner) in a tenement in Brooklyn in 1918 and she dreamed as a child of becoming a movie star. At commercial school she studied dress design and stenography, but on leaving became a model. A 'Saturday Evening Post' cover brought her to the attention of the Selznick studio, who tested her for Scarlett O'Hara. She was nixed but arranged for the test to be seen by Warners, who signed her and gave her some unbilled bit parts, then made her one of the *Girls on Probation* (38), a B with Jane Bryan and Ronald Reagan. That studio did not take up their option, but she hung on in the film city and eventually got a job at Paramount at $200 a week. There she replaced Frances Farmer (who insisted on doing a play in New York) in *Beau Geste* (39). She did not have much footage after the Geste brothers joined the Foreign Legion, but shared the fade-out with Ray Milland. She played the lead in a nervous B, *Our Leading Citizen*, a wretched study of labour relations (from a story by Irvin S. Cobb) which thudded badly, and Joe E. Brown's girlfriend in *$1,000 a Touchdown*. Then nothing. She fretted and complained; finally she heard of a good role going at Columbia and asked to be tested, and in *Adam Had Four Sons* (41) she gave a fine performance as a spoilt beauty. Burying her pride, she went to Republic to play second lead to Judy Canova (in Mabel Normand's old role) in *Sis Hopkins*; but Paramount, having read the reviews of *Adam*, starred her again, in a B, *Among the Living*, a good little melodrama – she was a tramp sharing a rooming-house with crazed killer Albert Dekker.

But Paramount saw her only as a useful second lead: *Reap the Wild Wind* (42), as the ingénue, Paulette Goddard's cousin; *The Forest Rangers*, as Goddard's butch rival for Fred MacMurray; and *I Married a Witch*, on loan-out, as Veronica Lake's more conventional rival. In *Star Spangled Rhythm* she did a short sketch as a wartime cutie who would rather have a girdle than a man. In response to her clamour for leading roles, Paramount loaned her out for some unexciting ventures: *Young and Willing* (43) with William Holden, a comedy about novice actors; *Hit Parade of 1943*; *Jack London*, as the sweetheart of that gentleman (Michael O'Shea); and *The Fighting Seabees* (44) with John Wayne. Then her performance as the spiteful nightmoth in *The Hairy Ape*, with William Bendix, brought much attention. James Agee thought she had a dazzling future playing vicious American women and the London 'Daily Herald' wrote: 'Provocative, heartless and enticing. As an exponent of the bad and the beautiful I do not know her equal on the screen.' Returning at last to her home studio, she was appalled to be cast simply as Loretta Young's rival in *And Now Tomorrow*; film-writers confirmed her view that Paramount underestimated her and she refused to renew her contract.

In 1945 she gave birth to twins (the marriage to Jess Barker – 1944–53 – ended in a barrage of stormy headlines); then returned to the screen as a freelance, in *Deadline at Dawn* (46), written by Clifford Odets and directed by Harold Clurman, playing a prostitute who helps Bill Williams prove he is not a murderer. Both Selznick and Walter Wanger were offering contracts and after hesitation she signed with Wanger, then releasing through Universal. He put her in the sort of parts which would – had the films been better – have made her the envy of other female stars. Still, the first was good: *Canyon Passage* with Dana Andrews, where her 'fiery beauty' contrasted with that of the imported, pallid Patricia Roc. And the second had a rich part: *Smash-Up, The Story of a Woman* (47). It was booze that did it (when husband Lee Bowman becomes a successful radio singer), the first of her two full-scale excursions into screen alcoholism. The 'New York Times' thought she performed 'with a solemn fastidiousness which turns most of her scenes of drunken fumbling . . . into offkey burlesque.'

Then: *They Won't Believe Me*, a footling little thriller at RKO with Robert Young; *The Lost Moment* with Robert Cummings, a decidedly foolish attempt to film 'The Aspern Papers'; and *The Saxon Charm* (48), a melodrama with Robert Montgomery, as John Payne's sensible wife. The latter came between two big-budgeters, *Tap Roots*, with Van Heflin, and *Tulsa* (49), in both of which she played aspects of Scarlett O'Hara, Southern belle and power-crazy beauty respectively. However, public response remained cool and Wanger unloaded her contract on to 20th, who put her into *House of Strangers*, an incomprehensible role as the girl Richard Conte is mad about. She went to Goldwyn for another drunken bout, plus romance with Dana Andrews, *My Foolish Heart*, her first real hit – though its take was much helped by a hit theme song. 20th were encouraged; they knew that Hayward had talent, but they did not know what to do with her. She was idle till Jeanne Crain became pregnant, taking over her role as the wife of minister William Lundigan in *I'd Climb the Highest Mountain* (51). Then she was a fiery ex-showgirl stranded with Tyrone Power in *Rawhide*, a good Western that suffered from the inability of either of them to suggest tension.

The Hairy Ape (*44*): *Susan Hayward first impressed critics as the tramp who becomes involved with tar William Bendix. Here she dallies with Bill Williams (in a very brief role; later in the 40s he had some leading-man assignments).*

Her swing into Hollywood's top stars probably began when 20th cast her as a go-getter in *I Can Get It For You Wholesale*, crawling her way ruthlessly to the top of New York's rag trade – followed by a co-starring assignment with Gregory Peck in *David and Bathsheba*. That indicated that she had reached the top of the 20th pile, even if her Bathsheba hardly justified David's passion (disguised

Darryl F. Zanuck never jibbed at copying the successes of others. His David and Bathsheba *(51) was an attempt to outdo Cecil B. De Mille: it had a much better director, Henry King, but was very dull. So were Gregory Peck and Susan Hayward in the title-roles.*

Susan Hayward in the witness-chair: I Want To Live! *(58), and her best film performance.*

though that was in Peck's performance). It was a hit and so was *With a Song in My Heart* (52), a biopic untouched by the slightest breath of originality, the story of Jane Froman, a singer crippled in a World War II air-crash. Her performance was at its best when doubled by Froman's warm contralto belting out the songs of the period, but she won a 'Picturegoer' Gold Medal all the same. And there was a third big hit, again with Peck, *The Snows of Kilimanjaro.* Exhibitors voted her one of the 10 top-grossing stars, and again in 1953. In 1953 she is said to have earned over $200,000.

Her films were mainly actioners and her heroines inevitably Stanwyck-like: *The Lusty Men* at RKO with Robert Mitchum; *The President's Lady* (53) – the president was Andrew Jackson (Charlton Heston) and the film was a flop; *White Witch Doctor* with Mitchum, as a determined doctor; *Demetrius and the Gladiators* (54) with Victor Mature, as the evil empress Messalina; *Garden of Evil*, where she was good every now and then, with Gary Cooper; and *Untamed* (55), with an astonished Tyrone Power: 'I can hardly believe it, *you* Katie, here in Africa fighting Zulus.' Overwork on that, said her studio, led to an overdose of sleeping pills in 1955. A while later Thomas Wiseman wrote: 'There are girls in Hollywood whose outer hardness conceals only an inner hardness. Miss Hayward, I would say, is not in this class. She has miscalculated too often to be accused of being calculating. She struck me as being an intelligent, gifted and blunt woman – down-to-earth without being earthy.'

Her last for 20th was *Soldier of Fortune*, looking for her husband in Hong Kong with Clark Gable. MGM offered her the biopic of another sad Show Business lady, Lilian Roth, *I'll Cry Tomorrow*, and that gave her a chance to combine two past performances, famous singer *and* alcoholic. The bookshop success of the memoirs was duplicated in cinemas and Hayward won a second 'Picturegoer' Gold Medal; but there were no medals around for her work in a John Wayne opus, *The Conqueror* (56), or a comedy with Kirk Douglas, *Top Secret Affair* (57). However, she confirmed her reputation as a dramatic actress in another real-life part, that of Barbara Graham, good-time girl and murderess: *I Want to Live!* (58). Her bid for sympathy was aided by a harrowing gas-chamber climax and sympathetic direction by Robert Wise; she probably never tried harder – and was suitably recompensed by the New York critics' award and a Best Actress Oscar.

Wanger had produced it and, still high on her, cast her as his Cleopatra – but 20th preferred Elizabeth Taylor. *I Want to Live!* was only a qualified success, but is presumably the reason Hayward turned up tenth among the top stars the following year, because both films that year were dreary flops: *A Woman Obsessed* (59) with Stephen Boyd and *Thunder in the Sun* with Jeff Chandler, as a Basque woman with a neat line in 'Excusez-mois'. This seemed a classic case of after Oscar, no place to go but down, and she plummeted again with *The Marriage-Go-Round* (60) with James Mason, another ill-advised fling at comedy, and *Ada* (61) with Dean Martin, as an ex-tart who becomes state governor. Maybe she no longer cared (she had married again, outside the industry in 1957; she was widowed in 1966), but she did not even attempt to eliminate the shade of other actresses in her subsequent films: *Back Street* with John Gavin, a totally computerized remake of that delicate old tale, no longer suffering as did Irene Dunne and Margaret Sullavan, but an ambitious dress-designer; *I Thank a Fool* (62), in a part designed once for Ingrid Bergman, with Peter Finch; *Stolen Hours* (63), a prettily photographed remake of *Dark Victory*, but colourless in Bette Davis's old part; and *Where Love Has Gone* (64), where Davis herself wiped the floor with her as her domineering mother. Hayward in this one was a famous modern sculptress with both mother and daughter problems (Harold Robbins's novel had been based vaguely on the case of Lana Turner's daughter) – which permitted her lots of tantrums, searing self-indictments, a large roster of lovers and some hollow laughter. The film was the only one of this batch to have much success.

After a longish absence she returned as one of Rex Harrison's three suitors in *The Honey Pot* (67), but it was an exceptionally wan performance; then at the last minute she replaced Judy Garland in *Valley of the Dolls*, as an ageing musical-comedy star in this cliché-packed tale of modern showbiz, based on a trashy bestseller of some notoriety – presumably the reason for the film's success. In 1968 Hayward attempted her first stage work by playing the title-role in the Las Vegas production of 'Mame'. She appeared opposite her old teenage co-star, William Holden, in *The Revengers* (72) – a part offered her when Mary Ure decided to do a Broadway play instead. And around the same time she did a TV film, *Say Goodbye Maggie Cole*, a tear-jerker about doctors. She died of cancer in 1975.

Audrey Hepburn

It was not till the war years that Britain discovered – more or less by accident – that it could build big stars without benefit of Hollywood. As a consequence the Rank Organization founded its Charm School for likely youngsters and Associated British started a stable of starlets. Among these forgotten and half-forgotten names are Carol Marsh, Susan Shaw, Natasha Parry, Joan Dowling, Patricia Plunkett, Honor Blackman, Jane Hylton, Patricia Dainton. Joan Rice and Hazel Court. These last two ladies were among several tested for the leading role – a beauty queen – in a 1951 comedy, *Lady Godiva Rides Again*, and so, thought 'Picturegoer', was a girl at Associated British called Audrey Hepburn. (The role went to an unknown – before and since – Pauline Stroud.) 'Picturegoer' had already written of Miss Hepburn: 'God's gift to publicity men is a heart-shattering young woman with a style of her own, no mean ability, and a photogenic capacity for making the newspaper pages among the first-nighters. The name is Audrey Hepburn; and the fact that some people have been twenty-four times to Ciro's to see her cabaret performance is a good enough start for Elstree [Associated British] to talk of signing her for the screen.' It was not that easy: few other people saw Hepburn as a potential star.

She was born in Brussels in 1929, of Irish-Dutch percentage. She spent the war years in the Netherlands and went to Britain later to complete her education and study ballet – she returned to Holland to play a minor role, an air stewardess, in *Netherlands in 7 Lessen* (48). She got into the chorus of the West End production of 'High Button Shoes' (48) and then into Cecil Landau's revue 'Sauce Tartare'. Landau gave her more to do in the follow-up, 'Sauce Piquante', and began plugging her. But whoever put 'Picturegoer' on to her was not very influential, nor was director Mario Zampi, then about to start a comedy for Associated British, *Laughter in Paradise* (51). He had, he said, been to see 'Sauce Piquante' 14 times because of her – but could get the studio to give her only one line in his film (he built it up to three), as a hat-check girl. Still, she got a contract from them and another bit part in *One Wild Oat* and another, on loan, in *The Lavender Hill Mob*, as the girl who spoke to Alec Guinness at the end. Mervyn LeRoy was in London looking for a girl to play the lead in *Quo Vadis?* and tested her, but despite his enthusiasm MGM turned her down. Her own studio had by this time got the message and gave her a bigger part in *Young Wives' Tale*, as a lodger with a hang-up about men. That led to another good part, in Ealing's *The Secret People* (52), as Valentina Cortese's sister. Her presence was fresh, if tentative; offscreen she continued studying acting under Felix Aylmer.

She was offered a part in a minor Franco-British co-production, *Nous Irons à Monte Carlo/Monte Carlo Baby*, and while filming in a hotel lobby was spotted by Colette, at that time considering a Broadway adaptation of her novel, 'Gigi'. She thought Hepburn looked right and producer Gilbert Miller agreed: in virtually one leap Hepburn went from West End obscurity to Broadway fame (51). Pausing in London on the way, she was tested by Paramount, who signed her for one film to be made after the play's run. William Wyler saw the test and demanded her for *Roman Holiday* (53) when Jean Simmons bowed out; it was actually filmed during the summer recess of 'Gigi', a squarely handled but beguiling story of a (modern) princess who escapes from surveillance and, believing herself incognito, falls for American newsman Gregory Peck. Paramount, when they saw the rushes, tried to buy Hepburn's contract, but Associated British cannily decided they could make more by renting her, exclusively, to Paramount, than by selling – or putting her in a film of their own.

Paramount's publicity machine ground into action, but there was no need. Dennis Myers summed it up in 'Picturegoer': 'So flowers,

On a rooftop in Rome, the morning after: Audrey Hepburn as a princess, and Gregory Peck as the American reporter who has innocently given her a bed for the night: Roman Holiday *(53).*

please, for the enchanting Audrey – for the girl that has shown that real stars are still to be found.' Even Sam Goldwyn pronounced: 'The most exciting thing since Garbo and our own Hepburn, Katharine.' She won the New York critics' award, a Best Actress Oscar and the 'Picturegoer' Gold Medal. Billy Wilder tried to explain the furore before directing her next film: 'After so many drive-in waitresses in movies – it has been a real drought – here is class, somebody who went to school, can spell and possibly play the piano. The other class girl is Katharine Hepburn. . . . She's a wispy, thin little thing, but you're really in the presence of somebody when you see that girl. Not since Garbo has there been anything like it, with the possible exception of Bergman. It's the kind of thing where the director plans sixteen close-ups throughout the picture with that dame – that curious, ugly face of that dame.' Wilder, in fact, made her glamorous, as the chauffeur's daughter fought over by William Holden and his older brother, Humphrey Bogart: *Sabrina* (54), a long version of a mild Broadway comedy.

And he confirmed her allure – the coltish movements, the big serious eyes, the sudden unexpected grin and her insecure manner. She was incandescent. You left the cinema haunted by her looks and by her voice (all the great stars have very individual voices). 'With its sing-song cadence that develops into a flat drawl ending in a child-like query, it has a quality of heartbreak' (Cecil Beaton). It also hints of artifice, but all would be forgiven: over the decade to come, she would often seem to be the only female star worth a light.

On Broadway she was in Giraudoux's 'Ondine', co-starring with Mel Ferrer, whom she married at the end of the run. He became Prince Andrei in *War and Peace* (56) and she was Natasha; according to director King Vidor no one else was even considered for the part (and he later said she was one of the three

'It was of course inconceivable to have anyone other than Audrey Hepburn as Natasha': King Vidor on his film of Tolstoy's War and Peace *(56).*

supremely talented actresses he had directed – the others were Laurette Taylor in *Peg o' my Heart* and Lillian Gish in *La Bohème*). William Whitebait in the 'New Statesman' concurred with the choice: 'She is beautifully, entrancingly alive, and I for one, when I next come to read "War and Peace" shall see her where I read Natasha.' The film was merely comic-strip Tolstoy, but compared with the other mammoth movies of the 50s a genuine colossus and it was popular. There were several projected versions at this time, but this Italian one went way ahead and was the only one made, because of Hepburn's participation; because of her Paramount released worldwide, except in Britain, where Associated British released, as their price for loaning Hepburn to Paramount, etc. Her fee was $300,000, then one of the top sums ever paid a film artist.

At MGM a revamp of the old Gershwin musical, *Funny Face* (57), was being prepared for her and Fred Astaire, but Paramount refused to loan her; fortunately he had a commitment to Paramount and in the end the MGM team moved there *en bloc*. Said Astaire of the prolonged negotiations: 'This could be the last and only opportunity I'd have to work with the great and lovely Audrey and I was not missing it. Period.' With the two of them the film, natch, had great charm, but did well only in the cities (it was also becoming clear that Hepburn, like Garbo, was more popular abroad than in the US). The next one, Billy Wilder's *Love in the Afternoon*, failed, because (it was reckoned) Hepburn was wooed by yet another ageing Romeo, Gary Cooper. In 1957 she also appeared in 'Mayerling' on TV with Ferrer, Raymond Massey and Diana Wynyard, and about this time 'Picturegoer' reckoned that Associated British had made £1½ million from the deal with Paramount. Her next would be the last under that deal; then she was contracted to Paramount for one film a year for six years.

The next was in fact made for Warners, *The Nun's Story* (59), tactfully directed by Fred Zinnemann and certainly the best-ever American movie dealing with religion. Hepburn's 'delicate and devoted performance' (Dilys Powell) won her the New York critics' Best Actress award and the BFA Best British Actress award. Stanley Kauffmann wrote: 'Audrey Hepburn is a good young actress – limpid, compassionate, intelligent and attractively dignified. She has generally been equal in talent and technique to what she had been asked to do. But her performance . . . is better than her sheer ability, as such, could make it: because her person is so right for the part. After she has done all she can with knowledge and design, her beauty speaks for her . . . the remarkable way it serves as an intensifying glass for the inner travail she is trying to convey.' The film's gratifying success at the box-office wiped out the memory of *Green Mansions*, an incredibly messy version of W.H. Hudson's novel directed by Ferrer in which she was, of course, Rima the Bird Girl. She might more profitably have done *The Inn of the Sixth Happiness* and *The Diary of Anne Frank*, both of which she turned down.

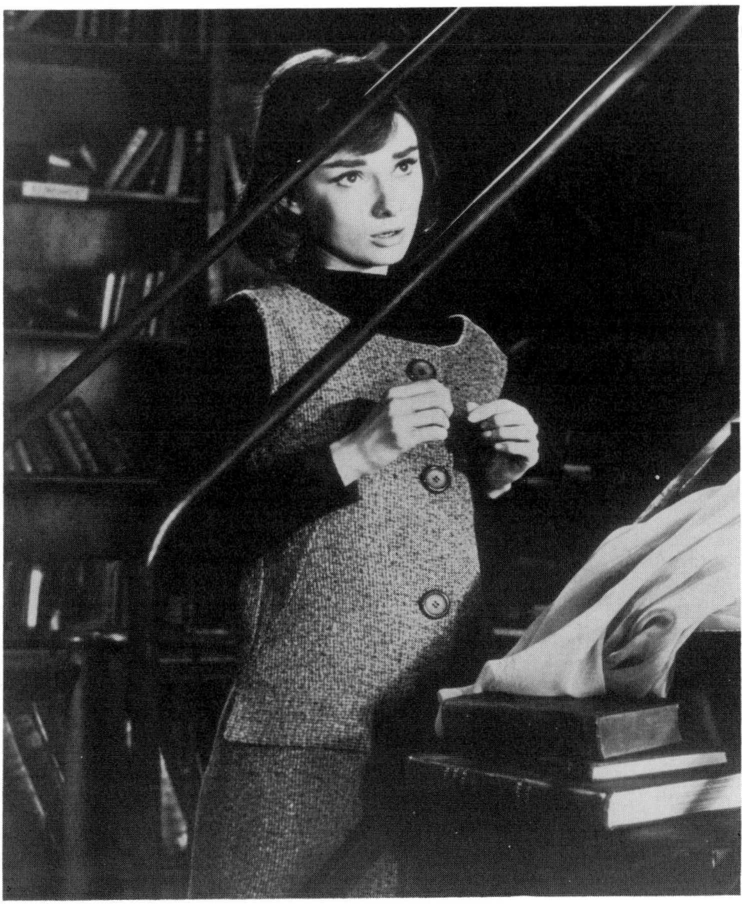

Hepburn in the title-role of Funny Face (57), *the supposedly plain Greenwich Village bookseller who is turned by fashion-experts into a top model. It is debatable whether she was more appealing before or after the change.*

She did a Western for John Huston, *The Unforgiven* (60), as Burt Lancaster's half-breed sister, and then took on a role abandoned by Marilyn Monroe, Holly Golightly in *Breakfast at Tiffany's* (61), from Truman Capote's novella. Capote described it as 'a mawkish valentine to Audrey Hepburn' and George Axelrod, who wrote the script, has said that it would have been better had Hepburn not refused to do or say anything which might make the character – a sort of feckless tramp – unsympathetic; but both film and performance were warmly received. *The Children's Hour* (62) was not. She and Shirley MacLaine did their best in this William Wyler remake of his own *These Three* with the play's original lesbian theme restored, but the script was lifeless and the direction ponderous. She then teamed with Cary Grant in a light-hearted thriller, *Charade* (63), which, while far from perfect, stood out among the year's films like Turkish Delight in a box of fudge. She won a second BFA award. *Paris When It Sizzles* (64) was pure fudge, an adaptation of Duvivier's *La Fête à Henriette*, with William Holden. It fizzled.

When Warners paid $5½ million (easily a record sum) for the rights to *My Fair Lady*, they passed over the stage Eliza, Julie Andrews, setting off her derisory fee and then lack of screen fame againt Hepburn's flat $1 million and box-office potency. It turned out to be good insurance, for the film made a mint, but, perhaps because of Andrews's shadow, Hepburn's generally entrancing Eliza was not, as it should have been, a peak in her career; and her dubbed singing voice had none of the throaty charm of her undubbed songs in *Funny Face*. Wyler directed her again in *How to Steal a Million* (66), a comedy with Peter O'Toole, but this time he diminished her and the film was not a big success. Stanley Donen (who had made *Funny Face*) then took her over, with sensational results, and the press sang her praises as they had not for years: *Two for the Road* (67) with Albert Finney, an artful and witty examination of marriage written by Frederic Raphael. She then returned to Hollywood (most of her 60s films were made in Europe) for a chiller, *Wait Until Dark*, which really was no great shakes, but she, as a blind girl, often made it seem so.

Julie Andrews famously played Eliza Dolittle in the original Broadway and London productions of 'My Fair Lady', but was passed over for the film version (64) just before she was on the verge of major film stardom. It must be said that Audrey Hepburn was a meltingly beautiful substitute.

Her marriage to Ferrer ended in 1968 and the following year she married an Italian psychiatrist; because she felt that a career was dangerous for marriage, she said she would not film again unless it could be on her doorstep (Rome and Switzerland). In the changing movie sphere there may not have been many offers, but she did turn down the lead in *Forty Carats*, because it could not be made in Europe. She had no intention of staying away – she was only tempted once or twice – she said, when she returned for *Robin and Marion* (76): though why *this* tempted her it is hard to say – other than that the role was suitable for her years. There is something to be said about an ageing Robin Hood and wife, and Hepburn and Sean Connery managed in their performances almost to save it, despite high jinks and incompetence all around them. She might have been in *A Bridge Too Far*, but her agent asked for $750,000 and they were able to get Liv Ullmann for less than $150,000. Hepburn did return to play an industrial heiress in *Sidney Sheldon's Bloodline* (79). Said 'Variety', speaking for all of us (except, presumably, Sheldon): 'Though it would take several pictures of the level of *Bloodline* to seriously damage her stature, it's a shame she picks something like this now that she works so seldom.' She explained that she liked the director, Terence Young, but the important thing was that the work did not take her far from her family (though she was divorced the following year). She said that she would make one last picture to go out on and Peter Bogdanovich's name may have been an inducement: but *They All Laughed* (81) was thin indeed – and she was wasted, as the object of suspicion to a detective agency in a comedy-thriller which was neither. The producers, Time-Life, dropped it and, though its writer-director reclaimed the rights, there were few further showings; in Britain it went direct to video.

In 1984 Ray Stark and Neil Simon were said to be preparing a vehicle for her, but nothing came of it. She eventually made a TV movie, *Love Among Thieves* (87), which caused John Leonard of 'New York Magazine' to remark: 'Audrey Hepburn can do no wrong, but wrong can be done to her' – citing both the script and co-star Robert Wagner.

Charlton Heston

Charlton Heston has starred in some of the most popular films ever made: in the 'Variety' tabulation of all-time box-office champs published in 1971, 11 Heston pictures were listed with a total take of $153 million. (John Wayne was first with 23 films taking $163 million and Julie Andrews third with 6 films totalling $144 million.) Yet Heston has never been voted into those top 10 stars lists by the showmen whose job it is to study these things. In fact, the statistics seem to indicate that in the right epic the public would turn up in droves to see Heston; and in the wrong ones you could not give him away.

Maybe the succession of saints and heroes he has played has, finally, been alienating, or maybe his god-like appearance qualifies him for some sort of unapproachable celestial position. Something seems to happen to him in most of his pictures: he looks interesting, but never is, very. A head-prefect reticence and conscientiousness creeps in. He told the 'Sunday Express' in 1960: 'It's a lot harder to be creative in an epic than in a low-budget picture. It's terribly easy to get swamped in a turgid sea of angry slaves brandishing spears. But it's worth it because of the characters you get to play. To be honest with you I consider Moses a more challenging role than, say, the hero in *Room at the Top*.' On occasion he has acted beautifully and for a while he proved himself to be one of the most intelligent actor-impresarios; if he can throw off his inhibitions and go into character acting he might yet do something worthwhile.

He was born in Evanston, Illinois, in 1923 and from junior school onwards was interested in theatricals; he majored in speech at Northwestern University and began his pro career on various Chicago radio stations. After three years with the air force (as a radio operator) he and his wife (Lydia Clark, married 1944) moved to New York City, but there were no breaks and they did stock in North Carolina. In 1947 he got a Broadway chance as a member of Katherine Cornell's 'Antony and Cleopatra'; then he was in stock again in Pennsylvania. He began to get some TV breaks – Antony in 'Julius Caesar', Heathcliff in 'Wuthering Heights', Petruchio in 'The Taming of the Shrew'. At university in 1941 he had played the title-role in an amateur film version of *Peer Gynt*, directed by David Bradley, who now asked him to play Mark Antony in *Julius Caesar* (48). This $11,000, 16-mm version of Shakespeare quickly acquired some small renown; but it was his Rochester in a TV 'Jane Eyre' which brought him to the attention of Hal Wallis, who signed him to a contract to embrace 10 films. He débuted for Wallis in a programmer with Lizabeth Scott, *Dark City* (50), as a crooked gambler, but continued to act on the stage in New York and on TV, notably as Macbeth opposite Judith Anderson in 1951.

He was reputedly walking across the Paramount lot (Wallis released through that company) when Cecil B. De Mille chose him to play the circus manager in *The Greatest Show on Earth* (52), a trite spectacular which became the second biggest-grossing picture in film history. He glowered to good effect as the tough hero, determined that the Show Must Go On. He was *The Savage*, a white man raised by the Sioux, which started a four-year fun of programmers – except for the next two: *Ruby Gentry*, as Jennifer Jones's bold, bad paramour, and *The President's Lady* (53) at 20th, as Andrew Jackson. Most of his films were the colour programme-fillers made for Paramount by Pine and Thomas, renowned opponents of originality: *Pony Express*, as Buffalo Bill Cody; *Arrowhead*, as a chief scout after the Apaches; *Bad for Each Other* – and for the audience, a *Citadel*-like sudser about a doctor, with Lizabeth Scott; *The Naked Jungle* (54), in which his plantation got eaten up by a plague of white ants in bad process work; *Secret of the Incas* – they really went all the way to Machu Picchu to film this?; and *The Far Horizons* (55), scanning them with Fred MacMurray, a strictly hackneyed account of the Lewis and Clark expedition. In fact, he must have been sorely depressed by the time he was loaned to Universal for a comedy, *The Private War of Major Benson*, a property which had been developed for Cary Grant and which Heston was mighty keen to do, playing a tough hero who has difficulty being human (not surprisingly, considering the nuns and kids who surrounded him). Then he was the solid rancher in love with Jane Wyman as *Lucy Gallant*, another Pine-Thomas effort.

To keep his spirits up he played Macbeth in Bermuda, Mister Roberts in Palm Beach and New York, and the hero of 'Detective Story' in stock; but he might have gone the way of all second-rate action stars if De Mille had not chosen him to play Moses in *The Ten Commandments* (56) – because, as he confided in a special trailer, Heston reminded him forcibly of Michelangelo's statue. The performance was hardly more animated, yet the film, for all its tedium, was hugely popular (at $7·5 million it was the most expensive film yet made; and *it* became the second biggest grosser in film history, but again after *Gone With the Wind*). Heston said later: 'if you can't make a career out of two De Milles, you'll never make it.' He worked out his contract with a Western, *Three Violent People*, with Anne Baxter, and then jumped at the chance of being directed by Orson Welles in *Touch of Evil* (57); there was a considerable make-up job to make him look Mexican (he was a detective), but it was also his least mechanical performance. He confirmed the favourable impression with an excellent account of Greg-

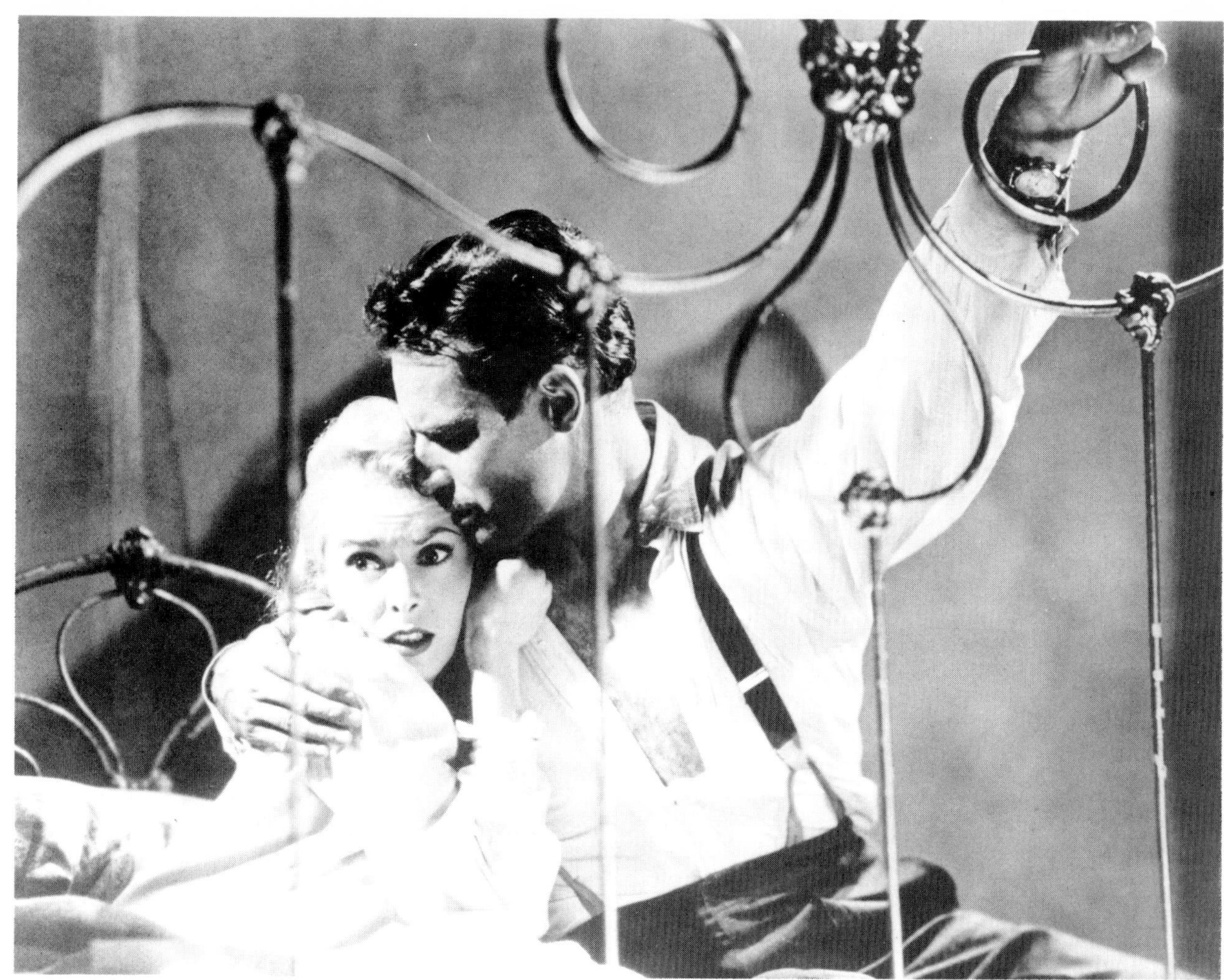

Not a very nice honeymoon: narcotics investigator Charlton Heston and his bride, Janet Leigh, getting caught up in mayhem, in Touch of Evil *(57), directed by Orson Welles with more power than cohesion.*

ory Peck's grinning rival in *The Big Country* (58), directed by William Wyler – after which it was back to more conventional stuff with De Mille's big-budgeted and unsuccessful *The Buccaneer*, again playing Andrew Jackson.

Then he was *Ben Hur* (59). The original casting was Cesare Danova, but MGM diplomatically announced that his English would not be good enough in time. The studio's fortunes were in a bad way when it was decided to gamble all (*this* became the most expensive film yet made, at $15 million) on a remake of their old Silent success. William Wyler was offered the earth to do it. The result was a long, painstaking, lavish and arid Sunday-school epic which more than accomplished its task: the studio was saved, the film took more money than *The Ten Commandments* (replacing it as the second box-office champ) and inevitably won a Best Picture Oscar. Heston got a Best Actor Oscar for his participation in it.

More enjoyable was *The Wreck of the Mary Deare*, with Heston as an obtuse and bad-tempered salvage expert, salvaging Gary Cooper among other things. He turned down *Let's Make Love* in order to work under Laurence Olivier's direction on Broadway in 'The Juggler', but it did not run. Then he was back on the epic trail as Spain's legendary hero, *El Cid* (61). Stirringly beautiful (Spanish locations, Sophia Loren, him), it spiralled downhill whenever anybody had to act anything. A change of pace, a comedy, *The Pigeon That Took Rome*, garnered no thanks, so he returned to his corner: *Diamond Head* (62), in fact a return to Ruby Gentry country, though literally Hawaii, as a proud, proud landowner; and *55 Days at Peking* (63), as an American marine combating (with help) the Boxer Rebellion. Considering their budgets, neither did well and by that same standard George Stevens's *The Greatest Story Ever Told* (65) was one of the biggest disasters in Hollywood history. Premièred at 225 minutes it was cut at least three times over the next two years, to 141 minutes; but still the public would not go. Max von Sydow played Christ and Heston had a key role as John the Baptist.

Cuts also affected *Major Dundee*, after trouble (the script was not ready) between Columbia and Sam Peckinpah, directing his first big-budget film. Heston championed the director, even offering to return his salary in an attempt to get things right (the studio, to his chagrin, accepted). Even so, the final film was not Peckinpah's conception but had merit and to spare. Heston's tough-nut Major, commanding a band of roughs in pursuit of the Apaches, was excellent, but demonstrated a crucial weakness in his heroic style: for all his craggy integrity, he is unable to create tension (as could Gary Cooper, Fonda, etc.). Co-star Richard Harris had another cause for complaint: 'Heston's the only man who could drop out of a cubic moon, he's so *square*. We never got on. The trouble is with him he doesn't think he's just a hired actor, like the rest of us. He thinks he's the *entire* production. He used to sit there in the mornings and clock us in with a stop-watch . . .' He had no more luck with a commercial venture, *The Agony and the Ecstasy*, flatly directed by Carol Reed from a bestselling novel about Michelangelo (Heston). Much more interestingly he backed another newish talent, Franklin Schaffner, enabling him to set up a film he had been wanting to make for four years, *The War Lord*; again it was mucked about with after star and director had left the studio, but was still Hollywood's best attempt out of many over the years to reconstruct medieval Europe (specifically, Norman France); and Heston again was fine in the title-role.

As General Gordon (with a Bible in one hand and a brandy in the other) he got better notices for *Khartoum* (66) than did Olivier: Richard Roud in the 'Guardian' found his performance 'first-rate. . . . For many years now he has been just about the only heroic actor we have had, the only one capable of even attempting the really big parts. Now, with his maturity, he adds to his natural physical prestige a fine grasp of character.' None of these films had done as well as had been hoped and the box-office doldrums continued (only more so): *Counterpoint* (67), as an American orchestral conductor *vs* the Nazis (it might have done better under its original title *Battle Horns*), and *Will Penny*, a critically admired Western and another example of his encouragement of new talent – in this case director Tom Gries.

20th's *Planet of the Apes* (68), directed by Schaffner, was, however, a huge success, with an almost naked Heston among the monkeys. Perhaps encouraged by this, he tried the first sexy love scenes of his career in *Pro* (69), a story of American football. Gries directed and it flopped badly (it has never been released in Britain). Heston had so wanted to do it that he had accepted a low salary and a participation deal; but with *The Hawaiians*, a sequel to *Hawaii* (which, as it happened, he had turned down) he was back to an announced $750,000 plus a percentage of the gross. He played Mark Antony again in the new, British version of *Julius Caesar* (70), once more taking off most of his clothes for the camera – but that did not stop the film from being universally panned: a third box-office dud in a row. Another sequel, *Beneath the Planet of the Apes*, was a success – but his role was

Charlton Heston in typical guise, as one of four astronauts who discover the Planet of the Apes *(68) – his most successful film of the 60s.*

Charlton Heston contemplative: as 'Chinese' Gordon in a British spectacular, Khartoum *(66).*

brief. He tried science fiction again, as *The Omega Man* (71), the last man on earth – and his salary was down to $300,000. He was on a participation deal then with a pet project, *Antony and Cleopatra* (72), as Antony, also directing and having prepared the screenplay. He reacted to the British press reception by saying, 'Critics? Who cares about critics?' It was too bad: in the credits and advertising he emphasized Shakespeare and underplayed his own role (a welcome facet at a time most directors seemed on ego-trip, *cf* Polanski and his *Macbeth*) – but the film was dull. His Cleopatra was Hildegard Neil and when he saw fit to publish the diary he had kept of his career (in 1978) he made it clear that he saw too late her inadequacy in the role; it was also apparent that the film's failure was a blow to him – and, curiously, that he has very little modesty about what most people feel is a very modest talent.

He was *Skyjacked* for MGM, as the pilot; and he had Clark Gable's old role in *The Call of the Wild* (73), but the British, West German, French, Italian and Spanish sponsors did not find that his name opened US cinemas to it. Again at Metro, he was in *Soylent Green*, as a man of the future; and he was a man of the past, Cardinal Richelieu, in *The Three Musketeers: The Queen's Diamonds* (74). There were two 'disaster' movies, *Airport 1975* and *Earthquake*, in which his roles were interchangeable, coming to the rescue; and the second look at his Richelieu, in *The Four Musketeers: The Revenge of Milady* (75). Since that was part of one venture divided into two, it was announced that the revised terms included a profit cut of this one. He was a gallant captain in *Midway* (76). His salary on *The Last Hard Men*, an MGM Western, was said to be $250,000 plus 10 per cent of the gross, but there was unlikely to be a profit. Nor was another disaster movie any more successful, *Two-Minute Warning*, in which he was the police chief directing operations against the sniper in the stadium. He was one of several names, playing Henry VIII, in *The Prince and the Pauper* (77), which closed the Carlton Cinema in London; retitled *Crossed Swords* later, it did the same to Radio City Music Hall (as a movie theatre) in New York. Another disaster movie, *Gray Lady Down* (78) – he was captain of a nuclear submarine – went the way of the others. He was an obsessed Egyptologist in *The Awakening* (80), which managed to be even worse than the 1971 Hammer horror, *Blood From the Mummy's Tomb*, which used the same source material; and he was a trapper in *The Mountain Men*, with a screenplay, full of vulgarities, by his son Fraser Clarke Heston.

The only stage work in years had been in Skokie, Illinois, as More in 'A Man for All Seasons' (65); and Macbeth in LA – scheduled to be repeated in London (and advertised) but cancelled at the last moment. Among TV appearances he was, less heroically, Essex in 'Elizabeth the Queen' (67). In 1981 in Los Angeles he played Sherlock Holmes in 'The Crucifer of Blood'. In Canada he directed and starred in, playing twin brothers, *Mother Lode* (82), again written by his son. It was yet another failure and his last cinema film to date. Reorganizing his career, he has kept a healthy profile: *Chiefs* (83), a small-town saga for CBS (mini-series) set back in the 20s-40s, as one of its leaders, at a fee of $750,000 for 10 weeks' work (*cf* Mitchum, who got $1 million for six months on *The Winds of War*); *Nairobi Affair* (84), again for CBS, as a big-game hunter; 'The Caine Mutiny Court Martial', as Queeg, in London in 1985; *Dynasty II: The Colbys*, the mini-series, from then to 1987; *Proud Man* (87), as a Wyoming rancher visited by his son (Peter Strauss), a Viet drop-out; and again in London, 'A Man for All Seasons'. In the teeth of poor notices he admirably expressed his commitment to good theatre (to be found in London rather than New York) and quoted Olivier's dictum that the reviews to worry about are the good ones. He filmed it for TV, a foolish thing to do in view of the Zinnemann-Scofield movie; and it has not to date been seen. Heston has been on TV, in *Original Sin* (89), as the grandfather of a boy kidnapped by the Mafia.

William Holden

William Holden in 1956, according to 'Picturegoer' was: 'Dependable, sturdy cornerstone of solid box-office winners. Likeable, man-in-the-street face and splendid physique, backed by consistent performances, rather than electrifying talent, mark his success.' He said that he did not enjoy acting: for which reason, said Billy Wilder, he was fond of Holden – he was never hammy He went on: 'He is the ideal motion-picture actor. He is beyond acting. . . . You never doubt or question what he is. Jimmy Stewart is a prime example of that sort of actor. So is Gary Cooper. There is no crap about them.' Yes, but Stewart and Cooper retained their individuality as they aged: having little to start with, Holden had only a certain weary integrity when his youthful charm had gone.

Holden was born in 1918 in O'Fallon, Illinois. The family moved to California and he studied at the Pasadena Junior College; while there he took part in radio plays and appeared at the Playhouse; in a play called 'Manya' (37) he played Madame Curie's 80-year-old father-in-law and so impressed a Paramount talent scout that he had the studio test him and they signed him at $50 a week. His first screen job was saying 'Thank you' in *Million Dollar Legs* (39). He might have languished had not Rouben Mamoulian screened his test when looking for a youngster for *Golden Boy* (released first). 20th had turned down his request for Tyrone Power, but Paramount did not mind loaning Holden; Columbia, producing, negotiated to take over half his contract, for the next 14 years – because the part was a very important one (but they did not raise his salary). He played a boxer who would rather be a violinist, one of Hollywood's pet themes and in this case based on a play by Clifford Odets.

Though nominally a star, neither company did much with him. He was loaned to Warners to play gangster George Raft's 'good' younger brother in *Invisible Stripes* (40) and to United Artists for the juvenile in *Our Town*, Sam Wood's screen version of Thornton Wilder's play. Paramount put him into *Those Were the Days*, campus cut-ups in the 90s, and Columbia into *Arizona*, much to the consternation of co-star Jean Arthur, who thought him much too young for her. He did not want to do *I Wanted Wings* (41), because he thought the part too small and nebulous (a scene of him filming this was incorporated into *Hold Back the Dawn*). He referred to these early parts as his 'Smiling Jim' roles, but short of striking there was no way of avoiding them: *Texas*, another Columbia Western; *The Fleet's In* (42), as a girl-shy sailor wagered by his buddies to kiss frigid nightclub queen Dorothy Lamour; *The Remarkable Andrew*, whimsical ghost stuff, with Brian Donlevy as Andrew Jackson; *Meet the Stewarts*, sentimental slosh in which rich Frances Dee adjusted to being married to hard-working him; and *Young and Willing* (43), a comedy about stage hopefuls with Susan Hayward. In 1941 he had married actress Brenda Marshall, who retired about the time he left for war service (they were divorced in 1970). He became a lieutenant in the army; and after the war returned to the same innocuous parts, starting with a loan-out to 20th for an air drama, *Blaze of Noon* (47), with Anne Baxter.

There was nothing remarkable about either the film or his performance, but *Dear Ruth* indicated a new ease in his acting and the film itself was a successful version of a Broadway hit about a soldier, a girl (Joan Caulfield) and the kid sister (Mona Freeman) who has been writing to him on her behalf. There followed a run of unobjectionable films; *Variety Girl*, in a guest spot; *Rachel and the Stranger* (48), as Loretta Young's husband and getting $14,000 for this loan-out, while Paramount picked up $250,000 for his services; *Apartment for Peggy*, as Jeanne Crain's; and *The Man from Colorado*, with his *Texas* buddy, Glenn Ford. He did get a change in *The Dark Past* (49), a remake of 1939's *Blind Alley*, as a desperate killer holed up in the house of psychiatrist Lee J. Cobb (just his luck), but it was no less implausible than others of its ilk. In *Streets of Laredo* he was an outlaw who reforms and joins the Texas Rangers (it was a remake of the film of that name). There were three comedies, *Miss Grant Takes Richmond* with Lucille Ball; *Dear Wife*, a sequel to *Dear Ruth*; and *Father Is a Bachelor* (50) with Colleen Gray.

His basic niceness was well used by Billy Wilder in *Sunset Boulevard*, to the extent that he was almost creepy as Gloria Swanson's gigolo, a scriptwriter down on his luck. It was the first time critics had taken much notice of him. He was the head of the railway police in a thriller, *Union Station*, and then had another choice part in *Born Yesterday*, as Judy Holliday's tutor, which he played without style but with rare good humour. He wanted to go to Broadway to replace Henry Fonda in 'Mister Roberts', but his two studios were more concerned with finding that film or part which would launch him into the forefront of Hollywood leading men. He was loaned to Warners for *Force of Arms* (51), a half-hearted remake of *A Farewell to Arms* with Nancy Olsen; it was their third film together and Paramount promptly re-teamed them in *Submarine Command*, a Korean War drama. *Boots Malone* (52), a horse-racing story, was his last for

William Holden when he was first under contract to Paramount, above. Left, Rachel and the Stranger *(48) was a comedy-drama about a nice backwoods couple – Loretta Young and William Holden, whose marriage is disturbed by a wayfaring stranger (played by Robert Mitchum).*

Columbia. He renewed with Paramount only, for 14 years (the negotiations took into account various suspensions for refusing roles), with the right to do one outside film a year, and the new contract kicked off with *The Turning Point*, a crime drama with Edmond O'Brien, as a racket-busting reporter.

His own turning-point came when Wilder chose him to play the sharp-boy hero of *Stalag 17* (53), an unsubtle but enjoyable prison-camp comedy. He got a Best Actor Oscar for it and began to get more meaty roles – if not quite yet: *The Moon is Blue*, as a wolf; *Forever Female*, as a bumptious supermarket clerk who writes a play, with Ginger Rogers; *Escape from Fort Bravo*, as a cavalry officer; and *Executive Suite* (54), as one of its inmates. Still, the films were better and distinctly A product. Over the next few years he was to appear in some mighty successful films, as a result of which he was one of the top 10 from 1954 through 1958, and in fact the box-office king in 1956. As 'Picturegoer''s appraisal hints, he was lucky, but he was certainly never bad – if invariable: *Sabrina*, as the happy-go-lucky younger brother, a suitor for Audrey Hepburn; *The Country Girl*, with Grace Kelly and Bing Crosby, as a theatre director; and *The Bridges at Toko-Ri*, as a naval officer in this Korean War drama, with Kelly as his wife. *Love is a Many-Splendored Thing* (55) kept him in the Far East, a love story between a Eurasian (Jennifer Jones) and an American journalist – a part written and played with no dimension whatsoever.

He was at his best in the sort of part in which Wilder had cast him, haf-hero/half-heel – the quintessential hero of the 50s. Earlier screen heroes were seldom completely despicable: the gangsters played by Robinson or Cagney were classified villains, while those done by Robert Taylor and Tyrone Power were mainly unfortunate. But from Marlon Brando's Kowalski onwards, the new hero was pushy, unmindful of charm, conscious only of hs virility. *Picnic*, directed by Joshua Logan from William Inge's play, embodied all the new clichés, all the wish-fulfilment and all the 'reality'. Holden was the no-good loafer who bums his way into town, treats the women like dogs, bares his torso and ships out on the freight-car just as the pack of them are fawning round his ankles. That he was in fact a *hero* might have been due to Hollywood exigencies: whether or not Inge's attitude to him was ambiguous, the film reduced the theme to boy-meets-girl, boy-loses-girl *but* boy-gets-girl in a nearby town, an ending tacked on for the screen.

Women at least lapped it up, but, when Holden played an out-and-out rogue in *The Proud and the Profane* (56), with Deborah Kerr, it flopped (it was not, however, a very good film). This was announced as the first of a new six-picture deal with Paramount over a seven-year period; but when Holden decided to produce, he went to Warners – *Toward the Unknown*, a sci-fier. He said he did not enjoy the experience of producing and acting and the piece was not very successful. *The Bridge on the River Kwai* (57) was a whopping hit and Holden's contractual arrangement, calling for a delayed percentage payment – for tax purposes – meant that he could retire at any time and be assured of an annual income. He was getting 10 per cent of the gross, paid out at $50,000 a year. As the film grossed $25 million, it was estimated that he would be paid over a 50-year period – and Columbia would make $2 million interest just holding it.

He did another war film, *The Key* (58) with Sophia Loren, basically a love story, profoundly unimportant and always several removes from reality. He signed for a John Ford Western, *The Horse Soldiers* (59), with John Wayne, the two of them to get $750,000 each, plus 20 per cent of the profits – up till then the biggest star salaries yet paid (soon Elizabeth Taylor would get more for *Cleopatra* and concurrently Brando was said to be getting $1 million against 10 per cent for *The Fugitive Kind*, but this was never confirmed). He almost did not make it: Para-

Trevor Howard and William Holden in The Key *(58), directed by Carol Reed. The key referred to was that to Sophia Loren's apartment, and the pointless plot had to do with Howard forcing a duplicate on Holden.*

mount had sued, saying that they wanted him for one of his contracted pictures. And it would have been as well if he had not: it was very dull and lost a fortune.

For Paramount he did *The World of Suzie Wong* (60), a tour of Hong Kong brothels which had been a successful novel and play, and was a successful film – at least, financially. According to Carl Foreman, who had produced the very profitable *The Key*, Holden turned down *The Guns of Navarone* because Foreman would not meet his new fee (see above). If that remained his fee for the next batch, it is unlikely that the producers got their money back: *Satan Never Sleeps* (62), with Clifton Webb, both as priests; *The Counterfeit Traitor*, a spy thriller; *The Lion*, a big-game hunting adventure in Africa; *Paris When it Sizzles* (64), a weak comedy with Audrey Hepburn; *The Seventh Dawn*, as a Malayan rubber-planter; and *Alvarez Kelly* (66), a Civil War Western. In 1966 he was convicted of manslaughter in Italy when a man died in a car accident; he was given a suspended sentence and paid the widow $80,000. He was one of the several names in *Casino Royale* (67), but, starring, was in another mediocre movie, *The Devil's Brigade* (68), a tired war story.

In 1968 he was on 'Variety''s list of over-priced stars. In 1960 he had said 'My blueprint is to make one very important picture a year – one that is artistically satisfying to me but successful at the box-office'. He finally got his wish – by which time he really needed it: *The Wild Bunch* (69), as their outlaw leader, Sam Peckinpah's violent and gratuitously bloody Western. Said 'Time Magazine': 'Holden hasn't done such good work since *Stalag 17*.' He then did a maudlin Franco-Italian effort, *L'Arbre de Noël/The Christmas Tree*, about a millionaire whose son is dying of the effects of radiation.

His name meant little at the box-office by the time he came to do *The Wild Rovers* (71), as an ageing cowboy, and *The Revengers* (72). It hardly mattered. In life he was a millionaire ('Golden Holden'), with business interests in the Orient and co-owner of a Mount Kenya safari club. Perhaps that is the reason he made a Swiss-Spanish co-production, *Open Season/Los Cazadores* (74), with Peter Fonda, set in the US, with Holden as a vengeance-happy killer. For NBC TV he did a four-part special, *The Blue Knight*, as a veteran police patrolman; cut to feature length, it received short shrift in British cinemas and Holden was little known to younger cinemagoers when he played the man who built what became *The Towering Inferno*. *Breezy* (75) was little seen: Clint Eastwood produced and directed this tale of a middle-aged man in love with a 'flower' girl (Kay Lenz). 'Aged' might have been the word for Holden's appearances in *21 Hours to Munich* (76), made for TV in the US and cinemas elsewhere, as the Munich police chief in this recreation of the shooting of the Israelis at the '72 Olympics, and *Network*, as an experienced TV executive. In the latter role, he was 'us', the voice of decency, and he had never been better in a serious role. It was a shame that he could not follow it with

William Holden's off-screen interest in big-game hunting has been reflected in only one picture – a mediocre effort called The Lion (62), *with Capucine.*

anything better than *Damien The Omen II* (78), replacing Gregory Peck, the ageing star of the first of this horror series; but he was concurrently in Wilder's *Fedora*, as a film producer with one last chance – if he can bring a reclusive star back to the screen. He was a mercenary helicopter pilot in *Ashanti* (79), having replaced James Coburn who had replaced Telly Savalas. He had a cameo role as a prisoner in a POW escape movie, *Escape to Athena*, starring Roger Moore and Savalas, and was the owner of a hotel chain *When Time Ran Out . . .* (80), a disaster movie which fizzled. He was a fatally ill curmudgeon in the Australian *The Earthling*, which did nothing to revive his career; but supporting Julie Andrews he had one last mild success, *S.O.B.* (81), as a studio executive.

His relationship with Stephanie Powers during his last years ended, she said, because of his drinking. In 1981 he fell in his apartment with a high level of alcohol in his blood; his corpse was not discovered for several days.

Judy Holliday

There are some who think Judy Holliday was the greatest comic actress of all time and some who think she was simply the greatest comic actress of the century. (Ssshh, dear, Beatrice Lillie was a *clown.*) Her touch was simply surer and lighter than any of the others. Hollywood knew this and treasured her talent; but, as if awed, was not prodigal with it. The legacy is small, but of shining burnished solid gold.

She was born in New York in 1922 and made her first contact with show business as telephonist for the Mercury Theater Group of Orson Welles. In 1940, with Betty Comden, Adolph Green and others, she formed a nightclub act, 'The Revuers', under her own name, Judith Tuvim. She went to Hollywood for a movie based on a radio programme, *Duffy's Tavern*, which was indefinitely postponed. While there, 'The Revuers' played the Trocadero and she was signed by 20th for seven years, starting at $400 a week. She insisted that her partners also be taken on and they filmed two numbers for *Greenwich Village* (44) which were cut from the final print (today, they would be worth all those of Vivian Blaine and Carmen Miranda put together). She had one line in *Something for the Boys* and then a goodish part as one of the wives in *Winged Victory*, Cukor's film of Moss Hart's play, billed eighth on the cast-list. Not long after that Zanuck invited her to join him on his office couch; she angrily refused and her option was not picked up when it next came up. She returned disillusioned to New York and starred in 'Kiss Them For Me', which won for her the Clarence Derwent award. The best break she could get was understudying Jean Arthur in Garson Kanin's 'Born Yesterday', but during the try-out Arthur took ill and she replaced her; and stayed with the play almost three years. If the dialogue was wittier than most, the part was an old comedy stand-by, the dumb broad with

the heart of gold. This variation had her leaving her ox-like 'protector' for the college boy employed to give her 'culture'. Holliday's Billie Dawn was by turns shrewd, petulant and sarcastic, all in a piercing Bronx whine; the face was vacuous but asinine when amused and glitteringly, childishly, touchingly triumphant when lover or learning was bested. She had created a comic masterpiece and it was, essentially, the only part she was to play. (She was offered a similar role in *My Friend Irma*, but turned it down in favour of Marie Wilson, who was playing it in the radio series of the same name – which did not prevent Wilson from campaigning for the role of Billie Dawn in the screen version.)

Columbia bought the play for Rita Hayworth, but she was at that moment in Europe, in love, and disinclined to return. They tested Jan Sterling, Gloria Grahame, Evelyn Keyes, among others and only *considered* Holliday, who was at that time at MGM playing a supporting role in *Adam's Rib* (49), written by Kanin and his wife Ruth Gordon and directed by Cukor. She played a dumb wife on trial for attempted murder, prosecuted by DA Spencer Tracy and defended by Katharine Hepburn. All of these people, and especially Hepburn, were determined that Holliday would repeat her stage triumph and press releases were issued to the effect that she was walking away with *Adam's Rib*. Columbia capitulated, not least because she would cost less than a name (she got $750 a week for six weeks' work). The film, *Born Yesterday* (50), was directed by Cukor and co-starred Broderick Crawford. Said C.A. Lejeune: 'Most of the film's pleasure is due to the accuracy of Judy Holliday. Only an actress of high intelligence could play a bird-wit woman so exactly. . . . Miss Holliday has some very funny situations and lines, and a most disarming way of using them.' She won a Best Actress Oscar against the stiffest competition in its history (including Bette Davis in *All About Eve*, Gloria Swanson in *Sunset Boulevard*).

Columbia signed her to a contract, one film a year for seven years, for the first of which she would get $5,250 a week. She in fact made only five films for them, all comedies. As befits a big star, she played women much less crass than her first, great broad. The first two were again directed by Cukor and written by the Kanins: *The Marrying Kind* (52), with Aldo Ray, a funny-sad look at a disintegrating marriage; and *It Should Happen To You* (54), possibly her best film, about a girl with an ambition to see her name on a billboard. Said co-star Jack Lemmon later: 'She was intelligent and not at all like the dumb blonde she

Left and above, Born Yesterday *(50) – four expressions of Judy Holliday. With her, Larry Olivier as a senator; Broderick Crawford as her loud-mouthed 'protector'; Howard St John as Crawford's aide; and William Holden as the reporter paid to tutor her. Said the 'New Statesman': 'Her naivety and her hoppity little xylophone notes end . . . by capturing us all. It is a wonderful display of the dead-pan vernacular, with unpredictable bum-wriggles and rounding of the eyes, and Miss Holliday's triumph is complete.'*

so often depicted. . . . She didn't give a damn where the camera was placed, how she was made to look, or about being a star. She just played the scene – acted with, not at. She was also one of the nicest people I've ever met.' There was a falling-off with *Phffft!*, with Lemmon, another marital comedy, but a return to form with *The Solid Gold Cadillac* (56), from a Broadway play about a sweet lady whose awkward questions upset the stockholders' meetings. Paul Douglas co-starred. *Full of Life*, with Richard Conte, was a weak comedy about pregnancy. None of them lit fires at the box-office and by a curious chance she never played opposite a star. Her leading men were either newcomers or reliable older actors, but Columbia never gave her maximum exposure by teaming her with a big gun, as was normal at that time.

She moved to MGM for *Bells Are Ringing* (60), which had been a second Broadway triumph for her, a musical written for her by Comden and Green, with a Jule Styne score. Minnelli directed, Dean Martin co-starred and it was about an answering-service girl who meddles in her clients' affairs. The 'Time Magazine' reviewer spoke of 'a comic gift that is a major wonder of the entertainment world. . . . For the beauty of Judy Holliday's talent lies not least in her meticulous control of it. She knows her type to a tee-hee, and she is never for an instant out of character.' However, the by-now faltering hand of Minnelli made the best of neither star nor material and she returned to the stage. A straight play, 'Laurette' (about Laurette Taylor), folded out of town and two years later a musical, 'Hot Spot' (62), was a quick flop. She had had a weight problem and there were rumours, as early as 1962, that she was fatally ill. From the time she left Columbia till she died in 1965 (of throat cancer) there were several projects which did not come off. During her last years, it had been expected that she would marry Gerry Mulligan; she had earlier (1948–58) been married to David Oppenheim.

Celeste Holm

Put to the top of the list of actresses wasted or neglected by Hollywood the delectable Celeste Holm, a warm and witty blonde who has graced only just over a dozen features. She only played three or four leads, always to excellent critical and public reaction. Perhaps if she had been more conventional, they would have capitalized on her blonde good looks; but very early on she won an Oscar for playing a wise-cracking dame and that, it would seem, was that.

She was born in New York City in 1919, studied acting, singing and dancing with a view to a career in the theatre and made her début with a stock company in Orwigsburg, Deer Lake, Pennsylvania, in 1936. She toured in 'The Women' (as Crystal), made her New York bow in 'Gloriana' (38) at the Little and was in 'The Time of Your Life' (39). She was a successful Broadway actress by the time of 'Oklahoma!' (43) and her Ado Annie in that show led to stardom in the next, 'Bloomer Girl' (44). 20th wanted her for a role in *Where Do We Go From Here?* but she turned them down; they were persistent and she finally went out to Hollywood under contract to them. They tried her out in *Three Little Girls in Blue* (46) – Vivian Blaine, June Haver and Vera-Ellen, three girls out to snag millionaire husbands (20th's old perennial), and she stole the film from them as a French visitor. As a result she got star-billing in *Carnival in Costa Rica* (47), also with Vera-Ellen and, despite a Lecuona score, a dim thing (the men were Dick Haymes and Cesar Romero). Her chance came with *Gentleman's Agreement* as the breezy spinster fashion editor, enormously understanding and witty. The part was well written and played to match (and today is the best thing in the film): she won a Best Supporting Oscar.

She did a rehash of that part, appearing intermittently as the *Road House* (48) cashier; and then was one of the unfortunate inmates of *The Snake Pit*. 20th decided to give her real star parts and made her Dan Dailey's loving but long-suffering wife in *Chicken Every Sunday*, a casserole of bits left over from *Life With Father, I Remember Mama*, etc. For another sentimental piece, *Come to the Stable* (49), she and Loretta Young donned wimples; then she played one of Young's old roles (*Wife, Husband and Friend*) in *Everybody Does It* with Paul Douglas, a diverting comedy about a vapid socialite who fancies herself a *diva*. But these were mainly double-bill fare and so was *Champagne for Caesar* (50) on loan-out to UA, where she was a vamp out to confuse a know-it-all quiz-winner, Ronald Colman.

There was virtually no one at this point who did not think Holm would be one of the biggest stars in the business – if not from the usual mould. 20th were confounded when, in 1950, she asked for release from her contract because she wanted to play all sorts of parts (there was talk of *Born Yesterday*). They had typed her as a wise-cracking blonde and she knew that few of that species ever made it to the very top. In that part again, as Bette Davis's one true friend in *All About Eve*, she received a third Best Supporting Oscar nomination. She left Hollywood for New York, where she did 'Affairs of State', written especially for her; at the end of its long run she did 'Anna Christie' and, for a short while, 'The King and I'. She was also in cabaret and TV (her own series, 'Celeste'), but was not in demand in Hollywood, which seldom forgives those who ask out of contracts. According to director Charles Walters, when her name came up at MGM for *The Tender Trap* (55) the head of the studio (Doré Schary) did not want her; Frank Sinatra did, so she became his confidante, making palatable once again her old role of the spinster with a yen-for-a-man. She partnered Sinatra again in *High Society* (56) but it was the same old part.

In 1957 she toured in 'Back to Methuselah' and since then has been mainly occupied in the theatre: 'Invitation to the March' (60) on Broadway, 'A Month in the Country' (63), 'Mame' (68) and (unsuccessfully) 'Candida' (70) on Broadway, among others. In films, she has given a lift to a couple of mild comedies: Frank Tashlin's *Bachelor Flat* (61), as Terry-Thomas's bewildered fiancée, and *Doctor You've Got to Be Kidding* (67), in another smallish role, as Sandra Dee's showbiz-fixated mother. Also that year some countries saw her – acting most poignantly – in *Cosa Nostra Arch Enemy of the FBI*, which had been part of the FBI TV series with Efrem Zimbalist Jr. Also for TV there was a movie, *The Delphi Bureau* (72), assisting government agent Laurence Luckinbill; they were reunited for the subsequent series, till her role was taken over by Anne Jeffreys.

It was good to have her back in a big role, as Aunt Polly, in *Tom Sawyer* (73), and she was, said 'Variety', 'just sensational . . . returns to the screen in personal triumph', but the film was not greatly admired and it did not lead to anything worthwhile in that area. Instead, she was in two tele-movies, *The Underground Man* (74), with Peter Graves as private eye Lew Archer, and *Death Cruise*, married to Eddie Albert, one of three couples marked for murder. She did 'Butterflies Are Free' and later 'Habeas Corpus' on Broadway, and was before the cameras again:

Four of the nicest people ever to appear in films: Bing Crosby, Grace Kelly, Frank Sinatra and Celeste Holm in a publicity shot for High Society *(56).*

Bittersweet Love (76), supporting Lana Turner; *Captains and the Kings*, a starry mini-series from Taylor Caldwell's novel about Irish immigrants, as a nun; *The Love Boat II* (77), the second pilot for the successful series; *The Private Files of J. Edgar Hoover*, in a cameo as a Washington hostess; and *Backstairs at the White House* (79), a mini-series, as Mrs Harding. After a one-night Broadway flop with 'The Utter Glory of Morrissey Hall' 'Variety' wrote 'It's inspiring, but also saddening to see a beautiful, talented, indomitable star like Celeste Holm try so valiantly to make something of such ludicrous material.'

She appeared off-Broadway in a one-woman show as Janet Flanner in 'Paris Was Yesterday' (80), in Philadelphia in 'Hay Fever' (a role she did in Los Angeles three years later), in Williamstown (Mass.) with a distinguished cast in the RSC play, 'The Greeks' (81), and in Nottingham, England, in 'Lady in the Dark'. In the television remake of *Midnight Lace* she had Myrna Loy's old role, now the mother (not the aunt) of the heroine (Mary Crosby); and in that medium she was another mother, Bess Armstrong's, *This Girl for Hire* (84), a flamboyant former starlet now living with Howard Duff. She was Lindsay Wagner's mother in an ABC series, 'Jessie' (84), and the following year went into *Falcon's Crest*, which she left to make a welcome return to the big screen – in *Three Men and a Baby* (88). She has been married three times.

TREVOR HOWARD

If Trevor Howard kept a press-cutting book, it was probably rather dull: no Oscars, no 'Photoplay' awards for the world's most beloved star, no scandalous headlines (despite a certain reputation as a roisterer), nothing but 40-odd years of good notices – 'reliable', 'excellent', etc. (those quoted in the following text are among the best). Like James Mason and Dirk Bogarde he mainly eschewed the boards of the Old Vic and avoided 'classical' status – normally not the best way for a British actor to hold his reputation and retain star rank. His parts grew smaller towards the end of his career but not his standing; it was absolutely no surprise, for instance, when Patrick Wayne (John's son) told the 'New York Times' that Howard was his favourite actor.

He was born in Cliftonville, Kent, in 1916 and educated at Clifton College and at RADA. He made his first stage appearance while still studying, in 'Revolt in a Reformatory' (34) at the Gate, and for the next couple of years acted mainly in London's 'little' theatres; in 1936 and 1939 he was at Stratford-upon-Avon, between which he did two years playing a student in the long-running 'French Without Tears'. It was not till he was invalided out of the Royal Artillery in 1943 that he had his first real success, playing Captain Plume in 'The Recruiting Officer' at the Arts. Shortly afterwards he starred for the first time in the West End, in 'A Soldier for Christmas'; in the cast was Helen Cherry, who became his wife. Carol Reed gave him a small part in *The Way Ahead* (44), as a naval officer, and he had another small part in *The Way to the Stars* (45), as an RAF officer. Noël Coward, on the basis of the first of these, chose him to play the lead in *Brief Encounter*, as the nice, married doctor who falls in love with married Celia Johnson. Against her anguish and emotion he had little to do but be manly and considerate, but he was established as a screen name. Two good thrillers for Launder and Gilliatt gave him a chance to add colour to his screen character: *I See a Dark Stranger* (46), as an English officer involved with Irish Deborah Kerr, and *Green for Danger* (47), as a surgeon and murder suspect. His image changed somewhat when he played a demobbed man turned crook in *They Made Me a Fugitive* – British 'social realism' but heavily theatrical at a time Hollywood was finding a new realism in such subjects. He was a drunken doctor in *So Well Remembered*, a heavy social drama, from a novel by James Hilton, that was part of a brief flirtation between Rank and RKO (who sent over director Edward Dmytryk and stars Martha Scott and Richard Carlson). And in David

Trevor Howard and Celia Johnson in Brief Encounter *(45). This is a posed still for publicity purposes, but it does convey the essential decency both of these players and the characters they portrayed.*

Lean's *The Passionate Friends* (48) he did a variation on his performance in *Brief Encounter*, as the gentle Other Man.

It was in a subsidiary role in *The Third Man* (49), as the British liaison officer, that he first demonstrated on screen that other aspect of his personality – sarcastic, cynical. These are qualities Hollywood has often demanded of British actors, but Howard was no George Sanders: he was blunt, forthright, trustworthy, an old hand. He was the intelligent hero of action thrillers: *The Golden Salamander*, as an archaeologist fighting gun-runners; *Odette* (50), as Captain Peter Churchill, a wartime hero for his exploits in Occupied France; and *The Clouded Yellow*, as an ex-British agent wrongly accused of murder. He went to seed convincingly in Carol Reed's version of Conrad, *Outcast of the Islands* (51), and in his performance were intimations of the good film this might have been. Then, after playing a disciplinarian skipper in *The Gift Horse* (52), he was superb in *The Heart of the Matter* (53), though this film of Graham Greene's novel was emphatically not. It was his own favourite among his films, perhaps for notices like these: 'Trevor Howard as Scobie is pity in the flesh; and, moreover, a spectator gets the sense that he is not one aspect of the hero in one scene, and another in another, but the whole man at every moment' ('Time Magazine'); and 'Trevor Howard, whose work seems to mature and expand with every performance, gives a magnificent study of a nice man tortured by the consequences of weakness he can recognize but not overcome' (Fred Majdalany in the 'Daily Mail').

Around this time he seemed to abandon the theatre; during these years he had played Petruchio at the Old Vic (47), the General in 'The Devil's General' (53) and Lopahin in 'The Cherry Orchard' (54); he would not return till 1962 in 'Two Stars for Comfort'. In 1964 he was in Strindberg's 'The Father'.

Graham Greene also wrote *Mano dello Straniero/The Stranger's Hand* (54), directly for the screen, but this 'entertainment' failed to do for Venice what *The Third Man* had done for Vienna. Howard stayed waterlogged, for *Les Amants du Tage*, made in France with Françoise Arnoul, as a rather extraordinary Scotland Yard Man. After that bleak year, he was in a big success, Warwick's routine war film, *Cockleshell Heroes* (55), as José Ferrer's laconic adjutant. This was perhaps the first time that he was widely seen by US audiences. Hollywood now called when Leo Genn did not like the script of *Run for the Sun* (56), so he was the sadistic baddie – played by Leslie Banks in an earlier version, *The Hounds of Zaroff*. He should have stayed on to do *Omar Khayyam* but this time he did not like the script and Michael Rennie played the part. In Britain he was in a worse film, *Interpol* (57),

The Heart of the Matter *(53): Elizabeth Allen as the restless and snobbish wife; Trevor Howard as the too fallible police commissioner; and Denholm Elliot as the civil servant who 'comforts' the wife. Howard's performance is unequivocally one of the best in the whole history of films.*

one of Warwick's amorphous thrillers, bolstering Victor Mature and Anita Ekberg. His playing, thought 'Picturegoer', 'made theirs look slightly silly', but his own comment was mild: 'I thought there was something more worthwhile in life than acting with an ex-beauty queen.' Also undistinguished was *Manuela* with Elsa Martinelli – apart from his playing: 'Perhaps it is only the depth and subtlety of Trevor Howard's playing which makes one conscious of a lack in his partner. . . . I can think of no actor like [him] for suggesting the heartbreak behind the bleak, the unwavering look' (Dilys Powell); and 'Trevor Howard gives the film an extra dimension with his painfully precise portrait of the anguished old man of the sea. This is a great performance' (Philip Oakes in the London 'Evening Standard').

He gave a genuine salty bite to *The Key* (58), another sea story, leaving Sophia Loren and William Holden stranded artistically after he died – and he won a BFA Best British Actor award; and he was the best of several names in the unsatisfactory *The Roots of Heaven.* He was the only good thing about *Moment of Danger* (60), a British thriller directed by Laslo Benedick with Dorothy Dandridge, as a crook. As for the version of D.H. Lawrence's *Sons and Lovers*, playing the father, 'Variety' said: 'Easily the outstanding feature of the production is the powerful performance by Trevor Howard. . . . Always a polished performer, Howard has rarely been better, giving a moving and wholly believable study of a man equally capable of tenderness and being tough.' He tolerated Brando in *Mutiny on the Bounty* (62), where his sober Captain Bligh could not eliminate memories of Charles Laughton's lip-smacking one, but this was nevertheless one of the most convincing delineations of one of the cinema's favourite characters, the martinet – unreasoning, apoplectic, as stubborn and dangerous as an ox.

Little of his subsequent work was as interesting. Too often he stood on the sidelines watching while lesser actors fought the battles; sometimes he smiled ironically, sometimes one could see him huffing and puffing with impatience. Mostly he was a British officer – and if not military at least militant, always gruff and worldly-wise: *The Lion* with William Holden, as a big-game hunter; *The Man in the Middle* (64), with Robert Mitchum, as a British military psychiatrist; *Father Goose* with Cary Grant, as a naval commander; *Operation Crossbow* (65) with George Peppard, as a British military adviser; and *Von Ryan's Express* with Frank Sinatra, as an English major.

Brando was sueing the 'Saturday Evening Post' for libel about his behaviour during the making of the Bounty film: thus Howard was offered a brief role with him in *Morituri*, as a British intelligence officer. It was only later that he realized his acceptance implied that Brando could not have behaved so badly that his co-star then refused to work with him again. Then: *the Liquidator* (66) with Rod Taylor, again as an intelligence officer; *The Poppy is Also a Flower*, the UN propaganda film, as a UN narcotics agent; *Triple Cross* (67) with Christopher Plummer, as a Winston Churchill-type figure; and *The Long Duel* with Yul Brynner, as an Indian police officer. At least *Pretty Polly* gave him a chance to bring something more to his usual authoritarian – something of a roué as a colonial rubber-planter, Hayley Mills's uncle.

He was a fiery British general, Lord Cardigan, in *The Charge of the Light Brigade* (68), and an air-vice-marshal in a later war, *The Battle of Britain* (69), from which it was a considerable drop to the small role of the roving grandfather of *Twinky* (70), a silly British sex farce. Coming up again he was very fine indeed as the village priest in David Lean's *Ryan's Daughter* (70). He was a detective in *The Night Visitor* (71), with Max von Sydow, not seen in his own country, and a Foreign Office diplomat in *Catch Me a Spy*, which starred Kirk Douglas. In *Mary Queen of Scots* (72) he was Lord Burleigh; in *Kidnapped* the Lord Advocate; and in *Pope Joan* Pope Leo. Since most of these wasted him, it was good to see him with important roles again in *The Offence*, with Sean Connery, and Visconti's *Ludwig* (73), as Wagner (originally announced for Alec Guinness), but neither film was successful. He was Dr Rank in the Jane Fonda *A Doll's House*, an experience he did not enjoy; but audiences enjoyed him as a monk in *Catholics*, an American TV film which actually merited the cinema showings it received abroad. But the next one marked a new low in his career: *Craze* (74), as a Scotland Yard man on the track of killer Jack Palance. Still supporting lesser (but younger, and Hollywood) talents, in this case Charles Grodin and Candice Bergen, he was a master crook in *11 Harrowhouse*; James Mason and John Gielgud were also there and Dilys Powell observed that the three performances 'aren't produced without years of devotion to the difficult business of acting'. But Howard was then involved with a lady who with as many years had never got the hang of it, Lana Turner, in *Persecution*: he was a politician who had once been her lover. He was a Soviet spymaster in *Who?*, with Elliott Gould, made around this time but not trade-shown till 1978.

Howard did a comic cameo in *Hennessy*

(75), which starred Rod Steiger and was back to real star-billing in *Conduct Unbecoming*, as a colonel in the Indian Army: but the film was too old-fashioned. He was the Squire (Hugh Griffith's old role) in an ill-advised musical, *The Bawdy Adventures of Tom Jones* (76); and in the next one the Abbé Farias, the aged prisoner who educates *The Count of Monte Cristo* – who was Richard Chamberlain. Well, if he could not get worthwhile roles, he could travel – to Africa for two West German co-productions directed by Jürgen Goslar, *Der Flüsternde Tod/Whispering Death*, with Christopher Lee, as a crusty farmer; and *Slavers* (77), with Britt Ekland. And to Australia for *Eliza Fraser* (76) and to Spain, where they photographed most of *The Last Remake of Beau Geste*, but he was in the English part, as father to the Gestes. He was 'The Man' in *Stevie* (78), explaining Glenda Jackson as the poetess Stevie Smith, and an Elder in *Superman*; then he went to the South Pacific to make *Hurricane* (79), playing the priest. *King Solomon's Treasure* finally turned up, made in South Africa some years earlier, and *Meteor* also took a while to turn up – since this New York disaster tale needed much special process work. In 1978 he told reporters that he considered himself a big man, a 'big' actor, and he would again like leading roles: this best of British film actors did find one in *The Shillingbury Blowers* (80), as an eccentric diehard in this bucolic comedy directed by Val Guest – but it seems never to have been publicly screened in Britain (it did find its way to US TV). After aiding Gregory Peck in an inane war adventure, *The Sea Wolves*, he had a similar role in *Sir Henry at Rawlinson End*, but this one was amateurish as well as offensively unfunny.

After that, it must have been a relief to be reunited with Celia Johnson, the two of them *Staying On* in India for a Granada telemovie. Still travelling, he was in Utah for *Windwalker* and in Eire for *Les Années Lumière/Light Years Away* (81), curiosities both. In the former he was an Indian chieftain returned to life to help his tribe, in whose language it was filmed; in the latter, filmed in English for a Franco-Swiss set-up, he was an eccentric recluse living in a junk-yard at some time in the future. Allegories were intended. For British TV he was Jonathan Swift in *No Country for Old Men* and in the US he was one of those *Inside the Third Reich* for a mini-series; others included Rutger Hauer as Speer and Derek Jacobi as Hitler. He did another of his aristocratic eccentrics in *The Missionary*, a period comedy with Maggie Smith; was a judge in *Gandhi*; co-starred with George Segal in a tele-film, *The Deadly Game*; was the king in as soon-gone Arthurian epic, *Sword of the Valiant* (84); and was Lord Fairfax in an American mini-series, *George Washington*. The depressing credits continued: *Dust* (85), a Franco-Belgian picture made in Spain but set in South Africa, where he is murdered by a spinsterish Jane Birkin after sleeping with a black woman; *God Rot Tunbridge Wells*, a tele-movie in which playwright John Osborne and director Tony Palmer proved they were meant for each other, as Handel; and *Time After Time*, a ghastly BBC tele-film about a strange Irish family whose members included his wife: he, in fact, had guest-star billing. After a stint as Isaac Newton being introduced to Olivier's also over-age William III in *Peter the Great* (86), the US mini-series, he supported Victor Banerjee, the *Foreign Body* – an Indian doctor being pursued by his female patients and another dated local comedy. There also turned up on video at this time a seven-hour epic, *Shaka Zulu*, made two years earlier in South Africa; the UN is said to have made a blacklist of the cast, since the film was thought to favour apartheid. He was Loretta Young's butler in an American tele-film, *Christmas Eve*; one of the Kenya colony in *White Mischief* (87); an Irish grandfather in *The Dawning* (88) with Jean Simmons; and a blind priest in *The Unholy*, filmed in Florida with Ben Cross. The last two were released posthumously, for Howard died – after a short illness, with bronchial complications – in 1988, while making *Silent Night Holy Night*, which concerned the composer of that carol: he was replaced by Anthony Quayle, another superb actor who has seldom received the recognition he deserves. At least Quayle had been knighted and perhaps David Lean was thinking of that sort of honour when he observed that it was 'a damned shame' that Howard had had such little recognition from either the industry or his country. Brian Baxter offered a more eloquent testimony: 'Simply a private man, married to an enchanting wife. He was also the greatest screen actor Britain has ever produced.'

ROCK HUDSON

Said the 'Sunday Chronicle' in 1954: 'Hudson is the latest rooster to be bred especially for the Hollywood barnyard. Coddled in a tray labelled He-Man (Romantic), he is the newest bobby-sox idol to be hatched out of the gilded egg of publicity and the movies' own brand of pre-filming technique.' Hudson's reaction to this situation was expressed in the same article: 'I don't like myself on the screen. I get embarrassed in the projection room. I can't make love very well. I just go in and mash the make-up. Riding is OK but horses still don't like me.' Thirteen years later he expressed himself (to the 'Sunday Express') on the televising of his early films: 'Most of them make me cringe, it's rather like having your old linen washed in public. But at least those lousy movies were good training. The only thing I can say in my defence is that I did the best I could. It was pretty rotten, I agree, but it was my best. . . . Oddly enough my greatest worry in those days was that I'd muff a line and waste film.'

It was a fact – if not a fault – of the old Hollywood system that many actors learnt their craft in full public glare; and there were others who learnt it in some obscure rep, became better at it and never came within scaling distance of the dizzy heights achieved by the Hudsons. Thus, Hudson was an easy target – and an early publicity tag, 'The Baron of Beefcake', did not help any. His work gradually improved, till Margaret Hinxman in the 'Sunday Telegraph' could write of *Ice Station Zebra* in 1969: 'The most convincing member of the cast is the modestly likeable Rock Hudson – but then he invariably is.'

He was born Roy Fitzgerald in 1925, in Winnetka, Illinois; he joined the navy on graduating from high school – he began the war as an aviation mechanic but finished as laundryman third class; and, on demob, became by turns a vacuum-cleaner salesman, a truck-driver and a postman. He delivered letters to agent Henry Willson, discoverer of Tab Hunter, Guy Madison, Rory Calhoun, Robert Wagner, John Saxon and someone called Race Gentry; Willson was impressed when he learnt that Hudson had acted in school plays (and did not like being a postman). He arranged a test at 20th, who for years showed it as a demonstration of inept acting; and then one with director Raoul Walsh, who gave him a bit in *Fighter Squadron* (48) at Warners. Warners offered a contract, but Willson advised him to turn it down; instead Hudson signed with Willson and Walsh jointly for $125 per week. Over a year later this contract was sold to Universal and thus Walsh and Willson got back their $9,500 investment. Universal put Hudson in small roles in their programmers: *Undertow* (49), a B starring Scott Brady; *I Was a Shoplifter* (50), with Brady and Mona Freeman; *One-Way Street* with James Mason; *Winchester '73*, well down the cast-list as 'Young Bull'; *Peggy*, with Diana Lynn and Charles Coburn; *The Desert Hawk* with Yvonne de Carlo and Richard Greene; *Double Crossbones* with Donald O'Connor; *Tomahawk* (51) with de Carlo and Van Heflin; *Air Cadet* with Stephen McNally; *The Fat Man*, a mystery story with J. Scott Smart in the title-role and Julie London; *Iron Man* with Jeff Chandler: and *Bright Victory*, a story of a blind ex-solider adjusting to his condition, with Arthur Kennedy (who won the New York critics' Best Actor award for his performance).

Hudson began to come into his own: *Here Come the Nelsons* (52) – Ozzie, Harriet and their radio-TV family; and *Bend of the River*, fourth-billed, as a gambler. He co-starred with Yvonne de Carlo in *Scarlet Angel*, as a tough sea-captain, and with Piper Laurie in a dim little comedy, *Has Anybody Seen My Gal?*, as a millionaire playboy. Then he starred in three Westerns: *Horizons West*, battling bad brother Robert Ryan; *The Lawless Breed*, directed by Raoul Walsh, as an unwilling killer trying to prevent his sons following in his footsteps; and *Seminole* (53), as a cavalry lieutenant. His best chance came when Walsh borrowed him for RKO's filmed-in-Britain *Sea Devils*, adapted from Victor Hugo's 'Toilers of the Sea': it was not a great improvement on what he had been doing, but it was almost the first of Hudson's films to be widely press-shown – unfortunately. After *The Golden Blade*, in old Baghdad with Piper Laurie, it was *Back to God's Country* – and back to all the clichés about the Frozen North. And after a loan-out to Columbia for *Gun Fury* he was, dopily, *Taza, Son of Cochise* (54).

These were strictly for undiscriminating halls. One that reached somewhat wider audiences was the harshly dated remake of *Magnificent Obsession*, opposite Jane Wyman, in Robert Taylor's old role as the playboy who causes a girl's blindness, then sticks around (secretly) till she is cured. His only impressive acting was when he took his shirt off to wash his hands, so he was shunted back to programmers: *Bengal Brigade*, as a British captain; *Captain Lightfoot* (55), made in Dublin, as a young Irish hothead; and *One Desire* with Anne Baxter. Fans were demanding, said Universal, a reunion with Miss Wyman, so they were teamed again in another soppy and successful soap opera, *All That Heaven Allows*, he as her gardener, Ron, and she as a socialite widow talked into not marrying him by her friends. It marked the start of a new contract at $3,000 a week. There was another tear-jerker, *Never Say Goodbye* (56), a remake of *This Love of Ours*, with Cornell Borchers.

It was a surprise to the trade when George Stevens borrowed him (for $250,000, though he himself was only getting $300 a week) for the demanding leading role in his film of Edna Ferber's *Giant*: a performance that is just the right side of competent but a vast improve-

One of the cinema's most famous tear-jerkers: Magnificent Obsession *(54) with Jane Wyman and Rock Hudson. An unbelievably glossy version of a novel by Lloyd C. Douglas.*

ment on anything he had done before. The film was the first he was proud of; it was the year's biggest grosser – and it brought him a whole new crop of fans. Universal began to give him if not better material, more exalted – like *Battle Hymn*, playing a flying parson. *Written on the Wind* (57) co-starred Lauren Bacall and was mainly notable for Dorothy Malone's (Best Supporting Oscar) performance. MGM borrowed him for what Willson said was a fee of $400,000, for *Something of Value*, for Robert Ruark's novel about the troubles in Kenya, with Sidney Poitier. *The Tarnished Angels*, with Malone, was a glossy picturization of Faulkner's novel 'Pylon' and, like all Hudson's films at this time, very popular. Exhibitors voted him 1957's biggest star.

Again, he leapt forward when he went outside his own studio (he turned down *Sayonara* to do it) – when Selznick chose him for *A Farewell to Arms* (58). He was not up to Gary Cooper in the 1932 version, but was sincere and thoughtful: he was gaining in confidence. The film was a hit (though less than Selznick hoped) and Hudson was fifth in the box-office poll. His position was doubtless helped by the film of Ernest H. Gann's novel, *Twilight for the Gods*, though he was hardly credible as a salt with 30 years' devotion to the sail. He was better as a landowner in *This Earth is Mine* (59), with Jean Simmons, and as a philanderer in *Pillow Talk* with Doris Day. The latter was a totally unexpected comedy hit and it put him back to first at the box-office that year. Due mainly to some follow-ups with Day, he was at the second spot in 1960, 1961, 1963; and third spot in 1964 and 1965 – as good a run as anybody has had. His popularity was due to the amiable personality displayed in this series of off-the-peg comedies; he certainly was not in the Jack Lemmon class as a technician and where, for example, William Powell used wit and malice in handling Myrna Loy, Hudson approached Doris Day with no more than a sense of mischievousness. Of all the actors who were considerable box-office champions he must be considered the least individual, the least positive – and he knew it (as Churchill said of Attlee, 'Of course, he has much to be modest about'). On-set, he became known as the most cooperative and hard-working of actors.

He might have had his pick of parts, but he preferred to stay with Universal – though when MGM wanted him for *Ben Hur* Universal would not spare him for the year that would take to make. He now restricted his appearances to around two a year: *The Last Sunset* (61), a Western with Kirk Douglas; *Come September*, a romantic comedy with Gina Lollobrigida (he showed a predilection for uninteresting Italian ladies over the next few years); and *Lover Come Back* (62), a reunion with Day – and 'Time Magazine', which had previously described them as like two shiny new Cadillacs parked side by side, now compared them to two cream-puffs. There were two adventure dramas, the silly *The Spiral Road* and *A Gathering of Eagles* (63), as a colonel in the Strategic Air Command. Then four leering comedies; *Man's Favourite Sport?* (64), with Paula Prentiss, directed by Howard Hawks; *Send Me No Flowers*, with Day, which he had not wanted to do; *Strange Bedfellows*, with Lollobrigida; and *A Very Special Favor* (65) with Leslie Caron. Hudson's brief was to scamper around furiously, in an effort either to bed the girl or to escape being bedded by her; his ruses to get Caron included posing as a gay. But the last two of these, at least, matched a complete predictability with a total lack of wit. The public had caught on and when a poor comedy-thriller flopped, *Blindfold* (66) with Claudia Cardinale, Hudson jumped at the chance of a drama.

This was John Frankenheimer's platitudinous *Seconds*, about an old man rejuvenated (Hudson). The director had wanted Olivier, but was offered Hudson as being more reliable at the box-office; in the event, the film took less than $1 million in the US, presumably because it alienated or failed to attract two opposite factions – the intellectual set and Hudson's fans. But he was, rightly, proud of it. It was his first film away from Universal for a decade; now he did his last there, *Tobruk* (67), which might have been a good war film, given the chance. In 1968 he was one of the stars considered overpriced by 'Variety', but an adventure tale, Alistair MacLean's *Ice Station Zebra* (68), did something to hoist his box-office again. Any good that did was undone by *Una Coppia Tranquilla/A Fine Pair* (69), a comedy with Cardinale. He co-starred with two big stars in two of their less successful efforts, with John Wayne in *The Undefeated* and with Julie Andrews in *Darling Lili* (70). *Il Vespaio/The Hornet's Nest*, a war film with Sylva Koscina, went entirely unnoticed.

The film crisis of this period left Hudson at low tide and he appeared without great éclat but fashionably moustached in Roger Vadim's first American film, *Pretty Maids All in a Row* (71), as college coach and murderer. But TV was exceptionally kind to him; he signed to do 'McMillan and Wife', rotating three-weekly, on NBC's 'Mystery Theater', with complete control and a proviso that none of his eight shows could be released theatrically. Univer-

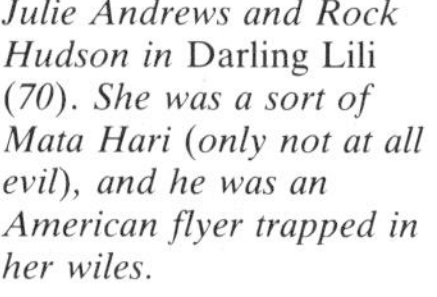

Julie Andrews and Rock Hudson in Darling Lili *(70). She was a sort of Mata Hari (only not at all evil), and he was an American flyer trapped in her wiles.*

sal produced and the deal included three films in two years, or four in two and a half if the series was dropped. He was reckoned to be getting $1,600,000 for these 90-minute shows (as opposed to $1 million each to Shirley MacLaine and James Stewart for their weekly 30-minute shows and $800,000 to Glenn Ford, $500,000 to Anthony Quinn for their 60-minute weekly shows). He returned to cinema films in *Showdown* (73), a Western with Dean Martin. It disappeared, as did *Embryo* (76), a horror film in which he was a meddling doctor. *Avalanche* (78), was more a return to his old beat, for he was heroic in this minor 'disaster' film. In 1979 he was in a big TV series based on Ray Bradbury's 'The Martian Chronicles' and in the National tour of 'On the Twentieth Century', after some contretemps as to whether his salary was too high to enable the theatres concerned to show a profit. During this period he also toured in 'I Do I Do'.

An Agatha Christie tale, *The Mirror Crack'd* (80), reunited him with Elizabeth Taylor, he as a movie director and she as the star to whom he is married. He was *The Star Maker* (81), a Hollywood producer with amorous designs, and the US president in *World War Three*, also a mini-series. He became a private eye for 'The Devlin Connection', a series postponed from 1981 to 1982 because of his open-heart surgery. His last cinema film was *The Ambassador* (84) with Robert Mitchum, as a security officer, and his last for television (discounting series, it was the only one he did in that medium) was *The Vegas Strip Wars*, as a casino boss. Dying, in 1985, he announced from his bed that he had AIDS; he was the first major show business figure to be killed by it and his statement brought with it revelations of his homosexuality – and the fact, for instance, that his marriage in 1955 had been a sham, arranged by the studio. He was perhaps then the most potent male sex symbol and had he been openly gay his career would have been ruined. Now it no longer seemed to matter.

Tab Hunter

Of all the pretty-boy teenage idols, Tab Hunter was probably the most appealing – by half an inch or so. He did at least have glimmerings of talent and might have gone further if he had kept his own name (Arthur Gelien) and not been landed with such a silly one. It might also have helped if he had not looked so much like a sugar candy-bar.

He was born in New York City in 1931 but the family moved to Los Angeles, where he went to school. He planned to be a professional ice-skater, but did various jobs – drugstore assistant, garage-attendant, cinema-usher, sheet-metal worker, packer. He had been interested in drama at school and 'when one day' – went a studio biography – 'somebody told him he ought to be in pictures, he decided to do something about it. He managed to get a very tiny role in a film.' That was *The Lawless* (50), but he was edited out on the cutting-room floor. He got himself an agent, Henry Willson, sponsor of some other handsome young male stars, like Rock Hudson, and Willson got him tested by director Stuart Heisler, who wanted an unknown to play opposite Linda Darnell in *Saturday Island* (52). He got the part to qualified approval. 'Variety': 'Hunter, as a young marine, displays a healthy torso, but not a great deal of talent.' But he now had a toe inside the glamorous door and producer Edward Small signed him to a three-picture deal: *Gun Belt* (53), a low-budget Western, as George Montgomery's brother; *The Steel Lady*, a low-budget war film with Rod Cameron; and *Return to Treasure Island* (54), opposite Dawn Addams as Jamesina Hawkins, descendant of you-know-who. The latter pair were directed by E.A. Dupont, the famous German Silent director, now mainly functioning as a Hollywood agent.

Warners signed him to a long-term contract. He played Robert Mitchum's younger brother in *Track of the Cat*, cowed at first but manly later. He was one of the male line-up, with Van Heflin and Aldo Ray, in *Battle Cry* (55), from Leon Uris's bestseller, as a nice young soldier in love with two girls (the one

Saturday Island *(52) – or* Island of Desire *in the US – was a desert island romance of splendid vacuity: three shipwrecked people, and a tug of war between Tab Hunter (left) and one-armed Donald Gray for Linda Darnell.*

here and the one back home). That one was a big box-office hit and Hunter was already a big noise in the fan magazines. After playing a German cadet (under John Wayne's command) in *The Sea Chase*, Warners decided to star him: *The Burning Hills* (56), a Western, and *The Girl He Left Behind*, miscast as a spoilt rich kid who resists discipline till he is broken in and becomes as tough a non-com as there is in this man's army. Natalie Wood was the girl in both: Warners saw them as a great new screen team, but no one else did.

Things were not good between Hunter and Warners. He had turned down a supporting role in the egregious Liberace *Sincerely Yours* and was suspended for refusing *Darby's Rangers*, reportedly in revenge when Warners refused to release an album he had made (he had some brief success as a singer). On TV he did 'Fear Strikes Out' and 'Hans Brinker on the Silver Skates'; and in 1957 he made this statement, 'I'm typical of where publicity is a zillion years ahead of career.' Warners took him back and dressed him in uniform again, a member of the *Lafayette Escadrille* (58), with Etchika Choureau, but this World War I drama was not a success. He was loaned out for a Western with Van Heflin, *Gunman's Walk*; and then was good in *Damn Yankees*, just the right side of obnoxious as the all-American youth – Faust as a baseball player – from a hit Broadway musical with the original cast (except for him). Despite much skill and the delicious virtuoso performance of Gwen Verdon, and good notices, it was a so-so hit in the US and a failure elsewhere. None of these films pleased Hunter much; his agent demanded better parts and better terms. According to Jack L. Warner's memoir, Hunter went down on bended knees asking for his release. He got it on payment of $100,000.

Which only goes to prove you never know when you are well off. A first he did okay: he was a young GI seeking to take *That Kind of Woman* (59) Sophia Loren from George Sanders, not knowing she was That Kind – only his heart did not seem to be in the part. He was better in *They Come to Cordura*, supporting Gary Cooper and Heflin, as a meanie; and excellent in *The Pleasure of His Company* (61), as a country boy bewildered by the prospect of losing bride Debbie Reynolds to the long-lost father who reappears at the wedding. In Italy he made *La Freccia d'Oro/The Golden Arrow* (62), some Oriental claptrap with Rosanna Podesta, playing the head of a gang of thieves. In New York he appeared in Tennessee Williams's flop 'The Milk Train Doesn't Stop Here Any More' with Hermione Baddeley. All Hollywood offered was an AIP war movie, *Operation Bikini* (63), supporting Frankie Avalon. In *Ride the Wild Surf* (64) he supported Fabian; the British *Troubled Waters* never seems to have been shown; in *The Loved One* (65) he was one of the stars in cameo roles, as a cemetery guide. Then he was in a British cheapie, *City Under the Sea*, supporting Vincent Price. Things did not get better: he supported TV comic Soupy Sales in *Birds Do It* (66).

In Spain he made a low-budget comedy-thriller for PRO, *The Fickle Finger of Fate* (67). It occasioned this review in 'Variety': 'Hunter is the major surprise, and his timing and momentum are mainly responsible for the film's fluid pace. More relaxed and charming than he has been for years, he seems to have conquered the stiffness he so awkwardly projected in his Warners contract days.' He was in an A.C. Lyles Western, *Hostile Guns*, with George Montgomery, and was then inactive. On his way to Europe to make *Quel Maledetto Ponte sull'Elba* (69) – as a veteran sergeant – he said this was the best time of his life: he was not under contract and could pick and choose his vehicles. Like *La Porta del Cannone*, a second Spanish-Italian war film, and *A Kiss From Eddie* (71) aka *Sweet Kill* aka *The Arousers* with Isabel Jewell, as a psycho who kills girls because he cannot make out with them. It was much better than it sounds.

Then he had a featured role in *The Life and Times of Judge Roy Bean* (72) with Paul Newman and he was rather good as a crook. He did not film again till he did one of the cameos in *Won Ton Ton the Dog who Saved Hollywood* (76).

With some other one-time names (Fabian, Vivian Blaine, Dorothy Malone) he supported Kim Basinger in a Hollywood tale, *Katie: Portrait of a Centerfold* (78), and then he supported the grotesque transvestite Divine in *Polyester* (81), as the nice drive-in owner who takes care of her when she ups and leaves home. It was an offensive, untalented movie but it knew its audience: kids at midnight matinees. Hunter capitalized on this renewed, if mild, burst of fame and toured in 'Chapter Two' at dinner theatres; he also observed, of his career going to pieces, 'One morning I woke up and couldn't get arrested.' Along with Eve Arden he was one of several former names in *Thursday the 12th* (82). He and Connie Stevens were teachers in *Grease 2*, set in the 60s when they were both luminaries. That one has the doubtful privilege of being Hunter's most important movie since *Judge Roy Bean*, but *And They're Off* seems never to have been seen. After another film with Divine, *Lust in the Dust* (84), in which he was 'the epitome of the straight-arrow hero' ('Variety'), he was absent till *Grotesque* (88), playing a plastic surgeon bent on revenge after Linda Blair is hospitalized. Made previously, but with release long delayed, was *Cameron's Closet* (89), more of same as Cameron's father, killed off early or by the diabolical child.

Glenda Jackson

Female stars, by and large, could at one time be divided into those who came from the stage and those picked out of the chorus-line. In the US, most good Broadway actresses got a chance in films. In Britain, very few of the good stage actresses appeared in films – a situation which reached an appalling low in the 50s, where girls picked from God-knows-where peopled the star dressing rooms at Elstree and Pinewood. While Dorothy Tutin, perhaps the best actress of her generation, made only three films, these anonymous blondes appeared in film after film – only to be forgotten as soon as they had made their last one (if not before). The situation changed in the 60s, when new producing and directing blood turned to the West End for acting talent. And thus arrived Glenda Jackson from the Royal Shakespeare Company, a plain-featured, strong actress. And she was not playing spinsters either – though she had a line in frustrated ladies; in fact, she was mostly to be seen rolling around in beds. 'Photoplay' called her 'Britain's First Lady of the Flesh'.

She was born in Liverpool in 1938 and brought up at Hoylake in Cheshire. After school she worked in Boots the Chemists for two years, began acting as an amateur and applied for a scholarship with RADA. After two years' studying, she made her professional bow in repertory in Worthing. She also acted in Crewe, where she met her husband, Roy Hodges, but there were long periods (two years, once) when she could not get work. Her breakthrough came when she was taken on by the Royal Shakespeare in 1964; within that company she worked with Peter Brook's experimental group and he chose her to play Charlotte Corday in 'The Persecution and Assassination of Marat as Performed by the Inmates of the Asylum of Charenton Under the Direction of the Marquis de Sade' (hereafter referred to as the 'Marat-Sade'). She had a small role in 'The Jew of Malta', larger ones in 'Squire Puntila and his Servant Matti' (65) and 'Hamlet' (Ophelia to David Warner's Prince). She made her New York début in the 'Marat-Sade'; and her film début in Peter Brook's film of it (67). She also appeared in another experimental film of Brook's, *Tell Me Lies* (68), delivering a speech of Mao Tse-tung. Neither film moved away from the specialized audiences for whom they were planned and the second – a muddled attack on America's Vietnam policy – must be considered a failure even by those standards.

Meanwhile, Jackson was signed by director Peter Medak for *Negatives* (68), screenplay by Peter Everett from his own novel, about a couple whose sexual fantasies have him impersonating Dr Crippen, etc. – till a German blonde intrudes and has him reincarnating the Baron von Richtofen. Peter McEnery and Diane Cilento completed the *ménage à trois* in this hazily constructed piece. It was released first in the US to limited success and limped into London for a couple of weeks after Jackson's next, *Women in Love* (69), which was worldwide success, a version of D.H. Lawrence's novel faithfully adapted by Larry Kramer. Her portrait of a 'free' woman was considerably praised – especially in the US: it brought her the New York critics' Best Actress award and – against thin competition – a Best Actress Oscar. Her fee had been a mere £3,000. The film's director, Ken Russell, eschewed most of the flashy tricks he had used in his TV documentaries; but he brought them back with a vengeance for *The Music Lovers* (71), a biopic about Tchaikovsky – or 'pornobiography' as one critic called it, the porn being about all that distinguished it from similar films in the past. Gary Arnold of the 'Washington Post' called it 'awful . . . the worst experience I ever had in a cinema'. There was some consolation in Richard Chamberlain's homosexual composer and Jackson as his frustrated nympho wife.

She was, however, at her best in *Sunday Bloody Sunday*, again a fiercely independent

Glenda Jackson in Sunday Bloody Sunday *(71), in which she and Peter Finch were in love with the same man. Some critics thought it brave at the time and perhaps it was in cinema terms: but it did not have anything profound to say on the subject of homosexuality.*

woman in love with a gay man (Murray Head); and John Schlesinger allowed her to use her talent instead of using her. She won a BFA Best Actress award for it. Around the same time she appeared in a ropey BBC series about Elizabeth I and, although monumentally miscast (the kindest conclusion to be drawn from her interpretation), Hal Wallis signed her to play that sovereign in *Mary Queen of Scots*, with, in the title-role, Vanessa Redgrave – who had accepted the role that Jackson had declined in Russell's *The Devils*. Jackson returned to Russell for an unbilled cameo role, that of the bitchy star whose place is taken by her understudy (Twiggy), in *The Boy Friend*, which was less a musical than Russell on another ego-trip, this time at the expense of Sandy Wilson's masterly pastiche of 20s musicals – perhaps among the crassest mishandling ever meted out by movies. Then Jackson was to have been another queen – *Isabella of Spain*, in the film which would have marked Samuel Bronston's return to the blockbuster field, but it was never made. Instead, she had *The Triple Echo* (72), playing a strong-minded countrywoman who hides an AWOL soldier dressed in drag, and *A Touch of Class*, going off to Spain for a spot of nookey with married George Segal but quarrelling, mostly, instead. At moments a secret smile suggested an acquaintance with comedy technique, but she was only too shrewish most of the time: if she had ever seen Carole Lombard, she – surely? – would never again have put her nose out of doors, let alone step on a soundstage. This unremarked-upon performance managed to win her, despite the competition of one of Joanne Woodward's best, a Best Actess Oscar; but the award did not urge any public interest in *A Bequest to the Nation*, in which she was Lady Hamilton.

She went to Italy to play a nun in a co-production with Britain, *The Tempter* (74), and then with Susannah York did the title-roles in Genêt's *The Maids* (75), which they had done on stage a month or two before; for Joseph Losey she was *The Romantic Englishwoman*, married to Michael Caine. In the US she toured as Hedda Gabler, a performance, said 'Time Magazine', which 'will certainly rank high in the annals of dramatic travesty'. That is curious, since Americans had always admired her work more than the British; as far as her films were concerned, all since *A Touch of Class* had been received with apathy by British press and public – including a film of *Hedda*, which, like *The Maids*, surfaced in its native country almost two years after its American première. Its producers were Brut, who had made the Oscar-winning film, and they had Jackson under a multi-picture contract; as did Readers Digest – another non-movie company diversifying – but they caught a cold casting Jackson as *The Incredible Sarah* (76) Bernhardt. Brut produced *Dirty Habits* and Jackson was a nun, again, in this 'ugly, unfunny travesty' (John Simon), based on Muriel Spark's 'The Abbess of Crewe' – which was Watergate retold in a convent. Filming for the first time in Hollywood, Jackson played opposite Walter Matthau in *House Calls* (78), a performance, said 'Variety', which 'would certainly suggest that comedy is not her bag.' In the theatre, she had done 'The White Devil' and 'Stevie', the latter about the British poetess Stevie Smith; and it was filmed. The producer was Robert Enders, who with Jackson co-owned Bowden Productions, collaborators on the Brut pictures – but by now Brut had gone out of the business. *Stevie* failed to impress British critics, but when it finally reached New York in 1981 it was a modest success and brought Jackson a Best Actress award from the critics there. A third Jackson film was around at this time, if briefly, *The Class of Miss MacMichael* with Oliver Reed, a school story which was regarded as the most ludicrous of the Jackson vehicles. On the stage more attention was being paid, since she was playing Shakespeare's Cleopatra for Peter Brook. *Lost and Found* (79) reunited her with Segal and the makers of *A Touch of Class*; and then she was reunited with Matthau, as an old flame in *Hopscotch* (80), a chase comedy. Robert Altman's *Health*, made earlier, finally surfaced to deservedly poor reviews – though it started well; Jackson played a boring woman with a fixation on Adlai Stevenson who fancies herself a candidate for the presidency of the health organization. In the West End she was in 'Rose' and there was talk of filming it; instead she played the lead in *The Patricia Neal Story*, a CBS tele-movie with Dirk Bogarde, with whom she was supposed to make *Buried Alive*. Instead, she did *The Return of the Soldier* (82), which had production difficulties when the money ran out. It turned out to be a mildly prestigious item for her, Julie Christie, etc., but was less satisfying then *Giro City*, a modest, intelligent drama about media manipulation and civic corruption. Jackson (at her best) and Jon Finch were partners making TV documentaries. It was made for television, but had a few prior scattered cinema bookings.

Theatre ventures included 'Summit Conference', about the mistresses of Hitler and Napoleon, and the German 'Great and Small', a more immediate flop; there was another setback when she discovered that the RSC owned the rights to 'Mother Courage', which she wanted to do – and they did not invite her to join them for it. In 1984 neither

'Strange Interlude' nor 'Phèdre' were particularly well received: yet the latter transferred from the Old Vic to the West End a year later, while the O'Neill play even more unaccountably was taken to New York – and even, later, filmed for video. Its producers had presumably not read John Simon's assessment in 'New York Magazine', which reasoned at length why Jackson is 'not an artist . . . nothing she says or does stems from genuine feeling, displays an atom of spontaneity, leaves any room for the unexpected. It is all technique – and not the most intricate technique at that'.

An Austrian-backed film on the Russian dissident *Sakharov* (84) evoked almost no interest anywhere. The British quite liked their own *Turtle Diary* (85), but others did not – a quaint piece in which a children's writer (Jackson) and a bookseller (Ben Kingsley) set out to rob the zoo of some of its prize possessions. Jackson returned to the US for another of Altman's failures, *Beyond Therapy* (87), as a psychiatrist in a movie often about that breed; and then she was the manageress of a Liverpool boutique sacked for complaining about sexual harassment – not to her (don't be silly) but to Cathy Tyson – in *Business as Usual*, which perhaps deserved more attention than it received. Theatre work during this period included 'Across From the Garden of Allah' and 'The House of Bernarda Alba' in London, and an unsuccessful trip to Broadway with Christopher Plummer to play the Macbeths. Films were unkind: two with Ken Russell, the horrible *Salome's First Night* (88), in a dual role as Herodias and a friend of Oscar Wilde (Nikolas Grace), and D.H. Lawerence's *The Rainbow* (89).

Glynis Johns

Glynis Johns was one of the more entrancing heroines of the 40s, one of the very few in British films who knew how to play comedy. With a deliciously husky voice and deceptively innocent eyes, she was most adept as vamps and impish schoolgirls; on the occasions she was properly handled and able to combine something of both aspects, she was irresistible. Not a powerful or especially versatile talent, it was, nevertheless, a highly individual one; and it is sad that, having survived some rather dreadful British films, it did not find a niche in Hollywood.

The daughter of Mervyn Johns, a British character actor, she was born in Pretoria, South Africa, in 1923 and went to Britain at the age of five. She studied with Adeline Genée and at the age of 12 danced at London's Garrick Theatre in 'Buckie's Bears' and understudied; she had an Old Vic engagement. She was 15 when she was chosen to play the hysterical schoolgirl in the film of Winifred Holtby's *South Riding* (38), and for a while continued to play mainly schoolgirls: *Murder in the Family, Prison Without Bars, On the Night of the Fire* (39) as a skivvy, *The Briggs Family, Under Your Hat* and *The Prime Minister* (40). She tested – successfully – for the lead in *Love on the Dole*, but did not play it because Powell and Pressburger were looking for a quick replacement for Elisabeth Bergner, who had walked out on *49th Parallel* (41); Johns did a creditable job as the timid Hutterite girl (it is still Bergner in the long-shots).

She was featured in *The Adventures of Tartu* (42), as a Czech patriot, and continued her stage career, including a much-liked Peter Pan the following year. She and her father played daughter and father in *The Halfway House* (43), an inn in Wales somewhat more than Outward Bound, bringing comfort to a group of guests including Françoise Rosay and Tom Walls. In Korda's *Perfect Strangers* (45)

Glynis Johns at the time she was under contract to the Rank Organisation in the late 40s.

she was a Wren who helps to modernize Deborah Kerr. Then she had the star role in a dank version of a West End success, *This Man Is Mine* (46), as a glamorous spitfire. Korda put her under contract and because he loaned her out frequently she seldom had time for the stage. There were ingénue parts in *Frieda* (47), with Mai Zetterling as a German bride married to British solider David Farrar ('Would *You* take Frieda into your home?'), and *An Ideal Husband*, as Mabel, for Korda.

Miranda (48) made her a star, as the innocently nympho mermaid who disrupts the home of doctor-discoverer Griffith Jones and wife Googie Withers: dimly made and every joke strictly anticipated, but a fair success. *Third Time Lucky*, with Dermot Walsh, was a hopeless little gambling melodrama which died the death. Somewhat better was a comedy, *Dear Mr Prohack* (49), and much better was a thriller for Korda (the only other film she made for him), *State Secret* (50), as a damsel in peril with Douglas Fairbanks Jr. That was seen a little in the US and so was *Flesh and Blood* (51), because it starred the then big Richard Todd; and seen much there was *No Highway*, with James Stewart, in which she played an air hostess (with featured-billing in the US and star-billing in the British market). *Appointment with Venus* was a nondescript comedy with David Niven and 'Gigolo and Gigolette' the weakest sequence in *Encore*, the third and last of the films taken from Somerset Maugham short stories. She also did a cameo that year in *The Magic Box*, one of the more memorable of the 60 stars featured in the film. Indeed, she was delightful, having brought her stock portrayal to the level of high comedy – as was demonstrated in *The Card* (52), with Alec Guinness.

Her only recent stage work had been in 'The Way Things Go' (50). In 1952 she was invited to Broadway to do 'Gertie' and on that trip met and married her second husband. She returned to Britain for a couple of Disneys with Richard Todd, *The Sword and the Rose* (53) and *Rob Roy the Highland Rogue* – competent stuff, but their drear successors can only have appealed to masochists: *Personal Affairs*, with Gene Tierney, a cheap novelette about a missing schoolgirl (Johns); *The Weak and the Wicked* (54), an exposé of life in a women's prison with Diana Dors; *The Seekers*, a muddled New Zealand pioneer story with Jack Hawkins, subdued and loyal while he has it off with a native girl; *The Beachcomber*, a particularly inept remake of *Vessel of Wrath* with Johns up against it in Elsa Lanchester's old part – and getting no help from either Robert Newton or the crude mixture of back projection and doubles in the location work; and *Mad About Men*, an unwelcome sequel to *Miranda*. Trifingly better was *Josephine and Men* (55), a comedy with Peter Finch, and then she flew off to Hollywood to be Danny Kaye's leading lady in *The Court Jester*. Back in Britain she was in a Graham Greene 'entertainment', *Loser Takes All* (56), with Rossano Brazzi, after which, understandably, she uprooted herself and settled in her husband's native land.

Her American career started promisingly, with 'Major Barbara' in New York and in Hollywood *All Mine to Give* with Cameron Mitchell; but the film was excessively weepy (the title in Britain was *The Day They Gave Babies Away*) – as well as being one of the last of the by-then defunct RKO. She was in *Around the World in 80 Days*, as a London tart. Few of her susbsequent parts have been of much consequence and she was ill-advised to accept subsidiary parts in a couple of American films made in Britain: *Another Time Another Place* (58), with Lana Turner, and *Shake Hands with the Devil*, with James Cagney. Still, as she explained in 1958 about being a star: 'It is not a pleasant way of earning a living. . . . I have not enjoyed being a star. It has made me ill, exhausted and unhappy.' In *The Sundowners* (60) she accepted a supporting part – with star-billing – as the Cockney barmaid who captures Peter Ustinov. She returned to Britain for *Spider's Web*, which had started life as one of the wettest of Agatha Christie's leaky plays.

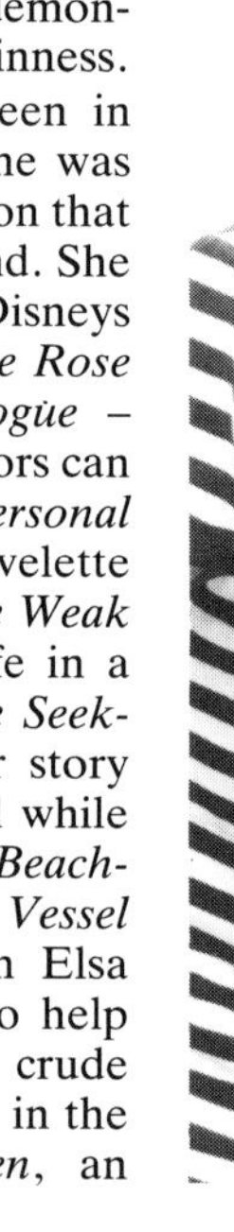

The Card *(52) was adapted from one of Arnold Bennett's novels about the Five Towns, with Alec Guinness as a back-street boy who rises by cunning to be mayor. There were three women in his life, including Glynis Johns, delicious as a designing little minx.*

In the US she was embroiled in a horror film called, for reasons best known to the management of 20th, *The Cabinet of Dr Caligari* (61), but then had her best part for years, in Cukor's *The Chapman Report* (62), as an arty lady after sex 'for experience'; she even made the role seem bigger than it was. After doing 'Too True To Be Good' in New York she did three featured mother-roles in succession: *Papa's Delicate Condition* (63), married to Jackie Gleason; *Mary Poppins* (64), married to David Tomlinson; and *Dear Brigitte* (65), married to James Stewart; there was a TV series, 'Glynis'. She played a bubbly writer of sex novels in a comedy with Robert Wagner and Mary Tyler Moore, *Don't Just Stand There!* (67).

She returned to London to co-star with Keith Michell in a play about Anne of Cleves, 'The King's Mare', and seemed to be pursuing her career, once again, in Britain. Her performance as the greedy and lecherous Mrs Squeezum was the best thing in the otherwise poor *Lock Up Your Daughters!* (69) and she was well cast in a British TV adaptation of Noël Coward's story 'Star Quality'. She appeared in some one-act plays, 'Come As You Are' by John Mortimer, and in *Under Milk Wood* (71), with featured-billing. In 1972 she starred on Broadway in 'A Little Night Music', from which it was a considerable drop to murdering Terry-Thomas in the British portmanteau *Vault of Horror* (73). She was announced for the Fairy Godmother (played by Annette Crosbie) in *The Slipper and the Rose*. She was divorced in 1973. Stage appearances included 'Cause Célèbre' in London in 1977 and 'An April Song', a musical version of Anouilh's 'Time Remembered' in stock in 1980. She was one of the battling women in an NBC mini-series, *Little Gloria . . . Happy at Last* (82), if (inevitably) overshadowed by Davis, Lansbury and Maureen Stapleton, and around this time she guested in an episode of 'Cheers'. She toured in a revival of 'The Boy Friend' (84), but had been replaced by Anna Quayle by the time it reached London. About the same time she was in a busted pilot for a series, *Spraggue*, as the nosey, helpful aunt of a professor (Michael Mouri) turned detective. A film went nowhere, *Zelly and Me* (88), who were respectively Isabella Rossellini and Alexandra Jones; Johns was the latter's grandmother. 'Coming of Age' was a CBS sitcom starring Paul Dooley and Phyllis Newman, with her and Alan Young as a couple with whom they are friendly. And ads have appeared for *Nukie*, but not the film itself.

She is due to appear at the Brooks Atkinson Theater in November 1989 with Rex Harrison and Stewart Granger in a revival of Somerset Maugham's 'The Circle'.

CELIA JOHNSON

Celia Johnson's range was narrow: the impeccably accented British gentlewoman, the backbone of 100 years of English fiction, from 'Cranford' to 'The Diary of a Provincial Lady'. But within that range she could work miracles; she was – the analogy is inescapable – the *petit pointilliste* supreme among actresses.

She was born in Richmond, Surrey, in 1908, studied for the stage at RADA and made her stage début at Hudersfield in 1928 as Sarah in 'Major Barbara'. She made her London bow a year later, succeeding Angela Baddeley in 'A Hundred Years Old'. Within five years she became one of the leading ingénues around Shaftesbury Avenue – notably in 'Cynara' (30) and the two-year run of 'The Wind and the Rain' (33). She made her New York début as Ophelia in 1931; consolidated her West End position in, among other plays, 'Pride and Prejudice', 'Old Music' and 'Rebecca' (40). In 1941 she made her first film, a propaganda short directed by Carol Reed for the American market, *A Letter from Home*; she appeared in another short which Reed made, *We Serve*, about the ATS.

Her screen fame would result from a series of Noël Coward heroines. Coward had been approached to make a big morale-boosting navy propaganda film and he fashioned *In Which We Serve* (42), which would look at some of the men above and below decks in HMS *Torrin*. He would co-direct with David Lean (whom he had brought from documentaries) and play the captain. Johnson, meeting him at a cocktail-party, asked him for the role of his wife: she tested and was cast. The film was a gigantic success in Britain and did useful business in the US (and today, mostly, stands up very well). She was in the film of Dodie Smith's matinée play, *Dear Octopus* (43), as the daughter having an illicit affair, and then returned to Lean and Coward, cooperating on a version of the latter's play, *This Happy Breed* (44). This was basically a working-class 'Cavalcade', fashioned by Coward's sure touch into an acceptable blend of sentiment and patrotism. Johnson was again the patient, anxious wife – this time to Robert Newton.

The third film she made with Lean and Coward, *Brief Encounter* (45), was from a short play by Coward, 'Still Life', and was something else again – an honest look at one of the cinema's favourite subjects, marital infidelity. Both the earlier films had been ecstatically received; here are some contemporary reviews of this one: 'Celia Johnson plays exquisitely in the part of a woman happily married, no longer very young, who by chance gets to know, on her weekly shopping expeditions to the neighbouring

Celia Johnson first made an impact on cinema audiences playing wives for Noël Coward, which is to say that in each case he wrote the screenplays. Here she is with Robert Newton in This Happy Breed *(44), the story of a suburban family from the Armistice to the eve of the Second World War.*

town, a doctor with a settled background like her own' (E. Arnot Robertson in the 'Daily Mail'). 'Much of the power of the love passages is due to the acting of Celia Johnson who, without manufactured glamour or conventional good looks, magnificently portrays the wife and mother meeting passion for the first time; who wants to die because of it and goes back to her husband and the books of Kate O'Brien, knowing that this golden brief encounter will die in the memory. This is perhaps the real twist of its everyday tragedy. Trevor Howard, more than good, is outshone by such a performance' (Richard Winnington). 'The performances of Celia Johnson (easily our best screen actress) and of Trevor Howard are faultlessly judged' (William Whitebait in the 'New Statesman'). Unprecedented for a player in a British film, she was nominated for an Oscar; and was judged the year's Best Actress by the New York film critics. Of the three Coward films this was the least popular, but it became accepted as a classic and one of the best loved and remembered of films. Because it captured so completely the essence of this actress, nothing she subsequently did was entirely separable from it.

The cinema, however, had little use for an actress of this kind, though on the stage she played Shaw's 'Saint Joan' (47) with the Old Vic. She put her home life first (she was married to the writer and explorer Peter Fleming; was widowed in 1971) and thus limited the runs of her plays and was selective over film-scripts. One can only speculate over *The Astonished Heart* (50), adapted by Coward from another of his short plays, but with a different director and producer. Another triangle drama, only she was in a different corner as husband Coward dallied with Margaret Leighton: artificial situations building into bilious melodrama (and recalled with a shudder by everyone concerned). She accepted the well-intended but hackneyed *I*

Celia Johnson with screen husband Cyril Raymond in Brief Encounter *(45).*

Believe in You (52), with fellow probation officer Cecil Parker, saving delinquents Joan Collins and Maxwell Reed in more ways than one. *The Holly and the Ivy* was minor West End fare with Ralph Richardson, set in a country vicarage; and *The Captain's Paradise* (53), a protracted joke with Alex Guinness – the only time on screen she was able to demonstrate her comedy finesse, a matter of blank looks and dithering. She could not manage the required accent for *A Kid for Two Farthings* (55), directed by Carol Reed from an East End fable by Wolf Mankowitz – not that it mattered. At least it was better than the remake of Priestley's story, *The Good Companions* (57), all tarted up and nowhere to go. No longer the adventures of a touring company but When Will Susie Dean Become a Star? (as played in this version, never). Johnson (as Miss Trant), Eric Portman and Joyce Grenfell went down with the ship.

It was an experience, perhaps, which kept her off the screen for 12 years. She had some notable West End seasons, among them: 'The Three Sisters' (51), as Masha; 'The Reluctant Débutante' (55); 'Flowering Cherry' (58); 'Tchin-Tchin' (62); at the National, 'Hay Fever' and 'The Master Builder'; and 'Relatively Speaking' (67). Television appearances included 'The Letter' and Ibsen's 'Ghosts'. Then, despite some opposition from 20th (who wanted Wendy Hiller), she played a featured role in *The Prime of Miss Jean Brodie* (69); as the embittered Scots headmistress she virtually stole the notices from Maggie Smith, won the BFA's Best Supporting Actress award and almost obliterated, finally, the image of a sad-eyed woman on a suburban train speeding away from her lover while the soundtrack thunders with Rachmaninov.

Her last three filmed performances were for television: *Les Misérables* (79), as a nun, *The Hostage Tower* (80), as the mother of the American president – both American productions, and *Staying On*, from Paul Scott's novel about post-Raj India, with Trevor Howard. Stage appearances included 'The Dame of Sark' and 'The Kingfisher' with Ralph Richardson. In 1982 she was rehearsing with him for 'The Understanding' when she was taken ill (Joan Greenwood replaced her) and she died shortly afterwards of a stroke.

Van Johnson

If you look very hard (and sometimes not so very) at that group of players labelled 'the boy (or girl) next door', you will usually find a performer so ordinary that even the experts in the publicity department are defeated in finding a more exciting description. Van Johnson was one such. Snub-nosed, freckled-faced, sandy-haired, he set aflame the hearts of countless bobby-soxers during the war years and just after. Critics did not like him (C.A. Lejeune wrote in 1952: 'Van Johnson does his best: appears') and it has to be admitted that his stock-in-trade, sincerity, was often merely an expression that resembled a sick calf. He was a moderately effective screen actor, but the wayward course of his career once his youth had gone was as inevitable as that first onslaught of fan mail.

He was born in 1916 in Newport, Rhode Island, into what was known as a 'broken home'. After graduation, he worked in an office for a while, but he already had the Broadway bug . . . he tried hard, and eventually landed a job in the chorus of 'New Faces'. He took dancing, singing and acting lessons; sang in vaudeville and then became what the hand-outs described as 'one of the famous Eight Men of Manhattan', entertaining at the Rainbow Room. He had small parts in two Rodgers and Hart shows, 'Too Many Girls' (39) and 'Pal Joey'. He toured in the lead of the first of these, but had only one line in the movie version (40). In the second he was also Gene Kelly's understudy and when he went on for him was seen by a Warner talent scout and given a contract: they starred him in a B with Faye Emerson, *Murder in the Big House* (42), as a reporter fearlessly uncovering it. When in six months his option came up it was not renewed. MGM took him on and gave him a short but showy role in *Somewhere I'll Find You*, as a GI explaining battle tactics to Clark Gable. Unfortunately, his eyebrows and lashes photographed white, but this was rectified. Happily, there was something about his manner suggesting he was everyone's idea of the boys out there fighting – not long ripped from mother's bosom, but eager to get the job done: so he was in uniform again, of on the home front, in *The War Against Mrs Hadley*, a sentimental comedy about a Republican dowager (Fay Bainter) who (at first) refuses to join the war effort. Reaction was favourable enough to have Johnson replace Lew Ayres as the thorn in Lionel Barrymore's side – *Dr Gillespie's New Assistant.*

That established him as one of the studio's bright young comers. He was Mickey Rooney's soldier brother in *The Human Comedy* (43); again in uniform alongside Gene Kelly in *Pilot No 5*; and opposing Barrymore again over *Dr Gillespie's Criminal Case*. He was considerably out of place in *Madame Curie*, in a featured role as a (French) journalist. *A Guy Named Joe* was a rousing war story in which dead fighter-pilot Spencer Tracy is sent back to earth by God (Lionel Barrymore, no kidding) to guide Johnson towards better pilotry and the bereaved Irene Dunne (so that a love like theirs cannot wither away). During its making Johnson was badly injured in a car crash and would have been replaced had not Tracy stepped in. Tracy was right: when the picture was shown, Johnson became an undisputed star. He was teamed with Dunne again, in another sentimental war drama, *The White Cliffs of Dover* (44), and was then rushed into a musical with two other youngsters for whom MGM had high hopes, June Allyson and Gloria De Haven – *Two Girls and a Sailor*. It was popular and made Allyson and Johnson a favourite team – to the extent that he was too 'big' to play the male lead in *Meet Me In St Louis* and was replaced by Tom Drake. He did his last two outings as a medico, *Three Men in White* and *Between Two Women*; with them the series was abandoned and Barrymore sought other employment. Between the two Johnson was a pilot in the interminable *Thirty Seconds Over Tokyo*, another of the year's most popular films.

And both the next two were among the year's top 10 successes: *Thrill of a Romance* (45), a musical with Esther Williams, and the starry *Weekend at the Waldorf*, where he was a debonair air force captain chasing stenographer Lana Turner. He had risen like a meteor and every studio in town was looking for similar types or remoulding those under contract – William Eythe at 20th, Dennis Morgan at Warners, Don Defore at Paramount – while wondering how the public would respond to their old heroes, now returning from the war; but none of the others really imposed themselves on the public, while Johnson trailed only Bing Crosby as the nation's favourite – nor was his popularity hurt (contrary to the predictions of the fan magazines) when the wife of friend Keenan Wynn divorced Wynn to marry him (1947; it lasted till about 1962 and they were divorced in 1968). In 1946 he was third at the box-office and even in Britain he scraped into the top 10. A 1946 poll of American critics and theatre-owners placed him after Greer Garson, Crosby and Ingrid Bergman, before Bette Davis, Humphrey Bogart, Gary Cooper, Spencer Tracy, Claudette Colbert, Judy Garland, Cary Grant and Irene Dunne in that order. But the 'Harvard Lampoon' voted him the year's worst actor. The relevant titles: *Easy to Wed* (46), a big-grossing comedy with Esther Williams; *No Leave No Love*, which brought the year's shortest review (from Lejeune), 'No Comment', and misused MGM's new contract star, Pat Kirkwood, so badly that they dropped her; and *Till the Clouds Roll By*, where guest Johnson did an embarrasingly bad dance. Then: *High Barbaree* (47), again as a soldier, with Allyson; *The Romance of Rosy Ridge*, demobbed – from the Civil War – as a schoolteacher, with the débuting Janet Leigh; and *The Bride Goes Wild* (48), a comedy with Allyson.

Those three did not do well and MGM put him in support of some of their old-timers: Tracy and Hepburn in *State of the Union* and Gable and Pidgeon in *Command Decision*. It was later admitted that Johnson had undergone a serious crisis of confidence in his talent (Hepburn is reputed to have helped him), but he was certainly good in the second of these films, funny as the general's wised-up orderly. Still, even if his salary was now $5,000 a week, the great days were over and he was loaned to 20th for a programmer with Loretta Young, *Mother Is a Freshman* (49), unconvincingly cast as a professor of English literature. He was learning to relax, however, and developing a comedy technique; and was at his charming bumptious best *In the Good Old Summertime*, with Judy Garland. *Scene of the Crime* – he was a cop – played double bills, an indication that the Johnson box-office path was now rocky. *Battleground* – he was a wise-cracking, scrounging rifleman – was a huge grosser, but the success of his films became dependent on the pull of his co-stars – and most of them lacked any. The films were pretty lacking too: *The Big Hangover* (50) with Elizabeth Taylor, a comedy about a man

In the Good Old Summertime *(49) was a pleasant remake, with music, of* The Shop Around the Corner*: here are Judy Garland and Van Johnson as fellow-employees and pen-pals. He's just found out she's the girl he's writing to; she won't discover the truth till the last reel.*

allergic to (even the smell of) alcohol; *The Duchess of Idaho*, an Esther Williams vehicle; *Grounds for Marriage* with Kathryn Grayson; and *Three Guys Named Mike* (51), with Jane Wyman (which Mike would she pick? Well, Johnson was billed over Howard Keel and Barry Sullivan . . .)

Go For Broke! was an attempt to repeat the success of *Battleground*, a tribute to the Jap-American combat team who fought in Europe, with Johnson as the Texan in charge. It did not restore him to the front rank of stars. Nor did: *Too Young To Kiss*, with June Allyson; *It's a Big Country*, as a priest in his episode; *Invitation* (52), with Dorothy McGuire, as an adventurer who discovers he has a heart; *When in Rome*, again as a priest; *Washington Story*, with Patricia Neal; and *Plymouth Adventure*, supporting Spencer Tracy. MGM seemed to give up – to judge from the quality of *Confidentially Connie* (53), with Janet Leigh replacing Nancy Olson when MGM realized that meant 'Olson and Johnson' on the marquees; and *Remains To Be Seen*, an infantile comedy-thriller with Allyson. He tried cabaret, not very successfully, and returned to Metro to appear with Williams in *Easy To Love*, but less as her co-star than as her leading man. In an attempt to give him a more virile image, he was loaned to 20th for a Western, *The Siege at Red River* (54), and made one of the *Men of the Fighting Lady*, a naval drama. He stayed in the navy, as Humphrey Bogart's First Officer, in a much better film, *The Caine Mutiny*, and was very good in that supporting role. Returning to Metro, he had a smallish role as Gene Kelly's sidekick in *Brigadoon*. The role in *Seagulls Over Sorrento* announced for him went to Kelly, but MGM offered what might have been a fond farewell, *The Last Time I Saw Paris*, a lush soap opera as Elizabeth Taylor's increasingly tipsy husband – but that was a bastardization of Scott Fitzgerald's 'Babylon Revisited' (using a silly, modernized script instead of the reputedly superb one he himself had done).

It was the last time he saw MGM – as a contract artist, anyway. Hollywood had always liked Johnson and trade talk was that as a freelance he would re-establish himself: but he started off disastrously in *The End of the Affair* (55), miscast as Deborah Kerr's lover, boring and boorish. He tried again with *Bottom of the Bottle* (56) with Joseph Cotten, directed by Henry Hathaway, tough as an escaped convict; the good *Miracle in the Rain*, as a soldier in love with Jane Wyman; Hathaway's *23 Paces to Baker Street*, as a blind amateur sleuth; and, back at MGM, a film about the *Slander* magazines, as a TV personality who is blackmailed. There were two minor films, *Kelly and Me* (57), as a small-time hoofer, and *Action of the Tiger*, with Martine Carol, rescuing refugees from the Commies. There was also a much-revived TV film, 'The Pied Piper of Hamelin' with Claude Rains. He signed a contract with Columbia for five films at $125,000 each, but three days before starting *Friday the Thirteenth* (a thriller written by Clifford Odets) he told the studio he did not want to do it. Columbia took the opportunity to release him from the contract.

After that, the only offers were British: *Subway in the Sky* (59), a romantic drama with Hildegarde Neff, ineptly directed; and *Beyond This Place*, from A.J. Cronin's novel, with Vera Miles and Jean Kent. And both, whatever their makers intended, were very unimportant. So were a couple made in France by Sam Katzman for Columbia, *The Last Blitzkreig*, and *The Enemy General*, a Resistance thriller with dialogue of that era ('French swine, they'll pay for this'). To all but the most diligent film-seeker, he had been off the screen for years; now he was definitely off and in the London production of 'The Music Man', which, as Tynan observed, was after Robert Preston's New York perform-

Van Johnson in The Caine Mutiny *(54), as the officer who unwillingly comes to believe that the captain is a paranoic and who, because he takes over command, is later court-martialled for mutiny. It is perhaps his best screen work – and the only time scars from an old accident were allowed to be seen.*

ance like ordering a steak and being served a thin slice of ham (to do it, he turned down the lead in TV's 'The Untouchables'). Undeterred, Johnson tried Broadway in Garson Kanin's 'Come On Strong', with Carroll Baker, and did both 'The Music Man' and 'Bye Bye Birdie' in stock.

He returned to the screen in a dated comedy produced by Hal Wallis, *Wives and Lovers* (63), as a nice author whose success turns him into a raving egomaniac. He got fine notices and it was announced that he had signed a five-year deal with Wallis, to start with *Boeing-Boeing* and *Decision at Delphi*: instead he worked much in TV – *The Doomsday Flight* (66) was later shown in cinemas – and was away from films till *Divorce American Style* (67), in an amusing cameo as a bouncy car salesman. He had a supporting role, as a wolf, at Lucille Ball's request in *Yours Mine and Ours* (68), and a guest spot in *Where Angels Go Trouble Follows* (69). He had changed but little since he had started, but his work had become more likeable, indicating a solid future as a character actor – though probably not if he made more films like *The Professional*, a cheapie shot in nine days and probably shown publicly for less time than that. *Company of Killers*, a Murder Inc thriller with Ray Milland, hardly got more bookings and after a TV movie, *San Francisco International Airport* (70), Johnson turned to Europe: *La Battaglia d'Inghilterra*, a Franco-Spanish-Italian effort about Germans in Britain after Dunkirk, with Frederick Stafford; and *Il Prezzo del Potere*, an Italian 'Western', made in Spain, set in Dallas in 1880, about a plot to assassinate President Garfield. Professional activity decreased, as he struggled against cancer; but he did appear in stock, adding 'Damn Yankees' and 'How To Succeed in Business Without Really Trying' to his repertoire.

Call Her Mom (72) starred Connie Stevens, with Johnson as the president of her college, reunited with Gloria De Haven as his wife (after Ann Miller and Cyd Charisse had worked on the role, that of an ex-chorus girl). It was the first of several films for television: *The Girl on the Late, Late Show* (74) with several other names – Walter Pidgeon, Yvonne de Carlo, Don Murray; *Rich Man Poor Man* (76), a mini-series, ditto – Dorothy McGuire, Ray Milland, Dorothy Malone; *Black Beauty* (78), another mini, ditto – Mel Ferrer, Farley Granger, Warren Oates; and *Superdome*, a thriller about a killer threatening the big game. Johnson's name was slipping down the cast-list, but he did play the father of the bride, Bess Armstrong, when she was *Getting Married* to Richard Thomas. He also appeared in an episode of 'Love Boat' with his old sidekick, Miss Allyson. Several European offers were turned down, till he finally accepted *Concorde Affaire 79* (79), as a pilot, and *Da Corleone ad Brooklyn*.

In the Canadian *The Kidnapping of the President* (80) he was the Vice-President; after doing 'Tribute' in stock he went to Italy for *Absurd (Anthropophagus II)* (81) with Laura Gemser and then again for a series, *The Mystery of the Etruscans* (82). He managed to be noticed (just) in another episode of *Love Boat* co-starring Ethel Merman, Carol Channing and Ann Miller, and was in a Spanish film with Giuliano Gemma, *La Muerte de un Presidente*. He was in stock in 'No, No Nanette' (83) and in a TV series which did not run, 'Glitter' (85). His career was seriously in trouble, unless he did that brief appearance in the film within the film, *The Purple Rose of Cairo*, for fun. But it then got a fillip, taking over the male lead (well, the butch one, anyway) in a Broadway musical, 'La Cage aux Folles'. Two other Italian ventures have been advertised in the trade press: *Down There in the Jungle* with Robert Powell and *Killer Crocodile* with Anthony Crenna.

JENNIFER JONES

Jennifer Jones was a nice young girl who got made into a star via one big part and wagonloads of publicity. Then, first time out, she even got an Oscar. She went on to play in some score of important movies with only medium success. Her chief virtue was that she was never quite the standard Hollywood female, her failing that she was not quite anything else, either. Given the roles she had, she was never quite magnetic or individual enough for them. She could sink herself into any part demanding a maximum of sensitivity and a modicum of characterization: on some occasions she was deceptively good. Her notices on the whole were mixed.

She was born Phyllis Isley in Tulsa, Oklahoma, in 1920, of theatrical parents; as a child she acted with their stock company, but they were not keen on her becoming an actress. She persuaded them, however, to let her study at the AADA in New York, where she met Robert Walker. They were married in 1939 and for a while worked on the Tulsa radio station; then they tried Hollywood, where Paramount tested them but turned them down. She did get some unimportant work at Republic – leading lady in a B Western starring John Wayne, *New Frontier* (39), and a role on one of their serials, *Dick Tracy's G-Men*, one of a series starring Ralph Byrd. There were no more offers, so they returned to New York where she did some modelling. She managed to get an audition with David O. Selznick's New York office – actually for *Laura*, which he was then contemplating – and was tested and signed to a long-term contract. At that time Selznick kept a small stable of important stars (e.g. Bergman, Joan Fontaine) whom he loaned out because his production programmes were too ambitious to be quickly realized. (After his 1939/40 triumph with *Gone With the Wind* he produced or actively participated in the production of only half a dozen films until his death 20 years later.) It was obviously a coup for Jennifer Jones (as he had renamed her) to be under his wing, though he thought she needed more experience; he got her into a local production of 'Hello Out There' by William Saroyan and sent her back to New York to study some more.

In 1942 he introduced her to the press as the probable star of *The Keys of the Kingdom*, as Nora, but he later sold that property to 20th, along with two other projects and their stars, *Jane Eyre* and *Claudia* – for both of which Jones had also been considered. But it was certainly in conjunction with 20th that Jones's name first became known, as the star of *The Song of Bernadette* (43). She was a 'brilliant new discovery' until a few sharp-eyed fans remembered her two films at Republic (her presence in which was denied for a while). Selznick and 20th combined to promote both star and film, the latter an expensive version of Franz Werfel's bestselling novel about Bernadette Soubirous, the French peasant girl who fought the Church in her insistence that she had visions of the Virgin and who was later canonized. The publicity campaign was Hollywood at its most pious – but the film's subject was compelling enough and Henry King's direction at least decent enough to justify it. It was one of the year's top grossers. Much lobbying brought in five Oscars, including one to Jones as Best Actress. The critics had given her warm but not sensational notices.

The day after the Oscar ceremony Jones announced that she was suing for divorce. She and Walker were then working on Selznick's paean to the woman who stayed at home, *Since You Went Away* (44), as the young sweethearts. Selznick had written the script himself, continually making her part bigger, and she is rather good in it – bright-eyed and bushy-tailed as the daughter who would rather work in a munitions factory than go to college. The film was another box-office hit – helped perhaps by its ad slogan, 'The four most important words since *Gone With the Wind*'. He then loaned her and Joseph Cotten to Paramount for *Love Letters* (45), a successful psychological drama about an amnesiac and the ex-soldier who had really written her husband's letters. The 'New York Times' described her performance as 'fatuous'; but it was generally agreed that she was good – with a vivacity she never again revealed – as *Cluny Brown* (46) at 20th, the British plumber's niece of Margery Sharp's comic novel. Sharp, in fact, insisted in her contract with the company that Jones play the role. Lubitsch directed, but it was not one of his major works.

Hollywood in religious mood: Jennifer Jones as the peasant girl from Lourdes who saw a vision: The Song of Bernadette *(43).*

Then came *Duel in the Sun*, a huge Western on which Selznick lavished almost as much on publicity as on production – and at a combined $6 million it was the most expensive film yet made. Despite critical put-downs his gamble worked: the film grossed $11 million and trailed only his own *Gone With the Wind* and Goldwyn's *The Best Years of Our Lives* among the all-time grossers. Jones played an impossible part, that of the tempestuous half-breed Pearl loved by both Cotten and Gregory Peck. Said Dilys Powell: 'Miss Jones, indeed, gives a performance beyond the range of any other young Hollywood actress I know. But . . . *Duel in the Sun* remains an enormous piece of dustbin.' (There have been later attempts to rehabilitate this film.)

Selznick's pride in his women stars had been obsessive and it was particularly so in the case of Jones. She, at first timid and then wary of him, became accustomed to his concern; and not long after his wife left him, he and Jones were married (1949). He subordinated all his activities to managing her career and indeed *Portrait of Jennie* (48) was the last film made by the Selznick studio. Her part was not big, but was choice. Cotten was again the man, an artist who meets a girl in Central Park at dusk who turns out to be a ghost . . . In that role Jones was feyer than ever and vaguely alienating. At least, the US public rejected the whole thunderingly romantic thing and it did not surface in Britain till three years later, as a dualler. It started a run of unsuccessful films for Jones – though none of them was without distinction. Her own work varied from the conscientious to the outstanding – though the 'New York Times' found her stiff in *We Were Strangers* (49), as a Cuban girl who loves revolutionary leader John Garfield. John Huston directed for Columbia and maybe the downbeat ending kept the public away.

At MGM Vincente Minnelli had a stab at *Madame Bovary*, with many fine effects and now and then that peculiar, acrid atmosphere of the novel. But. Jones was a but, though she did get as near to Emma as any Hollywood actress might. The 'Manchester Guardian' thought she 'certainly suggests a beautiful creature, of restless, silly, romantic and misdirected longings'. She was another lady from literature, the gypsy heroine of *Gone To Earth* (50), a co-production between Selznick and Korda and directed by Michael Powell, making the most of the Shropshire locations and the least of the preposterous story. But nothing jelled. The British première was

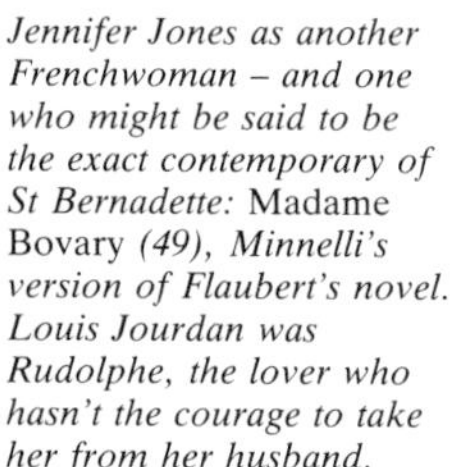

Jennifer Jones as another Frenchwoman – and one who might be said to be the exact contemporary of St Bernadette: Madame Bovary *(49), Minnelli's version of Flaubert's novel. Louis Jourdan was Rudolphe, the lover who hasn't the courage to take her from her husband.*

delayed because Selznick wanted to insert additional scenes; and after the apathetic reception there he had most of it reshot. But the revised version, called *The Wild Heart*, got even worse notices when shown in the US in 1952. Nor were there many takers for yet another literary lady, *Carrie* (52), Wyler's sober version for Paramount of Dreiser's novel; Jones's Carrie, thoughtless and light-hearted, might have seemed even better if not up against Olivier in full stream.

At 20th, *Ruby Gentry* (53) was a steamy small-town melodrama where Jones, as Richard Winnington put it, 'operating in her well-known primitive child-woman mood and spurned by her lover and local society, has only one answer – "to wreck a whole town" sin by sin, man by man'. In Europe Jones made *Beat the Devil*, directed by Huston from a script by himself and Truman Capote, a spoof thriller about a gang of curios (Bogart, Robert Morley, etc.) and a British couple – Jones as the wife, blonde, scatterbrained and a pathological liar. *Stazione Termini/Indiscretion of an American Wife* (54) was the disappointing result of Selznick having badgered Vittorio De Sica to make a film for him, a really long good-bye between Jones and Montgomery Clift in Rome's railway station (in the US it was not so long – Selznick cut it to 63 minutes; in Britain it was 75. He managed to sell it thus to Columbia for $½ million – but it can hardly have taken that). After the box-office receipts of this lot, it was not surprising that Jones tackled Broadway, in a dramatization of Henry James's 'Portrait of a Lady' (54); that too failed, thus cancelling Selznick's plans to film it (she might have been a perfect film Isabel).

20th signed her for three films and ironically the poor *Love is a Many Splendored Thing* (55) was a big hit (helped by a hit theme song); Jones was a Eurasian doctor in this version of Han Suyin's semi-autobiographical bestseller and William Holden the man she loved. *Good Morning Miss Dove* was a quiet study of a New England schoolteacher, too old-fashioned to find a large public. *The Man in the Grey Flannel Suit* (56) was a grey flannel film, with Gregory Peck as her husband. At MGM she was once more among the anti-macassars in *The Barretts of Wimpole Street* (57), directed by Sidney Franklin, who had made the more famous but inferior earlier version. Jones's reading of Elizabeth Barrett Browning was much more likely than Norma Shearer's and was up against the flesh and blood of John Gielgud's outstanding Papa Barrett – though the Browning (Bill Travers) would have been more at home in a rugger scrum.

The next two were novels which should have been left well alone. Selznick had long dreamed of a new version of *A Farewell to Arms* (57) and had seen his chance of getting it when Warners wanted the remake rights to *A Star is Born*: on top of the exchange, he paid them $25,000. He interfered so much with Huston, directing, that Charles Vidor took over and the result was a very dull drama indeed. Jones insisted that Hemingway get a percentage of the eventual profits and Selznick offered $50,000. Hemingway retorted that in view of her unsuitability (too old) for the heroine he doubted whether there would be any profits. There were: it was a success in the US, at least. 20th released and to them later Selznick turned over the rights to *Tender Is the Night* (61). It was no surprise to find Jones still cast as Nicole – or, rather, miscast. She was by no means as awful as Jason Robards Jr as Dick, but script, direction, indeed everything, were against them.

Selznick died in 1965 and not long afterwards Jones went to Britain at two days' notice, when Kim Stanley became indisposed, to make *The Idol* (66), in which she had an affair with her son's best friend. It passed unperceived. In 1967 she was taken to hospital after being found unconscious on a Californian beach, reputedly after an overdose of pills. No public statement was made, perhaps because she had always been aloof from the press. Hedda Hopper once observed that 'she is very nervous while acting, hating to be watched at work by anybody but the minimum crew, flinching at even routine questions when she is interviewed'. It was doubly a surprise when she elected to do a programmer for AIP, *Angel Angel Down We Go* (69). 'Playboy' observed that she 'has seldom reached lower depths professionally and is now asked to swallow her pride with such lines as "I made thirty stag films and never faked an orgasm."' Afterwards she entered a sanatorium. In 1971 she married millionaire Norton Simon; and she returned briefly to the screen as the wealthy widow who tries to save two children in *The Towering Inferno* (74). He bought for her Diana Trilling's book on the Jean Harris murder for $1 million, but it has not been filmed; another he bought for her, 'Terms of Endearment', he let go.

Louis Jouvet

'Crois-tu que je serais devenu ce que je suis s'ii n'y avait pas eu le cinéma?' said Louis Jouvet towards the end of his life. In fact, he was above all a man of the theatre – the greatest theatre man of his generation, an actor-manager whose achievements are legendary within France. But it is not thus that he is primarily remembered by those who throng the incessant revivals of his films in Paris, the *salles d'art et d'essai* – mainly stuffy cellars on the Left Bank. Laurence Olivier was posed the same problem: did he wish to be remembered as a great actor-manager or as a film star? Olivier replied that he used to be snobbish about it, but that he would be happy to be remembered as a film star. In a way, there is no choice. Descriptions of Jouvet in 'Dom Juan' do not have the strength of cinema reality – of Jouvet up on the screen in even his least film.

It was considered that he only acted in films for material gain; but the fact remains that on the evidence of those films this lean-featured, sloe-eyed man was one of the half-dozen great screen actors. Like Spencer Tracy or Walter Huston his range was not notably wide – making his last film, he said to the director, 'Si je suis trop Jouvet, tu m'arrêtes.' His characters were an extension of himself – cynical, wily, worldly. Few of them were admirable (one feels that Olivier in his sly mood had modelled himself on Jouvet) but there is a combination of two qualities which hits you right between the eyes – the attention to physical detail and the man's seemingly inexhaustible humanity. Virtually all of his screen portrayals are enriching experiences.

He was 46 when his film career started. He was born in 1887 at Crozon, Finistère, and educated *un peu partout* – Jouvet *père* travelled on government work till killed in an accident. After that the family lived mainly at Rethel (in the Ardennes) and Jouvet studied to be a pharmacist. He wanted to be an actor but was turned down three times by the Conservatoire. In 1907 he met the founders of the Groupe d'Action et d'Art and the following year they appointed him director of the theatre section: for them he played Coryphée in 'Oedipe-Roi' (10) and the title-role in 'Le Colonel Chabert', adapted from Balzac. When the group was disbanded he acted in Brussels and Liège; then in Paris appeared in 'Le Tour de Monde en 80 Jours', 'Michel Strogoff' and 'Les Frères Karamazov'. In 1912 he married. In 1913 he was in a film, *Shylock*, and was appointed director of the Théâtre du Vieux-Colombier. Called up in 1914 he was at the Front for three years, until Clemenceau decided that he would like a French troupe in New York for prestige reasons – so Jouvet and the Vieux-Colombier company were sent and remained at the Garrick on 35th Street for two years, 1919–21. In 1923 he became director of the Théâtre des Champs-Elysées and that year he created the title-role in Jules Romains's 'Knock'. In 1927 he received the Légion d'honneur; founded, with Georges Pitoëff, Charles Dullin and Gaston Baty, the 'Cartel', whose aim was to take their four theatres into the forefront of the avant-garde movement; and met Jean Giraudoux, whose first play, 'Siegfried', he produced the following year and whose prime promoter and interpreter he became. Over the new few years he directed and acted in, among others, 'Jean de la Lune', 'Amphitryon 38', 'L'Eau Fraîche', 'Un Taciturne' and 'Intermezzo' (33).

He made his film début in *Topaze* (33), from Marcel Pagnol's play. He wanted to do it on stage but did not care to risk comparison with André Lefaur, who had created the part – that of a meek schoolteacher who by virtue of circumstance and a good mathematical brain becomes the riotously successful frontman for a gang of crooks. He particularly relished the climax – where his eyes are opened and he decides to stay in business, this time for himself. Jouvet liked expediency; in his best film parts he bested or gulled the weak and the wicked. *Knock* was a satire on human credibility; he was a doctor of dubious qualifications who turned a run-down country practice into a roaring triumph. He played the part, as he had on stage, with a dry, laconic wit and co-directed with Roger Goupillères. Both films were basically photographed plays and, if they had attracted him for the philanthropic reason that he liked both plays and had wanted them to reach a wider audience, he was startled to find them so popular: it was their success rather than their merit which caused him to consider seriously the cinema as a medium.

In the meantime he directed and acted in 'La Machine Infernale' by Cocteau, 'Tessa' ('The Constant Nymph' adapted by Giraudoux) and 'La Guerre de Troie n'aura pas Lieu'; and began to teach at the Conservatoire. His return to films was a happy occasion: Jacques Feyder's *La Kermesse Heroïque* (35), with Françoise Rosay as the wife of burgomaster Alerme, welcoming the Spanish 'invasion' in her own way while the men of the town feigned death or departure. Jouvet was the Spanish chaplain, monumentally cunning, not averse to wine and revelling in the sale of indulgences. The film was ecstatically received (not least for the Franz Hals décor) and was the New York critics' Best Foreign Film. These factors, plus the empathy with Feyder, changed Jouvet's attitude to the cinema. He considered himself only a featured actor in films and took basically supporting roles, as in *Mister Flow* (36), though in the title-role – as a master con-man, posing as a valet, in love and in league with Edwige Feuillère before losing her to Fernand Gravey.

In Renoir's *Les Bas-Fonds* he was masterly

as the gambling count adjusting to the exigencies of poverty, proud but self-mocking; but he could not do much with Pabst's all-star (Dita Parlo, Pierres Blanchar and Fresnay, Dullin, Jean-Louis Barrault) *Mademoiselle Docteur* (37), as a German spy disguised as a Levantine fruit-merchant – but then the film was silly. He was at his most human in Duvivier's *Un Carnet de Bal*, as the shady ex-lawyer/club-owner wanted by the police, in one episode of this heavily romantic piece about an ageing beauty (Marie Bell) who finds an old dance-card and seeks out her partners. This was a great success abroad and also had a fine cast, including Harry Baur, Fernandel and Françoise Rosay. *Drôle de Drame* was similarly distinguished – Jean-Louis Barrault (as a homicidal maniac), Jean-Pierre Aumont (as an imaginative milkman) and Jouvet, nicely theatrical, as a sanctimonious bishop who terrorizes Michel Simon into thinking he had killed Mme Rosay: a freak farce about a murder that never was, set in an impossible Edwardian London, directed by Marcel Carné and scripted by Jacques Prévert from 'His First Offence' by Storer Clouston.

The next two were commonplace, even though *L'Alibi* at the time was considered the first successful French thriller, with Jouvet as a police commissioner on the trail of Erich von Stroheim: and even though *Forfaiture* was advertised 'Un immortel chef d'oeuvre'. That was in fact a remake of De Mille's ancient *The Cheat*, with Jouvet opposite another ex-Hollywood name, Sessue Hayakawa, as his *louche* Occidental secretary, conniving at the doom of Lise Delamare. Then: Renoir's vast, unsatisfactory Revolution tale, *La Marseillaise* (38), in but briefly as Dr Roederer; *Ramuntcho*, from a novel by Pierre Loti, as the head of a gang of smugglers, with Rosay, and Paul Cambo in the title-role; *La Maison du Maltais*, an underworld melodrama, mingling with Viviane Romance and Jany Holt, as an unscrupulous private detective; and Marc Allegret's *Entrée des Artistes*, an engaging if diffuse study of drama students (Claude Dauphin, Odette Joyeux, Bernard Blier), with Jouvet as their professor – a part he presumably played as himself. At all events he almost pulled the thing together and he was at his best again undertaking the *Education de Prince*, a smooth clubman living on his wits and offering to return said child and the queen mother (Elvire Popesco) to their realm in return for the oil concession – Carlo Rim's version of a popular boulevard play. He was not too hot, however, as the mysterious Russian villain of Pabst's *Le Drame de Shanghai*, a confused Chinesey drama with Raymond Rouleau.

The inhabitants of Carné's *Hôtel du Nord* were mainly up to no good, least of all Jouvet as a sleazy, boastful pimp – but unable to resist the gesture of letting himself be killed by the man he betrayed; perhaps his most finished pre-war performance. Michel Simon had the lead in *La Fin du Jour* (39), as an ageing thespian with a liking for boys; others in the home for old actors included Victor Francen and Jouvet – white-haired, *cabotin*, filled with regrets. Duvivier directed and he also directed *La Charrette Fantôme*, uneasily adapted from a Swedish novel by Selma Lagerloff (and filmed before, in 1920, by Victor Sjöstrom), with Jouvet as the crook turned Messenger of Death. This was shown in Scandinavia, but war interrupted showings in France. *Sérénade* (40) had similar difficulties, a musical of strictly limited charm, with Jouvet as the chief of the Vienna police losing his English dancer-mistress (Lilian Harvey) to Schubert (Bernard Lancret). Escapism was also the order of *Volpone*, adapted from the

Louis Jouvet in the title-role of Mister Flow *(36), a film described by George Sadoul as 'a remarkable pastiche of Lubitsch's famous* Trouble in Paradise*'. Robert Siodmak directed.*

Annabella and Louis Jouvet after they have left the Hôtel du Nord *(38). It was a shabby lodging-house on the Canal St Martin, brilliantly recreated in the studio by the art director, Alexandre Trauner.*

Jules Romains and Stefan Zweig version of Ben Jonson's play and begun two years earlier – but there were difficulties with the female lead (finally played by Jacqueline Delubac) and it was mostly remade just before the German occupation. Jouvet was Mosca, Harry Baur was Volpone, Dullin was Corbaccio and no one who saw them would ever accept anyone else in these roles.

In 1936 Jouvet had been offered the directorship of the Comédie-Française; he had refused but had directed plays there until the war. Now without any company at all he went to Nice to make *Untel Père et Fils* (not shown in Paris till 1945 but smuggled out to Britain and the US), intended by its director, Duvivier, to be a French *Cavalcade*, a story of a French fmaily through three generations and three wars, but overly ambitious; Jouvet had two parts – head of the family and an alcoholic ex-colonial. In the summer of 1940 he returned to Paris and tried to re-form his company, but found that the Germans had banned much of his repertoire (Romains, Giraudoux). He accepted an invitation from Switzerland to tour there in one of his great successes, 'L'École des Femmes', and began a film of that there, under the direction of Max Ophüls, whom he had smuggled across the border with his troupe. The film was also intended to be a look at Jouvet the actor (the camera would follow him offstage) but was abandoned after only a few shots (Jouvet and Ophüls were both in love with the same lady, Madeleine Ozeray). In 1941 he was in Lyons with his troupe and from there they sailed to Rio; and it was in South America that he spent the war, touring, often under conditions of great hardship.

He returned to Paris in 1945 and spent most of that year reclaiming his theatre, the Athénée, and preparing Giraudoux's posthumous play, 'La Folle de Chaillot'. Film offers were not lacking. In 1938 and 1939 he had been one of the top five box-office stars and in acknowledgment of that popularity he now accepted what were in fact star vehicles: *Un Revenant* (46), as a cynic bent on revenging himself on the crass family who destroyed his youthful love affair, with Gaby Morlay; and *Capie Conforme* (47), a comedy about a big-time swindler who uses a double, a mild little businessman, as an alibi. He also got to impersonate several other characters – a 'festival Jouvet'. René Barjavel wrote in 'L'Ecran Français': 'Jouvet étincelant d'intelligence métier de comédien, passe d'un rôle à l'autre avec maestria.' In the first French polls held since before the war, fans voted him their fourth male favourite and exhibitors their third.

Also that year he did his best postwar film, *Quai des Orfèvres*, a mordant thriller directed by Henri-Georges Clouzot, with Suzy Delair, Bernard Blier, Simone Renant and Charles Dullin (as the dirtiest old man on celluloid). Jouvet was the detective after one of them – relentless, seedy, grudging, disenchanted, with his little bourgeois moustache, living in one miserable room. In his theatre he was putting on 'Dom Juan' and Genêt's 'Les Bonnes'; on screen he virtually played himself again – a celebrated musician suspected by his wife of infidelity with one of his pupils (Dany Robin), met by chance when playing one of his compositions: *Les Amoureux sont Seuls au Monde* (48). The film caused a minor furore when shown with a happy ending and director Henri Decoin and scenarist Henri Jeanson sued because they had been promised that that was for foreign distribution only. It was also popular and Jouvet was voted the year's best actor in the Cinémonde poll.

None of his last films was particularly interesting: *Entre Onze Heures et Minuit* (49), again in a dual role, as a crook and as an inspector of police; Clouzot's *Retour à la Vie*, in the episode about a repatriated Frenchman and his former German captor; the third Talkie version of *Miquette et sa Mère*, not at his best as a pedantic, lecherous marquis who promises to help stage-struck Danièle Delorme in her career, and *Lady Paname*, directed by Jeanson – who had over the years given him some of his best screen dialogue – an affectionate study of theatrical life in the *quartier* Saint-Martin of the 20s, with Suzy Delair as a would-be *chansonnière* and Jouvet as the eccentric photographer determined to see she makes it. He went to New York with 'L'Ecole des Femmes' and played in a remake of *Knock* (50) – but the joke now seemed repetitious; and then in *Une Histoire d'Amour* (51), again as a police inspector, this time investigating a double suicide (Dany Robin and Daniel Gélin). It was shown post-

Quai des Orfèvres *(47) was a good thriller, a seedy tale of pimping, murder and jealousy, set around a third-rate music-hall. Louis Jouvet was the tired but weary Sûreté man; Simone Renant a pseudo-sophisticated procurer.*

humously: in 1951, while rehearsing a stage adaptation of Graham Greene's 'La Puissance et la Gloire', he was taken with a heart attack. *Les Etoiles ne Meurent Jamais* (57) was a compilation of extracts from his films and those of Raimu, Harry Baur, Marguerite Moreno, etc.

DANNY KAYE

Partly as a result of some sensationally successful in-person seasons at the London Palladium, Danny Kaye enjoyed for a while a preeminent position as a film comic. His popularity was somewhat greater in Britain, but the *cachet* held in the States. Audiences were captivated by the ease and charm of his personality, the modesty; they marvelled at his mimicry and patter songs, roared at his St Vitus-like antics. Said 'Time Magazine' once: 'Kaye is not naturally funny but more of a stuntman of humour who relies on glib footwork, a glibber tongue and a foxy aptitude for facial contortions. he has had to subdue these in "Two by Two" and concentrate on just being liked. He works long and arduously at it, and he is liked.' Those who found all of it completely resistible lived not to rue the day: his old films have not stood the test of time well.

He was born in Brooklyn (1913) as Daniel Kaminsky, started dancing and singing for audiences while still at school and after a spell in insurance did both professionally at summer camps. Between engagements he worked as soda-jerk and waiter, but there was a nagging need to find an outlet as an entertainer. He worked solo and in partnership; travelling to the Orient with an outfit called the A.B. Marcus Show; toured with Abe Lyman's Band; and in 1938 was in cabaret at the Dorchester in London, where he 'died the death' as he said later. He worked in the Catskills and while there met and married Sylvia Fine, who wrote much of his material; he first trod the New York boards in 'The Straw Hat Revue' (39) with Imogene Coca. That gave him a small reputation; he stopped the show with a song called 'Tchaikovsky' in 'Lady in the Dark' (41) with Gertrude Lawrence. Goldwyn looked him over and offered a contract, but Kaye did not think he was ready for films. Later that year he starred in Cole Porter's 'Let's Face It' and, after a long run in it, gave in to Goldwyn's blandishment and signed for five years, one film a year (earlier, he had turned down $3,000 a week from MGM because they wanted him only for speciality acts).

Goldwyn starred him in a lavish army comedy with Dinah Shore, *Up in Arms* (44). His success was instantaneous. The London 'Evening Standard' discovered 'a comedian who is really original . . . he has such a wide range in the art of entertainment . . . mimicry is witty, slapstick resounding'. A delighted Goldwyn made him the *Wonder Man* (45), the first of four in which his leading lady was Virginia Mayo. He had a double role, which demanded too much of him: nor did he manage to efface memories of Harold Lloyd in the remake of *The Milky Way*, now called *The Kid from Brooklyn* (46) – meek milkman turns boxer. (Of all the great comics Kaye is closest to Lloyd – the average, likeable guy. Lloyd offered fewer concessions, but more than Keaton, whose stone-face forbad any. What we like best in funny men are their failings – what one remembers best in Bob Hope are his cowardice and vanity.) *The Secret Life of Walter Mitty* (47) was a paintbox version of the Thurber story about a compulsive day-dreamer, giving Kaye a chance to do several impersonations: a personal and box-office success. But *A Song is Born* (48), a rehash of *Ball of Fire* plus some Big Bands, was poorly received and did less business than the others. Howard Hawks, who directed both, thought Kaye in Gary Cooper's old role as an unworldly professor 'as funny as a crutch'. Kaye's first London Palladium stint was in 1948 and he did another in 1949; in both years he was one of the top draws in British cinemas.

He was Goldwyn's prize property; Goldwyn had nurtured him. There was, therefore, some trade consternation when he did not renew with him but accepted a five-year contract with Warners. But after almost two years there emerged only one film and – with considerable publicity – they called it quits: *The Inspector General* (49), from Gogol's play, with Elsa Lanchester. It did not do well and was reissued as *Happy Times*, after one of its songs. (Two properties Warners planned for Kaye went to other actors – *Always Leave Them Laughing* to Milton Berle and *Stop You're Killing Me*, which was revamped for a different approach.) He went to 20th for *On the Riviera* (51), again in a dual role (it was a remake of *Folies-Bergère*, already remade as *That Night in Rio*); then returned to Goldwyn at a fee of $175,000 to help him fulfil a long-cherished dream, a life of *Hans Christian Andersen* (52) with Moira Shearer (who got pregnant and after much to-do was replaced by Renée Jeanmaire, at that time under contract to Howard Hughes). Richard Winnington thought that 'Kaye, unnaturally subdued on a reverent occasion, does in an odd way project a quality of innocence through the surrounding mush'. There were cartoons and

In The Kid From Brooklyn *(46) Danny Kaye amuses Fay Bainter but not Virginia Mayo: audiences today are more likely to side with Miss Mayo.*

ballet and sentiment, and the only relief was in Frank Loesser's score: it was a big hit.

Only one other Kaye film made more money, after he had moved to Paramount. He signed a one-picture deal with that studio and made *Knock on Wood* (53) with Mai Zetterling; and then he replaced the ailing Donald O'Connor (who had replaced Fred Astaire) opposite Bing Crosby in *White Christmas* (54) – 'Black Christmas' might have been better, a crock of Schmaltz to make Scrooges of us all. However, it was the biggest hit in which he appeared. Both encouraged Paramount to sign Kaye on a participation deal. Around the same time he made several highly publicized world tours on behalf of UNICEF and made both a TV and a cinema documentary – *Assignment Children* – about them, consisting mostly of him singing to kids of various races. He was given a special Oscar in 1954 'for his unique talents, his service to the Academy, the Motion Picture Industry, and the American people'. His own company produced for Paramount a costume merriment, *The Court Jester* (56), in which he played the title-role.

In 1950 he had signed with MGM for one film and there in 1953 he was about to start a musical version of *Huckleberry Finn* with Gene Kelly when it was postponed and then abandoned; he fulfilled his commitment with *Merry Andrew* (58), a musical with a circus background, but the ingredients did not jell. He accepted an invitation from Columbia to do a straight comedy part in *Me and the Colonel*, a version of the Franz Werfel and S.N. Behrman 'Jacobowsky and the Colonel', about a Jewish refugee and an anti-Semitic Polish officer (Curt Jurgens), but neither the two stars nor the director (Peter Glenville) had the necessary high comedy style. It was, in Kaye's own words, 'a financial disaster'. Its failure had the curious effect of cancelling a typical Kaye comedy which Paramount were preparing, *The Bamboo Kid*, to be made in Japan with Kay Kendall. Paramount put Kaye into a biopic of band-leader Red Nichols, *The*

Five Pennies (59), with Louis Armstrong. It did well, but *On the Double* (61) failed – Kaye as a GI in Britain and as a British baronet, and impersonating several other nationalities. He moved over to Columbia for *The Man from the Diners Club* (63), a return to slapstick. The 'MFB' thought him 'tired and ill-at-ease' and the film, too, failed.

He began a weekly series for CBS in 1963 and it ran four seasons. In 1967 he received a bad press in Britain for reneging on an agreement to play Goldoni's 'The Servant of Two Masters' at Chichester, because of the Six Days' War; he then returned to films in a character part, as the rag-picker in *The Madwoman of Chaillot* (69) starring Katharine Hepburn. He was then announced for the London production of 'The Last of the Red Hot Lovers' but was released from his contract when offered the lead in Richard Rodgers's musical, 'Two by Two' (70), in which he played Noah. He kept it running by interpolating his vaudeville act; the programme notes on him talked mainly of his efforts for charity. It is a pity he was not in life more charitable. Colleagues, especially those who could not answer back, often loathed him; witnesses have even spoken of him hitting children (when persistent in wanting an autograph). He made his TV drama début for CBS, in *Skokie* (81), as a concentration camp survivor protesting against neo-Nazis; but in 1976 he had been Captain Hook and Mr Darling to Mia Farrow's television *Peter Pan*. When he died in 1987 it was headline news in Britain but an also-ran item in the US.

Howard Keel

Hollywood, or at least MGM, rather underestimated Howard Keel. He was launched as a star in *Annie Get Your Gun* but then shuffled off sometimes into second leads or into second features. He was given boorish parts to play – modelled on his role in *Annie* – or stood up as the conventional leading-man prop. That he did so well despite this was due to the fact that this was the heyday of screen musicals, many of which he carried to success almost single-handedly. There was no other big-voiced baritone in films at the time: at his best he outclassed all the others of like ilk – Lanza, Eddy, Allan Jones. His voice was warm and lusty, he had a fetching grin and though few of his parts called upon him to do more than swagger he did it with a disarming ease. In these days when the MGM musical is seen in all its achievement, Keel is recognized as one of its cornerstones: the 'singing' musicals would never have been as good without him.

He was Howard Keel only after MGM found him. He was christened Harold in Gillespie, Illinois, where he was born in 1919. His father, a coal miner, died when he was young and his mother and he moved to California. In his teens he worked in an aircraft factory as a mechanic. He liked singing and a friend recommended a coach, who advised him to get a job in which he could practise; but being a singing busboy does not pay much and he went to work for Douglas Aircraft, who sent him on a concert tour for PR purposes. He won a singing competition and later first prize at a music festival, which got him an agent. The agent took him to see Oscar Hammerstein II, who gave him an understudy job in 'Carousel' and then the lead in the London production of 'Oklahoma!' (47). He shared that show's London triumph and was well known in Britain when offered a straight film role by producer Anthony Havelock-Allan: *The Small Voice* (48). He was an escaped convict holed up with the menacing householders Valerie Hobson and James Donald. During a holiday from the show he was tested by Warners in Hollywood without success.

MGM, however, needed someone to play Frank Butler in their film version of Irving Berlin's *Annie Get Your Gun* (50) and his tests there were successful. They changed his name and signed him to a seven-year contract starting at $850 a week. During shooting there were more changes – both director (Busby Berkeley) and star (Judy Garland) departed – and Keel also survived a broken leg. Opposite Betty Hutton his sunny personality and easy singing were relaxing, and took some of the essential bumptiousness out of the character. The film was a big success, but the next was not: *Pagan Love Song*, as Esther Williams's romantic interest. There were marvellous locations and no plot till the last few minutes when it became all plot and no locations; Keel had some good songs to sing and scored heavily – but said later that he thought the film had hurt his career. Producer Arthur Freed shrugged off the film: it was made just for fun, he said.

After being Van Johnson's rival for Jane Wyman in *Three Guys Named Mike* (51) Keel was in another Freed-produced film, the Technicolored and almost perfect version of *Show Boat* opposite Kathryn Grayson. Said C.A. Lejeune: 'Mr Keel is, perhaps, too much of a cheery modern to suggest the exquisite river dandy of Edna Ferber's book. But he has a friendly personality and *sings* his way into the story more winningly than any Ravenal I can recall. His voice is singularly warm and

'The House of Singing Bamboo' – Howard Keel singing a happy song in Pagan Love Song *(50), a pleasant and underrated musical filmed almost entirely in Tahiti (or what looked like it).*

accurate, with just the firmness necessary to correct the wobble in Miss Grayson's piercingly sweet high register.' For this he was rewarded with the mediocre *Texas Carnival*, supporting Esther Williams. He had a dual role – drunken movie cowboy and lookalike real cowboy – in *Callaway Went Thataway* with Fred MacMurray, and got good notices; but the film did poorly. Then he and Grayson sang more Jerome Kern songs in another remake, *Lovely to Look At* (52), but this was flat beer after the champagne sparkle of the old *Roberta*. He was noticeably patient with Grayson and Red Skelton, but his reward this time was a couple of Bs, *Desperate Search*, about an air-crash, and *Fast Company* (53), about horses. He supported Robert Taylor in a Western, *Ride Vacquero*, and between whiles guested in *I Love Melvin* – but was cut from the final print.

Two years earlier he had been first on the exhibitors' list of Stars of the Future and he seemed to have reasonably fulfilled hopes; but when MGM loaned him to Warners for *Calamity Jane* they did not seem to mind that his name was billed in smaller letters than that

Howard Keel and Kathryn Grayson were partnered three times by MGM in three musicals still endlessly revived – and justifiably so in the case of Kiss Me Kate *(54). It is probably her best performance, while it is impossible to imagine a better Petruchio or a better interpreter of the Cole Porter songs. All the songs Keel sang at Metro belong almost exclusively to him. Oh, and this still, by the way, is meant to show that the film was photographed in 3-D.*

of co-star Doris Day. Still, he was fine as Wild Bill Hickok and his popularity shot up. MGM's first choice for *Kiss Me Kate* was Laurence Olivier, but Grayson and director George Sidney insisted on Keel. The part was really brag-and-swagger again, as the egotistical husband of temperamental wife/co-star Grayson. 'Variety' thought him 'a dynamic male lead, in complete control of the acting role and registering superbly with the songs' (they were Cole Porter's).

He fought against another remake, that of *Rose Marie* (54), and was not wrong. It was not in the same league as the MacDonald-Eddy version and, further, this time the Mountie (Keel) lost the girl (Ann Blyth) to a fur-trapper (Fernando Lamas). However, he was then in another whopping hit, *Seven Brides for Seven Brothers*, one of the last original screen musicals. It was a 'dancing' musical but what was not choreographed was mostly Keel (with some good songs) and he rose magnificently to the occasion. His agent asked for new terms – he had been paid only around $10,000 for this – and he got a new contract starting at $3,000 a week. And a guest shot singing a Sigmund Romberg song in *Deep in my Heart.*

MGM's ceaseless search for new subjects for musicals led sometimes to mistakes like *Jupiter's Darling* (55), which had once been Robert E. Sherwood's 'The Road to Rome'. Keel was bearded again as Hannibal and Esther Williams was miscast as a temptress. A more unexpected flop was *Kismet*, which had run for years on Broadway. But the film was flawed by juvenile lead Vic Damone, by a script which did not know how lightly to take this old Oriental night and above all by terrible colour processing. Keel and Dolores Gray did their best with the songs, but otherwise director Vincente Minnelli never put them at ease.

Still, because of *Seven Brides*, Metro had big plans for Keel and a musical *Robin Hood* was well in preparation. When some other promising and big-budgeted musicals flopped the studio hesitated. Said Keel later: 'They threw a couple of things at me, but I didn't like them. I was stagnating there, had no chance to express myself.' With musicals out, MGM had no further use for Keel and bought up his contract. His best musicals for them did well in revivals and they had given him a popularity which was to last to the present – despite some straight parts in some very uninteresting films: the British *Floods of Fear* (58), again as an escaped convict; *The Big Fisherman* (59), an ill-advised participation, as St Peter, in a weak religioso; *Armored Command* (61); and a British sci-fier, *The Day of the Triffids* (62), from John Wyndham's novel – a film completed only after considerable production problems.

In 1960 he appeared on Broadway with Carol Lawrence in a disappointing Harold Arlen musical, 'Saratoga'; and continued in stock, nightclubs and TV. In 1963 he appeared in a BBC TV special with Patricia Morison: 'Kiss Me Kate' again, to remind one what a first-rate musical comedy star he is. He returned to Hollywood to star in some of A.C. Lyles's B Westerns, *Waco* (66), *Red Tomahawk* (67) and *Arizona Bushwhackers* (68). Before the latter he had a featured role as an Indian brave in the big-budgeted *The War Wagon* (67). He subsequently toured in 'Man of La Mancha' and had a very successful nightclub act with his old co-star Kathryn Grayson. In 1972 he was in London in a musical version of Henry James, 'Ambassador', with Danielle Darrieux; and its failure there did not prevent its promoters from inflicting it on Broadway later, with the same leads. In 1975, in St Paul, he starred in 'Gene Kelly's Salute to Broadway'; in 1977 he and Jane Powell appeared in stock in 'South Pacific', to huge audiences, and they broke records again the following year touring in a stage version of 'Seven Brides for Seven Brothers.' In 1980 they did 'I Do! I Do!' in Los Angeles. He told interviewers that he thought he had failed in Hollywood because he had been too naive and unable to play politics. Since he continued to prove on stage that his following, despite over 20 years away from MGM, remained enormous, you might have expected Hollywood to use him again: with him, *Man of La Mancha* probably would not have flopped.

When in 1981 he joined 'Dallas' – 'frankly, for the money' – he found himself again doing concerts to SRO business and the new albums he recorded were making the charts. Of course the MGM soundtrack records had never stopped selling. There were several reasons, including talent, why it was easier to programme seasons of Keel movies than those (Holden, Peck, Ford) considered bigger box-office at the time.

Keel has been married three times and throughout his career has insisted on keeping his private life private.

Gene Kelly

The career of Gene Kelly is something of an enigma. Just as he had confirmed his place as one of the most important talents ever to work in films he went downhill so fast you hardly saw him go. At the same time it became fashionable to decry the self-consciousness of his technique and belittle his screen personality. It seems unlikely that that his reputation will climb back to the position where it was, alongside Fred Astaire's, but, when the definitive history of the Hollywood musical comes to be written, he will be one of its heroes along with Astaire, producer Arthur Freed and perhaps Vincente Minnelli.

He was born in Pittsburgh in 1912 and majored in economics in that city's university. He had worked his way through college as an apprentice bricklayer, a soda-fountain clerk and, more importantly, dancing in local concerts with his brother Fred. Later they both taught dancing. In 1937 he tried without luck to get a job as a choreographer in New York; he tried again the following year and landed a job in the chorus of 'Leave It to Me' (he was one of the dancers assisting Mary Martin when her heart belonged to Daddy). He had a part of sorts in another revue, 'One for the Money' (39), and then a good part as the hoofer in Saroyan's play, 'The Time of Your Life'. Richard Rodgers saw him and cast him in the title-role of 'Pal Joey', the gigolo-hero of this trail-blazing musical; he left the cast when David O. Selznick signed him to a contract. Selznick, however, had no plans for a musical and was pleased to loan him to MGM for a lively vaudeville story, *For Me and My Gal* (42), as the Joey-type heel-hero ('You'll never be big time,' said Judy Garland, 'because you're small time in your heart.'). It was produced by Arthur Freed, who urged Metro to buy Kelly from Selznick.

MGM started him at $750 a week and put him into a straight part, *Pilot No 5* (43); into a musical but in an also-ran bit, as Red Skelton's rival, *Du Barry Was a Lady*; into a film loaded with guest stars, *Thousands Cheer*, as the romantic interest – with one dance; and into one of the better Resistance dramas, *The Cross of Lorraine*. Columbia borrowed him for a lavish musical built round the gifts of Rita Hayworth, *Cover Girl* (44), and agreed to let him do the choreography, with Stanley Donen, who had been in the chorus of 'Pal Joey'. The result was a series of dances with a freshness reminiscent of the Astaire-Rogers numbers. James Agee wrote: 'Kelly is limited and is capable of failure, as he occasionally proves here. But I can think of no one in Hollywood, just now, who is more satisfying or more hopeful to watch for singing, dancing or straight acting.' The film was a big hit with critics and public, but Kelly's new, glittering reputation was not helped by *Christmas Holiday*, on loan to Universal (in exchange for Turhan Bey!), as Deanna Durbin's no-good playboy husband.

Anchors Aweigh (45) teamed him with Frank Sinatra, as gobs on furlough in Hollywood, and confirmed his pre-eminence as dancer and choreographer, especially in a joyous dance with a mouse (Jerry of 'Tom and Jerry'). It all seems conventional now, but then it was the second-ranking box-office film of the year and brought Kelly a Best Actor Oscar nomination that was presumably an indication of the Academy's admiration for him. *Ziegfeld Follies* (46) had been made in 1944, before he joined the navy for a while; in it he and Fred Astaire teamed on the Gershwins' 'The Babbitt and the Bromide'. Certain efforts were made to present them as rivals, which was untrue and silly. Said Kelly: 'My style is strong, wide-open bravura. Fred's is intimate, cool, easy. He can give the audience pleasure just by walking across the floor.' He considered that Astaire had been able to transfer his stage technique to films because he was a unique artist, with a strong personal style. For himself, he needed to experiment: 'I felt the dancer in films and never had the opportunity to probe emotional and acting problems adequately.' His own dancing was not only technically good, but had a masculine and energetic grace; and his choreography was imaginative and seemingly spontaneous – he insisted that the numbers were worked into the plot.

He experimented somewhat in *Living in a Big Way* (47), a black-and-white musical about young marrieds with Marie McDonald; came into his own again with *The Pirate* (48), his first film with Minnelli and his first both with Freed and Garland since *For Me and My Gal.* As a team they strove for a cod costume epic (it had been a play by S.N. Behrman for the Lunts), with high jinks in the way of fights and dances. The result was bizarre, unlike any previous musical: critically admired but not popular (later, it acquired a coterie following). Kelly's buccaneer hero was fun and his solo ballet striking (it was reshot after Louis B. Mayer castigated it as too sexy). His next part was similar, d'Artagnan in the sumptuous and warmly received remake of *The Three Musketeers*, combining in the sword-fights a balletic flourish with a Fairbanksian athleticism. Simultaneously, he was dancing to 'Slaughter on Tenth Avenue' in *Words and Music* with Vera-Ellen, virtually the only thing in that film which made it worth seeing.

He and Donen (his assistant on most of these films) contributed the original story on which was based *Take Me Out to the Ball Game* (49), a period musical of considerable charm and energy – a good augury for *On the Town*, where some of the same cast (Kelly, Sinatra, Betty Garrett, Jules Munshin) were joined by Vera-Ellen and Ann Miller for a tale of three sailors and their girls in New York. Freed turned them loose on it – Kelly

Gene Kelly and Judy Garland in Summer Stock *(50). She was a farmer and he was a producer putting on a show in her barn, starring her sister (Gloria de Haven). When that lady walks out, Judy takes over as his co-star, as here.*

and Donen co-directing, from a screenplay by Comden and Green (who had written the original stage version – some of whose songs were jettisoned). They have all recalled that it was exciting to work on – but the studio was nervous. 'They thought,' said Kelly later, 'they had a disaster on their hands. . . . It's dated now, of course, but without that picture I don't think we would have had many pictures that followed: *West Side Story* might never have happened. I think there is no doubt that *Singin' in the Rain* and *An American in Paris* were bigger achievements – but . . . I think we broke new ground, we showed the way with that one.' It is his own favourite picture. Much of it was filmed on location and it had a gaiety and zest that film musicals – it was now apparent – had lacked till then. Dilys Powell thought it the best musical since *42nd Street* and Richard Win-

An American in Paris *(51) was not the best of the great MGM musicals, but it was the most acclaimed at the time: this is a publicity shot of Gene Kelly and Leslie Caron.*

nington wrote later that Kelly was 'one of Hollywood's half-dozen originals. Beyond the exuberant dancing style and a personality that comes over the screen in waves is the talent that made [this] the first homogeneous film musical'. Matthew Norgate: 'For which all thanks to Gene Kelly for his intelligence and inventiveness as director, actor and dancer (all he lacks is the personal attractiveness of Fred Astaire, and Fred Astaires don't grow on trees).' The film broke records at Radio City Music Hall, but did less well in the sticks.

He marked time with *Black Hand* (50), a drama about the Mafia, and *Summer Stock*, an agreeable Judy Garland musical. Then: *An American in Paris* (51), produced by Freed and directed by Minnelli – but a triumph for Kelly, particularly the 20-minute climactic ballet based on Gershwin. He received a special Oscar as dancer and choreographer, and among the picture's seven other Oscars was one for Best Picture. Unusually for a musical, it was a big hit worldwide and in the US was one of the year's top grossers. Fred Majdalany referred to it when reviewing the next, noting that it 'consummated the ideas with which he had been playing for some time; it confirmed him as the top song-and-dance man of the day and a greater film artist than Astaire'.

The next – excluding *It's a Big Country*, as a Greek store-owner in his episode – was *Singin' in the Rain* (52), a tale of Hollywood in the days of the transition from Silents to Talkies, co-directed with Donen and written with memorable wit by Comden and Green. Catherine de la Roche in 'Picture Post' spoke of 'Kelly's inventive genius. For Kelly telling a story means dancing it, or most of it. And, as he says himself, *every* dance must tell a story. That is what gives his pictures distinction . . . it would be hard to express the elation of a man who has won his heart's desire more eloquently than does Kelly in his literal interpretation of the title number. . . .' Penelope Houston: 'On Kelly himself, one has slight reservations; his dancing is as gay and inventive as ever, his screen personality is agreeable, but there seems some danger that his "good guy" characterization may become rather too much of a formula and its charm thereby overworked.' Few of the reviews suggested, however, that the film would become – and remain – most people's favourite screen musical. Said John Coleman in 1969, seeing it 'for the umpteenth time. This is surely the best movie musical ever made and Gene Kelly's dapper sauntering and splashing through a storm the most enchanting dance in history.' At the time it was – just – one of the year's top 10 grossers.

After that, nothing went very right. He was one of several stars working in Europe to qualify for tax exemption (available to US citizens employed abroad) – and getting $5,000 a week. In Germany he made an indifferent thriller *The Devil Makes Three*, and in Britain began *Invitation to the Dance*, having persuaded MGM to risk money on an all-ballet film. Four episodes were originally planned, but only three were filmed and one – a cartoon dance – was hived off and shown separately. Kelly's dancing was as good as ever, but when the film ws finally shown, in 1956, it was a critical and commercial disaster. In Britain he also made *Seagulls Over Sorrento* (54; *Crest of the Wave* in the US), as an old sobersides in this fair naval comedy; but he did not make *Brigadoon* in Scotland. Minnelli had this Highland village constructed on the backlot, which might have been the reason for its failure – though there were good things in this version of Lerner and Loewe's Broadway musical. Kelly's own contribution smacked of a forced gaiety. He did a guest spot with brother Fred in *Deep in My Heart*; was reunited with Freed, co-director Donen, and Comden and Green for *It's Always Fair Weather* (55), again the story of three guys in

Kelly in the third and last of his three great screen musicals, Singin' in the Rain *(52). It is usually reckoned the best, because it is also very, very funny. This therefore is not a typical moment – the rather arty transformation which follows his meeting with Cyd Charisse, illustrated on page 100.*

New York, this time ex-GIs – because Sinatra refused to do what was originally planned, a sequel to *On the Town*. Dismal colour, unsatisfactory casting and poor situations combined to confirm predictions that the screen musical was on its way out.

Sam Goldwyn, however, was preparing *Guys and Dolls* and wanted to borrow Kelly for the lead – but MGM refused (ironically, after Marlon Brando was signed, Goldwyn arranged for MGM to distribute). MGM let him direct as well as star in *The Happy Road* (57), a well-liked but unsuccessful picture about runaway children in France, but he had nothing to do with the creative side of *Les Girls*, playing a song-and-dance man under Cukor's direction. They had no more musicals planned; he was restless at working so little (and still angry about *Guys and Dolls*), so asked to be released from his contract – it had two more years to run. Free, Kelly announced several independent projects which came to nothing. At one point he was definitely set for *Gentleman's Gentleman*, a musical to be made by Rank at Pinewood. Instead, he went to Warners for *Marjorie Morningstar* (58), playing a composer who would rather be a big fish in a little sea (summer camp). He was a likeable enough reporter in *Inherit the Wind* (60). He worked in other fields: he directed a Broadway musical, 'Flower Drum Song' (58), and devised a ballet for the Paris Opera based on Gershwin's 'Concerto in F' (60). He appeared on TV, mostly in Specials, notably in a cartoon-live action 'Jack and the Beanstalk', a mere echo of former glories. He also did a TV series in the early 60s based on 'Going My Way'.

Two screen appearances showed him considerably aged: *What a Way to Go* (64), as a passé hoofer partnering Shirley MacLaine, a touching portrayal in what was that film's only good episode; and *Les Demoiselles de Rochefort* (66), which was a mistake. French *cinéastes* had always revered Kelly and when the success of his previous film permitted Jacques Demy a big budget he sent for Kelly to do a guest stint. But he was arch, a parody of his earlier self.

He had directed occasional movies: *The Tunnel of Love* (58), *Gigot* (62) with Jackie Gleason and *A Guide for the Married Man* (67) – each was terrible, but from external evidence they were doomed before they got on the floor. He did marvellously with a property that must have been nearer his heart, *Hello Dolly!* (69), with Barbra Streisand, and quite well with *The Cheyenne Social Club* (70). He played Liv Ullmann's ex-husband, an unsuccessful TV star, in *Forty Carats* (73) and the following year was in 'Take Me Along' in stock. He introduced excerpts from old MGM musicals in *That's Entertainment* (74), whose huge success led to him and Fred Astaire doing dancing introductions to same in *That's Entertainment Part Two* (76), which was not a success: the excerpts were sloppily chosen and put together, but the public, which had sensed a 'feast', a tribute, with the first film, recognized the second as a rip-off. Both films brought into the spotlight Kelly's contribution to films and there was a bid to revive interest in *Invitation to the Dance*: but admiration for him cannot disguise the fact that that one is not good. He has been married twice: to actress Betsy Blair (1940–57) and Jeanne Coyne (1960–73), who left him a widower. It was his children who persuaded him to play a role he had already turned down, that of a former motor-cyclist in *Viva Knievel* (77), with daredevil Evel Knievel as himself. He should not have listened to them: this was 'a credit best forgotten' said 'Variety'. The same is true of *Xanadu* (80), supporting – with star-billing – the anodyne Olivia Newton-John in this whimsy, as a former dance-band leader who opens a nightclub to show-case her talents. He has since done duty in two of the junkier mini-series, *North and South* (85), a Civil War saga, and *Sins* (86), a Joan Collins soap.

Grace Kelly

As Princess Grace, we saw her in photographs, elaborately coiffured, bespectacled, leading her children from airport lounges. As Grace Kelly, she really was a fairy-tale princess. Then, Hollywood was her kingdom, reviewers were her swains, audiences her subjects. Once upon a time . . .

She was born in Philadelphia in 1929, with – alas for fairy-tales – a silver spoon in her mouth. Uncle George (Kelly) was the author of some popular plays ('The Show-Off', 'Craig's Wife'), so the stage was not considered *infra dig*. She studied at the AADA and was sufficiently promising to be offered a film contract – which she turned down because she did not want to be a starlet. Instead she did TV, both commercials and drama, and some modelling. Her agent got her the part of Raymond Massey's daughter in a Broadway presentation of Strindberg's 'The Father' (49) and that, and bigger parts on TV ('Philco Playhouse', 'Treasury Men in Action'), brought her again to Hollywood's attention. 20th cast her in *Fourteen Hours* (51), almost unnoticed as one of the crowd, a would-be divorcee determined to try again after watching the man on the ledge.

Again she refused a contract because she

was not ready; but a year later she played Gary Cooper's Quaker wife in *High Noon* (52). She said: 'With Gary Cooper, everything is so clear. You look into his face and see everything he is thinking. I looked into my own face and saw nothing. I knew what I was thinking, but it didn't show.' As a result, she did not share in the film's success. No offers were forthcoming, but her agent got her tested at 20th for a programmer, *Taxi!* She was turned down in favour of Constance Smith and the agent hawked the test around Hollywood. Among those interested were John Ford and Hitchcock. Ford put in a bid and MGM, about to produce his *Mogambo* (53), offered a seven-year contract starting at $750 a week. She wanted to do the film for three things, she said – Ford, Clark Gable and a free trip to Africa; she signed, with the right to have a year off every two years to do a play.

Gable had to fall for her: her cool, English (in the film) manner had to divert him from the more obvious allure of Ava Gardner. And she had to succumb to a strong adulterous passion for him: the way she did it brought a Best Supporting Actress (Oscar) nomination. She had a curiously exciting quality and Hitchcock was to use it to perfection. He borrowed her for *Dial M for Murder* (54), a role once announced for Deborah Kerr, that of the unfaithful wife who inadvertently becomes the agent instead of the victim in a murder plot – never a damsel in such distress! He borrowed her again for *Rear Window*, as a Park Avenue career girl exuding impeccable breeding and a high moral tone; but there was no mistaking her ultimate intention when, clad in a night-gown, she announces to crippled fiancé James Stewart, 'Preview of coming attractions.' It was provocation with style, an unhavable girl who was not; serenity, then a giggle; hauteur, then a sexual invitation. She was, it was said, the perfect blonde whom Hitchcock had been seeking throughout his career. 'Time Magazine' observed that she distilled 'a tingling essence of what [he] has called "sexual elegance"'. Hitchcock himself told François Truffaut later: 'Sex on the screen should be suspenseful, I feel. If sex is too blatant or obvious, there's no suspense. . . . We're after the drawing-room type, the real ladies, who become whores once they're in the bedroom. Poor Marilyn Monroe had sex written all over her face, and Brigitte Bardot isn't very subtle either.' Audiences, anyway, sensed the element of personal mystery and every male spectator tried to fathom it out.

The stampede was on and Paramount was lucky: they had already arranged to borrow her – for $20,000 – for *The Bridges of Toko-Ri*, a very brief role as William Holden's wife. MGM wanted to cash in and slotted her into *Green Fire*, a jungle adventure drama that had been scheduled for Ava Gardner and then Eleanor Parker. But Paramount needed her urgently: Jennifer Jones had become unexpectedly pregnant as she was about to start *The Country Girl* and Garbo, contacted, declined to take her place. MGM refused to loan Kelly, but she fought like a tiger. In the end they let her go, for $50,000, plus a penalty for every day she was kept while *Green Fire* waited to roll. *The Country Girl* was a good part, that of an embittered but determined woman coping with an alcoholic husband (Bing Crosby). She got the New York critics' Best Actress award and the Oscar, which confirmed to Hollywood that she could do no wrong, for, good though she was, her work was not in the same league as Judy Garland's, up that year for *A Star is Born*. She was tinsel town's new golden girl and it was impossible to flick the pages of any magazine without coming across her name. Most journalists agreed that, along with Brando, Monroe and Hepburn, A., she was so far the only star of the 50s it was okay to rave about.

Grace Kelly had the good luck to star in three films for Alfred Hitchcock – then at his Hollywood peak (and, of course, he was equally lucky to have her). Here she is with James Stewart looking out of his Rear Window *(54).*

Grace Kelly in the last of her films for Hitchcock, To Catch a Thief *(55). She was a haughty American lady thawed out by Cary Grant – here, obviously, after the change.*

Green Fire finally limped into view, to be generally execrated. Kelly's own view of it was hardly soothed by its advertising slogan: 'Her fabulous career reaches a thrilling climax. . . .' MGM, in fact, had as little idea of what to do with her as they had earlier with Deborah Kerr. They proposed a Western with Spencer Tracy, *Tribute to a Bad Man*, but she loathed the script and refused. She was suspended until Hitchcock requested her for an amiable Riviera frolic with Cary Grant, *To Catch a Thief* (55). Then battle was joined again: she refused to be the heroine of *Quentin Durward*. She was suspended again. She went off to the Côte d'Azur to renew acquaintance with Prince Rainier of Monaco (they had met during the filming of *Thief*). As news of the royal romance leaked out, the box-office figures for 1955 were announced: of the five Kelly films going the rounds that year, four of them had done sensational business (the flop, natch, was *Green Fire*). She was voted the second box-office draw.

MGM magnanimously scrapped her old contract and drew up a new one which would promote her as a (home-grown) combination of Garbo and Bergman. *Cat on a Hot Tin Roof* was bought for her, but more significantly she would be in remakes of films that had starred Hollywood aristocracy of yesteryear: *The Swan* (Lillian Gish), *The Philadelphia Story* (Katharine Hepburn) and *The Barretts of Wimpole Street* (Norma Shearer). The last went to another actress and by the time *The Swan* (56) started shooting it was announced that Kelly would retire from the scene after her marriage. This and the other swan song, *High Society*, were to be, said Metro, entirely worthy of Hollywood's golden girl and the future Princess of Monaco. *The Swan* was Molnar's comedy about a princess with romanic complications, but despite a first-rate cast (Alec Guinness, Brian Aherne, Jessie Royce Landis, etc.) and Kelly's own delicate playing it was too languid for wide

Grace Kelly and Alec Guinness in The Swan *(56), Hollywood's last major attempt at Ruritanian romance. She was a princess and he her regal suitor – but only after she had flirted with her tutor (Louis Jourdan) did she realise she loved him.*

popular appeal. *High Society* ensnared the talents also of Bing Crosby, Sinatra, Celeste Holm and Cole Porter – and was enormously popular everywhere (in Britain, the top box-office film). Indeed, it was likeable and so was Kelly (especially if you had not seen Hepburn in the original).

There was a spectacular fairy-tale wedding in Monaco and the couple lived happily ever after – except, perhaps, for a spell in 1962 when Hitchcock announced that she would return to films in his *Marnie*. She had told him that she was longing to act again and had asked whether he had a part for her. The Prince approved, but the project was, apparently, frowned upon within the Principality. Kelly withdrew (and the part went to a Hitchcock discovery, Tippi Hedren). Similarly, she turned down *The Turning Point*, which Audrey Hepburn had accepted, conditional to her being the co-star. Occasional TV documentaries plugging Monaco, with appearances by Princess Grace, reminded audiences of what they were missing. She was killed in 1982 while at the wheel of a car, when a heart attack caused her to fall away from the Corniche.

KAY KENDALL

Kay Kendell died too soon. She did not make many films – and only a couple of them were much good – but she carved herself a special niche. The (London) 'Times' obituary described her as 'one of the cinema's few outstanding comediennes'.

It almost did not happen. She was a has-been before she ever started. She came from a show business family – her grandmother was Marie Kendall, a great star of the music hall, and her parents were a dancing team. She was born in Withernsea, near Hull, in 1927. At the age of 12 she was tall enough to join the chorus of the London Palladium and for the same management she toured in their spectacular revues. Later she began a music-hall act with her sister, Kim. They began to get small parts in films both as a team and separately: (Kay) *Fiddlers Three* (44) and *Champagne Charlie*, both starring comedian Tommy Trinder; *Dreaming* (45), another comedy vehicle; for Flanagan and Allen; and *Waltz Time*, Viennese schmaltz British style, with Peter Graves. As to musicals, Rank now attempted one in the Hollywood style, another of his reckless attempts to challenge the American film industry. Kendall auditioned for it and was chosen as one of the 'dozen-and-one' lovelies to surround Sid Field – and, when no one else proved suitable, was upped to being his leading lady. Wesley Ruggles was brought over to direct, there was a big budget and massive publicity – and the disaster was of the same proportions: *London Town* (46). Because he incorporated some of his stage routines, Field emerged comparatively unscathed, but Kendall sank with the ship. She was not, in fact, very good and the make-up they had plastered on her made her look like a dummy.

After that, no one wanted to know. She returned to Germany and Italy, where she had once toured with ENSA, and set about learning her craft. She turned legit and spent some time in provincial rep in Britain. After three years she was ready to try for the big time again, but was offered only small parts in *Dance Hall* (50) and *Happy-Go-Lovely* (51), with Vera-Ellen. Her chance came when she did a TV play, 'Sweethearts and Wives', and was seen by Launder or Gilliatt or both; they cast her in their amiable exposé of the beauty racket, *Lady Godiva Rides Again*, as the winner's elder sister, a *soignée* girl with some Eve Ardenish wise-cracks. She got good notices and two offers as a result, neither of them significant: *Wings of Danger* (52), a B starring Hollywood's fading Zachary Scott; and *Curtain Up*, a comedy about a provincial rep – she was its leading lady. She had another featured role in Rank's *It Started in Paradise*, which blatantly used the central theme of *All About Eve*, applied now to the London fashion world. The stars were Jane Hylton and Muriel Pavlow, and no one went to see it. But Kendall's performance as a bitchy socialite customer brought her a seven-year contract with Rank, starting at £100 a week.

Meanwhile, she did two more Bs: *Mantrap* (53), supporting Paul Henreid, and *Street of Shadows*, opposite Cesar Romero. At Ealing she was one of the girls cheering on the sidelines of *The Square Ring*, a boxing melodrama. The first picture under her contract was *Genevieve*, sharing the female lead with Dinah Sheridan, as the exasperated model brought along on the race by Kenneth More and forced by him into all sorts of indignities. She said later that the film was hardly fun to make and that no one dreamed it would be such a hit. Of all the raves, not the least of them were hers, though she still seemed inexperienced (also More, while filming, thought the film revealed only a fraction of her talent). While everyone was talking about her, the best that Rank could find for her were *Meet Mr Lucifer*, an Ealing satire on TV which misfired, in a small role as a TV star, and *Fast and Loose* (54), a feeble version of a Ben Travers farce ('A Cuckoo in the Nest'). Stanley Holloway starred in both.

The momentum of *Genevieve* was lost,

despite a special cameo in the successful *Doctor in the House*. She began to fight for better parts and was loaned out to play one of Rex Harrison's wives in *The Constant Husband* (55) – a role she later (1957) took on in life. She knew the next one would not be good, but did it to defy Rank: *Abdullah the Great*, as a model kidnapped by Oriental monarch Gregory Ratoff. It was made in Egypt and looked like it; and got a couple of bookings the following year – mostly, one imagines, on the strength of her name. She refused three Rank offered – *As Long as They're Happy, Value For Money* and *Doctor at Sea* – and was taken off salary (£120 a week), a fine reward for such admirable common sense. But they forgave her when MGM – faced with an equally intransigent Grace Kelly – needed her urgently for *The Adventures of Quentin Durward*, opposite Robert Taylor. She was hardly the obvious choice for a medieval heroine, but she clutched her jewel-box dauntlessly and fitted well into a film which beautifully caught Scott's neo-Gothic world. Further, MGM's make-up department rendered her more attractive than she had looked so far in films; that studio tried to buy her contract, but Rank was not selling.

Rank did find something worthy, a West End comedy about a husband-and-wife soap-opera team who do little but fight off-set: *Simon and Laura*, with Peter Finch. It threw away chances wholesale and Kendall 'missed' several lines – but it did exploit her special gift for sophisticated comedy, for remaining cool and elegant while tossing temperament around. MGM asked for her again when Leslie Caron refused to do *Les Girls* (57) and Gina Lollobrigida turned it down (Kendall herself insisted that *her* role was always meant for her; that Taina Elg got this part – which seems, on internal evidence, more likely than the press reports). Gene Kelly starred and one of les other girls was Mitzi Gaynor; but it was Kendall's film. She stole the notices and more than one critic raised the sacred name of Carole Lombard.

Hollywood was at her feet; she had more offers than she knew what to do with. Because her husband Harrison was in New York she refused to return to Britain to make a film for Rank. But Rank was only too happy to loan her again to MGM – at $100,000: she and Harrison were paid this each for *The Reluctant Débutante* (58), though she got only $28,000 – Rank kept the rest. It was again based on a West End play, was directed (clumsily) by Vincente Minnelli and she was a society wife launching her step-daughter into society. Said 'Variety': 'But it's really Miss Kendall's picture, and she grabs it with a single wink. She's flighty and well-meaning, snobbish and lovable . . . one of the best female comedy turns in years.'

She had leukaemia; Harrison knew she was dying but agreed to direct her in a play that he knew was terrible because she wanted to return to work, 'The Bright One': it ran a few days and Kendall returned to her doctors. Just prior to her death six months later (1959) Rank announced that they were suing her for breach of contract. 20th delayed release of her last film another six months – it had been made before 'The Bright One' and was from material equally dire: *Once More With Feeling* (60) with Yul Brynner. It was a curious epitaph – uncommonly unfunny, but suffused with her skill and charm. The 'Variety' review of it noted that she symbolized 'the grace, the complexities, the unpredictabilities and the beauty of woman'.

Kay Kendall's blazing talent for zany comedy was probably seen to best advantage in The Reluctant Débutante *(58). With her is Rex Harrison, her husband in the film and in life.*

DEBORAH KERR

'The camera', Deborah Kerr once admitted, 'always seems to find an innate gentility in me.' Hollywood marked her down as one of its good, sane ladies, one of the few of its citizens who could wear a tiara with ease or hobnob with the diplomatic set. In industry theory and practice, only a very select band of actresses was considered for all the 'class' parts. In the 50s Kerr was offered all the ladies of breeding that might in former days have gone to Irene Dunne, Bergman or Myrna Loy – or to Garbo or Hepburn or Bette Davis.

There are little bits of all these ladies within her, but she is somewhat less colourful than any of them: less flamboyant, obviously, than Hepburn or Davis, less melancholy than Garbo, less light-hearted than Dunne; not as radiant as Bergman in love, not as clear-sighted as Loy. Discretion is the keynote of her work.

In the event, she was only twice the châtelaine on screen, though you felt it was 'There but for the grace of God . . .', as she played somewhat deprived relatives – widows, spinsters, governesses, nuns. She might have been unlucky, but she was seldom neurotic. She was deceptively robust; her voice might choke with dry tears but she had no time for self-pity; brisk and British, she would never mope in a corner. Maybe she was lucky, in the 50s, in having this field virtually to herself, but it was and remains a very likeable talent; and has been acknowledged as such by six Oscar nominations – more than any other artist of those yet to win one, an omission compensated for by three Best Actress awards from the New York critics (for *Black Narcissus* and *I See a Dark Stranger* in 1947, *Heaven Knows Mr Allison* in 1957 and *The Sundowners* in 1960).

She was born in 1921 in Helensburgh, Scotland, and trained for the stage by an aunt who ran a drama school in Bristol. She intended to become a dancer and made her stage début among the corps de ballet in 'Prometheus' at Sadler's Wells in 1938, but changed her mind and turned to acting. She walked-on at the Open Air Theatre in Regent's Park during the 1939 season and then joined Oxford rep; her agent got her a bit, as a cigarette-girl, in *Contraband* (40) but it was left on the cutting-room floor. Later, Gabriel Pascal auditioned her for the role of the frail but forceful SA girl, Jenny Hill, in *Major Barbara* (41) and signed her to a long-term contract. Her performance in that film led to two co-starring roles at British National, both with Clifford Evans: *Love on the Dole*, a creaky if well-meant piece about the Industrial North, and *Penn of Pennsylvania*, a damp piece intended to solidify Anglo-American relations. When Margaret Lockwood became pregnant Kerr replaced her as Robert Newton's ill-used daughter in *Hatter's Castle*; then she was the Norwegian skipper's daughter in *The Day Will Dawn* (42), opposite Ralph Richardson.

Powell and Pressburger, who had cut her out of *Contraband*, signed her to play the three women in the life of Roger Livesey, in their chronicle of British mores over half a century, *The Life and Death of Colonel Blimp* (43) – a triple performance, thought Dilys Powell, of 'vivacity and discretion'. The film was both an important one and successful; and it made Kerr a star. On the stage she played Ellie Dunn in 'Heartbreak House'; then Korda – at that time head of MGM-British – signed her to co-star with Robert Donat in *Perfect Strangers* (45), a beguiling comedy

Perfect Strangers *(45) – or* Vacation from Marriage, *as it was retitled in the US: Deborah Kerr as a drab little wife who joins the Wrens, and Glynis Johns as the pal who teaches her a bit about lipstick, cigarettes and so on.*

about a dowdy shmoeish couple who blossom out while on active service. Partly as a result of that film's success in the US, MGM bought half of Kerr's contract from Pascal. She meanwhile was touring in 'Gaslight' for ENSA, during which she met and married Battle of Britain hero Anthony Bartley. MGM then decided to buy the rest of her contract, for a reputed total of $250,000. Her new deal with them was for seven years, 52 weeks a year, no options, with a guarantee of $3,000 a week; a clause was inserted to the effect that she would not be required in Hollywood till her husband was free of the RAF.

In fact, MGM lost interest. They had signed her partly to prevent another studio from getting her to rival their own Greer Garson and, as Garson was still going great guns, had no great use for her. She was loaned to Launder and Gilliatt to play an Irish girl in an enjoyable thriller with Trevor Howard, *I See a Dark Stranger* (46); and to Powell and Pressburger to play another colleen, now a nun, in *Black Narcissus* (47), a melodrama set in a convent in the Himalayas – its excesses redeemed by the colour photography and Kerr's 'quietly magnificent authority' (C.A. Lejeune). Metro finally sent for her to play Clark Gable's love interest, a Society widow, in *The Hucksters* (and much more circumspect than in the novel); then they cast her in a yesteryear weepie, *If Winter Comes*, finding last-reel happiness with Walter Pidgeon. The New York critics' award at this time cheered them and they gave her a good role in *Edward My Son* (49), filmed in Britain, as the genteel wife of tycoon Spencer Tracy, whose foibles drive her to drink. She became a much-courted heiress in *Please Believe Me* (50) – by Robert Walker, Mark Stevens and Peter Lawford.

Her anodyne presence hardly suggested to MGM that she was the successor to Garson that they were now seeking and she was cast in a series of adventure movies of variable quality, required mainly to smile winsomely at the leading man: Stewart Granger in *King Solomon's Mines*; Alan Ladd in *Thunder in the East* at Paramount, as a blind girl (made in 1951, released in 1953); Robert Taylor in *Quo Vadis?* (51); Granger again in *The Prisoner of Zenda* (52). She did play with something like her old verve in a comedy with Cary Grant, *Dream Wife* (53), but few people went to see it. She was unhappy about these insipid parts and realized that her career was dead if she did not reverse the trend. The last straw was *Young Bess*, originally announced as her first Hollywood vehicle: the title-role now went to Jean Simmons and she supported her, as Catherine Parr. Along with Garson, she graciously did a bit in *Julius Caesar* (as the wife of Brutus) and then asked MGM whether her contract could be amended so that she could freelance between assignments for them. They were not averse. Not one of her Hollywood roles had had any meat – and then suddenly a very juicy part was available, the embittered and nympho wife in *From Here to Eternity*. She begged Columbia to be allowed to test for it; the off-beat casting appealed to

A journey fraught with tension: Deborah Kerr in I See a Dark Stranger *(46). Next to her is Katie Johnson, a small-part actress who at the end of her life was given a leading role in* The Lady-Killers.

their publicity set-up and anyway it was a question of expediency (Joan Crawford had nixed the part at the last minute because she did not like the costumes). She got excellent notices, the film was a hit and it killed overnight the image of MGM's Kerr.

For the first time since she had arrived in the US she was inundated with offers, but she had already signed for a Broadway play, Robert Anderson's 'Tea and Sympathy', playing the teacher's wife who seduces one of his pupils (John Kerr) to prove to him he is not gay. She was released from its long run to play yet another unfaithful wife, in the hash made from Graham Greene's *The End of the Affair* (55), with Van Johnson; and was then a nurse seduced by William Holden ('My pleasures are physical . . . the men call me the Beast') in a war melodrama, *The Proud and the Profane* (56). The plum part of the indomitable governess in *The King and I* then fell into her lap and those who had seen the late Gertrude Lawrence create the part on Broadway did not feel too cheated (though Kerr's singing voice was part-dubbed). It was the best of the several stage-bound musicals which appeared at that time and with a $8½ million gross one of the most successful musicals yet made. The screen version of *Tea and Sympathy* retained both Kerrs but had been bowdlerized and was very silly.

She next did one of her favourite films, *Heaven Knows Mr Allison* (57), John Huston's revamping of his own *The African Queen* – another unlikely couple in the jungle, this time a nun and a rough diamond (Robert Mitchum) shipwrecked on a desert island. It gained immeasurably from their performances. She was at the peak of her career, heavily in demand – but the next batch were not very good: *An Affair to Remember*, a remake of *Love Affair*, with Cary Grant; *Bonjour Tristesse* (58), Preminger's heavy version of Françoise Sagan's first, bestselling novel, as a widow engaged to the philandering David Niven; *Separate Tables*, again with Niven, as the spinster crushed by mother Gladys Cooper and as good in the role as Margaret Leighton had been on the stage; *The Journey* (59) with Yul Brynner, as a British milady; *Count Your Blessings*, a comedy, discovering that husband Rossano Brazzi is unfaithful; and *Beloved Infidel*, a banal film version of the book by Sheilah Graham (Kerr) about her affair with Scott Fitzgerald (Gregory Peck). In 1959 she and Bartley were divorced; the following year she married Peter Viertel (one of the writers of *The Journey*).

More than anything, Kerr needed a good film and she got it with *The Sundowners* (60) a gentle study of Australian homesteaders, with Mitchum. Although directed by Fred Zinnemann it did not get much critical attention, but the public took to it and it was a particularly big hit in Britain (as well as Australia). With Mitchum and with Cary Grant again she did a weak comedy, *The Grass is Greener* – that was when she was the lady of the manor – and then she was Gary Cooper's British wife in a thriller, *The Naked Edge* (61). Then a brace of spinster governesses, where her tentatively declamatory acting style was singularly effective: *The Innocents* (62), Jack Clayton's impressive version of Henry James's 'The Turn of the Screw', and *The Chalk Garden* (64), a very poor version of Enid Bagnold's very good West End play. Kerr was again a spinster, a poetess, in Huston's fine version of Tennesse Williams's

The Sundowners *(60) was perhaps the best 'Australian' film made up to that time, and was, incidentally, a perceptive study of a marriage: Deborah Kerr was the wife who wanted to settle down, and Robert Mitcham the husband who didn't.*

'The Turn of the Screw' is the most imaginative of Henry James's ghost stories, and to judge from adaptations into other versions, the most popular. This 1961 film was called The Innocents, *with Deborah Kerr as the governess, Megs Jenkins as the housekeeper and Pamela Franklin one of the hallucinating children.*

The Night of the Iguana and was particularly touching, as willing and as eager as she ever was; her co-stars were Richard Burton and Ava Gardner, paid $500,000 and $400,000 respectively, as against her $250,000.

Unofficially, she retired – but Frank Sinatra insisted on her for his wife in *Marriage on the Rocks* (65), her first Hollywood-made film in six years (she lives in Switzerland). It was a pity she was persuaded; she got the first really bad notices of her career – an embarrassingly skittish performance, all mock-Lombard. Then David Niven talked her into doing *Eye of the Devil*, which had almost been completed when Kim Novak had an accident and a replacement was needed; she told interviewers she was glad to be working again – probably the only good thing about that benighted (in both senses) film. It got a few bookings in the US in 1967 and was shoved into Britain in 1968 as a second feature. She decided to go on workng, but took *Casino Royale* (67), she said, because nothing better was offered; and was very surprised when the critics lammed into everything about the film except her and most strongly agreed that she could play comedy after all. They liked her in another comedy – but not the film itself, *Prudence and the Pill* (68), with Niven again, as his unfaithful wife; then she had thin roles in two Hollywood films, *The Gypsy Moths* (69), being unfaithful with Burt Lancaster this time (for the second time in her career), and *The Arrangement* (70) where Kirk Douglas was unfaithful to her.

MGM president James Aubrey was quoted as saying that he would not be making pictures with Lancaster and Kerr 'groping with each other . . . It's obscene. It's like watching a couple of grandparents pawing each other.' The remark was much quoted and in an interview in 1971 she said that she was no longer being offered movie roles – or at least any she cared to do. There was talk in 1972 of a version of Iris Murdoch's *A Fairly Honourable Defeat*, but instead she returned to the West End in 'The Day After the Fair', which she also did in the US. She was later announced for the role in *An Eagle Has Landed* that Jean Marsh did. She restricted herself to stage work: 'Seascape' by Edward Albee in New York in 1975 and 'Souvenir' by her husband and George Axelrod in LA – both of them quick flops; and two revivals, 'Candida' in London in 1977 and 'The Last of Mrs Cheyney' on tour in the US. In 1979 she toured Australia in 'The Day After the Fair' and in London in 1981 was in Ustinov's 'Overheard'. She played the Elsa Lanchester role in the Hallmark Hall of Fame remake of *Witness for the Prosecution* (82) with Ralph Richardson, for TV, and returned to the big screen in a minor piece, *The Assam Garden* (85), as an ex-Raj widow who makes friends with an Indian family. It was even more undernourished than it needed to be and the actress, plump and ageing, revealed little grasp of character or even of the charisma which had once made her a star. She was reunited with Mitchum for an HBO tele-movie, *Reunion at Fairborough*, which recalled the Yanks in Britain, and received poor notices for 'The Corn is Green' (85) at the Old Vic in London, partly because she did not know her lines, despite a prior tour. Today's audiences perhaps know her best for a mini-series, *A Woman of Substance* (84), and its sequel, *Hold the Dream* (86).

Burt Lancaster

Burt Lancaster is one of those who learnt as they went along. In his first roles, ox-like convicts and gangsters, he merely looked morose; he moved over to swashbucklers, in a memorable series of movies, and here his physical attributes worked even more favourably for him – not only the rugged build, the huge frame and the penchant for startling athletics but the cheerful grin (all those teeth!) and the clear blue eyes. However, like other he-men stars he wanted to act. So he acted. 'Burt Lancaster!' said Jeanne Moreau: 'Before he can pick up an ashtray, he discusses his motivation for an hour or two. You want to say just pick up the ashtray and shut up.' He admits that Shirley Booth once told him, 'Burt, once in a while you hit a note of truth and you can hear a bell ring. But most of the time I can see the wheels turning and your brain working.' The results have been variable. He sometimes found the key and gave performances of sensitivity and some subtlety. When he did not, he bored audiences into the ground.

He was born in New York City in 1913, the son of a post-office employee. At school he showed a strong bent for athletics and acrobatics, and at 17 joined a circus troupe. He formed a duo with Nick Cravat, the little man who later was his sidekick in a couple of adventure films. They were not entirely successful and in 1941 Lancaster got a job in Marshall Fields' Chicago store, floorwalking in the lingerie dept. There were some more jobs before he joined the army. He acted and danced in army shows and decided to take up acting professionally. He got a job in a briefly-with-us Broadway play, Harry Brown's 'A Sound of Hunting' (later filmed as *Eight Iron Men*), and acquired an agent, Harold Hecht. Hecht got him a contract with Hal Wallis, who ran his own company within the confines of Paramount. He loaned him to Mark Hellinger at Universal, producing an adaptation of Hemingway's *The Killers* (46), a *danse macabre* consisting of the original anecdote plus a very long coda; Lancaster's tense ex-prize-fighter added something to its success. He stayed at Universal to play a convict in Hellinger's *Brute Force* (47) and returned to Paramount to guest in *Variety Girl*. He was a cop in an action-weirdie, *Desert Fury* (in fact his first film; release was delayed), and an ex-

The cinema public first became acquainted with Burt Lancaster in The Killers *(46), a tense adaptation of Hemingway's story. Ava Gardner was the woman who loved him.*

con trying to get back on the rackets in *I Walk Alone*, an arid melodrama with Lizabeth Scott. 'Burt Lancaster plays with all the blank-faced aplomb of Tarzan' said the 'New York Times'. At Universal he was Edward G. Robinson's embittered son in *All My Sons* (48) and at Paramount Barbara Stanwyck's two-timing husband in *Sorry Wrong Number*.

Then he and Hecht formed their own company and produced *Kiss the Blood Off My Hands*, a phoney London melodrama about a neurotic war veteran (Lancaster) and the nice girl (Joan Fontaine) who helps him. It was not a success, but the Hecht-Lancaster relationship became the first lasting actor-dominated production company, a concept which helped break up the old studio system. The two were later joined by Harold Hill and Hecht-Hill-Lancaster productions included not only those films with Lancaster, but films like *Marty* and *The Bachelor Party*. The team later split, but their early films, made in conjunction with the studios, were successful enough for them to get backing which rendered them completely independent. Lancaster worked in both systems, though like all stars of his stature he had, in any case, control over all facets of production – regardless of whether the film was produced by his own company, by another independent, or by one of the studios. (He probably lost overall control during the film crisis, 1969/70.)

Still, then he was just another tough-guy actor: *Criss Cross* (49), as an armoured-car guard who goes to the bad for love of Yvonne de Carlo, at Universal; and *Rope of Sand*, as a hunting-guide who returns to his home town bent on revenge and loot. At this point he signed an agreement with Warners, which left him free to do outside work (but they would not let him go back to Paramount later to play a trapeze artist in *The Greatest Show on Earth*; Cornel Wilde played it). For Warners he and Hecht produced *The Flame and the Arrow* (50), his first screen swashbuckling and his first success; then he went amiably if not skilfully through a comedy at 20th, *Mr 880*, which had Edmund Gwenn as a dear old forger. He and Hecht produced and he starred in *Ten Tall Men* (51) for Columbia, a Foreign Legion yarn that adopted the same tongue-in-cheek attitude as *The Flame and the Arrow*, but without like success. For MGM he did a Western, *Vengeance Valley*, and for WB *Jim Thorpe All American*, a biopic of the Indian athlete. Hecht-Lancaster produced *The Crimson Pirate* (52) for Warners, made in Europe under Robert Siodmak's direction: an enjoyable adventure spoof, visually witty and breathtaking. Lancaster recalls that time: 'they were fun days and we set the town on fire with every movie we did'.

Wallis reclaimed him for *Come Back Little Sheba*, as box-office insurance for a good

The Crimson Pirate *(52): Burt Lancaster's acrobatics were as stunning as anything Fairbanks Sr ever did, and he was aided in no small way by Nick Cravat, who had been his partner in his circus days.*

Broadway play that was doubtful film material, about an ex-alcoholic and his slatternly wife (Shirley Booth). When one could take one's eyes off her, he appeared to be giving a conscientious portrayal – his first 'character' part. Then, as a change, he appeared in sone nonsense with Virginia Mayo, *South Sea Woman* (53), rechristened in Italy *Il Sergente Bum*. He was now so firmly wedded to Hecht-Lancaster that when Columbia wanted him for *From Here to Eternity* they had no chance of getting him except by buying one of his commitments to Wallis; Wallis sold it for $150,000 (of which Lancaster got $120,000) but also insisted on Columbia taking from him for $40,000 *Bad for Each Other*, plus its stars, Charlton Heston and Lizabeth Scott. Lancaster's role as the bumptious sergeant in *Eternity* brought him the New York critics' award as the year's Best Actor, but it was followed by a notably weak one, *His Majesty O'Keefe*. He produced the latter, but could be forgiven because of *Apache* (54), in which he had the title-role, and more especially *Vera Cruz*, a bountiful Western, where his grinning bandit more than held its own against heroic Gary Cooper. Both were directed by Robert Aldrich, who found Lancaster 'not an easy man to get along with but quite responsive'. He noted that it was Lancaster's desire to become a director – till he failed at it: *The Kentuckian* (55), in which he also starred.

Wallis's *The Rose Tattoo*, with Anna Magnani, was an adequate version of a Tennessee Williams play; *Trapeze* (56) with Tony Curtis was a picayune circus drama directed by Carol Reed – and a big hit; and Wallis's *The Rainmaker* was another version of a Broadway play, with Lancaster as an itinerant con-man providing first – and temporary – love for ageing spinster Katharine Hepburn. At the end of 1956 he made one of only two appearances in the top 10 (the other was in 1962). *Gunfight at the OK Corral* (57) was his last for Wallis, a John Sturges Western with Kirk Douglas that cleaned up at the box-office. But *The Sweet Smell of Success* did not recoup its cost, despite a warm press – a flashy, gritty piece about the influence of a vicious gossip columnist, played by Lancaster with oily conviction. He stood up well to another veteran, Clark Gable, in *Run Silent Run Deep* (58), but it was not an interesting part. The next one was, the failed writer in *Separate Tables*, but he did little with it. Laurence Olivier was to have directed as well as co-starred, but after he had seen Lancaster 'try out' his (Olivier's) role he decided he could not direct him; and, as Hecht-Hill-Lancaster were producing, Olivier was relieved of his duties. (David Niven played his part; Rita Hayworth played the part which Vivien Leigh was to have taken.) The quarrel with Olivier was patched up when he agreed to play the general in *The Devil's Disciple* (59); Lancaster was the parson, Kirk Douglas was Dick and the film was spoiled, if not ruined, by an inadequate Mistress Anderson. These were the last four Hecht-Hill-Lancaster films.

John Huston's Western, *The Unforgiven* (60), was easier stuff and Lancaster had no difficulty with *Elmer Gantry*, Sinclair Lewis's charlatan evangelist, directed by Richard Brooks. He is reputed to have said that this was not acting but himself – cocksure, wheedling, swaggering, all conscious charm: it is still a perfectly right performance and won an Oscar and his second New York critics' citation. As if on a pogo-stick he then went down again: ineffectual in Frankenheimer's worthless teenage drama, *The Young Savages* (61), as an assistant DA; and hopeless as an elderly German war criminal in *Judgment at Nuremberg* (he tried too hard, as if awed by the fact that at the last minute Olivier had relinquished the role; and compounded his crime by disagreeing on-set with Maximilian Schell). He atoned again: with Frankenheimer's *Bird Man of Alcatraz* (62), a film he particularly wanted to do, the study of reprieved killer Robert Stroud who in a lifetime in goal became the world's leading expert on bird diseases. His performance is awkward and self-conscious – but somehow genuinely moving and the grip of the piece owes much to him. He was awarded Best Actor at the Venice festival. (The film had been started under director Charles Crichton

Burt Lancaster as Snow-White . . . Seriously, he is very good in Bird Man of Alcatraz *(62), an unusual picture – based on fact – about a prisoner who became an authority on bird diseases.*

before *Judgment* and abandoned; it was then a Hecht-Hill-Lancaster film – a company which now wound up heavily in debt.)

The next two emptied cinemas, although *A Child Is Waiting* (63), with Judy Garland, was a sincere attempt to say something in cinema terms about mongoloid children. Director John Cassavetes says producer Stanley Kramer interfered; then the distributors and some critics sold it short. What happened to *Il Gattopardo/The Leopard* is even more depressing. Giuseppe di Lampedusa's novel about an aristocratic Sicilian family during the Risorgimento required a big budget and to get US backing director Visconti had to consent to a big name – and Lancaster was anxious to do it. Filmed in a variety of languages, the result was nevertheless a masterpiece in its original Italian version; Lancaster, though dubbed, was mightily impressive. It was a box-office smash in Italy, France and other territories, but in the US and Britain 20th got cold feet. It was too long. Too foreign. Too long ago. The version shown had been hacked to pieces, was badly dubbed and the print re-processed and washed out. Critics who had seen the original were horrified and the film was generally ostracized; when shown on American TV it got lower ratings than any other movie that season. It is, along with *Elmer Gantry*, Lancaster's own favourite film.

Burt Lancaster at his best: as the Sicilian prince/patriarch in Il Gattopardo *(63) –* The Leopard *– Visconti's noble version of the posthumous novel by Giuseppe di Lampedusa.*

Frankenheimer directed *Seven Days in May* (64), with Kirk Douglas, an excellent political thriller in which Lancaster was a general plotting to overthrow the US president, a role which he played as a glassy-eyed mystic. At Lancaster's request, Frankenheimer took over direction of *The Train*, with Jeanne Moreau, an overrated war film but a success – which Sturges's Western, *The Hallelujah Trail* (65), emphatically was not. Then again Richard Brooks's *The Professionals* (66) was – due as much to a rousing cast: Lee Marvin, Robert Ryan, Jack Palance. Then again *The Swimmer* (68) was not, a muddled attempt to film John Cheever's novel of suburban dilemma. Somewhere along the middle line was Sydney Pollack's Western, *The Scalphunters*, but a war film Pollack directed, *Castle Keep*, was a giant flop. Lancaster told an interviewer that year: 'As an actor I know I can still improve. Oh God, yes. We've all got to keep trying to reach new horizons.' He added that he wanted to quit acting for producing: 'Some actors go on for ever, into the grave. Not me. I don't want to be like that. I want to get away from acting altogether.'

He might well have avoided Frankenheimer's *The Gypsy Moths* (69), which he described as 'pretentious' and which failed. On the other hand he called *Airport* (70) 'the biggest piece of junk ever made' and that turned out to be one of the biggest box-office hits ever made, an old-fashioned, star-studded action melodrama that rode triumphantly over the new-look films of the year. Lancaster, however, was an 'old' name; he went into a couple of Westerns budgeted at far less than he was used to: *Lawman* (71), publicized as the first Western made by a British director – and probably the only interesting thing about it; and *Valdez Is Coming*, much better, where his own performance as an ageing Mexican gunman was universally admired. Around the same time, on the West Coast, he played Walter Huston's old part in a revival of 'Knickerbocker Holiday'. In 1969 he was divorced from his wife of 23 years.

After an almost 20-year gap he returned to Aldrich for a Western, only the roles were reversed, for Aldrich was the boss and he the employee: in *Ulzana's Raid* (72) he was a grizzled Indian-fighter. He was a CIA man in *Scorpio* (73), for director Michael Winner, who discussed with him the lead in *Death Wish*, but the producers preferred Charles Bronson, who was much bigger box-office. In an attempt to get his career on the upgrade again, he produced, wrote and directed – all in collaboration with Roland Kibbee – *The Midnight Man* (74), designed to exploit his most frequent image, the solitary man given to terrible vengeance; he was an ex-cop turned security guard beset by mayhem and betrayal on all sides, but if the cards were stacked for audience sympathy – well, they were not large audiences. A return to Visconti augured better for the career, but *Gruppo di Famiglia in un Interno/Conversation Piece* (75) was barracked at the New York Film Festival and, as far as the US was concerned, never recovered: 'Embarrassing' said 'Variety', 'with its weirdo mix of boy stud, art professor, Roman upper-class tramps and radical chic philosophy', also predicting that it would not be seen again in the US. It was, re-edited, but briefly – which is a shame, for there was much good in it, headed by Lancaster in his least actory performance in years, as an ageing man confronted by the puzzling life-style of the young. Also in Europe, for an Italian-British TV combine, he played Moses in a spectacular series, which turned up later, cut, for cinemas – *Moses* (76); at least it was more honourable than his next European venture, playing the patriarch in Bertolucci's *Novecento/1900*, given things to do which should be asked of no self-respecting actor. Asked his opinion of the film, he would only repeat 'I think Sterling Hayden was wonderful in it.' From here his career could only go up, but it managed only half a notch with Robert Altman's muddled *Buffalo Bill and the Indians*, playing the journalist who outlined the myth of Buffalo Bill (Paul Newman). In both films Lancaster had an important role, but not the central one, and he took special billing: but it had been many a long year since he had not been top-billed.

In the all-star TV *Victory at Entebbe* he was the Israeli Minister of Defence and he also had weighty problems as an intelligence officer in *The Cassandra Crossing* (77), but there was no billing problem as he returned to the top of the cast-list, starting with *The Island of Dr Moreau*, daftly muted as the mad scientist – a role that Charles Laughton had once played so luxuriantly. He was villainous again, as an ex-Air Force general plotting his way to a huge ransom via atomic weapons in Aldrich's *Twilight's Last Gleaming*; and the few who went to see it found it an only-too-familiar Lancaster performance. Nor were there many takers for *Go Tell It to the Spartans* (78), in which he was an American military adviser in Vietnam, just before the war: he himself helped with the publicity, because he thought it his best film in years, and its seriousness was endorsed by some American critics – but their colleagues abroad felt otherwise. To do it, Lancaster had turned down a British adventure set in Africa, *The Wild Geese*, but he was there for the British (though it was a Dutch-American co-venture) in *Zulu Dawn* (79), as commander of the cavalry. He was a retired gangster in Louis Malle's Canadian-made *Atlantic City* (80), which Paramount bought (having had a minute investment) – an excellent convoluted thriller which brought Lancaster more attention than his last 10 films put together and which brought him the Best Actor citation from the New York critics. Two lesser enterprises were already in the can: *Cattle Annie and Little Britches*, in which he was a grizzled gangleader who adopts two girls looking for adventures in the old West, and Liliana Cavani's version of Malaparte's *La Pelle*, with under-title billing (Mastroianni starred), as General Mark Clark. The former, after a year on the shelf and some test engagements, was sold to cable; the latter got few export bookings – which will not surprise those who know the work of this director. After co-starring with Kirk Douglas in Los Angeles in 'The Boys in Autumn' Lancaster returned to Italy for an Italian-US mini-series, *Marco Polo* (82), to play the Pope. He then took a couple of choice roles with brief footage (but star-billing): Bill Forsythe's *Local Hero* (83), as the Texas oil boss who comes to see what has gone wrong in that remote Scottish fastness, and *The Osterman Weekend*, as the head of the CIA. Heart trouble cost him roles in *Maria's Lovers* (it went to Robert Mitchum), *Firestarter* (Martin Sheen) and *Kiss of the Spiderwoman* (William Hurt).

Recovered, he was a slippery, corrupt publisher in a tele-movie, *Scandal Sheet* (85), and a father visited by a stripper (Margot Kidder) in *Little Treasure*. He should have been in a film in France with Alain Delon, but it was cancelled when the director died. In Germany he was the patriarch in a co-production (France and Italy were also involved) mini, which became *Sins of the Fathers* when shown in its English version two years later: the sins were those of the I.G. Farben family and Julie Christie was also in the cast. There was another mini-series, *On Wings of Eagles*, in which he was a US army officer in Teheran at the time of the hostages crisis. A reunion with Kirk Douglas was one of the Disney studio's miscalculations, since few were curious to see these *Tough Guys* together again. Lancaster was *Barnum*, another mini, with Hanna Schygulla as his Jenny Lind, but *Rocket Gibraltar* (88) confirmed that his box-office standing had gone, for few went to see this tale of a family arriving on Long Island to help the old man celebrate his 77th birthday. But there were the usual big roles in prestigious projects for Italian television: *La Bottega dell'Orefice/The Jeweller's Shop*, from a play by Karol Wojtyla (Pope John Paul II) with Ben Cross and Olivia

Hussey, and *I Promessi Sposi/The Betrothed*, from Manzoni's novel, with F. Murray Abraham, Franco Nero and Helmut Berger.

When Paul Newman decided that his role in *Old Gringo* would be overshadowed by that of Jane Fonda, it was offered to Lancaster: he was not insurable, but there was a spoken agreement that he could solve that problem. The next thing he knew was that Gregory Peck had been cast, so he sued for $1.5 million, which is what he reckoned the film would have earned him over the next three years; and instead he supported Kevin Costner, in *Field of Dreams* (89).

Angela Lansbury

When Anglea Lansbury finally made it to the big time in the Broadway 'Mame', more than 20 years after starting in films, there can have been few filmgoers who were surprised and fewer still who were not pleased. She had been giving impeccable performances all that time, in a wide series of parts. Perhaps her trouble was that she was too versatile – and only big stars could afford to be (most of them, of course, did not try). She stayed firmly on the second or third rung, till justice was finally done.

Her mother was also a good character actress – Moyna McGill, who appeared in some Hollywood films of the 40s, e.g. *The Strange Affair of Uncle Harry* (and one grandfather was Labour leader George Lansbury). She was born in London in 1925 and taken by her mother to the US as an evacuee in 1940, where she continued her drama studies. A friend worked out an act for her (it included an impersonation of Beatrice Lillie's 'I Went to a Marvellous Party') and she got a job in a Montreal nightclub. Things did not go too well and they did not go too well after she joined her mother in Los Angeles in 1943: she was working in a store when she heard that MGM wanted an English girl for *The Picture of Dorian Gray*. She was auditioned and got taken instead to George Cukor to be interviewed for the part of the Cockney maid in *Gaslight*. He decided she was too young, but MGM signed her anyway, for seven years starting at $500 a week. And she got the part in *Gaslight* (44) after all, and an Oscar nomination. She played the flighty elder sister in *National Velvet* and then did *The Picture of Dorian Gray* (45), as a pathetic saloon-singer, loved and betrayed by Dorian (Hurd Hatfield) – and got another Best Supporting nomination. Albert Lewin directed.

She was just out of her teens and you would have thought that MGM might have taken this

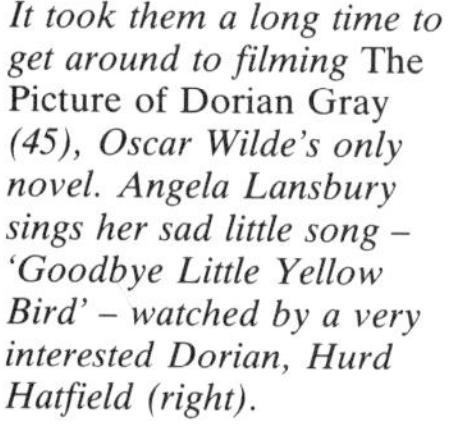

It took them a long time to get around to filming The Picture of Dorian Gray *(45), Oscar Wilde's only novel. Angela Lansbury sings her sad little song – 'Goodbye Little Yellow Bird' – watched by a very interested Dorian, Hurd Hatfield (right).*

further proof of her talent and built her into a star. But they had other ideas. As she said later, they had Esther Williams to swim, Judy Garland to sing, June Allyson to jitterbug and Lena Horne to lean against pillars. All she wanted to be was Jean Arthur. MGM saw her rather as a junior version of Claire Trevor or Ann Sheridan and in *The Harvey Girls* (46) she led the honky-tonk girls who tried to run nice Judy Garland out of town. She sang and she had a couple of songs in *The Hoodlum Saint* before being ousted from William Powell's affections by Esther Williams. In the same zesty manner she sang 'How'd you like to spoon with me?' in *Till the Clouds Roll By*. Lewin, now at UA, borrowed her to play a courtesan in *The Private Affair of Bel Ami* (47) with George Sanders, after which she was Walter Pidgeon's shrewish wife in *If Winter Comes*. She was a schoolteacher in *Tenth Avenue Angel* (48), who was Margaret O'Brien, and a tough career woman in *State of the Union*, bent on wresting Spencer Tracy from Katharine Hepburn; in the latter she effortlessly impersonated a woman 20 years older than herself and on the strength of her success she begged Louis B. Mayer to let her play Milady in *The Three Musketeers* – but the part went to Lana Turner and she had to be content with playing the queen.

If MGM felt she lacked that little extra something that makes a star, what about Turner? Certainly in retrospect it is difficult to see why MGM kept Lansbury as a featured player while making stars of Turner, or June Allyson, or Janet Leigh. . . . She supported Leigh (and others) in a silly Cold War drama, *The Red Danube* (49), playing a senior subaltern, and was then loaned to Paramount for *Samson and Delilah*, playing Delilah's sister, who gets bumped off on the point of becoming Mrs Samson. In 1949 she married – enduringly – for the second time (first marriage, to actor Richard Cromwell, 1945, lasted less than a year) and was off the screen for two years becoming a mother. She says herself of this period that after Doré Schary took over from Mayer as head of the studio she 'began to get lost in the shuffle'. She was starred in *Kind Lady* (51), with Maurice Evans terrorizing Ethel Barrymore in this second Talkie version of Hugh Walpole's story – but that was only a dualler. She was loaned out for *Mutiny* (52) with Mark Stevens, a mild piece about the War of 1812, and when there was no further work for her she went into summer stock – 'Affairs of State' and 'Remains to be Seen'. MGM shoved her into a quickie version of the latter (53), with Van Johnson, and she had the same – supporting – part, the mystery woman of the mystery. That concluded her contract.

She was off the screen till – she told Rex Reed later – she 'needed money so badly that I played a seamstress in a Tony Curtis film'; she forgot *Key Man* (54), a cheap little independent venture with Keith Andes. The Curtis film was *The Purple Mask* (55). 'Another low point' was a Randolph Scott Western, *A Lawless Street*, as his wife, but a high one was presumably *The Court Jester* with Danny Kaye, where she had a good role as the phlegmatic princess. In *Please Murder Me* (56) she obliged, co-starring in this B with Raymond Burr.

After a Broadway run in 'Hotel Paradiso' (57) with Bert Lahr the tide turned. She got two showy roles: as Orson Welles's kind-hearted mistress in *The Long Hot Summer* (58) and Kay Kendall's gossipy confidante and rival in *The Reluctant Débutante*. Her part in *The Summer of the Seventeenth Doll* (59) was even better, as one of two tarts who have their men for summers only; however, she was rather theatrical and the Australian emphasis of the original play was lost in the Anglo-American casting (Anne Baxter, John Mills, Ernest Borgnine). The film was not a success and when finally shown in the US was retitled hopefully *Season of Passion*. After that she returned to featured roles, though the first, at least, was a good one: the comforting, realistic beauty-salon friend of Robert Preston in *The Dark at the Top of the Stairs* (60). She was a Ruritanian princess, Sophia Loren's rival, in *A Breath of Scandal*. David Merrick inveigled her back to Broadway for 'A Taste of Honey', thinking she would be sensational as Joan Plowright's mother, and she was. In films she started a run of mother-roles: *Blue Hawaii* (61), as Elvis Presley's, a dithering Southern belle – a part turned down by Dolores del Rio; and *All Fall Down*, as Warren Beatty's. But it was as Laurence Harvey's mother in *The Manchurian Candidate* (63) that she got the best notices of her film career, as a vicious politicking bitch. She was Oscar nominated but lost to Patty Duke. And she was equally good as Peter Finch's spiteful wife in *In the Cool of the Day*. Her versatility was by now – or should have been – a byword. Not since the heyday of Bette Davis had there been an actress of this range and accomplishment. She was certainly one of the most talented half dozen women in Hollywood – but after all these years still not regarded as a star.

There were more good notices for *The World of Henry Orient* (64), a matron reluctantly falling for Peter Sellers, and *Dear Heart*, being jilted by Glenn Ford: 'Above all, one enjoys the easy skill with which Angela Lansbury suggests the plump, pampered and coolly self-centred Phyllis' (the 'MFB'). One could hardly enjoy her, however, in *The Greatest Story Ever Told* (65), 'a mere flash in

All Fall Down (61) *was described by its director, John Frankenheimer, as 'the story of a man's emergence from boyhood, the difficulty of becoming a man'. The boy/man was played by Brandon de Wilde; Angela Lansbury was his mother, and Warren Beatty his brother.*

the Panavision' as 'Variety' put it, glimpsed beckoning to Pontius Pilate. She was one of the few to emerge with credit from the Carroll Baker *Harlow* débâcle, as Mama Jean, but she went down with the rest in *The Amorous Adventures of Moll Flanders*, as a gay milady. And, finally, she helped James Garner, in difficulties as *Mister Buddwing* (66).

By the time that was shown she was literally the toast of Broadway. In 1964 she had been in a flop Broadway musical, 'Anyone Can Whistle', and had been well enough received to try for 'Mame' (66). Almost every actress over 40 was considered for the part and bigger names were turned down after she auditioned; she got raves and awards, and considered getting the part 'a terrific victory'. She was later praised for 'Dear World' (69), a flop musical version of 'The Madwoman of Chaillot', and for 'Prettybelle' (71), which folded out of town. Meanwhile, she had returned to films: as a wealthy countess in *Something for Everyone* (70), top-starred at last in this black comedy that was the film bow for Broadway producer-director Hal Prince; and Disney's *Bedknobs and Broomsticks* (71), as a kindly English witch. In 1972 she performed with the Royal Shakespeare Company in Edward Albee's 'All Over' and in 1975 with Britain's National Theatre in 'Hamlet', as the Queen; between the two engagements she was notably successful in the London première and (later) the New York revival of 'Gypsy', singing less well than Ethel Merman but acting better. She took over for a month in another Broadway revival, 'The King and I', while the leads were on holiday, and a few months later was back on the screen, in *Death on the Nile* (78), going outrageously but amusingly over-the-top as a tippling romantic novelist – and well-nigh stealing the film from the other stars. Also in Britain she was the sole reason for seeing the remake of *The Lady Vanishes* (79), the lady of the title; but she had meanwhile returned to Broadway in 'Sweeney Todd'. As Agatha Christie's Miss Marple in *A Mirror Crack'd* (80) she was billed above, among others, Elizabeth Taylor, whom she had supported in *National Velvet* – and who had been a superstar while Lansbury was (in the 50s) looking for offers. Lansbury herself was going from one to the next: *Little Gloria . . . Happy*

No one was quite sure what Angela Lansbury was doing in Death on the Nile *(78), but one thing was sure, that she was doing it outrageously – and making it one of the most taking over-the-top performances in the history of films. Not surprisingly, both David Niven and Peter Ustinov were bemused.*

at Last (82), a mini-series, as the Vanderbilt sculptress, teamed with some other formidable talents (Bette Davis, Maureen Stapleton); 'A Little Family Business', a Broadway play which did not run; *The Pirates of Penzance* (83), joining the members of the cast of the New York revival in a film which suffered the reverse of the success of that; *Sweeney Todd*, for cable; *The Gift of Love: A Christmas Story* for television, as Lee Remick's mother; and two mini-series, *Lace* (84), guest-starring as an aunt, with Bess Armstrong and Brooke Adams, and *The First Olympics – Athens*, one of a starry cast. In Britain she co-starred with Laurence Olivier in a television mystery, *A Talent for Murder*, and played Little Red Riding Hood's grandmother in a cinema movie, *The Company of Wolves*.

Rage of Angels: The Story Continues (86) was a return to Sidney Sheldon for Jaclyn Smith, Ken Howard and others; for Lansbury, who played a marchesa, it was a relief from sleuthing, which she has been doing in a TV series since 1984, 'Murder She Wrote', as a spinster not a million moves from Miss Marple. She had said that she likes the work and she likes the people, that she does not have to prove anything any more and that she will do it as long as the ratings remain high.

Mario Lanza

Mario Lanza was one of the screen's comets: his light dazzled briefly, then fizzled out. Today his records still sell and there are posthumous fan clubs; apart from their members, he is perhaps only remembered by some aged MGM accountants.

He was born Alfred Cocozza in 1921 in Philadelphia, where his dislike of discipline manifested itself early; he was expelled from high school. He sang as a child and studied voice; he was still studying and working temporarily as a piano-mover when Sergei Koussevitsky of the Boston Symphony Orchestra heard him sing (supposedly while shifting a piano). As a result he sang at the Berkshire Music Festival in 1942. During his army service he sang in the chorus of Moss

Hart's 'Winged Victory' and took part in the film version (44). In 1945 he was signed to an agreement by Sam Weiler, a real-estate man and amateur music-lover, who offered to spend $60,000 on training him in return for which he would become his agent and, if he clicked, get his money back. He got Lanza an RCA Victor recording contract, but, due in part to Lanza's squabbling with them, the first record was not issued till three years later (48). Lanza began a heavy schedule of concert tours; sang in a concert performance of 'Andrea Chénier' in the Hollywood Bowl (47) and made his opera début as Pinkerton in 'Madame Butterfly' (48). MGM executives saw another Bowl concert that year and signed him to a contract.

Joe Pasternak was given the job of producing his first film and came up with *That Midnight Kiss* (49), all about a barrel-chested piano-mover who has a glorious voice and turns out to be just what the Philly Opera needs! Special opera sequences were written, but could not save it at the box-office. Kathryn Grayson was the leading lady and MGM thought of them as a new Macdonald-Eddy. They were teamed again, after a year's hesitation, in *The Toast of New Orleans* (50), all about a fisherman who becomes a famous – guess what? This did use 'real' opera and was fractionally less inane. It still flopped; but about six months after its release one of the songs ('Be My Love') turned out to be a hit; and Lanza's Red Seal records were not only selling, but were highly regarded by (some) music buffs. MGM took a gamble: they would remake *The Jolson Story* with 'classical' music, starring Lanza. They called it *The Great Caruso* (51) and filled it with opera pops, like a pudding stuffed with plums. It made $10 million during its first year on release and perhaps the only one unhappy was Caruso's widow, who bitterly regretted selling her Caruso memoir to MGM. Lanza became the new golden boy. 'Metro has a natural,' said 'Variety', as the natural's earning for that year rose to $800,000.

There was one problem, but it was a major one: the star himself. Pasternak in his memoirs says that Lanza was difficult from the start: 'there was a wild, unpredictable streak in his nature'. Also he could 'put on fifty pounds as easily and quickly as most people add an ounce or two' – nor could he be persuaded to stop eating. His capacity for booze was equally sensational (later, drugs were added) and a 'Time Magazine' profile detailed a number of unpleasant habits, such

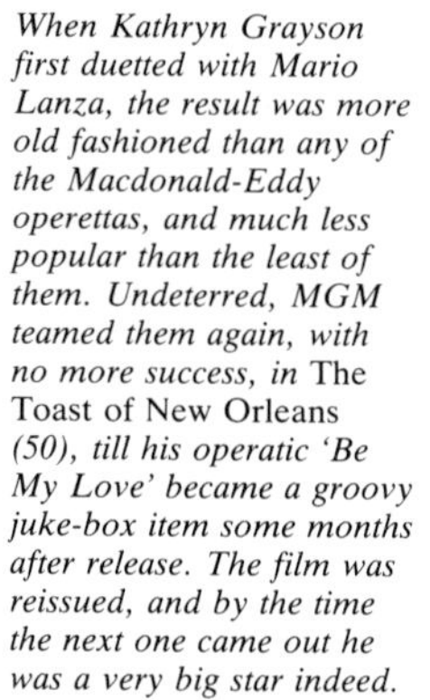

When Kathryn Grayson first duetted with Mario Lanza, the result was more old fashioned than any of the Macdonald-Eddy operettas, and much less popular than the least of them. Undeterred, MGM teamed them again, with no more success, in The Toast of New Orleans *(50), till his operatic 'Be My Love' became a groovy juke-box item some months after release. The film was reissued, and by the time the next one came out he was a very big star indeed.*

as a dislike of soap and water and not bothering to go to the men's room to take a leak. This article, understandably, made Lanza furious; he blamed MGM and refused to report for his next film. When he did, says Pasternak, he was 'writing a new definition of the word temperament'. Grayson had flatly refused to co-star and Lanza's behaviour towards his leading lady – Doretta Morrow, brought in hurriedly from Broadway – reached a new low. Still, the film, *Because You're Mine* (52), was a big success. An attempt was made to make Lanza more popular with male audiences by having him join the army in it, but by this time it was only too apparent that his abilities between arias were limited to bounce and beefiness. (In Britain the film caused a press uproar when chosen as the Royal Performance film.)

Lanza was not only fighting with MGM. In 1952 he replaced all his personal staff. Weiler's health was failing and he dissolved the contract, whereupon Lanza tried to bring suit against him for alleged fraud – but no attorney would take the case. In comparison, however, with what was to come, all these troubles were little ones. Lanza was cast as *The Student Prince*. Jane Powell refused to co-star and the part went to Ann Blyth. He recorded the songs, but never showed on the set. MGM cancelled his contract and sued for a sum variously reported but going as high as $7 million (the most likely break-up: $700,000 in actual cash losses including Blyth's $50,000 guarantee, plus $4½ million in estimated profits). Lanza claimed (wrongly) that they were trying to make the film during his free six months. In June 1953 studio and star made it up and some months later he actually began work, but there were reputedly differences as to how Prussian the prince should be and Lanza walked out again. An English actor, Edmund Purdom, was called in to mouth to Lanza's voice – the recordings were MGM's property. Such was the magic of Mario, the film (54) was a big hit. (Purdom became briefly the hottest new thing in Hollywood, but, after clashes over suitable vehicles and a poor box-office, MGM dropped him.)

This time MGM were not interested in a reconciliation. Paramount considered Lanza for a remake of *The Vagabond King*, but, coupled with his demand for 50 per cent of the profits, decided he was not worth the risk. Howard Hughes made an offer provided he could get down to 200 lb (just over 14 stone). In 1954 Lanza appeared on TV and there was a scandal because it was obvious that he was miming to one of his own records. His stock sank again when (in 1955) he failed to appear for a nighclub booking in Las Vegas. Eventually Warners signed him for two films at $150,000 each. The first was *Serenade* (56), from a novel by James M. Cain about a peasant boy who becomes an opera singer. . . . It did good business but WB preferred to pay Lanza not to make the second film.

He did concert tours and in Italy Titanus negotiated with him for a movie. *Arrivederci Roma/The Seven Hills of Rome* (58), which was all him plus a pictorial tour of the Eternal City (he described it as a 'terrible' film and said he was 'lousy' in it). Ironically, MGM had a distribution agreement with Titanus, so they made a bit from this, and from the next, which they also handled, also a co-production, filmed in Capri: *Serenade einer Grossen Liebe/For the First Time* (59), with Zsa Zsa Gabor, to be the first of a three-picture deal with a German company, CCC. Both films were largely critically ignored, though certain critics envied the heroine of the second one, who for plot purposes was deaf. Shortly after finishing it Lanza died in Rome of a heart attack; his wife, a non-professional, died a while later, with alcoholism a contributing factor. Hedda Hopper wrote of him: 'He recognized no authority, no discipline, no frontiers except his own gigantic appetite for food and drink and women.'

Jack Lemmon

'Happiness', said Billy Wilder, taking a leaf from that book extolling warm puppies, 'is working with Jack Lemmon.' On another occasion he said he rated him 'somewhere between Charlie Chaplin and Cary Grant'. Except in a couple of pictures, happiness is watching Jack Lemmon. He casts the old-time glow. People *like* Jack Lemmon, they go to Jack Lemmon pictures because he is in them, they talk about him in an affectionate way. He is Mr Average Guy, Junior Executive version, immeasurably committed to Right and Truth, and permanently insecure about the choice he has made. Corruption confronts him on every side. His voice will find new pitches to express astonishment, his face will crumple some more till it vaguely resembles a prune. He will stop in a sentence and start again, as if he could not believe the question or statement he is making. He is the most accomplished light comedian working in films.

He was born in Boston in 1925, son of a salesman who eventually became president of the Doughnut Corporation of America. He was a junior officer in the navy at the end of the war, simultaneously studying at Harvard, where his interest was focused on dramatics. When he left he did some stock work and learnt a lot at Knickerbocker Music Hall, where 'we did everything from old-time melodramas to waiting on tables to community sings to MC bits to oleo bits (meaning everything in one)'. He did TV – he estimates over 400 shows in a five-year period – and was in a flop Broadway revival of 'Room Service' (53). The head of Columbia casting caught him on TV and thought he would be ideal opposite Judy Holliday in *It Should Happen To You* (54), as the fellow roomer who tries to prevent her from making a fool of herself. He preferred to be in legit, but was persuaded by Garson Kanin's script and the prospect of working with Holliday and director Cukor. He signed for seven years and 'I did get things nobody had gotten before': the right to do four Broadway plays, to take a year's sabbatical and do an outside movie a year (provided he had done the two a year agreed upon).

The film effectively typed him: the desperately sincere young man, a bit naive, very good-hearted, always game but liable to panic. He also demonstrated a technique comparable to Holliday's and they were coupled again, less felicitously, in *Phffft!*. Then the studio wasted him in two musicals, *Three for the Show* (55), as one of Betty Grable's husbands, and the infinitely better *My Sister Eileen*, as Betty Garrett's suitor; the latter was directed by Richard Quine – who would make four more films with Lemmon – and it was also a good example of Lemmon making bricks without straw. Between the two, Quine directed him in a test for *The Long Grey Line*, which John Ford directed – and Ford insisted on Lemmon at Warners to play the wily, lecherous Ensign Pulver in *Mister Roberts*, a superb performance which netted him a Best Supporting Oscar. (A 1964 sequel, *Ensign Pulver*, starred Robert Walker Jr.) On TV he played John Wilkes Booth in 'The Day Lincoln was Shot', with Lillian Gish and Raymond Massey as the Lincolns. And then he marked time: the Gable role in an unpretentious musical version of *It Happened One Night* called *You Can't Run Away From It* (56); a supporting role to Rita Hayworth in a silly tropical melodrama, *Fire Down Below* (57); Quine's funny army comedy, *Operation Madball*, as the camp's most numble operator, with Ernie Kovacs; *Cowboy* (58), supposedly as Frank Harris, out West; and a supporting role, as a warlock, in *Bell, Book and Candle*, in which he was hard put to make his lines sound funny (it is one of the two films he has made which he dislikes: the other is *Three for the Show*). And he had little more to do in one of Doris Day's better comedies, *It Happened to Jane* (59), as the lawyer involved in her fight with the railroad. During this time Columbia's boss, Harry Cohn, insisted on casting him in *Joseph and His Brethren*, but the test, as Lemmon predicted, was a fiasco (the film was later cancelled).

But Billy Wilder had seen him in *Operation Madball* and offered him *Some Like It Hot* – a potentially dangerous career move, as he had to spend most of the film in drag. But he loved the script (planned by Wilder some years earlier for Bob Hope and Danny Kaye) and anyway was tired of doing films that Glenn Ford had turned down. So he became one of a couple of musicians who witness the St Valentine's Day Massacre and hide out in an all-girls band (whose vocalist is Marilyn Monroe). The reviews were sparkling: 'he is easily one of the most expert American actors of his generation. . . . His deft, hilariously agonized performance here sets the tone' (Stanley Kauffman). The film grossed $8 million, more than any comedy up to that time: quite justly. Lemmon was the BFA's Best Actor for it. He stayed with Wilder for another demonstration of his ability to be winning in unlikely circumstances ('surely the most sensitive and tasteful young comedian now at work in Hollywood' – 'Time Magazing') – as the careerist who loans his pad to his superiors for sexual dalliance: *The Apartment* (60). Shirley MacLaine beautifully partnered him as the girl in the case and the film was bitter-sweet, tragical-comical, sordid and sad: it was Oscared as the Best of the Year and netted over $9 million.

He did a guest spot in *Pepe*, and two very ordinary comedies for Columbia, *The Whackiest Ship in the Army* and Quine's *The Notorious Landlady* (62), around which time he was briefly on Broadway in 'Face of a Hero', an adaptation of a TV play he had once done. But Columbia would not back his pet project – only Warners would: the memorable *Days of Wine and Roses*, directed by Blake Edwards, with Lee Remick as his fellow alcoholic. He was good, drunk; when he was sober, he was gentle and effective. He was back being frenetic with Wilder and MacLaine in *Irma la Douce* (63), a musicless and rather dim version of the stage hit, but it racked up a total of $12 million, (again) the highest a comedy had yet done. For Columbia – to whom he was still under contract – he did two suburban farces, salacious but not fatally so: *Under the Yum-Yum Tree*, as a philanderer, and *Good Neighbor Sam* (64), as a harried husband. He formed his own company and did a similar piece, Quine's *How To Murder Your Wife* (65), and then got involved with a disaster called *The Great Race*, directed by Edwards, a hopelessly overdone slapstick to which his own cod performance contributed nothing. The prices were inflated and it grossed more than $10 million, but 'Variety' instanced it as a flop. Lemmon's salary was $1 million and he later said that it was partly because of the huge salaries paid to him and his co-stars that it had not broken even.

The next two failed: Wilder's *The Fortune Cookie* (66) and *Luv* (67), directed by Clive Donner for Lemmon's company, with Elaine May. Both got fairly poor reviews, but the Wilder was another skating-on-thin-ice job, funny and sad and always downbeat, about an injured baseball player conned into claiming the ultimate in insurance by his slob lawyer cousin, Walter Matthau. Lemmon did his first straight acting since *Days of Wine and Roses* in parts of it and gave a beautiful performance; but Matthau stole the notices. Wilder wanted to direct the next, *The Odd Couple* (68), again with Matthau, but Paramount thought him too expensive – and Lemmon could not contractually disapprove of their choice (Gene Saks). (Wilder has said that Lemmon is enormously inventive on-set and, unlike other actors, not insistent when his notions are turned down.) Lemmon was paid $1 million against 10 per cent of the gross for this version of Neil Simon's play about Two Gentlemen Sharing and this time Matthau was perhaps slightly the better. At all events, it made a fortune and put Lemmon back in the top 10 (where he had been, 1964/66 inclusive), at eighth. He was also at eighth in 1969 and 1970.

He produced *Cool Hand Luke*, with Paul Newman, who observed: 'Jack's one of the sharpest men in Hollywood. One of the few actors whom you can enjoy being around.' He did two more comedies, *The April Fools* (69), with Catherine Deneuve, which was poorly received, and *The Out-of-Towners* (70), with Sandy Dennis – from a Neil Simon script – which was very popular. He said that he looked hard for good scripts and added that he would like to play a small part in 'a little

Jack Lemmon, junior executive-style, in Billy Wilder's very fine The Apartment *(60), in which he gave a flawless comedy performance. (No, it wasn't set at the turn of the century, but the bowler hat or 'Derby' had briefly returned in vogue about that time.)*

Jack Lemmon in Irma la Douce *(63), a then-daring comedy about an ex-*flic *who falls for a* poule *and becomes her* mec*: but he cannot stand her going with other men.*

gem' but cannot, because he is a star and 'they'd wonder what the hell happened to Lemmon, he must be slipping.' His only objective he said, 'is to be the best actor I can possibly be, which means that I'd like to be better than I am, now'. There was another objective – to direct: *Kotch* (71), with Matthau and his second wife, Felicia Farr (his first wife was Cynthia Stone, 1950–56, who later married Cliff Robertson). 'Variety' described this as 'an outstanding directorial début'. Then he played a Thurber-man in *The War Between Men and Women* (72), based on some of Thurber's stories, and a businessman who falls in love with an English girl on Capri in Wilder's *Avanti*; the former received killing notices and the latter, though it was not Wilder on top form, deserved to have had bigger audiences.

From his first film onwards, Jack Lemmon was a superb light comedian, and obviously a very good actor. Twenty years later, he had become a superb actor, in Save the Tiger *(73), illustrated, and* The China Syndrome, *among others.*

Save the Tiger (73) concerned an LA garment manufacturer facing a number of crises: Lemmon loved Steve Shagan's script and later said he was prouder of the film than any he had done. When he found the studios uninterested, a deal was worked out at Paramount to do the film for no salary but a percentage only: the press endorsed Lemmon's view and while the public overall was not quite as keen, the film brought him a second Oscar, this time of course Best Actor. Following it proved difficult, for he was off the screen for almost two years, returning simultaneously in two comedies, Wilder's rather brash remake of *The Front Page* (74), reporter to Matthau's wily editor, and Neil Simon's rather grimmer *The Prisoner of Second Avenue*, jobless in New York. In LA with Matthau and Maureen Stapleton, he did a season of 'Juno and the Paycock'. On TV he played Olivier's role in an Americanized version of *The Entertainer* (76), shown in some cinemas abroad; but *Alex and the Gypsy* was hardly seen anywhere. Geneviève Bujold was the gypsy. Still, it was a mite sad to see Lemmon playing safe as the pilot in *Airport 77* (77), though he was as likeable as ever. After almost a year on Broadway in 'Tribute' he was the grizzled chief engineer of a nuclear power-plant in *The China Syndrome* (79), co-starring with Jane Fonda and Michael Douglas. Even his admirers were surprised by the new edge and authority in his acting.

On screen, *Tribute* (80), made in Canada (with Lee Remick as the wife and Rob Lowe as the son), turned out to be a sentimental and spurious family drama, but worse was to come: *Buddy Buddy* (81), a reunion with Wilder and Matthau. It was no secret that one of the greatest American film-makers was having difficulty (after several flops) in getting backing and Lemmon had always said that he would be there if Billy needed him. The kindest supposition is that the two actors suddenly found themselves free and Wilder did not have time to get the script into shape: it was both undernourished and vulgar, causing Lemmon to go into some frenzied effects to hold his own. He was a would-be suicide ruining the chance of would-be hit man Matthau and leading him into a series of adventures. The original, *L'Emmerdeur*, was funnier. *Missing* (82) more than made up for its failure, an impassioned and eloquent protest (based on fact) against the present regime in Chile, with Lemmon as a stuffy, right-wing father who arrives to seek his son, who disappeared during the coup in 1973. The fact that the US Embassy was involved in a cover-up operation is one reason why the State Department issued a rebuttal of the film's claims. *Mass Appeal* (84) was based on a play which would seem to be of the level of *Tribute*, but at least this was well made; Lemmon was a complacent priest in conflict with an earnest seminarian. *Macaroni* (85) was a concoction about two wartime buddies (the other was Mastroianni) meeting again in Italy, where it was filmed; Paramount took it for distribution during production, but were not much rewarded. Columbia similarly took *'That's Life!'* (86), Blake Edwards's serious, autobiographical comedy about an architect (Lemmon) with the male menopause. Miss Farr had a bit as a fortune-teller and Julie Andrews was Lemmon's screen wife, with secret troubles of her own. On the whole a nice movie, despite the usual Edwards vulgarities, but it is tempting to think what this star team might have done. What Lemmon did was to do 'Long Day's Journey Into Night' in New York and London, after by chance hearing Jonathan Miller say in an interview that that was a combination which might interest him in directing in America: but the venture was only moderately successful.

He returned to television as the State Governor in an excellent mini-series, *The Murder of Mary Phagan* (88), based on the Leo North case of 1913 which had been the source of *They Won't Forget*; and filmed *Dad* (89) with Ted Danson, after which he was expected to do another play in London, 'Veteran's Day' by Donald Freed.

JERRY LEWIS

Jerry Lewis falls down stairs and ladders, out of aeroplanes and windows, into holes and swimming pools. He is bullied by hotel clerks, waiters, cab-drivers and passers-by. But he catapults back.

There are millions of filmgoers who have never seen him. Like Rin-Tin-Tin and Elvis Presley, he appears in films devoted almost exclusively to himself and you know from reviews or trailers whether you are going to like him or not. In some countries it has been hard slogging, but in the US he was one of the top draws from 1951 to 1963 inclusive, with only one break (1960). For the first six of these years he was teamed with Dean Martin and they were joint top in 1952 and second on three other occasions. Critics were puzzled. Milton Shulman wrote in 1951: 'In more enlightened times it would be considered impolite, almost indecent, to be amused by such ugliness, lunacy and deformity'; and of the team he wrote: 'They represent a deterioration in humorous taste not far removed from what might be expected if the printing-press were suddenly abolished or if Attila the Hun reconquered Europe.' About 10 years later there was a move to have Lewis regarded as a genuine clown – mostly on the strength of some fine sight gags. These defenders point out how highly Lewis is regarded by some French critics – which impresses at least those who have not read the critics concerned.

He was born Joseph Levitch in Newark, New Jersey, in 1926 – the son of a couple of entertainers on the borscht circuit – and teamed up with Dean Martin exactly 20 years later, in Atlantic City, where he was doing a nightclub act (synchronizing to records). They had known each other for some time and he thought Martin would make a good feed. Their first routine was a flop; then they let rip and made people laugh. They did a successful season at the Copacabana in New York and some TV; Hal Wallis saw them at Slapsie Maxie's in Hollywood and signed them for five years – as a team, $50,000 the first year, $60,000 the second, $75,000 the third, to go to a ceiling of $175,000. He started them off in two quite modest films based on a radio series, in support of Marie Wilson, *My Friend Irma* (49) and *My Friend Irma Goes West* (50). In Lewis, Bosley Crowther recognized 'a genuine comic quality. The swift eccentricity of his movements, the harrowing features of his face and the squeal of his vocal protestations . . . have flair. His idiocy constitutes a burlesque of an idiot, which is something else again.' Other response was favourable enough for Wallis to star them: *At War With the Army*.

They began to go through the same old cut-ups which had worked for Abbott & Costello and others. The titles are mostly self-explanatory: *That's My Boy* (51), virtually stolen from them by Eddie Mayehoff, as Lewis's proud father; *Sailor Beware*, based on a 1933 play; and *Jumping Jacks* (52), as parachutists. Made before that – but released later as Paramount (Wallis's distributor) were not sure of it – was *The Stooge*, a more serious piece, about a vaudeville act. Their success

In two of their early films, Martin and Lewis joined the army and the navy. The formula was so successful that they joined a parachute brigade: Jumping Jacks *(52). Note the shadows in the sky: Hollywood was seldom so careless.*

brought a renegotiated Wallis contract – one film a year for seven years, with Wallis bidding up to any competing offers (in the event, as a team they filmed only for him). Also in 1952 they played a season at the London Palladium: they were booed on the first night and got terrible notices. (Later, none of their individual TV shows ever played Britain.) Then: *Scared Stiff* (53), a remake of *The Ghost Breakers*; *The Caddy*; *Money from Home*, from Damon Runyon's story; and *Living It Up* (54), which provoked the worst critical onslaught, being an adaptation of 'Hazel Flagg' which was a Broadway musical based on *Nothing Sacred* – Lewis had the Carole Lombard part. Around this time Martin and Lewis were reported as quarrelling. They did *Three Ring Circus*; *You're Never Too Young* (55). based on *The Major and the Minor*; and *Artists and Models*, directed by Frank Tashlin. Tashlin was almost the first of their directors to realize that their styles were incompatible. They had never been interdependent, like Laurel and Hardy, or even Abbott and Costello, and Tashlin siphoned off each to his specialities – Martin got the wise-cracks and Lewis the slapstick. All the same, 'Picturegoer' thought that this particular film 'hits a paralysing low. As a comedy team Martin & Lewis have become as dreary as Abbott & Costello.' After the split, Tashlin directed some of Lewis's best comedies. For the moment, the team simply broke from Wallis, but stayed with Paramount, with whom they signed a nine-picture deal. They only made two: *Pardners* (56), based on *Rhythm on the Range*; and *Hollywood or Bust*, with Anita Ekberg. Then they split. No official explanation was given.

Lewis's first solo effort was *The Delicate Delinquent* (57), which he also produced, with Darren McGavin in the part intended for Martin. Lewis was a janitor who yearns to be a cop and for almost the first time some merit was found in his funning. He was a misfit GI in *The Sad Sack* (58), also originally prepared for them as a team – and produced by Wallis. Wallis also produced *Rock-a-bye Baby*; Lewis produced *The Geisha Boy*; Wallis produced *Don't Give Up the Ship* (59) and *Visit to a Small Planet* (60), the latter a version of Gore Vidal's play. Vidal quickly went on record as being appalled by the casting; and the film pleased no one. With it Lewis finally left Wallis and became his own producer under a new contract with Paramount. Since the split with Martin either he or Wallis or Paramount had ensured that he was surrounded by some of the best supporting players in Hollywood and this continued to be the case; he continued to be billed alone above the title, less perhaps for reasons of economy or egotism than because no co-star was needed. Now he was also able to turn director: *The Bellboy* (in his youth he had been a bellboy). Martin was quoted by 'Variety' as saying: 'I still think he's on the wrong track. God gave him the gift to be the funniest comic the world ever saw, but whoever it was who advised him to direct, sing, dance, write and produce – what he's doing now is just plain stupid.' Tashlin directed *Cinderfella*, Lewis directed *The Ladies' Man* (61), set in a Hollywood studio, and *The Errand Boy*, one of his better films, and Tashlin directed *It's Only Money* (62). Dwight Macdonald called it 'a turgid farce' and added that 'only a Griffith or a Stroheim could have dominated Mr Lewis's irrepressible gift for over-mugging. The sad thing is that he has all the makings of a good clown, if only he didn't always Give It The Works.'

Lewis directed *The Nutty Professor* (63), and it looked as though he was breaking through (it was also his biggest commercial success *sans* Martin); but his later work became less controlled and riddled with curious attempts at pathos. *Who's Minding the Store?* (64; Tashlin), however, held a good inventive level and Tom Milne in the 'MFB' found both *The Patsy* (Lewis) and *The Disorderly Orderly* (65; Tashlin) 'patchily brilliant'. However, he wrote of *The Family Jewels*: 'it is a painful experience to watch him mugging on through seven characterizations and reams of gibberish talk without managing to raise a single laugh'. An attempt to fit Lewis into a more conventional framework, co-starring with Tony Curtis, *Boeing-Boeing*, provided Curtis with his first flop in years.

It was Lewis's last for Paramount: star and studio could not agree on terms. In 1966 he signed a non-exclusive multiple deal with Columbia – one a year, with no cut-off date. *Three on a Couch* was again conventional and flopped; Lewis returned to his usual stuff: *Way . . . Way Out!*, a space comedy for 20th, and *The Big Mouth* (67) for Columbia. Both got spotty bookings and *Don't Raise the Bridge Lower the River* (68), which he made in Britain (he was an American in London), played the lower half of double bills. His career had come full circle. *Hook, Line and Sinker* (69) hung to 'a straighter line of clowning than in his dimwit clowning days,' observed 'Variety', who noted later that it was the last of his Columbia pact: a dispute had arisen over Lewis's insistence on directing certain of his pictures – but the box-office was now very soft. Lewis told an interviewer: 'When Jerry Lewis is funny on screen, I swear to God I laugh louder than anyone. When he's funny, that is. When he's not he's the worst there is. Jerry Lewis is never just OK or adequate, he's either very funny or awful. . . .

I think of Jerry Lewis as being someone else, you see. I have to.'

He directed Peter Lawford and Sammy Davis Jr in *One More Time* in 1969, an unsuccessful sequel to their unsuccessful *Salt and Pepper*, and then moved to Warners to direct and act in *Which Way to the Front?* (70), described by 'Variety' as 'a witless self-indulgence'. There were virtually no bookings. During the latter years Lewis had tried TV, in a live two-hour show which flopped. He had also done marathons on TV for charity, which brought a blast in an interview from Elliott Gould, who said that Lewis had been a childhood idol: 'He blatantly tells you on network TV that he is the epitome of the socially conscious man, a great humanitarian. Entertainers who do something and don't tell you about it are far more admirable than he is. But to be told constantly about what he's done for muscular dystrophy! Lewis obviously needs to be loved by everybody and have them think he's wonderful. Actually, he's one of the most hostile, unpleasant guys I've ever seen. He's more diseased than the disease he's trying to combat. . . . He was an enormously talented, phenomenally energetic man who used vulnerability well. I've seen him turn into this arrogant, sour, ceremonial, piously chauvinistic egomaniac.'

In 1971 Lewis did a short season at the Olympia in Paris, after which he began a French film, in Sweden, *The Day the Clown Cried*, but it was abandoned. In 1975 he planned to do a Broadway musical, 'Feeling No Pain', but the idea was dropped; he was on Broadway the following year, after a short tour, in 'Hellzapoppin'', marked by backstage dissensions and recriminations which endured after its non-too-successful run. Producer Alexander H. Cohen sued, citing Lewis's refusal to rehearse with Lynn Redgrave as 'a primary cause of failure'. Lewis settled out of court for an estimated (by 'Variety') $100,000. But this was 'not an admission of guilt'. He returned to movies in the independently backed ($3 million) *Hardly Working* (80), directing and playing a clown. By the time it opened in Germany it had not found an American distributor and a second venture, also made in Florida and titled *That's Life*, was abandoned in 1982. In 1981 there was a bankruptcy hearing at which Lewis's annual income was estimated at $1 million annually. *Slapstick of Another Kind* (82) also premièred in Germany, with a PA by Lewis; based on a novel by Kurt Vonnegut, it turned out to be a one-joke idea with Lewis and Madeline Kahn as clever but ugly twins and their parents. Lewis got little up front but was to receive a share of the profits – which were likely to be minute as far as the US was concerned, though it did eventually open there. In the meantime Lewis had a deserved success in *The King of Comedy* (83), as the talk-show host bothered by aspiring TV star Robert DeNiro; he played him as a hollow man, one no longer likeable, though he might have been at one time. *Smorgasbord* was a sketch film with Lewis directing, producing and starring. This opened in Paris, was shelved in the US and then sold for the small screen. It certainly was a Lewis year in France, what with the première of *Retenez-moi ou je Fais un Malheur*, but 'Variety' put a damper on the occasion: 'designed to give its American star free-rein to his repertory of muggings, grimaces and idiot squeals . . . it's puzzling why he has committed himself to a film that will clearly not advance his critical or commercial fortunes'. Of *Par Où t'es Rentré on t'a Pas Vu Sortir* (84) the same paper said that Lewis 'seemed to touch bottom last year, but he has now appeared in another French-language farce (again as actor only) that reaches new depths in witlessness'. During this period his 30-year-old marriage broke up and he remarried. He also announced a sequel to *The Nutty Professor*, which has twice been postponed. He did eventually take another straight role, as the father of an epileptic girl, in *Fight for Life* (87), a tele-movie. In 1988 he and Sammy Davis Jr played Las Vegas together.

Gina Lollobrigida

The pneumatic delights of Gina Lollobrigida – what her countrymen call her 'busto provocante' – were celebrated long before those of her rivals. She was the first of the postwar European sex-bombs. Over a 20-year period she graced the cover of almost every non-specialist magazine in the Western world. The Italians fondly called her 'La Lollo' and she became famous everywhere. She has made films in her native Italy, in France, Spain, Britain and the US. She rated publicity in each country but outside Italy her box-office value was somewhat doubtful. Her achievements on-screen are less remarkable than her ability to get publicity *off* it – though she has not done that by a series of scandals. As an actress she was handicapped by a lack of intensity, lack of presence; the personality was somewhat lack-lustre. She switched from comedy to drama without varying her approach. Her sex appeal was basically that of an advertisement hoarding.

She was born in Subiaco, about 50 miles from Rome, in 1928, the daughter of a carpenter. The German retreat in 1943 dis-

Gina Lollobrigida in one of the first of her movies to be seen by foreign audiences – La Sposa non può Attendare *(49)* – The Bride Couldn't Wait.

rupted their lives and for a while the family of six – there were four daughters – lived in one room in Rome. Gina won a scholarship and studied to become a commercial artist 'but the movies found her one day when director Mario Costa stopped her on the street, and after patiently enduring her righteous tirade about men who accost respectable ladies, convinced her that all he wanted was to give her a screen test for a film he was casting' ('Film Fame'). This was *Elisir d'Amore* (46), starring Tito Gobbi. She stayed operatic for Costa through both *Follie per l'Opera* (47), with Gobbi and Beniamino Gigli, and *Pagliacci* (48), again with Gobbi, but this time in her first big part – that of Nedda (dubbed). It was her physical attractions that counted and these brought her several more offers: *Campane e Martello* (49) with Carlo Romano; *La Sposa non può Attendare*, as the bride, with Gino Cervi as a man late for his wedding when he saves a suicide from drowning; *Alina* with Amadeo Nazzari, as the wife of an elderly invalid who becomes involved with smugglers; *Miss Italia* (50), in the title-role, with Richard Ney; *Vita da Cani* with Aldo Fabrizi; and *Cuori senza Frontiere*, as a demure peasant girl, with Raf Vallone. British audiences first heard of her when she played opposite Bonar Colleano in the Roman episode of *A Tale of Five Cities*, but it was not the sort of film to which many of them wanted to go. US audiences first heard of her about the same time, when *Follie per l'Opera* was shown: she was billed as Lollo Brigida, but the same US distributor reverted to her full name on the next. In 1949 she married a Yugoslav refugee, Dr Milko Skofic, who took a series of 'sexy' stills of her (with a camera given him by Carlo Ponti). These were issued to magazines free, on condition that credit was given: Howard Hughes at RKO saw one and summoned her to Hollywood. She was there almost three months without a test; back in Rome the matter was settled by Hughes announcing that she was under contract for seven years. The actual details seem to have been vague – but she was prevented from filming in Hollywood for years.

There was plenty of work in Italy: *Achtung! Banditi* with Andrea Checchi; *Amor non ho . . . Però Però* with Renato Rascel; *La Città si Defende* (51), in a small role in her best film so far, Pietro Germi's study of the participants in a robbery; and *Enrico Caruso Leggende di una Voce* with Ermanno Randi and the voice of Mario del Monaco, a poor attempt to rival MGM's Caruso film (in the US it was called *The Young Caruso*; the posters distinguished Lollobrigida as 'Life Cover Girl'). She first attracted favourable attention internationally when Christian-Jaque chose her to co-star with Gérard Philipe in his gay swashbuckling *Fanfan-la-Tulipe*, as a daughter of the regiment. (She was dubbed into French – but this would not have alarmed her as most players in Italian films were automatically dubbed. She would use her own voice in Italian movies only after she had become an international star.) Back in Italy she did the final episode ('Phryné') of *Altri Tempi* (52), being defended on a murder charge by the amorous Vittorio De Sica, and *Moglie per una Notte*, a period comedy with Gino Cervi. The 'MFB' thought 'though quite competent and at times delightful [she] somehow fails to gain the sympathy and affection of the audience'. She returned to France to be one of the three women loved by Philipe in *Les Belles-de-Nuit*; in Italy she was *La Provinciale*, directed by Mario Soldati from a Moravia story, involved with two other men though married to professor Gabriele Ferzetti. But she did not have the weight for this sort of material. Then there was a small part in *Le Infideli* (53), as one of several women going off the rails because of Pierre Cressoy – among them Mai Britt, Anna Maria Ferrero, Irene Papas and Marina Vlady. Then she was leading lady to Errol Flynn in *Il Maestro di Don Giovanni/Crossed Swords*.

She had another good chance, in a British film, *Beat the Devil*, as Humphrey Bogart's sexy Anglophile wife. It did not do anything for her, but an Italian film increased her stock: *Pane, Amore e Fantasie* (54), as the village spitfire, with Vittorio De Sica as the local police chief. This was a worldwide success and she was inundated with offers. It was announced that she would do a film with Gregory Peck (she didn't). It was also made known that she was involved in seven lawsuits, one over Antonioni's 1953 *Donna senza Camelie*: she was sued for breach of contract when she changed her mind after reading the script – about a former Miss Italia who rises to film stardom without an ounce of ability. A former Miss Italia, Lucia Bose, in fact played the part; and it was a much better film than any that Lollobrigida made about this time.

There were three Bread, Love and . . . *movies, sparked off by the success of the first,* Pane, Amore e Fantasie *(54), with Gina Lollobrigida as the local beauty who is a thorn in the flesh of police chief Vittorio De Sica (he was in all three: Sophia Loren was the girl in the last of the trio).*

She chose to do Robert Siodmak's coloured and feeble remake of *Le Grand Jeu*, in the dual role once played by Marie Bell, with Jean-Claude Pascal in Pierre-Richard Wilm's old part of the obsessed legionnaire; and then *La Romana*, directed by Luigi Zampa from Moravia's novel. Partly because of its content – an artist's model takes to prostitution – this had been a bestseller worldwide, so the producers expected much of the film; but there was a qualified welcome, despite the participation of Daniel Gélin, Franco Fabrizi and Raymond Pellegrin as various lovers. More popular was a sequel with De Sica, *Pane Amore e Gelosia* (55), and the provocatively titled *La Donna più Bella del Mondo*, though the latter was a cobwebby biopic of soprano Lina Cavalieri, with Vittorio Gassmann as her princely lover and Robert Alda as her jealous music-master. Robert Z. Leonard directed this most banal of star-vehicles. It was a huge success in Italy – and remains Lollobrigida's

Gina Lollobrigida in her first big American film, made in Paris by an English director, Carol Reed: Trapeze *(56). On each side of her are two of the biggest leading men of the day, Tony Curtis and Burt Lancaster.*

biggest there. She announced after this that she would only make films in English – but because of her contract with Hughes these would have to be made in Europe.

It was news when she finally 'succumbed' – to United Artists for *Trapeze* (56), making with Burt Lancaster and Tony Curtis the most tiresome triangle on record (it was Curtis who was the bone of contention – strictly for the benefit of their 'act'). Her performance was not of the sort that elicits great offers; she stayed in Paris to play Esmeralda in a new version of *Notre Dame de Paris/The Hunchback of Notre Dame*, with Anthony Quinn. The year 1957 was mainly occupied in being pregnant, but she was back before the cameras in *Anna di Brooklyn* (58), with Dale Robertson, a film supposedly under the 'artistic' supervision of Vittorio De Sica. Despite the American leading men these were hardly international films and Lollobrigida was now suing Rizzoli for $300,000 damages because they had reduced their budget and plans on *Imperial Venus* from international to local 'status'. A French offer looked inviting, *La Loi* (59), what with an American director (Jules Dassin) and names like Yves Montand and Melina Mercouri (who reported that Lollobrigida ignored her on-set) . . . but it flopped.

Finally, she got into a run of American films. In Spain she made *Solomon and Sheba* for King Vidor with Yul Brynner, but the script turned it into a lesser Maureen O'Hara type vehicle – and Lollobrigida was not the actress to surmount such an obstacle. Nor was her part much livelier in *Never So Few* (60), as an Italian countess out East; Frank Sinatra starred and there was friction between them because he was a one-take man. She quarrelled with de Laurentiis over *Jovanke e le Altre/Five Marked Women*, so the part went to his wife, Silvana Mangano; and she was unfortunate with *Lady L*, began in Hollywood by George Cukor, with Tony Curtis. It was abandoned after some weeks (and later made with Sophia Loren, a lady whom Lollobrigida does not number among her friends). Instead MGM – having paid Hughes for her services – put her into *Go Naked in the World* (61), with Ernest Borgnine, as a call-girl ('Every man in town knew about Julie . . . except the man who wanted to marry her'). She had looked and acted better. *Come September*, with Rock Hudson, gave her career a lift, but not enough. She signed for three Italian films: *La Bellezza d'Ippolita* (62), as a blonde call-girl who 'settles down' with garage-owner Enrico Maria Salerno; *Venere Imperiale* (63), made at last, a dull biopic of Pauline Bonaparte, with Raymond Pellegrin as Napoleon and Stephen Boyd; and *Mare Matto*, the story of a Genovese widow who falls for a passing seaman (Jean-Paul Belmondo). We were promised a new Lollobrigida in that – an actress, not a glamour girl – and it was true that she looked plain.

There was a murky British melodrama, *Woman of Straw* (64), with Sean Connery inveigling her into helping him murder Ralph Richardson, a part which sums up the dilemma of this sort of actress. She is supposed to be mercenary (because she starved as a kid) and she is sexy (black lace underwear), but she is also sympathetic, loyal and decent-feeling (several times she leaves because she cannot go through with it). Too much of everything and not enough of anything. Connery said later that working with her was 'fraught'. In Italy she was in an episode of *Le Bambole* (65), 'Monsignor Cupido', a modernization of Boccaccio, seducing the secretary (Jean Sorel) of Monsignor (Akim Tamiroff); the film brought her and some of her co-stars into conflict with the Italian censor. Then again she and Rock Hudson were *Strange Bedfellows* and again she mistook a heavy pout for a comedy technique. She took part in the Italian film industry's all-star tribute to Alessandro Blassetti (who directed), *Io Io Io . . . e gli Altri* (66) – but like most of her recent Italian pictures it was hardly shown outside its country of origin. In France she made *Les Sultans*, a *Back Street*-type tale with Louis Jourdan, and *Hotel Paradiso*, in English, with Alec Guinness.

After that she seems to have given up great hopes of an American career: *Cervantes* (67) in Spain, with Horst Buchholz; *Le Piacevoli Notti*, with Gassmann; and *Morte ha Fatto l'Uovo*, where Jean-Louis Trintignant murdered her. She was invited back to Hollywood to play one of Bob Hope's playmates in *The Private Navy of Sgt O'Farrell* (68) and, more importantly, Mrs Campbell in *Buona Sera Mrs Campbell*, a comedy about an unmarried (Italian) mother and the three ex-GIs she has been milking for 20-odd years. Again this was a mercenary, rather nasty lady that she played for sympathy: without success. And she did not get any of the laughs going, either. Back in Italy she co-starred in Bolognini's *Un Bellissimo Novembre* (69) with Ferzetti, about a boy's passion for his aunt; and in *Stuntman* with Robert Viharo, a silly thriller where she had little to do as an avaricious divorcee. There was a European Western, *E Continuavano a Fregarsi in Milione di Dollari/Bad Man's River* (72), with Lee Van Cleef and James Mason, and a venture in Germany, *König, Dame, Bube/King, Queen, Knave* (73), with David Niven. But after two films made in Spain, the Italian *La Dove Volano le Pallottole/Where the Bullets Fly*, with Lionel Stander, and *No Encontre Rosas para Mi Madre*, with Danielle Darrieux, she left films to concentrate on photography – a hobby which had increasingly engrossed her. Some of her photographs were published between hard covers; and she was responsible for a 50-minute documentary, *Portrait of Fidel Castro* (75). She turned down a Broadway offer to appear with Jerry Lewis in 'Hellzapoppin'', but in 1977 accepted a film offer, to appear in *Widows' Nest*, in Spain; she left the project, however, a week before shooting when her contractual terms were not honoured, i.e. $75,000 to be paid into her account at that time. She made a come-back in an American mini-series, *Deceptions* (85), starring Stefanie Powers, but that was partly because Loren's asking price was much higher. And there was another, in the remake of *La Romana* (88), with Francesca Dellera in the role she played in 1954: she played her mother.

Her marriage ended in 1966, after which her name was coupled with those of several men, including Dr Christiaan Barnard's. But then, of all stars she was prone to publicity. The clue to her character may lie in another quote from 'Film Fame': '. . . an inward and self-reliant girl, she has never been dominated by a need to be liked, never made concessions to gain affection'.

Sophia Loren

In 1970 in New York Sophia Loren in a television interview talked about her marriage to producer Carlo Ponti. 'Variety' commented (7 October) 'Perhaps only Miss Loren could have made her liaison with Ponti, beginning when she was only 14, palatable to Middle America, and she did it with grace.' With Ponti behind her – and given her looks and her own iron ambition – it would have been remarkable had Loren *not* become a major screen name. But 'Variety''s remark indicates why she succeeded so much better than the other European sex-bombs launched around the same time: she is enormously sympathetic. Her physical endowments may have made her a joke on the 'Laugh-In' but she was never a figure of fun. She is an ex-beauty queen who became accepted as an actress – certainly the first ex-beauty contestant to win a Best Actress Oscar. She is not a particularly good actress. Even in the films where she has been good she has done little but project what 'Playboy' once called 'the earthy Italian super-girl'. But it just does not matter. Despite Ponti and despite too much publicity (in

The changing face of Sophia Loren. Reading top to bottom from left hand column, (1) as a starlet. *In (2) in* Aida *(53). In (3) around the time she became internationally famous. In (4) in* Boccaccio '70 *(62). In (5)* Judith *(66).*

common with all the superstars of her era) she remains Cinderella. She once made a fairy-tale, a specially concocted one – *C'era una Volta* – and it was more Perrault than Grimm or Hans Andersen. She is one of the most deliciously merry of heroines. She is gloriously alive. She was the most beautiful screen star of her generation. That is what matters.

In life, she was an illegitimate Cinderella, born in Rome in 1934. She and her mother lived in Pozzuoli, a run-down suburb of Naples, until she was 14, when she won a beauty contest; that encouraged her mother to take her back to Rome to try to push her into movies. They both worked as extras and Sophia registered as a model. Her face and figure guaranteed work, particularly in the *photo-romans* popular in Italy. Under her own name of Scicolone she was glimpsed – usually uncredited – in some dozen films, of which the first was, apparently, *Cuori sul Mare* (50), starring Jacques Sernas, followed by *Il Voto, Le Sei Moglie di Barbablu*, starring Toto, *Io Sono il Capataz*, starring Renato Rascel, and *Milano Miliardaria*. She had already met Ponti and he got her a small role in *Anna*, produced by himself and his partner for several years, Dino De Laurentiis, and starring Silvana Mangano. Mangano, coincidentally, had been an extra and when De Laurentiis fell in love and married her he made her a star – but unlike Loren, she loathed it and retired as soon as she could (she did return to films in the 60s). Whether Ponti yet had similar plans for Loren has not been disclosed: she continued in small parts, in *Il Mago per Forza* (52) with Tino Scotti, *Il Sogno di Zorro* with Walter Chiari, *E'Arrivato l'Accordatore* with Alberto Sordi and *Era Lui . . . Si Si* with Walter Chiari and Silvana Pampanini.

Ponti changed her name to Loren and got her a good part in *La Favorita*, starring Paolo Silveri, and a better one in *La Tratta della Bianche*, third-billed, after Silvana Pampanini and Eleanora Rossi-Drago – they were tarts, but she was a good girl in this white-slave melodrama. Then she starred in *Africa Sotto i Mari* (53), a silly film with underwater sequences and a trifling plot. She swam a lot. That led to *Aida*, miming to Tebaldi's voice, after which, 'officially', Ponti put her under contract. She was just another pretty girl, supposedly sexy in sweaters and low-cut blouses; technically a star, but in some dire pieces: Mauro Bolognini's *Ci Troviamo in Galleria*, a Ferraniacolor musical starring Carlo Dapporto, about a troupe of strolling players – she was the soubrette; *Carosello Napolitano* (54), a musical fantasy, in a bit role – made before 'stardom'; *La Domenica della Buona Gente*, about some Neapolitans in Rome on Sunday afternoon, with Renato Salvatori; *Il Paese dei Campanelli*, an operette in colour, with Carlo Dapporto; *Due Notti con Cleopatra*, a comedy with Alberto Sordi, as Cleo; *Pellegrini d'Amore* with Enrico Viarisio; and *Un Giorno in Pretura*, a pleasant sketch-film with Peppino De Filippo, Sordi, Chiari, etc. More and more frequently she was in the films produced by Ponti and De Laurentiis, and after starring her in *Miseria e Nobilità*, an adaptation of Scarpetta's Neapolitan comedy, a period piece with Toto, they put her in one of their early 'international' efforts, *Attila Flagello di Dio* (55), albeit in a small role, as a native girl tempting Hun Anthony Quinn. Then they put her in a film bound to attract critical attention outside Italy, because it was directed by Vittorio De Sica, his sketch-film *L'Oro di Napoli*, as a volatile Neapolitan shopkeeper.

Attila evoked little interest outside Italy and nor, more surprisingly, did the De Sica – partly because it was cut and dubbed by Paramount and other distributors, so that it was neither 'commercial' nor 'art'. But those critics who had seen the original were agreeably surprised that she had more to offer than just, um, a pretty face. She could act, she had presence. She was not just another sex-bomb – as which she was already known abroad, despite the fact that her movies had been either not distributed at all or dismissed. (Later, she always claimed that De Sica taught her all she knew of her craft.) Ponti took great care with the next. Mangano had become internationally famous paddling about in wet clothes in the rice-fields of *Riso Amaro*, so Loren would wear equally wet and revealing garments as *La Donna del Fiume* – also a study of bucolic passions – as she dithered, voluptuous and busty, between steady Gerard Oury and handsome muscular no-good smuggler Rik Battaglia. As hoped, and dubbed into English, the film was widely shown in the US and Britain; and, if not exactly creating a stampede, it did pave the way for: *Peccato che Sia una Canaglia*, a comedy directed by Blasetti and written by Moravia, as the daughter of crook De Sica pursued by honest Marcello Mastroianni; *Il Segno di Venere*, another comedy, in which De Sica, Raf Vallone, Sordi and Peppino De Filippo were all nuts about her; a new version of *La Bella Mugnaia*, the fable that was the basis of 'The Three-Cornered Hat', with De Sica as the governor and Mastroianni as the miller; and *Pane Amore e . . .* (56), with De Sica, replacing Gina Lollobrigida in the last of the 'Bread and Love' series, now that that lady had Hollywood offers. (It was perhaps inevitable, in any case, that there would be a rivalry between the two. Years later, Gina was to say: 'Sophia is a very pretty girl but she cannot threaten me because she is incapable of playing my roles'; and Sophia: 'Her personality is limited. She is good as a peasant but incapable of playing a lady.')

Ponti deemed that Loren was also ready for Hollywood, which – after considering the space she commanded in the world's magazines – was waiting with open arms. First, a Hollywood name, Charles Boyer, was engaged for *La Fortuna di Essere Donna*, a – tedious – comedy directed by Blasetti (De Sica and Mastroianni were also in it). Then she accepted a couple of American films locationing in Europe: *Boy on a Dolphin* (57), opposite Alan Ladd, as a Greek peasant diver after archaeological prizes (and how that dress clung to her as she climbed out of the water); and, actually filmed first, *The Pride and the Passion*, as Frank Sinatra's fiery Spanish peasant mistress, drawn to Cary Grant (she got $25,000 for it, replacing Ava Gardner, who turned it down). It could not be said that her screen personality was very interesting and she was equally lost in *Legend of the Lost* as an Arab slave-girl loved by John Wayne. In 1957 she and Ponti were married in Mexico and because he had been married before there was a long series of legal complications to placate Italian morality (one Italian Catholic magazine recommended its readers to avoid her films), including, later, the taking-up of French citizenship and a further ceremony in 1966.

Ponti, meanwhile, had negotiated a deal with Paramount (four films in three years; Paramount also distributed three further films which he produced in conjunction with them), but they were all mad to think she was up to the demands of Eugene O'Neill's *Desire Under the Elms* (58), with Burl Ives and Anthony Perkins as the father-son sides of the triangle. She progressed to adequate in *The Key*, for United Artists in Britain, but her ability hardly mattered in that particular film – she had become so beautiful. She improved in each of her Paramount films; it was as if she was shaking off a somnambulism induced by the shock of finding herself in Hollywood. A comedy with Cary Grant, *Houseboat*, did excavate some of her gaiety; and she gave capable performances in Martin Ritt's *Black Orchid* (59), as a widow wooed by widower Anthony Quinn – for which she was Best Actress at Venice, and Stanley Lumet's *That Kind of Woman*, as a kept woman wooed by GI Tab Hunter. Both were failures and so, more seriously, was Cukor's exquisite period Western, *Heller in Pink Tights* (60) with Quinn, in which she was the star of a troupe of strolling players. *It Started in Naples* did much better; she was cast, judiciously, opposite Clark Gable, as a Neapolitan who teaches him the ways of Old Europe – and got easily her best notices to date. But Paramount had lost faith in her and it was not restored by *A Breath of Scandal/Olympia*, a flat Italian-American-Austrian soufflé – based on a play by Molnar, about a self-willed Habsburg princess who falls for American John Gavin.

She did not actually work in Hollywood afterwards (being there was no longer essential to world stardom). A deal with Allied Artists fell through and Ponti set about getting the acclaim he wanted for her by other means. He sent her to Britain for a film which combined, hopefully, prestige and popularity, *The Millionairess* with Peter Sellers, directed – poorly – by Anthony Asquith, in a role that Shaw had written for Edith Evans. It was mildly popular and she looked devastating. In Italy he cast her in *La Ciociara* (61), with De Sica directing from a Moravia novel ('Two Women'), about a widow and her daughter in

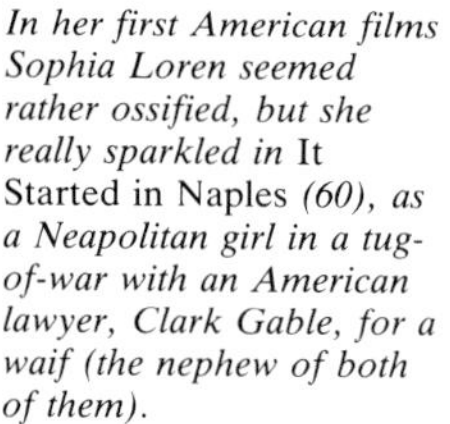
In her first American films Sophia Loren seemed rather ossified, but she really sparkled in It Started in Naples *(60), as a Neapolitan girl in a tug-of-war with an American lawyer, Clark Gable, for a waif (the nephew of both of them).*

Loren gave a fine, moving performance in La Ciociara *(61)* – Two Women – *as a woman coping with conditions in war-time Italy. Jean-Paul Belmondo played the student who silently worshipped her. Below, in a room above the Piazza Navona, call-girl Sophia Loren does a striptease for one of her visitors (Marcello Mastroianni):* Ieri Oggi e Domani *(64)* – Yesterday, Today and Tomorrow.

war-torn Italy. Stanley Kauffmann wrote: 'Physically, Sophia Loren is not as suited for the part as, say, Anna Magnani might have been [when originally announced, Magnani was to have played the widow, Loren the daughter; Eleanora Brown played the daughter]. But her beauty does not prevent her from giving a full-blooded performance, earthy and female, brimming with laughter and sex and devotion and selfishness. I hope – in vain, I know – that Miss Loren will never again make films outside Italy. On her own ground (like her heroine), and especially with the help of De Sica, she is splendid.' She won the Best Actress award at Cannes, a Best Actress Oscar – the first to go to a performer in a foreign-language film (though the dubbed version had been a hit in the US) – the New York critics' award and the BFA Best Foreign Actress.

Not heeding Kauffmann's advice, Loren made *El Cid* in Spain and was inhibited either by the cost of the thing or by the nobility of Charlton Heston; but was happily rumbustious again in De Sica's episode in *Boccaccio '70* (62), the best of the three (the others were Visconti directing Romy Schneider, Fellini directing Anita Ekberg), and in a new French version of *Madame Sans-Gêne*, with Robert Hossein as Napoleon. For the second year running she was the best Foreign Actress in the 'Cinémonde' poll. The Oscar had restored her international status, but three English-speaking efforts almost killed it again: *Le Couteau dans la Plaie/Five Miles to Midnight* (63), an absurd thriller with Anthony Perkins; *I Sequestrati di Altona/The Condemned of Altona*, De Sica's abused version of Sartre's play; and *The Fall of the Roman Empire* (64), as a Roman princess, the daughter of Alec Guinness. Ponti wisely took her back to Italy, for two De Sica efforts with Mastroianni: *Ieri Oggi e Domani*, a three-part film as (1) a pregnant Neapolitan slum wife, (2) the unhappy wife of a Milanese businessman and (3) a Roman call-girl; and *Matrimonio all'Italiana*, based on De Filippo's 'Filumena', as a Neapolitan whore who gets Mastroianni to the altar after 20 years. Both were mild entertainments, but they made plenty of coin for US distributor Joseph Levine, very high on the Ponti-Loren team after the success of *La Ciociara*.

Ponti, however, had made a production deal with MGM: *Operation Crossbow* (65), with Loren in a small role as a Dutch war widow; and *Lady L*, in a very big role as a Paris *poule* who marries into the British aristocracy. While he made other films for that company, she was more assorted nationalities for other producers: *Judith* (66), as the Jewish wife of a war criminal, helping the

Few people in Britain or the US went to C'era una Volta *(67), which was a pity for several reasons. For one, Sophia Loren had never looked so beautiful.*

Israeli underground; *Arabesque*, as the Arab mistress of Alan Badel, helping Gregory Peck; and Chaplin's *A Countess from Hong Kong* (67), in the title-role but in fact a Russian ex-whore, seducing Marlon Brando. If the press liked none of these films, they annihilated that one, though her own notices were, as usual, good. Returning to Ponti and MGM she did her fairy-tale concoction – peasant girl wooed and won by Prince Charming (Omar Sharif) – *C'era una Volta*, directed by Francesco Rosi; retitled *More Than a Miracle* for the US and *Cinderella Italian Style* for Britain, it proved to be too alien for these audiences. *Questi Fantasmi* (68) was called *Ghosts Italian Style* on its few B dates in New York: the critics who noticed it slaughtered it and it has never been shown in Britain. With it, the Ponti-MGM tie-up came to an end (and, presumably, the days of Loren's $1 million a picture fee).

Despite this dismal track record, in 1969 Loren was presented with the Golden Globe given annually by the US Press Association Foreign Corps to the world's most popular star (Sidney Poitier won for the men). Outside the Anglo-Saxon market her films had, by and large, remained popular; within it, she herself received proof of her own standing with the enormous interest and sympathy shown her when she gave birth to a baby (1969) after a series of miscarriages. For her return to the screen Ponti prepared a reunion with De Sica and Mastroianni, with Levine distributing, *I*

Girasoli (70), as an Italian war 'widow' seeking her husband in the USSR. Ponti proved as inept as ever in gauging Anglo-American taste, but it was a success in Italy; as was *La Moglie del Prete* (71) with Mastroianni – but that was an even bigger flop in the US and Britain, a sad augury as the first of a new deal with Warner Bros. *Mortadella* (72) was the second and she was a girl having trouble with Immigration because of some cheese: retitled *Lady Liberty*, it got few US bookings. Columbia had *Bianco, Rosso e . . .*, and rechristened it *White Sister* (Loren was a bereaved mother who falls in love after becoming a nun), but they never bothered to show it – partly because of the flop of *Man of La Mancha*: the fault was not Loren's, whose notices were not bad – but its box-office reception could hardly have justified her salary of $750,000 (and even less Peter O'Toole's $1 million). She had another child and made a French film with an admired actor, Jean Gabin: *Verdict* (74), in which she was a concerned mother. For an admired and loved director, De Sica, she made *Il Viaggio/The Trip*, based on a Pirandello novel about a woman who marries the brother (Ian Bannen) of the man she loves – who was Richard Burton. With Burton she did *Brief Encounter* for US TV and cinemas elsewhere – but after its American reception it was not chanced in cinemas anywhere, or at least in Britain where it was made: Rank (who owned the rights) sold it to TV, and though Loren did not get her share of the ridicule it was agreed that casting her as a plain, ordinary British housewife was *not* a good idea. *La Pupa del Gangster* (75), with Mastroianni, was another that did not make it to the US market. Nor did *Angela* (76), a Canadian modernization of 'Oedipus'.

Meanwhile, Ponti had announced various plans for her – including a Russian *Anna Karenina* – which had come to nothing; *The Cassandra Crossing* (77) was to have been the first Italian-Iranian co-production, the first of many – but this souped-up adventure came out instead with British and West German money: Loren was one of the endangered passengers. British audiences had not been kind for some time, having stayed away from the very few Loren pictures shown, and they refused to go to a dubbed version of *Una Giornata Particolare*: Americans who saw the original liked it more – in which she, as a housewife, wrested neighbour Mastroianni from homosexuality, if only temporarily. She was one of the few star actresses around who could make the situation believable; and the film's (guarded) US success and her enduring beauty reawakened Hollywood interest. Audience interest, however, was not stirred by two daft thrillers, *The Brass Target* with John Cassavetes, about a plot to assassinate General Patton, and *Firepower* (79) with James Coburn, a Caribbean chase story – despite a concurrent bestseller, 'Sophia: Living and Loving'. She made headlines with that, as she had being mugged and robbed in New York of $500,000-worth of jewellery, and being held by the Italian authorities for her and Ponti's supposed tax irregularities. However, in Italy she made a film for Lena Wertmuller (a compatriot whose US success is much harder to fathom), *Fatto di Sangue fra Due Uomini per Causa di Una Vedova, Si Sospetto Moventi Politici/Blood Feud* (80), playing a Sicilian widow caught between lawyer Mastroianni and American gangster Giancarlo Giannini. It was to have been the second of Wertmuller's three-picture English-language deal with Warners, but that had been cancelled after the failure of the first: it was taken up by Lew Grade despite that and its dismal flop on its home territory. It failed also in foreign territories.

The next venture was even more peculiar, a long tele-movie called *Sophia: Her Own Story*, based on her autobiography. She played herself in later life and her own mother, while Ritz Brown was her as a teenager. Playing herself, she said, was 'a strange sensation' and this stilted affair may have been a way of keeping her name before the public after a decade of movie failures. Only by the skin of her teeth did she retain her dignity (could you imagine Ingrid Bergman appearing in a movie about her affair with Rossellini?) – for this piece shows her living with Ponti while having an affair with Cary Grant, played by John Gavin (Grant was said to have been furious about this revelation in the book). It was true that Ponti in the book admitted to extramarital affairs; in January 1982 the 'Daily Mail' reported that she was estranged from him, that he had the children and that she was living with a French businessman. She has refused to comment on her marriage – when, for instance, promoting her book on beauty or the perfume named after her. One feature of her career at this point is the number of projects announced which never materialized – though the one she still hopes to do is play Maria Callas. Those which came to fruition were all for American TV: *Aurora* (84), in which she cheats some old lovers into paying for an eye operation for her son – played by her son Éduoardo, one of several members of her family involved; *Courage* (86), a mini-series, as a mother whose son has become hooked on drugs; and another mini, *The Fortunate Pilgrim* (88), from Mario Puzo's autobiographical novel, as wife and mother in a tapestry of Italian immigrant life through much of this century. By this time she was reconciled to Ponti, who arranged for her to play her old role, for television this time, in *La Ciociara* (89). She was now closer to the right age for it, but it is another credit of dubious value.

PETER LORRE

For almost 30 years Peter Lorre provided films with one of their most memorable villains. He was a whispering menace, with an indefinable European accent, moving silently into view with a deceptively friendly smile. There was nothing, however, very welcoming about *that*; his eyes remained sad. He was a man resigned to the follies of others, clasping to himself his own fastidiousness like a fetish. He occasionally played a hero or a good man, but one never quite warmed to him in that guise. He did not know how to make goodness interesting. There have been claims that he was limited by Hollywood's type-casting, but he seems rather to have been limited by his small stature and his individuality. He wanted to play better parts – but then, so did most of those other outstanding bogey-men. Perhaps by doing what they were made to do they left a more indelible mark on the movies of that era than the leading men.

Lorre was born Laszlo Löwenstein in Rosenberg, Hungary, in 1904; the family, a prosperous one, moved to Vienna. He left his studies at 17 to join a theatrical troupe and, except for a brief spell as a bank clerk, made a living for a while by entertaining in cafés and in one-man performances and readings. In 1924 he acted in repertory in Breslau and appeared in Zürich playing an old man in a production of Galsworthy's 'Loyalties'. He arrived in Berlin in 1929, reputedly with only 10 marks in his pocket, and apparently had little difficulty in getting the lead in 'Die Pioniere von Inglostadt', as a sex maniac. He also appeared in Wedekind's 'Spring Awakening' and, among other plays, Brecht's 'Happy End' and 'Mann ist Mann'. There have been reports that he appeared in the film of the Wedekind play, but he is not listed among the cast. His first film would seem to be *M* (31), in the lead – chosen by Fritz Lang on the strength of his work in the Wedekind. He played a psychopathic child-killer hounded by police and public, and finally tried by a kangaroo court: a subtle study in degeneracy (based on fact), with the cops-and-robbers conventions of the period. The film assured him a degree of success and he made several more movies: *Bomben auf Monte Carlo*, with Anna Sten; *Die Koffer des Herrn O.F.*, a small-town comedy, as a wily journalist; *Fünf von der Jazzband* (32), with Jenny Jugo, in a small role; *Der Weisse Damon*, a drug-running thriller, with Hans Albers, as a hunchback; *FPI Antwortet Nicht*, with Albers, as one of the team trying to destroy the landing platform in the middle of the Atlantic (he was also in the concurrent French version *FPI ne Répond pas*); *Was Frauen Traumen* (33); and *Unsichtbare Gegner*. After the Nazis came to power, he declined to make any more films for UFA; he was the favourite actor of Goebbels, who made representations to him to continue – this, despite the fact that he was a Jew (as a Hungarian citizen, he enjoyed immunity). He left voluntarily for Vienna, where he made *Schuss im Morgengrauen*, produced by another refugee from Berlin, Sam Spiegel; but when there was no more work to be had there, went on to Paris, where he appeared in Pabst's *De Haut en Bas* (34), with Jean Gabin. He arrived, and left, broke. The worldwide success of *M* had brought offers from Hollywood to play similar roles, but he was not interested.

He accepted an offer from Alfred Hitchcock in Britain to play the inhuman professional assassin in *The Man Who Knew Too Much* and Hitchcock built the part up (years later, Hitchcock recalled his 'sharp sense of humour'; earlier, Lorre had said that his English was not good enough to understand Hitchcock's jokes, but he laughed anyway). When he had learnt English, he sailed for the States. For eight months he sifted through offers before agreeing to do Karl Freund's remake of *The Hands of Orlac* at MGM, called *Mad Love* (35). Between them they managed a Gothic eeriness and, as expected from former cameraman Freund, it was visually impressive. Lorre's obsessed doctor, gleamingly pated and dandified, was a villain for connoisseurs. His second American film also met his standards: von Sternberg's elementary version of *Crime and Punishment*. He was too old as Raskolnikov, but suggested both the amplitude and the guilt-racked nerves. His pursuer, the inspector, was Edward Arnold. A French version with Pierre Blanchar and Harry Baur had been seen in New York some months previously and the American one suffered by comparison. Columbia, who produced, looked upon it solely as a prestige item; and offered Lorre a five-year contract at $1,000 a week. He refused and returned to Britain for another Hitchcock film, *Secret Agent* (36), with John Gielgud, as another agent – disguised as a mad Mexican general. Back in Hollywood, he was fun as the hypersensitive chief of a spy-ring (after the plans of a new airliner) in *Crack-Up* – and the plot did just that too. 20th produced and offered Lorre a three-year contract. This time, no doubt from expediency, he accepted.

He had a good role in an efficient melodrama about a kidnapping, *Nancy Steele is Missing* (37), as Victor McLaglen's cell-mate, a professor with homicidal tendencies. Then 20th put him into what was intended as the first of a series, *Think Fast Mr Moto* (37), as a wily and humorous Japanese detective, Mr Moto. The character had been invented by novelist John P. Marquand: 20th were interested in the books because they had another popular B series at that time, about a Chinese detective, Charlie Chan. (Monogram also had an Oriental detective, a Mr Wong.) After *Lancer Spy*, in which he played a German officer, there were three more: *Thank You Mr Moto*, perhaps the best of the series; *Mr Moto's Gamble* (38); and *Mr Moto Takes a Chance*. The second of this trio had begun as a Charlie Chan vehicle, but was made over for Lorre when the current Chan – Warner Oland – died, though retaining Keye Luke in his usual role as Lee Chan. It was directed by James Tinling, though Norman Foster was the usual director. Lorre then played with Warner Baxter in the remake of an Italian film written by Cesare Zavattini and Giaci Mondaini, *I'll Give a Million*, the two of them millionaires disguised as hobos on the Riviera. Then there were some more in the series: *The Mysterious Mr Moto, Mr Moto's Last Warning* (39), *Mr Moto on Danger Island* and *Mr Moto Takes a Vacation*.

Which was what Mr Lorre also did. Hs contract was up; after some months of idleness he returned as a freelance: *Strange Cargo* (40), with Clark Gable, as a crawly stool-pigeon, M'sieu Pig; *I Was an Adventuress*, with Erich von Stroheim an accomplice of Vera Zorina; and *Island of Doomed Men*, in which he owned a Pacific island and listened to Chopin when not flogging his slaves. The 'New York Times' observed that Hollywood only used 'his tricks but not his talent'. *Stranger on the Third Floor* – he had the title-role, as a murderer hiding out – might have been better: some critics thought it intelligent, some merely pretentious. He was hardly happier in *You'll Find Out*, with Boris Karloff and Bela Lugosi as the would-be murderers of band-leader Kay Kyser; or *Mr District Attor-*

Peter Lorre's distinctive but sinister screen personality was cleverly used on many occasions, but never more memorably than in The Maltese Falcon *(41), with a fine cast playing a* galère *of people chiefly up to no good. Of course, Humphrey Bogart and Mary Astor.*

ney, supporting Dennis O'Keefe, in this Republic thriller based on a radio series. And he was up to familiar tricks in *The Face Behind the Mask* (41), directed by Robert Florey, as an immigrant driven to crime to pay for plastic surgery. He was a double-crossing Chinese skipper – with a wispy beard – in *They Met in Bombay*, with Gable.

Then Warner Bros. asked him to play one of the dubious characters in *The Maltese Falcon* – not so much dubious as deadly, as long as there is a gun in his hand. Otherwise, cowardly and querulous with his spats and frizzy hair and perfumed calling-card: it is always a surprise (no matter how often you see it) when he turns out to be in league with Sidney Greenstreet. Warners kept him on to do *All Through the Night* (42), again with Bogart, this time partnering Conrad Veidt in Nazi skulduggery and murder in the US. And they liked him enough to sign him to a five-year contract. Meanwhile, he fulfilled two commitments: *The Boogie Man Will Get You*, hopefully a horror comedy with Boris Karloff; and *Invisible Agent*, about an invisible spy in Germany, as a baron.

His period at Warners was to be both productive and rewarding. He was, with Sidney Greenstreet, the ace villain of their stock company, but he also played a couple of heroes. He was his usual screen self in *Casablanca*, as a weaselly little man who can get stolen visas ('*Now* are you impressed with me?') and will be revealed as a murderer; but in *The Constant Nymph* (43), as a continental musician, he would not be an unworthy aspirant to the hand of the heroine. In *Background To Danger*, with George Raft, he was a Russian agent; in *The Cross of Lorraine*, at MGM, a German sergeant; in *Passage to Marseilles* (44) he was French, a fellow con of Bogart. He found himself the hero in *The Mask of Dimitrios*, a wary thriller-writer who becomes involved with the supposedly dead Dimitrios (Zachary Scott) and the mysterious Mr Roberts (Greenstreet): a good film which, despite wartime difficulties, captures both the cosmopolitan flavour and the sinewy quality of Eric Ambler's novel. He and Greenstreet were partnered again in *Conspirators* and *Hollywood Canteen*; he was back on familiar ground in *Confidential Agent* (45), as a measly Spanish exile who betrays Charles Boyer and is killed by him. He was no stranger to sudden death – or even a lingering one: in *Hotel Berlin* he was a sickly savant who drank himself to death. He starred, with Greenstreet, in *Three Strangers* (46), a modest mystery; was loaned out for *Black Angel*, as a shady saloon-owner, and *The Chase*, as the sardonic sidekick of gang-leader Steve Cochran. His Warner contract concluded with two starring parts: *The Verdict*, with Greenstreet, and *The Beast With Five Fingers*, a good thriller in which he was strangled by a disembodied hand.

Freelancing again, he hoped for varied parts to play; but in *My Favorite Brunette* (47) he was simply one of the baddies (the funniest, called Kismet) after Bob Hope. He was the police inspector in *Casbah* (48), a horrendous remake of you-know-what with Yvonne de Carlo, and Tony Martin as a singing (Harold Arlen songs) Pepe. He worked sparingly. In *Rope of Sand* (49), with Burt Lancaster, he was appropriately called 'Toady'; that year he appeared in vaudeville in New York, at the Paramount. His career at a low ebb, he appeared in a B thriller with Mickey Rooney, *Quicksand* (50), and in the British *Double Confession*, a silly thriller with Derek Farr and Joan Hopkins. He returned to Germany, where he wrote, produced and directed *Der Verlorene* (51), a study of Nazi mentality, and also played the lead – a scientist who becomes a homicidal maniac. It was an abject failure and not exported till later – it was perhaps too frank for the Germans to encourage its showing.

He remained off the screen till persuaded back by John Huston and Bogart, to play perhaps a distant cousin of the *Falcon*'s Joel Cairo, a fat (now) and foppish continental, pettishly insisting his name is O'Hara: *Beat the Devil* (53). After that he worked fairly regularly, sometimes in quite small roles: Disney's *20,000 Leagues Under the Sea* (54), as Paul Lukas's assistant; *Congo Crossing* (56), an idiotic 'political' tale with Virginia Mayo, almost saved by his hammy, smiling commander; *Around the World in 80 Days*, as a Japanese steward; *The Buster Keaton Story* (57), as a temperamental movie director; *Silk Stockings*, as a drunken commissar; and *The Story of Mankind*, as Nero. His career finished, unhappily, in a series of Bs, horror films and Jerry Lewis vehicles: *Hell Ship Mutiny*, with Jon Hall; *The Sad Sack*, with Lewis, as an Arab; *The Big Circus* (59), with Victor Mature, as a clown; *Scent of Mystery*, as a devil's advocate; *Voyage to the Bottom of the Sea* (61), as the commodore; *Tales of Terror* (62), a Roger Corman version of some Poe stories, in 'The Black Cat' (which incorporated 'The Cask of Amontillado'); *Five Weeks in a Balloon*, again as an Arab; *The Raven* (63), more Corman-Poe, as a magician; *Comedy of Terrors*, with Boris Karloff; and *The Patsy* (64), with Lewis, again as a movie director.

In 1959 while filming in Spain he was seriously ill with high blood pressure. He died of a stroke in 1964. He married four times; a divorce was pending at the time of his death.

SHIRLEY MACLAINE

When she appeared, there had never been anyone quite like her in films. She was, as Francis Wyndham once suggested, 'the first American crystallization of a type common in Europe – the Bohemian girl.' She was not at all like a movie star (there have been countless movie stars who were not like movie stars, who were photographed cooking or bathing the baby – Shirley MacLaine is not even like *them*). She is the friendly kookie (a word she loathes) girl you met at a party in the village – like Gittel in *Two for the See-Saw*. That is not to say that she played herself, but it was a supreme case of type-casting; most of the characteristics which William Gibson wrote into that part are common to most MacLaine characters – she is warm, off-beat, frank, enthusiastic, understanding, excitable, with a wry/funny disregard for her own ego and appearance. 'I guess I'm happiest when I'm looking reasonably like a slob,' she said once. Norma Shearer she is not.

The appeal is partly that of the waif. 'You haven't got enough sense to come in out of the rain unless someone holds your hand,' Sinatra said to her in *Some Came Running* and that summed up that character pretty well. She has within her, she says, pockets of compassion, which is why she plays doormats so well. But she is not so much plucky as enormously good-humoured. She is a delicious comedienne. When she played a Paris whore in *Irma-la-Douce* she had a cool line for one of her customers: 'I never remember a face.' 'Variety' observed that no other actress could make it so funny and so inoffensive – while retaining the obvious meaning.

She was born in Richmond, Virginia, in 1934 (Warren Beatrty is her brother). Her parents had been in show business and they put her in ballet class when she was three; she made her professional début in one of the Richmond Mosque recitals. In 1950, while still in high school, she applied for a job in a New York revival of 'Oklahoma!' and was taken on for the chorus. Things were tough after that and for a while she danced around a fridge at an electrical appliances show; some TV work followed, and modelling. She was in the chorus of 'Me and Juliet' and then 'The Pajama Game'; in that she also understudied Carol Haney, the second lead. Haney got sick and MacLaine went on for her and was 'discovered'. In the resulting brouhaha, there was only one concrete offer – from Hal Wallis, two films a year for seven years. She managed to beat him down to five years, starting at $600 a week.

Her first film was for Hitchcock, who saw a test that Wallis had had made: *The Trouble With Harry* (55) – the trouble was, he was dead and, like Cock Robin, several people claimed credit. MacLaine played the widow, the central character. There were no names, as Paramount had no faith in this *comédie noire* – and were proved right: despite the low budget, it was the only money-losing film of Hitchcock's in a long while. The press, however, had liked it and had warmly welcomed MacLaine. She later wrote: 'To me stardom was not a goal; it was a by-product. I wanted to do what I was able to do with all my might. To do otherwise seemed not only wasteful but dangerous.'

Wallis made her a model in *Artists and Models* – the one who got Jerry Lewis in the end. She found it an 'excruciating' experience because that team (Martin and Lewis) were breaking up – and she did not know what she was doing. 'Variety' said she played the role with 'bridling cuteness'. Still, she had qualities that Mike Todd needed for his campy Hindu princess in *Around the World in 80 Days* (56): she thought herself miscast. Wallis had lost interest. She did TV and tested unsuccessfully for the lead in *Marjorie Morningstar*. She toured in 'The Sleeping Prince' and when it came to Los Angeles Wallis saw it; as a result he cast her as Shirley Booth's daughter in *Hot Spell* (58). He managed to loan her to MGM for a programmer with Glenn Ford, *The Sheepman*, playing a tomboy, and to Paramount for another Shirley Booth vehicle, *The Matchmaker*, as the milliner. She was a critics' pet already, but Hollywood was unimpressed – except Frank Sinatra, who caught her on 'The Dinah Shore Show' singing 'Blue Moon' and thought her wistful quality right for a part for which they had failed to get Shelley

For most of Some Came Running *(58), Frank Sinatra is in love with a schoolteacher (Martha Hyer). Then, suddenly, he ups and marries a B-girl he has befriended, Shirley MacLaine.*

Winters – the woebegone but infinitely cheerful floozie of *Some Came Running*. MGM, producing, offered Wallis $75,000 for her services and he said they could have her at half that price (and he would pay her her normal salary of $10,600). As a result of rave notices and an Oscar nomination she was soon worth a helluva lot more; she and Wallis feuded throughout most of 1959 and at the last minute she refused to play another hooker, in *That Kind of Woman* (Barbara Nichols replaced her).

At MGM she got another good part, in *Ask Any Girl* (59) with David Niven, the good old Hollywood standby about the country chick who makes out in New York via a mixture of guile and guilelessness. Both she and the film were contemporary and droll; and she won a BFA award as the year's Best Actress. For Wallis she did *Career*, as a hard-drinking showbiz type who marries and then deserts Anthony Franciosa, a film which did nothing for *her* career (nor those of co-stars Carolyn Jones and Dean Martin). She was about to start *Who Was That Lady?* when Sinatra insisted on her as his co-star in *Can-Can* (60), and now Wallis asked and got $250,000 for her services. She played an independent saloon-owner and struggled gamely against overwhelming odds, including her costumes. For Sinatra she did a guest appearance, unbilled, in *Ocean's Eleven*. Her career revived when Billy Wilder had the notion to team her with Jack Lemmon in *The Apartment*, a bitter comedy concerned with the philanderings of some Park Avenue execs, including Fred MacMurray, who was taking lift-girl MacLaine to Lemmon's flat. Due to quite superlative work by both leading players (she was voted Best Actress at Venice and by the BFA again) the film won a Best Picture Oscar and was a huge box-office success.

After that it was sad to see her in a series of sub-standard efforts, beginning with a not unlikeable comedy with Dean Martin, *All in a Night's Work* (61), again as a naïve chick dodging men with designs. But *Two Loves*, from Sylvia Ashton-Warner's 'Spinster', about a New Zealand schoolteacher, was 'one of the year's more inexplicable films, remarkable . . . for its wanton misuse of Shirley MacLaine's talent' (Penelope Houston in the 'MFB'). The co-stars were Laurence Harvey and Jack Hawkins: it did dreadful business. *The Children's Hour* found her serious again and a teacher again – one who suspects that she has lesbian tendencies; her playing and that of Audrey Hepburn helped to make it

Jack Lemmon and Shirley MacLaine as friendly co-workers in The Apartment *(60); after an unhappy love affair and an attempted suicide, he realizes he loves her. With them at the office is Hope Holiday.*

bearable. *My Geisha* (62) was an overlong but pretty comedy about an American movie star who poses as a geisha in order to get the lead in her husband's version of 'Madame Butterfly', he, of course, not recognizing her. Yves Montand was the husband; MacLaine's real-life husband, Steve Parker, was one of the producers. (They had married in 1954 and remain married for a long time, though his home was in Japan and hers in the US and then Britain.)

There were four box-office successes, the first of which was good: *Two for the See-Saw*, where she teamed well with Robert Mitchum. Wilder put her and Jack Lemmon together again in *Irma-la-Douce* and she was fun, in the title-role, but the film was not (it is Wilder's least favourite of his films). Still, encouraged by the star names and the prospect of some brothel scenes – till then a rarity in American films – the public turned up in huge numbers. So they did, more surprisingly, for *What a Way to Go* (63), in which she had an unfortunate habit of getting widowed. All-star husbands included Mitchum and Paul Newman; and as it wound its unfunny way, a suspicion was formed – not for the first time – that MacLaine was exceptionally dependent on her material (this was written by Comden and Green but director J. Lee Thompson put the kiss of death on it). Certainly in the middle episode of *The Yellow Rolls-Royce* (64), hampered by Alain Delon and a feeble Terence Rattigan script, she was singularly unimpressive as a gangster's moll. She was well paid, though. Jeanne Moreau earned $67,660, George C. Scott and Omar Sharif each got $75,000, Alain Delon $99,000, Rex Harrison $240,000, Ingrid Bergman $275,000: but MacLaine took home $560,000.

Meanwhile, there was litigation with Wallis; at the end of 1962 he had summoned her for what she called a 'real tacky' subject, *First Wife*, claiming that her five-year contract was still in force as she had had so much time off for travelling. She did not make the picture. There was litigation over her next film, *John Goldfarb Please Come Home*, when the Notre-Dame football team sued 20th, claiming their name had been used without permission. They need not have bothered: when the film was eventually shown it sank immediately and has not been heard of since. Maybe that was why 20th cancelled the film of an old Broadway musical, *Bloomer Girl*, designed as a vehicle for MacLaine: she sued for, and got, her $750,000 fee.

She was off the screen for two years (discouraged?) and *Gambit* (66), a thriller with Michael Caine, proved to be no comeback vehicle; but it was scintillating entertainment beside *Sept Fois Femme/Woman Times Seven* (67), a French-American hybrid made by the once-great Italian team of De Sica and Zavattini. In seven witless episodes she essayed seven different Frenchwomen and was frequently blamed by critics for the tiresomeness of the whole picture. Nor was it evident that she was once a critics' pet when it came to reviewing *The Bliss of Mrs Blossom* (68), an obtuse British comedy with James Booth.

Rescue came at the eleventh hour, when Universal entrusted her with the title-role in their big-budgeted *Sweet Charity* – a part *made* for her – a trusting, misused but optimistic taxi-dancer. Gwen Verdon, who had done it on Broadway, helped coach her and Verdon's husband, Bob Fosse, directed. MacLaine got raves. 'Variety' thought it her 'finest and most versatile screen performance to date', adding 'Miss MacLaine's earlier highlights pale in comparison to her work here. Her unique talents as a comic tragedienne, or tragic comedienne, are set off to maximum impact.' The film was well received generally, but was a box-office failure (almost certainly due to the ending: most people found the last 30 minutes too good – too sad – too depressing). MacLaine was partly blamed and producer Mike Frankovitch singled her out as one of the many stars not drawing people into cinemas: 'Universal failed three times with Shirley MacLaine, yet still gave her $800,000 plus a percentage for *Sweet Charity*. . . .' She was incensed. She pointed out that only two of the Universal films had been released and one (*Gambit*) was a hit. She said: 'Frankly, when I see the amount of money flung into that cauldron called Hollywood I feel not one ounce of guilt about the money I get. . . . I made a movie in Mexico, *Two*

Shirley MacLaine as yet another lovable lady of easy virtue: as Sweet Charity *(68), with her fellow dance-'hostesses', about to go into its show-stopper, 'Hey! Big Spender'.*

Shirley MacLaine and Kenneth Mars in Desperate Characters *(71), written and directed by Frank D. Gilroy, 'a brilliant portrait of the state of things today' ('Newsweek').*

Mules for Sister Sara. I got my eight (800,000 dollars) and Clint Eastwood got whatever he gets, and we had only one set and a small crew – that's all. Now I learn that the film cost $4½ million. . . . They've always grumbled about the money they've paid us. But they keep on coming back. I can't tell you how often we've been offered subjects which belong strictly to the cesspool and which are sent to us in the hope that we can bail them out. But that's the name of the game. And if you need the money badly enough, you do it. Mike Frankovitch himself offered me one million dollars to do *Casino Royale*.' (She did not do it.) She played a whore disguised as a nun in the Eastwood film (70): it was not a success.

At this stage she published an admired and bestselling memoir, 'Don't Fall off the Mountain', and then signed for an Anglo-American TV series, made by the British company, ATV. The contract also specified two movies both filmed in New York: *Desperate Characters* (71) and *The Possession of Joel Delaney* (72). The title of the first of these referred to a New York couple and what that city had done to them. Frank D. Gilroy wrote and directed, Kenneth Mars was the husband and MacLaine's suburban housewife surprised and pleased even her warmest admirers. Despite its backing, it was not shown in Britain and the other film – a thriller, in which she was a divorcée – was not very popular. She turned to the stage and clubs, in her own act, which established her as a potent draw in that medium; in 1976 she played the London Palladium (twice), and in New York. The attention created re-interested Hollywood, though in fact there were indications again that the drought of good roles for women was over: the good one for her was as Anne Bancroft's old buddy in *The Turning Point* (77), an updating of the *Old Acquaintance* idea, set in the world of ballet. There were further prime roles in *Being There* (79), with Peter Sellers, and in two marital stories, *Loving Couples* with James Coburn and *Consenting Adults* (80) with Anthony Hopkins. These last two were quick failures, but *Being There* was much liked, perhaps because of the idea – that many sensible people could mistake a naïve ex-gardener for a political genius. As the wife of an elderly millionaire MacLaine became the first leading actress to masturbate in an American film – the point being that Sellers was too innocent to know that she was trying to excite him.

She had her own Special on CBS during the 82–83 season and appeared in two more movies, *Terms of Endearment* (83) and *Cannonball II*, in a cameo role as a gold-digging showgirl disguised as a nun. The other film, after being turned down by almost every Hollywood studio, became a big success even before winning a fistful of major Oscars, including Best Picture and Best Actress – to MacLaine for an unflattering portrait of middle-aged American womanhood, snobbish, self-satisfied and arrogant. The film itself was more successful in portraying her (amusing) relationship with her neighbour (Jack Nicholson) than the (maudlin) one with her daughter (Debra Winger). MacLaine also won a Golden Globe and the New York critics' award, and then embarked on a popular New York season of song and dance. During this period she published several volumes of autobiography, much of it about her brushes with mysticism. She also appeared in an ABC mini-series based on it, *Out on a Limb* (87). 'Of course there's no way of knowing how well she succeeds,' said 'Variety', of her playing herself, 'only how believable she makes it seem. Not very.' She then turned down several other films to make – 'for practically nothing', because she liked the role – *Madame Sousatzka* (88) for John Schlesinger, a role first meant for Vanessa Redgrave: that of an eccentric Russian-American teaching the piano in London, specifically to a young Indian boy. She was then one of several women whose lives are examined in a beauty parlour, in *Steel Magnolias* (89), and she has expressed a wish to play Louise Brooks – one trusts, in middle age.

GORDON MACRAE

In the 30s, Bing Crosby virtually had the field to himself. Over at Warners, Dick Powell also crooned, at RKO Fred Astaire sang as he tapped and at MGM Nelson Eddy gave out in stentorian tones. None of the other male singers made much impression or stayed long. In the 40s, after the success of Frank Sinatra, there was a new influx – Perry Como, Dick Haymes, Andy Russell. Crosby stayed way out in front. Gordon MacRae also came to movies via radio and records, and he developed into one of the best singing stars – almost as easy as Bing, more animated than Como or Haymes, more virile than was the Sinatra of the 40s.

He was born in East Orange, New Jersey, in 1921 of a theatrical family. He was a child singer on the radio, then a radio singer. He made his first stage appearance in 'Junior Miss' and did a season in stock at Roslyn, Long Island. While singing in the NBC Lounge, New York, he was discovered by Horace Heidt and began a successful recording career. He was also in a Broadway revue, 'Three to Make Ready'. Warners were looking for a male singer to replace their all-purpose Dennis Morgan, who had never really caught on. They signed MacRae, but he made his début in a straight film, *The Big Punch* (48), a corny B about boxing, starring Wayne Morris. Then he was cast as June Haver's leading man in *Look for the Silver Lining* (49), a big, happy biopic of Follies star Marilyn Miller. There was a respectable response – the film was a hit – but Warners wasted MacRae in a minor underworld melodrama with Virginia Mayo, Edmond O'Brien and Viveca Lindfors, *Backfire* (50). (Also in the cast was Sheila Stevens, who became his wife.)

He was reunited with Haver for *The Daughter of Rosie O'Grady*, playing restaurateur Tony Pastor in this piece of New York Irish blarney; it played dual situations and *Return of the Frontiersmen* was a B Western, with Julie London (neither of them sang). He was paired with Doris Day for the first time in *Tea for Two* and Warners liked them together so much that they were teamed again in *The West Point Story*, James Cagney's musical, and *On Moonlight Bay* (51), where he sang to her with a banjo (it was set in the 20s). The studio was not exactly falling over itself to use him: the following year he only made *About Face* (52), a remake of *Brother Rat* with music and Eddie Bracken. He serenaded Doris Day again *By the Light of the Silvery Moon* (53) and then played the Red Shadow in the third filming of *The Desert Song*, with Kathryn Grayson. The two films he had done without Day had not been successful and when he asked for his release the studio agreed with alacrity. He had hardly advanced, despite some hit records on the side, some with Jo Stafford. RKO took him on for a slight musical with Jane Powell, *Three Sailors and a Girl.*

He set his sights on getting the lead in *Oklahoma!* (55), the long-awaited film of what had been a revolutionary musical and the longest-running Broadway musical. Perhaps the only other likely candidate was the more popular Howard Keel – but Hollywood was surprised when MacRae was cast as Curly, especially as co-star Shirley Jones was completely unknown. They were both good, but the film stuck rigidly to the old-hat stage 'book', with the songs dropped in like tombstones. It was less profitable than anticipated. There was another Rodgers and Hammerstein musical in the offing, *Carousel* (56), not produced by themselves but by 20th, who held the rights. Still, Rodgers and Hammerstein had cast approval – Miss Jones again and

Shirley Jones and Gordon MacRae in the film-version of Oklahoma! *(55). The way it was done, everything about it seemed old-fashioned – except the songs, freshly orchestrated after too many Palm Court airings.*

Frank Sinatra; but Sinatra walked out on the first day of shooting (because each scene was to be filmed twice, once in CinemaScope, once in normal ratio) and MacRae was rushed into the part. He took the film: whereas *Oklahoma!* had been his co-star's picture, all gaiety and sweetness, the more sombre *Carousel* was his, in a convincing strong portrayal of fair barker Billy Bigelow, big-head and all-time heel. The picture was good too, till it sank in a quagmire of bathos.

He had arrived: the future looked rosy. 20th rushed him into a second film, *The Best Things in Life are Free*, an agreeable musical built around the songwriting team of Brown (Ernest Borgnine), de Sylva and Henderson (Dan Dailey). As the easy-going de Sylva, MacRae had the biggest part; he played it well and the film was a success. At that point musicals went out of fashion – almost overnight. MacRae had proved in *Carousel* that he could act and his casual personality might have served in light comedy, but he hardly filmed afterwards. 'Variety' said he admitted to being constitutionally lazy and that he only worked to pay for his hobby – gambling. He continued to work, in stock and nightclubs, in a very successful act with his wife until they separated in 1965 (they later divorced). In 1967 he took over from Robert Preston on Broadway in 'I Do! I Do!' He returned to films in *The Pilot* (79) and after a break was singing in clubs again – Toronto at New Year's in '79.

From the mid-50s onwards he had appeared frequently on TV discussing alcoholism, which had afflicted his career; in 1983 he was appointed national honorary chairman of the National Council on Alcoholism. He died of throat cancer in 1986.

Anna Magnani

Said Jean Renoir: 'Anna Magnani is probably the greatest actress I have ever worked with. She is the complete animal – an animal created for the stage and screen. . . . Magnani gives so much of herself while acting that between scenes . . . she collapses and the mask falls.'

She was born, illegitimate, in 1909, in Alexandria, Egypt, and brought up by a grandmother in one of the less elegant districts of Rome. She studied for the stage at the Corso Eleanora Duse at Santa Cecilia but began her career singing bawdy ballads in dives, from whence she moved to variety theatres and stock companies. She was singing in San Remo when she met film director Goffredo Alessandrini who was on location near there. They married (1933 and subsequently divorced). Now in contact with film people, she met Nunzio Malasomma, returning from Germany for one film; he gave her a star part, as the villain's mistress, in *La Cieca di Sorrento* (34), based on a 100-year-old novel about a blind girl (Dria Paola) in the Naples of King Bomba. Despite this, Magnani's own husband did not think she was suitable for films – though he did give her a role as a music-hall star in his *Cavalleria* (36), supporting Elisa Cegani and Amadeo Nazzari, a portrait of Italian high society at the turn of the century. Two years later she was in another period piece, *Tarakanova* (38), with Annie Vernay in the title-role and Pierre-Richard Wilm as Orloff, who left Catherine the Great's bed to marry her; there were two versions, French and Italian - Magnani was in the Italian one only (directed by Mario Soldati).

In the theatre she had established herself as a leading actress, in such plays as 'The Petrified Forest' and 'Anna Christie', but there were only small roles in films: *Una Lampada alla Finestra* (40) with Ruggero Ruggeri, *Finalmente Soli* (41) with Maurizio D'Ancora; and *La Fuggitiva* with Renato Cialente. Vittorio De Sica felt that she had film possibilities and fashioned a role in *Teresa Venerdi* for her. Said 'Variety' (later): 'Although sexy-looking Anna Magnani is billed as co-star, the femme standout is Adriana Benedetti.' Benedetti had the title-role, as an orphan who pinches a debt-ridden doctor (De Sica) from music-hall star Magnani, at her most temperamental. She returned to supporting roles, in *La Fortuna Viene del Cielo* (42) with Roberto Villa, and was inactive for a while giving birth to a son – by actor Massimo Serato (the child became a polio victim and was, Magnani said, far more important to her than her career). She could no longer act in plays, as most foreign plays were banned, so turned to revue – 'Cantachiaro No 2' (43). In films, there were star parts in two films with Aldo Fabrizi: *L'Ultima Carrozzella* (43), a thriller directed by Mario Mattoli, and *Campo di Fiori*, a comedy where he sold fish, she sold vegetables and he deserted her temporarily for a silly blonde. She also appeared in *T'Amero Sempre*, with Alida Valli.

In the chaotic conditions then prevailing in Italy, *La Vita e Bella* was abandoned, but Magnani was soon at work in a small part in *Il Fiore sotto gli Occhi* (44), with Claudio Gora. She was also working on Rossellini's *Roma, Città Aperta* (45), a study of the last days of the Occupation – indeed, it was started clandestinely even as the Germans were leaving the city. The Italian press disliked it and it flopped at Cannes, but Paris raved and from there it went on to be a world success, the first revelation of the Italian neo-realist movement – and of Magnani's powers. In Italy she had been regarded mainly as a comedienne; now the world regarded her as a great tragedienne (in the film she was a fierce, pregnant widow shot down by the Germans), though it should be noted that at that time lack of beauty/glamour/standard-film-features was an asset overprized by many critics.

Anyway, in Italy she was at last a star film actress: *Abbasso la Miseria*, a comedy with Nino Besozzi, directed by Gennaro Righelli; *Un Uomo Ritorna*, as the wife of Gino Cervi, coping with postwar problems; and *Davanti a lui Tremava Tutta Roma* (46), as a 'Tosca'-singing *diva* with a Scarpia of her own – a German officer (Tito Gobbi was in it and she was dubbed). There was another contemporary drama, Lattuada's *Il Bandito*, an often excellent treatment of the postwar dilemma, with Amadeo Nazzari this time as the returning soldier, driven by Magnani to banditry. Then Righelli's follow up to his earlier film, *Abbasso la Ricchezza*, with Magnani as a self-made woman who rents a villa from an impoverished count (De Sica) and is thus driven back to her old trade of street vendor. She was teamed again with De Sica in *Lo Sconosciuto di San Marino* (47), directed by Cottafavi, and with Cervi in *Quartetto Pazzo*.

Few of these were widely seen outside Italy, so *L'Onorevole Angelina* was for most foreigners their second look at Magnani. In that, directed by Luigi Zampa, she was the militant leader of some Rome tenement-dwellers protesting against their conditions; for it she won the Best Actress ribbon at Venice. In Britain, C.A. Lejeune thought her 'probably as fine an all-round actress as the current cinema has to offer' and Richard Winnington, after noting that she was 'unencumbered by glamour as we know it', proclaimed her 'the most potent female on the contemporary screen'. William Whitebait in the 'New Statesman': 'Again the performance dazzles in its overflowing naturalness. . . . In a crowd, in the distance, she may be nobody; but the moment she opens her mouth or makes a movement we are made to feel that vitality counts for more than beauty, that in fact – conforming to no ideal – it creates its own beauty. Supremely herself, she gets – or at any rate goes – her own way by nature, strong voiced, harassed and active, loving, spontaneous, the enforced heroine of a hard life as the Bovarys and Miss Julies are of ruinous dreaming.'

Assunta Spina (48) did not make much dent in the export market, a remake of Salvatore Di Giacomo's classic play – Neapolitan intri-

It was left to Luchino Visconti to make a movie about a subject which could have provided a good Hollywood satire: Bellissima *(51), about a mother desperate to have her child become a movie-star. Anna Magnani was the mother, a working-class Roman woman.*

gues, love and vengeance – with Eduardo De Filippo; but *Molti Sogni per le Strade* did, again revealing Magnani's gift for a certain sort of comedy, as a nagging wife who tags along when her husband (Massimo Girotti) tries to sell a stolen car. *Amore* was relentlessly bleak. Rossellini directed and it was 'dedicated to the art of Anna Magnani', as the subtitled version had it, a two-part film, consisting of Cocteau's telephone monologue, *La Voce Umana*, and *Il Miracolo*, a harrowing anecdote about a raped peasant woman who is convinced that her unborn child is the Messiah. Post-production difficulties were numerous: for most showings the Cocteau was lopped off and in the US, as *The Miracle*, there were difficulties with the censor. Still, everyone admired Magnani, Dilys Powell with caution: 'possibly a great actress, who can command anything of an audience except tears'. The relationship of Magnani and Rossellini took a bashing when he met Ingrid Bergman and the enraged Magnani commissioned a film to rival the one they were making, *Vulcano* (49), with Rossano Brazzi, directed in English by William Dieterle. It was, if anything, even worse than its rival and, like that, did no one's career any good.

But her next one was good, Visconti's *Bellissima* (51), a highly coloured comedy about a Rome mother determined to make her child a movie star. Then she was directed by her ex-husband, Alessandrini, in *Camicie Rosse* (52), as the wife of Garibaldi (Raf Vallone). Renoir directed *La Carosse d'Or/La Carozza d'Oro/The Golden Coach* (53), made in three different versions, from a short play by Prosper Mérimée about a Commedia dell'Arte actress and her admirers. Again, the praise: 'In the sort of extravagant comedy role that suits her better than any other, Magnani plays Camilla with her incomparable exuberance and pathos: a great performance' (Karel Reisz in the 'MFB'). All the same, after *Siamo Donne*, in its most amusing episode, directed by Visconti, about an actress and her pet dog (another included Bergman), there were no film offers and Magnani returned to vaudeville. (Her episode in this film turned up in the US attached to another sketch film, this new assembly being called *Of Life and Love.*)

Tennessee Williams had written *The Rose Tattoo* (55) with her in mind and though she had been afraid to tackle it on Broadway she agreed to do the film for Paramount: as a mourning widow succumbing to lusty Burt Lancaster she scored a hat-trick – Best Actress Oscar, New York critics' award, BFA award (with *Amore* and *Roma Città Aperta*, it was one of her three favourite parts). In Italy she was a nun, *Suor Letizia* (56), befriending a small boy, a lethargic piece galvanized by

Tennessee Williams was fond of writing about larger-than-life ladies and sexually-threatening young men, often in confrontation, and 'Orpheus Descending' was written for Anna Magnani and Marlon Brando, both of whom declined the roles in the original Broadway production. They played them in the film, however, when the opus was retitled The Fugitive Kind *(60). When, in life, he failed to respond to her advances, their relations on set hovered between the stormy and the icy.*

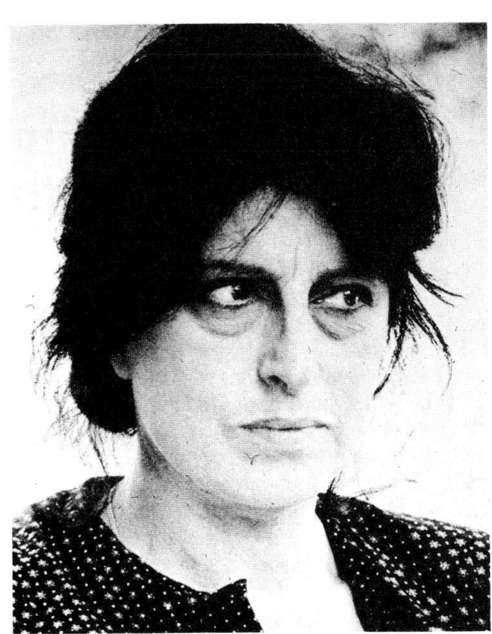

After three Hollywood films in the 50s, Anna Magnani worked in Europe for the next decade – until Stanley Kramer offered her the role of the mayor's wife in The Secret of Santa Vittoria *(69).*

her performance. Paramount, meanwhile, searched for another property and came up with the old cliché about the mail-order bride – Anthony Quinn's: *Wild Is the Wind* (57), expertly made, however, by George Cukor. It was not a success. Surprisingly, she accepted a supporting role in *Nella Città l'Inferno* (59), meant as a star vehicle for Fellini's wife, Giulietta Masina: but she so bullied the director, Renato Castellani, that by the time it was finished the roles were of reverse importance. It was a sanctimonious prison melodrama and although Masina was another actress thought potent to the foreign carriage trade, bookings outside Italy were few. Part of the trouble was that the force of Magnani was overpowering; like all volatile performers, her work stays with you so that each time round there is a creeping paralysis of non-appreciation – as in *The Fugitive Kind* (60), as a love-starved storekeeper who picks up, and keeps, Marlon Brando (another part Williams wrote for her).

Still, whatever strictures one applies to Magnani, the neglect of the 60s was surprising. True, the first two were failures: *Risati di Gioia* (61), as a film extra involved with American executive Fred Clark and con-man Ben Gazzara; and *Mamma Roma* (62), fashioned by Pier Paolo Pasolini especially for her. And the next two did not make the Anglo-American market: Autant-Lara's *Le Magot de Josefa* (63), in France with Bourvil, in which she was the village grocer and victim of a swindle; and *Volles Herz und Leere Taschen* (64), in Germany with Françoise Rosay. The only decent Italian offer was to do a sketch-film based on a TV series, *Made in Italy* (66) – and mostly it stayed there, despite other names (Nino Manfredi, Jean Sorel, Alberto Sordi, etc.). Magnani's episode 'La Famiglia', had her trying to cross a road. She returned to the stage, directed by Franco Zeffrelli (who had had a small part in *L'Onorevole Angelina*) – 'La Lupa', which toured Italy and visited London. Finally, Hollywood needed her for *The Secret of Santa Vittoria* (69), with Anthony Quinn as her husband: they were Italian villagers and her part was entirely made to measure – any other casting was unthinkable. In 1970 she embarked on a prestige Italian TV series, one of which was shown theatrically, *1870* (72), with Marcello Mastroianni; and she also appeared fleetingly as herself in Fellini's *Roma*. She died in 1973.

Jayne Mansfield

Jayne Mansfield wanted to be a movie star more than anything else in the world and while she was she enjoyed it. Reporters were taken on tours of her home, which was even more excessive than that of Mae West – one of the ladies who provided her inspiration. When her marriages went wrong she put on a happy face – it was all grist to the publicity mill. She was that super, fabulous, exciting being – a Hollywood star. Fortunately for her she happened along at the time when her only assets – big boobies – were prized in the film capital (Anita Ekberg had just been there and failed: but she had certainly got press coverage). 'Variety' said she always looked as though she was leaning out of a window and Alan King commented, 'She'll never drown.' Before, they would have been too much; afterwards, not enough. They were not enough to keep her in the forefront for long.

She was born in Bryn Mawr, Pennsylvania, in 1933. Her father died when she was small; her mother married again and the family moved to Dallas. At 16, in high school, she married Paul Mansfield and had a baby the following year. This was but a setback in her quest for stardom; she continued her drama studies at the Dallas Little Theater and her ballet classes. Her husband went to UCLA to study and, according to some reports, she was studying right along beside him; according to others she studied drama, languages, music, etc., 'all with a view to establishing her qualifications to be a famous film star'. She also did exercises to create the sort of body men talked about – 40-18½-36 – and that led to TV walk-ons, some publicity and an assignment to appear at the Florida première of a Jane Russell movie, *Underwater*. The resulting publicity got her a Warner contract, but

Jayne Mansfield *in* Too Hot to Handle *(60). Judgement suspended on whether this picture proves the point.*

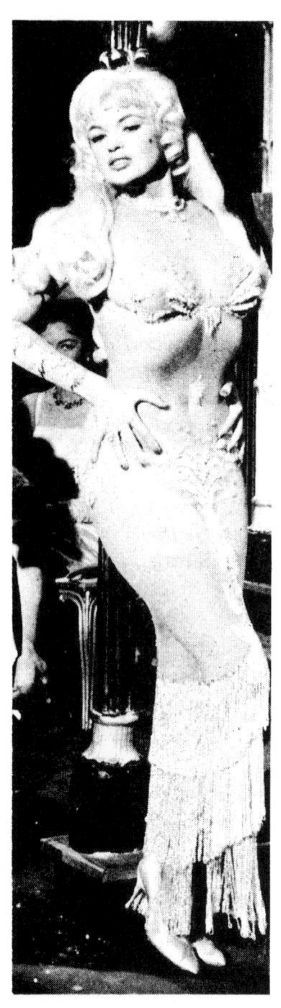

after small roles in *Pete Kelly's Blues* (55) and *Illegal*, fourth-billed as a moll, she was demoted to a bit in *Hell on Frisco Bay* and then dropped, which provided her with what she called the unhappiest day of her life. Around the same time she embarked on a second marriage, to muscle-man Mickey Hargitay.

She appeared in two independent films. *Female Jungle* (56), as a threatened model in this murder mystery with Lawrence Tierney, and *The Burglar* (57), as one of Dan Duryea's gang; and then went to New York to audition for the part of a Marilyn Monroeish blonde in George Axelrod's 'Will Success Spoil Rock Hunter?' Her notices were good and 20th, at that time feuding with a recalcitrant Monroe, signed her to a seven-year contract. She was written up, needless to say, as Marilyn's successor. The world did not exactly hold its breath, but when she made her first film for 20th comparisons were expected and made: 'Her range at this stage appears restricted to a weak imitation of Marilyn Monroe. A hint to her limitations is given in . . . the plot, which comes to the hopeless conclusion that she can do nothing more than make weird sounds' (Bosley Crowther). The film was *The Girl Can't Help It*, basically a rock-and-roll musical. Then came a dowdy version of Steinbeck's *The Wayward Bus*, as a bubble-dancer involved with travelling salesman Dan Dailey. Neither did great business, so hopes were pinned on the film of *Will Success Spoil Rock Hunter?*, but any success that had was due to Tony Randall's frantic performance as a New York copywriter.

20th tried again: *Kiss Them For Me* opposite Cary Grant, comforting GIs in wartime Manhattan – but she was 'more grotesque than funny' (the 'MFB'). The other leading lady, Suzy Parker, was negative and the film flopped – one of the few Grant films which did in a long career. 20th were worried and orders were given to go easy on publicity. Bette Davis commented: 'Dramatic art, in her opinion, is knowing how to fill a sweater.' Obviously audiences thought it was not enough. She was sent to Britain to play a saloon belle in *The Sheriff of Fractured Jaw* (58), opposite Kenneth More. She was off the screen for more than a year (pregnant) and then made two British independents, contrastingly teamed in both with two of Britain's more respectable actors (albeit not in respectable roles), Anthony Quayle in *The Challenge* (60) and Leo Genn in *Too Hot to Handle*. Both were Soho thrillers of the sort beloved by British B picture-makers. In the former she was a club singer by night and, laughably, the mastermind of a gang of crooks by day. In the other – 'Her acting is tepid and, at times, ludicrous' ('Variety') – she had a striptease sequence which had censorship problems, thus, Allah be praised, saving the film from instant oblivion.

In Italy she did *Gli Amore di Ercole*, with Hargitay, a 'Hercules' 'epic' never released in the US or Britain. She was loaned out again for *The George Raft Story* (61), made by Allied Artists with Ray Danton, as the sexy star who tangles with him as he is – understandably – touching rock-bottom. In Greece she played that country's greatest actress in 20th's *It Happened in Athens* (62) – absurd, obviously, but intentionally? Anyway, she was on the periphery of a tale built round the first modern Olympics in 1896. This was the end of 'the fabulous exclusive deal' with 20th – though there belongs to this period *Panic Button*, a mild comedy made in Italy with Eleanor Parker, with Mansfield as an amateur thespian taken up by Maurice Chevalier. It was started in 1961, shown in the US three years later (and never in Britain).

She still made headlines. Some publicity accrued when she tied herself to an italian impresario, Enrico Bomba, said also to be her romantic interest. Then she was shipwrecked in the Caribbean, but that was thought to be a stunt. She finally made a cheap little independent produced by Tommy Noonan, *Promises Promises* (63), with him, Hargitay and Marie McDonald, but it got few bookings. When there were no further offers, she did nightclub work and in the summer of 1964 she and her husband did 'Bus Stop' in stock, directed by Matt Cimber, who later married her. There were offers from Europe: the German-Italian *Einer Frisst den Anderen* (64), with Cameron Mitchell, which had a few bookings as *When Strangers Meet*; and, even more degrading, *L'Amore Primitivo*, in which she was an anthropologist showing her boring 'nature' movies to a professor and then stripping for him and two hotel porters. She was also in something called *Country Music USA* (65), with Mamie Van Doren, but it never appears to have been shown; and she was cut (so was Ruth Gordon) from the final print of *The Loved One*, in which she was a travel receptionist.

There were two more dudsville features, *Las Vegas Hillbillys* (66) and *The Fat Spy*, with Phyllis Diller, in which she was Brian Donlevy's daughter. And there were rumours of a pornographic movie, plus something called *Single Room Furnished*, directed by Cimber. Neither seems to have been shown publicly, nor does *Spree* (67), a revamp of something originally called *Here's Las Vegas* made in 1963. Mitchell Leisen is said to have had a hand in the direction: other names involved include Vic Damone and Constance

Hollywood lost interest in Jayne Mansfield fairly quickly, but she made a late guest appearance in A Guide for the Married Man *in 1967. Also guesting: Terry-Thomas.*

Moore. Further unreleased films she is said to be in are: *Dog Eat Dog* (65), *Mondo Hollywood* (67) and *The Wild, Wild World of Jayne Mansfield*. There was a last fleeting guest appearance in *A Guide for the Married Man* for 20th; and there are rumours of other credits – but again, none of these films seems to have been shown. In 1967 she was killed near New Orleans on the way to a TV engagement; she and her new fiancé, in a sports car, were decapitated in an accident with a truck.

Jean Marais

It is to Jean Marais that we are indebted for most of the excursions into film of Jean Cocteau. Cocteau, in an already varied career in art and literature, had made *Le Sang d'un Poète* in 1930, but it was not until he met Marais that he felt anxious to make more films. Marais was an aspiring film actor and it was to share his *métier* that Cocteau again began to flirt with the cinema. It is for the Cocteau films – made in the 40s – that Marais is best known to British and American filmgoers, but he was seldom away from the cameras subsequently. Nor, till age caught up with him, did he lose much of his hold upon French fans, first established as a young man with more than a passing resemblance to a Greek divinity.

Marais and Cocteau met in 1937, when Marais was 24. He was born in 1913 in Cherbourg, the son of a veterinarian. The parents' marriage was not happy and not long after the war the mother fled with one of her admirers, taking the children. They lived under a pseudonym in Le Vésinet, near Paris. Marais was a difficult child and a useless student. The official publicity line was that he was destined to be a photographer; he retouched photographs to earn a living, while hoping to get started as an actor. He was turned down by the Conservatoire but managed to get bit parts in seven films (six of them directed by Marcel L'Herbier): *L'Epervier* (33), *Dans les Rues, Le Scandale, L'Aventurier* (34) starring Victor Francen, *Le Bonheur, Les Hommes Nouveaux* (35) and *Nuits de Feu*. He auditioned without success for other movie-makers. He finally persuaded his mother to enrol him for a year in the course run by Charles Dullin and it was while there that he auditioned for Cocteau, for a secondary role in his 'Oedipe' (37). Cocteau was immediately enamoured and offered him the role of the king, but the rest of the troupe objected. According to one of Cocteau's biographers, Frederick Brown, 'he was the Dargelos of Cocteau's dreams, an insolent, untamable, excessively beautiful lad'. Brown also quotes Marais, keeping his head in retrospect about the admiration which now surrounded him: 'I believe that my physical appearance when I was young mysteriously answered the vague and fugitive taste of an era and fixed it, crystalized it for a time.'

The two men were soon living together (for Marais's sake, Cocteau gave up drugs) and Cocteau cast him as Galahad in his recently written play. 'Les Chevaliers de la Table Ronde'. The following year (1938) he appeared in 'Les Parents Terribles' which Cocteau wrote for him (basing it, he said, on Marais's relations with his mother). In 1939 Cocteau prepared to film it, but the venture was postponed because of the imminence of war. As Cocteau's protégé, Marais was being offered film roles and they were no longer small parts. In 1939 he turned down the part that François Perier eventually played in *La Fin du Jour*; he was ill and was replaced by Gilbert Gil in *Nuit de Decembre*; and he signed for *L'Embuscade*, but disliked the script so much that he paid not to do it. He was called to the Front at the outbreak of war and did serve, mainly as a chauffeur; so his real movie début was delayed until *Le Pavillon Brûle* (41), a melodrama with Pierre Renoir and Elina Labourdette, in which he was an engineer in North Africa. *Le Lit à Colonnes* (42) was hardly better, about an opera-composing prisoner (Marais) whose work is stolen by the governor (Fernand Ledoux). Marais's performance was somewhat excessive. Then he dyed his hair black to play Don José to the *Carmen* (43) of

Jean Marais when he first made the female hearts of France flutter: with Madeleine Sologne in L'Eternel Retour *(43), Cocteau's version of Tristan and Iseult.*

Viviane Romance – then France's biggest star: Bizet in the background, Italian studio locations and a Don José with the dash but not quite the virility for the part.

Cocteau, meanwhile, had written 'La Machine à Ecrire' (41) and Marais had played a double role in it as well as designing the décor. He also wrote for him 'Renaud et Armide', which Marais was to have done with the Comédie-Française, but his time as a *pensionnaire* was brief and unhappy – partly because of his looks and fame – and it was done without him (he did it in Brussels in 1946). He worked hard to improve as an actor and scored a success finally in 'Britannicus', a mock-classical tragedy written for him by Cocteau – around the same time that cinemagoers were crying their eyes out over *L'Eternel Retour*. This was Cocteau's modernization of the Tristan and Iseult legend, directed by Jean Delannoy, grimly Gothic and today absurd; but at the time audiences went gaga over the tragic fate of these blonde ice-cold lovers – the girl was Madeleine Sologne. There was another gloomy piece, Christian-Jaque's *Voyage sans Espoir*, as a fugitive embezzler having a night's fling with Simone Renant (then Mme Christian-Jaque). Cocteau wrote and directed the next, *La Belle et la Bête* (46), a sombre and fairly magical version of the fairy-tale, with extravagant décor by Christian Bérard. Beauty was Josette Day and Marais played both her shepherd lover and, heavily encased in a fur mask, the Beast – a beautiful creation. More than anything else this established him as France's No 1 heart-throb.

Jean Marais played both a village boy and the beast in La Belle et la Bête *(46); here he is as the beast – after his eventual metamorphosis into a fairy prince.*

He played a marquis in *Les Chouans*, after Balzac, with Pierre Dux and Madeleine Robinson, a film heavily cut by the distributors for religious reasons. Then he had another dual role, as a student and as a highborn bandit, in *Ruy Blas* (47) with Danielle Darrieux, adapted by Cocteau from the old romantic play by Victor Hugo. Cocteau's own romantic piece, *L'Aigle à Deux Têtes*, was ersatz, but, with Marais and Edwige Feuillère repeating their stage performances, a big success. Already, earlier in the year, in the first French filmgoers' polls since the war, he had been voted the country's most popular actor, with Pierre Blanchar as runner-up. After a love story with the most popular female star, Michèle Morgan, Delannoy's *Aux Yeux du Souvenir* (48), Cocteau directed him again, in *Les Parents Terribles*, filmed at last. This was far from the fantasies which had been Cocteau's films so far, a clinical stage-bound study of a family made miserable by the near-incestuous love of mother for son. As the mother Yvonne de Bray gave a magnificent performance and Gabrielle Dorziat was hardly less good as the aunt. Catherine de la Roche thought the whole cast acted flawlessly, but added, 'Nevertheless, the *casting* of Marais (a thing that seems unavoidable in Cocteau's dramas) was a pity – he is not young enough, nor is his physique frail enough for the part.' Cocteau himself wrote: 'If I keep Jean Marais till the last, it's because his performance escapes analysis. Not only is it prodigious; he *played* what he used to excite, instinctively, and tripled his effects by a fusion of passion and style.'

Marais's popularity meant that he had the pick of romantic parts. He elected to play the Crown Prince Rudolf in Delannoy's *Le Secret de Mayerling* (49), with Dominque Blanchar (the daughter of Pierre Blanchar) as his tragic partner. Some critics thought the film as good as the old Boyer-Darrieux version. Then Cocteau wrote and directed *Orphée* (50), a modern version of the Orpheus legend, with Marie Déa as Eurydice and Maria Casares (stunning) as Death. Marais looked magnifi-

Marais in the title-role of Orphée *(50), probably the most fascinating and enduring of Cocteau's several excursions into movies.*

Jean Marais and Michèle Morgan were teamed together twice at the peak of their popularity in France. Both films were stories of Impossible Love. This one is René Clement's Le Château de Verre *(51).*

cent – and properly bewildered – as Orpheus, in the midst of a barrage of continually surprising technical tricks and empty rhetoric, a cinema fantasy which outclassed anything that had gone before and which remains unrivalled. The young rival poet was played by Edouard Dermithe, an ex-miner who since 1947 had taken Marais's place in Cocteau's life and who was to be his legatee. Marais and Cocteau remained close, however, till the latter's death in 1963.

Marais again played a yearning but inexpressive hero, in both *Le Château de Verre* (51) with Morgan and *Les Miracles n'ont Lieu qu'une Fois* with Alida Valli. He spent some time with the Comédie-Française (welcomed now), then did the remake of an old swashbuckling favourite, *Nez de Cuir* (52) with Massimo Girotti, hidden by a leather mask to cover a battle scar. In Italy he played a member of the Maquis in Pabst's episode film, *La Voce del Silenzio*, then: *L'Appel du Destin*, basically a vehicle for child prodigy Roberto Benzi, reuniting his parents to music; *Les Amants de Minuit* (53), a pleasant light romance, an ideal Prince Charming to Dany Robin's modern Cinderella; *Le Guérisseur*, with Danièle Delorme; *Julietta*, again Prince Charming to Mlle Robin, in fact a lawyer to her dreamy teenager; *Dortoir des Grandes*, a thriller set in a girls' school; and *Le Comte de Monte Cristo* (54), an inferior remake of the Dumas story, released in two parts, part two under this title, part one as *La Trahison*. He was in two of Sacha Guitry's historical extravaganzas, *Si Versailles m'Etait Conté*, as a gracious Louis XV, with Micheline Presle as his Pompadour (Guitry himself was the older Louis XIV), and *Napoléon* (5), as one of his generals. The star-studded cameos made both films big in France, but none of this Guitry series would 'sell' abroad.

He played Higgins – and did the décor – in a successful run of 'Pygmalion' in France, but neither his screen roles nor his interpretations could any longer be considered important. He was edging towards the action movies and swashbucklers which were to be the mainstay of the rest of his screen career. He was a singer on whom girl students get a crush in *Futures Vedettes* and a marble-quarrier in love with gypsy Delia Scala in *Goubbiah*, a Franco-Italian-Yugoslav melodrama. The 'MFB' was not kind about his performance in that: 'Jean Marais's obsessed and overweight hero, though a fine legendary figure when on horseback, is otherwise merely depressing.' There was another Guitry pot-pourri, *Si Paris Nous Était Conté* (56), as François Ier, followed by: *Elena et les Hommes*, losing Ingrid Bergman to Mel Ferrer in Renoir's fantasy; *Toute la Ville Accuse* with Etchika Choureau, another fantasy – about a vacationing writer who finds himself the daily recipient of a lot of money; *Typhon sur Nagasaki* (57) with Danielle Darrieux; *SOS Noronha*; Visconti's *Le Notti Bianche* (58) with Marcello Mastroianni; *Un Amour de Poche* with Geneviève Page, as a scientist tempted by student Agnes Laurent – a sci-fi love story; and *La Tour, Prends Garde*, with Nadja Tiller, as a fighting troubadour. Said 'Variety': 'Jean Marais lacks the dash and stature to give a true breath of high adventure to the proceedings . . . result is that most of the derring-do falls flat.' *Chaque Jour a Son Secret*, with Danièle Delorme, was a 40s-type melodrama, with Marais as the 'dead' husband's brother. In *La Vie à Deux* he was in the episode with Lilli Palmer.

Le Bossu (60) was his first film for André Hunebelle, who was to direct him in many of his (mediocre) adventure films over the next few years. This one was the remake of an old Pierre Blanchar vehicle, set during the Regency of Louis XV, about an adventurer who masquerades as a hunchback; it featured Bourvil with him in a sort of Don Giovanni-Leporello relationship. He then appeared briefly in Cocteau's *Le Testament d'Orphée* (in which Dermithe had the leading role) and in Abel Gance's all-star return to film-making, *Austerlitz*, as Carnot, with Pierre Mondy as Bonaparte. Because of the success of *Le Bossu*, he and Bourvil were quickly reteamed in *Le Capitan*, another remake (of a 1946 movie). Then he climbed into costume again for a more dignified role in *La Princesse de Clèves* (61), which Cocteau had adapted from the classic novel by Mme de Lafayette. In 1946 Jean Delannoy was going to direct this screenplay with Marais and Michèle Morgan, in Czechoslovakia (so that it could be done in colour). The deal fell through and now Marais was too old to play the lover – which part went to Jean-François Poron. Marina Vlady was the unhappy princess and Marais the husband – and very grave, as if that might pass for acting.

There were two more cloak-and-sword remakes, *Le Capitaine Fracasse* (made most recently by Gance with Fernand Gravey in 1942), co-starring Gerard Barray, who also specialized in such films, and *Le Miracle des Loups*, a bit more lavish than usual and co-starring Jean-Louis Barrault as Louis XI plus Rosanna Schiaffino. Marais side-tracked for a duller bit of history (at least, in this version), *Napoléon II L'Aiglon* – which part was played by Bernard Verley; then travelled to Italy and much further back in time for *Ponzio Pilato*, in the title-role, with Jeanne Crain, and *Il Ratto della Sabine* (62), with Rosanna Schiaffino as the chief of the Sabine women. *Les Mystères de Paris* was another Hunebelle remake, with a good cast (Dany Robin, Raymond Pellegrin, Pierre Mondy, Jill Haworth) – high-life and low in the Paris of Louis-Philippe (from Eugène Sue's novel). Then after *Le Masque de Fer*, as d'Artagnan, Marais changed the formula and became *L'Honorable Stanislas Agent Secret* (63), involved in modern bravado with Geneviève Page and lots of disguises. Something similar went on in *Fantômas* (64). Hunebelle's weary attempt to resuscitate the famous arch-fiend of Louis Feuillade's 1912 serial, with Louis de Funès as Marais's sidekick.

Marais had his first real change in years in *Patate*, with Danielle Darrieux, a weak version of Marcel Achard's boulevard comedy that had run for six years in Paris: Pierre Dux had the title-role, that of a worm who turns, and Marais was miscast as his philandering friend. Then, after a picaresque adventure, *Le Gentleman de Cocody* (65), there was *Pleins Feux sur Stanislas*, a sequel; and after *Train d'Enfer*, there was *Fantômas se Déchaine* (66), another sequel, with de Funès. He then played the Saint in *Le Saint Prend l'Affut* (taking over from Felix Marten, who had played Leslie Charteris's detective in a French movie in 1959). *Sept Hommes et une Garce* (67) was a French-Italian-Romanian spectacle, set during the Napoleonic Wars, with Sydney Chaplin. Then: *Fantômas Contre Scotland Yard; Le Paria* (68), as a self-sacrificing gangster; *La Provocation* (69), with Maria Schell; and *Peau d'Ane* (70), Jacques Demy's fairy-tale with Catherine Deneuve, as the King.

In more recent years he has worked more frequently on the stage, in, among others, 'The Devil's Disciple' (69), as adapted by Cocteau, with décor and costumes by himself; 'Oedipe' with Madeline Sologne; and Guitry's 'L'Amour Masqué'. In 1977 he directed and played the father in 'Les Parents Terribles' – which he took to London. In 1979 he was in a popular TV series, a costume drama, 'Joseph Balsamo'. He was reunited with Feuillère for a couple of appearances and in 1981 was in 'Du Vent dans les Branches de Sassafras'. His only film in several years was *Lieu toi Parenté* (86), as a disagreeable old peasant who discovers that he has a mulatto grandson. Around the same time he and Jean-Louis Barrault supported Francis Huster in 'Le Cid'.

DEAN MARTIN

When Dean Martin was just Jerry Lewis's straight man, Daniel Farson wrote in 'Sight and Sound': 'His screen characterization is slick and cocksure, possessing all the unattractiveness of the professional charmer; he sings uninterestingly. He gave a convincing and unpleasant portrayal of a drunk in *The Stooge*, but otherwise his acting has been negligible.' Martin has seldom pretended to be an actor and over the years, as he mellowed, other critics have enjoyed his relaxed good nature: he appears as a lazy, amiable toper. Every comic makes jokes about his drinking. The image is completely unprofessional, but presumably a good deal of professionalism goes into it.

He was born (Dino Crocetti) in 1917 in Steubenville, Ohio. Before he teamed with Lewis he had been a prize-fighter, garage-attendant and gambling-house croupier among other jobs. He liked singing and got taken on by night-spots in and around his home town. The partnership began in 1946 and in December 1948 they signed a contract with Hal Wallis at Paramount. He tried them out among the cast of *My Friend Irma* (49), which was successful enough to spawn a sequel, *My Friend Irma Goes West*. He starred them in *At War With the Army*, which did well, and *That's My Boy* (51), which wound up the seventh biggest money-maker of the year. Both *Sailor Beware* and *Jumping Jacks* (52) were in the top 10 with a gross of around $4 million each. And most of these did very well: *The Stooge* (in which Martin was a big-headed vaudeville star); *Scared Stiff* (53); *The Caddy*; *Money from Home*; *Living It Up* (54); *Three Ring Circus*; *You're Never Too Young* (55); *Artists and Models*; *Pardners* (56); and *Hollywood or Bust*. No reasons were given for the break-up, but it was believed to be due to increasing animosity caused by Martin's refusal to drive himself as hard as did Lewis – the actual break came when he refused the role of the cop which Lewis had designated for him in *The Delicate Delinquent.*

As the straight man of the team, Martin was the one out in the cold. Lewis remained among the top 10 money-making stars; Martin promptly left the list. His first solo effort, a farce at MGM with Eva Bartok, *Ten Thousand Bedrooms* (57), was a financial fiasco. No further offers were forthcoming till Martin's agent, the all-powerful MCA, took the matter in hand. Two other clients of theirs, Marlon Brando and Montgomery Clift, were scheduled to appear in 20th's *The Young Lions* (58). According to 'Show Magazine', MCA told 20th that they would withdraw both unless Martin had the third star role, replacing Tony Randall. 20th complied. Martin said that Randall had not actually been signed 'and all I did was let my agents know I'd like to play it. There's nothing wrong with that. It's done every day in this business.' Martin's performance as the Broadwayite soldier went unremarked upon, as did his stint as Frank Sinatra's breezy buddy in *Some Came Running* (59), playing gin rummy with a Stetson on his head and no pants. Then when Montgomery Clift turned down the part of John Wayne's buddy in *Rio Bravo*, a Howard Hawks Western, MCA got Martin into the part.

All three films were successful and MCA got Martin signed to a $250,000 two-picture deal with Mirisch-United Artists, to be directed by Billy Wilder and by William Wyler (the Wyler one was never made). For the moment, Martin's films had a bumpy ride at the box-office: *Career*, as a selfish showbiz careerist, with Shirley MacLaine; *Who Was That Lady?* (60) with Janet Leigh and Tony Curtis; the agreeable *Bells Are Ringing*, as a lazy playwright, opposite Judy Holliday; and *All in a Night's Work* (61), leching after MacLaine. *Ocean's 11*, a jolly robbers' romp, was the first with the Sinatra clan, but the fillip it gave Martin's career was negated by *Ada*, playing a guitar-strumming man-of-the people candidate for State Governor, married to call-girl Susan Hayward. Some footage of Martin was inserted into the Italian *Canzoni nel Mondo* (62), giving him guest-star billing. Then came a clan Western, *Sergeants Three*; a comedy with Lana Turner, *Who's Got the Action?*; and a version of Lillian Hellman's Broadway success, *Toys in the Attic* (63), as the spoilt younger brother of Wendy Hiller and Geraldine Page. It underlined his ability to play a serious role, no more. Except in Westerns and thrillers he did not try subsequently.

He did a comedy with Elizabeth Montgomery, a fugitive from TV, *Who's Been Sleeping in My Bed?*, and it was stolen from them both by stage and TV star Carol Burnett as Montgomery's room-mate. The 'MFB' said 'Dean Martin give a tired, routine performance.' He was with Sinatra in *Four for Texas* – the other two were Anita Ekberg and Ursula Andress; with MacLaine in *What a Way to Go!* (64), as a playboy tycoon; and with Sinatra and the clan again in *Robin and the Seven Hoods*. Billy Wilder's *Kiss Me Stupid* was described once by Peter Barnes as a work of 'ferocious tastelessness . . . a brilliant satire on a cheap and vulgar society and crowned with an extraordinary performance by Dean Martin as a drunken lout who gets migraine if he does not go to bed with a woman every night.' For some reason the Martin character was a crooner and was called Dino, as he sometimes is offscreen. The film ran into troubles in the US; United Artists refused to handle it and passed it to their subsidiary, Lopert; and it was further boycotted by distributors. Wilder, to his shame, agreed that it had been a mistake.

Martin followed with a hit Western for Hal Wallis, with John Wayne, *The Sons of Katie Elder* (65), and a flop comedy with Sinatra – their last together – *Marriage on the Rocks*. In 1966 he jumped from nowhere to 11th on the box-office lists and for the next two years was safely among the top 10. The reason was a medium-budget actioner, *The Silencers* (66), with Martin as one of the pseudo James Bonds, Matt Helm, another secret agent with an extraordinary capacity for broads and mayhem – and in this case, booze. Martin kidded along and, after a Western, *Texas Across the River* (67), he did a prompt Matt

When Judy Holliday repeated her stage success in the film of Bells Are Ringing *(60), it was clear that her co-star would have to be a very unselfish fellow: Dean Martin.*

Helm sequel, *Murderers' Row*, with Ann-Margret. Around this time his TV shows made him one of the most popular stars working in that medium; in films, by turning to the bang-bang stuff, his career got a new lease of life: *Rough Night in Jericho*, a Western with Jean Simmons; another Matt Helm, *The Ambushers* (68); and *Bandolero*, a Western with James Stewart. A comedy with Stella Stevens did nowhere as well, despite an engaging and scene-stealing performance by Anne Jackson, as a girl resigned to being always the other woman, *How To Save a Marriage and Ruin Your Life*. There was *Five Card Stud* (69), a Western with Robert Mitchum, and a last weak Matt Helm, *The Wrecking Crew*, with Elke Sommer, proving that that vogue was really over. Then there was *Airport* (70), a dodo of a movie from a novel by Arthur Hailey, a *Grand Hotel* of the air with a few thrills in the tail. Burt Lancaster co-starred and the two of them were surrounded with semi-names (Van Heflin, Helen Hayes, etc.). Somehow it got through; to the extent that Martin, who worked on it for 10 per cent of the gross receipts, wound up just a year later with $7 million – believed to be the biggest personal take ever from a movie.

After a break, he made three more Westerns, *Something Big* (71), *Once Upon a River* (72) and, with Rock Hudson, *Showdown* (73). They all failed, as did a last star foray into films, *Mr Ricco* (75), called 'a tedious and corny hodgepodge' by 'Variety', which went on: 'Except for Martin, whose non-acting gets worse, the cast is rather good.' It was supposedly the first of a multi-picture deal as specified in his contract with the MGM Grand Hotel, Las Vegas. He returned to this medium teamed with Sammy Davis Jr in cameos in *The Cannonball Run* (81), the two of them as ageing swingers disguised as priests. They were seen to even less advantage in *Cannonball Run II* (83). Despite the débâcle of a London concert in 1983 (seven performances at an exorbitant £20 top ticket in a huge theatre, which could not sell out Shirley MacLaine for four) he returned to play the Palladium for a week in 1987. He has continued to appear on television. He has been married three times and has six children, some of whom have also gone into show business, with variable results.

Lee Marvin

Lee Marvin's career was not unlike Humphrey Bogart's: he first made his mark as a heavy, backing up or bucking leading actors much less forceful than himself. It took 10 years to get promoted to stardom and then five more years to become a superstar. Yet he was always good. He was a real mean villain, honest according to his own lights – quick to scrap, swifter with an unexpected fist. He never pussy-footed around. His sneers had humour – at least, his own sort of humour; and in his rare sympathetic portrayals he projected a gritty integrity – when he rejected buddy Jack Webb in *Peter Kelly's Blues*, you felt that Webb might as well give up.

He was born in New York City in 1924, the son of an advertising executive and a writer on beauty (mother), and was apparently a maverick as a child; he enlisted in the marines while still at school and was wounded on active service in the South Pacific. He spent over a year in hospital; he became a plumber's mate for a while, but was attracted to the theatre and studied at the American Theater Wing under the GI Bill of Rights. He made his début in a small part in stock in Woodstock; began to get bits in TV and off-Broadway; was on Broadway in 'Billy Budd'; and toured in 'A Streetcar Named Desire' and 'The Hasty Heart'. Director Henry Hathaway caught him on TV and gave him a small part in *You're in the Navy Now* (51), as one of the crew – 18th on the cast-list. No one else offered movie work, till a year later Hathaway gave him another part, as a military policeman in *Diplomatic Courier* (52). Hathaway induced a top agent to take him on and Marvin began to appear regularly in films. After small parts in *We're Not Married* and *Duel at Silver Creek*, an Audie Murphy Western, Stanley Kramer chose him for one of the leads in the starless *Eight Iron Men*, adapted by Harry Brown from his own play about soldiers under stress, 'A Sound of Hunting'.

That led to some supporting parts in mainly double-bill actioners: *Hangman's Knot*, as one of the baddies in this Randolph Scott Western; *Down Among the Sheltering Palms* (53), as a sailor; *Seminole*, as a cavalry sergeant; *The Glory Brigade*, as a corporal in Korea; and *The Stranger Wore a Gun*, another Scott Western; Then he was memorable as one of the most vicious villains yet seen on film: in Fritz Lang's *The Big Heat* – among other things, he stubbed out his cigarette on Carolyn Jones (it was a hobby) and threw a boiling coffee-pot at Gloria Grahame. The same studio, Columbia, wasted him in a Rock Hudson Western, *Gun Fury*, but gave him another good role, as Marlon Brando's overage gang rival in *The Wild One* (54). There was a beastly programmer, *Gorilla at Large*, with Cameron Mitchell and Anne Bancroft, then he was the easy-going ship's cook in *The Caine Mutiny*. There was another programmer with Bancroft, *The Raid*, then *Bad Day at Black Rock*, as the most threatening of the townsfolk who 'welcome' Spencer Tracy. John O'Hara wrote in 'Collier's: 'By the time he gets his head bashed in, you hate him so much that you could supply a supererogatory kick in the face.'

That film established Marvin as probably the leading heavy in films, but for the most part top-flight films just eluded him: *A Life in the Balance* (55) was a programmer with Bancroft again, but based on a story by Simenon now set in Mexico City, with Marvin as a psychotic – religious maniac – American killer. He was a killer again (with a cold) in *Violent Saturday*, starring Victor Mature. There were two hero's friends parts: *Not as a Stranger*, as a medical student with Robert Mitchum; *Pete Kelly's Blues*, in a band with Jack Webb. In *I Died a Thousand Times* he was one of Jack Palance's henchmen; in *Shack Out on 101* he was a cook in Cafe 101 who was actually a secret agent after scientist Frank Lovejoy's plans (and he got harpooned, literally, at the end). In *The Rack* (56) he was a fellow POW who testifies against Paul Newman.

Lee Marvin's long apprenticeship in movies was mostly spent playing thugs. This is the one he portrayed in Violent Saturday *(55).*

He was first star-billed in *Seven Men From Now*, another Scott Western, as the most arrogant of villains. Then: *Pillars of the Sky*, a Western with Jeff Chandler; *Attack!*, as the colonel; and *Raintree County* (57), as a hard-drinking, loud-talking type. He then moved, except for one film, into full-time TV for three years – 'M Squad', starring as a police lieutenant (later, in the 60s, he was to have a similar part in a series named after him). The one film he made was *The Missouri Traveller* (58), starring, with Brandon de Wilde: an unimportant piece where his sardonic bully was a relief from the general atmosphere of pastoral sentiment. On TV in 1960 he played Ira Hayes – the Iwo Jima hero – to great acclaim.

Medical students (they are listening to a lecture by Broderick Crawford) in Not as a Stranger *(55). Three familiar faces in the second row: Lee Marvin, Frank Sinatra and Robert Mitchum.*

He returned to films in *The Comancheros* (61), as John Wayne's half-scalped gun-running adversary, and their fights were among the film's high spots; they were enemies again in John Ford's *The Man Who Shot Liberty Valance* (62), but buddies (scrapping and boozing ones) in another for Ford, *Donovan's Reef*. With that one he was elevated to star-billing alongside Wayne and he was top-starred in *The Killers* (64), Don Siegel's remake of the Hemingway story, notable mainly for Ronald Reagan's last film appearance. It was also Marvin's last full-scale essay in screen villainy (originally *small* screen: it was made for TV but considered too violent, so was shown in cinemas instead). His old mentor, Kramer, then recalled him for *Ship of Fools* (65), to play the ex-baseball player with whom Vivien Leigh flirts: a warm performance, enriched by a keen comic sense – something he used to great advantage in *Cat Ballou*, with Jane Fonda. This spoof Western

In the Thirties, films about transatlantic liners were often great fun, but this late entry, Ship of Fools *(65), provided the dullest of crossings. Enlivening it, however, were Vivien Leigh and Lee Marvin (though Simone Signoret and Oskar Werner were even better value as another ill-assorted couple).*

cast him in a dual role – a small one, as the fastest and nastiest gun in the West, and a big one as the drunkest and oldest. . . . For his virtuosity he got the Best Actor Oscar (and the BFA award), which helped an agreeable picture to a huge gross. *The Professionals* (66), an adventure story with Burt Lancaster, was also a big one.

Lee Marvin as the tough Major Reisman who trained and led The Dirty Dozen, *a popular adventure film made by Robert Aldrich in 1967.*

And *The Dirty Dozen* (67) was a huge one: a well-made but over-violent – and basically meretricious – war/adventure film, it made almost $20 million in the US and was hardly less popular in Britain. Marvin led the dozen, both in action and on the bills, and jumped from nowhere into second position in both countries' top 10 draws – which presumably led Universal to release as a feature film *Sergeant Ryker*, which he had made for TV (Kraft Suspense Theater, 1963). Rightly, it got few bookings. *Point Blank* also had critics protesting against the violence, but cinemagoers liked it, a thick-ear thriller overdirected by John Boorman. He was voted into the top 10 again, but his position was imperilled by the flop of Boorman's *Hell in the Pacific* (68), which threw him and Toshiro Mifune on to a desert island as opposing survivors of the war. He thought it his best film but disliked the ending the producers insisted on.

Paint Your Wagon (69) was an old Lerner and Loewe musical which Lerner and Paramount brought to the screen, with a new book by Paddy Chayevsky and Lerner about two gold-rush partners (Marvin, Clint Eastwood) who share a wife (Jean Seberg). Trouble during location shooting (Joshua Logan directed) turned an already costly film into the third most expensive ever made (after *Cleopatra* and *Tora Tora Tora*). Marvin, as box-office insurance, was paid $1 million plus 10 per cent (said 'Time Magazine'. quoting his fee as being in only four figures before *Cat Ballou*) and it was well earned: the film had some good things going for it and Marvin's old hell-raker was the best of these, even if 'Playboy' was not entirely wrong in thinking he had 'plenty of vitality but very little charm to take the rough edges off a role made to order for the late Walter Huston'. If the film finally made a profit, it was due to him. He was seventh in the top 10 that year and the next, with *Monte Walsh* (70), as an ageing gunslinger. Co-star Jeanne Moreau said: 'Lee Marvin is more male than anyone I have ever acted with. He is the greatest man's man I have ever met and that includes all the European stars I have worked with.'

A gutsy, honest interview in 'Time Magazine' gave another indication of the reasons for his pre-eminence among the stars: 'There's an old adage in the business. Never shack up with anyone with lower billing than you. Now here I am, running out of shack-ups. But you know, when you reach 45 and are making enough money to retire, you still have to keep making the flicks. Yeah, you keep working at the masculinity thing, reconfirming it, always asking yourself, "Hey, Jesus, am I losing it?"' (he was married, 1952-65; remarried in 1972). He had considered retirement, he said; after a break (but he was still in the box-office 10 in 1971, at 10th), he returned to films in *Pocket Money* (72) with Paul Newman, a tired 'caper' film which needed their names to sell it. Newman produced, keeping the budget to just over $2 million with Marvin getting $500,000 plus 20 per cent. He turned down *Deliverance*, the role that Burt Reynolds eventually played, on the ground that he was too old. Script problems killed the next project, *Tender Loving Care*, and the reviews killed the next two: *Prime Cut*, as an underworld hand after Gene Hackman's blood; and *The Emperor of the North Pole* – which it was his ambition to be, as a train-hopping hobo hunted by Borgnine. In a filmed theatre venture, he was Hicky in *The Iceman Cometh*, which had limited showings; but it was the press reception – again – which limited showings of *The Spikes Gang* (1974) and *The Klansman* with Richard Burton. Because of the drinking of both stars, the film was a nightmare for the other participants. There was a minute improvement with *Shout at the Devil* (76), a British film made with South African money; Marvin was an Irish-American ivory poacher and he was the first half of *The Great Scout and Cathouse Thursday*, a Western with Oliver Reed, which did less than nothing to re-establish him. In 1979 he made news when his house companion of six years, Michelle Triola Marvin, sued him for half his earnings during their years together before his second marriage – i.e. $1,800,000. Since the case was liable to set a precedent for such relationships, it was followed with much interest, but the judge awarded only $104,000.

The recent films he had made had wrecked his position at the box-office and since his standing with directors was of the same level (due to on-set behaviour) the offers became fewer: *Avalanche Express* (78), as an agent escorting KGB defector Robert Shaw across Europe; *The Big Red One* (80), as a sergeant in this war movie; and *Death Hunt* (81), doggedly and drunkenly pursuing Charles Bronson. It was a pity that he was billed after Bronson, much inferior as an action hero – but his role, as an American entrepreneur favoured by the Russians, was smaller than that of William Hurt in *Gorki Park* (83). A French thriller, *Canicule* (84) found him as a footloose American bank robber on the run, but despite a distinguished supporting cast – including Miou Miou, Victor Lanoux and Jean Carmet – it was chiefly seen on video abroad (retitled *Dog Day*) and the *The Dirty Dozen: The Next Million* (85) was made for television. Between the two, financing of Losey's *Track 39* fell through at the last minute. In his final film, he and Chuck Norris led *The Delta Force* (86) to rescue hijacked passengers in the Middle East: Cannon made it and Marvin was again billed under a lesser light. He died in 1987.

Giulietta Masina

Giulietta Masina enjoyed an intense but brief vogue in the 50s, mainly because of two Chaplinesque (the adjective was ineluctable) roles written for her by her husband, Federico Fellini. She had button-eyes in a chalk-white golliwog face; she had short arms and puss-in-boots legs which kicked up when she was happy. You either liked her or loathed her. Critics loved her; she probably suffered more from overpraise than any other artist in film history. It is a pity; for her clowning for Fellini represented only one side of a generally likeable talent.

She was born in 1921 near Bologna, the daughter of a schoolteacher. She studied in Rome, where she took a degree in literature – and acted with the university drama group; she joined the Ateneo Theatre in Rome, then under the direction of Enrico Fulchignoni. Fellini was at this time a radio scriptwriter; he embarked on a series about a newly married couple, 'Cico e Pallina', and apparently chose Masina for Pallina on the basis of a photograph. They married in 1943 and she retired. After some years she returned to the stage and was recognized as an expert in Goldoni; but it was because she moved among movie people that she got her first film-role – Alberto Lattuada asked her to play a Livorno tart in *Senza Pietà* (48), the confidante to whom Carla del Poggio reveals her love for Negro John Kitzmiller. It was a fresh and funny performance and brought her a Silver Ribbon (Italy's major film award) for Best Supporting Actress. Her next role was in a film written by her husband and directed by him (his first step in that direction) and Lattuada: *Luci del Varietà* (50), a tale of a third-rate touring company. She was the mistress of star Peppino De Filippo.

Such, really, was to be her lot in films: friend or mistress. She was back among the bordellos – this time of Genova – in *Persiane Chiuse*, as the chum of Eleanora Rossi Drago. After *Sette Ore di Guai*, she was the chum of Elsa Merlini (a pre-war star making a come-back) in *Cameriera Bella Presenza Offresi*, the adventures of a housemaid among some other big stars – Vittorio De Sica, Aldo Fabrizi, Gino Cervi. She then did another film with Fellini, *Lo Sceicco Bianco* (52), the tale of a wife who leaves her husband on their honey-moon to pursue a pin-up magazine hero (Alberto Sordi) – and her husband's subsequent dilemma: a warped comedy, and boring, with grim jokes. Then she was back in her usual slot: friend to Ingrid Bergman – but a socialite one – in *Europa '51*; and friend to ex-whore Yvonne Sanson, involved in a romance with Frank Villard, as *Wanda la Peccatrice*. She had a break in *Romanza della Mia Vita*, as the faithful childhood friend of Luciano Tajoli, who becomes a famous singer; and she was a friend again in *Al Margini della Metropoli* (53) – Marlina Berti's, the girlfriend of condemned-to-death Massimo Girotti. She had a very good role, looking glamorous, as a girl thrilled by a man (Peppino de Filippo) whom she thinks has committed a *crime passionel: Via Padova 46*. She was a whore again in *Donne Proibite* (54), with Linda Darnell, and then in one of the episodes of *Cento Anni d'Amore*, six short stories of love directed by Lionello de Felice.

Fellini, meanwhile, had made a good film, *I Vitelloni*. Next he prepared a starring vehicle for his wife, *La Strada* (55), a story of some strolling players. She was the plain optimistic Gelsomina, a clown, who smiled up at the stars and laughed through her tears, no matter how much fortune or Anthony Quinn ill-treated her. The film was a great success and a personal triumph for her; she was much better, however, in *Il Bidone*, because she was not required to emote from A to Z, but stopped somewhere around L. In fact, the role was brief, as Richard Basehart's wife, in this best and least pretentious of Fellini. Around the same time she co-starred with Sordi in the mediocre *Buonanotte Avvocato!*; and Fellini was cooking up a follow-up to *La Strada* – *Le Notti di Cabiria* (57). She was Gelsomina's cousin or something, a whore on the Appian Way who smiled through all her misfortunes (it was the basis for 'Sweet Charity'). It was a better film, because it did not pretend to more than melodrama, and her performance was much more winning. Said 'Time and Tide': 'She is one of those performers you can't tear your eyes from, lest you miss a moment of her superb tragi-comic timing.' Isabel Quigly wrote in the 'Spectator' that she played 'Cabiria so individually, even

Giulietta Masina had been making films for seven years when she made La Strada *(55), which brought the critics of the world to her feet. 'Chaplinesque' was the usual adjective, and this picture gives an indication as to why. With her is Anthony Quinn.*

so eccentrically, that she never fails for a minute to convince one, almost painfully, of a real, rounded, solid Cabiria, with a past and a future, a house, a tatty fur coat, a gas-stove to swank about. yet she is touching and comprehensible on the broadest human level. . . . Even if there were no sub-titles, her walk and gestures and eyes would speak for her enough. . . . ' And Paul Dehn, who thought she 'deserves a single surname as surely as Chaplin or Garbo', added: 'She is a miniature version of the hope which still persists in a bloody world: and the world itself would be lost if it did not love her.'

Well, they did at Cannes, where she won a Best Actress award; and she was judged the year's Best Actress in Italy, Germany and Japan. But despite the additional presence of Paul Douglas, *Fortunella* (58) was given short shrift in Britain and the US – a pastiche of Fellini directed by Eduardo De Filippo, in which she played her by now familiar character. 'Variety' commented that 'all four expressions are outrageously overworked'. And that journal referred to 'grotesque facial distortions' in *Nella Città l'Inferno*, where she and Anna Magnani were convicts. She did a minor film, *La Donna Dell' Altro* (59), and then a big international co-production, *La Grande Vie/La Gran Vita/Das Kunstseidene Mädchen*, directed by Julien Duvivier, as a waif again, going from man to man. 'Variety' again: 'Actually Miss Masina has a tendency to mug rather than act, and it is hard to believe that she is physically appealing to the myriads of men in her life.' The film failed and sealed the doom of her career as an international name. She took a small supporting role in the French *Landru* (63), as one of his victims, and virtually disappeared from international view, except for Fellini's *Giulietta degli Spiriti* (65). Indeed, apart from the early whore films, only her films with her husband were known abroad; two of them at least had been designed to showcase her talents and had succeeded; but this one did nothing for her, although allegedly biographical/autobiographical, an ugly attempt at fantasy.

She did a cameo in *Scusi, Lei è Favorevole o Contrario?* (66), starring, written and directed by Sordi – with several other names: Anita Ekberg, Silvana Mangano, Bibi Andersson. And she had a supporting role in Lina Wertmuller's *Non Stuzzicate la Zanzara* (67) with pop star Rita Pavone in the leading role. At last, she appeared in an English-speaking film, *The Madwoman of Chaillot* (69), as one of the cronies of Katharine Hepburn. It was a brief role and she was reticent in it; remembering her in *Europa '51* and *Il Bidone*, one would like to have seen more of her.

After a long absence from films – though she did some television – she made two consecutively: *Frau Holle* (85), based on a German fairy-tale, and her husband's *Ginger e Fred*, with Mastroianni.

Marcello Mastroianni

Until *La Dolce Vita*, Mastroianni was unknown outside his native land except to the most assiduous follower of Italian flms. After *La Dolce Vita*, he was written up as the modern Boyer or Valentino, interviewed not on his career but on love, Italian men, love, American women, love, bed . . . all of which questions he answered wearily, repetitively and with great good humour. He is an amiable man. He pointed out that he had been married for many years (to actress Flora Clarabella in 1950), that he works too hard for much *amore* – and anyway he is lazy. He has no ambition; he says, he has been lucky. This, anyway, is nearer the truth. On the evidence of his screen portrayals you cannot make a case for Mastroianni as a great lover. Even as a leading man he is passive and not always interesting – in a business suit, as an executive, like Italy's answer to Gregory Peck. There are 40 good reasons why he was not famous before *La Dolce Vita* and each one of them is a film. However, as a character actor he is often superb and worth every sentence of those interminable interviews.

He was born in Fontana Liri, near Frosinone, in 1924, the son of a cabinet-maker. When he was five the family moved to Torino (Turin) and a few years later to Rome, where he started a career as a draughtsman. Towards the end of the war the Germans sent him to a labour camp in north Germany, but he escaped and hid out in an attic in Venice for the duration, earning a living by piece-work picture-painting. He returned to Rome and got a job in the accounts department of Eagle-Lion (Rank) films; he spent his evenings at a local drama group (where he met Giulietta Masina). A production of 'Angelica' was much admired; Luchino Visconti sent someone from his company to look at it and Mastroianni was offered a role in his production of 'As You Like It'. He joined Visconti's company and had parts in 'A Streetar Named Desire', 'Death of a Salesman', 'Troilus and Cressida', 'Uncle Vanya', etc. He was given a small role in a new version of Victor Hugo, *I Miserabili* (47), with Gino Cervi and Valentina Cortese, but his film career did not begin in earnest till 1949. Since then he has hardly stopped working.

He was in *Cuori sui Mare* (49), with Milly

Vitale, *Vent'anni*, with Liliana Mancini, and *Vita da Cane* (50), with Gina Lollobrigida. Then Luciano Emmer offered him one of the leads in his semi-documentary, *Una Domenica d'Agosto*, an affectionate look at Sunday by the Sea. He played a traffic cop in love and was liked enough to get one of the leads in *Atto di Accusa* (51), as an innocent man suspected of murder and incriminated by the lawyer husband of his mistress (Lea Padovani). It was a minor, shoddy picture and *Contro le Legge* was little better, a thriller with Fulvia Memmi. Emmer engaged him again to play a sports fan in Paris in *Parigi e Sempre Parigi*, with Lucia Bose; then he did two lurid melodramas: *L'Eterna Catena* (52), as one of two brothers fighting over Gianna Maria Canale, and the successful *Sensualità*. This was an incredible bucolic piece about a wife (Eleanor Rossi Drago) who cheats on Mastroianni with his earthy, virile brother (Amadeo Nazzari), which ends with a double murder and the survivor walking off to give himself up. . . .

There was another cross-section picture directed by Emmer, *Ragazze di Piazza di Spagna*, and then a host of forgotten, non-exportable items: *Tragio Ritorno* with Franca Marzi; *Lulu*, from a play by Carlo Bergolazzi, with Valentina Cortese; Dino Risi's good *Il Viale della Speranza* (53) with Liliana Bonfatti, a drama about two girls who are film extras; *Gli Eroi della Domenica*, a comedy-drama about a football team, with Raf Vallone; *Penne Nere* starring with Marina Vlady, a war film about the famous Alpine regiment of the title; *Febbre di Vivere*, a very fine contemporary drama, as the unfortunate pal of hero/heel Massimo Serato; *Non Amai Troppo Tardi*, a modern version of 'A Christmas Carol', with Paolo Stoppa as Scrooge and Mastroianni as his partner; and *La Valigia dei Sogni* with Maria Pia Casilia. He was then reunited with Lea Padovani for an episode ('Il Pupo') of *Tempi Nostri* (54), directed by Alessandro Blasetti, about a poor couple trying vainly to abandon their baby. He was poor again in *Cronaca dei Poveri Amanti*, Carlo Lizzani's study of a back street in Florence at the advent of the Blackshirts, a jolly, romantic film but irreproachable in its attitude to Fascism. These two stood out from the general run of Mastroianni's films and the former indicated a sure grasp of comedy. His idealist in the Lizzani film was not, however, very interesting. He returned to more conventional stuff: *Giorni d'Amore*, a comedy about marriage plans in southern Italy with Marina Vlady; and *Schiava del Peccato*, with Silvana Pampanini – she was an ex-whore and he her beau. He was Donizetti in *Casa Ricordi*, an all-star tribute to that Milanese family, punctuated with globules of music by the composers they sponsored (Paolo Stoppa was the founder; Maurice Ronet was Bellini; Gabriele Ferzetti, Puccini).

Then he worked with two people with whom his name would be linked professionally from time to time, Sophia Loren and Vittorio De Sica. In *Peccato che Sia una Canaglia* (55) they were father and daughter, both crooked, and he the nice taxi-driver who falls in love with her; Blasetti directed, from a story by Moravia. There were two programmers, *La Principessa delle Canarie*, a swashbuckler with Pampanini, and *Tam Tam* with Kerima, and then another with De Sica and Loren, *La Bella Mugnaia*, Mario Camerini's remake of his old movie of 1934. De Sica was Mastroianni's vain counsel in Emmer's comedy, *Il Bigamo* (56), about a young salesman falsely accused of bigamy. And De Sica and Loren were both in *La Fortuna di Essere Donna*, she as a budding movie star and Mastroianni as a photographer. Emmer directed *Il Momento Più Bello* (57) – a birth: a sleepy hospital drama about an obstetrician whose girl (Giovanna Ralli) becomes pregnant. Conversely, he and Fiorella Mari were a childless couple in *Padri e Figli*, another cross-section movie (parental misunderstandings), with De Sica, Antonella Lualdi, Franco Interlenghi, neatly directed by Mario Monicelli, but sticking to the tired formulas of Italian cinema. The same can be said of the German-Italian *Mädchen und Männer/La Ragazza delle Saline*, a melodrama of the salt-flats with newcomer Isabelle Corey; and *Il Medico e lo Stregone* (58), as a young medico opposed to wily faith healer De Sica.

Visconti then requested Mastroianni for one of his then rare excursions into films, *Le Notti Bianche*, designed in fact to showcase the talents of Maria Schell. Jean Marais was the other man, it was from a story by Dostoevsky and all too much an imitation of a pre-war Carné movie. Mastroianni mooned about – but there was little else he could do; he said later that this was the first time he became interested in filming. He had only a supporting role in Monicelli's *I Soliti Ignoti* as one of the gang – the unemployed photographer – but it was the first of his pictures to have a wide success overseas. *Un Ettaro di Cielo* was an undistinguished rural romance with Rosanna Schiaffino and so was Jules Dassin's *La Loi* (59), despite the presence of Yves Montand, Lollobrigida and others. The publicity for this film, coupled with the critical attention paid the Visconti film and the success of *I Soliti Ignoti*, meant that he was at last becoming known outside Italy. There should have been a wider audience for *Racconti d'Estate*, an account of summer in a resort on the Italian Riviera. True, four of the five episodes were dismal, but the one with Mastroianni and Michèle Morgan was splendid, a sensual, engaging piece about a policeman who succumbs to, and sleeps with, the woman handcuffed to him. Moreover, Mastroianni's quizzical cop was his liveliest, best performance to date. The next two were not seen outside Italy: *Tutti Inamorati*, a pleasant film about a widower in love with a schoolgirl (Jacqueline Sassard), and *Il Nemico di mia Moglie* with Giovanna Ralli.

It was perhaps because of Mastroianni's introvert, speculative qualities that Fellini chose him as the observer of *La Dolce Vita* (60), a long, episodic account of Rome's Via Veneto set – the wealthy, the party-givers and the party-goers. The film was as superficial as the life it pretended to portray, but excesses of symbolism (a statue of Christ hung from a helicopter over the Vatican, etc.), sexual variety (transvestites, 'orgies') and length made it a roaring success worldwide. Its title gave a new phrase to most languages. Mastroianni at last became a name.

Simultaneously on view were *Ferdinando il Re di Napoli* with Peppino and Eduardo De Filippo, a starring vehicle for them, and Mauro Bolognini's *Il Bell' Antonio*, a somewhat more pungent view of Italian mores than the Fellini film – marriage between a Sicilian count, impotent after over-sampling the *dolce vita*, and his sexually ignorant bride (Claudia Cardinale). He brought nothing to the part but a worried look, they all talked too much and audiences outside the peninsula found it all rather ludicrous. In *Adua e le Compagne* he was a car salesman philandering with ex-tart Simone Signoret – not a happy man, beset with insecurity, angry customers and a cold: but he played with a gaiety hitherto unexpected. He was expressionless again in Antonioni's *La Notte* (61), trapped in that loveless marriage with Jeanne Moreau. He had a double role in *Fantasmi a Roma*, a slight but enjoyable ghost comedy with Vittorio Gassmann.

Success had affected him: there was more confidence. His next two movies were – with *La Notte* – the best he had yet made and contain his best performances. In Elio Petri's *L'Assassino* he was a weak, oily philanderer, momentarily reforming when imprisoned for murder: his performance showed real fear, the film had real tension. In Petro Germi's *Divorzio all'Italiana* he was another Sicilian count, vain and down-at-heel, trying to murder his fat moustached wife because divorce was unheard of and he wanted to marry his pretty cousin. The joke was inventively sustained, with just the correct emphasis on its central – very real – problem. The film was a massive hit in Italy and won awards for Germi and Mastroianni; overseas the latter won the BFA Best Foreign Actor award, the film was extensively praised and spilled over from the art circuit. At this point Mastroianni was probably, with Belmondo, the most sought

Mastroianni became famous in Britain and the US in La Dolce Vita *and* La Notte. *He seemed a dull stick, however, until he played the conniving Sicilian husband in* Divorzio all'Italiana *(61). Daniela Rocca played the wife he wished to be rid of.*

after actor in Europe. His fee, according to 'Cinémonde', was 100 million lire a film, second among Italian actors (Alberto Sordi was first by a small sum; Mastroianni was followed by Ugo Tognazzi – 50 million – and Nino Manfredi, Peppino De Filippo, Renato Salvatore and Vittorio Gassmann in that order. Among the women Sophia Loren was top at 400 million, followed by Lollobrigida – 150 million, Silvana Mangano – 100 million, Claudia Cardinale – 60-80 million, Monica Vitti – 40 million).

He chose to do *Vie Privée* (62) with Brigitte Bardot; *Cronaca Familiare*, directed by Valerio Zurlini from a bestseller by Vasco Pratolini, a sad, intimate look at the relationship between two brothers – Jacques Perrin was the younger one; and Fellini's *Otto e Mezzo* (63). This was the much touted follow-up to *La Dolce Vita*, confessedly autobiographical; and Mastroianni walked through the fantasies again with an even more glazed expression. From which it must have been a relief to do a part with guts in a good picture, Monicelli's *I Compagni*, a sober account of the beginnings of the trade union movement in Torino. His dedicated agitator/professor, myopic, bearded, again increased his reputation.

His 'international' career was mainly in the hands of Loren's husband, Carlo Ponti, and/or Joseph E. Levine of Avco-Embassy, who had an agreement with Ponti to take many of his films. They, and De Sica and Loren, had two big hits: the three-part *Ieri Oggi e Domani* (64), in which Mastroianni indulged in caricature but won a BFA Best Foreign Actor award; and *Matrimonio all'Italiana*, unabashedly commercial stuff enhanced by the performances of the leads. Then Ponti produced Mastroianni in another three-episode picture, *Oggi Domani Dopodomani* (65) – 'L'Uomo dai Cinque Palloni' with Catherine Spaak, 'L'Ora di Punta' with Pamela Tiffin and 'La Moglie Bionda' with Virna Lisi. This was apparently offered to Levine as *Paranoia*, but turned down, as per the agreement, as not being 'a first-class motion picture'. The Tiffin-Lisi episodes turned up in the US as a two-part film, *Kiss the Other Sheik*; the Spaak episode arrived in 1968 as *L'Uomo dai Palloncini*, said to be a feature cut down for *Paranoia* but now restored to its original length. It was a mess anyway and so was the *Sheik*. Nor were there many takers Stateside for Monicelli's *Casanova 70*, with Mastroianni as a jaded NATO officer involved with Virna Lisi, etc. Ponti tried again with *La Deccima Vittima*, a sci-fier from a novel by Robert Sheckley, directed by Elio Petri with Ursula Andress, but that bombed in the US. Levine decided that Mastroianni dubbed and Loren-less was not worth a light in the US.

Not that there was not mileage to be had from Mastroianni's name in the right picture – though no distributor was much interested in the best film he made around this time, *Io Io Io . . . e gli Altri* (66), an all-star trifle (De Sica, Lollobrigida, Manfredi, Mangano, etc.), in which he played the humanitarian friend of the hero (Walter Chiari). There was still great interest when he went to New York to plug a new picture, though perhaps a falling off from his first visit to the US in 1962 when he received 37 firm offers. To protect himself from the temptations of an American career he claimed that he was too lazy to learn English, but he did speak a little in *The Poppy Is Also a Flower*, one of several stars in this film made originally for TV (they were each paid one token dollar by the United Nations, who produced). Levine handled the next one, *Spara Forte piu Forte Non Capisco*, written and directed by Eduardo De Filippo, from his stage play, a bizarre effort which co-starred Raquel Welch and which cast Masatroianni as a shabby junk-dealer; and that was the end of the agreement.

Worldwide interest, however, was expected in the next two. The first was never finished (or indeed started), *Il Viaggio di G. Mastorna*, produced by De Laurentiis and directed by Fellini; Fellini took a year to prepare it and spent $1 million, but they disagreed on the use of Mastroianni and Fellini walked out (the matter was settled out of court in January 1967). Visconti used him in his long-planned version of 'L'Etranger' by Camus (once announced for Belmondo): *Lo Straniero* (67), but it was cold, remote and one of Visconti's least successful films.

To maintain his salary – now around 350 million lire – Mastroianni had either to continue making Italian movies with (some) American backing or to make an American film. Dubbing had proved ineffective – and his English was improving. So he elected to make a film for Paramount in Britain, produced by Ponti, *Diamonds for Breakfast* (68), a comedy both tired and vulgar, about an impoverished White Russian (Mastroianni) bent on getting back the family jewels. It quickly disappeared. MGM backed *Gli Amanti/A Time for Lovers* (69), an old-fashioned piece about a love affair between a tubercular girl (Faye Dunaway) and a middle-aged Italian. De Sica directed and was roundly trounced. So was Mastroianni. 'Time Magazine' said he 'displays all the zest of a man summoned for tax evasion. He appears to be lip-reading his English. . . .' He himself admitted that he had learnt the first script phonetically: he described that film as 'ridiculous' and the second as

Mastroianni and Sophia Loren again, in La Moglie del Prete *(71)* – The Priest's Wife. *He was a priest and she a pop-singer – and they fall in love and want to marry; but the film did not make very much of the situation.*

'terrible'. He returned to his native Italian for *I Girasoli* (70), with Sophia Loren, and was back in Britain for John Boorman's allegorical *Leo the Last*, as an Italian prince living in Notting Hill Gate. That made his fourth big flop in a row – and it was even more deserving than the others.

The film with Loren had been popular in Italy and so was *Dramma della Gelosia: Tutti Particolari in Cronaca* – in fact, a comedy about jealousy with Monica Vitti, embracing just about every one of those modish, kinky clichés which had invaded Italian film-making. Again, Anglo-Saxon audiences resisted it with a vengeance. And they were not very warm to *La Moglie del Prete* (71) with Loren. After that, Mastroianni did a remake of an Italian perennial, *Scipio il Africano*; *Permette Roco Papaleo*, the adventures of an Italian in the US; and two films with his offscreen companion, Catherine Deneuve, *Ca N'arrive qu'aux Autres/It only Happens to Others* and *Melampo* (72). A TV film with Anna Magnani, *1870*, was released to cinemas. For Ponti, he did *Che?/What?*, directed by Roman Polanski in masturbatory mood – a daft Candy-in-Wonderland thing, with Sydne Rome as the innocent who strays into a house of weirdies, including Mastroianni as a retired pimp who is whipped by her when encased in a tigerskin and manacled to her on the beach when dressed as a carabiniere. Marco Ferreri's *La Grande Bouffe* (73) was equally pointless – and dull – a tale about four men who eat themselves to death. *Mordi e Fuggi* was a slight improvement: he was a businessman on a dirty weekend kidnapped by Oliver Reed. Then: *Rappresaglia/Massacre in Rome*, as a priest, with Richard Burton as a German colonel; *L'Evénement le Plus Important depuis que l'Homme a Marché sur la Lune*, an unimportant film itself, with Deneuve, as a pregnant man; Yves Robert's *Salut l'Artiste*, a study of a small-part Italian actor on the fringes of Paris show business; and *Touche Pas à la Femme Blanche* (74), reunited with Deneuve and Ferreri, as General Custer in a weak attempt at a Western parody. This made seven poor films in just over a year, surely no consolation for the cancellation of *Charlie Sugar I Love You*, a screenplay he had written and due to be filmed in Australia. After several months off the screen he found a good film – in the role originally meant for Maximilian Schell – the Taviani brothers' *Allonsofàn*, playing an 1816 aristocrat with revolutionary ideals. And, after *La Pupa del Gangster* (75), reunited with Sophia, there was another good film – Bolognini's study of a mental home in the days of Mussolini, *Per le Antiche Scale* (75): at least, there were good things in it, including his performance as the philandering head and Françoise Fabian's as the new-broom doctor.

In *La Donna della Domenica* (76) he was a

police inspector from the South; in *Signore e Signori, Buonanotte*, a sketch film, the compère; and in *Divina Creatura*, a period melodrama, he inducted Laura Antonelli into prostitution. He passed up a poor political film, *Une Femme à sa Fenêtre* (the role went to Philippe Noiret) to make a much better one, *Todo Modo*, with Gian Maria Volonté, directed by Elio Petri. He was a radio journalist in *Una Giornata Particolare* (77) and a homosexual until seduced by Sophia (and what better way for a gay to go!), he had sex problems too in Marco Vicario's *Mogliamante*, as a prosperous wine merchant who fakes death and then watches his wife's increasingly interesting love life. He was announced for a British (Box-Thomas) movie with Karen Black, *Persian Ransom*, but it was not made; instead he played a detective in *Doppio Delitto*, with Peter Ustinov. Unashamed, apparently, of his previous excursions with Ferreri, he went with him to New York to make *Bye Bye Monkey* (78), a French-Italian co-production with an English soundtrack, though that to date has not got this uneven farce-parody any Stateside bookings. On TV (in Italy) he played in Petri's version of Sartre's 'Les Mains Sales'; and in *Cosi Come Sei* he had an affair with a girl who might be his daughter. With Loren he did *Fatto di Sangue fra Due Uomini per Causa di una Vedova*, etc. (79); which he followed with Comencini's *L'Ingorgo*, about a giant traffic jam, with Sordi, Girardot, Tognazzi, etc., as himself, and *Giallo Napoletano*.

He seemed to be constantly working, though few of these movies were seen in the US or Britain: Scola's *La Terrazza* (80), as a magazine editor; Fellini's unsuccessful *La Città delle Donne* (81), once again as a surrogate of the director; Liliana Cavani's *La Pelle*; Risi's *Fantasma d'Amore* with Romy Schneider; and Scola's *La Nuit de Varennes* (82) as Casanova. Just as the Cavani film came out – to be described by 'Variety' as 'a poorly staged creepshow travesty' (of Malaparte's novel) – Mastroianni signed for another movie with this director, *Oltre la Porta*, after which he understandably went off to Brazil to work with the team which had had an international success with *Dona Flor and her Two Husbands*. The film in this case – much criticized on its home territory – was *Gabriela* (83), with Mastroianni as a Turkish-born bar-owner who has an affair with the heroine, Sonia Braga. Ferreri's *Storia di Piera* was hardly an improvement on past efforts, with Isabelle Huppert sleeping with both her parents (the mother was Hanna Schygulla). Mastroianni had the title-role in *Le Général de L'Armée Morte*, sent to exhume corpses left on the Albanian battlefield, and he remained in Paris to star in 'Tchin-Tchin' (84) with Natasha Parry, directed by her husband, Peter Brook. His two movies of the time were both adaptations of Pirandello, *Enrico IV*, directed by Bellochio at way below his best, and Monicelli's remake, *Le Due Vite di Mattia Pascal* (85). Neither film, surprisingly, found an international audience, but obviously the English-language *Macaroni* did; Mastroianni's co-star was Jack Lemmon. He was reunited with Fellini for a satire on television – two ageing dancers were reunited to appear on it (Giulietta Masina was the other) – called *Ginger e Fred*, which was followed swiftly by Monicelli's *I Soliti Ignoti . . . Vent' Anni Doppo* (86). Then to Greece, to play the title-role in *O Melissokomos/The Beekeeper*, wandering aimlessly to forget his incestuous love for his daughter; it was directed by Theo Angelopoulos, the country's best-known director, a fact likely to put you off Greek films for life.

There have been attempts to present Mastroianni as the great screen lover, which may be why he has so often elected to play men with sexual problems – as in Mogliamante *(77) –* Wifemistress *– in which he takes to spying on his own wife.*

Fellini's *Intervista* (87) was a salute to Cinecittà, albeit an egotistical one (or, if you prefer, a personal one), with Mastroianni and Ekburg appearing as themselves. The actor was prized at the Cannes Festival for his work in *Oci Ciornie*, 'one of the most outgoing, enjoyable performances in his long and illustrious career', as 'Variety' put it: he played a once-promising architect engaged in an extramarital affair. This compendium of Chekovian themes (it was partly a remake of *The Lady With the Little Dog*) was directed by Nikita Mikhalkov, who in Russia had made a film based on the author's early comedy 'Platanov'; he adapted this for Mastroianni under the title 'Pianola Meccanica', which later that year began a tour of the major Italian cities. *Arizona* (88) was a nightclub and the story, based on fact, found him and Hanna Schygulla as over-the-hill cabaret performers, she the widow of a Jew and he half-Jewish, coping with events in Europe from the end of World War I to the Anchluss: Pál Sandor directed, in two versions, and the Italian one was substantially different from the Hungarian one. And *Splendor* (89) was a cinema, whose ups and downs through the years are followed by Mastroianni, as the manager, and Marina Vlady.

Walter Matthau

Walter Matthau's emergence from supporting actor to star was one of the more agreeable aspects of cinemagoing in the 60s. He may not be as funny as W.C. Fields or even Bob Hope. He may, finally, lack that little extra something – paradoxically, for he has an especially subtle way of overdoing everything. He is always *more* surprised, *more* pained, *more* smug: his double-takes and his shudders are earth-shattering, his conceits awe-inspiring. He is not solely a comedy actor, though he has played little else since he became a star; he has a gift for character – but the badness of his bad guys pales beside the misanthropy of his good guys.

He was born in New York City in 1920 (he said once; 'Who's Who in the Theatre' says 1925). He became, by turns, a filing clerk, boxing instructor, basketball coach and, during war service, 1942-45, in the USAAF, a radio-operator. On demob he studied with Erwin Piscator at the Dramatic Workshop of the New York School for Social Research and did his first professional work in stock, at the Erie County Playhouse, in 'Three Men on a Horse' (46), as Charlie, and 'Ten Nights in a Bar Room'. He began to get small parts on Broadway – he was a candelabrum-carrier and understudy for seven others on 'Anne of a Thousand Days' (48) – and began doing TV, but attracted attention first on Broadway in 1951, in varied roles in a series of flop plays. The year 1955 was the turning point, when he played leads in City Center revivals of 'The Wisteria Trees' and 'Guys and Dolls', and scored a success in a featured part in George Axelrod's 'Will Success Spoil Rock Hunter?'. He also made his film début in 'a ridiculous part. . . . I did it because I was desperately short of money': *The Kentuckian* (55), as the heavy who tricked Burt Lancaster into a silly battle of whips. He was the chief villain in another Western, *The Indian Fighter*, with Kirk Douglas, and was upped to 'co-star' billing in *Bigger Than Life* (56), as the family friend of James Mason.

After the run of the Axelrod play and an appearance in 'Maiden Voyage' he returned to Hollywood: *A Face in the Crowd* (57), as the cynical but concerned reporter – written by Budd Schulberg and supposedly a self-portrait; *Slaughter on Tenth Avenue*, as the racketeer boss in this mild exposé of waterfront life, with Richard Egan; *Voice in the Mirror*, as a doctor trying to cure alcoholic Egan; *King Creole* (58), brilliant as the villain in this Elvis Presley vehicle; *Ride a Crooked Trail*, an Audie Murphy Western, as a boozy judge; and, still on the sauce, *Onionhead*, with Andy Griffith, as the tippling ship's cook. He livened up all these pictures and a Broadway play, 'Once More With Feeling' – a supporting performance which won the New York drama critics' award. He directed himself ('presumably on a dare,' says Steven H. Scheuer) in a B, *The Gangster Story* (60), an independent production that got mercifully few bookings, and the lows continued with yet another film he could only have done because he was short of money, *Strangers When We Meet*, playing a neighbourhood wolf bent on raping Kim Novak. On Broadway he was in 'Once There Was a Russian' and 'A Shot in the Dark' (for which he won a Tony); and in Hollywood, *Lonely Are the Brave* (62), as the sheriff.

He played a mother-loving, computerized racketeer in *Who's Got the Action?* and with Nita Talbot as his mistress left the nominal stars (Dean Martin and Lana Turner) without pants or shirt. He worked similar legerdemain in: *Island of Love* (63), as a Greek-born gangster bent on rubbing out Robert Preston; *Charade*, with James Coburn and George Kennedy, again bent on murder most foul; *Ensign Pulver* (64), as the ship's doctor; and *Fail Safe*, as a professor wearily urging the US to attack the USSR. During this period he was asked to do *The Thrill of It All*, in the part eventually played by Edward Andrews; Ross Hunter was furious when he asked $100,000. Matthau said the part was not even worth $10,000 – but it was a lousy role. He added that he had been averaging $150,000 over the last five years, but after 10 per cent to his agent, 10 per cent to his business manager and $60,000 a year in child support and alimony he could not afford to be out of work for more than a month. He was outstanding as the Mittel-European film producer of *Goodbye Charlie* and fine as the Hitchcock-styled private eye in *Mirage* (65). That year he played Oscar on Broadway in Neil Simon's 'The Odd Couple' and won another clutch of awards. His success was such that the only available Hollywood berth was labelled 'new star'.

He was fortunate in having Billy Wilder to guide him in *The Fortune Cookie* (66), as the slobbish, fast-talking conniving shyster lawyer, Whiplash Willie, brother-in-law to Jack Lemmon: the performance brought him a Best Supporting Oscar. He was amusing in *A Guide for the Married Man* (67), being instructed by Robert Morse in the art of infidelity – something, said Bosley Crowther, he approached 'with the ingenuousness of a clumsy bull moose'; but the film itself was laboured. Much funnier – and far more successful – was *The Odd Couple* (68), repeating his definitive portrait of an all-time slob, housekeeping with Jack Lemmon's very proper Felix. 'My admiration for Walter Matthau, the grown-ups' Yogi Bear, here padding in full dishevelment through a mess of innuendoes and somehow withdrawing one's attention from the worst of them, is without bounds' – John Coleman in the 'New Statesman'. Everyone went to see it; no one went to *The Secret Life of an American Wife*, except in Britain, where it got an exceptional press. He played a women-weary movie star 'inveigled' into adultery by a suburban housewife (the equally accomplished Anne Jackson). Some nice stuff; by George Axelrod. And the only mildly fetching sequence of *Candy* was Matthau's, as a bomb-happy general.

He was now established as one of the most jaded characters in films; experience had creased his expression into one of dire cynicism. Thus in deep gloom he meandered through *Hello Dolly!* (69), as the wealthy shopkeeper pursued by Barbra Streisand, and through *Cactus Flower*, as the philandering dentist finally cornered by Ingrid Bergman: in the former with some justification. He was defiantly miscast but funny as a Manhattan

The Secret Life of an American Wife *(68) was a funny comedy about a suburban wife (Anne Jackson) who one fine day sets out to bed a famous movie star (Walter Matthau).*

Another lady determined to have Walter Matthau was Barbra Streisand in Hello Dolly! *(69) – even to pursuing him when he is marching in the 14th Street Parade.*

Neil Simon's Plaza Suite *was three one-act comedies with only the set in common; as on the stage, one actor played the three leading parts – Walter Matthau in the film version, made in 1971 – but it was all too much like a photographed play to hold the attention for long.*

playboy in *A New Leaf* (70), written and directed by Elaine May and co-starring that multi-talented lady as the shy spinster he pursues. He was 10th at the box-office that year, seventh in 1971. Jack Lemmon directed him in *Kotch* (71), as a fugitive father who finds a new reason for living. He has, said Lemmon, 'talent that still hasn't been tapped. Films haven't yet touched on his depth.' Then he played three different parts in Neil Simon's *Plaza Suite*, as George C. Scott had done on stage; Maureen Stapleton repeated one of her three portrayals, but two other ladies were brought in for the others, Barbara Harris and Lee Grant. When the film was to have been made with three actors and he just one of them, his asking price was $1 million; in the event, he got $100,000 plus a participation fee which might go as high as 12½ per cent if the film took as much as $20 million. It did not and even he could not save it from being deadly dull. *Pete 'n Tillie* (72) was an interesting comedy about a couple getting on in life who marry and face tragedy; the lady was Carol Burnett in her first major screen role and they worked well together.

Charley Varrick (73) was, said the ads, 'A Siegel Film', and we may be glad that that director preferred Matthau to Donald Sutherland, his original choice – to play a crook in this clever-japes thriller – for the character needed all the sympathy he could get. Matthau elected to do two more thrillers: *The Laughing Policeman*, in which he and Bruce Dern were Frisco cops trying to solve a mass murder; and the excellent *The Taking of Pelham One Two Three* (74), in which he laconically masterminded the recovery of that abducted subway train. It was true that comedy was in short supply in Hollywood, but after doing a guest spot as a drunk in *Earthquake* (in which he was billed as W. Matuschanskayasky) he was in Billy Wilder's remake of *The Front Page*, with Lemmon – but the three of them could not make it second best of the three film versions. He was better served by the film of Neil Simon's *The Sunshine Boys* (75), permanently dyspeptic as he thunderingly traded insults with his old vaudeville partner, played by George Burns. And he had a similar situation going on with Tatum O'Neal in *The Bad News Bears* (76), he as an over-the-hill coach employed to coach a kids' baseball team. His salary for that was $750,000 against 10 per cent of the first $8 million gross receipts, then 12½ per cent of the next $5 million, then 15 per cent of everything over $13 million (this came to light when Paramount sold this and the two sequels to ABC for around $6 million each; and since of the three only this one was successful – with a gross of approximately $24 million – Matthau sued; the case was settled out of court). Matthau was with more kids, playing his sons, in *Casey's Shadow* (78), in which he was an impoverished and cantankerous Cajun horse-trainer: said 'Playboy'. 'If he keeps up his present pace as a grumpy, lovable slob, Matthau is going to have to admit that he's actually a reincarnation of Wallace Beery.' There was another felicitous teaming in *House Calls*, with Art Carney, he as a surgeon and Carney as the head of the hospital; but his episode in Simon's *California Suite* (with Elaine May) proved that to be in the same deprived annexe as *Plaza Suite*. In *Little Miss Marker* (80) he played the role done in earlier film versions by Adolphe Menjou and Bob Hope: Matthau in Runyon seemed ideal and there was promise in the teaming with Julie Andrews; but screenwriter Walter Bernstein, making his directorial début, made a hash of it. Matthau was presumably joking when he said it 'was too intellectual for the critics'.

He was no luckier with the next batch: *Hopscotch* and *The First Monday in October* (81), both directed by Ronald Neame, the first a chase comedy with the CIA trying to prevent former agent Matthau publishing his memoirs and the second a stagey courtroom clash between him and opposing lawyer Jill Clayburgh; Wilder's *Buddy Buddy* with Lemmon; and *I Ought to be in Pictures* (82), based on Neil Simon's play, with Matthau as a Hollywood screenwriter beseiged by the daughter (Dinah Manoff) who wants to be a star. He replaced Joseph Bologna in Michael Ritchie's *The Survivors* (83) for a happy teaming with Robin Williams, but this comedy about two men on the dole involved with cops was thin and it went direct to video in foreign markets. So did *Movers and Shakers* (85) and the teaming this time was with Charles Grodin, who wrote and co-produced – but he had surprisingly little to say about movie-making, leaving Matthau stranded as a studio head. At least most people heard of *Pirates* (86), a long-cherished project of high-profile director Roman Polanski, who needed American backing because of the cost – and because of a past indiscretion could not work in the US. Universal checked out during a change of management, with Cannon and De Laurentiis among those coming to the rescue – only to regret it, for after lethal notices this $31 million scatological swashbuckler took less than $1 million at the domestic (US) box-office. It was not surprising that Matthau observed that he felt himself a misfit in today's Hollywood, that things were easier in the theatre and television. For the first time in two decades he was not first cast of the players: in the case of Ritchie's *The Couch Trip* (88) both Dan Ackroyd and Grodin were signed before he was; he was guest-starred as a soul-mate of the former. An oft-announced remake of *Born Yesterday*, first with Whoopi Goldberg and then Bernadette Peters, would have been ideal casting, but it was eventually cancelled after one too many of Cannon's financial crises. Instead he went to Italy to appear in *Piccolo Diavolo* (88) co-starring Roberto Bergnini, who also directed.

VICTOR MATURE

'Actually, I am a golfer. That is my real occupation. I never was an actor; ask anybody, particularly the critics. This is my first Hollywood picture in ten years and I only did it because I was getting bored' – Victor Mature in 1968. Still, he must have had something to have got regular employment as an actor over a 30-year period. When he started, he was christened 'the Hunk' and had a strong shopgirl following. His name became a synonym for beefcake, 40s male sex-appeal. He had (therefore?) few fans among men, despite the fact that most of his movies were actioners. He was never a sympathetic hero, but on occasion made a convincing villain–tough, disdainful, sinister. He was impervious to the situations around him: you never got an inkling of what he was thinking or feeling. But in the sense that he moved comfortably before a camera and knew which chalk-marks to stand on, he was an actor.

He was born in Louisville, Kentucky, in 1916. Despite parental opposition he determined to be an actor and journeyed to California where he enrolled with the Pasadena Community Playhouse. He acted in over 60 plays before getting a leading part and that brought him to the attention of Hal Roach, who signed him to a long-term contract and gave him a part (10th on the cast-list) in a Joan Bennett vehicle, *The Housekeeper's Daughter* (39). Because of his physique Roach made him a prehistoric man in *One Million BC* (40), where he and prehistoric woman Carole Landis fled from huge magnified lizards and other reptiles: a later generation would call it 'camp', but meanwhile it did well on reissues. He was *Captain Caution* in a tale of the British-American War of 1812, with Louise Platt, and then was loaned to RKO for *No No Nanette* starring Anna Neagle – a teaming as curious in practice as theory. Roach and he parted company and he went to Broadway to be one of the men in the life of 'Lady in the Dark' Gertrude Lawrence. As a result of that, 20th offered a contract (he was to stay there for 14 years, though increasingly freelancing in the later years).

He started off more or less as a prop for the ladies: *I Wake Up Screaming* (41) with Betty Grable, as a murder suspect; *The Shanghai Gesture* at UA with Gene Tierney, as Mother Gin Sling's Arab companion; *Song of the Islands* (42) with Grable, a priceless piece of South Seas nonsense; *My Gal Sal* with Rita Hayworth, in a dim portrayal of Paul Dresser, songwriter brother of Theodore Dreiser; *Footlight Serenade* with Grable, as a boxer who conquers Broadway; and *Seven Days' Leave* at RKO, as a cocky corporal trying to marry highbrow Lucille Ball in order to collect an inheritance. 'Picturegoer', notably, disliked him. It said of his performance in *Song of the Islands* that he 'puts over his "you can't resist me" act effectively', and its Hollywood reporter, W.H. Mooring, told readers that he was disliked in the film city. He had, he said, set out 'to become Hollywood's self-avowed disciple of conceit and vulgarity. . . .'

At least he was patriotic and enlisted in the United States Coast Guard – for whom he starred in a review, 'Tars and Spars', which played New York in 1944. He returned to films as Doc Holliday in Ford's *My Darling Clementine* (46) with Henry Fonda. Then he was sinister in *Moss Rose* (47), a period melodrama with Peggy Cummins. The title *Kiss of Death* had nothing to do with the plot of that film unless it referred to Mature's performance – as a kid from the back streets who just could not help going bad, gee, he never had the breaks. He was out to restore his Dad's reputation in *Fury at Furnace Creek* (48), one of the hundreds of films that debased the Western tradition. Much better was *Cry of the City*, a good acrid thriller with cop Mature on the track of escaped con

Lost in a primeval forest: Victor Mature and Carole Landis as early inhabitants of our globe: One Million BC *(40).*

Richard Conte – and meeting up with Hope Emerson, the Miss Big behind the robbery. The next three were on loan-out: *Red Hot and Blue* (49) with Betty Hutton, as a theatre director; *Easy Living* with Lucille Ball, as a football player, and *Samson and Delilah*, as Samson. To get him for that Paramount paid $50,000 each to him and to 20th, plus the services of John Lund and Wandra Hendrix for one film. His Samson was ludicrous except, perhaps, physically, but then Hedy Lamarr was hardly a convincing Delilah – and the man who doubled for him in the fight with the lion did not even look much like him. Not that such considerations, nor the almost total boredom, prevented the film from being a huge box-office success.

It did not, however, give a noticeable fillip to his career: he went on to do conventional co-starring stints – with Betty Grable in *Wabash Avenue* (50), with Ann Sheridan in *Stella*. In *Gambling House*, 'Picturegoer' found him 'all teeth and bad manners, as the super spiv who reformed for the sake of . . . nice little Terry Moore'. He co-starred with Jane Russell in *The Las Vegas Story* (52), then took over from James Donald – who got tired of waiting around for the film to start – as the Roman centurion in *Androcles and the Lion*. He was considerably more at home in *Something For the Birds*, a comedy with Patricia Neal; *Million Dollar Mermaid* with Esther Williams; and *The Glory Brigade* (53), as a Greek-born commander in this Korean War story. Another comedy, *Affair With a Stranger*, with Jean Simmons, cruelly exposed his limitations: the 'MFB' found him 'an odd choice for light comedy. [He] wanders through the film with permanently raised eyebrows', and 'Variety' thought him 'less than credible as the playwright' (it was about a showbiz marriage). But 20th, not deterred by his earlier showing as a Roman soldier, made him another, that early Christian convert, Demetrius, and inheritor of *The Robe*.

Why is the lady laughing? Jean Simmons loathed the films she was forced to make at RKO after Rank sold her contract without bothering to inform her. This one was Affair With a Stranger *(53), in which she played the wife of a famous dramatist – who was Victor Mature, not only miscast but probably the dullest co-star she ever had.*

The Robe was rubbish with pretensions; *Veils of Baghdad* was merely rubbish. Mature played a rebel leader and he continued playing leaders, men of action, over the next few years: *Dangerous Mission* (54); *Demetrius and the Gladiators*, a sequel to *The Robe* and nowhere near as successful; *Betrayed*, supporting Clark Gable, as a Resistance leader and 'surprise' instigator of the title deed; *The Egyptian*, another confirmation of 20th's curious ability to see him as a denizen of the Ancient World, supporting Edmund Purdom; and *Chief Crazy Horse* (55), in the title-role. His last for 20th was *Violent Saturday*, about a small town bank heist, and it was probably his last decent film in a good while. After a Western, *The Last Frontier*, he went to Africa on *Safari* (56) for a British company, Warwick, which made actioners for Columbia release. He worked frequently for them over the next few years, which perhaps prolonged his career – but all his films were now strictly double-bill fare: *The Sharkfighter*; *Zarak* (57), as a native chief, with Anita Ekberg for Warwick; *Interpol*, also Ekberg and Warwick; and *The Long Haul*, still in Britain, with Diana Dors, as a truck-driver.

He returned to the US for a rather surprising liaison, with director Frank Borzage, making his first film for more than 10 years, to co-star with Li Li Hua, clearly the *China Doll* (58). His salary was $125,000 and it was announced that Mature and Borzage had formed a production company – but nothing came of it. Mature announced an independent venture, *Escape from Andersonville*, but nothing came of that either. Back at Warwick he did a war film, *No Time to Die*, and then returned to the US for *Escort West* (59). Meanwhile, Warwick were in trouble: public apathy if not antipathy to their product led to an announcement that they were cutting back to one film a year; then they announced that Mature had signed for six, which would put them back on the map. But *The Bandit of Zhobe* was a bad film even by their standards and turned out to be their last gasp (Mature was an Indian chieftain who turns bandit in revenge). These films were all nails in the coffin of a career: neither *The Big Circus* (as its impressario) nor *Timbuctu* (as an American trader) did anything to open it.

But if there was nothing in the Anglo-Saxon market, there was always Italy, which had already welcomed, among others, Jack

Palance, Guy Madison, Jeffrey Hunter, Edmund Purdom, Lex Barker, Ricardo Montalban, Jeanne Crain, George Nader, Robert Alda, John Derek, Rhonda Fleming, Orson Welles, Rory Calhoun, Debra Paget, Alan Ladd, Pedro Armendariz, Cameron Mitchell and John Drew Barrymore. Mature made *Annibale*, as Hannibal, with Rita Gam, and *I Tartari* (60) with Orson Welles. It was also in Italy that he made a come-back, satirizing his old screen self in a Peter Sellers comedy, *Caccia alla Volpe/After the Fox* (66); a while later he did a similar stint in a film starring a pop group called the Monkees, *Head* (68); and again after an interval appeared in *Every Little Crook and Nanny* (72), with Lynn Redgrave. He announced that he would retire after that, but was wheedled back for a spot in *Won Ton Ton the Dog Who Saved Hollywood* (76) and another in *Firepower* (79). And obviously he could not resist the role of Samson's father in a tele-movie, *Samson and Delilah* (84); Australian actor Antony Hamilton played his old role. Mature has been married four times.

DOROTHY McGUIRE

'Picturegoer' once observed that Dorothy McGuire belonged 'to that coterie of players – it includes Margaret Sullavan, Betty Field, Martha Scott and Barbara Bel Geddes – whose charm is uncommon, elusive. It is the charm of . . . frank, unpretty features that can for some, at times, take on an amazing beauty.' In other words, they were not the sort of Hollywood girl you would discover at the soda-fountain in a drugstore. They all came from the stage, they were all highly rated by critics and by the top Hollywood brass – at least *at first*: none of them had a prolific screen career. One might speculate on the reasons – lack of drive or determination, dislike of type-casting or of Hollywood or a combination of any of these. Being most of them very talented ladies, they were individual in style, but 'Picturegoer' was right: Sullavan played a tempestuous movie queen once and Field, memorably, a slut – but one thinks of them as very gentle and genteel heroines.

McGuire was born in 1918 in Omaha, Nebraska, and was so keen on drama at school that she was allowed to join the Omaha Community Playhouse. She made her début there at the age of 13 in Barrie's 'A Kiss for Cinderella', opposite Henry Fonda, who was visiting his home town after his first Broadway break. She continued her studies, in Indianapolis and Wellesley, Massachusetts, and decided to make the stage her career after being a maid-of-all-work with a summer stock company in 1937. She did the Broadway rounds without success till engaged as understudy to Martha Scott in 'Our Town' – and later took over the part of Emily (38). She toured with John Barrymore in 'My Dear Children' and did a revue with Benny Goodman, 'Swingin' the Dream' (39); there were several more parts and then an actress's dream role, 'Claudia' (41), a humorous look at a child-bride and how she is matured by marriage. It was a huge personal success for her and when Selznick acquired the film rights he signed McGuire to a long-term contract.

But first there were the obligatory Selznick tests: because of the publicity that accrued from finding the right Scarlett O'Hara, he had tested several famous actresses for *Rebecca* after deciding to give the part to Joan Fontaine, including Margaret Sullavan and Loretta Young. Now both they, and Fontaine, tested for *Claudia* (43); then he lost interest and sold the property, plus McGuire for that film only, to 20th. The film co-starred Robert Young and got her film career off to a flying start. When Gene Tierney became pregnant, 20th kept her for the pivotal role of the patient and hard-working mother in their film version of Betty Smith's bestselling *A Tree Grows in Brooklyn* (45); Elia Kazan directed (his first film) and it was a considerable critical and popular success. Selznick loaned her to RKO for *The Enchanted Cottage* with Robert Young, an updated version of the Pinero play about two plain people who find each other beautiful when they fall in love. Also for RKO she made one of her most popular films, *The Spiral Staircase* (46), a chiller about a mute servant girl menaced by a killer, and she had, thought C.A. Lejeune, 'given a good deal of care and imagination to her study of this hapless young woman.'

RKO also offered *Till the End of Time*, a sentimental drama in which she looked glamorous on the screen for the first time; Selznick had been against her doing it, but gave in when she agreed to do one that she had hitherto refused, a sequel to her first film, *Claudia and David*. She was nominated for an Oscar for her work in 20th's *Gentleman's Agreement* (47), a quite unremarkable performance except that her freshness makes this most understanding of heroines almost tolerable (there was never a *nicer* screen couple than she and Gregory Peck). She was very near the top of the Hollywood tree, but at this point took three years' sabbatical, during which time she did 'Tonight at 8.30' in stock and acted at the La Jolla Playhouse. Also, her contract expired (without having played Jo in *Little Women*, a pet project of Selznick's:

Till the End of Time *(46) was a glossy romance about a widow courted by three ex-servicemen. Dorothy McGuire was the widow and Guy Madison one of the men (the two others: Robert Mitchum and Bill Williams).*

some reports say he started it and abandoned it, selling the rights to MGM).

Her come-back was unexpectedly frivolous: *Mother Didn't Tell Me* (50) – but the audience could tell, an entirely predictable marital comedy with William Lundigan. There was a second comedy at 20th, *Mr 880*, with Burt Lancaster and then a serious film for Goldwyn, *I Want You* (51), a risible concoction about the effect of the Korean War on an 'ordinary' American family. She signed a two-film deal at MGM: *Callaway Went Thataway*, a comedy with Howard Keel, and *Invitation* (52), which unashamedly presented her as a dying heiress who learns that husband Van Johnston had been bribed to marry her by her father. On Broadway she did 'Legend of Lovers' (Anouilh's 'Eurydice') with Richard Burton. The only good offer for a while was a suspense programmer at Republic, *Make Haste to Live* (54) and its only asset was her performance. On TV she did 'The Philadelphia Story' and 'To Each His Own', with Gene Barry; she had not regained her early position in Hollywood, but at 20th did what was probably her biggest success, *Three Coins in the Fountain*, as one of three American girls (the others: Jean Peters, Maggie McNamara) finding European romance in a foully De Luxe-coloured CinemaScope Rome.

At MGM she had a nebulous role as Glenn Ford's secretary in *Trial* (55) and then began a series of continuing mother-roles: Wyler's *Friendly Persuasion* (56), with Gary Cooper; and *Old Yeller* (57), the first of three for Disney. She returned to Broadway for an adaptation of Sherwood Anderson's 'Winesburg Ohio' and then was another mother, as married to Clifton Webb, *The Remarkable Mr Pennypacker* (59). In *This Earth Is Mine* she had an unusual part for her (Barbara Stanwyck had turned it down), that of a woman of thwarted ambition. In Delmer Daves's *A Summer Place* she met up with old flame Richard Egan and when their respective spouses divorce them their kids (Troy Donahue and Sandra Dee) fall in love. Said 'Variety': 'With the single exception of Dorothy McGuire, who comes through with a radiant performance and is lovely to look at, the cast does an average job.'

In 1959 she and Fonda did a short charity run of 'The Country Girl' at the Omaha Playhouse; in films she had her best part for some time, in *The Dark at the Top of the Stairs* (60), as Robert Preston's long-suffering wife, but the trouble was that her role was so much less interesting than those of Angela Lansbury and Eve Arden. For Disney again she was a mother, in *Swiss Family Robinson*, with John Mills, one of the year's top-grossing pictures, and for Delmar Daves a grandmother: *Susan Slade*, passing off her daughter's baby as her own till, after many tribulations, the daughter (Connie Stevens) marries poor and faithful Troy Donahue – just as his first novel is being published. For Disney she was a mother, in *Summer Magic* (63), a musical remake of *Mother Cary's Chickens*; then for George Stevens she was the Greatest Mother of them all, in *The Greatest Story Ever Told* (65). After a long absence, she returned to the screen in an inferior but high-budgeted children's film, *Flight of the Doves* (71), as a young Irish grandmother.

Her ability to play such parts might well spring from a happy marriage to John Swope since 1943. Their daughter, Topo Swope, made her film début in 1971 in *Glory Boy*. McGuire herself worked little apart from some tele-movies: *The Runaways* (75); an ultra-long *Little Woman* (78) as – of course – Marmee; and *The Incredible Journey of Doctor Meg Laurel* (79). After a gap, there were three more: *Ghost Dancing* (83), as a widowed desert farmer taking on the water company; *Amos* (1985) with Kirk Douglas, and *American Geisha* (86), in a supporting role as a widow. In 1987 she appeared in a distinguished revival of 'I Never Sang for My Father', which toured.

Steve McQueen

Steve McQueen could act with the back of his head. He could act without doing anything. There is a moment in *Bullitt* when he is waiting under a clock for someone; his face is expressionless and for some reason he reminds you of Bogart. Stars (the concept of; as box-office bait) were supposed to be dead ducks years ago – just at the time McQueen turned up. He was a welcome change after the male models who peopled the films of the 50s; *of course* publicists raked up the names of Bogart, Cagney and Edward G. Not that he had dialogue as good as they did – or years to build up the image. He was his own invention. It is an instinctive cool; it is not a cynical cool like Bogart and the gangsters or the bland cool of a Crosby or Astaire. He was more self-aware than any of them, so he would overreach himself (overusing the grin). He was more casual, more freewheeling, more independent; he thought his own thoughts, went his own way – with a jaunty soft-soled walk quite unlike anyone else you can think of. His eyes are never still: he is looking for the main chance, looking for another way – or even the same old way – to buck authority, looking for a gamble. Whether he wears an executive suit, blue jeans and a sweater or a cop's raincoat he is going to do his own thing. His voice is not remarkable and he showed no sign of versatility. But versatility, where he was concerned, is immaterial. He had only to appear on the screen to fill it. He might have been doing nothing important – waiting under a clock, coasting along in a car, catching a ball in a baseball mitt – but there was never any doubt that he was a copper-bottomed gold-plated star.

His pre-movie experience was, again, a publicist's dream. It was almost too good to be true. 'Back-street brawler, reform-school hell-raiser – Steve McQueen was never groomed for stardom,' lied one Hollywood columnist. Born in Slater, Missouri, in 1930 (or in Indianapolis in 1932; reports vary) and deserted by his father while a baby, he did in fact go to a reform school (in Chino, California). He escaped and was gaoled; became a merchant seaman at 15, a lumberjack and a carnival barker before joining the marines. He arrived in New York in 1950 – was a docker, a bartender, a salesman, a bookie's runner and, intermittently, a beach-boy in Miami. He was a TV repairman when a chance meeting got him into New York's Neighborhood Playhouse; he graduated in 1952 and studied for two more years at the Uta Hagen-Herbert Berghof school. His first acting job was in stock, in 'Peg o' my Heart' starring Margaret O'Brien; in 1954 he toured in 'Time Out For Ginger' with Melvyn Douglas. His Broadway début was in 'The Gap', at which time he was studying with the Actors' Studio. His big break came when he replaced Ben Gazzara in 'A Hatful of Rain' (56), which led to a lot of TV work. He had already started in movies as a $19 a day extra, in *Somebody Up There Likes Me* (56).

With his wife, Neile Adams, he went to Hollywood in 1956. She, a Broadway dancer, gave a fetching performance in MGM's *This Could Be the Night* and retired (they separated in 1971). Allied Artists tested him and put him into *Never Love a Stranger* (58), a shoddy effort starring John Drew Barrymore, produced and written by novelist Harold Robbins. As the hero's boyhood chum McQueen's oddly innocent face – like a Botticelli angel crossed with a chimp – made him an appealing character in a screenplay of jerks; and his acting, though tentative, stood out from the appalling rest. The film's release was delayed for almost two years – by which time things really were happening. He got star spots in a couple of duallers, *The Blob* and the taut *The Great St Louis Bank Robbery* (59), as an ex-college-football hero. He was billed as Steven, but he dropped the 'n' after becoming nationally famous in a TV series, 'Wanted – Dead or Alive', a Western series he had begun in 1958. Frank Sinatra had seen him on TV and at the last minute asked him to be in *Never So Few*, when Sammy Davis Jr failed to make up with him after a quarrel. It was an undistinguished war film, but McQueen gave his best screen performance yet; and it led to his being chosen as one of *The Magnificent Seven* (60), as Yul Brynner's first recruit and second-in-command, third-billed above the title.

With the success of the film, MGM gave him top-billing in *The Honeymoon Machine* (61), one of a series of comedies featuring Paula Prentiss (who got raves but no career impetus, because they all flopped). He had a good war story, *Hell Is For Heroes* (62), but it was not a success – although he was good as a GI misfit; and another, *The War Lover* (62), made in Britain, an indistinct version of John Hersey's novel. It was the first film McQueen carried and he was not helped by a village institute performance by the leading lady. But his is a remarkable performance: he is a big-headed heel (he loves the bang-bang of war, is out to make his buddy's girl) but none the less conveys his own quirky dignity. A third war film, and a huge money-maker, really established him: *The Great Escape* (63), with his casual insolence towards the POW commandants and a memorable motor-cycle chase. There was a welcome chance of pace with the next three. The most welcome was the first, *Love With the Proper Stranger*, a touching New York story with McQueen as a shiftless, very independent musician who impregnates Macy's sales clerk Natalie Wood. Neither of the two that followed worked out: *Soldier in the Rain*, a comedy with Jackie Gleason, and *Baby the Rain Must Fall* (65), a sentimental drama with Lee Remick. Both were intelligently conceived, both had fine moments, but both set McQueen's box-office rating down a few rungs.

The Cincinnati Kid did excellent business – and was an excellent film, dominated by McQueen in the title-role – a young stud-poker gambler – except in the sequences where he was up against Edward G. Robinson. He then played *Nevada Smith* (66), a dullsville action melodrama spawned by the

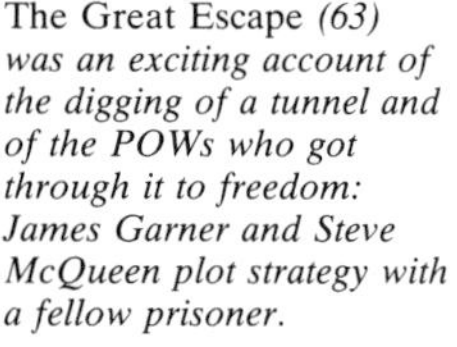

The Great Escape *(63) was an exciting account of the digging of a tunnel and of the POWs who got through it to freedom: James Garner and Steve McQueen plot strategy with a fellow prisoner.*

success of *The Carpetbaggers*, in which the part of Nevada had been played by Alan Ladd. McQueen had little more sense of character than Ladd, but had a tension which made the film watchable. Again, the grosses were good. 20th entrusted him with the lead in their expensive roadshow item, *The Sand Pebbles* (67), and he was good as an inscrutable loner in this overlong story: well, something, after downbeat reviews, must have carried it to a $13 million take – and it can be no coincidence that McQueen was voted fourth in the top 10 list that year. Something similar happened with a rainbow-hued bank robbery tale, *The Thomas Crown Affair* (68), with Faye Dunaway; as a result he was in both the US (seventh) and British (third) lists of the year's top stars. The film's director, Norman Jewison, said: 'I can honestly say he's the most difficult actor I ever worked with . . . God, he's got the power.'

Then came *Bullitt* (69). This was not in itself an extraordinary film, a *Big Sleep*-type thriller with 60s trimmings – colour, fine locations, violence; and well made – but no one could have foreseen that it would take over $15 million immediately (not Warners, anyway, who cancelled a six-picture deal with McQueen's company when the budget went over $5 million: his own salary was $1 million). McQueen had wondered whether his image would support his playing a cop, but this cop was in the classic tradition – independent, wary, jaded, chockful of integrity, ice-cold blue eyes in a head like a squashed walnut. Said the 'New York Times':

It was Bullitt *– both pictures – in 1969 which confirmed Steve McQueen's position as the best tough guy in movies. He played a San Francisco cop out to break an underworld syndicate, against pressure from that quarter and obstruction from his command.*

'McQueen embodies his special kind of aware, existential cool – less taut and hard-shell than Bogart, less lost and adrift than Mastroianni, a little of both.' McQueen himself said the film had found the perfect formula; it was an 'art actioner' and there is no doubt that it came at a good time, just as the action market had had the spy cycle; but its success was overall a giant justification for the star system.

He stayed at No 3 in 1969 and 1970, despite only one film during that time, the middlingly popular *The Reivers* (70), from William Faulkner's look back at old Mississippi, the picaresque adventures of a hired hand (McQueen), his Negro pal and a small boy. The rest of the time he was filming and part-financing *Le Mans* (71), which reflected his offscreen hobby, motor-racing, and his power: director John Sturges (*The Magnificent Seven, The Great Escape*) left and was replaced by Lee Katzin. McQueen also appeared in a documentary about motor-cycling, *Any Sunday*. In 1971, he was fourth at the box-office, but the next two, both directed by Sam Peckinpah, sent his stock tumbling – and the first of them managed to lose $2 million for ABC Pictures. It was *Junior Bonner* (72), the desultory adventures of a rodeo man who goes back to see Maw and Paw; the other was *The Getaway*, for that was what it was about. The other fugitive was Ali McGraw and McQueen gotaway with her in life; and later married her. The film itself was his first for First Artists (Newman, Poitier, Streisand), with whom he was now associated. For other companies he made two blockbusters: *Papillon* (73), in that role, escaping from Devil's Island; and *The Towering Inferno* (74), as the leader of the fire-fighters. Paul Newman was his co-star, after juggling with the billing, and they were a superb demonstration of star power – rightly, two of the lonely Hollywood people who were box-office. Of them, only Jack Nicholson had the talent and charisma of Gable or Tracy; the worst you could say of this pair was that they were a great improvement on Burt Lancaster and Kirk Douglas. In this film, any time they appeared the audience was reassured; their heroism was both devil-may-care and com-monsensical, in their initiative, stubbornness and humour a blend of Spencer Tracy in *North West Passage* and Dustin Hoffman in *The Graduate*.

Every age needs its heroes, and the disaster movies of the 70s needed a hero of steel – as McQueen in The Towering Inferno *(74), probably the best of them.*

The film's success kept McQueen in the box-office 10 in 1975, for the ninth consecutive year; he left it only because he did not work. Two films he did not make were *A Bridge Too Far* and *Apocalypse Now*, because his asking price was $3 million for three weeks' work. Said the director of the latter, Francis Ford Coppola: 'On the one hand, he makes the valid point that his appearance in the picture has a solid commercial value regardless of the number of weeks he works' – he had a choice of two roles, of three weeks and 16 – 'On the other hand, they all weigh how much other stars are getting per week.' After noting that James Caan had asked for $2 million, Coppola went on, 'I began to see that if this kept up the industry would some day be paying $3 million for eight hours, plus overtime and have to shoot at the actor's house.' But McQueen had become more interested in art than money. Privately buried in hair and beard, and rather corpulent (his marriage to McGraw had broken up), he was seen on screen thus, plus granny-glasses in *An Enemy of the People* (78). Ibsen, no less. Shelved for a year, it was then shown tentatively to schools before risking the critics – who promptly snubbed it. McQueen's next choice for First Artists was however first thumbsed-down by them: a film of Pinter's *Old Times*. After a lawsuit in 1977 it was agreed that he could take the property elsewhere.

However, he had singed his beard on Ibsen and chose to do the sort of films in which his public wanted to see him: *Tom Horn* (80) and *The Hunter*. In fact, both were the sort of films which had driven Clint Eastwood and Burt Reynolds to prominence in his absence; both have their moments, especially when McQueen is on screen, for he is quite touching, respectively as an Indian scout being 'used' by rival factions, all of whom would cheerfully destroy him, and a modern-day bounty hunter. As filming finished, he said that he would not even look at a script for less than $5 million upfront against 15 per cent of the gross; and he was reputed to have received $1 million for *Tai-Pan* before rejecting the project when no more money was forthcoming – and that was said to be anything from $3 million to $10 million. The Swiss producer had raised $18 million on the strength of his name, but the film was not to be (yet: when finally made, in 1986, after a dozen false starts, it flopped). McQueen was already losing a long battle with cancer, which took him in 1980.

MELINA MERCOURI

Melina Mercouri was once referred to (by Penelope Gilliatt) as 'the Attic Danny La Rue'. Her whole approach is too volatile, too strident, unrestrained. In interviews she indicates charm and intelligence as well as the forcefulness, but these are qualities the screen has exploited but fitfully – a riddle, considering that most of her pictures have been directed by her husband, Jules Dassin.

She was born in Athens in 1923, granddaughter of a mayor of the city, daughter of a politician and sometime Minister of the (Greek) Interior. She was married at 17, but found it dull (her book, 'I Was Born Greek', is graphic on her life and loves at this time). She took a drama course and made her début in an avant-garde play by Alexis Solomis. Her break came when she was offered the lead in a revival of 'Mourning Becomes Electra' and she went on to do several plays, including 'A Streetcar Named Desire' and 'The Seven Year Itch'. But Greece was not big enough for her and she went to Paris, where she appeared successfully in three plays, including 'Le Moulin de la Galette' (51) with Pierre Fresnay and Yvonne Printemps. She returned to Athens and Michael Cacoyannis offered the lead in his first film, *Stella* (55), a barnstorming melodrama filmed somewhat engagingly on location. As a Theda Bara of the Plaka, she had a ball: laughing, singing, dancing, crying, emoting, the lot. Some people took it seriously and among art buffs her name was made abroad.

In France she was offered the Mary Magdalene role in the film of a novel by Nikos Kazantzakis, *Celui qui Doit Mourir* (57), about a Greek village putting on a Passion play and becoming involved with parallel events. Surprisingly, it worked: director Dassin's good intentions encompassed compassion and an attack on inter-Christian intolerance. (Dassin and she began living together; they were married some years later). A while later, Britain's Rank sent for her to play the first half of a Regency drag directed by Joseph Losey, *The Gypsy and the Gentleman* (58): Keith Michell played the other half and seemed embarrassed by film and co-star. Dassin directed her and others (Yves Montand, Lollobrigida) in *La Loi* (59) and great things were expected of the English-dubbed version, *Where the Hot Wind Blows*, but it did not make a cent.

Melina Mercouri as the happiest whore on the waterfront: Never on Sunday *(60), directed by Jules Dassin, whom she later married. Its success gave both careers new impetus.*

They should care: by this time she and Dassin were riding high with the tale of a Piraeus whore who entertained like mad but *Pote Tin Kyriaki/Never on Sunday* (60). Filmed in English in Greece and technically a mess, it was hampered further – as he himself admitted – by an inept performance by Dassin as the American who grows to love her (Dassin is an American blacklisted by Hollywood in the McCarthy era). It only cost $150,000 and it would take that in one cinema alone. By a fluke perhaps it turned out a loud paean to life. She was a tonic (so was the music). UA, who had worldwide distribution, sat back amazed at the huge grosses everywhere and gratefully offered Dassin *carte blanche* provided Mercouri starred again. While he prepared something she slipped (noisily) into two all-star efforts, *Vive Henri IV Vive l'Amour* (61) and *Il Giudizio Universale* (62). Dassin had updated a tale already worked over by Euripides and Racine, *Phaedra*. She played that, Raf Vallone was the husband and Anthony Perkins the stepson for whom she conceives a forbidden passion – all clothed in pretension a yard thick. She did a stage stint in Paris and then an episode in

Carl Foreman's *The Victors* (63), comforting GI George Peppard in Brussels – more than one critic wondered whether she would eat him.

After the *Phaedra* débâcle, Dassin chose a good crime story – one of Eric Ambler's – and filmed it simply, in colour: *Topkapi* (64), about a heist from the museum of that name in Istanbul, with Mercouri as one of the conspirators. To offset the success of that, she was in three flops: *Les Pianos Mécaniques* (65), a Franco-Spanish drama directed by J.-A. Bardem with James Mason, as a cynical nightclub owner; *A Man Could Get Killed* (66), in Hollywood with James Garner, as a Portuguese vamp; and Dassin's *10.30 p.m. Summer*, from a novel by Marguerite Duras, with Romy Schneider, as the alcoholic wife of Peter Finch. On Broadway she appeared in a moderately successful musical based on *Never on Sunday* called 'Illya Darling'; at the end of its run she devoted time and money trying to drum up support against the Greek colonels' junta (which took power in 1967), travelling worldwide and pleading passionately for her countrymen. For her uncontrolled criticism, she was exiled and her citizenship withdrawn. She paused long enough to refill her coffers in Hollywood, in Norman Jewison's *Gaily Gaily* (69), as a madam in this extenuated tour of turn-of-the-century Chicago, with Beau Bridges as Ben Hecht (it was based on a memoir of his) and a good cast (Brian Keith, Hume Cronyn). In France Dassin directed her in another memoir – Romain Gary's of his Russian mother – *Promise at Dawn* (70) and again it was proved that meticulous period décor does not an entertainment make. In 1972 she was in New York in 'Lysistrata', which failed to run. Two years later she produced and starred in, and Dassin directed, *The Rehearsal*, a semi-documentary on the Greek junta's massacre of students, but the junta fell – which is why, apparently, the film was never shown. Under the new regime, Mercouri campaigned for and was elected to Parliament; but she found time – alas for all concerned – to have a clandestine lesbian affair with Alexis Smith in *Once Is Not Enough* (75). In Greece Dassin directed *A Dream of Passion* (78), which was 'Medea' updated, with Mercouri as a woman appearing in the play and Ellen Burstyn as a woman who had killed her offspring: the result – 'As one endures the spectacle of Mercouri baring her soul . . . it seems one has wandered into the home movies of a demented culture maven. Even as a vanity production for Mrs Dassin, the movie backfires: Mercouri's grotesquely inflated passions leave an ugly narcissistic aftertaste' – David Ansen in 'Newsweek'. In 1980 Dassin directed her in 'Sweet Bird of Youth' in Athens and the following year she was made Minister for Cultural Affairs by the Greek Government.

Toshiro Mifune

Toshiro Mifune first became known in the West when *Rashomon* was shown in the Venice Film Festival of 1951. It was the first Japanese film most Western filmgoers had seen and it won both the Venice Grand Prix and the Hollywood Oscar for a foreign-language film. It established its director, Akira Kurosawa, as one of the world's most exciting and accomplished film-makers. Because Mifune was often Kurosawa's leading actor his work also became appreciated in the West, till it became clear that he was not merely a fine interpreter for a great director but a notable talent in his own right. By the early 60s, he was established as the first Japanese star to become an international name since Sessue Hayawaka; as a consequence, it became possible to distribute in the West some of the films he made without Kurosawa. Japanese audiences, naturally, associate him less with that one director: to them he is a popular and extremely versatile actor, capable of taking on facets which in the West we associate with actors as disparate as Spencer Tracy and Jean-Paul Belmondo. He belongs absolutely with the great screen heroes.

We have seen him mainly in three sorts of roles – as the graceful, simple, ordinary man; as the contemplative executive or high-ranking officer; and as the samurai or medieval adventurer (literally, one of the military retainers of a feudal baron, often a mercenary). It is as the swashbuckling samurai that he has achieved his greatest fame; no Japanese Douglas Fairbanks, but a shabbily dressed warrior, absolutely invincible and fearless but canny and cautious – and sickened by killing and sick of war. He is somewhat theatrical, not least in his sardonic contempt for those around him; invariably the only sane man on whichever side of the fence he decides to fight – but remarkably patient of his allies. His physical dexterity is matched only by a rather jaded sensitivity. He is a man alone, unlike his fellows not of unquestioning loyalty to his certainly venal lord but as devoted as they to his sword: but unlike his contemporaries (that is, the other myriad actors playing samurai) he possessed an aggressive masculinity which suggested that a woman might win him away from it.

He was born in 1920 in Tsing-Tao, China. His father came from a long line of doctors.

He was brought up a Methodist and graduated from Port Arthur High School. When his parents were forced to return to Japan he went with them; and served in the army 1940–45. When the war ended he had no job, no profession and no money. A friend of his who was a cameraman with Toho suggested he try the 'new faces' competition at that studio. At that time Toho was losing ground to its chief rival Shintoho and such competitions as this and subsequent ones were meant to force interest on individual studios. Mifune was one of 4,000 entrants and was turned down, it was thought, because he said he was only interested in playing villains. One of the panel, however, was impressed. This was Kajiro Yamamoto, at that time a leading director. He had no immediate use for him, but turned him over to his ex-assistant Senkichi Taniguchi, who got him a small part in *Shin Baka Jidai/These Foolish Times* (46) and then the lead in *Genrei no Hate/Snow Trail* (47), as a gangster – Mifune himself suspected that the mountain work in this film was too hazardous for an established actor.

Kurosawa had also been an assistant of Yamamoto and had been directing since 1943. For one of the leads in his eighth film, *Yoidore Tenshi/Drunken Angel* (48), he chose the young actor he had seen in Taniguchi's film. Mifune was a young crook who grew ever more reckless on learning he had TB – until rescued by the alcoholic doctor of the title (Takashi Shimura, who also made several films for Kurosawa – the police chief in *The Stray Dog*, the wood-cutter in *Rashamon*, the dying man in *Ikiru/Living* and the head of the *Seven Samurai*). Kurosawa said later that he could not control Mifune; he found the film changing from his original concept, but did not want to suppress that vitality. He said: 'His reactions are extraordinarily swift. If I say one thing, he understands ten. He reacts very quickly to the director's intentions. Most Japanese actors are the opposite of this and so I wanted Mifune to cultivate this gift.' Until they quarrelled in the late 60s Kurosawa only made one film (*Ikiru* in 1952) in which Mifune did not appear.

Mifune made *Jakoman to Tetsu/Jakoman and Tetsu* (49) for Taniguchi, written by Kurosawa, then did two for Kurosawa. In *Shizukanaru Ketto/The Quiet Duel* he had the sort of part he would often play, that of a doctor who is accidentally infected with syphilis and who is destroyed not by the illness but by the knowledge of it. In *Nora Inu/Stray Dog* he was a detective searching for a missing revolver, a quest so remorseless as to seem allegorical. Kurosawa adapted from his own unpublished novel and now made the film over-technical. Mifune made a film for Yamamoto, *Datsugoku/Escape from Prison*, and then returned to Kurosawa for *Shubun/Scandal*, in which he was a young artist whose relationship with a famous singer (Yoshiko Yamaguchi) is destroyed by a muck-raking press.

During this time – little though he needed it – he was attending Toho's drama courses. He was under contract to Toho and was to film for them almost exclusively throughout his career. In 1950 he married (they have two sons). He made *Konyaku Yubiwa/Engagement Ring*; *Kaizoku-Sen/Pirates*, for Hiroshi Inagaki, perhaps the second-best of those directors with whom he worked consistently; *Ishinaka-Sensei Gyojoki/Conduct Report on Professor Ishinaka*; and with Kurosawa for the Daiei company, *Rashomon*. *Rashomon* was about the nature of truth: a nobleman (Masayuki Mori) and his wife (Machiko Kyo) are travellers attacked by a bandit (Mifune), who rapes her – their differing versions of what happened are the basis of the film. Daiei did not like it but it was not only a critical success in Japan but, somewhat surprisingly, a popular one. However, it would not have been entered for Venice if the then-head of Unitalia had not seen it and liked it; but its international success had no immediate effect on the careers of either the director or Mifune. With the exception of *Seven Samurai* it was not to be until the 60s that their films found wide appeal outside Japan.

Mifune, meanwhile, did *Ai To Nikushimi no Kaneta/Beyond Love and Hate* (51), which was written by Kurosawa; they were then reunited for *Hakuchi/The Idiot*, made for the Shochiku company. This was a modernized interpretation of Dostoevsky with Mifune as the Rogozhin character, the coarse friend and rival of Mishkin (Masayuki Mori); the film was badly received and was cut to half its length by the original distributor. Mifune overacted in this dull, excessive film (he can overact when he is unsure, and Kurosawa fails to restrain him in this). There followed: *Bakuro Ichidai/Life of a Horse-Trader*; *Sasaki Kojiro – Kanketsuhen/Kojiro Sasaki*; *Onnagokoro o Dare ga Shiru/Who Knows a Woman's Heart?*; *Tokyo no Koiboto/Tokyo Sweetheart* (52); and *Sengoku-Burai/Sword for Hire*, a samurai film for Inagaki, whose later films of this genre would provide Mifune with some secondary successes outside Japan. Mifune worked again with a first-rate director on *Saikaku Ichidai Onna/Life of O-Haru* – Kenji Mizoguchi, who fashioned an extraordinarily beautiful film – from a 17th-century classic about a samurai's daughter (Kinayo Tanaka) who is forced by circumstances to go from courtesan to whore to beggar. Mifune had a brief role as the seducer who sets her on the primrose path, and is soon decapitated. This was the second Japanese movie seen in the West and it impressed almost as much as *Rashomon*. Then Mifune made: *Keto Kagiya no Tsuji/Vendetta of Samurai*; *Muteki/Foghorn*; *Gekiryu/A Swift Current*; *Minato e Kita Otoko/The Man Who Came to the Port*; *Himawari-Musume/Love in a Teacup* (53); *Taiheiyo No Washi/Eagle of the Pacific*, a war film; *Fukeyo Harukaze/My Wonderful Yellow Car*; and *Hoyo/The Last Embrace*, in which he had a dual role.

Kurosawa, meanwhile, had been preparing *Shichi-Nin no Samurai/Seven Samurai* (54) and that expensive medieval adventure story was a year in production (and originally over three hours long: the one seen in the West was one of several cut versions). The seven are mercenaries hired by a war-weary village to protect them and Mifune was the odd man out and last survivor, a crazy, boasting fighter of peasant stock, posing as a samurai. Wrote Tony Richardson: 'Toshiro Mifune, gibing at the samurai, waving, in mocking triumph, a fish caught in a stream, and – another Falstaff – bullying his helpless recruits, brings to his portrayal a reckless and at moments out-of-hand gusto. It is a splendid performance. . . .' After *Mitsuyu-Sen/The Black Fury*, he appeared in a similar part, in the title-role of Inagaki's *Musashi Miyamoto/Samurai*, which was in colour but much more standard stuff. It won an Oscar for the Best Foreign movie – possibly helped by the commentary spoken by William Holden, who sponsored it in the US.

Mifune had a supporting role in Taniguchi's *Shiosai/The Surf*, as a wealthy man whose daughter runs off with a fisherman – but is finally forgiven. He made *Dansei No I/A Man Among Men* (55) and then Kurosawa's magnificent *Ikimono no Kiroku/I Live in Fear*, a satire that turned into tragedy – he was a successful ageing industrialist who, because he wants to move his family to Brazil to escape the next atom- or H-bomb, is committed to an insane asylum. Then: *Tenka Tahei/All is Well* and its sequel, *Zoku Tenka Tahei/All is Well Pt 2*; and *Otoko Arite/No Time for Tears*.

Toshiro Mifune (far left) in the second of his movies to be widely seen in the West: Seven Samurai *(54), Kurosawa's stunning adventure story. At the far right is Takashi Shimura, as the leader of the samurai.*

Inagaki then directed him in the two films which completed his *Samurai* trilogy, *Zoku Miyamoto Mushashi/Duel at Ichijoji Temple* and, the least good of the three, *Ketto Ganryu-Jima/Musashi and Kojiro* (56): throughout, he was Kusashi and Tatsuya Nakadai was his worthy opponent. Then: *Kuroobi Sangokushi/Rainy Night Duel*; *Ankoku-Gai/The Underworld*, as a detective; *Aijo no Kessan/Settlement of Love*; *Tsuma no Kokoro/A Wife's Heart*; *Narazumono/Scoundrel*; and *Shujinsen/Rebels on the High Sea*.

Kurosawa's next film was a version of 'Macbeth' which begins a trilogy of *jidai-geki* or period films. (Richie has pointed out that in Japan both industry and audiences divide films into period and modern; Japanese history does not seem to provide the sort of transition which gives us our 'period' films – and indeed most of the 19th century in Japan was still feudal.) This was *Kumonosu-Jo/Throne of Blood* (57), Noh-Shakespeare, a glittering, pounding drama with intimations of the supernatural. It had much less success in the West than one might have thought. Said 'The Times' (London) of Mifune: 'He brings to the part a combination of physical strength and irresolution that is in the best "Macbeth" tradition. His greatest asset is an expressiveness in face and eyes that mirrors every mood of the film.' From that he turned to the role of a truck-driver who falls in love with a widow, *Shitamachi/Downtown*; and returned to Kurosawa for *Donzoko/The Lower Depths*, as the thief in this Nippon adaptation of Gorki. He then did Taniguchi's *Arashi no Naka no Otoko/The Man in the Storm*; *Yagyu Bugei-Cho/Secret Scrolls*, Inagaki's version of an old legend, as a samurai with magic powers; *Kono Futari ni Sachi Are/Be Happy These Two Lovers*; and *Kiken na Eiyu/A Dangerous Hero*.

Muhimatsu no Issho/The Rickshaw Man (58) was Inagaki's remake of his own 1943 film and Mifune was a man who befriends a boy and (again) falls in love with a widowed mother. Its career in the West was due mainly to Mifune's performance after it was prized at the Karlovy Vary festival. The 'MFB' said that he had found a part 'admirably suited to his extraordinary power of translating every emotion from anguish to exaltation into violent physical fact'. Inagaki also directed *Soryu Hiken/Ninjutsu*, a sequel to *Secret Scrolls*, in which Mifune's role was brief. Both films were shown in a season of Mifune/Inagaki movies at the 55th Street Playhouse in New York in 1967/8, optimistically distributed by Toho's American branch; the second one, called *Secret Scrolls Pt 2*, in fact was totally incomprehensible to anyone who had not seen

Kurosawa's re-working of 'Macbeth' was perhaps in the end not so much a version of Shakespeare but a superior samurai epic: Throne of Blood *(57), with Toshiro Mifune and Isuzu Yamada.*

Part 1 – and that was confusing enough. Critics generally found the films inferior to Kurosawa's. The West was not to see *Tokyo no Kyujitsu/Holiday in Tokyo*; *Jinsei Gekijo Seishen-Hen/Theatre of Life*; or *Yajikita Dochuki/The Happy Pilgrimage*; but it did see *Kakushi-Toride no San Akunin/The Hidden Fortress*, the last part of Kurosawa's trilogy, and as unlike either of them as they were unlike each other. Mifune was a defeated warlord lumbered with an escaped princess in similar straits, in a feudal Japan that had affinities with both the primitive epics of Europe and the American Western. It was Toho's biggest hit till that time (thus justifying its huge budget) but only moderately successful in the US or Britain.

There were few export chances for: *Ankokugai no Kaoyaku/The Big Boss* (59); *Aru Kengo no Shogai/Samurai Saga*, a version of 'Cyrano de Bergerac', with Mifune very droll in that part; *Sengoku Gunto-Den/Saga of the*

As a samurai, Toshiro Mifune spends most of his time righting wrongs. In The Hidden Fortress *(58), he was the protector of a damsel in distress.*

Vagabonds; *Nippon Tanjo/The Three Treasures*; *Dokuritsu Gurentai/Desperado Outpost*; *Ankoku-Gai No Taiketsu/The Last Gunfight* (60); *Kunisada Chuji/The Gambling Samurai*; or *Otoko Tai Otoko/Man Against Man*. However, *Taiheiyo No Arashi/I Bombed Pearl Harbor* was shown in the West and 'Variety' said that Mifune, as Admiral Yamaguchi, gave a performance 'of great reserve, strength and dignity'. And there was a qualified Western welcome for Kurosawa's *Warui-Yatsu Hodo Yoko Nemuru/The Bad Sleep Well*, his first film for his own company (he had left Toho). This was a variation on 'The son-in-law also rises' theme. Mifune was the bastard son of a murdered company official bent on revenge – and unctuous, smart, he marries into the family to expose corruption: a drama of enormous power. He then went to Mexico at the behest of Ismael Rodriguez and starred in his *Animas Trujano* (61), as a Mexican Indian peasant who dreams of being the village chief. It was shown at Venice; and so was *Yojimbo*, which brought a Best Actor award for Mifune ('and no wonder!' – Hollis Alpert in the 'Saturday Review'). This was perhaps Kurosawa's most ambitious subject – about two warring factions equally heinous, with Mifune as the samurai who despises both but fights, honourably, for them both. It was an even bigger hit in Japan than *The Hidden Fortress* and, again, immeasurably exciting. Iagaki's *Osaka-Jo Monogatari/Daredevil in the Castle* was a much less distinguished samurai film, about two warring families, but it was in colour. Mifune made *Gen To Fudo-Myoo/The Youth and his Amulet* and then *Tsubaki Sanjuro/Sanjuro* (62), a modest sequel to *Yojimbo*. Kurosawa had not intended a sequel and indeed the samurai of this script had originally been much more cerebral; but the success of the earlier film suggested some modification, so Mifune played Sanjuro again.

He made *Doburoko no Tatsu/Tatsu*, in which he was an ordinary man; then he played a samurai in *Chusingara/The Loyal 47 Ronin*, a three-and-a-half-hour version of a Kabuki play about court life in the 18th century; it was packed with Toho's leading stars and famous Kabuki players, was directed by Inagaki and was expected to have great success in the West – but it did not. Then he played another high-ranking naval officer realizing the futility of war: *Taiheyo no Tasubasa/Attack Squadron* (63), directed, as the last time, by Matsubayashi. Kurosawa's *Tengoku To Jigoku/High and Low* was adapted from a novel by Ed McBain about a kidnapping, with Mifune as an industrialist in dilemma when his chauffeur's child is pinched for his own – a chase film of absorbing, intricate detail.

In 1963 he formed his own production company, releasing through Toho, and he directed as well as acted in *Goju Man-nin no Isan/The Legacy of the 500,000*. He has not tried directing since; he has personally produced some of his subsequent films; and, of the others, like an American star, his company usually has a piece of the action. *Dai-Tozuku/Samurai Pirate* was in colour, a 16th-century tale about a wealthy man who becomes a pirate after he has been unjustly imprisoned; AIP bought it, dubbed it and retitled it *The Lost World of Sinbad* – without appreciable results. He made only one film the following year, *Dai Tatsumaki/Whirlwind* (64), which starred Somegoro Ichikawa: he had only a cameo role as a legendary warrior. He produced and acted in *Samurai/Samurai Assasin* (65), as a bastard trying to solve the problem of his parentage; then appeared for the last time under the direction of Kurosawa, in *Akahige/Red Beard*, a long and ambitious film (it took two years to make) about a 19th-century doctor who takes to the sword – and the doctor, it must be said, was first cousin to Sanjuro. He won a second acting prize at Venice.

Kurosawa's own first film, the wartime *Sugata Shanshiro/Judo Saga*, already remade in 1955, was now remade – indifferently – with Mifune, a story of the rivalry between judo and ju-jitsu. After that he did *Taiheyo Kiseki No Sakusen Kiska/The Retreat from Kiska*, as an admiral; *Chi To Suna/Fort Graveyard*; *Abare Goemen/Rise Against the Sword* (66), the story of a shipwrecked diplomat, who rebels against tyranny in China; *Daibosatsu*

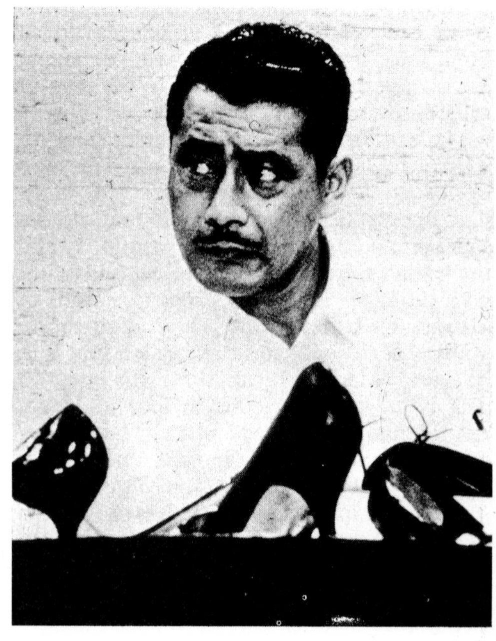

Toshiro Mifune in the last but one film he made for Kurosawa: High and Low *(63), as the shoe-manufacturing executive faced with a ransom demand for kidnapping.*

Toge/Sword of Doom, a poor but violent samurai film starring Tatsuya Nakadai, with Mifune in a cameo role; *Kiganjo No Boken/ Adventures of Takla Makan*; and, produced by himself, *Doto Ichi man Kairi/The Mad Atlantic*.

A Hollywood offer took him to Europe and the US to play the Japanese owner of a racing team in Frankenheimer's *Grand Prix* and he was asked, inevitably, why he had taken so long to accept an American offer. He said that in the days when he was under contract Toho's asking-price was unnecessarily high (adding that his American salary was the biggest he had yet got) and that two other projects had fallen through: *The Day Custer Fell*, as Chief Crazy Horse, for Fred Zinnemann and 20th, and *Will Adams*, for Paramount. Another reason must have been language: a newspaper report at that time said he spoke no English and a little Spanish – and he was dubbed in *Grand Prix*. He also said that he and Kurosawa planned another film together, but the samurai film he now produced, *Joi-Uchi/Rebellion* (67), was directed by Masaki Kobayashi – who, less well known in the West, ranks with Kurosawa as one of 'the great masters of Japanese cinema' (Satyajit Ray). Mifune was a retired naval officer forced into action when his daughter-in-law – once the overlord's mistress – is required to return to the palace. Said Philip Strick in 'Sight and Sound': 'The splendid Mifune scowl, and the instant authority with which he dominates the screen, give him such seemingly unquestionable heroic integrity that his glee at a fight is disturbingly easy to share . . .'

He was in two war films: *Nippon No Ichiban Nagai Hi/The Emperor and the General*, a documentary account of the Japanese surrender, as the war minister; and *Rengo-Kantai Shireichokan Yamamoto Isoruku/ Admiral Yamamoto* (68), as the admiral. Then he joined forces with another big star, Yujiro Ishiwara, to produce and co-star in *Kurobe no Taiyo/A Tunnel to the Sun*, as engineers involved in dam-building (locations were done at Kurobe Gorge, the world's third biggest dam). The huge budget was justified by the film's success in Japan, but it has been seen but fitfully abroad. He had a small role in *Gion Matsuri/Gion Festival* and was in a TV series. Paramount announced him for a Western to be made in Madrid, *Red Sun*; it fell through and he did *Hell in the Pacific*, in which he and Lee Marvin were shipwrecked enemy sailors unable to communicate – an ambitious subject which did not quite come off.

Inagaki directed *Furin Kazan/Samurai Banners* (69), a drama about the unification of Japan, with Mifune as the scarred and limping warrior who achieves it and is killed at the Battle of Kawanakajima in 1561. Mifune produced this and after *Nihonkai Daisakusen/ Battle of the Japan Sea* he produced another above-average samurai film, *Akage/Red Lion*. He did *Shinsen Gumi/Band of Assassins* and that, as directed by Tadashi Sawashima, was a subtle and violent historical drama, with

In battle: probably the image most people treasure of Toshiro Mifune. In Kobayashi's Rebellion *(67), duelling with Tatsuya Nakadai.*

Mifune as the leader of a gang of 'protectors': perhaps the best film he made without Kurosawa. He followed with another popular samurai film, *Zatoichi To Yojimbo/Zatoichi Meets Yojimbo*, playing his old role, with Shintaro Katsu as Zatoichi, a blind samurai who had already featured in about two dozen films. Then: *Eiko Eno 5000 Kiro/Safari 5000*; *Bakumatsu/The Ambitious* (70); *Aru Heishi No Kake/The Walking Major*; and *Gunbatsu/ The Militarists*.

Then Mifune went to Europe to film *Red Sun/Soleil Rouge* (71), at last, the story of a Japanese traveller in the US who is robbed by a bandit (Alain Delon) and sets off in pursuit. By this time most of his best films had passed into the repertory of film classics. In the early 60s, encouraged by the reception of Japanese films at festivals, Toho set up business in the US, but only the Kurosawas did much trade. Exhibitors in general believed the success of *Seven Samurai* to be a flash in the pan. It was probably *Yojimbo* and *Sanjuro* which changed the picture; neither was especially well greeted by the Western press, but the public began to realize that it enjoyed these films. Both *Red Beard* and *Rebellion* did well; so that by 1971 one New York cinema (the Bijou) was able to play Japanese films throughout the year, showing more during that time (including several premières) than had been seen over the past 20 years.

Mifune himself moved into television in an executive capacity and by 1975 had appeared in three series – in two as a samurai and in the other as a samurai detective. He was divorced in 1972, around which time he turned down the role that John Gielgud played in *Lost Horizon*. The producer (Ted Richmond) of *Red Sun* and the director (Terence Young) announced a number of projects, some to involve Kurosawa, whose attempted suicide greatly disturbed Mifune. He did appear for them in *Paper Tiger* (75), with David Niven, playing an executive whose son is kidnapped, but Young (to put it mildly) is no Kurosawa. In 1975, Mifune began *The New Spartans*, with Oliver Reed, and the following year *Winter Kills*, with Anthony Perkins, but both were abandoned; he did, however, appear in the Hollywood reconstruction of the Battle of *Midway* (76). In Japan he appeared in *Ningen No Shómei/Proof of a Man* (77), with Broderick Crawford, which turned out to be the second most successful Japanese film ever – thus ending a fallow period in Mifune's career; and *Nippon No Don – Yobohen/The Don of Japan – Big Schemes*, a dull gangster film.

Winter Kills (79) finally emerged – complete, though as Mifune only had one scene, as John Huston's butler, it was clear that his role had been written out. He was even less profitably employed in Steven Spielberg's dreadful spoof *1941*, as a Japanese submarine commander: this Universal-Columbia co-production cost $32 million, more than the cost of their entire output of 1941 put together. Little was recovered at the box-office. In Japan *Port-Arthur* (80) broke records: Mifune's co-star was Tatsuya Nakadai, who played the leads in the next two films of Kurosawa, *Kagamusha* and *Ran*. They were roles much more suited to Mifune, who has admitted that they were not offered to him. Neither actor nor director will publicly confirm rumours of a quarrel – on the contrary: but it would seem that Kurosawa did not forgive Mifune for turning down *Dersu Uzula* in 1975. That may be his greatest film, but one can sympathize with Mifune, who did not want to spend 18 months on locations in Siberia. He continues to say that he is prouder of his films with Kurosawa than all the others put together. Certainly these were hardly worthwhile: *Inchon* (81), directed by Terence Young, which few people have seen (hard to imagine Mifune and Olivier in the same film – and a very bad one); a 10-hour US mini-series, *Shogun*, with Richard Chamberlain, in the title-role; the Japanese-American *The Bushido Blade*, made two years earlier, with Richard Boone as a Kung Fuish Commander Perry, with Mifune again as the shogun; and *The Challenge* (82), directed by John Frankenheimer with Scott Glen, who played a prize-fighter drawn into Mifune's family dispute. He spent the next few years in television, including *Anataj* (84), an Italian mini-series on the building of the Trans-Siberian railway. He confessed that his work for TV was not of quality, but he felt responsible to the staff of his production company, looking to him to keep them employed. By general consent the Japanese film industry was only a shadow of its former self, producing little of calibre. When Mifune eventually returned to the cinema he made two movies which were outstandingly popular: *Otokowa Tsuraiyo: Shiretiko Bojo* (87), starring Kiyoshi Atsumi, the 39th film in the Tora-San series (two are usually made a year); and Ichikawa's *Taketori Monogatari/Bamboo Princess*, based on a 7th-century legend about a bamboo cutter (Mifune) who finds a baby girl with mystical powers.

ANN MILLER

Ann Miller never quite made it. She used to refer to herself as the near-click of show business. She tippy-tapped through some dozens of B musicals before going to MGM, at that time the maker of the best musicals. She played secondary roles, but MGM were so high on her at one point that they announced her for the lead in *Singin' in the Rain*. When the film was made two years later, Debbie Reynolds was the female star; but today, when people talk about those MGM musicals, it is not Reynolds they remember, but Miller. She was bright and effervescent – but never wearing. She had a natural modesty – it is no surprise to find her saying in 1953: 'As an actress I'm terrible . . . but if Ava Gardner and Lana Turner can act under a good director I think I have still got a chance.' One remembers her for her sexy legs. She was, as David Vaughan put it in 'Sequence' reviewing *On the Town*, a 'splendid animal'.

She was born in Houston, Texas, in 1923, the daughter of an attorney (studio handouts made her born in 1919 – because she lied about her age to get her first film job). She was taught dancing from the age of five onwards and at the age of 10 won a local 'personality' contest – which encouraged her mother to take her to Hollywood. She was an extra in *Anne of Green Gables* (34) and *The Good Fairy* (35); and was a chorus girl in *The Devil on Horseback* (36), a B with Lily Damita. She got a job at the Orpheum in LA, then at the Bal Tabarin, where she was seen by Lucille Ball, who recommended her to a talent scout at her studio, RKO (or, alternatively, and more probably, she was written up by Benny Rubin, on the basis of which an RKO scout was sent to look at her). Anyway, RKO signed her for seven years and she became one of their *New Faces of 1937* (37), starring Milton Berle. All she did was dance and that was all she did in *Life of the Party*, which starred Joe Penner and Parkyakarkus as themselves, and Gene Raymond and Harriet Hilliard. She went plummeting down the cast-line for *Stage Door*, as a stage aspirant – with two dances and some lines; but she was the top-billed female in *Radio City Revels* (38), with Milton Berle, Jack Oakie, Victor Moore, Bob Burns, Jane Froman and Kenny Baker. The revels were not soon enough ended, but on the credit side, noted the 'New York Times', was 'a nimble and beauteous little dancer named Ann Miller'. However, she had no dances in *Having Wonderful Time* (it was not a musical). Columbia borrowed her to play the daughter enthusiastically studying ballet in *You Can't Take It With You* – and she was very funny. However, she had little to do as the ingénue in the next two: *Room Service*, with the Marx Brothers, and *Tarnished Angel* – Sally Eilers as a fake evangelist who becomes a real one.

Hollywood, she said, treated her as too young and she asked RKO for her release. She herself thought there was difficulty in that the Wm Morris Agency were handling both her and Eleanor Powell, whose – more powerful – company were not happy about Miller's success. So she went to Broadway to appear in what was to be the last of the 'George White's Scandals' – which was not a success, though she was. When she returned, it was to the same sort of frivolous time-waster: *Too Many Girls* (40), as a trio of co-eds, with Ball and Frances Langford. It was at RKO, at $3,000 a week, and when nothing better was offered she signed for a couple at Republic: *Hit Parade of 1941*, with Mary Boland, Patsy Kelly, Langford and Kenny Baker, and *Melody Ranch*, as leading lady to Gene Autry in what Republic (erroneously) called a 'super-Western'. Then she signed for a couple at Columbia: *Time Out for Rhythm* (41), with Rudy Vallee, which, said the 'New York Times', 'except for the lovely and lively Ann Miller, who won't be suppressed, has the distinction of being one of the dullest diversions in months', and *Go West Young Lady*, supporting Penny Singleton. Then two for Paramount with Jerry Colonna: *True to the Army* (42), supporting Judy Canova and Allan Jones; and *Priorities on Parade*, top-billed, about a swing band in an aircraft factory.

She had signed for short-term deals, hoping for something better. Finally, she signed a three-year contract at Columbia, to make stuff which at best was double-bill material: *Reveille With Beverly* (43), as a disc jockey who mounts a show for servicemen; *What's Buzzin' Cousin?*, with Eddie 'Rochester' Anderson; *Jam Session* (44), with several name musicians, including Louis Armstrong; *Hey Rookie*, putting on another show for GIs, with Larry Parks; *Carolina Blues*, a Kay Kyser musical – she pursued him for a job and Victor Moore was her father; *Eadie Was a Lady* (45), a college girl by day and a burlesque queen by night; *Eve Knew Her Apples*, as a radio vocalist; and *Thrill of Brazil* (46), supporting Evelyn Keyes and Keenan Wynn as a divorcing couple who come together again. These deals were as reported at the time, but in her memoir Miller contradicts them by saying that after *Time Out for Rhythm* Columbia had signed her to a seven-year contract and as her friendship – from 1944 onwards – deepened with Louis B. Mayer, Harry Cohn proposed a big-budgeted musical, *The Petty Girl*, and then, suddenly, let her contract lapse. What she did not say was that Columbia kept her as a threat to Rita Hayworth, in case she became troublesome. That particular film was intended for Hayworth, as a follow-up to *Cover Girl*: but Miller married – the first of

three millionaire husbands – and he paid Cohn $150,000 when the studio sued her for refusing the film (which eventually surfaced in 1950 with Joan Caulfield and failed, despite an Arlen-Mercer score).

It is doubtful whether she was first-feature material; 'Picturegoer' said that readers' letters were very pro-Miller, but on the few occasions her movies were shown to the press, no critic exactly shouted that she was being wasted. At all events, she found that she did not like domesticity and the marriage lasted just a year. When Cyd Charisse tore a tendon someone at MGM thought Mayer would be pleased if Miller replaced her: it was the sort of role few stars will play, the conniving lady in *Easter Parade* (48), who deserts Fred Astaire for Broadway stardom and then tries to win him back. It did give her a chance to tread a few steps with him, as well as two showy solos, and it turned out to be a wise career move – for MGM signed her to a seven-year contract. She supported Kathryn Grayson in *The Kissing Bandit*, but then had a fine chance in *On the Town* (49), as the eager anthropology student. She danced like a dervish and her high spirits added much to the film; but despite fine notices, MGM did

The fighting spirit: Ann Miller in one of the manifold wartime musicals about an entertainer putting on a show for the troops, Reveille with Beverly *(43).*

Easter Parade *(48). Ann Miller had been in movies over ten years before she was asked to partner Fred Astaire – probably the peak for any screen hoofer.*

not know what to do with her. After a year's absence, she had a small role, losing Red Skelton to Arlene Dahl in *Watch the Birdie* (50), an inept reworking of Buster Keaton's *The Cameraman*. After another absence, she supported Esther Williams in *Texas Carnival* (51), as Sunshine Jackson, a somewhat addled Texas heiress, again partnered by Skelton. Along with Janet Leigh she was loaned to RKO for their attempt at a big musical, *Two Tickets to Broadway*: other names included Tony Martin and Gloria De Haven. She played second fiddle to Grayson again in *Lovely to Look At* (52) and to Jane Powell in *Small Town Girl*, playing a Broadway star. In the former at least she had two good dance numbers, and three terrific ones in *Kiss Me Kate*, compensating for playing second lead again to Grayson. Probably her numbers are what people remember best about that film – and her sizzling Charleston, 'It', was certainly the best number in *Deep In My Heart* (54). She was billed seventh in *Hit the Deck* (55), below the likes of the Misses Powell and Reynolds, and did her usual good supporting work in *The Opposite Sex* (56). She was completely wasted in *The Great American Pastime*, supporting Tom Ewell and Anne Francis. It was her last film. She had asked for and been promised the role Janis Paige eventually played in *Silk Stockings*, but Arthur Freed changed his mind, because she and its star, Cyd Charisse, were physically too much alike; so she asked to be released from her contract.

She married again, 1958–61 and 1961–62, both times to Texas oilmen. She retired, but returned for some guests shots in 'Laugh-In', in the late 60s, looking marvellous – she had started so young that few people realized she was under 50. She was warmly received on Broadway as one of the stars who followed Angela Lansbury as 'Mame' (69) and again in 1971 when she played 'Dames At Sea' on TV. In 1979 she co-starred with Mickey Rooney in 'Sugar Babies', which triumphantly returned burlesque to Broadway. They toured with it, as did Carol Channing and Eddie Bracken, who could not make it work. Rooney and Miller brought it to London in 1988, when her almost unique combination of verve, vulgarity and stylishness brought her some of the best notices of her career.

HAYLEY MILLS

Hayley Mills comes from a showbiz family. Father John is an actor, mother Mary Hayley Bell writes and sister Juliet acts. Though once described as the poor man's Redgraves, father John was one of Britain's top box-office stars when Hayley was born in 1946, in London. His career dimmed somewhat in the 50s, but he had a good chance in *Tiger Bay* (59), as a detective pursuing Horst Buchholz. The film required a frightened child witness, a boy, but the part changed sex after a friend of her father's had recommended Hayley to the producer. She got excellent notices, but might not have continued her career had not Walt Disney seen the film – father was making Disney's *The Swiss Family Robinson* at the time. He signed the child to a five-year contract, starting at $30,000 the first year and going to $75,000, and cast her in an old Mary Pickford part, as *Pollyanna* (60), a child who goes around spreading sweetness and light. Her performance did not have that effect on critics who, then and thereafter, simply referred to her presence without further comment (unless you are W.C. Fields, you don't hit a child when it's down). Still, she won a special Oscar, presumably for playing the part – like Mary Pickford earlier – matter of factly rather than cloyingly.

The film was not a box-office smash, but the next one was, *The Parent Trap* (61), playing twins who reunite parents Maureen O'Hara and Brian Keith. Back in Britain, she did *Whistle Down the Wind*, from a story of her mother's about some kids who mistake an escaped convict (Alan Bates) for Christ. Christ is right. Both films were among the top films in British cinemas that year and exhibitors voted little Mills the biggest box-office attraction (she dropped out of the top 10 two years later; in the US she was never quite in the top 10). She was offered *Lolita*, but either father or Disney nixed it (at the time, father was credited; later, Disney was blamed). For Disney she did a Jules Verne adventure with Maurice Chevalier, *In Search of the Castaways* (62), and one that was badly received, *Summer Magic* (63). Back home, but for Universal, she was a mixed-up kid playing in *The Chalk Garden* (64) – but without that child-like quality which might have redeemed both part and film. Indeed, in Disney's *The Moonspinners*, from Mary Stewart's novel about skulduggery in the Cyclades, it was quite clear that here was a strong contender for the title of least ingratiating child star. She made another outside film, with her father, *The Truth About Spring*, described by the 'MFB' as 'ponderously coy' and a great flop in Britain and the US. Her last for Disney, however, *That Darn Cat* (65), was a top-earner.

Conscious, perhaps, that she was a joke to many people (an occupational hazard of child stars), the Mills family plotted to have her accepted as a serious actress. Father produced and directed, and mother wrote: *Sky West and Crooked*, a fey fable about the mentally retarded Brydie (Hayley) and gypsy Roibin (Ian McShane). Slaughtered by British critics, it flopped there and managed only a few spotty bookings in the US. Father later opined that it was 'a bit ahead of its time'. She was, however, soon at work in Hollywood on *The Trouble With Angels* (66), all about a troublesome teenager and Mother Superior Rosalind Russell. Well, no one expected *that* to be a critics' picture. *The Family Way* was a British comedy in the old tradition about a young couple (Hywel Bennett was the boy) unable to consummate their marriage; father was in it; Roy Boulting directed; and it disclosed a 'new' Hayley, even to a brief nude slot. To many viewers, it was disappointingly like the old Hayley. But the film was a big success in Britain, due, presumably, to the very things which got it into censorship difficulties in the US. Not so *Pretty Polly* (67), from a corny but engaging Noël Coward story about a prim miss blossoming out and being deflowered under the influence of a trip to Singapore; she finally showed that she might make it as a talent, but it would be way after Lynn Redgrave, who had the part in a TV version.

Pretty Polly *(67) was a pleasant movie about a suburban girl, Hayley Mills, who learns about Life on a trip to Singapore. Trevor Howard played her reprobate uncle.*

Boulting made *Twisted Nerve* (68), an extremely nasty film about a psychotic (Bennett again) who will do anything to get possession of Hayley. Simultaneously, she and Boulting (born 1913) said in interviews that they were living together (they were married in 1970). In one interview she said: 'Now I feel as though I'm starting out my career again from the beginning but when I look about I see thousands of other girls thinner and prettier than me who can act just as well and who are after the same parts.' She tried the stage: 'Peter Pan' (69) and 'The Wild Duck' (70). One part she did get was in Jonathan Miller's film of Kingsley Amis's novel, *Take a Girl Like You* (71), her virginity threatened by Oliver Reed. It flopped. Also unfortunate was *Forbush and the Penguins*, made and remade several times (she came in for one of the remakes) and finally a failure. Then she made another film with Bennett, from Agatha Christie's *Endless Night* (72), as an American heiress. Little was heard of it and less of two films directed by Sidney Hayers, *Deadly Strangers* (75), a thriller with Simon Ward and Sterling Hayden, and *What Changed Charley Farthing?*, a comedy with Doug McClure. Around the same time she was in the West End in 'A Touch of Spring', in the role played in the prior screen version – *Avanti* – by her sister Juliet; in the cast was Leigh Lawson, who became her second husband.

After a family saga in South Africa with David McCallum, *The Kingfisher Caper*, she confined her activities to television and the stage, and was notably in an unsuccessful West End revival of 'Dial M for Murder' (83). Two years later she was in 'Toys in the Attic' in Croydon and in 1986 she left a production of 'The Innocents' in Bromley – the producers threatened to sue – when Disney offered a belated sequel: but *The Parent Trap II* (87) was made for cable. So *Appointment with Death* (88), based on an Agatha Christie mystery, was her first work for the big screen for a year.

JOHN MILLS

For almost 60 years John Mills has been the leading cinema representative of a certain kind of well-bred, well-mannered comfortable Englishman. As such, he was for a while one of the most popular actors in Britain. Later, he branched into character acting and playing comic Cockneys and little men, but he never seemed at ease except (figuratively speaking) in the officers' mess.

He was born in Felixstowe, Suffolk, in 1908, the son of a teacher. After school he worked as a clerk and joined an amateur drama group; his sister Annette Mills (later one of the first TV personalities of the postwar period) was already involved in the theatre professionally and recommended him to a dancing school in London; from there he went into 'The Five O'Clock Revue' (29), as a chorus boy. Then he got a job with a repertory company in Singapore; passing through that city was Noël Coward, who was persuaded to perform with them. He was so impressed with Mills's performance as Raleigh in 'Journey's End' that he promised to help him when he returned to London. He did; on his recommendation Mills got the lead in 'Charley's Aunt' (30) and Coward then cast him as the son of the family in 'Cavalcade' (31). When Fox bought the film rights, Mills was offered a seven-year contract, but he turned it down because he was set to appear in a Coward revue, 'Words and Music' (32). He made his film début in *The Midshipmaid* (32), as one of the sailors who welcome Jessie Matthews aboard, and was then in *Brittania of Billingsgate* (33), the film of a popular play about a Cockney mother (Violet Loraine) who becomes a film star. Mills was then solicited to appear in some of the quota quickies of the period: *The Ghost Camera*, a thriller with Ida Lupino; *River Wolves* (34), a waterfront story; *A Political Party*, a comedy with Enid Stamp-Taylor; *Those Were the Days* (considerably the best of this batch), as a schoolboy, Will Hay's stepson; *The Lash*, a silly drama in which he was a playboy whipped by his pa for deserting his wife; *Blind Justice*, a thriller in which he was murdered; and *Doctor's Orders*, as a medical student. His career was meant to look up with *Royal Cavalcade* (35), an ambitious effort made by Associated British to celebrate the Silver Jubilee of George V; but it was virtually ignored by critics and public. Mills was a soldier and the cast included such prestige stage names as Owen Nares, Seymour Hicks and George Robey. His career looked up with *Forever England*, a wartime adventure story adapted from C.S. Forester's novel, 'Brown on Resolution': this time Mills was a sailor. He was in another 'class' effort, *Charing Cross Road*, a theatrical story; and at the same time he was in a long-running musical comedy, 'Jill Darling'.

His films improved: he was in *First Offence* (36), with Lilli Palmer, a remake of *Mauvaise Graine*, which had starred Danielle Darrieux; and in *Tudor Rose*, as Lord Guildford Dudley, who was married to Lady Jane Grey (Nova Pilbeam). He was the lance-corporal hero of *O.H.M.S.* (37), an army drama directed by Raoul Walsh with Wallace Ford, and the chorus-boy hero of *The Green Cockatoo* (38), a good thriller adapted from a story by Graham Greene, with Robert Newton and René Ray. On the stage he appeared in 'Red Night' with Robert Donat; and he played Young Marlowe in 'She Stoops to Conquer' and Puck at the Old Vic. He had a small West End success in 'Of Mice and Men', around which time he was seen as a former pupil of Robert Donat's in *Goodbye Mr Chips* (39), courteous, crisp and self-effacing. Mills's trouble was that he was too self-effacing: he was a *nice* leading man, but not a very forceful one. Curiously, this was a type which would become pre-eminent under wartime conditions. The British did not desert Bogart or Gable or Cagney, but these were foreigners and supermen; they looked for someone more real but equally trustworthy; someone who would have been educated at a school like Mr Chips's, but did not lack the common touch. During the war Mills would advance to the forefront of British actors.

The young John Mills. As Lord Guildford Dudley, who married Lady Jane Grey, the Tudor Rose *(36). Nova Pilbeam played that role, and the film was called* Nine Days a Queen *in the US.*

For the moment he was playing a common soldier in *Old Bill and Son* (41), a propaganda effort built around a World War I cartoon character, 'Old Bill'; then an RAF pilot in a good thriller, *Cottage to Let* – only he turns out to be a Nazi agent in the end. In *The Black Sheep of Whitehall* he was a nice civil servant getting Will Hay to help him round up a gang of Nazi agents. In *The Young Mr Pitt* (42), with Donat, he was Mr Wilberforce; in *The Big Blockade* he was a merchant seaman in one sequence – the film was a series of vignettes about rotten Germans and brave Britishers made as propaganda, with an all-star cast. Better propaganda, and a better film, was Noël Coward's *In Which We Serve*, with Mills again as a chirpy young sailor. He was promoted to Skipper in *We Dive at Dawn*

(43), with Eric Portman. On stage he appeared in a war drama, 'Men in Shadow', written by his wife, Mary Hayley Bell (his first wife was Aileen Raymond, 1931–41). Coward chose him for the juvenile lead in *This Happy Breed* (44); and then he was in *Waterloo Road*, as the representative of every British tommy whose wife has been unfaithful while he is away. He co-starred with Stewart Granger; till then, his star-billing had varied, but the popularity of this film made him an undoubted draw in British pictures.

The next one was even more popular, *The Way to the Stars* (45), a drama about an RAF station with Michael Redgrave: it won the 'Daily Mail' Film Award (voted by its readers) and made Mills the most popular actor after James Mason. As the grown-up Pip in David Lean's much praised film of Dickens's *Great Expectations* (46) he won the 'Daily Mail' Film Award. He was No 4 at the British box-office and now under contract to the Rank Organization. Rank put him into its co-production with RKO, *So Well Remembered* (47), as the decent editor of a mill-town newspaper, and into *The October Man*, with Joan Greenwood, as an amnesiac. He moved

The Way to the Stars *(45) was probably the most popular British movie of the war years. John Mills played a young pilot, here comforting the widow, Rosamund John, of a fellow-flyer (Michael Redgrave).*

John Mills as that gallant English adventurer, Scott of the Antarctic *(48). Scott's reputation has suffered badly from revelations in recent years, including the fact that he refused to take heed of the advice and instructions which would almost certainly have saved his life and those of his men. This movie, being hagiography, would not have wanted to know, and it stands today as a dated tribute to one of the old heroes of Imperial days.*

over to Ealing (which worked independently within the Rank Organization) to play *Scott of the Antarctic* (48), a painstaking tribute to a modern British hero. For this Mills won a second 'Daily Mail' Film Award, playing with care and conscientiousness. But conscientiousness was virtually all he brought to *The History of Mr Polly* (49), an adaptation of a novel by H.G. Wells which marked Mills's entry into production. Mr Polly was Wells's little man, a humble draper's assistant who deserts his nagging wife and finds Arcadia with a plump innkeeper (Megs Jenkins). Mills appeared to have no grasp of the character, nor was he any better as the Cockney groom in *The Rocking Horse Winner* (50). This was a supporting part in his own production – the adaptation of a story by D.H. Lawrence – and a box-office flop. With it, he abandoned producing.

For Rank he made what turned out to be his last big popular film, *Morning Departure*, a drama about a submarine in distress, with Richard Attenborough. His Rank contract was up and he hesitated before signing for a film with Korda, *Mr Denning Drives North* (51), with Phyllis Calvert. It was a dud at the box-office and so were a couple for Ealing: *The Gentle Gunman* (52), an IRA thriller with Dirk Bogarde, and *The Long Memory*, a thriller which indeed seemed endless. For David Lean, Mills played Willie Mossop, the worm that turned, in *Hobson's Choice* (53), with Charles Laughton. It was a character part and did not restore him to the position of Britain's favourite British actor (his place was taken by Jack Hawkins, who would soon be succeeded by Kenneth More). The films he made were mainly for traditionalists: *The Colditz Story* (54), a POW escape tale with Eric Portman; *The End of the Affair* (55) with Deborah Kerr, a supporting performance as a Cockney private detective – and a fairly embarrassing one; *Above Us the Waves*, again as a submarine commander; and *Escapade*, with Alistair Sim. In *War and Peace* (56) he was Platon, the cheerful Russian peasant whose philosophies comfort Pierre (Henry Fonda); it was a cameo role, he played it with a Cockney accent and it can only be described as an unmitigated disaster. There cannot, either, be many good words to be said for these subsequent movies: *It's Great to be Young*, as a teacher whose pupils are mad about music; *The Baby and the Battleship*, a Service comedy with Attenborough; *Around the World in 80 Days*, as a London cabbie; *Town on Trial* (57), as a Scotland Yard man; and *Vicious Circle*, a double-bill thriller, as a murder suspect. For the next trio he relived yet again those wonderful days of World War II: *Dunkirk* (58), as a lance-corporal; *Ice-Cold in Alex*, as an army captain; and *I Was Monty's Double*, as a major. He changed into mufti to play a detective in *Tiger Bay* (59) with his daughter Hayley and then had his first real change in years, as an Australian in *Summer of the Seventeenth Doll* (60).

Things perked up a bit: *Tunes of Glory*, back in the Mess, but a good picture, with Alec Guinness; *The Singer not the Song* (61), in a clerical collar, with Dirk Bogarde; and Disney's *The Swiss Family Robinson*. But his career touched rock-bottom with *Flame in the Streets* (62), a so-called topical drama about a pro-Negro trade unionist who learns his daughter wants to marry one. Then: *The Valiant*, as a naval commander; *Tiara Tahiti*, with James Mason; *The Chalk Garden* (63), with Hayley, as a handyman; *The Truth About Spring* (64), also with Hayley, as a con-man; *King Rat* (65), with George Segal, as a British officer; and *Operation Crossbow*, as ditto. He directed daughter Hayley in *Sky West and Crooked* and then did a character part as a crusty old bachelor in *The Wrong Box* (66). He had a good role as a North Country dad in *The Family Way* (67), with Hayley, but was then inveigled into two dreary US-backed adventure tales: *Chuka*, with Rod Taylor, as a drunken martinet; and *Africa Texas Style* – originally a TV pilot – with Hugh O'Brian, as a Kenyan farmer.

He had one of the largest roles in Attenborough's *Oh What a Lovely War* (69), reputedly because it was his idea to film it in the first place; he played Field-Marshal Haig in a style which can most kindly be described as 'actorish'. After that he played a retired colonel in a boy-and-horse story, *Run Wild Run Free*. There were two offers from abroad: *Lady Hamilton Zwischen Schmach und Liebe*, a sexploitation look at that affair, with Richard Johnson and Michèle Mercier as the lovers, and Mills as the cuckolded Sir William; and the German-Italian *La Morte non Ha Sesso*, as a Hamburg police inspector. It was sad to see a once-liked actor descend to this. As for *Adam's Woman* (70), made in Australia, it does not seem to have left those shores (he played a 19th-century NSW governor). David Lean came to the rescue and cast him as the village idiot in *Ryan's Daughter*, with Robert Mitchum; the performance brought him a Best Supporting Oscar, a matter for the Ripleys of this world. Around the same time he had his first real starring part for ages in a British film: *Dulcima*, as a bone-headed old yokel who has an affair with a young girl (Carol White). It was shown two years later (72), to dire reviews. Then he supported in two historicals which flopped dismally, *Young Winston*, as Kitchener, and in *Lady Caroline Lamb*, as Canning.

Stage appearances during three decades were few and indeed since 1953, when he appeared in London in 'The Uninvited Guest', he did only three plays – 'Ross' (61) in New York and, in London, 'Power of Persuasion' (63) and 'Veterans' (72) with John Gielgud.

In 1974 he played Jess Oakroyd in a coolly received musical version of 'The Good Companions'; and was even less fortunate in his return to films: *The 'Human' Factor* (75), co-starring with George Kennedy, as his chum, in this unpleasant revenge thriller directed by Edward Dmytryk; and *Trial by Combat* (76), starring with Donald Pleasance, as a retired police commissioner on the track of some odd murders in what was supposed to be a comedy. In 1976 he was knighted, in the most controversial of Harold Wilson's Honours lists; the following year he attempted Eric Portman's old role(s) in a West End revival of 'Separate Tables'. He was a dying Monsignor in *Des Teufels Advokat/The Devil's Advocate* (77), written for a West German company by Morris West from his own novel about morality in the Abruzzi; but the film signally failed to duplicate the book's success. The remake of *The Big Sleep* (78) failed even to get up to the big toe of the original; it is not an error to say that Mills was a Scotland Yard man since the action had been foolishly transferred to Britain. He was killed off early in a marginally more welcome remake, *The Thirty-Nine Steps*; and was in a US TV film, *Mr Strange*, and then in *Zulu Dawn* (79).

In 1979 he played Professor Quatermass in a TV series which, adapted, became *Quatermass Conclusion* for American cinemas the following year – not that many of them booked it. After a TV series, 'Little Lord Fauntleroy' (81), he played the Viceroy in his chum Attenborough's *Gandhi* (82), one of many names; but he headed down the cast-list in Cannon's silly adventure vehicle for Brooke Shields, *Sahara* (83), playing English tutor to a young sheik (Lambert Wilson). He was in the Chichester musical version of 'Goodbye Mr Chips' and then for a goodish run in the West End in 'Little Lies', an adaptation of Pinero's 'The Magistrate'; American television employed him profitably in *The Masks of Death* (84), as Dr Watson; *A Woman of Substance*, a mini-series with Deborah Kerr; and *Murder with Mirrors* (85), an Agatha Christie mystery in which he was the lord of the manor and married to Bette Davis. With Rosemary Harris he did a two-character play, 'The Petition', scheduled for remarkably few performances at the National Theatre; promptly transferred to the West End, it played perhaps even fewer. *Hold the Dream* (87) was the sequel to *A Woman of Substance*. He was father to Eliza (Amanda Plummer) in a 'Pygmalion', starring Peter O'Toole, which transferred from Guildford to New York, around which time he did a cameo in *Who's That Girl?* The answer to the question was Madonna, but who cared?

Robert Mitchum

Robert Mitchum sort of crept up on us. In 1946 Katharine Hepburn considered she had the ill-luck to make a film with him: 'You know you can't act, and if you hadn't been good looking you would never have gotten a picture. I'm tired of playing with people who have nothing to offer.' In 1968, when working at a pitch which would have astonished Miss Hepburn, 'Time Magazine' commented: 'All three films do nothing to disturb the wide-spread image of Mitchum as a handsome side of beef, a kind of swaggering, heavy-lidded Victor Mature. That may be the public's view of Mitchum, but Hollywood knows better. At 51, after 64 pictures, Mitchum is still a star to contend with. More than that, he is one of the most respected professionals in the business, a no-nonsense actor who is never late on the set and knows his lines cold. Directors, writers and other stars admire the force and the surprising nuances he can bring to even the tackiest one-dimensional role. Just about the only one who continually puts down Mitchum is Mitchum himself.' 'Time Magazine' mentioned that Mitchum turned down *Town Without Pity* (61) even after UA upped their original offer from $500,000 to $750,000 – which surprises, because he has made more bad or negligible films than any other actor of his quality (in this case, he did not like the subject); if he had not, maybe he would earlier have been recognized. These run-of-the-mill pictures hampered his popularity, so that he has never, for instance, made the top 10. In a good film, one can feel the audience warm to this lethargic, easy, good-natured actor.

He is like Bogart or Gary Cooper or John Wayne – no-nonsense, tough-heroic. He is never *seen* to be acting. And yet not really like them: actors of this quality are not interchangeable, like the heroes of television Westerns. But again, like them, deceptively skilled: for instance, you do not notice Mitchum's sexual magnetism till it is pointed out. Like Bogart and Wayne, he was doing apprentice work in films for years – and Hepburn's outburst was as reasonable in 1946 as the 'Time Magazine' panegyric 22 years later.

His youth was marked by a certain amount

of mild delinquency. Unhappy at home (he was born in Bridgeport, Connecticut, in 1917) with a stepfather, he did various jobs – ditch-digging, coal-mining, factory work, songwriting – and by his own admission once rolled drunks in California and was once arrested for vagrancy. As a professional boxer he was in 27 fights. (In 1940 he married; of the Mitchums' three children, son Jim became an actor.) In Los Angeles he worked in the Lockheed aircraft factory. He was clerking in a shoe shop when an agent who had helped his sister – Julie Mitchum was a nightclub singer – got him a job as a studio writer. He decided there was more cash in acting and became an extra: *Hoppy Serves a Writ* (43). Most of his parts were microscopic, he was usually unbilled, but he normally had at least two lines: *The Human Comedy, The Leather Burners, Border Patrol, Follow the Band, Cold Comrades, Bar 20, We've Never Been Licked, Doughboys in Ireland, Corvette K-225, Aerial Gunner, The Lone Star Trail, The Dancing Masters, False Colors, Riders of the Deadline, Minesweeper* and *Beyond the Last Frontier* – a Republic Western and his first role of any substance. He was in two big war films, MGM's *Cry Havoc* and Universal's *Gung Ho!*, and then got featured parts in two Monogram Bs, *Johnny Doesn't Live Here Any More* (44), a farce with Simone Simon, and *When Strangers Marry*, an excellent thriller with Kim Hunter and Dean Jagger, as the faithful friend.

MGM had liked his work in *Cry Havoc* and re-engaged him for a small part in *30 Seconds Over Tokyo*. Meanwhile, RKO had signed him to a contract and he débuted for them in *The Girl Rush*, a B musical starring Frances Langford. He starred in two B Westerns, *Nevada* and *West of the Pecos* (45); then was loaned to UA to play the tough, weary captain in *The Story of GI Joe*, the William A. Wellman movie based on the war memoirs of Ernie Pyle (played by Burgess Meredith). Wellman directed Mitchum well enough to qualify him for a Best Supporting Oscar nomination; and while he was doing a spell in the army his agent used the nomination to renegotiate his contract. He persuaded RKO to share Mitchum with Selznick, who proceeded to loan him out between his RKO chores but never used him. Mitchum returned to RKO to play a returning soldier competing with two others for war widow Dorothy McGuire: *Till the End of Time* (46). The other veterans were Guy Madison and Bill Williams, and the publicity line on this was that these were RKO's three new stars of the future – of which Mitchum was considered by far the least promising.

He went to MGM for *Undercurrent*, the film with Hepburn; was then involved with kleptomaniac Laraine Day in *The Locket*; was out to revenge his father's murderers in *Pursued* (47), a good Western; and was one of the soldier suspects in *Crossfire*. MGM borrowed him again to play opposite Greer Garson no less in *Desire Me* and he was with another Greer, the talented Jane, in *Out of the Past*, a good private-eye thriller. Another top leading lady, Loretta Young, shared the title-roles with him, *Rachel and the Stranger* (48); William Holden was the jealous husband and Mitchum sang a couple of songs to an impressed Loretta. He had a similar role, the Shane-like stranger, in Robert Wise's violent, good Western, *Blood on the Sun*. It was in 1948 that he was convicted for smoking marijuana cigarettes and served a two-month gaol sentence. At an appeal two years later the verdict was set aside – it was widely believed, in any case, that he had been framed to make him more amenable to the industry bigwigs. His popularity, such as it was, survived the scandal intact, but Selznick took the opportunity to unload him and sold his half of the contract to Howard Hughes of RKO for

Howard Hughes's bid for the Great-Screen-Team stakes: Robert Mitchum and Jane Russell in His Kind of Woman *(51). The trouble was, she was not quite special enough for Mitchum.*

over $200,000. (A while earlier RKO had discouraged him from accepting a role on Broadway; it was a question of 'A Streetcar Named Desire'.)

He was loaned to Republic to play the hired hand in *The Red Pony* (49) and then started a long series of Hughes-inspired programmers, few of them the sort of pictures which people actually go to see: *The Big Steal*, again with Jane Greer and again a private eye; *Holiday Affair*, a sentimental comedy with Janet Leigh; *Where Danger Lives* (50), as a doctor smitten with sexy homicidal maniac Faith Domergue, 'introduced' in this film (Hughes thought she would be the greatest star ever/since Jane Russell); and *My Forbidden Past* (51), again as a doctor, with Ava Gardner. He was getting at this time $4,500 a week and was Hughes's top male star. It was time, Hughes thought, to team him with his top female star (he had given up on Miss Domergue), Jane Russell: *His Kind of Woman*, a woeful attempt at exotic melodrama. Hughes thought they could become one of the great screen teams and after diverting him with Lizabeth Scott in *The Racket* – he was a police captain – they were united again in *Macao* (52), more exotic melodrama and credited to Josef von Sternberg, who disowned it. The teaming was inspired by forerunners like Gable/Harlow and Bogart/Bacall and Mitchum was good – but Russell had not the personality to play a slangy femme fatale. Then: *One Minute to Zero*, a Korean War story; *The Lusty Men*, set among rodeos, with Susan Hayward; and *Angel Face*, as Jean Simmons's nice young fiancé.

20th borrowed him to play opposite Hayward in *White Witch Doctor* (53), as a gold-hunting adventurer; then he did a thriller in 3-D, *Second Chance*. Hughes wanted to reteam him with Russell in *The French Line*, but Mitchum refused; he played another doctor in *She Couldn't Say No* (54), a comedy with Jean Simmons, and it was his last RKO film. As long as he remained there he and Hughes feuded and he was suspended later in the year for refusing *Cattle Queen of Montana* (Ronald Reagan did it). He worked the remaining four

Robert Mitchum and Marilyn Monroe in River of No Return *(54), an outdoor adventure mainly concerned with an ex-con and a saloon girl fleeing the Indians.*

films of his contract on loan-out – a heavily imperfect quartet, but they opened him to popular and critical approval such as he had not yet known. He co-starred with Marilyn Monroe in *River of No Return*, as her laconic, sceptical escort. Wellman's *Track of the Cat* was more ambitious, a thriller whose colour photography was mostly black and white (a convenient snowy landscape) and described by the 'MFB' as 'CinemaScope's first real weirdie'. Stanley Kramer's *Not As a Stranger* (55) had been a bestselling novel about a doctor's career – ambitious, dedicated, priggish, callous; even Mitchum's careful underplaying could not make you like the man, but he gave a centre to this portentous rubbish. It was his biggest financial success up to that time. Conversely, the next may have been the least successful, just as it was, if not the best, the most original and stimulating he had made: *The Night of the Hunter*, directed by Charles Laughton, a very personal mixture of pure suspense and black comedy. Mitchum was a homicidal backwoods preacher, justifying Laughton's citation, 'one of the best actors in the world'. He added: 'He won't thank you for destroying the tough image he's built up as a defence. In fact he's a tender man and a very great gentleman.'

His next director – Wellman again – did not agree: Mitchum was dropped after some days' work on *Blood Alley* (John Wayne's company produced for WB and Jack L. Warner, having failed to interest either Bogart or Gregory Peck, insisted on Wayne's taking over). Mitchum, soured by this or by his foray into art movies, returned to programmers: *Man With the Gun*, a Western, as a retired hired gun; *Foreign Intrigue* (56), adapted from a TV series; and *Bandido*, his first self-produced film, for UA – gun-running in Mexico in 1916. He signed a three-year agreement with 20th, to begin with *Boy on a Dolphin*, but when Marlon Brando walked out on the part (intended originally for Clark Gable) they promptly stranded him instead on a desert island with nun Deborah Kerr: *Heaven Knows Mr Allison* (57). John Huston directed and both he and Kerr felt compelled to put on record their admiration for Mitchum (he is one of her two favourite leading men – the other was David Niven). The film was another example of how big Mitchum's box-office was when the ingredients were right. They were not there for *Fire Down Below* despite the presence of Rita Hayworth and Jack Lemmon, nor for *The Enemy Below* despite Curt Jurgens, at that time, in his own words, the greatest star in the world (20th had just signed Mr Jurgens to a contract, but events proved he was not quite as good as he thought).

Mitchum's second production was *Thunder Road* (58), for which he wrote the script and a couple of songs; Audie Murphy was cast in the lead but there were complications and Mitchum played it – a thriller involving a Korean War veteran. He was in the Korean War in *The Hunters* and then in World War II in *The Angry Hills* (59). They were the hills of Greece and *The Wonderful Country* was the American West, populated also by Julie London and Pedro Armendariz. *Home From the Hill* (60) was a Minnelli miss with Mitchum as a stern paterfamilias – another part meant for Gable. Raymond Stross, the British producer of *The Angry Hills*, had Mitchum for a second film, *A Terrible Beauty*, about the IRA; the title was taken from Yeats's poem, but as it was completely irrelevant most people took it to refer to leading lady Anne Heywood.

The Night of the Hunter *(55) was a cunning blend of the sinister aspects of Dickens, Mark Twain, Disney, the Brothers Grimm and Hans Andersen; Robert Mitchum played the killer at the heart of it all.*

Mitchum stayed on the other side of the Atlantic for *The Grass is Greener*, a drawing-room comedy with Kerr, Simmons and Cary Grant. They all sank together. He and Kerr travelled to Australia for *The Sundowners*, an affectionate portrait of a marriage, directed by Fred Zinnemann; for a Zinnemann film the reviews were only warm, but it did brisk business and brought new admiration for the stars – perhaps for Mitchum most of all, as a man who could not settle in one place. He then tried a comedy, *The Last Time I Saw Archie* (61), a military piece with Jack Webb, as a con-man, but it was so bad that it played the lower half of bills. *Cape Fear* (62) was an unpleasant melodrama with Gregory Peck and Mitchum was a sadistic killer-rapist. Dwight Macdonald thought him 'really *too* good' for it, noting how improved he was. He did a cameo in *The Longest Day*; was perfectly cast in *Two for the See-Saw*, as an out-of-town businessman having a casual affair with Shirley MacLaine; was one of the joky guests in *The List of Adrian Messenger* (63); and foolishly got involved in *Rampage* with Jack Hawkins and Elsa Martinelli, a tired Big Game Hunt tale, brought up to date by intimations of a *ménage-à-trois*. It was precisely the sort of film a major actor should not do (or a minor one, come to that), but the more sober *Man in the Middle* (64), about a military tribunal, was slightly better received. Mitchum was with MacLaine again, now one of her husbands, in *What a Way To Go* – almost the only one to play with the right sureness of touch. *Mr Moses* (65) was more jungle stuff and *The Way West* (67) a tired trail tale with Kirk Douglas; but *El Dorado* was the real thing – a Howard Hawks Western with Mitchum and John Wayne at the top of their bent as ageing gunmen. He observed later that it was not his way to have an entourage like Wayne (or Sinatra); and he recalled Wayne bawling his lot out for not being more Wayne-conscious. He also said that among the films he had turned down were *Gunfight at the O.K. Corral, The Misfits, Cat Ballou* and *Patton*.

He spent the next year in Europe: in Spain for *Villa Rides* (68), with Yul Brynner, as an aircraft pilot; in Italy for *Lo Sbarco di Anzio*/*Anzio*, with Peter Falk and Robert Ryan, as a war correspondent; and in Britain for *Secret Ceremony*, with Elizabeth Taylor, briefly as a bearded mystery man. Then he was town marshal in two light-hearted Westerns directed by Burt Kennedy, *Young Billy Young* (69) and *The Good Guys and the Bad Guys*. None of them was very successful, though Mitchum's fee for at least one of them was $200,000 plus 27 per cent of the gross. 'Photoplay' suggested, in 1969, that 'Mitchum's pull at the box-office is overtaking all his contemporaries' – all the same, he usually contented himself with second-billing. He was

Latter-day Mitchum: as the wronged husband in what may well be one of the last Establishment movies, David Lean's romantic Ryan's Daughter (*70*).

then the unfortunate man married to Sarah Miles in David Lean's *Ryan's Daughter* (70). Said Derek Malcolm in the 'Guardian': 'Had it not been for the presence – and the word is absolutely apposite – of Robert Mitchum, I do not believe there would have been a film at all. Everyone else acts like Trojans . . . Mitchum is simply and gloriously himself in spite of everything – one of the most powerful and expressive non-actors in the business. Even when off the screen . . . he casts his shadow. It makes everyone else, not least David Lean, look small.' Mitchum himself described the film as 'really David's love-affair with Ireland'. He spoke of retiring, but made a tough thriller, *Going Home* (71), as a wife-murderer who years later tries to make contact with his son. He was an unfrocked priest bumming in a banana republic in *The Wrath of God* (72) and a tired crook who turns fence in *The Friends of Eddie Coyle*, the most opposite of films. The first was messy, unnecessary, without tension; the second was sharply directed (by Peter Yates) and written, managing even some new slants on criminals – and it was that rarity among modern films, a good one completely without pretension. After which we will pass in silence over *The Yakusa* (75), except to say that it was a revenge drama set in Japan and Mitchum was an ex-GI. Before it, he had parted company from Preminger on *Rosebud* (Peter O'Toole took over) and since the film failed he could not have been sorry; after it, *The Jackpot* was abandoned (Richard Burton was in it at one point; but in 1978 its director, Terence Young, told 'Screen International' that he had 70 minutes' material with Mitchum and James Coburn; and was still hoping to finish it).

He had another good film in *Farewell My Lovely* (75), finally playing Philip Marlowe in this remake: 'finally' since it was a throwback to the sort of films in which he had started, when the role had been played by contemporaries like Bogart and Dick Powell. He was too old for the role and not really like Chandler's Marlowe; but he could be anybody else's idea of Marlowe – stoic, tired, Galahadish, and he certainly suited the re-creation of 1944 LA. He turned down *The Sailor Who Fell from Grace with the Sea* and stayed in the (recent) past for *Midway* (76), as Admiral William F. Halsey, and *The Last Tycoon*, as the studio boss. *The Amsterdam Kill* (77) found him involved with drug-dealers and is only notable as the intended first of six wholly funded Hong Kong films intended for the international market; *The Big Sleep* was notable only as one of the movies' biggest mistakes, i.e. remaking it. This time, doubtless due to inept direction, there were no bouquets for his Marlowe as he prowled around the 1977 Home Counties. In Australia he did a guest role in *Matilda* and in Germany he appeared in *Breakthrough*, also titled *Sergeant Steiner* (79); after which he was in Canada for *Agency* (80). Mitchum had first billing, but the role was small if pivotal in this thriller about the advertising world: he played a man who was trying to advance his political fortunes subliminally. After some test bookings the film went to cable two years later. Nor was much heard of *Nightkill* shot in Arizona by a German company.

In October 1980 Mitchum was given an award – for career achievement – by the Los Angeles critics and he observed that it was the first he had ever received. Equally surprising, movie offers were getting fewer, but he got $250,000 plus a percentage for Cannon's *That Championship Season* (82), ideally cast as the coach reunited with his 'boys', but the film was a deserved failure. He had finally looked to television, but the behaviour of Miss Dunaway sent him off the set of *Evita Peron* (and he was replaced by James Farentino). So he made his belated dramatic debut in that medium in *One Shoe Makes it Murder*, which started out even less promisingly as *So Little Cause for Caroline*. His role as a has-been private eye did not require much of him. He was in most of *The Winds of War* (83), an 18-hour mini-series based on a book by Herman Wouk, and as the lead he received a million dollars for his participation. He returned to the big screen in two productions for Cannon, *The Ambassador* (84), in the title-role, with Ellen Burstyn and Rock Hudson, and *Maria's Lovers*, replacing an ailing Burt Lancaster, as Maria's father-in-law. Then he was with television for a few: *The Hearst/Davies Affair* (85), as William Randolph and Virginia Madsen as Marion; a *Reunion at Fairborough* for him and Kerr; *North and South*, one of several stars guesting in this mini-series; *Promises to Keep*, acting with son Christopher and grandson Bentley; and *Thompson's Last Run* (86), as a safe-cracker whom boyhood pal-cum-lawman Wilford Brimley wants to bring in. He did not wish to play his old role in the sequel to *The Winds of War*, so ceded it to George C. Scott, while the dying John Huston asked that Mitchum should replace him in *Mr North* (88).

Marilyn Monroe

More has been written about Marilyn Monroe, both during her lifetime and since, than any other figure in movie hagiography. Almost 30 years after her death, the Marilyn-memorabilia industry seems insatiable the world over: she remains the queen of posters, postcards, calendars and books, her image ubiquitous (along with the less deserving James Dean) in the places where these items are sold. Of the full-length biographies published in her lifetime the most intensive is that by Maurice Zolotov, published in 1960, which contains long analyses by colleagues and critics as to what constituted her appeal and talent. One must wonder to what extent such scrutinies led to the final tragedy – though that did, when it happened, have an air of inevitability. Marilyn fascinated the world while she lived – more than any other star since Garbo, to whom she was sometimes compared. Garbo worked mostly in tragedy and Monroe in comedy, and they were enormously different in temperament, but both could turn dross into gold. The camera found incandescent qualities in them both and in return they surrendered themselves completely to it; from both of them there was an extraordinary love directed towards the camera, to the leading man and to the audience. Both were instinctive actresses. Joshua Logan thought Monroe 'the most completely realized and authentic film actress since Garbo. Monroe is pure cinema. Watch her work. In any film. How rarely she has to use words. How much she does with her eyes, her lips, her slight, almost accidental gestures.'

Audiences were never in any doubt as to what she was thinking or when, more often, she was not thinking at all. Billy Wilder quotes an instance in *Some Like It Hot* 'when she comes undulating down the station platform. She comes on with her two balconies sticking out, and you know she's killing everybody with her looks, but she always seems surprised that her body is kicking up such an excitement. Now this is a real comic attitude. It's not anything that I, as a director, showed her.' When she first became a star, it was said that she kidded sex, like Mae West earlier. She certainly was not serious, as she half-closed her eyes and half-opened her mouth, as she wiggled her chassis ('There's a broad with a future behind her' commented Constance Bennett during the filming of *As Young As You Feel*): a strip-cartoon blonde come to life. But she never threw sex at audiences. She was tentative and vulnerable. Laurence Olivier once said she had 'a cunning way of suggesting naughtiness and innocence at the same time', but the naughtiness was really in that smashing physical appearance: looking like that, she should have been wised-up about men, but you knew she was utterly dependent on them.

Much was said after her death about her potential as a great actress. It is doubtful whether she could have been and certain that she did not need to be. Perfect in at least half a dozen of her portrayals, she had no cause to extend a limited range. Her last completed film was a drama and in it she was little more than a luminous presence – which of course was enough. It is impossible to think of her now, in her major films, without being reminded of the way she glowed, like a moth in candlelight.

The facts of her early life are well known. She was born (Norma Jean Baker) in Los Angeles, illegitimate, in 1926, of a mother who spent most of her life, subsequently, in mental institutions. The child was raised in a series of orphanages and by foster-parents, and was raped at the age of eight by a lodger in one house where she lived. She was married when she was just 14 (her foster-parents asked a Jim Doughterty to marry her since they had to move and did not want her to return to an orphanage); during the later war years she worked in a munitions factory and began to be photographed in tight sweaters and shorts by local photographers. By late 1946 she was accredited to a successful model agency and was appearing in national magazines. When Howard Hughes expressed an interest, her agency got her an agent who got her a screen test at 20th, who signed her at $125 a week; but, as Mark Harris put it, that company 'paid a great many young ladies $125 a week, [and] she was only one blonde girl in a world of blonde girls where even here or there an uncommon blonde was common enough'. She was edited out of a bucolic frolic called *Scudda Hoo! Scudda Hay!* but did have a bit in a C picture about juvenile delinquents, *Dangerous Years* (47). Then 20th dropped her.

It has been claimed that she was a prostitute *toute simple*; certainly colleagues who worked with her as she was heading for stardom believed that she had serviced executives and visiting firemen. She did cultivate friends in high places during these years – but then so, probably, did the other blondes. When, later, the searchlight turned on her, she spoke candidly of these friends (they included Joseph Schenck) – and said proudly that none of them helped her. Certainly she struggled on for two more years. Columbia signed her and gave her the lead with Adele Jergens in a B, *Ladies of the Chorus* (48), but despite the 'Motion Picture Herald' decree that she was 'promising', dropped her when her first option came up. She returned to bits – being leered at by Groucho in *Love Happy* (49) when she complained to him that men were following her; playing a chorus girl in a mild musical with Anne Baxter, *A Ticket to Tomahawk* (50). By this time she had got a good agent, Johnny Hyde, who fell in love with her and who is generally credited with first recognizing that 'extra something' and plugging it to producers. Through him she landed the role of Louis Calhern's Lolita-ish mistress in John Huston's *The Asphalt Jungle*, a good part in a fine thriller which brought her first recognition – as well as an offer to return to 20th for *All About Eve*, as an aspiring actress, 'a graduate of the Copacabana School of Dramatic Art' as George Sanders put it. (Later, in his memoir, Sanders said he knew that Monroe would become a star – because she *needed* to so much.)

At 20th she vamped Mickey Rooney in a programmer, *The Fireball*; at MGM had an unbilled bit in *Right Cross*; and for General Motors was top-featured in a 'commercial' film, *Home Town Story* (51), with Jeffrey Lynn and Marjorie Reynolds (MGM bought it for distribution to cinemas). Hyde, before he died, arranged a six-month deal with an unenthusiastic 20th; nothing happened till, simply by being there, she caused a sensation among exhibitors at a studio dinner – when she was offered a new contract starting at $500 a week going to $1,500 after seven years. Darryl F. Zanuck still did not see her potential and merely ordered that she was to be written into any picture which could use a sexy blonde. Accordingly, she was rushed into *As Young As You Feel* with Thelma Ritter, as a secretary (and given some extraneous primping in mirrors to extend her role); *Love Nest*, as June Haver's neighbour; and *Let's Make It Legal* with Claudette Colbert. RKO borrowed her to play the juvenile lead in a Barbara Stanwyck vehicle, *Clash by Night*, and Alton Cook, in the 'New York Telegram and Sun', noted 'a refreshing exuberance, an abundance of girlish high spirits . . . a gifted new star, worthy of all that fantastic press agentry'.

Her status had improved phenomenally, unhelped by the studio (except by mailing out cheesecake stills). She did it, literally, herself – though helped by a lucky accident when it was discovered that she had posed two years earlier for a nude calendar. This made headlines, but few outside the industry censured when she confessed that she had been near the breadline; and the world laughed at her answer when asked whether she had anything on at all – 'Yes, the radio.' Her comments to the press, her public appearances and the photographs – her obvious delight in it all – had sold her to the public in a bigger way than any publicity machine could have devised; her very appearance on the screen, even in the revivals where she walked-on, set audiences abuzz; and exhibitors visiting the 20th lot wanted to meet not the established stars but Marilyn. Her name on the billboards was estimated to add $500,000 to the gross (and when RKO, who had borrowed her for only $3,000, made overtures for *The Big Heat* a few months later, the asking price was $100,000). Zanuck finally got the message and rushed her into a quickie with Richard Widmark, *Don't Bother To Knock* (52), as a psychotic baby-sitter with (ironically) a background of mental illness. Unsurprisingly, she was inept, but it was a part even Duse could not have mastered. Simultaneously she was safely included in two all-star films, *We're Not Married*, improbably married to David Wayne, and *O. Henry's Full House*, in a bit as a streetwalker in the Charles Laughton episode. She was more happily cast in *Monkey Business* with Cary Grant, as a stenographer whose only assets were physical.

But 20th still did not know what to do with her. At the beginning of 1953 her agent renegotiated her salary, from $750 a week to $1,200. Finally, Charles Brackett devised a cod melodrama, *Niagara* (53), directed tongue-in-cheek by Henry Hathaway. Clad mostly in a skin-tight red dress she sang a

Niagara (53). *Predictably, Marilyn Monroe was a honeymooner. Less predictably, she wanted her husband (Joseph Cotten) bumped off – and here she is discussing her scheme with her lover.*

Marilyn Monroe started out as just another blonde starlet. She became a sex-symbol and then a much-praised comedienne. In the end she probably engaged more real affection than any other star of her generation.

Marilyn Monroe in Gentlemen Prefer Blondes *(53). The film was not up to much, but she had some good lines. In the second picture she and Jane Russell are enlivening a Paris café with a song called 'When Love Goes Wrong'.*

sulky song called 'Kiss' and tried to lure her latest conquest into killing her new husband (Joseph Cotten). A.H. Weiler wrote in 'The New York Times': 'Obviously ignoring the idea that there are Seven Wonders of the World, 20th Century-Fox have discovered two more and enhanced them with Technicolor . . . making full use of both the grandeur of the Falls and its adjacent areas as well as the grandeur that is Marilyn Monroe. The scenic effects in both cases are superb.'

The two comedies she did next established her. *Gentlemen Prefer Blondes* was a garish adaptation of a good Broadway musical, bought for – or at any rate announced for – Betty Grable, who had been kicking up about her material; but one reason that 20th preferred Monroe was that Grable's fee, at $150,000, was more than ten times hers. Monroe was a better choice for Lorelei Lee, the archetypal dumb blonde who knew that diamonds are a girl's best friend, and Jane Russell partnered her well as her partner in gold-digging. Monroe was also dumb – and short-sighted – in *How to Marry a Millionaire* (the second film photographed in CinemaScope), with Grable and Lauren Bacall this time as fellow gold-diggers. In both pictures audience and critical attention were focused on her – and she justified it with a comedy sense as yet uneven but already effective. Both films were among the year's top grossers, and she was among the top 10 stars, the biggest female draw – a position she retained the following year, despite being laden with two poor films: Preminger's *River of No Return* (54), which she categorized as a 'Z cowboy movie, in which the acting finishes third to the scenery and CinemaScope' – but it exploited her limited range; and *There's No Business Like Show Business*, a banal and tasteless musical with Irving Berlin songs. She was only one of several stars (Ethel Merman, Dan Dailey, Mitzi Gaynor, Donald O'Connor) and had little to do – as a hat-check girl who longed to play Chekhov – but exhibitors sold it on her name. It grossed a princely £5 million. In between the two films she made world headlines by (a) marrying baseball star Joe di Maggio, (b) singing for the troops in Korea and (c) failing to turn up on the set of *The Girl in Pink Tights.*

Her troubles seem to have begun in 1952, when she started to appear late on the set. There had already begun that succession of coaches and advisers who were such a bane to her directors. *Pink Tights* caused the first of a series of suspensions because she did not like the material (and was probably right: it was never made and two others she refused, *The Revolt of Mamie Stover* and *The Girl in the Red Velvet Swing*, were flops). She was also grieved that her proposed co-star, Frank Sinatra, was to receive $5,000 a week as against her $1,500. In June 1954, 20th revised her contract – seven years, going from $75,000 to $100,000 per film. The suspension was lifted when she agreed to do *Show Business*, but she only did that as she was promised *The Seven Year Itch* (55) afterwards, a prime

Monroe got her best notices to date in the film of George Axelrod's comedy, The Seven Year Itch *(55). Tom Ewell was the man with the itch (for infidelity), Marilyn the unbelievable girl who just happens to live upstairs.*

And Monroe was well received again as a roadhouse singer in Bus Stop *(56), here giving out with her inimitable version of 'That Old Black Magic'.*

Broadway comedy, here sluggishly directed by Billy Wilder. Still, as the girl upstairs who innocently tempts grass widower Tom Ewell, she was, as Paul Dehn wrote, 'incomparable' and the public flocked to see it. Then there was another row, when she refused *How to Be Very Very Popular*; she fled to New York where she studied at the Actors' Studio, whose director, Lee Strasburg, later described her as 'one of the two or three most sensitive and talented people I've ever met'.

Pressure from their stockholders and from her debts caused 20th and Monroe to patch things up. Yet another contract was drawn up and signed, for non-exclusive services, four pictures over a seven-year period, at $100,000 per film plus $500 a week expenses, and director approval. Also, she liked the new property 20th had bought for her, *Bus Stop* (56), William Inge's Broadway play. She was a lonely chantoosie who finds romance with cowboy Don Murray, 'a wonderful role, and she plays it with a mixture of humour and pain that is very touching' (William K. Zinsser in the 'New York Herald-Tribune'). All the reviewers agreed she had matured as an actress and she won over a couple of hold-outs. Incredibly, she was not nominated for an Oscar.

The co-starring combination of Laurence Olivier and Marilyn Monroe – for The Prince and the Showgirl *(57) – occasioned several much-written-up press conferences. With them here – in London – is Arthur Miller, to whom she was then married. Below, Monroe in the last film she completed,* The Misfits *(61).*

In 1956 she married dramatist Arthur Miller and announced that she would co-star with Olivier in her own production (that is, she had artistic control and would get 75 per cent of the profits), *The Prince and the Showgirl* (57). Olivier directed and Monroe had never looked so beautiful or been so appealing – despite friction between them on the set. Not surprisingly, the film was not the soufflé it should have been, nor the great hit (the publicity had been fantastic; her arrival to film in Britain had found that country breathless with excitement and was noticed by both the BBC news bulletin and 'The Times', neither of whom was often aware of movie stars in those days).

Back in Hollywood she rejected 20th's silly project to remake *The Blue Angel* and agreed to do Billy Wilder's *Some Like It Hot* (59) – though the part was smaller than those of Tony Curtis and Jack Lemmon – as the vocalist with an all-girl orchestra loved by both of them. All three players and the film got raves, easily her most successful film (and the only one of her profit-sharing films to help pay her debts after her death). At 20th, Cukor's *Let's Make Love* (60) was of another order, a poor showbiz tale of love between an actress and a millionaire (Yves Montand). Cukor commented later that she had difficulty in concentrating. Her reliance on stimulants and sleeping-pills was by now well known. Her next director, John Huston, said: 'It was as though a tide had turned in her life, and was now beginning to run out.' The film was *The Misfits* (61), written by Miller for her as their marraige fell apart, with Clark Gable, a drama of some lonely people coming together in the Mid-West. Miller was accused of squandering his talent and some hazarded that the story behind the filming – Monroe's delays were only part of the problems – was more interesting than what was on the screen. Public approval was qualified; but it looks today, with its strange combination of despair and hope, as though it might have been before its time.

Apart from Monroe's fights with her directors and co-stars, she had acquired a reputation for unreliability and was frequently hospitalized – in what were admitted after her death to be psychiatric clinics. It was hardly surprising therefore when 20th fired her for seldom showing on the set of *Something's Got to Give*: in 32 days she was only there 12 times, during which she had alienated all her co-workers, who believed her behaviour due to her insistence on having her own way in even the smallest matter. The studio, after the expensive antics of Elizabeth Taylor on the *Cleopatra* set, were not prepared to indulge another star and Marilyn was slapped with a

$750,000 lawsuit. Two months later (August 1962) she died from an overdose of barbiturates. She had been drinking heavily and was apparently worried about ageing. The mystery surrounding her death has never been cleared up and may be sinister. She had been having an affair with the President, John F. Kennedy, and seems genuinely to have believed that he would divorce his wife to marry her. When that proved not to be so and when he stopped taking her calls to the White House she rang other government departments. He sent his brother Robert, the Attorney-General, to reason with her, but this Kennedy also began an affair with her, with precisely the same results. She told friends that she was going to call a press conference to publicize her treatment by the Kennedy brothers and she may have told Robert this when they came to blows in her garden on the afternoon of her death – having been brought there, at her wish, by Peter Lawford, so often the Kennedys' Hollywood pander, and indeed, it was he who had introduced her to Jack Kennedy in the first place. Lawford answered the telephone that night to a friend of hers, so he was in the house after she died. None of this was revealed at the time, which does not of course prove that the lethal dose was not self-administered.

A week before her death she had told 'Life Magazine': 'I never understood it – this sex-symbol – I always thought symbols were things you clash together. That's the trouble, a sex symbol becomes a thing – I just hate to be a thing. But if I'm going to be a symbol of something, I'd rather have it sex.' (Another observation at this time, to 'Newsweek': 'Only the public can make a star. It's the studios who try and make a system out of it.')

There was a worldwide sorrow – and then an outcry: Hollywood was blamed. Certainly no movie star except perhaps Judy Garland was mourned by so many. There was a sense of loss and she was missed. A year later, 20th put out a compilation film, *Marilyn*, and were promptly trounced for not (apparently) trying to get sequences from the three late films she made for other companies. It included the five or so minutes salvaged from *Something's Got to Give* and the 'ageing' Monroe was revealed as being ethereally lovely. For the last time, and for very different reasons from the days of *Niagara*, audiences caught their breath.

Yves Montand

'Le bonheur, c'est avant tout ma carrière,' said Yves Montand once. He has been lucky. He is probably the most successful French actor of his generation. No continental actor since Boyer had played opposite so many big Hollywood stars – Ingrid Bergman, Marilyn Monroe, Shirley MacLaine and Barbra Streisand. He will be remembered, however, for his participation in four or five native productions.

In fact, he is not French at all. He was born in Monsumagno, near Milano, in 1921 and his real name is Ivo Livi. He was the youngest son of a Jewish peasant family, who fled Italy when Mussolini came to power. Montand grew up in the back streets of Marseilles and left school at 11. He was a *garçon du café*, a barman, a factory hand and a barber's assistant; and at 18 a music-hall entertainer. He had sung and done impressions as an amateur and was taken on by the Alcazar in Marseilles, from which it was but a small step down to the suburban cinemas and music halls in which he subsequently sang. When he could not get work he signed on as a docker, but was sufficiently self-confident to breach Paris in June 1944. The ABC Music Hall took him on to close the bill (i.e. to follow the star, hopefully to prevent a mass-exit) and he did well. There were club engagements and while he was singing at the Moulin Rouge he met Edith Piaf, whose protégé and lover he became. It was she who got him into a film she was making, *Etoile sans Lumière* (46), as the provincial boyfriend she leaves behind when she becomes a star – after dubbing and replacing Silent star Mila Parély (shades of *Singin' in the Rain*). It was a made-to-measure musical for her, he was unimpressive.

However, Marcel Carné signed him for the part meant for Gabin in *Les Portes de la Nuit*, with Nathalie Nattier (signed at the very last minute and very bad). He played a Spanish

Yves Montand's film career for years lagged behind his fame as a singer. This is a still from his third movie, L'Idole *(47).*

workman in France in the winter of 1945 and again was poor; and the film, despite all expectations, was not a success (its detractors rechristened it 'Les Portes de L'Ennui'). Over the next few years he made only one film, with Danielle Godet, *L'Idole* (47) – of prize-fighting. He might, had he chosen, have gone to Hollywood. At the beginning of 1947 he signed a contract with Warner Bros; it was in English and when he later had it translated he realized that he would become totally the property of Hollywood. He sued for breach of contract and one franc damages; Warners counter-attacked and the matter was settled out of court.

He moved to the fore, however, of French ballad-singers. In 1948 he appeared in an operette, 'Le Chevalier Bayard', and in 1951 presented his first one-man show in Paris, at the Theâtre de l'Étoile. In the meantime he had married Simone Signoret and made a film, *Souvenirs Perdus* (50), an episode picture, as a street-singer in the sketch with Bernard Blier. He guested in two more: *Sempre Parigi* (51), with Marcello Mastroianni, in which he sang two songs; and *Paris Chante Toujours* (52), a Cook's Tour of Paris in which he sang, along with Piaf and others. He became a film actor of importance with Clouzot's *Le Salaire de la Peur* (53), a lengthy thriller about a convoy of trucks bearing nitro-glycerine over a succession of rough or bumpy roads. Possibly because the drivers were society's throw-outs there was a move to see significance in it; but as a hair-raising, cliff-hanging (literally) thriller it was well-nigh faultless – and it became the most successful French film yet in the export market (it was the first foreign-language film to play as top attraction on the British circuits). Montand's leading protagonist, weary and cynical, showed little real ability but was a stalwart principal. It netted him some more movie roles: *Tempi Nostri*, another episoder, in Italy, in a sketch, 'Mara', with Danièle Delorme, as a schoolteacher; Guitry's *Napoléon* (55); and *Les Héros sont Fatigués*, 'wooden and lifeless' ('Variety') as pitted against Curt Jurgens in this sour melodrama of violence and corruption, set in Liberia. He starred opposite Michèle Morgan in *Marguerite de la Nuit* (56), as Mephistopheles, and opposite Silvana Mangano in the Italian *Uomini e Lupi* (57), an Eastmancolor drama of two men out to destroy marauding wolves in the Abruzzi hills, with Pedro Armendariz.

Between film engagements he had toured the world with his one-man show and had broken records in Paris, again at the Étoile, in 1953–4 – a six-month run – and again the

Montand's first big movie success was Le Salaire de la Peur *(53), a taut thriller directed by Henri-Georges Clouzot. Vera Clouzot (the director's wife) had a brief role as 'relaxation' for Montand.*

following year. He and Signoret then put on Arthur Miller's 'The Crucible' in Paris; after playing it for a year they filmed it, as *Les Sorcières de Salem*, but his John Proctor, undoubtedly heroic, was as steadfast in expression as behaviour. There was another film in Italy, *La Grande Strada Azzurra/Un Dénommé Squarcio* (58), with Alida Valli, as a fisherman, Gillo Pontecorvo's first film, from a novel by Franco Solinas; and then *Premier Mai*, a comedy with Nicole Berger, a silly tale about a father who has to explain the facts of life when a second baby is expected. Much publicity attended *La Loi* (59), directed by Jules Dassin from the Prix Goncourt novel by Roger Vailland, but it turned out to be an expendable peasant drama about a racketeer (Montand) with the hots for a village maiden (Gina Lollobrigida) who had eyes only for a nice boy from the North (Marcello Mastroianni). A concert tour of the USSR he made was filmed by the Russians and shown in Paris under the title *Yves Montand Chante* (60).

There was a Hollywood offer, for a film opposite Marilyn Monroe, *Let's Make Love* (they did, admitted Montand later, confirming newspaper gossip at the time). It was her then-husband, Arthur Miller, who suggested Montand when there were difficulties with other actors – billing complications, conflict of schedules, a reluctance to play second fiddle to Monroe or pander to her very personal working conditions. (Norman Krasna's script was written with Yul Brynner in mind and at one point Gregory Peck was set; among others offered the part were Charlton Heston, Cary Grant, William Holden, Rock Hudson and James Stewart). Thus Montand was the poor little rich boy who tried to enter show business after falling in love with a showgirl; despite Bing Crosby, Gene Kelly and Milton Berle, brought in (as guests) to teach him the rudiments of the trade, he remained talentless – and the film made it seem only too true, due either to his usual underplaying or to unfamiliarity with the language.

20th, who produced, had signed him for three more pictures, but they agreed to scrap the contract if he would do *Sanctuary* (61), which he had refused: he could not see himself as a bootlegger who seduces the Governor's daughter, Lee Remick. In the event, his performance is dour, but as Remick admitted later, he had learnt his dialogue phonetically. Nor was he any more exciting as Ingrid Bergman's husband in *Aimez-vous Brahms?/Goodbye Again*, filmed in Paris. His American career looked doomed, therefore, when he played opposite Shirley MacLaine in *My Geisha* (62): despite leaden direction he gave a performance of much delicacy and charm (outclassing almost all those leading men who had turned down *Let's Make Love*). But he did not film for three years, when he and Signoret (and Jean-Louis Trintignant, Charles Denner, Jacques Perrin, Michel Piccoli plus several guest stars) backed novice Costa-Gavras, scripting and directing *Compartiment Tueurs* (65), an exhilarating black mystery story. Montand's police inspector, coping with a cold, confirmed that he had found a new ease before the cameras. He then played a Spanish revolutionary in *La Guerre est Finie* (66), directed by Alain Resnais from a screenplay by Jorge Semprun. The point was that the war was not finished for the exiles in Paris, some thugs, some idealists, living on vicarious admiration, conscious that in Spain events had overtaken them. The film worked equally as a thriller. From Montand it demanded firstly his world-weary look, but required from him beautiful playing beyond that, and got it.

He had a guest spot in *Paris Brûle-t-il?/Is Paris Burning?* and made another American film, *Grand Prix*, second lead to James Garner. He was really – for the first time – entrenched as a film name, much in demand.

Goodbye Again *(61) was a Franco-American version of a novel by Françoise Sagan, 'Aimez-vous Brahms?' Yves Montand was a man in the dilemma of losing his mistress (Ingrid Bergman) to a younger man (Anthony Perkins).*

He starred in *Vivre Pour Vivre* (67), with which Claude Lelouch followed his over-praised and record-breaking *Un Homme et une Femme* – but vengeance was reaped and it was accused everywhere of modishness and shallowness. Still, Montand was fine as a leading TV journalist, unfaithful to wife Annie Girardot with Candice Bergen. He did *Un Soir . . . Un Train* (68) with Anouk Aimée, as a professor who gets into 'Outward Bound' territory: but a haunting picture as directed by André Delvaux. Then there was a guest appearance – Capitaine Formidable – in a pretentious satire directed by a fashion photographer, *Mr Freedom*. He was a Corsican gangster in *Le Diable par le Queue*, proving himself, said 'Variety', 'a gifted comedian'. The film itself was delightful, Philippe de Broca's witty comedy about a family (including Maria Schell) who turn their crumbling château into a hotel.

Irene Papas and Yves Montand as husband and wife in Z (69), obviously not the first political thriller, but there had never been one before to so successfully indict closet fascists and the thugs they unscrupulously hired. It did open up a new era of such movies, several of which were also directed by Costa-Gavras with Montand. They also made a love story together which was the reverse of these: terrible.

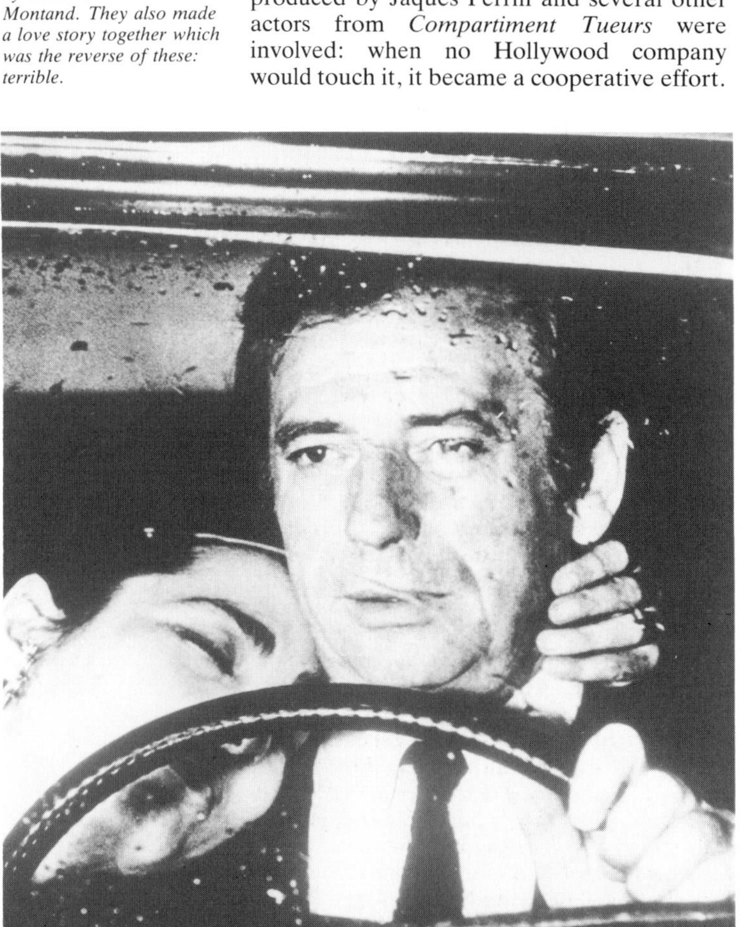

Costa-Gavras's third film, *Z* (69), was produced by Jaques Perrin and several other actors from *Compartiment Tueurs* were involved: when no Hollywood company would touch it, it became a cooperative effort. Jorge Semprun wrote it, from a novel by Vassili Vassilikos. Set in North Africa, the plot paralleled a political assassination in Greece some years earlier. As the murdered leader Montand, with the minimum of dialogue, was commanding and sympathetic; and equally good were Trintignant, Denner, Irene Papas, Renato Salvatore, Marcel Bozzufi, etc. As a thriller it had the kick of a power-house piston and as political propaganda it was hardly less effective: either way, it had its priorities right. In France the Académie du Cinéma voted it the year's Best Film and so did the New York film critics; it was the first foreign-language film ever nominated for a Best Picture Oscar; and it won the Best Foreign Picture Oscar.

Its success revived Hollywood's interest in Montand and Paramount cast him opposite Barbra Streisand in *On a Clear Day You Can See Forever* (70). Said Joseph Morgenstern in 'Newsweek', after recalling Montand's 'disastrous' American début: 'It would be easy to conclude that Montand destroys the movie single-handedly.' But who needs Hollywood when Costa-Gavras is offering *L'Aveu?* – based on the rigged Czech trials of the early 50s and a harsh indictment of democracy as practised in communist countries. (Communists felt betrayed, as Montand and Signoret were notable left-wingers.) Like good journalism, it concerned itself with the mechanics of what happened rather than the reasons and used Montand's sympathy and power to great advantage (as the chief victim he had little to act but harassment). Then he played a gangster in *Le Cercle Rouge* (71), with Alain Delon, with Bourvil (his last film) as a police inspector; it was a big success in France – but the English version, though supervised by the director, Jean-Pierre Melville, was so awkward as to kill it in Britain and the US. Montand was in another local success, teamed with another French favourite, Louis de Funès, in a historical caper, *La Folie des Grandeurs*, loosely based on 'Ruy Blas'. Then he appeared with Jane Fonda in Jean-Luc Godard's *Tout Va Bien* (72), but it was an act of philanthropy that benefited no one. Also on a percentage he returned to that territory annexed by Costa-Gavras, the political thriller, *Etat de Siège* (73); he was an American attaché kidnapped by an underground organization in South America – in actuality one in Uruguay, while the film was made in Chile just before the Revolution: as a study of American infiltration in that continent it was magnificently biased – and magnificently entertaining, a hat-trick for director and actor.

Obviously what followed was more conventional, but the first three were good: Granier-

Deferre's *Le Fils*, in which he was an American gang boss who returns to Corsica to see his dying mother; and *César et Rosalie* and *Vincent, François, Paul et les Autres* (74), both directed by Claude Sautet. Montand was César, in love with Rosalie (Romy Schneider), and Samy Frey also loved her; and he was Vincent, while the others were his *copains* all adjusting to middle age. It was at this time that Chris Marker made *La Solitude du Chanteur de Fond*, a documentary on Montand's recital at the Olympia on behalf of Chilean refugees. Montand was a middle-aged writer in Labro's *Le Hasard et la Violence*, stuck in a menacing, violent town and in love with a young doctor (Katherine Ross); in *Le Sauvage* (75) he was on an island with Catherine Deneuve; in *Police Python 357* (76) he was a police inspector and Signoret was his boss's crippled wife; and in *Le Grand Escogriffe*, with Agostina Belli, he was a con-man. He turned down his original role in William Friedkin's remake of *Le Salaire de la Peur* –a $20 million flop called *Sorcerer* – which was also turned down by Jean Yanne, Lino Ventura and Serge Reggiani. *La Menace* (77) was French-Canadian, an ingenious enough thriller in which a former mistress throws the blame for her suicide on his new wife. Few of these films were seen outside France, but there seemed a better chance for *Les Routes du Sud* (78), since it was directed by the sporadically admired Joseph Losey and written by Semprun; it did not matter so much that the plot resembled *La Guerre est Finie*, but the direction . . . 'well, he's not known as lousy Losey for nothing (James Morton). Montand returned to Costa-Gavras for a romance, *Chair de Femme* (79), from a novel by Romain Gary and co-starring Romy Schneider. The film was so pretentious and pointless that it could have been made by any hack.

There followed: *I Comme Icare* (80), as a DA involved in a Kennedy-like assassination; *Le Choix des Armes* (81), as a retired crook, with Gérard Depardieu as a young thug; *Tout Feux, Tout Flamme* (82), involved in a father-daughter conflict with Isabelle Adjani; and *Garcon!* (83), Sautet's study of a waiter's lot. During this period (1981–82) his one-man show at the Olympia did sell-out business for its three-month run. Claude Berri next claimed him for the two companion pieces based on a film (and novel) of Marcel Pagnol, *Jean de Florette* (86) and *Manon des Sources*, which, with an eight-month shooting schedule at a cost of the equivalent of $16 million, needed an American pre-sale. Orion took them up, to find that they repeated the success they had had on their home ground, while in Britain too they enjoyed greater popularity than any French movie in a generation. His performance as the scheming Provençal uncle of simple peasant Daniel Outieuil, who together cheat Gérard Depardieu out of his land, is Montand's greatest performance to date. There is unlikely to be a similar welcome for *Trois Places pour le 26* (88), one of Jacques Demy's increasing miscalculations, with Montand as himself arriving in Marseilles to star in an autobiographical musical. 'Embarrassing' said 'Variety'.

AGNES MOOREHEAD

The movie moguls always assumed that the public would not pay to see ageing female stars, unless they had watched them grow old, painlessly, with a lot of help from the make-up department. (In *Since You Went Away* Claudette Colbert, a year older than Moorehead and in the film mother of a grown-up daughter, is seen without a single line or wrinkle; but Moorehead is photographed plain, as it were.) Agnes Moorehead started in films with the disadvantage of being over 35: in her first film she played a mother and in her second an aunt. The critics raved, but it was too late. Besides, she was not beautiful and she was obviously intelligent – which facts clearly disqualified her from playing any but supporting roles. No one complained, least of all the lady herself, and she sometimes enlivened up to half a dozen films a year. Five times out of six she acted everyone else off the screen and out of sight, often in parts which can hardly have existed on paper. Her versatility was one of the pleasures of picturegoing in the 40s and 50s. Now and then she hammed, if only in circumstances which would deem her contemptuous of her material; for the most part she was the most careful and subtle of actresses – certainly in *The Magnificent Ambersons* she gives a performance among the best ever put on celluloid.

She was born in 1906 in Clinton, Massachusetts, the daughter of a Presbyterian minister (she was religious and believed her work was God-inspired). She was educated at the University of Wisconsin and taught English for a while; but she had had the theatre bug since the age of three when she had first appeared on the stage. In 1917 she appeared with the St Louis Municipal Opera Co., and she decided to study at the AADA. She made her New York début in 'Scarlett Pages' (29), doubling as a maid and a secretary, and after several more plays got some radio work, including 'The Seth Parker Family Hour' on NBC; she later toured in a play based on that saga. For three years, 1933–36, she toured in vaudeville with Phil Baker in a sketch called 'Baker Bottles Beetle'. In 1940 she joined Orson Welles's Mercury Theater Group and Welles took her with him when he went to Hollywood to make *Citizen Kane* (41): her role as Kane's mother was small.

Her part in his *The Magnificent Ambersons* (42) was, however, vital. 'Sight and Sound' in a later article (1955) said it 'confirmed the scope of her talents. The lonely, hysterical, inescapably spinsterish Aunt Fanny became, in her performance, like a character in a classic novel. This extraordinary power – of developing a complete, full character, of extracting the secret from the moment, of judging and placing the personality she is playing, so that we can see it in embracing perspective – has never been allowed, in succeeding films, to be so richly displayed.' There is a breathtakingly good sequence (filmed in one long take) where she watches Tim Holt eat – which alone would have justifed the Best Actress award bestowed on her by the New York critics. The industry recognized her achievement to the extent of nominating her for a Best Supporting Oscar, but the award that year went to Mrs Miniver's daughter, Teresa Wright.

The sad ladies of the two Welles films determined to some extent her status – she would mostly be mean, hard-working and, if not bitter, at least resigned. When she broke out, it was often as a busybody, as in her third film for Welles, *Journey Into Fear*. She remained at RKO for *The Big Street*, playing Eugene Pallette's wife, and then signed a five-year non-exclusive contract at MGM. Around the same time she first did the radio thriller that became a classic, 'Sorry Wrong Number'. She was in *The Youngest Profession* (43), a comedy about autograph hounds with Virginia Weidler, as a meddlesome governess; *Government Girl*, as a society hostess; *Jane Eyre* (44), as Mrs Read; *Dragon Seed*, as a shrewish Chinese woman; and *Since You Went Away* as a selfish, gossipy do-gooder, a part turned down by Ruth Gordon and in Moorehead's hands the best performance in the film. She did a cameo as a daffy theatrical costumier who helps Spencer Tracy in *The Seventh Cross*; but was much more in evidence in *Mrs Parkington*, as the witty and vivacious Frenchwoman who teaches Greer Garson the social graces. This was a performance so much praised that she was expected to win the Best Supporting Oscar that year,

Family group: The Magnificent Ambersons *(42). In the foreground, Dolores Costello as Isabel Amberson; Agnes Moorehead as Aunt Fanny; Joseph Cotten as Isabel's lifelong beau, Eugene; Tim Holt as Isabel's son George Minafer; and Anne Baxter as Eugene's daughter.*

but the award went instead to Ethel Barrymore for *None But the Lonely Heart*. In *Tomorrow the World* she was Fredric March's nasty spinster sister.

In: *Keep Your Powder Dry* (45) she was Lana Turner's CO; *Our Vines Have Tender Grapes* Edward G. Robinson's long-suffering wife; and *Her Highness and the Bellboy* a countess. He part in *The Beginning or the End?* was cut from the release print, but there was compensation with *Dark Passage* (47) at Warners, one of her best roles, as a would-be *femme fatale* and murderess. She acted under a rubber mask in *The Lost Moment*, as the centenarian keeper of the treasure in this (poor) version of 'The Aspern Papers'. In *Summer Holiday* (48) she was the gay spinster cousin sought by Frank Morgan, in *The Woman in White* married to Sydney Greenstreet. Almost without exception these had been 'quality' pictures – films if not good, at least of big budget: now she did a Dick Powell Western that was poor in all ways, *Stations West*, as the owner of a gold-mine.

The next batch were variable, but mainly good: *Johnny Belinda*, as Jane Wyman's harsh aunt; *The Stratton Story* (49), as James Stewart's worried mother; *The Great Sinner*, as the pawnshop hag; *Without Honor*, as Franchot Tone's resigned, sophisticated wife; and *Caged* (50), as the sympathetic warden of a women's prison – one of her best performances. In Europe she made *Black Jack* with George Sanders, playing a crook pretending to be a millionairess pretending to be a policewoman – not, considering the film, that anyone cared much. The next three were fine: *Fourteen Hours* (51), as another worried mum and in this case a hysterical one – Richard Basehart's; *Show Boat*, as Parthy Ann, Joe E. Brown's vinegary wife; and *The Blue Veil*, very funny as another silly socialite. But what made her do this lot only she and her agent knew: *The Adventures of Captain Fabian*, wasted as a pipe-smoking aunt; *The Blazing Forest* (52), a John Payne adventure in which she was another aunt; *The Story of Three Loves* (53), in a minute part, again as an aunt

Agnes Moorehead in Mrs Parkington *(44), one of the early films which revealed her versatility. In the centre of the picture is Greer Garson.*

Fourteen Hours (*51*) *was a well-made, gripping movie about a disturbed young man (Richard Basehart) who balanced on a ledge high above New York threatening suicide. Involved were: Howard da Silva as a police lieutenant; Paul Douglas as another cop; and Agnes Moorehead and Robert Keith as the man's parents.*

– Moira Shearer's; *Scandal at Scourie*, as a nun; *Main Street to Broadway*, as a predatory agent; and *Those Redheads from Seattle*, as their mother. Presumably she was getting artistic satisfaction from the 'Don Juan in Hell' readings that she had begun in 1951 and with which she toured for four years intermittently, along with Charles Laughton, Charles Boyer and Cedric Hardwicke. In 1954 she began to tour solo, under the title 'The Fabulous Redhead', reading from Proust, Ring Lardner, 'Sorry Wrong Number', etc.

But she was still greatly in demand in Hollywood: *The Magnificent Obsession* (54), as Jane Wyman's nurse-companion, in what appeared to be an impersonation of Edith Evans; *Untamed* (55), as governess to the kids of Susan Hayward; *The Left Hand of God*, as the wife of doctor E.G. Marshall; *All That Heaven Allows* (56), as Wyman's country-club friend; *Meet Me in Las Vegas*, as Dan Dailey's mother; *The Conqueror*, as Genghis Khan's mother – *he* was John Wayne; and *The Revolt of Mamie Stover* with Jane Russell, by far the best performance in the film as a tough 'madame' (or dance-hall proprietor, as this film had it). She had a good part in a goodish film, *The Swan*, as the dowager queen, Alec Guinness's mother; but the films after that were even worse than the last lot: *Pardners*, as Jerry Lewis's dominating mother; *The Opposite Sex*, excellent in the old Mary Boland part in this remake, as a much-married divorcee; and *Raintree County* (57), as Montgomery Clift's mother.

There were occasions when Moorehead's style seemed to be becoming theatrical and *The True Story of Jesse James* was one of them – Nicholas Ray's retelling of that story, with Robert Wagner and Jeffrey Hunter as the James brothers. She was their mother. She was good as a drama coach in *Jeanne Eagels*, supposedly teaching Kim Novak to act, and also in her brief apparition in *The Story of Mankind*, as Elizabeth I. In *Night of the Quarter Moon* she was yet another mother – John Drew Barrymore's – a socialite in this sleazy miscegenation story produced by Albert Zugsmith and directed by Hugo Haas. Possibly depressed by that experience she stayed away from films for more than a year, but returned in something equally dire: *La Tempesta/The Tempest* (59), an Italian version of a Pushkin story, starring Van Heflin and Silvana Mangano. Then she did *The Bat*, from a play by Mary Roberts Rinehart, with Vincent Price, as a writer of mystery novels who rents an old dark house.

She was noisy and not very good in Disney's *Pollyanna* (60), as an eccentric; and seen but briefly in *Twenty Plus Two* (61) – but not at all in Britain, where a 30-minute cut lost both her and William Demarest. She was a judge in *Bachelor in Paradise*; a fierce Sicilian matriarch in *La Sage-Femme le Curé et le Bon Dieu/Jessica* (62); and a pioneer woman in

How the West Was Won (63). In *Who's Minding the Store?* she was a mother horrified that her daughter wanted to marry Jerry Lewis and was funny in what seemed this time to be an impersonation of Bette Davis. She was Davis's slatternly maid in *Hush Hush Sweet Charlotte* (64) and was somewhat obvious; but was back at her best in improbable circumstances, *The Singing Nun* (66), making something out of that hackneyed character, the grumpy nun with a heart of gold. For the next few years she devoted herself mainly to TV: in a sit-com called 'Bewitched' she had a supporting role that called for regular appearances, as the heroine's witch mother. When the series folded she made her first appearance in a tele-movie, *The Ballad of Andy Crocker* (69) – he was Lee Majors and she was the shrewish mother of Joey Heatherton, whom she had forced to marry during his absence in Vietnam.

Her remaining credits are not on a par with earlier ones: *Pufnstuf* (70), a movie version of a popular TV children's show; *What's the Matter With Helen?*, excellent in her few minutes as an evangelist; *Suddenly Single* and *Marriage Year One*, both for television, in the latter as Sally Field's grandmother; *Dear Dead Delilah* (72), dying in a mansion while the rest of the cast (or most of it) search for money hidden in its grounds; and again for television, *Night of Terror* with Martin Balsam, *Rolling Man*, as another grandmother, and *Frankenstein the True Story* (73). In 1973 she was on Broadway in 'Gigi', the first of several attempts to turn the MGM film into a stage musical.

She was married twice, 1930–52 and 1953–58. She died in 1974.

Kenneth More

Kenneth More was *the* big British star of the 50s; he might be claimed to be the last solely British star. With the 60s Hollywood took over the British production field, in some years financing as much as 90 per cent of production. British players became 'international' (and henceforth shall be). Maybe More was the right person for the role. He said once: 'I seemed fated to be either the stiff-upper-lip war hero or the hearty back-slapping beer-drinking idiot' – the typical Englishman, in fact.

He was born in Gerrards Cross, Buckinghamshire, in 1914. On leaving school he was apprenticed to an engineer for two years; then he went to Canada to be a fur-trapper. When that did not work out he got a job as a stage-hand at London's Windmill Theatre (the owner, Van Damm, was a friend of his father) and there, occasionally, stooged and understudied – the Windmill specialized in revue (with nudes) and in 1936 More was featured in a sketch. He remained on the bill for a year, then moved into legit via rep in Newcastle. He did his war service in the navy as a lieutenant and on demobilization was with the Wolverhampton rep for a while. In London he was in 'And No Birds Sing' (46) and in the first play televised after the war, 'The Silence of the Sea'. He worked constantly in TV (Badger in 'Toad of Toad Hall' some years running) and got his stage break in 'Power Without Glory' (47). Noël Coward saw it and gave him a part in 'Peace In Our Time' and by the time that had finished he was getting small parts in films.

The first was in *Scott of the Antarctic* (48), Ealing's worthy tribute to that explorer (John Mills). He got £500 for playing Lt 'Teddy' Evans. Then: *Man on the Run* (49), about any army deserter (Derek Farr), as a colonel; *Now Barabbas Was a Robber*, as one of the prisoners; *Stop Press Girl* (Sally Ann Howes), a comedy so silly that it was not released; and *Morning Departure* (50), again as one of Captain John Mills's crew. *Chance of a Lifetime* was an independent film about factory life that was only released because the government stepped in. By this time More was starring in a West End success, 'The Way Things Go' with Ronald Squire – from whom he learnt, he said, his comedy technique. His parts in films became bigger: *The Clouded Yellow* with Jean Simmons, as a Secret Service man pursuing Trevor Howard; *The Franchise Affair* (51), a modest thriller with Michael Denison and Dulcie Gray, as a friendly garage mechanic; *No Highway*, as one of the aircrew; and *Appointment With Venus*, with David Niven, as an artist who loses his pacificism – and the film's best performance.

On stage he was lucky – one of those cases of the perfect actor and the perfect part: 'The Deep Blue Sea' (52) by Terence Rattigan, as a feckless, breezy and sane ex-RAF type, involved with a married woman whose emotionalism and possessiveness is just too much for him. During its run he starred in two unpretentious 'class' programmers, *Brandy for the Parson* (52), a comedy about a holiday-maker (James Donald) and a smuggler (More); and *The Yellow Balloon*, as the father of a small boy caught in the clutches of a crook. He tested for the role that Nigel Patrick played in *The Sound Barrier* and played Clark Gable's journalist pal in *Never Let Me Go* (53).

Director Henry Cornelius saw 'The Deep

Genevieve (53) *was a modest-seeming comedy which got rave notices, made a mint for its makers, and established the reputations of its four leading players – especially Kay Kendall and Kenneth More.*

Blue Sea' and offered More one of the four leading roles in *Genevieve* (and £3,000 to do it), a tale of two couples on the old crocks' race to Brighton and back. More would be a loud-mouthed London smartie taking model Kay Kendall; the others were married (Dinah Sheridan and John Gregson); none of them was a star. The writer was an American, William Rose, and he managed to combine the sort of wit which was Hollywood's prerogative with the idiosyncratic humour of the best Ealing comedies. The critics were knocked for six (Richard Winnington: 'A landmark in British film comedy') and the public responded with delight. The film became a classic overnight and one of the most successful British pictures ever made.

Prior to its release, More had signed for *Our Girl Friday*, a desert-island comedy which foundered on the notion that Joan Collins was adored by her three fellow shipwreckees. The public held its breath, but with *Doctor in the House* (54) fell over themselves to see Mr More (and Mr Bogarde) as medical students. His role was more or less a repeat of his *Genevieve* one, but it obviously had staying power – it copped the BFA award as Best British Actor. Korda signed More to a five-year contract and put him into a slight comedy about a grass widower coping with kids, *Raising a Riot*, which his popularity made into a big box-office hit. Then, the film of *The Deep Blue Sea* (55), which brought him a Best Actor award at Venice and this appreciation from Dilys Powell: 'the flawless performance we expected'. He said later: 'This was in every way a disappointing film for me. . . . I think there was a great deal of miscasting, particularly Vivien Leigh. All the intimacy and tenseness of the play was lost.'

For Rank he took on a part turned down by Richard Burton, in *Reach for the Sky* (56), based on a bestselling biography of war hero Douglas Bader, who triumphed over a double leg amputation. It became Britain's top-grossing film of the year and More's biggest hit; it made him the year's top star and brought him a 'Picturegoer' Gold Medal. That journal said: 'More's popularity isn't just phenomenal. It's unique, unique because he's a star – by public demand only.' In New York the film was badly received, recognized as an atrociously made piece of patriotism. Hollywood, however, was now interested, but More refused to go because he felt his very British personality would fit badly there; but he wisely directed his career towards the US – his next film would be backed by Columbia and the one after that would be based on an American bestseller; the next five after that would all have American names as co-star.

Korda had died and Columbia willingly took over a pet project of his and More's – *The Admirable Crichton* (57), with More totally admirable as J.M. Barrie's perfect butler turned desert-island chieftain. It was not just that he had superb comic timing: one could see absolutely why the family trusted their fates to him. No other British film actor had come so close to that dependable, reliable quality of the great Hollywood stars – you would trust him through thick and thin. And he was more humorous than, say, Gary Cooper, more down to earth than, say, Cary Grant. Obviously he was ideal as Lightoller, one of the few people to emerge from the sinking of the Titanic with honour: *A Night to Remember* (58), scripted by Eric Ambler from the book by Walter Lord, easily the best of the several films on that subject. It was the first of a new Rank contract – seven films in five years; his fee at this period was £40,000 per film. There was a half-failure, Cornelius's *Next to No Time*, with Betsy Drake, an odd mixture of farce and whimsy, as a ship's engineer. He was an Englishman out West, *The Sheriff of Fractured Jaw*, filmed in Spain with Jayne Mansfield for 20th, and getting 5 per cent of the profits. Rank brought over Taina Elg for *The 39 Steps*, generally considered inferior to the Hitchcock version, and Lauren Bacall for *North-West Frontier* (59), a decent Indian yarn. These were big-budget productions, but still the US grosses were nothing sensational.

More did have a surprise hit in the US, *Sink the Bismarck* (60), with Dana Wynter for 20th; but Rank was not trying again and the best they would do for a leading lady this time was Shirley Ann Field – *Man in the Moon*, a space travel comedy. That flopped in Britain – More's first real flop. Carl Foreman offered him the role that David Niven subsequently played in *The Guns of Navarone*, but he was prevented from doing it by John Davis, the head of Rank, due to what was possibly a misunderstanding. According to More's own account, he personally insulted Davis and as a result was paid not to do the last two films of his Rank deal. But Rank were in every respect the losers as a result, for More remained No 1 at the British box-office. He changed his image slightly, to play the mystery visitor (smuggler? thief?) in *The Greengage Summer* (61) and you could see why the children, including Susannah York, adored him. He was No 3 at the box-office for this year and No 4 in 1962, but you could feel the chill – neither of his pictures that year made much mark: *Some People*, built round the Duke of Edinburgh's award scheme (in the cast was Angela Douglas, who became his second wife); and *We Joined the Navy*, a naval farce. And *The Comedy Man* (63) did not do well – a downbeat tale of a seedy actor and More's own favourite role.

After Genevieve, *More's beautifully relaxed comedy playing was utilized far too seldom (there were several serious films): but he was amusing in* The Sheriff of Fractured Jaw *(58). The lady is Jayne Mansfield.*

British producers seemed no longer interested and he himself thought that the reason was because he had left his wife for a younger woman; anyway, he returned to the stage: 'Out of the Crocodile' (63) and 'Our Man Crichton' (64), a musical. He worked in TV again and valiantly told reporters that he preferred it to any other medium. Certainly he had a big success as Young Jolyon in 'The Forsyte Saga' (1967/8), perhaps compensating for some film disappointments, notably *The Collector*; he agreed to play a supporting role in the 35-minute prologue to the main action at William Wyler's special request, but all of it was cut from the release prints. He had a supporting role to Rod Taylor in *The Mercenaries* (67), as a drunken doctor, and then went off to Italy to play in Lattuada's unnecessary rehash of *Fräulein Doktor* (68), made in English with Capucine, etc. He played a colonel.

But his future was assured; he was in a West End success, 'The Secretary Bird' (68), and got personal notices which must be among the best accorded any light comedian during this century. In films he did three cameo parts: *Oh What a Lovely War!* (69), as the Kaiser; *The Battle of Britain*, as the CO; and *Scrooge* (70), as the Ghost of Christmas Present, in romping good form. In 1971 he played the advocate in a revival of 'The Winslow Boy' and then – beautifully – an MP in Alan Bennett's play 'Getting On'. He continued to appear regularly on TV and gave an exceptional performance in Terence Rattigan's 'In Praise of Love'; but films were not kind. He was wasted as the Lord Chamberlain in *The Slipper and the Rose* (76), a Cinderella story; and his old friends, the Box-Thomas team, could not get backing for *The Donkey Rustlers*. There was a Spanish venture, *Viaje al Centro de la Tierra/Where Time Began* (77), as a professor who discovers a strange manuscript (the film went direct to TV in Britain) and one in Canada, *Leopard in the Snow* (78) in a supporting role; and then a British Disney, replacing David Niven (who was taken ill), *The Spaceman and King Arthur/The Unidentified Flying Oddball* (79), as the latter half of the title in this new version of Mark Twain's story, which also starred Jim Dale. In 1980 he announced his retirement due to ill-health, but he was persuaded to play Mr Lorry in a version of *A Tale of Two Cities* (80) made for American television. He died of Parkinson's Disease in 1982.

JEANNE MOREAU

In the early 60s, by common consent, Jeanne Moreau was the finest contemporary screen actress. 'Time Magazine''s cover profile in 1965 said that 'film directors all over the world have to struggle to praise her hard enough', dragging in the wake of that remark the names of Orson Welles, Tony Richardson, Satyajit Ray, Carl Foreman and François Truffaut. 'Time Magazine''s own panegyric included this: 'There is no actress in Hollywood who can match the depth and breadth of her art. There is no personality in films so able to withstand the long, lingering look of the movie camera, no one whose simple presence on the screen evokes such a variety of moods. Her love scenes are among the most intense ever filmed, her suffering agonizingly acute. She is an actress of infinite complexity and conviction. . . .'

With the exception of Marilyn Monroe, no actress since Garbo had been so relentlessly dissected in all the best journals; there was no actress it was more okay to admire – and not only for her 'infinite complexity and conviction'. She was the art-house love-goddess. Maybe, in the end, she was not that remarkable, but there had been a dearth of interesting women on the screen. You knew you were in the presence of no common or garden actress.

It is her appearance that makes her so immediately compelling: that tenebrous face and those dark unsmiling eyes. Among movie stars, the decisive factor – the dividing line between effectiveness and the lack of it – is the eyes; there are ladies who are conscientiously passionate, but when you look at the eyes there is nothing happening behind them. With Moreau, there is almost too much. Cast, inevitably, as some modern Emma Bovary or Delilah, her thoughts might be tantalizingly unfathomable – but you are never in any doubt that there is a hell of a lot of them (she could never have played the last scene of *Queen Christina*).

She was born in Paris in 1928, the daughter of a Lancashire chorus girl who had been dancing at the Casino de Paris, and a French barman; the parents divorced in 1939 and she stayed with her father. She determined to be an actress after seeing Anouilh's 'Antigone', was accepted by the Conservatoire and became a star pupil; made her stage début at the Avignon festival in 'La Terrasse de Midi' and while still at the Conservatoire was taken on by the Comédie-Française to play Veroutchka in 'A Month in the Country'. She stayed four years and in her early films was billed as 'pensionnaire de la Comédie-Française'. Not long after joining them she was offered a good film role in *Dernier Amour* (49), third-billed, suspected by Annabella of vamping her husband, Georges Marchal. She was the ingénue in *Meurtres* (50) with Fernandel and in a musical, *Pigalle-Saint-Germain-des-Prés*. As she was – in a way – in *L'Homme de ma Vie/L'Uomo della mia Vita* (52), as the daughter of a whore (Madeleine Robinson), whose fiancé brutally beds her *sans* marriage when he learns the truth about Maman. For the next 10 years she would receive little more respect on the screen – though she was good (but very bad) as a young nurse in *Il Est Minuit Docteur Schweitzer*, with Pierre Fresnay, a cheap allegory of colonial 'goodness', based on a play.

In 1952 she joined the TNP for a season; among other roles she played the princesses in both 'Le Prince de Hambourg' and 'Le Cid' opposite Gérard Philipe. It was Philipe who persuaded her to take one of the two leading roles, a tart, in a boulevard comedy, 'L'Heure Eblouissante' (53) – and she became famous when she played the other one as well, the wife, when Suzanne Flon became ill. Her films did not improve though: *Dortoir des Grandes* (53), a murder mystery with Jean Marais, playing a waitress, and *Julietta*, again with Marais, where she was, thought 'Variety', 'delightful as his sharp-tongued and bewildered fiancée'. Somewhat better was *Touchez Pas au Grisbi*, as a *poule*, with Gabin, but well below par were: *Secrets d'Alcove* (54), in the episode with Richard Todd, 'Le Billet de Logement'; *Les Intrigantes*, as the ambitious, scheming and unfaithful wife of theatre director Raymond Rouleau; and *La Reine Margot*, in the title-role of this cut-price Dumas (though in colour), with Françoise Rosay as Catherine de Medici. In the theatre her stock increased via 'La Machine Infernale', as the Sphinx, and 'Pygmalion', as Eliza.

On film she was not especially dynamic. She was plumpish and pretty and sulky-looking, and was on her way to becoming, as Truffaut put it later, 'the Edwige Feuillère of B pictures'. By 'B', he meant simply cheap or undistinguished: *Les Hommes en Blanc* (55), a hospital drama with Raymond Pellegrin; *Gas-Oil*, with Gabin; *M'sieur la Caille* with Philippe Lemaire, as a *poule* of Pigalle; *Le*

Salaire du Péché (56), with Jean-Claude Pascal; *Jusqu'au Dernier* (57), as a dancer in this underworld story; *Les Louves*, as the heroine of this sickly greed melodrama by Boileau and Narcejac, with Micheline Presle as a murderess (and Madeleine Robinson and Pierre Mondy); *L'Etrange Monsieur Steve*, as the only convincing character, an underworld schemer who ensnares Philippe Lemaire; and, top-billed over Serge Reggiani, *Echec au Porteur*, a confused melodrama about a bomb hidden in a football.

Most of these films she was offered because of a sensational success in the Paris production of a play by Tennessee Williams, 'La Chatte sur un Toit Brûlant', in 1956. They were not good films, but Louis Malle, till then a director of shorts, saw her in the play and decided that no one had used her properly. He was the first director to see Moreau clear – sensual, tired, the Woman Who Had Lived (he also became her lover). As such he used her in his first feature – also the first ripple of the *nouvelle vague* – *Ascenseur pour l'Echafaud* (58), as the accomplice of her lover (Maurice Ronet) when he murdered her husband and spending most of the film wandering over Paris looking for him. It opened in Paris in April and so did two other Moreau films, the minor *Trois Jours à Vivre* and the good *Le Dos au Mur*, another thriller and again superb as an unfaithful wife, proudly mink-coated and wanton. In Paris she consolidated her new star status in 'La Bonne Soupe', as a tart; and world audiences first became aware of her in Malle's *Les Amants*, type-cast again as a bored wife taking a lover, Jean-Marc Bory. It was the sex-film *par excellence*, love its *raison d'être* – the first half cynical, the second lyrical, with the camera erotically holding Moreau's face, the microphone catching the occasional phrase mur-

Jeanne Moreau's screen image was built around her care for, and need of, men. Gas-Oil (55), *above, is an early example where she provided relaxation for Jean Gabin, as a long-distance truck-driver.*

She became world-famous with Les Amants (58), *as a bored wife who leaves her husband's bed to moon around the grounds (and then some) with her lover, Jean-Marc Bory.*

mured in her scratchy voice. Because of the sex the film became internationally famous – a harsh, but commercially useful, fate for so simple an anecdote.

For similar reasons the next became famous: Roger Vadim's updating of Choderlos de Laclos's *Les Liaisons Dangereuses* (59), with Philipe. For some time the government refused an export licence, but it turned out to be an empty thing, Vadim at his most vacuous. She did a workmanlike film of Bernanos's story of nuns confronted by the Revolution, *Le Dialogue des Carmélites* (60), not altogether convincingly cast, with Jean-Louis Barrault, Pascale Audret and Madeleine Renaud; and then, now in demand outside France, an 'international' film, *Jovanke e le Altre/Five Branded Women*, with Silvana Mangano and Barbara Bel Geddes. She said later that she had only done it to pay back taxes: it was her last really bad film in a long time.

She fascinated and was loved by two men, Oskar Werner and Henri Serre, in Jules et Jim *(61), and over the years she shared her favours with them, uncertain which to choose. In the second of these pictures she is seen with Monsieur Serre.*

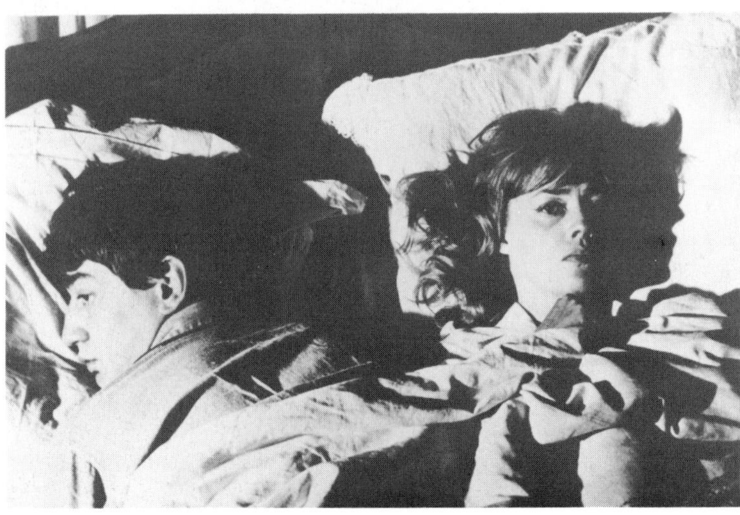

Indeed, she began a series of films which, for continuing quality, can hardly be rivalled in the history of films (if variously successful commercially). First was Peter Brook's version of Marguerite Duras's *Moderato Cantabile*, again bored and developing a fixation on one of her husband's workmen, Jean-Paul Belmondo. It was the year's most complete and haunting performance and presumably pleased Brook, who had said he did not care who disliked the film – it was made only to please two people, Moreau and Duras. While making it, Moreau saw *L'Avventura* and wrote to its director, Antonioni, saying if he ever had need of her. . . . The result was *La Notte* (61), his highly personal study of a disintegrating marriage, with Marcello Mastroianni. In the event, she disliked Antonioni, the film and her character: he and she could not communicate and she found it all unbearably pessimistic – but admitted to carrying the film's attitude off the set (she is renowned for a total response to her material). One reason why her films of this period were so good is that she chose them on the strength of the director: 'If I get concerned with what kind of part I would like to play, I would then start to wonder what roles would be good for me, good for my career, pleasing for the public. Life does not invite this choice and neither should films.' She had also become acquainted with the Young Turks who had revitalized the French movie industry: after unbilled bit appearances in *Les Quatre Cents Coups* (59, Truffaut) and *Une Femme est une Femme* (61, Godard) she and Truffaut did a film together, with their own money, *Jules et Jim*, a popular trifle (from an old novel by Henri-Pierre Roche) about two pals, Oskar Werner and Henri Serre, in love with the same woman. She was gay in this one, utilizing her little girl sudden laugh as well as her little girl pout.

She did a cameo role in Orson Welles's *The Trial/Le Procès* (62) and was then in Joseph Losey's *Eva/Eve*, some sort of apotheosis as a contemporary courtesan. In France it was advertised as 'le rôle de ma vie – Jeanne Moreau': she sued, claiming she had never said that, and lost. Abroad, it suffered from disputatious cuts (Losey and the distributors) and was not widely seen – no great loss, for at its fullest it was muddled and pretentious. Moreau's international reputation was in fact better served by Jacques Demy's anecdote about a compulsive woman gambler, *La Baie des Anges* (63), dazzlingly blonde. By this time the world waited breathlessly for her first Hollywood film, but the one she chose, Carl Foreman's *The Victors* – actually made in Europe – gave her only a wan role, one of several names, as a war victim. She had only

But in Baie des Anges (63), Moreau's first love was playing the tables.

a brief role, a cameo, Malle's brilliant study of a suicide (Maurice Ronet), *Le Feu Follet*, and had sunk herself so deeply into the part that she was virtually unrecognizable.

After a weak imitation of pre-war Hollywood comedies with Belmondo, *Peau de Banane*, she bounded back with Buñuel's gloomy but absorbing remake of Mirbeau's ironic *Le Journal d'une Femme de Chambre* (64). She made two more ventures into international territory, *The Train* with Burt Lancaster and *The Yellow Rolls-Royce*, the episode with Rex Harrison; tentative ventures – her English was perfect, but it looked as though she had strayed into both by accident. She was back on form as *Mata Hari Agent H-21* (65), directed by her ex-husband (1948–55), Jean-Louis Richard, and partly written by Truffaut – but the film was considerably less lively than the Garbo version. Malle directed her again in *Viva Maria!*, and because she partnered Brigitte Bardot the publicity was terrific; but after a good start this tale of two vaudeville artists getting bogged down in a Mexican revolution itself got bogged down and did not become the expected worldwide hit.

For Orson Welles she was Doll Tearsheet in *Campanadas a Medianoche/Chimes at Midnight/Falstaff* (66) and was, once again in English, only quietly competent. The next two were, in theory, her best try at an international career: *Mademoiselle*, from a story by Jean Genet about a schoolmistress-pyromaniac in a small French village; and *A Sailor From Gibraltar* (67), from a novel by Marguerite Duras about a wandering woman and her several lovers. Tony Richardson directed both; the reviews for both were disastrous and those audiences who were not bored into the ground sniggered. Both lost a mint for United Artists and critics began to question her talent – though in fact she was about the best thing in both films. Indeed the failure was of such proportions that when she appeared in a cheap little episoder about prostitution, *Le Plus Vieux Métier du Monde*, no one gave a damn. Nor was her reputation restored by her subdued rendering of *Great Catherine* (68) of Russia, opposite Peter O'Toole, or by Truffaut's *La Mariée était en Noir*, a particularly silly sub-/Hitchcockian essay in suspense.

For Orson Welles again she made two films, one of which has never been completed. The other was *L'Histoire Immortelle/The Immortal Story*, made for French TV and dubbed for cinemas abroad, from a tale by Isak Dinesen, as a woman hired for sex – a role she played with hypnotic intensity. Then: *Le Corps de Diane* (69), directed by her ex-husband, as a lesbian who kills her neurotic husband when she learns he wants to kill her. It was her first film in 10 years to find no takers in the Anglo-American market. She toured France in

Moreau was beautifully cast as a chambermaid in Journal d'une Femme de Chambre *(64), a young lady whose presence disturbs, or excites, all the male members of the household. This particular male is the brutish handyman Joseph, played by Georges Géret.*

vaudeville (after a song in *Jules et Jim* she had become a popular recording artist) and accepted a brief role in a Hollywood film, *Monte Walsh* (70), as Lee Marvin's girlfriend, a tart with a heart . . . but, again playing blandly in English, this time you wanted to know more about her. Also in Hollywood, she did a cameo, as herself, in *Alex in Wonderland* (71); and then, in France, was a tired gangster's girlfriend in *Comptes à Rebours*, an equally tired gangster piece, with Serge Reggiani. There were rumours that she would play on Broadway in Edward Albee's 'All Over' but instead she did *L'Humeur Vagabonde* with Michel Bouquet, who played 13 different roles. Shown in some French cinemas at this time was *Le Petit Théâtre de Jean Renoir* (made earlier for TV), in which she sang. She played a 40-year-old schoolteacher-divorcée in love with an adolescent (Julian Negulesco) in *Chère Louise* (72), carefully directed by Philippe de Broca, followed by *Nathalie Granger*, written and directed by Marguerite Duras, an introspective study of two women – the other was Lucia Bose – and the film seemed destined to end the days of the cinema. No one could feel kindly to any of the participants, so who cared when Moreau travelled abroad to make two more flops?: *Joana la Francesca* (73) in Brazil, playing a madam who marries and moons around the old plantation; and *Je t'Aime* (74), an inept Canadian film.

More than ever she rejected the standards of the commercial cinema, lending her name to films to help new talent, or accepting roles with people she wanted to work with. Consequently she had supporting roles in all of the following: *La Race des Seigneurs*, with Alain Delon; *Les Valseuses*, as a strange woman who shoots herself after spending the night with the two heroes, Gérard Depardieu and Patrick Dewaere; *La Jardin Qui Bascule* (75), a murder drama with Delphine Seyrig; *Souvenirs d'en France*, a family saga – and easily the best of these films; and *Hu-Man*, a science-fiction tale with Terence Stamp as himself and she as an old mistress. On stage she was Wedekind's Lulu and 'greeted nightly by howls of derision' (according to the 'Evening Standard''s Paris correspondent); but her mistakes of the past few years were forgotten with *Lumière* (76), which she also wrote and directed. Since she also played a movie star, we may suppose the piece to be semi-autobiographical, but unlike most autobiographical films this was light-hearted, the reverse of maudlin and egotistic; and she shared the screen with several other actresses. It was also the first of her films in years to be widely seen in the US. After a brief stint in *Mr Klein*, as the country house lady who may or may not know the real Klein, she did another, in the US, in *The Last Tycoon*, not in her element this time as another star. On this trip she presumably met the young American director, William Friedkin, and they married (but divorced in 1979); it was because of this, she said, that she was turning down offers from Europe. In any case, she was writing screenplays with a view to again directing – and *L'Adolescente* (79) was even more successful than *Lumière*, capturing some of the feeling of Pagnol and much of the essence of that last golden pre-war summer of 1939. It had taken her six months to raise the money – the equivalent of $1 million, which she got from German sources.

She went to Canada to appear in a ghastly movie with Richard Harris, *Your Ticket is No Longer Valid*, playing a Paris madam, and in that city in 1981 began an 18-month run in 'L'Intox'. During its run and afterwards some very poor Moreau films appeared: Verneuil's *Mille Milliard de Dollars* (81), a political thriller in which she was fourth-billed but had a brief role as a minister's drunken wife; *La Venexiana* (82), in the lead; Fassbinder's *Querelle*; and Losey's *La Truite*, which eclectically also starred Isabelle Huppert, Alexis Smith, Eiji Okada and Daniel Olbrychski. The only one of these to be seen much abroad was *Querelle*, from Genet's novel, which seemed to restrict its pornographic content only because Gaumont had put up 3 million francs and the German government 770,000 DM, i.e. it needed to be widely accepted to recover its costs. It was a ludricrous exercise, with Moreau looking embarrassed throughout, and who can blame her? – since as the bar-owner she would seem to be the only heterosexual in the place, which does not prevent her from bedding sailor Querelle himself. Understandably, she stayed away from movies for a while, making a film for Japanese television about the Impressionists and beginning a series of TV interviews with American actresses. In 1985 she appeared for the BBC in 'Huis Clos' with Omar Sharif, the two of them seemingly vying to see which could bring the least conviction to their lines; a Broadway venture, the spinster role in a revival of 'The Night of the Iguana', closed out of town. She chose her films more carefully: Deville's *La Paltoquet* (86), with husband Michel Piccoli running a café in a strange coastal town; *Sauve-toi, Lola*, with Sami Frey, as a diplomat's terminally ill wife; and Mockey's satire on Lourdes (they were not allowed to film it there), *Le Miraculé*, as the platonic girlfriend of Jean Poiret, reteamed with Michel Sarrault in a film once meant for Benny Hill. By this time she was starring in a play which translates as

'The Narrative of the Servant Zerline', based on a chapter in Hermann Brock's novel 'The Irresponsibles': it was virtually a one-woman show and a huge success – the first of its kind that she had experienced.

Michèle Morgan

Michèle Morgan once confessed to 'Cinémonde' that as a young girl it had been her ambition to be a great international actress and that it was a disappointment to her that she had never achieved this. On her native heath, however, she has the others licked. For most of her career she was consistently voted the most popular actress in France. Seven times 'Cinémonde' readers voted her Actress of the Year. The French find in her qualities which perhaps Anglo-Saxon audiences prize somewhat less. True that most of her English-speaking pictures have been appallingly bad, but in her good ones, and in her French pictures, she is usually a remote, spiritual figure. She is serenely beautiful; her emotions are rarely called into play. She is to a flesh-and-blood woman what a Turner painting of Venice is to Venice itself. Her later films have presented her rather more as she is in life – *chic*, radiant, composed – but most of them have been poor. They have hardly been seen abroad and for many a middle-aged American or Englishman Mlle Morgan remains a warm, fond memory – something tenuous, exquisite, glimpsed, inevitably, through the mist of *Quai des Brumes*.

She was born in Neuilly-sur-Seine, a suburb of Paris, in 1920 but was brought up mainly in Dieppe. At 15 she returned to Neuilly and lived with her grandmother while trying to get into films. She also studied drama under René Simon. As an extra she appeared in *Mademoiselle Mozart* (35), *Une Fille à Papa* (36) and *Mes Tantes et Moi*. A fellow student, a niece of Jean Gabin, had got a small part in *Le Mioche* when Gabin wanted her for *La Belle Equipe*; she suggested Morgan as her replacement and director Léonide Moguy agreed, so she played a schoolgirl in this sentimental school drama starring Lucien Baroux and Madeleine Robinson. She was billed under her own name, Simone Roussel, but became Michèle Morgan when offered a big part opposite Raimu in *Gribouille* (37). Again, a friend had recommended her, to director Marc Allégret, discoverer of, among others, Simone Simon, Odette Joyeux and Jean-Pierre Aumont. She played a girl accused of a *crime passionel* and befriended by Raimu, one of the jury, and who, when acquitted, is loved by both him and his son. 'La Cinématographie Française' said that Raimu 'a comme partenaire à sa taille une toute jeune fille, revélation non seulement du film, mais de la saison'.

Her success was instantaneous. Allégret hurried her into *Orage* (38), about an illicit affair between a respectable businessman (Charles Boyer) and a drifter (Morgan). She was dreadful in it – because, she said later, she was terrified of Boyer. Still, her salary had risen from 12,500 to 25,000 francs – and for her next would go to 75,000 francs. This would *not* be in Hollywood where agent Charles K. Feldman had arranged a contract with RKO, but would be Carné's *Quai des Brumes*, as the sad, knowledgeable, waxen, raincoated waif who enslaves Gabin. Hollywood could wait while there were so many good offers in Europe – two from UFA in Berlin for Franco-German productions: *Le Récif de Corail* (39), set in Australia, in a small part as a girl who shelters a fugitive Gabin; and *L'Entraineuse*, good in the title-role as a dance-hostess on holiday trying to hide her profession from Gilbert Gil. After this series of shady heroines she was too good to be true for the first time in *Les Musiciens du Ciel* (40) – and died of it, in this honest film about the Salvation Army.

The war affected the fate of her next three films. Jacques Feyder's *La Loi du Nord* was begun in February 1939 but not shown until 1942, when the censor changed the title to *La Piste du Nord*; it turned out to be only a fair thriller about another fugitive from justice, Pierre-Richard Willm, after a shooting based on the Stanford White-Harry Thaw incident. Morgan was the secretary who flees with him to the Canadian snows. *Remorques* was begun in July, not finished till late 1940 and premièred a year later. She was an unhappily married woman drawn to Gabin, whose marriage is good in this excellent triangle drama set in Brest and brilliantly directed by Jean Grémillon – and, she said later, she and Gabin were briefly in love at the time. She made *Untel Père et Fils* in Nice for Julien Duvivier, the story of a French family through three wars with Germany (she was a young wife, *circa* 1914). The Germans banned it and destroyed every print but one – which was buried in a garden. Later it was unearthed, smuggled to the US and reassembled by Duvivier, with some new scenes made in Hollywood (with the help of Boyer); it was thus the first 'new' French film seen in Britain and the US since the outbreak of war – in 1944 – but turned out to be undistinguished. It was shown in France in 1945.

Morgan herself went to Hollywood where RKO eagerly awaited her, but she waited around over a year while they debated what

Michèle Morgan and Jean Gabin representing for most people the screen lovers of pre-war French films. Here they are in Grémillon's Remorques *(41), described thus by 'Time Magazine': 'Tugboat captain Gabin, married for ten years to a nice, affectionate little blonde, suddenly finds that he is mad about Mlle Morgan. The actors act as though they had never heard of the standard movie triangle and have no idea that it must be played in a standard way.'*

*Michèle Morgan, Hollywood style (*Higher and Higher *(43), with the young Frank Sinatra. Unsurprisingly she was not a success in Hollywood, and for a while wondered whether to make her career in Britain, where she could remain the international name she wanted to be. In the event she only made two British films, one of which was destined to be a classic: Carol Reed's* The Third Man *(49) with Ralph Richardson and Bobby Henrey.*

to do with her. *Journey Into Fear*, bought for her, went to Dolores del Rio. Finally, with great publicity, they made her *Joan of Paris* (42), a Resistance drama where she sacrificed herself to help British flyers. It was not very good. She married actor William Marshall and went to Universal to make *Two Tickets to London* (43), a silly espionage drama with Alan Curtis, Barry Fitzgerald and inappropriate overtones of *Quai des Brumes*. At RKO she was co-starred with Frank Sinatra in *Higher and Higher*, virtually unrecognizable – lower and lower, playing a maid forced to impersonate a deb. Her face, her hair (now darkened), were arranged like the hard-faced Goldwyn Girls of the period and with the new look went a new personality, or rather lack of. She looked more her old self in *Passage to Marseilles* (44), opposite Humphrey Bogart, one of the several follow-ups to *Casablanca*. It was by no means as good, nor was Morgan's part as big or as interesting as Ingrid Bergman's had been – ironically, for *Casablanca* had been intended for her till Warners balked at RKO's huge fee. Now no one was talking huge fees or even offers for Morgan and after being off the screen, pregnant, she accepted an offer from France, for a film to be made in Switzerland.

This was a version of Gide's *La Symphonie Pastorale* (46), directed by Jean Delannoy, as the blind girl in love with priest Pierre Blanchar. It re-established her in France: at Cannes she won the Best Actress award and in the postwar polls held by 'Cinémonde' and Radio Luxembourg she and the film walked away with Best Actress and Best Film. Back in Hollywood she played a distraught wife in a melodrama with Robert Cummings, *The Chase*, and then returned to Europe.

She was an international name if hardly a star. The Hollywood offers were few, the French plentiful, but she compromised and went to Britain. In 1947 she was said to be about to start *Daughter of Darkness*, but Siobhan McKenna made it. She was also said to be about to sign a three-year contract with Korda. For Korda she did make *The Fallen Idol* (48), as Ralph Richardson's mistress. The part was only a cipher but the hint of melancholy, of sophistication, recalled the pre-war Morgan. Then there was an Italian offer, for *Fabiola*, Blasetti's rambling remake of one of the famous early Italian spectaculars. It was the most expensive production yet made in Italy – though it did not give her, as a patrician lady, much of a part. Opposite her was Henri Vidal, playing a gladiator. Offset she and Vidal fell in love and were married as soon as her divorce from Marshall came through. (Marshall later married Morgan's compatriot Micheline Presle, who after a successful career in French films had signed a contract with 20th and made her American début in *Under My Skin* in 1950; in 1952, disillusioned after a series of unsuitable parts, she too returned to France but, unlike Morgan, never quite recovered her former glory.)

Morgan appeared opposite Jean Marais in *Aux Yeux du Souvenir* – an unhappy love affair between a pilot and a drama student which is revived when she becomes an air-hostess; and then she did another film for Korda, Allégret's remake of *Maria Chapdelaine* called *The Naked Heart* (49). It had been started in 1946 on location in Canada with Barbara White (a new British 'star') and Trevor Howard (failing Michael Rennie, the original choice). Morgan had been the original choice for the girl, but had been unavailable. Korda disliked what he saw of the rushes and closed it down. Maybe there was a jinx on the film: the Morgan version was also beset by production troubles. Kieron Moore, now playing the man, was wildly inadequate and the film, when finally shown, soon sank from view. This setback to her international hopes was perhaps offset by the chance to do two films with her husband. *La Belle que Voilà* was a Hollywooden concoction (by Vicki Baum) about a dancer deserted by her sculptor lover; he returns and shoots her wealthy protector, whereupon she takes to the streets to buy his release; when that day comes she dies in his arms. Grémillon's *L'Etrange Madame X* (50) was equally hackneyed (his worst film, undertaken for money after years during which his grand projects had died). Morgan was a society woman adulterously in love with a workman – who thinks she is a housemaid. In 1951 when *Fabiola* reached Los Angeles (badly dubbed and cut by an hour for the US), 'Picturegoer' reported that Morgan and Vidal, during their promotion trip, were tested by all the major studios.

But it was in France that she continued to work: in René Clément's slight *Le Château de Verre* (51), again with Marais; and in *Les Sept Péchés Capitaux* (52), in its best episode, Autant-Lara's 'L'Orgueil' with Françoise Rosay – aristocratic mother and daughter down on their luck, discovered secreting *canapés* at a society reception. In the US she did 'Camille' on television and did some TV work in France. But she consistently refused stage offers. She reappeared with Gabin in *La Minute de Vérité*, as his wife; and was Joan of Arc in one of the episodes of *Destinées* (53) – scripted by Aurenche and Bost, directed by Delannoy, and looking like a village pageant. In Yves Allégret's fine, atmospheric *Les Orgueilleux* she was stranded in a run-down Mexican coastal town and drawn to a drunken Gérard Philipe; and in *Obsession* (54) the man

Philipe and Morgan were teamed again in other circumstances, gay and elegant, in René Clair's Les Grandes Manoeuvres *(55) but the outcome would be equally uncertain. He was a young officer compelled by a wager to make her love him.*

was Raf Vallone – a turgid circus melodrama; they did their own trapeze work. It was her first in colour. As Josephine she loved Guitry's *Napoléon* (55) – Daniel Gélin as the younger Bonaparte, unconvincingly metamorphosing into Raymond Pellegrin. Maria Schell was Marie-Louise. And in *Oasis* Morgan loved Pierre Brasseur in the French version and Carl Raddatz in the German: a co-production, the first French film in CinemaScope (and released by 20th), an adventure tale filmed in Morocco, from a novel by Joseph Kessel.

The generally low standard of these films was tempered considerably by Clair's *Les Grandes Manoeuvres*, opposite Philipe, but another notable director failed her – Autant-Lara on *Marguerite de la Nuit* (56): Faust in the 20th century, with Marguerite-Morgan as a cabaret singer of indifferent virtue and Jean-Francois Calvé as the young Faust. She was Gabrielle d'Estrées in *Si Paris Nous Etait Conté* and then *Marie Antoinette* for Delannoy, a film notable merely for her beauty (not the Marie Antoinette of history but of legend). Hollywood beckoned and she was crisp and sun-tanned as the unhappy wife of Leif Erickson in *The Vintage* (57) for MGM; but the film was silly stuff and a box-office dud. *Retour de Manivelle*, with Daniel Gélin, was a twisty melodrama from a novel by James Hadley Chase in which she plotted to murder her husband – her first villainess – and got murdered herself. *Le Miroir à Deux Faces* (58) was a Peg's Paper melodrama directed by André Cayatte, about a bourgeois marriage which founders when the ugly wife undergoes plastic surgery and emerges as the Michèle Morgan we all expected; as her manner and dress-sense are equally transformed, incredulity takes over and one is simply left with a good performance by Bourvil as the husband. It was a wow in France. She was with Boyer again in *Maxime* (he was paid to woo her by the young, unworldly Félix Marten) and with Mastroianni in an episode of *Racconti d'Estate* (59). And she was with her husband in *Pourquoi Viens-tu si Tard?*, a melodrama about reformed alcoholics (she was an alcoholic lawyer). They had separated their careers since 1950 and this was to be their last teaming, for Vidal died of a heart attack later in the year. She has not remarried.

Again in Italy she was in *Vacanze d'Inverno*, with Georges Marchal, and in Germany she played Garbo's old role of the ballerina in the remake of *Grand Hotel* called *Menschen im Hotel* (60), a silly mistake to make. O.W. Fischer played the Barrymore part. *Les Scélérats* was typically French of its period: directed by and co-starring Robert Hossein, about a wealthy, miserable couple – lots of infidelity, drinking, misunderstandings, plottings and car accidents. Also too conventional, but more likeable, was a reteaming with Bourvil, *Fortunat*, with, again, a deliberate emphasis on the contrast between their screen personas; set in 1940, she was a wealthy refugee from Paris and he an uncouth peasant upon whom she relies and whom she finally loves. Overall it was too sentimental.

As with Mlle Presle and Danielle Darrieux she was now being called upon to play an ageing beauty. In *Le Puits aux Trois Vérités* (61) she had a grown-up daughter (Catherine Spaak); Jean-Claude Brialy was the young man who flirted with both of them. *Les Lions Sont Lachés* was another blatantly commercial piece, with Brialy, a fable about a little country girl in Paris – played by Claudia Cardinale. Morgan, as her confidante, and Darrieux, as a lionizing *grande dame*, took what were basically supporting roles and glittered: Cardinale did not hold a candle to them. After years of rivalry the paths of Morgan and Darrieux crossed frequently at this time. Morgan was in *Rencontres* (62), a triangle drama with Pierre Brasseur and Gabrielle Ferzetti; then she and Darrieux were both in *Le Crime ne Paie Pas* and were both victims of *Landru* (63). It had become more than ever customary for French 'commercial' movies to cram in several names and after a trip to Italy for *Il Fornaretto di Venezia* with Jacques Perrin she and Darrieux were both in *Méfiez-vous Mesdames*, she as Paul Meurisse's conniving wife.

The mediocre level continued: *Constance aux Enfers* (64), as a piano-teaching widow conned by a vicious young couple; *Les Pas Perdus* with Jean-Louis Trintignant, a May–September romance, young worker and society woman; and *Les Yeux Cernés*, directed by and co-starring Robert Hossein, about a harassed woman being blackmailed after the murder of her husband. As long as she was, in all the polls, France's favourite actress, producers were tempted to offer her films which were simply Michèle Morgan vehicles; but she was less and less happy with them and the following year made only one film, *Dis-moi Qui Tuer?* (65), with Paul Hubschmid, a silly tale about diving for Nazi treasure. Another Hollywood offer resulted in another dud movie – *The Lost Command* (66), as a countess, with Anthony Quinn. She made a rare TV appearance, in 'La Bien-Aimée'; and then did *Benjamin ou les Mémoires d'un Puceau* (68), as another countess, the sympathetic aunt of Pierre Clementi. It was, she said, the only one of her recent films that she had liked.

Since then she has taken an increasing interest in the fashion business, where she has money invested. In 1968 she became a Chevalier of the Légion d'Honneur. She said she was not worried about filming again; but she would presumably still have the pick of parts – for her popularity had not diminished. In both 1969 and 1970 she was found to be (by L'Institut Français d'Opinion Publique) France's favourite female star. (In 1970 she got 27 per cent of the votes, followed by Brigitte Bardot with 17 per cent, Jeanne Moreau 13 per cent, Danielle Darrieux 9 per cent, Marlène Jobert 7 per cent, Annie Girardot 6 per cent, Catherine Deneuve 4 per cent, Edwige Feuillère 3 per cent.) Finally, in 1972, she accepted an offer to appear in another menopausal romance, *Les Amis de Mon Fils*. She returned to films in a thriller for Claude Lelouche, *Le Chat et La Souris* (75), and was scheduled to make *Ames Fortes*, from the novel by Jean Giono, for Jean Delannoy, but the material was considered too strong. She did a guest appearance for Lelouche in *Robert et Robert* (78), and shortly afterwards made her first stage appearance since her student days, in 'Le Tout pour le Tout' with Jean-Pierre Bouvier. They co-starred again in a revival of 'Cheri' (82) with which she toured the following year. She told a reporter that there were no film offers, and she has since done some television work, including *Le Tiroir Secret* (85), a mini-series.

ROBERT MORLEY

Robert Morley has some reputation as a wit and conversationalist, which skills he does not deny to the television-viewing public on both sides of the Atlantic. He heaves himself before the TV cameras with great aplomb and is wise, expansive, iconoclastic, outrageous, modest, smug and tolerant, with a happy and epigrammatic turn of phrase. Strangely, all these qualities are to be found in his film performances: normally cast (perhaps because of his physical bulk) as an aristocratic buffoon or a pompous ass, he manages nevertheless to suggest both wit and intelligence. Or at any rate it seems like it. He can act, though he usually prefers to do his Robert Morley thing – whichever way, he is a great scene-stealer; and you know a film is bad (and most of his films are) when critics make comments of this order: 'Not even Robert Morley can save it.'

Not that Morley is a leading actor on the screen, though he has been top-billed on several occasions; but he had a successful stage career. He was born in 1908 in Semley, Wiltshire, into a moneyed family; but his father, an army officer, gambled away most of what he had and consequently Morley's schooling, including Wellington and spells on the Continent, was rather chequered. He persuaded his parents to let him go to RADA and he subsequently made his first appearance on the stage at Margate in a small part in 'Dr Syn' (28). For the next seven years he trouped the provinces in a ragbag of plays, including a season with Sir Frank Benson's Co. (a period which provided the best of the several plays he has written or co-authored, 'Goodness How Sad!'). In 1935 he established a summer rep at Perranporth in Cornwall with Peter Bull (who wrote all those funny books). London success came in 1936 when he played 'Oscar Wilde'; in 1937 he played Dumas in 'The Great Romancer' and Higgins in 'Pygmalion' – the former was seen by an MGM executive looking for an actor to play a role originally intended for Charles Laughton, Louis XVI to Norma Shearer's *Marie Antoinette* (38). (He had been sacked from two previous British pictures, he says in his memoir.) He stayed in the US to play Wilde in New York.

He was probably the only actor in *Marie Antoinette* to get good notices, but he returned to Britain and a couple of years later began his prolific British film career with *Will You Remember?* (40), a biopic of songwriter Leslie Stuart, as Stuart, and *Major Barbara* (41), as Undershaft. He was in several wartime subjects: *This Was Paris* (42); *The Big Blockade*, as a particularly self-satisfied Nazi officer; *The Foreman Went to France*, as a traitorous French mayor; and *The Young Mr Pitt*, as Charles James Fox – a characterization which had more Morley than Fox in it. He was still regarded as mainly a stage actor; during the decade he appeared in only four plays, but three of them were long-runners: 'The Man Who Came to Dinner' (41), 'The First Gentleman' (45), as the Prince Regent, and 'Edward My Son' (47), which he also subsequently did in New York, Australia and New Zealand. He co-authored it with Noel Langley and he wrote the fourth play, 'Staff Dance' (44). His other films around that period were *I Live in Grosvenor Square* (45), supporting Anna Neagle; *The Ghosts of Berkeley Square* (48), with Felix Aylmer in the title-roles of this minor effort based on a comic novel by Brahms and Simon; and *The Small Back Room* (49), from Nigel Balchin's novel, as a very stupid senior civil servant.

A backstage musical with Class: The Story of Gilbert and Sullivan *(53), with Maurice Evans as Sullivan; Peter Finch as D'Oyly Carte; and Robert Morley as W.S. Gilbert.*

On his return from the Antipodes Morley settled into another long run, 'The Little Hut' (50), and began his film career in earnest: *Outcast of the Islands* (51), from Conrad's novel, as the greedy Almayer, a part he played as a petty-minded buffoon. There was some brief exposure as Katharine Hepburn's missionary brother in Huston's *The African Queen*; then the lead in an unimportant comedy about a provincial rep, *Curtain Up* (52), felicitously teamed with Margaret Rutherford. *The Final Test* (53) had been a TV play by Terence Rattigan about a boy more interested in poetry than in his father's last cricket match; Morley, as the boy's idol, satirized to some extent the TV 'personality' he later himself became. He played another famous poet, this time a real one, W.S. Gilbert in *The Story of Gilbert and Sullivan*, a prestige production which marked London Films's 21st anniversary; it was, withal, an unpretentious backstage musical with great globs of the G & S pops beautifully done, helped a bit by Morley's grumpy, sometimes touching, Gilbert but not by Maurice Evans's flat Sullivan. The public, in any case, was indifferent, as they were again in the case of another classy musical biopic, *Melba*. Patrice Munsel was the *diva* and Morley her impresario, Oscar Hammerstein. Then he was funny as a crook in Huston's *Beat the Devil* (and flattered to be in another film of Huston's: 'They don't usually ask me back again,' he said once).

He was a baronet, the unfortunate father of Laurence Harvey, in *The Good Die Young* (54); then a lord in a racing comedy, *The Rainbow Jacket*; by natural progression, he played a couple of kings, first in *Beau Brummell*, as the mad George III – which caused a minor fuss in Britain when the film was selected as the Royal Performance film and someone realized it was tactless to show it to the Queen. The second king was French and hardly less mad, and again at MGM (for whom he had already been a later Louis) – Louis XI this time, in *The Adventures of Quentin Durward* (55). He was a kind-hearted business executive in *Loser Takes All* (56); then a judge in *Law and Disorder* (58), starring opposite Michael Redgrave in this weak comedy. He was out West with Kenneth More in *The Sheriff of Fractured Jaw* and still far afield in *The Journey* (59), as a Blimpish British traveller. He supported Dirk Bogarde in a couple. *The Doctor's Dilemma*, as B.B., and *Libel*, as a QC.

After playing another business executive, a Scottish one, in *The Battle of the Sexes* (60), he was starred again, in a film that was usually referred to as 'The Other' *Oscar Wilde* – the one which was rushed through in an attempt to compete with the Peter Finch film on the same subject. It was wise of its producers to engage Morley to recreate one of his most famous roles, but beyond that the film – unlike the Finch version – had little distinction. The comparison was unlikely to worry Morley, who wrote later (in his funny memoir, 'Robert Morley Responsible Gentleman'): 'Fortunately, I am not an actor who has ever got into the habit of refusing film roles, holding that if one does not read the script in advance, or see the finished product, there is nothing to prevent one accepting the money.' Hence, presumably, his participation in most of his films in the 60s, starting with *Giuseppe Venduto dai Fratelli/Joseph and his Brethren* (61), as Potiphar, with Belinda Lee and Geoffrey Horne (as Joseph).

Further, perhaps, Morley's interest in the theatre was tempered by some half-successes and failures in the 50s – notably 'Fanny' (56), as Panisse in this London production of an American musical: he has said, however, that he enjoyed enormously the experience of poor and indifferent audiences – he found the task of communicating to them far more stimulating than acting in a hit play. The film roles offered him kept him busy and for a while he averaged four films a year. He was a scoundrelly millionaire in *The Young Ones*, sensibly trying to dissuade son Cliff Richard from putting on a teenage musical: pop singer Richard was at that time Britain's top box-office attraction. This film was strictly for home consumption. So, come to that, were most of the following: *Go To Blazes* (62), a comedy starring Daniel Massey in which Morley played 'Arson Eddie'; the Hope-Crosby *Road to Hong Kong,* in a guest spot; *The Boys*, in the legal profession again, opposing Richard Todd in the court-room, *Nine Hours to Rama* (63) with José Ferrer, as an Indian; *Murder at the Gallop*, with Margaret Rutherford, as a cat-hating recluse who gets murdered; and *Ladies Who Do*, as a colonel involved in the doings of charwoman Peggy Mount. Also in 1963 he was in a remake of the James Whale classic, *The Old Dark House*, as the sinister Uncle Roderick; neither he nor Joyce Grenfell could amuse much in the depressing circumstances and the film was held up for some years before being released as a B.

He returned to Hollywood – after 25 years – to support James Stewart in *Take Her She's Mine* and he and John McGiver provided the film's only humour. And he was one of the few bright spots in *Hot Enough for June* (64) with Dirk Bogarde, as an SS chief, and *Of Human Bondage*, as Laurence Harvey's tutor. But even in the lively, well-cast *Topkapi* his own characterization – he was a con-man – stood out; and he was agreeably spirited in two overblown pieces, the international *Genghis Khan* (65), as the Emperor of China, and *Those Magnificent Men in Their Flying Machines*, as the newspaper baron who sponsors the race. There were a couple of detective stories: *A Study in Terror*, as Mycroft Holmes to John Neville's Sherlock, and *The Alphabet Murders* (66), as a Scotland Yard man helping Tony Randall as Hercule Poirot. After *Life at the Top* (Laurence Harvey again) he went to Hollywood to play Sir Ambrose in *The Loved One* and then to Paris for *Hotel Paradise* with Alec Guinness. In Hollywood again he was an American scientist in Jerry Lewis's *Way Way Out* and in France again a pompous Englishman in *Tendre Voyou*, a Belmondo vehicle which was not exported. He appeared in another Cliff Richard musical, *Finders Keepers*, as the owner of the Spanish hotel who employs Richard and his pop group; but filmgoers' interest in Richard was exhausted (and he disappeared from films as fast as he had come).

In 1967 Morley returned to the stage, in Peter Ustinov's 'Halfway Up the Tree'. His autobiography (1966) said that he wanted to concentrate more on the stage; and it ended on a significant note – a note on the film he was then making: 'it will be, I trust, at least no worse than the ones I usually appear in'. If he meant *The Trygon Factor* (67) it was no worse – or so thought the 'MFB', totting up the promising ingredients, including a 'Robert Morley pouting petulantly'. If he meant *Sept Fois Femme/Women Times Seven* . . . well, it was not his fault: his part was small. After that, he briefly enlivened *Hot Millions* (68), with Ustinov, as a pop-eyed computer expert; but as another expert, a cookery writer called Miss Mary – camp relief – he could do nothing to save a dire attempt to resurrect Bulldog Drummond (in the person of Richard Johnson), *Some Girls Do* (69). He was a kilted Duke of Argyll in *Sinful Davey*, but arrived too late this time to salvage it, a tired imitation of *Tom Jones* directed – inexplicably – by Huston. There were two more films of unbelievable awfulness: *Twinky* (70), the adventures of a 'swinging' teenager, as a judge; and *Doctor in Trouble*, the last faint gasp of the 'Doctor' series with Leslie Phillips doing locum for Dirk Bogarde, as the ship's captain. His role in *Cromwell* was, as written, a libel on the real Duke of Manchester who had been Cromwell's ally, but Morley compounded the crime by playing him as a bully and an idiot. Nor was he much of a relief in *Song of Norway*, as a snobbish brewing magnate, in this lavish life of Greig (Torval Maurstad) based on an old Broadway musical. Small wonder that around that time he returned to the theatre: 'How the Other Half Loves' (70) in which he also toured Down Under. In fact, he stayed on the boards for the next years, except for *Theatre of Blood* (73), killed off by eating his pet poodles; *Great Expectations* (74), for US TV, as Uncle Pumblechook; and *Someone is Killing the Great Chefs of Europe* (78), as one of the chefs, and 'for once working within the limits of his preposterousness' (Ian Hamilton in the 'New Statesman'). Perhaps encouraged by that, he did two films almost simultaneously, *Scavenger Hunt* (79), as lawyer to prankster Vincent Price, and *The Human Factor*, as a senior civil servant. *Oh Heavenly Dog* (80) starred Benji in the title-role; though made in Britain it was not screened there. In *Loophole* (81) Morley was a bad-mannered banker and for the BBC he was one of *The Old Men at the Zoo* (82), a mini-series. Though a frequent guest on talk-shows, he has rarely acted in TV, but he was there again, suddenly, supporting George Segal in *The Deadly Game*. After plotting against Tom Selleck in *High Road to China* (83) he returned to the small screen for an American *Alice in Wonderland* (85), as the King of Hearts. *The Trouble With Spies* (87), made for HBO, turned up after three years on the shelf, understandably: Morley played the boss of Donald Sutherland, a member of British Intelligence. After a break he played a lord in the two-part *Little Dorrit*; during this time the trade press carried ads for the still unseen *Second Time Lucky* with Roger Wilson (star of *Porky's*) and Robert Helpmann.

He is married to Joan Buckmaster, daughter of Gladys Cooper.

PATRICIA NEAL

It is not simply a question of talent or lack of it, of being used well or mishandled. In 1950 Warners released *Three Secrets*, an item about three women with illegitimate babies. It was intended as a showcase for three of their younger leading ladies, Patricia Neal, Eleanor Parker and Ruth Roman, none of whom had got quite as far as Warners had hoped. The film, which was middling, did not help. The ladies had shown ability and star-quality to varying degrees before and they would again; but within a few years they had all lost their stellar positions and it was touch and go whether they would survive at all. Miss Parker left Warners after *Three Secrets* and she later signed an MGM contract – but her performances varied as much as her parts until, by the 60s, she was relegated to supporting roles. Miss Roman remained for a couple of years, getting better parts; but once free of Warners was offered only indifferent material and gave up in 1961 (except for one supporting part in 1965). Miss Neal left Hollywood; and returned to win an Oscar.

She partly explained it when she spoke later of these years: 'I don't think I really knew what I was doing. I was too young. There was no one I could ask for advice. Not another actress, anyway. Think what I was like. Bette Davis was queen of the studio, and you couldn't go up to her and ask her to solve your problems. They were real stars in those days, babe. There's no doubt I was difficult. I didn't turn out to be the star they hoped. They had me dye my hair blonde, but I decided to let it go back to normal, and when it did they just let me go.' Warners must have been disappointed: they had boosted her to the skies and she was good, as she herself said, in only a couple of the pictures she made for them. Yet the qualities were always there – the presence, the warm personality, the soothing deep corncrake voice.

They had found her on Broadway. She had been born in Packard, Kentucky, in 1926 and had studied drama at Northwestern University and – after a fruitless round of the New York agents – at the Barter Theater, Eaglemore, Pennsylvania. While there she got a job understudying Vivian Vance in 'The Voice of the Turtle' and as such made her Broadway début (46); there was a scout in the audience and she was offered the lead, the young Regina, in Lillian Hellman's 'Another Part of the Forest'. Her success in that brought the Warner contract; they banged the big drum and very carefully prepared her launching. The first would be a guaranteed hit, the film version of a long-running Broadway farce; the second would be a drama, where she would stake her claim as the logical successor to their own (ageing) Bette Davis. She did not, however, impress the critics in *John Loves Mary* (49), as the American fiancée of Ronald

Reagan, who was trying to smuggle a British GI bride into the US. In *The Fountainhead* director King Vidor got her to posture like Davis (and she was photographed like same and made-up like same), as a moody and sophisticated columnist who falls madly and secretly for Gary Cooper (but marries Raymond Massey). It was no wonder 'The New York Times' described her performance as 'affected'.

She was much better as the sympathetic nurse in *The Hasty Heart*, with Reagan and Richard Todd. She guested in *It's a Great Feeling*; co-starred with Cooper again in *Bright Leaf* (50), as a rich bitch who marries and betrays him. Then, *Three Secrets*. She was really good, peroxided, as the loose lady who befriended John Garfield in *The Breaking Point*. Like all screen tart parts, it was conceived in cliché, but she played it a new way – with pathos and a sense of mockery directed at herself as much as Garfield. However, it was back to standardization in *Operation Pacific* (51), divorced from John Wayne because he loved the navy too much, and *Raton Pass*, married to Dennis Morgan in an attempt to get hold of his family fortune. At that point Warners dropped her.

20th used her in a good science-fiction story, *The Day the Earth Stood Still* with Michael Rennie, but her part was ordinary; and she hardly had a better chance over at Universal, in a weak comedy with Van Heflin, *Weekend With Father*. 20th signed her again, to play a smooth Commie agent in *Diplomatic Courier* (52) with Tyrone Power. She was good and so were her notices; they hurriedly booked her for two more films. At MGM she was a journalist and Van Johnson a senator in *Washington Story*; and at 20th she remained in that city for *Something for the Birds* with Victor Mature. The film was appropriately named; it was clearly time to turn her back on Hollywood – also because she realized that, for the sake of his wife, she must put an end to her love affair with Gary Cooper. She did not do the other film for 20th.

In New York she played in the 1953 revivals of 'The School for Scandal', as Lady Teazle, and 'The Children's Hour'. Her notices were excellent, but the only film offers were for a British B, *Stranger from Venus* (54), with Helmut Dantine, and an Italian picture with Massimo Girotti and Lea Padovani, *La Tua Donna* (55). In New York she enrolled at the Actors' Studio and made two more stage appearances, in 'A Roomful of Roses' and, while Barbara Bel Geddes was on vacation, 'Cat on a Hot Tin Roof'. Elia Kazan was among those impressed and he offered her the part of the protective girl reporter in his harsh study of the rise to fame of a TV personality

Patricia Neal as the nurse in The Hasty Heart *(49), one of the two films she made with Ronald Reagan. It was made in Britain and when they were not filming they were sent everywhere and anywhere for publicity purposes. She says in her autobiography that this was pleasant, as she enjoyed his company anyway, but when the conversation turned to politics it became a monologue.*

In her days as a contract player at Warners, Patricia Neal was seldom very well received, but she did get good notices for her performance as a hooker in The Breaking Point *(50), opposite John Garfield.*

(Andy Griffith): *A Face in the Crowd* (57). Her notices were marvellous and Hollywood was castigated for wasting her earlier – but the film was not popular, so Hollywood did not want to know. Anyway, she disappeared again from films.

In fact, she had married novelist Roald Dahl ('Kiss Kiss') in 1953 and had settled in Buckinghamshire (England) to look after their children (son Theo had been injured as a baby and survived eight brain operations; a daughter died of measles in 1962; there are three other girls). She came out of retirement occasionally to do TV – 'Royal Family', 'Biography', etc., in the US; 'Clash by Night' for BBC TV – and 'Suddenly Last Summer' on the London stage. Sam Spiegel saw her (magnificent) performance in the latter and bought the screen rights for her. For a year, she has said, she talked with the various directors he was considering – until she learnt in a newspaper that Elizabeth Taylor was to play the role. She finally returned to films in a featured role, as the moneybags keeping George Peppard in *Breakfast at Tiffany's* (61); again, the part was conventional but not her playing of it; and the film was a big hit, which meant further offers. She elected to do the weary but loving housekeeper in *Hud* (63), with Paul Newman, and a couple of melodramas in Britain. *The Third Secret*, however, left *all* of her part on the cutting-room floor (and much else besides, one assumes from the final hodge-podge it was) and *Psyche 59* wasted her, as Curt Jurgens's blind wife, suspecting he is carrying on with her sister, Samantha Eggar. But the laugh was on their producers: both films could have done with a boost and *Hud* had meanwhile brought Neal Best Actress statuettes from both the American and British academies – following critical raves. Said Penelope Gilliatt in the 'Observer': 'Patricia Neal as the family housekeeper, humorous and 100 per cent intelligent, made me think how badly we need an actress like this in England. The scenes of her slow, sexual fencing with Paul Newman would be a nightmare to cast here.' England did not seem to need her; but the BFA gave her a second award, for her performance as a navy nurse in *In Harm's Way* (65), with John Wayne.

Patricia Neal left Hollywood in 1952, and her subsequent film career was rather chequered. In 1963 she returned to give a superb performance in Hud *(it brought her an Oscar). Paul Newman was Hud.*

At that time she was dangerously ill. She had just started making *Seven Women* for John Ford in Hollywood, when she had three consecutive strokes, all damaging her brain (and she was pregnant). She was semi-paralysed; speech and movement were impaired. Without undue publicity she fought back, but it looked as though her career was ended. It was not by any means only the soppier journalists who admired her courage; in 1968 President Johnson presented her with the 'Heart of the Year' award. Though not entirely recovered, that year she did another beautiful acting job, in *The Subject was Roses*, which, said Judith Crist in 'New York Magazine', 'has sent us groping for superlatives to surpass all the superlatives we had applied in the past to the performances of Patricia Neal'. Despite such notices (and the fact that the film won a Best Supporting Oscar for Jack Albertson) MGM hardly bothered to distribute the film abroad – certainly not in Britain. It was in Britain that she returned to the screen, in a film specially written by her husband, *The Night Digger* (71), which had few bookings in the US and has not been shown in Britain. In a tele-movie, *The Homecoming – A Christmas Story*, she gave what many consider one of the finest performances ever given in that medium, as the mother of John-Boy (Richard Thomas); this piece, as remake of *Spencer's Mountain*, would become the long-running series, 'The Waltons' (but not with her). *Baxter* (72) was the study of a small boy traumatized by divorce and she was his speech therapist. *Happy Mother's Day, Love George* (73) was a gothic horror tale filmed in Canada and retitled *Run, Stranger, Run* for the US; in the cast was Miss Neal's daughter, Tessa Dahl, and the director was Darren McGavin. That actor returned to the front of the cameras in a political thriller made in Spain by José Luis Borau, *Hay Que Matat a B/B Must Die* (74); Neal was the plain, ageing landlady with whom he is half in love and others implicated were Burgess Meredith and

Stephane Audran. Released in its own country by CIC (the export arm of Universal and Paramount), it was not of sufficient merit to be seen much abroad.

She mothered for television, as often as not Emmy-nominated: *Love Leads the Way*, based on fact, and the boy (Timothy Bottoms, was blind); *Things in Their Season*, dying of leukaemia among Wisconsin dairy farmers; *A Love Affair, the Eleanor and Lou Gehrig Story* (75), with Edward Herrmann as the baseball-playing son (a role once played by Gary Cooper); and *Eric*, again based on a true story, with a son dying of cancer. *Tail Gunner Joe* (77) was Peter Boyle as Joseph McCarthy for television and she was another Senator, just for a change. *The Bastard* (78) was a mini-series, the first of a trilogy based on John Jakes's novels about a hero of the American Revolution. (Eleanor Parker was also in the cast, but so, if it comes to that, were many names, including Barry Sullivan, Keenan Wynn and Buddy Ebsen.) Neal returned to Spain for *Widows' Nest* and to the US, permanently, after the break-up of her marriage (about which she is very bitter, according to her memoir, published in 1988). She was married to James Mason in *The Passage* (79) and mothered Richard Thomas again in a mini-series, *All Quiet on the Western Front*; then she was married to Fred Astaire in *Ghost Story* (81) and was a nun in *Shattered Vows* (84) for television – class all the way, still, even in rotten movies. And her roles were brief. But you cannot see her without wishing she had had the chance to leave a legacy as rich as Miss Davis's. After several years' absence she returned in *An Unremarkable Life* (89) with Shelley Winters.

Paul Newman

'Paul Newman is the last star,' said George Segal. 'He's the link. We're just actors.' Newman is too handsome and too limited to be just an actor. He had to be a star. In a 'Playboy' interview he agreed that he was type-cast: 'My God, yes. There are few actors who can avoid that. Only the great, great actors have an inexhaustible source of variety. Brando, when he's interested, when he's involved, can do it. So can Olivier and Guinness. My wife, Joanne, can do it. But not me.' The public, if it noticed the limitations, did not seem to mind: on the way to his 50s Newman was easily and certifiably the world's most popular actor.

Let us say the looks guaranteed superstar status, that physically he has been endowed with all that is required for a Hollywood leading man. The plus must be the wry, pawky sense of humour, the twinkle in his eyes; he is casual and very much his own master. So was Gable, but there is a touch of the juvenile delinquent about Newman: 'Life's a gas, man,' he seems to say, whether as outlaw or Ivy-league businessman. He is not at all like any of the great stars of the 30s, though one can see the tradition in him, filtered as it has been through the opportunistic, insolent heroes of the 50s. There are hardly any of the usual adjectives that do not apply – he is tough, stubborn, sensitive, honourable, taciturn, etc., etc. Coupled with a varied selection of roles in a highly successful series of pictures, all this suggests that if he is not exactly versatile he is at least adaptable. He never gets bad notices. What more could anyone want?

He was born in 1925 in Cleveland, Ohio, where his father owned a sports shop. After war service as a radio man, second class, he returned to Kenyon College, Ohio, whither he had gone on an athletic scholarship. A knee injury kept him out of sports and he turned to acting. After majoring in economics, he joined a summer stock company in Williamsburg, Wisconsin, and then moved on to Woodstock, Illinois (47), where he met actress Jacqueline Witte, whom he married. When his father died he went to mind the store, but sold his interest to his brother and enrolled at the Yale School of Drama. In the vacation he went to New York to seek work, was taken on by CBS TV for a series, 'The Aldrich Family', and did not go back to Yale. He did a lot of TV over the next few years ('The Web', 'You Are There', 'Danger') and in 1952 auditioned for and was accepted by the Actors' Studio. He auditioned also for a Broadway play, 'Picnic' (53), and was taken on as Ralph Meeker's understudy; during rehearsals he was upped to second male lead.

Someone at Warners saw him and he was signed to a five-year contract starting at $1,000 a week. Warners began to make a lot of 'Second Brando' noises and the 'Second Brando' was unveiled to the filmgoing public in a $41 million flop. *The Silver Chalice* (54), as the Greek craftsman who made it for St Luke. The film was adapted from a pious bestseller and was categorized thus by Newman later: 'I had the privilege of doing the worst motion picture filmed during the fifites.' Further, he thought he was 'very, very bad'. The press thought so too, but this did not deter the studio from forcing him into a new contract as their price for letting him do a Broadway play – seven years, two films a year with an option on a third. The play was 'The Desperate Hours', in the part Bogart played in the film version.

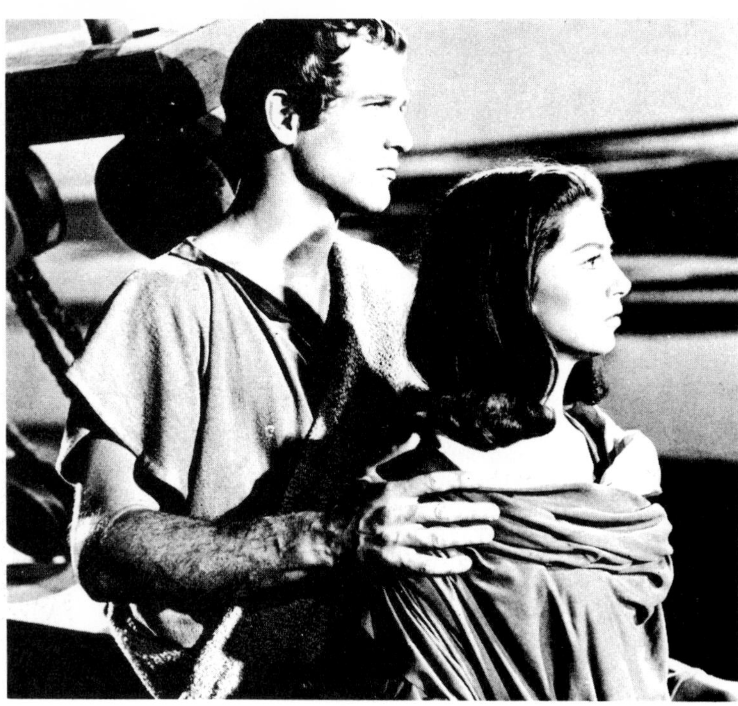

Paul Newman in his first film, The Silver Chalice *(54), with Pier Angeli. Many years later, when it was telecast in Los Angeles, he took an ad in a local paper disclaiming all responsibility.*

Back in Hollywood, MGM borrowed him for a role destined for Glenn Ford, who was too busy: *The Rack* (56), as a captain court-martialled for collaborating with the Chinese. His notices were again cool – not 'second Brando' but 'sub-Brando' – and the film was withdrawn, to be reissued after the next, which MGM were convinced would be a big hit. Director Robert Wise had persuaded Metro to keep Newman on to play boxer Rocky Graziano in the autobiographical *Somebody Up There Likes Me*. It was a hit and caused Newman to be much talked about – which is more than can be said for his participation in *The Helen Morgan Story* (57), at Warners, as that lady's racketeer lover, and *Until They Sail*, at MGM, as an American officer visiting New Zealand and falling for Jean Simmons. At 20th he showed how he could dominate a film, *The Long Hot Summer* (58), as that familiar figure, the rolling stone who proves to be a catalyst – in this case to a William Faulkner family (it was based on two of his short stories). Also in the film was Joanne Woodward, who became his second wife.

At Warners he played Billy the Kid, stupid but inevitably still glamorous, in Arthur Penn's fine and then underrated *The Left-Handed Gun*. The failure of that was perhaps compensated for by his first real box-office success, *Cat on a Hot Tin Roof*, directed by Richard Brooks from Tennessee Williams's play. Williams is on record as disliking the film, but he liked Newman as Brick, the man who is not quite sure that he wants to sleep with his wife (Elizabeth Taylor). He was similarly afflicted, for different reasons (i.e. Joan Collins), in *Rally Round the Flag Boys*, a weak comedy at 20th with his real wife as his screen wife. At Warners he did the plushly old-fashioned *The Young Philadelphians* (59) – from tarnished parentage to the city's leading lawyer: it was their price for letting him do Williams's 'Sweet Bird of Youth' on Broadway.

Not long after returning to the Coast he was given the chance of buying himself out of his contract – at this time, he said, Warners were paying him $17,500 per film, including those on loan-out, for which they charged $75,000 for his services. The price he paid them was reckoned to be as high as $500,000. At least he would quickly earn it back: after the next one became a big hit – an endless version of a John O'Hara bestseller, *From the Terrace* (60), with Woodward – he was able to ask $200,000 per film. At least, that is what he got for *Exodus*, as a freedom fighter in this 'epic' story of the birth of Israel, based on another bestseller (by Leon Uris). He did not exactly, at this point, *need* a good film, but one came in handy – Robert Rossen's *The Hustler* (61) – and it belatedly justified the better claims of his early publicity. As a small-time pool-room con-man he got great notices and was expected to win an Oscar (it went to Maximilian Schell). He did win the BFA Best Foreign Actor award. The next had once been destined for Brando: *Paris Blues*, with Woodward and Sydney Poitier. Expatriate Americans and young love – and he may have been a jazz trombonist, but it was really an old friend in disguise, the Concerto movie. At MGM, for $350,000 plus a percentage, he did *Sweet Bird of Youth* (62) and though he may have done it on the stage he was not right as the gigolo – too much the golden-beauty ne'er-do-well instead of the desperate ageing boy, too often the mocking smile instead of the mirthless sneer.

Still, by this time Newman was giving confident star performances – though not in Hemingway's *Adventures of a Young Man* (played by Richard Beymer), where he deliberately elected to do a character part, as a bruised old boxer. He was especially good as Hud in *Hud* (63), brother to *The Hustler*, and not coincidentally rhyming with 'stud': 'The man with the barbed wire soul,' said the ads. The film was good too, a study of a farming family, directed by Martin Ritt. But another film with Woodward disappointed, *A New Kind of Love*, an old kind of comedy. It was as if their screen partnership was jinxed. *The Prize* was an entertaining pseudo-Hitchcock thriller, but *What a Way to Go!* (64) seemed

destined to speed the end of entertainment (he was one of Shirley MacLaine's all-star husbands). All the same, it made money. Ritt's *The Outrage* (64) lost a packet, after a hostile press reception – a Hollywood version of *Rashomon*, set in Mexico, with Newman in Mifune's old role of the bandit. Newman has said that it is a pity it disappeared, as it contains his best work: but the 'MFB' thought him 'hopelessly miscast . . . laughably melodramatic'. He was a Paris apache in *Lady L* (65) with Sophia Loren.

Those two films kept him out of the box-office 10 in 1965. He had gone in at No 9 in 1963, stayed there in 1964 and was to be there again in 1966. His fee was now up to $750,000 against 10 per cent of the gross; after that – profit participation. His status improved via two popular thrillers, Hitchcock's *Torn Curtain* (66), with Julie Andrews, and a pseudo-Chandler, *Harper* – basing his characterization, he said, on Bogart and Robert Kennedy. That one had him joining the smashed-up, beaten-up heroes and he took two more excursions into screen masochism via Ritt's *Hombre* (67), as a part-Indian, and Stuart Rosenberg's *Cool Hand Luke*, as a member of the chain-gang. Ritt's film was only a moderate success, but *Luke* was a hit, an allegorical prison drama, with a performance by Newman which was 'brilliant' (Tom Milne in the 'MFB'). It brought him his fourth Oscar

Left, Paris Blues *(61) was a tale of four Americans in Paris: Paul Newman played a jazzman who, after thinking it over, opts for Paris and jazz rather than the US and Joanne Woodward. Above, Arthur Penn directed (his first feature)* The Left-Handed Gun *(58), an attempt to look more closely at the myth of Billy the Kid (it was based on a play by Gore Vidal). Paul Newman was Billy Bonney, and Lita Milan was the girl.*

Harper *(66) – or, as it was called in Britain,* The Moving Target. *This photograph does not denote a bedroom scene; for, like most movie detectives of the 60s, Harper lived apart from his wife (Janet Leigh). It was never quite clear why.*

nomination and raised his box-office – No 5 in 1967, No 2 in 1968. As a change of pace he did a comedy, *The Secret War of Harry Frigg*, as a sad sack soldier, but it was not very funny.

In 1968, to help his wife's career get back on an even keel, Newman directed her in *Rachel Rachel*, with spectacularly good results for both of them – he won the New York critics' award for Best Director. When they next appeared in a film together, *Winning* (69) – a good motor-racing drama – one critic referred to them as 'this rather special couple'. Meanwhile, as 'Playboy' put it: 'Both the Newmans are serious, down-to-earth professionals, but they also feel that their responsibility to society doesn't end there.' In 1968 Newman campaigned full-time for Presidential candidate Eugene McCarthy; both have been at the forefront of the Hollywood figures involved in the Civil Rights movement. He has denied that he wants to move into politics, but has, like Brando, expressed dissatisfaction with acting: 'It's silly, stupid and nothing to do with being an adult.' Brando had, by the way, been offered the lead opposite Newman in almost every film over which the latter had production control and certainly turned down the part Robert Redford played in *Butch Cassidy and the Sundance Kid*. They were opportunistic robbers and something about the teaming provoked huge public response; the film was pleasant but over-extended (the public of, say, John Ford's heyday would have given it short shrift), but it became the highest-grossing Western in film history. Newman became No 1 at the box-office in both 1969 and 1970. He was equally big in Britain.

W.U.S.A. (*71*): *Paul Newman as the drifter-hero, a 'survivor'. 'You gotta run faster, you gotta hassle' was his motto.*

He and Woodward appeared in *W.U.S.A.* (71), which he produced, a good allegory of the political chaos in the US, which flopped at the box-office. Because of its subject it was reckoned to have had enemies. True or not, the failure was a pity: it had faults, but it was jagged and rich, full of allusions, and Newman was at his best as a drifter, a spieler who works for the radio station of the title. In *Sometimes a Great Notion* he played again the hard-hearted hard-headed young rip who is his own worst enemy and as well as producing this lumberjack-family saga he also directed when the director he had chosen did not work out.

With Sydney Poitier, Barbra Streisand and Steve McQueen he formed First Artists, to produce their own films independently, rather as Pickford, Chaplin and Fairbanks had once done. His first film for the company was *Pocket Money* (72), trailing cattle in Mexico with Lee Marvin; but it was an inauspicious start, since the public were not attracted to the film. He directed Woodward again in *The Effect of Gamma Rays on Man-in-the-Moon Marigolds* and, as with *Rachel Rachel*, it was happily devoid of the pseudo-political message that had tried to surface from several of the films in which he had been involved as a producer. Both *The Life and Times of Judge Roy Bean* and *The Mackintosh Man* (73) were simple entertainments, but neither found director John Huston at his best; the former was supposedly a return to movies about lovable Western eccentrics and the latter an underrated return to Cold War spy stories. But, in the right story, with the right co-star, Newman was still a power-house attraction: *The Sting*, a Chinese box crime tale, set in the 20s, with Redford; and *The Towering Inferno* (74), as the architect of the skyscraper, with Steve McQueen (both got $1 million, plus 20 per cent of the gross). The success of both films kept Newman in the box-office 10 till 1976, making a run of 10 consecutive years; but in the last of those years he was hardly there by virtue of *The Drowning Pool* (75), an incomprehensible mystery in which he was detective Harper again. After an unbilled guest stunt in *Silent Movie* (76) he was in Robert Altman's even less comprehensible *Buffalo Bill and the Indians*, as B. Bill – a critical disaster as total as *The Silver Chalice*, and this time the public stayed away. Meanwhile, Newman owned the rights to *The Front Runner*, aiming to play the coach, but, he said, no studio would back a homosexual love story. He did play a coach in George Roy Hill's *Slap Shot* (77), an overlong piece with one sole proposition – that hockey players are goons. It had a certain popularity, but did not restore Newman to the box-office stars; but he probably did not care, since he was quoted in an interview in 'Ciné-Revue' as being completely disenchanted with and uninterested in his career and everything that went with it. Which would account for his presence in Robert Altman's *Quintet* (79), perhaps 'the most aggressively self-indulgent motion picture made in the last twenty years by a major American director' as Vincent Canby put it in 'The New York Times', '. . . as [it] droned on in its settings of surreal, frozen beauty, and as the characters, the last survivors on earth, play a mysterious kind of backgammon called quintet, or slink around the ruins cutting each other's throats, or talk about life, death, hope ("an obsolete word") and the mystical meaning of the numerical five, I was reminded of all the terrible little-theater plays I'd seen in my youth.'

The film, needless to say, was a complete bomb and with no real hit in five years Newman was still reported as commanding a fee of $2 million for *When Time Ran Out* (80), a soggy Irwin Allen disaster movie – and $3 million for *Madonna Red*, directed by Joseph L. Mankiewicz and originally scheduled (in 1976) for Robert Redford. It was not made with Newman either, who at this time was turning down several scripts of *Cannery Row* (made with Nick Nolte). He directed Woodward in a tele-movie, *The Shadow Box*, and told several interviewers that he was completely fed up with movies, the industry and acting – which was not surprising, given the script of the last-named and everything about *When Time Ran Out*. And *Quintet*. The films could only get better, and *Fort Apache the Bronx* (81) was a tough, if aimless, thriller with Newman as the street-wisest cop on the beat – though he later sued Time-Life (who produced) for 15 per cent of the gross receipts of sales and 12½ per cent of foreign. *Absence of Malice* partnered him with Sally Field in a gripping tale of journalistic ethics in which she tried to connect him, a Miami warehouseman, with the Mafia; he was on even better form in *The Verdict* (82), replacing Redford, as a derelict lawyer offered a last chance to prove his integrity. He directed *Harry and Son* (84), once again in this capacity choosing a tale of working-class family life, but it foundered, curiously, on one otherwise beautiful sequence between him and Woodward, widower and old flame – since it concerned their own film starriness rather than the roles they were playing. *The Color of Money* (86) was a sequel to *The Hustler*, with Tom Cruise as the youngster learning the rules and Newman as the old pro. There was not, alas, much more to it than that. Earlier in the year Newman had been given an honorary Oscar 'in recognition of his many memorable and compelling screen performances and for his personal integrity and dedication to his craft'. For this film he received a Best Actor Oscar. He stayed away from the ceremony from superstition, because he had not won on six prior nominations. He directed his wife in a remake of *The Glass Menagerie* (87), with backing from Cineplex Odeon, a film he made, he claimed, to atone for the two Tennessee Williams films in which he had starred.

In 1987 he signed a three-year non-exclusive pact with Disney (producer of *The Color of Money*) and changed his mind about co-starring with Jane Fonda in *Old Gringo*; but after an absence he made three films on the go: *Fat Man and Little Boy* (89), *Blaze* and *Mr and Mrs Bridge* with Woodward, the last-named financed by Merchant Ivory and Paul Halmi, and acquired by Cineplex Odeon on negative pick-up.

DAVID NIVEN

David Niven was a star for almost 50 years. One of the most accomplsihed of light comedians, he never quite attained the renown of, say, Cary Grant or Rex Harrison. The magic that great players have just eluded him. In his chosen field he was urbane, unruffled and frivolous (it is basically 'Anyone for tennis?' – the well-bred stage juvenile of the years between the wars); it does not matter that he played with predictability and a lack of heart – that is part of the pattern; but he had a soft centre – he seemed anxious to be liked, anxious not to offend. This is not fatal, and it does not matter a jot in drama: for instance, *The First of the Few* only survives today because of his and Leslie Howard's formidable charm. In first-rate mataerial (which that, for its time, very nearly is) he is unbeatable; in second-rate material he is not very interesting, though indeed he held together more dud pictures than any other actor of his standing. It was not difficult for Cary Grant to have a long career, given the material he was given; given the material Niven had to work with, to be there after 40 years was miraculous.

He was born in Kirriemuir, Scotland, in 1909; his father was killed at the Dardanelles. He was schooled for the army at Stowe and Sandhurst, and served with the Highland Light Infantry for a while. After resigning he went to Canada with a friend, where, among other jobs, he was a bridge-builder and a barman. At the back of his mind was the idea (suggested to him by director Edmund Goulding) that he could always earn a living as a film extra and in due course he landed in Los Angeles and registered with Central Casting. According to Niven's own account (which has varied) he was an extra on *Mutiny on the Bounty* (35) and the director of that film, Frank Lloyd, arranged a test at MGM, which was inconclusive. At Paramount Mae West auditioned him for the lead in *Goin' to Town* and he was tested for *The Gilded Lily*. Nothing came of either; but in any case the truth is that Niven was Merle Oberon's 'escort' – and she was under contract to Goldwyn. All stories regarding being an extra and MGM's interest were camouflage. Goldwyn signed him. He would certainly have noticed a certain resemblance to his erstwhile top star, Ronald Colman (English 'breeding', the moustache).

He did not, however, act as if he was very impressed: he loaned him out for a one-liner, *Without Regret* (35). Then he made him a Cockney sailor in *Barbary Coast*. He loaned him out again to play a party guest in *A Feather in her Hat*... Niven was then one of the hero's friends in *Splendor* and one of a crowd of Jeanette MacDonald's admirers in *Rose Marie* (36). A loan-out again, to Wanger, for *Palm Springs*, brought a few more lines; then he was starred in a B by 20th, *Thank You Jeeves*, as Bertie Wooster, with Arthur Treacher – who else? – as Jeeves. Goldwyn made him a gigolo who dallies on shipboard with Ruth Chatterton in *Dodsworth*; then he auditioned (one of 12) for an important role in *The Charge of the Light Brigade* and got it – the gallant young officer who dies trying to get through enemy lines. (During filming he and Errol Flynn became friends and they shared house for a while.) As a result Goldwyn cast him as the third side of the triangle, a staff officer, in *Beloved Enemy*, with Merle Oberon and Brian Aherne.

At Universal he supported James Dunn and Sally Eilers in *We Have Our Moment* (37), a late reunion after their films at Fox, and he had only a small role – light relief – in support of Ronald Colman in *The Prisoner of Zenda* at his home studio. 20th, who had given him his first starring role, gave him his second, in an A picture this time – if made in Britain: *Dinner at the Ritz*, primarily a showcase for their new and delightful French acquisition, Annabella, but giving him a good role as a debonair and flippant man-about-town (really a detective in disguise, surprise, surprise). In the US he was little more than an amiable stooge to Gary Cooper and Claudette Colbert in *Bluebeard's Eighth Wife* (38); at 20th he was one of four English brothers, the *Four Men and a Prayer*, with Richard Greene and directed by John Ford; and then in support of Loretta Young and Joel McCrea in *Three Blind Mice*. At one point he was in support of Oberon in *The Cowboy and the Lady*, but he disappeared when it was reshot. His best chance yet came as Errol Flynn's jocular buddy in the good remake of *The Dawn Patrol*, as another gallant British officer – and the one for whom Flynn sacrifices his life. It is probably the best of his early performances though he did surprisingly well as the weak but well-meaning Edgar Linton in *Wuthering Heights* (39), a part he thought the worst ever written for an actor.

He finally got a star role and a chance to show his worth in comedy, opposite Ginger Rogers in *Bachelor Mother*, one of the year's best – as opposed to *Eternally Yours* with Loretta Young, an assembly-line assembly of marital misunderstandings. Equally dire was the one before, Goldwyn's *The Real Glory*, in which he was a gallant ladies' man in uniform, with Gary Cooper. His contract was up and he hesitated before re-signing, for he resented the fees which Goldwyn pocketed when loaning him out. But Goldwyn planned a new version of *Raffles* (40), originally intended for Cary Grant; they both knew what the last version had done for Ronald Colman – and the new Ronald Colman was precisely what Goldwyn and Niven himself wanted Niven to be. So he played that famous cracksman opposite Olivia de Havilland; then Goldwyn suspended the new contract for the duration.

He was released from the British Army to make: *The First of the Few* (42), as Leslie Howard's test pilot; and Carol Reed's *The Way Ahead* (44), as a good-egg officer in this propaganda piece about life in the wartime army, made almost believable by fine craft in all departments. On demobilization he donned RAF uniform to play a dying pilot in *A Matter of Life and Death* (45), some Powell and Pressburger whimsy in which a Very High Court debated a hero's right to live out his normal life span. Much attention was paid to it and it was frequently ingenious, but it is probably only remembered as the first selection for that odd British institution, the Royal Film Performance.

All the same, it was to be many years before Niven was again in a film of that calibre. In the US to finish his contract (a sojourn that began tragically when his wife fell downstairs

The hero of another age: David Niven in Garson Kanin's Bachelor Mother *(39). Ginger Rogers had the title-role, as a salesgirl who 'adopts' a stray baby; Niven played her boss's son, suspected of being the father.*

at a party and was killed; he married again in 1948), Goldwyn either put him into, or loaned him out for, rubbish, beginning with *The Perfect Marriage* (46), a reunion with Loretta Young which seemed composed of left-overs from *Eternally Yours*. He was with Barbara Stanwyck in a supposedly stark piece, *The Other Love* (47), turned down by Ronald Colman, and was then with Young again, and Cary Grant, in Goldwyn's *The Bishop's Wife*. Amid fanfares he returned to Britain to play *Bonnie Prince Charlie* (48); it was known that he was not Korda's first choice for this expensive epic and critics congratulated the unknown actors who had turned it down. Later, Niven said he tried to forget the experience – as did audiences. He was quarrelling with Goldwyn and his next for that gentleman (and last, as it turned out) was a flop: *Enchantment* (a lying title, if ever), as a Guards officer in the Victorian part of that tale.

He played a concert pianist in some slapstick with Jane Wyman, *A Kiss in the Dark* (49), and then returned to Britain for another Korda spectacular, *The Elusive Pimpernel*, Michael Powell directing him in Leslie Howard's old role of the British milord who rescued aristoes from the French Revolutionaries. Goldwyn had an agreement to take it for the US and there was litigation when he refused it. It did not come out in Britain till 1951, a few months before the Bonnie Prince finally made it to the US (via a very minor distributor). There was some debating among critics as to which was the worse of the two films. Filming of the *Pimpernel* had taken so long that he had taken off in the middle of it to do *A Kiss for Corliss* with Shirley Temple, as a middle-aged roué on whom she gets a crush. At this point, with two years to go, the Goldwyn contract was dissolved by mutual consent. Then he freelanced – and these were not good news either: *The Toast of New Orleans* (50), supporting Mario Lanza; *Happy-Go-Lovely*, a British musical with Vera-Ellen; *Soldiers Three* (51) as their captain, a belated attempt to film Kipling; and *The Lady Said No*, trying to seduce Joan Caulfield – because she had written a bestseller about how not to be seduced. He was finally free of his contract and it was announced that he had refused all offers to make two films for the company he had formed with Gene Markey and Douglas Fairbanks Jr. Instead, he went to Britain to make *Appointment With Venus* with Glynis Johns, a pleasant tale about a cow in the occupied Channel Islands.

The truth was, after six years of bad films, he was a wreck at the box-office. In New York he did a play with Gloria Swanson, 'Nina', and some TV work. Otto Preminger saw him in the play and thought he might do for the movie version of *The Moon is Blue* (53). So Niven appeared in the West Coast production of that play (he hated stage work, he said later) and then did the movie. Said 'Variety': 'Niven's middle-aged playboy is mighty fancy laugh-acting.' His salvage work had never been more needed than in this concrete piece and it was especially needed by those who went to it on the strength of its being denied a seal by the Motion Picture Association (up to this time it was thought that without this seal of approval no film could get bookings). What they saw was a smirking Broadway comedy about a professional virgin (Maggie McNamara), daring only in its use of words like virgin.

The smile on Mr Niven's face does not seem quite genuine, but then when this was taken in the early 50s, his career was not going so well. He appeared on a series of British stamps in 1985 to celebrate British cinema, along with Hitchcock, Chaplin and Vivien Leigh, but except for the war years he only worked in Britain when there were no Hollywood offers. Something similar might be said of Hitchcock and Chaplin, so we might ask if the Post Office considered Leslie Howard and Robert Donat, both of whom turned his back on Hollywood to make films in Britain.

The film's success restored Niven to favour, but he had to wade through more mediocrities before getting a film he deserved: in Britain, *The Love Lottery* (54), as a Hollywood-British film star won as a prize by Anne Vernon; *Happy Ever After*, as the villain in this comedy with Yvonne de Carlo; and *Carrington V.C.*, a court-roomer with Margaret Leighton. In the US: *The King's Thief* (55), a run-down swashbuckler, as the heavy; and *The Birds and the Bees* (56), a ham-fisted remake of *The Lady Eve* with Mitzi Gaynor and George Gobel – and getting the only good notices of the three of them, in the old Charles Coburn part. Then Mike Tood cast him as the intrepid Phileas Fogg in *Around the World in 80 Days*. Launched with unprecedented ballyhoo (it was one of the first of the 50s roadshow films) and containing some valuable production assets (including about 80 guest stars) it was in fact a very pedestrian trip. Still, it won a Best Picture Oscar and at one time trailed *Gone With the Wind* as the most financially successful film ever made.

Its success brought no more exciting offers: *The Silken Affair*, in Britain with Genevieve Page, about a meek accountant on a fling; *The Little Hut*, a former stage success which critics almost jeered off the screen; *Oh Men Oh Women* (57), a farce with Ginger Rogers; and the remake of *My Man Godfrey*, called in at the last minute when the German O.W. Fischer left the cast and playing the now-German butler 'with his usual smoothness and practised charm' (the 'MFB'). *Bonjour Tristesse* (58) was the mess that Preminger made of a Françoise Sagan novella, with Niven as a philanderer; nor was *Separate Tables*, from Terence Rattigan's play, a very distinguished film – but it brought Niven an Oscar and the New York critics' Best Actor award, as the bogus retired major with a weakness for molesting women in cinemas. He followed with *Ask Any Girl* (59) – Shirley MacLaine –

Around the World in 80 Days *(56) got most of its entertainment value not from the race-against-time aspect or world views, but from a parade of innumerable guest stars, most of whom knew that it was all right to be aboard when Noël Coward was the first to be signed. It certainly also helped the ailing career of David Niven, the leading character, seen here with the Mexican comic Cantinflas, who played his valet.*

as her lecherous boss, at last getting dialogue it was a pleasure to hear. There was also some good stuff in *Happy Anniversary* with Mitzi Gaynor and *Please Don't Eat the Daisies* (60) with Doris Day, but neither was in the same class.

During the 60s his reputation rose considerably, but in common with most players *not* in the superstar category the fortunes of his films varied (by the end of the decade even the superstars trembled). *The Guns of Navarone* (61) was successful, a war film in which he was a commando-guerilla. But two more war films, made in English and Italian, played the lower half of bills on their few foreign dates: *I Due Nemici/The Best of Enemies*, with Alberto Sordi; and *La Città Prigioniera/The Captive City/Conquered City* (62), a melodrama set in 1945 Athens. Nor was he luckier with a chase drama, *Guns of Darkness*, with Leslie Caron. He supported Charlton Heston in *55 Days at Peking* (63): 'Of a large and largely expendable star cast only David Niven manages to transcend the absurdity of his lordly role with practised authority' – Peter John Dyer in 'MFB'. He was an elegant jewel thief in *The Pink Panther* (64), a popular film, with Peter Sellers, and had a similar role in *Bedtime Story* – Marlon Brando's own choice as co-star and their styles surprisingly jelled as con-men working the Côte d'Azur. He did the French-Italian *Lady L* (65), backed by MGM, with Paul Newman and Sophia Loren, as the English aristocrat who marries her; and the British *Where the Spies Are* (66), said to be the first of a series of secret-agent films about a Dr Jason Love, but there was no demand for others.

Neither of the next two were released for a couple of years: the British *Eye of the Devil* was a black-magic disaster with Niven as a mixed-up wine-grower; and the American *The Extraordinary Seaman*, a comedy directed by John Frankenheimer, was described by 'Variety' as 'strictly steerage cargo'. The James Bond farce, *Casino Royale* (67), managed with several directors and a name cast to cost $12 million; since no one emerged with the least credit it must be marked a failure – as well as a strong contender for the worst film ever made. But the next two were successful, if only in their countries of origin: the British *Prudence and the Pill* (68), as a philandering husband encouraging his wife to stray; and the American *The Impossible Years*, a generation-gap comedy. The latter played Britain first, to devastating reviews and poor business, but did well Stateside after being Radio City's Christmas attraction. *Prudence* was also panned and critics complained that Niven deserved better material. But he hardly got it with *Before Winter Comes* (69), an army drama with Topol; nor with *Le Cerveau/The Brain*, as a master-crook, with Belmondo, Bourvil and Eli Wallach. Gerard Oury, who directed, had had a series of hits in France which had flopped, if shown, in Britain and the US. This was no exception: and Britain and the US were right.

Niven should then have started Zinnermann's version of Malraux's *Man's Fate* and the chances are that it would have been the best part and the best movie of his career; but MGM cancelled it – after $1 million at least had already been spent – among other economies at the end of 1969. He was not idle long; he went to Rome to make *The Statue* (70), a comedy about a man searching for the man who posed for the private parts of his wife's statue of himself. 'I find this whole affair degrading,' he said at one point: so did audiences. There were not many of the latter for the next trio: *König, Dame, Bube/King, Queen, Knave* (72), made in Germany with Gina Lollobrigida; *Vampira* (74), a lamentable British attempt at a horror spoof; and *Paper Tiger*, a Far East adventure, with Niven as a self-fantasizing Old Colonial. Disney came to the rescue and he was grandfather to the infant heroes of *No Deposit, No Return* (76); also in Hollywood, he was the Nick Charles character in a wan spoof, *Murder by Death*. There were more Disney tots and he was a butler prone to disguise at the mansion called *Candleshoe* (77); and then he was sidekick to Hercule Poirot Ustinov in *Death on the Nile* (78). *Escape to Athena* (79) marked the first time he had worked with David Niven Jr, but the critical reception accorded this POW tale would not suggest that the latter was a valuable addition to the industry's producers. *A Man Called Intrepid* was made for TV in the US, with a cut, feature-length version to be shown in cinemas elsewhere: since it was of the standard of Niven's other recent films, 10 minutes proved too much, but as he often said, his first question on receiving a script was 'Where?' and then 'How much?' The where is obvious with *A Nightingale Sang in Berkeley Square*: and an amount is certainly involved, since the subject is a bank heist.

In 1971 Niven published a memoir, 'The Moon's a Balloon', which became perhaps the most successful book ever written by an entertainer, and the sequel was also a bestseller, 'Bring on the Empty Horses', despite the comment of 'Variety': 'Old, Borrowed, Blue, But Very Little New.' Both books confirmed the impression of a genial spirit, as expected, and so perhaps he once was: later colleagues found him a deeply unpleasant man – a fact always hidden by the press, perhaps because he always knew who to be nice to. He played a Scotland Yard man out to nail jewel thief Burt Reynolds in *Rough Cut* (80) and he sued Paramount because his contract called for his image to appear in the ads alongside the star and Lesley-Ann Down; it was the first lawsuit in a long career and it was settled out of court in his favour. It was a feeble movie, if not quite as abysmal as those of the previous decade. The last two were of their level: *Trail of the Pink Panther* (82), as a jewel thief reminiscing about Inspector Clouseau (Peter Sellers), and *Better Late Than Never* (83), as a down-and-out song and dance man competing with Art Carney for the affections (and money) of a child who is the granddaughter of one of them. It was in fact made before the Pink Panther film and premièred as an in-flight movie – to the chagrin of the director, Bryan Forbes, who believes himself an underrated talent. It was also shown posthumously, for Niven died in August of that year, of a rare wasting disease – the reason why Rich Little was hired to dub him in the Pink Panther job.

Kim Novak

Was Harry Cohn pleased? Columbia's fortunes were made by one man, the director Frank Capra; when he departed Rita Hayworth arrived and they continued in high gear. Though she was recalcitrant Cohn still depended on her, so Cohn was delighted to discover that he had Kim Novak under contract as her box-office appeal declined. As it happened, Miss Novak's was of brief duration.

For a brief period Kim Novak looked like being one of the cinema's goddesses. At the beginning of 1955 she was virtually unknown; by the end of the following year she was second only to Marilyn Monroe as the biggest female draw in pictures. You could hardly move without being confronted by pictures of her or articles in the press (like Grace Kelly a while earlier). 'Time Magazine' profiled her. Director Richard Quine was only one to analyse her appeal: she had, he said, 'the proverbial quality of the lady in the parlour and the whore in the bedroom. Kim has a ladylike quality, but it goes a step further. She has a combination of that with sex appeal and a childlike quality.' She was beautiful, not unlike a Botticelli woman, with a haunting quality reminiscent of the young Dietrich. She was the sort of girl of which Hollywood dreamed.

And understood. She was one of the few manufactured stars who made it big. Harry Cohn, the head of Columbia, reckoned that he had 'made' Rita Hayworth and Novak was designed to replace the by-then fading Hayworth. She had come to Los Angeles from Chicago, where she was born in 1933, the daughter of a railroad worker; she had run an elevator, worked in the five-and-dime and was now a model demonstrating refrigerators. In LA someone from RKO saw her and she got a walk-on in a Jane Russell movie, *The French Line* (54). Columbia's casting director gave her the once-over; she was tested and showed signs of ability as well as the stuff from which glamour stars are made. They gave her a contract, starting at $75 a week, and a star part in *Pushover*, as a blonde moll for whom police dick Fred MacMurray goes bent. As a performance it was only fair, but there was a certain mystery to her presence; Columbia cancelled plans to borrow Sheree North to play the Other Woman in *Phfft!*, a Judy Holliday vehicle, and cast Novak instead. Then they had her replace Mary Costa, playing a nightclub singer in *Five Against the House* (55), a heist thriller with Guy Madison and Brian Keith. The rumblings continued favourable, so Cohn gave her the plum role – Kim Stanley's stage part – in *Picnic*, as a wistful country girl seduced by bum-in-town William Holden. She did quite nicely till she had to go into a dance with him, to the tune of 'Moonglow' – and then suddenly she was the most desirable thing in the world. Around the same time Otto Preminger borrowed her (for $100,000, though her salary from Columbia was only $100 a week) to play opposite Frank Sinatra in *The Man With the Golden Arm*. Both films were big successes.

Still no one was screaming about her *acting*, but she acted more than she was wont to – and looked ethereally lovely – in *The Eddy Duchin Story* (56), as Tyrone Power's first wife. Power commented on working with her:

'Confusion between temperament and bad manners is unforgivable.' George Sidney, who directed this and Novak's next picture, when questioned, spoke of 'the hopeless poison that gets into actresses when they become big stars'. The next one was the awful *Jeanne Eagels* (57), a carefully made biopic of that famous actress of the 20s who died of drink and drugs. It was advertised with pictures of Novak and the slogan. 'This *too* is Jeanne Eagles', but her performance indicated no such variety. She was now earning $1,000 a week and thus made a total of $13,000 for this film, while co-star Jeff Chandler was borrowed for $200,00. Her agent reckoned she was worth at least $300,000 per film, a view borne out by an intensive poll carried out by the magazine 'Box Office' at the end of 1956, when she was named the most popular star in the US (followed, in order, by William Holden, Doris Day, Marilyn Monroe, Susan Hayward, Deborah Kerr, Marlon Brando, Frank Sinatra, Grace Kelly and Elizabeth Taylor). Columbia fought against a raise, claiming they had $12 million bound up in her.

But critics had begun to snipe. She gave them plenty of ammunition in *Pal Joey*, a performance of such inadequacy that it soon became legendary (she contorted both her lines and her body as if embarrassed). 'Photoplay' (March 1958) considered her career over: she 'has no personality beyond a publicity handout, and has outstripped her meagre talent'. Still, she got Hayworth's dressing-room. And Hitchcock was interested. He had considered her for *The Trouble with Harry* but thought her too sultry; now he cast her for *Vertigo* (58) when Vera Miles became pregnant (he had intended to make Miles a big star in *Vertigo*; later, he said, he lost interest). He prophesied publicly that she would 'act' for the first time, but her performance – in a dual role – was little more than competent. Her co-star was James Stewart and Columbia had loaned her on condition that he came to them on his usual terms; he and Novak were teamed again in a poor version of a hit play, *Bell Book and Candle* (Rex Harrison had refused to co-star). She made a brave stab as a youngster attracted to an older man (Fredric March) in *The Middle of the Night* (59), but it was not a success. *Strangers When We Meet* (60) was a tale of adultery in the suburbs with Kirk Douglas (when Glenn Ford refused to co-star) and they fought – according to journalist Bill Davidson – because she insisted on telling him how to play his scenes. The film, as Davidson put it, 'ended up in chaotic mediocrity'.

For Joe Levine/MGM she did a comedy, *Boys' Night Out* (62), as a sociologist studying extramarital activity, but the press slaughtered it. It had been made as the result of much squabbling with Columbia over material; now they tried her in another comedy, *The Notorious Landlady*, but she was little help to Jack Lemmon and the rest of the cast, struggling to make it funny. The studio and she did not patch up their quarrel; and she left Columbia. In that film she had struggled vainly with a Cockney accent; but her complete failure did not deter Seven Arts/MGM, who cast her as the Cockney waitress in the remake of *Of Human Bondage* (64), directed by Ken Hughes after Henry Hathaway had resigned. (Hathaway said later he had planned the film for Marilyn Monroe and Montgomery Clift, 'they made it with Stupid – what's her name – Kim Novak . . . I worked one day with her and quit'.) The film's publicists admitted that she was no Bette Davis, but insisted she would bring her own qualities to the part – but little could be discerned of her original qualities, at least. Critics roasted her and co-star Laurence Harvey, and the film died the death. So did *Kiss Me Stupid*, but mainly perhaps because

Tyrone Power and Kim Novak, husband and wife in The Eddy Duchin Story *(56). The first hour was the best, with nothing much happening except some piano-playing and Novak's beauty.*

Billy Wilder was attacked for bad taste and many exhibitors refused to play it. Wilder later said they were right. Some British critics thought it up to his best work and Novak, as a waitress hired for a one-night-stand, gave strong indications that she should not be written off.

But hopelessly miscast, she was uninteresting as the eponymous heroine of the British *The Amorous Adventures of Moll Flanders* (65), an atrociously made and cheap-jack attempt to cash in on the success of *Tom Jones*. One of her co-stars, Richard Johnson, was briefly her husband (1965-66). After a long absence, Robert Aldrich cast her as a movie star in *The Legend of Lylah Claire* (68), the film version of a play that Tuesday Weld had done a while back. She was well cast as an amalgamation of several movie queens, but the film, in the opinion of 'Time Magazine', was a poor thing when measured against Aldrich's other work (for which, it indicated, it had little estimation). In the US it took less than $1 million, or one-quarter of its cost, and was not seen in Britain till 10 years later. Warners tried with Novak, in a comedy wth Zero Mostel, *The Great Bank Robbery* (69), but the only bookings it could get were B dates.

Hollywood, decidedly, had lost interest, but TV offered a movie, *The Third Girl From the Left* (73), with Tony Curtis. So did the British, when Hayworth walked out of *Tales That Witness Madness;* 'Variety' described Novak's performance as 'awful' and the film was not released in its country of origin. Her fee for it was $100,000; she was in another tele-movie, *Satan's Triangle* (74), shipwrecked in the Bermuda triangle, and when she returned to the large screen she got $50,000 for just three days' work on *The White Buffalo* (77), another disaster: but this time the fault was not hers, since obviously she had only a small role. Charles Bronson had a big one. In 1976 she remarried – her vet. The Germans were the next takers: *Schöner Gigolo Armer Gigolo/Just a Gigolo* (78), seducing the hero (David Bowie) over the body of her dead husband. She was one of several passé names (Maria Schell, Curt Jurgens, David Hemmings, who also directed – badly), as she was again when the British called: *The Mirror Crack'd* (80), playing a movie star among the likes of Elizabeth Taylor, Rock Hudson, Tony Curtis. Both films indicated that she had not been attending acting school during her absences from the screen. Colleagues in a mini-series, *Malibu* (83), included George Hamilton, Troy Donahue, Anthony Newley; she returned to television when she joined the successful soap opera, 'Falcon's Crest', starring Jane Wyman, in 1986.

MAUREEN O'HARA

The wide-eyed, red-haired beauty of Maureen O'Hara started her on her career and, fading hardly at all, kept her there – plus a realistic assessment of her own abilities and position in the Hollywood hierarchy. She was content to work – but regularly – in undemanding parts, a star of the second rank just as she was an actress of the second rank (if that); but her crisp and somehow innocent competence combined with that beauty to make her one of the most eternally welcome of leading ladies (and, presumably, her on- and off-the-set niceness has prolonged her career while those of more illustrious ladies have declined).

She was born in Dublin in 1920. A success at school reciting persuaded her mother to enrol her for dramatic training and she later broadcast regularly on Dublin radio. At 14 she was a minor member of the Abbey Players. She reputedly won every award the Abbey Theatre School handed out and was destined for leading roles. But films intervened. She was introduced to Harry Richman, the American singer, and he got her a small role in a British film he was making, *Kicking the Moon Around* (38). Also under her own name, Maureen Fitzsimmons, she had a bit in *My Irish Molly* (39). She returned to Dublin, but her agent had fixed another film deal; after some weeks in London working on it, it was abandoned, but what was in the can was seen by Charles Laughton and his partner Erich Pommer, looking for a heroine for their *Jamaica Inn*, to be directed by Hitchcock. They signed her to a personal contract, changed her name and made her a 'star'.

At Laughton's request RKO signed her to play opposite him again in his next film and she followed him and his wife to Hollywood: *The Hunchback of Notre Dame*. She was wildly miscast as a wild gypsy girl, but RKO liked her enough to buy up her contract. They considerably overestimated her by giving her Katharine Hepburn's old role in the second remake of *A Bill of Divorcement* (40), with Adolphe Menjou as the father; and as a result she was reduced to a couple of Bs, *Dance Girl Dance*, an idiotic backstage story with Lucille Ball, and *They Met in Argentina* (41) with James Ellison (but it had a Rodgers and Hart score). In 1941 her first marriage was annulled and she married producer Will Price. Her career also took an upturn when John Ford chose her to play the female lead in *How Green Was My Valley*, swopping her Irish accent for a Welsh one as the daughter in this family of miners; she was sincere and direct, and the film itself, from Richard Llewellyn's bestseller, won a Best Picture

Oscar and became one of the year's half-dozen top-grossing films. 20th, who produced, negotiated with RKO to share O'Hara's contract; and Ford, who directed, was to turn to her again and again when he needed a leading lady.

It cannot be said that 20th gave her much to get her acting teeth into: *To the Shores of Tripoli* (42), as the colonel's daughter, with John Payne and Randolph Scott; *Ten Gentlemen from West Point*, as a local restaurant-owner who comforts and flirts with some of them, including George Montgomery and John Sutton; *The Black Swan*, as the haughty lady won over by buccaneer Tyrone Power; and *The Immortal Sergeant* (43), as the 'girl back home'. With Laughton she gave one of her best performances, as the beset schoolmistress of Renoir's Resistance drama, *This Land is Mine*. Still at RKO she did another good contemporary drama, *The Fallen Sparrow*, helping ex-Spanish Loyalist John Garfield battle against Nazi agents in New York. Then she returned to escapism: *Buffalo Bill* (44) with Joel McCrea and *The Spanish Main* (45) with Paul Henreid. She was particularly incongruous in the former, impeccably groomed and enamelled out West as a senator's daughter. In *Sentimental Journey* (46) she was a fatally ill childless wife who adopts a child to whom she will communicate instructions from the Beyond, for the benefit of widower John Payne. Then she was a prim bespectacled miss brought up to date via Dick Haymes and swing, *Do You Love Me*?: no one did. In *Sinbad the Sailor* (47) she was a damsel in distress rescued by Douglas Fairbanks Jr.

Maureen O'Hara as she was most often wont to be: rescued from danger by a handsome lout. He is Paul Henreid, and the film was a cardboard caper called The Spanish Main *(45).*

A.E. Wilson in the London 'Star' summed up O'Hara at this time: '. . . no great actress. Her perfect clear-cut features register no shades of emotion, and her poise in any circumstance remains correct and undisturbed. She is ravishing in Technicolor. and who can give thought to horses . . . when she adorns the screen?' The film was *The Homestretch* (neatly rechristened *L'Amour au Trot* in France), with Cornel Wilde. But she was charming in *Miracle on 34th Street*, a much-liked attempt at whimsy – now badly dated, with Edmund Gwenn as Macy's Kris Kringle and O'Hara and Payne as the love interest. However, she was a liability to *The Foxes of Harrow*, as Rex Harrison's wife – by this time one had simply seen her too often playing these hoity-toity beauties who succumb to the hero's wiles. Much better were the next two: *Sitting Pretty* (48), as Robert Young's wife, employing Clifton Webb as governess; and *Britannia Mews* (49), filmed in London, as the suffering heroine of this version of Margery Sharp's panoramic novel, with Dana Andrews. She did the last under her contract: *A Woman's Secret* at RKO, a melodrama with Melvyn Douglas, in which she murdered Gloria Grahame; and *Father Was a Fullback*, a comedy with Fred MacMurray.

At Universal she did a medium-budget swashbuckler, *Baghdad*, as an English-educated daughter of the desert pitted against wicked pasha Vincent Price. She returned to RKO for *At Sword's Point*, as the daughter of Athos, with Cornel Wilde as d'Artagnan Jr. This went into production at the end of the year, but was not shown in the US till three years later – by which time it was clear that O'Hara was stuck in such things. Especially in colour, she had all the prerequisites for these roles, called upon only to scream at the villain or spit at the hero (till tamed by him). Thus: *Comanche Territory* (50) with Macdonald Carey; *Tripoli* with Payne, directed by her husband; and, infinitely better, John Ford's *Rio Grande*, with John Wayne. *Flame of Araby* (51) was either her or a horse – it was never quite clear – and Jeff Chandler was the man, after which Ford rescued her again and made her the wilful colleen wooed and won by Wayne in *The Quiet Man* (52). After Eire, Australia – for Milestone's *Kangaroo* with

Maureen O'Hara in another familiar situation: comforting the hero. He is Cornel Wilde, and the film was called At Sword's Point *(52) in the US, and* Sons of the Musketeers *in Britain.*

Peter Lawford – after which remissions she returned to a steady run of third-class fare: *Against All Flags* with Errol Flynn: *The Redhead from Wyoming*, notably ill at ease as a saloon belle with Alex Nicol; and *War Arrow* (53), with Chandler. She did turn down *Veils of Baghdad* with Victor Mature.

There was an offer from Britain, but it was more of same: *Malaga* (54) with Macdonald Carey, as a modern Mata Hari. Said the 'MFB': 'Maureen O'Hara looks very handsome in Technicolor, but her expressions are limited – mostly to disgust at shooting smugglers or pulling knives from dying men.' Ford put her into *The Long Gray Line* (55), as Tyrone Power's loving wife, but then it was back to dime-magazine stuff: *The Magnificent Matador*, as an American society girl involved with same – Anthony Quinn; and *Lady Godiva*, a medieval hotch-potch where she remained discreetly covered. Yes, she told reporters, she would like more meaty roles but they were not offered her; no, she had no objection to being called 'The Queen of Technicolor'. The next, however, was in that old process known grandly and erroneously as 'Trucolor by Consolidated': *Lisbon* (56), a melodrama with Ray Milland.

The years roll by and like other stars Miss O'Hara begins to play mothers – in this case, she is Hayley Mills's. The film is a confection cooked up by the Disney studio, The Parent Trap *(61).*

As a change, there was a minor comedy, *Everything but the Truth* with John Forsythe: 'They were caught with their scandals showing,' said the ads, in an only too obvious reference to the 'Confidential Magazine' trials, where O'Hara was one of the bandied-about names. It was back to Class then, as Wayne's loving wife in *The Wings of Eagles* (57), but that was run-of-the-Ford and did not tempt O'Hara to continue. She stayed away till there was a good offer – and an urgent one, when Lauren Bacall was held up on *North-West Frontier* – from Carol Reed, to do *Our Man in Havana* (59), not a big role, but a key one. She waited again for another good one – Hayley Mills's mother in Disney's *The Parent Trap* (61), opposite Brian Keith. She and Keith were partnered again in a good Western – Sam Peckinpah's first feature – *The Deadly Companions* (62): she was a dance-hall keeper. A new phase had begun in her career. She was James Stewart's wife in *Mr Hobbs Takes a Vacation*, Henry Fonda's in Delmer Daves's *Spencer's Mountain* (63) and Wayne's again in *McLintock!* – but, as before memorably with Wayne, a lady of decided spirit. Daves chose her for the lead in his soap opera version of a Rumer Godden novel, *The Battle of the Vila Fiorita* (65), as a lady who leaves her kids for the sake of a fling with Rossano Brazzi. It was not a success. She was a widow out West wooed by James Stewart in *The Rare Breed* (66).

In 1968 O'Hara married for the third time (her second marriage had ended in divorce in 1953). She did not film again till *How Do I Love Thee*? (70), a flop domestic comedy, as Jackie Gleason's wife. The ads said, 'They do not make them like this anymore', which was a pity, whichever way you looked at it. Then she was married to – if separated from – John Wayne in *Big Jake* (71), only they were grandparents now. She hardly looked the part.

Ryan O'Neal

'Esquire' magazine once published an article on Ryan O'Neal called 'The Sheik of Malibu', which its subject did not care for, since it pictured him as a ladies' man and suggested he was obsessed with his looks and his body. But such things make him a rare bird among today's top players. Unlike most stars of the post-Hoffman era he is very handsome, especially when moustached; he has blond curly hair and a toothpaste smile; he seems to lead an interesting life. What is on screen is, er, less interesting, but still agreeable. Maybe he would really come on if he had the apprenticeship of the stars of the 30s: for he is, to underline the point, a throwback to that era. There are no nervous tics, solemnity is at bay; his is an easy, genial presence, and thank heaven for it!

He was born in Los Angeles in 1941, the son of writer Charles O'Neal and actress Patricia Callaghan. He left LA University High School to move to Germany, where his father was working on 'Tales of the Vikings', and while still at school (the US Army School in Munich) he did bit-parts and stand-in on that. Returning to the US he found employment in a commercial and again in bit-parts and stunt work, graduating to bigger roles. If there are re-runs of any of the following, you might glimpse him: 'Dobie Gilliss', 'Our Man Higgins', 'The Untouchables', 'Perry Mason' and 'My Three Sons'. He co-starred with Richard Egan in a short-lived series, 'Empire'; in 1965 he had a large role in 'Peyton Place', as Rodney Harrington, and by the time that plastic soap opera had completed its run almost five years later he was a national name. He had also been divorced from actress Joanna Moore and married Leigh Taylor-Young, one of his co-stars in 'Peyton Place'. That marriage did not last and one of its more unpleasant memories would be the press reception of the film they made together, *The Big Bounce* (69). It was put together (at breakneck speed, to judge from the results) to cash in on their TV success, a crime tale in which he played a drifter. The next people to attempt to cash in were the promoters of *The Games* (70), a flop drama of the Rome Olympics in which he was a marathon runner from Yale with a heart condition. He was approached to make a film for Jerry Lewis at a fee of $125,000: it was never made, but he was much more interested in the mere $25,000 offered to play Oliver in *Love Story*, because he wanted to change his image. His parents, he said, had supported him till he made it to the top and he liked this script (among those who did not – at least, they turned it down – were Beau Bridges, Jon Voight, Michael Sarrazin, Michael York and Michael Douglas): it was not a foolish move since the script then became a book which became a bestseller – and its avid readers were joined by many a cinemagoer, to the extent that the film became the third top-grossing film of all time. Admittedly the director, Arthur Hiller, soft-pedalled the more egregious aspects of what was only pap; O'Neal's partner in love and suffering was Ali McGraw, who hitherto was no more box-office than he.

If he was: *The Wild Rovers* (71) with William Holden (they were respectively old and young cowboys) was not rapturously received. On TV, O'Neal was in *Love Hate Love*, being dogged by his new love's ex; then he was a shy musicologist dogged by 'whacky' Barbara Streisand in Peter Bogdanovich's *What's Up Doc?* (72). The film was dogged, too, being an attempt to revive the screwball comedies of the 30s – and to that extent O'Neal was an appropriate choice, even if he lacked the ability of a Grant or Powell to make believable eccentricity and illogical behaviour. The film was popular, but the public did not particularly want to see *The Thief Who Came to Dinner* (73), with Jacqueline Bisset, in whch O'Neal was a computer programmer who doubles as a cat-burglar. *Paper Moon* was originally to have been directed by John Huston with Paul Newman and his daughter Nell; Bogdanovich took it over and cast O'Neal and his daughter Tatum.

There were the Barrymores, John and Diana, the Fondas, Henry and Jane, and the Redgraves and so on: but Ryan O'Neal and Tatum O'Neal are different – for one thing, he had not been a star very long, and she was only a kid. Director Peter Bogdanovich met her when he went to discuss Paper Moon (73) *with Poppa – and cinemagoers were mightily glad that he did.*

He was a con-man working the Middle West – 'a high water mark in his career to date' ('Variety') – and she his more than wary accomplice; and *this* was a reminder of the old days when movies were fun. You might say commercial cinema at its best and certainly it was the only film in years that people wanted to hug – the reverse exactly of *Barry Lyndon* (75), commercial film-making at its most absurd and a giant audience turn-off. The producer-director, Stanley Kubrick, presumably chose O'Neal as the nearest thing we have to Errol Flynn, but instead of blithely swashing a buckle, he was buried beneath decor, pretensions and a hopelessly ignorant attempt to turn Thackeray's sprightly satire into a rediscovery of the 18th century. The film was long in gestation and O'Neal hesitated: but he went into another 'disaster' (his word for it), Bogdanovich's *Nickelodeon* (76), an affectionate and ramshackle nod to the early days of movies. Burt Reynolds played his rival and partner, and daughter Tatum their factotum, and they were all nice and lively; in truth the film was no worse than *What's Up Doc?* and if the press had not slaughtered it it might have found a public.

Along with most of the players, he was not impressive in *A Bridge Too Far* (77), 'one of my more vulgar endeavours, I think' he said; although the Brigadier-General he played was very young, he was still, to put it kindly, unconvincing. They had wanted him for his name-value; he had done it for the money – estimated at $500,000. In *The Driver* (78), he was The Driver and since the cast-list was all like that, you may have some idea of the film – you probably did not go to see it, having by now realized that car chases were the *sine qua non* of mindless thrillers; and this one had little else on offer. O'Neal then had a chance to erase the mistakes of the last few years, in box-office terms, at least – since he was needed for *Oliver's Story*, the sequel to you-know-what. It was clear that Paramount wanted him, and only him, and he said he would only do it if the script was right; he turned it down and reported for Wallace Beery's old role in the remake of *The Champ* – then thought again, leaving the champ to Jon Voight. As 'Photoplay' put it, 'Wonder if 3 million dollars helped to change his mind.' The money, alas, was wasted, since the reviews – though indeed no more scathing than for its predecessor – created a disaster area wherever the film was shown. O'Neal smiled bravely (with reason) and went to work on *The Main Event* (79), forgetting earlier reservations about his co-star, Streisand. She played an executive who takes him, an over-the-hill prize-fighter, as a tax loss.

That was something which would happen to the next two: *Green Ice* (81), one of Lew Grade's British flops, about emerald smuggling, which found no US distributor and went eventually to cable; and *So Fine*, a comedy about the fashion business. He and John Hurt were the *Partners* (82), straight and gay respectively, but pretending an affair in order to crack a homosexual murder case; and it was he and Shelley Long having *Irreconcilable Differences* (84), a marital comedy set against the movie business – about which it was both sharp and very funny. If all O'Neal's screen work was as good as this he would not have to admit (as he did to journalist Roderick Mann) that there had been no further offers: but he really could not be blamed for *Fever Pitch* (85), Richard Brooks's horrendously old-fashioned drama about gambling. The pity was that O'Neal, as a journalist up to his neck in debts, was sole-billed, thus taking the blame. He was offscreen till he appeared in an independent production, written and ludicrously directed by Norman Mailer, *Tough Guys Don't Dance* (87), as an unsuccessful writer; this fared no better with either critics or the public. *Sam Found Out* (88) was a three-part television showcase for Liza Minnelli and he was with her in one of the episodes; and *Chances Are* (89) was a star vehicle for Robert Downey Jr, playing a dead man who returns to life: Cybill Shepherd was his wife and O'Neal, third-billed, an old boyfriend of hers.

TATUM O'NEAL

To say that Tatum O'Neal was grave-faced is to summon up memories of Margaret O'Brien. She was like no other child star before and is probably the only film child W.C. Fields would have liked. Like him, she is cunning; she sulks; she does not signal her tricks. Or, at least, we saw her thus in her first film, *Paper Moon*; only three films later she was into adolescence – and remarkably pretty, which compensated for the loss of her gruff freshness.

She was born in Los Angles in 1963 and was chosen by director Peter Bogdanovich to co-star with her father Ryan (for a fee of $16,000) in *Paper Moon* (73) – which brought her a Best Supporting Oscar, the youngest artist ever to win one (the child stars of the 30s and 40s were awarded 'special' statuettes at the Awards ceremony). Since she did not like acting and the family did not need the money – and whatever the other reasons were for the child stars of the past, including their contracts with the studios – it was uncertain whether she would film again. Her parents' attitude was

Kristy McNichol, received by far the best notices; the plot had them trying to lose their virginity at summer camp.

She had turned down *Pretty Baby*; she told 'Time Magazine' in 1979 that she 'had been interviewed too many times'; she still was not keen on a movie career – though *Circle of Two* was a mistake, even at $500,000 plus a percentage. In this Canadian production she and middle-aged Richard Burton were mutually attracted. In New Zealand she fell for Colin Friels, one of the *Prisoners* (82) under the jurisdiction of her father, David Hemmings; Shirley Knight was her bickering mother, but none of these names helped the film to travel. O'Neal returned North of the Border for *Certain Fury* (85), a sleazy tale of two girls –the other was Irene Cara – on the lam. It brought no kudos. When she is pictured now it is usually as the wife of John McEnroe, the bad boy of tennis, but she returned to show business in a movie for CBS, *Getting Straight* (89), about a girl in a drug rehabilitation centre with Drew Barrymore, the child player of *The E.T.*, who herself had such problems not long after entering her teens.

Paper Moon *was a joy, but when Bogdanovich used father and daughter again in* Nickelodeon *(76) the result was much less happy.*

that she would, but only if she wished to and the script was right. The money was right – $350,000 – but the script was not: *The Bad News Bears* (76) had difficulty sustaining its one idea – a foul-mouthed kids' baseball team being whipped into shape by a broken-down ex-pro, Walter Matthau. It was a good idea and it was a good idea to have young Tatum 'on' to him – sassing him as she sassed her dad's con-man in *Paper Moon*. They might have been a wonderful team; but there was far too little of her – a criticism also to be applied, among a mountain of others, to Bogdanovich's *Nickelodeon*, with father, as the movie-company's all-knowing general factotum. This time a number of good ideas went wrong, but making a sequel to *National Velvet* was one of the daftest ideas movies ever had: when MGM announced *International Velvet* (78), a good many people thought it a joke. The movie was no joke and Tatum got poor notices and a real box-office disaster as the American girl who comes to Britain to ride a horse. It did better in Britain, where it was made, and Tatum at least outclassed its writer-director's wife, Nanette Newman, in Elizabeth Taylor's old role, now grown-up (which actress spurned it, as did, said writer-director, Julie Andrews and Audrey Hepburn). Tatum's seventh place in the box-office listings, in 1976, had not been sustained by these last two movies and *Little Darlings* (80) did not restore her to favour. The other darling,

PETER O'TOOLE

With his presence, his stature and his looks (though somewhat remodelled for stardom) it seemed certain that Peter O'Toole would reach the top of his profession. What was nice about this was that the talent was there as well, reaching out in all directions, till it took a turn towards neurotic or obsessed roles. After some dozen of these it was no longer so attractive.

He was born in Leeds in 1933, though some sources specify Connemara in Eire. On leaving school he went into journalism and in the evenings dabbled in acting in the rep theatres in and around Leeds. When he left the navy after national service he applied for a scholarship to RADA; from there he went to the Bristol Old Vic, during which time he appeared in London in two of their productions, 'Major Barbara' (56) and a musical, 'Oh My Papa' (57). He started in small parts, but graduated to the big ones, like Jimmy Porter, John Tanner and Hamlet. He toured in 'The Holiday' (58), whose cast included Sian Phillips, who became his wife. His break came with 'The Long and the Short and the Tall' (59), a virtuoso display as the barrack-room lawyer; it was announced that he would repeat it on film but the part went to Laurence Harvey because he was supposed to have a reputation in the US. Meanwhile, director

Robert Stevenson saw the play and signed O'Toole for Disney's nicely Scottish *Kidnapped* (59), in a good supporting part. As it happened, he had already made one film, *Ombre Bianche/The Savage Innocents/Les Dents du Diable* (60), with Anthony Quinn, as a Canadian trooper – dubbed and uncredited; he described the film as 'a disaster'. He got third-billing for *The Day They Robbed the Bank of England*, with Aldo Ray, playing an obtuse Guards officer; the producer was Jules Buck, with whom he later formed his production company. When the film came out he was on the threshold of a season at Stratford-upon-Avon which was to make him the new white hope of the British Theatre: he played Petruchio, Thersites and Shylock. The last was particularly admired.

Sam Spiegel and David Lean were looking for someone to play in a projected super epic about T.E. Lawrence ('How the East Was Won'). Marlon Brando had turned it down and so had Albert Finney. Spiegel began to think in terms of another Finney, a dynamic young Britisher without an international reputation, but he did not want O'Toole, who had offended him while testing for the Montgomery Clift role in *Suddenly Last Summer*, by ad-libbing – 'It's all right, Mrs Spiegel, your son will never play the violin again.' But Lean insisted on O'Toole who, unlike Finney, could see no objection to a long-term contract (he worked most of it on loan-out); and when *Lawrence of Arabia* (62) came out, he became world-famous. He was as good as could be expected within the limits imposed – this was Lawrence of the legends, with just a hint of his mental complexities – and the film was a critical and popular success and the winner of a Best Picture Oscar: perhaps the best of the 60s epics (not high praise).

He planned to follow with a $50,000 version of *Waiting for Godot*, but instead played another twisted historical figure, Henry II to Richard Burton's *Becket* (63) – another hit; but Richard Brooks's version of Conrad, *Lord Jim* (64), was a failure – partly because it was not Conrad at all. Peter John Dyer said that O'Toole in the title-role was simply 'a winsom blond mystic in search of something transcendental always just out of camera range – hence, presumably, his oft-profiled expression of sometimes grim, sometimes grinning vacuity'. Nor had O'Toole exactly covered himself with glory as Brecht's 'Baal' (63) or later that year as Hamlet in the National Theatre's opening production. Nor would he do so in 'Ride a Cock Horse' (65). In films he turned down the role of a Southerner in *The Chase* (another Britisher, James Fox, played it); and his reputation stood still through *What's New Pussycat* (65), a scatty sex-

The uncomfortable character of T.E. Lawrence has fascinated film-makers for years, and various projects were announced, including one with Leslie Howard and another with Dirk Bogarde. Peter O'Toole finally played him in Lawrence of Arabia *(62). With him is Anthony Quinn as an Arab ally.*

comedy with Peter Sellers; *La Bibbia/The Bible . . . In the Beginning* (66), effective in a small role as three angels; and *How To Steal a Million*, a comedy-thriller with Audrey Hepburn. His notices were downright bad for Spiegel's *The Night of the Generals* (67), playing a scar-faced, neurotic Nazi officer. The film did spotty business, but *Casino Royale* – he was unbilled but one of several stars – did well.

He returned to the historical field with *Great Catherine* (68), produced by his own company, Keep Films: Jeanne Moreau as the Tsarina and a Shaw squib extended unmercifully, though his own high spirits compensated, as a visiting British officer. It flopped. He had dropped many accumulated mannerisms in a tough and virile reprise of Henry II, older now and in a different context: *The Lion in Winter* with Katharine Hepburn. He got $750,000 plus 10 per cent of the gross and his enthusiasm for the whole project repaid him handsomely. However its producer. Joseph E. Levine, was less enthusiastic, refusing the percentage on the grounds that his 'disgraceful conduct . . . excessively drunk' had caused the costs to soar: but he lost the case. 'Variety' commented on the next one: 'as an acting exercise, it demonstrates his seemingly limitless range and enormous energy as an actor'. This was *Goodbye Mr Chips* (69), a musical remake with Petula Clark of what seemed in theory a singularly dated piece; but both players attacked with verve and charm the script of Terence Rattigan, a touching but wholly unsentimental improvement on the original, and Herbert Ross directed with a fond feeling for times remembered. A very likeable piece, dismissed in some quarters as old-fashioned and thus not realizing MGM's hope for it.

Country Dance (70) spanned three changes of régime at MGM but was finally butchered in release and became 'meaningles' – in O'Toole's own words; at any rate, a poor thing, badly made (Ireland deputizing for the Highlands) from a florid script about an aristocratic Scotsman (O'Toole) as he degenerated into alcoholism, insanity and incestuous passion (for Susannah York). The new régime cancelled O'Toole plan to film *The Merchant of Venice* on location; ironically, he refused to play Wellington in *Waterloo* because it was to be made in Italy (he did not think any film worth the pestering by the paparazzi). Another project – of Spiegel's – which came to nothing was O'Toole as John Barrymore in *Good Night Sweet Prince*. As it happens, he did not film in the US for many years, though he went to Venezuela for most of *Murphy's War* (71), a flat rendering of the *African Queen* idea with his wife as co-star. It was the first time he had played an Irishman on screen. He played a Welshman, Captain

Literally dozens of stars were announced for MGM's long-projected musical remake of Goodbye, Mr Chips (69), *including Rex Harrison and Julie Andrews. None wanted to court comparison with a much-loved original and there was a sense of desperation in the casting of Peter O'Toole and Petula Clark: he was not a singer and she was not a movie name. Both – on other occasions resistible – were charming and the film effortlessly superior to the original: though you would not have known it from the reviews. With them is Michael Bryant, a fine stage actor making a rare movie appearance.*

Cat, in the film of Dylan Thomas's *Under Milk Wood*.

In Dublin he played in 'Arms and the Man' and 'Waiting for Godot' and was reported as being through with films. Certainly audiences did not regard as beneficial either *The Ruling Class* (72) or *Man of La Mancha*, both based on doubtful but successful stage originals; Peter Medak directed the former and O'Toole produced and starred, as another mad aristocrat; in the latter (made in Italy!) he was a singing Don Quixote, for a reported $1 million, with Sophia Loren. Visiting New York to promote it, 'The Times' of that city described his recent credits as 'lamentable': but they got worse, partly because the failure of the much-touted *La Mancha* closed a number of Hollywood doors. One that opened was Otto Preminger's after Robert Mitchum left the cast of *Rosebud* (75), but O'Toole's 'Newsweek' reporter/CIA man did not restore his flagging movie reputation. Nor did his Robinson Crusoe in a pretentious item with Richard Roundtree, *Man Friday*, the last film of O'Toole's agreement wth Jules Buck, which was formally concluded three years later. He played another decadent aristocrat, Russian this time, in *Foxtrot* (76), a Mexican-Swiss co-production which does not seem to have been seen beyond those countries' borders; he was in Canada for a salary of $125,000 on *Power Play* (78), playing an enigmatic colonel in this duff military tale; and in Toronto he played the leads in 'Present Laughter' (which he had done for BBC TV in 1966) and 'Uncle Vanya'. In South Africa he played another military man in *Zulu Dawn* (79).

None of the last four films got more than minimal bookings and if more was heard of *Caligula* (79) it was because of a troubled production history (beginning in 1976) and the subsequent litigation – some of it due to the fact that the producers, 'Penthouse' magazine, inserted into it some pornographic sequences. The publicity about these brought in customers, but not enough to justify the $16 million cost (escalating from $3.5 million, on Italian locations). Malcolm McDowell played the title-role and O'Toole was Tiberius, acting 'with raw ham' said Tom Milne.

Worse – much worse – was to come. O'Toole played Macbeth, under Bryan Forbes's direction, at the Old Vic in 1980 to perhaps the worst notices in theatrical history; and toured in this fiasco. Already in the can were *Masada* (81), a seven-hour Biblical mini-series cut to two for foreign showings, as *The Antagonists*, and *The Stunt Man*, filmed in Canada two years earlier. The role of a temperamental movie director seemed made for him, as did a drunken movie star (based on Errol Flynn) in *My Favorite Year* (82), but as the scripts of both flailed around, so did O'Toole. He was *Svengali* (83) to Jodie Foster's updated Trilby (now a rock star) for television, and ruler of the planet where *Supergirl* (84) was born, a small role but one to which his other-worldly acting was suitable; he was Paul Lukas's old role in a television *Kim*. He was a scientist trying to reawaken his dead wife in *Creator* (85) and Governor General of a Caribbean island in *Club Paradise* (86), more controlled than in other recent outings. Stage work was confined to Shaw: 'Pygmalion' (London, 84; New York 87), 'Man and Superman' (London, 83), 'The Apple Cart' (London, 86). O'Toole also appeared in the first of these for Pay TV in 1983 and the second for British television: anyone who has seen these performances will not be surprised – as were some naive New Yorkers – that he was not even nominated for a Tony Award for what was his Broadway début.

He appeared catatonic as the British tutor to *The Last Emperor* (87) of China, John Lone, and it is not surprising in view of the incompetence all about him, especially the direction, by Bernardo Bertolucci, who nevertheless won an Oscar for it (and there was a fistful of other Oscars, including Best Picture). A further Anglo-American venture, *High Spirits*, written and directed by Neil Jordan, found him as the drunken owner of an impoverished Irish castle which he turns into a tourist attraction by claiming that it is haunted. Steve Guttenberg, as an American tycoon, and Darryl Hannah, as a real ghost, were also billed above the title. Both films were dangerously expensive, though since O'Toole was no longer a box-office name his salary would not have been a great factor in that: but while the first did well, because of the awards, the second failed miserably. But O'Toole was in demand: for *Helena* (89) with Kris Kristoffersen, *Wings of Fame* with Colin Firth and *The Pit and the Pendulum*.

Geraldine Page

It can be only a matter for surmise how Geraldine Page might have fared on screen in the days of long-term contracts and build-ups. As it happens, she was there, fleetingly, in the old days and nothing much did happen to her; she returned intermittently once her Broadway work demonstrated her ability. She was a star of the new breed, working in films, in TV and in the theatre, with no great fuss about status.

She was born in Kirksville, Missouri, in

1924 and started acting in her teens with a local Methodist amateur group. She went on to study at the Goodman Theater School and acted in stock in the Mid-West for the next five years (1945-51) – Lake Zurich, Woodstock and Shadylane – with some TV work and one minor film appearance, in *Out of the Night* (47), produced by the Moody Bible Institute. She went to New York and took acting lessons under Uta Hagen; she got a small role in 'Yerma' (51) at the Circle in the Square, off-Broadway, and there a year later starred in Tennessee Williams's 'Summer and Smoke'. This led to a role on Broadway in 'Midsummer' and two film offers – a very small role in the New York-located *Taxi* (53), starring Dan Dailey, and leading lady to John Wayne in *Hondo* (54), a role turned down by Katharine Hepburn. She played a fading spinster – but one more sturdy than the one in 'Summer and Smoke'. The Warner Bros. disliked her appearance so much that they recalled her to shoot a scene, explaining that she knew she was homely. Still, she got an Oscar nomination – and no further movie offers.

In 1954 she appeared on Broadway in 'The Immoralist' and in 'The Rainmaker', in the latter again as a spinster. She toured in it and played it in London in 1956. She appeared in Chicago in 'A Month in the Country', 'Desire Under the Elms' and other plays; on Broadway she took over from Margaret Leighton in 'Separate Tables' (57). In 1959 she was a Broadway sensation in Williams's 'Sweet Bird of Youth', which brought her several awards and two worthwhile movie offers – both for adaptations of plays by Williams. Hal Wallis had finally decided to make *Summer and Smoke* (61), but, miserably directed by Peter Glenville and with Laurence Harvey co-starring, it was both a bore and a flop; in other circumstances, Page's bruised, lovelorn Alma might have been affecting. MGM engaged her for *Sweet Birth of Youth* (62), with her stage gigolo, Paul Newman (the cast included Rip Torn, who became her second husband in 1963). In these happier conditions – Richard Brooks directed – she tore the place apart: a coruscating performance full of enthralling detail, causing Dwight Macdonald to write: 'Whenever she is on, one concentrates on her exclusively. She has all the attributes of a great actress – style, presence, wit, timing, emotional nobility – and she is also able to imitate an actual person . . . able to express the grandiose phoniness of the ageing star and at the same time to let us glimpse the human being underneath . . . tough and frightened and vulnerable.' The part had been written for Bette Davis and had Page followed it up with two more hits she might have inherited Davis's mantle. Instead, these both flopped: a version of Lillian Hellman's *Toys in the Attic* (63), as Dean Martin's snobbish spinster sister; and *Dear Heart* (64), as a spinster librarian who falls for out-of-towner Glenn Ford.

Broadway performances during this time included revivals of 'Strange Interlude' (63),

Ageing movie-star and gigolo: Geraldine Page and Paul Newman in Sweet Bird of Youth *(62). She had played the part on the stage, and the film remains memorable for her performance.*

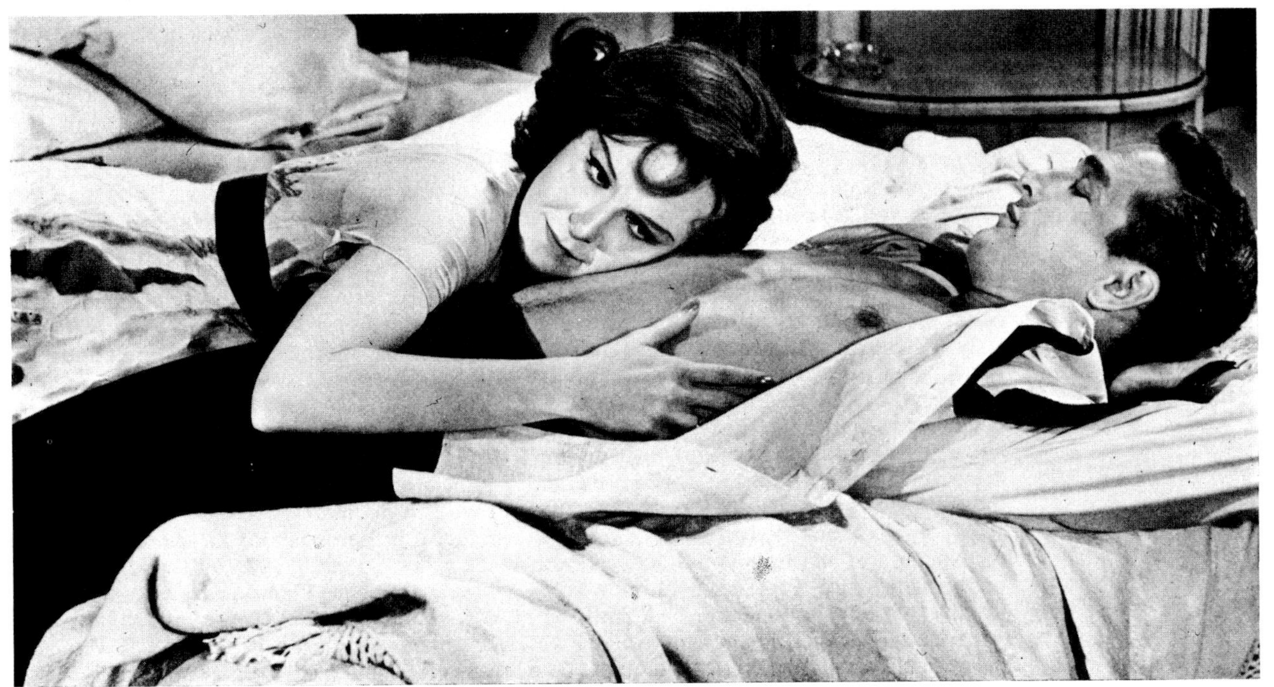

'The Three Sisters' (64), 'PS I Love You' and 'Black Comedy' (67). She returned to films in *Monday's Child* (67), made in Puerto Rico with American backing, directed by Argentina's baroque Leopoldo Torre Nilsson; she was a blowsy selfish mother with an understandably neurotic daughter and Arthur Kennedy was her weak husband. It was not one of Nilsson's successful films and has never been shown in the US. Better was *You're a Big Boy Now*, Francis Ford Coppola's freewheeling look at growing up in New York; the boy's parents were played in correct zany fashion by Page and Torn. She took a good supporting part in Disney's *The Happiest Millionaire*, as the snobbish prospective mother-in-law of the millionaire's son. After a break she accepted a part meant for Bette Davis and played it with a Davis-like relish – a superb performance as a murderess, matched by Ruth Gordon as her prospective victim: *What Ever Happened to Aunt Alice* (69), and it was somewhat more fun than the two Grand Guignol predecessors which Davis had done.

On TV she had had a success in Capote's 'A Christmas Story'. It was transferred to the screen as one part of *Truman Capote's Trilogy*; but had few bookings. After another absence, she appeared opposite Clint Eastwood in *The Beguiled* (71), as a neurotic schoolteacher who nurses him when wounded, and played Cliff Robertson's mother in *J.W. Coop* (72). She was very funny in *Pete 'n' Tillie* (73), as the matchmaking lady who brought them together, but with good offers lacking she made a tele-movie, *Live Again Die Again* (74), about a woman (Donna Mills) threatened with murder after years in suspended animation. Then: *The Day of the Locust* (75), as a Revivalist preacher, one of several players rendered ineffective in a misconceived attempt to film Nathaniel West's satire; *Nasty Habits* (76), religious again, as a nun, with Glenda Jackson; *Something for Joey* (77) for TV and based on fact, as the mother of the Capelletti brothers, one a football star and the other stricken with leukaemia; and *Hazel's People* (78), a tale of the Mennonites of Pennsylvania (made four years earlier and now getting a few belated showings). She had her best film role in a long time in Woody Allen's *Interiors*, as the elegant mother who heads towards breakdown when her husband (E.G. Marshall) leaves her; and there was another good role in *Harry's War* (81), a comedy about man and the taxman, as Edward Herrmann's aunt. Release had been delayed for over a year and in the interim she played Zelda Fitzgerald in Williams's 'Clothes for a Summer Hotel'. She was on Broadway again in a French farce, 'A Woman of Paris'; simultaneously you might have seen her as a nun again, in John Schlesinger's much-abused *Honky Tonk Freeway*. As such she was promoted – to Mother Superior in 'Agnes of God' (82), again in New York. She supported Jill Clayburgh in a drama about Valium-addiction, *I'm Dancing As Fast As I Can*, and was one of several names in a mini-series, *The Blue and the Gray*: among the others was Torn, but they had no scenes together.

Then she was a mother three times, the first two for television: *The Parade* (84), to Michael Learned in a small Kansas town; *The Dollmaker*, to Jane Fonda in Kentucky, replacing Jessica Tandy, who accepted a Hollywood offer; and to a crooked cop in *The Pope of Greenwich Village*, one of the colourful characters encountered by Mickey Rourke and Eric Roberts in their adventures. Page supported Sting and Jennifer Beales (in the title-role) in one of the greatest flops in movie history, *The Bride* (85), a loose remake of *The Bride of Frankenstein*, while New Yorkers could have seen her in a repertory of three plays, including 'The Madwoman of Chaillot' and 'Vivat! Vivat Regina'. Cinemagoers could find her as Philip Bosco's co-star and mother in *Flanagan* aka *Walls of Glass* and as Baryshnikov's agent in *White Nights*. She starred again as the Texas widow determined to revisit her birthplace one more time, *The Trip to Bountiful*, based on Horton Foote's play done originally on TV and then on Broadway by Lillian Gish. She was nominated for her eighth Osar and reflected that if she lost she would have had more nominations without winning than any other performer: but she did win (the Best Actress award). She replaced Geraldine Fitzgerald (whose son directed) as a survivor of the concentration camps in *Nazi Hunter, The Beatie Klarsfeld Story*, based on fact. There were only two more screen credits to come, neither of consequence, though the intentions were worthy: *My Little Girl*, as a grandmother, with Mary Stuart Masterson as a social worker; and the remake of Richard Wright's novel, *Native Son*, with Victor Love in the title-role. She was, however, making *Single Room* with Don Ameche when the financing ran out; and in 1987 she was playing Madame Arcati on Broadway in 'Blithe Spirit', with Richard Chamberlain, when she died suddenly of a heart attack.

Gregory Peck

Gregory Peck was the postwar dream man: tall, dark and handsome, with a deep brown voice. He was supposed to make fans forget their pre-war idols, now returning from the services. Critics thought him an exceptional actor. He got four Oscar nominations within six years. Because he was grave and sincere – not flippant like Cary Grant, not casual like Gable, not cynical like Bogart – he seemed a better actor than he actually was. He did not live up to the initial furore and in the interim there have been better-looking actors and indeed better actors. But he is a strong survivor. He seems to represent some sort of ethos, the sort of man you would like as your bank manager or your kid's tutor, a solid, likeable, kindly, self-effacing – and very American – actor. Someone once said he was the nicest man in Hollywood (adding, 'and the dullest'). He has no great gift for illuminating a script; he said himself, 'When I'm wrongly cast, or in a poor script, I sink with the ship.' (There have been, however some very good scripts.)

He was born in La Jolla, California, in 1916. He was educated at San Diego State College and planned to go on to Berkeley but he could not afford it and became a truck driver. He eventually did study at Berkeley and while there began acting. He went to New York and was a barker at the 1939 World's Fair; then won a two-year contract to the Neigborhood Playhouse. His first professional work was with the Cornell-McClintic company, with a notable first Broadway appearance in Emlyn Williams's 'Morning Star' (42). During its run David O. Selznick tested him and turned him down. There were occasional film offers during the next two years (he was refused for the army), most of which time he was playing a double role in 'The Willow and I'; finally he accepted an offer from scriptwriter Casey Robinson, who wanted him to co-star with his then fiancée, Tamara Toumanova, in *Days of Glory* (44), as a Russian guerrilla. The film was memorable only for him and every studio scurried after him; the winner was 20th, who cast him as the gentle and noble missionary in the film of A.J. Cronin's *The Keys of the Kingdom*. Said the ads: 'Never before has the screen so daringly unlocked the scret sanctuary of a man's heart', but in fact the novel's point – how the priest's Christianity was tempered by his years in China – was completely missed. Peck gave this ambitious, poor film a centre and was notably good as the aged priest.

He was paid $750 a week for it, making his 1944 earnings $26,000 after taxes. His earnings the following year would be $48,000 after taxes. It was recognized that this was only the beginning. He was in the enviable position – almost unique up to that time – of being able to pick his own roles. Under the guidance of agent Leland Hayward, he refused to be tied down to one studio or sign a long-term contract. It was announced that he had commitments to Casey Robinson, to RKO, to 20th and to Selznick. MGM, and in particular Louis B. Mayer, wanted to get in on the act and fortunately for them Peck wanted to do *The Valley of Decision* (45), as a wealthy mill-owner who marries servant Greer Garson; to get it he agreed to do three more films for them at $45,000, $55,000 and $65,000. Playing opposite Garson accelerated his box-office and after her, Bergman, in Selznick's *Spellbound*, directed by Hitchcock: he was an amnesiac – a performance which brought him a 'Picturegoer Gold' Medal. He went into two more even more important ones, *The Yearling* (46) at MGM, from Marjorie Kinnan Rawlings's novel, as a homesteader; and Selznick's grandiose *Duel in the Sun*, a none too happy stab at portraying a lecher. He was more successful as the cynical hunter in *The*

Now, now, now: Gregory Peck may look like the butler, but actually he is the son of a wealthy Pittsburgh family. He is looking admiringly at Greer Garson who is the maid, but one so wise, beautiful and lovable that the family conspires to have him marry her. Yes, it was the sort of situation beloved at old MGM, but they got it from a bestseller by Marcia Davenport: The Valley of Decision (*45*).

Macomber Affair (47), from a story by Hemingway, and as the crusading journalist in Kazan's *Gentleman's Agreement*, a superficial (he was a Gentile 'posing' as a Jew) an already obsolete study of anti-Semitism that seemed bold enough to be voted a Best Picture Oscar. At the end of the year Peck made the first of two appearances in the top 10 list (the other was in 1952).

He was a British lawyer in Selznick's *The Paradine Case* (48), in love with client Alida Valli: perhaps Hitchcock's worst film (Hitchcock had wanted Olivier) and a box-office flop. He went from vice to virtue in *Yellow Sky*, a good Western, at 20th, as a bank-robber who reforms after falling for Anne Baxter; and took somewhat the reverse journey in *The Great Sinner* (49), as a writer who becomes a compulsive gambler after falling for Ava Gardner – a rather silly version of a story by Dostoevsky. At this point he signed a favourable deal with 20th, for four pictures over an eight-year period at around $1 million (in fact, he made six films for them during that time). The first two were good (both directed by Henry King): *Twelve O'Clock High*, as a general in charge of a bombing mission – a performance which brought a citation from the New York Critics as the year's Best Actor; and *The Gunfighter* (50), as Jimmy Ringo, retired hired gun, forced against his will to defend his reputation. He did another Western, *Only the Valiant* (51), at Warners, as part of his commitment to Selznick, who got $150,000 for his services (of which Peck got $60,000). Selznick had also sold several of his star commitments to Warners at a fee of $1½ million, as a package deal, including Peck (the others: Jennifer Jones, Shirley Temple, Joseph Cotten, Louis Jourdan, Betsy Drake and Rory Calhoun); so he remained with that company to do *Captain Horatio Hornblower*, a rousing tribute to C.S. Forester's Nelson-like hero. They sent him and director Raoul Walsh and Virginia Mayo (injudiciously cast) across the Atlantic to do it, a package which some Britishers confused with Marshall Aid.

The World in His Arms *(52), and it was Gregory Peck who had it. Since even Universal could not manage to show it there, they substituted Ann Blyth, who anyway was smaller and prettier.*

For 20th, he was the front part of *David and Bathsheba* with Susan Hayward, every inch a king in an overblown piece that was one of the year's top grossers; and for Universal, a well-born sea-captain in *The World in His Arms* (52), from a Rex Beach story. He turned down *High Noon* because he thought it too much like *The Gunfighter* (but then, years before, Gary Cooper had turned down *Stagecoach*); instead did one of his best-liked films, *The Snows of Kilimanjaro*, a Hemingway story directed by King, with Gardner and Hayward. In order to qualify for tax exemption, he spent the next eighteen months in Europe, first for Paramount, in Wyler's *Roman Holiday* (53), as an amiable journalist to Audrey Hepburn's princess; he was on a percentage, thought soon to be worth $350,000 – even though 'Variety' reported that business was 40 per cent below expectations. For 20th, he was a high-ranking officer again, stationed in Germany, in *Night People* (54), a weak anti-Red thriller. He went to Britain to make two pictures for Rank – virtually the first American to act for a British company while at the peak of his career and certainly the first since the great days of Korda, but then, his fee was uncommonly hefty (said to be $350,000 for the two films). Neither did much business in the US, and it is doubtful whether Rank got his money back – ironically, for both were above the Rank average; *The Million Pound Note*, from Mark Twain's comic novel about a man who finds one; and *The Purple Plain* (55), from H.E. Bates's war novel – a survival trek from a crashed plane.

In the US his box-office was restored by a version of Sloan Wilson's bestselling *The Man in the Gray Flannel Suit* (56), but it was dimmed again by John Huston's *Moby Dick*, a forthright attempt at the impossible, considerably weakened by his conscientious Ahab, likeable but never pitiable (he did it against his will to help Huston get backing). After that, his limitations were exposed more cruelly by *Designing Woman* (57), a comedy about a sports columnist and his fashion-designer wife (Lauren Bacall) that deliberately courted comparison with earlier work by Tracy and Hepburn (and this he only did to get Ava Gardner for his own independent venture, *Thieves' Market*, which finally he did not do). He and Wyler co-produced, and he starred in, *The Big Country* (58); they did not get on – but it was a popular film. Another Western, *The Bravados*, supported by Stephen Boyd and Joan Collins, was also, more surprisingly, a success. However, Lewis Milestone's Korean War story, *Pork Chop Hill* (59), was not up to much, due, in Milestone's opinion, to the fact that much of the footage which did not feature Peck was cut out – at the suggestion of Mrs Peck (the second, 1955, a French journalist; the first, 1942-54, had been Finnish). King's *Beloved Infidel* was a disaster – but then, Peck should never have attempted to play Scott Fitzgerald. (He did not agree: when the author, Sheilah Graham, asked him what he thought of the film he said, 'I thought I was wonderful'.) Nor, for different reasons, should he have done *On the Beach*, Stanley Kramer's entirely inadequate study of the world on the brink of extinction after a nuclear war; of his performance, Stanley Kauffman wrote: he 'embodies Gordon Craig's ideal of an actor: an Uber-marionette, wooden to the core'.

At this sticky point, he starred (with David Niven, Anthony Quinn and others) in *The Guns of Navarone* (61), a World War II adventure story that became one of the biggest grossers in film history. Its success almost made people forget the incredibly nasty *Cape Fear* (62), about ex-con Robert Mitchum out to revenge himself on lawyer Peck by raping his wife and daughter (it was poorly written and directed into the bargain). Dwight Macdonald found Peck 'his usual vapid self – how did Henry King get that superb performance out of him in *The Gunfighter*?' He was also poor in the Cinerama *How the West Was Won* (63), as a pioneer, but complaints about his acting were silenced by the film of Harper Lee's bestselling *To Kill a Mocking Bird*: as a liberal Southern lawyer he won a Best Actor Oscar (and, because he was on a participation salary, made at least $1 million).

That was his last real success. Right from the start he had been able to pick his subjects – originally the only actor of his generation who could. If not always credited as producer, he had great power; for his failures he could perhaps blame no one but himself. Fred Zinnemann directed *Behold a Pale Horse* (64), his one dud in an otherwise splendid track record, but the cast did not help, including Peck as a Spanish Loyalist (sincerity was no longer enough; the time had gone when audiences would accept star American actors as any nationality they wanted to be). *Captain Newman MD*, a comedy with Tony Curtis, did fairly well, but two thrillers,

Gregory Peck in perhaps his most fondly remembered film, Roman Holiday *(53), in which he was an American reporter following the exploits of a European princess doing the town incognito. Every so often there is talk of a remake or a musical version: they could find another Peck, but they would never find another Audrey Hepburn.*

To Kill a Mocking Bird *(63) was set in the South during the Depression, and Gregory Peck played a lawyer defending a Negro on a charge of rape. Mary Badham was his daughter.*

Mirage (65) and *Arabesque* (66) with Sophia Loren, passed almost unnoticed. He began filming *The Bells of Hell Go Ting-a-Ling-a-Ling* on location in Switzerland, but shooting was abandoned after two weeks with no public explanation offered. Thus there was a break – and it lasted three years, till four Peck films appeared at once: *The Stalking Moon* (69), a good Western; a feeble adventure tale, called *The Most Dangerous Man in the World* in Britain, where it was made, and *The Chairman* in the US (both titles referred to Mao Tse-tung); and *Mackenna's Gold*, made, as the ads reminded us, by the *Navarone* team. Said 'Time Magazine': 'Peck, all dignity, stalks senselesly through the film lke a man in someone else's nightmare. The dreamer is Carl Foreman, whose shoddy special effects and flaccid production turn *Mackenna's Gold* into solid dross.' The fourth film was *Marooned* (70), a very expensive space-age epic which was perhaps the biggest flop of all.

There was another failure, *I Walk the Line*, with Peck miscast as a middle-aged sheriff tempted by Tuesday Weld. 'Variety's' review summed up Peck's career: 'Peck is, as always, brooding American Gothic, essentially "a good man" as Miss Weld says.' After that, he did *Shoot-Out* (72), directed by Henry Hathaway, who accepted him against his will, 'Worst son of a bitch in the world for the picture. He's such a cold, indifferent actor; he has no love in him.' Audiences, it seemed, had no love for Peck, for they refused to go to it and to another Western, made in Israel, *Billy Two Hats* (74), and indeed that was described by its director (Ted Kotcheff) as 'a disaster in commercial terms'. Peck played a grizzled old Scot out West. It was probably very sage of him at this point to turn producer: in 1972 he offered *The Trial of the Catonsville Nine*, in protest against the Vietnam War, and in 1974 *The Dove*, about a youngster who sails round the world. Peck was in neither; but public and critical reception did not suggest that he had a future in that line. It was perhaps in desperation that he did a horror film that Charlton Heston had turned down, *The Omen* (76), playing an American ambassador to Britain who finds Satanism in the family: and it was perhaps in desperation that patrons of this genre of film made it a huge, huge hit. That reawakened studio interest and he was offered $250,000 (the same as Charlton Heston at that time, though the latter was also getting a percentage) to play General *MacArthur* (77), but that signally failed to approach the success of an earlier film about *Patton*. The role had been once suggested for Laurence Olivier, who co-starred with Peck in *The Boys from Brazil* (78), as a Jewish pursuer of one-time Nazis; as the chief of these, Peck played his first screen villain: said the 'New Yorker', when he speaks 'you can't keep from laughing'.

He spoke 'British', unconvincingly, one of several geriatric names, in a World War II sabotage adventure, *The Sea Wolves* (80), and remained back then for his TV acting début, in *The Scarlet and the Black* (82), playing an Irish-born monsignor who uses his position in the Vatican to help Allied soldiers. In a mini-series, *The Blue and the Grey* (83), he was – who else? – Abe Lincoln. He coveted another of Walter Huston's parts – in *Dodsworth*, and although he was reported as having bought all screen and TV rights no remake has appeared. Nor has *Judgment Day*, due to begin in 1985, with him getting $500,000 plus 10 per cent of the profits. He sued the production company for $2.5 million plus $10 million punitive damages, claiming that the pay-or-play deal was contingent on the signing of director William Friedkind. His only screen work in a while was to play the US president in a pointless anti-nuke movie, *Amazing Grace and Chuck* (87), though he was scheduled to do a TV remake of *Inherit the Wind* with Kirk Douglas – but it went ahead with Jason Robards, while he went into *Old Gringo* (89) when Jane Fonda could not get Paul Newman to co-star.

ANTHONY PERKINS

Anthony Perkins started in films as an uncertain adolescent, taking his mumbling and bumbling a step or so further than the young James Stewart. His subsequent career has been bedevilled by a series of unlikely or unsuitable roles, some of which have obscured a very real talent.

He was born in New York City in 1932, the son of actor Osgood Perkins, who died when the boy was five. He began acting at 15, in 'Junior Miss' at a summer theatre in Vermont. He was studying in Florida when he heard that MGM were looking for a young actor to play Jean Simmons's boyfriend in *The Actress* (53); he hitch-hiked to Hollywood to test and got the part. He returned to New York and studied at Columbia; and began getting parts on TV (Kraft Television Theater). He auditioned for the James Dean part in *East of Eden*: Kazan turned him down, but chose him to take over from John Kerr in 'Tea and Sympathy', opposite Joan Fontaine. When the run ended, William Wyler offered him the part of Gary Cooper's son in *Friendly Persuasion* (56), which he did beautifully.

He was then engaged to play the lead in a low-budget film version of a much admired

TV play, *Fear Strikes Out* (57); there were several such projects at this time and this one was directed by Robert Mulligan, a quiet little drama based on baseball player Jim Piersall and the father fixation which led to his breakdown. The film was a mild success and Perkins much praised; Paramount had him for four more pictures, of which the first two were Westerns, *The Lonely Man*, as Jack Palance's son, and *The Tin Star*, as an inexperienced sheriff helped by Henry Fonda. He was injudiciously cast as the boy in love with his father's wife (Sophia Loren) in *Desire Under the Elms* (58); but was somewhat better as another mixed-up kid in a peculiar Italo-US hybrid, *La Diga sul Pacifico/This Angry Age*, made in Saigon by René Clément from a novel by Marguerite Duras ('Barrage Contre le Pacifique'/'The Sea Wall'). He had Jo Van Fleet as his mother, Silvana Mangano as his sister and brilliant support from Alida Valli and Nehemiah Persoff. He returned to Paramount for the last picture of his contract, *The Matchmaker*, and was somewhat better served there than before – as the disobedient shop clerk (Robert Morse was the other). But he should never have played the fey young adventurer in *Green Mansions*, even if Audrey Hepburn was in it (and she should not have been either). By the time this was shown Perkins was in the middle of a year's run in 'Look Homeward Angel'; he had worked non-stop in films and Hollywood thought him mad to turn down further films for Broadway. But by the time the play finished, his work in at least two of these pictures had considerably cooled the ardour. He said later: 'I went through many years of giving performances of great limitation. I fail to understand how I come to be around today after the flat, one-dimensional, safe performances I gave for many years.'

He returned to films in Stanley Kramer's *On the Beach* (59), as a worried young Australian officer; then appeared in *Tall Story* (60), a mild campus piece with Jane Fonda, where his main talent seemed to consist of 'gulping and twitching', according to the 'MFB'. Those were characteristics not incompatible with his role in *Psycho*, the twisted psychopathic motel-keeper in Hitchcock's accomplished and startling exercise in horror. The film's enormous critical and box-office success would in time haunt and hurt Perkins, but for the moment, in Paris, he played opposite three big European ladies: with Ingrid Bergman in *Aimez-vous Brahms?/Goodbye Again* (61), with Melina Mercouri in *Phaedra* (62) and with Sophia Loren in *Le Couteau dans la Plaie/Five Miles to Midnight* (63). They were all poor films and he was unconvincing as the adolescent passion of Bergman and Mercouri (though for the former he won an acting prize at Cannes). He was better as Sophia Loren's sinister conniving husband. In New York he had done Frank Loesser's flop musical 'Greenwillow' (60), and 'Harold' (62), but he had made his home in Paris. There he played the protagonist in Orson Welles's *Le Procès/The Trial*; and there he was on trial again in *Le Glaive et la Balance*, along with Renato Salvatori and Jean-Claude Brialy, an over-ingenious thriller directed by André Cayatte. He was virtually the first 'big' American player to star in a

Hitchcock's Psycho *(60). Janet Leigh is a typist who has run off with her firm's bankroll in order to be with her lover; Anthony Perkins runs the motel where she puts up for the night.*

Sophia Loren and Anthony Perkins in Le Couteau dans la Plaie *(63)* – Five Miles to Midnight. *He was her husband feigning death to collect the insurance, and she was the wife forced into coercion.*

wholly French film – and was remunerated accordingly (but a dubbed version of the film had no success in the US). He also played opposite Brigitte Bardot in *Une Ravissante Idiote* (64).

He returned to the US for *The Fool Killer* (65), a low-budgeter about a runaway orphan (Edward Albert, son of Eddie Albert and Margo) who thinks Perkins is the title-character. He was only in the last third of the film. On Broadway he was in Neil Simon's 'The Star-Spangled Girl'; then returned to France for *Paris Brûle-t-il?/Is Paris Burning?* (66), as a GI, and Claude Chabrol's *La Scandale/The Champagne Murders* (67), as an ex-gigolo, made in French and English, with Maurice Ronet and Stephane Audran – and not one of Chabrol's more incisive works. Hollywood recalled Perkins to play another psychopath, in *Pretty Poison* (68). 20th threw it away, but a New York critic attempted salvage of this clever and compassionate piece about a boy caught up with a girl even more dangerous than he – Tuesday Weld, in a performance equalling Perkins's own virtuosity. He was equally impressive in a slight role, that of the meek, well-meaning padre in *Catch-22* (70). In New York he directed a play called 'Steambath' and at one point played the lead; he co-starred with Paul Newman and Joanne Woodward in *W.U.S.A.* (71), excellent again as an ineffectual do-gooder. He returned to France for *Quelqu'un Derrière la Porte/Someone Behind the Door*, a thriller with Charles Bronson, and *La Décade Prodigieuse/Ten Years' Wonder*, with Orson Welles, both actors trapped in self-parody – Welles grandiloquent and Perkins neurotic – and this time the film was one of Chabrol's occasional turkeys. In the US he played opposite Tuesday Weld in *Play It As It Lays* (72), as a burnt-out film producer described by 'The New York Times' as 'a suicidal homosexual with a penchant for kinky sado-masochistic sex'; and he did a cameo as a shifty priest in *The Life and Times of Judge Roy Bean*. He co-wrote (with Stephen Sondheim), but did not appear in, *The Last of Sheila* (73) and loved *Lovin' Molly* (74), who was Blythe Danner, sharing her affections over a 40-year span with Beau Bridges. As the dead man's secretary he was one of those suspected of *Murder on the Orient Express* and as a mad fashion photographer he had murderous intent in *Mahogany* (75) – a feeling shared by any spectators of this vehicle for Diana Ross. Another intent was rape: 'I understand the needs of a woman' he told her. He took over the lead in the Broadway production of 'Equus' and said farewell to what had been considered firm bachelorhood.

In 1976 the trade press carried ads for *Winter Kills*, with John Huston, from Richard Condon's novel about a presidential assassination, but it was abandoned and Perkins was off the big screen till he played a construction worker (marriage had clearly changed him) in *Remember My Name* (78), with Geraldine Chaplin, Alan Rudolph's not-too-satisfactory second feature. That was the beginning of a burst of activity: *First, You Cry*, a tele-movie all about Mary Tyler Moore having a mastectomy; *Les Misérables* (79), as Javert, for US TV and cinemas elsewhere; the Dutch *Twee Vrouwen/Twice a Woman*, made in English, as the smarty theatre-critic husband of a woman (Bibi Andersson) engaged in a lesbian affair – and of course he beds down with the partner; the reactivated *Winter Kills*, in the umpteenth repeat of his *Psycho* performance; the Disney *The Black Hole*, as the captain of the space-ship which gets lost therein; *North Sea Hijack* with James Mason, as one of the hijackers, a psychopath; and *Double Negative* (80), a Canadian thriller starring Michael Sarrazin, as the villain, a blackmailer.

That year he was in 'Romantic Comedy' on Broadway, from which it was quite a switch to *The Sins of Dorian Gray* (83), a tele-movie for which Dorian had had a sex-change. *Psycho II* had Norman released from the asylum, making one sigh for the good old days when the Hays Code insisted that *all* killers died for their crimes – from which Perkins went to an Australian mini-series, *For the Term of His Natural Life*, a term many might like to apply to Ken Russell, whose *Crimes of Passion* (84) was his usual zilch movie. Perkins, in easily his worst movie, was a paranoiac priest hung up on harlot Kathleen Turner. He directed *Psycho III* (86) not badly, given that someone had made the decision to make the approach campy, after which he played Talleyrand – oh, for some class after so long – in a mini-series, *Napoleon and Josephine: a Love Story* (87). Then there were two more excursions into fear, though the first does not seem to have been publicly seen to date: *Shadow of Death* (88), a last-minute replacement for the ailing Roddy McDowall, as a perverse newspaper editor, and the British *Edge of Sanity* (89), a travestied remake of *Dr Jekyll and Mr Hyde* in which Mr Hyde is revealed as Jack the Ripper.

Gérard Philipe

You can find Greta Garbo in mosaic on the floor of the National Gallery, but for a long time the only film stars of a major country to have appeared on the postage stamps (give or take an Eva Peron or so) were Raimu and

Gérard Philipe, in a series of great French actors in 1961. Philipe was a special, unique actor, the most admired and loved French player of his generation. As a classical actor, in Racine and Corneille, Paris audiences marvelled; and as a movie star, an international name on the art circuit, he was the chief favourite of postwar filmgoers. Said Serge Reggiani: 'Il a été le seul à être à la fois honnête et solide malgré son talent et malgré sa réussite. Il a été pour nous qui sommes de sa génération une justification. Nous avons chacun un nombre de qualités, lui, il les avait toutes à la fois.' Said Georges Sadoul: 'Au niveau du génie (où se situait Gérard Philipe) le Personnage composite exprime les courants profonds d'une époque donnée. Talma fut une explication de la Révolution et de l'Empire, Frédérick-Lemaître du Romantisme. Philipe est une explication de notre pays et de notre temps – l'après-guerre.'

It could not be said that Philipe on screen exhibited the range of an Olivier or a Brando – he was in no sense a character actor – but he did act with great sensitivity the romantic young men he was given to play. Sometimes he was moody, engrossed, even psychotic; normally he was light-hearted, impish, even frivolous. Had he lived he might well have hesitated before taking on the sort of solid businessmen played by Jean Gabin or Pierre Brasseur. One thinks of him, even in his last films, as the eternal, the perfect, *jeune premier*.

He was born in 1922 in Cannes. His father was a hotel director and he was brought up mainly in Grasse, a dreamy, imaginative child, very close to his mother and sister. He was destined to be a doctor, but after being asked to recite at a Red Cross benefit he knew that he wanted to be an actor. He said later that he chose through vanity. He tested for, but did not get, a role in *Les Cadets de l'Océan*. He sought advice from Marc Allégret and got a small role at the Cannes Casino in 'Une Grande Fille Tout Simple' by André Roussin, starring Claude Dauphin. Allégret's brother Yves directed him in a small role in *La Boîte aux Rêves* (43; premièred 45) – it had been started by Jean Choux but there were differences between him and star – and *scenàrist* – Viviane Romance. Then Allégret himself gave him a bigger part in *Les Petites du Quai aux Fleurs* (44), a tale of four sisters (Yves did the exteriors). Philipe got a part in 'Une Jeune Fille Savait' and toured with it – and that took him to Paris. He auditioned for Edwige Feuillère who okayed him for the part of the angel in Giraudoux's 'Sodome et Gomorrhe' (43). At the same time he began to study at the Conservatoire. In 1944 he was in 'Fédérigo' by René Laporte.

Director Georges Lacombe saw him in this and chose him to enact the anguished young men in both parts (1830 and the present day) of *Le Pays sans Etoiles* (46), where he was overshadowed somewhat by Pierre Brasseur – though 'L'Ecran Français' thought it notable for 'surtout un Gérard Philipe à qui l'on peut confier sans craintes des rôles prestigieux'. Someone did, Georges Lampin, in his academic version of Dostoevsky, *L'Idiot*. The stars were Feuillère and Lucien Coëdel, and he was billed below the title; but he dominated the film as Myshkin, the idealist who destroys unwittingly because he cannot understand that other people are motivated by creeds that are greedy and irrational. For all the gentleness, there was a gleam of paranoia in his eye, suggesting the Dostoevskyan paradox. Richard Winnington wrote: '. . . over all this is Gérard Philipe's tremendous playing of Myshkin, tragic, romantic, full of pathos, stupefaction and nobility; evoking the essence, the Christ-like goodness, if not the full complexity of Dostoevsky's "Idiot".' Feuillère played the courtesan and relations between them became strained as he grew more exacting over his own performance (but she remembers him fondly, as 'charmant et espiègle').

But it was Micheline Presle who was indirectly responsible for making him world-famous. At that point perhaps France's biggest female star, she chose both the subject and her leading man: *Le Diable au Corps* (47), adapted by Aurenche and Bost from Raymond Radiguet's novel, directed by

Gérard Philipe, said Kenneth Tynan once, has a flair for reproducing 'the most touching transports of adolescence'. This he did to perfection in Le Diable au Corps *(47). The lady he loved was Micheline Presle.*

Claude Autant-Lara, the story of a youth who has an affair with a woman whose husband is away at the Front (World War I). Both played beautifully. Dilys Powell wrote after he died: '. . . impossible to forget Philipe's portrait of the schoolboy in love, awkward, furtive, desperate, triumphant, at last alone, a sad pariah forbidden even the luxury of mourning'. (She added: 'I think of him as a supremely elegant actor, but he had passion, he had pathos, he had rage.') 'Cinémonde' readers voted the film the year's best, and Philipe and Presle the best players. He was judged Best Actor at the Brussels Film Fesitval, 1947. He refused to go to Hollywood, but went to Italy for *La Chartreuse de Parme*, a 'poetic', overstuffed version of Stendhal directed by Christian-Jaque and enlivened by his sprightly, seductive Fabrice. Maria Casarès was his co-star and they were togther in 'Epiphanies' at the Noctambules. After another play, 'KMX Labrador' (a version of *Petticoat Fever*) he concentrated on movies. (In 1945 his father had been imprisoned for almost a year for collaboration with the Germans; he was pardoned, but tried again and condemned to death; he escaped to Spain.)

Une si Jolie Petite Plage (49), directed by Yves Allégret, cast him as a murderer wandering on a Normandy beach, one of the lost souls in a winter-time resort: conventional and atmospheric, with the rain which raineth all the time. *Tous les Chemins Mènent à Rome* was a confused comedy about an actress (Presle) 'protected' by Professor Philipe because he thinks she is in danger from reporters. The next did lead to Rome – it was filmed there: Clair's *La Beauté du Diable* (50), an alternately clumsy and witty retelling of the Faust legend, with Michel Simon as Mephisto. Its success was strictly qualified. He was amusing as the monocled, beplumed officer in *La Ronde*, moving from actress Isa Miranda to whore Simone Signoret; but was hard-pressed to do much with the homicidal maniac of *Souvenirs Perdus*. Marcel Carné's *Juliette ou la Clé des Songes* (51) was another disappointment, a revamping of 'Peter Ibbetson' (he stole for his girl, found her again in his dreams, in prison).

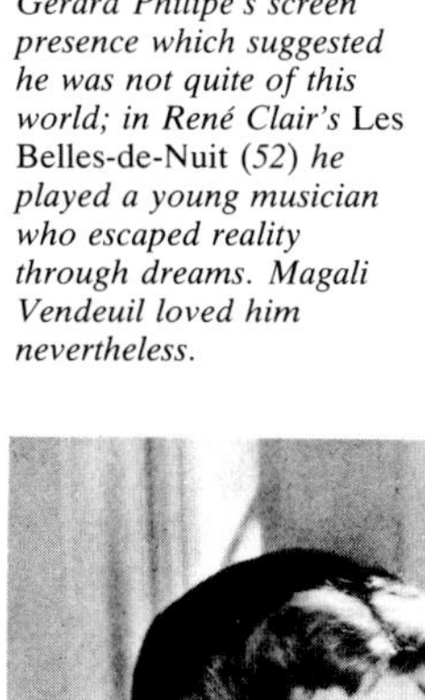
There was something about Gérard Philipe's screen presence which suggested he was not quite of this world; in René Clair's Les Belles-de-Nuit *(52) he played a young musician who escaped reality through dreams. Magali Vendeuil loved him nevertheless.*

He began work on *Stazione Termini*, but it was abandoned (later, Montgomery Clift did it); and refused to do a film of 'Le Grand Meaulnes' because he felt it would betray the novel. Suddenly he asked Jean Vilar to let him join the newly formed Théâtre Nationale Populaire (TNP), at a salary of 30,000 francs a month (instead of the 30 millions he could earn per film). He began by playing 'Le Cid' and 'Mother Courage', in a small role; later he was in 'Le Prince de Hambourg', 'Lorenzaccio', etc. His film career became secondary. Also in 1951 he married and his wife became, it was believed, the guide his mother had been. He was a retiring, private person, so that colleagues were astonished when he spoke out against the war in Korea and when he worked on behalf of the staffs of the national theatres when they went on strike. In 1957 he was to consent to head the Comité des Acteurs, a newly formed trade union in rivalry with the existing one.

Meanwhile, he had a worldwide hit, *Fanfan-la-Tulipe*, an engaging swashbuckler directed by Christian-Jaque – the adventures of a country boy wth His Majesty's army; and *Les Sept Péchés Capitaux* was also a success, though all he did was MC the seven episodes. Korda announced him for a British movie, but nothing happened. He worked for Clair again in *Les Belles-de-Nuit* (52), as a provincial pianist who dreams his way into three centuries and the arms of three beautiful women. This was a typical *bonne-bouche*, grudgingly admired by some; but its eventual reception did not match early expectations (in Paris a gala première at the Opéra, in Britain a première attended by the Queen). Philipe left levity awhile for *Les Orgueilleux* (53), as a drunken doctor in Mexico with Michèle Morgan. He played d'Artagnan in *Si Versailles m'était Conté*, the first and most popular of the all-star Guitry historical films and the first French movie to be made in a decent colour system (Eastmancolour); then went to London for *Knave of Hearts/Monsieur Ripois*

(54), René Clément's ironic look at a young Frenchman on the make (Joan Greenwood, etc.) and one of the most honest pieces till then made in Britain (the British press did not care for it).

He moved to Italy for a sketch in the French-Italian *Villa Borghese*, again as the lover of unfaithful Micheline Presle – but this was a different thing from *Le Diable au Corps*. The next two were among the first French movies in Technicolor and the second in particular used it exquisitely. *Le Rouge et le Noir* was adapted by Aurenche and Bost from Stendhal's novel, concentrating mainly on Sorel's affair with Mme de Renal (Danielle Darrieux). As directed by Autant-Lara, Philipe was subdued, neither enough the dreamer nor the idealist. Clair directed *Les Grandes Manoeuvres* (55), a *conte* about a lieutenant in the Dragoons who wagers that he will make the next woman to enter the room fall in love with him. She (Michèle Morgan) does; he falls genuinely in love with her; she hears about the bet. . . . He, elegant, handsome, gay; she, proud, meltingly beautiful; a provincial garrison town in the Belle Epoque; a waltz theme tune; complete enchantment. Abroad, critics complained that Clair was old-hat; in France the film was a huge success. The critic of 'Le Monde' (Jean de Baroncelli) wrote that it represented 'everything I love in my country. . . . Here are clarity and modesty, lucidity and tenderness, irony and elegance.'

With the exception of *L'Idiot*, Philipe once said, he never chose a film because he liked the part. The chief attraction was the subject or scenario (and he regretted agreeing to *Le Rouge et le Noir*: it was only made because he agreed to do it and he found the responsibility too great). However, it is difficult to see what attracted him to *La Meilleure Part* (56), an ambitious drama about building a dam (he was a dedicated engineer) that went out without a director credit (Yves Allégret was responsible). Then: *Si Paris Nous était Conté*, as a troubadour. He had dreamed for years of making a film about Till Eulenspiegel – at one point in 1951 the cameras were ready to roll when the producers changed their mind. Finally, he began *Les Aventures de Till l'Espiègle* (57), shot in Sweden, with himself directing. It was badly received and did poor business. He was depressed by its failure and cancelled plans to direct what would have been the first Franco-Chinese co-production. Instead he did Duvivier's *Pot-Bouille*, based on Zola, as an amorous adventurer of infinite resource and charm – the sort of part he could play blindfold.

Montparnasse 19 had at one time been set with Mel Ferrer, and Max Ophüls was about to start it when he died; Jacques Becker took over and made of it a romanticized but touching version of the life of the painter Modigliani. Both the film and Philipe were at their best towards the end, embittered by failure. The film failed and was retitled *Les Amants de Montparnasse*. He made another sketch-movie, *La Vie à Deux* (58), and returned profitably to Dostoevsky – *Le Joueur*, directed by Autant-Lara, with Françoise Rosay as the old lady. Another classic, *Les Liaisons Dangereuses* (59), as updated by Vadim, found him miscast as lecherous, wily Valmont. And he was little more impressive, again as an idealist, in *La Fièvre Monte à El Pao* (60), one of the lesser Buñuels, an exposé of a South American police state, with Maria Felix. He became ill during shooting and died six months later of a heart attack, towards the end of 1959. He was buried near his property at Ramatuelle, near Saint-Tropez: a simple grave which became a place of pilgrimage to all who cherished his glowing spirit.

Among movie lives of painters, Montparnasse 19 *(57) was easily one of the better ones. Philipe was Modigliani, and Anouk Aimée was Jeanne Hébuterne, who left her bourgeois family to live with him.*

Sidney Poitier

Sidney Poitier was the first Negro superstar. The timing, of course, was right – others never had the same chance (Bert Williams, a Negro comedian, was starred in some early Silents, which did not go; no one tried hard to 'push' the great Paul Robeson). Talking about it bores him: 'I'm an American, first and foremost. Then, I'm an actor. Finally, if you like, I'm a Negro.' He seems to be such a nice, modest fellow that one would not wish on him the albatross of colour round his neck; but wear it he must; and when there are dozens of other Negro stars, he will be the Elder Statesman.

There are reasons why he reached his high position which have little to do with colour. Over the years the public grew to like and respect and trust him. Like all the best screen actors he has presence and integrity. He is not especially versatile: he is only really good playing those lithe Ivy-League-suited Negroes. But his face is expressive; he usually understates, but he can flash his eyes to suggest a brooding mood or a tense restlessness. Maybe others could do better, but he was there first, tried and trusted at the time Hollywood finally put paid to the Amos 'n' Andy stereotype and recognized the black as a human being.

He was born in 1924 in Miami, Florida, of West Indian parents. He returned with them – his father was a tomato-farmer – to Nassau, but was sent back to Miami when he was 15 to live with his brother. Having American citizenship, he served in the army (as a physiotherapist) and was discharged in 1944. He could not see himself as a manual labourer and auditioned for a study course with the American Negro Theater; while studying, he did odd jobs. He was hired to play Polydorus in an all-black 'Lysistrata' (46), which led to an offer to understudy all the young actors in a Broadway revival of 'Anna Lucasta'; including a subsequent tour, he was with that production two years and in the end had played most of the parts.

No Way Out *was made in 1950, and it does not stand up too well today – but it was significant then as the first major movie dealing with colour prejudice. Sidney Poitier was a nice young doctor and Richard Widmark the racialist out to 'get' him.*

His first film part was in an Army Signal Corps documentary, *From Whence Cometh My Help* (49), and then 20th called him to Hollywood to test him for an important part in Mankiewicz's good *No Way Out* (50). He got the part, and a fee of $7,500, as a young doctor in danger from a colour-bigot (Richard Widmark) who swears he killed his brother. He played it with humour and understanding with a capital U; it was a blue-print for many of the parts he would play later. But if the reviews were good, work was sparse: the British film version of Alan Paton's novel *Cry the Beloved Country* (51), as an Anglican priest in South Africa; and a couple of potboilers, *Red Ball Express* (52), supporting Jeff Chandler, and *Go Man Go* (54), supporting the Harlem Globetrotters (that one was directed by James Wong Howe, the cameraman). A year later MGM needed a Negro for Richard Brooks's *The Blackboard Jungle* (55); Poitier looked young enough to play a student, one with a colour complex, caught between decency and delinquency. In that he really made his mark and whenever a producer needed a Negro actor he came to mind.

He was in a boy-meets-dog movie, William Wellman's *Goodbye My Lady* (56), and then in the film version of a TV play which he had done, 'A Man Is Ten Feet Tall', rechristened *Edge of the City* (57), a lead role as John Cassavetes's buddy, an ebullient, ingratiating performance. In *Something of Value* he was the embittered young Kikuyu brought up alongside Rock Hudson. And he got uptight halfway through *Band of Angels*, as Clark Gable's bailiff and protégé, knocking out Patric Knowles after he has tried to rape half-coloured Yvonne de Carlo: a film with something for everyone – which nobody wanted, and his worst performance. In Britain he played an African administrator married to Eartha Kitt, in *Mark of the Hawk*; it was trade-shown in the US early in 1958, but does not appear ever to have been publicly shown. His next big advance came when Stanley Kramer felt compelled to make some statement on the race problem: *The Defiant Ones* (58) were he and Tony Curtis, two convicts on the run, chained together. . . .

In Britain he played Cassavetes's buddy again in *Virgin Island*, satirizing the Jolly West Indian. Meanwhile, the huge success of the Kramer picture caused Goldwyn to redouble his efforts to get him for *Porgy and Bess* (59) – material which Poitier considered outdated. Rouben Mamoulian, who had

directed the original stage production and was scheduled to do the film, talked him into it. Unfortunately, Goldwyn and Mamoulian differed over interpretation and Otto Preminger took over; the result was predictably overblown and heavy-handed, and the film was stolen from Poitier and Bess (Dorothy Dandridge) by Pearl Bailey and Sammy Davis Jr. Commercially, too, it was a write-off. Poitier was no better served by a silly Alan Ladd war film, *All the Young Men* (60), as a sergeant: he loathed making it and presumably hoped the day would come when he could turn down such stuff. He did not like *Paris Blues* – with Paul Newman – either, but said that the original script was vastly different; he was a jazzman in love with Diahann Carroll. Neither film did well. On Broadway he had a big success in an all-Negro play by Lorraine Hansberry, which Columbia hastily decided to film, *A Raisin in the Sun* (61); it did not cost much, being virtually a photographed play – and a verbose and meretricious one at that. The Poitier character was half-baked, which did not help. There was yet another failure, *Pressure Point* (62), as a Jewish doctor (at least, in the original script) helping mixed-up Bobby Darin.

A modest budgeter (except for his fee – $300,000), a sloshy piece about a surly young man who melts while helping some nuns, *Lilies of the Field* (63), was entered for the Berlin Film Festival and won Poitier a Best Actor prize – which put him in line for an Oscar and he got it (the film was then reissued with much success). The award brought nothing better for a while: *The Long Ships* (64), the Vikings *v* the Moors, with Poitier panned as head villain; *The Greatest Story Ever Told* (65), a one-shot appearance, inevitably as Simon of Cyrene; and *The Bedford Incident*, as a reporter on board Richard Widmark's ship. As in *The Greatest Story*, he went on befriending people: a blind girl (Elizabeth Hartman) in *A Patch of Blue* and a potential suicide (Anne Bancroft) in *The Slender Thread* – he was social worker and psychologist respectively. It was part of Hollywood's new 'liberal' conscience that it wanted to have Poitier seen doing the Utmost Possible good. He did a Western, *Duel at Diablo* (66), and then returned to the genre: the Pollyanna part this time was a schoolteacher in London's East End, *To Sir With Love* (67). It was released first in Britain, where it was mildly received; but in the US it really broke through – unexpectedly and so much so that Columbia conducted a poll to find out why cinemagoers wanted to see it: 'Poitier' was the answer. (He was on a percentage and someone reckoned his heirs would get payment for 200 years.) Concurrently he was in *In the Heat of the Night*, as Northern detective Virgil Tibbs, pitted against Rod Steiger's bigoted Southern police chief; the film and Steiger won Oscars and Poitier was also outstanding – arguably his best performance. The year 1967, his *annus mirabilis*, also included *Guess Who's Coming to Dinner*, and he was committed emotionally – for almost the first time on screen – *and* to a white girl. Three box-office giants and Poitier became the third biggest draw in the US. In 1968 he was first.

Inevitably there were snipers and remarks about Sidney Superspade. Now that he had

The problem of colour inevitably loomed large in many of Sidney Poitier's movies. Another (if facile) attempts to handle it was The Defiant Ones *(58) which found him and Tony Curtis chained together as escaping convicts.*

The most satisfying of Poitier's films was perhaps In the Heat of the Night *(67), because it dealt with prejudice quietly in a thriller context. Rod Steiger was the Southern cop confronted with a Northern detective – Poitier.*

autonomy over his pictures, Poitier prepared one and made this statement: 'I'm the only Negro actor who works with any degree of regularity. I represent 10 million people in this country and millions more in Africa; I'm the only one for these people to identify with. . . . Wait till there are six of us; then one of us can play villains all the time.' He wrote the original story for *For the Love of Ivy* (68), a comedy where black–white relationships were only incidental – and, that aspect apart, the critics found it hopelessly dated. It did good business, but *The Lost Man* (69) got somewhat lost, a remake of *Odd Man Out* (concurrent with another Irish novel/movie updated, Americanized and blackened: *The Informer* as *Uptight!*). Still he remained in the top 10, at No. 6. He was committed to UA for a second film about detective Tibbs and he turned down several scripts; he reputedly rewrote much of the one that finally emerged, *They Call me MISTER Tibbs!* (70), but no one thought it a patch on the original. A second film that year sank without trace, *Brother John*, a mystical story of a man who could predict death. *The Organization* (71) was a third Tibbs film.

By this time other Negro actors were starring in films; James Brown appeared in a series of medium-budget actioners and James Earl Jones was Oscar-nominated for his magnificent performance in *The Great White Hope*. But the only other one then who might be said to have made it is Harry Belafonte, a nightclub singer who had acted in some big films of the 50s; for various reasons he found clubs and TV more profitable, but after a 12-year absence he returned to the screen co-starring with Poitier in a Western, *Buck and the Preacher* (72). Belafonte produced and after some weeks Poitier took over direction from Joseph Sargent. He also directed the next two: *A Warm December*, a black love story about an American doctor visiting London; and *Uptown Saturday Night* (74), in which he and Bill Cosby were innocents in the big city, running across such fly fellows as Belafonte, Flip Wilson and Richard Pryor. He returned to the 'message' film with *The Wilby Conspiracy* (75), with Michael Caine, playing a revolutionary African leader, but its damp reception caused him to play safe with two more modest and agreeable comedies with Cosby, *Let's Do It Again* and *A Piece of the Action* (77), both of which he also directed. In both they were involved with gangsters, firstly as innocents trying to raise money for their lodge and secondly as likeable petty criminals. In 1976 he married Joanna Shimkus (star of *The Virgin and the Gypsy*, etc.), after long hesitation, in view of his leadership of the black community – at least, such was speculation, since he is reticent on his private life. Whether because of that, or whether because he was tired of such leadership, he has carried his career into a lower notch with his middlebrow comedies for blacks – or, of course, he may just have tired of the pseudo-liberal tracts which had mainly been his lot.

In his capacity of director only he made *Stir Crazy* (80) and *Hanky Panky* (82), conceivably on the grounds that his experience as an actor might help Gene Wilder – who starred in both – to be either charming or funny. He failed. In 1982 he signed a three-year contract with Columbia to produce and direct – and to act, too, if he found the right script: but nothing emerged. There were reports of a remake of *A Double Life*, directed by Stanley Kramer, but nothing came of this; he eventually returned to acting in *Little Nikita* (88) and *Shoot to Kill*, in both as a veteran FBI man. They were made in reverse order, but his come-back evoked little interest in the public, though the critics were kind; he had been too long away.

Jane Powell

Jane Powell was a (fairly) popular singing star during the great days of MGM musicals. She appeared in some of the lesser of them. Her voice was quite sweet.

She was born in Portland, Oregon, in 1928; and not long after she began singing lessons her voice was discovered. She sang on local radio stations and had her own programme. Her parents took her to Los Angeles on a 'new talent' show, 'Hollywood Showcase', as a result of which she was taken on for the Chase and Sanburn programme. Within a week MGM had taken her on and put her in the care of Joseph Pasternak, who had nurtured Deanna Durbin's career. He agreed to loan her to United Artists for a minor musical with Edgar Bergen and Charlie McCarthy, *Song of the Open Road* (44). 'Introducing Jane Powell,' said the ads. 'Discovered by the man who brought Deanna Durbin to the screen.' No one was impressed. UA kept her for *Delightfully Dangerous* (45), in which she was ashamed that sister Constance Moore was a stripper. At Metro, Pasternak instituted a series of Powell movies, all escapist, Technicolored, frothy, and Durbin-inspired (the last, in fact, was a remake of *It's a Date*): *Holiday in Mexico* (46) with father Walter Pidgeon; *Three Daring Daughters* (48) with mother Jeanette MacDonald; *A Date With Judy* with father Wallace Beery; *Luxury Liner* with father George Brent; and *Nancy Goes to Rio* (50) with mother Ann Sothern, plus Roddy

McDowall as her puppy-love interest (Nancy was also supposed to go to Rome and Paris but the proceeds did not justify a sequel). The formula was varied slightly in *Two Weeks With Love*, with mother Ann Harding: it was set at the turn of the century.

Powell had sung in support of a couple of MGM films at Loew's State, New York, but had made little more impact than in films. Her chance came when June Allyson and then Judy Garland could not do *Royal Wedding* (51): she was a last-minute replacement and okay, but her winsome personality clashed with Fred Astaire's more urbane one. She returned to vehicles tailored specially for her: *Rich Young and Pretty*, which, like all her films, got only ho-hum reviews and did only so-so business – but it had a fine score and Danielle Darrieux to play her mother. Similarly, Ann Miller enlivened *Small Town Girl* (53), the remake of a Janet Gaynor vehicle – but it was too small town and played Bs. Warners borrowed her for *Three Sailors and a Girl*, but that did not do much either. However, when MGM had trouble casting *Seven Brides for Seven Brothers* (54), they gave the lead, Howard Keel's bride, to Powell; it was an enormous hit and gave indications that she was beginning to relax on the screen at last. But it was virtually the end. *Athena*, a silly musical about a health cult with Edmund Purdom, played Bs; she merely guested in *Deep in My Heart*, singing songs from 'Maytime' with Vic Damone; and was only one of several stars in *Hit the Deck* (55). MGM were no longer making musicals.

They had not let her grow up, Powell complained, as she signed a three-picture deal with RKO, who made her *The Girl Most Likely* (57) in a remake of *Tom Dick and Harry*. Kaye Ballard, who was also in it, later cracked that it closed the studio; in fact, it was one of the last films made there and was sold off after it closed, to Universal. At Universal she went dramatic as the daughter of Hedy Lamarr, *The Female Animal* (58), with drunk scenes. Then she was a native girl in *Enchanted Island*, with Dana Andrews, directed by Allan Dwan, who said later: '. . . I suffered through it with a drunken actor and a nice girl who didn't belong in it – Jane Powell – she looked false as hell.' It was her last Hollywood film in a long, long while and she was later to admit that it was a profound shock to find how very tightly the studio gates were closed on her. On TV she appeared in two specials, 'Ruggles of Red Gap' (57) with Michael Redgrave and 'Meet Me in St Louis' – the Judy Garland role – with Myrna Loy, Walter Pidgeon, Ed Wynn, Jeanne Crain and Tab Hunter.

She has appeared frequently on TV since, in nightclubs and in tent shows ('The Sound of Music', 'The Merry Widow', etc.). At least one film plan (*Girl on the Gran Via* in the early 60s) came to naught. She does not mind: 'I left film work because I didn't want to fight to be a star any more. I adore all the domestic things' – she has been married five times, in 1949, 1954, 1965, 1978 and 1989. 'You can't combine those with the anxiety of fighting for jobs, the fear of not being on top. It's a full-time job being a star. It's all-absorbing – and human relationships suffer from it. I'm past the point of champing at the bit, desiring this or that. I think now I've found my own happy ending without the help of a script.' She made one tele-movie, *Mayday at 40,000 Feet!* (76), while her repertory for summer stock also includes 'The Boy Friend', 'Meet Me in St Louis', 'Brigadoon', 'Irene', 'The Unsinkable Molly Brown', as well as 'South Pacific' and 'I Do! I Do!', which she did with Keel on several occasions – certainly in 1977 and 1980 respectively. Her voice is on the track of *Tubby the Tuba*, an animated feature advertised in the trade press in 1982 but not publicly seen; and she did appear as 'Singer at Rally' (a political one) in *Marie* (85) with Sissy

Jane Powell had been in movies ten years when she had her biggest hit – and the movie for which most people remember her: Seven brides for Seven Brothers *(54) opposite Howard Keel.*

Spacek, but if you closed your eyes you may have missed her. About the same time she played a tough matriarch in an ABC soap, 'Loving', and for ABC in 1988 she had an occasional role in Alan Thicke's series, as his mother.

ELVIS PRESLEY

Elvis Presley stands apart from the normal Hollywood pattern: his films were unashamedly Presley vehicles, made exclusively for his fans. Other artists from other media who infiltrated films were helped on by other artists, but from the start Presley never appeared with a star of equal stature (the only precedent is among comics like The Three Stooges; Jerry Lewis is the only recent example). Some fine talents (e.g. Barbara Stanwyck, Angela Lansbury) played featured roles in his films, but most of his leading ladies were never heard of before (and have seldom been heard of since). His directors were usually competent craftsmen from the 30s and 40s (Norman Taurog directed nine of his 31 feature films) and his scriptwriters something less – but it was their brief merely to tailor a screenplay which would put the star through familiar paces and let him sing half a dozen songs.

It is probable that, like Jerry Lewis, most cinemagoers never saw him. Few critics cared for either him or his films; and there were no efforts by his studios to sell him to other than convinced fans. There were, once, millions of these: what was originally a teenage public stayed faithful till they and he grew older. He has been a fantastic record-seller and a huge earner, from the sullen, side-burned youth he was to the smiling but ageing juvenile he had become before he died – which event caused his diminished popularity to explode again, often with ghoulish side-effects. His early success coincided with the impact of the rock 'n' roll form on popular music; later he became a capable performer, significantly the only rock idol to have a prolonged success in pictures.

He was born in 1935 in Tupelo, Mississippi, where his father worked in a paint factory. He became a truck-driver in Memphis, Tennessee, then a centre for a certain type of 'country' music. As a present for his mother he cut a disc at the Sun Record Company, who offered him a contract. His first commercial disc was heard by a Colonel Tom Parker, who became his agent and who promoted him subsequently. It was he who negotiated the recording deal with RCA Victor, who paid Sun the then unprecedented price of $35,000 for him – but Presley repaid it, by quickly becoming the biggest money-spinner that company had ever had. And it was Parker who arranged the triumphant p.a.'s and decided which of the several Hollywood offers to accept: all of them.

He did deals with 20th, Hal Wallis at Paramount and MGM before Presley had even stepped before a camera; and from then on he kept him moving from studio to studio – though this is not evident in either the style or content of the movies, which are predictable to the *n*th degree. Apart from singing, the star woos or is wooed and has several obstacles to overcome, usually his detractors, with whom he will, before the eighth reel, have a punch-up. The happy end is inevitable – though oddly, in the first, *Love Me Tender* (56), he died; he did reappear at the end as a ghost, still singing and strumming his guitar. Still, in this Civil War Western, he played second fiddle to Richard Egan. 20th rushed it into exhibition and fans and the curious made it one of the year's biggest grossers. The next did less well, *Loving You* (57), all about publicist Lizabeth Scott discovering a rock singer in order to get ex-husband hillbilly band-leader Wendell Corey back into the big time. He was real rough in *Jailhouse Rock* and that was a big one for him. These three films lifted him into fourth position among the top 10 stars of 1957.

His appeal was demotic – the kid in the parlour pool-room or pin-table arcade, a junior Victor Mature, tough but basically harmless: a street-corner Casanova whose greatest need is to be mothered. With the possibility of military service within the near future the image was softened and the new family-package-size Presley was found making albums of 'inspirational' songs. Hal Wallis

Elvis Presley in his first film, Love Me Tender *(56), a drama about a feuding family in the aftermath of the Civil War. It was very silly, but no matter – crowds flocked to it.*

tried to make a really good film out of *King Creole* (58), he said – but it was not very popular (an adaptation of 'A Stone for Danny Fisher' by Harold Robbins; with Carolyn Jones). By this time Presley's very future was doubtful: he had been unable to get exemption and it was thought unlikely that his public – family or otherwise – would remember him two years later. It did, via careful releases of records (some made during furloughs) and a career in itself as the most publicized GI in the world (serving in Germany). It was announced during his army service that he had been signed to make a film for 20th for either (reports varied) \$200,000 or \$250,000 plus in both cases 50 per cent of the profits.

His come-back film was for Wallis and was appropriately titled *GI Blues* (60): 'from . . . the outset to the last fade-out, Elvis is front and centre and singing,' said the 'MFB', also observing sourly that co-star Juliette Prowse deserved a leading man 'with more genuine fire than Presley'. But this was not apparent to his fans; by the end of the following year Presley was back in the top 10 and he stayed there through 1966; he also began getting into the British list. These are the films which kept his popularity popping: *Flaming Star*, directed by Don Siegel, as a half-breed Indian; *Wild in the Country* (61), written by Clifford Odets, as a literary genius beset by Doubts; *Blue Hawaii* (62), the biggest grosser among his Wallis films; *Follow That Dream*, virtually the only Presley film the press liked; the remake of *Kid Galahad*, in the title-role with Lola Albright in the old

In Jailhouse Rock *(57), Presley was a young thug (well, he had accidentally killed a man) who learns in jail to do things like this.*

Follow That Dream *(62) was strictly for Presley fans, but anyone chancing on it might have found it more rewarding than most of his other movies. He played an amiable oaf accidentally outwitting the people trying to stop the family settling in a new house.*

Bette Davis role; *Girls Girls Girls* – who included Stella Stevens, and one of his better pictures; and *It Happened at the World's Fair* (63). In *Fun in Acapulco* his co-star was Ursula Andress; in *Viva Las Vegas* (64) it was Ann-Margret; in *Kissin' Cousins* it was himself, in a double role; and in *Roustabout* he was supported by Barbara Stanwyck. That film demonstrated all aspects of Elvis, as if devised by the Colonel's computer: he was a sort of maverick, liking motor-cycles, guitars, being a loner; he is said to have a chip on his shoulder but is by no means bitter; he tangles – innocently enough – with older women, but gallantly courts the ingénue, rather in the style of the young John Wayne, he resents the phoniness and bossiness of other people, especially his elders; and is quick with the karate on three college toughs who try to rough him up.

Girl Happy (65) and *Tickle Me* continued him on his anodyne way. In *Harum Scarum* he was a movie star who goes to the Orient to plug his latest picture. However, as opposed to these family/trade entertainments, *Frankie and Johnny* returned somewhat to the primitive quality of his early films. Hal Wallis tried reviving the formula of *Blue Hawaii* for *Paradise Hawaiian Style* and then, after *Spinout* (66) at MGM, gave up with *Easy Come Easy Go*, leaving the field clear to others. Presley had survived Beatlemania, but his cinema reputation was faltering: after *Double Trouble* at Metro, he did *Clambake* (67) for United Artists, who booked it into the lower half of double bills. Few artists could have survived such standard vehicles: *Speedway* (68) with Nancy Sinatra; *Stay Away Joe*, supported by Joan Blondell; and *Live a Little Love a Little*, with Rudy Vallee. The latter was never distributed in Britain, nor was *Charro* (69), a belated attempt to change his image – tough and unshaven now, but Wanda Hale in The 'New York Daily News' told him to 'stop trying to act, and sing'. *The Trouble With Girls* again did poor business, so *Change of Habit* hoped for more than slight change, with the new Elvis involved with a breed often encountered by Hollywood heroes – nuns, chief among whom was Mary Tyler Moore. In Britain its distributor did not bother with it, but sold it to the BBC, the first American film to have its British première on TV.

It did not get into the ratings, though it was clear that most of Presley's fans had by now grown older and deserted films for their television set. Some younger writers, who had grown up while Presley dominated that pop scene, began to consider him the king of that fabled world; and they and some others treated him with respect when he appeared in a documentary based on a personal appearance in Las Vegas, *Elvis – That's the Way It Is* (70). But for most cinemagoers, he was now but a name from the past. Another such, *Elvis on Tour* (72), was strictly for nostalgics, but his death in 1977 – from a heart attack, perhaps brought on by drug abuse – sparked off a huge wave of interest, uncooled by unseemly reminiscences by companions and reports of his last concerts, when he was obese but metaphorically a mere shadow of his former self.

Robert Preston

With almost 40 pictures to his credit, and leading roles in all of them, Robert Preston was much less well known as a movie actor – even in the sticks – than as a Broadway star. He was not one of Hollywood's glories and only in the light of later events can one say that Hollywood was wrong. He was a virile, attractive, capable leading man, but the spark revealed later by 'The Music Man' had not then been ignited.

Preston was born in Newton Highlands, Massachusetts, on 8 June in 1913 or 1918 or some point in between. The family moved to California, where he did school dramatics; on leaving he joined the Pasadena Playhouse. He was playing the lead in 'Idiot's Delight' (38) and was seen by a Paramount scout. Paramount were not impressed, but their B picture czar, Harold Hurley, was and he signed Preston to a six-month contract at $100 a week. After hanging around for a few weeks Preston returned to the stage; he heard that the said czar was planning *King of Alcatraz* (38) to star J. Carroll Naish and he asked for a part – and was given a crewsman on a tanker. That got him into two more Bs, *Illegal Traffic* and *Disbarred* (39), which starred Gail Patrick as a lawyer and featured him as an assistant DA. He might have stayed in Bs had De Mille not chosen him to play the heavy, Barbara Stanwyck's husband, in *Union Pacific*, after which he was one of the younger Gestes, the self-sacrificing Digby, in *Beau Geste*. Paramount then starred him with Dorothy Lamour – but only because Jon Hall was not available – in *Typhoon* (40), which he loathed. He was one of De Mille's *North West Mounted Police*, the one whose obsession with half-breed Paulette Goddard gets them all into so much trouble; and was then wooing Lamour again under the *Moon Over Burma*, again from the higher realms of idiocy and even more dizzying than *Typhoon*.

In 1940 he married Paramount starlet Catherine Craig and his career took an upswing when Loretta Young asked for him over at Universal for *The Lady From Cheyenne* (41); not so good was *Parachute Battalion* with Edmond O'Brien at RKO, one of the cheap recruiting posters the studios were churning out that year. In *New York Town* he was second lead, a millionaire playboy pursuing Mary Martin; then he was in two more Bs, *Night of January 16th*, a mystery with Ellen Drew, and *Midnight Angel*, whose title was hastily changed to *Pacific Blackout* because the US had entered the war (but the change had no effect on the box-office). He was second lead again in De Mille's *Reap the Wild Wind* (42), a jolly tar in love with Susan Hayward, and he was the detective hero of *This Gun for Hire*. He had his best chance in some time in *Wake Island*, with two more of Paramount's reliables, William Bendix and Brian Donlevy. He appeared very briefly in *Star Spangled Rhythm* and did another B, *Night Plane From Chungking* (43), a topical remake of *Shanghai Express*, with Ellen Drew, before joining the USAF, Intelligence branch.

Demobbed, he returned to Paramount to support Alan Ladd in *Wild Harvest* (46), as a hired hand almost corrupted by Dorothy Lamour; he was loaned to UA for *The Macomber Affair* (47), one of his favourite parts, as Joan Bennett's unfortunate husband; guested in *Variety Girl*; and refused to play the heavy in *Unconquered* (Howard Da Silva did). At MGM he gave one of his best performances, as the Protestant minister in *The Big City* (48) with Margaret O'Brien; then he played a couple of heavies in Westerns, *Blood on the Moon* at RKO, pitted against Robert Mitchum, and *Whispering Smith*, pitted against Ladd. But he did not want to support Ladd; nor, he said, did he want to play parts turned down by Ladd or Ray Milland. His fights with Paramount over these ended when he asked for release from his contract; they refused, but Louella Parsons took his stand and accused them of ill-treating a war veteran. Paramount let him go.

Leaving them turned out to be a mistake. Preston did get the leading roles he wanted, but not in good films. Four of the next five were for Eagle-Lion, the British (Rank)-owned company, and they got the poor distribution, in both countries, that was the lot of the films of that short-lived studio. The first, however, was big-budget and in colour, *Tulsa* (49), opposite Susan Hayward. At Universal he played Barbara Stanwyck's husband in *The Lady Gambles*. For Eagle-Lion: *The Sundowners* (50), a Western; *My Outlaw Brother* (51), with Robert Stack as the outlaw, Mickey Rooney as the brother and all of them, according to 'Variety', giving 'mechanical interpretations'; and *When I Grow Up*, with Bobby Driscoll thinking about it, and Preston and Martha Scott as his parents. These killed any draw that Preston had had at the box-office and he was hardly better served by *Best of the Bad Men*, as a crook, with Robert Ryan, or by the two-part *Face to Face* (52) in 'The Bride Comes to Yellow Sky', from the Stephen Crane story, with Marjorie Steele (her millionaire husband, Huntingdon Hartford, produced it). A British picture did nothing to help, *Cloudburst*, made by a company, Exclusive, whose studio was a converted country house (as was usually evident from their films). He played a retired colonel of the European Resistance.

Tulsa *(49) was a 'spectacular Technicolor drama of the Oklahoma oilfields', so there had to be a climactic fire. Watching it are Lloyd Gough, Pedro Armendariz, Susan Hayward and Robert Preston.*

Meanwhile, he had returned to the stage, taking over from José Ferrer in 'Twentieth Century' (51). The following year he was in another hit revival, 'The Male Animal', and soon, with good reason, he was both a critical favourite and a popular draw in New York: 'The Magic and the Loss' (54), 'The Tender Trap', 'Janus' (55) and 'The Hidden River' (57). He returned to Hollywood to play a paranoid disciplinarian in *The Last Frontier* (55), a Victor Mature Western. His career at last took wing with 'The Music Man' (57), which had been turned down by Danny Kaye, Milton Berle, Art Carney, Gene Kelly, Ray Bolger, Phil Harris and Dan Dailey. Fortunately for all of us. Preston auditioned and went on to one of the biggest personal successes of the decade, as Professor Harold Hill, the fast-talking con-man who charms a small Iowa town and is charmed by it in return. Meredith Willson's score contained some speak-songs which he did irresistibly.

When its three-year run ended, Preston

accepted a Hollywood offer; he returned clean-shaven (the old moustache had qualified him for all those heavies, or vice versa), as the father in the film of William Inge's *The Dark at the Top of the Stairs* (60), with Dorothy McGuire. Warners produced, and it might have been their way of preparing audiences for his screen repeat as *The Music Man* (62). Certainly both Fred Astaire and Cary Grant were mentioned for it and both Bing Crosby and Gene Kelly had instructed their representatives to buy it. But Willson and Co. stuck out for Preston and Warners took him as part of the package. Commercially, it was not wise: outside the US the film did so-so business and in some territories Warners did not bother to release it. Added to Preston's lack of lure was its entrenched Americana; and Preston, if vital and persuasive, was revealed by the camera to be a mite aged. Otherwise, it was a prime example of the filmed Broadway hit. Morton da Costa, who had directed the stage show, did the film; and he directed Preston again, playing a movie director in his 'Music Man' style, in *Island of Love* (63), filmed in Greece with Tony Randall and Georgia Moll. It was a complete disaster. *How the West Was Won* of course did well – and Preston's was one of its better performances – but there was no better box-office for *All the Way Home*, James Agee's story, as the father, with Jean Simmons.

But on Broadway, Preston had successes in 'Too True to Be Good' (63), 'Nobody Loves an Albatross', 'Benjamin Franklin in Paris' (64) and 'I Do I Do' (67), with Mary Martin. He returned to films as Steve McQueen's father in *Junior Bonner* (72) and replaced Marlon Brando in *Child's Play* when Brando and the producer, David Merrick, did not get on. His playing of the jovial but finally demonic teacher was only too realistic, underlying the dilemma of Preston's film career: he is too *strong* for the screen. He stays well below the ham-level, but his personality demands too much of us – so that he tends to be an especially unlikeable villain.

Robert Preston was a Hollywood has-been when he landed the lead in a fine Broadway musical, 'The Music Man'. It was a spectacular example of the right part and the right talent – as screen audiences saw when he repeated in the movie version (62). Opposite him was Shirley Jones.

He and Lucille Ball did not get on when he played her Southern admirer in *Mame* (74): and in view of her notices, he had the last laugh – though he himself had a musical flop with 'Mack and Mabel', despite the fact that this Broadway piece about Mack Sennett deserved a better fate. Turning again to father roles, he dominated a TV movie, *My Father's House* (75), as *père* to Cliff Robertson, who throughout it remembered him; and he had an important cameo in *Semi-Tough* (77), as 'Big Ed', manager of a baseball team and father to Jill Clayburgh – with whom players Burt Reynolds and Kris Kristofferson are in love. He had a large role again in *The Chisholms* (79), a mini-series with Rosemary Harris. They played a pioneer couple and he was killed off in the first episode of the subsequent series. Blake Edwards cast him as a cynical, permanently hung-over doctor in his sour Hollywood tale, *S.O.B.* (81), one of several names supporting Julie Andrews. His reward for that was to get a large role and some songs with Andrews and solo in *Victor/Victoria* (82), as the down and out vaudevillian who persuades her to drag up. As long as the two of them were on-screen everything was fine. He led Broadway's showfolk in discovering why a movie star died when due to make her stage début, in *Rehearsal for Murder*, made for TV, as was *September Gun* (83), in which he was Billy Sunday, an ex-gunfighter who helps a nun (Patty Duke Astin) look after some Apache kids. He was back on the big screen in *The Last Starfighter* (84), as the inventor of a video game who takes its champion player (Lance Guest) on a guided tour of Outer Space. There were two more prime tele-movies, *Finnegan Begin Again* (85), as a married newspaperman drawn into an affair with a younger woman (Mary Tyler Moore), a widowed teacher, and *Outrage!* (86), as a man who turns himself in after shooting the man who raped and killed his daughter. He died of lung cancer in 1987, 'the finest song and dance man of the last forty years' as Mark Steyne said in the 'Independent', pointing out that he could neither sing nor dance: but the songs from the five show albums that he cut can be heard (in Britain, at least) as often as any of those sung by Bing Crosby or Perry Como.

VINCENT PRICE

Said Vincent Price in 1964: 'You know I have made about eighty films so far and only a relatively small proportion of them have been horror subjects. I suppose it's true that I have been mainly identified as a terror specialist and if that is to be my public image I've no objection.' He had been a star for 20 years when his career deviated into low-budget horror films and that period can be regarded as a lengthy apprenticeship for the ultimate in ghouls that he played until recently. He was seldom cast as a nice man. At his best he was an egotist or a dilettante; at his worst he was sadistic, lecherous, covetous or just plain murderous. He usually had it in for the hero or heroine or both. Like the best villains of the Talkie period, Price patterned himself on the Sir Jaspers of Victorian melodrama, the landlord who was about to foreclose – devious, dandyish, wheedling. Silent melodrama preferred the gorilla-like, primitive villain, patterned after Caliban or the half-human creatures of Harrison Ainsworth: actors like Lon Chaney and Wallace Beery were physically more intimidating. Talkies restored the subtle menace of voice. Claude Rains, George Sanders, Basil Rathbone and Price (the only American of the four of them) – each had/has a dry, light-toned, well-accented voice, each had a patina at least of superiority, a conviction born of conceit or riches. Price, who has certainly steeped deeper into blood than the others, is the joker of the bunch. It is hard to take him seriously. The relish with which he invests even the meanest line is to be savoured: he understands the degree to which the material can submit to his idiosyncrasies.

He was born in 1911 in St Louis, Missouri, into comfortable circumstances. At the age of 16 he was sent to Europe alone on a grand tour; he studied at Yale and after graduation enrolled at the University of London – studying Fine Arts at the Courtauld. He received his MA around the same time as he was making his stage début: he had done some amateur Gilbert and Sullivan, so acting won out over painting and he auditioned for the Gate Theater, which gave him two small parts in 'Chicago' (35). The Gate was a (small) club theatre and therefore able to present an evening of Laurence Housman's one-act plays about Queen Victoria under the title 'Victoria Regina' (stage and film portrayals of that lady were still banned). Price was chosen to play Prince Albert and when Gilbert Miller decided to present the plays on Broadway with Helen Hayes he asked Price to repeat. When the run finished (1937) Price played leading roles in stock ('Eden End', 'Parnell', 'The Wild Duck', 'Elizabeth the Queen', etc.); he returned to Broadway for three plays – including two with Orson Welles's company, then went out to Hollywood under contract to Universal.

His first picture was a Constance Bennett comedy, *Service de Luxe* (38), as the troublesome nephew of Charlie Ruggles, who hires her to keep Price from visiting him. He returned to Broadway for a revival of 'Outward Bound' starring Laurette Taylor; then in Hollywood he was loaned to Warners to play a shallow and vainglorious Raleigh in *The Private Lives of Elizabeth and Essex* (39). He played another unfortunate Englishman, the vacillating Duke of Clarence, in *The Tower of London*, drowned by order of Richard III (Basil Rathbone). He was another weakling, Joan Bennett's husband in *Green Hell* (40). These were supporting parts; Universal had not liked him enough opposite Constance Bennett to keep him in leads. His contract finished with two films directed by Joe May, *The Invisible Man Returns*, heard but hardly seen, and *The House of Seven Gables*, opposite Margaret Lindsay – they were young lovers and George Sanders was the villain.

Price moved over to 20th on a seven-year contract and played two more historical characters: Mormon Joseph Smith in *Brigham Young Frontiersman* and Charles II in *Hudson's Bay*. Like his previous contract it allowed for stage work and in 1941 he began a long run starring in 'Angel Street' ('Gaslight'). He returned to 20th to play the most sceptical of all Jennifer Jones's unbelieving opponents in *The Song of Bernadette* (43) – the prosecutor who tries to get her put away. He was: a Southern soldier spouting Shakespeare in *The Eve of St Mark* (44); Senator Gibbs McAdoo, contemporary and son-in-law of President *Wilson* (Alexander Knox), one of the most ambitious films 20th ever attempted and one of its costliest flops; the most suave and equivocal of the various admirers of *Laura*; the student friend of Gregory Peck who becomes a worldly, politicking monsignor in *The Keys of the Kingdom*; the French ambassador seduced by Tallulah Bankhead in *A Royal Scandal* (45); and the smooth DA in *Leave Her to Heaven*.

His first star role was in a programmer, *Shock* (46), as a psychiatrist who shuts up Lynn Bari in his asylum when she sees him murder his wife; then he starred in an A feature, *Dragonwyck*, as Gene Tierney's sadistic husband – an uninteresting villain. He began *Forever Amber* with Peggy Cummins, as Charles II, but when it was stopped and restarted he was replaced by George Sanders. He and Cummins were in *Moss Rose* (47), an Edwardian melodrama in which he was a

Up in Central Park (*48*) *had been Sigmund Romberg's last Broadway musical. The movie version starred Deanna Durbin as an Irish colleen, and Vincent Price as Boss Tweed, that corrupt force behind Tammany Hall in the 1870s.*

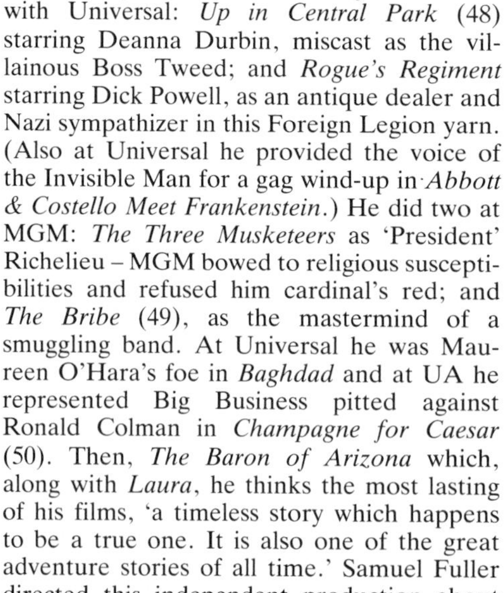

Scotland Yard man. On release at the same time were *The Long Night* from UA, a remake of *Le Jour se Lève*, in the Jules Berry role; and *The Web* from Universal, in which he was the wicked tycoon who spun it, trapping Edmond O'Brien. His contract with 20th expired and was not renewed.

After a year's absence, he signed for two with Universal: *Up in Central Park* (48) starring Deanna Durbin, miscast as the villainous Boss Tweed; and *Rogue's Regiment* starring Dick Powell, as an antique dealer and Nazi sympathizer in this Foreign Legion yarn. (Also at Universal he provided the voice of the Invisible Man for a gag wind-up in *Abbott & Costello Meet Frankenstein*.) He did two at MGM: *The Three Musketeers* as 'President' Richelieu – MGM bowed to religious susceptibilities and refused him cardinal's red; and *The Bribe* (49), as the mastermind of a smuggling band. At Universal he was Maureen O'Hara's foe in *Baghdad* and at UA he represented Big Business pitted against Ronald Colman in *Champagne for Caesar* (50). Then, *The Baron of Arizona* which, along with *Laura*, he thinks the most lasting of his films, 'a timeless story which happens to be a true one. It is also one of the great adventure stories of all time.' Samuel Fuller directed this independent production about James Addison Reavis, who almost worked a fantastic scheme to cheat the government out of Arizona Territory. Contemporary notices were poor.

In both *Curtain Call at Cactus Creek* and *His Kind of Woman* (51) he played a ham actor – and in the latter, as a Hollywood star, his was very much a supporting part (to Jane Russell), with billing to match. In *The Adventures of Captain Fabian* he was a wealthy Southerner used by Micheline Presle and vanquished by Errol Flynn. Howard Hughes liked his work in the Russell picture and signed him to a starring contract. It was announced that he would star in a new version of *Topaz*, but he only did a featured role for the mercurial Hughes – *The Las Vegas Story* (52), as Russell's supercilious husband. As a relief from such tosh he turned back to the stage – 'The Cocktail Party' in San Francisco, 'The Lady's Not for Burning' at La Jolla and the reading of 'Don Juan in Hell', replacing Charles Laughton, on tour. But the success of his next picture was to have a far-reaching effect on his career: *House of Wax* (53). This was Warners' remake in 3-D and colour of their old *Mystery of the Wax Museum*, with Price as the impresario whose wax effigies are filled with corpses. Every old trick of the horror-flick was exploited (plus a few new 3-D ones) and the public lapped it up: the film was one of the year's big grossers and probably in commercial terms the most successful horror film yet made. Price's crazed, exultant, sinister 'professor' was exactly right (if not as original as Lionel Atwill in the earlier version) and it ensured that he was offered similar roles. After playing a hired killer in *Dangerous Mission* (54), in 3-D, and Casanova in

Vincent Price was seldom an admirable figure, and in The Las Vegas Story (*52*), *with Jane Russell, he played a big-time embezzler and gambler. It was difficult to know whether he was meant to be funny or sinister.*

Casanova's Big Night, with Bob Hope, he was *The Mad Magician*, also in 3-D, and produced by Brian Foy, who had made *House of Wax*. This was a cheap little programmer, redolent of what was to come.

Around this time he played Buckingham in 'Richard III' at New York City Center and was in a play called 'Black-Eyed Susan': these were his last stage appearances for 14 years, but he was frequently on TV. His films were a weird bunch indeed: *Son of Sinbad* (55) with Dale Robertson, playing a poet called Omar Khayyam; *Serenade* (56) with Mario Lanza, as an opera impresario; *While the City Sleeps*, as a newspaper baron; *The Ten Commandments*, as a whip-wielding slave-driver; and *The Story of Mankind* (57), as the Devil, disputing with Ronald Colman – as the Spirit of Man – as to whether mankind should continue. Colman's arguments included Moses (Francis X. Bushman), Hippocrates (Charles Coburn), Joan of Arc (Hedy Lamarr) and Shakespeare (Reginald Gardiner), while Price summoned up Nero (Peter Lorre), Cleopatra (Virginia Mayo), Josephine (Marie Windsor) and Peter Minuit (Groucho Marx). Someone was joking.

Price loaned little more than his presence to *The Fly* (58), a fairly literate horror film about a scientist (Al Hedison) whose experiments cause a part-mutation into a fly; but despairing perhaps of better roles – he had worked little in recent years – he warmly embraced horror. Learning that his wife plans to murder him, he hires the *House on Haunted Hill* (59) and turns the table on wife and her lover. . . . Producer-director William Castle added a presumed box-office gimmick called 'Emergo', whereby an illuminated skeleton, on wires, moved out over the audience. Price had only a brief role, as a ring-master, in *The Big Circus*; he returned to Horror with *The Bat* starring Agnes Moorehead, *Return of the Fly* and Castle's *The Tingler* (60). Castle's gimmick this time was a device attached to the cinema seat which tingled at opportune moments, but like 'Emergo' few exhibitors were buying.

Among the bankrupt melodramas of the 50s, The Big Circus *(59), would rate a high place. Vincent Price gave it style if not class.*

Price's flamboyant acting was for the most part of little interest; then he gave a fairly arresting performance as Roderick of *The House of Usher*, underplayed and albino. The film was adapted from Edgar Allan Poe by Richard Matheson, photographed by Floyd Crosbie and directed by Roger Corman. Corman was a young man who had been turning out low-budget exploitation films and who here found a new bent for his own resourcefulness. Pleased by its (relative) success, the producers – AIP – allowed Corman (and usually Matheson) to do a series of Poe adaptations and all but one of them (*Premature Burial*) starred Price. Price worked mainly for AIP in the 60s and his salary was probably the biggest single item in their budgets. Most of his other films were equally cheap, done for independents and almost all of them were horror stories. The Corman/Poe films stand apart. There are imperfections (more than a touch of amateurishness, poor performances) but they have a certain resource and imagination.

For instance, Matheson wrote but Corman did not direct *Master of the World* (61), a messy and anachronistic version of two Jules Verne stories. Price loved it because 'it had a marvellous moralising philosophy. . . . A man who sees evil and says "Destroy it" . . . and if it's the whole world, then it's got to go.' Then he did Corman's *The Pit and the Pendulum*, of which the 'MFB' said, 'Only Vincent Price ("This room" – indicating the torture chamber – "was my father's life") has the right kind of scenery-caressing style, a blend of oily solicitude and cissy sadism ideally suited to the orotund dialogue.'

In Italy, he was the villain of both *Gordon il Pirata Nero* with Ricardo Montalban and *Nefertite Regina del Nilo* starring Jeanne Crain. He seemed bored; nor did he have much relish in Albert Zugsmith's *Confessions of an Opium Eater* (62), supposedly as a descendant of Thomas de Quincey in this compendium of old-fashioned Chinese melodrama. His last 'normal' part for some time was in *Convicts Four*, with Ben Gazzara, 'as a highly improbable art-expert' ('MFB'). Then he remade *The Tower of London*, playing Richard III this time, and directed by Corman for a company called Admiral. He and Corman returned to AIP for *Tales of Terror*, four Poe stories made into three episodes, with Peter Lorre and Basil Rathbone, and *The Raven* (63), with Lorre and Boris Karloff. The latter was based only loosely on Poe and gleefully sent up the whole genre. Admiral produced the next two, excruciatingly shabby efforts that must have given even Price cause to pause: *Diary of a Madman*, based on the de Maupassant stories about an evil spirit called The Horla (Price was the man possessed); and *Twice Told Tales*, three episodes based on three stories by Hawthorne, one of which – coming full circle – was a concise 'House of Seven Gables'.

Comedy of Terrors added Joe E. Brown to Price, Lorre, Karloff and Rathbone; *Beach Party* added Price, as Big Daddy, to Frankie Avalon and Annette Funicello; and Corman's *The Haunted Palace* grafted H.P. Lovecraft's 'The Case of Charles Dexter Ward' on to Poe's poem, with Price in a dual role as a warlock and one of his descendants. Corman had virtually mastered the genre – after a fashion – and Price must have felt let down by *L'Ultimo Uomo della Terra/The Last Man on Earth*, which was Matheson's good science-fiction novel ruined by inept handling. But he returned to Corman for the last – and perhaps best – of the Poe series, *The Masque of the Red Death* (64) and *The Tomb of Ligeia* (65), both filmed in Britain. Most of his subsequent films were made in Britain, like *City Under the Sea*, also from Poe, but directed by Jacques Tourneur. *Dr Goldfoot and the Bikini Machine* cast him as a mad scientist (in Britain the *Goldfoot* of the title was shortened to *G* when a doctor of that name complained – not that many heard of the film under either title). There was a sort of sequel, Italian and equally infantile, *Le Spie Vengono dal Semifreddo/Dr Goldfoot and the Girl Bombs* (66), whose real stars were a popular, prolific and unexportable team, Franco Franchi and Ciccio Ingrassia. *Der Haus der Tausend Freuden* (67) was a Spanish-German production set in Tangier, with Price and Martha Hyer as an illusionist act who as a sideline run an expensive brothel with white-slave victims – till investigator George Nader comes on the scene and Price falls to his death.

He made *The Jackals* for 20th, a B remake of *Yellow Sky*, and then in Britain *Witchfinder General* (68), in the title-role, terrorizing the innocent in the aftermath of the Civil War – a tense, eerily atmospheric tale, imaginatively directed by the very young Michael Reeves (who died shortly afterwards from a drug overdose). In the US it was retitled *The Conqueror Worm* and sold, erroneously, as another adaptation of Poe – and without indication that it was Price's best film in 20 years. For a change, he had a sympathetic role in a Clint Walker Western, *More Dead Than Alive*, as a travelling tent showman – and he had a similar part in *The Trouble With Girls* (69), starring Elvis Presley. Then there were three more indifferent British creepies, all directed by Gordon Hassler, *The Oblong Box* (70), *Scream and Scream Again* and *Cry of the Banshee*. He was in an American TV movie, *What's a Nice Girl Like You . . .?* (71), and then, in Britain for AIP was *The Abominable Doctor Phibes*, a wealthy 'musical genius'. It was successful enough to spawn a sequel, *Dr Phibes Rises Again* (72).

Price made no secret of the fact that he made such films for money and would only act for a hefty fee. He acted for the BBC in 'The Heiress' but was not interested when Katharine Hepburn asked him to play Prospero for $500 a week for eight weeks. He was said to be the highest-paid lecturer on art in the US and he served on several national committees, including the Art Committee of the White House. He was art-buyer for Sears Roebuck and has a notable collection of pre-Columbian art. In the 50s he and Edward G. Robinson were pitted as experts on 'The $64,000 Challenge'. He has also published several books, including an autobiography, 'I Like What I Know' (58), and a gourmet cookbook with his wife Mary. They were married in 1949, after his first marriage (1939–48) failed. He also did a TV series on cookery, conceivably one of the most embarrassing in the history of that medium.

He played actors in *Theatre of Blood* (73) and *Madhouse* (74), both made in Britain; in the former he enacted deadly revenge on a 'name' cast and in the latter he and an equally tired Peter Cushing vied via horror tricks for a TV show on Dr Death – a role identified with the Price-character till he became a Hollywood recluse. AIP, who produced, packed it with clips from old AIP-Price movies and the self-parodying masturbatory effect may have been the last straw for Price, who did not make any more horror movies for some years. Following the lead of one-time co-star George Sanders, he played a supporting role in a dim little British sex comedy – *Percy's Progress*, as a Greek oil tycoon who considers taking hero Percy as his heir. Made after *Madhouse*, it appeared first, but neither film was much noticed – nor Price's presence in them. Almost equally unheeded was *Jour-*

ney Into Fear (75), a remake of Orson Welles's old thriller. Price turned away from movies: in 1974 he and his third wife, Coral Browne, revived, unsuccessfully, Anouilh's 'Ardèle' in London; in 1976 he played 'Damn Yankees' in stock and a while later toured in a one-man show on Oscar Wilde, which failed in Manhattan to repeat its provincial welcome. In 1979 the *Percy* film turned up in the US retitled *It's Not the Size That Counts*, but that was just one more soft-porn item in a market surfeited with them. Around the same time he and his wife commenced a four-part film series made for TV, which was entitled 'Time Express'.

He guested at the beginning of a raucous American comedy, as the dying games manufacturer responsible for the *Scavenger Hunt* (79), and as a vampire hosted *The Monster Club* (80), a collection of three horror stories which never made it across the Atlantic – at least to US cinemas. Back in the US he did a cameo as a wino in a Richard Pryor vehicle, *Bustin' Loose*, but the producers decided that he was unrecognizable and left him on the cutting-room floor. He returned to Britain for three: a video *Ruddigore* (82); *House of the Long Shadows* (83), haunting it along with Peter Cushing, Christopher Lee and John Carradine or just upsetting resident Desi Arnaz, probably the sixth and certainly the worst version of *Seven Keys to Baldpate*; and *Bloodbath at the House of Death* (84), as 'Sinister Man' frightening Kenny Everett in this dire spoof, penned by Everett's TV writers. Price was compère again, a decapitated head, in the schlock *From a Whisper to a Scream* (87) and then his film career touched class again, after a period longer than he or anyone could remember, when he supported Bette Davis and Lillian Gish in *The Whales of August*, a role meant originally for John Gielgud. But it was back to the usual with *The Offspring*, despite its claim that it was a horror story with a difference. An ad in the trade press also claimed record takings, but none of the papers concerned has been able to find it to review it. Perhaps Price will be luckier with Dennis Hopper's *Backtrack* (89).

ANTHONY QUINN

Anyone with a penchant for watching 'The Late Late Show' is liable to keep coming across Anthony Quinn in the 50 or so supporting parts he did before attaining stardom. He crops up, sometimes for only a few minutes, as any species of Red Indian or Latin-American and invariably up to no good. There is seldom any indication that he would rise from Mexican bandit to Pope, that he was made of that magic stuffing of which real stars are made – and that, unfortunately, remained the case. He has a certain gift for projecting ox-like virility and strength, but not without some modicum of monotony; he is never as rewarding to watch as, say, Clark Gable, whose actual range was far smaller. It could be argued that movies became much less engaging when actors without star-power took over.

He was born in Chihuahua, Mexico, in 1916, of mixed Irish-US-Mexican descent. The family moved to Los Angeles, where the father was killed in a car accident; because of this, Quinn's upbringing was varied and by his own admission he had little education. He was determined to be an actor, but was turned down by a local drama group because of a speech impediment; he had an operation to cure this (for which he paid over a five-year period). He got a job as a janitor at a drama school and managed to get a role in their 'Hay Fever', which led to parts in other amateur plays. 'Clean Beds' brought him to the attention of John Barrymore, because his role – an ageing drunken actor – was said to resemble that gentleman; as a result he became a junior member of the Barrymore clan. Via a friend he got a walk-on part in a B at Universal, *Parole* (36), as a convict. Then he heard that Cecil B. De Mille was looking for Indians for *The Plainsman*; De Mille gave him a small part and offered a contract. Instead, Quinn signed with Paramount (who distributed De Mille's movies).

Before *The Plainsman* was released, he was briefly seen as a blackmailer in a B, *Partners in Crime*. Afterwards, he had small parts in *Swing High Swing Low* (37), as a Panamanian interested in Carole Lombard; *Waikiki Wedding*, as a native employed by Bing Crosby; and *The Last Train From Madrid*, as a Spaniard in love with Dorothy Lamour. After another B, *Daughter of Shanghai*, he returned to De Mille to play one of Fredric March's French pirates in *The Buccaneer* (38). During its making, he dated De Mille's daughter, Katherine, and married her. The connection did nothing to advance his career and indeed he became a member of Paramount's B stock company, along with Anna May Wong, Lloyd Nolan, Lynne Overman, William Henry, Akim Tamiroff, Mary Carlisle, etc.: *Dangerous to Know*, a version of Edgar Wallace's 'On the Spot'; *Tip Off Girls*; *Hunted Men*; *Bulldog Drummond in Africa* with John Howard; *King of Alcatraz*; and *King of Chinatown* (39). Most of the time he was set-decorational and when he did emerge from the shadows it was to sneer or scoff. He was also villainous in De Mille's *Union Pacific*, after which he returned to Bs: *Island of Lost Men*, a remake of *White Woman*, as a spy – on the 'good' side; *Television Spy*; and *Emergency Squad* (40). He had a bit in *Road to Singapore* and was a gangster in *Parole Fixer*, another B. After playing a Cuban assassin in *The Ghost Breakers*, after Bob Hope, he broke his contact because he disliked being known as 'the son-in-law'. (The marriage lasted till the mid-60s, when he married an Italian girl, the mother of his sons.)

He freelanced: *City for Conquest* at Warners, as Ann Sheridan's dancing partner; *Texas Rangers Ride Again* (41), a Paramount B, with John Howard; and *Blood and Sand* at 20th, as Tyrone Power's friend who sours on him. He spent a year at Warners: *Thieves Fall Out*, as a gangster who cons heir Eddie Albert; *Knockout*, as the promoter of boxer Arthur Kennedy; *Bullets for O'Hara*, a B, as a gangster; *The Perfect Snob* at 20th, as Cornel Wilde's buddy; *They Died With Their Boots On*, as Chief Crazy Horse; and *Larceny Inc* (42), as an ex-con, a really nasty piece of work, who mucks things up for Edward G. Robinson and company. He returned to Paramount to play Dorothy Lamour's chieftain suitor and implacable foe of Hope and Crosby in *Road to Morocco*; then began a two-year stint at 20th: *The Black Swan*, as a one-eyed pirate; the *Ox-Bow Incident* (43), as one of the men – Mexicans – who are lynched; *Guadalcanal Diary*, as the Mexican-born marine; *Buffalo Bill* (44), again as an Indian warrior; *Ladies of Washington*, a B, as a spy in that city; *Roger Touhy Gangster*, another B, as a fellow con of that real-life murderer; *Irish Eyes are Smiling*, as the pal of songwriter Dick Haymes; and *Where Do We Go From Here?* (45), as the Indian who sold Manhattan to the Dutch. At RKO he got two bigger parts, but he was unconvincing in the first of them, as a Chinese, a guerrilla leader, in *China Sky*, with Randolph Scott. He was second-billed, after John Wayne, in *Back to Bataan*, as a Filipino general; but was then off the screen for 18 months before playing a small part, as a Spaniard, in *California* (46), a big Western at Paramount. He was an emir,

Anthony Quinn in one of the myriad movies he was in while just a supporting actor: The Perfect Snob *(41), with Cornel Wilde, a minor 'college' epic.*

the mortal enemy of Douglas Fairbanks Jr as *Sinbad the Sailor* (47), and a Spaniard again, a pianist, in *The Imperfect Lady*, with Ray Milland and Ann Todd.

Quinn's ambitions led him to a deal with Allied Artists for a starring vehicle for himself and his wife, *White Gold*, a true story about an Indian couple who discovered oil and became millionaires; but it was a shoddy film and passed unnoticed. After a featured role as Laraine Day's cousin in *Tycoon*, he decided to try the stage. Sam Wanamaker invited him to New York to star in 'The Gentleman from Athens', which flopped, but he was offered the part of Kowalski in the road company of 'A Streetcar Named Desire'; a year later, when the play was revived at the City Center, the critics took a look at Quinn and were impressed. He also played the uncouth tycoon in 'Born Yesterday' on tour, but after a couple of Broadway failures returned to Hollywood.

It was as if he had never been away: the parts and the films were interchangeable with the earlier ones and the salary for his return film, he said later, was 'peanuts'. This was *The Brave Bulls* (51), Robert Rossen's brave but unsuccessful film about the *corrida*, with Mel Ferrer as a nervy matador and Quinn as his hustling manager. He did *Mask of the Avenger* at Columbia, pitted against John Derek, as an Italian military governor in league with the Austrians, and was then offered a good part by Elia Kazan, who had directed him in 'Streetcar', that of Marlon Brando's eldest brother in *Viva Zapata!* (52). He got good notices, but returned to a series of indifferent action pictures: *The World in His Arms*, as Gregory Peck's rival; *The Brigand*, as a rascally Spanish prince, the foe of Anthony Dexter (his flop follow-up to his unsuccessful *Valentino*); *Against All Flags*, as Errol Flynn's enemy, a pirate captain; and *Seminole* (53), as a leader of that tribe defying Rock Hudson. Meanwhile, he won a Best Supporting Oscar for *Zapata*; it is not an Oscar that invariably leads to stardom and he stayed in featured roles: *Ride Vacquero!* with Robert Taylor, as a savage Mexican bandit; and *East of Sumatra* with Jeff Chandler, as the ruler of a Pacific island. At least he got away from villainy in *Blowing Wild*, as Barbara Stanwyck's husband – murdered by her because she has the hots for pal Gary Cooper.

At that time Ponti and De Laurentiis were making their bid for the international market and they offered Quinn a three-picture deal, starting with *Ulisse/Ulysses* (54) – Kirk Douglas in the title-role and Quinn again as the heavy. Also in Italy, but not under that deal, he did *Donne Probite*, some Italian sentiment about whores with Linda Darnell, Giulietta Masina and Valentina Cortese, and *Cavalleria Rusticana*, a non-operative version of the old melodrama with Mai Britt and Kerima. He returned to Hollywood to play the detective hero of *The Long Wait*, a mediocre thriller from a Mickey Spillane story, and then went back to Italy to fulfil his contract to Ponti and De Laurentiis, first as *Attila Flagello di Dio* (55), scenery-chewing in a humdrum epic that was rescued from well-deserved oblivion by Clive James in the 'Observer' in 1979: 'Some experts place it among the All-Time Bottom Ten, along with *Zarak, Written on the Wind* and *The Swarm*. For admirers of Anthony Quinn, this is perhaps the key film in his oeuvre. In *Zorba the Greek* he is Zorba the Greek, in *Lust for Life* he is Zorba the Frog, but in *Attila the Hun* he is Zorba the Hun. Attila is a rough diamond but he is imbued with energy. "Lissename allayou" he tells the Huns. "This is an arpatoonity to carnker Rome!" . . . More macho than he they don't come. Attired in top-knot, ear-rings, green tights, gold-studded jockstrap and apres-ski boots, he is one stunning hunk of Hun.' The four Italian films had so far been disasters and

Anthony Quinn as Yellowhand in Buffalo Bill *(44). He had dialogue like this: 'Yesterday the buffalo was as many as the leaves of grass upon the earth. Today the buffalo is as few as the leaves of the oak trees in winter'.*

had simply served to make American audiences forget his existence. The fifth, *La Strada*, undid all their evil work. Fellini directed this picaresque tale of three strolling players – Quinn, Richard Basehart and Giulietta Masina – and it was primarily a vehicle for her. For unfathomable reasons, it was a big success everywhere, the 'art' film *par excellence* – and as such won the Best Foreign Film Oscar. Quinn's career got a big boost (any Hollywood actor in such a film *must* be good), even if his bank balance did not – originally on a 25 per cent percentage, he sold out for $12,000 before it began to build.

In Hollywood he could now get star-billing, even if the films were no better than the Italian batch: *The Magnificent Matador*, as Mexico's greatest; *The Naked Street*, as a gang-boss; and *Seven Cities of Gold*, as a Spanish explorer. He got featured billing in *Lust for Life* (56), playing Gauguin to Kirk Douglas's Van Gogh. That brought him a second Best Supporting Oscar, but for the moment no better pictures – though *Man From Del Rio*, a minor Western, is one of his own favourites. There followed three programmers: *The Wild Party*, as a neurotic beast involved with sensation-seeking socialite Carol Ohmart; *The River's Edge* (57), made in Mexico, as a rancher murdered by Ray Milland; and *The Ride Back*, a good offbeat Western, as a murderer. In France he played Quasimodo in *Notre Dame de Paris/The Hunchback of Notre Dame* with Gina Lollobrigida and was considered inferior to both Chaney and Laughton – but coming after his second Oscar it drew some attention to him. He had almost despaired of making it to the top and announced that he was giving up acting for directing; he did direct a remake of *The Buccaneer* (with Yul Brynner) for De Mille, but its failure presumably put paid to that ambition. He also, throughout the next few years, announced prolific plans for independent productions, none of which came off.

But he became at last a star: a star with top-billing in A features. And stardom brought a new image. For 20 years he had been villainous, soft-talking, suave and rather stupid. Now he was elemental – the Earth Father: gusty, lusty, unshaven, loud-talking, arm-waving, slobbery-eating, vigorous. Such he had been in his two biggest successes, *La Strada* and *Lust for Life* (to an extent, at least: in the former he was still the villain, and a rather brutish one; he was of course sympathetic as Gauguin). And such he was in *Wild Is the Wind*, co-starring with Anna Magnani, both as Italian immigrants in this rehash of *They Knew What They Wanted*. He was Shirley Booth's loutish husband in *Hot Spell* (58) and an extrovert Italian-American widower wooing widow Sophia Loren in *The Black Orchid*. There followed three Westerns: *Last Train From Gun Hill* (59), as Kirk Douglas's opponent; the overlong *Warlock*, as Henry Fonda's partner; and *Heller in Pink Tights* (60), as the manager of a troupe of strolling players, which included Sophia Loren. In an attempt to widen his appeal he did a soap opera with Lana Turner, *Portrait in Black*, helping her to kill her husband and then the man they suspect is blackmailing them. One he should not have done was an international effort about Eskimos (for one thing, he was too tall) directed by Nicholas Ray, *Ombre Bianche/The Savage Innocents/Les Dents du Diable*.

In 1960 he returned to Broadway, co-starring with Laurence Olivier in 'Becket' and at some point in the run they exchanged roles; he was not outclassed by the more experienced Olivier. He returned to Europe for three all-name spectacles: *The Guns of Navarone* (61), as a Greek Resistance officer; the Italian *Barabba/Barabbas* for De Laurentiis in the title-role, the thief whose place Christ took on the cross; and *Lawrence of Arabia* (62), as an Arab chief, one of his best performances. The first and third of this trio were enormously successful; the indifferent *Barabbas* was indifferently received. In the US he made one of his own favourite films, *Requiem for a Heavyweight*, as a broken-down ex-pug: he rather overdid the inarticulate bit. He crossed the Atlantic again for another co-production (between France, Italy, Yugoslavia, Egypt and Afghanistan!), *La Fabuleuse Aventure de Marco Polo* (64), as a shaven-headed Kubla Khan to the Marco of Horst Buchholz. Hardly more successful was the more sensible *Behold a Pale Horse*, as an officer of the Guardia Civile out to get Gregory Peck. Another failure was *Der Besuch/The Visit*, as the mayor upon whom Ingrid Bergman revenges herself.

Then came *Zorba the Greek* (65), a minor film backed by 20th and made in Greece by a Cypriot, Michael Cacoyannis, about a shy young Britisher (Alan Bates) who learns what Life is All About from the gusty, lusty (see above) Zorba (quintessential Quinn). As with *La Strada* you either loved it or loathed it (they loathed it in Greece), but there could be no reproach against Quinn, who made the character at least lively. It was a hit on the art circuit and it oddly established Quinn as a superstar – doubly oddly, as the majority of the films he made immediately before and afterwards were among the decade's biggest money-losers. Undoubtedly producers overestimated his box-office pull, but at the same time Quinn must be blamed for accepting

Quintessential Quinn: Anthony Quinn in his most famous role, Zorba the Greek *(65), from the novel by Kazantzakis about a pallid Englishman (Alan Bates) who inherits some land in Greece, and the consequences thereof (mainly Zorba, as it turns out).*

films which, in general, could not have looked good on paper. Still, it was a pity about *A High Wind In Jamaica*, a somewhat misguided version of Richard Hughes's marvellous novel about children's fantasies, with Quinn as a pirate chief.

He was announced for an American remake of Kurosawa's *Sanjuro*, but instead he did *The Lost Command* (66), oddly cast – in this day and age – as a French officer (the film was adapted from 'Les Centurions' by Jean Larteguy). He played a Romanian peasant in Henri Verneuil's *La Vingt-Cinquième Heure/The 25th Hour* (67), a wartime drama with Virna Lisi and Serge Reggiani; in the US, he was a kidnapped bigwig who takes over the gang who have got him, in *The Happening*; for Verneuil, again, he was a Mexican patriot in *La Bataille de San Sebastian/Guns for San Sebastian*. Also that year he made in Italy *L'Avventuriero/The Rover*, with Rita Hayworth, directed by Terence Young from a story by Conrad; it was announced for the San Francisco festival but withheld for 'technical reasons' and it seems to have been withheld from public showings ever since. One would have wished a similar fate for *The Magus* (68), which transformed an intriguing novel into pap cinema – and Quinn was foolish to accept a role which required a combination Olivier/Picasso/Chaplin. No better liked was another expensive version of a bestseller, *The Shoes of the Fisherman*, with Quinn as a Russian peasant who becomes Pope; it was written off by the MGM accounts department (and could have caused red faces in the Vatican, which had offered locations: the triteness of its message was awesome). In 1968 Quinn was one of the nine stars listed by 'Variety' – on the basis of recent box-office receipts – as overpriced.

It was no surprise to find him cast as an Italian in *The Secret of Santa Vittoria* (69), with Anna Magnani, and yet another filmed novel, but the critics were not kind. Said 'Playboy': '. . . the ubiquitous Anthony Quinn, as the drunken mayor . . . acting more Italian than any self-respecting native would dare.' John Coleman in the 'New Statesman': 'Mr Quinn goes on doing his personal impression of the life force. Once more and some of us won't be around tomorrow.' Quinn had usually got good notices, but now the critics turned. Said 'Playboy' of the next: 'Role after role, regardless of the name they give him, Anthony Quinn continues to play Zorba.' Well, in that one, *A Dream of Kings* (70), he at least played a Greek immigrant. He was a Tennessee Zorba in *A Walk in the Spring Rain* with Ingrid Bergman, relentlessly coy as her farmer lover, mad about squirrels and flowers. Neither film stood a chance in the upheavals which shook the film industry at this time and the next two also sank without trace. The first was adapted from a novel called 'Nobody Loves a Drunken Indian' and was, after several title changes during production, finally called *Flap* in the

US and *The Last Warrior* in Britain, but few people heard of it under any title. Said Dilys Powell: 'There is a persistent tendency, when somebody is wanted to play an Eskimo, or a gypsy, or a drunken Italian, or a Mexican, or just another throaty character, to send for Anthony Quinn (he has, in fact, Mexican Indian blood). Okay, but I wish they would not ask me along to watch.' The second was *R.P.M.* (71) and Quinn was a professor. Said 'Time Magazine': 'Anthony Quinn, as usual, yells and mugs a lot.'

It was announced that he was in charge of Four Star Television and several projects with the BBC were announced which came to nothing. He said he planned to direct a movie called *What About Cleopatra?* In the end he did a TV series, 'The Man and the City' (71), which was quickly dropped. A British company announced him for a war film, *Three Men Went to War*, but instead he made a police thriller in New York, *Across 110th Street* (72). There was an Italian Western with Franco Nero, *Los Amigos/Deaf Smith and Johnny Ears* (73), playing an ageing, deaf troubleshooter; during its production Quinn announced a film of *Across the River and Into the Trees* and a biopic of Haiti's Emperor Henri-Christophe, with himself in that role, to be called *Black Majesty* and directed by Brando. Instead, he played a 'godfather' in *The Don is Dead*, which proved only that both Mafia movies and Quinn were dead at the US box-office. (The film has since been rechristened *Beautiful but Deadly*.) In France he was an American embassy official who employs hit-man Michael Caine to kill James Mason: the film was called *The Marseille Contract* (74). In Italy he was conman and patriarch in two period pieces, comedy and drama respectively, *Bluff: Storia de Truffe e di Imbroglioni* (76) and Mauro Bolognini's quietly splendid *Eredita Ferramonti*. For the Arab world (the piece had Lebanon nationality and was filmed in Libya after expulsion from Morocco) he was a famous Moslem leader at the time of Mohammad in *Al-Risalah/The Message (Mohammad Messenger of God)*, a fair-sized epic. Like the Italian films, Quinn's name was no help in getting US bookings and, failing a distributor, the producers opened it there themselves – to scant interest; in London the tourists kept it running awhile. Quinn moved South, for a South African film, *Tigers Don't Cry* (77), for which Warners had world rights outside the US; but they withdrew during shooting (over the casting of the female lead) and no one else seems to have picked them up. He donned burnous again to play a judge in the TV *Jesus of Nazareth/Gezu di Nazaret*, singled out with Rod Steiger in the otherwise rave review in the London 'Daily Telegraph' for 'the bathos of their performances.

That apart, Quinn was virtually a new face to young American cinemagoers when he played *The Greek Tycoon* (78), a fictionalized, opportunist account of the Onassis-Jackie Kennedy (Jacqueline Bisset) marriage which Universal bought for the US – and if publicity meant success, this would have been the year's biggest film: but after a good start, business fell away. This was a project Quinn has talked about for years (since he had apparently promised Onassis he would play him in the film) and so was *The Children of Sanchez*, i.e. in 1973, 'I, as a Mexican, feel bad about the pictures that are made there.' This was made there. *Caravans* was made in the Middle East, being Persia's biggest onslaught yet on the world markets; its source was a novel by James A. Michener and Quinn was an Arab chieftain. The burnous was replaced by beret for *The Passage* (79), as a Basque shepherd who helps professor James Mason escape the Nazis, but returned for another epic for the team which made *The Message*, called *Omar Mukhtar Lion of the Desert* (81), at $30 million one of the most expensive films ever made – but it took only $1½ million at the US box-office. Franco Nero, Claudia Cardinale and Martin Balsam were among other names in *The Salamander*, based on Morris West's novel about a coup d'état, but Universal, who had first call on this Italian-US-British co-production, did not want it and it went direct to HBO. Quinn did a cameo as a revolutionary bandit leader in a mindless action movie, *High Risk*, and should then have started *Tai-Pan*, one of the most off-on projects in the history of the cinema. It was to have been an Italian-Yugoslav co-production financed by two French banks – and $10 million had been spent when it was cancelled. John Guillerman was to have directed and Roger Moore to have played the lead: he had not signed the contract but Quinn had. Quinn did *Regina* (82) in Italy with Ava Gardner and in Spain he was the village priest in both *Valentina* and its sequel, *1919* (83).

In 1983 he was conscripted to play in 'Zorba', a revival of the musical based on the film (along with Lila Kedrova, who had also been in it). His fee was $25,000 a week plus 10 per cent of all receipts over $250,000. He was still touring in it in 1986 when Cannon announced a film version, to be directed by Robert Wise, but nothing further has been heard of this. Instead, Quinn went to Italy to play Long John Silver in a sci-fi mini-series, *L'Isola del Tesoro* (87), and he stayed there to star in *Stradivari* (88), whose cast included several of his family. For television he was, appropriately, the father of *Onassis: The*

Richest Man in the World, rejecting him (Elias Koteas; Raul Julia took over for the older Onassis) for having an affair with a Turkish officer. *Mi Abuelo y Yo* found him as a Bohemian artist and then he was in *The Actor* (89), after which he was scheduled to be in *The Old Man and the Sea* for television and to tour the university circuit in a one-man show on Picasso.

Raimu

Arletty: 'Le plus grand comédien de tous les temps.' Marlene Dietrich: 'In my book, the greatest actor.' Zero Mostel: 'For me, the greatest actor in history was Raimu.' Orson Welles: 'He was the greatest actor in the world.' No younger actor today – or filmgoer or professional critic – would dare be so certain, for the films of Raimu are not revived, except those he made with Pagnol – and then to remind us more of an era than an art. 'Marcel Pagnol, Raimu: les deux hommes sans qui le cinéma français, pour la période de son installation dans le "parlant" n'aurait pas été ce qu'il fut' (Jeanne and Ford). The films of Marcel Pagnol are intellectual folk-art, metropolitan memories of a rural past. Pagnol's two great parts for Raimu (le boulanger, César) – though they were in fact the same person – were indeed beautifully played by the actor: earthy middle-aged Provençeaux, with their pride, their poverty, their truculence, their human failings. Or, as Pierre Leprohon similarly put it in his excellent monograph on Raimu: 'Sous la plume de Pagnol, César, c'est l'homme – tout entier avec sa bonhomie, sa vérité, ses feintes, ses colères, sa tendresse, sa mesure, son tact, son émotion, sa force – c'est l'homme.'

He was born Joseph Muraire (Raimu was devised from 'Muraire') in Toulon in 1883, the son of a shopkeeper. As a child he was difficult and overbearing, and troublesome at school. His motive was to be noticed and he made a start as an amateur performer, singing the songs of Polin. At 15, his father died and he felt free to go on the stage; he made his professional début at the Casino de Toulon in the winter of 1899/1900. The manager there gave him a part in a play; then he moved to Marseilles and worked as prompter at the Alhambra. He joined a touring British mime troupe and formed a double-act for a while. In 1902 he was in a revue in Grenoble, but in 1905 was working as a croupier, after which he joined his brother in his salt business. But a slight reputation had accrued and Félix Mayol, a well-known singer and also from the Midi, opened a café-concert in Paris and engaged him. He was an instantaneous success; Sacha Guitry, among others, advised him to try the legitimate stage – but he was as yet content. Between 1912 and 1914 he made a couple of films, *L'Homme Nu* and *L'Agence Cacahuete*, but the elementary slapstick did not appeal to him. After war service – he was invalided out after a year – Rip engaged him for a revue, 'Plus ça Change!' (15), and then he did a revue partly written by Guitry. He made his legit bow when Feydeau chose him for a revival of 'Monsieur Chasse' (16); he starred with Guitry in 'Faisons un Rêve' and with Yvonne Printemps in an operette, 'Le Poilu' (17). His first great hit was 'L'École des Cocottes' in 1918, followed by a succession of revues, operettes and comedies, including 'Un Homme en Habit' (20), 'Le Blanc et le Noir' (22), 'Edith de Nantes' (23), 'La Huitième Femme de Barbe-Bleue', 'La Flambée' (24) and 'Vive L'Empereur' (26). Despite his popularity and the critical acclaim he was never invited to work for any of the great actor-managers of the time.

In fact, his first serious part was in Pagnol's 'Marius' (29), a play about a sea-struck barman who hesitates when he realizes that a local girl, Fanny, loves him. Pagnol wanted him to play Panisse, the girl's middle-aged suitor, but he preferred to play César, the boy's father – provided the part was built up. Charpin played Panisse and Pierre Fresnay the title-role; the play, considerably more 'realistic' than was customary in Paris, was a huge success – and there were offers to film it from a French industry about to move into talking pictures. Meanwhile, Roger Richebé and Pierre Braunberger asked Raimu to appear in *Chotard et Compagnie* (done by Charpin on the stage), to be directed by Robert Florey, recently returned from Hollywood. Florey realized that Raimu was not really enthusiastic and asked him what he wanted to do. Raimu chose *Le Blanc et le Noir* (31), the Guitry play he had done some years before; most of the cast was reassembled, plus Fernandel. It was little more than a filmed play – a comedy about infidelity. (*Chotard* was later filmed by Renoir with Charpin.) Before it was premièred Raimu began work on *Mam'zelle Nitouche*, as the convent organist who secretly writes songs.

Then came the film of *Marius*, backed by Paramount, whose European head of production (Alexander Korda) directed it with Charpin, Fresnay and, as Fanny, Orane Demazis. French critics (wrongly, for it looks very fresh today) found it stagey, but it was enormously popular – even abroad (though not in Britain or the US, where it was banned on moral grounds till 1949; a version without subtitles was, however, shown in New York in 1933).

It had a success which, being on film, was physically beyond that of a stage play, a revelation that delighted Raimu; further he was impressed with the possibilities that a camera offered an actor: 'En ce qui me concerne, les possibilités que me fournit le cinéma sont incomparablement plus vastes. Car un artiste, à mon avis, n'a de réelle valeur que par la mobilité de ses traits et surtout par l'expression des yeux.' There is no question that he had a marvellous instinct for film acting. He virtually abandoned the theatre – at the time he should have been in a sequel to 'Marius' called 'Fanny', but was replaced by an even greater actor, Harry Baur, when he failed to show for a rehearsal. His professional life was fraught with dissension – at least, as long as he was surrounded by colleagues equally stubborn; as the years went by he worked increasingly with directors who were docile and obedient. One of the reasons he made few good films was that he insisted on being the boss; he considered that he had learnt all there was to know about timing a laugh or making effective an expression and would have no truck with anyone who might, literally, cut. Most of his films were, deliber-

Raimu (left) in the first of the Pagnol trilogy, Marius *(31), a study of some people in and around a quayside bar in Marseilles. Raimu was César, the proprietor, and Charpin was Panisse, old* copain *and fellow card-player.*

Another scene from Marius. *Alida Rouffe played Honorine, the mother of the unfortunate Fanny (Orane Demazis). Fanny loves the feckless Marius (Pierre Fresnay) but is courted by the wealthy – if middle-aged – Panisse. Honorine discusses the situation with César.*

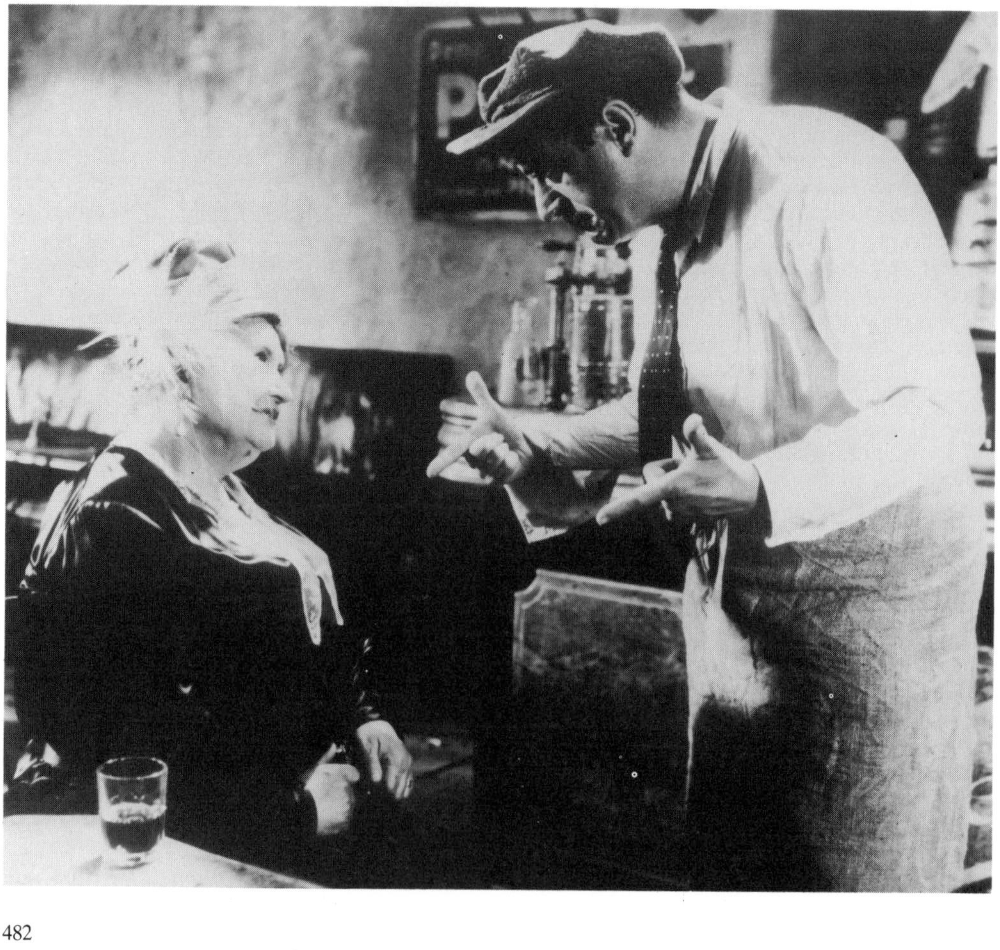

ately, filmed plays. None of them as such was as important as his performance, nothing was allowed to obscure the glory of his acting. Few actors so tyrannized it on set: he was authoritarian, petty, obstinate; his fits of temper were legendary.

Marc Allégret directed him in a light comedy which he had done on stage, *La Petite Chocolatière* (32), and Maurice Tourneur in *Les Gaités de l'Escadron*, an army comedy where he was Captain Hurluret, hypocritical, huge, bibulous, vain and bombastic. The creation was loved as much as praised and the film a great popular success (the print at the première was hand-coloured). Then Allégret directed *Fanny*, in which he played César again. This was in fact one of his serious roles: most of his films were as frivolous as the plays he had done. There were: *Theodore et Cie* (33), a heavy piece notable only for his *tour de force* as a corrupt businessman who has seven different disguises; *Charlemagne*, as the stoker of a private yacht who becomes temporary ruler of a desert island, with Marie Glory as his queen; *Ces Messieurs de la Santé* (34), which he had done on the stage, as an unscrupulous banker, with Edwige Feuillère; *Tartarin de Tarascon*, a charmless version of the Alphonse Daudet novel, scripted by Pagnol, about a chronic boaster who tries to make good his claims of big-game hunting; *J'ai une Idée*, based on an English farce and film, *Tons of Money*; and *Minuit Place Pigalle* (35), based on a novel by Maurice Dekobra, with Ginette Leclerc. He filmed two of the plays he had done, *Faisons un Rêve*, directed by Guitry, with Jacqueline Delubac, and *L'École des Cocottes*, as a lecherous old man; and then did the serious *Gaspard de Besse*, with Berval in the title-role, a drama about the oppression of the peasants and the coming of the Revolution.

There were yet two more versions of stage successes, *Le Secret de Polichinelle* (36), with Françoise Rosay, and *Le Roi*, a popular farce, with Raimu as a wily politician who extends to a visiting king (Victor Francen) such local amenities as wife Gaby Morlay and mistress Elvire Popesco. The French cinema as a whole had been obsessed by words and resigned to triviality since the advent of Talkies, but around this time there was a move towards something more adventurous. Raimu benefited with a comparatively subtle comedy, *Les Jumeaux de Brighton*, playing both twins and their father. Then he played *César* again, with Pagnol turned director for this last of his trilogy, taking place 20 years later, with Fanny widowed and reunited with Marius – but it was a contrived effort compared to the other two. That was the top box-office film of the year and *Le Roi* was third; but Raimu was only 10th among the male stars (followed by Jean Gabin). Also in 1936 he married. He made seven films the following year: *Vous n'avez Rien à Déclarer?* (37), as an eccentric entomologist; Guitry's *Les Perles de la Couronne*, the only one of the many names in the cast billed with Guitry above the title, but in a very brief role as the Marseilles industrialist who buys one of the pearls for his unfaithful wife; *La Chaste Suzanne* (filmed in Britain, at Ealing), repeating another stage role, a hypocritical and debauched professor; *Les Rois du Sport*, as a waiter who becomes a *champion du boxe*, with Jules Berry and Fernandel – and popular because of this teaming; and *Le Fauteuil 47*, from a comedy by Louis Verneuil that he had done on stage, as an instructor of *gymnastique* who is the father of the daughter of actress Françoise Rosay. The other two were well above average: *Gribouille*, as the kindly jury-man who ensures the Michèle Morgan is acquitted of murdering her elderly protector, but finds that in sheltering her with his family the problems come from all sides: and *Un Carnet de Bal*, in the episode about the village mayor who marries his maid.

Conversely, *Les Héros de la Marne* (38) was one of his worst films, as he suffered the afflictions of Job – as a French patriot who joins up with his three sons. Better was *L'Etrange Monsieur Victor*, made by UFA in Berlin – among the best works of Jean Grémillon, one of Raimu's few distinguished directors. In it he was a happily married businessman with a guilty past and the cast included Pierre Blanchar, Madeleine Renaud and Viviane Romance: it was a big success. He and Michel Simon were *Les Nouveaux Riches*, lottery-winners, in this mediocre comedy with Betty Stockfield. Then came the famous baker, with Ginette Leclerc as the young, unfaithful wife: *La Femme du Boulanger*, adapted from a Jean Giono story by Pagnol, who directed (and who announced that he had signed Raimu to a four-year deal). *Noix de Coco* (39) was something else that Raimu had done on stage (in 1935, his only stage appearance since 1931), a boulevard comedy by Marcel Archard about a wealthy horticulturist who discovers his wife had once been a saloon singer – Marie Bell in the title-role. It was filmed in Berlin in the shadow of Munich. Then he was in another familiar role – cuckolded husband – *Monsieur Brotonneau*, a banker whose wife has fallen for a subordinate. Pagnol wrote it. *Dernière Jeunesse* was written and directed by Jeff Musso from a novel by Liam O'Flaherty and filmed in Rome – but emerged very French: the story of a wealthy ex-colonial who picks up a stray (Jacqueline Delubac), worships her and

Raimu in another film he made for Pagnol, La Femme du Boulanger *(39), again a study of Provençal life – and in particular the loving, cuckolded husband. With, on the right, Odette Roger.*

strangles her when she is unfaithful. He was in the first French film started after the declaration of war: *L'Homme qui Cherche la Vérité* (40), a drama about a wealthy banker who pretends to be deaf and dumb to test his family.

When the Germans invaded, he retired to his home at Bandol and most of his wartime films were made in Nice or Marseilles or on location in Provence – which pleased him, because he had always considered himself merely a visitor in Paris. He played the picturesque uncle in *Untel Père et Fils* (not shown till 1945) and then the well-digger who disowns his daughter when she becomes pregnant in Pagnol's *La Fille du Puisatier*, the filming of which was interrupted by the war – and when finally finished and shown in 1942 it suffered from the necessary modifications. Also shown in 1942 was *Le Duel*, begun before the war, directed by Pierre Fresnay with himself, Raimu and Yvonne Printemps. (A casualty of the war was *La Rue de la Gaieté*, which René Clair was writing for him and Michèle Morgan.) The only new project he undertook in a while was *Parade en Sept Nuits* (41), with Micheline Presle and Jean-Louis Barrault, as a curé.

Raimu's last film for Pagnol was La Fille du Puisatier *(42), the story of a well-digger and what happens when his daughter (Josette Day) is seduced by the son of a local shopkeeper.*

Meanwhile, in Paris the Germans had started a French film company, Continentale, under a man called Grevin, who was particularly anxious to have Raimu in one of his films. He agreed to do *Les Inconnus dans la Maison* (42), which was neither Germanic nor propaganda, but a good film about a drunken lawyer defending his daughter's lover and uncovering the real murderer. Henri-Georges Clouzot wrote as if to demonstrate every facet of Raimu's art, using as source a novel by Simenon (and it as heavy with atmosphere as all good films from Simenon). He did another adaptation of Daudet, *L'Arlésienne*, as the patron Marc, with Gaby Morlay. As a result of the success of *Les Inconnus*, Grevin insisted on three more films, but Raimu's secretary (and later, biographer) Paul Olivier managed within 48 hours to get him signed for three others which would prevent that: *Monsieur la Souris*, again from a Simenon story, as an innocent hobo involved in a murder hunt (the British remade it, as *Midnight Episode* with Stanley Holloway); and *Le Bienfaiteur*, as a philanthropist who doubled as a gang-leader. Before making the third, he made *Les Petits Riens*, in a sketch about an old man marrying his young secretary, and played in a revival of 'Fanny' in Paris, for the first time on stage. The third film was based on a novel by Balzac, *Le Colonel Chabert* (43), about a man who returns having long been believed dead. Jacques Becker was to have directed, but after a conflict on interpretation he suggested Raimu test; an incensed Raimu countered that Becker should test for him. The film was eventually directed by someone called René le Hénaff.

Continentale were clamouring for him to begin a film for them in January 1944 and he signed for them exclusively; he was due to appear in *L'Affaire des Poisons*, but fell ill just before shooting. Then – rather to his surprise – he was invited to join the Comédie-Française. He played in 'Le Bourgeois Gentilhomme', 'Le Malade Imaginaire' and a weak modern comedy, 'L'Anglais tel qu'on le Parle' (in 1945). The accolade was not an unmixed blessing for all concerned: his acting conflicted with the atrophied style of the *pensionnaires* and his temper made life very difficult for them. Meanwhile, he made the undistinguished *Les Gueux au Paradis* (46), written by André Obey, in which he and Fernandel were saints with Provençal accents – St Anthony and St Nicholas respectively. Then, when offered another film he renounced his role in 'Le Voyage de M. Perrichon'. The film was *L'Homme au Chapeau Rond*, directed by Pierre Billon from 'L'Eternal Mari' by Dostoevsky, a morbid study of an alcoholic widower bent on revenge against the man who cuckolded him. Jean Queval thought him 'admirable' but not Russian – 'et tous ses efforts pour échapper à la Canebière tendent, au plus, à le faire ressembler à Winston Churchill. Sans cette erreur de latitude, il serait parfait.'

In March 1946 he was involved in a car accident which left him weak and he was unable, six months later, to start *Monsieur Ramatuelle* (it was never made). He did not survive an operation a while after that. Earlier that year (January) L'Institut Français d'Opinion Publique had named him as the most popular star in France (followed by Fernandel, Louis Jouvet and Pierre Blanchar at second place, Jean Gabin and Danielle Darrieux at third place and Jean-Louis Barrault, Gaby Morlay, Edwige Feuillère and Charles Chaplin at fourth place). René Clair had another film for him, *Le Silence est d'Or*: the part was played by Maurice Chevalier.

Robert Redford

The shake-up of the old star-system at the end of the 60s had the curious effect of throwing up a handful of stars – all men – who were probably more powerful and more popular than any who had gone before; and if they were not so much idolized and loved as the Gables and Coopers it was perhaps because those elements had escaped from fan worship. The three big ones were Paul Newman, Steve McQueen and Clint Eastwood; hovering just below were a few others, including Robert Redford – and it was his own fault (he chose badly) that he was not top of the heap. In time he succeeded, the latest dream man in a line which starts with Gregory Peck. Of course the Gables and Coopers made the ladies in the audience dream, but they could also act. Now, Redford can act: he is a nice guy to have around – amused, modest, intuitive, intelligent, helpful – but then so are the star-heroes of most TV series and TV movies. Since Redford has never been more than moderately interesting and yet for a long time was probably the most sought-after star of all, we cannot be blamed for feeling that his face is his fortune.

He was born in Santa Monica, California, in 1937 and went to high school in Van Nuys. He went on to the University of Colorado on a baseball scholarship, but dropped out with the intention of discovering Europe. To pay for his trip he worked in the LA oil-fields. He spent a year in Europe, mainly in Paris. He married in 1958 and began to study acting, at the AADA. He was still there when he got an agent and a small part in 'Tall Story' (59) on Broadway, followed by increasingly good roles in 'The Highest Tree', 'Little Moon of Alban' (60) and 'Sunday in New York'. He chose to make his movie début in a low-budget (it was shot in 15 days) independent movie made by Terry and Dennis Sanders, who had made their name with a short fiction piece set during the Civil War, *Time out of War*. Thereafter they had little luck in films and *War Hunt* (62) was no happier. It was again an anti-war piece, about tensions in a front-line unit in Korea – but in the end all it seemed to amount to was a struggle between the good Redford and the neurotic John

Robert Redford and Jane Fonda in Barefoot in the Park (67). *The comedy ran downhill, but the first part was good, with Fonda unabashedly enjoying being newly wed and thereby somewhat embarrassing her more reticent husband.*

Butch Cassidy and the Sundance Kid (69). *Paul Newman was Cassidy and Redford was the Kid. Katherine Ross was the girl they both love (cf.* Jules et Jim) *and cart around from the West to Bolivia, as they go about their business of bank-robbing.*

Saxon for the affections of the unit mascot, a Korean boy. Redford was notable, digging beneath his blond looks to mine into the nature of goodness itself.

The film did nothing for him. He first came to prominence in the lead of the Broadway 'Barefoot in the Park' (63) opposite Elizabeth Ashley and that led to two films: *Situation Hopeless But Not Serious* (65), as an American GI hidden away in a German cellar by Alec Guinness; and *Inside Daisy Clover* (66), as a Hollywood star who runs out on Natalie Wood on their wedding-night because he is gay. He was offered the role that Brando played in *The Chase*, but instead chose to do the role of the convict on the run. Then he chose to play a Southern railroad boss in *This Property Is Condemned*, opposite Wood, and directed by Sidney Pollack, who had been in *War Hunt*. They were all flops. He was offered one certain hit, by its director, Mike Nichols, who had directed him on stage; this was *Who's Afraid of Virginia Woolf?*, but he refused it because he did not like the play (he said, 'They said, don't you want to film with the Burtons?' – but he thought the film bad and them bad in it). Instead, he went to Spain, to relax. He said later, 'I don't like working a lot and I don't respect the profession, the business of being a star. All through my career people have been telling me, "In three years you're going to be the biggest star in Hollywood." I've got all these plaques naming me the star of tomorrow. But I never did believe it.'

On returning to the US he was surprised to find himself offered his stage role in the film of *Barefoot in the Park* (67), this time opposite Jane Fonda. They were terrific and funny together as a young married couple and the film was a big success. Then he turned down *The Graduate*, because he thought himself unsuitable, and *Rosemary's Baby*. He signed to make a Western at Paramount, *Blue*, but one week before shooting changed his mind. Paramount sued and he sued them. He was penniless and for a long while jobless. With only one success among his credits he was considered a risk. However, Paul Newman wanted a partner for *Butch Cassidy and the Sundance Kid* (69), a sidekick and rival – a sort of cool, straight, Western version of the old Crosby-Hope relationship. Up before him had been Brando, Steve McQueen, Warren Beatty. But Redford was ideal, sardonic and playful. He got great notices and in Britain was voted by their Film Academy the year's Best Actor; co-star Katherine Ross was the Best Actress among an unaccountable nine awards given to this overlong adventure. Still, with some reason, it was a huge success; and Redford was elected superstar. Unfortunately, the next two failed: *Tell Them Willy Boy Is Here*, as a sheriff relentlessly after a renegade Indian in this cold drama, directed by Abraham Polonsky (his first since he was blacklisted); and *The Downhill Racer*, directed by Michael Ritchie, as a laconic ski champion. He had persuaded Paramount to back it at the time of their dispute and among films about sport it was distinguished; but the public was not interested enough in the subject to go to it.

He made another film about sport, *Fauss and Big Halsey* (71) – this time about motorcycling with Michael J. Pollard – but that proved to be something else which did not turn the public on. Then with George Segal he appeared in *The Hot Rock* (72), a 'caper' thriller which on TV is indistinguishable from any 'Kojak', 'Starsky and Hutch', etc., except for its undynamic lead – Redford, who seemed to think that by looking bright and wearing his hair long he could pass for a master-crook. He made a similar mistake as a mountain man in Pollack's *Jeremiah Johnson*: he was not a natural man of the West and since this study of same – from novice to figure of legend – had little else to offer, it was, well, no *Shane*. It was pretty, though, and his fee was $5500,000 plus a percentage. Harvard Lampoon's Kirk Douglas Award for the year's Worst Actor went to him in *The Candidate*, but, released between the two, it was by far the best of his three performances that year: he was a Kennedy-like candidate for the Senate and the film was one of director Ritchie's always-lively looks at contemporary America. Pollack's *The Way We Were* (73) looked at America's recent past, following Redford from college jock to naval officer to Hollywood writer, and through marriage and divorce to Barbra Streisand: but since they were clearly mismatched in the first place, their split-up had, to say the least, its longueurs. *The Sting* went even further back, to (the Chicago of) the 30s, and the script in this case was a real bummer: but the co-star (Newman) and director (George Roy Hill) of *Butch Cassidy* were on hand to help it towards a certain lightness. The public, anyway, again found the Newman-Redford team – as con-men – irresistible and since both films were popular Redford moved into the box-office 10 at No. 5. Since Redford moved up to the No. 1 spot in the following year, and retained it in the two years that followed, it may have been unwise of Warren Beatty to have turned down both roles; he also turned down *The Great Gatsby* (74), which almost certainly Jack Nicholson should have played (and could have; but he said later that Redford's crowd wanted it so badly for him that he let it go). Redford lacked the slightly raffish, slightly sinister quality which Scott Fitzgerald's enigmatic hero needs, though he was quite touching in his gallantry and his pursuit of Daisy (Mia Farrow). The film was overstuffed and overlong, and when the public failed to turn up in the expected numbers, the pre-première ballyhoo was blamed.

Redford stayed in the 20s for *The Great Waldo Pepper* (75), a tale of daredevil stunt pilots, directed by Hill, which offered undemanding and mechanical entertainment as a price for perfecting the Redford image – gently, self-mockingly daring and romantic: he was genuinely the golden boy by this time, seemingly apologetic, as if aware that the times demanded a younger and more swinging 'superstar'. His salary had gone from $1,200,000 plus a percentage for *The Way We Were* via a mere $250,000 for *Gatsby* to a reputed $1½ million for *The Three Days of the Condor*, directed by Pollack, a CIA thriller in which he was the hunted man and his second unnecessary film that year. But then he really came up with something: he bought (for

Robert Redford in The Sting (73). *Note the tousled hair, the tilt of the hat, the glimpse of what Americans call suspenders and the British braces:* très à la mode *in several Redford movies and the sort of thing which gives a star his 'image'.*

$425,000) the film-rights to and produced *All the President's Men* (76), playing with Dustin Hoffman the two 'Washington Post' journalists who helped to break the Watergate affair. Since he was playing a living man, his nice, hesitant, customary performance was more appropriate than usual and the film, as directed by Alan J. Pakula, was absorbing from start to finish. So it should have been, given the subject, but it was also Hollywood's most intelligent film in many a long year: thus, since press and public endorsed Redford's urge to bring the book to the screen, this must be his finest hour.

Financially, he may never do better than *A Bridge Too Far* (77), since Joseph E. Levine paid him $2 million for four weeks' work; according to Levine when selling territory rights pre-production, the Japanese were talking of that sum and insisting on Redford – so from his point of view the deal was a sound one. Redford's view was that if Levine were foolish enough to offer it. . . . The public's view was that huge salaries and a bevy of star names do not a masterpiece make: as a commando, this particular star got lost and the public that initially went to the film let the word out: a clinker is a clinker. However, since producers seeking investor-distributors the world over need the few stars of Redford's clout as come-on, he was worth every cent: but when another such upped with a $2 million plus a percentage for the title-role in *Superman* he declined – because, he said, the script was 'inept'. (Other roles he turned down at this time include *Kramer vs. Kramer*.) Despite his one duff film, he stayed in the box-office 10 in 1977, at No. 5; but stayed off the screen for two years, before returning in Pollack's *The Electric Horseman* (79), as a has-been cowboy exploited by Jane Fonda, and *Brubaker* (80) – which was to have been directed by Bob Rafaelson, but he left not long after shooting began and was replaced by Stuart Rosenberg. Redford himself was at his best as a humane prison governor fighting the system. He himself directed – but did not appear in – *Ordinary People*, with Mary Tyler Moore and Donald Sutherland as the parents with problems, including themselves; this was a family drama which never delved beneath the surface (though it thought it did) and yet won a Best Picture Oscar and another for the direction. Redford was to have been directed in *The Verdict* by Arthur Hiller, but Sidney Lumet took over when Redford was sacked after two days' work (he was to have been paid $2 million). He wanted the script changed to suit his personality, but producers Zanuck-Brown disagreed. The incident bears out a comment made by Arthur Laurents, who wrote *The Way We Were*: 'Redford doesn't want to be an actor but a film-star.' This is also apparent from Redford's screen wardrobe, perhaps the most lavishly designed and inappropriate since Joan Crawford's: what he wears in all his period movies, though vaguely correct, is exactly what is the 'in' gear at fashionable boutiques. This was true again of *The Natural* (84), in which he is a baseball champ of the 1930s, as based on Bernard Malamud's novel, so rearranged (and much of its point destroyed) as to make a star vehicle. It was the first production of Tri-Star, the company formed by Columbia, CBS and HBO.

Curiously, Sydney Pollack saw in Denys Finch Hatton – Karen Blixen's lover – a role for Redford, who physically and in every other way is the antithesis of the Oxford-educated *bon vivant*. Meryl Streep played Blixen and both stars did their shtick, which was to blandly exchange amorous remarks, out-acted by Klaus-Maria Brandauer as Blixen's husband. Redford's fee was a reported $3 million of a $30 million budget, which was justified by the box-office and seven Oscars, including Best Picture: *Out of Africa* (85). He and Deborah Winger were the *Legal Eagles* (86), fighting over the accused (Darryl Hannah) and falling in love, in both cases behaving more like spoilt children than top lawyers in this efficient thriller. The domestic take of over $27, against a cost of $38 million, proves the drawing power of the stars and makes probable (since the budget could not be discerned from the screen) the claim in 'Los Angeles Magazine' that Redford was paid $6.5 million. He then turned his back on such worldly matters, to direct and produce a tale of Hispano-Americans fighting land developers in *The Milagro Beanfield War* (88), but with a starless cast it cost $18 million, of which just over a third was recovered from the domestic box-office.

Lynn Redgrave

It looked for a while as if the younger Redgrave, Lynn, would spend her career in the shadow of Vanessa. There was such acclaim for Vanessa. Then Lynn bounded forth with a fine comic performance in *Georgy Girl*, acting in such a different style that no comparisons were made. She will probably leave the big romantic stuff to Vanessa. She will – hopefully – make us laugh.

She was born in London in 1943 and was, she has said, so mad on horses that she never expected to make the stage her career; but she did study at the Central School of Music and Drama. With her famous name, she had little difficulty in getting jobs – and was Hermia in 'A Midsummer Night's Dream' (62) at the Royal Court. Then: Dundee rep, in plays like 'The Merchant of Venice' and 'Rookery Nook'; a tour of 'Billy Liar' and 'The Tulip Tree' in the West End. Her film début was no more spectacular, being a brief role as a serving wench (screaming 'Rape') in *Tom Jones* (63), directed by her brother-in-law Tony Richardson. For the same company she played Rita Tushingham's chum in *Girl With Green Eyes* (64) and was very funny, with her eager smile for men, her hair-primping, her self-confidence and a greedy use of all the latest slang. She did a season at the National Theatre, playing among other parts Jackie in 'Hay Fever' and Miss Prue in 'Love for Love'. Screen success came when Vanessa at the last minute turned down *Georgy Girl* (66) and she, by coincidence, stepped in. A modern variant on some old themes ('The Ugly Duckling', 'Daddy Long Legs'), it still provided a honey of a part, that of a pudgy, good-natured also-ran – the sort of girl who is left holding the baby (and here, literally, is). Redgrave was touching and deliciously funny. The film was a success in Britain and it ended up (and it had not cost very much) among the top 10 money-makers in the US; it also netted her a Best Actress citation from the New York critics (shared with Elizabeth Taylor). She accepted in person, as she was appearing on Broadway in 'Black Comedy'.

She had done an amusing cameo, as an eager young actress, in *The Deadly Affair*; then she co-starred with pal Tushingham in a vapid tale about two Northern girls in Swinging London, *Smashing Time* (67). She married John Clark (a former English child actor who had subsequently made a career in North America) in 1966 and became pregnant just as she was about to start *Hot Millions* (Maggie Smith did it). She had been much in demand, but after the baby was born she did not film till *The Virgin Soldiers* (69), as the RSM's daughter in this dead-accurate comedy about conscripts in Singapore, from a novel by Leslie Thomas. The film was a huge success in Britain, but was apparently much more parochial that *Georgy Girl*, for it attracted little attention in the US. Redgrave went there to appear in *Blood Kin*, an adaptation of Tennessee Williams's 'The Seven Descents of Myrtle', directed by Sidney Lumet; she played a slobby semi-whore who married an impoverished Southerner (James Coburn), with consequent melodramatics. The film was poorly received and did business to match. On the stage, in London, Redgrave appeared in 'The Two of Us' and after another absence made three films – and it must be assumed that the first of these she did because there were no better offers: a Spanish-German-Italian Western *Viva la Muerte . . . et Tua* (72), with Franco Nero and Eli Wallach, which turned up in the US two years later as *Don't Turn the Other Cheek*. The others were made in Hollywood: *Every Little Crook and Nanny*, an unfunny comedy about kidnapping, with Victor Mature; and Woody Allen's *Everything You Always Wanted to Know About Sex, But Were Afraid to Ask*, in a chastity belt in one of the sketches. Clearly she needed a good film, and a British comedy, *The National Health* (73) went a way in that direction: based on Peter Nichols's National Theatre play, it juxtaposed hospital reality with soap-opera parody – a sort of adult *Carry On*. Redgrave was splendid as a nurse, but her role was small – a pity, since she and Jim Dale would have made a fine team.

Alan Bates and Lynn Redgrave in Georgy Girl *(66). She was the plain friend of the glamorous Meredith (Charlotte Rampling), but in the end Bates decides it is her he loves after all. Their playing made the material seem better than it was.*

Her husband is also her agent and manager, and he decided that her career lay in the States: she agreed, to stop – as she put it – being in Vanessa's shadow; and while appearing on Broadway in a British play, 'My Fat Friend', she adroitly accepted two contrasting roles, the governess in *The Turn of the Screw* (74), three hours of it for television, and the title-role in *The Happy Hooker*. Xaviera Hollander's notorious memoir of her days as a madame had become a light comedy, thus initial surprise at Redgrave's participation was stilled. She herself said that she regarded the role as a challenge, but the film was not of a quality to be of benefit to her career. She was one of the stars in cameo roles in *The Big Bus* (76), still showing proof of her comedy skill as an ultra-British fashion designer who travels on it; but her subsequent work for a while was in the New York theatre – in 'Mrs Warren's Profession' and 'Saint Joan' (78). She should have been in *The Europeans* and she should have been so lucky, but her husband was in dispute with Merchant-Ivory over scheduling and salary: the film cost only $750,000 and Lee Remick replaced her, at less than her usual salary.

She also established herself in television: *Sooner or Later* (79), as a teacher whose pupil has that dilemma, when to lose her virginity; *Centennial* – 26 hours of it, the making of America, as taken from Michener's novel; *Beggarman Thief*, as Jean Simmons's sister-in-law, widow of her murdered brother in this mini; *Gauguin the Savage* (80), as the wife of the painter (David Carradine); and *The Seduction of Miss Leona*, as a shy spinster who falls in love with her handyman (Brian Dennehy). Then she was one of the *Sunday Lovers* in this four-part French-Italian-US-British co-production, with an episode set in each country (more, perhaps, than actually saw it), and a film star who is murdered while attempting a Broadway come-back, in *Rehearsal for Murder* (82), with Robert Preston as her playwright fiancé. During this period – since 1979 – she had played Glenda Jackson's old role in 'House Calls', a sitcom based on the film of that name, and it had made her nationally popular; but when she differed with Universal TV over renewal fees and the right, apparently, to bring her baby to the set, the quarrel was much publicized: her suit was dismissed and the case never settled – but as the case dragged on she was said to be suing her lawyers for malpractice, to the tune of $30 million. The next two seasons found her in another sitcom, 'Teachers Only', but it did not enjoy the same success.

In New York she took over the lead in a double bill, 'Sister Mary Ignatius Explains It All for You' and 'The Actor's Nightmare' (83) and two years later starred with Rex Harrison and Claudette Colbert in 'Aren't We All?'; between the two there was a BBC series, 'The Fainthearted Feminist'. In a television remake, *The Bad Seed* (85), she was the mother; in another tele-movie she was a lesbian, one of Mariette Hartley's *My Two Loves* (86) – the other, more orthodox, was Barry Newman; and she was a mother again in *Morgan Stewart's Coming Home* (87). Broadway saw her again, in 1986, in 'Sweet Sue' and Los Angeles two years later admired her in 'Les Liaisons Dangereuses'. For the BBC she did a stunning job as a mother tracking down a drug-dealer in *Death of a Son* (88) and about the same time she could be seen on PBS in *Tales From the Hollywood Hills*. Still to be seen are *Midnight*, with Tony Curtis, and *Getting It Right*, directed by Randall Kleiser, with John Gielgud and Helena Bonham-Carter.

Vanessa Redgrave

Vanessa Redgrave became a big name in films so quickly and the object of so much publicity – not all of it invited by her – that it was soon forgotten that for some time she had been one of the most admired stage actresses of her generation. The auguries were good: her birth in 1937 was announced by Laurence Olivier over the footlights of the Old Vic where father Michael Redgrave was Laertes to his Hamlet. Mother was Rachel Kempson, who was in semi-retirement while the children (also Corin and Lynn) were growing up (but she emerged to prove on TV she was one of the best actresses of *her* generation). Vanessa studied at the Central School and made her stage début in 1957 at Frinton Summer Theatre. She made her London bow in 'A Touch of the Sun' (58), re-enacting the daughter-father relationship, and she played Michael Redgrave's daughter a second time in *Behind the Mask* (58), a minor drama with a hospital setting. She later called the film 'a stinker' and said it left her frightened of trying again. Certainly no one was impressed, but the later admired qualities of luminous presence and grace are tentatively there. She appeared on TV and had small parts with the Royal Shakespeare Co. at Stratford in 1959. She did some modern plays and when the bigger parts started coming – mostly with the Royal Shakespeare, 1960-62 – it was clear that this was an actress touched with magic. Kenneth Tynan thought her acting as (Boletta) in 'The Lady From the Sea' the best in London. Of her Rosalind, Bernard Levin wrote: 'Nothing at once more beautiful and more accomplished has ever met my sight.' She did Katharine in 'The Shrew' and Nina in 'The Seagull', but was not considered film material – too tall, too plain, too high-brow.

The first indication that she could be a marvellous film actress came with a BBC version of 'A Farewell to Arms' with George Hamilton and the impression was confirmed some months later by *Morgan: A Suitable Case for Treatment* (66). It was her personality in life (rather than her stage work) which encouraged director Karel Reisz to sign her to play the wealthy wife of poor demented Morgan, a Marxist fantasist – beautifully played by David Warner; because the three of them worked together so well, the film changed as they went along. It was a big international success and brought her much praise. She turned down the part of More's daughter in *A Man for All Seasons*, but asked to do a one-shot no-dialogue bit as Anne Boleyn. Further, it was now discovered that she was not only beautiful but sexy. The sexy image was maintained when Antonioni used

David Warner and Vanessa Redgrave in Morgan: A Suitable Case for Treatment *(66), a quite funny picture about a crazy artist and the wealthy wife who does not want to divorce him but thinks she should.*

her in *Blow-Up* (67), in a small but teasing part as a mystery girl who tangles once with photographer David Hemmings – Antonioni's first English-language film and a runaway success for reasons separate from his disenchanted view of so-called 'swinging' London. On stage she gave a remarkable performance in 'The Prime of Miss Jean Brodie', but with it she lost interest in the theatre – partly because of the role, that of a Scots teacher with Fascist tendencies (in life, Redgrave had been noted for her espousal of left-wing causes). She went over to movies and noted: 'Films are where the art and excitement are today. And being a movie star – it's super.'

Being a movie star has not yet been – unlike her stage career – an unqualified success. She made bold decisions, but her films have in the main been either commercial or artistic failures and frequently both; her choice suggested the least egotistical of actresses, but no matter how thin the role her thoughtfulness contributed something to the character. For instance, she had little screen time in *The Sailor from Gibraltar*, but this was the definitive study of a jilted girl – in an otherwise execrable film directed by her then husband, Tony Richardson, and starring Jeanne Moreau (who was named in the divorce suit). Also for Richardson she made *Red and Blue*, playing a cabaret singer. Designed as one part of a three-episode film (other parts were directed by Lindsay Anderson and Peter Brook; the Brook sequence has never been publicly shown), it was shown on its own after a delay – supporting *The Graduate* in London, when it was literally laughed off the screen (it has not been heard of since). She went to Hollywood to play her second consort, in *Camelot*, Joshua Logan's consistently vulgar screen version of the Lerner-Loewe musical; she, Richard Harris as Arthur and Franco Nero as her lover, Lancelot, contrived to lift it to an acceptable level, but it was by no means the success that Warners had hoped for. Nor, outflanked by carping reviews, did audiences fight to see Richardson's *The*

If any movie epitomized the London of the 'Swinging Sixties' it was Blow-Up *(67), but since it did not like what it saw it has not dated an iota. It was also made by a film-maker of genius, Michelangelo Antonioni, so that you can still peel layer and layer from the plot and still find something there, which may surprise those who found it merely modish at the time. With Vanessa Redgrave and David Hemmings.*

Isadora (69). *The real Isadora was a decidedly tiresome lady, but Vanessa Redgrave's interpretation concentrated on her idealism rather than her eccentricities.*

Charge of the Light Brigade (68), a superb evocation of Victorian England: Vanessa did wonders with a minor, nothing role, a young bride.

The failure, also, of Reisz's *Isadora* (69) then spelled practical doom to such subjects. Both films, historical and biographical, were light-years in advance of the old ways of doing such things, but this honest and painstaking film about dancer Isadora Duncan was no more than that. However: 'For star Vanessa Redgrave, this is a major acting triumph, reflecting mastery of a broad emotional spectrum' ('Variety'); 'Vanessa's physical magnificence and mastery of a sketchy part are reminiscent of Garbo way back when' ('Playboy'); and 'There has not been an actress of this calibre since Garbo' (Penelope Mortimer in the 'Observer').

As another Lady with a Mission, Mrs Pankhurst, she brought the only moments of passion to *Oh! What a Lovely War!*; then with Franco Nero (the father of one of her children) did *Un Tranquillo Posto di Campagna/ A Quiet Place in the Country* in Italy. The romping in black underwear looked less like enfranchisement than exhibitionism, especially as the film itself was a pretentious attempt at a psychological thriller – and a box-office flop. Commercially, Redgrave was no luckier with Sidney Lumet's film of *The Seagull*, improving immeasurably on her earlier performance as Nina and once again well partnered by David Warner, as Konstantin. With Nero, in London, she made *Drop Out* (70), an Italian picture – about a hobo and not apparently shown outside that country. Tinto Brass directed and he directed them both again in *La Vacanza* (71), which was shown – without great acclaim – at Venice that year, about the same time as surfaced the two Anglo-US films which Redgrave had made in the interim. One was *The Trojan Women*, as Andromache, adapted from Euripides and directed by Michael Cacoyannis, with Katharine Hepburn as Hecuba. The other was *The Devils*, adapted from a play by John Whiting and a novel by Aldous Huxley, about an outbreak of sexual hysteria in Loudon (France) in 1633; Redgrave was the deformed Mother Superior who thought herself in love with a worldly cleric (Oliver Reed). As directed by Ken Russell, it gave a new dimension to screen vulgarity – but as junk, it was childish. 'One can really only sympathize with the players' said 'Punch'. It had a certain success commercially, presumably because of the anti-clerical theme and the sensationalism.

There followed a more orthodox historical film, made by Hal Wallis, the only producer with faith left in the genre: *Mary Queen of Scots*, with Glenda Jackson as Elizabeth and Redgrave in the title-role. As it happened, the faith was misplaced – but then he had assigned a plodder to the direction. Redgrave returned to the stage, in, among others, 'The Threepenny Opera', directed by her ex-husband, and 'Design for Living'. Among the

Mary Queen of Scots (*71*) *provided Vanessa Redgrave with another real-life heroine – and another tiresome lady. But, following the script, Vanessa played her as the Mary of legend rather than the foolish woman of the history books. That being so, why not add a confrontation with Elizabeth I (Glenda Jackson)? After all, Schiller did.*

others was Shakespeare's Cleopatra in a tent in London: that brought no kudos and around the same time Redgrave's career hit a low when a US visa was refused – for political reasons – which would have allowed her to cross the Atlantic for *Gone Beaver* with Bruce Dern, to have been directed by Jim McBride for BBS-Columbia. She was therefore something of a back number when she agreed to be one of the star suspects of the *Murder on the Orient Express* (74), predictably one of the year's biggest hits; equally predictably, *Out of Season* (75) was one of the year's failures, a moody-talkie piece set in a resort in winter, with Cliff Robertson as Redgrave's one-time fiancé. The predictability, though, is a pity, for the cinema needs both kinds of film; but neither of these were good examples of those kinds.

Redgrave played Lady Macbeth, her visa restored, to Charlton Heston's thane in LA and the following year she played 'The Lady from the Sea', now in the title-role, in New York – and repeated the role in Manchester in 1978 to restore her British reputation. Meanwhile, the reputation was pushed neither way by the role of the anguished kidnapped actress in Herbert Ross's Sherlock Holmes romp, *The Seven-Per-Cent Solution* (76), but it soared with the title-role in Zinnemann's *Julia* (77). Julia was the idealistic, left-wing friend of Lillian Hellman (Jane Fonda), helped financially by the latter – but involving her in a number of dangers: she was well-cast but damaging, since in the film her behaviour corresponded to her much reported political activities offscreen, which hardly seem to have relationship to commonsense, practicality, etc., and therefore in the film it was difficult to be patient with her. Her political views got aired at the 1978 Oscar ceremony, when she used her award (Best Supporting Actress) to support the anti-Zionist struggle in the Middle East: the discernible reaction of industry and press indicated that the matter had been far better left unsaid – and the American producer of the British *Yanks* (79), then shooting, said that he was considering sacking her from the film – though as the director, John Schlesinger, said, what was important was Redgrave's talent, and there was an awful lot of that. She had meanwhile played Agatha Christie in *Agatha*, a tale of that lady's disappearance in the 20s, one of the most litiginous of all movies: the Christie estate had tried to get an injunction in New York; co-star Dustin Hoffman and First Artists were suing each other over it; and the BBC, who had put money into it, were suing the EMI circuit for refusing to book it (EMI's grounds being that the BBC intended to break the five-year British rule keeping movies off TV). Redgrave herself was in court, having sued the 'Observer' for libel when that journal reported unfavourably on the conduct of the Workers Revolutionary Party; but the court found against 'Vanessa and her loonies', as Bernard Levin christened them, and the costs were in the region of £70,000. However, *Julia* had made her again a demanded name and she was in Canada to star in *Bear Island* (80), an Alistair MacLean thriller with Donald Sutherland. It did so badly in its British showings that it went direct to cable in the US.

She won the 'Evening Standard' award for her performance in 'The Lady From the Sea' and the Emmy award in the US for *Playing for Time* (81), as adapted from Fania Fenelon's book by Arthur Miller. Redgrave was Fenelon, one of the survivors of Auschwitz; this was one of the occasions when television did not trivialize and there were also Emmys for the production and Jane Alexander. *My Body, My Child* (82) was endeavour of the same order – and in the same medium – with Redgrave as a mother uncertain whether to have her child born deformed or aborted. After making a documentary, *Occupied Palestine*, she had the misfortune to be the wife of *Wagner* (83) – Richard Burton – in a ghastly British mini-series and then was the Wicked Queen in a *Snow White and the Seven Dwarfs* made for video. She should have made *Track 39* in the US for Joseph Losey, but the financing fell through, enabling Merchant-Ivory to grab her for *The Bostonians* (84) to play Olive, who engages in battle with cousin Basil (Christopher Reeve) over Verena (Madeleine Potter) – though no more than in the book are Olive's feelings made explicit. It is a rather dull battle, since only Redgrave brought any intelligence to it. Reeve was merely amiable, as he was again when he and Redgrave were reunited in a further version of Henry James, 'The Aspern Papers', as adapted by her father and revived in London in 1984. Boston, as it happened, was giving Miss Redgrave trouble: in 1982 because of her Zionist views the city's Symphony Orchestra cancelled her $31,000 contract to narrate Stravinsky's 'Oedipus Rex'. She sued the orchestra's management for $5 million for the damage to her reputation and said in court that the only work offered was not 'financially solid' and she therefore did not work for 14 months. She would not otherwise have appeared naked in *Steaming* (85), Ladies' Night in a Turkish Bath, but that was an odd remark from a woman noted for unorthodox beliefs – and in this case the film was based on a highly respected play by Nell Dunn and directed by Joseph Losey, who may have been a hack but his reputation was otherwise.

Wetherby, written and directed by David Hare, cast her as a teacher who becomes hung up on a strange young man and then on the detective (the excellent Stuart Wilson) investigating his suicide: her daughter Joely Richardson played her in the flashbacks (her other daughter, Natasha Richardson, is also an actress). There was work in American television, in two mini-series, *Three Sovereigns for Sarah*, an account of the Salem witch trials, with Kim Hunter and Phyllis Thaxter as her sisters, and *Peter the Great* (86) with Maximilian Schell, as his scheming sister; and in *Second Serve*, based on fact, as Dr Renee Richards, the transvestite tennis player who deserted manhood for frocks. Redgrave had a guest role in *Comrades*, a long plod through the saga of the Tolpuddle Martyrs, and then was involved with deviants again, as the agent of the homosexual writer Joe Orton in *Prick Up Your Ears* (87), in some ways an odd choice, since she is tall and the lady concerned is diminutive: it was also her least mannered performance in years, as was recognized by Bafta and the New York critics, both of whom voted her the year's Best Supporting Actress. From that, it was a falling-off to a grim, much-panned black comedy, *Consuming Passions* (88), where her performance as a sexually ravenous Maltese woman, chasing Tyler Butterworth, was less like the next Garbo than the last Barbara Windsor. Obviously, her role as Thomas More's wife in the Charlton Heston TV remake of *A Man for All Seasons* (89) was not going to help her any, but she escaped Peter Greenaway's *The Cook, the Thief, His Wife and Her Lover* at the last minute and was replaced by Helen Mirren. Stage appearances during these last years include 'The Seagull' as Arkadina, 'Antony and Cleopatra' and 'The Taming of the Shrew' in repertory with Timothy Dalton, 'Ghosts' and 'Orpheus Descending'.

Oliver Reed

During the ten years in which he waited for screen stardom, you always knew that Oliver Reed would make it. He looked, simply, dynamic. He did not look like any other British star; you would have to look way back to find anyone else with that same scowling magnificence and you would come up with only James Mason – whose bearing and appearance was, in any case, much less plebeian. Reed looked capable of playing the sort of parts once played by Wallace Beery or Clark Gable and in which you could not imagine any other British film star, from Ronald Colman to Robert Powell. He could play, you thought, a regimental sergeant-major, a bouncer for a strip-club (which he was, briefly, at 17), a lumberjack or a monster. As it turned out, as a star he has the old-time starriness: looks, presence, but not an actual abundance of real acting talent.

He was born in Wimbledon, in south

London, in 1938. His uncle was Carol Reed, the director; one set of grandparents were performers, but there were no other show-business connections. Apart from the bouncing, he worked as a medical orderly before national service, for which he did his stint in the Medical Corps. He decided to become an actor and disregarded the advice of his uncle, who told him to study. He thought his army training had equipped him better for the profession than any acting school might – nor was he interested in the Theatre, with a capital or any other sort of 't'. He began as an extra in films: *Beat Girl* (59; released late 60), as a teenage layabout in this dim picture about 'wild' youth, with David Farrar as one of its fathers; *The Angry Silence* (60), as a factory worker; *The League of Gentlemen*, as a ballet dancer; *The Two Faces of Doctor Jekyll*, a poor Hammer remake of the Stevenson story, with Paul Massie, as a bouncer; *The Bulldog* Breed (61), as a teddy-boy who threatens Norman Wisdom; and *No Love for Johnnie*. He managed then to get billing for his bit parts in: *His and Hers*, as a poet; *The Rebel*, as a fellow painter of comedian Tony Hancock; and *Sword of Sherwood Forest*, as a wicked earl. The last was an attempt by Hammer to cash in on the popularity of a TV Robin Hood series starring Richard Greene, who repeated here. The Hammer casting director was impressed by Reed's sullen appearance and thought he would do to play the werewolf in *The Curse of the Werewolf*; it was the star part, with billing to match, but as a film – 'Even by Hammer standards this is a particularly repellent job of slaughter-house horror' ('MFB').

Hammer kept him for a series of films: *The Damned* (61; released 63), a science-fiction thriller directed by Joseph Losey, in a performance – as the leader of a motor-cycle gang – described by the 'MFB' as 'inept'; *The Pirates of Blood River* (62), starring Kerwin Matthews, as a pirate; *Captain Clegg*, with Peter Cushing, as a smuggler; *The Scarlet Blade* (63), with Lionel Jeffries, both of them as baddies; and *Paranoiac*, as a murderer in that condition, trying to drive mad his sister (Janette Scott). He was also in *The Party's Over*, as the leader of what were described as a 'gang of Chelsea beatniks', leading astray the American daughter of Eddie Albert. The British censor ordered cuts, which director Guy Hamilton refused to make; it did not come out till 1965, with cuts and minus director credit – and it turned out to be arty and empty.

Meanwhile, a then B picture director, Michael Winner, saw Reed in a TV play. He had tried to get him for his *West Eleven*, but the producers had refused. For his first independent production he put Reed in the lead – a promenade Casanova in a dim little comedy-drama, *The System* (64). He returned to Hammer to play the villain, a rebel leader, in *The Brigand of Kandahar* (65), a tale of the Bengal Lancers (briefly, Hammer tried to find new formulas: when few of them were successful, they returned to horror). Then he got the lead in an A picture, *The Trap* (66), opposite Rita Tushingham, as a brutish fur-trapper in this Canadian-made film. It was not a success. He was a village layabout who terrorizes Carol Lynley in *The Shuttered Room* (67), supposedly set in New England but filmed in old England. Then Winner put him into a pair of flashy comedies, *The Jokers* (67), with Michael Crawford, and *I'll Never Forget What's-'is'-name*, with Orson Welles. Winner's talent for film-making is far exceeded by his talent for publicity, so each time there was excessive publicity for 'A Michael Winner film' it became likely that a few more people would hear of Reed. The second of these two films had a – surprising – success, but he was not generally known till he was signed to play the dastardly Bill Sikes in *Oliver!* (68). This had been a British musical based on 'Oliver Twist', a success on Broadway as well as in London; Columbia backed the film, Reed's uncle directed – and it turned out to be a big hit. It won a Best Picture Oscar.

Reed went into *The Assassination Bureau*, a period black comedy based on a story by Jack London, and then did another film for Winner, *Hannibal Brooks*, about two men (the other was Michael J. Pollard) who take an elephant over the Alps. On TV he had

There seemed no good reason to remake 'Oliver Twist', but a musical version had been successful on the stage. It came to the screen more than somewhat improved: Oliver! *(68), with Oliver Reed as Sikes and Ron Moody as Fagin.*

done two semi-documentaries for Ken Russell nd his career got a big boost when Russell put him into his film of D.H. Lawrence's *Women in Love* (69), with Glenda Jackson. It was a success, but the next few were not: *Take a Girl Like You* (70), with Hayley Mills; *La Dame dans l'Auto avec des Lunettes et un Fusil/The Lady in the Car* (71), a dull French-made thriller, directed by Anatole Litvak, with Samantha Eggar; and *The Hunting Party*, a Western, made in Spain, with Candice Bergen. Another film made at this time, *Z.P.G.*, made in Copenhagen with Geraldine Chaplin, was not shown till 1972. He was in Russell's *The Devils*, with Vanessa Redgrave; and around this time he told a New York reporter: 'Do you know what I am? I'm successful. Destroy me and you destroy the British film industry. Keep me going and I'm the biggest star you've got. I'm Mr England.' There were other, similar remarks, including his estimate of his irresistibility to women (his marriage to Kathleen Byrne lasted 10 years, 1960–70). *Sitting Target* (72), with Jill St John, was unfortunately titled; *The Triple Echo* was simply unfortunate – a pretentious trifle with Reed as a bull-necked sergeant too dim to notice that the girl he is pursuing is a guy in drag.

Oliver Reed was villainous, as usual, in The Hunting Party *(71): doing the hunting was Gene Hackman, because Reed and his gang had kidnapped and raped his wife, Candice Bergen – though in this still she seems to have forgiven him.*

Glenda Jackson was in the latter, which needed any of the business her name might drum up – since Reed was not, despite his boast, exactly a popular star. With another player of some clout, he was noticed; but neither *Z.P.G.* nor *Sitting Target* had attracted any attention. Nor were there any showings in his native land of two Italian films, *Il Giorno del Furore*, with Claudia Cardinale, a historical tale of revolt in Russia; and *Mordi e Fuggi* (73), where he kidnapped Marcello Mastroianni while on a dirty weekend. He returned to Britain to do an unbilled guest spot in one of Ken Russell's idiotic biopics, *Mahler* (74), with Robert Powell in that role; and he had his first hit in a long while as Athos in *The Three Musketeers: The Queen's Diamonds*. In Italy he was a prison officer blackmailed by Fabio Testi in *Revolver*, which turned up briefly in New York (but nowhere else) as *Blood in the Streets*. The next batch were even less fortunate. *Rider* was being filmed in Greece (with Orson Welles in the cast) when it was abandoned; its director, Andrew Sinclair, had earlier directed Reed in *Blue Blood*, in which he was a sinister butler to a dotty family. Trade-shown finally at the end of 1974, plans seem to have been abandoned to show it publicly; and something similar happened to *And Then There Were None*; nominally British (though made in Iran) it has never been theatrically screened in that country but was sold direct to US TV – as *Ten Little Indians*: Reed had the role played by Louis Hayward in the 1945 version. However, the public could see him in a spin-off of an earlier film, *The Four Musketeeers: The Revenge of Milady*, but the box-office indicated that it had not liked that film enough to bother this time. It, the public, did go, or the youthful portions of it, to *Tommy*, a 'rock opera' and Russell's only popular film in a run of flops: Reed did a billed guest spot as Tommy's father. He was, of course, no more responsible for its success than he had been for the failures he had had: there had been bad scripts, directors, co-stars – and it says much for his presence on screen that he continued to be in great demand. It might be argued that *Royal Flash* was one of the few 'quality' films he had elected to do, but that proved unfortunate once the critics got at it – doubly unfortunate from Reed's outlook, since he revealed a nice comic sense in his role of a power-crazy Prussian baron. Later that year Jack Starrett was directing him and Toshiro Mifune in *The New Spartans* when, after nine days' shooting, its (German) financing fell through. (Earlier Reed projects are also sometimes listed in his credits: *Undersky* in 1972 with Genevieve Bujold, which was probably made; and *The Captive* in 1974 with Curt Jürgens, which seems to have been cancelled at the last minute.) A run of bad luck was not lifted by a British-Italian co-production with Richard Widmark, *The Sellout* (76), yet another CIA thriller set in Israel; Reed was a double agent.

Hollywood called, but the results did little to help him and he was certainly hammy as an

Indian half-breed buddy of Lee Marvin's in *The Great Scout and Cathouse Thursday*; and he was ineffective in *Burnt Offerings*, behaving oddly as he and wife (Karen Black) are done in by a malevolent house. In the international *The Prince and the Pauper/Crossed Swords* (77) he was a soldier of fortune who befriends the boy – the role played by Errol Flynn in the 1937 version. He was an American police 'hit' man in *Assault on Paradise*, another unlucky one – since it has not surfaced to date. It is, however, difficult to sympathize with Reed's choices: director Peter Collinson had already lumbered him with two flops (*And Then There Were None* and *The Sellout*), but he elected to do another with him, the Anglo-Canadian *Tomorrow Never Comes* (78), which turned out the same way; as the upright police chief, Reed was appreciated by John Gillett (in the 'MFB'): 'Although saddled with an impossibly clichéd role, [he] plays with an uncharacteristic, banked-down authority which at least makes his scenes watchable.' There was virtually no comment on his performance as the nightclub owner in *The Big Sleep*, since reviewers were too busy waxing indignant on a fifth-rate director (Winner) remaking a classic ('Have you seen it?' someone asked Lauren Bacall. 'Has anyone?' she replied); but Reed's disciplinarian teacher in *The Class of Miss MacMichael* provoked mainly irreverence. Miss Jackson was his co-star in this third and least of their teamings. Reed went to Canada and began *Mad Trapper*, which folded after two weeks' shooting due to 'lack of green stuff' in the words of 'Photoplay'. That might be why (as reported in 'Variety') he was discovered drunk and trouserless one December afternoon in a Toronto thoroughfare. Certainly that country bore no grudge, since he stayed on to make *The Brood* (79) with Samantha Eggar. David Cronenberg directed and it was ludicrous.

From there it was quite a step to Disney, but Reed was still being evil in *Condorman* (80), as a KGB man trying to capture a children's book author (wimpy Michael Crawford). He was *Dr Hekyl and Mr Hype* in a dire modernized spoof produced by Cannon, from which he moved to Zambia for *A Touch of the Sun*, which also wasted Keenan Wynn and Peter Cushing. He moved North to Libya to play the Italian military commander in *Omar Muktar, Lion of the Desert*, who was Anthony Quinn, and then returned to Britain to play Sterling Hayden's chauffeur in *Venom* (82), a title which referred either to a black mamba or the spirit in which critics reviewed it – the few that bothered, that is. *Al-mas a la Al-Kuba/Clash of Loyalties* (83) was a large-budget Iraqi production which first announced itself in the trade papers with an ad in which David Niven led the cast; a further ad, a week later, apologized to all concerned without explanation. Despite heavy British participation – it concerns their activities in the region after World War II – its only British showings were at the London Film Festival. Well, it flopped on its home territory. Another failure was *The Sting II*, in which Reed's role was modelled on – but shorter than – Robert Shaw's in the original; but after a Hollywood mainstream production he was reduced to Harry Alan Towers's cheapjack version of an infamous Victorian pornographic novel, *Fanny Hill*. Reed was an unctious lawyer and he was a KGB boss in *Masquerade*, a tele-film with Rod Taylor. He remained in the US to play a Lucifer figure in *Two of a Kind* and then flew to Italy for one of the leading roles in a starry mini-series, *Christopher Columbus* (84). *Spasms* was a Canadian horror film made two years earlier and it starred Peter Fonda; Reed overacted as a cripple with telepathic powers. He returned to Mr Towers to play one of the villains in an adaptation of Robert Louis Stevenson for cable, *The Black Arrow*, in fact a co-production with Disney and hence a union between one of the least and one of the most fastidious producers in the business. He was then in two prestige productions by former collaborators (of each other), Paul Mayersburg's *Captive* (86) and Nicolas Roeg's *Castaway*, in the former as a wealthy tycoon whose obsessive love for his daughter is threatened when she is kidnapped by terrorists and in the latter, based on fact, as a publisher who places a small ad for a woman to spend a year with him on a desert island. Neither was of a quality to help Reed's career or his box-office standing; nor was *Wheels of Terror* (87), a war film made in Yugoslavia with David Carradine and Bruce Davison, with Reed in a cameo as an officer. More for Towers: *Gor* (87) as a high priest; *Dragonard* and *Master of Dragonard Hill*, as the garrison commander in these slave melodramas set in the Caribbean, with Eartha Kitt. *Rage to Kill* was made by the equally wretched Action International Pictures and then it was back to Towers: *Captive Rage* (88) with Robert Vaughan; and two made in South Africa to benefit from government subsidies, *Skeleton Coast* with Ernest Borgnine, as a wicked diamond merchant, and *Rage to Kill* (89), supposedly set in old Grenada, as a chieftain who seizes an island. Although Reed was listed in 'Variety' in 1989 as one of the busiest of actors, if only in low-budget movies, it is probable that the last film of his that any but a hard-case buff could name would be *Oliver!*; but he has kept in the public eye with occasional arrests for drunkenness; and his career may have taken an upward turn with *The Lady and the Highwayman*, a tele-film with Claire Bloom, and Lester's *The Return of the Musketeers*.

LEE REMICK

For a long time Lee Remick's looks were against her. Pretty, doll-like, she looked more like the last blonde starlet than the next Oscar winner and thus was usually cast as some sort of sex-pot – giddy, breathless, carefree, teasing. . . . But people *noticed*; she is probably one of the half-dozen most respected actresses in films.

She was born in 1935 in Boston; her mother was an actress. She learned dancing at school and got her first job after an audition, dancing at Hyannis, near Cape Cod; she did summer stock while still at school. There was a five-performance Broadway play, 'Be Your Age', and then about 40 TV shows. Elia Kazan saw her in one, 'All Expenses Paid', dancing the samba, and chose her for the small but important role of the drum majorette in *A Face in the Crowd* (57). She attracted some attention and 20th signed her to a short-term contract. In a cast of some merit, she attracted more attention to herself in *The Long Hot Summer* (58), as Orson Welles's daughter-in-law, the flighty, giggling wife of Anthony Franciosa. She was paid $30,000 for it, a good sum for a beginner. 20th announced *The Jean Harlow Story* for her when Marilyn Monroe refused to do it, but in the end it was cancelled. *These Thousand Hills* (59) was a dreary Western, where she was a sad, clinging little whore who offers all her savings to Don Murray; then she got her big chance when Lana Turner did not like her costumes for Preminger's *Anatomy of Murder*. Fortunately – for the film was dull enough even *with* Remick's lively performance of a woman crying rape while appearing to enjoy it.

Baby the Rain Must Fall *(65) was a flawed but still notable film about a convict on parole and his wife's attempts to stabilize him.*

Kazan then starred her in one of his few failures – and her own favourite film – *Wild River* (60), as a newly widowed woman drawn to Montgomery Clift. Taken from two novels by different writers, it showed it, but both stars gave beautiful performances. She appeared on TV in 'The Tempest', with Richard Burton and Maurice Evans, then did her last for 20th, *Sanctuary* (61), directed by Tony Richardson (but publicly denounced by him, for studio interference). It was adapted from William Faulner's novel and Remick made a real figure of the prim little flapper who discovers she likes being raped and getting drunk. Blake Edwards directed *Experiment With Terror* (62), a conventional thriller with Glen Ford where she had little to do but looked frightened; but Edwards then gave her some meat, as Jack Lemmon's wife drawn to drink because of his addiction to it: *Days of Wine and Roses*, an excellent study of an alcoholic marriage (and Edwards's best film). Lemmon was memorable; Remick was unforgettable.

In the brouhaha which followed Marilyn Monroe's sacking from *Something's Gotta Give*, 'Newsweek' asked John Ford for a comment. He said: 'Marilyn Monroe? Hell, Lee Remick's a lot sexier than she is and a much better actress to boot.' 20th sat up and signed Remick as Monroe's replacement; but co-star Dean Martin claimed that his contract was to star only with Monroe and the film was shelved. Instead, Remick was wasted in a couple: Carol Reed's thriller, *The Running Man* (63), with Laurence Harvey, and *The Wheeler Dealers* with James Garner. On Broadway she appeared in a Sondheim musical with Angela Lansbury, 'Anyone Can Whistle'. The next two films failed, the first undeservedly: *Baby the Rain Must Fall* (65), a rambling tale about a restless ex-con (Steve McQueen) and his loving wife. 'Lee Remick, temperamentally ideal for the role, gives a kind of faultlessly low-key performance that is, in itself, sufficient reason to see the film' – 'Sight and Sound'. She was also good in the other, *The Hallelujah Trail* with Burt Lancaster, cast against type as a temperance campaigner.

She returned to Broadway, playing a blind girl in 'Wait Until Dark' for over a year; and in New York she was the bubbly heroine of *No Way To Treat a Lady* (68), with George

Segal and Rod Steiger. *The Detective* found her as Sinatra's nympho wife and it was typical of that nasty film that (a) she was not nympho in the original novel and (b) Sinatra did not take advantage of the fact. She had a similar role in *Hard Contract*, with James Coburn. In 1968 she and husband Bill Colleran, a TV producer, divorced; in Europe filming she met and later married an Englishman, Kip Gowans and settled in London. The film she was making was *A Severed Head* (71), an absurd comedy adapted from Iris Murdoch's novel; she and Ian Holm, as a particularly silly couple of socialites, almost made it work. A second British film was much better, *Loot*, from Joe Orton's stage farce, where she was more than game as the doll-like nurse. She returned to the US to appear opposite Paul Newman in *Sometimes a Great Notion*.

In 1972 she played Alma in 'Summer and Smoke' on BBC television, to outstanding reviews.

For selected US cinemas only, she was with Katharine Hepburn and Paul Scofield in a filmed play (it was one of Edward Albee's), *A Delicate Balance* (73), and for another limited audience – televiewers – she did: *And No One Could Save Her*, as an heiress whose husband disappears en route to Ireland; *The Blue Knight*, as William Holden's patient girlfriend; *QB VII* (74), a starry mini-series with Ben Gazzara, as a British milady; *Hustling* (75), as a reporter investigating prostitution in New York; and *A Girl Named Sooner* with Richard Crenna as her husband, a childless couple who adopt an unwanted child. Cinemagoers could see her only in some inferior thrillers: *Hennessy*, as an IRA widow who shelters Rod Steiger; *The Omen* (76), as Gregory Peck's wife (though the film was a popular one); *Telefon* (77), as an American contact for KGB agent Charles Bronson; and *The Medusa Touch* (78), as ambiguous psychiatrist to Richard Burton. She was wasted in all of them, but during this period – in 1976 – she appeared in the first West End production of 'Bus Stop'. Unsurprisingly, she returned to television: *Breaking Up*, as a woman stunned to hear that her husband plans to leave her; *Arthur Hailey's 'Wheels'*, as the bored wife of executive Rock Hudson in this mini; *Torn Between Two Lovers* (79) – they were Joseph Bologna (in fact, her husband) and George Peppard, and it was she who had the dilemma; and *Ike*, another mini-series, as the mistress-chauffeuse of that general (Robert Duvall). At last she found the good cinema role for which her admirers had long hoped, in the Ivory-Merchant version of Henry James's *The Europeans*, as the capricious American-born baroness confronting her fellow-Americans.

Lee Remick and Ian Holm after the ceremony in The Severed Head *(71) – an ironic flashback, for the film was mainly concerned with their (and others') infidelities.*

Much as we love her, she could not come near the magic of Margaret Sullavan when she played her in a mini-series based on the memoir by that lady's daughter, Brooke Hayward, *Haywire* (80), which was otherwise sound. She was then the leading feminist in a tele-movie based on Marilyn French's novel, *The Women's Room*, and then teacher to Amy Irving in a film about concert pianists, *The Competition*. While she was making both of these there were negotiations for her to play Jack Lemmon's wife (for the second time) in *Tribute* – for although the role called for an American the film was made in Canada and the authorities originally wanted a Canadian actress. In 1981 she left a Broadway-bound play with Geraldine Page, 'Agnes of God', due to 'artistic differences'. She had by now moved back to California at her husband's suggestion, since the offers coming in were fewer than she had a right to expect. She had never become a first-rank star, but as far as the US was concerned she had the reputation of selecting her tele-movies more intelligently than most – although a remake of *The Letter* (82) was a mistake from most points of view. It was the first of a two-picture deal her husband had made for her. Better was *The Gift of Love: a Christmas Story* (83), in which she played a depressed woman who visits her mother (Angela Lansbury) in order to revive memories of her childhood. *A Good Sport* (84) was Ralph Waite and she was a fashion editor in this TV reworking of *Woman of the Year*. She was an American patron for whom painter Stacey Keach deserts Stefanie Power in another mini-series, *Mistral's Daughter*, which was soap, while *I Do! I Do!* for cable proved chiefly that what this material needs is Mary Martin and Robert Preston; Hal Linden had Preston's old role. In *Rearview Mirror*, a TV thriller, Remick was a wife trying to save a baby from a psychopath; in *Toughlove* (85) she and Bruce Dern were parents of a teenage junkie. It was in Australia that she lived *Emma's War* (86), as Emma's San Francisco-born mother: the film told how both were affected by World War II. It was her first for cinemas since *Tribute*, but since her television movies continued to be of a high standard it is possible that she always had first refusal: *Of Pure Blood* (86), as an American career woman who goes to Germany to find why her son was killed there; *Nutcracker: Money, Madness and Murder* (87), based on fact, as a socialite who likes men and booze too much; *The Vision*, for the BBC with Dirk Bogarde, as the scheming head of a TV channel; *Jesse* (88), again based on fact, as a nurse who believes in practical, rather than theoretical, medicine; and *Bridge To Silence* (89), as a domineering woman who interferes in the affairs of her deaf daughter (Marlee Matlin) and her grandchild.

Debbie Reynolds

Debbie Reynolds was one of those who got into films via a beauty contest. She was living in Hollywood, actually in beautiful downtown Burbank (whither the family had moved from El Paso, Texas, where she was born in 1932), and she was elected Miss Burbank 1948. Also at Burbank was the Warner studio and it was only natural that Miss Burbank should find herself there at $65 a week. She was given a brief bit in *June Bride* (48) and then nothing till *The Daughter of Rosie O'Grady* (50), in a good little role as one of June Haver's sisters. She lit up the screen with her young good looks, freshness and vivacity, but Warners let her go. After an approach by her agent, the lucky company who picked her up was MGM, who gave her a song in *Three Little Words*; she did not even sing, but mimed to Helen Kane's voice. The boop-boop-a-doop gestures and Charleston kicks got her plenty of notice and they made her Jane Powell's peppy kid sister in *Two Weeks With Love*. It was apparent that here was no ordinary starlet and MGM, such is the optimism of film companies, or their publicity department, saw her as a new Judy Garland: she became Marjorie Main's niece in *Mr Imperium* (51), with just a couple of scenes.

She was upped to star-billing opposite Gene Kelly in the imperishable *Singin' in the Rain* (52), and against his will. She said later: 'Gene knew the movie was going to be classic, and I was an amateur then.' Apart from a couple of songs, she had little to do but ape a flapper, which she did with a will, and gaily. Three minor musicals followed: *I Love Melvin* (53) with Donald O'Connor; *The Affairs of Dobie Gillis*, a campus comedy with Bobby Van as Dobie; and *Give a Girl a Break* with Marge and Gower Champion. She was only getting $400 a week and thus got $4,000 for ten weeks' work on *Susan Slept Here* (54), a cutesy comedy with Dick Powell, on loan to RKO – but RKO paid $80,000 for her. After her success in it, MGM gave her a new seven-year contract with improved terms. They did not give her improved films. *Athena* was a musical satire on health fads which missed by a mile and *Hit the Deck* (55) was a so-so version of the old musical. But she had a good chance in *The Tender Trap*, with Frank Sinatra, as a fey and ingenuous starlet whose ambition is to be married, and in *The Catered Affair* (56), as the bride whose wedding causes all the fuss. It was a nicely judged performance, causing 'Time Magazine' to remark: 'Debbie is astonishingly believable – a Hollywood butterfly turned into an authentic urban grub.'

In 1955 she had married singer Eddie Fisher and RKO now starred them in *Bundle of Joy*, a musical remake of *Bachelor Mother*. At Universal she put on a Pollyanna hat and made *Tammy and the Bachelor* (57), which was so popular that Universal asked her back for *This Happy Feeling* (58), a mood its heroine shared with Tammy, involved in a spring-winter romance with retired actor Curt Jurgens. At MGM she did a film for which she had at one time been suspended for refusing, *The Mating Game* (59), H.E. Bates's 'The Darling Buds of May' Americanized, with Tony Randall. She did three more unappetizing films: *Say One for Me*, as Father Bing Crosby's most devoted parishioner; *It Started With a Kiss*, with Glenn Ford, as a nightclub dancer; and *The Gazebo*, as Ford's wife. Then, as a change from all this sweetness and light, she did the disappointing film version of Garson Kanin's *The Rat Race* (60), almost consenting to become a call-girl for Don Rickles (but only so that Tony Curtis can have a new saxophone). She was also one of the guests in *Pepe*, an attempt to make an international star out of the Mexican comic, Cantinflas. Except for that, her roles were mainly too young for her and she leaned increasingly on her experience of being cute and 'peppy' in her roles ten years earlier; but her expertise – all too noticeably – had fled.

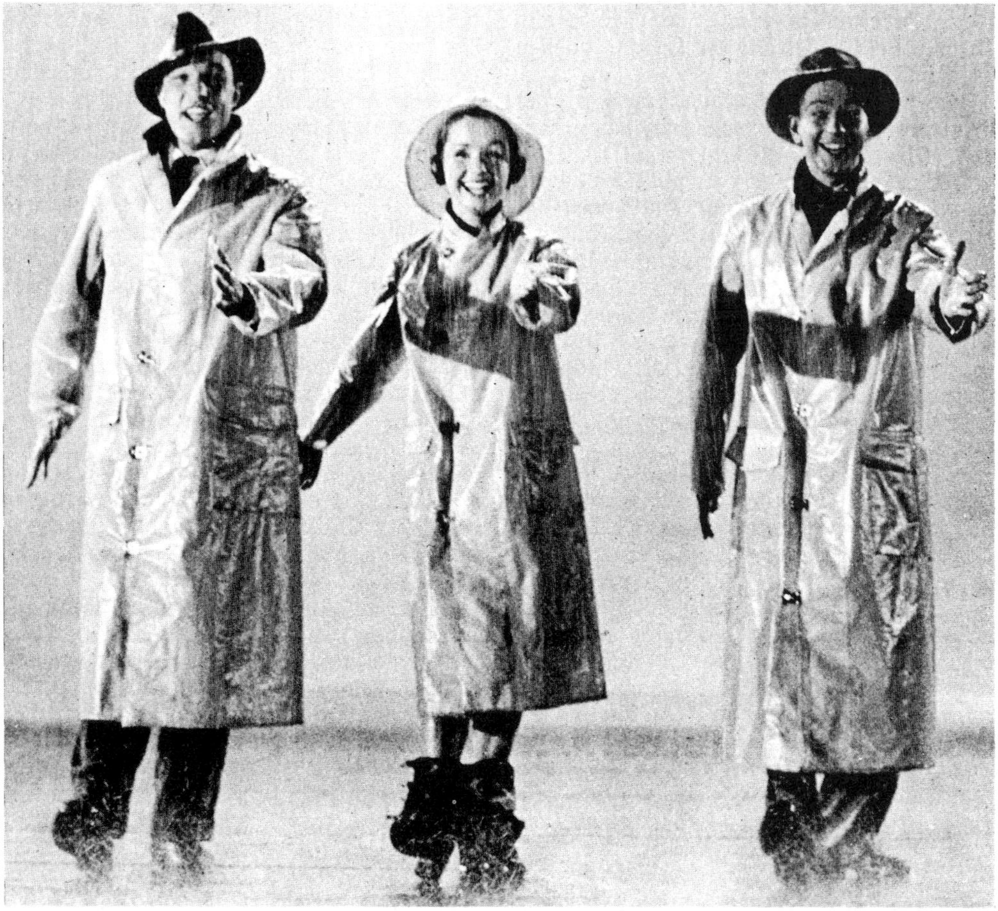

Gene Kelly, Debbie Reynolds and Donald O'Connor singing one of the most famous songs in the history of movie musicals (it was originally featured in The Hollywood Revue of 1929). *This shot was featured before the credits of the movie named after it (52).*

When MGM dominated the field of musicals they put out some cheerful, low-budget ones, including this one, I Love Melvin *(53), in which Debbie Reynolds is a sweet young thing wanting to be a star and Donald O'Connor a photographer's assistant who rashly promises to help her achieve her ambition by getting her face on the cover of 'Look' Magazine. With them, as her sister, is Noreen Corcoran, one of the least ingratiating of Hollywood children.*

However, popular she was. Both in 1959 and 1960 she was one of the top 10. The fan magazines called her 'The New First Lady of Hollywood' and one of them stated that her salary had risen from $75,000 to the millions. 'Maybe,' ventured the same source, 'the cloud of her break-up from Eddie Fisher had this silver-lining because it won her great public sympathy.' She had lost him to Elizabeth Taylor in 1959; in 1960 she married shoe-manufacturer Harry Karl. Outside the US, the trend was if anything in the reverse direction, particularly after both *The Pleasure of His Company* (61), as Fred Astaire's daughter, and *The Second Time Around*, as a small-town widow, gave renewed and depressing evidence of her limitations. She was in an episode of *How the West Was Won* (63) and then in *My Six Loves*. That one failed to do much business off its home ground, so it was surprising that Warners picked her to play *Mary Mary* in their film of the stage hit: predictably, the New York critics found her inferior to Barbara Bel Geddes and the London ones to Maggie Smith.

However, Hollywood had faith in her (Hollywood reads fan magazines, not critics) and, when MGM could not come to terms with Shirley MacLaine, they put Reynolds to carry an expensive musical, *The Unsinkable Molly Brown* (64). She tried hard, but she was not in that league. 'Energy is insufficient and she falls into the trap which waits for all the more feminine American comediennes from Lucille Ball downwards: that of exaggerating the mask of little-boy doggedness . . . "indefatigable" is the safest adjective to describe her performance' ('Sight and Sound').

What's the Matter With Helen? *(71) starred Debbie Reynolds and Shelley Winters as two mothers who escape to Hollywood after a murder trial involving their offspring. But they find they have not left murder behind.*

After a weak comedy, *Goodbye Charlie* (Lauren Bacall had done it on stage and 20th had bought it for Marilyn Monroe originally), she played what she has described as her favourite part, *The Singing Nun* (66), an impressive contender for the most nauseating film ever made. It did little business and her performance was to blame. The next two found her acting her age, but she remained saccharine, even if, on first glance, she played a squabbling wife in *Divorce American Style* (67), with Dick Van Dyke. She was a flirtatious wife in the other one, *How Sweet It Is* (68). In 1969 she started her own TV series, 'The Debbie Reynolds Show', to terrible reviews, and it lasted only half a season. She returned to the big screen in *What's the Matter With Helen?* (71), a camp horror film with Shelley Winters in which she played a Hollywood bitch: a performance good enough to suggest she had been miscast over the years. She has not filmed since, but has done a number of popular nightclub and stage appearances, including 'Irene' (74) in New York, also in a solo turn in Australia and London – though a stint at the latter's Palladium did not bring rave reviews. In 1977 she did 'Annie Get Your Gun' in San Francisco. Two years later she was to have done 'Gypsy' in that city, but the project was cancelled after a run in LA. Cancelled two years later was a New York appearance as Colette, but in this case because she opted to appear in a TV series (which did not run), 'Aloha Paradise'. In September 1981 she opened the bill at MGM's Grand Hotel in Las Vegas, which was demotion – but she could claim to be the only genuine MGM player to star there. She continued to do cabaret – once in tandem with Donald O'Connor (87) – and TV, till returning to dramatic work in a tele-film, *Sadie and Son* (89). In 1988 she published her autobiography, which revealed that her second husband, Karl, had died bankrupt, having spent all her money and his own; she had worked for seven years, she said, to pay off his debts.

Thelma Ritter

Thelma Ritter was one of the few character players to get star-billing (if not consistently). She was, said 'Variety', one of that 'too-small army of character people considered in films as "box-office insurance" '. She was almost certainly more enjoyed and better liked than most of the big stars she bossed around in her usual role of mother or maid. They certainly did not dazzle *her*. Fixing the heroine (or, less often, the hero) with a baleful eye, she would offer in her gravelly Brooklyn voice some down-to-earth advice which emerged as withering contempt. (It was because of artists like her that we took the Hollywood nonsense for so long.) Even with a poor line, she was very funny.

She came to films late in life. She was born in New York in 1905. Her father was an office manager and amateur singer. She first appeared on stage at the age of 11 as Puck in a semi-professional 'A Midsummer Night's Dream'. After high school she worked in a candy-store and was a telephone operator until she had saved enough to study at the AADA; she worked in stock in New York and New England – mostly playing maids – and made her Broadway début in 'The Shelf' (26). She married an actor (Joseph Moran), but he went into advertising during the Depression – he later became a vice-president of Young and Rubican. Ritter retired, but in the early 40s began to work regularly in radio. To amuse her, director George Seaton, an old friend, offered her a bit part in *Miracle on 34th Street* (47), as a harassed housewife haranguing a

Bette Davis, Thelma Ritter and Celeste Holm in Joseph L. Mankiewicz's All About Eve *(50). It is about this point in the film – because of the witty, pungent dialogue – that you realize that this is an exceptional entertainment: in fact, it is the very first sequence.*

department-store Santa Claus for promising her son a pair of skates. Zanuck was so impressed with the rushes that he ordered the part built up; and when the film came out her success was such that he offered her a contract.

It started badly when her footage in *Call Northside 777* (48) was cut to practically nothing, but Mankiewicz gave her a good part in his *A Letter to Three Wives*, as the gossipy, beer-guzzling neighbour of Linda Darnell's mother, Connie Gilchrist. She was upped to second-billing on *City Across the River* (49), as the ringleader's mother (from Irving Shulman's novel about juvenile delinquents, 'The Amboy Dukes'), but was demoted to family maid in *Father Was a Fullback* – father was Fred MacMurray. Warners borrowed her to play a common housewife while fellow jurors and *Perfect Strangers* (50) Ginger Rogers and Dennis Morgan fell in love; then she was a maid again, Bette Davis's and memorably, in Mankiewicz's *All About Eve* – the first of six Oscar nominations (a record in the Supporting category; she never won). She was in a June Haver musical, *I'll Get By*; then loaned to Paramount for the key role in *The Mating Season* (51), the mother-in-law who poses as the maid without wife Gene Tierney being aware of her identity: 'Miss Ritter is sockeroo' said 'Variety'. Her social status was less doubtful in *As Young As You Feel*, as Monty Woolley's daughter-in-law, an ex-dancer reminiscing over her past. The two of them were top-billed (his part had been meant for Clifton Webb) over Jean Peters, Constance Bennett, etc. She was poor in it, for some reason, but she was good in *The Model and the Marriage Broker*, with Jeanne Crain and sharing the title with her.

Producer Charles Brackett at least thought that with the right handling she could become as big an attraction as had been Marie Dressler and *The Late Christopher Bean* was bought for her – but not made (she later did it as a TV film, for 20th). It was clear that there was more to her than an ability to make acid cracks, but *With a Song in My Heart* (52) was the first picture in a long while to give her the chance to do more than that: she played, very warmly, the firm nurse who helps Susan Hayward and later becomes her companion. It was only a supporting part; exhibitors may have voted her the second most likely star of tomorrow (after Howard Keel) but 20th had not been impressed by the grosses of her two starring pictures. They made her a millionairess on the *Titanic* (53) – the same original that inspired 'The Unsinkable Molly Brown'; a friendly neighbour of Betty Grable's in *The Farmer Takes a Wife*; and what Synopsis called 'a lovable old underworld character' in *Pick-up on South Street*. She was murdered in that; what with the *Titanic*, these were dangerous times. She then played James Stewart's nurse in Hitchcock's *Rear Window* (54). She was equally sceptical as Fred Astaire's secretary in *Daddy Long*

Legs (55), her last for 20th – she asked for release from her contract.

On TV she played in 'The Catered Affair' by Paddy Chayevsky, who said later: 'The first act . . . was farce, the second was character comedy, and the third abruptly drama. There aren't a dozen actresses in the world who could make one piece out of all that, and Miss Ritter did. The fact is she was never properly appreciated as an actress. She was blessed – or cursed – with a tough, urban wit, and a voice to match, and so she got all the gravelly 10th Avenue parts. But she could reveal to an audience the tragedy of the human condition, and do it by being a supreme comedienne – she was a consummate technician. She was also a kind and gentle woman who was esteemed by everyone who ever worked with her.'

She signed for two with Paramount: *Lucy Gallant* with Jane Wyman, as a boarding-house keeper who becomes a customer of that couturier; and *The Proud and the Profane* (56) with Deborah Kerr; after which, understandably, she accepted a Broadway offer – Dressler's old part in a musical version of 'Anna Christie' called 'New Girl in Town'. It brought her a Tony award; earlier, rehearsals had prevented her returning to 20th for *Will Success Spoil Rock Hunter?* and Joan Blondell took on the part. At the end of the run Ritter announced her retirement – not for the first time – but returned to do *A Hole in the Head* (59), as Edward G. Robinson's wife, and *Pillow Talk*, as Doris Day's tippling maid. Her retirement continued – but she continued to receive offers which she considered irresistible: *The Misfits* (61), as a kindly fellow divorcee who befriends Marilyn Monroe; *The Second Time Around*, with Debbie Reynolds; *Bird Man of Alcatraz* (62), as Burt Lancaster's mother; *How the West Was Won* (63), as a pioneer woman; *For Love or Money*, with Mitzi Gaynor; *A New Kind of Love*, as Joanne Woodward's colleague, full of admirable common sense; and *Move Over Darling*, with Doris Day. In *Boeing-Boeing* (65) she was, as at the beginning of her film career, a harassed maid (Tony Curtis's). Larry Peerce's *The Incident* (67) happened in a subway and was a pretty stark drama (it was never shown in Britain). Ritter's last screen appearance ws an unbilled bit in *What's So Bad About Feeling Good?* (68). She died of a heart attack early in 1969.

Jason Robards

Jason Robards is a complete actor, as you might expect from someone who made his New York début as the rear end of a cow in 'Jack and the Beanstalk' and went on to be the country's leading exponent of Eugene O'Neill. He made his reputation in the original production of 'Long Day's Journey Into Night', as the elder son: and he recognized in the father something of his own father, since he had been a travelling actor. Jason Jr was born in Chicago in 1922; shortly after that Jason Sr began to get fairly regular employment as a character player in Hollywood and it was at the Hollywood High School that the boy was educated. He was in the navy during the war and subsequently studied at the AADA; there was a brief appearance in Delaware before playing half that cow in 1947, followed by walk-ons, understudies and jobs as ASMs, including a tour in 'Stalag 17'.

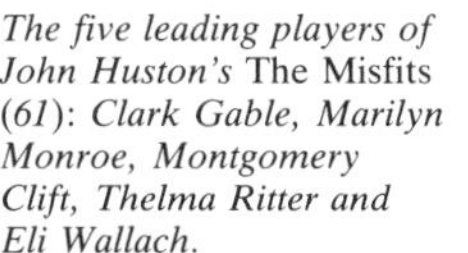

The five leading players of John Huston's The Misfits *(61): Clark Gable, Marilyn Monroe, Montgomery Clift, Thelma Ritter and Eli Wallach.*

He was in 'American Gothic' at the Circle-in-the-Square in 1953 and at the same theatre three years later was Hickey in a revival of 'The Iceman Cometh' (which he repeated on TV in 1960), which led in turn to 'Long Day's Journey' and the critics' award for the year's most promising actor. When its run finished he was at the Stratford, Ontario, Festival as Hotspur and Polixenes ('The Winter's Tale') and later that year, 1958, in another prized Broadway performance, the Scott Fitzgerald role in 'The Disenchanted'. Just prior to that he made his first film, *The Journey* (59), heading the supporting cast as the Russian refugee all the fuss is about – Deborah Kerr is trying to smuggle him in and Yul Brynner is trying to catch him: it could not be said that he was very impressive.

He played Macbeth in Cambridge, Mass., and won another New York drama critics' award for his performance in Lillian Hellman's 'Toys in the Attic', which reawakened Hollywood interest: he played Lana Turner's impotent husband in *By Love Possessed* (61), referred to him as 'By Love Depressed'. He married Lauren Bacall (the third of his four wives; according to her memoir, it was a marriage killed by his drinking, a problem he later licked) and by his own admission was tenth choice for the role of Dick Diver in *Tender Is the Night* (62); he had sincerity, but nothing of the required dash or charm. The film was terrible and few cared that Robards failed along with it. However, to fail in the lead role of an important movie might have spelt finis to screen aspirations had he not already done the film of *Long Day's Journey Into Night*, the only one of the stage cast to repeat – and consistently the best of the screen cast, self-loathing mixed with a boozy good nature. Undoubtedly physical likeness helped him get the role of George S. Kaufman to the Moss Hart of George Hamilton in the film of Hart's memoir, *Act One* (63): the fastidious finickety, dour dramatist was a good role and Robards seized it – underplaying. He was so good, and touching, that it is a pity this made yet another film that few people saw. It was made in New York, where he was appearing in a play (so successfully that he dropped the junior from his name): and he was the only choice for the film version – *A Thousand Clowns* (65), playing the drop-out TV writer who is a Bad Influence on his kid nephew (Barry Gordon). In fact, since he is a Life Force, he really is a good influence and such was the message of this folksy, cutesy piece; fortunately the author (Herb Gardner) also had wit and malice, and Robards had both ease and charm. In time the film became a minor cult, since from the box-office view Robards had not been the right choice. As far as the industry was concerned, he had now shown in his last three films that his work in his first three was not what was to be expected: he was, in fact, a subtle but strong screen actor. His lack of film-star looks precluded big screen stardom, but he would be a useful name above the title, presumably in character roles. He was the chief poker-player against Henry Fonda in *A Big Hand for the Little Lady* (66) and the millionaire executive keeping Jane Fonda in *Any Wednesday*.

He managed to be dull in both *Divorce American Style* (67), as one of the divorcees, and Roger Corman's *The St Valentine's Day Massacre*, as Al Capone: he seemed, with justification, to be uninterested in what he was doing, but he said later that he liked working with Corman. He also liked *Hour of the Gun* because it was closer to the truth than any previous film: he was Doc Holliday to the Wyatt Earp of James Garner. In *The Night They Raided Minsky's* (68) he was Minsky's top banana, good if soulful in that role, but less successful offstage as a lecher; he had more woman trouble in the next – in the shape of *Isadora* (69) Duncan (Vanessa Redgrave), whose first, prim lover he played, the millionaire Paris Singer. That was the first of a number in Europe: *C'era una Volta il West/Once Upon a Time in the West*, partnered with Charles Bronson as the two mysterious outlaws; a British *Julius Caesar* (70), a poor thing compared to Mankiewicz's version and one of the things which made it so was Robards's slightly worried Brutus; and *Rosolino Paterno, Soldato*, directed by Nanni Loy. He had one of his best roles in Sam Peckinpah's *The Ballad of Cable Hogue*, as Hogue, an essentially good man, surviving both his own

Divorce American Style (67); *(left to right) Dick Van Dyke as the one divorcing (Debbie Reynolds); Jean Simmons as the divorcée he's interested in; Jason Robards as her ex-husband; and Van Johnson as the man after Miss Reynolds.*

stupidity and the hazards of Western life: it is a film that he himself is fond of and thinks Warners threw it away. Warners were right, since there had already been far too many supposedly comic Westerns (i.e. the stars running around in longjohns); and the public was right to avoid *Fools*, despite its views of San Francisco: Robards as a horror movie star and Katherine Ross as a much younger and married woman mooned around in them. And to complete a bad year, Robards was a general in Fox's flop version of Pearl Harbor, *Tora Tora Tora*.

As he said himself, around this time he did 'junk', not referring specifically to Dalton Trumbo's plea for peace, *Johnny Got His Gun* (71), but that was the view of several critics; he did mean *Murders in the Rue Morgue* – in Bela Lugosi's old role – which he did because he got a percentage, but it was one horror film, as he lamented, which did not make a cent. In *The War Between Men and Women* (72) he was Barbara Harris's ex and Jack Lemmon's rival for her; in *Pat Garrett and Billy the Kid* (73), he headed down the cast-line to play the Governor. In the German-Israeli *Tod eines Fremden/The Execution* he was a police inspector who warns Jewish lawyer Hardy Kruger about his affair with an Arab terrorist. Seemingly desperate, he made two more dubious movies – not that either were with us more than briefly: *A Boy and His Dog* (75), as the chief of a futuristic (World War 3 has just ended) robot-like tribe and reading 'his fatuous lines with an expression of distate' ('Variety'); and *Mr Sycamore*, as a postman inspired by Greek mythology to turn into a tree.

Whatever his stage abilities, Jason Robards was a fairly uninteresting film-actor when he started, but by the time he made Julia *(77) he was one of the best in the business. He was Dashiell Hammett to Jane Fonda's Lillian Hellman, with little footage and no help from the script, managing one of the cinema's best portraits of a writer.*

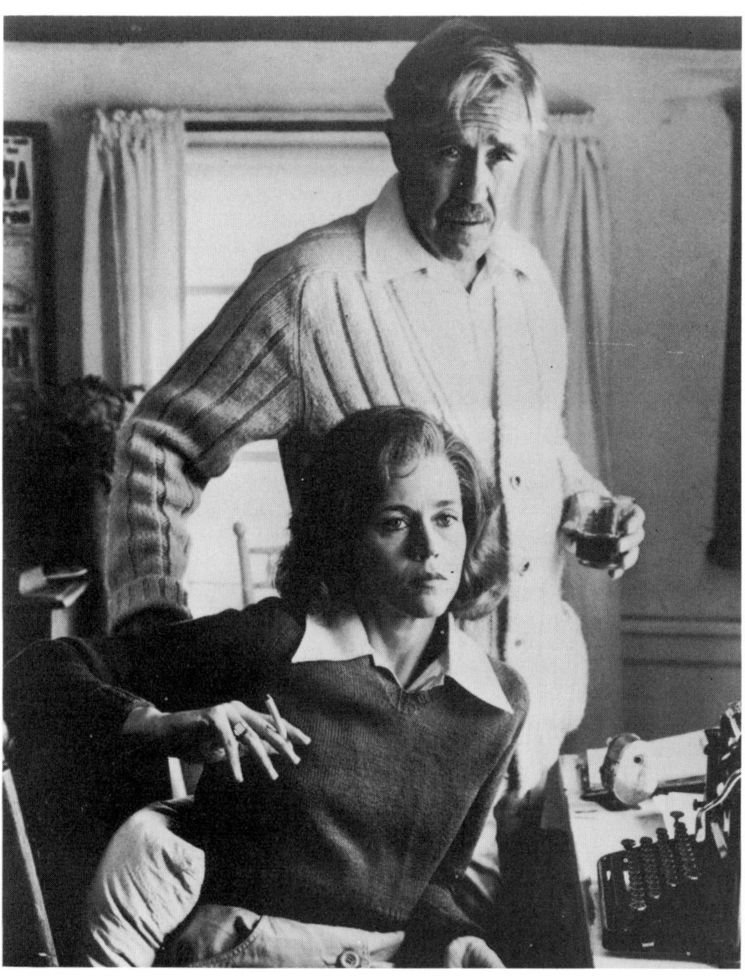

Clearly it was time to turn again into a stage actor; a year earlier he had done 'A Moon for the Misbegotten' in New York and in 1976 he played the father in 'Long Day's Journey Into Night' in Brooklyn; the following year he revived 'A Touch of the Poet' on Broadway. Returning to films, he was offered two plum supporting roles (both based on people he had known) – the hustling editor Ben Bradlee iin *All the President's Men* (76) and the gentle writer Dashiell Hammett in *Julia* (77), and if one invokes the name of Walter Huston it is because for too long there had not been in films an actor able to give both detail and warmth to roles one-dimensionally written. For the first he won the New York critics' award for Best Supporting Actor; for both he won consecutive Best Supporting Oscars.

There was also widespread praise for his portrait of a Nixonian president in *Washington: Behind Closed Doors*, a mini-series, but in the Huston-like role of the old rancher in *Comes a Horseman* (78) he was, as John Coleman put it, 'preposterous'. It was the beginning of much activity: *A Christmas to Remember* for TV with Eva Marie Saint as his wife, a middle-aged couple who during the Depression take, unwillingly, a city boy into their farmhouse; the very expensive and unpopular remake of *Hurricane*, which he did, he said, for 'sheer greed', playing the Governor, Raymond Massey's old role; *Caboblanco* (80), an inept imitation of Casablanca starring Charles Bronson, as a Nazi; and *Melvin and Howard*, as Howard Hughes in Jonathan Demme's sweet tale of the factory worker (Paul Le Mat) who believed – with reason – that he was going to inherit that gentleman's fortune. There were two more real people to enact: agent Leland Hayward, Margaret Sullavan's husband in *Haywire*, and you-know-who in *FDR: The Last Years*, also for TV, with Eileen Heckart as Mrs Roosevelt; then he was in two of Lew Grade's more expensive disasters, in face-savingly cameo roles, *Raise the Titanic*, as an admiral, and *The Legend of the Lone Ranger* (81), as a campaigning General Grant. In Peru he began work – at $16,667 a week for a minimum of

15 weeks – on Werner Herzog's *Fitzcarraldo*, but with 40 per cent of it in the can he left and was replaced by Klaus Kinski. Herzog sued first, for $83,334 plus interest 'for services never rendered'. Robards counterclaimed for much more, claiming 'illness from hazardous tropical working conditions'. Since Robards's doctors supported him, the matter was settled in his favour. Evidence might have been demonstrated in an American documentary on the making of the film, *Burden of Dreams*, which suggests both that Herzog's method of working would have alienated any professional and that his ego is far less limited than his talent. Robards must have felt happy to return to *Hughie* (82), Eugene O'Neill's monologue, for cable; the Disney version of Ray Bradbury's clever *Something Wicked This Way Comes* (83), as the town librarian, father to one of the two small heroes; and Neil Simon's *May Dugan Returns*, as Max, an old reprobate trying to purchase his daughter's love with dubiously acquired gifts. After playing the grandfather in a revival of 'You Can't Take It With You' in Millburn, NH, he was a professor in a controversial tele-film about the effect of a nuclear war on a small Kansas town, *The Day After*, much watched at home and much criticized abroad; simultaneously seen was a mini-series, *Kennedy*, with Martin Sheen as the president. Little seen – and even less liked – was a film about the Russian dissident, *Sakharov* (84), in the title-role, with Glenda Jackson as his activist wife.

There were two more mini-series: *The Atlanta Child Murders* (85), based on fact, opposing Rip Torn across the court-room; and *The Long Hot Summer*, from William Faulkner, as the patriarch, and infinitely better than Orson Welles in the 1958 film. In *Johnny Bull* (86) for TV he and Colleen Dewhurst were a Tennessee couple not happy with the British bride their GI son has brought home; but he was transplanted himself, to Australia, for another mini, *The Last Frontier*, where Linda Evans was a lone American woman coping. After playing a gruff grandfather in *Square Dance* (87), he was on Broadway in a British play, 'A Month of Sundays', but it did not run. Then: *Norman Rockwell's Breaking Home Ties* for TV, so called because it was meant to be Americana, with Miss Saint again as his wife; *Bright Lights Big City* starring Michael J. Fox, in a cameo as a boozy old bore who boasted of hobnobbing with the greats of American literature; *Inherit the Wind* for TV with Kirk Douglas, in the role played previously by Paul Muni (Broadway), Spencer Tracy (film) and Melvyn Douglas (TV, 1965); *The Good Mother*, third-billed, as a lawyer; *The Christmas Wife*, a tele-movie, as a widower who meets the equally lonely Julie Harris; and *Dream a Little Dream* (89), an odd fish in which an adolescent (Corey Feldman) absorbs his 'spirit'. Said Walter Goodman in 'The New York Times': 'Even if you don't quite understand what [Robards] is supposed to be doing, he does it with a charm – a touch laid on, to be sure – that cannot be easily transported into another body.' *Reunion* has a Pinter script and Berlin locations; and it will be followed by *Black Rainbow* and *Parenting*, with Steve Martin.

Cliff Robertson

When Cliff Robertson won his 1968/9 Oscar for *Charly*, he commented that hitherto he had not been considered important enough to be even invited to the Awards ceremony: it was a classic case of perseverance and ambition triumphing over a lot of rotten breaks – i.e. a career composed mainly of films made to keep his name before the public and/or to pay the rent.

He was born in La Jolla, California, in 1925 and studied at Antioch College, where he decided to become an actor. After war service with the merchant marine, he tried New York for acting jobs and finally got into a small troupe touring the Catskills with 'Three Men on a Horse' (47). Then it was back to odd jobs for a bit (cab-driver, longshoreman), till he got into one of the road companies of 'Mister Roberts'. He was two years with it and from 1950 onwards got regular work on – and off – Broadway and in TV. In 1952 he was in 'The Wisteria Trees', which Joshua Logan had adapted from 'The Cherry Orchard', and that led to Logan casting him as the second male lead in *Picnic* (55) at Columbia. That studio signed him to a contract, two films a year, and put him into *Autumn Leaves* (56), as Joan Crawford's mentally unstable and much younger husband – an excellent performance, in a different style from hers but not clashing: but it was the sort of sudser which could further her career and not his. He went to Broadway to appear in 'Orpheus Descending' and returned to Hollywood to play opposite Jane Powell in *The Girl Most Likely* (57).

He was better served by *The Naked and the Dead* (58), but that, decent though it was (Raoul Walsh directed), fatally conventionalized Norman Mailer's novel about the antagonism between officers and men on a Pacific outpost. It passed almost unnoticed and the best Columbia offered Robertson then was a teenage surf pic, *Gidget* (59), which did well in the US but not elsewhere. After that, he was reduced to *Battle of the Coral Sea* and a German effort with Maria Schell, set in

Greece, *Raubfischer in Hellas/As the Sea Rages* (66). He was strictly the loser in *All in a Night's Work* (61), with Shirley MacLaine and Dean Martin, and, as far as the films were concerned, with *Underworld USA*, as a Cagney-type ex-con who goes straight in this Samuel Fuller film, and *The Big Show*, dead-and-circuses with Esther Williams. He was top-billed in Columbia's popular medico melodrama, *The Interns* (62), as one of them, but was merely decoration in a dog-collar in *My Six Loves* (63), some slush with Debbie Reynolds.

Robertson's name first made the world's press in a big way when he was personally selected (it was said; Warren Beatty had certainly refused the part earlier) by President Kennedy to play his younger self in the film of his war memoir, *PT 109*: it failed at the box-office and fared no better when reissued in the wake of the worldwide sympathy which followed JFK's assassination. However, it got Robertson into another A picture, *Sunday in New York* (64), as Jane Fonda's Lothario-brother, and, more importantly, into *The Best Man*, as Henry Fonda's younger, more ruthless rival – which may have been very witty casting. This was the saddest of the failures, for it was an exceptional film, an accusation not to be levelled at any of the following: *633 Squadron*, a war film made in Britain; *Love Has Many Faces* (65), a Lana Turner romance; *Masquerade*, a British thriller with Jack Hawkins; and *Up from the Beach*, 20th's 'sort-of' sequel to *The Longest Day*. Robertson did have a good part in *The Honey Pot* (67), as Rex Harrison's secretary, an actor/gigolo, and he made it both sympathetic and sinister. There was another good role in a mediocre war film, *The Devil's Brigade* (68), with William Holden. *The Sunshine Patriot* was a tele-movie about spying, directed by Joseph Sargent.

Cliff Robertson and Claire Bloom in Charly *(68). He gave a good performance as a mentally backward man who is shown to have a large IQ after a brain operation. Miss Bloom was the woman who helped and loved him.*

The story behind *Charly* became doubly romantic with the awarding of the Best Actor Oscar. Robertson had been in two TV plays which had become successful movies for other actors ('The Hustler' and 'Days of Wine and Roses'); so when he did 'The Two Worlds of Charly Gordon' on TV in 1961 he bought the screen rights. It took him seven years to get backing – from Cinerama; finally there were fine notices (for him) and good business for this drama about a mentally retarded man who becomes a genius after an operation and then regresses. Said 'Time Magazine' about his Oscar victory: 'Competitors like Alan Arkin and Alan Bates may have been content to rest on their performances; Robertson knew better. Starting in October 1968, ads on his behalf were placed in the trade papers. "Best actor of the year – the National Board of Review" they reminded readers. . . . The campaign culminated in a giant double-page foldout inserted in Daily Variety. Its contents: 83 favorable mentions from a spectrum of journals. Publicly, the Academy frowned. Privately, many members agreed that Robertson's victory was based more on promotion than on performance.'

When the Oscar was announced, he was making *Too Late the Hero* (70), with Michael Caine, of whom the director approved, referring to 'his asshole of a co-star' because Robertson tried to upstage him. Robertson indicated that if he now got the expected choice of better scripts, it would probably be his last war film. However, the Oscar had no discernible effect on his career. He wrote, produced and directed *J.W. Coop* (72), about a rodeo rider rehabilitated after some years in prison, and though made before a number of similar films it was the last released – though none of them much interested the public. Nor did either *The Great Northfield Minnesota Raid*, about the James brothers, or *Ace Eli and Rodger of the Skies*. He was *The Man Without a Country* (73), a drama of the 1812 war, for TV; and also for that medium were a remake of *A Tree Grows in Brooklyn* (74) with Diane Baker, in James Dunn's old role; and *My Father's House* (75), in which he reflects on life and growing up with father Robert Preston after a heart attack. He was one of several names in *Midway* (76), but had only one scene, as a commander; and had his best part in years in the Canadian *Shoot* – and took it: as a partly deranged military man he was 'superlative' said 'Variety'. *Obsession* was a confused and Hitchcock-influenced horror film, though it increased the cult for its young director, Brian De Palma: Robertson and Genevieve Bujold were the husband and wife at the centre of the mystery.

It was clearly time to return to television:

Return to Earth, as the astronaut Buzz Aldrin, who wrote about his own nervous breakdown; *Washington: Behind Closed Doors* (77), as President Kennedy; and *Overboard* (78), in which Angie Dickenson is shipwrecked and remembers their marriage in flashback. Robertson planned to direct himself again in a film of Maxwell Anderson's *Morning, Noon and Night*, but financing fell through early in 1978; and he postponed his film version of James Kirkwood's *Good Times, Bad Times*, when offered the alcoholic title-role in *The Pilot* (81). He was one of its writers and took over the direction some way into shooting. The film had been made two years earlier – very slowly, according to 'New York Magazine', referring not only to the Kirkwood project but also *Charly II*, which was started but abandoned: 'Each of the [three] pictures has either collapsed or been dogged by budget problems, leaving equipment suppliers, contractors, and crews out in the cold for hundreds of thousands of dollars.' Robertson himself, according to the same source, had 'angered Hollywood's sultans by blowing the whistle on [executive] David Begelman's fiscal indiscretions', including forging a cheque in Robertson's name. The scandal was considerable and occasioned a major book on the subject; it was rumoured that Robertson had been boycotted by Hollywood, whatever his wrongs, and the fact is that he had been absent from Hollywood for a long while before returning – ironically for MGM, where the forgiven Begelman now reigned: but then, Robertson had been working for four years on the project with the director, Douglas Trumbell. *Brainstorm* (83), however, was a dud; Robertson played the boss of the company responsible for the sci-fi breakthrough which provided the plot. It was released after *Two of a Kind* (82), a tele-movie in which he puts his father (George Burns) into a home; and *Class* (83), in which as Jacqueline Bisset's husband he is cuckolded by a schoolboy; and before *Star 80*, Mike Nicholls's study of the 'Playboy' centrefold murdered by her husband. Robertson played Hugh Hefner. In 1983 he also joined 'Falcon's Crest' for a salary estimated by 'People Magazine' to be in the same range as Jane Wyman's, perhaps between $35,000 and $50,000 weekly. Then: *The Key to Rebecca* (85), a mini from Ken Follett's thriller, as a British army major pitted against a Nazi spy in North Africa; *Dreams of Gold: the Mel Fisher Story* (86), based on fact, as Fisher, the underwater treasure seeker, for TV; *Malone* (87) as a megalomaniac whose plans to dominate America are foiled by Burt Reynolds; and *Ford: the Man and the Machine*, a mini-series.

Gail Russell

Gail Russell was a frail and beautiful heroine of the 40s and one of the movies' most pathetic creatures. She was born in 1924 in Chicago and moved to California with her parents in her teens. She was educated at Santa Monica High and it was a chance meeting between two schoolmates and a Paramount executive which brought her into films: they boasted of her looks – 'the Hedy Lamarr of Santa Monica' – and he arranged a test. She was painfully shy and had had no acting experience, but she photographed well enough for Paramount to offer the standard seven-year contract. They gave her a small role as a high school beauty in *Henry Aldrich Gets Glamour* (43), with Jimmy Lydon, one of their B series about the Aldrich family. They also gave her a drama coach. A year later, she had a bit as Ginger Rogers's rival in *Lady in the Dark* (44), though that was in fact released a few days after her first starring role, in *The Uninvited*, a Cornish ghost story with Ray Milland and a film with a rather endearing 'atmosphere'. She played a girl apparently possessed: not a role which required much emotional depth. But the film was very successful and she was regarded as Paramount's next big female star.

Gail Russell at the time she was still regarded as one of the brightest new stars in Hollywood: as John Wayne's leading lady in The Angel and the Badman (*47*).

With another Paramount hopeful, Diana Lynn, she was paired in *Our Hearts Were Young and Gay*, a comedy about two US flappers coping with Europe in the 20s, from a bestseller by Cornelia Otis Skinner (who was in *The Uninvited*) and Emily Kimbrough. There was a sequel after the next three: *The Unseen* (45), another supernatural tale, with Joel McCrea; *Salty O'Rourke*, leading lady to Alan Ladd; and *Duffy's Tavern*, in a guest spot. It was called *Our Hearts Were Growing Up* (46) and was by no means as well liked as the earlier film. Paramount loaned her out to play one of a quartet of gold-diggers in *Bachelor's Daughters* (the others were Claire Trevor, Jane Wyatt, Ann Dvorak) and then again to be John Wayne's love interest in an indifferent Western, *The Angel and the Badman* (47).

No studio loaned out its star properties for two consecutive films unless things were not entirely satisfactory and the truth was that Russell's screen personality, because of her inhibitions, was rather blah. They tried her as a villainess, opposite Alan Ladd in *Calcutta*, but she did not have the 'fatal beauty' appeal of a Mary Astor, or even that of a Hedy Lamarr. She guested in *Variety Girl* and then, after a year's absence, was again a haunted heroine, in *The Night Has a Thousand Eyes* (48), a confused melodrama with Edward G. Robinson. She returned to John Wayne and Republic for *Wake of the Red Witch*, a sea story, and became mired in a series of indifferent action melodramas: *Song of India* (49), filmed in sepia tones by Columbia, with Sabu, as Princess Tara; *El Paso*, a Cinecolor Western with John Payne, produced by Pine-Thomas for Paramount; and *The Great Dan Patch*, also in sepia, at United Artists, a racing story with Dennis O'Keefe. At Republic she was in Frank Borzage's *Moonrise*, an unsuccessful mood piece about a young man (Dane Clark), haunted by murder, who falls in love with a schoolteacher. Her last two films for Paramount were *Captain China*, a Pine-Thomas junk in which she was fought over by John Payne and Jeffrey Lynn, and *The Lawless* (50), a Joseph Losey-directed story of mob violence in which she was a newspaperwoman. Losey later spoke of 'poor, desperate, lonely, tragic Gail Russell's eyes' as contributing to the film.

The Night Has a Thousand Eyes (*48*). *Edward G. Robinson played an ex-vaudeville magician with clairvoyant powers. Having predicted that Gail Russell will die shortly, he sets out to prevent it. John Lund was also helping.*

Paramount did not renew her contract, because, for one thing, Russell was drinking heavily – a habit begun as early as *The Uninvited*, when she found that alcohol stilled her nerves. It was hoped she might stabilize when she married Guy Madison, a young actor of strictly pin-up-boy appeal. After a long courtship they were married in 1949. A year later she was convicted on driving charges. Universal took a chance on her and let her play Stephen McNally's estranged wife in *Air Cadet* (51), but she did not make *Flaming Feather* for Paramount, as announced, nor *Loan Shock*, opposite George Raft: the latter was to have been her 'come-back' film – a B – but she suffered nervous shock when her brother was in a car crash and withdrew. She was out of the news till John Wayne's wife named her in her divorce suit (1953): both Wayne and Russell denied this, but the flurry of scandal sent Russell into a sanatorium. In 1954 she and Madison were divorced. She was in and out of sanatoria and now when she was on a driving charge (one in 1955 was said to be the sixth in two years) there was no studio to cover up the fact that she was an alcoholic. Hollywood tried to help. A cure was said to be effected and Wayne put her into a film being made by his company, *Seven Men From Now* (56), a Western with Randolph Scott. She looked much older. Universal used her now rather dramatic appearance in a full-blooded role, in *The Tattered Dress* (57), where she lied under oath and shot her lover (Jack Carson) on the courthouse steps. For Republic she did an incredible flying story, *No Place to Land*, with Mari Blanchard and John Ireland.

As these films went the rounds she was fined again for drunken driving and given a suspended gaol sentence. In an occasional interview she spoke humbly of her alcoholism, saying it was caused because 'everything happened so fast'. In 1961 20th gave her top-billing in a B, *The Silent Call*, a boy-and-dog picture (she was the boy's mother). In August of that year, she was discovered dead in her one-room apartment, surrounded by empty bottles. She had died some days earlier, from natural causes. She was 36.

JANE RUSSELL

Jane Russell first appeared among us looking surly on a pile of straw. Her lips were set petulantly, her eyes were scornful but inviting, her dress pushed off the shoulder so that it stretched against what were thought to be the biggest boobs in the business. 'Mean! Moody! Magnificent!' ran the legend under the stills. Schoolboys and dirty old men anticipated her first film and licked their lips. It took a long time in coming – five years – but it arrived carrying blazons of censorship and the promise of at last giving the low-down on the proverbial roll in the hay. Thus Russell acquired a name in film-lore largely unjustified by what happened on screen. When they let her play comedy she – and we – discovered that she could do funny lines with verve; she had, then, a warm, likeable personality. Her advent made and marred her.

She was born in 1921 in Bemidji, Minnesota; her mother was a minor actress, but Russell was at first not ambitious in that direction. She became a chiropodist's assistant and did some occasional modelling. However, in 1940 she enrolled in Max Reinhardt's Theatrical Workshop and afterwards studied under Maria Ouspenskaya. Meanwhile, Howard Hughes had seen some of her model photos and wanted to test her for a Western he planned about Billy the Kid. Hughes was a millionaire who liked to dabble in films and he was going to produce and direct this one, *The Outlaw* (43); he wanted a couple of unknowns in the leads and signed Russell and Jack Buetel. Filming began in 1941 and proceeded, with retakes, for nine months, with Hughes taking over direction from Howard Hawks. Whether the breast fetish or Jane came first is not known, but the film's publicity (organized by an expert, Russell Birdwell) soon began to emphasize her front. By the time the picture opened, the bluenoses were ready for it: it opened and closed very quickly in San Francisco. The Hays Office disapproved of both the Russell cleavage and the adverts; the Code seal of approval awarded back in 1941 was revoked; and there was much litigation. A Baltimore judge observed that Russell's bosom 'hung over the picture like a thunderstorm over a landscape' (quoted by Murray Schumach, 'The Face on the Cutting Room Floor'). In 1946 the film finally played a few cities: it shocked some, bored others (today, it only bores).

Critics found Russell's acting unexceptional, to say the least – a view confirmed by *Young Widow* (46). Hughes had loaned her to United Artists for it; the fuss about *The Outlaw* did not help and there, pending any future Hughes plans, her career might have languished. But Paramount were planning a spoof Western for Bob Hope, with Ginger Rogers as Calamity Jane. They baulked, however, at her fee – $325,000 plus a percentage – and simultaneously realized that fun could be made out of Russell's mammary attractions. In *The Paleface* (48) she proved to be an excellent foil in more ways than two and a future as a comedienne seemed assured.

Hughes had now bought into RKO and was running it. He sold half of Russell's contract to RKO and each time she made a film he picked up in the region of $200,000 for her services: *His Kind of Woman* (51) – Robert Mitchum's, but the title had little to do with the plot; *Double Dynamite*, with Frank Sinatra, a last-minute title change from *It's Only Money*; *The Las Vegas Story* (52), a triangle drama with Vincent Price (husband) and Victor Mature (old flame); and *Macao* directed by von Sternberg, with Mitchum, playing yet again a clip-joint crooner mixed up in thuggery. These followed on the delayed US release of *The Outlaw*, a film already forgotten by the rest of the world – though it was, everywhere, a big money-maker. Hughes was having trouble with RKO: ex-chairman Arnold M. Grant said the studio was now losing $6 million a year and a group of stockholders filed suit, claiming 'it is the consensus of motion-picture critics that the acting ability and talent of Jane Russell are of a minor nature and the payment of $100,000

Jane Russell in The Outlaw *(43). This photograph was once considered very shocking.*

Jane Russell in (above) Gentlemen Prefer Blondes *(53) and* Gentlemen Marry Brunettes *(55). Like the two novels on which they were based, the original was more popular than the sequel. As far as the films were concerned, this might have had something to do with the fact that Miss Russell's partners were Marilyn Monroe and Jeanne Crain respectively.*

for her services constitutes a waste of corporate funds'. (In fact, she got that for *The Outlaw* and was now getting twice that sum.) Hughes resigned, but after selling some shares – at government decree – returned as production head. Russell also surfaced: 'Picturegoer' reported that a Miami nightclub was suing her for $1 million because she was disappointing in the flesh, but Bob Hope again came to her rescue and she co-starred with him in *Son of Paleface*. Paramount liked her so much that they planned a musical for her and Danny Kaye, but their schedules did not fit (it was made, *Red Garters*, with Guy Mitchell and Rosemary Clooney).

For the moment, however, Hughes contented himself with a movie made, like *Double Dynamite*, back in 1948: the Trucolored *Montana Belle* with George Brent, in which she played Belle Starr (Hunt Stromberg had made it and Hughes bought it from him for $600,000, to keep it out of distribution till he had made her a star himself). He loaned her to 20th to play Dorothy – her favourite part – to Monroe's Lorelei Lee in *Gentlemen Prefer Blondes* (53), a big hit and the provider of the best notices of her career. There were again censorship problems with Hughes's *The French Line* (54), specifically about the camera angles (it was shot in 3-D) and the costume in a song-and-dance number: it was later shown with some cuts, flat (very flat). *Underwater* (55) did no better, despite a much-publicized première under water in Florida. It was her last film for Hughes, although she signed a new contract for six pictures with him over a 20-year period. None was ever made (even though he retained her contract when he sold RKO), but they could hardly have been worse than the ones she did make: *Foxfire* at Universal, as Jeff Chandler's stuffy, disapproving wife (a part meant for June Allyson); *The Tall Men* with Clark Gable – and with her increasing confidence, they made a good team; *Gentlemen Marry Brunettes*, produced by her husband and by its scripter, Richard Sale, a poor sequel to an earlier film, with Jeanne Crain; *Hot Blood* (56); an absurd gypsy melodrama with Cornel Wilde; and *The Revolt of Mamie Stover*, a cleaned up but vulgar version of William Bradford Huie's novel, 'a commercial film about a commercial dame' in the words of 'Variety'. *The Fuzzy Pink Nightgown* (57) she produced herself and it served her right.

On film she had evidenced a good singing voice and she now accepted singing engagements on TV and in nightclubs, sometimes with one or two female partners. Sometimes they sang religious songs: she was renowned for her religious beliefs. She also made some unimportant appearances in legit. She did not return to movies till *Fate Is the Hunter* (64), playing herself in an unbilled bit. A while later she starred in a couple of B Westerns for A.C. Lyles, *Johnny Reno* (66) and *Waco*. She had a guest spot in one of AIP's motor-cycle pics, *Born Losers* (67), as the mother of a raped girl. In 1968 she told a reporter: 'Sure, I'd like to do movies again. But the studios can't forget the old image of Jane Russell'; instead she did a singing act in British clubs with Beryl Davies. She also made headlines by divorcing her husband of 25 years (former football-player Bob Waterfield) and marrying again – but the groom died within months of the wedding. She had a good role in *Darker Than Amber* (71), starring Rod Taylor, and then made her Broadway début, taking over from Elaine Stritch in the musical 'Company'. She was still receiving $1,000 a week under her contract to Hughes, which he renewed in 1974 for a further 10 years, but it was presumably cancelled on his death. She married again; and in 1978 was jailed for drunken driving.

Margaret Rutherford

James Mason once, on being asked who was his favourite leading lady, said that he had tried rating them all by stars and the only five-star lady was Margaret Rutherford. The interviewer suggested he was being diplomatic; Mason only half agreed. The fact is that Margaret Rutherford was a rather special actress. She had, it must be admitted, a funny face. Unattractive, no; but funny, yes. She had the demeanour of a startled turkeycock, the jaws of a bloodhound (all British character actors are compared, sooner or later to animals). This element of *grotesquerie*, allied to a rather unwieldy frame, restricted her for a while to weirdies. When her comic skill was recognized, she played a variety of eccentric English spinsters, intense, gushing and woolly-minded – all of which she embraced with a non-patronizing warmth. It was this sublime comic gift which lifted her from the serried ranks of featured players: even when being mishandled by those manifold incompetent British directors, she imposed on her material an elegance of timing which made almost every line amusing.

She was born in London in 1892 and started out as a teacher of elocution and of the piano. But she wanted to be an actress and studied at the Old Vic School, making her début in the Old Vic pantomime of 1925, 'Little Jack Horner', as the Fairy with the Long Nose. She worked in rep, at Croydon and Oxford, and was back on the London boards in 'Wild Justice' (33). She gained some small fame over the next few years on the stage and made her screen bow in a quota quickie, *Dusty Ermine* (36), when 'Picturegoer' thought she scored as the wily agent of a gang of forgers. She was in *Talk of the Devil*, a comedy and one of Carol Reed's first films, and *Beauty and the Barge* (37), as Gordon Harker's landlady and romantic interest. *Catch as Catch Can* was the only film she made with James Mason, as a passenger on an Atlantic liner; then she was in the equally unmemorable *Missing Believed Married*, as an irritable grandmother.

Her career first took off when she played Bijou in the long-running 'Spring Meeting' (38) and that was followed by three more successes: 'The Importance of Being Earnest' (39) with John Gielgud, as Miss Prism, 'Rebecca' (40), as Mrs Danvers, and Noël Coward's 'Blithe Spirit' (41), as the irrepressible medium, Madame Arcati. Meanwhile she returned to films: *Quiet Wedding* (40) with Margaret Lockwood, as a village busybody; *Spring Meeting* (41) with Nova Pilbeam, in her stage role; and then *Yellow Canary* (43), with Anna Neagle, as a dotty old lady – a part that was built up during filming because she was so effective; *The Demi-Paradise*, with Laurence Olivier, as the doyen of the village fête; and *English Without Tears* (44), as an English matron campaigning before the League of Nations on behalf of migratory birds. If Terence Rattigan wrote this, as credited, he did so in a few days and it was filmed in less, but it was amusing and mildly successful. New York critics in particular noticed her; and her next film made her perhaps the favourite

Blithe Spirit *(45). Rex Harrison and Constance Cummings were a couple who play at spiritualism and get more than they bargain for – the ghost of his first wife. Margaret Rutherford was the medium not displeased at this manifestation.*

character actress of the time. This was the film *Blithe Spirit* (45), in her stage role, 'What a part!', said William Whitebait in the 'New Statesman'. 'And Miss Margaret Rutherford fits it like a glove – or should I say a meal-sack? Every moment of her presence is memorable.'

On the stage she played a pair of queens in 'Alice in Wonderland' (44) and was in Ivor Novello's 'Perchance to Dream' (45). Also in 1945 she married actor Stringer Davis. 20th signed her for a leading role in *Meet Me at Dawn* (46), starring Britain's Hazel Court and Hollywood's William Eythe, the first of a series of 20th-British pictures (but its failure, and that of the subsequent products, soon curtailed the project). After a cameo role in the film of Rattigan's long-running play, *While the Sun Shines* (47), starring Ronald Howard (Leslie's son) and Bonar Colleano, she went to New York to play Lady Bracknell and subsequently toured in that part in the US. Returning to Britain, she was at her most energetic as a mermaid's nurse in *Miranda* (48), a fair comedy carried to huge success in Britain on the tide of euphoria washing over native films at that time, among both critics and public alike. *Passport to Pimlico* (49) was, however, a genuinely funny comedy, made by Ealing, about a London community which threw off postwar restrictions on learning that their 'village' was in fact French territory; brilliantly scripted by T.E.B. Clarke, it assembled a recognizable bunch of Londoners (Stanley Holloway, Hermione Baddeley, etc.) including Rutherford as the enthusiastic expert who verified the authenticity of the medieval charter on which the plot depended.

The Happiest Days of Your Life (50) was more conventional but also pretty terrific, with Rutherford repeating her recent stage role as the headmistress of a girls' school inadvertently billeted on a boys' school; a stroke of genius brought Alastair Sim as the

Michael Redgrave and Margaret Rutherford in The Importance of Being Earnest *(52). James Agate wrote of her Miss Prism in an earlier stage production: 'Miss Margaret Rutherford couldn't miss perfection – even if she aimed wide of it'.*

boys' headmaster. Said Whitebait: '. . . but headmistress or anything else, she's a world in herself, the counterpart in loose-lipped virtuosity of M. Michel Simon. . . . The duel between Miss Rutherford and Mr Sim – she bluff and soldierly, he with a sinuous crushed charm – is a confrontation or long-drawn-out skirmish that should not be missed.' It was not; in Britain the film was a big hit and it did well in the US art houses. It now occurred to producers that Rutherford, billed above the title, was a considerable box-office asset – though no one could have helped *Her Favourite Husband*, an Anglo-Italian comedy with Jean Kent and Robert Beatty, whose disapproving mother-in-law she played. She did a cameo, as an aristocratic client of the photographer hero, in *The Magic Box* (51), while appearing in another West End success, Anouilh's 'Ring Round the Moon'.

There were more successful stage appearances, including 'The Way of the World' (53), as Lady Wishfort, and 'Time Remembered' (54) by Anouilh – presumably compensating for as dire a bunch of pictures (with one exception) as can be imagined: *Curtain Up* (52) with Robert Morley, as a would-be dramatist; *Castle in the Air* with David Tomlinson, as a lodger in a stately home that is trying to pay its way; Anthony Asquith's enjoyable *The Importance of Being Earnest*, perfect as Miss Prism and beautifully matched by Miles Malleson as Chasuble; *Miss Robin Hood*, as the eccentric meddling fan of a mild writer of girls' stories; and *Innocents in Paris* (53), as an elderly British artist. Yet worse was to come: *Trouble in Store* (54), as a shoplifter, supporting comic Norman Wisdom in his first film. Undeterred, she accepted a similar assignment – bolstering comic Frankie Howerd in his first movie, *The Runaway Bus*, even more of an endurance test for audiences and much less successful (though Howerd was considerably more talented than Wisdom). After *Mad About Men*, a sequel to *Miranda*, she co-starred with another comic, Ronald Shiner, in *Aunt Clara*, but this was rather a starring film for *her*, as a pious old girl left some dubious enterprises by a reprobate uncle.

She was the pet-shop owner in *An Alligator Named Daisy* (55) and a romantic usherette in *The Smallest Show on Earth* (57), a charming comedy about a flea-pi , with Virginia McKenna and Bill Travers as its young owners – and her only good film in a while. She was with Wisdom again in *Just My Luck*, as a racehorse-owner, ridiculously caparisoned and surrendering to the mugging going on wholesale about her – and still stealing every scene. In 1957/8 she toured Australia with her husband, in 'The Happiest Days of Your Life' and 'Time Remembered'. She returned to the West End in 'Farewell Farewell Eugene' (59), which she also did in New York the following year. In films she played a pair of daffy aristocrats, Ian Carmichael's aunt in *I'm All Right Jack* (59) and Danny Kaye's in *On the Double* (61), in Hollywood. All but two of her subsequent film appearances were for Hollywood companies, starting with *Murder She Said*, a dualler for MGM, as Miss Marple, Agatha Christie's elderly spinster detective. When Peter Sellers declined to replay the Grand Duchess in the sequel to *The Mouse That Roared*, called *The Mouse on the Moon* (63), it went to Rutherford, under the direction of Dick Lester. The film was nowhere as successful as the original, but another sequel, *Murder at the Gallop* with Robert Morley, as Miss Marple again, did even better business than the first. In *The V.I.P.s* she was a querulous plane passenger, a certain joy in this uneven film – and received a very popular Best Supporting Oscar. Her international reputation reached a peak: MGM did two more Miss Marple thrillers, *Murder Most Foul* (64) and *Murder Ahoy* (65). Programmers both in intent and content, and both poor, they were hugely popular in certain European countries.

In 1962 she was in an acclaimed production of 'The School for Scandal', but her last stage performance, in the long-delayed British première of 'The Solid Gold Cadillac' (65), was not too well received. In 1966 she was made a Dame of the British Empire and appeared in cameo roles for two famous film-makers: as Mistress Quickly in Orson Welles's *Campanadas a Medianoche/Chimes at Midnight/Falstaff* (66), a touching performance – unsurprisingly, but unexpected, as she had seldom been allowed to play seriously on screen; and as a greedy passenger in Chaplin's *A Countess from Hong Kong* (67), perhaps the sole bright spot in that film. In Italy she made *Arabella* (69) with Terry-Thomas, as a lady in tax difficulties, helped out by larcenous granddaughter Virna Lisi. Afterwards she was announced for several movies, including *The Virgin and the Gypsy* and *Song of Norway*, but serious back and hip injuries often kept her hospitalized. She died in 1972: a lady who will never be replaced.

Robert Ryan

The word to describe Robert Ryan was 'dependable' – which is not to suggest exactly that he was a second-stringer. He was not 'a shimmering, glowing star in the cinema firm-a-ment' – as Jean Hagen described herself in

Singin' in the Rain – but belongs in a category unique to himself (or almost – Van Heflin would belong to this category and perhaps Arthur Kennedy): the second-billed leading man. For 25 years. He never went from star to supporting player. He remained a star, but usually as the hero's friend or the heavy. His leads were mainly in programmers. To achieve a career of such longevity, without undulation, and to sustain it when most ageing actors fall away, suggests an even and reliable talent, one respected by producers and critics. He was a sympathetic, relaxed, forceful but rather tentative hero, limited by what he calls his 'long, seamy face': Cary Grant, he once pointed out, because of his charm and gifts, got the glamorous locations, but he did his films 'in deserts with a dirty shirt and a two day growth of beard'. The eyes which in his pleasant parts could show a crinkly humour could also suggest paranoia, someone withdrawn from the warm ways of the world. He was a glinting, wiry, villain. Few actors of his stature have cared to risk unsympathetic parts and he liked to point out that he had not done that many. Still, he said: 'I have been in films pretty well everything I am dedicated to fighting against.'

He was born in Chicago in 1909, where his father was an executive of the Ryan Contracting Co. As a child he was taught boxing and at Dartmouth he was college heavyweight champion; he majored in dramatic literature and planned to go into journalism. But these were the Depression years. He refused to go into his father's business and did various jobs – ship's stoker, ranch-hand, sand-hog, salesman and even debt-collector for two weeks. Back in Chicago he did some modelling and became interested in amateur dramatics. A friend of his mother's got him a municipal appointment, but a lucky oil investment enabled him to seek professional drama training; he went to California to enrol at the Pasadena Playhouse but instead joined Max Reinhardt's Theatrical Workshop (he married fellow pupil Jessica Cadwalader in 1939; she gave up acting but published some children's books and mystery stories). After graduating, he got a job in a local musical, 'Too many Husbands', based on a Maugham play, and that resulted in a Paramount contract worth $75 a week. He had bit parts in *Golden Gloves* (40), directed by Edward Dmytryk, as a boxer; *Queen of the Mob*; *North West Mounted Police*; and *Texas Rangers Ride Again* (41). Paramount dropped him.

He got an unbilled bit in *The Feminine Touch* and then a job in stock on Cape Cod, where he was in 'A Kiss for Cinderella' with Luise Rainer. Her ex-husband, Clifford Odets, saw him and offered him the juvenile in his 'Clash by Night' on Broadway, and he was seen in that by Pare Lorentz, then working for RKO. Lorentz had made a number of award-winning documentaries and was preparing his first feature, a Depression story called *Name Age and Occupation*. Ryan was signed to play the lead opposite Frances Dee, on a long-term contract starting at $600 a week. After months of preparation it was decided that wartime audiences would not want a Depression picture and it was cancelled. Instead, Ryan made a series of war-themed movies: *Bombardier* (43) starring Pat O'Brien and Randolph Scott, as a student bombardier; *The Sky's the Limit*, as Fred Astaire's airforce buddy; *Behind the Rising Sun*, directed by Dmytryk, with Margo and J. Carroll Naish, as an American boxer in Japan; *The Iron Major*, as a priest, with O'Brien as a (real) World War I hero; and *Gangway for Tomorrow* – which was the assembly-line where the chief characters worked.

Ginger Rogers then asked for him as her leading man – the 'dead' husband in flashback in *Tender Comrade*, which was notable only because it gave him a *cachet* among studio workers – because of his diplomatic handling of the rightist star and the left-wing director and writer (Dmytryk and Dalton Trumbo respectively). At Pat O'Brien's request he was given co-star billing alongside him in a programmer, *Marine Raiders* (44). Then he joined the marines in actuality. He returned to RKO to play Randolph Scott's comrade-in-arms in a Western, *Trail Street* (47), and then had his best film role to date, in *Woman on the Beach*, as the mixed-up coast-

Crossfire *(47) was a much admired thriller in its day because it dealt with racial prejudice – the murdered man was Jewish. Robert Ryan was one of the suspects; Robert Young the detective in charge of the case.*

guard egged on by Joan Bennett to murder her blind husband (Charles Bickford). Jean Renoir directed, with an untypical lack of cohesion – but Ryan liked working with him. His next film also advanced his career: *Crossfire*, directed by Dmytryk and based on a novel by Richard Brooks (whom Ryan had known in the marines), about three army buddies, one of whom murders a homosexual. In the film the victim became simply a Jew and the film was thus praised as a tract on anti-Semitism. It benefited, rather, from the new, postwar realism, but today on any count is merely a conventional thriller. Ryan was mean and ugly as the murderer.

He did two more programmers, *Berlin Express* (48), a Nazi melodrama with Merle Oberon, and *Return of the Badmen*, a Randolph Scott Western in which he was a sadist called the Sundance Kid. Then he played a psychiatrist in *The Boy with Green Hair* (played by Dean Stockwell), a pretentious allegory – directed by Joseph Losey – which was supposed to Mean Something. But *Act of Violence* at MGM was a good film – perhaps the best that Ryan was in – about an ex-veteran, a solid citizen (Van Heflin), suddenly plagued by an old buddy. Ryan was fine as this limping Nemesis; Fred Zinnemann directed. Ryan had another good director, Max Ophüls, on *Caught* (49), but the corn was high – a multi-millionaire (based on Howard Hughes, as Hughes recognized, without rancour) given to tantrums and locked in a loveless marriage with Barbara Bel Geddes. *The Set-Up* brought him the most acclaim, as a washed-up boxer who latches on to integrity in his come-back fight: Robert Wise directed and it is still the best film on the fight game.

The next flopped: *I Married a Communist*, with Laraine Day as the 'I'; after some months it was reissued as *The Woman on Pier 13* and did no better. He did not have much to do in *The Secret Fury* (50), as Claudette Colbert's bemused spouse in this silly mystery; or in *Born To Be Bad*, losing Joan Fontaine to Mel Ferrer. RKO were not at this stage doing much worthwhile, but these were modestly entertaining: *Best of the Badmen* (51), as a Yankee officer in peril when there is no murder evidence; *Flying Leathernecks*, as John Wayne's second in command; *The Racket*, with Robert Mitchum, as a racketeer/killer; and *On Dangerous Ground* (52), with Ida Lupino, as a disillusioned fist-happy cop. Fritz Lang's version of *Clash by Night* knew the level of its material: Ryan played the embittered lover, Barbara Stanwyck was the tramp-wife and Keith Andes had the part Ryan had played on the stage. His RKO contract finished with another study of depravity, *Beware My Lovely*, based on Mel

About Mrs Leslie *(54) was a sentimental drama about a tycoon who escapes from work and family every year to spend some weeks with the woman he really loves: Robert Ryan and Shirley Booth.*

Dinelli's play 'The Man', as the handyman who terrorizes housewife Ida Lupino.

As a freelance he played the same sort of parts in the same sort of pictures – only some of them were bigger-budgeted. He was a cattle-rustler in *Horizons West*; a killer in *The Naked Spur* (53), with James Stewart; a deep-sea diver in *City Beneath the Sea*; and a millionaire playboy left to perish in the desert *Inferno* (by faithless wife Rhonda Fleming). At the end of *Alaska Seas* (54) – a remake of *Spawn of the North* – he was, deservedly, killed beneath an avalanche. *About Mrs Leslie* was a soap opera with Shirley Booth, made touching by the playing of the two of them: he was 'a splendid partner' to her, thought 'Variety'. In *Her Twelve Men* he won Greer Garson and, again at MGM – after a quick trip to New York to play Coriolanus – was another killer bent on blowing out Spencer Tracy, spending his *Bad Day at Black Rock*. That was a high and Ryan's career hit a low with the next two, *Escape to Burma* (55), maybe the worst film either he or Barbara Stanwyck did (painted studio jungles), and Samuel Fuller's *House of Bamboo*, which was even more needlessly vicious than most of Fuller's films. Ryan, a GI turned gangster, was top-billed and the combination of him, Robert Stack and Fuller was a drag at the box-office.

20th, who produced, gave him something more deserving: *The Tall Men*, with Clark Gable, as the double-crossing businessman who hires him. There followed: *The Proud Ones* (56) with Virginia Mayo, as the (good) town marshal; *Back From Eternity*, as a drunken pilot; and *Men in War* (57), as the platoon looey who eventually succumbs to truculent sarge Aldo Ray ('Okay, Montana, we can use you'). For the same director, Anthony Mann, and company, Ryan and Ray did *God's Little Acre* (58), from Erskine Caldwell's bestseller. Ryan was the Georgia farmer convinced he would find gold on his farm: 'the performance of his career' said 'Variety', adding, 'he opens a whole vista of roles for himself by this portrayal, as remarkable, perhaps, as Walter Huston's performance in *The Treasure of Sierra Madre*'. The film did not do well, but was one of Ryan's own favourites. He was wooden as the editor in *Lonelyhearts*, seemingly unconvinced by the cynicisms given him as dialogue. There was a good, bleak, Western, *Day of the Outlaw* (59), and then another disquieting study in prejudice – the nigger-hating thug in Wise's *Odds Against Tomorrow*, involved in a bank heist with Harry Belafonte. It flopped.

He had begun to appear on TV, notably in the leads of 'The Great Gatsby' (58) with Jeanne Crain and 'The Snows of Kilimanjaro' with Ann Todd. In 1960 at the Stratford, Conn., festival he played Antony to Katharine Hepburn's Cleopatra, around which time he moved North for two films: *Ice Palace* (60), playing a character called Thor Storm (it was based on a novel by Edna Ferber), and *The Canadians* (61), a British-quota picture which could be described as a North-Western. He was a mountie and opera singer Teresa Stratas was a squaw. He was ludicrously miscast in Samuel Bronston's Spanish-made *King of Kings*, but so was everyone else – Jeffrey Hunter no less in the title-role, Brigid Bazlen as Salome and Siobhan McKenna as the Virgin. He was John the Baptist – and he only did it because he got $50,000 for a week's work, he said. Nicholas Ray directed. His films for a few years were lensed in Europe: *The Longest Day* (62), as a brigadier-general; Ustinov's *Billy Budd*, excellent as the vile Claggart, a role he found difficult because there was no reason for Claggart's villainy; *The Crooked Road* (64), with Stewart Granger, as a journalist; and *Battle of the Bulge* and *La Guerre Secrète/The Dirty Game/The Secret Agents*, in both as a general, in both with Henry Fonda. However, in the midst of them he returned to New York to play the title-role in an Irving Berlin musical, 'Mr President'.

In Hollywood, he was one of several names in the next three: *The Professionals* (66), with Burt Lancaster; *The Busy Body* (67), a B starring Sid Caesar, uninterested as a crime-boss; and *The Dirty Dozen*, as a colonel. He was a cattle-rustler again in *Hour of the Gun*, then had a brief bit as a deserter in *Custer of the West* (68), made not in the West, but in Spain, with Robert Shaw as Custer. He remained there for the Spanish-Italian *Escondido/Un Minuto per Pregare Un Instante per Morire*, with Arthur Kennedy. His general's uniform was dry-cleaned for *Lo Sbarco di Anzio/Anzio*, directed by Dmytryk. After playing Othello and Father Tyrone in 'Long Day's Journey Into Night' at Nottingham, he returned to the US for *The Wild Bunch* (69), at his best as the reluctant head of the bounty-hunters. He was back in Britain to play Nemo in *Captain Nemo and the Floating City*; then was back in the West, with Burt Lancaster, in *Lawman* (71). In contrast, he played a tycoon in *The Love Machine*, with Dyan Cannon, an unsuccessful soap opera based on an even sillier and 'sexier' book by Jaqueline Susann, supposedly about a TV exec (John Phillip Law). Then he appeared in *Pancho Villa* (72), with Telly Savalas, made in Spain, and René Clément's *La Course du Lièvre à travers les Champs*, made in Canada. After opposing Rod Steiger in *The Lolly Madonna XXX* (73), he was in a film-play, *The Iceman Cometh* which starred Lee Marvin, and *The Outfit*, with Robert Duvall, in which he was a crime syndicate boss. The latter two were released posthumously and his last screened work was a TV movie, *The Man Without a Country*, with Cliff Robertson. He died of cancer in 1975.

Eva Marie Saint

Eva Marie Saint is an elegant blonde with a very limited list of credits. She probably is not worth a light at the box-office, but she is one of those actresses everyone seems to like, with a warmth and candour not usual in elegant blondes. At no time were looks and talents like hers common and one feels that if she had come up earlier – when stars were all contractees – things might have been different.

She was born in Newark, New Jersey, in 1924; she intended to become a teacher and studied at the University of Ohio, where she became involved in dramatics. During a vacation she got a summer job as a Guidette at the NBC Studios in New York – so when she left college she had some knowhow about getting a job in radio. She became established in radio and in 1946 made her television début. She did a number of major TV drama shows and in 1951 married one of her directors, Jeffrey Hayden. One play she did, 'A Trip to Bountiful' with Lillian Gish, was so much liked that it was done again on Broadway; two weeks after the opening night she was signed for *On the Waterfront* (54), as the gentle girl who befriends Marlon Brando. The performance netted her fine reviews and a Best Supporting Actress Oscar.

Her fee had been around $6,000. The Oscar made a difference and in 1955 her fee was said to be $75,000. She did not make a film that year, presumably because she was sifting through the hundreds of offers – though she did two TV plays, 'Yellow Jack' with Broderick Crawford and 'Our Town' with Paul Newman. The role she chose to do was very different – the glamorous leading lady to Bob Hope in *That Certain Feeling* (56), a part meant originally for June Allyson. It did not enhance her reputation, pleasant though she was, nor did the supporting role she took in *Raintree County* (57), with Elizabeth Taylor. This was the first of an MGM contract for three pictures over a three-year period, guaranteeing $350,000. She signed a similar deal with 20th, worth $450,000 – but her credits reveal that she filmed little for that company. For them she did do *A Hatful of Rain*, as a wife of junkie Don Murray. Fred Zinnemann directed, but the dialogue retained lines from Michael V. Gazzo's original (hit) play (like, 'Paw, you never loved me . . . and I *needed* you'). Again the film did nothing for her; she lost *The Long Hot Summer* to Joanne Woodward because she was pregnant, but she was sleek and sexy and everything a Hitchcock heroine should be in his *North By Northwest* (59), opposite Cary Grant. She was a fine example of heroinism in *Exodus* (60), with Paul Newman; and she had almost the charisma which the role required as Warren Beatty's girl friend in *All Fall Down* (61).

Not long after that she did herself no good when she used a four-letter word only too audibly at a Hollywood function. It was not for some years that she was again in a film – *36 Hours* (64), with James Garner. Then she lost husband Richard Burton to other woman Elizabeth Taylor in *The Sandpiper* (65). She was good as a Maine housewife in *The Russians Are Coming The Russians Are Coming* (66), but hardly more than decorative in *Grand Prix* (67), a film with ambitions to the sort of 'class' she has as an actress. She was announced as the glamorous insurance sleuth in *The Thomas Crown Affair*, but the part was played – uninterestingly – by Faye Dunaway. A year later, Miss Saint had a difficult role in *The Stalking Moon* (69), opposite Gregory Peck: she was a white woman who had spent 10 years in Indian captivity – and it was her best performance in years. She was also outstanding as George Segal's loving and loyal wife in *Loving* (70), giving the role both the patina and the probing. After another interval, she appeared with Bob Hope in *Cancel My Reservation* (72). Later that year 'The Lincoln Mask' failed to run on Broadway; the following year she did a stock tour of 'Summer and Smoke' and in 1979 she toured with Henry Fonda in 'The First Monday in October', in the role played in New York by Jane Alexander.

Marlon Brando and Eva Marie Saint in On the Waterfront *(54). They both won Oscars for their performances, part of a clutch of eight major Academy awards which went to that film.*

During this period she was appearing regularly in tele-movies: *The Macahans* (76), forming a pioneer couple with James Arness – but as she died she was not in the series that followed; *A Christmas to Remember* (78) with Jason Robards; *When Hell Was in Session* (79), as wife to Hal Holbrook, who had suffered in a Vietnam POW camp; *The Curse of King Tut's Tomb* (80), as a reporter; *The Best Little Girl in the World* (81) with Charles Durning, as parents of an adolescent daughter afflicted with that nervous disease which causes self-starvation: the remake of *Splendor in the Grass*, as the mother of the Natalie Wood character, now played by Melissa Gilbert; *Malibu* (83), a mini-series about life in the smart set, with Kim Novak; *Jane Doe*, as a psychiatrist to an amnesiac someone is trying to murder; *Love Leads the Way* (84), about the first blind American (Timothy Bottoms) to benefit from a Seeing Eye dog; and *Fatal Vision* (84) a superior mini-series with Karl Malden, as the parents of a girl murdered by her husband, a medic with the Green Berets, based on fact. In 1982 she appeared in Chicago in 'Duet for One', which

Irvin Kershner's Loving *(70), was a bitter comedy about a commercial artist whose idiosyncrasies include a penchant for extra-marital affairs. George Segal and Eva Marie Saint were very good indeed as the husband and wife.*

she did in New York the following year. She returned to cinemas in *Nothing in Common* (86), a title which referred to father Jackie Gleason and son Tom Hanks; she completed the family. For television again she did *The Last Days of Patton*, as George C. Scott's wife; *A Year in the Life* – of a Seattle family; *Norman Rockwell's Breaking Home Ties* (87) with Robards; and then she joined 'Moonlighting', to play Cybill Shepherd's mother. *I'll Be Home for Christmas* (88) found her and Hal Holbrook as parents of a large family during World War II.

Maximilian Schell

Oscar is a funny brute, as has often been remarked. One of the few Oscar victories unanimously anticipated, and much approved of afterwards, was Maximilian Schell's, for *Judgment at Nuremberg*; but apart from those character actors for whom the Oscar could only be a temporary fillip (Victor McLaglen, Paul Lukas, Broderick Crawford, Ernest Borgnine, F. Murray Abraham) none has got so little out of it as Schell. He was unlucky, it is true – particularly as his other performances had demonstrated that that one was no flash in the pan. In after years he said: 'I had to restart after that, I couldn't go up. I had to go down in order to scale the mountain again.'

He was born in 1930 in Vienna of theatrical parents. At the age of three he appeared in a play by his father. He was brought up in Switzerland, where the family fled after the Anschluss (1938). He studied at the universities of Zürich, Munich and Basle, during which time he acted in college productions. His sister Maria (born 1926) had begun acting at 15 and by the time he began professionally had scored several successes, notably in the two versions of *The Angel With the Trumpet* (the original German one and the Korda remake a year later). He acted in the Swiss provinces, in Germany, Austria and France; and made his film début in a supporting role as an army officer in *Kinder Mütter und ein General* (55), an anti-war piece (a mother visits the Russian front), among the stronger films in the baffling career of American-Hungarian director Laslo Benedek. Then he had a good part (eighth-billed) as a member of the Kreisau Circle – the young group of aristocratic anti-Hitler intellectuals – in *Der 20 Juli* (56), one of the two concurrent films on the attempted assassination of the Fuehrer (Pabst made the other). The next two were both minor: *Reifende Jügend*, with Christine Keller, and *Ein Mädchen aus Flandern* with Nicole Berger.

He had his first star role in *Ein Herz Kehrt Heim* with Maria Holt, followed by *Taxichauffeur Bäntz* (57), a *gemütlich* Swiss comedy, as the taximan's daughter's suitor, and *Die Letzten Werden die Ersten Sein*, as a weak murderer protected by lawyer brother O.E. Hasse. He was engaged for a Broadway play, 'Interlock', and that brought him to the attention of 20th, looking for German actors to support Marlon Brando in *The Young Lions* (58); it was a good role, as the CO whom Brando cuckolds. He returned to Germany to make *Ein Wunderbaren Sommer* with Barbara Rütting; but meanwhile his work in the Brando film brought a couple of US TV offers – to play d'Artagnan and the intense defence lawyer, all swoop and cunning, in Abby Mann's play 'Judgment at Nuremberg'. On German TV for Eurovision he was a notable *Hamlet* (60).

When Stanley Kramer came to film *Judgment at Nuremberg* (61), he assigned Schell to repeat his performance and he was quite outstanding in a film notable (only) for its acting. Apart from the Oscar, the New York critics judged his the year's best male acting. He had already found another role that seemed ideal, that of the German tutor who acts as catalyst to the family of Peter Shaffer's *Five Finger Exercise* (62), but the film was a travesty of the play and a giant flop – though his performance (as against Rosalind Russell, Jack Hawkins, etc.) had a measure of force and truth. He was even less lucky with *The Reluctant Saint*, about a peasant boy who becomes a priest and then levitates, a film he later described as 'the one that is closest to my

Maximilian Schell in his first English-language movie, The Young Lions *(58). He and Marlon Brando played fellow German officers.*

heart'. The failure was complete and total, and not a little to blame was Edward Dmytryk, who directed it in Italy. It was Dmytryk who persuaded Schell to dub his *Hamlet* into English and show it at the San Francisco Film Festival: not a very good idea. His international career continued gloomily with De Sica's film of a Sartre play, *The Condemned of Altona/I Sequestrati di Altona* (63), as the guilt-racked son who has holed himself up in the attic since the war.

He remained, obviously, a resourceful performer and it was a pity therefore that his one good film, *Topkapi* (64), demanded so little of him – he was a master-thief. Nor was *Return from the Ashes* (65) – playing a particularly nasty murderer in this thriller botched by poor direction – any more demanding, nor even Lumet's good *The Deadly Affair* (67), in a one-dimensional role as a master-spy. (The international flavour of these last four films can be indicated by the nationalities of their leading ladies; Italian – Sophia Loren; Greek – Melina Mercouri; Swedish – Ingrid Thulin; French – Simone Signoret.) He remained a master-spy, the Austrian Redl whose homosexuality betrayed him, in John Osborne's play 'A Patriot for Me', which he did in London and which kept his name alive in show business circles, something not done by his next two movies. *The Desperate Ones* (68) was a Spanish-US production, from Alexander Ramati's 'Beyond the Mountains', about two Polish brothers (the other was Raf Vallone) waiting somewhere to cross the border: a pointless film, not helped by Schell's tentative performance. *Counterpoint* was a flop Hollywood drama in which he was Charlton Heston's Nazi captor and *Heidi* was a television version of that tale with Jean Simmons, Michael Redgrave and Jennifer Edwards in the title-role.

He started shooting a film of his own in 16 mill. called *Pedestrian*. When ideas ran out he was glad to be offered the banalities of *Krakatoa East of Java* (69), a Cinerama adventure story filmed off and on over a two-year period. He accepted this because it was the highest salary ever offered him and

There have been so many 'heist' films in recent years that it is pleasant to recall the time when they were a pleasant rarity. One of the best was Topkapi *(64), in which Maximilian Schell and Melina Mercouri planned to steal jewellery from the Istanbul museum of that name.*

enabled him to finance *Das Schloss/The Castle* – adapted from Kafka, directed by Rudolf Noelte and filmed in Spain with Schell producing and starring. (The German version has the ending Kafka envisaged; the English version has the published ending.) He was in another spectacle, *Simon Bolivar*, a biopic of the great South American liberator, directed by Alessandro Blasetti; several countries were involved in the filming – neither Britain nor the US has ever seen it. Schell then directed a version of Turgenev, in English. *First Love/Erste Liebe* (70), with John Osborne acting; then he took Osborne's play about Redl to Broadway, to qualified approval. He collaborated on the screenplay of a German film, *Trotta* (71), with the director Johannes Schaaf, a story of the Austrian aristocracy during World War II. He was then the romantic object of attention for two ladies of the past, the British *Pope Joan* (72), who in the film was German and played by Liv Ullmann, and the French *Paulina 1880*, who was Italian and played by Olga Karlatos (who is German): he was monk and Italian count respectively and the films were bad and good in the same order.

He directed but did not appear in an old project restarted, *Der Fussganger/The Pedestrian* (74), which failed to get international distribution despite a cast including Françoise Rosay, Peggy Ashcroft, Lil Dagover, Peter Hall and Elisabeth Bergner. Its subject was Nazi guilt and Schell tackled it again, as actor only, playing a former SS officer in *The Odessa File* as pursued by journalist Jon Voight, and in *The Man in the Glass Phone Booth* (75), as the haunted Jew. The latter was a film of a play based on a novel by Robert Shaw, who co-starred with Martin Ritt in Schell's next film as a director, *Der Richter and sein Henker/The End of the Game*, from the play by Friedrich Dürrenmatt; despite a prize at San Sebastian and a supporting cast including Jacqueline Bisset, Donald Sutherland and Jon Voight – who used his clout to get financing from 20th Century-Fox – it was not released in the US or Britain. Nor has the Yugoslav-Czech co-production, *Atentat u Sarajevu/The Assassination at Sarajevo*, in which he was one of the conspirators and Christopher Plummer the Archduke Franz Ferdinand. Less profitably employed, he was a villainous psychiatrist mixed up with Charles Bronson in *St Ives* (76) and he then donned uniform again to play the battalion commander in *Cross of Iron* (77). He has repeatedly said that he does not want to play Nazi roles, 'my greatest cross to bear as an actor', but this was a good role, deadlocked against the sergeant hero, James Coburn. 'Hollywood is the only place that still digs up movies about Nazis', he said, though strictly speaking all his recent jobs on Nazis had had British nationality – as *A Bridge Too Far*, where he and Hardy Kruger as the two best-known 'German' actors were the high-salaried representatives of the Wehrmacht. Kruger was to have directed him in the Israeli-German-Italian *Horizons*, but instead Schell played the shy, bespectacled stranger contacting Jane Fonda on behalf of *Julia*. He had special billing, but this indicated that he would accept supporting roles (and he was the New York critics' Best Supporting Actor). After directing 'Tales From the Vienna Woods' by Odön von Horvath for Britain's National Theatre he was a KGB commissar in *Avalanche Express* (79); but he starred again, in Italy, with Jacqueline Bisset in *Amo Non Amo/Together?*, fulfilling a long-cherished aim to play romantic comedy. The producers of *Players* needed him for a small but special role, the suave lover of Ali McGraw; he was announced simultaneously for *Sidney Sheldon's Bloodline* and Disney's *The Black Hole*, and did the latter, ceding his role in the former to Gert Froebe. In the Disney, which was not the success hoped for – indeed bargained for – he was the Captain Nemo of Outer Space. A busy year concluded with his film – he directed (only) – of the von Horvath play, *Geschichten aus dem Wiener Wald*, which was much liked on its home ground but little seen abroad.

He appeared in the TV remake of *The Diary of Anne Frank* (80) with Joan Plowright, with Melissa Gilbert as their daughter, and was then a New York Zionist in *The Chosen* (81), opposing rabbi Rod Steiger, though the piece was basically about the friendship of their sons. After appearing in a French movie, *Les Iles* (82) with Marie Trintignant, he returned to US TV for a remake, *The Phantom of the Opera* (83), in the title-role, only now it was the Budapest Opera he terrorized – most effectively. he was an investigative lawyer in *Morgen in Alabama* (84), which premièred at the Berlin Festival at the same time as his documentary on *Marlene* Dietrich, in which, unseen but in good voice, she managed to be rude to him and about most of her screen work. *The Assisi Underground* (85) may have been a more pleasurable experience, at least for him – but audiences had little chance of finding out, because it disappeared after test showings. Ben Cross, Irene Papas and Simon Ward co-starred in this war story, directed by Alexander Ramati for Cannon – surprisingly, in view of the quality of Ramati's previous work. Schell was no luckier with *Laughter in the Dark*, a remake which he began in 1986; Mick Jagger exited early with his contract unsigned; there existed 25 minutes of edited footage, but the production company filed for bankruptcy when Vestron (with a one-third stake) pulled out because Myriam D'Abo replaced Rebecca De Mornay. He himself was much seen in the title-role of a very expensive mini-series, *Peter the Great* (86).

ROMY SCHNEIDER

If you travelled on the continent of Europe in the late 50s, it was impossible to escape the name of Romy Schneider. Her name was there on cinema hoardings but also her face seemed to be on every other magazine; stationery shops seemed stuffed with picture postcards of this smiling, chubby fraulein. She was the first German-speaking star since Marlene Dietrich to win such wide acceptance; her films were not, in general, exported to the US or Britain, but she had broken through in Italy and France, normally resistant to German movies. Obviously, sooner or later she would arrive on the international scene.

She was not, in fact, German but Austrian; she was born in Vienna in 1938, the daughter of Magda Schneider, a famous pre-war Austrian movie star, and Wolf Albach-Retty, a well-known Viennese actor. She grew up in Germany, in Berchtesgaden. Magda Schneider was still making movies in the 50s, mainly of the same kind as she made 20 years earlier – romantic German-Viennese comedies with music. One of these, however, *Wenn der Weisse Flieder Wieder Blüht* (53), required her to have a young daughter: the director, Hans Deppe, talked Miss Schneider into letting Romy (the name is a contraction of Rose-Mary) play the part. The film was in Gevacolor and Romy photographed prettily. Against her will, Miss Schneider agreed to let Romy make another picture, *Feuerwerk* (54), with Lilli Palmer, a charmless musical with a circus background, based on a stage hit. That led to *Der Zigeunerbaron*, another musical, with Georges Guetary. Romy was already a star and there was nothing for mother to do but to give in gracefully.

She supported her daughter when director Ernst Marischka cast her in *Mädchenjahre einer Königin* (55), a silly romance (in Agfacolor) which cast Romy unconvincingly as Queen Victoria and Adrian Hoven as Albert. It was popular enough for Walt Disney to buy the American rights and for him to call Romy over to test. The film quickly flopped in the States and she was so angry at being asked to test in Tyrolean costume against a twee mountain background that she walked off the set. Meanwhile, Marischka put her into a period musical with her mother, *Die Deutschmeister*, made in Austria (her previous films were made in Germany). She did a serious role, as the daughter of Hans Albers, in *Der Letzte Mann*, a remake of the famous Emil Jannings film (only now the *mann* was not a commissionaire but a head waiter). Then Marischka starred her as *Sissi* (56) – the name by which the Empress Elizabeth was affectionately known; it was an attempt to repeat the success of the Victoria film, with Magda Schneider in the cast and Karl-Heinz Böhm as the Emperor Franz-Josef – and, commercially, it more than surpassed expectations. 'Variety' described Romy as 'a heavy-set Teutonic looker whose main plus factor is a gurgling innocence. Her gauche girlishness manages to be acceptable.'

She did a comedy with Böhm, directed by Alfred Weidenman, *Kitty und die Grosse Welt*, about a young secretary discovering romance in Vienna. It was in Eastmancolor: colour was still rare in German or Austrian films of the time, but it had been proved that the grosses of Romy Schneider's films justified it; at the same time, it added to the air of dreamland which pervaded them all. The success of *Sissi* wrought a sequel, *Sissi Die Junge Kaiserin*, done by the same team and again produced by the Neue Deutsche Filmgesellschaft. That company had put Schneider under contract and it now cast her opposite Germany's leading young romantic actor, Horst Buchholz, in *Robinson Soll Nicht Sterben* (57), a version of a play set in London in 1730, about a young couple who help Daniel Defoe. The two of them were promptly costarred in *Monpti*, a tragic tale of young lovers in modern Paris, she as a shop-girl and he as a penniless Hungarian artist (the title referred to her name for him – a contraction of 'mon petit'). Then there was a third Sissi film, *Sissi Schicksalsjahre einer Kaiserin*, and again it was a wow throughout the Continent. Paramount, encouraged by this reception, bought the three Sissi films, dubbed them, cut them and rolled them into one, retitled *Forever My Love*; but it was just too lilac-time for American audiences.

Schneider continued in such stuff: *Scampolo* (58), a German remake of an Italian film made four years earlier (with Maria Fiore; it was from a novel by Dario Niccodemi), about a waif who guides tourists round Ischia, including Paul Hubschmid. There was a change with *Mädchen in Uniform*, Geve von Radvanyi's remake of the famous old German film, with Lilli Palmer – but Schneider was hammy as the aristocratic orphan. Then she did a remake in France of her mother's best film, Max Ophüls's bitter-sweet romance,

Romy Schneider made her name in horrible kitschy movies – oh yes, about Queen Victoria and the Empress Elizabeth, both of whom emerged as terminally coy fairy-tale princesses. She eventually said, Enough is Enough, but before then she insisted on something more substantial, a remake of Mädchen in Uniform *(58), in which she and Lilli Palmer were pupil and teacher caught up in an 'unnatural' attraction. It was by no means, however, as effective as the original.*

Leibelei, rechristined *Christine* (59) – and it was just as well to attempt to ward off comparisons. Jean-Claude Brialy co-starred and the cast included Alain Delon. Her relationship with Delon and with the new French agent she acquired, Georges Beaume, were to influence her life and career considerably. Meanwhile, in Germany, she escaped schmaltz somewhat in *Die Halbzarte*, a comedy about a family who write a naughty play – she was the daughter who, as a result, becomes involved with Carlos Thompson. However, in *Ein Engel auf Erden*, directed by von Radvanyi, she was an angel sent – disguised as an air hostess – to help Henri Vidal. She insisted on co-productions with France: *Die Schöne Lügnerin* was a comedy with Jean-Claude Pascal, in which she was a liar; and *Katja die Ungekrönte Kaiserin* (60) was the remake of an old film with Danielle Darrieux, with Curt Jurgens as her emperor lover.

The French strain was as yet the closest Schneider could get to the sort of films she wanted to make; she asked for and got a cameo role in *Plein Soleil*, which starred Delon, and refused all offers from Germany. She was not entirely surprised when the student body of Erlangen College voted her the world's worst actress (followed by Diana Dors and Jayne Mansfield). German exhibitors were still clamouring for her films, so *Die Sendung der Lysistrata* was released, made originally for TV, a version of Aristophanes directed by the great German actor Fritz Kortner. In France she set out to change her image and it was not easy; the only work offered her that she wanted to do was a stage production with Delon of an English play. ''Tis Pity She's a Whore' (in French). Visconti directed. Visconti had never deemed it necessary to work with actors of ability and he cast Schneider in his episode of *Boccaccio 70* (62) – 'Il Lavoro', an anecdote about a wife who gets her marriage going again when she charges the husband (Thomas Milian) for her favours. She did not quite escape her old image: Visconti made her drop a tear as she accepted the money. Then she did *Le Combat dans l'Ile*, a murky drama about a woman who leaves her terrorist husband (Jean-Louis Trintignant) for a pacifist (Henri Serre). She played the nymphomaniac, Leni, in Orson Welles's *Le Procés/The Trial* and appeared briefly, unbilled, in *L'Amour à la Mer*. In 1962 she toured France in Chekhov's 'The Seagull'.

Her appearances in films by Welles and Visconti had not brought her much acclaim, but they had made her a 'prestige' actress. She was to benefit further by the increased interest which Hollywood took in European players in the 60s (there were several reasons for this, but both are related to the realization that the European film festivals were useful commercially and the fact that a European reputation – for director or player – could reverberate across the Atlantic). At this particular moment Carl Foreman needed a bevy of European actresses to play opposite his GI heroes, *The Victors* (63): Schneider was a demure violin student forced by the war to become a whore. Columbia, who produced, signed her for two more films: Otto Preminger's *The Cardinal*, as a Viennese student who tries to seduce the priest (Tom Tryon) and is later a victim of the Gestapo; and *Good Neighbor Sam* (64), as a girl who has to pretend – to inherit a fortune – that Jack Lemmon is her husband. She returned to Europe to two projects which might have gone some way to compensating for both her uninteresting showing in these films and the recurrent attacks which had appeared in the German press since she had left: Visconti's life of the Countess Tarnovska, which was never made, and Clouzot's *L'Enfer*, with

Serge Reggiani, which was abandoned during production.

In *What's New Pussycat?* (65) she was Peter O'Toole's true love, but just one of a job lot of minor screen beauties roped into that enterprise; in *10.30 p.m. Summer* (66) she was swamped by Melina Mercouri. She returned to Germany for *Schornstein Nr 4*, directed by a Frenchman, Jean Chapot, and written by Marguerite Duras, an unsuccessful fable about an unmarried mother who wants her baby back after she marries. Then she played a countess in *Triple Cross* (67), with Christopher Plummer. She herself married – German impresario Harry Meyen – and retired temporarily. Pregnancy caused her to refuse Losey's *Accident* (earlier she had had to turn down his *Modesty Blaise*). She took stock of her career and remained as ambitious as ever. She said later: 'The most important thing to me is that I am an actress. It would be a lie to say that acting was just my job or something I did for fun. It is my life. I couldn't live without it.' The film she chose to return in was *Otley* (69), with Tom Courtenay, because, she said, it was made by 'young talented people'. The trouble was, her part was not large and she still concealed – if she had it – that spark which makes the difference; she had to be both beautiful and enigmatic, but could only fulfil one of the conditions.

In France she did a thriller with Delon, *La Piscine*. She returned to Britain for what must be the fastest movie flop on record – or rather, off (it played a couple of dates for a couple of days): *My Lover My Son* (70), an insipid drama about incest in which she was ridiculously cast as the mother of Dennis Waterman. In France she played Michel Piccoli's mistress in Claude Sautet's study of a motor accident and the victim's last days, *Les Choses de la Vie*. It was a success in France, which led to two more pictures for the same company, both thrillers, and both directed by Sautet: *Qui?*, with Maurice Ronet, which was good; and *Max et les Ferrailleurs* (71), which was better – Piccoli as a flic who turns crook and Schneider as the *belle-de-nuit* who aids him. Her notices were good, compensating once more for critical indifference towards her work in *Bloomfield* with Richard Harris (made, in fact, before the last two). She had an excellent part in the Italian *La Califfa*, written and directed by Alberto Bevilacqua from his own novel about the changes in modern Italy – as an aggressive worker who becomes the mistress of capitalist Ugo Tognazzi; but she disliked the film.

Then she at last made a film for Losey, *The Assassination of Trotsky* (72), as the mistress of the assassin (Delon). She then played the Empress Elizabeth again in *Ludwig* (73), Visconti's film about Ludwig II, with Helmut Berger as the Emperor – and it was strange that the aristocratic Visconti should have cast two players capable only of expressing a shop-girl mentality. Because of their dialogue (filmed in English), they shared the worst sequences, but the good things in the film did not prevent it from flopping everywhere. It was a joke in New York, as MGM kept slicing sequences from its three-hour running-time; they never bothered to open it in London, but later sold it off to a minor distributor. Since the Losey also failed, international interest dimmed and Schneider stuck to the French cinema: Sautet's *César et Rosalie*, with Yves Montand; Granier-Deferre's *Le Train*, on it as a Jewish refugee in May 1940, loved by Jean-Louis Trintignant; Jean-Claude Brialy's *Un Amour de Pluie* (74), having a holiday romance with Nino Castelnuovo as a mysterious Italian; Deville's *Le Mouton Enragé*, as a wife committing adultery with timid bank clerk Trintignant while Jean-Pierre Cassel rearranges his life; and a lumpish piece of Grand Guignol, *Le Trio Infernal*, with Michel Piccoli and her film sister murdering and graphically disposing of the bodies. She was with Fabio Testi in Andrzej Zulawski's *L'Important c'est d'Aimer* (75) and the important thing, one would have thought, was to avoid pretentious rubbish like this: but, incredibly, the French Film Academy voted Schneider a Best Actress Award, a César, in the first year they were issued. Still, she was not in that a positive irritant, as she was in Chabrol's *Les Innocents aux Mains Sales*, playing the bored (weren't we all?) wife of Rod Steiger, given to shoving a bottle up her privates. She supported in Enrico's *Le Vieux Fusil*, with

Romy Schneider returned to the role of the Empress Elizabeth for Visconti, in his Ludwig *(73). This picture was taken off the set.*

Philippe Noiret as a surgeon bent on avenging his family wiped out by Germans, and she ruined *Une Femme à sa Fenêtre* (76), also with Noiret. She went through the entire film with two expressions – one with a supercilious smile and one without; the script required her to have a magnetic and mysterious (hence the smile) personality and she registered a void.

She had only a cameo role in Sautet's *Mado*, as the alcoholic ex-wife whose life still centres on Piccoli; and she had another pretentious bore in Aleksander Petrovic's mishandling of Heinrich Boll's novel, *Gruppenbild mit Dame* (77) – her first German film (discounting *Ludwig*) in 18 years, though in 1972 she had planned a new version of Wedekind's 'Lulu' there, directed by the second of her three husbands, Meyen (she married again in 1975); this was later planned with Liliana Cavani directing, while another German project (announced in 1974) was another version of another movie perennial, *Die Tarnowska*. In 1977 the readers of 'Ciné-Revue' voted her their favourite star and the following year she won a second César – suggesting that the French found in this inexpressive actress something invisible to mere foreigners. The César was for Sautet's *Une Simple Histoire* (78), their fifth film together (counting *Mado*) and written expressly for her. Sautet spoke of 'her beauty, talent and her inner force', all of which disappeared in the Channel crossing. Without her, this tame tale of a middle-aged woman and her crowd might have had some meaning, but with her, it was a *rien*. She supported Audrey Hepburn in *Sidney Sheldon's Bloodline* (79), as the unfaithful wife of executive Maurice Ronet, and played a housewife to Montand's middle-aged businessman in a Costa-Gavras adaptation of Romain Gary, *Clair de Femme*, the two of them moping around making soppy, solemn generalizations about love, death and life. Tavernier's *Death Watch/Le Mort en Direct* (80), filmed in English in and around Glasgow, could only be an improvement, a sci-fier about a publishing employee (Schneider) who, dying, is followed around by Harvey Keitel because he has a TV camera in his head. No more than *Bloodline* did it to do anything to restore Schneider to favour with foreign audiences. She had the title-role in *La Banquière*, a banker whose unorthodox methods are so successful that her rivals plot to destroy her. Then she co-starred with Mastroianni in Risi's *Fantasma d'Amore* (81) and did a 10-minute cameo in Claude Miller's thriller, *Garde à Vue*, as the wife of suspected murderer Michel Serrault. Her last film was *La Passante du Sans Souci* (82) with Piccoli, from a novel by Joseph Kessel. She died of a heart attack in May of that year; from the obituaries we learned that her son had impaled himself on a railing the previous year, that her first husband had committed suicide and she had recently separated from her third.

PAUL SCOFIELD

There must remain speculation about the acclaimed stage actors with few or no film credits – since, at least, the cinema has been a respectable medium. Some were never asked; some tried films but did not come across; others, clearly, preferred the stage. Paul Scofield has apparently been in all three situations during his career. In the theatre it has been a resplendent career, but there have been only a small number of films.

He was born in Hurstpierpoint, Sussex, in 1922, the son of a headmaster; he was educated at a grammar school where, at the age of 13, he played Juliet with the school dramatic society. He left at 17 to join the Croydon Repertory Theatre School, moved on to the London Mask Theatre and made his London début in 'Desire Under the Elms' in 1940. He worked in several reps and toured; a tour of 'Young Woodley' led to an invitation to join Birmingham rep to play Horatio. In 1943 he married actress Joy Parker. There were more tours; then he returned to Birmingham for two seasons, 1944/6, where he made a vast local reputation – which became a national one during three consecutive seasons at Stratford-upon-Avon, playing, most importantly, Henry V, the Bastard in 'King John', Troilus and Hamlet. Between these three seasons he appeared in London: in 'A Phoenix Too Frequent' (46), as Mercutio and Aguecheek (47), and in 'The Relapse' (48); but his West End period really began with 'Adventure Story' (49), Terence Rattigan's play about Alexander the Great. Among the plays he did over the next few years were: 'The Seagull', 'Ring Round the Moon' (50), 'Much Ado About Nothing' (52), as Don Pedro, 'Richard II', 'Venice Preserv'd' (53) and 'Time Remembered' (54). Critics and public adored him; he could be as still as a tombstone or as tense as a caged lion; he was virile, baleful and exciting, with an odd, mannered voice, either squeaky or rusty; he had a lined, ageless face; it was generally accepted that he was the only one who might snatch the laurel from Olivier's brow.

Britain's film heroes of this period were anonymous, standardized performers, including, among many, Anthony Steel, Tony Wright, Donald Sinden, John Gregson. Possibly it was Scofield's old-young ugly-handsome face which prevented film offers; he finally made his film début in a featured role, playing an old man, in *That Lady* (55), a British production backed by 20th, with Olivia de Havilland. He was Philip II of Spain and it was ironic that the hero was Gilbert Roland, entirely inadequate in a role for which Scofield was better equipped. Darryl F. Zanuck was so impressed when he saw the rough cut that he ordered production re-started to get more footage of Scofield – three days to get six more minutes of screen time. Rank then chose him to play the British instructing officer in *Carve Her Name With Pride* (57); Virginia McKenna was Violet Szabo, a (real) war heroine, and the film was vastly popular in Britain. Scofield, however, seemed embarrassed – and not merely by the clichés. During filming he said that he had been stand-offish regarding films but had relented and would do almost anything to make more films, even to baring his chest. In 1961 he was more cautious: 'I would like to work in more films, if I could be sure of the director. But I've got the stamp of the classical actor, and I don't know whether the film people want that.' He did agree to play Brother Martin in Preminger's *Saint Joan*, but backed out at the last minute (Kenneth Haigh played it).

Meanwhile, on the stage, he was no longer a young comet, but a steady sun-like luminary. In an adaptation of Graham Greene's 'The Power and the Glory' (56) he gave a performance which many years later Laurence Olivier said was the finest he had seen in the theatre. Also: 'The Family Reunion', Rodney Ackland's 'A Dead Secret' (57), 'Expresso Bongo' (a musical), 'The Complaisant Lover' (59) and 'A Man for All Seasons' (60), by Robert Bolt. After a season at Stratford, Ontario (61), playing Coriolanus, and Don Armado in 'Love's Labour's Lost', he took the Bolt play to New York, where he collected a Tony to add to several British awards. In 1962 he played Lear under Peter Brook's direction and in 1963/4 he took the production to several European capitals and to New York. He made his third film for a good director, John Frankenheimer: *The Train* (64), with Burt Lancaster, as a German officer. It was not a huge part or even well written, but he played it confidently.

When Fred Zinnemann was preparing to film *A Man for All Seasons* (66), Scofield indicated that he would be interested in playing his stage role. The subject was Sir Thomas More and his fealty to his religion rather than his king – unlikely film fare. Columbia had allocated a modest budget and preferred Scofield to a bigger name. The result was handsome and arguably the most accurate and sensitive historical film made in English. It got raves, won a Best Picture Oscar and made a mint of money. And Scofield's beautiful performance brought him Best Actor awards from the British and American motion picture academies and from the New York critics. The film entirely changed his unsympathetic attitude towards films, he said, but he refused the flood of offers and returned to the stage: 'The Government Inspector' (66), 'Staircase', 'Macbeth' (68) and 'A Hotel in Amsterdam'. In 1968 he resigned from the board of the Royal Shakespeare Co. and three years later joined Olivier at the National Theatre. In the interim he appeared in 'Uncle Vanya' (70) and made two films. Peter Brook directed *King Lear* (71) as an Anglo-Danish co-production, and one sensed disaster when release was long delayed and then arrived without fanfares; it was mitigated only by Scofield's gritty performance. Much earlier a *Macbeth* had been announced under Peter Hall's direction, but

Paul Scofield as Sir Thomas More in A Man for All Seasons *(66), Fred Zinnemann's successful film version of Robert Bolt's stage play. Scofield chooses his film parts with discrimination, and he has made only very few movies since his first in 1955.*

that project quietly died when the stage production was poorly received and Scofield was dissatisfied with his performance. The second film was *Bartleby*, an adaptation of Herman Melville's story of the clerk who mentally disintegrates; Scofield was the boss. He thought the script exciting if 'way-out for cinema audiences' and preferred to work with the tyro talents involved than for the Hollywood companies still soliciting him. So much for idealism: after faint praise from the press the film did not have a chance. He did a spy thriller with Burt Lancaster, *Scorpio* (73), playing a KGB agent, but was more gainfully employed at the National Theatre, in 'The Captain from Kopenick' and 'Rules of the Game'. He co-starred with Katharine Hepburn in a filmed play, *A Delicate Balance*, and hoped to play Prospero in a film of *The Tempest*, but financing fell through. He played the role in Leeds and in London, and did some television, in adaptations of Henry James ('The Ambassadors') and Graham Greene ('When Greek Meets Greek'). He returned to the NT to play Volpone in 1977 and was also in 'The Madras House'; and was announced for *The Riddle of the Sands*, but Alan Badel played the role. When a 'Daily Mail' interviewer brought up a rumour of a declined title in the Honours list, he refused to comment.

He was to have been in *The Shooting Party*, but a runaway pony-and-trap accident on the first day of filming brought the role to James Mason. A year later he was Karenin in a US tele-movie, *Anna Karenina* (85), with Jacqueline Bisset and Christopher Reeve, but he was less profitably employed in a messy, inconclusive BFI-Channel 4 co-production, *Nineteen Nineteen*, with Maria Schell, the two of them as former patients of Freud, reminiscing as to the reasons why they were. After a return to the stage in 'I'm Not Rappaport' (86) he was in an excellent one-hour TV drama, *Mr Corbett's Ghost*, and also in that medium he was Otto Frank in *The Attic: the Hiding of Anne Frank* (88). Filming continued to occupy him: *The Conspiracy* (89) with Raf Vallone and Robert Mitchum, as Pope John Paul I, and filmed in Yugoslavia because the Italian authorities would not permit shooting there; *Why the Whales Come*; and Kenneth Branagh's *Henry V*, as the King of France.

George C. Scott

By common consent, George C. Scott is one of the best actors in the world. He has explained his approach: 'You've got to be three different people. You have to be a human being. Then you have to be the character you're playing. And on top of that you've got to be the guy sitting out there in Row 10, watching yourself and judging yourself.' It is a cautious philosophy, not paradoxically at odds with his first, immediate, striking characteristics – his presence and his energy. Without care, these are useless; like Laurence Olivier, Scott understands when to discipline them. José Ferrer, who directed him on stage, spoke of 'a concentrated fury, a sense of inner rage, a kind of controlled madness'. Scott sublimates – and then dares, dares that sort of detailed and regulated impersonation associated with those few actors commonly considered 'great', Olivier, Brando, Scofield.

He learnt, he said, from Muni, Tracy, Cagney, Robinson and Bette Davis – by watching them; but, he said, Tracy, Cagney and Robinson eventually became 'symbol actors'. 'The great danger with most actors is that the more successful they become, the less risk they will take with their careers. They forget why they became actors in the first place.' Scott himself became an actor when he could not make it as a writer; he admits to being a movie buff as a boy, says now that he is unhappy when he is not acting, even if – apropos of his remarks above, 'it's a pretty spooky way to earn a living'.

He was born in 1926 in Wise, Virginia, the son of a mine-surveyor. (The C. in his name stands for Campbell.) He was raised in Detroit and joined the Marine Corps at 17. After serving for four years, he spent another four years at the University of Missouri where, under the GI Bill of Rights, he majored in journalism. There, he played the lead in 'The Winslow Boy' – and from then on wanted only to act. Instead, he taught – at a women's college in Columbus, Mo. He continued to act there as an amateur and married his first wife. He got a job in summer stock, in Detroit, 'everything from Coward and Anouilh to potboilers like "Come Out of the Kitchen" '. Between whiles, he did manual work; he finally joined a semi-professional troupe doing 'Six Characters in Search of an Author', where he met his second wife. Then Joseph Papp, the director of the New York Shakespeare Festival, chose him to play Richard III (57) – and some claimed he was the finest living Richard, defying you to think of any other. Three months later he was acclaimed again as the demonic Lord Wainwright in 'Children of Darkness', with Colleen Dewhurst (whom he married, his third wife, in 1960; they divorced and remarried twice – they were last married in 1967). This success brought him a small role as a vengeful hellfire-preaching maniac in *The Hanging Tree* (58), starring Gary Cooper.

He returned to New York and stole much of 'Comes a Day' from Judith Anderson. He did some TV, including an 'Omnibus', when he played Robespierre: Otto Preminger saw this and cast him as the sarcastic, cold, special attorney in *Anatomy of a Murder* (59). He starred on Broadway in 'The Andersonville Trial' (he directed a TV revival in 1970) and in 'The Wall', meanwhile gaining a reputation on Shubert Alley for his anger and after-hours boozing. It was *The Hustler* (61) which first brought him to the forefront of film players, as the fast-talking, sharp-eyed promoter. His iron-hard power, his driving authority and his rasping voice made him instantly alienable, but one paused: there was a dry wit and a harsh common sense. When he was nominated for a Best Supporting Oscar, he asked to be withdrawn because he considered the Oscar ceremony bull. In New York, he directed, co-produced and acted in 'General Seeger'; and played Shylock (62) and Ephraim in a revival of 'Desire Under the Elms' (63) with his wife. Television appearances included a couple that were released to cinemas abroad: 'The Power and the Glory', as the police chief, starring Laurence Olivier, and an episode of 'The Virginian' called *The Brass Bottle* (62), notable only for his rendering of 'The Ballad of Reading Gaol'.

His first film lead was in John Huston's *The List of Adrian Messenger* (63), as the unruffled but irascible Scotland Yard man, a performance which went some way to giving solidity to that fey entertainment. He then played the classic Pentagon general, Buck Turgidson, in *Dr Strangelove or How I Learned to Stop Worrying and Love the Bomb*, a portrayal of obtuse self-righteousness in a movie which gave him 'one of the best times I've ever had'. During this time he was in a TV series, 'East Side West Side', as a social worker, and in 1965 he played Vershinin in 'The Three Sisters' in London. He was also in a British movie: his vulpine, dandyish, show-off gangster on vacation enlivened one episode of *The Yellow Rolls-Royce* (65). He was not in *How To Steal a Million*: he showed up late on the first day of shooting and was replaced by Eli Wallach. In Italy he acted magisterially the underwritten and generally impossible part of Abraham in Huston's *La Bibbia/The Bible . . . In the Beginning* (66) – at which time his name was linked with co-star Ava Gardner.

His stint in a Tony Curtis comedy, *Not With My Wife You Don't*, he did, he said, only because he needed the money; nor did his career pick up with *The Flim-Flam Man* (67), as a hobo-cum-con-man, with Michael Sarrazin, a film that was just out of synch with public taste. He was in a Lincoln Center revival of 'The Little Foxes' and then took on another impossible part, in *Petulia* (68), that of the harried married-but-separated doctor drawn illogically to Julie Christie. He not only brought it off, but played with a warm, comforting authority reminiscent of middle-period Spencer Tracy. *The Savage Land* is a feature built on his TV guest appearances in 'The Road West'. That year he was on Broadway in Neil Simon's 'Plaza Suite'.

George C. Scott as the American general, Patton *(70). The film, as it happened, had several things in common with* Lawrence of Arabia: *inordinate length, correct locations, some insights into the way modern wars are fought, and a central character, a soldier, of some complexity.*

A film about General Patton had been first mooted by Warners in 1951 and was later planned for Tracy. Later, when 20th decided to do it – *Patton A Salute to A Rebel* (70) in the US, *Patton Lust for Glory* in Britain – Burt Lancaster was considered, Rod Steiger and Lee Marvin (among others) were offered it, and John Wayne asked for it. This exasperating, vain, unreasonable and brilliant World War II soldier attracted Scott because 'he was a professional and I admire professionalism. And for whatever else he was, good or bad, he was an individual. And that's what's most important to me today, when everybody around seems to be some kind of ostrich.' He told another interviewer it was an unactable part 'and I'm not doing it too well. It's an inadequate script' – though, according to the producer, Scott did *not* improve it by making Patton more sympathetic. It was not the performance expected from this actor, being that crusty old cliché, the martinet with the heart of gold. And the film, as directed by Franklin J. Schaffner, seldom rose – for all its care – above a boy's guide to modern warfare. Still, it appealed to both hawks and doves, did well at the box-office at a time when 20th really needed the money and picked up a fistful of Oscars, including Best Film and Best Actor. Scott refused to accept his, having not changed his attitude to Oscars or the ceremony; when his wife accepted for him the New York critics' award which he also won, she said he said 'this was the only film acting award worth having'.

The controversy hardly mattered; the success of the film ensured a run of offers, starting with *They Might Be Giants* (71) opposite Joanne Woodward, a much underrated fantasy in which he played a lawyer convinced that he is Sherlock Holmes. In Britain he was forceful if insufficiently romantic as Rochester, to Susannah York's *Jane Eyre* – a film which in the US went straight to TV. In Spain he made *The Last Run*, a thriller 'in the tradition of Hemingway and Bogart', as the ads said – a statement with which no one argued, or conspicuously agreed. Bogart's old director, Huston, started off directing, but clashed with Scott on the script and the casting of Tina Aumont; when he left, she was replaced by Trish Van Devere and Richard Fleischer took over direction. Huston observed that Scott is 'one of the best actors alive. But my opinion of him as an actor is higher than my opinion of him as a man.' The film was medium-successful, but Scott's fourth film that year was a huge success: *The Hospital*, with Diana Rigg, a grim comedy written by Paddy Chayevsky centred on a surgeon whose professional life is as empty as his personal life. In 1971 he was No. 5 at the US box-office. Then, with Fleischer again directing, he made *The New Centurians* (72), as a grizzled LA cop matched with hot-shot rookie Stacey Keach; he himself directed *Rage* – which described his situation in the film, a rancher-father bent on revenge when he and his son are sprayed with poison gas. Both bombed and so did: *Oklahoma Crude* (73); battling in the oil wells under Stanley Kramer's direction; *The Day of the Dolphin*, scientifically studying fish under Mike Nichols; and *The Bank Shot* (74), masterminding a heist under Gower Champion.

The only real surprise flop of the bunch was *Dolphin*, since it was heavily publicized and the director was supposedly fashionable; its producer, Joseph Levine, castigated Scott, calling him 'a jerk' and saying that he lost days of filming – at a salary of $750,000 plus a percentage; he also instanced Scott's bringing in his own directorial effort under its $1 million budget (half of which was Scott's own money). He was referring to *The Savage Is Loose*, with Van Devere (now Mrs Scott); as with *Rage* it had a Message for Society, though quite what was not discernible, since it dealt with a shipwrecked couple (Scott, Van Devere) and the son growing up without a mate. Ridicule greeted it; ligitation followed and Scott lost every penny.

To recoup, he turned to television: the excellent *Fear on Trial*, as Louis Nizer, defending a blacklisted broadcaster (William Devane); and *Beauty and the Beast*, as the beast, with his wife. And since he was 'cool' in Hollywood, he did a Broadway revival of 'Death of a Salesman' with Teresa Wright, which he also directed. Returning to films, he

It is probable that only a handful of screenwriters are known to the public at large, and Paddy Chayevsky was one of them, partly because he was both affectionate and funny about the inarticulate working people of this world. A couple of his celebrated television plays were filmed in the 50s, but he had been away awhile before he came back with The Hospital *(71) – angry now, about incompetence and corruption, but still with compassion, for one troubled doctor, a role beautifully realized by George C. Scott.*

played a worried German Luftwaffe colonel in charge of security on *The Hindenburg* (75) – and chalked up another flop, singularly unlucky, it seems, with director or script or both. He did a long Broadway run in a version of 'Volpone' called 'The Sly Fox' and put in a guest appearance as an outlaw in *The Prince and the Pauper/Crossed Swords* (77). *Islands in the Stream* was supposed to restore him to favour, but though his Hemingway-like hero (that gentleman had written the original novel) was warmly received, the film itself was not. *Movie Movie* (78) was Stanley Donen's attempt to revive the movies of the 30s, a two-part film with Scott in each part – as a Broadway producer in 'Baxter's Beauties of 1933' and a boxing promoter in 'Dynamite Hands'. 'Variety' called it 'awful awful', but, among other reviewers, 'The New York Times' liked it: its principal pleasures, said Vincent Canby, were Scott and Miss Van Devere, who 'by bringing a laser-beam intensity to this material come close to transforming parody into farce'. *Hardcore* (79) tackled that subject, with Scott as a father setting out to find why his daughter chose it for a career. Neither of the latter had been released when 'Variety' pondered Scott's run of failures, querying 'fiscal confidence' in Scott by a Canadian company, about to pay him what would amount to over $1 million for *Changeling* (80). He played a widowed musician who comes to believe that the Seattle mansion he has rented has a ghost. Van Devere co-starred. Together in October of that year they had a one-night Broadway flop, 'Tricks of the Trade'; then he was a fearless cop trailing all over Europe, always a body too late, to find why a colleague was killed – in the aptly named *The Formula*, with Brando and Marthe Keller (who according to 'Time Magazine' replaced Dominique Sanda, on a salary of $350,000, because Scott believed that her English was not good enough).

He was: a deranged military martinet, a cameo role, in *Taps* (81), set in a military academy; Fagin in a TV *Oliver Twist* (82); a flamboyant playwright in a revival of 'Present Laughter', which ran successively on Broadway; a businessman searching with Ali McGraw for his son lost in the Cultural Revolution in *China Rose* (83), reputedly getting a record fee for a tele-movie (along with George Segal and Peter O'Toole); a crazy, charming but deadly government operative in yet another of Hollywood's flop versions of Stephen King's dafter bestsellers, *Firestarter* (84), and doing 'a terrific salvage job', according to 'Variety'; and the old miser in a TV *A Christmas Carol*. Said John Leonard in 'New York Mgazine': 'Scott is wonderful. His is not only a Scrooge for all time . . . it renders obsolete all the other Scrooges the movies and television have evoked.' British critics were equally enthusiastic, but the two Dickens films did only minimal business when released to cinema in that country. *Mussolini: the Untold Story* (85) was an unfortunate mini-series in which Scott's galvanic performance as Il Duce could not disguise the dreadful dialogue. *Choices* (86) found him as a retired judge whose much younger second wife (Jacqueline Bisset) and daughter (Melissa Gilbert) both have unwanted pregnancies; also in television he was in *The Last Days of Patton*, in his old role, and *Murders in the Rue Morgue*, as the Sûreté man trying to solve them. On Broadway a play, 'The Boys in Autumn', failed to run and on television, a sitcom, 'Mr President' (87), failed to take off; but in that medium he and Don Ameche were *Pals*. Illness kept him inactive for a while, till he joined Warren Beatty in *Dick Tracy* (89).

Jean Seberg

Jean Seberg started her career as a has-been and a never-was at the same time. When she was 17 Otto Preminger chose her, after a nationwide search, to play Saint Joan, but she was critically roasted. The film died at the box-office. It seemed already the end for this wholesome girl from Marshalltown, Iowa. She was born in 1938 and wanted to be an actress when she saw Marlon Brando in *The Men*. She studied drama in her home town and played in 'Our Town', 'Picnic', etc. Columbia and Preminger launched their search with much fanfare and it was genuine; Graham Greene adapted from Shaw's *Saint Joan* (57) and it was filmed in England. It was not, in any case, a good movie, partly because of her performance and partly because Preminger approached the subject with his customary stolidity. Notorious for bullying even established talents, he completely demoralized Seberg, who later believed that she never recovered from his treatment. Defiantly, he used Seberg again in *Bonjour Tristesse*, as a French girl (again!), a spoilt young thing who embroils herself in the (love) affairs of father David Niven. The reaction was equally discouraging and he loaded her contract on to Columbia, who dejectedly put her into *The Mouse That Roared* (58). That might have been the end if Jean-Luc Godard had not requested her for *A Bout de Souffle* (59) – opposite Jean-Paul Belmondo, as an American girl living in Paris – having seen in her qualities which others missed (he was also an admirer of Preminger). She was a 'name' and

Jean Seberg at the start of her career, as Saint Joan *(57).*

Godard's backer reasoned – correctly – that Columbia would loan her for practically nothing. As it happened, she was living in Paris, having married a young lawyer, François Moreuil, whom she had met during the filming of *Bonjour Tristesse*. The success of the Godard film was so great that Columbia recalled her for *Let No Man Write My Epitaph* (60) – drug addiction on skid row; she was a rich kid looking on.

Hollywood remained unimpressed, but there were plenty of offers in France: Philippe de Broca's *L'Amant de Cinq Jours* (61), as a loose, neglected wife having an affair with a gigolo (Jean-Pierre Cassel) – Micheline Presle's; *Les Grandes Personnes*, as an American girl living in Paris, sharing car-racer Maurice Ronet with career woman Presle; and *La Récréation*, in a similar role, encouraged to have an affair with Christian Marquand by his mistress, Françoise Prévost. Only the first of these three keyhole peeps at Paris life was at all distinguished; the third was from a story by Françoise Sagan and was directed by Seberg's husband (he had turned director). For Godard she made a film in Marrakesh in three days, but he lost interest and did not even cut it. For a further change of scene she chose *Congo Vivo* (62), a squalid melodrama set in Brazzaville with Gabrielle Ferzetti, then did a British/American/Paris romance, *In the French Style* (63), with Stanley Baker. Columbia distributed and she returned to Hollywood to make her last film for them, Robert Rossen's *Lilith*, with Warren Beatty – giving her best performance, as a mental patient; the film itself, intelligent but over-ambitious, was a failure. She was reunited with Belmondo for the mediocre *Echappement Libre* (64) and was then in a torpid crime comedy with Claude Rich, *Un Milliard dans le Billard* (65).

She continued to skip back and forth between French and American movies with not quite the monotony of a metronome: *Moment to Moment* (66), the last film directed by Mervyn LeRoy, a run-down and freakish soap opera set on the Côte d'Azur; *A Fine Madness*, made in New York, as a spoilt wife being unfaithful with Sean Connery; Claude Chabrol's *La Ligne de Demarcation*, an espionage drama set in Vichy France, as Maurice Ronet's English wife; and *Estouffade à la Caraibe* (67) with Frederick Stafford, all about guerrillas and revolutionaries on a tropical isle. Chabrol directed her and Ronet in *La Route de Corinthe*, an undisciplined and tenuous thriller *à la* Hitchcock. Her second husband, the novelist Romain Gary, wrote and directed *Les Oiseaux Vont Mourir au Perou* (68), in which she played a nymphomaniac. She was a big star in France, but none of her American films had been successful enough to establish her as an international name; and *Pendulum* (69) would not do it, a thriller with George Peppard (the only one of her leading men she disliked).

Her best chance came when Alan Jay Lerner asked her to play the female lead in *Paint Your Wagon*, as the woman shared by Lee Marvin and Clint Eastwood. It was a nice reward for a girl who, by diligence and determination, had eclipsed a bad beginning; but she was hardly more than okay in a part which required someone like the young Ann Sheridan. She was better in a film she did not like, in a part she did not like, *Airport* (70), as Burt Lancaster's stewardess girlfriend – but, for all her charm, she lacked the individuality which might have made the role more than a stereotype. She had a good chance in *Ondata di Calore* (71), made in Italy by Nelo Risi, holding the screen throughout its length, as an American girl who murders her elderly husband. In Mexico she did an English-speaking Western, *Macho Callahan*, with David Janssen and Lee J. Cobb. When she later became pregnant she told friends the father was a Mexican she had met during the making of the film, but 'Newsweek' wrote that the father was an American black activist and went on to suggest that Gary – from whom she was divorced – would remarry her to legitimize the child. The two of them sued in the Paris courts for 500,000 francs for invasion of privacy and settled for one-tenth of that amount, long after she had lost the baby.

She returned to Italy to be Ugo Tognazzi's anxiety-ridden wife in *Questa Specie d'Amore*, written and directed by Alberto Bevilacqua, a study of a businessman coming to terms with his Antonionesque existence; and then Gary directed her in *Kill* (72), an English title for a French-Italian-Spanish-German co-production, made in Spain, with Stephen Boyd ('ick' she said) and James Mason, who did it as a favour to Gary, after turning down those Peruvian birds as too pretentious. He played an Interpol man and Seberg was his wife in this absurd drugs story, considered by her friends as further 'sadomasochistic erotica' exploiting her. Yves Boisset directed her in *L'Attentat*, a *Z*-like thriller based on the Ben Barka affair with Jean-Louis Trintignant, her last good film and the last at a good salary, approximately $40,000. She reckoned to have earned over $2 million, but had no assets beyond a cottage in Greece, a farm in Iowa which cost more to run than it brought in and half an apartment in Paris, though it was not in her name. She married again, Dennis Berry, the son of the expatriate American director, John Berry. Juan Bardem in Spain put her into an undistinguished horror movie, *The Corruption of Chris Miller* (73), in which she and her stepdaughter murder the randy hippy who has been living with them; and about this time one of her lovers, Hakim Jamal, was murdered. She fell in love with Fabio Testi while making *Camorra* with him in Italy and was then in more mayhem in *Mousey*, when Kirk Douglas turned psychotic killer for ABC television after she, his wife, left him.

For a friend, Philippe Garrel, she appeared in an impenetrable amateur effort made in the streets of Paris, *Les Hautes Solitudes* (74), and was involved in the production of a short, *Ballad for the Kid*. *Bianchi Cavalli d'Agosto* with Frederick Stafford concerned an American couple in marital difficulties while in Italy and *Le Grand Délire* (75) concerned a wealthy family which turns its home into a brothel; Seberg was the American madame, Berry wrote it and the real star was Isabelle Huppert. Seberg went to Vienna to play Gena in *The Wild Duck* (76), in English, but it did not hit the international market. Problems with drink and drugs prevented her from doing a TV film, *Je Parle d'Amour*, and Gary was making her an allowance as she had no money. After hospitalization she began an affair with an Algerian restaurateur and it was apparently more serious than the many other affairs at this stage of her life, for they exchanged vows – since she was still legally married. Georges de Beauregard, who had produced *A Bout de Souffle*, offered a last chance, nine days' filming for $10,000 in *La Légion Saute sur Kolnezzi*, but Seberg's agent refused to have anything to do with the deal since she did not think she was fit to do it. Before filming began Seberg took a lethal overdose; her body was not found till 10 days later, in a car parked in a suburban street in Paris. Gary filed claim that she was not being well looked after at the time of her death, in 1979, and himself committed suicide the following year.

George Segal

When the movie industry was shaken up like a kaleidoscope in 1969/70 there emerged strange new patterns and George Segal was discovered to be one of the big new names. He certainly had not been before, though he had been in films for almost 10 years. Only a few names were not in a perilous position – the old, driving, guard like Burt Lancaster and (natch) John Wayne and the bright, over-publicized boys like Dustin Hoffman and Elliott Gould. Segal had not quite had the breaks – not great parts in smash-hits that Hoffman and Gould had, as Alan Arkin almost had in *Catch-22*: and worse, he had a face as nondescript as Arkin's, altering with the character he played. He represented – rather than projected – the new hero. He was not an anti-hero, as has been claimed, but a new creature in movies – the urban-dweller, the new Manhattanite, buffeting off the new horrors of fun-city with an ironic humour and pushing aside the roar of the rat-race with a couldn't-care-less shrug. He offers to others in the same situation as himself a care and an honesty, with only a wry backward nod to the age of chivalry.

Segal's own background is very much like that of his films. He was born into the smart New York suburb of Great Neck on Long Island in 1936 and educated at a Quaker school in Pennsylvania – where he formed a noted jazz band – and then went to Columbia University where he received his BA in 1955. He started in the theatre off-Broadway, at the Circle in the Square, then at the height of its reputation – but he never went on (he understudied in 'La Ronde'). His professional début was in Molière's 'Don Juan', with Peter Falk, at New York's Downtown Theatre: it lasted one night. However, he returned to the Circle for a leading role in 'The Iceman Cometh' (56), with Jason Robards Jr. He married (a story editor at CBS) and was drafted. When he left the army in 1957, he played in the New York Shakespeare Festival 'Antony and Cleopatra'; was in the off-Broadway revival of Jerome Kern's 'Leave It to Jane'; formed a nightclub singing act with Patricia Scott; and was one of the original cast of 'The Premise', the improvised revue which ran for some years. Columbia producer Larry Turman saw him in that and signed him for a brief role in *The Young Doctors* (61), with Fredric March; and he signed a non-exclusive long-term Columbia contract. He was taken on for one of the cameo roles *The Longest Day* – a 30-second appearance that was originally uncredited but is now billed on reissue.

He was also working steadily in TV; and was later to appear in three Specials – 'Death of a Salesman', 'Of Mice and Men' and 'The Desperate Hours'. He established himself on Broadway in Paddy Chayevsky's 'Gideon' and in 'Rattle of a Simple Man', the latter a two-hander. He had a small role in Doré Schary's *Act One* (63), a flop version (it never opened in most countries) of Moss Hart's bestselling memoir; then had his first considerable film role, in *Invitation to a Gunfighter*, produced by Stanley Kramer and starring Yul Brynner. He played a young landowner deprived of his land. After returning to medicine in the dreary, over-busy *The Young Interns*, Columbia gave him a star part, finally, in *King Rat* (64), an otherwise all-British film – made

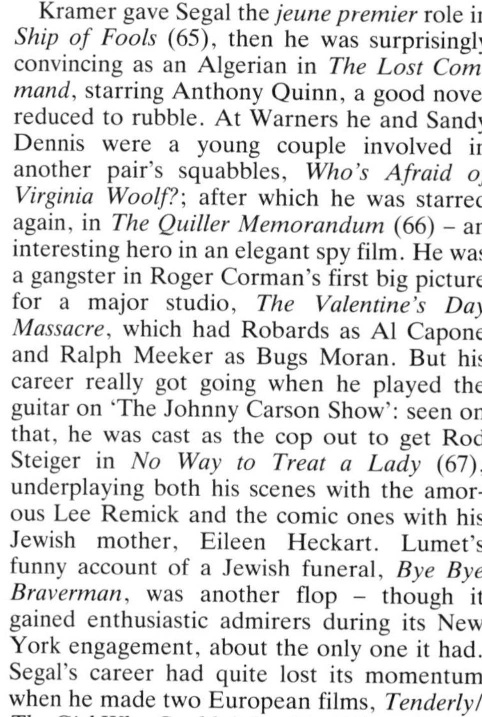

in Hollywood and set in a Singapore gaol during the war. He had the title-role, that of an arch-scrounger, cheat, thief, etc., and was highly effective. James Clavell, who wrote the original novel, called the film 'a deserved box-office failure'; Bryan Forbes, who directed, thinks it 'way ahead of its time'.

Kramer gave Segal the *jeune premier* role in *Ship of Fools* (65), then he was surprisingly convincing as an Algerian in *The Lost Command*, starring Anthony Quinn, a good novel reduced to rubble. At Warners he and Sandy Dennis were a young couple involved in another pair's squabbles, *Who's Afraid of Virginia Woolf?*; after which he was starred again, in *The Quiller Memorandum* (66) – an interesting hero in an elegant spy film. He was a gangster in Roger Corman's first big picture for a major studio, *The Valentine's Day Massacre*, which had Robards as Al Capone and Ralph Meeker as Bugs Moran. But his career really got going when he played the guitar on 'The Johnny Carson Show': seen on that, he was cast as the cop out to get Rod Steiger in *No Way to Treat a Lady* (67), underplaying both his scenes with the amorous Lee Remick and the comic ones with his Jewish mother, Eileen Heckart. Lumet's funny account of a Jewish funeral, *Bye Bye Braverman*, was another flop – though it gained enthusiastic admirers during its New York engagement, about the only one it had. Segal's career had quite lost its momentum when he made two European films, *Tenderly/The Girl Who Couldn't Say No* (68), an Italian comedy with Virna Lisi, and the French *L'Etoile du Sud/The Southern Star* (69), a facetious African adventure with Orson Welles which did not come off. Also in Europe he did an undistinguished war film, *The Bridge of Remagen*, with Ben Gazzara.

How To Steal a Diamond in Four Uneasy Lessons *was how they rechristened* The Hot Rock (*72*) *for British audiences. Chief of the four thieves were Robert Redford and George Segal.*

Nor could *Loving* (70) be considered a great success, though by far the best – both the most honest and the funniest – of the crop of investigations into American commuter marriages, with Eva Marie Saint matching his own work. This got him the lead opposite Barbra Streisand in *The Owl and the Pussycat*, which was, coincidentally, a second engaging 'New York' picture; underplaying in the face of her exuberance, he still more than held his own. Another good comedy did not do well, Carl Reiner's manic *Where's Poppa?* (71), where his avowed will was to get rid of his Jewish mother (Ruth Gordon) by fair means or foul. He took the failure of this stoically. He had said, 'I've been party to everything I've done. I don't think you can go up now and not be involved. There's no Big Daddy any more, no studio to take care of you, to say this script is for you. That was a fascist dictatorship. This is just scuffling. But we're all together now, and it's producing more intelligent movies.' If the next two were intelligent, no one told the public, which preferred to stay at home and watch old movies on TV: *Born To Win*, another *film noir* with laughs, in which he was a New York junkie; and *The Hot Rock*, just another caper film. The public did desert TV for Melvin Frank's *A Touch of Class* (73), which kept harking back to old (and better) movies; what nuggets of intelligence on display were mostly in Segal's performance as a married executive who becomes besotted with a prim Englishwoman (Glenda Jackson). Simultaneously he had more emotional troubles in Paul Mazursky's *Blume in Love*, adjusting to becoming divorced.

As a change of pace he played a mechanical man who turns murderer in *The Terminal*

The family at war: Where's Poppa? (*71*). *Ruth Gordon was the dominating mother and George Segal the son out to be rid of her by fair means or foul. Ron Leibman played the brother who liked walking about in the nude.*

Man (74), one of several similar tales which failed, again, to find an audience; and there should have been bigger audiences for Robert Altman's fine, idiosyncratic study of two compulsive gamblers, *California Split*. In fact, if Segal was popular – and he was, in the same manner as Jack Lemmon, for his humour and humanity and comedy technique – it was clear that the public was only interested if the notices were good. Hence, there were two more flops: *Russian Roulette* (75), a Cold War thriller with laughs in which he was a corporal in the Mounties; and *The Black Bird*, with Stephane Audran, as Sam Spade Jr – supposedly a parody of Spade Sr's still (infinitely) more entertaining 1941 film. During the making of the latter Segal suddenly acquired a behaviour on set described by 'Photoplay' as 'eccentric . . . temperamental' and indeed even his agent believed that he would not work again. Still, he was offered and at the last moment declined *Lucky Lady*. Meanwhile, Frank was hoping to reunite Segal and Jackson, and came up with a comic Western, *The Duchess and the Dirtwater Fox*, but that lady refused the role and Goldie Hawn played it: since this looked like one of the felicitous comic teamings so rare today, much was expected – but Frank let them down. In *Fun With Dick and Jane* (77) he and Jane Fona were marginally more profitably teamed; but *Rollercoaster* never got off the ground – despite the addition of 'Sensurround'. Segal played a safety inspector who suspects a crash was murder. *Who Is Killing the Great Chefs of Europe?* (78) was a mild murder tale with Jacqueline Bisset; *Lost and Found* (79) was Frank's long-planned reunion for Segal and Jackson. Segal was then set to do *'10'*, opposite Julie Andrews, and one might have supposed him glad to act with an English lady who could play comedy; but he ankled the role at the last minute, with talk of litigation. His decision was understandable, given the script: but ironically and incredibly it was a big hit for his replacement, Dudley Moore. (Do we have Segal to blame for Moore's 'stardom'?)

Segal and Natalie Wood were *The Last Married Couple in America* (80), not that anyone cared. In the promising but ultimately disappointing *Carbon Copy* (81) he was a Jewish father confronted with a grown-up black son (Denzel Washington). Financing fell through for *Not a Penny More*, to have co-starred Rod Steiger and to have begun in London in June; and when in 1982 a Canadian film (see below) stopped and started, Segal said he waited for it to resume because there were no other offers. He made his TV dramatic début, for a record fee, as the detective in charge in *Trackdown: Looking for the Goodbar Killer* (83), and he stayed in that medium for *The Cold Room* (84), co-financed by Australia and HBO, and *The Deadly Game*, a co-production between Ely Landau and the BBC, also filmed in Britain and also meant for cable in the US; as far as the second was concerned, Segal also had cast approval. Neither worked – not the former, which set Segal and estranged daughter in today's East Berlin but also in a time warp which allowed for threatening Nazis, and not the latter, a barren Dürrenmatt essay on espionage. A busy year began with *Not My Kid* (85), a tele-movie in which he and Stockard Channing were parents of a daughter on drugs; and *Stick*, as the villain, a crass millionaire in this Burt Reynolds vehicle. Reynolds's career had also declined, but he had held his stellar status: since he also directed, was he remembering the time when they were in competition for the same roles in encouraging Segal to give one of the most overblown, embarrassing performances in all movie history? Segal also toured in 'Requiem for a Heavyweight', but it did not last in New York. He had the role formerly played by Jackie Gleason; John Lithgow had the role played in the film by Anthony Quinn. Also for TV – at least in Britain – Segal was a comic *Robin Hood*. In the meantime the Canadian film turned up, now titled *Killing 'Em Softly*. It had started out as a vehicle for Peter O'Toole, who was too busy, based on the same novel as *Atlantic City* – 'The Neighbor' by Laird Koenig, which was not credited on screen: Segal was a retired Broadway prop man who allows Irene Cara's boyfriend to be accused of a murder he has committed. It would not have mattered if it had not started again. A telefilm was a considerable improvement: *Many Happy Returns* (86), also made in Canada and teaming him with Ron Leibman (for the third time), as fighting in-laws in this bright comedy about the terrors created by the IRS. He tried a sitcom, 'Take Five' (87), and toured in a play by Alan Ayckbourn, 'Henceforward . . .'. *Run for Your Life* went on the shelf and, alas, *All's Fair* (89) did not: he was the trigger-happy owner of a candy company and Sally Kellerman was the wife trying to get hold of it by divorcing him. Bad luck held as he went into an Italian-backed mini-series with Albert Finney, *The Endless Game*.

Peter Sellers

Peter Sellers had questionable resources as an actor. An outstanding mimic, it is soon apparent that he has little else to offer. He promised more than he delivers. There is nothing unusual in this – there are actors who are uninteresting after four minutes, even without his gift for mimicry (just as, it is increasingly clear, there are those with few gifts other than 'personality' who continually fascinate). But if the varied characterizations of Sellers have nothing, no colour under the surface, is there anything there at all? How long can you laugh at a cardboard cut-out, however brilliantly executed? Does Sellers make people laugh? Do people sit there merely expecting to laugh at him (the secret of most TV comics) or do they genuinely find him funny? If they find him funny, do they find him funny like Buster Keaton is funny – silent, black and white, po-faced, but with a heart and mind which seem omitted from the meticulous masterwork of Sellers? He has been called a 'genius' by some and the grosses of his films suggest that he enjoyed, at least for a time, a wide and admiring popularity.

He first surfaced as a stand-up teller of embarrassingly unfunny lavender jokes. Born in 1925 in Southsea, into a theatrical family, he started as a callboy and was a camp entertainer during his RAF service. He also toured with Ralph Reader's wartime 'Gang Show'. Demobbed, he got some London breaks, notably in radio and at the Windmill Theatre. In 1949 he began, with three other comedians, a BBC series called 'The Goon Show', which ran for seven years. During this time he was frequently on TV and was making assorted shorts with and without fellow Goons, starting with *Let's Go Crazy* (50). His first feature was a B with Goons Harry Secombe and Spike Milligan, *Penny Points to Paradise* (51), playing an elderly colonel. They were each paid £100. They were together again in the appropriately titled *Down Among the Z-Men* (52). His film career really began with *Orders Are Orders* (54), a dull army farce in which Tony Hancock, in another small part, 'provided the only moments of real brightness' ('MFB'). He was one of a large bunch of British eccentrics in a syrupy concoction about two kids wanting to see the coronation, *John and Julie* (55), but really made his mark in *The Lady-Killers*, very correct as the spiv member of Alec Guinness's gang. Guinness was his idol, he told reporters (frequently), and in the field of face and voice disguises he emulated him.

Alec Guinness, Peter Sellers and Danny Green as three of the gang in The Lady-Killers *(55). They utilise the house and kindness of a dear little old lady (Katie Johnson) while planning what they hope is their 'big job'.*

He was engaging as an elderly and sentimental cinema projectionist in *The Smallest Show on Earth* (57), and 'Variety' thought he took 'top honours' as a quick-change artist in *The Naked Truth*. Both established him as the sort of crowd-pleaser often needed in British comedies; certainly his portrait of an enterprising bo'sun was some consolation amid the dire goings-on of a naval farce, *Up the Creek* (58). Now, says Peter Evans in his biography of Sellers, 'he was slowly developing a reputation for being difficult. The ruthless selectivity and fickle pirouetting around a decision, later to enrage producers who suspected temperament or the victimizing vanity of stardom, was already an integral part of his suspicious, self-protective instincts.' He and Terry-Thomas made a droll pair of robbers in *Tom Thumb*, made by MGM in Britain with Russ Tamblyn in the title-role; and they were effectively teamed in *Carlton-Browne of the F.O.* (59), with Thomas in that role and Sellers as a wily wog premier. It was the first of a run of comedies which were going to make it a Sellers marquee on all British cinemas: at the end of the year he was voted one of Britain's top 10 draws and he would stay there till 1965, on two occasions rising to second position.

The Mouse That Roared, after an ignominious start, did just that on the US art circuit: a fable about a minor duchy which declared war on the US – and won – it had Sellers as the grand duchess, as a treacherous prime minister and as the hero – the first time he had appeared more or less as himself on the screen. He was a truculent shop steward in *I'm All Right Jack*, a comic look at trade unions and an enormous success in Britain; for Sellers the performance was his biggest personal hit to date and it brought him a deserved BFA Best British Actor award. In

Two-Way Stretch he was a convict, one of his weakest performances, and in *The Battle of the Sexes*, a none-too-happy version of Thurber's 'The Cat-Bird Seat', an elderly Scottish accountant. Also being enjoyed at this period was a freewheeling short entitled *The Running Jumping and Standing Still Film*.

Some experiments did not come off. In *Never Let Go* (60) he essayed a straight part, as a villain, but neither critics nor public cared for it; which was equally true of *The Millionairess*, despite the presence of Sophia Loren – but as the Indian doctor he was able to use one of his staples, his 'funny' Indian accent. He then took it upon himself to direct as well as star in the fourth movie version of Marcel Pagnol's old play, *Mr Topaze* (61), and came a good fourth after Louis Jouvet, Fernandel and John Barrymore. Fortunately, his next film and performance, as a lecherous Welsh librarian, were much liked, *Only Two Can Play*, from a novel by Kingsley Amis. Basically, though, both pace and jokes were clodhopping and it did not repeat its success outside Britain; nor did *The Waltz of the Toreadors* (62), an equally clumsy version of Anouilh's play – and in another straight part, the lecherous general, Sellers was uneven. Then he did a guest spot in *The Road to Hong Kong* with Hope and Crosby, where he did a guest shot.

His American reputation had been waiting in the wings since the *Mouse* film. It came with a bang when Stanley Kubrick chose him to play the ubiquitous pursuer, Quilty, in *Lolita*. He did three British films: *The Wrong Arm of the Law*, as the mastermind of a gang of crooks, 'perhaps the worst to date of that fast-breeding species, the Peter Sellers film' (Dwight Macdonald); *The Dock Brief*, a serious version of John Mortimer's one-act play which passed unnoticed; and *Heavens Above* (63), a send-up of clerics. In the States, his reputation fully asserted itself with *The Pink Panther*, directed by Blake Edwards, as the bumbling French police inspector, Clouseau – a role originally meant for Peter Ustinov, who instead played the role intended for Sellers in *Topkapi* (he had heard that Maximilian Schell was unprofessional and when Jules Dassin repeated this to Schell he refused to co-star with Sellers; so United Artists, who were funding both films, arranged a straight swop). Sellers returned to Kubrick for the second triple role of his career, the US president, an RAF officer and the scientist of the title – *Dr Strangelove Or How I Learned To Stop Worrying and Love the Bomb* (64), a highly praised and probably brilliant anti-war/anti-bomb/anti-military fantasy that was big box-office. Even bigger was *A Shot in the Dark*, where the original French play was altered slightly by Blake Edwards and collaborators to accommodate Inspector Clouseau. Then he had somewhat less success with his first Hollywood-filmed film, *The World of Henry Orient*, as an egomaniacal concert pianist pursued by two teenage girls.

Sellers never made the US top 10 list (though he was 13th in 1965 and 15th in 1966) but he was at this time probably the most sought-after actor in the world. He elected to do *Kiss Me Stupid* for Billy Wilder, but had a series of heart attacks during filming and was replaced by Ray Walston. Recovered, he gave an interview criticizing Hollywood, which brought this response, signed by Wilder and the whole company, 'Talk about unprofessional rat finks'. Sellers took a full-page ad in 'Variety' explaining that he did not like Hollywood as a place to *work*. (His biographer wondered whether he was not 'the most unpopular chap in Hollywood'.) His career recovered quickly with *What's New Pussycat?* (65) – or at least that testified to his drawing power: a feeble piece, it was carried to success by him, Peter O'Toole and plenty of smirking sex-jokes.

The next years were fairly bleak; his own personal notices were poor and few of the films did well. Certainly, as he admitted himself, everyone lost interest halfway through the filming of *Caccia alla Volpe/After the Fox* (66), written by Neil Simon and directed by Vittorio De Sica, in which he was a crook posing as an Italian film director. He did a guest stint in *The Wrong Box*, as a cat-crazy doctor. *Casino Royale* (67) was the James Bond film not made by the normal Bond-makers and Sellers was one of the many tricks shoved into it in order to persuade the public it did not matter that Sean Connery was

Sellers played three roles in Kubrick's Dr Strangelove *(64): an American president – being urged on by a military fanatic (George C. Scott); an RAF officer – being comforted by another odd military man (Sterling Hayden); and a mad scientist.*

Sellers's seesawing career was chiefly his own fault, for he was not, to put it mildly, the most considerate of colleagues. He went through a very bad patch before achieving a minor triumph in Hal Ashby's Being There *(1979), as a simple-minded gardener thought to be a political genius. He was nominated for an Oscar and his failure to win may well have contributed to his fatal heart attack, since his lifelong insecurity about his talent could make him rage for days on end. Here he is about to receive an injection, from Richard Dysart.*

not in it – he was one of the Bonds. He did it, he said, because he was flattered to be offered $1 million, but that did not apparently persuade him to film his scenes with Orson Welles *with* Welles (they were spliced together). He was originally set to direct *The Bobo*, but fortunately did not, for the press was unkind enough, claiming he had overreached himself in trying to add singing and Keatonesque pathos to his normal mugging. (The leading lady was Britt Ekland, who was briefly the second Mrs Sellers; he married for the third time in 1971.) A second excursion into Indian territory, as an Indian extra in Hollywood, Blake Edwards's *The Party* (68), was equally disastrous, though he might have been better with less sustained gags. However, as a respectable man turned hippie in *I Love You Alice B. Toklas*, both performances – his and the box-office – returned more or less to form.

He turned down both *Oliver!* (Fagin) and *The Fixer*. After an absence he turned up as star and co-adapter of Terry Southern's comic novel, *The Magic Christian* (69), supposedly a satire on money – Sellers was Ringo Starr's millionaire father. A horrible film. He played an obsessed lover in *Hoffman* (70), which flopped, and a homosexual – a guest performance – in *A Day at the Beach* made in Denmark and still, apparently, unshown. *There's a Girl in My Soup* was adapted from a stage success, with Goldie Hawn as a waif pursued by Sellers, playing a big-headed and lecherous TV personality. It was a surprisingly amateurish performance, but did go some way towards reflecting the dilemma of the latter-day Sellers: he could not decide whether to play it for laughs or romance, as character actor or leading man. As directed by Roy Boulting, the film and he were repellent together. In 1970 'Newsweek' reported that Sellers, who had once been getting $750,000 per film, was now being offered for $50,000 plus a small percentage.

He returned to the US to play a crooked hospital administrator in one of a spate of comedies about such institutions, *Where Does It Hurt?* (72) – and the answer came at the box-office. The answer was similarly dusty with all the following – or those of them that managed to get shown in the first place: a British remake of *Alice's Adventures in Wonderland*, one of several 'names', as the March Hare; *The Blockhouse*, made in the Channel Islands with Charles Aznavour, a rare serious role as one of a group of men (in fact, a teacher) trapped underground by bomb damage, and not publicly screened to date (though it was trade-shown in 1978); Boulting's *Soft Beds, Hard Battles*, as six different people, including Hitler, and described by 'Variety' as 'embarrassingly crude' when it turned up briefly in the US as *Undercovers Hero*; *The Optimists of Nine Elms*, probably the best of this batch, as written and directed by Anthony Simmons from his own novel, as a busker (a role meant for Danny Kaye) involved with two children; and *The Great McGonagall*, as Queen Victoria, no less, to the Scottish poet of old-partner Milligan, who co-scripted with the director, Joseph McGrath, who had earlier perpetrated *The Magic Christian*. There was no doubt that Sellers was unlucky in choosing his scripts, but there could be little sympathy in view of the lavatorial and other lesser forms of humour; and they were not seemingly chosen other than to display the Sellers skills. In fact, after the press had savaged them and the public avoided them, Sellers was very much a back number. However, he still behaved like a big star, absent apparently on whim from the set of *Ghost in the Noonday Sun*: the diplomatic director, Peter Medak, fell over backwards without getting anywhere and thought the result so predictably awful that he wanted his name off the credits: but in the event the film went unseen till 1984, when it surfaced on cable in Canada. Sellers played a cook on a pirate ship. His box-office rating and the offers coming in were virtually nil, so he accepted an offer from Lew Grade to do 26 episodes of Clouseau for TV. Edwards had several times sworn never to work with Sellers again, but his career was also at a low ebb. He decided to participate, pushing aside the TV series because he believed that the public was ready for *The Return of the Pink Panther* (75): United Artists did not think so, despite the success of the earlier Clouseau films, but agreed to release and via owning the character retained a part of the action; they were rewarded with some of the largest grosses in their history. Thus, after Sellers had done the Charlie Chan role in *Murder By Death* (76), UA had a much bigger stake in *The Pink Panther Strikes Again* and since the strike was also made at the box-office, more was on offer: *The Revenge of the Pink Panther* (78). Sellers's salary was now back to $750,000 plus a percentage. The Mirisch Co. was also involved with these films and had in 1976 signed Sellers to a three-picture deal, to begin with an exceptionally ill-advised new version of *The Prisoner of Zenda* (79).

The industry, which had not – apparently – heard patrons' comments on this or the last of the Pink Panthers, decided that Sellers was hot again and was prepared to pay him the $3 million he was now asking. Hal Ashby's *Being There*, with Shirley MacLaine, certainly attracted attention to him and was a huge hit: he played an ex-gardener considered to be a genius though he was in fact naive, ignorant and hollow – a role said by some to be much like the real Sellers. He was nominated for an Oscar and the fact that he did not get it (bad notices sent him into rages for days) may have contributed to his death, of a heart attack, in May 1980. He had been scheduled for a series of remakes of hoary old properties, despite the complete failure of *Zenda*. That, like *The Fiendish Plot of Fu Manchu*, had gone through a number of directors, amidst much-publicized disputes – and had ended up with Sellers helming most of it himself. He planned to co-write and direct *The Romance of the Pink Panther* – though that might have been cancelled after the notices and receipts of *Fu Manchu* had been examined. There did emerge *The Trail of the Pink Panther* (82), a collection of out-takes from earlier films put together by Edwards, with a linking story in which a reporter (Joanna Lumley) was researching for a programme on Clouseau. Sellers's widow, who had remarried, asked for, and got, $1 million damages for what she considered his false cooperation.

There were many revelations now available: the Boulting brothers said that he had been 'a human disaster area', as capricious as a spoilt child, with a life which 'teetered between total narcissim and total insecurity'.

Omar Sharif

Omar Sharif is the only Egyptian to become a front-rank world movie star. He was born in Alexandria in 1932 of Lebanese and Syrian stock; his father was a wealthy timber-merchant – wealthy enough for the boy to be raised speaking only French (he did not learn Arabic till he began making films). He became interested in acting while at Victoria College in Cairo, but worked five years in his father's business until given the chance to act; he had, in fact, persuaded the family to let him apply to RADA when an old friend, Jusef Shahine, offered him the lead in *Sina Fil Wadi/The Blazing Sun* (54). He was billed as Omar el Cherif. The star was Faten Hamama, then the biggest female attraction in the Middle East. Some time after it was completed, they were married (1955-66). That film was shown at the Cannes festival, but none of his subsequent Egyptian films was seen outside the Arab countries: *Ayamina El Hilwa/Our Happy Days*, with Hamama; *Chitane es Sahra/Devil of the Sahara:* and *Sinâ Fil Nina/Struggle on the Pier* (55), *Ard el Salam/Land of Peace* and *La Aname/No Sleep* (56), all with his wife. He was also appearing on the stage. He was offered a featured role in *La Châtelaine du Liban* (billed as Omar Cherif), a silly desert adventure tale starring Jean-Claude Pascal and Gianna-Maria Canale. As a result he starred in the Franco-Tunisian *Goha* (58), a sad little love story directed by Jacques Baratier; it had some success at the Cannes festival and was seen in most English-speaking countries. Meanwhile, Sharif continued his Egyptian career: *Chati el Asrar/Shore of Secrets* (57); *Galtet Halibi/My Lover's Mistake; Min Ajl Imraa/For the Sake of a Woman* (58); *Saidate el Kasr/The Lady of the Castle* with his wife; *Mouid Maâ el Majhoul/Rendezvous with a Stranger*; *Fediha fil Zamalek/Scandal at Zamalek*; *Ehna el Talamza/We the Students* (59); *Sinâ fil Nil/Struggle on the Nile*; *Eshaet Hob/Love Rumour* (60); *Laât el Hob/The Agony of Love*; *Hobbi el Wahid/My Only Love; Jharan el Asyad/I Love My Boss; Bidaya wa Nibaya/*

Beginning and End; and *Fi Baitina Rajul/A Man in Our House* (61).

It was not till he was touted to David Lean to play Sherif Ali Ibn Kharish in *Lawrence of Arabia* (62) that a break from Egyptian films became possible. His engaging performance as Lawrence's friend brought a supporting Oscar nomination and a Columbia contract. Meanwhile, he played a sheik in *La Fabuleuse Aventure de Marco Polo* (left uncompleted; finished and premièred in 1964), then returned to Egypt to star in *El Mamaleak/The Mameluks* (63). He resumed his international career somewhat tentatively, with featured roles in *The Fall of the Roman Empire* (64), as Sophia Loren's Armenian husband, and *Behold a Pale Horse*, as a Spanish priest. He was good in that one, but much less interesting in *The Yellow Rolls-Royce* (65), as Ingrid Bergman's Yugoslav lover. He was then involved in another international 'spectacular' *Ghenghis Khan*, this time in the title-role.

Doctor Zhivago (65) *was a huge, panoramic and very dull version of Boris Pasternak's novel about some characters just before, during, and after the Russian Revolution. Chief of them were Zhivago (Omar Sharif) and Lara, the girl he loves (Julie Christie).*

His nationalities proliferated. Next, Russian. David Lean, who had once got some sensitive acting from him, tried again in *Doctor Zhivago*, in the title-role – this time without success. There is a hollow at the centre of the film, perhaps the reason the film was not critically liked; but it astounded its makers (or, rather, MGM, who distributed) by going on to be an immense popular success (the book no one could read became the film everyone wanted to see). He popped up in *The Poppy Is Also a Flower*, an expanded version of the United Nations feature originally intended for TV, and then played a Nazi officer in *The Night of the Generals* (66). That finally killed any doubt in anybody's mind that he really looked like an Arab and, coupled with the continuing success of *Zhivago*, made him available to play any nationality.

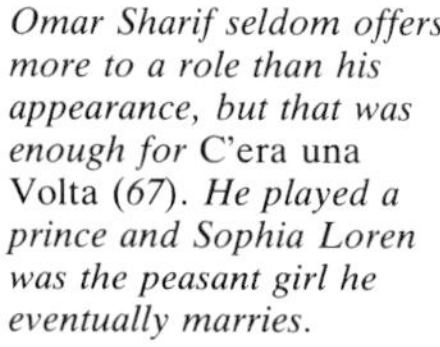

Omar Sharif seldom offers more to a role than his appearance, but that was enough for C'era una Volta (67). *He played a prince and Sophia Loren was the peasant girl he eventually marries.*

Over the next two years he was the busiest actor in the business. He was contracted for six pictures and was making the last of them when the first was shown. This was *C'era una Volta* (67), sumptuous-looking but dull as Sophia Loren's Spanish prince. He played an American-Jewish con-man, Barbra Streisand's husband, in *Funny Girl* (68) – basically a supporting role, though with co-star billing. He did it on condition that Columbia release him from his contract. As Sheilah Graham observed, 'the reviewers who noticed him merely did it to murder him'. He played an Austrian prince in *Mayerling*; 'I have no authority, I'm just the puppet prince,' he said, which 'Time Magazine' quoted gleefully, adding, 'It shows.' He was the Mexican villain of *Mackenna's Gold* (69) and an Italian lawyer, Anouk Aimée's lover, in *The Appointment*. 'Variety' found the latter 'burdened additionally by an uninspired performance by Omar Sharif . . . over-rigid' and 'Cinéma '69' though it confirmed Sharif 'est bien le plus mauvais acteur de toute l'histoire du cinéma'. He was an Argentinian revolutionary, Che Guevara, in 20th's opportunistic and inadequate biopic, *Che!*, with Jack Palance as Fidel Castro.

Of that sextet, only *Funny Girl* was a success; at least three of them were flops of gigantesque proportions – certainly the last two. Sharif had explained his approach to film-making when asked about Prince Rudolph on the set of *Mayerling*: 'I haven't a clue. I'm not that kind of actor. If a director wants Omar Sharif to play a part he gets Omar Sharif, not the reincarnation of some nutty prince. I play Rudolph like I play all my parts. Prince Rudolph is me. I don't give a damn how his mind works. All I care about is getting to the studio on time and remembering my lines.' Later he said that filming was boring, that the most important thing to happen him in his film career was learning chess (he is also a champion bridge-player and in 1964 represented Egypt in the Olympic bridge tournament).

Despite the flops, 'Photoplay' reported Sharif's salary as around $750,000 while he was making *The Last Valley* (71), with Michael Caine, as a German priest, and Frankenheimer's *The Horsemen*, with Jack Palance, as an Afghan warrior. Both flopped. After that he played a heavy in a French movie starring Jean-Paul Belmondo, *La Casse*, and then was a hot-headed revolutionary on a prison island with Florinda Balkan, in *Le Droit d'Aimer* (72); he crossed the Pyrenees for a new version of Jules Verne, *L'Isola Misteriosa*, as Captain Nemo. There were starring roles in two British films, *The Tamarind Seed* (74), as the Russian military attaché who falls in love with British widow Julie Andrews; and *Juggernaut* with Richard Harris, as the captain with a bomb on board ship. He had special billing and brief footage in *Funny Lady* (75), a sequel to *Funny Girl*, and had a guest spot in *The Return of the Pink Panther*. *An Ace Up My Sleeve* (76) co-starred Karen Black and was based on a novel by James Hadley Chase: it was, said 'Variety' later, when it turned up retitled *Crime and Passion*, a 'dreary sexy murder comedy attempt' and Sharif was 'an investment counsellor who gets horny when tense'. Invited to appear in an African adventure with Michael Caine, *Ashanti* (79), Sharif ceded his leading role to the Indian actor Kabir Bedi (who mistakenly announced that this would make him a world star) and instead did a cameo, as the Prince. This was a compromise, because he feared that after this Israeli-backed adventure his films might be banned in the Arab world: and he did it, he explained, because he had been out of work for three years.

The offers which now came in could not have been tempting: the foolish *Sidney Sheldon's Bloodline*, as a member of Audrey Hepburn's board, married to Irene Papas; the German-backed *S-H-E* (80), which was fortunate to find itself sold to CBS TV for its première, as the head of an international spy ring, with Anita Ekburg and Cornelia Sharpe; *The Baltimore Bullet*, as an ace pool-player challenged by James Coburn; *Oh Heavenly Dog!*, in which Chevy Chase returned to earth as Benjy; *Pleasure Palace*, a tele-film mysteriously retitled *Crime Club* in Britain, as a big-time gambler; and *Green Ice* (81) as the villain, an Italian exiled to Mexico doing wrong to Ryan O'Neal. In Chichester and London, to mediocre notices, he was 'The Sleeping Prince' (83) and he remained royal, though Indian this time, in a lavish British tele-film, *The Far Pavilions*. He returned to Egypt to star in *Ayoub* (84), subtitled *Psychodrama of a Millionaire*, which was a success there but has not arrived among us; and did a cameo in *Top Secret!*, as a mystery man in this spy (and much else) spoof. He was in a dire BBC 'Huis Clos' with Jeanne Moreau and in two US mini-series, *Harem* (86) with Ava Gardner, as its ruler, and *Anastasia: The Mystery of Anna*, partnered with Claire Bloom as Nicholas and Alexandra in the flashback sequences. He was in Wajda's *Les Possédés* (88), based on Dostoevsky, as the intellectual father of the hero, and in a Franco-British tele-movie, *Grand Larceny* with Louis Jourdan, as a wealthy Arab playboy. In *Les Pyramides Bleues* he was a magnate who loses Arielle Dombasle – who also wrote and directed – to a nunnery. Then: *Mountains of the Moon* (89), Bob Rafelson's biography of the explorer, Sir Richard Burton; *Keys to Freedom*, made in Malysia with Jane Seymour and Denholm Elliott; and *Michelangelo and Me*.

Simone Signoret

During the early part of her career Simone Signoret usually played prostitutes or kept women; even on those occasions when she was not taking money for it, her love was illicitly sought. As she aged she turned to playing bourgeois wives, frumps and, once or twice, *grande dame* actresses. But whatever her range – and her overall skill as a screen actress is impressive – she was unbeatable as a woman in love; her eyes would light up when the designated man appeared, she would fondle him sensuously as she offered him her lips to kiss, she hovered over him like a mother cat – and she was still vulnerable, like all the great screen mistresses. Think of Garbo's best performance as a woman racked with love and Signoret equalled it at least twice.

She was born in 1921 (Simone Kaminker) in Wiesbaden, Germany, where her father was a member of the Occupation forces. She was brought up in Paris and planned to be an actress, but when her father left to join de

Gaulle in London – 18 June 1940 – there was no option but to become a typist. It did not last long; she fell in with a *rive gauche* group of actors and writers, who persuaded her that she could support the family more comfortably by becoming a film extra. Her film début was in *Le Prince Charmant* (42) and she can be glimpsed in *Boléro*, where she had one line, *Les Visiteurs du Soir* and *Adieu Léonard* (43), the Prévert *frères* comedy with Charles Trenet. At the same time she was getting acting experience in a small cellar theatre and she studied under Solange Siccard. She had a bit in *Béatrice devant le Désir* (44), a heavy drama starring Fernand Ledoux and Jules Berry, and around this time met and married director Yves Allégret, who gave her another small part, as the mistress of Henri Bry, in *La Boîte aux Rêves* (45). She was featured in *Le Couple Idéal*, a comedy starring Raymond Rouleau, and then her husband gave her the female lead in *Les Démons de l'Aube*, an honest account of the French commandos who took part in the Southern invasion. Her part was small but she was not unnoticed.

When Sophie Desmarets became pregnant Jacques Feyder replaced her with Signoret in his *Macadam*, a conventional Montmartre story starring Françoise Rosay. Signoret was the *pensionnaire* who shifted her love from a guilty Paul Meurisse to an innocent Jacques Dacqumine and she was, said 'The New York Times', 'saucy and alluring'. She had been noticed in Britain, too: after playing the heroine in a new version of *Fântomas* (47), the old World War I Feuillade serial, now starring Marcel Herrand, she went to Ealing for *Against the Wind*. This was a preposterous and dull thriller about the Belgian Resistance, somewhat enlivened by her performance as a patriot – though that was little commented upon at the time.

She first imposed herself on the French public in *Dédée d'Anvers* (48), a conventional study of brothel life in Antwerp, directed by Allégret (considering the postwar French cinema's obsession with prostitution, she had to play whores if she wanted to stay in business). She was an actress in *L'Impasse des Deux Anges*, but had two lovers – Meurisse from the past and Herrand in the present. And she was a Very Bad Lot indeed in *Manèges* (49), a cheap slut who ensnares landowner Bernard Blier into marriage and leads him a dog's life – all told in flash-back, which gave the film a dubious weight. Allégret directed and not long afterwards they were divorced. In 1951 she married singer Yves Montand.

Meanwhile, she became an international name: not in the Swiss-locationed *Four Days Leave* (50), vamping Cornel Wilde, but in

It is unlikely now that any movie could provoke the furore that greeted La Ronde *(50) when it arrived in London. Because it was about a series of lovers moving on to the next one, the popular press thundered, as though such things never happened; on top of that, the critics were unanimous in calling it a masterpiece. By the time it arrived in New York in 1954, there had been too many censorship rows about European movies for this one to be news, and American critics were somewhat less impressed. A notable cast included Gérard Philipe as the Count and Simone Signoret as the prostitute.*

Max Ophüls's delicious, famous *La Ronde*, in the first and last of the 10 sequences – inevitably as a tart. A Franco-American effort, *Le Traqué/Gunman in the Streets* – Dane Clark as an ex-GI on the run in Paris – did little for her, but she had a very good role in *Ombre et Lumière* (51), as a pianist, with Maria Casarès – sisters in love with the same man. What made her really famous abroad was the title-role in Jacques Becker's *Casque d'Or*, a turn-of-the-century courtesan of the underworld, with Serge Reggiani as her doomed lover. Lindsay Anderson wrote that the two performances 'are remarkable above all for their complete fusion, at a level of great intensity, of their personalities and acting styles into a shared conception. . . . Signoret's Marie, in particular, shows a radiant blossoming of talent: a creature entrancingly feminine, with a range of institution that encompasses the arrogant (and irresistible) wilfulness of the earlier sequences as persuasively as the later warmth of a woman passionately and constantly in love. Superbly confident of her power of attraction. . . .' In a rare poll, London critics voted her overwhelmingly the year's Best Actress and the BFA voted her Best Foreign Actress.

After that she deliberately restricted her

Casque d'Or (51) *was directed by Jacques Becker, who said he had attempted a fusion of Eugène Sue and Auguste Renoir. Serge Reggiani and Simone Signoret were the underworld lovers who have one brief idyll in the country, and both were memorable. The title referred to Signoret's nickname in the film, in turn a reference to her hair-style.*

film appearances, claiming that her career was subservient to that of her husband. She returned in Carné's straightforward modern version of *Thérèse Raquin* (53) with Raf Vallone – not exactly Zola's lovers, but the couple seen a thousand times in French movies, ill-used and haunted by bad luck. She played a teacher, Paul Meurisse's murdering mistress, in Clouzot's *Les Diaboliques* (54), one of the most gripping and most cunning of horror films – and one of the first foreign-language films to be widely distributed in the US and Britain. She was a prostitute stuck in the jungle in Buñuel's seldom-revived *Le Mort en ce Jardin* (56), after which she and Montand did the film of Arthur Miller's 'The Crucible', which they had been playing on the stage: *Les Sorcières de Salem* (57), directed, at their insistence, by Raymond Rouleau, who had staged it. She won a second BFA award for her performance – and then another, plus an award at Cannes and a Hollywood Best Actress Oscar, for her portrait of the rejected older woman in Jack Clayton's *Room at the Top* (58). It was a unique Oscar – the first major acting award ever to go to an artist who had never made a Hollywood picture and the second to go to a performer in a non-American film (Olivier in *Hamlet* was the first). The film's worldwide success would be due partly to Signoret's notices – somewhat ironically, for the original character in John

Simone Signoret and Raf Vallone as the guilty lovers in Marcel Carne's modernization of Thérèse Raquin (*53*).

Vera Clouzot as the wife and Signoret as the mistress – partners in crime in Les Diaboliques *(54). Charles Vanel was the detective who calls at an unnerving time – as they begin to wonder whether their very dead victim is dead after all.*

Braine's novel was a Yorkshire housewife (no British actress was thought to have sufficient sensuality).

Signoret was inundated with American offers, some of which were just silly, such as the roles played by Hope Lange in *Wild in the Country* and by Nicole Courcel in *High Time*; most of them required her to repeat her *Room at the Top* performance and she turned them all down (a later, sensible idea, for an American film of Colette's 'Chéri', was abandoned). She was compelled under an old contract to make a film in Italy and with ill grace went into *Adua e le Compagne* (60), a tale of four girls (including Emmanuèle Riva) who set up a restaurant – just like a Hollywood movie of the 30s (there are Capra-like businessmen who try to break it up), except they are all ex-prostitutes. The British title was *Hungry for Love* and it deserved better. She said she was too lazy to go to Hollywood and did two French movies: *Les Mauvais Coups* (61), an extended marital drama, again desperately in love – with her husband – but wise and cynical; and *Les Amours Célèbres*, in 'Jenny de La Cour', the best episode, as a Second Empire poisoner. Neither was seen much abroad and the next two turned out unhappily. She did not like playing Olivier's shrewish wife in *Term of Trial* (62), and *Le Jour et l'Heure* (63) was a disappointment. Made by René Clément in French and English on the strength of her name and Stuart Whitman's (as Resistance worker and downed flyer respectively), the English version got a few bookings in the US and none at all in Britain. (Yet it is one of the best of an unhappy breed, the Resistance movie.)

Yves Montand and Signoret in Les Sorcières de Salem *(57), the French movie version of Arthur Miller's play 'The Crucible'.*

She made a second stage appearance, in 'Les Petits Renards', which she had also translated as an act of homage to Bette Davis ('The Little Foxes'), but her Regina was in all ways too small. Her bit, as a call-girl, with Belmondo, was the only bright spot in another sketch-film, the draggy *Dragées au Poivre*, done to please friends. She began *Zorba the*

Greek, as the old whore, but decided after a few days that the part was not right for her – it went to Lila Kedrova, who won an Oscar for her performance. (Ten years earlier, she is said to have begun a German film of 'Mother Courage' which was abandoned.) She finally went to Hollywood for Stanley Kramer's *Ship of Fools* (65), as a drug-addicted countess having a passing affair with ship's doctor Oskar Werner, and the two of them, beautifully, acted the rest of the cast below deck and out of sight. Again among friends, she graced *Compartiment Tueurs*, with Montand, as a phoneyish actress, and dominated her few scenes; she also had just a couple of scenes, with Montand, as a bar-owner in *Paris Brûle-t-il?/Is Paris Burning?* (66). Looking by now chubby and, by movie-star standards, somewhat older than her years, she nevertheless brought magic to Sidney Lumet's excellent thriller, *The Deadly Affair*, as a concentration-camp survivor living in a London suburb. In Britain again she essayed Lady Macbeth opposite Alec Guinness in a much-despised production of that play; anxious to forget the experience she accepted a Hollywood film, *Games* (67), directed by Curtis Harrington. She did it, she said, to encourage new talent. Thanks: the film, a stylish if unoriginal chiller, was relegated to the bottom half of double bills. She was a weird woman who visits, and stays. . . .

Lumet reassembled many of the team of *The Deadly Affair* to make a version of Chekhov's *The Seagull* (68), including James Mason. Signoret was Arkadina and said that making the film was a very happy experience for all of them involved; but reviewers were not too happy and the film virtually disappeared. In fact, since *Room at the Top* she had not had a picture which was a box-office success in either the US or Britain, but her critical and cognoscenti reputation remained unrivalled; it had not, for instance, been challenged by the younger Jeanne Moreau. If she was no longer getting offers except from French film-makers it was probably because her appearance now restricted her to character roles. She looked old as a Resistance leader in *L'Armée des Ombres* (69), with Lino Ventura and Paul Meurisse, Jean-Pierre Melville's unexciting reworkings of some old themes. The next films, again, were made among friends: *L'Américain* (69), directed by actor Marcel Bozzufi, with Jean-Louis Trintignant, as a local bar-owner; *L'Aveu* (70), with Montand, as his agonized wife; and *Comptes à Rebours* (71), directed by actor Roger Pigaut, as an old gangster's moll who acts as mediator when gang warfare breaks out. As with the earlier *Compartiment Tueurs*, Signoret loaned her name and presence to enable these films to get off the ground (the same names recur in all four films, plus *Z*), and took either a small fee or none at all (but with a participation).

She returned to more conventional film-making with two very agreeable ones made by Pierre Granier-Deferre after Simenon, *Le Chat*, as a housewife of the *faubourgs* who loathes her husband (Jean Gabin), and *La Veuve Couderc*, as a country woman who shelters a man (Alain Delon) who confesses to an old murder. There as another film with Delon, *Les Granges Brûlées* (73), in which she was a peasant matriarch and he an inspector investigating a murder. She was a frumpish housewife in *Rude Journée pour La Reine*, on a participation fee, and she said she would have paid to be in it – though she presumably changed her mind when she saw the result, a messy proliferation of dreams as directed by René Allio; she coasted through her role and the film flopped. She was one of several names in supporting roles, playing a blowsy ex-actress, in *La Chair de L'Orchidée* (75), a tale about the travails of Miss Blandish's daughter (Charlotte Rampling); and she was with her husband in *Police Python 357* (76), as a cripple. As an aged prostitute looking after a small boy she had her best role in years – and it brought her a César (the French Oscar) for Best Actress: *La Vie Devant Soi* (77) was also the first of her films in years to be widely seen in the US. That she looked her years (unlike most American actresses of her age) shocked some viewers, but she talked cheerfully if resignedly of her lines when promoting her memoir, 'Nostalgia Isn't What It Used To Be', easily one of the best of the species. There were more good roles: in *Judith Therpauvre* (78), as a retired school-teacher who takes over a newspaper; in a TV movie, *Madam le Juge*; and in Jeanne Moreau's *L'Adolescente* (79), as the country-wise grandmother.

Moshe Mizrahi, who had directed *La Vie Devant Soi*, used Signoret again in *Chère Inconnue* (80), based on Eunice Rubens's novel, 'I Sent a Letter to My Love', now set in Brittany: she looked after crippled brother Jean Rochefort and became his pen pal without either of them knowing who the other was. The film, incidentally, has not been seen in Britain, perhaps because of the contemptuous press reception accorded the earlier Mizrahi-Signoret collaboration – which as *Madame Rosa* has become a staple in US art-houses. She was a Belgian landlady and Philippe Noiret was a French-Egyptian dreamer staying with her – 'The Tenant' of Simenon's novel, now retitled *L'Etoile du Nord* (82). She was ill during filming and around the same time a French TV series was cancelled. Her last film role was as the writer's mother in Michel Drach's *Guy de Maupassant*, though televiewers saw her posthumously, after her death of cancer in 1985, in a mini-series set in Paris in 1938, 'Music Hall'.

Alastair Sim

Among the eccentrics who people the casts of British pictures, Alastair Sim has pride of place. An enjoyable supporting actor for the early part of his career, he found stardom – by public demand – in the 40s, whereupon he began to refine his art. This is an appraisal by J.W. Lambert in the 'Sunday Times': 'Above all, it would be monstrous not to salute yet again the comic genius of Alastair Sim. His battery of twitches and scowls, his sudden alarming grins, his accelerandi, his glissandi, his awful pauses are all perfectly familiar. Yet, put to the service of a charter, even in a farce, they come up new-minted. All human tremors, timidities, qualms and sudden ecstasies flicker across that vast face, now beaming like a rising sun, now drooping like a moon dismayed by the impertinence of approaching astronauts' (on the occasion of the 1969 revival of Pinero's 'The Magistrate'). Mr Lambert might have made more of the voice, which must be an ornithologist's delight – in the cause, normally, of dismay or disapproval, he would cluck like a hen, hoot like an owl, coo like a dove. One may tire of such analogies, but in this case no others will do.

He was born in 1900 in Edinburgh, where he started out as a tailor in the family firm; an interest in the theatre intervened – in the end, too much. He ran a school for poetic drama; taught elocution; trained as a teacher; and was appointed to the Fulton lectureship at New College, Edinburgh. He acted in London as an amateur and was advised by John Drinkwater to make acting his career. He made his professional bow in London as a walk-on in Paul Robeson's 'Othello' (30) and played small parts, including a season at the Old Vic. Among the plays he did: 'As You Desire Me' (33), in the part Eric Von Stroheim took in the film; 'The Rose Without a Thorn'; and 'Alice in Wonderland' (34), appropriately as the Mad Hatter. Fox, chief source of quota quickies, offered him a good part in *Riverside Murder* (35) and he was thereafter kept too busy in the studios to appear often on the stage. The films he made were either quota quickies or modest vehicles for star comics: *A Fire Has Been Arranged*, with Flanagan and Allen, as the villain; *The Private Secretary* starring Edward Everett Horton, from a farce by Sir Charles Hawtrey; *Troubled Waters* and *Late Extra*, both with James Mason, in the latter as a Scottish housekeeper. He was a Scottish minister, the father of Florence Nightingale (Fay Compton) in a slight story about that family, *Wedding Group* (36); then he had the star role in another Fox quota quickie, *The Big Noise*, a comedy about big business. He was in another Edward Everett Horton vehicle, *The Man in the Mirror*, as an interpreter; then was in a George Formby picture, *Keep Your Seats Please*; followed by star roles in *The Mysterious Mr Davis*, directed by Claude Autant-Lara, and *Strange Experiment* (37). He played Constance Collier's manservant in *Clothes and the Woman*, which starred Rod la Rocque; and was a detective in both *Gangway*, starring Jessie Matthews, and *The Squeaker*, starring Edmund Lowe, the latter a part he had played earlier in the year in a successful revival of this Edgar Wallace piece.

His fame was now respectable, even if the films, still, were not: *A Romance in Flanders*; *Melody and Romance*, as a professor; *Sailing Along* (38), with Matthews, as an eccentric artist; and *The Terror*, another bash at Edgar Wallace – and a very silly film, with Wilfred Lawson as a mad, organ-playing monk and Sim as a crook disguised as a priest. He had a good role in *Alf's Button Afloat*, as a wizard in W.A. Darlington's famous piece refurbished for the Crazy Gang. He played an excitable news editor in *This Man is News*, supported Matthews in *Climbing High* (39) and was Sergeant Bingham in *Inspector Hornleigh*, with Gordon Harker. Two of these three occasioned sequels: *This Man in Paris* and *Inspector Hornleigh on Holiday*. He supported husband-and-wife team Barry K. Barnes and Diana Churchill in *Law and Disorder* (40); then did the third and last of the Scotland Yard pictures, *Inspector Hornleigh Goes to It* (41). Said Max Breen in 'Picturegoer': 'If you don't know Sim on the films you've missed one of the greatest treats that British films have to offer.' The Inspector Hornleigh films were quite important to Sim: they were written by the scriptwriting team of Launder and Gilliat who, as producers-directors, would be responsible for some of his biggest screen successes (meanwhile, Inspector Hornleigh continued as a BBC radio detective). On stage and then on screen he had a good part in an enjoyable thriller, *Cottage To Let*.

On stage, he played Captain Hook in 'Peter Pan' for the first time and began his association with the plays of James Bridie; over the next decade he appeared in – and sometimes directed – half a dozen; he championed Bridie to the extent of appearing on TV, one of the first big stars to use that medium. For the moment he made fewer films: *Let the People Sing* (42), popular propagandist stuff written by J.B. Priestley, top-billed and rather artificial as a bearded foreign professor; Launder and Gilliatt's *Waterloo Road* (44), with Stewart Granger, and their *Green for Danger* (46), as a detective again. That might be considered the one that did the trick; he got better notices than ever before – 'The New York Times' found him 'altogether captivating'; and he would henceforth have no difficulty in getting over-the-title billing.

Ealing's *Hue and Cry* (47) was an engaging comedy about a group of boys who realize that their favourite comic series is being used for code messages; Sim was its innocent and bewildered author. Then he did three more for Launder and Gilliatt: *Captain Boycott*, with Stewart Granger, as a priest; *London Belongs to Me* (48), as a phoney spiritualist; and *The Happiest Days of Your Life* (50), opposite Margaret Rutherford, as a headmaster. He had a small part in Hitchcock's *Stage Fright*, Jane Wyman's father, partnered by an equally befuddled Sybil Thorndike; and teamed well with another funny lady, Joyce Grenfell – as his gauche fiancée – in *Laughter in Paradise* (51), a film that the Ealing comedies had rendered old-fashioned. But it was popular. He had a guest spot in Launder and Gilliatt's *Lady Godiva Rides Again*; was miscast as *Scrooge* – but the film was poor anyway; and filmed Bridie's 'It Depends What You Mean' under the title of *Folly To Be Wise* (52), in his original part as the hearty Scots padre. It was an odd choice, for it was easily the least distinguished – and most dated – of the Bridie plays he had done and, as made by Launder and Gilliatt, a very tame movie.

He then got involved in a horror called *Innocents in Paris* (53), as a Treasury official who gets drunk in that city with a Russian diplomat. Much more satisfying was a minor and stagey version of one of J.B. Priestley's best plays, *An Inspector Calls* (54), as a quizzical Scotland Yard man. When Ronald Searle's schoolgirls came to the screen as *The Belles of St Trinian's*, he doubled as the majestic headmistress and her crooked brother: Launder and Gilliatt again, and one joke carried much too far in such elementary treatment – but Sim and fellow mistresses (Joyce Grenfell, Irene Handl, Hermione Baddeley, Beryl Reid, etc.) were funny and the film and its sequels huge successes in Britain. He brought a lift to both *Escapade* (55), as a headmaster again, and *Geordie*, as a laird; and was practically the only virtue of *The Green Man* (56), a version of a play by Sidney Gilliatt, as a professional assassin.

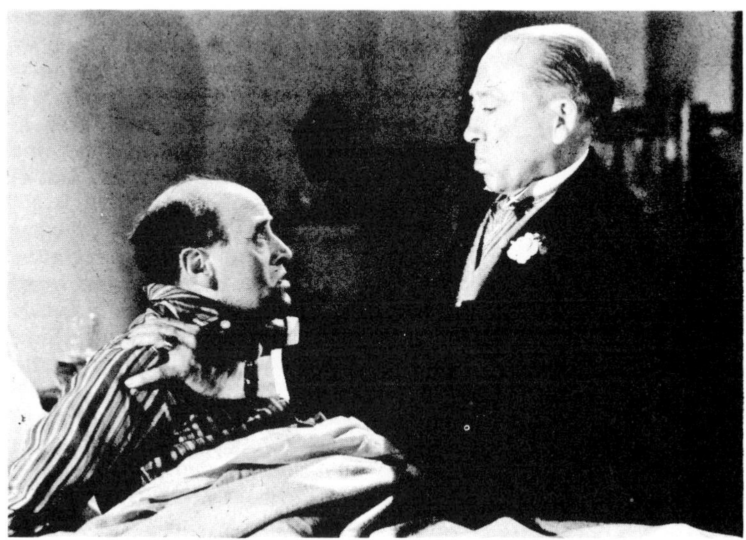

He played Sir Cutler Walpole in *The Doctor's Dilemma* (59), the Shaw play directed by Anthony Asquith; and the enterprising owner of an impoverished stately home in *Left Right and Centre*, a Launder and Gilliatt spoof of electioneering, with Ian Carmichael. He and Carmichael were together again in *School for Scoundrels* (60), Sim as its headmaster – Robert Hamer's comedy based on Stephen Potter's 'Oneupmanship' manuals. Then he did another Asquith version of Shaw, *The Millionairess*, with Sophia Loren. He did not film again for more than a decade, though the theatre was not entirely profitable, with two misfires at a serious level – Prospero at the Old Vic in 1962 and Shylock in Nottingham in 1964. However, he was well received in a revival of 'Too True To be Good' in 1965; and rapturously received in that revival of 'The Magistrate'. Among his occasional TV work

Alastair Sim and Gordon Harker, sparring-partners in a British crime series, written by Launder and Gilliatt. This one was Inspector Hornleigh on Holiday *(39). Below, Sim and Margaret Rutherford, headmaster and headmistress in* The Happiest Days of Your Life *(50). Due to an error in Whitehall, her school was billetted on his – for some of the funniest screen comedy ever.*

was more Bridie, including 'The Anatomist' (61), which played US TV as a feature film; and A.P. Herbert's 'Misleading Cases'. He returned to films co-starring with Peter O'Toole in *The Ruling Class* (72), as a comic bishop. He was one of several comic eccentrics in a Victorian adventure spoof, *Royal Flash* (75), and was an ennobled mine-owner in *Escape from the Dark* (76), a Disney film about Yorkshire pit ponies. He died in 1976, a few hours before a scheduled BBC transmission of one of his lesser films, *An Inspector Calls*.

JEAN SIMMONS

Jean Simmons has always been taken for granted. As a child player in Britain she was expected to be one of the best child players and she was; she was expected to become a big international name and she did. In Hollywood for over 20 years she was given good roles because she was reliable and she played them, or most of them, beautifully, and got good notices, and was liked. But she was never a cult figure, one of those who adorn magazine covers, or someone the fan magazines write about all the time. It was not or is not that she simply did or does her job – she is much better than that; she is not a competent actress, she is a very good one – by Hollywood standards a great one, if you take the Hollywood standard to be those ladies who have won Oscars. She was not even nominated for a Best Actress Oscar till 1969. She was not nominated even for *Elmer Gantry* (and that year Elizabeth Taylor won). Maybe it does not help to have been so good so young.

She was born in London in 1929 and educated at the Ada Foster School, a training-ground for child actors. Like most of the kids there, she was picked from time to time for modelling jobs and bits in films: *Give Us the Moon* (44), a comedy with Margaret Lockwood, as her sister; *Mr Emmanuel*, from Louis Golding's novel about a Jew who returns to Germany, with Felix Aylmer, unbilled as a landlady's daughter; *Kiss the Bride Goodbye*, a comedy with Patricia Medina, as her sister; and *Meet Sexton Blake* (45), who was David Farrar. She was glimpsed as a harpist in *Caesar and Cleopatra*, but by that time the people at Rank had tested her for a couple of roles and were excited about her. In *The Way to the Stars* she sang a song ('Let him Go Let Him Tarry') in the village dance-hall, with great aplomb, and she was delightful in a short, *Sports Day*. Rank signed her to a contract and really began beating the publicity drum in a big way when David Lean chose her to play the young Estella, pert and spoiled, in *Great Expectations* (46). After that, she had only a small part in *Hungry Hill* – a film version of a long Irish novel by Daphne du Maurier – as the youngest daugh-

The young Pip (Anthony Wager) meets Miss Havisham's uppity ward Estella (Jean Simmons) for the first time: a scene from David Lean's first-rate film version of Great Expectations *(46).*

Jean Simmons and Donald Houston in The Blue Lagoon, *a silly piece of escapism once taken seriously – but not at the time this second movie version was made, in 1949. They were a couple shipwrecked on a desert island as children.*

ter of the family who lived there, but then a bigger one in *Black Narcissus* (47), as an Indian minx with a jewel in her nose. The publicity was reaching a crescendo, so it was fortunate that critics thought she had the talent to sustain it, even in a film they did not much like: *Uncle Silas*, her first starring part, in this excellent version of Sheridan Le Fanu's Victorian mystery classic, with Katina Paxinou as the sinister governess; and *The Woman in the Hall*, as a girl who embezzles for mummy (Ursula Jeans).

It was said that no pressure was brought by Rank on Laurence Olivier to use her as Ophelia, in *Hamlet* (48), but Olivier, in any case, was keen. Simmons was flattered but nervous and was, among the veterans, 'the only person in the picture who gives every one of her lines the bloom of poetry and the immediacy of ordinary life' (James Agee). She was awarded a Best Actress decree at Venice and nominated for a Best Supporting Oscar (only the second actress ever nominated for a British film). A happy Rank sent her to Hollywood on a publicity trip; there was little fear that she would remain there as she was under contract for years yet. But the problem was to find films the whole world would want to see. There was *The Blue Lagoon* (49), from an antique novel about a couple of shipwrecked kids who grow up and have a baby without knowing anything of love, marriage or – it maintained – sex; the critics scoffed, but the colour locations were indeed an island amid the gloom of contemporary British films. There was *Adam and Evelyne*, a grim comedy where she was Stewart Granger's ward, but she was 'as bright and sunny as a day in May' said 'The New York Times'. There was *So Long at the Fair* (50) with Dirk Bogarde, a slight mystery based on the famous disappearance at the Paris Exposition of 1889. There was *Cage of Gold*, a silly drama made at Ealing, about a girl married to a bounder (David Farrar). There was *Trio*, three Maugham stories, literally in the 'Sanatorium' with Michael Rennie.

British critics were becoming vociferous about these poor vehicles, but the public was responding warmly enough: at the end of 1950 Simmons was the fourth biggest attraction, British or American, in British cinemas – even after a 21st birthday which received as much coverage as a royal wedding. She was not only younger than other British female stars, but fresher, warmer, gayer. There was one setback: a stage venture with Stewart Granger, 'The Power of Darkness', by Tolstoy, which flopped; and Rank were worried about her image when it was clear that Granger was going to leave his wife to marry her, which he did in 1950 Meanwhile, they put her into a (fairly) good film. *The Clouded Yellow*, an adventure tale with Trevor Howard. Granger was on the verge of his American career and Rank let her go to Hollywood to play Lavinia in *Androcles and the Lion* (52), which Gabriel Pascal was to make for RKO. She waited around months for it to start – during which period it was announced that Rank had sold the remainder of her contract to RKO, much to the displeasure of the party concerned, and of her husband, who wanted her to go to MGM with him. It was all very frustrating; every Hollywood studio wanted her and the filming of *Androcles* took forever – and the result was pasteboard G.B.S. She announced that she would not re-sign with RKO, but that studio claimed the commitment and rushed her into a quickie, *Angel Face*, whose sole distinction was her performance as a murderess. RKO had bought her contract when it had only six months to run – but claimed that she had made an oral agreement to stay on there.

At MGM she was *Young Bess* (53) with Granger, just in time for the Coronation, a good historical novel about Elizabeth I (by Margaret Irwin) converted into Metro pap. At RKO, just to get things over with, she did *Affair With a Stranger* with Victor Mature, after which MGM yelled for her again. Debbie Reynolds was held up on *Give a Girl a Break* and they needed Simmons to play Spencer Tracy's stage-struck daughter in *The Actress*, based on an autobiographical play by Ruth Gordon and directed by George Cukor. None of her previous work had quite prepared audiences for her brilliance here; as Virginia Graham said in the 'Spectator', she was 'adolescence personified'. The film was not a success and there's the rub: she was wan as the heroine of *The Robe* with Richard Burton, a tremendous success – the first film in CinemaScope, a rotten version of a rotten Biblical novel by Lloyd C. Douglas. With something like genius RKO wasted her again in another programmer, *She Couldn't Say No* (54), a comedy with Robert Mitchum, as an heiress.

Jean Simmons was in some of Hollywood's biggest films in the 50s, but few of them were very good. One small film was very good indeed: The Actress *(53), with Anthony Perkins and Teresa Wright.*

She had sued RKO for release and after lengthy litigation it was announced that Howard Hughes could no longer use her in his own films, but could loan her out for three pictures at a fee of $200,000. (She also got a $250,000 lump sum.) One of these was *A Bullet is Waiting*, a melodrama at Columbia with Rory Calhoun. That was sandwiched between a couple of historical turkeys at 20th, *The Egyptian*, as a tavern wench in love with a truth-seeking Edmund Purdom, and *Desireé*, as the beloved of Napoleon Brando. Back in Britain she did an Edwardian thriller with her husband, *Footsteps in the Fog* (55), impressive as a slyboots tweeny. Then she was with Brando again in *Guys and Dolls*, as the Salvation Army heroine, singing a couple of songs and being transformed by him from sweet and innocent to something more mature. At 20th she was a restless vamp, *Hilda Crane* (56), going nowhere – it got no further in Britain, even after they had prefixed *The Many Loves of* to the title. At MGM she was involved with gangsters in an agreeable comedy, *This Could Be the Night* (57); 'Variety' thought her 'terrific as a clean, pure, but not necessarily naive grade-school teacher'.

Still at Metro, she did *Until They Sail* with Paul Newman, a wartime story by James Michener about some sisters in New Zealand, and then went over to William Wyler for *The Big Country* (58), with Gregory Peck and Charlton Heston. Heston years later said that she was an exception among leading ladies: 'There's a girl who has managed to succeed in a profession that has destroyed femininity.' She was a very big leading lady at this time, big enough to 'carry' an important film, *Home Before Dark*, a drama about the rehabilitation of a mental patient. She played that part with her usual sensitivity and something new had crept into her acting, a sort of heartbreak, a longing for things unexpressed – but the film itself dithered between ambition and hokum. She was little more than decorative in *This Earth is Mine* (59) – it was Rock Hudson's – but was simply stunning in *Elmer Gantry*, ambiguous as an Aimée-Semple MacPherson-like evangelist. Richard Brooks, who directed and adapted Sinclair Lewis's novel, found her 'a remarkable human being and an incredible actress'. Later, after her divorce from Granger, he married her (1960-77).

To protect this marriage and to bring up her children, she began to refuse work; but went into *Spartacus* (60) when director Stanley Kubrick replaced Anthony Mann and threw out all the footage of a German actress, Sabina Bethman. She was conscientious, little more, as a slave-girl, and the same might be said of her work as the next-door vamp in *The Grass is Greener* (61) – but then no one could have erased the memory of Joan Greenwood's stage performance. She was superb again as the mother in *All the Way Home* (63), with Robert Preston, but this adaptation of James Agee's gentle 'A Death in the Family' was death at the box-office (and played only a couple of cinemas in Britain). And she got excellent notices for the British *Life at the Top* (65) as Laurence Harvey's wife, the role played in the earlier film by Heather Sears. In the meantime she had made her American stage début in a play which did not reach New York, 'Big Fish Little Fish'. Then there was another huge failure, *Mister Buddwing* (66), as a wealthy blonde who gets involved with James Garner.

Around this time Simmons realized that she was not getting any offers and it disturbed her. In an attempt to take up her career again she did a Western with Dean Martin, *Rough Night in Jericho* (67), and accepted a small part and fourth-billing in *Divorce American Style*, but in revenge for billing, maybe, she properly fouled up the plot, looking serenely beautiful and sexy and making it unbelievable that anyone would leave her arms for those of Debbie Reynolds. In 1968 she played the governess in a TV *Heidi* with Michael Redgrave. Being out of work over the next few years she described as 'depressing'; her husband brought her back by creating *The Happy Ending* (69) for her, a study of a failing marriage (to John Forsythe). On the strength of her personal notices and maybe the Oscar nomination the film was a mild success – but it was platitudinous stuff. In Britain she was a housewife who has a brief encounter with a much younger man, *Say Hello to Yesterday* (70), but this time good personal notices did not offset dreadful reviews for the film itself.

There was another dud, *Mr Sycamore* (75), with Jason Robards, where she 'has nothing to do but stand around and look ravishing' according to 'Variety'. She had to sing and dance on the US tour and in the London production of 'A Little Night Music'; she did indeed look ravishing and she also brought more personal magic and sheer stage enchantment than has been seen since Gertrude Lawrence. She was, in fact, everything that the frumpish Glynis Johns was not in the Broadway version, but since her notices were not, on the whole, as good, we can only assume the two actresses react differently to first nights. Her enjoyment of her role and her gaiety were contagious: thus she again demonstrated versatility in a six-part TV movie with James Coburn, *The Dain Affair* (78) playing a black-garbed and ruthless ex-actress.

Leading men, films, times, conditions change: Jean Simmons in Uncle Silas *(47), with Derek Bond – and with Laurence Olivier in* Spartacus *(60). Only she hardly seems to age.*

Joseph L. Mankiewicz, who directed *Guys and Dolls* and a passionate student of Hollywood stardom, has called Simmons 'a dream . . . in terms of talent so many heads and shoulders above most of her contemporaries'; he concluded that she did not become the star she might have been because it was not important to her. Granted the limited movie roles for actresses of her age, we may feel it a pity that she has confined her activity chiefly to television, if usually top-billed: *Beggarman Thief* (79), a mini-series about the movie industry with Glenn Ford, based on the novel by Irwin Shaw; *Golden Gate* (81), a busted pilot about the world of publishing, as Perry King's mother; *Jacqueline Susann's 'Valley of the Dolls 1981'*, another mini, in the role played in the film by Susan Hayward; *A Small Killing*, as a professor teaming up with an undercover cop; and *The Thornbirds* (83), as the loving wife of Richard Kiley. She said that she had asked for the part – the only time in her life she has done that – after reading the book. After Barbara Stanwyck left this mini-series Simmons was the only reason to watch it – giving an astonishing performance as she aged and as an old lady being more convincing perhaps than any other younger actress ever when asked to play 'old'; she was awarded an Emmy for Best Supporting Actress in a series. *Midas Valley* (85) was a pilot for a Dallas-type epic with Robert Stack, and *North and South* and *North and South Book II* (86) were mini-series about the Civil War with a dozen guest names each: she was a South Carolina matriarch. She was an old flame of Raymond Burr, *Perry Mason: the Case of the Lost Love* (87) and Kirk Douglas's wife in *Inherit the Wind* (88), about which time she returned to cinemas for the first time in 13 years: *Going Undercover* with Chris Lemmon and, in Britain, *The Dawning*, as the Irish aunt of the heroine (Rebecca Pidgeon). Then she was offered the role of the eccentric Miss Havisham – played in the earlier version by Martita Hunt – in a television remake of *Great Expectations* (89): the news of this made many of her first admirers feel very, very old and she herself said, 'I thought they'd gone crazy. I fell out of bed laughing', but decided there was no reason why she should not do it – especially as she loves working and does not plan to retire.

Frank Sinatra

Most movie stars are described, sooner or later, as a legend in their lifetime. Some are. Frank Sinatra has a better claim than most, though less for anything he does or did on the screen than as a singer, tycoon, hitter of world headlines and, generally, one of the most successful all-rounders in show business. He has moved from being a band crooner to the man whom some observers consider the most powerful in Hollywood. He is very, very famous: a consistently bestselling recording artist, a TV performer who carries both ratings and prestige, a box-office film star, a power-house draw in nightclubs – none of which seems affected by a rather unfortunate public image. Arnold Shaw summed that up in his detailed and sympathetic biography (1968): 'Sinatra wants avidly to be in the papers but he has consistently fought reporters and photographers who could put him there. He wanted to be the last word in charm, but was frequently an explosive porcupine of ill-temper. He prided himself on his exquisite tastes, but he couldn't help using his fists and four-letter words in public. He wanted to move gracefully among the cultured and social élite, but he could not resist associating with pugs and hoods.' His press has been so bad through his career that it is improbable that his popularity is leavened by much actual *liking* for the man – which is perhaps what makes his apologists so arrogant and so generous with their superlatives. However, at least when he sings – and his choice of material is usually superb – it is hard to dislike him and impossible not to admire.

He was born in a cold-water flat in Hoboken, New Jersey, in 1915, of Italian parents, and educated in the high school of that town; he worked for a while on a local paper, in a humble position, and concentrated on singing in any amateur talent contest he could lay his hands on. He idol was Bing Crosby. He eventually got on the Major Bowes Amateur Hour in 1935, as one of the 'Hoboken Four'; he toured with Bowes and sang solo on local radio stations. Harry James heard him in a New Jersey roadhouse and invited him to join his band as vocalist; he moved over to Tommy Dorsey a few months later and with that outfit made two brief appearances in films – *Las Vegas Nights* (41) and *Ship Ahoy* (42). He began to have some success as a solo disc singer and as such was invited for *Reveille With Beverly* (43), a Columbia B with Ann Miller; his turn (one song) went unnoticed, but was the reason the film was reissued some months later. An appearance at the Paramount, New York, in the winter of 1942/3 indicated an unexpected and huge following among teenage girls – the bobby-soxers; hysteria began to accompany his personal appearance tours, which caused unfavourable comment among showbiz observers. Indeed, he looked soppy: skinny, emaciated, with a kiss-curl and a penchant for oversize bow-ties. In Britain, critics considered his voice and style infinitely inferior to the Crosby he was then emulating (he had much less popularity there till after his 1953 renaissance).

But as his following showed no sign of diminishing, Hollywood became interested. RKO signed him to a long-term contract. *Higher and Higher* was a feeble attempt to showcase him, though taken from a Rodgers and Hart original – an interpolated song ('I couldn't Sleep a Wink Last Night') was a hit for him, but the film was not. Nor was *Step Lively* (44), a musical remake of *Room Service* with a lustreless Gloria De Haven. His contract permitted him to make one outside film a year and he arranged to do two at MGM. The first, *Anchors Aweigh* (45), was built round Gene Kelly, but as his sailor-buddy Sinatra showed enough promise as a song-and-dance man for MGM to negotiate to take over his contract – despite some unpleasant publicity when he told a reporter 'Hollywood stinks!' The contract guaranteed $1½ million over a seven-year period, still allowed him an outside film each year and unusual concessions regarding music publishing and broadcasting.

His concerts and records continued to do

well and in 1945 he made a short with Mervyn LeRoy about racial intolerance, *The House I Live In*, which won a special Oscar. But his features were something else. He appeared at the end of *Till the Clouds Roll By* (46) in a pink suit, singing 'Ol' Man River' on top of what looked like a giant wedding-cake (for which he atoned, later, by learning to sing that song really well). There was a minor musical with Kathryn Grayson, *It Happened in Brooklyn* (47), and some unpleasant squabbles with the press, including a nightclub brawl with a columnist. His image was not improved by playing a priest – at RKO and against MGM's wishes – in *Miracle of the Bells* (48), but mostly because of comments like that in 'Time Magazine': 'Frank Sinatra, looking rather flea-bitten as the priest, acts properly humble or perhaps ashamed.' *The Kissing Bandit* with Grayson also brought poor personal notices – and a lot of red ink in the MGM ledgers. Things perked up considerably with two breezy musicals, *Take Me Out to the Ball Game* (49) and *On the Town*, in both teamed felicitously with Kelly again, and with Betty Garrett and Jules Munshin.

He had become an amiable enough actor, but there was still no indication that he would ever be a major asset to MGM. Consequently, there was no surprise when they announced the parting of the ways, officially so that he could be in New York to appear on TV. He was unhappy with his roles – he wanted to be a serious actor – and MGM were unhappy over his deteriorating relations with the press, his contempt for Louis B. Mayer (he admitted later that he was fired after joking on the set that Mayer, who was in plaster after falling off his horse, had in fact fallen off Ginny Simms) and his pursuit of Ava Gardner (there was a brief and stormy marriage, with excruciating headlines, 1951–52 – though no divorce till 1957). He did not appear on TV till nine months later, after a poor two weeks at the London Palladium (50) – nor was the half-hour 'Frank Sinatra Show' very special. A programmer at RKO was at the last minute rechristened *Double Dynamite* (51) to emphasize that it was mainly built round co-star Jane Russell. Universal signed him to a pact which gave them a non-exclusive option on his services for three years, but when so few responded to the invitation to *Meet Danny Wilson* (52) they dropped him (it was about an egocentric fist-happy crooner, with Shelley Winters). Then, CBS TV dropped him, his agent MCA dropped him and Columbia Records, after 10 years of hits, did not renew his contract.

He was on his uppers when he pleaded with Columbia for the part of Maggio in *From Here To Eternity* (53); he offered to do it for $8,000 (i.e. $1,000 a week) instead of the $150,000 he had asked for his last two films. At that price Columbia was interested and, when first choice Eli Wallach decided to do a Broadway play, he got the part – and a Best Supporting Oscar. During his downfall he had become kind to the press, which now talked of a comeback – but certainly his Maggio had more depth and fire than his previous screen work. As a result he was offered *Suddenly* (54), as a killer in this minor piece about the assassination of a president. Again he showed mettle, but the film was a flop. What really brought him back to favour was the series of records he had begun to make for Capitol; he had found a new determined style, at its peak in the 1955 'Songs For Swinging Lovers', one of the first bestselling LPs. At last he had reached Crosby's level. He sang in *Young at Heart* with Doris Day, as one of those pianists with a chip on his shoulder and his tie-knot at his navel. He was big enough again to turn down a sequel to *On the Town* (rewritten, it became *There's Always Fair Weather*). Then, after playing Robert Mitchum's loyal buddy in Stanley Kramer's *Not As a Stranger* (55), he

The first time Frank Sinatra and Gene Kelly played sailors 'on the town' the town was Hollywood, and the film was Anchors Aweigh *(45).*

There was much speculation as to who would get the leads in Goldwyn's film version of the hit musical, Guys and Dolls (55): *Marlon Brando, Jean Simmons, Frank Sinatra, and – to repeat her Broadway success – Vivian Blaine.*

returned to MGM for *The Tender Trap*, the first of his swinging bachelor roles. More than anything else it established him as a major screen star. He gave a sprightly performance as Nathan, the second male lead, in *Guys and Dolls*, teamed with another – but temporary – revenant, Vivian Blaine; and a considerable one as a junkie on Otto Preminger's *The Man With the Golden Arm*, the okay film of the month, made almost viable by his work in it. One he did not do was *Mister Roberts* – the Jack Lemmon part – because the producers thought him too old.

Another he did not do was *Carousel*; he walked off the set the first day because it was to be shot in two processes and he refused to do everything twice. Presumably he had not behaved like this at the time of *From Here To Eternity*, but by 1956 he refused to rehearse; when he became really powerful he insisted on only one take and employed only directors and crew who respected his feeling for 'spontaneity'. He produced as well as starred in *Johnny Concho* (56), which was not very successful; but was in a big hit, *High Society*, as a happy-go-lucky reporter sent to report on Grace Kelly's wedding to John Lund – and he had a fine carousing duet with Crosby. He got $250,000 for that and for *The Pride and the Passion* (57), a historical effort filmed in Spain for Kramer (who had sworn not to use him after friction on *Not As a Stranger*, but needed him when Brando turned down the part).

In both of those Sinatra was only second lead, but at the end of 1956 he turned up at ninth among the top 10 money-making stars; he stayed in the top 10 till 1960 – and was just out of it thereafter. His salary went down to $125,000 for his next two pictures, but a Sinatra-owned company owned 25 per cent of the action: *The Joker Is Wild*, a standard biopic – of nightclub comic Joe E. Lewis; and *Pal Joey*, a transcription of the Rodgers and Hart classic, perfectly cast as the go-get'em, disarming heel/hero – indeed, he was almost the sole redeeming feature (but not enough to compensate for the tinkering with the score). It was still a big hit. Not so *Kings Go Forth* (58), a souped-up war romance set on the Côte d'Azur, with Natalie Wood; but *Some*

Came Running was, with Sinatra at his most aggressive as James E. Jones's idealist hero. He was a widower with romantic and business problems in *A Hole in the Head* (59) directed by Frank Capra from a Broadway comedy; and a hard-drinking, hard-bitten army captain in another dim war drama, *Never So Few* (60), this time set in Burma.

A Sinatra film had come to mean middle-brow entertainment of little distinction. His control over his material, be it films, records or TV, was king-size – either revenge or security after his 1952 low-point. It was also doubtful. *Can-Can* – which he did for 20th in settlement for their suit over *Carousel* – had been a less exciting and distinguished Broadway original (by Cole Porter) than *Pal Joey* and the film version was equally vulgarized and bowdlerized. It was also a box-office disappointment. And there is little to be said for the series of jokey movies which Sinatra made with various members of his so-called clan (Dean Martin, Sammy Davis Jr, Peter Lawford, Joey Bishop), though the first was probably the best: *Ocean's Eleven*, about an attempted heist in Las Vegas. Lewis Milestone, who directed, said that if you understood Sinatra he was easy to handle. He did a guest spot in *Pepe* and played a cynical convict in *The Devil at Four O'Clock* (61), which did poorly, despite the presence of Spencer Tracy, who deeply resented the fact that Sinatra refused to pay him the usual co-star's privilege of reacting to his close-ups from behind the camera. Sinatra obliquely denied this later by claiming that he had watched Tracy from the sidelines when not required himself for a scene. The clan reassembled for *Sergeants Three* (62), a remake of *Gunga Din* in Western guise that was a box-office biggie; but *The Manchurian Candidate*, from Richard Condon's novel and unquestionably the critics' favourite among the later Sinatra films, somehow did not appeal. Sinatra was a Korean veteran puzzled by the behaviour of ex-comrade Laurence Harvey. He did an undistinguished stint as a hip philanderer in *Come Blow Your Horn* (63); another in a guest spot in *The List of Adrian Messenger*; and another as a comedy cowboy in *Four For Texas*, with Dean Martin. Critics dubbed that just another expensive home movie and accusations of mass exhibitionism also hurt the next one at the box-office – *Robin and the Seven Hoods* (64), with Martin, Davis, Crosby *et al.* – which was a pity, for it was an amiable, if derivative, musical about Chicago gangsters.

He produced and directed *None But the Brave* (65) and acted in it, as a hard-drinking marine doctor; it was set in the Pacific and he continued his investigation of the theatres of war in World War II by going to Italy for *Von Ryan's Express*, as a colonel masterminding commando raids. That was perhaps the most successful of his war films and its grosses looked huge, anyway, beside this miserable quartet: *Marriage on the Rocks*, a comedy with Martin and Deborah Kerr; *Assault on a Queen* (66) – Mary, a thriller; *Cast a Giant Shadow*, in a guest appearance; and *The Naked Runner* (67), a spy thriller. He seemed much happier in three private-eye thrillers, *Tony Rome*, *The Detective* (68) and *Lady in Cement*, as a hard, cynical, disillusioned law-enforcer – clearly challenging the shade of Bogart. Bogart he was not, but there was no trace of the flowing ninny of his early films and there was something greatly compelling and likeable about his performance(s), with his beaten-up mug and wry smile. Nat King Cole once suggested that the trouble with Sinatra's singing was that often he did not try – which was often the trouble with his acting. When he did, and retained that marvellous Sinatra ease, he was unbeatable. The three films did well, especially *The Detective*, tarted up with silly sensationalism (a nympho wife, homosexual suspects, gratuitous blood). Still, Sinatra stayed off the screen, though still making headlines for concerts, clubs and TV work: he returned in *Dirty Dingus McGee* (70), a jokey Western, and reputedly became the first star to take a low fee and a big participation deal after the industry crisis that year. It did not do well and in 1971 Sinatra announced, amidst great fanfares, his retirement from all media of show business. In 1972 there was talk of an original film musical written by Lerner and Loewe, *The Little*

Frank Sinatra changed his image several times during his career: perhaps he was at his best as the pugnacious tough guy he played in the 60s – as here, in The Detective *(68), with Lee Remick.*

Prince, at a salary of $200,000 plus a participation, but he was wise to decline, since the result – with Richard Kiley – was a disaster with both critics and public.

It was clear that Sinatra had decided to go before he was pushed: it was better to go out big than to be seen in films which did progressively less well than the one before. When he came out of retirement in 1974 – 'Old Blue Eyes Is Back' – he restricted himself to records, TV and concerts, the latter at often ridiculously inflated prices (£17.50 in London in 1975). Even so, and even though the voice was not what it was, he could, he found, play to SRO business; but there was trouble in Melbourne. He refused to give a press conference and as a result of press hostility he insulted journalists at his first concert; in the resulting row the second concert was cancelled. He was persuaded to issue a sort of apology so that the tour could continue. He was encouraged to act again, in a very long tele-movie, *Contract on Cherry Street* (77), and in *The First Deadly Sin* (80), in both cases as a police inspector. The second – turned down by Brando – did not cause a stampede to the box-office. In 1981 the Nevada State Gambling Control Board heard his 'pleas to have his licence restored': speaking on his behalf were such luminaries as Gregory Peck and Kirk Douglas. Press reports on this matter remarked that Sinatra's Mafia connections were being discussed at a high level. He was one of the stars playing cameos in *Cannonball Run II* (83), in his case playing himself.

In 1988 he toured with Dean Martin and Sammy Davis Jr, probably the dullest of the century's first-rate singers: whether there was an audience for either without Sinatra was unclear. There is for him, for he is a great one, if less controlled than Crosby and much less imaginative, within the confines of his material, than Nat 'King' Cole or Tony Bennett. When he appeared in London in 1989, with Liza Minnelli replacing the indisposed Martin, the trio played the Royal Festival Hall for five nights at hugely inflated prices, which soared even higher on the black market: but when one critic asked who you would rather hear sing the best songs ever written the answer was obvious: Mr Bennett.

Rod Steiger

Rod Steiger spent the first decade of his screen career in semi-eclipse. If the part was good, the film was not, and vice versa. Finally, he broke through, reaping notices like this one in 'Time Magazine': '. . . one of the most convincing character actors in Hollywood history. Although a stratum of burly menace seems to underlie all his performances, there is an uncommon variety in his characterizations. His recent range includes an evocation of Pope John XXIII in the semi-documentary *And There Came a Man*; the simpering mortician in *The Loved One*; the lascivious Komarovsky in *Doctor Zhivago*; and his favourite role, the guilt-racked Nazerman in *The Pawnbroker*.' Steiger noted, in talking to 'Time Magazine' at this point, that he was the same age as Brando and Paul Newman but looked like everybody's father. His Hollywood precursor, Charles Laughton, was playing fathers while still in his early thirties and, though Steiger had not (then) played father-roles, he was equally restricted by his girth and round features. He has said that he would like to have been a romantic hero, again like Laughton. Their styles are very different, though there is the same compulsion to go over the top in the way that great and bad actors have and good ones do not. Like Laughton, Steiger is professionally conscientious to a neurotic degree. In television interviews he has revealed himself emotional and passionate; and, despite his range, one thinks of him at his best as some sort of Dostoevskyan haunted figure.

He was born in 1925 in Westhampton, Long Island, to a song-and-dance team playing roadhouse shows who split a year later. He enlisted in the US Navy at 16 and after the war worked for the Veterans Administration. He joined a Little Theatre group and found that he liked acting, so took advantage of the GI Bill of Rights to study at the New York Theater Wing and the Actors' Studio. His professional bow was with a small company in 'The Trial of Mary Dugan', but it was TV rather than the theatre which provided essential experience, and which pushed him on. He reckoned that between 1948 and 1953 he made over 250 live TV appearances, playing everything from Rasputin to Romeo. Meanwhile, he made his Broadway début in a revival of 'An Enemy of the People' (50), in a small role, and had got great notices for a good part in a revival of Odets's 'Night Music', as a 56-year-old detective. Around the same time he had a small part in Fred Zinnemann's *Teresa* (51), filmed in New York. In 1952 he was on Broadway in 'Seagulls Over Sorrento'.

By the following year he had become well known via his portrayal of people like Vishinsky and Rudolph Hess in a non-fiction TV series, 'You Are There', and more especially for his performance in the title-role of Paddy Chayevsky's TV play, 'Marty'. As a result of that he was auditioned by Budd

Schulberg and Elia Kazan for *On the Waterfront* (54), as Marlon Brando's racketeer brother; their scene in the taxi '(You shoulda looked after me, Charley') soon became one of the most famous of all film scenes and Steiger got an Oscar nomination. He was offered a co-starring role in *The Big Knife* (55), an Odets play brought to the screen by Robert Aldrich, with Jack Palance as a movie star on his uppers; Steiger was a Hollywood studio chief – which considerably upset several such moguls (Steiger based the tears on Louis B. Mayer, the tantrums on Harry Cohn). He was again the heavy, the lovelorn pore Jud in *Oklahoma!*, but his Sophoclean approach brought conviction only at the expense of the film. He was much more at home as the dispassionate and unctuous prosecuting counsel in *The Court Martial of Billy Mitchell*, starring Gary Cooper, and was exceptional as a sadistic cowhand in a Glenn Ford Western, *Jubal* (56). There was another good villain, the twisted cheating boxing promoter in *The Harder They Fall*, Bogart's last film.

Around this time Jerry Wald told him that if he would lose 30 lb he would become a great screen lover and David O. Selznick discussed with him the lead in *A Farewell to Arms* – but Steiger was not interested in the accompanying long-term contract (which is why, earlier, he had lost the film of *Marty*). Instead, his career hit a bad patch, starting with *Back from Eternity*, John Farrow's studio-bound remake of his own successful 1939 B, *Five Came Back*, about some survivors of a plane crash stuck in hostile country. It now seemed monumentally silly, but, thought the 'MFB', 'of the variable cast, Rod Steiger impresses as the condemned revolutionary: less mannered and exaggerated than before, his performance provides . . . a much-needed central point of interest'. Then there was a nasty Samuel Fuller Western, *Run of the Arrow* (57), as a Yankee-hating Southerner who joins the Sioux after the Civil War. Steiger prefers to forget the film; Fuller said in an interview: 'I suppose you mean that you think he's bad in Kazan's films (*sic*). I agree entirely. He overdoes it. We discussed the part a lot, and I had to keep an eye on him. He has lots of talent but he doesn't know how to use it. He could have done everything a Baur, a Gabin and a Jannings did. He gets carried away and needs to be closely directed.' Finally, there was the husband of *The Unholy Wife*, conceivably his first sympathetic role on screen, plotted against by Diana Dors in her first American film; his Method acting did not improve a film which he regards as the low point of his career.

He accepted a British offer, at £35,000 plus expenses, *Across the Bridge*, adapted from a Graham Greene story about a crooked financier hiding out in Mexico; he got good notices and the film was one of the better British efforts of the time – but not a great success. Back in the US he was the heavy, a gang-boss, in a conventional thriller, *Cry Terror* (58), and then *Al Capone* (59) for a minor company, Allied Artists, which he agreed to do provided the cast and the director were people he 'respected artistically' (at that time few actors liked to work outside the major studios). John Gillett in the 'MFB' said the film confirmed the 'impression of an undeniably gifted actor who requires extremely close supervision and control'. During this period, 1957–59, Steiger made some occasional TV appearances, for which he won two Emmys. In 1959 he returned to Broadway in an adaptation of 'Rashomon', with Claire Bloom, who became his second wife.

To pay off his alimony in one fell swoop he went against his rule and signed a long-term contract with 20th, starting with *Seven Thieves* – who included himself and father Edward G. Robinson – a quite genial thriller. When it came out, however, he was 'sick for days'. The contract was cancelled at the time of the actors' strike, shortly afterwards, and in Britain he did a minor drama, *The Mark* (61), as the understanding psychiatrist of a potential child-molester (Stuart Whitman). His own notices were superb, but those for the film were mixed and it did poor business. On British TV he had done 'A Town Has Turned to Dust' for Alvin Rakoff (he had also done the US TV version, for John Frankenheimer) and he agreed to do a film Rakoff was making in Germany, *An Einem Freitag um Halb Zwölf*, as a Marseilles gang-boss; James Hadley Chase wrote the original story, Ian Bannen was also in it and it was a dud in Britain as *On Friday at Eleven* and in the US as *World in my Pocket*. In the US, depression for him continued with a play about Hemingway by A.E. Hotchner, which flopped on tour, and two movies: *13 West Street* (62), as a sympathetic police detective in this Alan Ladd dualler, and *Convicts Four*, in a guest role as a sadistic head warder.

There was another guest spot in *The Longest Day* and then, like other has-beens, he hit the Italian trail; but, like Anthony Quinn before him, went not into sand-and-sex epics, but into class stuff: *Le Mani sulla Città* (63), a story of graft in Naples (Steiger was a corrupt businessman), directed by Francesco Rosi with less cohesion than passion. The other was less well thought of and much less seen (not at all in Britain): *Gli Indifferenti* (64), with Claudia Cardinale and Paulette Goddard, from a Moravia novel. Rescue came from Sidney Lumet, who had worked with him a decade earlier in television: the title-role in *The Pawnbroker* (65), at $25,000 plus a percentage. That was the maximum fee as no major studio would touch it, a study of a Jewish pawnbroker in Harlem whose war-time experiences had isolated him from his fellow beings. The reviews were staggering and it was a great success on the art circuit; in Britain the press dubbed it pretentious, but all agreed that Steiger was superb; he was judged Best Actor at the Berlin festival, was nominated for an Oscar and once again in demand.

He was also good, playing more broadly, in Tony Richardson's unlucky *The Loved One*, as the gross mother-loving Mr Joyboy – but few people saw it: MGM had spent more on it than they wanted to and did not like it when finished; encouraged by critical thumbs-down, they gave it a spotty distribution. In fact, it was a genuinely eccentric movie, from Evelyn Waugh's satiric tale of Californian cemetery customs (and infinitely better than the travesty of 'Decline and Fall' made three years later). Also unlucky was *E Venne un Uomo*, Ermanno Olmi's attempt to tell the life of Pope John as semi-documentary – since this great film-maker did not get it quite right.

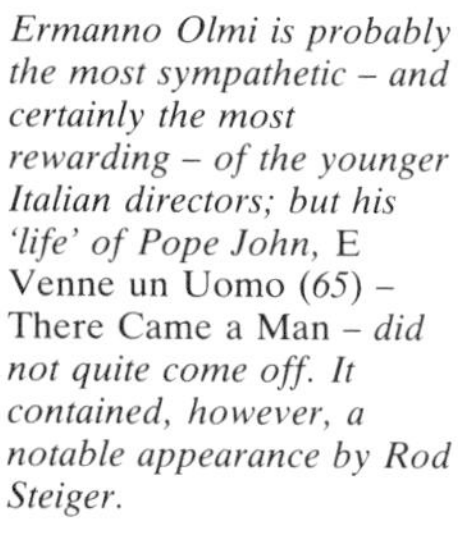

Ermanno Olmi is probably the most sympathetic – and certainly the most rewarding – of the younger Italian directors; but his 'life' of Pope John, E Venne un Uomo (65) – There Came a Man – *did not quite come off. It contained, however, a notable appearance by Rod Steiger.*

He went from Olmi to the very different David Lean, *Doctor Zhivago* (66), and that was enormous box-office; altogether it did more for Steiger's reputation than anything hitherto – for one thing, of the starry cast he was the only one to get consistently good notices. He was excellent in a BBC TV 'Death of a Salesman' and got his just deserts, finally, in *In the Heat of the Night* (67) as a bigoted fascist Southern cop who comes to accept and then admire Negro detective Sidney Poitier; the scene where he confesses to him his loneliness had some beautifully controlled emotional acting and perhaps more than anything contributed to the several awards, including a Best Actor Oscar, and citations by the New York Film critics and the BFA. The film also won a Best Picture Oscar and was a huge box-office success.

No Way To Treat a Lady *(68) was a black comedy about a mass murderer who utilized various disguises to go about his deadly work, and Rod Steiger was at ease in all of them. Lee Remick was also fine as one of his intended victims.*

The Oscar and the resulting publicity did not help its makers to find distribution in the US or Britain for *La Ragazza e il Generale*, which Steiger had returned to Italy to make before *Heat* was shown. He played a German general, says he did it for money and prefers not to talk about it. He could now take his pick of offers and, when offered the role of the Jewish detective in *What a Way to Treat a Lady* (68), chose to play the villain, a multiple strangler, instead. Said Tom Milne in the 'Observer': 'Starting off as a red-haired Irish priest with a leering eye for pretty girls, and working his way in rapid succession through W.C. Fields, a camp wig-fitter, a hearty cop and a trembling prostitute, he gives a virtuoso display of characterization and comic timing which all but turns a minor black comedy into a masterpiece.' Steiger's new status enabled him to get backing for *The Sergeant*, which he had wanted to do for years; it turned out too

The Sergeant (*68*) *treated of a subject – and a little tragedy – not common to movies about military life. Rod Steiger was a non-com who gets hung-up over an enlisted man, John Philip Law.*

dated – and too grey – for general acceptance, a drama about a latent homosexual (Steiger) who falls for one of the enlisted men. Nor did things go right with *The Illustrated Man* (69), from Ray Bradbury's science-fiction novel. And they went very wrong with *Three Into Two Won't Go*, a marital drama ineptly directed by Peter Hall; Steiger's performance as a philandering British executive was badly received. Claire Bloom was in both films; they were divorced after the second was finished.

He went on to play Napoleon in the gigantic Russo-Italian *Waterloo* (70), after which there was some talk of his playing Galileo for Zeffirelli. Instead he played a Mexican peasant caught up in Revolution for Sergio Leone: *Giù la Testa* (71), which turned up variously as *Duck You Sucker* and *A Fistful of Dynamite*, proof enough that no one much wanted to see it. The same fate awaited *Happy Birthday Wanda June*, from Kurt Vonnegut Jr's play about the explorer who returns home to his wife (Susannah York) to find that things are not what they used to be. In Italy, Steiger replaced Yul Brynner in *Gli Eroi/The Heroes* (72), a World War II tale with Rod Taylor; and he had another US failure with *The Lolly Madonna XXX* (73), a modern Hatfields and McCoys feudin' tale, with Robert Ryan as the opposing patriarch. Returning to Francesco Rosi should have lightened the gloom, but *Lucky Luciano* was not one of that director's better films and Steiger's role as the pursuer of Luciano (Gian Maria Volonté) was poorly defined. No one, including Henry Fonda, was very lucky with *Mussolini Ultimo Atto/Mussolini Dead or Alive* (74): but Steiger as Mussolini added to his gallery of historical portraits. *Les Innocents aux Mains Sales* (75) was one of the occasional bad films of Claude Chabrol, but in truth not helped by Steiger's performance as a wealthy, impotent and alcoholic paranoiac: he was as monotonous as Romy Schneider as the unfaithful wife. Chabrol said later that it was soon clear that the film would be a disaster, since neither player would accept that it was supposed to be a comedy. In life his third marriage (1972) ended.

However, the Steiger career revived somewhat with *Hennessy* in Britain: the film itself was not too hot, but he was in his best form as a modern Guy Fawkes – an Ulster Catholic one. And Hollywood needed him to do an extended version of his Fields in *W.C. Fields and Me* (76), based on a memoir by the comic's mistress, Carlotta Monti. In that role, Valerie Perrine had this to say: 'I don't know how someone playing W.C. Fields could be so totally without humour. *Everybody* on the picture was so serious. Steiger wouldn't even loan me his car to drive to the supermarket.' No one was driving to see the film, either, but had they done so they might have seen a biopic as full of clichés and lies as was, say, *The Buster Keaton Story*, and a performance by Steiger which seemed to confuse Fields and Pagliacci. He was Pilate in Zeffirelli's *Jesus of Nazareth/Gesu di Nazaret* (77) and a gangster chieftain who hires Jack Palance in *Portrait of a Hitman*, then the tic-ridden Head of a Senate Investigations Committee in *F.I.S.T.*

(78) with Sylvester Stallone. In Germany he had prepared his role of a Brigadier-General in *Breakthrough* (79) with care, which is more than Richard Burton had done – but the film was taken from them by Robert Mitchum, underacting. Steiger was Father Delaney, uncle to a young couple experiencing a true ghost 'happening', in *The Amityville Horror*. This 'rabid performance . . . merits the Sarah Bernhardt award for wretched excess' said David Ansen, so who knows what the copywriters meant (when it first turned up on British TV) by claiming it was 'played with the type of performance you'd expect from Rod Steiger'? At least the film was widely seen, which could not be said for: *Klondike Fever* (80), based on a story by Jack London; *Abakarov*, made in Germany with Alan Howard; *The Lucky Star*, in which Steiger was a German colonel captured by a Dutch Jewish boy in 1940; *Omar Mukhtar – Lion of the Desert* (81), which starred Anthony Quinn, as Mussolini again; and *Cattle Annie and Little Britches*, a Western starring Burt Lancaster. Most of these films sat on the shelf awhile, as did *Wolf Lake*, filmed in Chihuahua in 1977, but set in Canada: Steiger was a hunter bitter because his son was killed in Vietnam – and coming across a Viet deserter. Beside most of these *The Chosen*, though not a good film, seems like a masterpiece. Steiger was a rabbi. *Der Zauberberg* (82), from Thomas Mann's novel, was the most expensive film yet made in Germany, which would also see it later in an extended television version. The magic mountain itself was beautifully photographed and Steiger, as the rich Dutch colonial in the sanatorium, headed an international cast, but none of these factors helped it move beyond the three countries providing the backing (the others were France and Italy).

He ceded the lead in *Uncommon Valor* to Gene Hackman and then was Peary to Richard Chamberlain's Cook in a tele-movie, *Cook and Peary: the Race for the Pole* (83). *The Naked Face* (84) starred Roger Moore (a shrink), Steiger (a cop), as directed by Bryan Forbes from a novel by Sidney Sheldon, a combination of talents which did not result in many bookings: one person who did see it, Tony Sloman, thinks it a candidate for the worst film ever made. Steiger took refuge in a ghastly mini-series from a Jackie Collins novel, *Hollywood Wives* (85), playing an executive, and was hardly better served by the mysterious *Sword of Gideon*, which may be an Italian mini-series, and which may have Israeli backing but which is officially a telefilm shot in Montreal. Its subject is revenge for the Israeli athletes killed at the Munich Olympics. He was: a mad scientist in *The Kindred* (87), a poker-faced sci-fi horror; the head of a Buenos Aires drug-ring in *Feel the Heat*, written by Stirling Silliphant as a vehicle for his wife, Tiana Alexandra; and with Yvonne de Carlo the head of a family of homicidal maniacs in the Canadian *American Gothic*. Of the first of these Alan Frank wrote in 'Photoplay' that it was 'ludicrously bad', adding that Steiger 'delivers his most ludicrously bad performance ever'.

Most of these credits had devalued his standing and he turned, understandably, to television: *Desperado: Avalanche at Devil's Ridge* (88), playing a cruel and pompous ranch-owner; and he had a good supporting role in *The January Man*, which was at least meant to be a major movie. Kevin Kline had the lead, as an unorthodox cop rehired to solve some serial killings, who beds Mary Elizabeth Mastrantonio, daughter of his old enemy, Steiger, the Mayor of New York. There was another murder in *Passion and Paradise* (89) – that of Sir Harry Oakes (Steiger) in the Bahamas in 1943 and never solved, though some theories were offered in this telefilm. Also on the stocks with Steiger are *Celluloid*, in Italy with Gian Maria Volonté, *White Roses* with Tom Conti and *Tennessee Waltz* with Julian Sands.

Steiger says he loves acting; and that after three weeks of not working he gets uptight. He observed that he had refused *Patton*, because he thought it pro-military – and was then being offered parts that George C. Scott had turned down. The changed condition of the film industry suited him well. He once made a good statement on Hollywood to 'Playboy': 'I've never played the Hollywood games. I'm not a member of the A or B or C party group. I don't usually go to openings. . . . Nobody really knows anybody here. Above all, Hollywood is a community of lonely people searching for even the most basic kind of stimulation in their otherwise mundane lives. I've met too many people in Hollywood who sacrifice personal happiness for professional gain. They have big swimming-pools and more money than they can spend, and then at two a.m. they go to pieces. They turn their souls inside out and become bitterly disillusioned.'

Barbra Streisand

If she had no other claim to fame, the $20 million gambled by Hollywood on Barbra Streisand at the start of her career would be enough. There are less stratospheric examples of financial confidence being invested in unknown talent – it was the amount which was unprecedented. True, she had been acclaimed for her stage work and had been equally successful with records and TV, but she was untried as a movie player: and there were contracts for three films before the first of them was shown – all of them blockbusters/ road-shows/top-budget musicals. (Her salary would be $200,000 for *Funny Girl*; $350,000 for *On a Clear Day You Can See Forever* – contracted for next; and $750,000 plus a percentage for *Hello Dolly!*.) And it was a gamble, because for all her undoubted brilliance – *and* because of it – she was unlike any star who had gone before. She was most like Fanny Brice, whom she portrayed in *Funny Girl*: both were physically plain, both were essentially Jewish comediennes, both sang, equally adept in comic-numbers and torch-songs. But Fanny Brice did not make it in pictures. Streisand did. The film of *Funny Girl* opened and in it Streisand sang 'I'm the greatest star' – and not only she but a lot of other people believed it.

She came not from the lower East Side, like Brice, but from Brooklyn. She was born there in 1942. At the age of 14 she saw 'The Diary of Anne Frank' and nothing thereafter could prevent her becoming an actress. She got her start singing in an amateur talent contest in Greenwich Village, which led the nightclub engagements in the Village – during which time she appeared on TV in 'The Mike Wallace Show' and was auditioned for a Broadway musical. 'I Can Get It For You Wholesale' (62). It was a small part, but she got raves (and married the leading man, Elliott Gould) – and was offered 'Funny Girl' (64). Anne Bancroft had in fact been signed, but Jules Styne wrote the songs for Streisand, whom he had been seeing in a Village *boîte*: and Bancroft realized she could not sing them. She played it in New York and London; Ray Stark, who produced it on the stage, produced the film version and insisted on her (he was/ is, coincidentally, married to Fanny Brice's daughter). William Wyler was engaged to direct.

The film of *Funny Girl* (68) brought Streisand more fine reviews and eventually a Best Actress Oscar (tying with Katharine Hepburn). It was a dazzling display, not least in her mastery of the innumerable self-depreciatory jokes. Dilys Powell observed that she delivered a crack as well as Groucho Marx, but added that there was every talent 'except the indefinable quality – some interior feeling, perhaps – by which a Judy Garland can involve the audience too'. Unfortunately, the film relied over-much on pathos: at the climax, Streisand's rendering of 'My Man' was harsh and mechanical, in no way comparable to Brice's own, or Alice Faye's in an earlier version of the Brice story, *Rose of Washington Square* – but then, it seemed to be of the same vintage (or some sort of 40s rehash of *A Star is Born*). 'Miss Streisand's talent is very poignant and strong' said Renata Adler in 'The New York Times', 'but the movie almost does her in.' To what extent she herself was responsible is not known: there were reports that she was directing the director and it is on record that she fancies herself primarily as a dramatic actress. It might be significant that several (excellent) numbers not featuring her had disappeared in the transition from stage to screen.

There were further reports of dissension on the set of her second film, *Hello Dolly!* (69), specifically with co-star Walter Matthau, quoted later as saying: 'I had no disagreements with Barbra Streisand. I was merely exasperated at her tendency to be a complete megalomaniac.' At one time on the set he yelled at her to 'remember what happened to Betty Hutton'. Around the same time the 'Sunday Times' reported: 'There's a market on late night TV shows for anti-Streisand anecdotes. . . . She scares people. She could

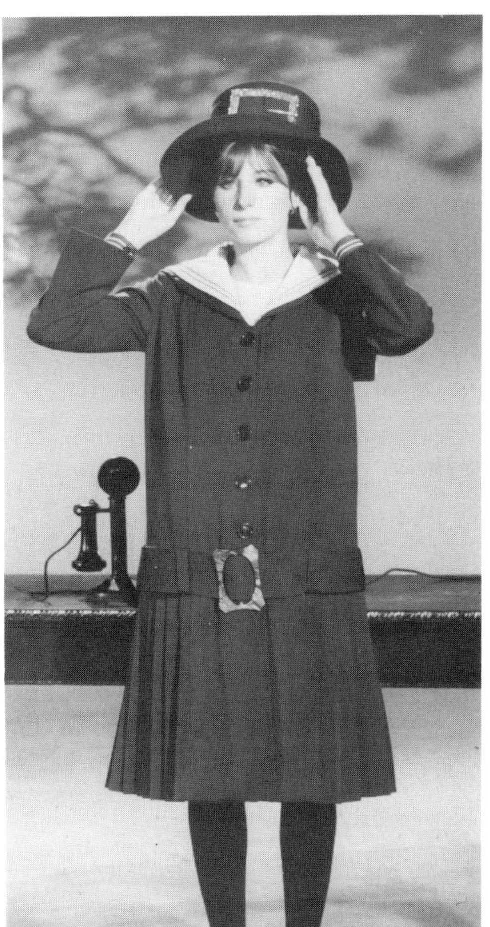

Barbra Streisand in Funny Girl *(68). It was not funny –in more ways than one – but cinema audiences were offered the chance to see Streisand in the role in which she had triumphed in New York and London.*

be Madame Guillotine the way some speak of her.' An article in 'Life Magazine' suggested she had a star-complex as powerful as Joan Crawford's – on top of which, her reviews for *Dolly* were not too good. As the match-making widow, 'Time Magazine' found 'her mannerisms . . . so arch and calculated that one half expectes to find a key implanted in her back'. 20th watched anxiously; the film cost around $22 million (about the same amount as her first film had taken in the domestic market – and most of it due to her). In the event, it took about $13 million – a fancy sum under other circumstances, but clearly a disappointment.

Streisand's third film, *On a Clear Day You* Can See Forever (70), was yet again from a Broadway musical and was directed by the veteran Vincente Minnelli. Reviews were mixed, but were generally downbeat, and the film failed at the box-office. She did better with a neat comedy, produced by Stark, *The Owl and the Pussycat*, as a noisy hooker who becomes involved with a meek book-clerk, George Segal. In 1969 she was 10th at the US box-office, and in 1970, ninth. It was announced that she would take over *A Glimpse of Tiger*, which had been abandoned by Gould (from whom she was now separated). Instead, under director Peter Bogdanovitch, with Ryan O'Neill she did *What's Up Doc?* (72), said to be a return to 30s screwball comedy in the style of *Bringing Up Baby*. Said 'Newsweek': 'Unlike Katharine Hepburn, gossamer charm is not Miss Streisand's long suit. Where Hepburn was cunnning, Miss Streisand tracking O'Neill smells of desperation.'

She had become one of the four cornerstones of First Artists Corporation (with Newman, Poitier, McQueen) and during 1971 about a dozen 'definite' projects were announced for her, including a life of Sarah Bernhardt to be directed by Ken Russell. Instead she did *Up the Sandbox* for First Artists, about a neglected young New York mother who indulges in fantasies; in *The Way We Were* (73) she was a militant left-winger, at one point married to Robert Redford, some of whose scenes, apparently, she had cut. Her singing of the title song gave her a hit record and the unlikely teaming of the two stars was big box-office. John Simon spoiled things (as he invariably did when reviewing a Streisand movie: the director, he said, had 'tried to tone down her brashness and shrillness, but has hardly made a dent in that basic pugnacious charmlessness that is beyond redemption. The difficulty is that even when Miss Streisand labors to appear sensitive and vulnerable, she cannot conquer our impression that, were she to collide with a Mack truck, it is the truck that would drop dead.' *For Pete's Sake* (74) was a so-so comedy in which she was Michael Sarrazin's enterprising wife; and *Funny Lady* (75) was a sequel, with Herbert Ross's direction desperately trying to disguise script problems. Around this time Columbia commissioned a poll to find the nation's most popular star and it was Streisand; but while they were about it they polled for the least popular star, which was also Streisand. However, despite the patchy box-office of three of the last four films (*Up the Sandbox* did significantly bad business, thus helping towards the demise of First Artists), exhibitors liked her: with the exception of Goldie Hawn in 1972 she was the only female star in the box-office 10: 1972 (No. 5), 1973 (No. 6), 1974 (No. 4), 1975 (No. 2).

And she had the last laugh over *A Star is Born* (76). Though it remained clear that she would never hold a candle to Judy Garland, she wanted to remake it, though changing the milieu to rock concerts. Epic battles between her and co-star Kris Kristofferson and director Frank Pierson marred the filming and when it came out cynics dubbed it 'A Bore is Starred' and 'A Star is Still-Born'. Seldom in the history of films had manic vanity been so indulged: critic after critic turned off, but the public seemed to like it – huge numbers of them. They were surely desperate for entertainment, but there it was: taking inflation into account, it was seen by less people than the Garland version – but the gross was still enormous. And exhibitors voted Streisand again No. 2 at the box-office in 1977. (She also got an Oscar for helping to compose a Best Song.) The producer was her friend, Jon Peters, who worked again in that capacity on *The Main Event* (79), a reunion with Ryan O'Neal, despite his comment in the interim

On a Clear Day You Can See Forever *(70) was a curious musical about a girl able to transport herself into the past. Barbra Streisand was the girl, and her brother in the modern sequences was Jack Nicholson.*

(quoted in 'Ciné-Revue') that she was the most pretentious woman the cinema had ever known. He was a broken-down prize-fighter inherited by her, a cosmetics executive, a performance which must have had even her fans agreeing with Mr Simon's diatribe, which began, 'This summer may go down in cinema history as the summer of the horror movies, but none of these can match Barbra Streisand and her latest offering . . .'

She took second-billing to Gene Hackman on *All Night Long* (81) because she wanted to play his son's kooky mistress, to whom he was attracted – and thus Lisa Eichhorn, who was already playing the role, left after 'artistic differences': the true story is in William Goldman's book, 'Adventures in the Screen Trade', where he notes that the director's wife was Streisand's agent. Of course, she was the bigger star, able to command $4 million instead of Eichhorn's $250,000, 'so what the studio had done was to take a frail, $3 million film and turn it into a $15 million film that was a total disaster and that, when you add in prints and advertising, probably lost them $20 million' (Goldman). When the budget of *Yentl* (83) escalated from $14 million to $18 million, MGM/UA tried to protect themselves by selling shares to private investors – though with a take of $19.7 domestic, not otherwise unrespectable, there was probably little profit. The star co-wrote, co-produced and directed, giving one of her more pleasing performances as a young Polish girl who in 1904 dresses as a boy to study the Talmud, with consequent romantic complications. Its chief fault was its treacly, seemingly unstoppable score. That particular aspect particularly annoyed the author of the original story, Isaac Bashevis Singer, who wanted to say 'Do me a favour. Stop it'; Streisand he referred to as 'Miss What'shername' and added that Garbo could not play Anna Karenina, but that film 'in comparison to *Yentl* . . . is a masterpiece'.

When Streisand showed an interest in playing in *Nuts* (87), which Universal had backed on Broadway, that studio passed – but then it had also produced *All Night Long*: so for Warners and director Martin Ritt she played a Park Avenue belle turned whore turned mental who is defended in court by Richard Dreyfuss – and the stars' fees may be one reason why this mild-looking film cost a whopping $25 million, of which only just over $14 million were recovered from the domestic box-office. When 'Variety' observed that she was thrust at the audience 'with endless close-ups as if she were too lovable to deny', it was one of the kinder notices, while Kenneth Turan in 'Premier' thought she tried hard to act 'on the edge' but achieved only 'the kind of whiny, irritating petulance a Beverly Hills matron might exhibit if someone grabbed her parking space . . . [and the role is] so close to the woe-is-me-do-I-have-troubles Streisand persona we've seen in just about every one of her films that the idea of her being a real character barely enters our minds'.

Elizabeth Taylor

As one of the Dell fan magazines once pointed out, the name Elizabeth Taylor has come to be 'synonymous with beauty, talent, intrigue and excitement'. More than any other star in the history of the cinema, her private life has been public property; during the 60s it was almost impossible to pick up a newspaper without some item about her. This was intriguing. Her life was, and probably still is, exciting. Her beauty is unquestioned. Her talent is something else.

Richard Burton said in 1968, 'You may not agree, but I think she's by far the best actress in films.' Her career divides neatly into two, with her marriage to him as the dividing-line. Before, no one took her acting very seriously, including herself: 'The first time I considered *acting* when I was young was in *A Place in the Sun*' (in her memoirs, 1966). She went on to say that most of the subsequent films were 'lost under a morass of mediocrity. Not just the scripts. I was mediocre too.' Once she began to take her job seriously, she began acting with a capital A. She did not attempt the sort of parts once considered show-off pieces (spinsters, nuns, alcoholics), but played as many adulterous and/or over-sexed wives as she could cram into the time; certainly they were the parts – after those much-publicized love affairs and marriages – in which the public expected to see her. Views were divided about her effectiveness. Wilfred Sheed, writing in 'Esquire' (October 1969), found her still 'a sub-average film actress. They have tried to exploit her fiery, earthy womanliness again and again . . . but every time it comes out air and water, because she hasn't the idiosyncrasy of voice and manner that colourful women have in real life. She can shout and lunge about with the best of them but this isn't interesting, just noisy. . . . There is nothing drearier than eccentricity without wit or personality.'

She was born in London in 1932 and went with her parents to the US at the beginning of World War II. They settled in Hollywood and, according to Hedda Hopper, manœuvred the support of a friend, a big Universal stockholder, to get her a contract at that studio; she had a small part in a B, *There's One Born Every Minute* (42), and supported

Alfalfa (of 'Our Gang') in a short, *Man or Mouse*. A while later her father was fire-watching with an MGM producer, as a result of which she was taken on to play Roddy McDowall's little girlfriend in *Lassie Come Home* (43), an agreeable film version of Eric Knight's bestseller about a little boy and his courageous collie-dog. It had an English setting and, as MGM were very fond of English settings around that time, they took Taylor under contract. They loaned her to 20th for *Jane Eyre* (44), to play young Jane's sad consumptive friend; then put her to playing with McDowall in *The White Cliffs of Dover*, as June Lockhart as a child. Then she starred with Mickey Rooney in *National Velvet*, from Enid Bagnold's novel about a girl determined to ride her horse in the Grand National. She was a pale-faced, big-eyed, husky-voiced kid.

MGM did not exploit her and she grew into her teens in a series of middling, mainly featured parts: *Courage of Lassie* (46), supporting that dog again: *Cynthia* (47), in the title-role as a pampered child; *Life With Father*, on loan to WB, as a visiting cousin; and *A Date With Judy* (48) – Jane Powell, as her sister. Her first grown-up role was opposite Peter Lawford in support of Greer Garson, in *Julia Misbehaves*. She was the petulant Amy in *Little Women* (49) and then had her first romantic lead opposite Robert Taylor in *Conspirator* (50). 'Harvard Lampoon' gave her its annual award 'for so gallantly persisting in her career despite a total inability to act', naming her 'the most objectionable ingénue' and one of the two 'most objectionable movie children'. She did not exactly counter that onslaught with her work in three comedies, *The Big Hangover* with Van Johnson and *Father of the Bride* and *Father's Little Dividend* (51), in both as Spencer Tracy's daughter. However, she was convincing as a spoilt rich girl in George Stevens's *A Place in the Sun*: 'For Miss Taylor, at least, the histrionics are of a quality so far beyond anything she has done previously, that Stevens . . . must be credited with a minor miracle' ('Variety').

MGM had nothing better for her than *Love Is Better Than Ever* (52), a comedy with Larry Parks, and a supporting role in *Ivanhoe*, as the unfortunate Rebecca. Richard Winnington thought he would long cherish the image of her being sentenced to death 'with the expression of a girl who has been stood up on a date'. In 1952 when her contract expired she was getting $1,500 a week. She re-signed on condition that it went to $5,000. A year later it was revised – five more years without options, three films a year. Meanwhile, she had begun that marital life which would

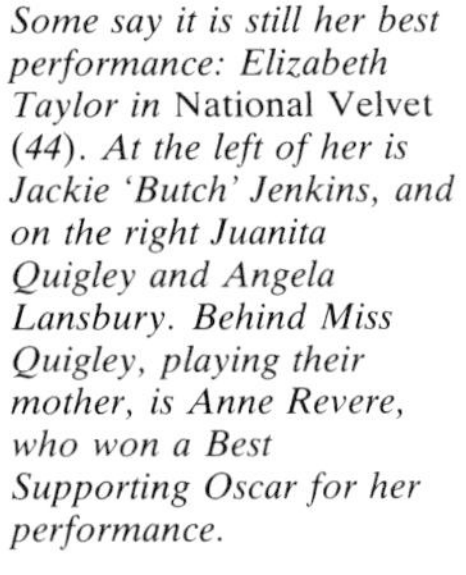

Some say it is still her best performance: Elizabeth Taylor in National Velvet *(44). At the left of her is Jackie 'Butch' Jenkins, and on the right Juanita Quigley and Angela Lansbury. Behind Miss Quigley, playing their mother, is Anne Revere, who won a Best Supporting Oscar for her performance.*

eventually transform her into a world star: Nicky Hilton (1949–51), Michael Wilding (1952–57). For the moment her box-office remained minimal: *The Girl Who Had Everything* (53) – prophetic title, with Fernando Lamas; and *Rhapsody* (54), with Vittorio Gassmann. She took over from the ailing Vivien Leigh on *Elephant Walk* with Dana Andrews, but only after the part had been turned down by Jean Simmons, Olivia de Havilland and Katharine Hepburn. She was then in *Beau Brummel*, with Stewart Granger. Said Taylor of this period: 'The films I did then in *Beau Brummell*, with Stewart Granger. because they were so distasteful to me. . . . A lot of them I haven't seen, but I must have been appalling in them. *Beau Brummell*: I was so embarrassing in it.' A dim period finished with *The Last Time I Saw Paris*, a soap opera with Van Johnson which hit the bathos trail with a vengeance.

The early films of Elizabeth Taylor went mainly unregarded by both press and public. An outstanding exception was George Stevens's A Place in the Sun *(51), adapted from Theodore Dreiser's 'An American Tragedy'. Montgomery Clift played the young man who wanted a place in the sun.*

Her career began moving when she was loaned to Warners and George Stevens (who had wanted the just-retired Grace Kelly) for *Giant* (56), from Edna Ferber's bestseller. It took a lot of money and so did *Raintree County* (57), with Montgomery Clift. Both, however, had been dangerously expensive, to the extent the very future of MGM depended on the second film – a future which it did not secure for it just broke even, but that particular problem was solved by the surprise success of *Jailhouse Rock* with Elvis Presley. Still, the grosses suggested to MGM that Taylor was a major draw, especially as her performance as a Southern belle was remarked upon, if at all, unfavourably – but it garnered her an Oscar nomination. There had begun a sort of groundswell which was to lead to her being considered an important star and this was doubtless something to do with her new husband, master-showman Mike Todd. Ironically, his death a year later (1958) in an air crash paved the way to greater fame: she became involved in a triangle battle with Debbie Reynolds and won ('I'm not taking anything away from Debbie Reynolds because she never really had it'). He was a singer, Eddie Fisher, who had been married to Reynolds since 1955. The fan magazines devoured them, screaming, and if Reynolds got the sympathy, Taylor seemed to take her place with the great courtesans of history, which is to say that she behaved selfishly and splendidly in an amorous matter. It was the way movie stars were supposed to behave, and with the exception of the less suitable Ingrid Bergman there had not been a Hollywood scandal in too long a while. Taylor's salary rose to $500,000 against 10 per cent of the gross – for *Two for the See-Saw*, announced as her next but one, postponed, and later done with Shirley MacLaine. The next was *Cat on a Hot Tin Roof* (58) from Tennessee Williams's play, as Paul Newman's sexually frustrated wife. *Suddenly Last Summer* (59) was again from a Williams play and another step in the cinema's move towards themes of sexual hang-up. Joseph L. Mankiewicz directed and Dwight Macdonald spoke of one 'directorial triumph: he has somehow extracted from Elizabeth Taylor a mediocre performance, which is a definite step up her dramatic career'. Artistically, the film failed partly because she did not convey any suggestion that the character might be mentally disturbed. Both these films were big commercially and she was rated at the box-office for the first time, second in 1958.

MGM issued a lot of pictures of Elizabeth Taylor looking like this in Cat on a Hot Tin Roof *(58): utterly desirable. The point was, of course, that her husband in the film did not find her so, for he was hung up on a dead chum of his.*

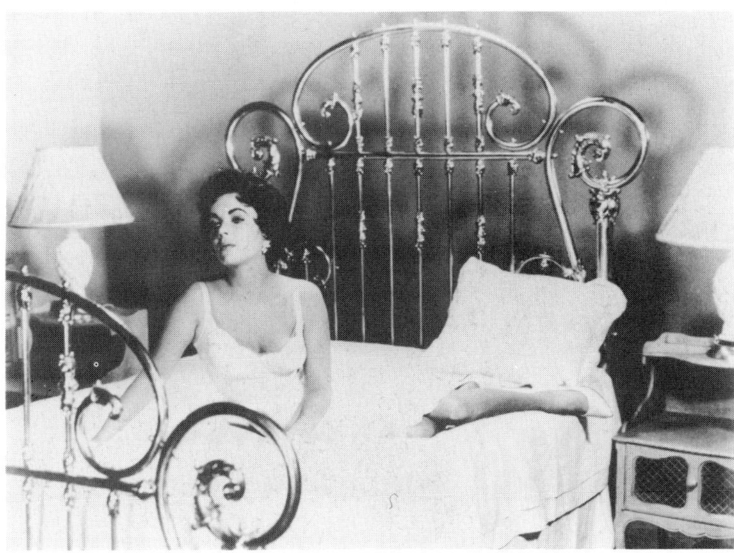

Unwillingly, she did her last film under her MGM contract, *Butterfield 8* (60), from John O'Hara's novel – unwillingly, because she did not want to play a call-girl. Then Walter Wanger and 20th signed her to play *Cleopatra* (63), at a (much-) publicized fee of $1 million. In fact, she was to get $125,000 for 16 weeks' work, plus $50,000 for every week afterwards if it ran over schedule, plus $3,000 a week expenses plus 10 per cent of the gross. Before the film was even started it was estimated that it would go over schedule so that she would earn at least $2 million (at one point she refused to start work until she received her daily cheque of $10,000; Fisher was paid $1,500 daily just to see she got to work on time). In fact, the picture took years, not weeks, to make. It was begun in London and abandoned after $5 million had been spent, when Taylor was ill in the London Clinic. At that point she won a Best Actress Oscar (for *Butterfield 8*), about which she later said – echoing earlier comment, 'I knew my performance hadn't deserved it, that it was a sympathy award.' Lloyds, the insurers, suggested several other actresses to replace her, but Wanger refused ('She came through to me as the one young actress who could play Cleopatra. She is the only woman I have ever known who has the necessary youth, power and emotion.'). The film was restarted in Italy with director Mankiewicz replacing Rouben Mamoulian, Rex Harrison replacing Peter Finch and Richard Burton replacing Stephen Boyd. Soon, in life, Burton had replaced Fisher for what must be the most publicized romance of all time. No film was ever so pre-sold, pre-advertised. It turned out to be a $37-million fiasco, the most expensive film ever made and one of the dullest. The curious kept it running for a while and, by dint of high seat-prices and an eventual $5 million sale to TV, it did eventually go into the black. The notices were generally derisive. John Coleman in the 'New Statesman' took the occasion to discuss star-quality (chance had it that he was reviewing Monroe and Garbo in the same issue): 'Whatever it is, and the compressed history of film has seen a variety of offers, Elizabeth Taylor surely lacks it, registers a signal and absolute deficiency in that enigmatic private business that a "star" can't help disclosing on cellulois. . . . Monotony in a split skirt, a pre-Christian Elizabeth Arden with sequinned eyelids and occasions constantly too large for her. Plumply pretty, she gives herself womanfully to the impersonation of the world's prime seductress, yet nary a spark flies.'

Attempts to film Shakespeare were for years doomed to box-office and/ or artistic failure. Laurence Olivier's films were exceptions, and so were the two which Franco Zeffirelli made in the 60s. This is the first of them, The Taming of the Shrew *(67), with Elizabeth Taylor and Richard Burton.*

A bad press and bad personal publicity had not hurt Burton or Taylor. They were married in 1964, in the midst of a run of successful films together; *The V.I.P.s*, as his wife, illicitly in love with Louis Jourdan; Minnelli's execrable *The Sandpiper* (65), as his mistress; Mike Nichols's film of Edward Albee's *Who's Afraid of Virginia Woolf?* (66), as his wife, fat, blowsy and spitting out some hitherto banned-in-films words, a performance that won her a second Oscar and a New York critics' award (in a tie with Lynn Redgrave); and *The Taming of the Shrew* (67), directed by Franco Zeffirelli (his first film). However, another semi-philanthropic bash at the classics, *Dr Faustus* – she had a few apparitions as Helen – was pronounced poor and was not widely distributed. She had retained her place in the magic 10 (fourth in 1960, first in 1961, sixth in 1962 and 1963, ninth in 1965, third in 1966, eighth in 1967, tenth in 1968) but was about to leave it. Neither of the next two did very well. *Reflections in a Golden Eye*, with Marlon Brando, was in fact a fine film, blemished by her superficial – and by now monotonous – vulgar-beldame act. *The Comedians*, with Burton, was a poor version of a good novel by Graham Greene, who considers her performance the worst in any film of his books. Her presence in the cast, he told the 'Guardian', 'was apparently to do with Mr Burton's presence, and the necessity therefore of paying her hotel bills on location anyway'. Coleman observed that 'the Burtons are not the Lunts and it is time they kept their private relationship out of the realms of art'. (For this they might have; it was said that Taylor took half her normal salary after it was suggested that the part be offered to Sophia Loren.)

But both grosses looked good beside those of *Boom!* (68), with Burton, a version of Williams's play 'The Milk Train Doesn't Stop Here Anymore'. It raked in less than one-quarter of its cost, what 'Variety' called 'one of the biggest box-office losers of the year'. Joseph Losey directed, as he did *Secret Ceremony* (69), where she played an ageing whore on whom Mia Farrow gets a crush. That too played to empty cinemas. Losey spoke warmly of Taylor, though said 'she'll make life hell as a way of testing you'. Most of her colleagues have spoken warmly of her – though that would not bring back the days of the million-dollar salary. She would get that once more, for *The Only Game in Town* (70) with Warren Beatty, directed by George Stevens in Paris – though set in Las Vegas, a fact which considerably upset 20th stockholders, especially when it got back only a minute proportion of its $8 million cost (of which the Burtons got $2.5 million). She played a chorus girl and 'Playboy' found her 'hopeless in the part. . . . Liz resembles a well-heeled suburban matron having a fling at community theatricals.'

Thereafter she worked for no salary but a cut of the profits: *Under Milk Wood* (71) with Burton, in a small part; *Zee and Company* (72), from a story by Edna O'Brien, revenging herself on husband Michael Caine by bedding his mistress, Susannah York; and *Hammersmith Is Out*, with Burton. There could not have been any profits, certainly not with the latter, which was quickly laughed off the screen. If you chance upon it on TV you will find both stars neck-deep in self-parody, she as a hash slinger and uttering dialogue jumping from late Joan Crawford to would-be significance: a fitting finish to this professional partnership – if one does not include a two-part TV film, *Divorce His, Divorce Hers* (73). Separated, then, professionally, Taylor had no more luck: *Night Watch* was a lacklustre thriller in which she was a frightened wife (Laurence Harvey's) and later a double murderess; *Ash Wednesday* was a vapid soap opera about an ageing beauty who goes in for rejuvenation and has an affair with Helmut Berger; and the Italian *Identikit/The Driver's Seat* (74) found the star as a neurotic spinster fascinated by a killer. Despite the fact that these films were hardly seen, Taylor headed the 'Observer' readers list of bores (Burton was third) in 1975 – though, of course, her divorce had made headlines. She and Burton were remarried and her memoir of that event appeared in syndicated magazines the week the second separation was announced.

Professionally, the Taylor saga remained absurd. She played several roles in the US – *The Blue Bird* (76), which, despite its budget and all the publicity, disappeared as quickly as her other recent films; there was an appearance, at a fee of $100,000, in the all-star TV *Victory at Entebbe*, as a worried mother; and there was a guest role in *Winter Kills*, which was temporarily abandoned when the money ran out (her fee was another $100,000). Then there was Hal Prince's version of his own Broadway success, *A Little Night Music* (77), which, said Brian Baxter in 'Films Illustrated', 'brings a whole new concept to the term "disaster movie" '. Derek Malcolm in the 'Guardian' did not quibble about the reason: it was Taylor. Her fee had been only $50,000 (as Burton obligingly explained: because she needed a good film) – which may be the reason why Prince grabbed her, in which case the film deserved its trouncing and dire business, since the role (that of an actress) needed qualities of charm and talent that Taylor had not yet indicated in her career. In 1978 she was in a TV film, *Return Engagement* and there turned up finally *Winter Kills* (79), in which her wordless cameo as a Washington procuress had, due to 'contractual provisions', also become creditless: 'The rest of the cast should have been so lucky' said 'Variety'. In Britain she played an American movie star, a possible murder victim, in an Agatha Christie tale, *The Mirror Crack'd* (80).

Since film offers were not plentiful, she turned to the stage and at one point it was reported that she would be doing 'Much Ado About Nothing' in New York, London and for cable. She in fact chose 'The Little Foxes', which she did in New York (81) and the following year in London – where one section of the press welcomed her as a 'megastar', but another – the critics – were not so kind: 'She has no vestige of star quality,' wrote Mark Amory in the 'Spectator', 'If you saw her in Reading rep you would think she was having a decent stab at a big role and not bother to check the programme.' 'For the most part, as an actress, she teeters on the brink of competence,' said Jack Tinker in the 'Daily Mail'. The 'Daily Mirror' reported a first night audience, at £25 a ticket, as unimpressed: 'There was little applause and even a few boos.' The limited run, said to be entirely sold out, was soon being advertised on TV and then it was cut short; but this London engagement was a triumph beside a Broadway revival of 'Private Lives' (83) with Burton, which managed to survive – just – some of the worst personal notices in theatre history. There was a spell (later) in the Betty Ford Clinic for Alcoholism and drug addition, and there would be a future for Taylor in telemovies. She once said on TV, 'I think you should know your business before you get out there' i.e. on the set. This still was not apparent – incredibly, given her years of experience – in what she chose to do: *Between Friends*, with Carol Burnett, as divorcees who form a friendship; *Malice in Wonderland* (85), an inept account of the careers of Louella Parsons (Taylor) and Hedda Hopper (Jane Alexander), for a reputed fee of $500,000; *North and South*, one day's work, for $100,000, in a cameo as a madame; *There Must Be a Pony* (86), from James Kirkwood's novel, as a film star making a comeback and having trouble with her son; and *Poker Alice* (87) with Tom Skerritt and George Hamilton, in the title-role, as a lady who likes the tables. A real film offer proved tempting: *Il Giovane Toscanini/Young Toscanini* (88), playing a diva for Zeffirelli, but it was literally laughed off the screen at the Venice Film Festival and has been heard of no more. Then: *Sweet Bird of Youth* (89) for television.

Rod Taylor

Handsome and brawny, Rod Taylor has nevertheless played comedy with some finesse and drama with considerable sensitivity; but he seems less to want to act than to blaze away as the beefy, breezy hero of what 'Variety' called 'middle-budget action pictures'. While the fan magazines refer to him as a Tough Guy, critics call him 'underrated'. The public likes him. He says he waits for parts that interest him; then adds that he has 'little patience with stars who sit around demanding the earth in exchange for their services. If I get the rate for the job I'm satisfied.' Perhaps that is what has kept him from reaching that area where all the best parts are offered around.

He was born in Sydney, Australia, in 1929 and in that city's Technical and Fine Arts College set out to study art and engineering. But he wanted to act and was swayed finally by the Australian visit of the Old Vic and Laurence Olivier. He began acting as an amateur, while doing design work for a department store; then studied at the Independent Theatre School in Sydney. A part in Shaw's 'Misalliance' at the Mercury Theatre paved the way towards some fame; and he had roles in a couple of local movies, *The Stewart Expedition* (51) and *King of the Coral Sea* (54) starring Chips Rafferty, in the latter playing an American. An Australian company decided to make a sequel to *Treasure Island*, again with Robert Newton as *Long John Silver*, and Taylor was cast as Israel Hands, the blind madman. 20th distributed and when he stopped off in Los Angeles on his way, hopefully, for a career in Britain, that company gave him a small part in *The Virgin Queen* (55). He decided to stay in Hollywood.

He got small parts in a Sterling Hayden Western, *Top Gun*, and in *Hell on Frisco Bay* with Alan Ladd; then a better one in *World Without End* (56), as one of four scientists in this Allied Artists sci-fier starring Hugh Marlowe. MGM tested him for the lead in *Somebody Up There Likes Me*, but found him unsuitable. However, they liked him enough to place him under long-term contract. His first for them was *The Catered Affair*, an uncommonly likeable performance as Debbie Reynolds's bespectacled fiancé. He was loaned to Warners to play a British baronet in *Giant*; then was a Southern boss in *Raintree County* (57). He was loaned out again for *Step Down to Terror* with Charles Drake, an ill-advised low-budget remake of *Shadow of a Doubt*, in MacDonald Carey's role, a cop disguised as a reporter; and for *Separate Tables* (58), playing the juvenile – a student – opposite Audrey Dalton. Then he was one of the three men chasing Shirley MacLaine in *Ask Any Girl* (59), superb as her would-be seducer. His reward was the sole starring credit on George Pal's pleasant adaptation of H.G. Wells's *The Time Machine* (60).

The current MGM management had done nothing to promote him and, just as he had attained stardom, they let him do a TV series, 'Hong Kong'. That disposed of, they permitted him to go off to Italy for *La Regina delle Amazzoni*, billed after Gianna Maria Canale and Ed Fury, and then again for *Seven Seas to Calais* (62), a jolly Italo-American biopic of Sir Francis Drake, with Keith Michell as his mate and Irene Worth – giving the film some distinction – as Elizabeth. At that level he might have languished had Hitchcock not chosen him to play the lead in *The Birds* (63) opposite Tippi Hedren and, even if the part allowed him little scope, he was a comforting hero in the frightening circumstances. Universal kept him on for one that, despite the title, had no similarity or connection, *A Gathering of Eagles*, as Rock Hudson's commanding officer and friend; then MGM gave him a couple of good chances – *The V.I.P.s*, a particularly engaging portrait of a young Australian tycoon, and *Sunday in New York* (64), alternately pursuing and being pursued by Jane Fonda. In life, he had pursued and now married model Mary Hilem. At 20th he was a dead pilot whose heroism is investigated by friend Glenn Ford in *Fate Is the Hunter*; at MGM he did the last two under his contract, *Thirty-six Hours*, a good wartime thriller, as a Nazi posing as an American, and *Young Cassidy* (65), good (though not physically right) as the young Sean O'Casey.

He had established himself as an imaginative man of action, a romantic junior executive, very self-confident, rather in the manner of Don Ameche or Ray Milland 20 years

*'*The Birds *is coming' said the ads, in a publicity campaign apparently planned by Hitchcock himself. The film (63) certainly confirmed his propensity at that time to go to outrageous lengths in the cause of thrills, as the entire ornithological population of California attack the humans there. Hardly surprisingly Tippi Hedren takes comfort in Rod Taylor's arms.*

earlier. As such, Doris Day beckoned, for two comedies, *Do Not Disturb* and *The Glass-Bottom Boat* (66), but he could do little with such weak material. Ditto for *The Liquidator*, some British variations on espionage themes. *Hotel* (67) was a good one for him – in the pivotal role as its manager – but the programmers that followed were undistinguished: *Chuka*, produced by his own company; *Dark of the Sun/The Mercenaries* (68), a US-British adventure story; and *A Time for Heroes* with Claudia Cardinale. All the same, they looked pretty good when stacked against *Nobody Runs Forever*, a thriller he made in Britain for Betty Box and Ralph Thomas, from which he went to the other end of the director spectrum, working under Antonioni in his first US-made film, *Zabriskie Point* (70). The leads were two amateurs, Mark Frechette and Daria Halprin, playing Los Angeles dropouts who meet in Death Valley: Taylor was the girl's tycoon lover. It was a case of less than meets the eye and was savaged by some critics – especially those who found it anti-American. But it was visually stunning and quite unlike anything but itself. It failed to salvage MGM's fortunes as hoped, but did not do as badly as its detractors hoped.

From there Taylor dipped to a silly drama with a Swinging London setting, *The Man Who Had Power Over Women*. It did no better than his other recent films. There was another action yarn, *Darker Than Amber* (71), as sailor of fortune Travis McGee, and then he returned to television, in a series called 'Bearcats!', of which the two-hour pilot played cinemas abroad, much abridged, as *Powder Keg*. Another TV film followed, *Family Flight* (72), and then he and Rod Steiger were in the desert for World War II in *Gli Eroi/The Heroes*. He was one of John Wayne's confederates in *The Train Robbers* (73) and the baddie shot down by Richard Harris in *The Deadly Trackers*. Neither of these Westerns was successful, nor was the film between them, *Trader Horn*, a 'laughably inane remake' ('Variety') by MGM of their old success. In other circumstances Taylor would have been fine in Harry Carey's old role of African adventurer. In Yugoslavia he made *Partisani* (74), in which he and Adam West were partisan leaders having love affairs: titled *Hell River* it turned up in the US four years later. He returned to television: *A Matter of Wife . . . and Death* (75), as the private eye Shamus (a role played earlier on the big screen by Burt Reynolds); and *Oregon Trail* (76), as a pioneer patriarch in this pilot, which was followed by a brief season. He did supporting roles in the French *Blondy* (76), starring Bibi Andersson, as a UN official, and the Australian *The Picture Show Man* (77), as rival to the title character – a travelling cinematograph showman (John Meillon) of the 1920s. In between, he was reported making *On a Dead Man's Chest*, from his own script, in Jamaica. Taylor was a CIA man in *A Time to Die*, with Rex Harrison, filmed in 1979 and sent direct to video (in Britain) in 1982. He thereafter concentrated mainly on television: *Cry of the Innocent* (80), based on a story by Frederick Forsyth, as an American businessman seeking revenge for the death of wife and child in Eire; *Hellinger's Law* (81), a busted pilot for Telly Savalas, as front man for the mob; *Jacqueline Bouvier Kennedy*, as her father, Black Jack, with Jaclyn Smith in the title-role; and another 'factual' tale, *Charles and Diana: a Royal Love Story* (82), as the Queen's press secretary. He returned to Australia to appear in *Go for Broke* and while there was asked to make *On the Run* (83) with Paul Winfield, but he was not at his most convincing as an international hit man. Back

Doris Day's comedies of the 60s were very successful at the time – and have been much derided since. Rod Taylor was her co-star in two of them – this one is The Glass-Bottom Boat *(66).*

in the US he starred in *Masquerade* and *Outlaws* (86), both done with anticipated series to follow; and in 1987 he joined the cast of 'Falcon Crest'.

TERRY-THOMAS

In the 30s the 'typical' Englishman was represented by Sir C. Aubrey Smith, among others. So the world turns, and later when Hollywood wanted a 'typical' Englishman they sent for Terry-Thomas, who has the same County bearing but belongs rather to the comedies of P.G. Wodehouse. The 'Silly-ass' Britisher is part of the comic tradition. It was the luck of Terry-Thomas to be doing it at a time when tradition was crumbling, when comic eccentrics, by and large, were disappearing. By the late 50s, most of the marvellously funny artists who had supported the stars in American films had gone, which left people like Terry-Thomas and Margaret Rutherford to know a popularity in the US undreamt of before by British players. The truth is, that Terry-Thomas's 'act' was done with a great deal of skill and, what is more essential, good humour.

Curiously, as a stand-up comic he was not very funny. He traded on his gap-teeth, elaborate cigarette-holders and fancy waistcoats – props which do not seem to have a great deal of humour built into them. It was more or less by chance that he got into films and more or less in the same way that he got into show business. He was born Thomas Terry Hoare-Stevens in Finchley, north London, in 1911 and educated at Ardingly, a public school in Sussex. He worked for a while as a buyer for a grocery firm and drifted into films as an extra. He met a small-time impresario who got him a job compèring in cabaret: in 1938 he started appearing on radio. He joined the Royal Signals on the outbreak of war and became one of the 'Stars in Battledress'. When the war was over, he got a break in a West End revue supporting Sid Field, 'Piccadilly Hayride', which led to much radio work and later his own television programme, 'How Do You View?' – meant to suggest his catch-phrase, 'How do you do?', said in an ineffably upper-crust manner. During this period he had a small part in a dim Rank farce starring David Tomlinson, *Helter Skelter* (49). His real film début was in a Boulting Brothers' farce, *Private's Progress* (56), as the infinitely disgusted CO, a performance of immense skill; no one else could have mouthed his disdainful 'You're an absolute shower' quite as delicately. His success in that led to the role of one of the hotel guests in *The Green Man*, a fastidious gentleman coping with a popsie; then the Boultings cast him in the second of their comic films about British institutions, *Brothers-in-Law* (57); taken to task this time was the law, with T-T as a wide-boy defended by Ian Carmichael. The Boultings cast him as the fatuous, bearded professor in *Lucky Jim*, with Carmichael in the title-role: a baggy-pants version of a fairly serious book – by Kingsley Amis – about life in a provincial university.

Private's Progress (56) *was an army comedy distinguished by the performance of Terry-Thomas as an officer not given to faith in the men under his command. The objects of his disdain here are Ian Bannen and Jill Adams.*

With these four films, Terry-Thomas was established as one of the most valuable character actors in Britain. He was in heavy demand, often in the leading role; *The Naked Truth*, a comedy about a scandal magazine, as a pompous peer embroiled in its machinations; *Happy Is the Bride*, a strident remake of *Quiet Wedding* with Janette Scot and Carmichael, in its only funny sequence – as an obtuse country policeman; and *Blue Murder at St Trinian's*, as the crafty boss of the coach firm which takes the St Trinian's girls into Europe. In general, American audiences first got to know him when he played a crook in MGM's filmed-in-Britain *tom thumb* (58) paired with Peter Sellers. His British films became marginally better: *Too Many Crooks* (59), where he was very funny as a rascally businessman who refuses to ransom his wife – kidnapped by an incompetent gang of crooks; *Carlton-Browne of the F.O.*, in the title-role, a red-tape-bound official trying to cope with the ways of wily natives like Sellers – and perhaps his best British film; *I'm All Right Jack*, with Sellers, as the factory personnel manager; *School for Scoundrels* (60), with Carmichael and Alastair Sim, as an insufferably superior man-about-town; and *Make Mine Mink*, as a retired major who organizes

The films of writer-director Frank Tashlin are of variable quality, but Bachelor Flat *(61) had a goodly share of funny moments. Terry-Thomas was an English professor, here accosting Tuesday Weld after being dosed with some sort of magic elixir.*

crime for some old ladies, including Athene Seyler. His luck ran out with *His and Hers* (61), an excruciating comedy about a writer who changes after being lost in Africa, with Janette Scott as his wife; and *A Matter of WHO*, as a civil servant trying to find the source of an outbreak of smallpox – perhaps the worst idea ever thought up for a comedy.

He was saved by Hollywood: Frank Tashlin at 20th called him over for a star role in *Bachelor Flat*. He played an English professor and had little to do but chase about trouserless for most of its length – an old comic idea inventively done. The film was not a great success, but he had stood up in the US and been counted. The two British films he did were abysmal – though once again he almost salvaged them: *Operation Snatch* (62), as a clumsy army major involved with the Barbary apes in wartime Gibraltar; and *Kill or Cure*, as a private detective stuck in a nursing-home. He played a British secret agent in *Mouse on the Moon* (63) and the lecherous boss of Nancy Kwan in *The Wild Affair*, another poor thing – and not released for a couple of years. He returned to Hollywood to get lost in a couple of biggies, *The Wonderful World of the Brothers Grimm* and *It's a Mad Mad Mad Mad World*. Also in Hollywood, he did a cameo, as a mortician, in *Strange Bedfellows* (64). In Britain he was the villain of *Those Magnificent Men in Their Flying Machines*; in Hollywood he was Jack Lemmon's Jeeves-like valet in *How To Murder Your Wife* (65), his own favourite film.

He filmed almost non-stop – not only in Britain and the US, but also in Europe. Few of the films, it must be said, were distinguished, but he brightened most of them: *You Must Be Joking*, a comedy about an army initiative test, with a member of the ASAF (Michael Callan) and several stock British farce figures; *Our Man in Marrakesh* (66), a nitwitted comedy-thriller, with Tony Randall, as an Anglophile Arab; *Munster Go Home!*, a black comedy with Yvonne de Carlo, as the son of Hermione Gingold; *The Sandwich Man*, a flop comedy with a host of British clowns, including T-T as a scout-master; *La Grande Vadrouille*, with Louis de Funès and Bourvil, as a British squadron leader who bails out over Paris – probably the most successful French comedy ever made, in France, but a flop in the US and Britain in its dubbed versions; *Se Tutte le Donne del Mondo/Kiss the Girls and Make Them Die*, a dismal spy-spoof with Raf Vallone, as an aristocratic explorer: *The Perils of Pauline* (67), yet another spoof (no relation to the Pearl White serials) with Pat Boone as the richest man in the world, as the villain; *Jules Verne's Rocket to the Moon*, a cheapjack version of that tale with Burl Ives and Troy Donahue, with Lionel Jeffries and T-T as the heavies; *I Love a Mystery*, for TV; and *The Karate Killers*, a 'Man from UNCLE' TV programme, shown in cinemas abroad. He made three films in Italy: *Top Crack*, in which he and Gastone Moschine were comic kidnappers; *Arabella*, with Margaret Rutherford and Virna Lisi, in a triple role – which he considers his best work; and *Danger Diabolik* (68), yet another crime comedy, with John Phillip Law, as a politician.

Asked at this time why he did so many small parts, he said he did not have time for big ones. He enlivened a couple of conventional pieces: *Don't Raise the Bridge Lower the*

River, with Jerry Lewis, as a typical bowler-hatted Britisher; and *Where Were You When the Lights Went Out?*, with Doris Day, as a Hungarian film director. *2,000 Years Later* (69) was released two years late, an amateurish satire on modern life (an ancient Roman returns to earth) with Edward Everett Horton. Then: *Sette Volte Sette*, another Italian crime comedy, with Moschine and Lionel Stander; *Quei Temerari sulle Loro Pazze Scatenate Scalcinate Carriole/Monte Carlo or Bust*, with Tony Curtis and Bourvil; *Una su Tredici*, with Vittorio Gassmann; *Le Mur de l'Atlantique* (70), with Bourvil (his last film) and Peter McEnery; and *The Abominable Dr Phibes* (71), with Vincent Price. In 1971 he began *The Cherry Picker* with a pop-singer, Lulu, which was unseen till released to video 10 years later (possibly incomplete, since it was reported at the time that the money had run out).

In Italy, he supported Rod Steiger and Rod Taylor in *Gli Eroi/The Heroes* (72), but their names were not enough to get bookings in the US or Britain; in *Vault of Horror* (73) he married Glynis Johns, nagged her and got chopped up by her – one of several stories in this omnibus film; then he returned to Italy to make *Colpo Grosso . . . Grossissimo . . . Anzi Probabile*, with Nino Castelnuovo. He must have been depressed by his material: Hollywood was no longer making comedies where he had once done sterling supporting roles and, though Britain was still making comedies, there was a considerable falling-off from the days when he had started in films – though he himself was a saving grace in the dire *Spanish Fly* (76), as the expatriate (it was set in Minorca) aristocrat and unwitting manufacturer of that aphrodisiac which has such a startling effect on an underwear salesman (Leslie Phillips). Possibly even more embarrassing were: *Side by Side*, as the nightclub-owning uncle of Australian Barry Mackenzie (Bruce Beresford directed in Britain, which has not yet seen it; Australia has); and *The Bawdy Adventures of Tom Jones*, a musical version with Nicky Henson as Tom, as one of his tutors. He began work in Africa on *King Solomon's Treasure*, but was felled by a heart attack and did not work again till the small role of the prison governor in *The Last Remake of Beau Geste* (77). He returned to Italy to take the star role in *Le Braghe del Padrone* (78), as the boss himself; and was then the villain in *The Hound of the Baskervilles*, with a comic team, Cook and Moore – which achieved the no mean feat of being the worst of this particular batch. His last film was a German-Italian co-production, *Buon Compleanno Harry* (80). Not long after completing it he announced that he had suffered from Parkinson's disease for 10 years and was retiring. In 1988 it was discovered that after years of huge medical bills he was living in poverty; the profession put on a gala at the Theatre Royal, Drury Lane, to benefit him and other sufferers from the illness.

GENE TIERNEY

Gene Tierney was as sleek and as beautiful as a lynx – a shade warmer, but nowhere near as agile. Once she emerged from the miscasting which almost wrecked her career at the outset she was neither very good nor very bad. She was simply there, on the screen – which, when you come to look at her, was not at all a bad place for her to be.

Although she hailed from Brooklyn (born 1920) it was a select part of it; her father was an insurance broker and could afford to have her educated in Connecticut and Switzerland. She met Anatole Litvak socially and he was so struck by her beauty that he had Warner Bros do a screen test; a contract was offered but the salary was so low that her parents decided she would never rise above bit-player status and dissuaded her. She did get a part on Broadway in 'Mrs O'Brien Entertains' (38), which George Abbott directed; and Columbia offered a six-month contract. But they did not put her into a film and she returned to New York, where she auditioned for and got the ingénue role in 'The Male Animal'. MGM decided she would be just right for the little girl in *National Velvet* and brought her out to Hollywood at $350 a week. The film was postponed and she found herself free to take up a long-term offer from 20th, who cast her opposite Henry Fonda in Fritz Lang's Western, *The Return of Frank James* (40), in a fairly nothing role. She had an even smaller role as the aristocratic British heroine of *Hudson's Bay*, from which she went to the other extreme, playing the backward Georgia farm-girl, Ellie May, in Ford's *Tobacco Road* (41). The 'Harvard Lampoon' listed her 'The Worst Discovery of the Year'.

20th, however, had detected a more positive response to their discovery, so they decided to give her a big star-role: but how they detected in her the wildcat qualities necessary for *Belle Starr* was and remains a mystery. Randolph Scott and Dana Andrews were the men in Belle's life. But it was not only 20th who were impressed: United Artists borrowed her to play a native girl in both *Sundown* and *The Shanghai Gesture*, which struck 20th as such a happy idea that they cast her as another girl in *Son of Fury* (42). In fact, she was good in none of them. 'The New York

Times' said of the first: 'As an actress of worldly wise glamour Miss Tierney continues to create a distinct impression of adolescent weltschmerz.' There was something cynical in the use of this good-looking New York girl as a sort of tropical Theda Bara (in fact, in *Sundown* she was an African mystery woman who turns out to be English; in *Gesture* a high-class English dame who turns out to be a half-caste and, especially ludicrous, going to the dogs in Mother Gin Sling's; in *Son of Fury* a 19th-century – but Max-Factored – South Seas mantrap). However, if she had proved proficient in comedy on Broadway, 'The New York Times' was to be no kinder about her efforts in a trifle called *Rings on Her Fingers*: 'An actress, we suspect, should have a little more equipment than Expression A for rapture, B for apprehension, etc. A slight sense of timing helps, too. . . . Maybe Miss Tierney will learn these things in time.'

At least *Thunder Birds* made few demands on her, as a socialite living near the training-field (being trained were British pilots in the US, Preston Foster and John Sutton); then she was back again in exotica as a Vassar-educated *China Girl*, in love with George Montgomery in Burma. But in another comedy, Lubitsch's sparkling *Heaven Can Wait* (43), she had very obviously made little progress. However, there was a 'goddess' phase beginning – when Hedy Lamarr turned down the lead in *Laura* (44), a fairly intriguing mystery from a novel by Vera Caspary. She was supposed to be dead at the outset and became a figure of mystery rather by the way she was discussed (by Clfiton Webb, Dana Andrews and Vincent Price) than by anything she brought to the part. But she looked lovely and the film became quite famous. (The lyric of the theme tune – 'Laura is the face in the misty glow . . .' – was not written till later.) *A Bell for Adano* (45) had been John Hersey's novel about the liberation of an Italian town by GIs, the chief of whom was now John Hodiak; Tierney was so wildly miscast as a blonde Italian peasant girl as to sabotage the film – despite Hodiak's beautiful performance as the guy who tells her about American democracy. She then played a *femme fatale* in a lurid Technicolor novelette, *Leave Her to Heaven*, pinching her sister's boyfriend, allowing her brother-in-law to drown, killing her unborn baby and finally driving her husband back to her sister's arms – as is the wont in such films; then she in turn was victimized by husband Vincent Price in their Gothic mansion *Dragonwyck* (46), based on a novel doubtless inspired by the vogue for Brontë-type situations.

Leave Her to Heaven was probably Tierney's biggest commercial success of those films where she was the major star. She was no longer to dominate any film – if that is the word to use about so gentle a creature; from now on she was little more than just another leading lady. She took very much a back seat to Tyrone Power in *The Razor's Edge*, though she did then have one last really major role, in *The Ghost and Mrs Muir* (47), as a widow who falls in love with sea captain Rex Harrison. She was Dana Andrew's concerned wife in *The Iron Curtain* (48); an heiress who revenges herself on reporter Power in *That Wonderful Urge*; and a wealthy kleptomaniac trapped into murder by evil José Ferrer in *Whirlpool* (49). She went to London to co-star with Richard Widmark in *Night and the City* (50) and was rewarded with about 10 lines and

For some reason Gene Tierney was often cast as a native girl in her early films. She played a well-bred English girl in The Shanghai Gesture *(41) – until revealed as an Eurasian, after which she was made up as such. The man was Victor Mature.*

The Razor's Edge *was 20th Century-Fox's prestige offering of 1946. As befitted the occasion, there were several stars above the title, including Gene Tierney as the aristocratic Isabelle, and Anne Baxter as the unfortunate Sophie.*

half a song – dubbed (she was supposed to be a saloon singer). Then there was another thriller with Andrews, *Where the Sidewalk Ends*, improbable as the daughter of a cab-driver. She was loaned to Paramount for a comedy with John Lund, *The Mating Season* (51); and was Danny Kaye's leading lady, a society intriguer, in *On the Riviera*. She was a pioneer woman in *The Secret of Convict Lake* with Glenn Ford and Ray Milland's wife, trying to adopt a waif, in *Close to my Heart* at Warner Bros. Her last under her contract was *Way of a Gaucho* (52), a soap opera, in the Argentine with Rory Calhoun.

Her career got a lift with two at MGM, opposite their two biggest stars – and it might have been a bigger lift if the films had been better: *Plymouth Adventure* with Spencer Tracy, torn between love of him and Leo Genn (she solved it by drowning herself); and *Never Let Me Go* (53) with Clark Gable, as his Russian ballerina wife, rescued by him from the USSR. Her accent was convincing and in a tutu she was everyone's dream dancer. It was made in Britain and she stayed there to play schoolteacher Genn's American wife in a dud thriller, *Personal Affair*. She wanted to stay in Europe because of a romance with Prince Aly Khan; when that broke up she returned to Hollywood where 20th gave her star-billing but in what were merely supporting parts: *Black Widow* (54), as the wife of suspected murderer Van Heflin; *The Egyptian*, as Michael Wilding's haughty sister; and *The Left Hand of God* (55), as a nurse in love with Humphrey Bogart.

Then, voluntarily, she entered a mental institution, the Menninger Clinic in Topeka, Idaho. The trouble may have started when her first child, Daria, was born – retarded, because of German measles which Tierney contracted during pregnancy from a fan who insisted on speaking to her. She said herself that she might have coped with the situation better if the said fan had not decided to inform her of her illness years later. She had a second daughter and soon after divorced Oleg Cassini, her dress-designer husband (1941–52). But most papers commented that her breakdown followed the break-up of her European romance – though in fact she had had anxiety symptoms for some time. She said later: 'By the time of my breakdown I was a very frightened girl. I was scared to death, dazed.' As far as fans were concerned, she merely disappeared, until discovered working in a small Mid-West store, but this was, in fact, therapy. 20th was anxious to lend a hand and for them she started *Holiday for Lovers*, but quit after a few days (Jane Wyman took over) to return to the clinic.

The following year, 1960, she married a Texas oil millionaire (he had once been married to Hedy Lamarr) and in interviews seemed very happy. In 1961, 20th, still faithful, gave her another chance of a come-back, *Return to Peyton Place*, but just before she started work it was announced she was pregnant. She finally returned in the smallish role of a Washington hostess in *Advise and Consent* (62), made by Otto Preminger, who had directed three of her earlier films. She had featured roles in *Toys in the Attic* (63) and *The Pleasure Seekers* (64). It could not be said that she was any more of an actress, but her beauty, though lined, was undimmed and her presence was serene. She had retired, 'but once in a while they offer me a role I can't resist'. She added: 'I used to write some columns for the local paper in Houston. That was a year ago. I told my story, my experiences in show business, my life in Texas, my work with the Cancer Crusade, mental health and retarded children's charities, which are very important to me. I keep busy.' Rather surprisingly, she turned up in a tele-movie with Ray Milland, *Daughter of the Mind* (69), and she made another come-back, rather stout, in *Scruples* (80), a mini-series based on Judith Krantz's book.

Richard Todd

Richard Todd's peculiarly stiff screen presence has yielded at least one fine performance, but it has been mainly a distinct disadvantage in a career that once seemed full of promise.

He was born in Dublin in 1919, the son of an army doctor, and was educated at Shrewsbury and, during the war, at Sandhurst – he volunteered in September 1939. Before the war he had studied acting with Italia Conti and had been one of the founder-members of the Dundee rep; he returned to Dundee on leaving the army. In 1948 he was offered a screen test by Robert Lennard, formerly his agent and now casting director for Associated British; it was successful and he made an unimpressive screen bow in a minor melodrama, *For Them That Trespass* (49). Then he was cast as the dour young Scot, Lachie, dying of an incurable disease in a field hospital in Burma: *The Hasty Heart*. Every heart-tugging trick known to man was thrown in except dogs and children, plus Patricia Neal and Ronald Reagan – the play had been a success on Broadway as well as in London, and Warners had sent over two contract players and a financial director (Vincent Sherman) as a result of their interest in Associated British. They released in the US and Todd became a sensation in two continents; in Britain he won a 'Picturegoer' Gold Medal. Only an exceptionally able actor could have prevented the rest of his career from being a prolonged anticlimax.

And Todd was far from that: his work in *The Interrupted Journey* – a thriller that turned out to be a dream – was quite inadequate. Still, it was thought, that is only a cheap little British number, made before stardom gave him confidence; but he was equally poor in Hitchcock's British-made *Stage Fright* (50), as the boyfriend whom Jane Wyman refuses to suspect of murder. Hitchcock later said 'the villain was a flop'. Warners produced and, after playing one of Margaret Johnston's three husbands in *Portrait of Clare*, they sent for him for *Lightning Strikes Twice* (51) with Ruth Roman, one of the lurid melodramas which King Vidor was then making for them. This time he was a dour Englishman living in Texas and suspected of murder. He was not good, but the British *Flesh and Blood*, in his dual role as two boorish young doctors (one the grandson of the other), again suggested that there was something there if only the right director could mine it. And Disney found something – boyish enthusiasm – when he cast him in the lead of *The Story of Robin Hood and His Merrie Men*, generally considered closer to the legends but less enjoyable than the Errol Flynn version.

Despite its chain of cinemas, Associated British had not been much of a force in British film-making until with Todd they had a world star; now, ambitious, like other British companies before them, they sought a co-production deal with an American studio. Instead of tying up with their US partner, Warners, they made a deal with Allied Artists. The first result was *24 Hours of a Woman's Life* (52), a version of Stefan Zweig's novel with Merle Oberon and Todd, as her lover and a compulsive gambler. It flopped and nothing more was heard of the deal. Todd made a minor thriller, *The Venetian Bird*, playing a private eye, and then Disney came to his rescue again: *The Sword and the Rose* (53), a dull picture distantly based on some trouble between the Tudors, and the better, spirited *Rob Roy the Highland Rogue*, based on Sir Walter Scott. He was a TV Heathcliff and then, inexplicably, the possessor of a small role in a French episode film, *Les Secrets d'Alcove* (54).

Then 20th signed him to a long-term non-exclusive contract, mainly because they thought him the only actor who could play Scots-born minister Peter Marshall in the film of his wife's bestselling memoir, *A Man Called Peter* (55). 'This is the story of a man . . . and his close friendship with God,' said the foreword – at which point today most televiewers switch off. Filmgoers then were hardly less discriminating. And *The Virgin Queen* was virgin where most audiences were concerned – he was Raleigh and Bette Davis was the queen. But the British *The Dam Busters* would easily lead the British box-office that year, with Todd as war-hero Wing Commander Guy Gibson – a mannered performance, but a warmly human one, proving that he could rise to the occasion when required. 20th's *D-Day the Sixth of June* (56), with Robert Taylor, did not do comparable business; with it Todd abandoned tin hat and gas mask for powdered wig and cane – the Swedish Count Fersen to the *Marie Antoinette* of Michèle Morgan, made in France. It surfaced in the Anglo-Saxon lands a while later, if only in a very few cinemas.

While receipts from *The Dam Busters* still mounted, Herbert Wilcox engaged Todd for another picture based on (war) fact, the escape of the 'Amethyst', a Royal Navy frigate, in 1949: *The Yangtse Incident* (57). Todd played Commander Kerans. It was too late: the picture did not make a penny profit. Todd was then a sturdy Dunois in Otto Preminger's travesty of *Saint Joan*. He did a modest thriller with Anne Baxter, *Chase a Crooked Shadow*, and *The Naked Earth* (58), one of 20th's barren efforts to make Juliette Greco into a screen actress – he was an Irish farmer in Africa, she his French wife. His last for 20th was another slight British thriller,

The Hasty Heart *was one of the most popular pictures of 1949 – in part because of the performance of Patricia Neal, but mainly because of Richard Todd, as a Scottish soldier with a fatal disease.*

with Betsy Drake, *Intent to Kill*, as a brain surgeon. Then there was *Danger Within* (59) a POW camp, where fellow-inmates included Bernard Lee, Richard Attenborough, Michael Wilding and Donald Houston, a sparkling cast. There followed: *Never Let Go* (60), very good as a failed cosmetics salesman, with Peter Sellers; *The Long and the Short and the Tall* (61), as the earnest patrol sergeant; *Don't Bother to Knock*, which he produced, as a Cassanovering travel agent; *The Hellions*, a South African Western, as the police sergeant hero; and *The Longest Day* (62), as a British Major. He donned his British Warm again to play another officer in *Le Crime ne Paie Pas*, opposite Danielle Darrieux in one episode.

After that, he surrendered unconditionally to Bs and programmers: *The Boys*, as a barrister defending some of them; *The Very Edge* (63), a silly melodrama with Anne Heywood; *Todestrommeln am Grossen Fluss/Death Drums Along the River* (64), a West German-British co-production based on Edgar Wallace's 'Sanders of the River', as district commissioner Sanders; *The Battle of the Villa Fiorita* (65), in support of Maureen O'Hara and Rossano Brazzi, as the other man – O'Hara's stern husband; and *Coast of Skeletons*, with Dale Robertson, another offshoot of 'Sanders of the River'. Both 'Sanders' films were produced by Harry Alan Towers, who hovers prolifically on the outer verges of British B picture production – usually from some offshore base (probably because he was in legal difficulties in the US and Britain). Todd had become a successful dairy farmer, so there was some puzzle why he continued when the film offers, clearly, were so uninteresting. He did get a good part in *Operation Crossbow*, as a wing commander, and he played Lord Goring in a return to the boards – 'An Ideal Husband', an embarrassingly inflexible, unflippant performance.

He returned to the US to play a professor turned hippie in Sam Katzman's low-budget *The Love-Ins* (67) with James MacArthur, which was banned in Britain. In 1968 he made a B movie called *Subterfuge* with Gene Barry, playing a secret service officer; it had hopes for US TV and turned up in British cinemas three years later. He also made *The Last of the Long-Haired Boys*, playing an RAF pilot, never publicly shown; in Italy he played Basil in an exploitation version of Oscar Wilde, *Il Dio Chiamato Dorian/Dorian Gray* (70), which starred Helmut Berger. He toured in revivals of old favourites like 'The Winslow Boy' (71), but later returned to films, one of several names, in *Asylum* (72), before going off to Australia to appear in 'Sleuth'. In Spain he made *The Sky is Falling* (75), with Carroll Baker, directed by Silvio Narizzano, but their combined reputations were not enough to get any bookings in the US or the UK. *No 1 of the Secret Service* (78) had been a couple of years on the shelf and received no belated welcome; the star was Nicky Henson and Todd played an unhinged toy millionaire. He was a Scotland Yard man in *The Big Sleep*; and then made *Home Before Midnight* (79), fifth-billed in this lame tale about a rock musician's affair with a teenage girl, before touring South Africa in 'Nightfall'. In 1969 he married for the second time. He had a cameo as a publisher in a horror spoof starring Vincent Price, *House of the Long Shadows* (82), before taking over in a West End play, 'The Business of Murder'. He explained his absence as being a decade of taking theatre to the provinces. During the play's long run he incurred the wrath of the original star, Gerald Harper, by claiming it was a flop till he took over.

Jean-Louis Trintignant

He is an unassuming man, pale-skinned, with luminous, sensitive eyes, a leading man in French films for 30 years. There was never any question that he was a likeable actor – but most young French actors are likeable, endowed with (for want of a better phrase) Gallic charm. Of this generation only Belmondo seemed gifted with that extra, charismatic thrust. But this one, Jean-Louis Trintignant, from time to time broke out from his reserved shell: in *Le Cœur Battant* he gives a performance of relaxed, masculine charm which must be one of the best of its kind in the history of films. He did it again in *Un Homme et une Femme*, which made him famous throughout the world; and with the films that followed he established himself as one of the two young French actors who matter.

He was born in Piolenc, Vaucluse, in 1930 and he grew up there and in Aix-en-Provence. He arrived in Paris in 1950 to study under Charles Dullin and Tania Balachova, and made his Paris bow in 'A Chacun Selon sa Faim' (51) by Jean Mogin, followed by Schiller's 'Marie Stuart'. In 1953 he toured in 'Britannicus' and 'Don Juan', and in 1954 got his first big role in Paris, in 'Responsabilité Limité' by Robert Hossein. In 1955 he made his first film, a short, *Pechineff*, directed by Marcel Ichac. Then Christian-Jaque picked him for one of the leads – sixth-billed – in *Si Tous les Gars du Monde* (56), an adventure story about the efforts to get some serum to a fishing-smack off the coast of Norway. He was one of the concerned; Jean Gaven was the official star and Gaven starred in *La Loi des Rues*, where Trintignant was a reform-school boy who teams up with him – but the real villain in this underworld story was Raymond Pellegrin. He was seduced by Brigitte Bardot in *Et Dieu Créa la Femme*, which made him a name; and he starred with Nicole Courcel and Ivan Desny in *Club des Femmes*, the remake of a pre-war film with Danielle Darrieux. Then he went to do his military service.

He had not enjoyed any of the films he had made (and would not like any for two or three years yet); when he left the army he planned to abandon acting, but he was given the chance to play Hamlet in Paris. He did it for only 15 performances but it established him; he was invited to join the TNP and he returned to films in Vadim's *Les Liaisons Dangereuses* (59), as Darceny, a small but key role – he murders Gérard Philipe for seducing his beloved (Jeanne Valerie). He went to Italy for *L'Estate Violente* (60), a story about life in Riccionne (a resort on the Adriatic) in the summer of 1943, directed by Valerio Zurlini; Trintignant was a youngster seduced by an older woman (Eleanora Rossi Drago). In France he was the juvenile in *La Millième Fenêtre*, a comedy about an old man (Pierre Fresnay) refusing to leave his home to go to a new estate. He played one of Napoleon's generals (Ségur) in Gance's *Austerlitz* and was then in Franju's *Pleins Feux sur l'Assassin* (61), an original whodunit by Boileau and Narcejac (only not very original: a series of murders involving the legatees of a will). For the ex-critic Doniol-Valcroze, he made *Le Cœur Battant*, a sunny, unpretentious comedy about a couple at the seaside – she (Françoise Brion) waiting for her lover to turn up, he (Trintignant) in love with her but not going to admit it. It was the most enchanting French comedy in years and almost the first of his films which Trintignant liked.

He must have been at a low ebb to go to Italy for a remake of a famous old French silent, *L'Atlantide*, about the adventures of two Frenchmen in the lost city of Atlantis. This version, *Antinea L'Amante della Città Sepolta*, as directed by Edgar G. Ulmer and Giuseppe Masini, was just another confused sex-and-sandal epic with Haya Harareet. Then: *Le Jeu de la Verité*, a thriller starring Robert Hossein, in a featured role; *Horace 62* (62), a modern Greek tragedy – Corsican vendettas in Paris, with Charles Aznavour and Raymond Pellegrin; *Les Sept Péchés Capitaux*, in Jacques Demy's sketch, 'La Luxure', with Laurent Terzieff – they were students who liked to imagine girls nude; and *Le Combat dans l'Ile*, with Romy Schneider, as a cheap little killer. He was offered the role which James Fox played in *The Servant*, but turned it down because he did not speak English (three years later, he turned down a supporting role in *Two for the Road*). However, the exigencies of the Franco-Italian film agreement sent him to Italy to play a student impressed by the flashy Vittorio Gassmann in *Il Sorpasso*. It was such a success that he was recalled some months later for a follow-up, *Il Successo* (63), this time as Gassmann's friend. In France he co-starred with Monica Vitti in Vadim's ponderous version of a Françoise Sagan comedy, *Château en Suède*.

His films over the next months were a mixed bag, on the whole undistinguished: *Les Pas Perdus* (64), as a young man in love with Michèle Morgan; *Merveilleuse Angelique*, one of a series of historical romances – by Serge and Anne Golon, with Michèle Mercier as a sexy marquise, as a poet; *Mata Hari Agent H21* (65), as a young man who gets shot for

Et Dieu Créa la Femme . . . *(56) was few people's idea of a good movie, but it was popular because in those days it was unusual to have a heroine who slept around. She was of course, Brigitte Bardot – and the unfortunate man who married her was Jean-Louis Trintignant.*

Le Coeur Battant *(61) does not seem to have been shown in Britain or the US: a pity, for it had wit and gaiety, and pleasing performances by Françoise Brion and Jean-Louis Trintignant.*

love of Jeanne Moreau; *La Bonne Occase*, a sketch-film about an automobile; *Io Uccido Tu Uccidi*, an Italian sketch-film about murder, in its best episode, 'La Donna che Viveva Sola', with Emanuèle Riva – he was the layabout she falls in love with; and, by far the best of this batch, *Compartiment Tueurs*, with Yves Montand, as one of the murder suspects. Three Trintignant films were shown at the Cannes festival the following spring: *La Longue Marche* (66), Alexandre Astruc's adventure about the Maquis, with Hossein, Trintignant and Maurice Ronet as three of its members; *Le Dix-Septième Ciel*, a gentle comedy about a window-cleaner and a maid who pretends to be her own mistress; and *Un Homme et une Femme*, which was a romance between a widow and a widower who meet when their children go to the same school – she was Anouk Aimée, he was a racing-driver. The first of this trio was of uncertain quality and did so-so business; the second was considered old-fashioned and failed; the third was an enormous success in France and became the most successful French film ever to play in foreign markets. For Trintignant it was a justification: the film was mainly improvised and its success gave him confidence – till then he had never considered himself a good actor. He was offered the role, he thought, because he had told the director, Claude Lelouch – hitherto unsuccessful – that he had admired one of his films.

The next was simply a commercial chore: *Safari Diamants*, with Marie-José Nat, as a bored ex-para who turns to crime. He was a partisan in *Paris Brûle-t-il?/Is Paris Burning?*, then he made a real 'art' piece, Alain Robbe-Grillet's *Trans-Europ-Express* (67), in which he was the sadistic criminal hero of the film within a film. It was a failure, but was the sort of film he liked doing; he told 'Variety' in 1968 that he would like to be an international star, but not if it meant giving up movies like Robbe-Grillet's. He was also working with his wife, Nadine (Nadine Trintignant *née* Marquand, the sister of actor Christian Marquand; Trintignant's first wife was Stephane Audran, who later married Claude Chabrol): Nadine had directed Jean-Louis in a short, *Fragilité ton Nom est Femme*, and she followed up with a feature, *Mon Amour Mon Amour*, a Lelouch-like romance about an architect in love with a girl (Valérie Lagrange) who wants to be a pop singer. He made a thriller, *Un Homme à Abattre*, about the search for an ex-Nazi in Spain, and then travelled to Italy for a couple – though the first was actually set in London: *Col Cuore in Gola*, about a disillusioned man who meets a girl with no illusions (Ewa Aulin). Tinto Brass directed and it was not shown in France. The other picture was *La Morte ha Fatto L'Uovo*, where he was a chicken-farmer married to Gina Lollobrigida but acting out his fantasies in a local brothel.

Increasingly, Trintignant was to play men of dubious mentality or strange sexuality: without contouring his features or adopting much more than a hangdog expression he was to make a corner in mixed-up heroes. In *L'Homme qui Ment* (68), Robbe-Grillet's anthology of fake-enigmas, he was a pathological liar; in Chabrol's acrid *Les Biches* he was the dilettante who consciously comes between the two lesbians of the title. In Italy, he was fairly normal in a Western set among the snows of Mexico, *Il Grande Silenzio*, and then he was a shy young doctor in *La Matriarca* – till asked by Catherine Spaak to indulge in kinky games, which turn out to be very much to his liking. In *Una Ragazza Piuttosto Com plicata* (69) he and Miss Spaak indulged in murder fantasies. But he was noble in *Z* (69) – indeed, quite movingly so, as the honest and determined young lawyer kicking against corruption, in the second of his films to have a great success abroad. In *Le Voleur de Crimes*, directed by his wife, he was the psychopathic witness to a suicide who claims it was a murder – committed by him. He was in another good film, Eric Rohmer's *Ma Nuit chez Maud*, as a lonely young Catholic engineer caught between Françoise Fabian and Marie-Christine Barrault. It was about much more than that – about the nature of belief and fate (its key is a remark of Lenin's, that it is better to take that chance in a million than no chance at all). The film was all talk, most of it wide-ranging and stimulating. So was the next all talk, but it was not much good: *Metti una Sera a Cena*, directed by Patroni-Griffi from his own play about a blasé set of lovers.

He was *L'Américain* – in fact a Frenchman returning to his home town, with Simone Signoret; then he was unprofitably involved in another Italian sex thriller, *Cosi Dolce Cosi*

Françoise Fabian and Jean-Louis Trintignant in Ma Nuit chez Maud *(69) – written and directed by Eric Rohmer (the third in his series of* contes moraux*) and a reminder that the French have no peers in the matter of cerebral comedy.*

Perversa, with Carroll Baker. He explained his presence in this cruddy movie thus: he had made so many successful 'intellectual' films that he asked his agent to find him 'the most stupid film' then being made in Italy, on the understanding that the most stupid films were made in Italy. He returned to Lelouch to play a petty gangster in *La Voyou* (70), a pretty, tricksy thriller with a neat idea about kidnapping. In Spain he made *Las Secretas Intenciones*, playing an architect who becomes involved with a suicidal woman – for no salary, since he liked the script and director, who told him that he could not pay him; he had an agreement, however, to take the French rights if the film was successful – but, as he ruefully admitted, it was far from that. Then he returned to the world of jump-cuts, flash-forwards and dazzling photography, in Bertolucci's *Il Conformista* (71), a fascinating Pandora's Box of a movie – if a betrayal of the Alberto Moravia novel on which it was based; Trintignant played an Italian Fascist who turns to murder – because, as it turns out, he never had the courage to indulge his true sexual preference. Then he played a police inspector of a good workmanlike thriller – from a novel by Ed McBain, now set in Nice – *Sans Mobile Apparent*, one of his biggest successes, in France and abroad. In 1971 he played Hamlet again in Paris, but without success. For René Clément in Canada he made the unsuccessful *La Course du Lièvre à travers les Champes* (72), during the filming of which it was announced that he would turn director. That was delayed, however, while he made *L'Attentat* for director Yves Boisset, with Gian-Maria Volonte: a thriller based on the Moroccan politician who disappeared in Paris, scripted by Jorge Semprun. There was another transatlantic venture, Jacques Deray's *Un Homme est Mort/The Outside Man*, filmed in LA with Ann-Margret, Roy Scheider, etc., but one not likely to suggest a future for Franco-American co-productions; Trintignant played a hit man.

He directed, but did not appear in, *Une Journée Bien Remplie* (73), and his wife directed *Défense de Savoir*, in which he was an idealistic lawyer coming up against politicking. Both *Le Train* and *Les Violons du Bal* (74) were set at the German invasion of France; in the former, Trintignant was a humble radio repair man, as originally written by Simenon, and in the latter the father of a Jewish household and married to Marie-José Nat – whose husband, Michel Drach, wrote and directed from an incident in his own childhood. Trintignant had his life changed by a chance meeting with Jean-Pierre Cassel in *Le Mouton Enragé* and he had a supporting role in the Swiss *L'Escapade*, which he did to help it get launched. In *Le Secret* he had escaped from a mental home, becoming involved in the mountains with Philippe Noiret and Marlène Jobert – and, as directed by Robert Enrico, a thriller like they used to make, daft and riveting at the same time. *Le Jeu avec le Feu* (75) was, maybe, one of the sort of films no one should make – one of the minimal cinema exercises of Robbe-Grillet. Trintignant then made: *L'Agression*, as a bereaved husband bent on revenge; *Flic Story*, with Alain Delon, as a psychopath; *Il Pleure Sur Santiago*, a French-Bulgarian co-production, as a Chilean senator; *La Donna della Domenica* (76), as a wealthy homosexual murder suspect; and *L'Ordinateur des Pompes Funèbres*, as a henpecked insurance clerk who finds a perfect way to cause accidents. *Le Voyage de Noces* was directed by his wife and concerned a second honeymoon, in North Africa; *Il Deserto dei Tartari* was directed by Valerio Zurlini and concerned an army outpost – Trintignant was the doctor. He was a father menaced by another driver in *Les Passagers* (77) and in the Swiss *Repérages* he was involved in a production of 'Three Sisters'. In *L'Argent des Autres* (78) he had his biggest success in years – and the film won the Prix Delluc and the César for Best Film – as a bank executive who becomes the victim of an examination of corrupt practices. Trintignant was at his best, nervy and edgy; but in an era which has seen financial scandals

There is both a charm and edginess about Trintignant's screen persona which have caused him to be often cast as sexual misfits. In Bertolucci's Il Conformista *(71) he played a wealthy young Italian flirting with Fascism and turning to murder – all because, so we learnt from the final scene, he wished he had responded as a child to the chauffeur's advances.*

proliferate – certainly in Britain, France and the US – the film was superficial and far below films like *Z*, which it was emulating.

Trintignant returned to directing with *Le Maitre-Nageur* (79), starring Stefania Sandrelli as a girl fascinated by riches; he played the small role of the gardener. Then: *Melancoly Baby* in Switzerland, with Jane Birkin as a bored wife who wants to seduce him, her husband's best friend; Ettore Scola's *La Terrazza* (80), as a screenwriter; *La Banquière* with Romy Schneider; Claude Berri's *Je Vous Aime* (81) with Catherine Deneuve; *Un Assassin qui Passe* with Carol Laure, as a sexually repressed police inspector; Scola's *Passione d'Amore*, in a supporting role as an army doctor in this drama about a soldier (Bernard Giraudeau) falling in love with an ugly woman at a lonely outpost; de Challonge's *Malévil*, from a novel by Robert Merle (who asked for his name to be removed from the credits), as a Fascist survivor of a nuclear holocaust; *Eaux Profondes* with Isabelle Huppert, from a Patricia Highsmith story; *Une Affaire d'Homme* with Claude Brasseur as a police commissioner investigating the death of his best friend (Trintignant); *Le Grand Pardon* (82), an underworld melodrama in the style of *The Godfather*, as a xenophobic police inspector pursuing a family of Jewish criminals; Scola's *La Nuit à Varennes*, unbilled till the end credits, as the man who apprehended Louis XVI; *Colpire al Cuore*, in Italy, as a professor in conflict with his son; Philippe Labro's *Coverup 'Le Crime'* (83) with Brasseur, as a government minister implicated in crime; and *Under Fire* with Gene Hackman, playing a French double agent with an edgy, raddled charm. He said around this time that he preferred doing supporting roles and he had certainly chosen well for his first wholly English-language film. He had not had a real art-house success abroad since *Il Conformista*. He did have a leading role in *Vivement Dimanche!*, that of an estate agent whose secretary (Fanny Ardant) decides to go sleuthing. This was seen in foreign cinemas, since it was directed by Truffaut, but it was a poor thing compared to the Hollywood comedies it was emulating. Then: *Le Bon Plaisir* (84), as the French president, confronted by Deneuve who says he is the mother of her son; *Femmes de Personnes*, as a successful businessman loved by a doctor (Marthe Keller); Lelouch's *Vive la Vie* with Aimée, Michel Piccoli and Charles Aznavour; *L'Eté Prochaine* (85), directed by his wife, as a struggling playwright married to Ardant; Lelouch's absurd *Partir Revenir*, married to Annie Giradot and sheltering some Jews (Piccoli, Françoise Fabian); Téchiné's *Le Rendezvous*, as the father-in-law of the heroine (Juliette Binoche); *David, Thomas et les Autres/Sortüz Egy Fekete Biralyert*, a Franco-Hungarian co-production directed by Laszlo Szabo, as a schoolteacher in a small village just after the war; *Un Homme et une Femme: Vingt Ans Déjà*, with Aimée; *L'Homme aux Yeux d'Or*, again as a police inspector; *La Femme de ma Vie* (86), as an industrialist who helps the violinist hero (Christophe Malavoy); *Le Moustachu* (87), a spy thriller; Alain Tanner's autobiographical *La Vallée Fantôme*; and *Bunker Palace Hotel* (89), made in Belgrade.

Liv Ullmann

Liv Ullmann, to put it succinctly, is a superb actress. You would not know it from her films in English, but it is different with Ingmar Bergman. Bergman is one of the authentically great film creators of our time, not with range, but within his chosen field capable of exploration – notably in the field of male-female relationships. He has needed, and found, a team of wonderful actors for his expression of same: among the actors, Birger Malmsten, Gunnar Björnstrand, Jarl Kulle, Max von Sydow and Erland Josephson, and among the actresses Eva Dahlbeck, Harriet Andersson, Bibi Andersson, Ingrid Thulin and Gunnel Lindblom. Since he discovered Miss Ullmann – she became his mistress and the mother of their daughter – she became his own preferred interpreter of his female roles. It would be impossible to say whether she is better than his other players, but we can say that she constantly managed to surprise us, to take us off our guard. Probably no film actress hitherto had been asked to expose her thoughts and emotions so completely to us and she seems to do it without craft. She has, wrote A. Alvarez in the 'Observer', 'that undefinable quality which is neither a matter of looks nor even of acting ability; it is, instead, a weird chemical relationship with the camera, so that what appears on screen is not just a marvellous face or style but a complex, compelling presence, full of depths and indisputably alive.'

She was first alive in Tokyo, in 1938; her parents were Norwegian and her father was working in Japan designing aircraft. When Germany invaded Norway the family moved to Toronto and then New York; her father was killed in an accident before the war ended and his widow later went to live in Trondheim. When Liv was 17, she sent her to study acting at the Webber-Douglas School in London: what she learnt there did not get her accepted for the state theatre school in Oslo, but the repertory company in Stavanger took her and promptly put her in the lead of 'The Diary of Anne Frank'. She later starred on the Oslo stage, and on TV, and in 1960 married a psychiatrist. Her film career had started in a small role in *Fjolls till Fjells* (57), directed by Edith Carlmar, who later put her in the lead of *Ung Flukt* (59), as a loose young girl taught the joys of country life by her student lover – though one of them turns out to be the local farmer. As *The Wayward Girl*, this surfaced briefly in Britain in 1962; none of her pre-Bergman films was shown in the US.

She was Tonny's girlfriend in *Tonny* (62), who was one of society's misfits; after which she went to Sweden to do a film for Bjorn Henning-Jensen, *Kort ar Sommaren* (*Short is the Summer*), based on Knut Hamsen's novel 'Pan'. The leading roles were taken by Bibi Andersson and Jarl Kulle, he as a lieutenant with whom she is in love; Ullmann was her father's mistress, who also falls for the soldier. In Norway she was in *Der Kalte Ham Skarven* (65), the tale of a fisherman (Per Christensen) who has an accident; but meanwhile she had met Bergman – while walking in Stockholm with Miss Andersson. He had asked her whether she would like to be in one of his movies; the role he wrote for her was small, in a script he discarded when he became ill: but during his illness he fashioned *Persona* (66) for her and Andersson. She played a one-time actress confined to a clinic since an incident had deprived her of speech; Andersson was the nurse who shares with her a summer by the sea. There was perhaps madness here, and contagious: and similarly von Sydow was a troubled artist in *Vargtimmen* (*Hour of the Wolf*; 68), set again against seas and skies. Ullmann was his wife, unable to help him. In *Skammen* (*The Shame*) they were again husband and wife, isolated farmers, caught up in civil war: the film is an experience of war and a masterpiece – which leaves no word for *En Passion* (*A Passion; Passion for Anna*; 69), but then how do you summarize a Bergman film in one sentence? This one concerns a marriage and the accompanying pain and misery. The married couple were again Ullmann and von Sydow, joined in their lonely hell by (Bibi) Andersson and Erland Josephson, a quartet of matchless players in one of the densest and greatest of all films.

Ullmann returned to Norway to play the title-role in *An-Margrit*, directed by Arne Skouen from 'Nattens Bröd' by Johan Falkbergets, about an impoverished orphan girl coping with difficulties in a mining town in the 1600s. It was in Denmark and Sweden that she made *The Night Visitor* for director Laslo Benedek, an inauspicious beginning to her international career – but appropriate, in that to date it has been studded with disasters: this supposed thriller about a man who leaves a mental clinic to murder – von Sydow, heading a team of British and Scandinavian actors – received a couple of scattered dates two years later, in 1971, and was then sold to TV. She and von Sydow should have been in *Man's Fate*, with David Niven, when MGM cancelled it – on the morning shooting was to begin. *Da la Part des Copains/L'Uomo dalle Ombre/Cold Sweat* (71) was a thriller which wasted her and James Mason, if not Charles Bronson, whose wife she played. In fact, Ullmann's name first became widely known through two Swedish epics directed by Jan Troell, *Utvandrama* (*The Emigrants*; 72) and its sequel *Nybyggarna* (*The New Land*), each three hours long and based on four novels by Vilhelm Moberg, set back in the 19th century and, after an opening in Sweden, in the US. Ullmann's husband was again von Sydow – and Troell indeed got little from either player, in what seemed a very sluggish trek indeed. The first was so much disliked in Britain that the second was never imported – in contrast to the very warm welcome in the US.

In Britain, Ullmann played *Pope Joan*, a historical fiasco; but Bergman meanwhile had decided to renew his relationship with Ullmann – professionally, that is. With Thulin and Harriet Andersson she became one of three sisters in a household of death: *Viskningar od Rop* (*Cries and Whispers*) was an elegant chamber-work, but often too much like self-parody. Its press reception was better than for any Bergman film in years, which did not surprise cynics, aware that his reputation fluctuated while those of the myriad lesser directors did not – and had been at its lowest while making his finest films. The raves in the US coincided with a 'Time' cover for Ullmann, at that time embarked on her second Hollywood movie. The pathetic musical remake of *Lost Horizon* (73) was first . . . from which it had to be a step up to *Forty Carats*, in the role Julie Harris had taken on Broadway. Since that required a lady of a certain age, the publicity went – doubtless truthfully – that a great many stars had begged to play it (including Audrey Hepburn and Elizabeth Taylor). With Liv, the lady looked much younger, which destroyed half the point: what is clear is that both the producer and the begetters of *Lost Horizon* were less aware of Ullmann's abilities than hoping for another, younger, Bergman (i.e. Ingrid). Both ladies were Scandinavian; but it was imperceptive of them. *Forty Carats* failed because it threw out farce for Great Romance – spring-summer variety – which it handled in clumsy fashion; young Edward Albert and Ullmann brought conviction, but her role

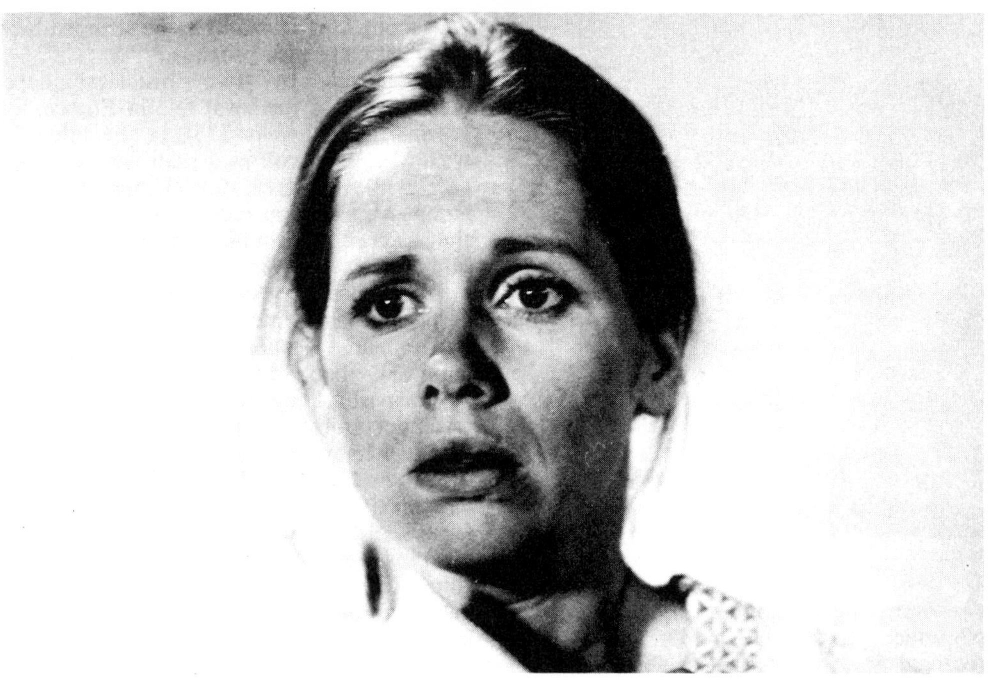

Liv Ullmann, peerless interpreter for a great film-maker: in Face to Face *(76), the study of a failing marriage.*

needed the sort of comedy expertise it took the great American comediennes years to acquire. The industry, not understanding that, blamed Ullmann for the film's failure: and, alas, she had already signed for two more English-language movies – neither of which, to put it mildly, were well received. She was at least sensibly cast in the title-role of *Zandy's Bride* (74), arriving mail-order for Gene Hackman: but the thing was another ghastly Hollywood idea, having brought over Troell to direct it. Maybe her English was not good: she was not competing with Garbo when she played Queen Christina, since *The Abdication* found that lady in Rome, but, as the 'New York Daily News' put it, 'The dialogue is so silly it could easily have been written by Yoko Ono.' Bergman again came to the rescue, with *Scenerur ett Aktenskap* (*Scenes From a Marriage*), a six-part TV series which he recut and shortened for cinemas. It was a marriage – to Josephson – which failed and the film was often a painful experience (in a different way from *Lost Horizon*) as he stripped bare these basically nice people.

Undeterred by two historical flops, Ullmann did a medieval tale in France, for Juan Buñuel, *Leonor* (75), in the title-role, with Michel Piccoli as a man who makes a pact with the devil. 'Liv Ullmann as the vampirish love figure, is more effective than she has been in most pix outside Scandinavia,' said 'Variety'. *Ansikte mot Ansikte* (*Face to Face*; 76) had also been a TV series – in four parts – but this time had been planned with the cinema version in mind. Bergman admitted that the central character, a psychiatrist (Ullmann), was suffering from a crisis not unlike some unexplained anxieties that had happened to himself. This woman tried to find meaning in her real world (work, daughter, grandparents, absent husband, friends, colleagues) while increasingly escaping into the dreams of a would-be suicide: physician, heal thyself, examined in detail and complexity – and 'searingly impersonated by one of the greatest actresses of our age', as John Coleman put it in the 'New Statesman'. She received the New York critics' Best Actress award for both this and *Scenes From a Marriage*. But: again from the heights to the pits, playing a Dutchwoman helping Our Boys in a war film of searing simplicity, *A Bridge Too Far* (77). By now it was an accepted fact that between the Bergmans, Ullmann would make some of the worst films of our time: she began to decline the offers, turning instead to the theatre – 'Anna Christie' in New York at this time. When she rejoined Bergman, it was in Munich and in Norway – after his self-imposed exile which followed a clash with the tax authorities. He had permitted – for the first time – *Face to Face* to be premièred abroad in a dubbed version; both *The Serpent's Egg/Das Schlangerei* and *Autumn Sonata* (78) were filmed in English. The former was a compendium of received opinion about Berlin in the 20s, with Ullmann in frilly garters as a cabaret performer involved with (a phrase this time most accurate) an American Jew, David Carradine; and the film itself was a curate's egg, astonishingly good in parts. The latter was another chamber-piece, with Ingrid Bergman as the concert-pianist mother in full confrontation with her somewhat inhibited daughter (Ullmann), now married to a country parson. Impossible to say which actress was the more mesmerizing, but perhaps in the end it is Ullmann's face one best remembers, eyes strained behind round glasses, trying, as ever, to make sense out of life.

In Australia in 1978 she did a double-bill of Chekhov's 'The Bear' and 'The Human Voice', and she repeated the latter in New York in 1979, for one week at $100 a ticket, giving her services free – and all proceeds to charity. She was in Manhattan warming up for Richard Rodgers's musical version of 'I Remember Mama', which did not run as long as anyone would have liked. She did 'The Human Voice' for TV and then went to Britain to make a telefilm (though it did play briefly in cinemas), *Richard's Things* (80), adapted by Frederic Raphael from his own novel. It remains among the best things she has done in English, playing a recently bereaved widow amazed to find that her husband had a mistress and then that she is sexually attracted to her. In Canada she wrote, directed and acted in her own sequence of a feminist movie, *Love*, which does not seem to have been shown; in Washington, DC, she was in 'Ghosts' (82) and there was more Ibsen waiting in Australia, *The Wild Duck* (83), in a modern transposition with Jeremy Irons, directed by Henri Safran. A tele-movie, *Prisoner Without Name, Cell Without Number*, misused her, Roy Scheider and its source, Jacobo Timerman's account of his newspaper attack on the Argentine Government and his subsequent fate. Better was Daniel Petrie's autobiographical *Bay Boy* (84), set in Nova Scotia in 1936, with Keifer Sutherland as her son, but hers was a thankless role; and she was hardly better served by *La Diagonale du Fou* (85), a Swiss film about chess with Leslie Caron and company, or Harold Pinter's 'Old Times', with which she made her London stage début. It was true that she had difficulty finding superior material now that Bergman had retired from film-making, though she had told him that she did not want to work with him again – not for any personal reason, but because what he required her to do was too agonizing: and if the script she sent back unread was *Fanny and Alexander* then it was her loss as well as ours.

Still, it was a shame to see her in a superficial Italian comedy, *Speriamo che sia Femmina* (86), as the estranged wife of a philandering count (Philippe Noiret). She remained in the peninsula for *Mosca Addio* (87), playing a Jewish dissident in Moscow: the producer said he turned down an offer from Joanne Woodward, and others by Kazan, Coppola and Zinnemann; Mauro Bolognini directed, as he did a mini-series from Moravia, *Gli Indifferenti*. *Gaby, a True Story* was American, but set in Mexico, in the 30s, with Ullmann as an Austro-Jewish refugee with a paraplegic daughter, and then she travelled South for a German-Argentine production, *L'Amiga* (88), the tale of two friends in Buenos Aires over the years: one (Ullmann) remains to oppose the regime while the other is an actress who seeks refuge in Germany. Since then she has made *The Rose Garden* (89), with von Sydow and Eli Wallach.

Ullmann in The Serpent's Egg *(77), as a cabaret performer in the Berlin of the 20s; and, (below), with Ingrid Bergman in* Autumn Sonata *(78), a portrait of a mother-daughter relationship.*

Peter Ustinov

Peter Ustinov can do almost anything in show business. He has written plays ('The Banbury Nose', 'Halfway Up the Tree', a dozen others) and directed them; he has directed movies and operas; he has written screenplays, fiction ('The Loser', 'Add a Dash of Pity', etc.) and he has had considerable success as a conversationalist and raconteur on TV programmes. All of which bespeaks a formidable intelligence – though, to put it mildly, opinion has been divided as to the merits of the plays (at least). Where acting is concerned, there has never been any dissent: the unwieldly Ustinov has consistently had raves and is solidly entrenched as one of the few character actors who is also a star attraction.

The multi-talents are perhaps inherited: his father was a journalist and his mother a writer, both White Russians. His uncle was Alexandre Benois, Diaghilev's designer. He was born in London in 1921 and trained to be an actor under Michel St Denis. He made his first stage appearance at a small theatre in Shere as Waffles in 'The Wood Demon' (38), was in rep for a while and made his London reputation in a series of revues, 1940–41, 'Diversion', etc. An article by James Agate about a play he had written did not hurt him either. He made his screen bow in a short, *Hullo Fame* (40), followed by *Mein Kampf My Crimes*, a semi-documentary in which he played that unhappy Dutchman who took the rap for the Reichstag fire. He played a German schoolboy in *The Goose Steps Out* (42) and a Dutch Resistance worker in *One of Our Aircraft is Missing*, and then joined the army. During his service career he worked on the screenplay of, and acted in, *The Way Ahead* (44), the semi-official army film; after demob, he directed and wrote *School for Secrets* (46), starring Ralph Richardson, and *Vice Versa* (47), with Roger Livesey. On the stage he acted in 'Crime and Punishment' and in 'Frenzy,' his own version of the Swedish film of that name (*Hets* in Swedish); he returned to films with his own version of Eric Linklater's novel *Private Angelo* (49), co-directing and starring as the conniving, bumbling Italian soldier of the title, in this soporific account of some wartime wanderings.

Great things had been expected of that movie, as they usually are of one-man-bands who get involved with films; Ustinov retreated to a supporting role in someone else's movie: *Odette* (50) with Anna Neagle, as a kindly Frenchman. Afterwards, however, he had a lead in *Hotel Sahara* (51) with Yvonne de Carlo and David Tomlinson, and was very funny as the harassed, compliant Arab hotelier; in *The Magic Box*, the Festival of Britain film, he was wordless as a dandified film industryite. He made his international reputation with his light-hearted interpretation of Nero in the otherwise unendurable *Quo Vadis?* (52), around which time he had his biggest playwriting success, in London (where he acted in it) and New York (with Rex Harrison), 'The Love of Four Colonels'. Because of his Nero, there were Hollywood film offers: *Beau Brummell* (54), as that gentleman's 'fat friend', the Prince Regent;

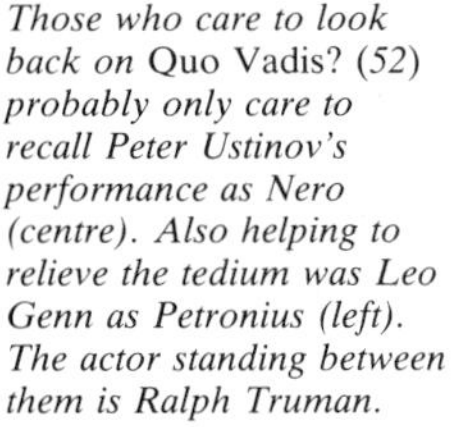

Those who care to look back on Quo Vadis? *(52) probably only care to recall Peter Ustinov's performance as Nero (centre). Also helping to relieve the tedium was Leo Genn as Petronius (left). The actor standing between them is Ralph Truman.*

The Egyptian (55), as Edmund Purdom's opportunistic servant (a film he loathed making so much that he refused to see it and which he had only agreed to do because Brando was originally cast); and *We're No Angels* (55), making that claim along with fellow convicts Humphrey Bogart and Aldo Ray.

He returned to Europe to play the ringmaster in Max Ophüls's beautiful study of the 19th-century courtesan *Lola Montez*, with Martine Carol, made in three versions (French, English, German) and a great flop in all of them; the cost had been envisaged at 150 million francs, but it went to over 650 million – then the final print(s) were hacked about, sometimes reducing Ustinov's role (Ophüls framed the story in a circus). He made three more films on the Continent: *I Girovaghi* (57), with Abbe Lane, as an itinerant puppeteer in Sicily; *Un Angel Paso sobre Brooklyn/Un Angelo Passò per Brooklyn*, a vehicle for the Spanish child star Pablito Calvo, as the heavy; and Clouzot's *Les Espions* (58), as a Russian espionage chief, with Curt Jurgens as a scientist. These were made during intervals from his own play, 'Romanoff and Juliet', which he played in London, New York and on tour in the US over this period. After *Spartacus* (60) in Hollywood, as a Roman slave-dealer – a performance which won him a Best Supporting Oscar – and *The Sundowners* (61), as an Australian layabout, he persuaded Universal to back a film of *Romanoff and Juliet* on the strength of its American success (and also because he had worked, uncredited, on the script of *Spartacus*). He directed and produced this so-called satire on Cold War relations, about the offspring of the Russian and American ambassadors in a mythical country – and acted in it, fortunately, as the local prime minister.

Conversely, he could only get backing from a very minor company for *Billy Budd* (62), which he had prepared from Melville's novel, and it turned out infinitely better than anything else he had done as writer or director, beautifully acted by himself, Robert Ryan, Terence Stamp, Melvyn Douglas, Paul Rogers and John Neville. In Britain, the only country where it was properly exploited, it did well. Then he acted in his own play, 'Photo-Finish', damply received in London (62) and New York (63). He gave another typical performance, one of his sly, clumsy rogues, in Jules Dassin's *Topkapi* (64), and it was so hugely enjoyable that he got a second (Best Supporting) Oscar. But he, as an Arab chieftain, and Shirley MacLaine were felled by the script of *John Goldfarb Please Come Home*. MGM entrusted to him the script and direction of *Lady L* (65), with Sophia Loren, and he entrusted to himself a brief minor role, an absent-minded prince: but he played it as predictably as his other work on the film. The theatre engaged him, till he played a South American ambassador, Elizabeth Taylor's husband, in *The Comedians* (67), progressively losing interest in the proceedings. He had the title-role in a Disney fantasy, *Bluebeard's Ghost* (68), and was a lovable larcenist who beats the computers in *Hot Millions*: he played delightfully and is perhaps responsible for what is best in a script which underwent many vicissitudes. Changing his nationality again, he was a Mexican general in an unsuccessful spoof of US history, *Viva Max!* (69). In 1971 he was in Israel making an American-backed film, *Big Mack and Little Claire*, which has never been publicly seen. Robert Ellis Miller directed this romance with Francesca Annis and Perry King; Ustinov played a taxi-driver and he says he is 'very proud' of his performance. Whatever his contribution to another film with the Burton-Taylor team, *Hammersmith Is Out* (72), he cannot be exonerated; for he not only acted but directed it. Another Disney fantasy, *One Of Our Dinosaurs Is Missing* (75), found him

Peter Ustinov's film of Herman Melville's Billy Budd *(62) is easily the best he has made as writer and director. It also contains his best serious performance, as the Captain, and an excellent one by Robert Ryan as the bullying master-of-arms Claggart.*

as a Chinese Intelligence man in London in the 20s, a role he attacked with relish; in *Logan's Run* (76) he was a senile old man several years from hence – and this sci-fi tale with Michael York and Jenny Agutter was not a success. There was another for Disney, *Treasure of Matecumbe*, as a medicine man once again making up for patches of dullness.

He played a mysterious German in *Un Taxi Mauve/A Purple Taxi* (77), a French film made in Eire, with Charlotte Rampling and Edward Albert: a success in France (the book had been a bestseller), it had a sole US booking and none in Britain till sold to TV. Would we had been so lucky with *The Last Remake of Beau Geste*, some gags indiscriminately assembled and directed by Marty Feldman! Most of them seemed to be about the wooden leg of the villainous Foreign Legion sergeant – who was Ustinov, once more consoling us in poor material. He played a screenwriter in *Doppio Delitto*, with Marcello Mastroianni, and was said to be writing a screenplay of 'Gulliver's Travels'; he published a memoir, 'Dear Me'. As Hercule Poirot, Agatha Christie's Belgian sleuth, he gave a scrupulous, understated performance in *Death on the Nile* (78), an improvement on its predecessor (*Murder on the Orient Express*); but from that comparative high he hit low – twice, in two Oriental adventures – *Ashanti* (79), as the wicked slave-trader, and *The Thief of Bagdad*, the worst of the four film versions, as the Caliph and father of the heroine (played by his own daughter, Pavla). He has been married twice to actresses, Isolde Denham and Suzanne Cloutier, and remarried in 1972.

A French movie, *Nous Maigrirons Ensemble*, was described by 'Variety' as 'an embarrassment', a description equally applicable to the American *Charlie Chan and the Dragon Queen* (81). He guested in *The Great Muppet Caper* and provided a voice for one of the animated characters in the Australian *Grendel, Grendel, Grendel*. He returned to Poirot for *Evil Under the Sun* (82), definitely not the best of the series, and it may have been a relief after a West End play which flopped, 'Overheard' – and the same might be said of a BBC-West German co-production, *Imaginary Friends* (83), after 'Beethoven's Tenth', in which this time he also appeared. Yet the biggest disappointment of Ustinov's career may be *Memed My Hawk* (84), based on the novel by Yashar Kemal, which he had dreamed of filming for 20 years. He was star, producer, director and writer – as well as backer, to the tune of £250,000 when there was trouble with the financiers (the total cost was £1.5 million, with Yugoslavia standing in for Turkey). The reviews in Britain were devastating – and they were not even kind towards his performance, as an incompetent, tyrannical landowner in conflict with young rebel Memed (Simon Dutton); a belated reception in the US was no kinder. It was back to Poirot: *Thirteen for Dinner* (85), *Dead Man's Folly* (86) and *Murder in Three Acts*, all for television. He reprised the Belgian detective for the big screen in *Appointment With Death* (88), but its reception suggested that the public fascination with Mrs Christie's tired tales was finally dwindling. In Paris he was one of many names, chiefly French, in a bicentennial tribute to *The French Revolution* (89) and in Rome he co-starred with Roberto Alpi in *Paradiso dei Cani*.

Alida Valli

If you stopped going to the cinema around 1950 you will probably remember Alida Valli – or mere 'Valli' as she was billed – as one of Hollywood's least impressive continental imports. If, however, you have seen her in any two or three of the films she has made since, you will probably regard her as one of the half-dozen best actresses in the world. Being basically a romantic player she specializes in ageing women-in-love, women obsessed, desperate, anguished women. The smile is melancholy, but the expression is hopeful, anxious to help: this is a woman, like Garbo, who wants to give. It was as a latter-day Garbo that Hollywood publicized her; and it is a matter of mystery why she so signally failed to live up to it.

When she went there she was Italy's leading female star. She was born in Pola in 1921, the daughter of a journalist of Austrian descent. In 1928 the family moved to Como; when she was 15 Valli went to Rome to study at the motion picture academy founded by Mussolini (the Centro Sperimentale di Cinematografia). She was given a one-reel test and as a result a small part – bottom of the cast-list – in *Il Cappello a Tre Punte* (35), one of the many screen versions of 'The Three-Cornered Hat' by Pedro de Alarcon, with Peppino and Eduardo De Filippo. That got her a more important part in *I Due Sergenti* (36), with Gino Cervi, from Aubigny's play about love and espionage during the Napoleonic Wars, followed by roles in *Il Feroce Saladino* (37), starring Angelo Musco, and *L'Ultima Nemica*, starring Fosco Giachetti as a doctor struggling against disease. She was the thoughtless daughter in a family comedy with the De Filippo brothers, *Sono Stato Io*, and also with them she appeared in another comedy, *Ma L'Amore mio Non Muore* (38).

The same company, Amato, kept her on for one of the leads in *La Casa del Peccato* which starred Assia Norris and Amadeo Nazzari (then and for some years Italy's leading male star). The director was Max Neufeld, who gave her her first star role, in a social comedy, *Mille Lire al Mese*, as a girl with rival suitors, Umberto Melnati and Renato Cialente. Mario Mattoli directed her in *L'Ha Fatto una Signora*, and thus she was in one of the last 'white telephone' films (the expression used to describe the frivolous Italian films of this era); and *Assenza Ingiustificata* (39), with Nazzari and Paolo Stoppa.

Her first star part in a serious role was as *Manon Lescaut*, the Abbé Prevost's trollop, with Vittorio De Sica as des Grieux, and Puccini's music, serviceably directed by Carmine Gallone. 'The New York Times' found her 'not only tremulously beautiful but emotionally sincere'. Italciné signed her to a five-year contract and put her into two films directed by Neufeld, *Ballo al Castello*, a sort of musical, with Antonio Centa, and *Taverna Rossa*, a comedy. They then loaned her out for Carmine Gallone's *L'Oltre l'Amore* (40), opposite Nazzari, a version of Stendhal's 'Vanina Vanini' with Verdi's music. There followed *La Prima Donna che Passa*, a comedy directed by Neufeld with Carlo Lombardi; then Mario Soldati's almost perfect version of a novel by Antonio Fogazzaro, *Piccolo Mondo Antico*, a genuinely touching period piece, with Massimo Serato as the wealthy scion cast out by his family for marrying her. What, however, made it memorable was her performance (she won an acting award at the – wartime – Venice festival that year). Because of both critical raves and box-office success, she became Italy's leading female star.

She was loaned out for Gallone's *L'Amante Segreta* (41), with Giachetti, and then she made three films for director Mattoli: *Ore Nove Lezione di Chimica*, a stagey drama in which she was a schoolgirl in love with professor Andrea Checchi; *Luce nella Tenebre*, with Giachetti, and *Catene Invisibile* (42), a heavy drama about an industrialist's cynical young daughter, and her problems with her engineer lover (Carlo Ninchi) and half-brother (Andrea Checchi). *Le Due Orfanelle* was a popular French sob-story already filmed several times – this time by Gallone, with Toto; Valli and Maria Dennis were the unfortunate orphans in the France of Louis XV. *Noi Viva* was directed by Goffredo Alessandrini and adapted from a novel by Ayn Rand ('We the Living') set during the Russian Revolution. The cast included Fosco Giachetti, Rossano Brazzi and, most notably, Valli in a shawl to give it a Russian flavour. A second part was released the following year, *Addio Kira!*, and was, needless to say, equally anti-Communist. She played Nedda in a poor version of *I Pagliacci*; then a singer turned prostitute in Mattoli's *Stasera Niente di Nuovo*, in love with alcoholic journalist Carlo Ninchi (it ended tragically – she died). Then Italciné was closed down for political reasons. Valli did two movies for another studio, both romantic dramas directed by Mario Camerini, *Apparizone* (43) with Massimo Girotti and *T'Amero Sempre* with Cervi as the accountant who loves her, an abandoned, unmarried mother.

The Nazis entered Rome after Italy signed the armistice with the Allies and Valli was petitioned by the reconstituted Nazi Party in Venice to go there to film but preferred to go into hiding; Continentale in Paris also made approaches but she claimed she had retired. In 1944 she married pianist and composer Oscar de Mejo (who went with her to Hollywood where he composed 'All I Want for Christmas is My Two Front Teeth'). In 1945 her mother was shot as a collaborator. She returned to films, under contract to Minerva-Savoia: *Il Caneto della Vita* (45) and *Giovanna*, both directed by Gallone; and *La Vita Ricomincia*, which started well with the return of a POW (Fosco Giachetti), but descended to melodrama when he discovered that wife Valli had killed the man she had 'given herself to' to save their baby's life. Mattoli's *Circo Equestre Za-Bum* was escapist stuff, as was Soldati's careful version of Balzac, *Eugenia Grandet* (47), very good as that sad, proud lady.

Hollywood beckoned. More than any other producer, David O. Selznick was obsessed with Garbo and when that lady showed a reluctance to sign any contract with him he looked at dozens of European movies to find a substitute. Impressed by Valli in the Balzac film, he signed her to a long-term contract. All the same, he did not put her into *The Paradine Case* (48) until negotiations with Garbo broke down completely. She played a wife accused of murder with whom defending counsel Gregory Peck falls in love. Hitchcock, directing, has said that Selznick insisted on using her – though it must have been apparent from the first day's rushes that the vivacious Valli of Italian movies had been converted to a non-expressive frump. Critics and filmgoers were unimpressed and *The Miracle of the Bells*, on loan to RKO, did not help any, as a Polish girl who rises from burlesque to great movie star (she was dead when it started and was only seen in flash-back). After a year, she appeared in *The Third Man* (49), as the ballerina who had loved Harry Lime: a better performance, but wan, and it really seemed that she had not much command of the English language. Selznick loaned her out for two films and then dropped her. She was better in these two, for RKO: *The White Tower* (50) with Glenn Ford, as a girl with ambitions to climb the Alp of the title; and *Walk Softly Stranger*, as a girl in a wheelchair who reforms Joseph Cotten.

There was an offer from France: Yves Allégret's *Les Miracles n'ont Lieu qu'une Fois* (51) with Jean Marais, the story of two students in Paris in 1939 who meet again in Italy in 1950. Said 'Variety': 'Alida Valli does a fine job of etching the young, ardent girl and the disillusioned woman.' She returned to Italy for a reunion with Nazzari – playing her husband: *Ultimo Incontro*, from Marco Praga's 'La Biondino', about an erring wife blackmailed into working part-time in a high-class bordello (the title refers to what happens when Nazzari finds her there). This was by far her best performance since her pre-Hollywood days. In that city she was sought for the role of the countess in *Five Fingers*, but she claimed that she loathed flying and could not get there in time. That sealed her Hollywood career. In private life her marriage had broken up (they were officially separated in 1952) and she had shared an apartment with compatriot Valentina Cortese until the latter married Richard Basehart in 1951. (Cortese was under contract to 20th, for whom she did some good work – *Thieves' Highway, The House on Telegraph Hill*, etc. The two of them were among some notable European talents – Signe Hasso, Viveca Lindfors – who failed to make out in the US at this time. Cortese and Basehart later worked mainly in Italy.) In 1953 Valli left the US with her two sons and resumed her European career.

It cannot be said that *The Lovers of Toledo/ Les Amants de Tolède* (53) did much for her, a grandiose co-production (filmed in English, French, Spanish and Italian) which was an 'extremely tedious' ('MFB') version of Stendhal's 'Le Coffre et le Revenant', directed by Henri Decoin. She was a fiery Spanish belle, Pedro Armendariz was the police chief obsessed with her and Françoise Arnoul was her rival. In Italy she did *Il Mondo le Condanna*, as an ex-whore trying to go straight with Nazzan; and *Siamo Donne*, an episode film with Magnani, Ingrid Bergman and Isa Miranda. Valli's was by far the best; she played herself – with both delicacy and self-parody – in an anecdote about a star slumming, tempted to steal her hairdresser's boyfriend. In *The Stranger's Hand/La Mano dello Straniero*, written and part-produced by Graham Greene, she played a hotel receptionist in a way that did nothing to further her reputation.

But then she gave a sensitive and haunting portrayal in Visconti's *Senso* (54), as a Venetian countess who falls adulterously in love with an Austrian officer (Farley Granger) and hands over to him the party funds. Gavin Lambert thought it 'a remarkable performance, both credible and frightening in the stages of decline' and it won her the Best

Alida Valli in the caserne: she has fallen passionately in love with a young Austrian officer and so forgets herself as to go, if veiled, to look for him. A scene from Visconti's deeply romantic Senso *(54), in which she gives one of her greatest performances.*

Actress award at the Venice festival. The film itself was cut for political reasons in Italy and then hacked and badly dubbed for showing in the US and Britain as *The Wanton Countess*. Later, the complete version was to reveal itself as the peak of romantic film-making. Around the same time Valli was the chief movie name to be involved in the Montesi scandal (1954–57); a girl was found dead on a beach and Piero Piccioni, the son of a former Foreign Minister, was accused among rumours of drugs and sex. Valli claimed that Piccioni was with her at the time of the murder, in Carlo Ponti's villa.

Perhaps because of the scandal she did not film for some time and her next two parts were small – though the one in Antonioni's *Il Grido* (57) was the key role, refusing to marry the man she lives with (Steve Cochran) – so that he sets out on the odyssey which will lead him to disintegration. It could not be said that she was convincing as a working-class woman, but she was marvellous in *La Diga sul Pacifico/This Angry Age*, as the floozie who 'befriends' Anthony Perkins in a cinema. She co-starred with Yves Montand in *La Grande Strada Azzura/Un dénommé Squarcio* (58) and then supported Brigitte Bardot in *Les Bijoutiers du Clair de Lune*, as her Spanish aunt. In Spain she did *Tal Vez Manaña*; in Italy *L'Uomo dai Calzoni Corti*, the adventures of a small boy; and in France *Les Yeux sans Visage* (59), Franju's undistinguished horror film, as the assistant of 'mad' professor Pierre Brasseur. She appeared on the Paris stage in 'Vu du Pont' with Raf Vallone and filmed mainly in France: *Signé Arsène Lupin*, an attempt to resurrect that gentleman thief, with Robert Lamoreux and Valli as his rival-cum-mistress. Then she was a moving Mother Superior in *La Dialogue des Carmélites* (60), with Jeanne Moreau; and one of the victims of *Le Gigolo*, a modestly entertaining piece with Jean-Claude Brialy in the title-role. She returned to Italy for two: *Treno di Natale*, a 'train' thriller, with Nazzari again, and Jack Palance as the criminal who has taken over that train, and *I Peccati degli Anni Verdi* (61), a poor romantic drama with Maurice Ronet.

Once more there came a fine film and a great performance: Henri Colpi's *Une Aussi Longue Absence*, a gentle picture about a saloon-keeper who recognizes in an amnesiac clochard (George Wilson) the husband she lost in the war. The sensitivity and sensibility of her performance were matched by Wilson. After which it was a shame to see her supporting Rita Hayworth in *The Happy Thieves* (62), as a duchess – not that you might have seen her at all in *La Fille du Torrent*, which seems to have disappeared after one booking in Nice. In that she was a possessive mother. And the next was not so lucky – one she went to South America to do – a co-production (Brazil-France-Argentine) directed by Leopoldo Torre Nilsson from a play by his wife Beatriz Guido, *Homenaje a la Hora de la Siesta/Quatre Femmes pour un Héros*, in which Paul Guers was investigating the deaths of four martyred men and she was the widow of one of them – not one of Torre Nilsson's more persuasive films. And a Spanish venture was not seen abroad: *Al Otro Lado de la Ciudad*, directed by Alfonzo Balcazar. But Claude Chabrol cast her as Gertrude in a black joke called *Ophélia*, about a young man who insists on finding the Court of Denmark on his country estate: perhaps too clever, because it too failed at the box-office.

George Wilson and Alida Valli in Une Aussi Longue Absence *(61). He was a* clochard *probably suffering from amnesia, she was the* patronne *of a suburban bar who insists that he is her long-lost husband.*

Le Désordre/Il Disordine (63) was a tedious tale of high life that wasted her, as a mother obsessed by jealousy, along with George Wilson, Susan Strasberg, Jean Sorel, Curt Jurgens and Renato Salvatori. Then she crossed the Atlantic again for *El Hombre de Papel*, a sombre Mexican drama about a deaf-mute who finds that wealth does not bring happiness. She went to Spain for a dim role in *The Castilian*, with Broderick Crawford, and was there again for a French film, *L'Autre Femme* (64), a triangle drama about a visiting Frenchwoman (Annie Girardot), Valli and Richard Johnson. Then she was in *Umorismo Nero* (65) in the episode 'La Cornacchia', with Folco Lulli. Her only appearance in some years was in a minute part in Pasolini's *Edipo Re* (67) and there were reports of personal problems. She returned to filming in *Le Champignon* (70), a drama about a doctor who takes to drugs, directed by Marc Simenon (George's son) and starring his wife, Mylène Demongeot, and Jean-Claude Bouillon. But then Valli had a marvellous part in Bertolucci's *Strategia del Ragno* (made for TV, but shown abroad in cinemas), from a novel by Jorge Luis Borges, as the mistress of a dead hero trying to persuade his son to avenge his death. It was a film heavy with enigma, but her equivocal performance kept the balance right. Then she did *Concerto per Pistola Solista* (71), with Anna Moffo, a crime story filmed in Suffolk, and was on the stage in Milan in 'Lulu'.

After playing the mother of a young conscript (Donatello) in *Diario di un Italiano* (72) and Alain Delon's mother in Zurlini's *La Prima Notte del Quiete*, she was again up to her ears in horror, this time drug-induced: *L'Occhio nel Labirinto* (73), as a strange woman who opens her door when Rosemary Dexter is looking for her boyfriend. She and Fernando Rey were the wealthy parents of a megalomaniacal David Hemmings in *No Es Nada Mama, Solo un Juego* (74), a Spanish-Venezuelan co-production, directed by a veteran from the latter, José Maria Forque, and received in the former territory with very mixed notices. She was the wife of Peter Cushing, a 'horror' actor who is trying to retire, in *La Grande Trouille*, a comedy; and she remained in France to do supporting chores in *La Chair de l'Orchidée* (75), a thriller, and *Ce Cher Victor*, based on a long-running stage comedy about a gay couple (Bernard Blier, Jacques Dufilho), one of them murderous. In the first she had just one scene as a madwoman who talks to Charlotte Rampling at a railway station. Both *L'Anticristo* and *La Casa del Exorcismo* were rip-offs of *The Exorcist*; the former starred Mel Ferrer as a prince and Arthur Kennedy as a bishop; in the latter Robert Alda was the priest, Telly Savalas the butler who arranged the wax dummies and Elke Sommer the girl with demons. Valli, in this one, was the possessive mother in this house of horror and the film itself had a history: it was directed in 1972 by Mario Bava under a pseudonym and had had about 10 title changes before being offered to an unastounded public. The level stayed low with Bertolucci's *Novecento* (76), as an impoverished widow, now mad, who ends impaled on the railings; but it rose with *Il Caso Raoul*, the case history of a mentally sick man (Stanko Molnar) – she was his adoptive mother. And *Le Jeu du Solitaire* was a film of moods and nuances, if few of them new: about a Paris psychiatrist (Sami Frey) drawn to the orphan boy he thinks killed his son. Valli owned the Provence farm on which it all took place. She was one of the passengers making *The Cassandra Crossing* (77) and one of the schoolteachers suspected of horrors in *Suspiria*, lending, said Scott Meek in the 'MFB', 'exactly the right sort of overblown presence'; after which she did a minor comedy with Roberto Benigni, *Berlinguer, Ti Voglio Bene*. Her best film in some time was *Cuore Semplice*, from Flaubert's story, as the wealthy widow who takes its heroine (Adriana Asti) as her servant; that was followed by a weird French abstract, *Zoo Zèro* (79), playing an ogress, *Porco Mondo* with Arthur Kennedy and Bertolucci's *La Luna* with Jill Clayburgh. *Suor Omicidi* starred Anita Ekburg, and was the tale of that Belgian convent-lady who had been indulging in just about every crime in the book. A busy year concluded with *Indagine su un Delitto Perfetto* with Leonard Mann and Anthony Steel.

In Dario Argento's *Inferno* (80) she plunged to her death in flames; and after Comenici's *Tutti gli Volevano Tanto Bene* she was in Madrid, playing a schizoid in another (above average) horror movie, *Aquella Casa en las Afueras*. *Sezona Mira u Parizu* (81) was a Yugoslav film set in Paris, also engaging the services of Erland Josephson and Maria Schneider, but Valli was back in Italy for *La Caduta degli Angeli Ribelli*, which starred Clio Goldsmith as a girl who has an affair with a terrorist; Valli's performance as the housekeeper brought her the Donatello award (equivalent to an Oscar) for Best Supporting Actress. *Aspern* (82) was a Portuguese version of a Henry James story in French directed by Eduardo de Gregorio, with Bulle Ogier, Jean Sorel and Valli as the old lady whose letters he was after. But with the youngsters miscast and the action transferred from Venice to Lisbon in the present-day, even she could not make it watchable. Understandably, she was off the screen for some time – till there was a good offer from Giuseppe Bertolucci (Bernardo's brother) to play in *Segreti Segreti* (85), four parallel stories concerning terrorism. Her next two films were made in France: *Le Jupon Rouge* (87), as the survivor of the concentration camps, a human rights worker, whose life is shattered when her protégée (Marie-Christine Barrault) begins a lesbian affair; and *A Notre Regrettable Epoux* (88), a regrettable black comedy, as the widow of Jean-Pierre Aumont.

Raf Vallone

The American cinema has flirted only occasionally with Raf Vallone (or vice versa), which is strange, because he has more sex-appeal than almost any other actor you can think of. One thinks of him as one of those sons of the soil he used to play, tanned and lusty after a day in the fields (not tired), grinning to reveal teeth as white as his skin-tight, snow-white singlet (no Cinécittà myth, this). He can glower, too, as in *Les Possédées* – from Ugo Betti's 'Isle of Goats' – where his very presence, capricious, marauding, stirs the female cast to all sorts of passion (as a wayfaring stranger who happens on a household of women – not goats, but a ram and three sheep). Even in his roles as a middle-aged businessman he seems about to burst out of his clothes – though that is probably because of his bulk. One of the reasons (just one) that *Phaedra* failed so miserably was that you just could not believe that Melina Mercouri would desert him for Anthony Perkins.

But whereas several actresses have made longish careers out of their physical appearance, no actor can rely on that solely. He needs presence and that Vallone has, almost in excess. It limits him. He cannot, literally, disappear inside a part; but beyond that – except for a couple of times when he seemed like an Italian William Bendix – his ability is not betrayed by his appearance.

His background is urban, though he was born in the country, in Tropea, Calabria, in 1917. His father, a lawyer, moved to Turin shortly after the Armistice. As a boy he showed an aptitude for music and football; his father opposed a career in football, but in his teens he played for a club which competed in the Student World Championships in Vienna in 1939. He was studying at the University of Turin (law and philosophy) and after he had graduated was an actor for a brief while. He then became a sports journalist and later music and film critic on the same paper. In Italy there has always been a closer accord between critics and producers than operates elsewhere and Vallone was in the office of Giuseppe De Santis when the latter offered him a featured role, the sergeant in *Riso Amero* (48), a stark melodrama about deprived workers toiling in the rice-fields. It was also the first big role for Silvana Mangano and stills of her went round the world – thick-thighed and big-busted, knee-deep in the paddy-fields. It helped make the film, as *Bitter Rice*, a successful 'art' movie in English-speaking territories.

De Santis and his producers (Lux) liked Vallone's performance and offered him the leading role in *Non c'è Pace Tra gli Ulivi* (49), as a peasant wronged when local bigwig Folco Lulli commandeers his sheep and rapes his sister. This was again a success (as *No Peace Among the Olives* in some countries) and Vallone embarked on a serious film career. Lux put him into Luigi Zampa's *Cuori senza*

Raf Vallone in Non c'è Pace Tra gli Ulivi *(50), directed by Giuseppe de Santis. Called* No Peace Among the Olives *in some countries, it offered, said the 1952 Film Review, 'a fascinating glimpse of a primitive community – whose people live close to the earth and whose simple passions are violent and raw'.*

Frontiere (50), opposite Gina Lollobrigida, as a Yugoslav refugee in this preachment against war; and then into Pietro Germi's *Il Cammino della Speranza*, a good film about the right to work – Sicilian miners seeking work in France when their mine is closed. 'As the group leader Raf Vallone was never better,' said 'Variety'. In the cast was Elena Varzi, who appeared with him in several more films and became his wife in 1952.

After a poor thriller, *Il Bivio*, he made *Il Cristo Proibito* (51), playing a moody POW returning to Tuscany bent on revenging his brother's death, an inflexibly poetic film written and directed by Curzio Malaparte the novelist. It was a complete disaster at the box-office (and did not reach Britain till 11 years later). *Camicie Rosse* (52) was an ambitious and confused film about the Risorgimento, with Vallone perfectly cast as Garibaldi, with Anna Magnani as his wife. Then Lux (Ponti and De Laurentiis) reunited Vallone and Mangano in *Anna*, directed by Alberto Lattuada. It was not good, but it was popular: she was a nun recalling her past – as a cabaret singer – and particularly Vallone as the decent farmer who fought the sneaky Vittorio Gassmann for her honour. Even more lurid was *Carne Inquieta*: when fiancée Marina Berti becomes a nobleman's plaything the honest Vallone sets fire to the village. In *Le Avventure di Mandrin*, a shoddy swashbuckler, he was a soldier of Louis XV who becomes a buccaneer.

Roma Ore II, directed by De Santis, was based on fact (one of several made on the subject): a staircase collapsed, killing several of the 200 girls on it queueing to get a job. The film concentrated on a handful of them, including Lucia Bose, married to artist Vallone. He and his wife went to Spain for *Los Ojos dejan Huellas* (53) and then he did a couple of mediocre pieces, *Gli Eroi della Domenica*, as an ageing footballer, and *Perdonami*, as a man bent on revenging his brother; after which he went to France to play Simone Signoret's truck-driver lover in *Thérèse Raquin* and Martine Carol's husband (she was Lysistrata) in *Destinées*. Carol followed him to Italy for *La Spiaggia/La Pensionnaire* (54), Lattuada's pleasant film about a whore on vacation and the left-wing mayor (Vallone) who befriends her. His leading ladies remained French: Françoise Arnoul in *Delirio*, a remake of *L'Orage*, which had starred Charles Boyer and Michèle Morgan; and Morgan herself in *Obsession*. His wife played opposite him in *Siluri Umani* (55), a World War II story based on fact, and Sophia Loren was his co-star in *Il Segno di Venere*, in which he was a level-headed fireman. The French interest returned with *Andrea Chenier*, the poet who was guillotined during the Revolution: Michel Auclair played the title-role and Vallone was a revolutionary leader. *Les Possédées* (56) was French – though the original play was Italian – and his co-star was Madeleine Robinson. Also in France he did *Le Secret de Sœur Angèle*, as a murderer in love with a nun, Sophie Desmarets.

Les Possédées (56) *was a French version of a play by the distinguished Italian dramatist Ugo Betti. Its theme was a common one in European movies of the time: the arrival of a (male) stranger in a household of women. The stars were Magali Noel and Raf Vallone.*

The next batch suggest that he was too busy packing and unpacking to bother much about scripts – but the first was good: *Guendalina* (57), with Sylva Koscina, about a teenage love affair, with Vallone as the girl's eye-roving papa. And *Rose Bernd* was intended as the most important German film of the year, Wolfgang Staudte's modernization of the Hauptmann play, with Vallone as a labourer, one of the men loved by Maria Schell: her notices wrecked the film's chances and just about wrecked her career – but not before she and Vallone co-starred again in *Liebe*. He travelled south to Spain, for *La Venganza* (58), directed by Juan-Antonio Bardem with Carmen Sevilla, a revenge drama set among migratory farmworkers; and *La Violetera*, primarily a vehicle for Sarita Montiel – from gypsy to grande dame in colour. In France he did two: *Le Piège* with Magali Noel, a shallow piece about an escaped murderer having it off with a widow whose father-in-law also leches after her; and Laslo Benedek's disappointing *Recours en Grâce* (60), as an army deserter, with Annie Girardot as his old love, Emmanuèle Riva as his new. He returned to Italy for *La Garconnière*, with Eleanora Rossi Drago. During this time, in Paris, he adapted, directed and played – for two years – Arthur Miller's 'A View from the Bridge', which he regards as the peak of his career.

He left his play to do a brief bit, unbilled, in *La Ciociara* (61), as the cheerful truck-driver who befriends Sophia Loren; then went on to Spain to make *El Cid* with her, as Charlton Heston's traitorous rival for her hand. He was top-featured in this, his English-language début, then was starred in *Vu du Pont/A View from the Bridge* (62), filmed in French and English by Sidney Lumet on New York locations with a cast including Maureen Stapleton, Carol Lawrence, Jean Sorel and (especially good) Raymond Péllégrin. It was one of the first films to justify co-productions, keen and clear and beautifully acted. Vallone repeated his stage role – a difficult part in a modern context – of the obsessed and agonized immigrant father. The film was picked at by critics and was not a great success; but it netted Vallone the role of the husband in *Phaedra*, which he got away with by simply looking bewildered.

Otto Preminger starred him in his over-long religioso *The Cardinal* (63), as the bald confidant – of Tom Tryon in the title-role. He was held up on this and his part in *Le Mépris* went to Michel Piccoli. Then he did *The Secret Invasion* (64), with Stewart Granger, and two Italian movies, *Una Voglia da Morire* with Annie Girardot and *La Scoperta dell' America* with Giovanno Ralli. In Hollywood he did two films for Avco-Embassy: *Harlow* (65), as that lady's brutish stepfather, and *Nevada Smith* with Steve McQueen, as a sympathetic monk. In Spain he starred in *Volver a Vivir*, a drama about football, but in American films he continued in supporting parts: *Se Tutte le Donne del Mondo/Kiss the Girls and Make Them Die* (66), with Dorothy Provine, as a mad industrialist; *The Desperate Ones* (68), as brother to Maximilian Schell; *The Italian Job* (69) with Michael Caine, as a Mafia leader: and *The Kremlin Letter*, as a trainer of spies – a second consecutive waste of his talents. Most of these years he spent on the stage, notably in a play which he wrote and directed, 'Proibito per Chi?'. In France he did Arthur Miller's 'All My Sons' on TV and he played another obsessive father in *La Morte Risale a Ieri Sera* (70) – with more pathos than the part was worth, in this thriller about a girl abducted into white slavery and then murdered. Then: *Cannon for Cordoba* (71) with George Peppard, as Cordoba, the Mexican general; *Perchè Non ci Lasciate in Pace?/Por Que No Nos Dejais en Paz?*, a Spanish-Italian thriller with Sylva Koscina; *La Villa*; and *A Gunfight*, in Mexico with Kirk Douglas, as a local entrepreneur. *Un Verano para Matar/The Summertime Killer* (72) was a Spanish-Italian-French revenge thriller whose ambitions were not realized at the box-office: he was a retired Mafia man, Chris Mitchum was the man after him and Karl Malden was a detective. There was a similar role in an American TV film, *Honor Thy Father* (73), from Gay Talese's book: 'As the senior Bonanno, [he] was strong, and persuasive in all his scenes' ('Variety'). As a change, he toured France in 'Six Characters in Search of an Author', which left time for one movie, *Grazie Amore Mio* with Lea Massari, and two more American tele-films, *The Small Miracle*, based on Paul Gallico's story 'Never Take No for an Answer', with Vittorio De Sica, and *Catholics*, with Trevor Howard.

Arthur Miller's play 'A View from the Bridge' was a strong drama about Italian immigrants working on the docks in New York; the film (62) improved upon the original by eliminating the Greek chorus device. Raf Vallone and Carol Lawrence as father and daughter.

L'Histoire de l'Oeil/Simone, Story of the Eye (74) was directed in Belgium by Patrick Longchamps and the names of Laura Antonelli and Patrick Magee also in the cast would seem to assure this version of the porn classic of respectability: but it seems never to have been publicly shown. Alas, that the next few were: Preminger's *Rosebud* (75), with Peter O'Toole, as the exiled Greek father to Isabelle Huppert; *That Lucky Touch*, with Susannah York, as an Italian general with NATO; and *The Human Factor*, with John Mills, as a Neapolitan police chief. Hollywood again offered a plum role in *The Other Side of Midnight* (77), a big, boring film from a big, boring bestseller. Hollywood continued to be taken in by such things – though the cinema public refused to be: the few that ventured along found a tale about a French girl (Marie-France Pisier) ever-loving an American pilot (John Beck) and married in the meantime to a millionaire Greek shipping tycoon (Vallone). Perhaps there was something about Vallone's outsize presence which made him suitable for the banalities of paperback best-sellerdom: for he was there again in *Des Teufels Advokat/The Devil's Advocate* (78), made in Germany with John Mills, as a bishop. Again, the readers of the novel failed to support it; and no amount of publicity could help *The Greek Tycoon*, in which he was Anthony Quinn's chief rival.

Thus was Vallone type-cast – either as priest or Greek or Italian bigwig; but at last he was in a goodish film, Michael Ritchie's study of adultery at the Cannes Film Festival, *An Almost Perfect Affair* (79), with Monica Vitti: as her 'wronged husband, a flamboyant but sympathetic producer, Raf Vallone is so appealing that it is hard to know why Vitti would forsake him. Whether he is arguing on the phone about Burmese distribution rights or comforting his wife in time of need, the serpentine Vallone is a grand old charmer' (Frank Rich in 'Time Magazine'). After that he went into René Allio's *Retour à Marseille*, with Andrea Ferreol (80), a thriller about a man returning to his home town, and *Omar Muktar – Lion of the Desert* (81) with Anthony Quinn, as a sympathetic Fascist. Also made at this time, but not released to cinemas, was *A Time to Die*, with Rex Harrison and Rod Taylor. In the Yugoslav *Sezona Mira u Parizu* with Valli, he was a Nazi living in Paris, obsessed with uniforms. He packed his bags again to go to Africa for a Japanese film with James Stewart, *Afurika Monogatari* (82), and yet again for an American tele-movie set in the Vatican, *The Scarlet and the Black* (83) with Gregory Peck. He was one of several names in an Italo-American mini-series, *Christopher Columbus* (85), and about the same time he returned to the film studios for Zanussi's *Paradigme* with Gassmann, as the director of the laboratory. His last seen movie was *La Nuit de l'Océan* (86), as the captain of a ship which loses a crewman, son of Jeanne Moreau; but he is also in *The Conspiracy* (89), with Paul Scofield.

VERA-ELLEN

Vera-Ellen was one of the screen's best dancers and, after a poor start, an attractive performer in musicals. Her career, however, never really got into first gear. She was born in Cincinnati, Ohio, in 1926; her mother sent her to dancing class and while still young she became a dance instructor; in New York for a convention of dancing instructors she got herself on Major Bowes's Amateur Hour, as a result of which she toured with his show. She became a Rockette for a while and danced at Billy Rose's Casa Manana Club, going from there to Broadway musicals: 'Very Warm for May' (39), 'Panama Hattie' and the Rodgers and Hart 'By Jupiter' (42). She was in a featured role in another Rodgers and Hart show, 'A Connecticut Yankee' (43), and was seen by a Goldwyn agent: Goldwyn signed her to a long-term contract.

He started her off in a Danny Kaye vehicle, *Wonder Man* (45), as second female after Virginia Mayo, a leading lady of iron charm; Vera-Ellen danced a bit and smiled so relentlessly that she was in the end hardly more fetching than Mayo. The two of them were with Kaye again in *The Kid From Brooklyn* (46), then she was loaned to 20th to play the third girl (and very much the third girl) in *Three Little Girls in Blue*, with Vivian Blaine and June Haver. They kept her on for a *Carnival in Costa Rica* (46), which was more like a wake, what with Dick Haymes singing and her smiling while he sang. Still Bosley Crowther in 'The New York Times' found her 'a pleasant chick who dances with stimulating vigor and has a nice way with a song'. Well, good. Later she gave the readers of the 'New York Journal-American' advice on what was needed for a Hollywood career: '. . . now more is required. You've got to be able to act and sing.' In fact, her singing voice was always dubbed in films and she certainly could not act. As Goldwyn made so few musicals her opportunities were limited and after a year of inactivity she asked for and got release from her contract.

MGM stopped her grinning and put her in a long blonde wig for the 'Slaughter on 10th Avenue' ballet with Gene Kelly in *Words and Music* (48) – which proved that as long as she stuck to dancing she was sensational; as a result the producers of *Love Happy* (49) inserted a sexy dance for her to do – but that was about all she had to do as the ingénue in this Marx Brothers farce. As a further result, MGM offered a seven-year contract, to begin with *On the Town*, as one of the three girls pursued by the three sailors – in her case, Kelly again. As 'Miss Turnstiles' she had undergone a metamorphosis, prettier and fresher and less addicted to levity; and she proved almost worthy of her new partner, Hollywood's other great male dancer, Fred Astaire, in *Three Little Words* (50) – though after she hung up her dancing shoes in reel two all she did was smile for the rest of the film. Then she took a risk and did a British musical, *Happy Go Lovely* (51) with David Niven, dancing round a painted Piccadilly with young men in bowler-hats (it was all on that level).

Astaire, fortunately, was waiting for her – for the charming but unsuccessful *The Belle of*

New York (52), directed by Charles Walters, who later referred to her as 'a moving piece of putty'. And 20th borrowed her – at a fee of $40,000 – to play the princess in Irving Berlin's *Call Me Madam* (53), dancing with diplomat Donald O'Connor. MGM decided that her acting had improved enough to put her in a straight film, *The Big Leaguer*, after which Paramount borrowed her to play another second lead in another Berlin musical, *White Christmas* (54), opposite Danny Kaye again. She had begun to look quite lovely and there was every reason to think that she would move on to bigger things; indeed, MGM announced her for the leads in *Seven Brides for Seven Brothers*, *Hit the Deck* and *Athena* – all of which Jane Powell eventually played.

Meanwhile, she had returned to the stage: in 1953 she had done stock, 'I am a Camera', with Tom Drake. In 1954 she married for the second time (she had been married briefly during her teens), Victor Rothschild, who was in oil. She did not need to work. She told MGM that she would not renew her contract and when asked to do a film called *Tennessee's Partner* preferred to do cabaret in Las Vegas. She made one more film, *Let's Be Happy* (56), with Tony Martin, a musical version of

Vera-Ellen and Fred Astaire in Three Little Words (*50*), a musical built round the songs and careers of Kalmar and Ruby. Astaire was Bert Kalmar, and Vera-Ellen played the girl he married.

By virtue of being the first studio to use Technicolor regularly in musicals and because the immensely popular Betty Grable was under contract, 20th Century-Fox was for a while the leader of the field: then MGM took over and, except in quantity, 20th was not even in the running. Its response was to copy MGM and buy some big Broadway shows. This is one of the latter, Call Me Madam (*53*), *but for the juveniles they borrowed Vera-Ellen from MGM and signed Donald O'Connor, who had just made his biggest screen impact in MGM's* Singin' in the Rain.

'Jeannie' (a play about a Scots girl who inherits a fortune, filmed in 1940 with Barbara Mullen), which was a hybrid of 1940s Hollywood and 1930s Shaftesbury Avenue and even worse than her previous British musical. It must have made her regret that her decision to retire had not been made some months earlier. She died of cancer in 1981.

Monica Vitti

As long as the films of Michelangelo Antonioni are shown, Monica Vitti will not be forgotten. Her cool, attentive gaze hides, normally, a tender compassion for the poor males she encounters. She is intensely giving – she will give as much as the oppressive circumstances will allow. Progressively, Antonioni pushed her into a world which can be summed up – simplistically – as one of alienation. In *Il Deserto Rosso* she was, as he said, 'a neurotic woman who has lost touch with reality'. He added, 'she certainly inspires me, because I like to watch and to direct her, but the parts I give her are a long way away from her own character: Monica, c'est la joie de vivre.' Other directors later gave her roles which corresponded to her real character and as a comedienne she achieved in Italy a popularity unthinkable in the days when she was Antonioni's muse.

She met him, not as generally recorded when she dubbed for actress Dorian Gray in *Il Grido*, but when she joined the company at the Teatro Nuovo di Milano in 1957, at that time directed by him. She had been born in Rome in 1931 (Maria Luisa Ceciarelli), but was brought up in Milan. She was studying at Pitman's when she played the role of the teenage protagonist in a charity performance of Niccodemi's 'La Nemica' – which encouraged her to enrol at the Accademia d'Arte Drammatica in Rome. After graduating she toured Germany with an Italian company and made her Rome début in 'La Mandragola' by Machiavelli, followed by roles in 'Mother Courage' and 'L'Avare'. In films, she was given small roles in *Ridere Ridere Ridere* (55), a minor comedy with several minor comics including the then-unknown Ugo Tognazzi, and *Une Pelliccia di Visone* (56) with Giovanni Ralli. After joining Antonioni's company she appeared in *Le Dritte* (58), with Franco Fabrizi. She said later that she did not want to be in films, because she had seen what happened to some of the Italian girls who were. She did work in TV. For Antonioni she appeared in his production of 'I Am a Camera' and a play he had written in collaboration, 'Scandale Segreta'. It was he who persuaded her to do the dubbing job for him; they became inseparable and he planned to star her in his next film.

He had made five films, with varying degress of unsuccess – though the most recent one (*Le Amiche*) was very fine indeed. *L'Avventura* (60) was rough going: location work (Sicily and the Lipari islands) was difficult and money ran out. When the finished film was shown at the Cannes festival it was booed. In it, Antonioni refined some of the ideas he had been practising – he revolutionized cinema form in that plot became subsidiary to theme and theme subservient to technique which in turn was used, rather than words, to tell a drama of emotion. The plot was merely one aspect of this 'adventure'. On a cruise, Anna (Lea Massari) disappears; looking for her is her boyfriend (Gabriele Ferzetti) and a girlfriend (Vitti). During the search their relationship develops and they learn some not pleasant, not conclusive things about themselves and each other. No one who saw it when it came out will forget the excitement of seeing it for the first time; Dwight Macdonald observed that one measured one's friends by their reaction to this and the two other big Italian films of that year (which were, of course Visconti's *Rocco e i suoi Fratelli* and Fellini's *La Dolce Vita*).

A while later, Antonioni gave Vitti a subsidiary but telling role in *La Notte* (61), as the fey rich girl who 'comforts' Marcello Mastroianni. He co-starred her with Alain Delon in the most arid of his films, *L'Eclisse* (62). The reception of his films in Paris brought Vitti some offers from France: *Les Quatre Vérités* (63), in the episode 'Le Lièvre et la Tortue', a frenzied comedy with Rossano Brazzi, where she was animated but did not

Vitti in Il Deserto Rosso *(64), in which her troubles were marital, but then no marriage in an Antonioni film is a happy one.*

act; *Dragées au Poivre*, a chaotic attempt at satire, where she and Roger Vadim (acting) sent up the 'smart' films they supposedly both made; and *Château en Suêde*, directed by Vadim, weak as a *femme fatale* in this version of a Françoise Sagan play. She did a sketch-film in Italy, *Alta Infideltà* (64), in 'La Sospirosa', as the over-jealous wife of Jean-Pierre Cassel; and then for Antonioni his first in colour, *Il Deserto Rosso*, and another attempt to chart the malaise of a certain kind of wealthy Italian. She was the frustrated and lonely wife of a Ravenna factory tycoon in love with Richard Harris.

She was in *Le Bambole* (65), in the episode 'La Minestra', as a wife desperate to get her husband bumped off; and then in *Il Disco Volante*, as one of the population (others: Alberto Sordi – in four different roles, and Silvana Mangano) comically concerned when a flying saucer lands nearby. There had been feelers from abroad and she signed to appear in *The Defector* with Montgomery Clift, but changed her mind at the last minute. Thus she made her English-speaking début in *Modesty Blaise* (66), Joseph Losey's story of a glamorous karate-conscious lady spy, based on an English comic strip, with Dirk Bogarde. She was ludicrously miscast and the film was a clear miss. Antonioni reportedly loathed it – though the relationship broke up not long afterwards. He was said to be about to direct her in an American film, *Identification of a Woman*, but she indicated in interviews that, much as she admired his work, she wanted to be in comedy (he eventually made it in Italian in 1982, with two minor actresses in the roles meant for her). She got her way: *Le Fate*, yet another sketch-film, as a mini-skirted hitch-hiker – unwilling to be seduced but willing to seduce; *Fai in Fretta ad Uccidermi . . . Ho Freddo!* (67), a facetious comedy about a couple (Jean Sorel and Vitti) who set up con-schemes together; and *La Cintura di Castita*, a period comedy with Tony Curtis. Her experience of working with Curtis, and the failure of both this and *Modesty Blaise*, made her cautious of working again for the Anglo-Saxon market. After *Ti Ho Sposato per Allegria*, a comedy with Giorgio Albertazzi, she was *La Ragazza con la Pistola* (68), a betrayed Sicilian who chases her man – who had gone to work in a spaghetti restaurant – over much of Great Britain; despite a guest appearance by Stanley Baker as a professor it was neither exported or exportable as messily directed by Monicelli. 'Variety''s comment on her next performance also applies here.

In France she did a mad comedy with Maurice Ronet, *La Femme Ecarlate*, in which she was a suicide. Said 'Variety': 'Miss Vitti acts coy, gay, pouts and cavorts with good spirits but does not have the true comic mien and expressiveness.' This did not worry cinemagoers in Italy, where she was now as popular as Sophia Loren. They turned up to see: *Amore Mio Aiutami*, a marital comedy with Alberto Sordi as her jealous husband; *Vedo Nudo*, an episodic sex comedy, with Nino Manfredi; *Dramma della Gelosia: Tutti i Particolari in Cronaca* (70), a vapid triangle tale with Mastroianni; and *Le Coppie*, in two episodes of this study of marriage, again with Sordi. If sometimes the old moody Vitti could be glimpsed, the one who now appeared was changed beyond recognition: as *Nini Tirabuscio La Donna che Invento la Mossa* (71), she was a small-time actress of the Neapolitan music halls and very noisy in this period comedy. She co-starred with Tognazzi in *La Supertestimone*, as a woman who has a man condemned for murder and then marries him.

Monica Vitti as the Antonioni heroine, with Gabriele Ferzetti in L'Avventura *(60): they were unexpected lovers in this, the director's masterpiece – and voted one of the ten best films of all time in the 'Sight and Sound' polls of 1962 and 1972.*

She returned to more serious problems in *La Pacifistica*, the first film directed outside his native Hungary by Miklós Jancsó, about a woman TV interviewer who becomes involved in a student revolt in Rome: a striking but shadowy piece. *Noi Donne Siamo Fatte Cosi* found her up to her old tricks, playing a variety of – comic – women; and she had a certain problem in *Gli Ordini Sonto Ordini* (72), as an apparently contented wife who takes it upon herself to take a lover during her vacation. Stark drama followed: *La Tosca* (73), in the title-role; and *Teresa la Ladra*, ditto – a fisherman's daughter drawn into a life of petty crime, as drawn from Darcia Maraini's critical biography. *Polvere di Stella* (74) was a happy reunion with Sordi, the two of them as a vaudeville team during World War II and she in love with an American sailor (John Philip Law); *Le Fântome de la Liberté* was Buñuel's least film, a 'surrealist' jumble, in which she and Jean-Claude Brialy had a mere bit as parents of a troubled child; and *A Mezzanotte va la Ronda del Piacere* (75) found her the working-class wife of Giancarlo Giannini, on trial for murder – their lives compared with that of lawyer Gassmann. There followed: *L'Anitra all'Arencia* (76) with Tognazzi (who replaced at the last minute George Segal, who turned down the role when Vitti refused to act in English); *Qui Comincia L'Avventura*, with Claude Cardinale as Sancho Panza to Vitti's modern, female Don Quixote; *Mimi Bluette; Basta Che Non si Sappia in Giro*, another episode film; and *L'Altra Metà del Cielo* (77) with Adriano Celentano. In France Vitti made *La Raison d'Etat* (78) with Jean Yanne, André Cayette's facile study of the political responsibility of supplying arms to Africa; and there were two more mediocre vehicles, *Amore Miei* and another episode film, *Per Vivere Meglio Divertitevi con Noi*.

With the exception of the Buñuel and *Teresa la Ladra* (which turned up in the US in 1979), none of these recent films was seen in Britain or the US, but Vitti remained a big star on her home ground – and therefore reasonable in her terms for *Bloodline*, e.g. control over a certain number of close-ups. The producers refused to agree, but after *Letti Selvaggi* (79), a sketch film (hers was about a con-girl who poses as a nun and an old lady), she was seen in an American film, Ritchie's *An Almost Perfect Affair* (79), deserting De Laurentiis-like husband Raf Vallone for independent film-maker Keith Carradine: she 'has rarely seemed as radiant and emotionally full-blooded as she is here' said Frank Rich in 'Time Magazine', thinking Carradine inadequate to her 'smokey eyes and voice to match'. Yes: she was hardly the young innocent of *L'Avventura* and Antonioni had a very different role for her to play – that of a Ruritanian queen in *Il Mistero di Oberwald* (80): he had, incredibly, not been able to get backing for other projects and had – even more incredibly – fallen back on Cocteau's 'L'Aigle à Deux Têtes', which in this version had little more than curiosity value.

Then she pursued comedy with a vengeance: *Camera d'Albergo* (81) with Gassmann; *Il Tango della Gelosia*, an old-fashioned marital tale which she also produced, as a woman who tries to make her horse-loving husband jealous by having an affair with her bodyguard, and a big success; *Io So che Tu Sai, che Io So* (82), as Alberto Sordi's wife; *Infidelmente Tua* (83) with Ugo Tognazzi; and *Quando suona Veronica*, as a lady married to a schizoid (Jean-Luc Bideau) for many years. Then she stayed away from films for several years, though she flirted with Diane Kurys's *Un Homme Amoureux* (Claudia Cardinale replaced her): but in 1987 she did the female version of 'The Odd Couple' on the stage.

Monica Vitti and Marcello Mastroianni in a film whose full title was Dramma della Gelosia: Tutti i Particolari in Cronaca *(70). In the US they called it* The Pizza Triangle, *in Britain* Jealousy Italian Style: *it flopped as both.*

ROBERT WALKER

The mild-mannered Robert Walker was not among Hollywood's more versatile actors, but he embodied the same friendly, helpful boy-next-door qualities as James Stewart and Van Johnson. Between the image and the reality of being a movie star there developed the conflict that destroyed him.

He was born in 1914, 1918 or 1919 in Salt Lake City, Utah, where his father was editor of a local paper. He was sent to the San Diego Military and Naval Academy, where his acting prowess encouraged him to study at the AADA. There he met the girl who became film star Jennifer Jones and married her in 1939. They got a few acting jobs, mostly in radio, and tried Hollywood. He did walk-ons in three or four films, most noticeably in

Winter Carnival (39) where he asked Ann Sheridan to dance. They returned to the East and Walker returned to radio, though he did get the chance to play at the Provincetown Playhouse, in 'Springtime for Henry'. At one bleak point he became a sailor on a freighter, but by 1942 was steadily employed in the radio serial, 'Myrt and Marge'. When David O. Selznick signed Jones, Walker accompanied her to Hollywood; he worked again in radio, acted at the Pasadena Playhouse and was taken on by MGM for a brief stint as the garrulous novice sailor in *Bataan* (43). The company liked it enough to sign him to a contract.

He had another brief (unsuitable) role in *Madame Curie* and was then starred in *See Here Private Hargrove* (44), as the bumbling PFC hero of Marion Hargrove's bestselling army memoir. Keenan Wynn was also in it and it was a big hit. Walker was clearly every mother's son in uniform and was type-cast as long as the war lasted. During this time he was fined $500 for a hit-and-run accident, but that did not prevent Selznick from borrowing him to play a West Point drop-out who becomes a dead hero in *Since You Went Away* – though the part was a variation on Pvt Hargrove, the shy soldier who backs into doors and knocks things over. Jones was also in it and the title expressed all too well their real-life relationship. He was a corporal in both *Thirty Seconds Over Tokyo* and *The Clock* (45), in the latter on 48-hour furlough in Manhattan and gently romancing Judy Garland. From there he went into another uniform with a very different leading lady – Hedy Lamarr: *Her Highness and the Bellboy*, but the girl he got at the end was June Allyson. *What Next Corporal Hargrove* was a slapstick rehash of the original (author Hargrove sued and got $100,000 damages); then he was with Allyson again in *The Sailor Takes a Wife*.

There was the first of a brace of composers in two appalling films: reverentially, Jerome Kern amidst a flock of stars in *Till the Clouds Roll By* (46), inspired to write 'Ol' Man River' by a glimpse of the Mississippi. He was Katharine Hepburn's ne'er-do-well bastard son in *The Sea of Grass* (47) and involved in the development of the atom bomb in *The Beginning or the End?*, with Brian Donlevy and Tom Drake. Then he was an appropriately beardless Brahms to Hepburn's Clara Schumann, exhorted by her: 'You must go on to write wonderful music – music the angels will want to sing.' Paul Henreid was Schumann and Henry Daniell Lizst: *Song of Love*. After a year's absence he was loaned to Universal, along with Ava Gardner, for *One Touch of Venus* (48).

Troubles were besetting this seemingly placid young man. He and Jones had been divorced in 1945, but gossip-columnists insisted that he was carrying the biggest torch in Hollywood. In 1948 he married again (a daughter of John Ford) but they separated after five months. There had already been reports of an emotional crack-up and there were several much-publicized alcoholic escapades (drunken driving, assaulting a policeman). MGM cast him as a fortune-hunting playboy in *Please Believe Me* (50) starring Deborah Kerr; and further tried to refurbish his image in a light comedy with Joan Leslie, *The Skipper Surprised his Wife*. His salary at this time was $2,000 a week.

He was demoted to supporting status, as Burt Lancaster's no-good foster-brother in *Vengeance Valley* (51), after which came Hitchcock's memorable *Strangers on a Train*, part-written by Raymond Chandler from Patricia Highsmith's novel. Farley Granger was the tennis star to whom stranger Walker proposed a murder pact, each to kill for the other's benefit . . . the perfect crime. Milton Shulman wrote in the 'Evening Standard' (London) that Walker 'carries his sinister purposes with so charming and attractive an air that it could start a vogue in lovable maniacs'. It did; and this one performance

Robert Walker and Judy Garland in the Metropolitan Museum in New York. He was a soldier on furlough, she was the girl he meets: Vincente Minnelli's The Clock *(45), the best of all those wartime romance movies.*

might have created a new career for Walker. He was scheduled also for *Clash by Night* when he died, of respiratory failure after an overdose of sedatives on top of alcohol – and because he had been drinking, and knew the combination fatal, he had begged the medics to spare him; but he had been held down. He had almost finished Leo McCarey's *My Son John* (52), as a secret Communist subversive with beliefs alien to America, and they managed to complete it without him – laughably, with inserts from the Hitchcock film and a wholesale rearrangement of the last reel. It was not a film of which much notice was taken.

Clifton Webb

Clifton Webb might have been MGM's answer to Fred Astaire. Instead, he did not become a movie star till he was middle aged, as an acidulous, Pecksniffian character actor. He found stardom as Mr Belvedere, a hardly forbearing literary gentleman who, employed as a nursemaid, used strictly personal methods to keep the kids seen but not heard. His contempt for both the children and the fond parents must have struck a responsive chord, for he kept audiences rolling in the aisles for years. Presumably people vicariously enjoyed his superiority.

His screen character represented Hollywood's normal distrust of intelligence. Screen heroes were cunning or quick-witted; a few actors like Lionel Barrymore and Lewis Stone were permitted – indeed expected – to be wise; but it took a rare actor like Edward G. Robinson to get away with the suggestion of intellectualism. Brains were not in demand, except for absent-minded professors – and Clifton Webb. Webb, in the three films he made before he became Mr Belvedere, was like nothing so much as an animated ad from the 'New Yorker' – sardonic, suave, dandyish, immensely pleased with himself, witty (at the expense of others), celibate and selfish. He knew about books and wine. This, incidentally, was what Hollywood considered the Noël Coward syndrome; and not much like Fred Astaire.

Laura (44) was a smart New York thriller, with a lot of smart New York people: Gene Tierney as the mystery woman of the title, and Clifton Webb and Vincent Price as two of her obsessed admirers.

Webb was born in Indianapolis, in 1891. He was taught dancing as a child and made his first stage appearance in 1902 as one of the children in 'Huckleberry Finn'. He left school in 1904 and studied singing, appearing in 'Mignon' at the Boston Opera in 1911 and other operas. He made his New York bow in 'The Purple Road', partnered Bonnie Glass in nightclubs and taught dancing; he became a successful musical-comedy leading man: 'Town Topics' (15), 'See America Thirst' (16), 'Love o' Mike' (17), 'As You Were' (20), 'The Fun of the Fayre' (21) in London, 'Jack and Jill' (23) and 'Sunny' (25), which he played for three seasons. He also played supporting roles in some movies: *Polly With a Past* (20), at Metro, with Ina Claire making her movie début in a part she had made famous on the stage; *Let Not Man Put Asunder* (24), with Pauline Frederick and Lou Tellegen, a sophisticated drama about wandering husbands and wives; *New Toys* (25), a farce with Richard Barthelmess at First National, as an actor-manager; *The Heart of a Siren*, also at First National, playing the secretary of the star, Barbara La Marr; and *The Still Alarm* (26), a programmer at Universal starring William Russell. He partnered Beatrice Lillie in 'She's My Baby' (28) and Gertrude Lawrence in 'Treasure Girl'; and was in the first 'Little Show', in 'Three's a Crowd' (30) and 'As Thousands Cheer' (33). At this point MGM offered him a guest appearance in *Dancing Lady*, but Webb demanded equal billing with Joan Crawford, so they said forget it and gave the part to Astaire. But they did not lose interest: in 1935 they signed him to a star contract, as an avowed rival to Astaire. His first film was announced as *Elegance*, co-starring Crawford and Franchot Tone, to be followed by a film with Jessie Matthews. Neither was made and after 18 months Webb was dropped from the pay-roll.

He appeared in 'The Importance of Being Earnest' (36), in, inevitably, 'The Man Who Came To Dinner' and in Coward's 'Blithe Spirit'. He was in Los Angeles in that play in 1944 when 20th were casting *Laura* (44). Rouben Mamoulian was to have directed and he wanted Laird Cregar to play Waldo Lydecker, Laura's possessive dilettante admirer. But when Otto Preminger took over the film he contacted Webb, an old friend. Webb's performance brought a five-year contract with 20th (who later renewed: during his 18-year film career he worked exclusively for that company). He played a version of Waldo in *The Dark Corner* (46) starring Lucille Ball; instead of dashing off a bit of *belles-lettres* he dabbled in modern art. As Somerset Maugham's insufferable snob Elliott Templeton he was so perfectly cast that it was tempting to suppose they had bought *The Razor's Edge* only because he was under contract.

On Broadway he played in Coward's 'Present Laughter'; he returned to 20th for *Sitting Pretty* (48), starring Maureen O'Hara. Here he was Mr Belvedere and the reception was such that a sequel was concocted, *Mr Belvedere Goes to College* (49) – naturally more learned than the tutors but (invention drying up) then playing cupid to Shirley Temple and Tom Drake. A whole host of Mr Belvedere films was promised – imagine the possibilities! – but instead he played the bossy paterfamilias of a family of 12, including Jeanne Crain, *Cheaper By the Dozen* (50). He died at the end – adored by them all – so could not be in the later sequel, *Belles on Their Toes* (though his voice was heard – from heaven). Meanwhile, he descended from heaven, along with Edmund Gwenn, for a sticky comedy, *For Heaven's Sake*: he was a Texan angel sent to save the marriage of Joan Bennett and Robert Cummings. The suggestion of supernatural omniscience was not entirely coincidental: his stock at 20th was indicated by a report that Darryl F. Zanuck, who hero-worshipped him, predicted that Webb would become one of the great film directors – in about 10 years, when the public had tired of Mr Belvedere. And that was sooner than expected: *Mr Belvedere Rings the Bell* (51) was rather a case of tolling the knell.

He made *Elopement*, with Anne Francis as the daughter who eloped; *Dreamboat* (52), opposite Ginger Rogers, as a ham actor – one of his best performances; *Stars and Stripes Forever*, a biopic of John Philip Sousa which mercifully proved there is only a small cinema audience for brass bands; and *Titanic* (53), opposite Barbara Stanwyck, a *Grand Hotel* afloat with a smash finale. *Mister Scoutmaster* was Mr Belvedere thinly disguised (there must have been good reasons why it was not called 'Mr Belvedere Joins the Boy Scouts'): he was the usual misanthropist, taking on a scout troop in order to understand children. He found he liked little boys more than he knew and the end was particularly mawkish.

He was the older man Dorothy McGuire fell for in *Three Coins in the Fountain* (54), top-billed and the most popular film he made; and a top executive in *A Woman's World*. Both were star-filled, which was one way – lining 'em up across it – to fill the new CinemaScope screen. Then he was in *The Man Who Never Was* (56), filmed in Britain, a wartime suspense story which had been one of the many true-war bestsellers. This was almost the only normal part he played in films, though he was somewhat restrained in a familiar part – a collector – in *Boy on a Dolphin* (57). *The Remarkable Mr Pennypacker* (58) was *Cheaper by the Dozen* all over again, firmly set among Victoriana, with Dorothy McGuire as his wife; and *Holiday for Lovers* (59) – in the part Don Ameche had done on stage – was more 1950s formula (love and locations), though with situations that went back to Will Rogers. This version was merely embarrassing. His last picture was also the last picture of Leo McCarey, once one of the best of comedy directors, but now offering this distasteful spectacle of a couple of priests up against it in revolutionary China: *Satan Never Sleeps* (62), with William Holden. Webb's performance was rather moving, suggesting his range had never been exploited. He died in 1966.

Clifton Webb as the insufferable Mr Belvedere, in one of the three comedies built around that character – in a way, all *his films were. . . . Anyway,* Mr Belvedere Goes to College *(49), with Shirley Temple.*

Raquel Welch

If stardom was measured in mileage of newsprint, Raquel Welch would have been the greatest star since Marilyn Monroe. The articles, mind you, were repetitive: (a) how she became famous before the public had seen her on screen, (b) how popular she was despite a series of bad and poorly attended pictures and (c) how she felt about being the new sex-goddess. 'Playboy' interviewed her and 'Time Magazine' wrote her up not once but twice – once with a cover picture. It has always been difficult to decide whether the people on 'Time Magazine' covers are supposed to be men of achievement or merely newsworthy, but as Miss Welch qualifies in neither category one must conclude that he is what the American public wants to read about. Ezra Goodman said that 'Time Magazine' had discovered that their sales rose each time there was a movie star on the cover and, so as not to appear frivolous, they strictly rationed them. Welch joins a company which includes Jeanne Moreau, Humphrey Bogart, Marlon Brando, Bob Hope, John Wayne, the Redgrave sisters, Burton and Taylor, Marilyn Monroe, the Fondas, Mia Farrow and Dustin Hoffman, and – for Broadway achievements – Rosalind Russell, Rex Harrison, the Lunts and Shirley Booth. (It does not include Laurence Olivier, Bing Crosby, Judy Garland, Katharine Hepburn. . . .)

Welch belongs with 'Time Magazine'; and with 'Playboy', Kleenex, Coca-Cola and all the other pre-tested, pre-packaged goods of modern American society. She is ardently what statistics prove we want of our movie stars: statuesque, curvaceous, beautiful, young and healthy (though, said George Masters – 'make-up king to the stars' – to the 'Washington Post', 'she's silicone from the knees up'). In a Hollywood hopefully threatened with a take-over by the likes of Anne Jackson and Carrie Snodgress, she was a comforting throwback – a girl who was Miss La Jolla, Miss San Diego and Maid of California. She was born in Chicago in 1940, the daughter of a Bolivian-born engineer. As a child she took dancing lessons and in her teens started entering beauty contests. When her parents divorced she married a tuna-fisherman called Welch and they had two children. They were divorced after five years, in 1963, and she went to work in Dallas, modelling and serving cocktails. She also had her nose fixed before heading back to California and what Ruth Buzzi called 'tinsel-town'. There, after only three days, she met man-about-Hollywood Patrick Curtis. Curtis had started in show business as Olivia de Havilland's baby in *Gone With the Wind*; he became one of the children of Ma and Pa Kettle and changed his name to Curtis after his idol, Tony; he had played in 'Leave it to Beaver' on TV for six years and had made a documentary about musclemen. He was now working for a promotions firm and the thing he decided to promote was Raquel; within three weeks Curtwell Enterprises had been formed.

Raquel Welch as Prehistoric Woman in One Million BC *(66). It was certainly better to look at than the earlier version, but no more convincing.*

Her picture appeared in 'Life Magazine', in a bikini. She got a regular walk-on in 'Hollywood Palace' on ABC TV and a small unbilled bit in Elvis Presley's *Roustabout* (64). That was followed by a brief role as a hooker in *A House is Not a Home* and another unbilled bit in *Do Not Disturb* (65). Curtis got her the female lead in a two-bit pop musical, *A Swingin' Summer* (66), where she did a brief striptease. 20th signed her to a contract and put her into a medium-budget sci-fier, *Fantastic Voyage*, starring Stephen Boyd – the voyage was inside a human body and we did not see much of hers because she wore a rubber suit. She was then loaned to a British company, Hammer.

Hammer, in the course of making their horror pictures, had discovered there was a commercial advantage in familiar titles like *The Phantom of the Opera*; clinging to the cinema's bizarre past they had had a hotsy item with a (for them) lavish production of *She* with Ursula Andress and John Richardson. They planned a remake of *One Millon BC* with the same stars, but Andress said no: 20th, who had the US rights, sent over Welch. Curtis got her publicity by claiming she was America's answer to Andress – and she was certainly striking in the stills, in a few strategic tufts of fur. Of the film, 'Time Magazine' later said: 'No one who has seen *BC* will ever forget it. It was a ghastly, primeval *Romeo and Juliet. . . .*'

Publicity or no, 20th were not about to call her to make her contracted films, so Curtis fixed up four in Europe; an international effort with Edward G. Robinson and Vittorio De Sica, *The Biggest Bundle of Them All*, as a lady crook; *Le Fate* (67), an Italian episoder with Monica Vitti, Claudia Cardinale and Capucine in the other segments (rechristened *The Lovely Ladies* in the US, *Sex Quartet* in Britain and *Les Ogresses* in France – not that anywhere many went to see it); *Spara Forte più Forte non Capisco* with Marcello Mastroianni, as a whore; and *Le Plus Vieux Métier du Monde*, kinky-games time with an elderly German (Martin Held) in this execrable prostitute film. In 1967 she married Curtis in Paris, wearing a crocheted mini-dress which got plenty of news-space – as did the pictures released the same day of the two of them in bed together (some sort of nadir in the annals of movie publicity). 20th used her in two of their minor European products: *Bedazzled*, as Lust, a weak whimsy written by and featuring Dudley Moore and Peter Cook; and *Fathom*, a thriller with Anthony Franciosa.

Finally, she went home. 20th were cautious: more or less as window-dressing they put her into *Bandolero* (68) starring James Stewart and *Lady in Cement* with Frank Sinatra; then into a Spanish-made Western, *100 Rifles* (69), with Jim Brown – but notable only for offscreen feuds with him and Burt Reynolds, who later described her as 'plastic'. She paused on the way home to guest in *The Magic Christian*; then in Hollywood made another gimcrack thriller, *Flare-up*, playing a go-go dancer. Her first real star part was as *Myra Breckinridge* (70), the hero/heroine of Gore Vidal's novel, tastelessly filmed by Mike Sarne and a body-blow at human decency, no less – it was not exactly planned that way but Sarne's on-set antics apparently caused chaos. Welch's alleged differences with Mae West, making a come-back, also caused gossip and in the event the only good notices the film gleaned were directed towards Miss West. At the New York première she was mobbed and Welch ignored. It is hard for a sex-goddess to be passed over in favour of an old lady your grandfathers drooled over.

Smarting, perhaps, Welch went to Cyprus to make an art film for her own company, *Restless*, with Richard Johnson: 'a hot-blooded drama of adultery and vengeance' 'Playboy' called it – it was based on 'Thérèse Raquin' – but not till 1978, when it finally achieved a press show. Somewhat more in evidence were: *Hannie Caulder* (71), a mediocre Western co-starring Richard Culp; *Fuzz* (72), a thriller with Burt Reynolds in which she was a police detective; and *Kansas City Bomber*, about roller derby rivalries. The bomb was at the box-office and in her marriage, which ended in 1973. In Europe she was one of the wives of *Barbe-Bleue/Bluebeard* (73) Richard Burton and one of the suspects in the American-backed *The Last of Sheila*; she did not, apparently, get on with any of the other names in the cast and James Mason, after a lifetime of professional discretion, told a reporter that he had never met anyone as 'badly behaved'. The (well-publicized) rows on the next were with Oliver Reed and Faye Dunaway: *The Three Musketeers: The Queen's Diamonds* (74) and its sequel, *The Four Musketeers: The Revenge of Milady* (75); as Constance, Welch did her lines and her pratfalls like an automaton. The Merchant-Ivory team made her a movie queen of the 20s in *The Wild Party*, their ill-fated and ill-fitting rip-off of the Fatty Arbuckle affair; they had trouble with her – and with the distributor, who refused to show their version. Hollywood tried for the last time to date with *Mother, Jugs and Speed* (76), an overdone black farce about three ambulance drivers (Welch, Bill Crosby, Harvey Keitel). Welch remained the reigning sex queen of movies, but it was certainly *faute de mieux*: if men drooled over her photographs, they did not bother to go to her movies. She turned to nightclubs, concerts and TV, and in an interview 'Photoplay' commented: 'Raquel also feels that her versatility as an entertainer will help dispel her sex goddess image'; the magazine also reported that she had bought the rights to *Woman of the Dunes* and hoped to get Louis Malle to direct her in a Mexican version. There were two more films in Europe; *The Prince and the Pauper/Crossed Swords* (77), produced by the Salkinds (of *Musketeers* fame); and *L'Animal*, opposite Jean-Paul Belmondo.

In 1980 she remarried and began *Cannery Row* at a salary of $250,000, but was sacked a month later and replaced by Debra Winger, not then a name to conjure with. In February 1981 Welch sued for $20 million, claiming that she was being made a scapegoat for other movie personalities whose temperament was causing delays. She was, she said, always on the set on time – and MGM's case was, in part, that she breached her contract by applying make-up at home. She considered that her career was irreparably damaged and the award of $11 million was upheld, after the studio appeal, in August 1986. In the meantime she had substituted for the vacationing Lauren Bacall in 'Woman of the Year' – so impressively that she was asked to take over (82) when Bacall left to tour: Welch on Broadway played to SRO business (so, okay, it was on twofers), but this triumph led to no new career move. Indeed, that seemed stalled: *The Legend of Walks Far Woman*, a tele-film made in 1979 and a personal project which she had persuaded EMI, the British company, to back, finally made it – but cut and incomprehensible. She played a 19th-century Indian from youth to extreme old age.

Raquel Welch and Jim Brown in 100 Rifles *(69). He was an American lawman and she a Mexican Indian in this European-made Western, directed by Tom Gries.*

Her agent failed to get backing for a mini-series based on *Forever Amber* and she was away from public view till *Scandal in a Small Town* (88), a tele-film in which she was a waitress coping with anti-semitism.

TUESDAY WELD

It was widely assumed that no one with a name like Tuesday Weld was to be taken seriously. Besides, she made films with titles like *Rock Rock Rock* and *Sex Kittens Go To College*. She was/is blonde and cute-faced, like Sandra Dee. There was consternation, if not alarm, when, about her tenth film, critics started talking about her as an actress.

The name came about because she was a model. She was born in New York City in 1943; her father died when she was four and her mother found it easy to get the child jobs modelling children's clothes (she was christened Susan and nicknamed 'Tu-Tu', which became 'Tuesday' when she was older). As she grew, she progressed from mail-order catalogues to TV commercials, but she did not like modelling and wanted to act; her first experience was the star role in *Rock Rock Rock* (56), in which her singing voice was dubbed by Connie Francis. There were 30 musical numbers; it was shot in a studio in the Bronx in nine days and looked like it. Then, still less than 15, she understudied two roles in 'The Dark at the Top of the Stairs' on Broadway (57). She went on for one of them and an agent got her a contract at 20th – $350 a week to go to $1,500 over a seven-year period. They called her 'Fox's threat to Sandra Dee' and cast her in *Rally Round the Flag Boys* (59), as a precocious teenager called Comfort Goodpasture, who suddenly discovers she likes boys. That might suggest that someone had already realized her potential, but in fact 20th dropped her (though she worked intermittently for that studio for the next few years).

Pretty Poison *(68) was a sleeper, pushed out without fanfare by its distributors and rescued by a couple of critics. It managed to say something new and disturbing about that old movie cliché, neurotic youth: Tuesday Weld and Anthony Perkins.*

She played Danny Kaye's polio-stricken daughter in *The Five Pennies*; then Columbia sought her for the female lead in a campus drama, *Because They're Young* (60), directed by Paul Wendkos., She stayed on campus for *High Time*, at 20th, with Bing Crosby, and *Sex Kittens Go to College*, an Albert Zugsmith movie which, like the next, *The Private Lives of Adam and Eve*, was never shown abroad. This cruddy level continued with *Return to Peyton Place* (61), where she took on the part played by Hope Lange in the original, that of the girl who killed the man who tried to rape her. Also at 20th she and Lange were in something similar, *Wild in the Country* with Elvis Presley. Weld was a sluttish unmarried mother who played the guitar.

20th kept her on for a third film, *Bachelor Flat*, and she brought something more than looks and high spirit to her role, that of a thorn-in-the-flesh of Terry-Thomas. She turned down *Lolita* and began to study at the Actors' Studio. She returned to Hollywood for *Soldier in the Rain* (63), as a hip, bubblegum teenager used by Steve McQueen to persuade Jackie Gleason of the pleasures of civilian life. Urged on by director Ralph Nelson, she was touching and funny. She announced her intention of playing no more teenage roles, but after a two-year absence she played Bob Hope's wilful daughter in *I'll Take Sweden* (65). She was also learning her craft in TV dramas (earlier, she had been in a series, 'Dobie Gillis'). In *The Cincinnati Kid* she was McQueen's girl, yielding in her absence to Ann-Margret – and no prizes for who got audience sympathy. Weld's was, in fact, a really original performance, coupling a sense of wonder that he loved her with a matter-of-factness towards his idiosyncrasies.

Her best chance came with *Lord Love a Duck* (66), with Roddy McDowall, a bright satirical comedy about an innocent college girl granted her wishes by a student magician. It was overlooked by all but a few cinema buffs; those who saw it raved about Weld – and so did George Axelrod, who wrote and directed. She herself said it was the first film on which she had a chance to be creative; Axelrod said: 'Tuesday's a great actress and can become a great star because she doesn't fake anything. And the reason she doesn't fake anything is because she simply can't.' That year she married George Harz, McDowall's secretary, and because of a baby later turned down *Bonnie and Clyde* (later she turned down *Bob & Carol & Ted & Alice*, *Cactus Flower* and *True Grit*).

She got fine notices again for *Pretty Poison* (68) – which surprised her, for she had not enjoyed making it and thought it her 'worst performance'. But she was superb, in a difficult part, that of a completely amoral girl goading on Tony Perkins and not averse to a little matricide herself. More than any actress since Louise Brooks, she was able to suggest both a cherubic innocence of spirit and a satanic enjoyment of evil for its own sake. With Gregory Peck, she played a moonshiner's daughter in *I Walk the Line* (70). During this period she was reported as having retired and living in Britain. She returned to films in *A Safe Place* (71), written and directed by an old friend, Henry Jaglom, and based partly, it was said, on her own life – an excruciating, inpenetrable piece about a girl locked in dreams. *Play It As It Lays* (72) was better (what wasn't?), but there were few more takers for this tale of a weird Hollywood marriage; the husband was Anthony Perkins. Weld's own husband for a while was a British comic, Dudley Moore, and her only work was in television: *Reflections of Murder* (74), a remake of *Les Diaboliques*, with Joan Hackett and Sam Waterston; and *F. Scott Fitzgerald in Hollywood* (76). She returned to films in *Looking for Mr Goodbar* (77), in a supporting role as Diane Keaton's sexually-experimental sister, and was a high-flying divorcee accused of killing her child in *A Question of Guilt* (78). She and Nick Nolte, as a Vietnam veteran, were on the lam in *Who'll Stop the Rain?*, adapted from a novel called 'Dog Soldiers', to which title it reverted overseas, one of countless movies featuring foul-mouthed, vicious cops and sympathetic hard-drug pedlars: a critic or so tried to see it as something more, but the public knew better. United Artists distributed and it was reported that Weld was suing for $15 million over billing.

Then: *Mother and Daughter, the Loving War* (80), which made her the daughter of the underrated Frances Sternhagen, helping her with her daughter, for TV; *The Serial*, based on Cyra McFadden's satire on life in Marin County; and the seventh *Madam X* (81) but the first for television, in the title-role, with Eleanor Parker as the scheming mother-in-law. Much had been expected of *The Serial*, but it attracted little attention, and the same may be said of *Thief* and *Author! Author!* (82), respectively girlfriend to James Caan and married to Al Pacino (who has an affair with Dyan Cannon: in the plot, that is). She supported Donald Sutherland and Terri Garr in a telefilm based on John Steinbeck's last novel, *The Winter of Our Discontent* (83), which did her more good than a leading part in Serge Leone's self-indulgent *Once Upon a Time in America* (84): she was jeweller's clerk, gangster's assistant and raped by Robert DeNiro en route to prostitution and eventual retribution. After that, it was small fry to be *Scorned and Swindled* for TV – but getting revenge for same, with the help of Keith Carradine. The small screen would detain her for two more: *Circle of Violence* (86), turning on her demanding mother (Geraldine Fitzgerald), and *Something in Common*, allowing Ellen Burstyn's much younger son to fall in love with her. She returned to the big screen inauspiciously in a poor Disney, *Heartbreak Hotel* (88), as the dizzy mother of a boy who brings Elvis Presley (David Keith) to stay.

Richard Widmark

When Richard Widmark deserted villainy the screen lost one of its best villains. He was never so entertaining as a hero. As a hero, to be blunt, he is second-rate – oh, likeable, full of integrity, conscientious and all that, but when he is tough and cocky it is a long way after Cagney, when he is jaded he is way behind Bogart and he has hardly a hint of the bravura that made Errol Flynn so attractive to women. Nor – though he is probably a better actor – does he fill the screen quite so well as Burt or Kirk or Chuck. He is, in a word, self-effacing. His interviews make it clear that this is a man who loves his craft rather than the aura of being a big film actor. He was not content to play psychopathic killers throughout his career.

He was born in Sunrise, Minnesota, in 1914, the son of a travelling salesman. He grew up mainly in Sioux Falls, South Dakota, and went to school in Princeton, Illinois. He studied at Lake Forest College, where he was active in debating and drama (he appeared in about 30 plays). After graduating in Speech and Political Science he stayed on for two years as instructor in the Drama department. In 1938 he tried New York and began getting work in radio soap operas; he married a college friend, Jean Hazelwood, in 1942, when he was turned down for war service; in 1943 he made his stage début, due to the intervention of Arlene Francis, with whom he had worked in radio – in the Broadway

Richard Widmark and Victor Mature in Kiss of Death *(47), one of several crime melodramas made by 20th Century-Fox during the postwar period.*

production of 'Kiss and Tell', in a leading role. Most of the subsequent plays he did were flops, though he did have a run in the Chicago production of Elmer Rice's 'Dream Girl'. He got into films when someone heard him auditioning for a radio show and sent him over to see Henry Hathaway, looking for a villain for his next movie. Widmark wanted to be in movies and had already planned to do two a year – one for a studio, one for himself. However, to get the part that Hathaway promised, he had to sign a seven-year contract with 20th Century-Fox, with one-year options and no outside work.

The film was *Kiss of Death* (47), made in New York, an underworld thriller mostly about Victor Mature trying to go straight. The success of the film spawned a cycle of underworld movies at 20th, none of which attained the renown of those earlier Warner Bros thrillers (possibly because the players could not compare to Cagney, Robinson or Bogart). Widmark's assignment was to play an unbalanced giggling thug who at one point pushes a frail old lady down a flight of stairs to her death. His skullshead appearance and falsetto laughter made him famous overnight, though it is not a performance that today strikes you with its subtlety. (It was a type first established by Dan Duryea, following on the tight-lipped nattily suited gunmen of Lloyd Nolan. Duryea's contribution was the thin voice, the sneer and the nonchalant pose: Widmark refined the character to a point where it emerged as his own creation.) After appearing in stock in 'Joan of Lorraine' (his last stage appearance to date) he did a variation on it in *The Street With No Name* (48), with trilby, ankle-length open overcoat and catarrh-inhaler, the leader of the gang which is infiltrated by FBI agent Mark Stevens; and again in *Road House*, as the layabout lover of Ida Lupino; and in *Yellow Sky*, out West and hunted by Gregory Peck.

Paul Douglas and Richard Widmark look suitably grim as they face the prospect of bubonic plague in New Orleans: Panic in the Streets *(50), a thriller directed by Elia Kazan (who has called it his 'only perfect film').*

Widmark turned nice for Hathaway's remake of *Down to the Sea in Ships* (49), a look at life in the New England whaling ships, owing less to the Silent original than to *Captains Courageous*: Dean Stockwell played the Freddie Bartholomew part and Lionel Barrymore (hurrah) Lionel Barrymore. Widmark stayed nice for *Slattery's Hurricane*, playing a super species of weather forecaster; and he was then a cheap American con-man working the Soho joints in *Night and the City* (50): 'I just want to be somebody,' he says at the beginning, and, at the end, 'All my life I've been running.' He was very noble indeed as the medical officer helping detective Paul Douglas in Kazan's *Panic in the Streets* – perhaps his best sympathetic performance. Then he reversed again, to the low-down nigger-hating skunk of *No Way Out*, vowed to 'get' Sidney Poitier. This was a chilling performance, but determined him not to play any more such parts – and he was sufficiently strong at the box-office for 20th to give way.

He did Lewis Milestone's war drama, *Halls of Montezuma*, which, coming along just after a reissue of *All Quiet on the Western Front*, was a great disappointment; *The Frogmen* (51), an underwater melodrama, as a commander who goes by the book; *Red Skies of Montana* (52), pitted against a vengeful Jeffrey Hunter in this forest-fires melodrama; *Don't Bother to Knock*, as the drifter unluckily embroiled with psychopath Marilyn Monroe; and *O. Henry's Full House*, in the episode 'The Clarion Call', as a conceited killer. He was so fed up with playing villains or hard-faced heroes that he resolved to throw up his $3,500 a week contract – then they offered him a part he liked: *My Pal Gus*, his first screen comedy, a sentimental thing about a widower/tycoon who discovers (what else?) that money is not everything. There were four programmers: *Destination Gobi* (53), a war story; *Pick-Up on South Street*, a suspense-less crime story, marked by some good photography and good slangy dialogue – as a pickpocket (if he would not be a villain for 20th, at least they would make him an outsider); *Take the High Ground*, miscast as a tough training sergeant; and *Hell and High Water* (54), a conspicuously silly anti-Red film, as a submarine pilot. His contract wound up supporting Gary Cooper in *Garden of Evil*, playing a gambler with a neat line in cynical cracks, and Spencer Tracy in *Broken Lance*, as his maniacal and evil son Ben.

He did not wish to be tied down any longer by a contract and there were as many offers as he could cope with: the British *Prize of Gold* (55), as an American sergeant drawn into crime in West Berlin; Minnelli's *The Cobweb*, as the nicest and healthiest of the doctors, almost drawn into an affair with Lauren Bacall; *Backlash* (56), a Western; and *Run for the Sun*, along with Jane Greer on the run from Trevor Howard. After a Western at 20th, *The Last Wagon*, he made a stab at the Dauphin in Preminger's *Saint Joan* (57), but the performance was more embarrassing than intended. He redeemed himself with *Time Limit*, which he produced, a no-nonsense version of a Broadway court-martial play, well acted by himself (as a sympathetic colonel), Richard Basehart (as a man who may have collaborated with the Reds in Korea), Rip Torn and Martin Balsam. Karl Malden directed. Then there were two at MGM: *The Law and Jake Wade* (58), at his most nefarious in this Robert Taylor Western; and *The Tunnel of Love*, a domestic 'comedy' with Doris Day. He made *The Trap* (59), playing an attorney after killer Lee J. Cobb; *Warlock*, a Western with Henry Fonda; and John Wayne's *The Alamo*, playing a drunken Jim Bowie.

Widmark produced and his wife scripted *The Secret Ways* (61), a Cold War thriller based on a novel by Alistair MacLean; despite good locations it was the old business of an American journalist involved in Old–World skullduggery and his own harassed performance hardly helped. Further – like several other actors who became their own producers – the beatings up seemed rather more masochistic than necessary (*per ardua ad* Oscar?). He was an American in Europe under different circumstances in *Judgment at Nuremberg* – an entirely conventional performance as the prosecuting attorney. Between the two he and James Stewart were

Maximilian Schell and Richard Widmark, defence lawyer and prosecuting attorney respectively, in what might have been the biggest courtroom drama of them all: Judgment at Nuremberg (*61*).

in *Two Rode Together*, directed, at much less than his best, by John Ford. Then Widmark was in the third section of *How the West Was Won* (62). He turned up as a Viking in a turgid British-Yugoslav co-production, *The Long Ships* (64), supported by an equally lost cast including Sidney Poitier, Russ Tamblyn and Rosanna Schiaffino. He had two more failures that year: *Flight From Ayisha*, as a pilot, with Yul Brynner, and Ford's grandiose *Cheyenne Autumn*. Like most of Ford's recent work the story-line was tenuous and the whole unsatisfactory. Widmark loved working for Ford and deeply regretted the failure.

He turned to producing again, in conjunction with James B. Harris (who had been Kubrick's producer), who directed: *The Bedford Incident* (65), a sea story, as the skipper. It was only moderately successful and like other ageing stars Widmark put his faith in actioners: *Alvarez Kelly* (66), with William Holden, as a ruthless gunslinger; *The Way West* (67), with Robert Mitchum and Kirk Douglas; Don Siegel's excellent *Madigan* (68), a day or so in the life of a cop; and *Death of a Gunfighter* (69), notable chiefly because Lena Horne played his mistress and no reference was made to colour; it was also the scene of much distress, since Widmark did not get on with the first director, Robert Totten, and Siegel, who took over, disliked the experience so much that he refused credit (it is not the only film credited to the fictitious Allen Smithee). In Spain he made *A Talent for Loving* with Genevieve Page and Topol, directed by Richard Quine from a comic novel by Richard Condon about land claims in the old West: it was sold direct to TV. Quine also directed *The Moonshine War* (70), with Widmark as a struck-off dentist turned bootlegger, second-billed after TV player Patrick McGoohan, playing a lawman. Widmark made his own TV début as the President in *Vanished* (71), an over-three-hour version (it was the first tele-movie shown in two parts) of

Fletcher Knebel's novel about an aide who disappears. He had his best chance in years, and was superb, in *When the Legends Die* (72), as a drunken and ageing ex-rodeo star who becomes guardian to an Indian boy; but the film died too, at the box-office. In the tele-film *Brock's Last Case* he was a big city cop who relocates only to find, disillusioned, that he has not left crime behind.

In Britain, he played the American collector who is *Murdered on the Orient Express* (74); and after another TV movie, *The Last Day* (75), playing an ex-gunman who gets his rifle out again when the Dalton gang invades, he crossed the Atlantic again to do a dud horror film, *To the Devil a Daughter* (76), playing an occult novelist, and *The Sellout*, a spy thriller set in Jerusalem with Oliver Reed. Of the first of this pair he said 'I should never have gotten involved. I should have known better': he might have said as much of both. Returning to American films after five years, he began to establish himself as a star supporting actor: *Twilight's Last Gleaming* (77), as a top military man; *The Domino Principle*, with Gene Hackman; *Rollercoaster*, as an FBI agent investigating a crash of same; *Coma* (78), as chief surgeon in this hospital chiller, and a return to master villainy; and *The Swarm,* 'once again playing one of those cardboard military officers' ('Variety').

David Carradine was *Mr Horn* (79), a mini-series – that same bounty hunter whom Steve McQueen was incarnating for the big screen, with Widmark second-billed as his Indian scout chum; he supported Vanessa Redgrave and Donald Sutherland in a daft action adventure, *Bear Island*, as a repentant Nazi professor. He was a judge pronouncing on bussing for TV, in *All God's Children* (80), and an old salt, supporting Peter Strauss, in *A Whale for the Killing* (81), another tele-film of quality: at least, it was while he was on screen, giving authority and warmth to the role, proof that he had learnt from masters when he himself was younger. His co-star from those days, Poitier, directed him in a featured role, that of a menacing government agent, in *Hanky Panky* (82) starring Gene Wilder and Gilda Radnor – and if Widmark and Wilder had changed roles it might have been endurable for more of its length. Third-billed, he was the US Secretary of State in another British action adventure, *Who Dares Wins*: the star this time was Lewis Collins, who was famous for all of five minutes. *National Lampoon Goes to the Movies*, shot early in 1981, finally made it to HBO (83); Widmark was in the third of its three episodes, all of them terrible. He was a private eye in *Blackout* (85), made in Vancouver, in Volker Schlöndorff's superior *A Gathering of Old Men* (87) and a lawman on the trail of robber Willie Nelson in *Once Upon a Texas Train* (88), all made for television, but the first two were shown at the Cannes Film Festival.

Cornel Wilde

Cornel Wilde became a competent producer/director/actor, but for years he was a sort of male Maureen O'Hara, confined to medium-budget swashbucklers and action melodramas. Like her, his acting career was at its peak in the 40s, but unlike her, his charm was limited. Ditto his acting ability. In his marshmallow period, this hardly mattered, but in the harsher days of the 50s he had to struggle. It is much to his credit that he staved off oblivion by becoming a director.

He was born in New York City in 1915, the son of a Hungarian immigrant. The family returned to Budapest while he was still a boy, but not for long; he was educated at Townsend Harris High School in New York and at Columbia University for a while. He intended to become a surgeon, but became interested in Theatre; he had a job with a stock company in Saugerties, New York, and got a Broadway break with 'Moon Over Mulberry Street', after which he had assorted jobs, including ASM and translating plays from Hungarian and German. There were some Broadway engagements at the end of the decade: 'Pastoral' and 'White Plume' – and 'Romeo and Juliet'. He was a champion fencer and his prowess helped him get the part of Tybalt in Laurence Oliver's star-crossed 1940 production. As Olivier was filming in Hollywood, the cast was rehearsed there and Wilde was offered a contract by Warners to start at the end of the run. It was brief.

So was the contract. Warners gave him small parts in three pictures: *The Lady With Red Hair* (40); *High Sierra* (41), as a Mexican hotel clerk; and a B known variously as *Knockout* or *Right to the Heart*, with Arthur Kennedy and Anthony Quinn. They dropped him, but 20th took him up and put him into a B, *The Perfect Snob*, as a college athlete. They gave him a long-term contract and he supported Lloyd Nolan in *Manila Calling* (42), a minor war drama. He was the juvenile lead in *Life Begins at 8.30*, the film of Emlyn Williams's 'The Light of Heart', the neighbour who helps an old ham (Monty Woolley) to a come-back and falls for his crippled daughter: 'You may have a twisted-up foot, but Venus de Milo was mutilated, too,' he tells her. Then he was Sonja Henie's romance in *Wintertime* (43), which was some sort of progress – but it was Columbia who made him a star. They were planning a life of Chopin, a film they had had long on the shelf (it was originally a cherished project of Frank Capra); the use of some Tchaikovsky in a couple of wartime films and its subsequent popularity convinced them that the time might be right for Chopin. Wilde applied for the part and was cast after testing. Columbia had no intention of making a star for the benefit of 20th, so a deal was worked out whereby they could have him on favourable terms for three more films; also part of the deal was Alexander Knox, whom 20th wanted to borrow for *Wilson*. The film, *A Song to Remember* (45), turned out to be a big hit despite many deficiencies (such as its inability to suggest which song, if any, was to be remembered) and fans went wild about Wilde.

The notices, however, were not kind and, failing any favourable comment on Chopin's acting, Columbia cast him as Aladdin in *A Thousand and One Nights*, a Maria Montez vehicle which lacked Maria Montez. 20th grabbed him back for a steamy melodrama with Gene Tierney, *Leave Her to Heaven*, while Columbia waited patiently to turn him into a third folk-hero, Robin Hood (strictly speaking, Robin's son) in *The Bandit of Sherwood Forest* (46). 20th, not quite sure whether he would supplant Tyrone Power, tried him out in a musical with Jeanne Crain, *Centennial Summer*, and a horse-opera, *The Homestretch* (47). He was Amber's true love in *Forever Amber* and extremely dull about it. Columbia tried him in a comedy, *It Had to Be You*, with Ginger Rogers; then he did two dramas for 20th: *The Walls of Jericho* (48), as a county attorney saddled with a drunken wife (Ann Dvorak), and *Road House*, as a prison parolee hooked on Ida Lupino. Those concluded his contract.

He did a minor picture for Columbia, *Shockproof* (49), this time as a parole officer, with his then-wife, Patricia Knight (1937-51). At RKO he defended Maureen O'Hara *At Sword's Point* – but that was not released till 1952. He was a GI on *Four Days Leave* (50) in the Alps with Josette Day and Simone Signoret – a Swiss film made in English. Back at 20th, he moved *Two Flags West* with Linda Darnell. An ailing career got a shot in the arm when he played with a poor French accent the star trapeze artist in *The Greatest Show on Earth* (52), De Mille's big money-maker. The injection did no good, though it was said he was deluged with offers – from the evidence, they were all programmers, like *California Conquest*, with Teresa Wright, in which he was the leader of the Spanish-Americans seeking annexation by the US. It was a mild success and Columbia offered $100,000 each for two more films. At Warners he was a US major serving with the Maquis, in *Operation Secret*; at 20th he had Tyrone Power's old role in a remake of *Son of Fury* now transferred to South America, *Treasure of the Golden Condor* (53). There was much talk of him playing Sir Walter Raleigh for that studio, but instead he did a pair for MGM – *Main Street to Broadway*, their tribute to the Theatre, and *Saadia*, some Albert Lewin kitsch in which he was a Moroccan chieftain. Even more depressed was a cheap British costumer produced by Raymond Stross and directed by Arthur Lubin, *Star of India* (54), in which he was a French nobleman. It was the first of several with his second wife Jean Wallace (1951) and they were, said the 'MFB', both 'barely adequate'.

He had a good role as a nice junior executive in the star-studded *Woman's World*, married to June Allyson, but was back among the corn in *Passion*, as an outlaw in love with Yvonne de Carlo. He was an honest cop out

Centennial Summer *(46): the scene where sweet Jeanne Crain realizes that her flighty sister, Linda Darnell, is trying to pinch from her her new beau, handsome French Cornel Wilde. Miss Darnell's own fiancé, William Eythe, will provide momentary consolation.*

Woman's World *(54) was built around the premise that a tycoon (Clifton Webb) would choose his successor on the strength of a country weekend with three executives and their wives. Lauren Bacall was one of the wives and Cornel Wilde one of the husbands.*

to get Brian Donlevy and Richard Conte, *The Big Combo* (55), and a colonial spy in *The Scarlet Coat*, a part which Stewart Granger had refused to do – rightly, for the film flopped. The first film he produced and directed – for United Artists – was *Storm Fear* (56), a routine melodrama with himself, his wife and Dan Duryea. The reviews were not encouraging, but he would try again. As an actor only he did: *Hot Blood*, with Jane Russell; the British *Beyond Mombasa*, a cruddy adventure tale with Donna Reed; and *Omar Khayyam* (57), in the title-role of this Arabian Nights tale, lazily directed by William Dieterle. Paramount made the latter, in Technicolor and Vista Vision, and they gave the same lavish appendages to Wilde's own productions: *The Devil's Hairpin*, a motor-racing drama, and *Maracaibo* (58), an odd gallimaufry of fire-fighting and flamenco. His direction had got better and his acting worse. He returned to his old alma mater, Columbia, for Don Siegel's *Edge of Eternity* (59) – it was actually the edge of the Grand Canyon – a good thriller not enhanced by his own colourless performance.

He journeyed to Italy for one of the sand-and-sandal spectaculars, *Constantino il Grande in hoc Signo* (60), 'dreadfully uninspiring' in the title-role, thought the 'MFB'. He took much time and trouble setting up *Lancelot and Guinevere* (63), a pet project, with his wife sharing the title chores (Brian Aherne was Arthur). Filmed in Britain, distributed by Universal, the end result was tedium. Its bookings were spotty, but he came on strong with *The Naked Prey* (65), filmed in South Africa – a white man ('Man') hunted by a tribe of natives (these were the bad old days). Heavily allegorical, but both performance and direction were honest, a distinct improvement on what he had done before in both fields. Encouraged by favourable reviews, he showed increasing confidence in his handling of *Beach Red* (68), a rather bloody war film. He appeared in, but did not direct, *The Comic* (69), which starred Dick Van Dyke, whose 'personality' he, a Silent screen idol, steals; and he directed, but did not appear in, *No Blade of Grass* (71), a science-fiction thriller made in Britain with his wife and Nigel Davenport. It was not a success, nor was there a warm welcome when he made his television dramatic début as an anthropologist whose life and work (a book on demonology) are threatened by the *Gargoyles* (72) in the garden. In the years of *Jaws*, he had his own contribution to make – as writer, director, producer and actor: *Shark's Treasure* (75). He supported Lee Majors, *The Norseman* (78), as his aide, worrying whether they would make it back across the Atlantic – and worrying was one of the few things he was ever any good at. In Austria he was D'Artagnan in *The Fifth Musketeer* (79), based on 'The Man in the Iron Mask' – with a script unchanged from the 1939 version – that stayed long on the shelf.

ESTHER WILLIAMS

Esther Williams swam. For approximately 10 years (from the mid-40s to the mid-50s) MGM's script department was commanded to turn out two or three stories a year set round a swimming-pool. Imagination flagged: the star invariably played a swimming instructor. At intervals she jumped into the pool, coyly followed by an underwater camera. 'I can't honestly say that Esther Williams ever acted in an Andy Hardy picture,' said Mickey Rooney, 'but she swam in one.' It was enough. In 1949 and 1950 she was the biggest money-making female star after Betty Grable. In Singapore, for instance, where a week's run was considered a success, an Esther Williams musical could expect to run at least four.

She could not dance, she could not sing (when she did they dubbed her) and she never learned to act. She was pretty, cheerful and healthy. 'Wet she is a star. Dry she ain't,' commented Fanny Brice. To be fair, she never wanted to be one and MGM laid siege to her for over a year before she would sign a contract. She was born in Los Angeles in 1921 and was working in a department store when she first attracted the attention of sports-page writers. In 1938 at the Senior National Championships in Santa Barbara she broke the world record in her lap of the 880 yards relay. In Des Moines she broke another record – for the 100-metres free style. She should have been in the 1940 Olympics but in the meantime Billy Rose hired her for his 1939 Acquacade in San Francisco. An MGM talent scout was impressed: she was unimpressed, but eventually agreed to sign. She was tested with Clark Gable as a replacement for Lana Turner when Turner ran off to New York to marry Artie Shaw, but when Turner returned Williams lost the part (in *Somewhere I'll Find You*). The test was fine, but Williams reputedly claimed she was not ready for a star part and so became one of Rooney's romances in *Andy Hardy's Double Life* (42). A year later she had another small part in *A Guy Named Joe* (43).

Having got her feet wet, the studio decided to launch her as a star and in *Bathing Beauty* (44) they bolstered her with comic Red Skelton and guest stars like José Iturbi and Ethel 'Tico Tico' Smith. After her own guest spot in *Ziegfeld Follies* (shown in 1946; Fanny

Brice was in it but cut from the British version) there was another lavish Technicoloured vehicle, *Thrill of a Romance* (45) with Van Johnson and guest Lauritz Melchior. A 'straight' Esther was clearly out of her depth in a drama with William Powell, *The Hoodlum Saint* (46), and in Myrna Loy's old part in a musical remake of *Libeled Lady*, *Easy to Wed* with Van Johnson. In *Fiesta* (47) she left her pool to fight bulls – she was a toreador. Then: *This Time for Keeps*, supported by Melchior and Jimmy Durante; *On an Island with You* (48) with Durante and Peter Lawford; and *Take Me Out to the Ball Game* (49), by far the best film she made – and one of the least successful. She was the owner of a baseball team whose members included Gene Kelly and Frank Sinatra and she only swam once.

Between pregnancies (1949 and 1950) she kept the box-offices clicking merrily: *Neptune's Daughter* with Skelton; *Duchess of Idaho* (50) with Johnson; *Pagan Love Song* with Howard Keel; *Texas Carnival* (51) with Keel and Skelton; *Callaway Went Thataway*, in briefly, as herself; and *Skirts Ahoy!* (52), where the waves were not water but female gobs. Indeed, the emphasis was no longer on swimming, but she reverted increasingly to it as receipts declined: *Million Dollar Mermaid*, a heavily fictionalized biography of Annette Kellerman, and *Dangerous When Wet* (53) with Fernando Lamas, which had her swimming the English Channel. But *Easy to Love*, with Johnson, was just another musical – though she did play a swimming star. As for *Jupiter's Darling* (55), a neo-Roman musical with Keel, neither MGM nor anyone else liked it.

Her contract had four years to run and was reportedly revised in 1956 to run until 1961, for three films only. But Williams never made another film for MGM. She said later: 'All they ever did for me at MGM was to change my leading men and the water in the pool.' In 1956 she did a song-and-dance nightclub act with her husband, Ben Gage, and appeared in some Swim Spectaculars, including the 'Aqua Spectacle of 1956' at London's Empire Pool, advertised as 'Water Queen of the World'. As such she appeared on TV, swimming. She continued to receive royalties from a line of Esther Williams bathing-suits, but another venture, swimming-pools, failed.

As an actress, she at last began to take herself seriously and at Universal did *The Unguarded Moment* (56), from a story by Rosalind Russell and Larry Marcus, in which she was a schoolteacher supposedly attacked in the dark by a sexually maladjusted student (it turned out to be his father). No more successful was *Raw Wind in Eden* (58), where she was the object of contention between Jeff Chandler and Carlos Thompson – though she herself showed a slight flair for playing silly lines for comedy. Her name was linked romantically with Chandler for a brief while and then, after her divorce, with Fernando Lamas. They both went to live in Spain and it was in Europe that Williams made *The Big Show* (60), a psychological circus drama with Cliff Robertson that got only limited bookings. A year later Lamas directed himself and her in *La Fuente Magica*, but it seems never to have been publicly shown. They were married in 1963, but she was widowed in 1982.

Thrill of a Romance *(45) was a conventional postwar froth, with pilot Van Johnson falling for swimming instructress Esther Williams. Thrilled by the romance are Lauritz Melchior and Ethel Griffies.*

The titles and the leading men changed but the plots did not: naval officer Peter Lawford falling for swimming film-star Esther Williams in On an Island with You *(48). She went on location to Hawaii – and diverted him from duty.*

SHELLEY WINTERS

She was once an engaging blonde cutie, to be seen in tights in saloon bars, mouthing remarks like 'The noirve of the guy – inferring that I'm not a lady.' Then she began to Act, shifting her image only slightly – not so cute but even more tarnished, a succession of 'no-better-than-she-should-be' roles, usually from the lower strata of society and invariably victimized. Shelley Winters on screen is the prime example of the Hollywood truism that fast and flighty girls end up unhappy. She was a born loser – either her man (*He Ran All the Way*, *I Am a Camera*) or her life (*The Night of the Hunter*, *A Double Life*, *A Place in the Sun*) or both. Very often her lover murdered her. She has carried over this sad propensity for doom into the third and present stage of her career, playing blowsy and promiscuous American matrons. The range of her parts over 40 years does not suggest that she had fought very hard against type-casting, though 'Picturegoer' categorized her thus in 1955: 'Believes it pays to be tough – on and off the screen. She's truculent, frankly temperamental, but feels the draught when she's out of the headlines.' But she did fight for *better* parts, realizing after a while that she would never be a star of the first magnitude so it was better to be known as an actress. When the breaks were right, she was able to create living characters; more than most, she is a credible actress.

She was born (Shirley Schrift) in 1922 in St Louis, daughter of a tailor's cutter; the family moved to Long Island and then to Brooklyn. She became a Woolworths salesgirl, moved on to the Garment Center and a bit of modelling on the side. At that time the International Ladies Garment Workers Union were putting on an amateur revue, 'Pins and Needles'; it became the rage of New York and ran, with changes, for almost four years. Winters went into it during its run and did not go back to clerking by day. She had always wanted to be an actress and managed to get a small part in a 'trying-out' musical, 'Conquest in April' (40). By sheer persistence, apparently, she got a part on Broadway in 'The Night Before Christmas'; there were a couple more small parts before a good one in 'Rosalinda' (42), a version of 'Die Fledermaus', in which she was seen by Harry Cohn, who offered her a Columbia contract starting at $150 a week. She only got bits, most of them unbilled – and because most of them were sometimes no more than 'extra' bits, there is some controversy about her early credits. She herself admits to being in: *What a Woman!* (43), *Sailor's Holiday* (44), *She's a Soldier Too*, *Tonight and Every Night* (45) and *A Thousand and One Nights*; and she might also have been in: *Nine Girls* (44), *The Racket Man* and *Two-Man Submarine*. She was certainly in *Knickerbocker Holiday* (44), probably her second film, billed as Shelley Winter – feature-billed (fifth on the cast-list) and good as a bouncy ingénue in this United Artists musical starring Nelson Eddy and Constance Dowling. But Columbia were not remotely impressed: after her series of decorative bits, they dumped her.

She managed to get a part in a Long Beach production of 'The Merry Widow' (46) and tested at Warners, 20th and MGM. MGM made her a poolside lovely in *Living in a Big Way* (47); that was all. She got a bit as a nightclub chanteuse in *The Gangster* at Allied Artists, with Barry Sullivan and Belita, and she danced in a barn dance in *Red River* (48). By the time the latter was shown (it was long delayed) she had been seen in the part which made her a star. It came about when she asked Garson Kanin to let her understudy Judy Holliday in 'Born Yesterday'; instead he recommended her for a film he had written, to be directed by George Cukor. Cukor later said that she phoned him ceaselessly – this despite the fact that, by the time he eventually signed her, she had taken over the role of Ado Annie in 'Oklahoma!' in New York and was doing quite well in it. The part in the Cukor-Kanin film, *A Double Life*, was a showy one, that of Ronald Colman's waitress-mistress-victim, and Universal had wanted a name actress – but Winters received excellent notices and Universal offered a seven-year contract. They saw her, however, as a lower-case Lana Turner and made her a gangster's moll called Tory in *Larceny*, a B starring John Payne, Dan Duryea and Joan Caulfield. They loaned her to 20th for a good cameo role in *Cry of the City*, an old flame of escaped con Richard Conte, and then to Paramount to play the pathetic Myrtle in *The Great Gatsby* (49). She was killed off again in *Take One False Step* and was a moll again in *Johnny Stool Pigeon* with Howard Duff. She had the lead in *South Sea Sinner* (50), as a sister or cousin of Sadie Thompson, and, though 'Variety' found her performance 'vivid . . . reminiscent of Mae West in gestures and speech', 'The New York Times' thought she had 'no more command, either of glamour or of humor, than might be had by an apple blossom queen'. She was a dance-hall floozie in both *Winchester 73*, opposite James Stewart, and *Frenchie*, and the latter was a real vehicle for her (made perhaps because the press was clamouring for better roles for her) as a lady gambler out West, in love with Joel McCrea.

It was a very different Winters in *A Place in the Sun* (51) for George Stevens at Para

Above left Shelley Winters proved in her first important role – in A Double Life *(48) – that she could act, but for the next few years she became more familiar in poses like this.*

Above Shelley Winters reaffirmed her ability as an actress in George Stevens's A Place in the Sun *(51), as the sad little girl seduced by Montgomery Clift.*

Her roles matched the image: she played a saloon queen in South Sea Sinner *(50) – curiously retitled* East of Java *in Britain. (The piano-player, for those who care, is Liberace.)*

mount: no longer a sexy peroxide blonde, but a drab little factory girl made pregnant by Montgomery Clift. There was no longer any doubt that this was one of Hollywood's better performers. She begged for better parts. Before *A Place in the Sun* was released, UA asked for her for *He Ran All the Way*, as a naive and ingenuous girl who shelters murderer John Garfield. Universal refused, as they had *Little Egypt* lined up, a cheap extravaganza about that famous hip-dancer; according to Winters, she deliberately got so fat that Rhonda Fleming was cast instead, whereupon she quickly reduced and reported to UA. 'Picturegoer', reporting this, said that she was reckoned to be the most temperamental star since Katharine Hepburn or Luise Rainer – but she herself pointed out her films were always on schedule. In later years, she was not noted for temperament and it has to be said that this batch was enough to make anyone bad-tempered: *Behave Yourself*, a grim comedy at RKO with her then-fiancé, Farley Granger, as his dizzy wife; *The Raging Tide*, a waterfront drama based on Ernest K. Gann's 'Fiddler's Green', with Richard Conte; *Phone Call From a Stranger* (52) at 20th, an episode film, very good as a luckless but optimistic showgirl: *Meet Danny Wilson*, with Frank Sinatra; *Untamed Frontier*, a dull Western with Joseph Cotten; and MGM's weird *My Man and I*, with Ricardo Montalban as my man, a Mexican migrant worker, and Winters as I, a ridiculous drunken heroine.

Around this point Universal suspended her for dallying in New York with her new fiancé, Vittorio Gassmann (she had been married before, 1943-48, to a salesman). The marriage lasted two years (1952-54) and was stormy, with headlines at its demise. She was off the screen becoming a mother and also because of further suspensions. In June 1953 she told Universal that she wanted to film overseas (because of Gassmann) and asked for and got a new contract, non-exclusive (reportedly for seven years, but she did not film for that company after 1954). She returned with a whole rash of films, only the first of which was any good. *Executive Suite* (54), as Paul Douglas's more-than-a-secretary. The others: *Tennessee Champ*, a programmer blend of boxing and God, as the wife of promoter Keenan Wynn; *Saskatchewan*, as Alan Ladd's love interest; and *Playgirl*, where she got shot but did not die, as the brassy over-protective sister of Colleen Miller. Universal loaned her out for *To Dorothy a Son*, with John Gregson, as a gold-digger in this foolish British comedy. She stayed in Europe to make *Mambo* (55), an Italian-American venture by Robert Rossen, with Gassmann, and she was dead at the end of it. Critics wrote her off, but she was back on her old form in Charles Laughton's *The Night of the Hunter*, as a widow wooed, won and knifed by Robert Mitchum. The next two were supporting parts, presumably the reason she was billed as 'Miss Shelley Winters': the British *I Am a Camera*, touching as the German girl too cowardly to marry a Jew; and *The Big Knife*, a really incisive performance as the pathetic Dixie, Hollywood extra and girlfriend and, again, murdered. After which it was downhill again: *I Died a Thousand Times* with Jack Palance, an indifferent remake of *High Sierra*; and *The Treasure of Pancho Villa*, miscast as an American idealist caught up in the revolution.

She decided that Hollywood was taking her for granted and returned to the theatre. Earlier, she had toured in 'Born Yesterday' (50) and played Stella in 'A Streetcar Named Desire' (52) in Los Angeles. Now her sights were on Broadway; after 'Wedding Breakfast' in stock, she starred in New York in 'A Hatful of Rain', with Anthony Franciosa, who became her third husband (for three years). She was on Broadway again in 'Girls of Summer' (56) and made a couple of appearances in stock. She also did TV: 'The Women' (55), in the Joan Crawford part; 'A Double Life' (57) – her film part with Eric Portman; and 'Beyond This Place', with Farley Granger. She did not go back to filming till 1958, when she persuaded George Stevens to let her play the slobbish, frightened neighbour, Mrs Van Daan, in *The Diary of Anne Frank*, his version of the book and Broadway play that was mortally compromised by the casting of an ex-model, Millie Perkins, as Anne; apart from her the film was notably well-acted and Winters won a Best Supporting Oscar.

Now she met Hollywood on her own terms. It did not matter what the film, so long as the part was good (it did not have to be big). She continued to be variable, but there were seldom occasions when she was not interesting: *Odds Against Tomorrow*, in an older version of her waitress in *A Double Life*, more vulnerable but resilient; *Let No Man Write My Epitaph* (60) and *The Young Savages* (61), in both as the mother of delinquents – and fairly delinquent herself; *Lolita* (62), outstanding as that young lady's mother, vulgar, affectionate and sluttish; and *The Chapman Report*, hardly less so as a married woman hopelessly attracted to a narcissistic young man (Ray Danton). She continued to work from time to time in stock ('Two for the Sea-Saw', 'The Country Girl', etc.) and in 1962 took over from Bette Davis in the New York production of 'The Night of the Iguana'.

She played the madame in Joseph Strick's adaptation of Jean Genet's *The Balcony* (63), one of the first important films to emerge from the new 'independent' movement in Hollywood – but it was a dull thing, neither art nor entertainment, and it did not exactly help the cause. Winters was too casual and, for her, subdued: she herself considered her performance misconceived and said later that she wanted to forget the film, which she had hoped would be artistic. She returned to the conventional fold in *Wives and Lovers*, stealing the notices from the better-billed Van Johnson and Janet Leigh. She went to Italy to make *Gli Indifferenti* (64), as Rod Steiger's former mistress; in Hollywood was a madame again in *A House Is Not a Home*, the film of Madam Polly Adler's memoir. She was one of the many stars with cameo parts in Steven's *The Greatest Story Ever Told* (65) and a sluttish mother again in *A Patch of Blue*, which netted her a second Best Supporting Oscar. As a greedy ex-child star she gave a lift to her scenes in *Harper* (66) and she gave a positive wallop to those in *Alfie*, a beautifully humorous portrayal of a middle-aged American living in London with an eye for young Londoners and specifically Michael Caine. She was good as the prototype Jewish mother in *Enter Laughing* (67) and particularly pleasing in *The Scalphunters* (68), as a camp-follower who finally goes off with the Indians.

She was one leading player not affected by the industry crises, 1968/70, and not affected by the reduction in the number of films made. Indeed, she is a stronger survivor than almost all of her contemporaries. Possibly none of them – if asked – would have wanted to play in *Wild in the Streets*, because it was an AIP film, but the role was superb, as the obsessive mother of the first 'youth' US President; possibly none of them wanted to play her small role in *Buena Sera Mrs Campbell*, as Phil Silvers's harassed wife. Maybe no one ese wanted to play the vulgarian widow in *The Mad Room* (69), an undistinguished version of *Ladies in Retirement*. She then did *Arthur! Arthur?*, a black comedy with Donald Pleasence which has never been shown; then *How Do I Love Thee?* (70), as Jackie Gleason's mistress; AIP's *Bloody Mama*, in the title-role, the diabolical Ma Barker, gangster extraordinary; and *The Last Warrior* with Anthony Quinn, as a whore. She returned to Broadway for a short-lived musical about the Marx Brothers, as their mother, 'Minnie's Boys'; and then did two of Curtis Harrington's horror films, *What's the Matter with Helen?* (71), opening a school for kids in the Hollywood of the 30s, with Debbie Reynolds, and *Who(ever) Slew Aunti Roo?* as 'witch' to a modern Hansel and Gretel. She was seen simultaneously in two tele-films, in both as a mother, *Revenge*, exacting just that because her daughter was raped, and the much better *Death of Innocence*, attending the trial (for murder) of another daughter, in New York. The level did not rise much with a busted pilot, *The Adventures of Nick Carter* (72), co-starring Robert Conrad.

Miss Winters's later career has been mainly spent playing a certain type of American woman, perhaps best described as a middle-aged broad. In good circumstances, such as Kubrick's Lolita *(62), with James Mason, she could be very funny and accurate.*

Indeed, there remained no consistency in this actress's choice of roles or her playing of them, and, similarly, the films themselves ranged from those you never heard of to big successes – as in the first of them. *The Poseidon Adventure*, married to Jack Albertson in this shipwreck tale; made earlier, *Something to Hide* (73) found her married to Peter Finch and murdered by him after one big alcoholic scene. *The Devil's Daughter* was not her, but Belinda J. Montgomery, whom she has come to claim for Satan-worshipping rites: for television. The *Blume in Love* was George Segal and she had a cameo as a wealthy lady accustomed to her husband's infidelities; *Cleopatra Jones* was black narcotics agent Tamara Dobson and she was a dope pedlar. *Big Rose* (74) was her, a private detective in partnership with the much younger Barry Primus, and it was a pilot for a series which came to nought. *The Sex Symbol* was Connie Stevens, laughably cast as Marilyn Monroe, and Winters was a bitchy gossip columnist: scheduled for ABC TV, it was cancelled due to content, but shown in a couple of British cinemas the following year. *Journey Into Fear* (75) never reached them – nor many in the US: a Canadian film made on various European locales (and not a patch on the 1942 version), it began a particularly peripatetic phase in Winters's career: *That Lucky Touch*, with Susannah York and Roger Moore, as nagging wife to NATO general Lee

J. Cobb; *Diamonds*, a heist movie with Robert Shaw, made in Tel Aviv by Menahim Golan, in a dispensable cameo as an American tourist; *Next Stop Greenwich Village* (76), as an archetypal Jewish mother – to the young hero (Lenny Baker) who wanted to be an actor: *Le Locataire/The Tenant*, the most mistaken of all Roman Polanski's films, as a Paris concierge; and *Tentacoi/Tentacles*, as Henry Fonda's meddling sister. The latter was the first of four in Italy: *Mimi Bluette*; *Fiore del Mio Giardino*, with Monica Vitti; *Gran Bollito*, with Max von Sydow and Rita Tushingham, directed by Mauro Bolognini, as a mass murderess; and *Un Borghese Piccolo Piccolo* (77), as the scolding wife of mild-mannered Alberto Sordi, who leaves her to find the man who killed their son in a bank raid. *Pete's Dragon* was a live-action Disney with an animated dragon, with Jim Dale and Helen Reddy, and Winters was a backwoods woman up to no good in her five minutes of screen time; she was a local witch in a telemovie about college sororities, *The Initiation of Sarah* (78); and *King of the Gypsies* was, according to Frank Pierson, who directed, 'a Greek tragedy set in the Bronx'. As Queen of same, she was, said 'Variety', 'very bad.' She was the mother of *Elvis* (79), in a three-hour TV movie which had hopes of cinema showings overseas, and was then in the Canadian *City on Fire*, a dull disaster story, as a nurse, and the German-Israeli *The Magician of Lublin*, with Alan Arkin, and baring her breasts (which might have been worthwhile 30 years earlier).

Then: *Redneck County*, which originally had *Rape* appended and which does not seem to have been seen; a mini-series, *The French Atlantic Affair*; Blake Edwards's film à clef, *S.O.B.* (80), again as a conniving Hollywood agent; *Looping* (81), a German film made in English with Sydne Rome and 'a disaster from start to finish' ('Variety'), as an ageing carnival lady; *My Mother, My Daughter*, a feminist film made in 16mm, as a possessive mother; Harry Alan Towers's *Fanny Hill* (83) in Britain, as a madame; and *Over the Brooklyn Bridge* (84), as a Jewish mama – Elliott Gould's. Even the least of these were major credits compared to the quartet which followed: *Ellie*, a sex comedy, as Big Mama to Sheila Kennedy (1983 Penthouse Pet) who gets her revenge on her for marrying and murdering her father by seducing all her sons before killing them; *Déjà Vu* (85) with Jaclyn Smith, as a spiritualist; and *Witchfire*. On television she was the Dodo in all-star *Alice in Wonderland* and she had another fairly respectable credit with *The Delta Force* (86), in which she and Martin Balsam were a Jewish couple among many others hijacked by Middle East terrorists – till rescued by Charles Bronson. But *Very Close Quarters*, filmed three years earlier, went direct to video, an unfunny sex comedy set in Moscow with Winters as a single mother trying to get her daughter married to her boss. *Single Room* was abandoned when the money ran out and she was off the screen till *An Unremarkable Life* (89) with Patricia Neal and *Purple People Eater* with Ned Beatty.

NATALIE WOOD

In *Inside Dairy Clover* Natalie Wood played a young screen idol of the 30s, genus Judy Garland. At no point was she convincing. One critic said, 'She's brassy and mechanical, with wind-up emotions.' When James Mason discovered Garland in *A Star is Born* the audience is as convinced as he that here is a girl with that extra something. It is precisely that which Wood lacked. She was pretty and vivacious, she was competent and always watchable. If she was a star, why should she have been so wrong as Daisy Clover? It could be maintained that she was lucky, that she happened to be around in an era deficient in leading ladies.

She was certainly fortunate, if that is the word, in being one of the few child performers who made it big as a grown-up. She was born in San Francisco in 1938 and was discovered by director Irving Pichel when she was five. The family had moved to Santa Rosa, California, where he was filming *Happy Land* (43) on location; she was one of the neighbourhood kids and he put her into the film, with credit (as Natasha Gurdin). Her mother got her on to an agent's books and changed her name. Pichel gave her a good part in *Tomorrow is Forever* (46), as Orson Welles's adopted daughter, after which she got a bit part in *The Bride Wore Boots*, as Barbara Stanwyck's niece. Universal announced they had signed her to a seven-year contract – but she never made a film for them. A year later she turned up in two films for 20th: *Miracle on 34th Street* (47), as Maureen O'Hara's daughter, and *The Ghost and Mrs Muir*, as Gene Tierney's. She went to Republic for *Driftwood*, as an orphan adopted by doctor Dean Jagger; returned to 20th for *Scudda Hoo Scuda Hay* (48), as June Haver's sister, and *Chicken Every Sunday*, as Celeste Holm's daughter. She was Walter Brennan's daughter in *The Green Promise* (49), produced by Texas oilman Glenn McCarthy to boost the 4-H Club movement.

The demand continued for 'family' films: *Father Was a Fullback*, as Fred MacMurray's pet daughter; *Our Very Own* (50), as Ann

The young Natalie Wood, being comforted by Claudette Colbert in Tomorrow is Forever *(46), a weepie about a woman (Colbert) whose husband (Orson Welles) returns after twenty years' absence. And Natalie Wood growing up: as the nice girl who tried to help mixed-up James Dean in* Rebel Without a Cause *(55).*

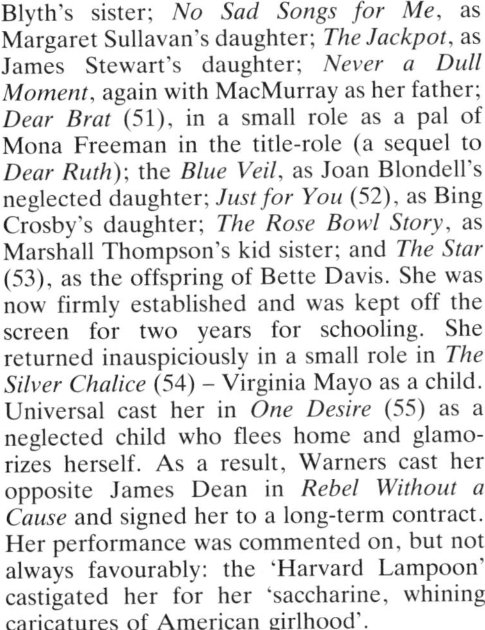

Blyth's sister; *No Sad Songs for Me*, as Margaret Sullavan's daughter; *The Jackpot*, as James Stewart's daughter; *Never a Dull Moment*, again with MacMurray as her father; *Dear Brat* (51), in a small role as a pal of Mona Freeman in the title-role (a sequel to *Dear Ruth*); the *Blue Veil*, as Joan Blondell's neglected daughter; *Just for You* (52), as Bing Crosby's daughter; *The Rose Bowl Story*, as Marshall Thompson's kid sister; and *The Star* (53), as the offspring of Bette Davis. She was now firmly established and was kept off the screen for two years for schooling. She returned inauspiciously in a small role in *The Silver Chalice* (54) – Virginia Mayo as a child. Universal cast her in *One Desire* (55) as a neglected child who flees home and glamorizes herself. As a result, Warners cast her opposite James Dean in *Rebel Without a Cause* and signed her to a long-term contract. Her performance was commented on, but not always favourably: the 'Harvard Lampoon' castigated her for her 'saccharine, whining caricatures of American girlhood'.

Warners began to build her into a star: *The Searchers* (56), as the white girl kidnapped by Indians; *The Burning Hills*, again as a half-breed, with Tab Hunter; *A Cry in the Night*, a silly melodrama in which she was kidnapped by sex maniac Raymond Burr and rescued by father Edmond O'Brien; *The Girl he Left Behind*, again with Hunter; and *Bombers B-52* (57), with Efrem Zimbalist Jr. There was little enough response and Warners tested several other actresses before assigning her to the film of Herman Wouk's bestseller, *Marjorie Morningstar* (58), as a Jewish girl among Gentiles. Gene Kelly co-starred: a flabby romantic drama that had some small success. She was at least in the star bracket and appeared with Frank Sinatra in *Kings Go Forth*, as a French girl with Negro blood. She co-starred with James Garner in *Cash McCall* (59) and with her then-husband (1957-63) Robert Wagner in *All the Fine Young Cannibals* (60). In the latter she took to drink; neither film did anything for her.

She knew it. She refused to be loaned out for *This Earth is Mine* and was suspended. This was said at the time to be over salary disagreements; later she said the quarrel was over parts: 'You get tough in this business, until you get big enough to hire people to get tough for you. Then you can sit back and be a lady.' She said she was suspended for 18 months; but she was back on the screen in two important films before too long. *West Side Story* (61) was the Robert Wise-Jerome Robbins film version of the Robbins-Bernstein stage hit. She was top-starred, alone, but like the male lead (Richard Beymer) there was an impression of *faute de mieux*: her singing voice was dubbed and her acting uninteresting. The film was a calculated milestone in screen musicals and a big, big hit. She was a teenager warned off sex in Kazan's *Splendor in the Grass* with Warren Beatty (her companion for a while in 1962), a film curiously translated into French as *La Fièvre dans le Sang* – but a better description of its overheated style and contents.

These followed another transferred Broadway musical and another plum part: *Gypsy* (62). She survived the onslaught of Rosalind Russell, playing her mother, but the real Gypsy Rose Lee *had* to have had more than this to arouse audiences. She turned down *Term of Trial* in Britain and did *Love With the Proper Stranger* (63) with Steve McQueen – and it was the closest she had yet come to projecting the ordinary American girl. She was certainly seen to better advantage in that

Natalie Wood as an adult: as a Macy's shop-girl loved and seduced by jazz musician Steve McQueen in Robert Mulligan's Love With the Proper Stranger *(63).*

film than in two frenzied comedies with Tony Curtis, *Sex and the Single Girl* (64) and *The Great Race* (65). *Inside Daisy Clover* followed, one of those wayward adaptations in which the bad things are retained and the good things jettisoned (and the author of the original novel, Gavin Lambert, did the screenplay). Audiences wisely eschewed this fake-poetic piece; nor were they interested in *This Property is Condemned* (66), an expansion of a one-acter by Tennessee Williams – who disowned the film. Wood was hopelessly out of her depth as the by-now archetypal Williams heroine (despite the fact that, in the words of Francis Ford Coppola who had worked on the script, she had 'gone through' several directors). Nor were there many takers for *Penelope*, a minor comedy with Ian Bannen. It was not surprising, therefore, when 'Variety', examining her track record in 1968, intimated that she was hardly worth the huge salary she then commanded. She was off the screen for three years and after many well-publicized affairs married again, British agent Richard Gregson. She returned as one of the players in a wife-swapping comedy, *Bob & Carol & Ted & Alice* (69). She worked for a percentage and when the film became a smash hit is reckoned to have made $2 million. Plans to produce her own films came to nothing and in 1972 she and Robert Wagner remarried. For TV, they were *The Affair* (73), he a lawyer and she a songwriter with polio: it was directed by Gilbert Cates, whose work usually deserves more than the one-off of this medium – but when shown in British cinemas the following year, the critics did not agree. There was unanimity on *Peeper* (75), a private-eye thriller with Michael Caine: it was a waste of time for all concerned; and on the TV *Cat on a Hot Tin Roof* (76), with Laurence Olivier and Wagner: Wood was hopeless as Maggie the Cat (like the earlier celluloid Maggie, Elizabeth Taylor, here was another one-time child-star who seemed to have learnt nothing in a long career). She was adequate in the Deborah Kerr role in *From Here to Eternity* (79), a mini-series which caught both the book and the time more faithfully than the film version – and was, indeed, way ahead of most TV adaptations. Also in that medium she was a suburban housewife recovering from a nervous breakdown in *The Cracker Factor*.

Natalie Wood, married to Robert Culp, but good friends with Dyan Cannon and her husband Elliott Gould, indulges in a spot of spouse-swapping in Bob & Carol & Ted & Alice *(69).*

She returned to the large screen in *Meteor*, followed by *The Last Married Couple in America* (80) with George Segal. A telemovie, *The Memory of Eva Ryker*, found her playing mother and daughter – and the memory concerned being torpedoed in the war. She had 'too many commitments' and was replaced in *The Mirror Crack'd* by a more potent name, Elizabeth Taylor. There were some striking parallels in their careers: at this point both were about to make their stage débuts – Wood in 'Anastasia' in Los Angeles. But this was not to be.

She was in the middle of a film for MGM, *Brainstorm*, when she died mysteriously in 1981. Husband Wagner was reputedly quarrelling with co-star Christopher Walken when she left their yacht, to be found hours later drowned with a high blood-alcohol level. Her ambition, she once said, was to be like Bette Davis, getting better all the time by playing all sorts of roles: but where a Davis performance stays with you for days you have forgotten Wood as soon as you have left the cinema.

JOANNE WOODWARD

Such is the way that the publicity machines and fan magazines work, most husband-and-wife teams have been written up out of all proportion to the results on screen. In fact, very few married couples have been either prolific or successful as a team and it is ironic that one of the most prolific – and most talented – should have been the least successful in commercial terms. Most of the films co-starring Paul Newman and Joanne Woodward have been poorly received and she never *quite* made it on her own; had it not been for his commanding stellar status she might well have been forgotten long ago, lost in the wash with the many other intelligent and admired actresses who never quite came to terms with Hollywood stardom. When, eventually, Newman decided to *direct* his wife, the shift in her career was decisive: the reception accorded *Rachel Rachel* prompted 'Variety' to comment that it represented 'as much as any picture can the truth of the old Show Biz maxim that real talent is never "dead". Despite her 1957 Oscar for *The Three Faces of Eve* Woodward has been considered a forlorn box-office cause by the industry. Her last six films had been flops . . . and the publicity "line" on her had been that she deliberately curtailed her acting schedule in order to concentrate on her roles as wife and mother. Now she can be expected to once again have her pick of scripts.'

She was born in Thomasville, Georgia, in 1931 and was stage-struck from childhood; she acted in college plays while studying at Louisiana State University, subsequently training in New York at both the Neighborhood Playhouse and the Actors' Studio. The break came when she got a Broadway understudy job, for William Inge's 'Picnic' in 1953 – it was then she met Newman. In 1954 she had a role in Leslie Stevens's 'The Lovers'. She also did about a hundred TV shows, including 'The 80 Mile Run' with Newman. In one 'Four Star Playhouse' her performance as a lonely adolescent caught the attention of Buddy Adler, then head of production at 20th. He signed her to a long-term contract.

She was loaned to Columbia for her film début, *Count Three and Pray* (55), co-starring with Van Heflin, as a gun-totin' orphan girl reformed by him; it received the scanty attention paid to that genre of film (the sentimental Western). The next was also bypassed, after an ad campaign which ran into censorship trouble; it was withdrawn and later sneaked into release, a capable version of Ira Levin's thriller, *A Kiss before Dying* (56). Robert Wagner did the kissing, Woodward was the one who died – after the first 20 minutes – and the film, really, died with her. Producer-director Nunnally Johnson wanted her for the lead in a movie based on a true story about a woman with schizophrenia-plus – a whale of a part; 20th said no until just about every important actress (including Judy Garland, Carroll Baker, June Allyson and Susan Hayward) had refused it. Thus she got *The Three Faces of Eve* (57) and her Best Actress Oscar; it was a creditable performance anyway – magnificent in view of the dim writing and direction. 20th were delighted but did not quite know what to do with her; she could act, but there was no guarantee that the public would respond as it had to more glamorous figures like Grace Kelly and Marilyn Monroe. Apart from which, she was selective over scripts and turned down film after film.

In the meantime she had been assigned to *No Down Payment*, with a bevy of the studio's hopefuls, all of them as young marrieds in the suburbs. As a new wife, Southern and already slatternly, she walked off with the film (though some of the others did not deserve their subsequent oblivion, notably Barbara Rush). *The Long Hot Summer* (58) was an overheated Southern tale; her part – that of Orson Welles's stubborn daughter – was typical of such pieces, but she played it without cliché and with that warm humour which has marked all her work. Newman was in it and they were married that year; she turned down the Shirley MacLaine role in *Some Came Running* (because she thought she was not ready for Sinatra's one-takes) and did a comedy with him, *Rally Round the Flag Boys*, which foundered on the unlikelihood of

From the Terrace *(60) was a typical John O'Hara examination of a marriage – if coated with a heavy Hollywood gloss. As the unhappy couple both Paul Newman and Joanne Woodward tried to behave like real people.*

his leaving her and the domestic nest for the plastic charms of Joan Collins. She was a Deep South Jane Eyre in *The Sound and the Fury* (59) with Yul Brynner, derived (like *The Long Hot Summer*) from William Faulkner, and was an asset to a movie which could have done with a few more. After that, *The Fugitive Kind*, with Marlon Brando, suggested that she might be making a corner in weirdies; but *From the Terrace* (60) at least saw her looking attractive. Her 'taunting, soulless, physically frustrated society girl glints as sharply as the tiara she appears to reserve for wear in taxis,' said Peter John Dyer. The film was lustreless, but it did well at the box-office. Newman co-starred and they were together again in *Paris Blues* (61), the first of the series of flops listed by 'Variety'. Deservedly; though Woodward did try to suggest a character where none existed – the sort of woman who would take Newman, jazz and Paris all in her stride.

It is less easy to account for the failure of the next, except that 20th lost its nerve and threw it away. From Inge's play 'A Loss of Roses', it became the catch-penny *The Stripper* (63) in the US and the meaningless *Woman of Summer* in Britain (the French title, *Les Loups et l'Agneau*, is incomprehensible). Brilliantly directed by the débuting Franklin Schaffner, it made something touching of an old situation: mutual attraction between a teenager (Richard Beymer) and his mother's house guest, a blowsy, good-natured showgirl, ageing but optimistic (the part had once been intended for Monroe). Like the film itself, Woodward's finely etched performance went conventional at the edges – perhaps the price that Hollywood exacts of real talents.

She freelanced after this: *A New Kind of Love* with her husband, an ooh-la-la look at Paris in the style of the Doris Day comedies, lightened by her comic skill; and *Signpost to Murder* (64), which seemed equally antique – the sort of B flick thought to have been abandoned. Accepting it suggested that she despaired of getting good offers and after it she was off the screen for two years. She returned in two decent pictures and was stunning in both of them: *A Fine Madness* (66), a serious New York comedy with Sean Connery, and *A Big Hand for the Little Lady*, a comedy-drama about a poker game, as Henry Fonda's wife. But both lacked the ingredients for wide popularity. Early in 1967 Universal announced that they had signed Woodward to an *exclusive* contract, which surprised the industry; later it was admitted there was no such contract, but no explanation was given for the announcement.

Both she and Newman admitted that *Rachel Rachel* (68) was the result of a long search to attempt to rehabilitate her career. Warners agreed to back it, provided that he would commit himself to a film for them – and then only to the tune of $3 million. He decided to direct, the story of an old-maid school-marm and how the experience of love changes her. He, she and it got raves: 'The most perceptive, heart-rending study I have ever seen of a girl in her thirties faced with spinsterhood. . . . Miss Woodward, in the performance of her careeer, gives her the shining inner spirit under her mushroom pallor' (Felix Barker in the London 'Evening News'). 'An actress who inhabits her part as a soul does a body. . . . It is in the transcendent strength of Joanne Woodward that the film achieves a classic stature. There is no gesture too minor for her to master. She peers out at the world with the washed-out eyes of a hunted animal. Her walk is a ladylike retreat, a sign of a losing battle with time and diet and fashion. Her drab voice quavers with a brittle strength that can command a student but break a parent's will. By my reckoning, it is Actress Woodward's best performance' ('Time Magazine'). She won the New York critics' Best Actress award; and the film did hefty business.

Before it had been shown, she had played an ordinary part – an unfaithful wife – in *Winning* (69), a racing drama with her husband. With him she appeared in *W.U.S.A.* (71), as a semi-whore who shacks up with him, a credibly touching performance. She was a psychiatrist in *They Might Be Giants*, with George C. Scott. None of them was very successful and Newman stepped in again, to direct her in *The Effect of the Gamma Rays on the Man-in-the-Moon Marigolds* (72), based on an off-Broadway play by Paul

Below, Rachel Rachel *(68) was directed by Paul Newman and was a fine example of those movies about spinsters having one last love affair. Joanne Woodward gave a beautiful performance, and James Olsen was equally good as the man.*

Zindel. If, from his point of view, *Rachel Rachel* atoned for *The Silver Chalice*, this atoned for *From the Terrace*; both films showed him a film-maker who cares about everyday predicaments – loneliness, old age, growing-up and just coping. Woodward was a sharp-tongued, slovenly and trashily dressed mother (of two daughters, including her own, Nell Potts), indicating along with her dreams an honest and realistic care for them. Stewart Stern, who had done the screenplay of *Rachel Rachel*, wrote one specially for her, but Newman declined to direct, because he did not want to make a career out of making women's pictures; so Gilbert Cates helmed *Summer Wishes Winter Dreams* (73), with Woodward this time at the menopausal stage of her marriage to Martin Balsam, facing a number of crises, including the death of her mother and the homosexuality of their son. The three performances form a remarkable triumvirate, unique in American cinema: daughter, mother, wife, done by Woodward with a blend of wit and compassion unmatched by any other screen actress of her generation. The three films themselves, though not devoid of melodrama or the thrills of women's pictures, do cover areas neglected by the cinema; the last two – *Rachel Rachel* has moments to set you cheering – had too much hurt in them to be wildly popular.

Perhaps that is why Woodward returned to a conventional role in a conventional thriller with her husband, as an old flame of his, *The Drowning Pool* (76), and then turned to TV. 'As Hollywood movie stars Paul and I were both colossal flops,' she told 'Photoplay'. 'I could never stand the place. There were so many things I loathed about [it].' She told another reporter, 'I used to have great traumas about not presenting a star image. But I'm not a star. A star is someone whose personality transcends anything. Mine doesn't transcend anything. That's why I like acting – so I won't have to come on as myself.' She observed that she lost interest in movies after the failure of *Summer Wishes Winter Dreams* and added, 'Parts for my age – middle-aged ladies – don't exist in movies, but they do in television.' She started off in that medium in terrific style, in a three-hour-plus piece reminiscent of *Three Faces of Eve*, *Sybil*, in which she was the psychiatrist and Sally Field the teenager with a multiple personality: Field, who has worshipped her ever since, won an Emmy for Outstanding Actress, which in a just world should have been shared. *Come Back Little Sheba* (77) at least gave her a chance to work with an idol, Laurence Olivier, in Britain, and also for television she was a housewife who rebels against her family and runs the marathon, in *See How She Runs*

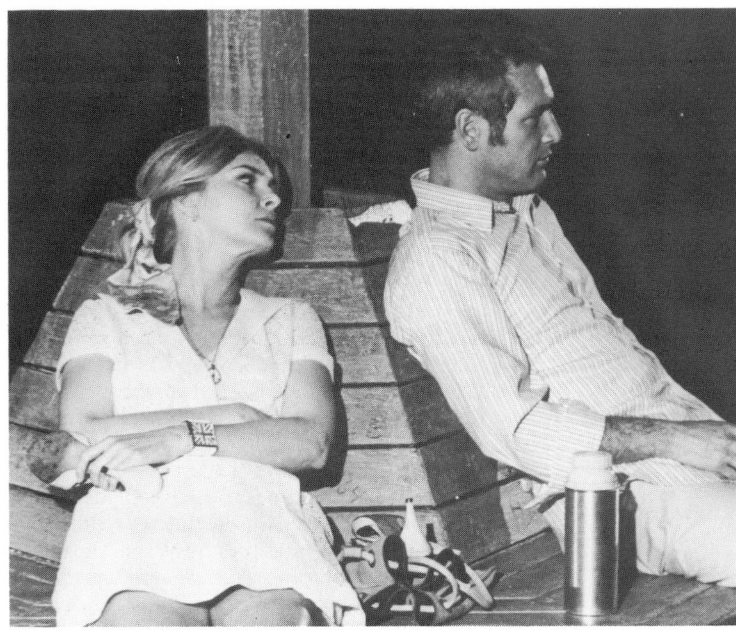

Above, Woodward and Newman in W.U.S.A. *(71). This was also familiar territory to her – part-time floozie, too old for the Five and Ten, hopefully waiting for a job slinging hash – but she had seldom played with more depth.*

(78), which won her her first Emmy. For cinemas, she was the wife separated from Burt Reynolds in *The End*, 'poorly utilised but adroitedly cast' said 'Variety'. On television she did a cameo, as the young hero's mother, in *A Christmas to Remember* and turned vigilante to chase the thugs who have slashed her tyres on *The Streets of L.A.* (79).

Newman directed her in *The Shadow Box* (80), which spoils their record in these capacities and her choice of TV properties: as a play it won a Pulitzer and a Tony, but the piece is a vapid thing about some terminally ill people, including Christopher Plummer as her gay ex-husband. Visiting him, she comes on like a cross between Blanche du Bois and Shirley MacLaine at her kookiest. But *Crisis at Central High* (81) was compensation, a beautiful job – which won her another Emmy – as Elizabeth Huckaby, the teacher who set down an account of the turmoil when Little Rock High School, Arkansas, was integrated. Woodward returned to the stage, in 'Candida' in Ohio and on Broadway, in 'Hay Fever' (83) and in 'The Glass Menagerie' as Amanda – on the same stage on which she had played Laura 35 years earlier. She had a gratifyingly large cameo role with Newman, again as an old girlfriend, in *Harry and Son* (84), which he also directed, and then returned to television: *Passions*, as the wife of Richard Crenna and meeting his younger mistress (Lindsay Wagner) after he dies; and the superior *Do You Remember Love?* (85), as the teacher wife of Richard Kiley, who does not know how to react when she discovers that she has Alzheimer's Disease – a performance which brought her her third Emmy. For cinemas, Newman set forth her definitive Amanda, in *The Glass Menagerie* (87), and it is hard to imagine the (entire) play better done. They are to act together again in *Mr and Mrs Bridge* (89).

JANE WYMAN

Jane Wyman has undergone almost every permutation available to a Hollywood actress: extra; bit-player; starlet; B-picture queen; glamour girl; heroine's friend/brash blonde/second lead; actress; Oscar winner; star; great actress; has-been; TV star in soaps. The Wyman that toiled so long in the Warner Bros vineyards is not tremendously interesting, though hindsight detects an intelligence and spirit not adequately appreciated at the time. Once she reached the top, however, she made as affecting a heroine as there had ever been, with her big curious eyes and squirrel cheeks.

She was born in St Joseph, Missouri, in 1914, to a family which took a prominent part in civic affairs. Her mother wanted her to become a movie star and to that end she trained as a dancer while still a child. When she was eight they tried an uninterested Hollywood; and they tried again when she was 15. Living in Los Angeles was no help, so Wyman returned to Missouri and became a singer under the name Jane Darrell (she was born Sarah Jane Fulks and took the name Wyman from her first husband, whom she divorced in 1931). She travelled the US singing mostly blues on radio stations – until she wound up in LA once more. She got a job dancing with Le Roy Prinz, the dance director, and began to see the inside of the studios. Universal tested her and gave her a bit in *My Man Godfrey* (36), but she got left on the cutting-room floor. She applied to Warners for a test and was offered a contract; unbilled, she had one line as a chorus girl auditioning for Dick Powell in *Stage Struck*: 'My name is Bessie Fuffnik, I swim, ride, dive, imitate birds and play the trombone.' After a similar role in *Cain and Mabel*, she was upped to seventh billing in *Smart Blonde*, the first of the studio's Torchy Blane B series. She was one of the *Gold Diggers of 1937*, unbilled, and then in the chorus – of the Folies-Bergère – with Joan Blondell in *The King and the Chorus Girl* (37). She was a pal of Ruby Keeler in *Ready Willing and Able*, Stuart Erwin's girl in *Slim* and one of the admirers of *The Singing Marine* Dick Powell.

Warners liked her enough to put her opposite radio singer Kenny Baker in his screen bow, *Mr Dodds Takes the Air*, a remake of *The Crooner*. She was delightfully daffy and was given the star spot in a B, *Public Wedding*, with William Hooper. Then she was loaned to Universal for another B, with William Hall, *The Spy Ring* (38), about espionage on a California airbase. After supporting Carole Lombard in *Fools for Scandal*, she returned to Bs: *He Couldn't Say No* and *Wide Open Faces* opposite Joe E. Brown at Columbia. Also on loan she supported Robert Taylor, as the friend of his beloved, Maureen O'Sullivan in *The Crowd Roars* and was then cast as a bouncy, bespectacled blonde in *Brother Rat*, a hit film from the Monks-Finklehoffe Broadway comedy about life at a military academy; the boys included Eddie Albert, Wayne Morris and Ronald Reagan, their girl were respectively Jane Bryan, Priscilla and Wyman. She was loaned to 20th for *Tail Spin* (39), as Alabama, one of Alice Faye's fellow flyers, then played a lady dick in *Private Detective No 1*, a B, with Dick Foran. She was now firmly typed as a peppy blonde, an obvious successor to Joan Blondell and Glenda Farrell, both of whom were leaving the studio. She was with Blondell in *The Kid from Kokomo*, a boxing yarn, and then took over Farrell's girl detective, Torchy Blane, in *Torchy Plays With Dynamite* – which series was then quietly dropped. In *Kid Nightingale*, another B, she coped with singing boxer John Payne.

She had been married briefly (1936-37) and was now seen around with Ronald Reagan (they were married, 1940-48; she remarried, 1952-54 and 1961-65, musician Fred Karger). To capitalize on the romance, Warners put them into two films: *Brother Rat and a Baby* (40), a sequel that in no way equalled the success of the first, and *An Angel From Texas*, again with Albert, a version of George S. Kaufman's old play, 'The Butter and Egg Man'. In a B, *Flight Angels*, she and Virginia Bruce were stewardesses; in *My Love Came Back* she and Olivia de Havilland were violinists. *Tugboat Annie Sails Again* was an attempt to refloat Marie Dressler's old barge, with Marjorie Rambeau in that part, Alan Hale in Wallace Beery's and Reagan and Wyman as the ingénues. She stayed seaworthy for *Gambling on the High Seas* and then was part of the *Honeymoon for Three* (41) with Ann Sheridan and George Brent. She helped Dennis Morgan tackle the *Bad Men of Missouri*; said *You're in the Army Now* to Jimmy Durante and Phil Silvers; and was perplexed with Jeffrey Lynn each time *The Body Disappears*, an imitation of *Topper* – and as far as audiences were concerned, the same fate might have overtaken these films.

Things improved with *Larceny Inc* (42) which, if only a programmer, at least starred Edward G. Robinson; she was no longer being sold as a leggy, busty broad and her quiet but perky charm was here nicely set off by Jack Carson's ox-like ditto – the first of several teamings. There was a loan-out to RKO that did nothing for her, *My Favorite Spy*, a B musical with Kay Kyser, but she was much noted as Betty Grable's sidekick in *Footlight Serenade* at 20th, telling her *almost* prophetically, 'You have as much chance of doing that routine as I have of being the First Lady.' She was off the screen becoming a mother and returned to the screen with her hair back to its natural brunette; and her role in *Princess O'Rourke* (43), though merely as Olivia de Havilland's sidekick – and again with Carson – was a good one. Billy Wilder saw it and it was to lead to great things. Meanwhile, she and Carson were detectives disguised as domestic help in *Make Your Own Bed* (44) and she was an amateur one in *Crime by Night* with Faye Emerson, her last B. She was a nitwit in *The Doughgirls*, loving and squabbling with Carson, and in *Hollywood Canteen* they dueted 'What are you doin' the rest of your life?'.

Wilder got Paramount to borrow Wyman for a small but telling part in *The Lost Weekend* (45), that of Ray Milland's faithful but suspicious fiancée; it did not require great histrionics, but proved that Warners had got her all wrong. They teamed her again with Carson (and others from *The Doughgirls* – Ann Sheridan, Eve Arden) in *One More Tomorrow* (46); and cast her as a showgirl – with a couple of songs – in *Night and Day*. However, on the strength of *Lost Weekend*, MGM borrowed her for *The Yearling* to play the embittered, patient wife of Gregory Peck. With her plain-scrubbed, tired face and her hair scraped back in a bun, it was the sort of performance which always impresses the film colony and gets an Oscar nomination. The press agreed; Fred Majdalany in the 'Daily Mail' (London) called it 'an outstanding performance' and added that she 'most subtly conveys the impression that love, not shrewishness, is behind her discipline'. A joyful Warners announced that they had signed her to a new 10-year contract (though seven was the legal limit), but ignored her notices and dumped her into a Dennis Morgan Western, *Cheyenne* (47). Let out again, she gave an excellent account of herself (new style) in RKO's *Magic Town*, opposite James Stewart.

It was producer Jerry Wald who thought she could be trusted with the central role of *Johnny Belinda* (48), a melodrama about a deaf mute who is raped and made a mother without being able to confess or comprehend what has happened. Director Jean Negulesco has said the film was made with great love, and it shows – but Jack Warner disliked it so much that Negulesco was sacked and the film shelved. When finally previewed, it became a huge success and garnered 10 Oscar nominations (Wyman made Warner take a trade ad apologizing to cast and crew). Wyman's reviews were so lyrical (Bosley Crowther: 'sensitive and poignant . . . brings superior insight and tenderness to the role . . . makes the pathetic young woman glow with emotional warmth') that almost overnight she became the hottest property in films. A Best Actress Oscar – plus the 'Picturegoer' Gold Medal – confirmed her new position. The performance did not, in fact, indicate an overwhelming new talent, but it would probably have been a lesser film with any other actress; in subsequent films she played always with understated intelligence and charm. The days of the blonde cutie were forgotten and the public responded with warmth to this new 'class' actress (as to which was the real Jane Wyman, probably a bit of both; interviews suggest taste, intelligence, zest and professionalism of a high order).

Warners tried to capitalize on the demand for Wyman by hurrying her into two mediocre comedies, *A Kiss in the Dark* (49) with David Niven, as a photographer's model, and *The Lady Takes a Sailor* with Dennis Moran, as a researcher defending her reputation: that they did not put her back where she started is due to the size of the *Belinda* triumph. She

Jane Wyman in the days when she was type-cast as a dizzy blonde, usually the heroine's best friend: My Love Came Back *(40) with Eddie Albert. At the time she was married to Ronald Reagan and since she also made some films with him you might have expected us to include a still from one of those, but we just could not bring ourselves to do it.*

Lew Ayres as the kindly doctor and Jane Wyman as the deaf-mute in Johnny Belinda *(48). The plot is so melodramatic that at one time the film seemed dated; but today the care that went into its making is its most evident quality. After* Johnny Belinda, *Jane Wyman was offered several movies which required her to suffer nobly throughout. One of the better ones was* The Blue Veil *(51), in which she played a nanny continually sacrificing herself for her charges. In this picture she is turning down Richard Carlson.*

guested in *It's a Great Feeling* and then Hitchcock's *Stage Fright* (50) found her convincingly a RADA student in London (though he found her difficult because she did not care to look as plain as was necessary for the part, or so he claimed: she says the remark has puzzled her for years). She took a few more years off her age to play the shy, club-footed Laura of Tennessee Williams's *The Glass Menagerie* and in that fairly satisfactory film version was as good as the part will allow, tremulous and pathetic. She did a comedy at MGM, as an air-stewardess loved by the *Three Guys Named Mike* (51) and was more than game ('a wow' in the words of 'Variety') as Bing Crosby's wayward leading lady in *Here Comes the Groom* (they had a genial duet, 'In the Cool, Cool, Cool of the Evening'). These she liked; but was upset when Warners proposed the lead in a Kirk Douglas Western. Instead she was loaned out again for a part turned down by both Garbo and Ingrid Bergman and played by Gaby Morlay in the original version, *La Maternelle: The Blue Veil*, ageing through 10 reels minding other people's babies. 'Variety' said it was 'a personal triumph that ranks with, if not surpassing, any for which she has previously been kudoed'. In Britain she was voted a second 'Picturegoer' Gold Medal.

She sang one song in *Starlift*, guesting; did another with Crosby, *Just for You* (52); and then had her first failure in quite some time, the maudlin *The Will Rogers Story*, with Rogers Jr as his pa. One American trade paper put her second at the box-office, after Gary Cooper, and followed by Susan Hayward, Crosby, June Allyson, Doris Day, Gregory Peck, Esther Williams, Cary Grant and John Wayne. There were three remakes: *Let's Do It Again* (53) with Ray Milland, an awful musical version of *The Awful Truth*; *So Big*, from Edna Ferber's weepie and her last for Warners; and *Magnificent Obsession* (54), another weepie, with Rock Hudson at Universal. The latter had lots of pianos which no one played and in more ways than one resembled an ad in 'Ladies Home Journal' – but the public liked it enough (Wyman won a third 'Picturegoer' medal) for Universal to team her with Hudson again in *All That Heaven Allows* (55), which was even more sudsy. In between, she did another woman's picture, *Lucy Gallant*, and afterwards, yet another, *Miracle in the Rain* (56), back at Warners, with Van Johnson. That one was decently written (by Ben Hecht) and directed (by Rudolph Maté, on location in New York) and was in many ways touching; but it came at the end of the cycle and hastened Wyman's demise at the box-office. She was resolved, she said, to do only comedies in future.

Instead, she turned to TV, with her own series, 'The Firestone Theater'; she worked very hard, she said, and when it was through she was happy to settle into semi-retirement. She left it when 20th needed a replacement for Gene Tierney in *Holiday for Lovers* (59), as Clifton Webb's wife, and later let Disney talk her into playing the stern aunt in *Pollyanna* (60), but was weak in a strong cast because she was unable to disguise her natural warmth (though that was not a bad quality to find in that particular film). For Disney again she co-starred with Fred MacMurray in the high-grossing *Bon Voyage* (62) and then stayed away till Bob Hope persuaded her to demonstrate with him *How to Commit Marriage* (69), a welcome if unremarked-upon return. In a

Wyman suffered quite a lot in her films of this period, usually in Technicolored splendour. This one is Lucy Gallant (55), *in which she owned a chic boutique in Texas but did not make it to the altar with Charlton Heston till the last reel.*

TV movie, *The Failing of Raymond* (71), she was a teacher threatened by a mental Dean Stockwell. When seen after an absence of some years – in a TV tribute to Crosby – she was grey-haired, in contrast to just about every other female star of her generation, and you wanted to cheer because she looked so much better than most of the others (poor Merle Oberon could not smile). Also on TV, she returned to acting, in a major role, as the local healer who opposes an idealistic young medico, Lindsay Wagner, in *The Incredible Journey of Dr Meg Laurel* (79). In 1981 she was lured back to television, to play the matriarch in a classy weekly soap opera, 'Falcon Crest' – because of the attractive high fee, said by 'People Magazine' in 1986 to be $60,000 per episode (28 a year = $1,600,000).

SUSANNAH YORK

Susannah York is blonde, blue-eyed and very engaging: intermittently during her film career she has given evidence of a talent as positively agreeable.

She was born in 1941 in London, but brought up mainly in Scotland; she studied at RADA (where she met her husband, Michael Wells) and had no difficulty, when she left, in getting both an agent and a job. She went into rep at Worthing and did some TV and worked in pantomime in Derby. The agent got her the ingénue role – Alec Guinness's daughter – in *Tunes of Glory* (60); Guinness called her 'the best thing in films since Audrey Hepburn'. She played a sweet young thing in a weak comedy with Norman Wisdom, *There Was a Crooked Man*, and then a schoolgirl in Rumer Godden's gentle story, *The Greengage Summer* (61), with a crush on Kenneth More. It was less a performance than a smile, a glance, a movement of her head: only a curmudgeon could fail to be captivated. Veteran Victor Saville, who produced, was: he signed her to a one picture a year contract (but never made another film). So were the Americans: the film was an unexpected success in the States and as a result John Huston signed York to play one of the key patients of Montgomery Clift *Freud* (62).

The film that made her well known, however, was *Tom Jones* (63), the ideal picture-book heroine, peaches-and-creamy, capricious, with just the right degree of sex dancing in her eyes. In the West End she starred in an adaptation of Henry James's 'The Wings of the Dove' and got rave notices; as in her film performances, she betrayed inexperience, but also that quality of stillness that great stars have. Unfortunately, she proceeded to make three rotten (American) films: *The Seventh Dawn* (64), her least favourite film, a jungle drama with William Holden, as the Governor's daughter; *Sands of the Kalahari* (65), stuck in the desert with Stuart Whitman and almost raped by Nigel Davenport; and *Kaleidoscope* (66), a 'swinging' comedy-thriller with Warren Beatty, as a society ninny. The latter should have starred Sandra Dee, but to qualify for Eady plan money (it was technically a British film) Miss Dee ceded to Miss York. Only *A Man for All Seasons*, playing Meg Roper, gave her any chance to show that she was growing as an actress; and her quiet strength was in refreshing contrast to her work in the two stinkers that followed, *Sebastian* (67) with Dirk Bogarde and *Duffy* (68) with James Coburn. In fact, she was increasingly tiresome in such parts. Both these roles, and that in *Kaleidoscope*, were much of a muchness: the modern, liberated British miss, well connected and dolled up in the latest modes. She was also batty and amorous and self-willed in a way that recalled Carole Lombard – not a wise thing to do. It was one thing to avoid the inevitable English rose type-casting, another to be over-ambitious. She was unwise to do *Lock Up Your Daughters* (69), a vastly inferior copy of *Tom Jones*, where she was again chaste but scheming.

Nor is there much to be said for her participation in *The Killing of Sister George* and its famous lesbian love scene. She explained her reasons for doing it (to 'The New York Times', among others) and to an extent it was 'safe' in the hands of two such impeccably respectable actresses as herself

Susannah York in Robert Altman's Images *(72), in which she seeks solace from an impending nervous breakdown by thinking about her lovers past and present – and future. No one, except perhaps Altman, was sure what it all meant.*

and Coral Browne; but that was not reckoning with producer-director Robert Aldrich, who inserted this unnecessary scene and otherwise vulgarized the original text almost beyond recognition; bits only of Frank Marcus's touching and funny play remained, mostly in Beryl Reid's repeat of her stage role. The film did the sort of business hoped for.

York was happier in the all-star *Oh! What a Lovely War!*, as a bored member of the top-drawer set, and *The Battle of Britain*, looking anachronistic as the WAAF officer wife of RAF officer Christopher Plummer, with a very silly scene in which their first sex in ages is interrupted by the start of the Blitz. She returned to Hollywood to play a Harlow-type movie aspirant in *They Shoot Horses Don't They?* (70) with Jane Fonda; then she made *Country Dance* in Ireland, married to Michael Craig, loved incestuously by Peter O'Toole and sleeping with the local bobby. As some atonement for their sins, she and O'Toole did 'Arms and the Man' in Dublin. For US TV and cinemas elsewhere she was a pretty, competent Jane in a handsome new version of *Jane Eyre*. Then there was another Hollywood film, *Happy Birthday Wanda June* (71) with Rod Steiger and an every-which-way triangle drama with Michael Caine and Elizabeth Taylor, *Zee and Company* (72). After this she was in *Images*, with Marcel Bozzufi, directed by Robert Altman, who said he had considered both Julie Christie and Sandy Dennis for what was reckoned to be the best female part in years, but chose York after seeing her in *Jane Eyre*.

That puzzle picture led only to a so-so adventure film, *Gold* (74), with Roger Moore, playing granddaughter to tycoon Ray Milland – and just another movie heroine. Better chances offered with *The Maids* (75), sharing the title-roles with Glenda Jackson in this version of Genet which found its audience even less than the minority one it was seeking, and *Conduct Unbecoming*, as the promiscuous army widow who is the cause of all the fuss. Teamed again with Moore, she sparred with him as a 'Washington Post' reporter in *That Lucky Touch*, but both failed to find the light touch needed for comedy like this. It would be too cruel to call her Moore's female equivalent, but this once-promising actress was merely decorative in *Sky Riders* (76), albeit she was kidnapped for the purposes of the plot; it was photographed in Greece and James Coburn played her ex-husband. Taking a plunge, she was one of the first 'names' to try the Australian cinema and she played *Eliza Fraser*, Victorian woman extraordinary: but it is not one of the Aussie films that has travelled. She stayed there, acted in 'Private Lives' and her marriage went to pieces; the idyll over, she returned to Britain to co-star with Alan Bates in *The Shout* (78) and then went to Toronto to play colleague and lover to Elliott Gould in *The Silent Partner*. She was then wife to Marlon Brando, and hence mother of *Superman*, and then a nun helping cop David Janssen to solve *The Golden Gate Murders* (79) for television.

Cinema films were less kind: *The Awakening* (80), as the assistant of Egyptologist Charlton Heston – though hers was the only decent acting around; *Falling in Love Again* – with Elliott Gould; and *Superman II*, with little footage. She admitted (to the 'Telegraph Magazine') that she did the second of these, an independent production, for a deferment, because she had a compulsive need to work – which may be why she appeared in two British mini-series, as Mrs Fitzherbert and as a wartime wife in 'We'll Meet Again'. She also appeared in Paris, in Jean-Louis Barrault's theatre, in 'Apparences', which she did briefly in London; in that city she was a 1982 Hedda Gabler. She was in a Polish-British musical version of Lewis Carroll, *Alice*, which seems never to have been seen, and in: *Loophole*

And Susannah York saving a poor movie from complete dreariness, simply by looking like this: Duffy *(68).*

(81), as Martin Sheen's wife; *Yellowbeard* (83), a horrendous pirate spoof with some doubtful comic talents (Peter Cook, Marty Feldman, Cheech and Chong), in a walk-on as a milady; and the George C. Scott *A Christmas Carol* (84), as Mrs Cratchit to David Warner's Bob. On stage, she was in 'The Human Voice' (New York) for a limited run, 'Multiple Choice' (Guildford) and 'Fatal Attraction' (London, 85) – the latter at the Theatre Royal, Haymarket, and she stayed on there to do 'The Apple Cart' (with Peter O'Toole), for which Glynis Johns was first announced. Films offered this talented, still beautiful, actress nothing better than *Prettykill* (87), starring Season Hubley, as a madame; and *Barbablú, Barbablú*, an Italian tele-movie with John Gielgud as a psychiatrist whose deathbed wish (apparently) is to jaw, jaw, jaw with the offspring of his five marriages. Also available at this time was *Mio in the Land of Faraway*, a co-production between Norway, Sweden and the USSR. She got special billing on *A Summer Story* (88), based on Galsworthy's tale, 'The Apple Tree', as the lady in whose house the young lovers (Imogen Stubbs, James Wilby) meet and stay; and she stole the notices of *Just Ask for Diamond* (formerly *The Falcon's Malteser*, till the Hammett estate objected), as cabaret singer Lauren Bacardi in this affectionate tribute to private-eye movies.

TITLE CHANGES

All British and American films which suffered a title-change when they crossed the Atlantic (those, that is, which are mentioned in the text) are listed below, except when noted in the text. Foreign language movies are only listed where (a), the film has been in exhibition within the last few years, and (b), the English-language title is not a literal translation of the original. For a note on multi-national productions see the introduction. This index is arranged alphabetically according to the changed or alternative title – with the original title, country of origin and date appearing on the right. No account has been made where films were re-titled for television showings.

Ace in the Hole (alternative title)	*The Big Carnival*, US (51)
Advance to the Rear (alternative title)	*Company of Cowards*, US (64)
Adventure for Two, US	*The Demi-Paradise*, GB (43)
Adventures of Sadie, US	*Our Girl Friday*, GB (53)
The Adventuress, US	*I See a Dark Stranger*, GB (46)
Affair in Monte Carlo, US	*24 Hours in a Woman's Life*, GB (53)
Affairs in Versailles, US	*Si Versailles m'était Conté*, F (54)
Agent 8¾, US	*Hot Enough for June*, GB (64)
All at Sea, US	*Barnacle Bill*, GB (57)
All This and Money Too, GB	*Love is a Ball*, US (63)
Always in My Heart, GB	*Mr Imperium*, US (51)
The Amorous Mr Prawn, US	*The Amorous Prawn*, GB (62)
And Nothing but the Truth, US	*Giro City*, GB (82)
And Suddenly It's Murder, US	*Crimen*, It (61)
Angels and the Pirates, GB	*Angels in the Outfield*, US (51)
Angels of Darkness, US	*Donne Proibite*, It (55)
Any Number Can Win, US	*Mélodie en Sous-Sol*, F (63)
Appointment With a Shadow, GB	*The Midnight Story*, US (57)
Armoured Command, GB	*Armored Attack*, US (61)
The Assassin, US	*The Venetian Bird*, GB (52)
Baby Be Good, GB	*Brother Rat and a Baby*, US (40)
Bachelor Girl Apartment, GB	*Any Wednesday*, US (66)
Bad Sister, US	*The White Unicorn*, GB (47)
The Battle of Austerlitz, US	*Austerlitz*, F (60)
Beautiful But Dangerous, GB	*She Couldn't Say No*, US (54)
Beauty and the Devil, US	*La Beauté du Diable*, F (50)
The Bed, GB	*Secrets d'Alcove*, F (54)
Bengal Rifles, GB	*Bengal Brigade*, US (54)
Best Shot, GB	*Hoosiers*, US (86)
Beyond the Limit, US	*The Honorary Consul*, GB (83)
Beyond the River, GB	*The Bottom of the Bottle*, US (56)
The Big Bankroll, GB	*King of the Roaring Twenties*, US (61)
Big Deal at Dodge City, GB	*A Big Hand for the Little Lady*, US (66)
Big Deal on Madonna Street, US	*I Soliti Ignoti*, It (58)
The Big Heart, GB	*Miracle on 34th Street*, US (47)
The Big Risk, US/GB	*Classe Tous Risques*, Fr (59)
The Big Snatch, GB	*Mélodie en Sous-Sol*, Fr (63)
Bizarre! Bizarre!, US	*Drôle de Drame*, Fr (37)
Black Flowers for the Bride, GB	*Something for Everyone*, US (71)
Blonde Sinner, US	*Yield to the Night*, GB (56)
Blood Money, GB	*Requiem for a Heavyweight*, US (62)
Blood on His Sword, GB	*Le Miracle des Loups*, F (61)
Blood on My Hands, GB	*Kiss the Blood off My Hands*, US (48)
Bluebeard, US/GB	*Landru*, F (63)
Bonaventure, GB	*Thunder on the Hill*, US (61)
Both Ends of the Candle, GB	*The Helen Morgan Story*, US (57)
Brainwashed, US	*Schnachnovelle*, G (60)
The Brave and the Beautiful, GB	*The Magnificent Matador*, US (55)
Breaking the Sound Barrier, US	*The Sound Barrier*, GB (52)
Breakout, US	*Danger Within*, GB (59)
Breathless, US/GB	*A Bout de Souffle*, F (59)
Brink of Hell, GB	*Toward the Unknown*, US (56)
Brotherly Love, US	*Country Dance*, GB (70)
Build My Gallows High, GB	*Out of the Past*, US (47)
Cactus Jack, GB	*The Villain*, US (79)
Caged, GB	*Nella Citta L'Inferno*, It (58)
Californian Holiday, GB	*Spinout*, US (66)
Canyon Pass, GB	*Raton Pass*, US (51)
Captain Blood, US	*Le Bossu*, F (60)
Carnival in Flanders, US	*La Kermesse Héroique*, F (35)
Cash on Delivery, US	*To Dorothy a Son*, GB (54)
A Christmas Carol, US	*Scrooge*, GB (51)
The Circle, US	*Vicious Circle*, GB (57)
Circle of Love, US	*La Ronde*, F (64)
City After Midnight, US	*That Woman Opposite*, GB (54)
The City Jungle, GB	*The Philadelphians*, US (59)
Come Dance With Me, US/GB	*Voulez-vous Danser avec Moi*, F (59)
Commando, US	*Marcia o Crepa*, It (62)
Confessions of a Counter Spy, GB	*Man on a String*, US (60)
Constantine and the Cross, US/GB	*Constantino il Grande in hoc Signo*, It (60)
The Counterfeiters, GB	*Le Cave se Rebiffe*, F (61)
The Courageous Mr Penn, US	*Penn of Pennsylvania*, GB (41)
Court Martial, US	*Carrington VC*, GB (54)
The Crimson Blade, US	*The Scarlet Blade*, GB (64)
The Crucible, US	*Les Sorcières de Salem*, F (57)
A Curious Way to Love, GB	*La Morte Ha Fatto L'Uovo*, It (67)
Curse of the Demon, US	*Night of the Demon*, GB (57)
Damn the Defiant, US	*H.M.S. Defiant*, GB (62)
Danger Grows Wild, GB	*The Poppy Is Also a Flower*, US (66)
Dark of the Sun, US	*The Mercenaries*, GB (67)
A Date With a Lonely Girl, GB	*T. R. Baskin*, US (71)
Daybreak, US	*Le Jour se Lève*, F (39)
Deadlier Than the Male, US	*Voici les Temps des Assassins*, F (56)
Desert Attack, US	*Ice Cold in Alex*, GB (58)
Desert Patrol, US	*Sea of Sand*, GB (58)
The Detective, US	*Father Brown*, GB (54)
The Devil Never Sleeps, GB	*Satan Never Sleeps*, GB (62)
The Diamond Earrings, US	*Madame De. . .*, F (53)
The Domino Killings, GB	*The Domino Principle*, US (77)
Double Cross, US	*Il Tradimento*, It (51)
Dulcimer Street, US	*London Belongs To Me*, GB (48)
Dynamite Man from Glory Jail, GB	*Fools Parade*, US (71)
The Earrings of Madame De . . ., US (alternative title)	*Madame De. . .*, F (53)
East of the Rising Sun, GB	*Malaya*, US (50)
The Easy Life, US	*Il Sorpasso*, It (62)
End as a Man, GB	*The Strange One*, US (77)
Everybody's Cheering, GB	*Take Me Out to the Ball Game* , US (49)
Evils of Chinatown, GB	*Confessions of an Opium Eater*, US (62)
Farewell, Friend, US	*Adieu l'Ami*, F (68)
Fast and Sexy, US	*Anna di Brooklyn*, It (58)
Fatal Desire, US	*Cavalleria Rusticana*, It (54)
Fernandel the Dressmaker, US/GB	*Le Couturier de ces Dames*, F (56)
The Fifth Chair, GB	*It's in the Bag*, US (45)
The Final Option, US	*Who Dares Wins*, GB (82)
Fine and Dandy, GB	*The West Point Story*, US (50)
Fire Over Africa, US	*Malaga*, GB (54)
The Fire Within, US	*Le Feu Follet*, F (63)
Fitzwilly Strikes Back, GB	*Fitzwilly*, US (67)
Five Angles on Murder, US	*The Woman in Question*, GB (50)
Flame Over India, US	*North West Frontier*, GB (59)
Flaming Frontier, US/GB	*Old Surehand*, G (65)
Flesh and the Woman, US	*Le Grand Jeu*, F (54)
Forbidden Streeet, US	*Britannia Mews*, GB (49)
The Forgiven Sinner, US	*Léon Morin, Prêtre*, F (61)
Four Ways Out, US	*La Città si Defende*, It (51)
The French Conspiracy, US	*L'Attentat*, F (72)
The French Detective, US	*Adieu Poulet*, F (75)
French Provincial, US	*Souvenirs d'en France*, F (75)
Frenzy, US	*Latin Quarter*, GB (45)
Freud – the Secret Passion, GB	*Freud*, US (62)
Frontier Hellcat, US	*Unter Geiern*, G (65)
The Game is Over, US/GB	*La Curée*, F (66)
The Gay Adventure, US	*Golden Arrow*, GB (53)
The Gentle Art of Murder, GB	*Le Crime ne Paie Pas*, F (62)
The Girl-Getters, US	*The System*, GB (64)
Girl in His Pocket, US	*Amour de Poche*, F (58)
Girls for the Summer, GB	*Racconti d'Estate*, It (59)
The Girls He Left Behind, GB	*The Gang's All Here*, US (43)
Glory at Sea, US	*The Gift Horse*, GB (52)
The Great Manhunt, US	*State Secret*, GB (50)
The Greatest Love, US	*Europa 51*, It (52)
The Great Gilbert & Sullivan, US	*The Story of Gilbert & Sullivan*, GB (53)
The Grip of Fear, GB	*Experiment in Terror*, US (62)
Gypsy Girl, US	*Sky West and Crooked*, GB (65)
The Hardcore Life, GB	*Hardcore*, US (79)
Harem Holiday, GB	*Harum Scarum*, US (65)
The Haunting of Julia, US	*Full Circle*, GB (77)
He, She or It, GB	*La Poupée*, F (62)
Heaven Fell That Night, GB	*Les Bijoutiers du Clair de Lune*, F (58)
Hell Bent for Glory, GB	*Lafavette Esquadrille*, US (58)
Her Man Gilbey, US	*English Without Tears*, GB (44)
Her Panelled Door, US	*The Woman With No Name*, GB (51)
The Hideout, US	*The Small Voice*, GB (48)

High and Dry, US	*The Maggie*, GB (54)
Hollywood Cowboy, GB	*Hearts of the West*, US (75)
Horror Chamber of Dr Faustus, US	*Les Yeux sans Visage*, F (59)
The House in the Square, GB	*I'll Never Forget You*, US (51)
The House of Lovers, GB	*Pot-Bouille*, F (57)
How to Steal a Diamond in Four Uneasy Lessons, GB	*The Hot Rock*, US (72)
I Became a Criminal, US	*They Made Me a Fugitive*, GB (47)
I Like Money, US	*Mr Topaze*, GB (61)
If You Feel Like Singing, GB	*Summer Stock*, US (60)
Immediate Disaster, US	*Stranger from Venus*, GB (54)
Immortal Battalion, US	*The Way Ahead*, GB (44)
Indiscreet, GB	*Christmas in Connecticut*, US (45)
Infidelity, GB	*L'Amant de Cinq Jours*, F (61)
The Inheritance, US	*Uncle Silas*, GB (47)
Innocence is Bliss, GB	*Miss Grant Takes Richmond*, US (49)
Inspector Maigret, US	*Maigret Tend un Piège*, F (58)
The Invaders, US	*The 49th Parallel*, GB (41)
Island of Desire, US	*Saturday Island*, GB (52)
The Island Princess, US	*La Principessa delle Canarie*, It (55)
Island Rescue, US	*Appointment with Venus*, GB (51)
It Started in Tokyo, GB	*Twenty Plus Two*, US (61)
It's a Great Life, GB	*Toller Hecht auf Krummer Tour*, G (61)
It's Magic, GB	*Romance on the High Seas*, US (48)
The James Brothers, GB	*The True Story of Jesse James*, US (57)
Jennie, GB	*Portrait of Jennie*, US (48)
Johnny in the Clouds, US	*The Way to the Stars*, GB (45)
Jungle Fighters, US	*The Long and the Short and the Tall*, GB (61)
The Keepers, GB	*La Tête Contre les Murs*, F (58)
Killer on a Horse, GB	*Welcome to Hard Times*, US (66)
Lady Liberty, US/GB	*Mortadella*, It (72)
A Lady Surrenders, US	*Love Story*, GB (44)
Lady Windermere's Fan, GB	*The Fan*, US (49)
Land of Fury, US	*The Seekers*, GB (54)
The Last Warrior, GB	*Flap*, US (70)
Leda, GB	*A Double Tour*, F (59)
The Legion's Last Patrol, GB	*Marcia o Crepa*, It (62)
The Libertine, US/GB	*La Matriaca*, It (68)
The Light of Heart, GB	*Life Begins at 8.30*, US (42)
Live for Life, US/GB	*Vivre Pour Vivre*, F (67)
The Long Ride Home, GB (alternative title, US)	*A Time for Killing*, US (67)
The Lost Kingdom, GB	*Antinea, L'Amante delle Citta Sepolta*, It (61)
A Loss of Innocence, US	*The Greengage Summer*, GB (61)
The Loudest Whisper, GB	*The Children's Hour*, US (62)
Love Eternal, GB	*L'Eternel Retour*, F (41)
Love in Las Vegas, GB	*Viva Las Vegas*, US (64)
Love is My Profession, GB	*En Cas de Malheur*, F (58)
Love on a Pillow, GB	*Le Repos du Guerrier*, F (62)
A Lovely Way to Go, GB	*A Lovely Way to Die*, US (68)
Lovers, Happy Lovers, US	*Monsieur Ripois/Knave of Hearts*, F/GB (54)
The Lovers of Isadora, US	*Isadora*, GB (69)
The Lovers of Montparnasse, US	*Montparnasse 19*, F (57)
The Lovers of Paris, US	*Pot-Bouille*, F (57)
Madame, US/GB	*Madame Sans-Gêne*, F (62)
Madame Rosa, US	*La Vie Devant Soi*, F (77)
Magnificent Sinner, US	*Katja, die Ungekrönte Kaiserin*, G (60)
Malaga, US	*Moment of Danger*, GB (62)
Male Hunt, US	*La Chasse à l'Homme*, F (64)
Mam'zelle Pigalle, US/GB	*Cette Sacrée Gamine*, F (56)
A Man Called Sledge, GB	*Sledge*, It/US (70)
A Man Called Sullivan, GB	*The Great John L.*, US (45)
The Man in the Cocked Hat, US	*Carlton-Browne of the F.O.*, GB (59)
A Man is Ten Feet Tall, GB	*Edge of the City*, US (57)
Man of Bronze, GB	*Jim Thorpe, All American*, US (51)
Man of Evil, US	*Fanny by Gaslight*, GB (44)
The Man Who Came Back, GB	*Swamp Water*, US (41)
The Man Who Wagged His Tail, US/GB	*Un Angel Paso sobre Brooklyn/Un Angelo Paso por Brooklyn*, Sp/It (57)
Man With a Million, US	*The Million-Pound Note*, GB (64)
Marching Along, GB	*Stars and Stripes Forever*, US (52)
Marco the Magnificent, US	*La Fabuleuse Aventure de Marco Polo*, F, etc. (64)
A Matter of Innocence, US	*Pretty Polly*, GB (67)
McGuire, Go Home, GB	*The High Bright Sun*, US (65)
The Mean Machine, GB	*The Longest Yard*, US (74)
Meet Whiplash Willie, GB	*The Fortune Cookie*, US (66)
Mississippi Mermaid, US	*La Sirène de Mississippi*, F (69)

Mr Lord Says No, US	*The Happy Family*, GB (52)
Mrs Loring's Secret, GB	*The Imperfect Lady*, US (47)
The Most Wanted Man in the World, US	*L'Ennemi Public No 1*, F (54)
Mother Knows Best, GB	*Mother Is a Freshman*, US (49)
The Moving Target, GB	*Harper*, US (66)
The Murder in Thornton Square, GB	*Gaslight*, US (44)
Murder on Diamond Row, US	*The Squeaker*, GB (37)
My Heart Goes Crazy, US	*London Town*, GB (45)
Never Give an Inch, GB	*Sometimes a Great Notion*, US (71)
New Face in Hell, GB	*P.J.*, US (67)
Night Ambush, US	*Ill Met By Moonlight*, GB (57)
Night Creatures, US	*Captain Clegg*, GB (62)
The Night Fighters, US	*A Terrible Beauty*, GB (59)
The Night Heaven Fell, US	*Les Bijoutiers du Clair de Lune*, F (58)
Nine Days a Queen, US	*Tudor Rose*, GB (36)
No Highway in the Sky, US	*No Highway*, GB (51)
No Sleep Till Dawn, GB	*Bombers B-52*, US (57)
Notorious Gentleman, US	*The Rake's Progress*, GB (45)
Nutty, Naughty Chateau, US	*Château en Suède*, F (63)
Of Flesh and Blood, US	*Les Grands Chemins*, F (62)
Oh for a Man!, GB	*Will Success Spoil Rock Hunter?*, US (57)
One Born Every Minute, GB	*The Flim-Flam Man*, US (67)
One-Man Mutiny, GB	*The Court-Martial of Billy Mitchell*, US (55)
The One-Piece Bathing Suit, GB	*Million Dollar Mermaid*, US (52)
One Step to Eternity, US	*Bonnes à Tuer*, F (55)
One Woman's Story, US	*The Passionate Friends*, GB (49)
Open City, US/GB	*Roma, Città Aperta*, It (45)
Operation Disaster, US	*Morning Departure*, GB (50)
Operation Snafu, US	*On the Fiddle*, GB (61)
O'Rourke of the Royal Mounted, GB	*Saskatchewan*, US (54)
Outcry, US	*Il Grido*, It (57)
Pantaloons, US	*Don Juan*, F (55)
Paradise Lagoon, US	*The Admirable Crichton*, GB (57)
Paris Does Strange Things, US	*Elena et les Hommes*, F (56)
The Passionate Thief, US	*Risati di Gioia*, It (61)
Pay the Devil, GB	*Man in the Shadow*, US (57)
The Phoney American, US	*Toller Hecht auf Krummer Tour*, G (61)
Pickup Alley, US	*Interpol*, GB (57)
The Pistolero of Red River, GB	*The Last Challenge*, US (67)
Please, Not Now, GB	*Le Bride sur le Cou*, F (61)
Port of Shadows, US	*Quai des Brumes*, F (38)
Portrait of a Sinner, US	*The Rough and the Smooth*, GB (59)
The Possessors, US	*Les Grandes Familles*, F (58)
The Promoter, US	*The Card*, GB (52)
The Proud and the Beautiful, US	*Les Orgueilleux*, F (53)
Purple Noon, US	*Plein Soleil*, F (60)
Pursuit of the Graf Spee, US	*The Battle of the River Plate*, GB (57)
Queen of the Nile, US	*Nefertite, Regina del Nilo*, It (61)
Race for Life, GB	*Si Tous les Gars du Monde. . .*, F (55)
The Rage of the Buccaneers, US	*Gordon, il Pirata Nero*, It (61)
Rampage at Apache Wells, US	*Der Ölprinz*, G (65)
The Randolph Family, US	*Dear Octopus*, GB (43)
The Red Dragon, US	*Das Geheimnis der Drei Dschunken/A009 Missione Hong Kong*, G/It (65)
The Reluctant Spy, US	*L'Honorable Stanislas, Agent Secret*, F (63)
Remember That Face, GB	*The Mob*, US (51)
Reprieve, GB	*Convicts Four*, US (62)
The Rich Full Life, GB	*Cynthia*, US (47)
Richer Than the Earth, GB	*The Whistle at Eaton Falls*, US (51)
Rock Around the World, US	*The Tommy Steele Story*, GB (57)
Rough Company, GB	*The Violent Men*, US (55)
Royal Flush, GB	*Two Guys from Milwaukee*, US (46)
The Saboteur, Code Name Morituri, US (alternative title)	*Morituri*, US(65)
The Sabre and the Arrow, GB	*The Last of the Comanches*, US (52)
Saraband, US	*Saraband for Dead Lovers*, GB (48)
Scandal in Sorrento, US/GB	*Pane, Amore, e. . .*, It (56)
School for Love, US	*Futures Vedettes*, F (55)
Season of Passion, US	*The Summer of the Seventeenth Doll*, GB (59)
Separate Beds, GB	*The Wheeler Dealers*, US (63)
The Shadow Man, US	*Streets of Shadows*, GB (53)
Sidewalks of London, US	*St Martin's Lane*, GB (38)
The Silent Stranger, GB	*Step Down to Terror*, US (58)
The Sleeping Car Murder, US/GB	*Compartiment Tueurs*, F (65)
Sons of the Musketeers, GB	*At Sword's Point*, US (52)
Sophie's Place, US	*Crooks and Coronets*, GB (69)

South West to Sonora, GB	*The Appaloosa*, US (66)
Speaking of Murder, US	*Le Rouge est Mis*, F (57)
Spin of a Coin, GB	*The George Raft Story*, US (62)
Spinster, GB	*Two Loves*, US (61)
Spirits of the Dead, US	*Histoires Extraordinares*, F (68)
Spitfire, US	*The First of the Few*, GB (42)
Spy in the Pantry, US	*Ten Days in Paris*, GB (39)
Stairway to Heaven, US	*A Matter of Life and Death*, GB (45)
The Star Said No, GB	*Callaway Went Thataway*, US (51)
Stop Train 349, US	*Verspäting in Marienborn*, G (63)
Stowaway Girl, US	*Manuela*, GB (57)
The Stranger in Between, US	*Hunted*, GB (52)
Strictly for Pleasure, GB	*The Perfect Furlough*, US (58)
Stronger than Fear, GB	*Edge of Doom*, US (50)
Such Men are Dangerous, GB	*The Racers*, US (54)
Summer Manoeuvres, US/GB	*Les Grandes Manoeuvres*, F (55)
Sweet and Sour, GB	*Dragées au Poivre*, F (63)
The Swindle(rs), US/GB	*Il Bidone*, It (55)
Take the Stage, GB	*Curtain Call at Cactus Creek*, US (50)
A Tale of Five Women, US	*A Tale of Five Cities*, GB (50)
The Tall Women, US	*Las Siete Magnificas*, SP (67)
The Taming of Dorothy, US	*Her Favourite Husband*, GB (50)
Tank Force, US	*No Time to Die*, GB (58)
Target for Scandal, GB	*Washington Story*, US (52)
Terror on a Train, US	*Time Bomb*, GB (52)
Their Secret Affair, GB	*Top Secret Affair*, US (57)
There's Always a Price Tag, US	*Retour de Manivelle*, F (57)
These Are the Damned, US	*The Damned*, GB (63)
The Thief of Paris, US	*Le Voleur*, F (67)
This Is My Affair, GB	*I Can Get It For You Wholesale*, GB (51)
This Woman is Dangerous, GB	*Perfect Strangers*, US (50)
Three Moves to Freedom, GB	*Schnachnovelle*, G (60)
Three Murderesses, US	*Faibles Femmes*, F (59)
Three Sinners, US	*Meurtres*, F (51)
Thunder in the Dust, GB	*The Sundowners*, US (60)
Tiger in the Sky, GB	*The McConnell Story*, US (55)
Tight Little Island, US	*Whisky Galore*, GB (49)
Time of Indifference, US	*Gli Indifferenti*, It (64)
Time Out for Love, US	*L'Amant de Cinq Jours*, F (61)
Time Running Out, US	*Le Traqué/Gunman in the Streets*, F/GB (50)
A Time to Live and a Time to Die, GB	*Le Feu Follet*, F (63)
Tonight's the Night, US	*Happy Ever After*, GB (53)
Too Bad She's Bad, US/GB	*Peccato che Sia una Caniglia*, It (55)
Too Dangerous to Love, GB	*Perfect Strangers*, US (50)
Too Many Chefs, GB	*Who is Killing the Great Chefs of Europe*, US (78)

The Treasure of Kalifa, GB	*The Steel Lady*, US (53)
Trial and Error, US	*The Dock Brief*, GB
The Trouble Shooter, GB	*Man with the Gun*, US (55)
Two Women, US/GB	*La Ciociara*, It (61)
Under the Clock, GB	*The Clock*, US (45)
Up to His Ears, GB	*Les Tribulations d'un Chinois en Chine*, F (65)
The Upper Hand, US	*Du Rififi à Paname*, F (66)
Vacation from Marriage, US	*Perfect Strangers*, GB (45)
Viva Las Vegas, GB	*Meet Me in Las Vegas*, US (66)
Wall of Death, US	*There is Another Sun*, GB (51)
War-Gods of the Deep, US	*City Under the Sea*, GB (65)
The Warriors, US	*The Dark Avenger*, GB (55)
Waterfront Women, US	*Waterfront*, GB (50)
The Way of Youth, US	*Le Chemin des Ecoliers*, F (59)
The Wayward Wife, US	*La Provinciale*, It (52)
Web of Evidence, US	*Beyond This Place*, GB (59)
Web of Fear, US	*Constance aux Enfers*, F (64)
Web of Passion, US	*A Double Tour*, F (59)
Wedding Bells, GB	*Royal Wedding*, US (51)
Wedding Breakfast, GB	*The Catered Affair*, US (56)
Wee Geordie, US	*Geordie*, GB (55)
Weekend at Dunkirk, US/GB	*Weekend à Zuydcote*, F (65)
What Lola Wants, GB	*Damn Yankess*, US (58)
Where the Hot Wind Blows, US/GB	*La Loi*, F (59)
Where the River Bends, GB	*Bend of the River*, US (52)
White Slave Ship, US	*L'Ammutinamento*, It (61)
Why Bother To Knock, US	*Don't Bother To Knock*, GB (61)
Wild for Kicks, US	*Beat Girl*, GB (60)
The Wild Heart, US	*Gone To Earth*, GB (50)
The Winning Way, GB	*The All American*, US (53)
A Woman Like Satan, US/GB	*La Femme et le Pantin*, F (59)
Woman of Dolwyn, US	*The Last Days of Dolwyn*, GB (49)
The World and His Wife, GB	*State of the Union*, US (48)
X, Y and Zee, US	*Zee and Co*, GB (72)
You Belong to My Heart, GB	*Mi Imperium*, US (51)
Young Man of Music, GB	*Young Man with a Horn*, US (60)
Young Scarface, US	*Brighton Rock*, GB (46)
Your Past Is Showing, US	*The Naked Truth*, GB (57)
Zero Population Growth, GB	*Z.P.G.*, US (72)